What's New in This Edition?

This book is completely revised and updated for DB2 version 4 and version 5, and includes coverage of the following:

- How to effectively implement DB2 stored procedures
- How to access DB2 via the Internet and where to find information about DB2 on the World Wide Web
- Application development and SQL programming changes, such as outer joins, in-line views, CASE expressions, column renaming, new functions (`NULLIF`, `STRIP`, and `COALESCE`), and dynamic reoptimization of static SQL
- Dynamic SQL changes, including new authorization and caching techniques
- Data sharing and how to effectively share data across the parallel Sysplex
- Locking changes including row locks, Type 2 indexes, selective partition locking, dirty reads, and read stability isolation
- DDl changes that impact database design, such as Type 2 indexes, check constraints, user-defined defaults, large tablespaces, `UNIQUE WHERE NOT NULL` indexes, and table renaming
- The different types of query parallelism and how they impact access path selection and performance
- Changes to how partitioned tablespace scans operate
- New features and performance enhancements made to the DB2 utilities, including online `REORG`, reorganizing the DB2 Catalog, and `RUNSTATS` sampling
- How to effectively implement data warehouses using DB2

Additional revisions were made to the entire book to expand the techniques that were previously covered, and to add new tips, tricks, and techniques for developing performance-oriented, stable DB2 application systems. New and revised SQL and DDL tips, dynamic SQL usage considerations, and DB2 subsystem performance and reporting techniques will prove to be invaluable to DB2 version 4 and 5 sites. The sections on DB2 tools and vendors were combined into a single, completely revised chapter. Although these changes include three new chapters, the entire text has been expanded and completely revised.

PRISM
THE BOOK SHOP
No. 16, 11th Main, IV Block, Jayanagar
Bangalore - 11 Ph : 663 7527

Accolades for *DB2 Developer's Guide*:

"Craig's no-nonsense approach to DB2 topics could only come from the knowledge of having worked in the pits in depth with DB2, the real-world technical information coming from real-world experiences. I found the information on DB2 very significant and timely, and Craig is able to demystify the new features and workings of this release so that they are both meaningful to an application developer as well as a seasoned DBA. His sections of performance guidelines should form the basis for standards in every company. If DB2 is your profession, this book belongs on your desk."

—Richard Yevich

"*DB2 Developer's Guide* presents literally everything programmers and DBAs need to know about advanced DB2."

—Jonathon Sayles
Relational Database Journal

"Now that much of the industry is using DB2, I believe that Craig Mullins' book will become a classic reference that most of you will want to keep on your desks."

—Steve Loesch
PLATINUM Sysjournal

"...the book is not only the size of a small encyclopedia, it is also just about as comprehensive."

Books & Bytes News & Reviews

"*DB2 Developer's Guide* has the potential to pay for itself many times over if you follow its useful design and performance advice. If you use DB2 in your workplace, the most recent edition of *DB2 Developer's Guide* should definitely be on your bookshelf. Read it to save yourself an enormous amount of pain and suffering."

—Ron Shirey
Relational Database Journal

"...instead of rummaging through various DB2 reference materials when looking for DB2 information, I have been reaching for Craig's book."

—Chris Foot
Database Programming & Design

"This is an excellent book...It is chock-full of DB2 technical information, design and tuning approaches, and database administration guidelines...In an organized and coherent way, Mullins seems to have dumped his entire DB2 life experience into *DB2 Developer's Guide.*"

—Jonathon Sayles
Relational Database Journal

DB2®

Developer's Guide

Third Edition

Craig S. Mullins

Techmedia

Munish Plaza, 20, Ansari Road, Darya Ganj, New Delhi-2

SAMS Developer's Guide

FIRST INDIAN EDITION 1998

Distributors:

MICRO BOOK CENTRE
2, City Centre, CG Road,
Near Swastik Char Rasta,
AHMEDABAD-380009 Phone: 6421611

COMPUTER BOOK CENTRE
12, Shrungar Shopping Centre, M. G. Road,
BANGALORE-560001 Phone: 5587923, 5584641

MICRO BOOKS
Shanti Niketan Building, 8, Camac Street,
CALCUTTA-700017 Phone: 2426518, 2426519

BUSINESS PROMOTION BUREAU
8/1, Ritchie Street, Mount Road,
CHENNAI-600002 Phone: 834796, 8550491

DECCAN AGENCIES
4-3-329, Bank Street,
HYDERABAD-500195 Phone: 4612280, 593826

MICRO MEDIA
Shop No. 5, Mahendra Chambers, 150 D.N.
Road, FORT, **MUMBAI-400001**
Phone: 2078296, 2078297, 2002732

BPB PUBLICATIONS
B-14, Connaught Place, **NEW DELHI-110001**
Phone : 3325760, 3723393, 3737742

INFO TECH
G-2, Sidhartha Building, 96 Nehru Place,
NEW DELHI-110019
Phone: 6438245, 6415092, 6234208

INFO TECH
Shop No. 2, F-38, South Extension Part-I
NEW DELHI-110049
Phone : 4691288, 4641941

BPB BOOK CENTRE
376, Old Lajpat Rai Market,
DELHI-110006 Phone: 2961747

INFO TECH
B-11, Vardhman Plaza, Sector-16,
Electronics Nagar, **NOIDA-201301**
Phone: 8531346

This book is dedicated to my parents, Giles and Donna Mullins, whose constant support and guidance is the reason fo rmuch of my success today.

THIRD EDITION

Composed in Adobe Garamond and MCP digital by Macmillan Computer Publishing.

TRADEMARKS

Printed in India by arrangement with
Macmillan Computer Publishing, USA.

ISBN 81-87105-40-2

Published by G. C. Jain for Techmedia, Munish Plaza, 20, Ansari Road, Darya Ganj, New Delhi-110 002 and Printed by him at Akash Press, Delhi.

Overview

VI DB2 Utilities and Commands

VII The Ideal DB2 Environment

VIII Distributed DB2

IX Appendixes

Contents

II DB2 Application Development

V DB2 Performance Tuning

VI DB2 Utilities and Commands

Acknowledgments

The writing and production of a technical book is a time-consuming and laborious task. Luckily, I had many understanding and helpful people to make the process much easier. First, I would like to thank the many folks who have reviewed and commented upon the text for each of the three editions. Sheryl Larsen has been especially helpful in reviewing the access path and complex SQL components of the book. Chuck Kosin, Sheryl Larsen, Bill Backs, and Roger Miller have pored over each chapter of various incarnations of the manuscript and this book is much better thanks to their expert contributions.

I would also like to thank the many people who provided suggestions for improvements on the first and second editions of the book. Special thanks go to Chuck Kosin and Tim McAllister for their sharp eyes and useful comments.

Additionally, many thanks to the many understanding and patient folks at Sams who have worked with me on each of the three editions. And finally, a thank you to all of the people with whom I have come in contact professionally at USX Corporation, Mellon Bank, Barnett Technologies, Duquesne Light Company, Gartner Group, and PLATINUM *technology, inc.* This book is surely a better one due to the fine quality of my coworkers, each of whom has expanded my horizons in many different and satisfying ways.

If you have any questions or comments about this text, you can contact me at `CMullins@compuserve.com` or `cmullins@platinum.com`. You can also write to me in care of the publisher.

About the Author

Craig S. Mullins is vice president of Marketing and Operations for the database tools division of PLATINUM *technology, inc.* He has extensive experience in all facets of database systems development, including systems analysis and design, database and system administration, data analysis, and developing and teaching DB2 and Sybase classes. Craig has worked with DB2 since V1 and has experience in multiple roles, including programmer, DBA, instructor, and analyst. His experience spans industries, having worked for companies in the following fields: manufacturing (USX Corporation), banking (Mellon Bank), utilities (Duquesne Light Company), commercial software development (PLATINUM *technology, inc.*), consulting (ASSET, Inc.), and computer industry analysis (Gartner Group). Additionally, Craig authored many of the popular "Platinum Monthly DB2 Tips" and worked on Platinum's DB2 posters.

Craig is also a frequent contributor to computer industry publications, having over five dozen articles published during the past few years. His articles have been published in magazines like *Byte*, *DB2 Update*, *DB2 Magazine*, *Database Programming & Design*, *DBMS*, *Data Management Review*, *Relational Database Journal*, *Enterprise Systems Journal*, *IDUG Solutions Journal*, *Sybase Technical Journal*, *Mainframe Client/Server*, and others. Complete information on Craig's published articles and books can be found on the World Wide Web at `http://www.platinum.com/craigm`.

Craig graduated cum laude with a degree in Computer Science and Economics from the University of Pittsburgh.

Tell Us What You Think!

As a reader, you are the most important critic of and commentator on our books. We value your opinion and want to know what we're doing right, what we could do better, what areas you'd like to see us publish in, and any other words of wisdom you're willing to pass our way. You can help us make strong books that meet your needs and give you the computer guidance you require.

Do you have access to the World Wide Web? Then check out our site at `http://www.mcp.com`.

NOTE

If you have a technical question about this book, call the technical support line at 317-581-3833 or send e-mail to `support@mcp.com`.

As the team leader of the group that created this book, I welcome your comments. You can fax, e-mail, or write me directly to let me know what you did or didn't like about this book—as well as what we can do to make our books stronger. Here's the information:

Fax: 317-581-4669

E-mail: Rosemarie Graham

Mail: `enterprise_mgr@sams.mcp.com`
Sams Publishing
201 W. 103rd Street
Indianapolis, IN 46290

Introduction

Welcome to the third edition of *DB2 Developer's Guide.* I have been overwhelmed by the success of the first two editions of this book. The data processing community obviously needs a practitioner's view of DB2 development issues and concerns. The second edition covered DB2 through V3; this third edition expands coverage to include the latest release of DB2, version 5. Be advised that this incorporates two new versions of DB2: V4 and V5. For a summary of the changes made to DB2 for each of these releases, please refer to Appendix J.

Other books about DB2 are available, but they discuss the same tired subjects: SQL syntax, basic relational database design, and embedded SQL programming techniques. *DB2 Developer's Guide, Third Edition* unlocks the secrets of DB2, picking up where the DB2 tutorial books leave off. It delves into subjects not covered adequately elsewhere—not even in IBM's DB2 manuals. This book clarifies complex DB2 topics, provides performance and procedural advice for implementing well-designed DB2 applications, and describes what DB2 does behind the scenes. Using *DB2 Developer's Guide, Third Edition* as a blueprint, your administration and development staff can implement optimized DB2 application systems.

This is not an introductory text on DB2 and SQL, but much of the advice contained herein is useful to the beginner as well as to the advanced user. It does not teach SQL syntax, relational theory, normalization, or logical database design, but it does provide suggestions on how and when to use these and other techniques. If you are interested in the intricacies of complex SQL instead of syntax diagrams, this book is for you. Other areas covered include the following:

- Comprehensive coverage of new DB2 V4 and V5 features including stored procedures, data sharing, outer joins, in-line views, column renaming, dirty reads, online REORG, utility enhancements, row locks, Type 2 indexes, large tablespaces, ODBC, ASCII support, the World Wide Web, and more
- Tips, tricks, and guidelines for coding efficient SQL
- Guidelines for building performance-oriented DB2 databases
- Environmental options for developing DB2 applications using TSO, CICS, IMS/TM, CAF, and RRSAF
- Description of what goes on in DB2 behind the scenes, including logging, locking, and a roadmap for using the System Catalog and Directory
- Comprehensive techniques for achieving and maintaining optimal DB2 performance
- In-depth performance monitoring and tuning guidelines from both an application and a system perspective
- Using EXPLAIN and interpreting its output
- Procedures for using the DB2 Catalog to monitor DB2
- DB2 application development guidelines

- In-depth advice on using the DB2 utilities
- Guidelines for assigning bufferpool sizes and strategies for implementing multiple bufferpools and hiperpools
- DB2 disaster recovery scenarios and recommendations
- How and when to use DB2 views
- How to use DB2 in a client/server environment including discussion of stored procedures, access to DB2 over the Internet, and ODBC
- Coverage of DB2's support for distributed databases including a discussion of DRDA and distributed two-phase commit
- In-depth coverage of how to deploy DB2-based data warehouses
- Comprehensive coverage of add-on tools for DB2, including a description of the types of tools and a listing of vendors and their offerings (useful if you must evaluate DB2 tools)
- Discussion of DB2 organizational issues including roles and responsibilities, design review guidelines, and political issues

How To Use This Book

This book serves as a tour guide for your adventurous journey through the world of DB2. To obtain the most benefit, you should read the book from cover to cover. The book's usefulness does not diminish after your initial reading, however. It is probably best used as a reference text for your daily workings with DB2.

The book is organized to function in both capacities. Each chapter deals with a particular subject and references other chapters or DB2 manuals when appropriate. In short, the book is designed to optimize the performance of both planned and ad hoc access, much like DB2!

The Importance of DB2

Why is DB2 so important to the long-term success of your organization? First, DB2 is a strategic product from IBM. It is available on all of IBM's key platforms. Although this book covers DB2 for MVS (OS/390) only, versions of DB2 are now available for PC workstations using Windows NT or OS/2, UNIX workstations using AIX, HP/UX, Solaris, and Seimens Nixdorf, midrange systems using VM or VSE, and the AS/400.

However, each of these DB2 products is not 100% compatible or portable. Why would IBM either rename old products (SQL/DS and SQL/400) or create new DB2s? First and foremost, because the name DB2 carries with it the aura of a successful product. However, to be a little less cynical, plans are also in the works to make DB2 implementations as consistent as possible, regardless of the platform.

Furthermore, IBM's Information Warehouse architecture employs DB2 as a key component This means that IBM is committed to DB2—and support for DB2 continues to grow. To gauge just how fast DB2 is being accepted as an industry standard, consider that there were fewer than 1,800 worldwide DB2 licenses in 1988. Today there are in excess of 8,000 licenses and that number is continuing to grow even in the face of mounting competition from the client/server DBMS vendors such as Oracle, Informix, and Sybase.

Another factor in DB2's success is that it is based on the relational model. The relational model is founded on the mathematics of set theory, thereby providing a solid theoretical base for the management of data. Relational databases are typically easier to use and maintain than databases based on nonrelational technology. DB2's foundation in the relational model also provides it with improved data availability, data integrity, and data security because the relational model rigorously defines these features as part of the database, not as part of the processes that maintain the database.

Because DB2 is a relational database management system, it more easily lends itself to a distributed implementation. Tables can be located at disparate locations across a network and applications can seamlessly access information in those tables from within a single program using DB2. As distributed processing and client/server technology continue to gain market presence, DB2 will coexist within that framework operating as the ultimate server.

DB2 uses SQL, which is the de facto standard language for maintaining and querying relational databases. Even many non-relational databases (such as, Adabas, IDMS, and some object-oriented DBMS products) provide SQL access to data. IBM developed SQL, and DB2 was one of the first databases to use SQL exclusively to access data. SQL provides the benefits of quick data retrieval, modification, definition, and control. It is also transportable from environment to environment. This is good news for both SQL professionals and managers of SQL professionals. SQL professionals can quickly translate their skills from job to job because SQL is used at many installations. Managers can easily replace SQL professionals because their skills are so transportable.

The last factor that should convince you that mastering DB2 is a worthwhile goal is the marketplace. As DB2 grows, the need for experienced DB2 professionals increases also. The acceptance, performance, and usability of DB2 are increasing. DB2 is the predominant database in the mainframe marketplace, and is rapidly gaining acceptance and market share in the workstation and midrange markets. So let's get down to business and begin understanding how to use DB2 to its maximum.

I

SQL Tools, Tips, and Tricks

Part I provides a bag of SQL tools and tricks that will help you squeeze every bit of performance out of the SQL code in your DB2 applications.

Chapter 1, "The Magic Words," introduces SQL and provides tools for the SQL practitioner. The remaining chapters in Part I provide five categories of SQL tricks. Chapter 2, "Data Manipulation Guidelines," provides a collection of simple suggestions to speed data access and modification; it suggests tips for both simple and complex SQL statements.

Chapter 3, "Data Definition Guidelines," guides you through the maze of physical parameters that you must choose when implementing DB2 databases, tablespaces, tables, and indexes with DDL statements.

In Chapter 4, "Miscellaneous Guidelines," the "Authorization Guidelines" section provides tips on effective security implementation. Additionally, the benefits and pitfalls of DB2 view creation and use are covered in Chapter 4 under "View Guidelines." Finally, Chapter 4 provides general hints (not easily categorized) that assist you in achieving an optimal DB2 environment.

The information in these chapters is based on my experience and should be consistent with DB2 V5. Sometimes, the guideline does not apply to every release of DB2. In these cases, the DB2 release level to which that guideline applies is stated and, if necessary, examples are provided to show the different options.

1

The Magic Words

Once upon a time there was a kingdom called Userville. The people in the kingdom were impatient and wanted to know everything about everything—they could never get enough information. Life was difficult and the people were unhappy because data was often lost, and even when it was available, it was often inaccurate and not easy to access.

The King decided to purchase DB2, an advanced tool for storing and retrieving data that could be processed by the Users and turned into information. "This," he thought, "should keep the people happy. DB2 will solve all my problems." But he soon found out that special knowledge was necessary to make DB2 work its wonders. Nobody in Userville knew how to use it.

Luckily, a grand Wizard living in a nearby kingdom knew many mystical secrets for retrieving data. These secrets were a form of magic called SQL. The King of Userville summoned the Wizard, offering him many great treasures if only he would help the poor Users in Userville.

The Wizard soon arrived, determined to please. Armed with nothing more than SQL and a smile, the Wizard strode to the terminal and uttered the magic words:

```
SELECT E.EMPNO, E.EMPNAME, D.DEPTNO, D.DEPTNAME
FROM   DSN8510.DEPT  D,
       DSN8510.EMP   E
WHERE  E.WORKDEPT = D.DEPTNO
```

A crowd gathered and applauded as the desired information began pumping out of the terminal. "More, more," shouted the data-starved masses. The Wizard gazed into the screen, and with amazing speed effortlessly produced report after report. The King was overheard to say, "You know, this is just too good to be true!" Everybody was happy. The Users had their share of information, the King had a peaceful kingdom, and the Wizard had his treasures and the respect of the Users.

For many months, the Users were satisfied with the magic of the great Wizard. Then, one day, the Wizard disappeared...in a jet to the West Coast for 100 grand a year. The people of the kingdom began to worry. "How will we survive without the magic of the Wizard? Will we have to live, once again, without our precious information?" The Wizard's apprentice tried to silence the crowd by using his magic, but it wasn't the same. The information was still there, but it wasn't coming fast enough or as effortlessly. The apprentice was not yet as skilled as the great Wizard who had abandoned the kingdom. But, as luck would have it, one day he stumbled upon the great Wizard's diary. He quickly absorbed every page and soon was invoking the Wizard's magic words. And all was well again.

Well, life is not always that simple. Departing Wizards do not often leave behind documentation of their secrets. The first part of this book can be used as a "Wizard's diary" for efficient SQL. This chapter is an overview of SQL, not from a syntactic viewpoint, but from a functional viewpoint. This chapter is not intended to teach SQL, but to provide a framework for the advanced issues discussed in the remainder of this text. This framework delineates the differences between SQL and procedural languages and outlines the components and types of

SQL. Chapters 2 through 4 delve into the performance and administrative issues surrounding the effective implementation of SQL for DB2.

So continue and take the next step toward becoming a DB2 Wizard…

An Overview of SQL

Structured Query Language, better known as *SQL* (and pronounced "sequel" or "ess-cue-el"), is a powerful tool for manipulating data. It is the de facto standard query language for relational *database management systems* (R*DBMSs*) and is used not just by DB2, but also by the other leading RDBMS products such as Oracle, Sybase, and Informix. Indeed, every relational database management system—and many nonrelational DBMS products—provide support for SQL. Why is this so? What benefits are accrued by using SQL rather than some other language?

There are many reasons. Foremost is that SQL is a high-level language that provides a greater degree of abstraction than do procedural languages. Third-generation languages (3GLs), such as COBOL, and older fourth-generation languages (4GLs), such as FOCUS, require that the programmer navigate data structures. Program logic must be coded to proceed record-by-record through the data stores in an order determined by the application programmer or systems analyst. This information is encoded in the high-level language and is difficult to change after it has been programmed.

SQL, on the other hand, is fashioned so that the programmer can specify what data is needed but cannot specify how to retrieve it. SQL is coded without embedded data-navigational instructions. The DBMS analyzes SQL and formulates data-navigational instructions "behind the scenes." These data-navigational instructions are called *access paths.* By forcing the DBMS to determine the optimal access path to the data, a heavy burden is removed from the programmer. In addition, the database can have a better understanding of the state of the data it stores, and thereby can produce a more efficient and dynamic access path to the data. The result is that SQL, used properly, provides a quicker application development and prototyping environment than is available with corresponding high-level languages.

Another feature of SQL is that it is not merely a query language. The same language used to query data is used also to define data structures, control access to the data, and insert, modify, and delete occurrences of the data. This consolidation of functions into a single language eases communication between different types of users. DBAs, systems programmers, application programmers, systems analysts, systems designers, and end users all speak a common language: SQL. When all the participants in a project are speaking the same language, a synergy is created that can reduce overall system-development time.

Arguably, though, the single most important feature of SQL that has solidified its success is its capability to retrieve data easily using English-like syntax. It is much easier to understand

```
SELECT    LASTNAME
FROM      EMP
WHERE     EMPNO = '000010';
```

than it is to understand pages and pages of COBOL, FORTRAN, C, or PL/I source code or the archaic instructions of Assembler. Because SQL programming instructions are easier to understand, they are easier also to learn and maintain—thereby making users and programmers more productive in a shorter period of time.

The remainder of this chapter focuses more fully on the features and components of SQL touched on in this overview.

The Nature of SQL

SQL is, by nature, a flexible creature. It uses a free-form structure that gives the user the ability to develop SQL statements in a way best suited to the given user. Each SQL request is parsed by the DBMS before execution to check for proper syntax and to optimize the request. Therefore, SQL statements do not need to start in any given column and can be strung together on one line or broken apart on several lines. For example, the following SQL statement:

```
SELECT * FROM DSN8510.EMP WHERE SALARY < 25000;
```

is equivalent to this SQL statement:

```
SELECT   *
FROM     DSN8510.EMP
WHERE    SALARY < 25000;
```

Another flexible feature of SQL is that a single request can be formulated in a number of different and functionally equivalent ways. This flexibility is possible because SQL provides the ability to code a single feature in several ways. One example of this SQL capability is that it can join tables or nest queries. A nested query always can be converted to an equivalent join. Other examples of this flexibility can be seen in the vast array of functions and predicates. Examples of features with equivalent functionality are:

- `BETWEEN` versus `<= / >=`
- `IN` versus a series of predicates tied together with `AND`
- `INNER JOIN` versus tables strung together in the `FROM` clause separated by commas
- `CASE` expressions versus complex `UNION ALL` statements
- Single-column function versus multiple-column functions (for example, `AVG` versus `SUM` and `COUNT`)

The flexibility of SQL is not always desirable as different but equivalent SQL formulations can result in extremely differing performance. The ramifications of this flexibility are discussed in the next few chapters, which provide guidelines for developing efficient SQL.

As mentioned, SQL specifies what data to retrieve or manipulate but does not specify how you accomplish these tasks. This keeps SQL intrinsically simplistic. If you can remember the set-at-a-time orientation of a relational database, you will begin to grasp the essence and nature of SQL. The capability to act on a set of data coupled with the lack of need for establishing *how* to retrieve and manipulate data defines SQL as a non-procedural language.

A procedural language is based, appropriately enough, on procedures. One procedure is coded to retrieve data record-by-record. Another procedure is coded to calculate percentages based on the retrieved data. More procedures are coded to modify the data, rewrite the data, check for errors, and so on. A controlling procedure then ties together the other procedures and invokes them in a specific and non-changing order. COBOL is a good example of a procedural language.

SQL is a non-procedural language. A single statement can take the place of a series of procedures. Again, this is possible because SQL uses set-level processing and DB2 optimizes the query to determine the data-navigation logic. Sometimes one or two SQL statements can accomplish what entire procedural programs were required to do.

NOTE

Several major RDBMS vendors have extended SQL to support procedural logic, except DB2 (as of version 5). For example, Sybase SQL Server provides procedural support in Transact-SQL, Oracle in PL/SQL. Procedural SQL will look familiar to anyone who has ever written any type of SQL or coded using any type of programming language. Typically, procedural SQL dialects contain constructs to support looping (`while`), exiting (`return`), branching (`goto`), conditional processing (`if...then...else`), blocking (`begin...end`), and variable definition and usage. Procedural extensions enable more of the application to be written using only SQL.

SQL was extended to enable stored procedures and triggers to be written and deployed using SQL alone. DB2 avoids procedural SQL requiring that stored procedures are written using a 3GL or 4GL; DB2 does not yet support triggers. Look for this to change in a future release of DB2, but probably not until a standard method of extending SQL for procedural support has been accepted.

Set-at-a-Time Processing

Every SQL manipulation statement operates on a table and results in another table. All operations native to SQL, therefore, are performed at a set level. One retrieval statement can return multiple rows; one modification statement can modify multiple rows. This feature of relational databases is called *relational closure*. Relational closure is the major reason that relational databases such as DB2 generally are easier to maintain and query.

See Figure 1.1 for a further explanation of relational closure. As the figure shows, a user of DB2 issues the SQL request, which is sent to the DBMS. (This request may need to access one or many DB2 tables.) The DBMS analyzes the SQL request and determines which pieces of information are necessary to resolve the user's request. This information then is presented to the user as a table: one or more columns in zero, one, or many rows. This is important. Set-level processing means that a set is always used for input, and a set is always returned as output. Sometimes the set is empty or consists of only one row or column. This is appropriate and does not violate the rules of set-level processing. The relational model and set-level processing are based on the laws of the mathematics of *set theory*, which permits empty or single-valued sets.

FIGURE 1.1.
Relational closure.

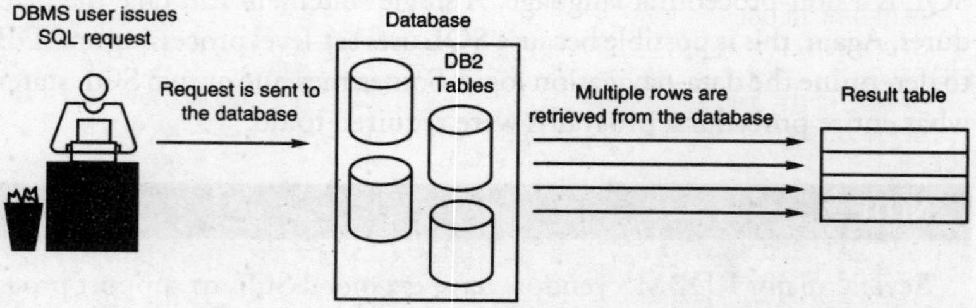

Contrast the set-at-a-time processing of SQL with record-at-a-time processing as depicted in Figure 1.2. Record-level processing requires multiple reads to satisfy a request, which is hard-coded data navigation. Set-level processing, on the other hand, satisfies the same request with a single, non-navigational statement. Because fewer distinct operations (`read`, `write`, and so on) are required, set-level processing is simpler to implement.

The power of SQL becomes increasingly evident when you compare SQL to COBOL (and flat files to relational databases). Consider the following SQL statement:

```
UPDATE    DSN8510.EMP
SET       BONUS = 1000
WHERE     EMPNO = '000340';
```

This single SQL statement accomplishes the same job as the following, comparably complex COBOL psuedo-code program:

```
Must set up IDENTIFICATION and
    ENVIRONMENT DIVISIONS.
DATA DIVISION.
FILE-SECTION.
    Must define input and output files.
WORKING-STORAGE SECTION.
    Must declare all necessary variables.
01  EMPLOYEE-LAYOUT.
    05  EMPNO          PIC X(6).
    05  FIRSTNME       PIC X(12).
    05  MIDINIT        PIC X.
    05  LASTNAME       PIC X(15).
    05  WORKDEPT       PIC X(3).
    05  PHONENO        PIC X(4).
    05  HIREDATE       PIC X(10).
    05  JOB            PIC X(8).
    05  EDLEVEL        PIC S9(4) COMP.
    05  SEX            PIC X.
```

```
    05  BIRTHDATE      PIC X(10).
    05  SALARY         PIC S9(7)V99 COMP-3.
    05  BONUS          PIC S9(7)V99 COMP-3.
    05  COMM           PIC S9(7)V99 COMP-3.
77  EOF-FLAG           PIC X      VALUE 'N'.
PROCEDURE DIVISION.
MAIN-PARAGRAPH.
    PERFORM OPEN-FILES.
    PERFORM PROCESS-UPDATE
        UNTIL EOF-FLAG = 'Y'.
    PERFORM CLOSE-FILES.
    STOP RUN.
OPEN-FILES.
    OPEN INPUT INPUT-DATASET.
    OPEN OUTPUT OUTPUT-DATASET.
PROCESS-UPDATE.
    READ INPUT-DATASET
        INTO EMPLOYEE-LAYOUT
        AT END MOVE 'Y' TO EOF-FLAG.
    IF EOF-FLAG = 'Y'
        GO TO PROCESS-UPDATE-EXIT.
    IF EMPNO = '000340'
        MOVE +1000.00 TO BONUS.
    WRITE OUTPUT-DATASET
        FROM EMPLOYEE-LAYOUT.
PROCESS-UPDATE-EXIT.
    EXIT.
CLOSE-FILES.
    CLOSE INPUT-DATASET
         OUTPUT-DATASET.
```

Indeed, many required lines in the COBOL program have been eliminated. Both the SQL statement and the sample COBOL program change the bonus of employee number 000340 to $1,000.00. The SQL example obviously is easier to code and maintain because of the limited size of the statement and the set-level processing inherent in SQL. The COBOL example, though straightforward to a COBOL programmer, is more difficult for most beginning users to code and understand.

NOTE

Set-level processing differs from record-level processing because:

- All operations act on a complete set of rows.
- Fewer operations are necessary to retrieve the desired information.
- Data manipulation and retrieval instructions are simpler.

The set-level processing capabilities of SQL have an immediate and favorable impact on DB2's capability to access and modify data. For example, a single SQL `SELECT` statement can produce an entire report. With the assistance of a query-formatting tool, such as QMF, a general SQL processor, such as `DSNTEP2`, or one of many Windows-based query tools, hours of coding report programs can be eliminated.

FIGURE 1.2.
Record-at-a-time processing versus set-at-a-time processing.

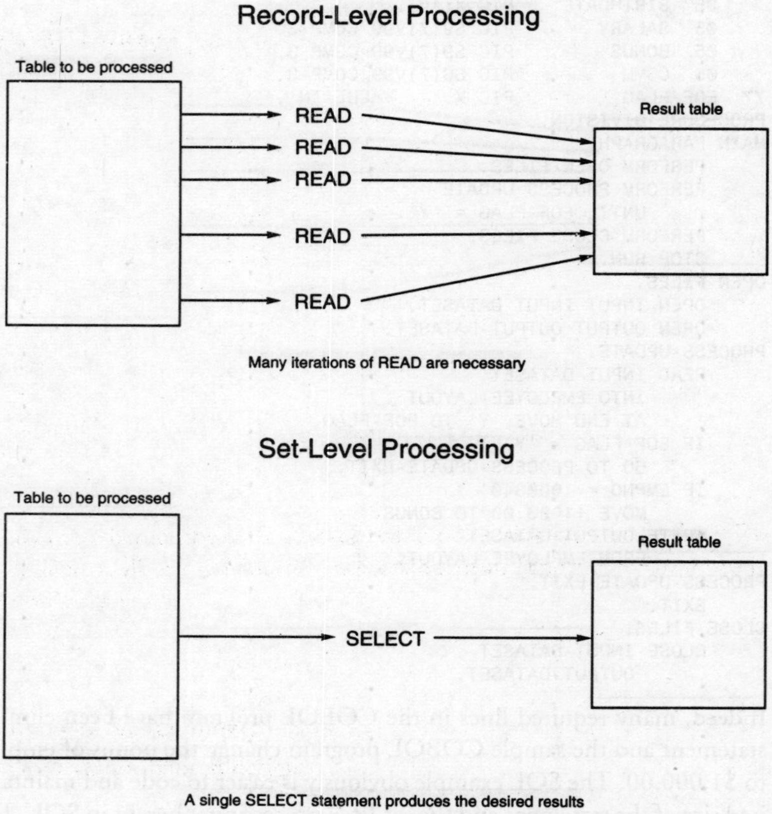

In addition, all of the data-modification capabilities of DB2 act also on a complete set of data, or, more simply, on a DB2 table. For example, consider the following statement:

```
INSERT
INTO DSN8510.EMPPROJACT
    (SELECT   EMPNO, '222222', 1, 0.10,
              '1991-12-30',  '1991-12-31'
     FROM     DSN8510.EMP
     WHERE    WORKDEPT = 'E21');
```

Another benefit of the set-level processing capabilities of DB2 is that SQL can append rows to one table based on data retrieved from another table. The preceding statement assigns every employee of department E21 to activity 1 of project 222222.

A final example of the set-level benefits of SQL is shown in the range of the SQL UPDATE and DELETE statements, which can act on sets of data. This allows the user to use a single SQL statement to update or delete all rows meeting certain conditions.

Types of SQL

SQL is many things to many people. The flexibility of SQL can make it difficult to categorize. Definitive SQL types or categories, however, can be used to group the components of SQL.

Perhaps the most obvious categorization of SQL is based on its functionality. SQL can be used to control, define, and manipulate data, as follows:

- The *Data Control Language* (*DCL*) provides the control statements that govern data security with the GRANT and REVOKE verbs.
- The *Data Definition Language* (*DDL*) creates and maintains the physical data structure with the CREATE, DROP, and ALTER SQL verbs.
- The *Data Manipulation Language* (*DML*) accesses and modifies data with the SELECT, INSERT, DELETE, and UPDATE verbs.

Figure 1.3 depicts this breakdown of SQL statements by functionality.

FIGURE 1.3.
SQL statement types.

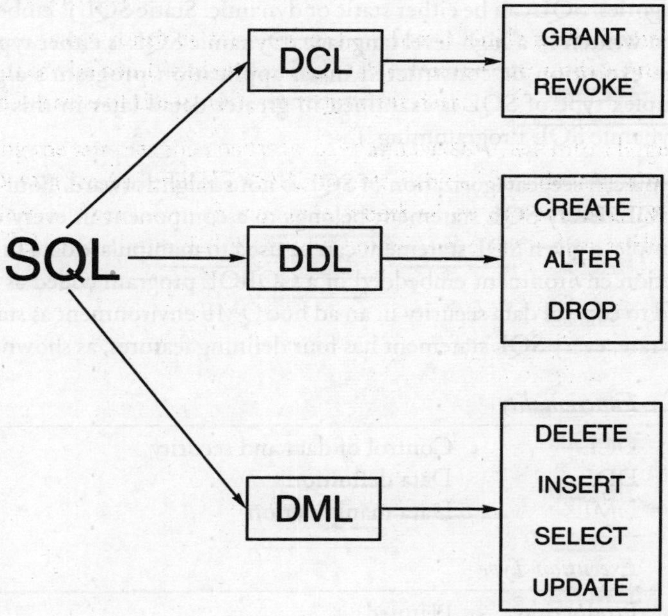

Another way to categorize SQL is by execution type. SQL can be planned and executed as embedded SQL in an application program, or it can be unplanned (ad hoc). The execution of planned SQL usually is referred to as a *production environment.* The production environment is stable and well-defined and can be planned before the execution of the SQL. This approach to data processing is the traditional one, and SQL fits into it nicely. Batch processing, online transaction processing (OLTP), canned reporting, and administrative jobs typify the common production SQL environment. Typical applications in the production environment include accounts receivable, order entry, and inventory control systems.

Ad-hoc SQL, on the other hand, usually is undefined until an immediate need is identified. Upon identification, an unplanned or, at best, hastily planned query is composed and executed. Decision-support processing, data warehouse queries, information-center queries, online analytical processing (OLAP), and critical unplanned reporting needs typify the common ad hoc SQL environment. The ad hoc environment is just as critical, if not more so, to ongoing business of the organization as the production environment.

Another type of SQL can be thought of as existential SQL. SQL has an existence that relies on the vehicle that maintains and supports it. SQL statements can exist either embedded in an application program or as stand-alone entities.

Yet another way to categorize SQL is according to its dynamism. This fourth and final category is probably the most difficult to define and provides the greatest flexibility of all the categories. SQL can be either static or dynamic. Static SQL is embedded in an application program written in a high-level language. Dynamic SQL is either typed in at a terminal for real-time execution or constructed in an application program's algorithms at runtime. This complex type of SQL is examined in greater detail later in this chapter (and in Chapter 6, "Dynamic SQL Programming").

As you can see, categorization of SQL is not straightforward. Four categories define the nature of SQL. Every SQL statement belongs to a component in every one of these categories. For example, a given SQL statement can be used to manipulate data functionally in a planned production environment embedded in a COBOL program coded as static SQL. Or, it could be used to control data security in an ad hoc QMF environment as stand-alone dynamic SQL. At any rate, every SQL statement has four defining features, as shown in the following groupings:

Functionality	
DCL	Control of data and security
DDL	Data definition
DML	Data manipulation

Execution Type	
Production	Planned
Ad hoc	Unplanned

Existence	
Embedded	Requires a program
Stand-alone	No program used

Dynamism	
Dynamic SQL	Changeable at runtime
Static SQL	Unchangeable at runtime

SQL Tools of the Trade

SQL, as a relational data sublanguage, must support certain basic functions. These functions, or tools of the trade, implement the basic features of set-theory functions. You must have a basic understanding of the capabilities of SQL before you can explore the deeper issues of efficiency, development environments, performance, and tuning.

The basic functions of SQL are described in the following sections. Use these sections as a refresher course; they are not meant to teach SQL syntax or provide in-depth coverage of its use.

Selection and Projection

The *selection* operation retrieves a specified subset of rows from a DB2 table. You use predicates in a WHERE clause to specify the search criteria. The SQL implementation for selection is shown in the following example:

```
SELECT    *
FROM      DSN8510.PROJ
WHERE     DEPTNO = 'D01';
```

To retrieve all rows from the PROJ table, simply eliminate the WHERE clause from the statement.

The *projection* operation retrieves a specified subset of columns from a given DB2 table. A DB2 query can provide a list of column names to limit the columns that are retrieved. Projection retrieves all of the rows but only the specified columns. The following statement illustrates the SQL implementation for projection:

```
SELECT    DEPTNO, PROJNO, PROJNAME
FROM      DSN8510.PROJ;
```

Simply, the selection operation determines which rows are retrieved, and the projection operation determines which columns are retrieved.

The SQL SELECT statement is used to implement both the selection and projection operations. In most cases, queries combine selection and projection to retrieve data. The following SQL statement combines the selection and projection operations in the preceding two examples:

```
SELECT    DEPTNO, PROJNO, PROJNAME
FROM      DSN8510.PROJ
WHERE     DEPTNO = 'D01';
```

Joins and Subqueries

The capability to query data from multiple tables using a single SQL statement is one of the nicer features of DB2. The more tables involved in a SELECT statement, however, the more complex the SQL. Complex SQL statements sometimes cause confusion. Therefore, a basic understanding of the multiple table capabilities of SQL is essential for all users.

Joining Tables

The capability of DB2 to combine data from multiple tables is called *joining.* A join, also referred to as an inner join, matches the data from two or more tables, based on the values of one or more columns in each table. All matches are combined, creating a resulting row that is the concatenation of the columns from each table where the specified columns match.

The most common method of joining DB2 tables requires SQL SELECT statements having the following:

- A string of table names separated by commas in the FROM clause
- A WHERE clause comparing the value of a column in one of the joined tables to the value of a column in the other joined table (this is usually an equality comparison)

For example, to query employees and their department names, the EMP table is joined to the DEPT table as follows:

```
SELECT   EMPNO, LASTNAME, DEPTNO, DEPTNAME
FROM     DSN8510.EMP,
         DSN8510.DEPT
WHERE    WORKDEPT = DEPTNO;
```

This method of coding joins, however, has confused many novice SQL programmers. No join verb need be coded explicitly in the SQL SELECT statement to implement table joining. A join can be specified by the presence of more than one table in the FROM clause of the SELECT statement. It is sometimes difficult to grasp the concept of joining tables without a specific JOIN keyword being used in the SQL join statement.

Version 4

DB2 version 4 introduced the JOIN keyword and an alternate method of coding joins. The following two join statements are equivalent to the previous join statement:

```
SELECT   EMPNO, LASTNAME, DEPTNO, DEPTNAME
FROM     DSN8510.EMP JOIN DSN8510.DEPT
ON       WORKDEPT = DEPTNO;
```

or:

```
SELECT   EMPNO, LASTNAME, DEPTNO, DEPTNAME
FROM     DSN8510.EMP INNER JOIN DSN8510.DEPT
ON       WORKDEPT = DEPTNO;
```

Note that the comma-delimited list of tables is replaced with the keyword JOIN or INNER JOIN. The INNER keyword is used to differentiate a normal, or inner, join from an outer join. Outer joins will be discussed in a moment. The INNER keyword is implicit and will be assumed if not explicitly coded.

Likewise, note that using the JOIN keyword requires that the JOIN clause is coded specifying ON instead of WHERE. Additional local predicates can be applied with an additional WHERE clause if so desired.

When coding joins, remember to keep in mind that SQL is a set-level language. If the value of the data in the columns being matched is not unique, multiple matches might be found for each row in each table. Even if the data is unique, many rows could still match if the operation specified in the join criteria is not an equality operation. For example:

```
SELECT  EMPNO, LASTNAME
FROM    DSN8510.EMP,
        DSN8510.DEPT
WHERE   WORKDEPT > DEPTNO;
```

(Admittedly, this example is contrived.) Many rows will match, and could result in the join returning more rows than either table originally contained.

You do not have to join tables based only on equal values. Matching can be achieved with any of the following operations:

=	Equal to
>	Greater than
>=	Greater than or equal to
<>	Not equal to
<	Less than
<=	Less than or equal to

Take care to ensure that the proper join criteria are specified for the columns you are joining. Base the predicates of a join on columns drawn from the same logical domain. For example, consider the following join:

```
SELECT  EMPNO, LASTNAME, DEPTNO, DEPTNAME
FROM    DSN8510.EMP,
        DSN8510.DEPT
WHERE   WORKDEPT = DEPTNO;
```

This is a good example of a join. The employee table is joined to the department table using a logical department code that exists physically as a column in both tables (WORKDEPT in the employee table and DEPTNO in the department table). Both these columns are pooled from the same domain: the set of valid departments for the organization.

You must consider the possible size of the results table before deciding to join tables. Generally, the more data that must be accessed to accomplish the join, the less efficient the join will be. Note that this does not necessarily mean that joining larger tables will result in poorer performance than joining smaller tables. It all depends on the formulation of the query, the design of the database, and the organization of the data. Guidelines for the efficient coding of SQL joins are presented in Chapter 2, "Data Manipulation Guidelines."

More than two tables can be joined in a single SQL statement. As many as 15 DB2 tables can be joined in one SQL statement. This is not usually practical, but it is possible. The order of magnitude for the join is determined by the number of tables specified in the FROM clause. For example, the following join is a three-table join, because three tables—EMP, DEPT, and PROJ—are specified:

```
SELECT  PROJNO, EMPNO, LASTNAME, DEPTNAME
FROM    DSN8510.EMP,
        DSN8510.DEPT,
        DSN8510.PROJ
WHERE   EMPNO = RESPEMP
AND     DEPTNO = WORKDEPT;
```

This example of an equijoin involves three tables. DB2 matches rows in the EMP table with rows in the PROJ table where the two rows match on employee number. Likewise, rows in the EMP table are matched with rows in the DEPT table where the department number is the same. This example produces a results table listing each project number along with information about the employee responsible for the project, including his or her department name.

Version 4

The following is an equivalent formulation of the prior statement using the INNER JOIN keyword, and it would perform similarly:

```
SELECT  PROJNO, EMPNO, LASTNAME, DEPTNAME
FROM    DSN8510.EMP INNER JOIN DSN8510.DEPT
          ON DEPTNO = WORKDEPT
        INNER JOIN DSN8510.PROJ
          ON EMPNO = RESPEMP;
```

The join criteria are specified in the ON clause immediately following the table join specification. Contrast this with the looser, comma-delimited formulation. It is much easier to determine which predicate applies to which join specification when the INNER JOIN syntax is used.

Tables can be joined to themselves also. Consider the following query:

```
SELECT  A.DEPTNO, A.DEPTNAME, A.ADMRDEPT, B.DEPTNAME
FROM    DSN8510.DEPT   A,
        DSN8510.DEPT   B
WHERE   A.ADMRDEPT = B.DEPTNO;
```

This join returns a listing of all department numbers and names, along with the associated department number and name to which the department reports. This listing would not be possible without the capability to join a table to itself.

Joins are possible because all data relationships in DB2 are defined by values in columns instead of by other methods (such as pointers). DB2 can check for matches based solely on the data in the columns specified in the predicates of the WHERE clause in the SQL join statement. When coding a join, you must take extra care to code a proper matching predicate for each table being joined. Failure to do so can result in a *Cartesian product*, the subject of the next section.

Cartesian Products

A *Cartesian product* is the result of a join that does not specify matching columns. Consider the following query:

```
SELECT  *
FROM    DSN8510.DEPT,
        DSN8510.EMP;
```

This query combines every row from the DEPT table with every row in the EMP table. An example of the output from this statement follows:

```
DEPTNO DEPTNAME          MGRNO  ADMRDEPT EMPNO  FIRSTNAME MIDINIT LASTNAME WORKDEPT ...
A00    SPIFFY CO.        000010 A00      000010 CHRISTINE I       HAAS     A00      ...
A00    SPIFFY CO.        000010 A00      000020 MICHAEL   L       THOMPSON B01      ...
A00    SPIFFY CO.        000010 A00      000030 SALLY     A       KWAN     C01      ...
A00    SPIFFY CO.        000010 A00      000040 JOHN      B       GEYER    E01      ...
A00    SPIFFY CO.        000010 A00      000340 JASON     R       GOUNOT   E21      ...
B01    PLANNING          000020 A00      000010 CHRISTINE I       HAAS     A00      ...
B01    PLANNING          000020 A00      000020 MICHAEL   L       THOMPSON B01      ...
B01    PLANNING          000020 A00      000030 SALLY     A       KWAN     C01      ...
B01    PLANNING          000020 A00      000040 JOHN      B       GEYER    E01      ...
E21    SOFTWARE SUP.     000100 E01      000340 JASON     R       GOUNOT   E21      ...
```

All the columns of the DEPT table and all the columns of the EMP table are included in the Cartesian product. For brevity, the example output does not show all of the columns of the EMP table. The output shows the first four rows of the output followed by a break and then additional rows and breaks. A break indicates data that is missing but irrelevant for this discussion.

By analyzing this output, you can see some basic concepts about the Cartesian product. For example, the first row looks okay. Christine I. Haas works in department A00, and the information for department A00 is reported along with her employee information. This is a coincidence. Notice the other rows of the output. In each instance, the DEPTNO does not match the WORKDEPT because we did not specify this in the join statement.

When a table with 1,000 rows is joined as a Cartesian product with a table having 100 rows, the result is 1,000 × 100 rows, or 100,000 rows. These 100,000 rows, however, contain no more information than the original two tables because no criteria was specified for combining the tables. In addition to containing no new information, the result of a Cartesian product is more difficult to understand because the information is now jumbled, whereas before it existed in two separate tables. Avoid Cartesian products.

Subqueries

SQL provides the capability to nest SELECT statements. When one or more SELECT statements are nested in another SELECT statement, the query is referred to as a *subquery.* (Many SQL and DB2 users refer to subqueries as nested SELECTs.) A subquery enables a user to base the search criteria of one SELECT statement on the results of another SELECT statement.

Although you can formulate subqueries in different fashions, they typically are expressed as one SELECT statement connected to another in one of three ways:

- Using the IN (or NOT IN) predicate
- Using the EXISTS (or NOT EXISTS) predicate
- Specifying the equality predicate (=) or the inequality predicate (<>)
- Specifying a predicate using a comparative operator (<, <=, >, or >=)

The following SELECT statement is an example of a SQL subquery:

```
SELECT   DEPTNAME
FROM     DSN8510.DEPT
WHERE    DEPTNO IN
         (SELECT   WORKDEPT
          FROM     DSN8510.EMP
          WHERE    SALARY > 50000);
```

DB2 processes this SQL statement by first evaluating the nested SELECT statement to retrieve all WORKDEPTs where the SALARY is over 50,000. It then matches rows in the DEPT table that correspond to the WORKDEPT values retrieved by the nested SELECT. This match produces a results table that lists the names of all departments where any employee earns more than $50,000. Of course, if more than one employee earns over $50,000 per department, the same DEPTNAME may be listed multiple times in the results set. To eliminate duplicates, the DISTINCT clause must be used. For example:

```
SELECT   DISTINCT DEPTNAME
FROM     DSN8510.DEPT
WHERE    DEPTNO IN
         (SELECT   WORKDEPT
          FROM     DSN8510.EMP
          WHERE    SALARY > 50000);
```

The preceding statements use the IN operator to connect SELECT statements. The following example shows an alternate way of nesting SELECT statements, by means of an equality predicate:

```
SELECT   EMPNO, LASTNAME
FROM     DSN8510.EMP
WHERE    WORKDEPT =
         (SELECT   DEPTNO
          FROM     DSN8510.DEPT
          WHERE    DEPTNAME = 'PLANNING');
```

DB2 processes this SQL statement by retrieving the proper DEPTNO with the nested SELECT statement that is coded to search for the PLANNING department. It then matches rows in the EMP table that correspond to the DEPTNO of the PLANNING department. This match produces a results table that lists all employees in the PLANNING department. Of course, it also assumes that there is only one PLANNING department. If there were more, the SQL statement would fail, because the nested SELECT statement can only return a single row when the = predicate is used.

The capability to express retrieval criteria on nested SELECT statements gives the user of SQL additional flexibility for querying multiple tables. A specialized form of subquery, called a *correlated subquery*, provides a further level of flexibility by permitting the nested SELECT statement to refer back to columns in previous SELECT statements. An example:

```
SELECT   A.WORKDEPT, A.EMPNO, A.FIRSTNAME, A.MIDINIT,
         A.LASTNAME, A.SALARY
FROM     DSN8510.EMP  A
WHERE    A.SALARY >
         (SELECT   AVG(B.SALARY)
          FROM     DSN8510.EMP  B
          WHERE    A.WORKDEPT = B.WORKDEPT)
ORDER BY A.WORKDEPT, A.EMPNO;
```

Look closely at this correlated subquery. It differs from a normal subquery in that the nested SELECT statement refers back to the table in the first SELECT statement. The preceding query returns information for all employees who earn a SALARY greater than the average salary for that employee's given department. This is accomplished by the correlation of the WORKDEPT column in the nested SELECT statement to the WORKDEPT column in the first SELECT statement.

The following example illustrates an alternative form of correlated subquery using the EXISTS predicate:

```
SELECT   A.EMPNO, A.LASTNAME, A.FIRSTNAME
FROM     DSN8510.EMP  A
WHERE    EXISTS
         (SELECT '1'
          FROM    DSN8510.DEPT  B
          WHERE   B.DEPTNO = A.WORKDEPT
          AND     B.DEPTNAME = 'OPERATIONS');
```

This query returns the names of all employees who work in the OPERATIONS department.

A *non-correlated subquery* is processed in bottom-to-top fashion. The bottommost query is materialized and, based on the results, the topmost query is resolved. A correlated subquery works in a top-bottom-top fashion. The topmost query is analyzed, and based on the analysis, the bottommost query is initiated. The bottommost query, however, relies on the topmost query to evaluate its predicate. After processing for the first instance of the topmost query, therefore, DB2 must return to that query for another value and repeat the process until the results table is complete.

Both forms of subqueries enable you to base the qualifications of one retrieval on the results of another.

Joins Versus Subqueries

A subquery can be converted to an equivalent join. The concept behind both types of queries is to retrieve data from multiple tables based on search criteria matching data in the tables.

Consider the following two SELECT statements. The first is a subquery:

```
SELECT  EMPNO, LASTNAME
FROM    DSN8510.EMP
WHERE   WORKDEPT IN
        (SELECT  DEPTNO
         FROM    DSN8510.DEPT
         WHERE   DEPTNAME = 'PLANNING');
```

The second SELECT statement is a join:

```
SELECT  EMPNO, LASTNAME
FROM    DSN8510.EMP,
        DSN8510.DEPT
WHERE   WORKDEPT = DEPTNO
AND     DEPTNAME = 'PLANNING';
```

Both of these queries return the employee numbers and last names of all employees who work in the PLANNING department.

Let's first discuss the subquery formulation of this request. The list of valid DEPTNOs is retrieved from the DEPT table for the DEPTNAME of 'PLANNING'. This DEPTNO list then is compared against the WORKDEPT column of the EMP table. Employees with a WORKDEPT that matches any DEPTNO are retrieved.

The join operates in a similar manner. In fact, the DB2 optimizer can be intelligent enough to transform a subquery into its corresponding join format before *optimization*; optimization is covered in depth in Chapter 14, "The Optimizer."

The decision to use a subquery, a correlated subquery, or a join usually is based on performance. In earlier releases of DB2, the performance of logically equivalent queries could vary greatly, depending on whether they were coded as a subquery or a join. With the performance changes made to DB2 from V3 through V5, worrying about the performance of joins and subqueries is usually not worth the effort.

As a general rule, I suggest using joins over the other two types of multitable data retrieval. This provides a consistent base from which to operate. By promoting joins over subqueries, you can meet the needs of most users and diminish confusion. If you need to squeeze the most performance from a system, however, try rewriting multitable data retrieval SQL SELECT statements as both a join and a subquery. Test the performance of each SQL formulation and use the one that performs best.

Union

The *union* operation combines two sets of rows into a single set composed of all the rows in either or both of the two original sets. The two original sets must be *union-compatible.* For union compatibility:

- The two sets must contain the same number of columns.
- Each column of the first set must be either the same data type as the corresponding column of the second set *or* convertible to the same data type as the corresponding column of the second set.

In purest set-theory form, the union of two sets contains no duplicates; but DB2 provides the option of retaining or eliminating duplicates. The UNION verb eliminates duplicates; UNION ALL retains them.

An example of the SQL UNION verb follows:

```
SELECT  CREATOR, NAME, 'TABLE   '
FROM    SYSIBM.SYSTABLES
WHERE   TYPE = 'T'
UNION
SELECT  CREATOR, NAME, 'VIEW    '
FROM    SYSIBM.SYSTABLES
WHERE   TYPE = 'V'
UNION
SELECT  CREATOR, NAME, 'ALIAS   '
FROM    SYSIBM.SYSTABLES
WHERE   TYPE = 'A'
UNION
SELECT  CREATOR, NAME, 'SYNONYM'
FROM    SYSIBM.SYSSYNONYMS;
```

This SQL UNION retrieves all the tables, views, aliases, and synonyms in the DB2 Catalog. Notice that each SELECT statement tied together using the UNION verb has the same number of columns, and each column has the same data type and length. This statement could be changed to use UNION ALL instead of UNION, because you know that none of the SELECTs will return duplicate rows. (A table cannot be a view, a view cannot be an alias, and so on.)

The ability to use UNION to construct results data is essential to formulating some of the more complex forms of SQL. This is demonstrated in the next section.

One last comment about unions: When results from two SELECT statements accessing the same table are combined using UNION, remember that the same result can be achieved using the OR clause. Moreover, the use of OR is preferable to the use of UNION because the OR formulation:

- Is generally easier for most users to understand
- Tends to outperform UNION

Consider the following two queries:

```
SELECT  EMPNO
FROM    DSN8510.EMP
WHERE   LASTNAME = 'HAAS'
UNION
SELECT  EMPNO
FROM    DSN8510.EMP
WHERE   JOB = 'PRES';
```

and:

```
SELECT   EMPNO
FROM     DSN8510.EMP
WHERE    LASTNAME = 'HAAS'
OR       JOB = 'PRES';
```

After scrutinizing these queries, you can see that the two statements are equivalent. If the two SELECT statements were accessing different tables, however, the UNION could not be changed to an equivalent form using OR.

> **NOTE**
>
> A literal can be used in the UNION query to indicate which predicate was satisfied for each particular row—for example:
>
> ```
> SELECT   EMPNO, 'NAME=HAAS'
> FROM     DSN8510.EMP
> WHERE    LASTNAME = 'HAAS'
> UNION
> SELECT   EMPNO, "JOB =PRES'
> FROM     DSN8510.EMP
> WHERE    JOB = 'PRES';
> ```
>
> The result set from the query using OR cannot include a literal. However, if rows exists that satisfy both predicates, the results of the UNION query will not match the results of the OR query because the literal will cause the duplicates to remain (when the literal is added, the row is no longer a duplicate).

Outer Join

Version 4

As discussed previously, when tables are joined, the rows that are returned contain matching values for the columns specified in the join predicates. Sometimes, however, it is desirable to return both matching and non-matching rows for one or more of the tables being joined. This is known as an *outer join*. Prior to version 4, DB2 did not explicitly support outer joins. Instead, users were forced to accommodate outer join processing by combining a join and a correlated subquery with the UNION verb.

Before we progress to discussing how to code an outer join, let's first clarify the concept of an outer join. Suppose that you want a report on the departments in your organization, presented in department number (DEPTNO) order. This information is in the DEPT sample table. You also want the last name of the manager of each department. Your first attempt at this request might look like this:

```
SELECT   DISTINCT
         D.DEPTNO, D.DEPTNAME, D.MGRNO, E.LASTNAME
FROM     DSN8510.DEPT   D,
         DSN8510.EMP    E
WHERE    D.MGRNO = E.EMPNO;
```

This example, using an inner join, appears to satisfy your objective. However, if a department does not have a manager or if a department has been assigned a manager who is not recorded in the EMP table, your report would not list every department. The predicate D.MGRNO = E.EMPNO is not met for these types of rows. In addition, a MGRNO is not assigned to the DEVELOPMENT CENTER department in the DEPT sample table. That department therefore is not listed in the result set for the preceding query.

The following query corrects the problem by using UNION to concatenate the non-matching rows:

```
SELECT   DISTINCT
         D.DEPTNO, D.DEPTNAME, D.MGRNO, E.LASTNAME
FROM     DSN8510.DEPT  D,
         DSN8510.EMP   E
WHERE    D.MGRNO = E.EMPNO
UNION
SELECT   DISTINCT
         D.DEPTNO, D.DEPTNAME, D.MGRNO, '* No Mgr Name *'
FROM     DSN8510.DEPT  D
WHERE    NOT EXISTS
         (SELECT  EMPNO
          FROM    DSN8510.EMP  E
          WHERE   D.MGRNO = E.EMPNO)
ORDER BY 1;
```

By providing the constant '* No Mgr Name *' in place of the nonexistent data, and by coding a correlated subquery with the NOT EXISTS operator, the rows that do not match are returned. UNION appends the two sets of data, returning a complete report of departments, regardless of whether the department has a valid manager.

This was the standard way to code an outer join with DB2 SQL for DB2 version 3 and all previous releases. DB2 version 4 simplifies this query significantly:

```
SELECT   DEPTNO, DEPTNAME, MGRNO, LASTNAME
FROM     DSN8510.EMP LEFT OUTER JOIN DSN8510.DEPT
           ON EMPNO = MGRNO;
```

The keywords LEFT OUTER JOIN cause DB2 to invoke an outer join, returning rows that have matching values in the predicate columns, but also returning unmatched rows from the table on the left side of the join. In the case of the left outer join example shown, this would be the EMP table, because it is on the left side of the join clause.

Note that the WHERE keyword is replaced with the ON keyword for the outer join statement. Additionally, the missing values in the result set are filled with nulls (not a sample default as shown in the previous example). Use the VALUE (or COALESCE) function to fill in the missing values with a default, as shown in the following SQL query:

```
SELECT   DEPTNO, DEPTNAME, MGRNO, VALUE(LASTNAME, '* No Mgr Name *')
FROM     DSN8510.EMP LEFT OUTER JOIN DSN8510.DEPT
         ON EMPNO = MGRNO;
```

Types of Outer Joins

Version 4

There are three types of outer joins supported by DB2 V4:

- LEFT OUTER JOIN
- RIGHT OUTER JOIN
- FULL OUTER JOIN

The keywords LEFT OUTER JOIN, RIGHT OUTER JOIN, and FULL OUTER JOIN can be used in place of the INNER JOIN keyword to indicate an outer join.

As you might guess, the keywords RIGHT OUTER JOIN cause DB2 to return rows that have matching values in the predicate columns but also return unmatched rows from the table on the right side of the join. So the following outer join is 100 percent equivalent to the previous query:

```
SELECT   DEPTNO, DEPTNAME, MGRNO, LASTNAME
FROM     DSN8510.DEPT RIGHT OUTER JOIN DSN8510.EMP
             ON EMPNO = MGRNO;
```

The only code change was swapping the position of the DEPT and EMP tables in the FROM clause and changing from a LEFT OUTER JOIN to a RIGHT OUTER JOIN. In general practice, it is wise to avoid RIGHT OUTER JOIN statements, instead converting them to LEFT OUTER JOIN statements.

The remaining outer join option is the FULL OUTER JOIN. It, like all previous outer joins, returns matching rows from both tables, but it also returns non-matching rows from both tables, left and right. A FULL OUTER JOIN can use only the equal (=) comparison operator. Left and right outer joins are able to use all the comparison operators. An example of the FULL OUTER JOIN follows:

```
SELECT   EMPNO, WORKDEPT, DEPTNAME
FROM     DSN8510.EMP FULL OUTER JOIN DSN8510.DEPT
             ON WORKDEPT = DEPTNO;
```

In this example, all of the following will be returned in the results set:

- Rows where there are matches indicating that the employee works in a specific department (for example, where WORKDEPT in EMP matches DEPTNO in DEPT).
- Employee rows where there is no matching department in the DEPT table (for example, where a WORKDEPT in EMP has no matching DEPTNO in DEPT). This could occur when an employee is temporarily unassigned to a department or the employee is assigned to an invalid department.
- Department rows where there is no matching work department in the EMP table (for example, where a DEPTNO in DEPT has no matching WORKDEPT in EMP). This could occur when a department has no employees assigned to it.

This section outlines the basics of the outer join. For suggestions on proper implementation, refer to Chapter 2.

Sorting and Grouping

SQL also can sort and group retrieved data. The ORDER BY clause sorts the results of a query in the specified order (ascending or descending) for each column. The GROUP BY clause collates the resultant rows to apply functions that consolidate the data. By grouping data, users can use statistical functions on a column (discussed later) and eliminate non-pertinent groups of data with the HAVING clause.

For example, the following query groups employee data by department, returning the aggregate salary for each department:

```
SELECT    DEPTNO, SUM(SALARY)
FROM      DSN8510.DEPT
GROUP BY DEPTNO;
```

By adding a HAVING clause to this query, you can eliminate aggregated data that is not required. For example, if you're interested in departments with an average salary of less than $17,500, you can code the following query:

```
SELECT    DEPTNO, SUM(SALARY)
FROM      DSN8510.DEPT
GROUP BY DEPTNO
HAVING    AVG(SALARY) < 17500 ;
```

Note that the report is not necessarily returned in any specific order. The GROUP BY clause does not sort the data for the result set; it only consolidates the data values for grouping. To return the results of this query in a particular order, you must use the ORDER BY clause. For example, to order the resultant data into descending department number order, code the following:

```
SELECT    DEPTNO, SUM(SALARY)
FROM      DSN8510.DEPT
GROUP BY DEPTNO
HAVING    AVG(SALARY) < 17500
ORDER BY DEPTNO ;
```

The ORDER BY, GROUP BY, and HAVING clauses are important SQL features that can increase productivity. They are the only means of sorting and grouping data in SQL.

The Difference Between HAVING and WHERE

The WHERE and HAVING clauses are similar in terms of functionality. However, they operate on different types of data.

Any SQL statement can use a WHERE clause to indicate which rows of data are to be returned. The WHERE clause operates on "detail" data rows from tables, views, synonyms, and aliases.

The HAVING clause, on the other hand, operates on "aggregated" groups of information. Only SQL statements that specify the GROUP BY clause can use the HAVING clause. The predicates in the HAVING clause are applied after the GROUP BY has been applied.

If both a WHERE clause and a HAVING clause are coded on the same SQL statement, the following occurs:

- The WHERE clause is applied to the "detail" rows.
- The GROUP BY is applied to aggregate the data.
- The HAVING clause is applied to the "aggregate" rows.

Consider the following SQL:

```
SELECT   WORKDEPT, AVG(BONUS), MAX(BONUS), MIN(BONUS)
FROM     DSN8510.EMP
WHERE    WORKDEPT NOT IN ('D11', 'D12')
GROUP BY WORKDEPT
HAVING   COUNT(*) > 1;
```

This query will return the average, maximum, and minimum bonus for each department except 'D11' and 'D12', as long as the department has more than 1 employee. The steps DB2 takes to satisfy this query are:

- Apply the WHERE clause to eliminate departments 'D11' and 'D12'
- Apply the GROUP BY clause to aggregate the data by department
- Apply the HAVING clause to eliminate any department groups consisting of only one employee

Relational Division

A very useful, though somewhat complex SQL statement is relational division. Because of its complexity, developers often avoid relational division, but it is wise to understand relational division because of its power and usefulness. The *relational division* of two tables is the operation of returning rows whereby column values in one table match column values for *every* corresponding row in the other table.

For example, look at the following query:

```
SELECT   DISTINCT PROJNO
FROM     DSN8510.PROJACT  P1
WHERE    NOT EXISTS
        (SELECT ACTNO
         FROM   DSN8510.ACT  A
         WHERE  NOT EXISTS
               (SELECT PROJNO
                FROM   DSN8510.PROJACT  P2
                WHERE  P1.PROJNO = P2.PROJNO
                AND    A.ACTNO = P2.ACTNO);
```

Division is implemented in SQL using a combination of correlated subqueries. This query is accomplished by coding three correlated subqueries that match projects and activities. It retrieves all projects that require every activity listing in the activity table.

NOTE

If you execute this query, no rows are returned because no projects in the sample data require all activities.

Relational division is a powerful operation and should be utilized whenever practical. Implementing relational division using a complex query such as the one depicted above will *almost* always outperform an equivalent application program using separate cursors processing three individual SELECT statements. However, this query is complicated and may be difficult for novice programmers to understand and maintain as your application changes.

CASE Expressions

Version 5

The CASE expression, new to DB2 version 5, is similar to CASE statements used by many popular programming languages. A CASE statement uses the value of a specified expression to select one statement among several for execution. A common application of the CASE statement will be to eliminate a multitable UNION statement, for example:

```
SELECT  CREATOR, NAME, 'TABLE'
FROM    SYSIBM.SYSTABLES
WHERE   TYPE = 'T'
UNION
SELECT  CREATOR, NAME, 'VIEW '
FROM    SYSIBM.SYSTABLES
WHERE   TYPE = 'V'
UNION
SELECT  CREATOR, NAME, 'ALIAS'
FROM    SYSIBM.SYSTABLES
WHERE   TYPE = 'A';
```

It can be coded more simply as

```
SELECT CREATOR, NAME,
CASE TYPE
  WHEN 'T' THEN 'TABLE'
  WHEN 'V' THEN 'VIEW '
  WHEN 'A' THEN 'ALIAS'
END
FROM SYSIBM.SYSTABLES;
```

The WHEN clause of the CASE expression replaces the predicates from each of the SELECT statements in the UNION. When CASE is used in place of multiple UNIONs, performance most likely will be improved because DB2 will make fewer passes against the data to return a result set. In the preceding example, one pass is required instead of three.

There are two types of CASE expressions: those with a simple WHEN clause and those with a searched WHEN clause. The previous example depicts a simple WHEN clause. Simple WHEN clauses only test for equality of an expression. Searched WHEN clauses provide more complex expression testing. An example follows:

```
SELECT EMPNO, LASTNAME,
   CASE  WHEN SALARY < 0. THEN 'ERROR'
     WHEN SALARY = 0. THEN 'NONE '
     WHEN SALARY BETWEEN 1. AND 20000. THEN 'LOW  '
     WHEN SALARY BETWEEN 20001. AND 50000. THEN 'MID  '
     WHEN SALARY BETWEEN 50001. AND 99999. THEN 'HIGH '
     ELSE '100+ '
   END
FROM DSN8510.EMP;
```

In this case, the SALARY column is examined by the CASE expression to place it into a specific, predefined category. CASE expressions also can be specified in a WHERE clause, for example:

```
SELECT  EMPNO, PROJNO, ACTNO, EMPTIME
FROM    DSN8510.EMPPROJACT
WHERE   (CASE
           EMPTIME=0. THEN 0.
         ELSE
           40./EMPTIME
         END) > 25;
```

This query returns data for employees who are allocated to spend more than 25 hours (of a typical 40 hour work week) on a specific activity. The CASE expression is used to avoid division by zero. The EMPTIME column ranges from 0.0 to 1.0 and indicates the ratio of time to be spent on an activity. When EMPTIME is zero, the CASE expression substitutes zero and avoids the calculation.

Another valuable use of the CASE expression is to perform table pivoting. A common requirement is to take a normalized table and produce denormalized query results. For example, consider the following table containing monthly sales numbers:

```
CREATE TABLE SALES
  (SALES_MGR     INTEGER          NOT NULL,
   MONTH         INTEGER          NOT NULL,
   YEAR          CHAR(4)          NOT NULL,
   SALES_AMT     DECIMAL(11,2) NOT NULL WITH DEFAULT);
```

The table contains 12 rows, one for each month, detailing the amount of product sold by the specified sales manager. A standard query can be produced using a simple SELECT statement. However, many users prefer to see the months strung out as columns, showing one row per sales manager with a bucket for each month. This is known as table pivoting and can be produced using the following SQL statement, using the CASE expression in the SELECT list:

```
SELECT SALES_MGR,
  MAX(CASE MONTH WHEN 1 THEN SALES_AMT ELSE NULL END) AS JAN,
  MAX(CASE MONTH WHEN 2 THEN SALES_AMT ELSE NULL END) AS FEB,
  MAX(CASE MONTH WHEN 3 THEN SALES_AMT ELSE NULL END) AS MAR,
  MAX(CASE MONTH WHEN 4 THEN SALES_AMT ELSE NULL END) AS APR,
  MAX(CASE MONTH WHEN 5 THEN SALES_AMT ELSE NULL END) AS MAY,
  MAX(CASE MONTH WHEN 6 THEN SALES_AMT ELSE NULL END) AS JUN,
```

```
    MAX(CASE MONTH WHEN 7 THEN SALES_AMT ELSE NULL END) AS JUL,
    MAX(CASE MONTH WHEN 8 THEN SALES_AMT ELSE NULL END) AS AUG,
    MAX(CASE MONTH WHEN 9 THEN SALES_AMT ELSE NULL END) AS SEP,
    MAX(CASE MONTH WHEN 10 THEN SALES_AMT ELSE NULL END) AS OCT,
    MAX(CASE MONTH WHEN 11 THEN SALES_AMT ELSE NULL END) AS NOV,
    MAX(CASE MONTH WHEN 12 THEN SALES_AMT ELSE NULL END) AS DEC
FROM SALES
WHERE YEAR = ?;
```

The results will be spread out across a single row for the year specified. Other uses for CASE include rounding numeric data (containing positive and negative numbers), performing different calculations based on type indicators, and converting two-digit dates.

Column and Scalar Functions

Two types of functions can be applied to data in a DB2 table using SQL: *column functions* and *scalar functions*. You can use these functions to further simplify the requirements of complex data access.

Column Functions

Column functions compute, from a group of rows, a single value for a designated column or expression. This provides the capability to aggregate data, thereby enabling you to perform statistical calculations across many rows with one SQL statement. To fully appreciate the column functions, you must understand SQL's set-level processing capabilities.

The column functions are AVG, COUNT, MAX, MIN, and SUM:

AVG — The AVG function computes the average of the column or expression specified as an argument. This function operates only on numeric arguments. The following example calculates the average salary of each department:

```
SELECT   WORKDEPT, AVG(SALARY)
FROM     DSN8510.EMP
GROUP BY WORKDEPT;
```

COUNT — The COUNT function counts the number of rows in a table, or the number of distinct values for a given column. It can operate, therefore, at the column or row level. The syntax differs for each. To count the number of rows in the EMP table, issue this SQL statement:

```
SELECT   COUNT(*)
FROM     DSN8510.EMP;
```

To count the number of distinct departments represented in the EMP table, issue the following:

```
SELECT   COUNT(DISTINCT WORKDEPT)
FROM     DSN8510.EMP;
```

MAX The MAX function returns the largest value in the specified column or expression. The following SQL statement determines the project with the latest end date:

```
SELECT   MAX(ACENDATE)
FROM     DSN8510.PROJACT;
```

MIN The MIN function returns the smallest value in the specified column or expression. To retrieve the smallest bonus given to any employee, issue this SQL statement:

```
SELECT   MIN(BONUS)
FROM     DSN8510.EMP;
```

SUM The accumulated total of all values in the specified column or expression are returned by the SUM column function. For example, the following SQL statement calculates the total yearly monetary output for the corporation:

```
SELECT   SUM(SALARY+COMM+BONUS)
FROM     DSN8510.EMP;
```

This SQL statement adds each employee's salary, commission, and bonus. It then aggregates these results into a single value representing the total amount of compensation paid to all employees.

NOTE

The result of the MAX or MIN function has the same data type as the column or expression on which it operates. You cannot apply the MAX and MIN functions to long string columns and long graphic columns.

This list shows some rules for the column functions:

- Column functions can be executed only in SELECT statements.
- A column function must be specified for an explicitly named column or expression.
- Each column function returns only one value for the set of selected rows.
- If you apply a column function to one column in a SELECT statement, you must apply column functions to any other columns specified in the same SELECT statement, unless you also use the GROUP BY clause.
- Use GROUP BY to apply a column function to a group of named columns. Any other column named in the SELECT statement must be operated on by a column function.
- The result of any column function (except the COUNT function) will have the same data type as the column to which it was applied. The COUNT function returns an integer number.

- The result of any column function (except the COUNT function) can be null. COUNT always returns a numeric result.
- Column functions will not return a SQLCODE of +100 if the predicate specified in the WHERE clause finds no data. Instead, a null is returned. For example, consider the following SQL statement:

```
SELECT    MAX(SALARY)
FROM      DSN8510.EMP
WHERE     EMPNO = '999999';
```

  There is no employee with an EMPNO of '999999' in the DSN8510.EMP table. This statement therefore returns a null for the MAX(SALARY).
- When using the AVG, MAX, MIN, and SUM functions on nullable columns, all occurrences of null are eliminated before applying the function.
- You can use the DISTINCT keyword with all column functions to eliminate duplicates before applying the given function. DISTINCT has no effect, however, on the MAX and MIN functions.
- You can use the ALL keyword to indicate that duplicates should not be eliminated. ALL is the default.

Scalar Functions

Scalar functions are applied to a column or expression and operate on a single value. Contrast this with the column functions, which are applied to a set of data.

There are 22 scalar functions, each of which can be applied to a column value or expression. The result is a transformed version of the column or expression being operated on. The transformation of the value is based on the scalar function being applied and the value itself. Consult the following descriptions of the DB2 scalar functions:

CHAR	Converts a DB2 date, time, timestamp, or decimal value to a character value.
COALESCE	For nullable columns, returns a value instead of a null (equivalent to the VALUE function). Version 4
DATE	Converts a value representing a date to a DB2 date. The value to be converted can be a DB2 timestamp, a DB2 date, a positive integer, or a character string.
DAY	Returns the day portion of a DB2 date or timestamp.
DAYS	Converts a DB2 date or timestamp into an integer value representing one more than the number of days since January 1, 0001.
DECIMAL	Converts any numeric value to a decimal value.
DIGITS	Converts a number to a character string of digits. Be aware that the DIGITS function will truncate the negative sign for negative numbers.

`FLOAT`	Converts any numeric value to a floating-point value.
`HEX`	Converts any value other than a long string to hexadecimal.
`HOUR`	Returns the hour portion of a time, a timestamp, or a duration.
`INTEGER`	Converts any number to an integer by truncating the portion of the number to the right of the decimal point. If the whole number portion of the number is not a valid integer (for example, the value is out of range), an error results.
`LENGTH`	Returns the length of any column, which may be null. Does not include the length of null indicators or variable character-length control values, but does include trailing blanks for character columns.
Version 5 `NULLIF`	Returns a null when two specified expressions are equal; if not equal, the first expression is returned.
`MICROSECOND`	Returns the microsecond portion of a timestamp.
`MINUTE`	Returns the minute portion of a time, a timestamp, or a duration.
`MONTH`	Returns the month portion of a date, a timestamp, or a duration.
`SECOND`	Returns the second portion of a time, a timestamp, or a duration.
Version 5 `STRIP`	Removes leading, trailing, or both leading and trailing blanks (or any specific character) from a string expression.
`SUBSTR`	Returns the specified portion of a character column from any starting point to any ending point.
`TIME`	Converts a value representing a valid time to a DB2 time. The value to be converted can be a DB2 timestamp, a DB2 time, or a character string.
`TIMESTAMP`	Obtains a timestamp from another timestamp, a valid character-string representation of a timestamp, or a combination of date and time values.
`VALUE`	For nullable columns, returns a value instead of a null (equivalent to `COALESCE` function).
`VARGRAPHIC`	Converts a character string to a graphic string.
`YEAR`	Returns the year portion of a date, a timestamp, or a duration.

Some rules for the scalar functions follow:

- Scalar functions can be executed in the select list of the SQL `SELECT` statement or as part of a `WHERE` or `HAVING` clause.
- A scalar function can be used wherever an expression can be used.
- The argument for a scalar function can be a column function.

Definition of DB2 Data Structures

You also can use SQL to define DB2 data structures. DB2 data structures are referred to as *objects*. Each DB2 object is used to support the structure of the data being stored. There are DB2 objects to support groups of DASD volumes, VSAM data sets, table representations, and data order, among others. A description of each type of DB2 object follows:

`ALIAS`	A locally defined name for a table or view in the same local DB2 subsystem or in a remote DB2 subsystem. Aliases give a DB2 location independence because an alias can be created for a table at a remote site, thereby freeing the user from specifying the site that contains the data. Aliases can be used also as a type of global synonym because they can be accessed by anyone, not only by their creator.
`COLUMN`	A single, non-decomposable data element in a DB2 table.
`DATABASE`	A logical grouping of DB2 objects related by common characteristics, such as logical functionality, relation to an application system or subsystem, or type of data. A database holds no data of its own but exists to group DB2 objects. A database can function also as a unit of start and stop for the DB2 objects defined to it or as a unit of control for the administration of DB2 security.
`INDEX`	A DB2 object that consists of one or more VSAM data sets. To achieve more efficient access to DB2 tables, these data sets contain pointers ordered based on the value of data in specified columns of a table. For partitioned tablespaces, an index is required to assign rows to the appropriate partition.
`STOGROUP`	A series of DASD volumes assigned a unique name and used to allocate VSAM data sets for DB2 objects.
`SYNONYM`	An alternative, private name for a table or view. A synonym can be used only by the individual who creates it.
`TABLE`	A DB2 object that consists of columns and rows that define the physical characteristics of the data to be stored.
`TABLESPACE`	A DB2 object that defines the physical structure of the data sets used to house the DB2 table data.
`VIEW`	A virtual table consisting of a SQL `SELECT` statement that accesses data from one or more tables or views. A `VIEW` never stores data. When you access a `VIEW`, the SQL statement that defines it is executed to derive the requested data.

These objects are created with the `DCL` verbs of SQL and must be created in a specific order. See Figure 1.4 for the hierarchy of DB2 objects.

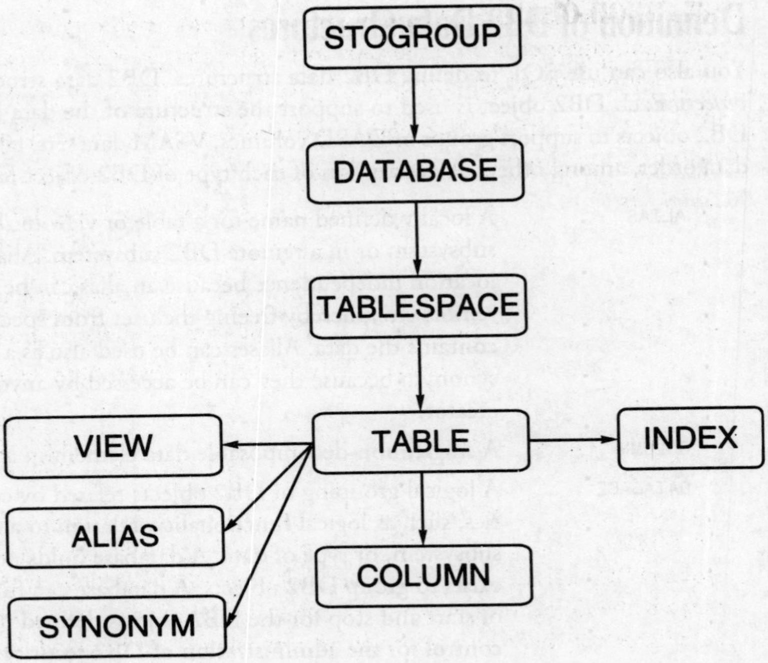

FIGURE 1.4.
The DB2 object hierarchy.

Security Control over DB2 Data Structures

The data-control feature of SQL provides security for DB2 objects, data, and resources with the GRANT and REVOKE verbs. The hierarchy of DB2 security types and levels is complicated, and can be confusing at first glance (see Figure 1.5).

You can administer group and individual levels of DB2 security. A group-level security specification is composed of other group-level and individual security specifications. Individual security is a single authorization for a single object or resource.

The group-level authorizations are enclosed in boxes in Figure 1.5. This list shows these authorizations:

INSTALL SYSADM	Authority for the entire system at installation time
SYSADM	Authority for the entire system
INSTALL SYSOPR	Authority for the entire system at installation time
SYSOPR	Authority for the entire system
SYSCTRL	Authority for the entire system
BINDAGENT	Authority for the entire system
PACKADM	Authority for all packages in a specific collection or collections

DBADM	Authority for a specific database
DBCTRL	Authority for a specific database
DBMAINT	Authority for a specific database

FIGURE 1.5.
DB2 security levels.

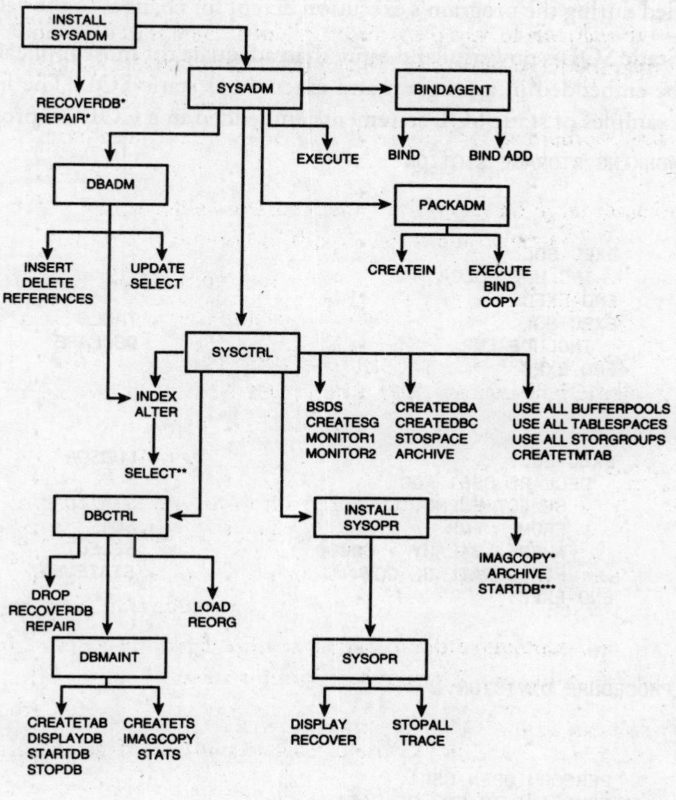

* This security applies to the DB2 Directory Database (DSNDB01) and the DB2 Catalog Database (DSNDB06). Install SYSADM can also run CATMAINT.

** This security applies only to the DB2 Catalog tables.

*** Cannot change ACCESS mode.

Each group-level authorization is composed of the group and individual security levels connected by arrows in Figure 1.5. For example, INSTALL SYSOPR is composed of IMAGCOPY authority for the DB2 Catalog and SYSOPR authority, which in turn is composed of the DISPLAY, RECOVER, STOPALL, and TRACE authorities.

The effective administration of these levels of security often is a job in itself. Guidelines for the efficient utilization and administration of DB2 security are in Chapter 4.

Static SQL

Most DB2 application programs use static SQL to access DB2 tables. A *static SQL statement* is a complete, unchanging statement hard-coded into an application program. It cannot be modified during the program's execution except for changes to the values assigned to host variables.

Static SQL is powerful and more than adequate for most applications. Any SQL statement can be embedded in a program and executed as static SQL. The following listing shows several examples of static SQL statements embedded in a COBOL program.

```
WORKING-STORAGE SECTION.
          .
          .
          .
     EXEC SQL
       INCLUDE SQLCA
     END-EXEC.
     EXEC SQL                                           TABLE
       INCLUDE EMP                                      DECLARE
     END-EXEC.
          .
          .
          .
     EXEC SQL                                           CURSOR
       DECLARE CSR1 FOR
         SELECT EMPNO, COMM                             STATIC
         FROM   EMP                                     SQL
         WHERE  SALARY > 60000                          SELECT
         FOR UPDATE OF COMM                             STATEMENT
     END-EXEC.
          .
          .
          .
PROCEDURE DIVISION.
          .
          .
          .
     PERFORM OPEN-CSR1.
     MOVE 'N' TO END-OF-DATA.
     PERFORM FETCH-AND-MODIFY
       UNTIL END-OF-DATA = 'Y'.
     STOP RUN.
FETCH-AND-MODIFY.
     EXEC SQL
       FETCH CSR1 INTO :HOST-EMPNO,                     EMBEDDED
                       :HOST-COMM                       FETCH
     END-EXEC.
     IF SQLCODE < +0
       PERFORM ERROR-ROUTINE
     ELSE
       IF SQLCODE = +100
         MOVE 'Y' TO END-OF-DATA
       ELSE
         PERFORM MODIFY-COMM.
MODIFY-COMM.
     IF HOST-COM < 1000
```

```
    COMPUTE HOST-COMM = HOST-COMM + 100.
  EXEC SQL
    UPDATE  EMP                                 STATIC
      SET COMM = :HOST-COMM                     SQL
    WHERE CURRENT OF CSR1                       UPDATE
  END-EXEC..                                    STATEMENT
  IF SQLCODE < 0
      PERFORM ERROR_ROUTINE.
OPEN-CSR.
  EXEC SQL
    OPEN CSR1
  END-EXEC.                                     OPEN &
CLOSE-CSR.                                      CLOSE
  EXEC SQL                                      CURSOR
    CLOSE CSR1                                  STATEMENTS
  END-EXEC.
```

To embed static SQL in a host program, you must prepare for the impedance mismatch between a high-level language and SQL. *Impedance mismatch* refers to the difference between set-at-a-time processing and record-at-a-time processing. High-level languages access data one record at a time, whereas SQL accesses data at a set level. Although DB2 always accesses data at the set level, the host program uses a structure called a *cursor* to access the set-level data one row at a time. SQL statements are coded with cursors that are opened, fetched from, and closed during the execution of the application program.

Static SQL is flexible enough that most application programmers never need to know any other means of embedding SQL in a program using a high-level language. Coding methods and guidelines are covered comprehensively in Chapter 5, "Using DB2 in an Application Program," where embedded SQL programming is discussed.

Sometimes, static SQL cannot satisfy an application's access requirements. For these types of dynamic applications, you can use another type of SQL: *dynamic SQL*.

Dynamic SQL

Dynamic SQL is embedded in an application program and can change during the program's execution. Dynamic SQL statements are coded explicitly in host-language variables, prepared by the application program, and then executed. QMF and SPUFI are two examples of programs that execute dynamic SQL statements.

Recall that the two types of SQL are static SQL and dynamic SQL. The primary difference between static and dynamic SQL is described capably by their names. A static SQL statement is hard-coded and unchanging. The columns, tables, and predicates are known beforehand and cannot be changed. Only host variables that provide values for the predicates can be changed.

A dynamic SQL statement, conversely, can change throughout a program's execution. The algorithms in the program can alter the SQL before issuing it. Based on the class of dynamic SQL being used, the columns, tables, and complete predicates can be changed on the fly.

As might be expected, dynamic SQL is dramatically different than static SQL in the way you code it in the application program. Additionally, when dynamic SQL is bound, the application plan or package that is created does not contain the same information as a plan or package for a static SQL program.

The access path for dynamic SQL statements cannot be determined before execution. When you think about it, this statement makes sense. If the SQL is not completely known until the program executes, how can it be verified and optimized beforehand? For this reason, dynamic SQL statements are not bound, but are prepared at execution. The PREPARE statement is functionally equivalent to a dynamic BIND. The program issues a PREPARE statement before executing dynamic SQL (with the exception of EXECUTE IMMEDIATE, which implicitly prepares SQL statements). PREPARE verifies, validates, and determines access paths dynamically.

A program containing dynamic SQL statements still must be bound into an application plan or package. The plan or package, however, does not contain access paths for the dynamic SQL statements.

DB2 provides four classes of dynamic SQL: EXECUTE IMMEDIATE, non-SELECT PREPARE and EXECUTE, fixed-list SELECT, and varying-list SELECT. The first two classes do not allow SELECT statements, whereas the last two are geared for SELECT statements.

Dynamic SQL is a complex topic that can be difficult to comprehend and master. It is important that you understand all aspects of dynamic SQL before deciding whether to use it. Dynamic SQL is covered in-depth in Chapter 6.

SQL Performance Factors

This chapter discussed SQL basics, but little has been covered pertaining to SQL performance. You need at least a rudimentary knowledge of the factors affecting SQL performance before reading a discussion of the best ways to achieve optimum performance. This section is an introduction to DB2 optimization and some DB2 performance features. These topics are discussed in depth in Part V, "DB2 Performance Tuning."

Introduction to the Optimizer

The DB2 optimizer is integral to the operation of SQL statements. The optimizer, as its name implies, determines the optimal method of satisfying a SQL request. For example, consider the following statement:

```
SELECT  EMPNO, WORKDEPT, DEPTNAME
FROM    DSN8510.EMP,
        DSN8510.DEPT
WHERE   DEPTNO = WORKDEPT;
```

This statement, whether embedded statically in an application program or executed dynamically, must be passed through the DB2 optimizer before execution. The optimizer parses the statement and determines the following:

- Which tables must be accessed
- Whether the tables are in partitioned tablespaces (to determine whether query I/O, CPU, and Sysplex parallelism is feasible)
- Which columns from those tables need to be returned
- Which columns participate in the SQL statement's predicates
- Whether there are any indexes for this combination of tables and columns
- What statistics are available in the DB2 Catalog

Based on this information (and system information), the optimizer analyzes the possible access paths and chooses the best one for the given query. An access path is the navigation logic used by DB2 to access the requisite data. A tablespace scan using sequential prefetch is an example of a DB2 access path. Access paths are discussed in greater detail in Part V.

The optimizer acts like a complex expert system. Based on models developed by IBM for estimating the cost of CPU and I/O time, the impact of uniform and non-uniform data distribution, and the state of tablespaces and indexes, the optimizer usually arrives at a good estimate of the optimal access path. Remember, though, that it is only a "best guess." Many factors can cause the DB2 optimizer to choose the wrong access path, such as incorrect or outdated statistics in the DB2 Catalog, an improper physical or logical database design, an improper use of SQL (for example, record-at-a-time processing), or bugs in the logic of the optimizer (although this occurs infrequently). In addition, the optimizer does not contain optimization logic for every combination and permutation of SQL statements.

The optimizer usually produces a better access path than a programmer or analyst could develop manually. Sometimes, the user knows more than DB2 about the nature of the data being accessed. If this is the case, there are ways to influence DB2's choice of access path. The best policy is to allow DB2 initially to choose all access paths automatically, then challenge its decision only when performance suffers. Although the DB2 optimizer does a good job for most queries, you might need to periodically examine, modify, or influence the access paths for some SQL statements.

NOTE

As a general rule of thumb, be sure to review and tune all SQL statements prior to migrating the SQL to the production environment.

Influencing the Access Path

There is no way for a user to force DB2 to use a specific access path. DB2's optimizer determines the best method based on the information discussed previously. However, users can influence the DB2 optimizer to choose a different access path if they know a few tricks.

To influence access path selection, users can tweak the SQL statement being optimized or update the statistics in the DB2 Catalog. Both of these methods are problematic and not recommended, but can be used as a last resort. If a SQL statement is causing severe performance degradation, you could consider using these options.

The first option is to change the SQL statement. Some SQL statements function more efficiently than others, depending on the version of DB2. As you learned previously, SQL is flexible; you can write functionally equivalent SQL in many ways. Sometimes, by altering the way in which a SQL statement is written, you can influence DB2 to choose a different access path.

The danger in coding SQL to take advantage of release-dependent features lies in the fact that DB2 continues to be enhanced and upgraded. If a future DB2 release changes the performance feature you took advantage of, your SQL statement may degrade. It usually is unwise to take advantage of a product's undocumented features, unless it's as a last resort. If this is done, be sure to document and retain information about the workaround. At a minimum, keep the following data:

- The reason for the workaround (for example, for performance or functionality).
- A description of the workaround.
- If SQL is modified, keep a copy of the old SQL statement and a copy of the new SQL statement.
- The version and release of DB2 at the time of the workaround.

The second method of influencing DB2's choice of access path is to update the statistics in the DB2 Catalog on which the optimizer relies. DB2 calculates a filter factor for each possible access path, based on the values stored in the DB2 Catalog and the type of predicates in the SQL statement to be optimized. *Filter factors* estimate the number of accesses required to return the desired results. The lower the filter factor, the more rows filtered out by the access path and the more efficient the access path.

There are two methods of modifying DB2 Catalog statistics. The first is with the RUNSTATS utility. RUNSTATS can be executed for each tablespace that requires updated statistics. This approach is recommended because it populates the DB2 Catalog with accurate statistics based on a sampling of the data currently stored in the tablespaces. Sometimes, however, accurate statistics produce an undesirable access path. To get around this, DB2 allows SYSADM users to modify the statistics stored in the DB2 Catalog. Most, but not all, of these statistical columns can be changed using SQL update statements. By changing the statistical information used by the optimization process, you can influence the access path chosen by DB2. This method can be used to

- Mimic production volumes in a test system to determine production access paths before migrating a system to production
- Favor certain access paths over others by specifying either lower or higher cardinality for specific tables or columns
- Favor indexed access by changing index statistics

Examples of this are shown in Chapter 14 along with additional information on access paths and influencing DB2.

Directly updating the DB2 Catalog, however, generally is not recommended. You might get unpredictable results because the values being changed might not accurately reflect the tablespace data. Additionally, if RUNSTATS is executed any time after the DB2 Catalog statistics are updated, the values placed in the DB2 Catalog by SQL UPDATE statements are overwritten. It usually is difficult to maintain accurate statistics for some columns and inaccurate, tweaked values for other columns. To do so, you must reapply the SQL updates to the DB2 Catalog immediately after you run the RUNSTATS utility and before you run any binds or rebinds.

In order to update DB2 Catalog statistics, you must have been granted the authority to update the specific DB2 Catalog tables (or columns) or have SYSADM authority.

As a general rule, updating the DB2 Catalog outside the jurisdiction of RUNSTATS should be considered only as a last approach. If SQL is used to update DB2 Catalog statistics, be sure to record and maintain the following information:

- The reason for the DB2 Catalog updates
- A description of the updates applied:
  Applied once; RUNSTATS never run again
  Applied initially; RUNSTATS run without reapplying updates
  Applied initially; RUNSTATS run and updates immediately reapplied
- The version and release of DB2 when the updates were first applied
- The SQL UPDATE and INSERT statements used to modify the DB2 Catalog
- A report of the DB2 Catalog statistics overlaid by the UPDATE statements (must be produced before the initial updates)

DB2 Performance Features

Finally, it is important to understand the performance features that IBM has engineered into DB2. Performance features have been added with each successive release of DB2. This section is a synopsis of the DB2 performance features discussed in depth throughout this book.

Sequential Prefetch

Sequential prefetch is a look-ahead *read engine* that enables DB2 to read many data pages in large chunks of pages, instead of one page at a time. It usually is invoked when a sequential scan of pages is needed. The overhead associated with I/O can be reduced with sequential prefetch because many pages are read before they must be used. When the pages are needed, they then are available without additional I/O.

Sequential Detection

DB2 can dynamically detect sequential processing and invoke sequential prefetch even if the optimizer did not specify its use.

List Prefetch

When the DB2 optimizer determines that an index will increase the efficiency of access to data in a DB2 table, it may decide also to invoke *list prefetch.* List prefetch sorts the index entries into order by *record identifier* (*RID*). This sorting ensures that two index entries that must access the same page will require more than one I/O because they now are accessed contiguously by record identifier. This reduction in I/O can increase performance.

Index Lookaside

The *index lookaside* feature is a method employed by DB2 to traverse indexes in an optimal manner. When using an index, DB2 normally traverses the b-tree structure of the index. This can involve significant overhead in checking root and nonleaf index pages when DB2 is looking for the appropriate leaf page for the given data. When using index lookaside, DB2 checks for the RID of the desired row on the current leaf page and the immediately higher nonleaf page. For repetitive index lookups, it is usually more efficient to check recently accessed pages (that are probably still in the bufferpool) than traversing the b-tree from the root. Index lookaside, therefore, generally reduces the path length of locating rows.

Index Only Access

If all the data being retrieved is located in an index, DB2 can satisfy the query by accessing the index without accessing the table. Because additional reads of table pages are not required, I/O is reduced and performance is increased.

RDS Sorting

DB2 sorting occurs in the Relational Data Services (RDS) component of DB2. (See Part III, "DB2 In-Depth," for in-depth descriptions of DB2's components.) DB2's efficient sort algorithm uses a *tournament sort* technique. Additionally, with the proper hardware, DB2 can funnel sort requests to routines in microcode that significantly enhances the sort performance.

MVS Exploitation

DB2 exploits many features of MVS, including cross memory services, efficient virtual storage use with a minimum of memory consumption below the 16-megabyte line, hiperspace usage with DB2 V3 hiperpools, and effective use of expanded storage, enabling the use of very large buffer pool and EDM pool specifications.

Stage 1 and Stage 2 Processing

Sometimes referred to as *sargable* and *nonsargable* processing, Stage 1 and Stage 2 processing effectively split the processing of SQL into separate components of DB2. Stage 1 processing is more efficient than Stage 2 processing.

Join Methods

When tables must be joined, the DB2 optimizer chooses one of three methods based on many factors, including all the information referred to in the discussion on optimization. The join methods are a merge scan, a nested loop join, and a hybrid join. A *merge scan* requires reading sorted rows and merging them based on the join criteria. A *nested loop join* repeatedly reads from one table, matching rows from the other table based on the join criteria. A *hybrid join* uses list prefetch to create partial rows from one table with RIDs from an index on the other table. The partial rows are sorted, with list prefetch used to complete the partial rows.

Lock Escalation

During application processing, if DB2 determines that performance is suffering because an inordinate number of locks have been taken, the granularity of the lock taken by the application might be escalated. Simply stated, if a program is accessing DB2 tables using page locking, and too many page locks are being used, DB2 might change the locking strategy to tablespace locking. This reduces the concurrency of access to the tables being manipulated, but significantly reduces overhead and increases performance for the application that was the beneficiary of the lock escalation.

Data Compression

As of V3, DB2 provides Ziv-Lempel data compression, employing hardware-assist for specific high-end CPU models or software compression for other models. Additionally, data compression can be directly specified in the CREATE TABLESPACE and ALTER TABLESPACE DDL, thereby avoiding the overhead and restrictions of an EDITPROC. Edit procedures were the most common method of implementing compression in earlier releases of DB2.

Data Sharing

Version 4

DB2 V4 provides the ability to couple DB2 subsystems together, enabling data to be shared between multiple DB2s. This allows an application running on more than one DB2 subsystem to read from and write to the same DB2 tables simultaneously. This was not possible in prior releases without using DB2's distributed data capabilities. Additionally, data sharing enables nonstop DB2 processing. If one subsystem becomes unavailable, workload can be shifted to other subsystems participating in the data sharing group. Refer to Chapter 12, "Data Sharing," for an in-depth discussion of data sharing.

Query Parallelism

As of V3, DB2 can utilize multiple read tasks to satisfy a single SQL SELECT statement. By running multiple, simultaneous read engines, the overall elapsed time for an individual query can be substantially reduced. This will aid I/O-bound queries.

Version 4

DB2 V4 improves on query I/O parallelism by enabling queries to utilize CPU in parallel. When CPU parallelism is engaged, each concurrent read engine will utilize its own portion of the central processor. This will aid processor-bound queries.

Version 5

DB2 V5 improves parallelism even further with Sysplex query parallelism. With Sysplex query parallelism, DB2 can spread the work for a single query across multiple DB2 subsystems in a data sharing group. This will further aid intensive, processor-bound queries.

Partition Independence

Using resource serialization, DB2 has the capability to process a single partition while permitting concurrent access to independent partitions of the same tablespace by utilities and SQL.

Limited Partition Scanning

Version 4

As of DB2 version 4, DB2 limits partitioned tablespace scans to a specific range of partitions based on the specified predicates.

DB2 V5 further modifies partition scanning to allow skipping partitions in the middle of a range.

Version 5

Uncommitted or "Dirty" Read

When data integrity is not an issue, DB2 can bypass locking and enable readers to access data regardless of its state. The "UR" isolation level provides a dirty read by allowing a SELECT statement to access data that is locked, in the process of being deleted, inserted but not yet committed, or, indeed, in *any* state. This can greatly enhance performance in certain situations.

CAUTION

Never use DB2's dirty read capability without a complete understanding of its ramifications on data integrity. For more information on uncommitted read processing, refer to Chapter 2, "Data Manipulation Guidelines," for statement level usage, and Chapter 7, "Program Preparation," for plan and package level usage.

Runtime Reoptimization

Version 5

DB2 version 5 can reoptimize static and dynamic SQL statements that rely on input variables in the WHERE clause during processing. This feature enables DB2 to optimize SQL statements after the host variable, parameter marker, and special register values are known. Runtime reoptimization can result in better access paths (albeit at a cost).

Online Reorganization

Version 5

As of DB2 V5, data can be queried and modified concurrently with the REORG utility. DB2 accomplishes this by reorganizing to a shadow copy of the tablespace. For more information on the online reorganization capabilities of DB2, consult Chapter 26, "Data Organization Utilities."

Summary

Now that you have obtained a basic understanding of SQL and the performance features of DB2, proceed with this guide to DB2 development!

2

Data Manipulation Guidelines

In Chapter 1, "The Magic Words," you learned the basics of SQL, but you can gain a deeper body of knowledge on the proper way to code SQL statements. Any particular method of coding an SQL statement is not wrong, per se, as long as it returns the correct results. But, often, you can find a better way. By *better*, I mean

- SQL that understands and interacts appropriately with its environment
- SQL that executes more efficiently and therefore enhances performance
- SQL that is clearly documented and therefore easily understood

You should pursue each of these goals. The guidelines introduced in the following sections are based on these three goals. These guidelines enable you to write efficient SQL and thereby limit the time programmers, analysts, and DBAs must spend correcting performance problems and analyzing poorly documented SQL and application code.

A Bag of Tricks

Understanding the ins and outs of DB2 performance can be an overwhelming task. DB2 tuning options are numerous and constantly changing. Even the number of SQL tuning options is staggering. And the differences in efficiency can be substantial. For example, coding a query as a join instead of as a correlated subquery sometimes results in a query that performs better. The same query, however, might result in degraded performance. Plus, to make matters worse, a new version or release of DB2 can cause completely different results.

The release level of DB2 is not the only factor that can cause performance problems. Changes to the MVS operating system, the DB2 database environment, the application code, or the application database can cause performance fluctuations. The following is a sample list of system changes that can affect DB2 query performance:

- Enterprise-wide changes
  Distributing data
  Moving data from site to site
  Replicating and propagating data
  Downsizing, upsizing, and rightsizing
  Changing to a new hardware environment
- MVS system-level changes
  Modifying DB2 dispatching priorities
  Modifying CICS, IMS/TM, or TSO dispatching priorities
  Installing a new release of MVS, CICS, IMS/TM, or TSO
  Implementing parallel sysplex
  Modifying TSO parameters

Adding or removing memory

Installing additional hardware that consumes memory

Increasing system throughput

- DB2 system-level changes

Installing a new DB2 version or release

Applying maintenance to the DB2 software

Changing DSNZPARMs

Modifying IRLM parameters

Incurring DB2 growth, causing the DB2 Catalog to grow without resizing or reorganizing

Ensuring proper placement of the active log data sets

Implementing data sharing

- Application-level changes

Increasing the application workload

Adding rows to a table

Deleting rows from a table

Increasing the volume of inserts, causing unclustered data or data set extents

Increasing the volume of updates to indexed columns

Updating variable character columns, causing storage space to expand and additional I/O to be incurred

Changing the distribution of data values in the table

Updating RUNSTATS information (see Chapter 1 for more information on RUNSTATS)

Rebinding application packages and plans

Enabling parallel processing

- Database-level changes

Adding or removing indexes

Converting from Type 1 to Type 2 indexes

Changing the clustering index

Altering a table to add a column

Reorganizing tablespaces and indexes

Compressing data

Moving physical data sets for tablespaces or indexes to different volumes

Luckily, you can prepare yourself to deal with performance problems by understanding the dynamic nature of DB2 performance features and keeping abreast of SQL tricks of the trade.

Use caution when implementing these tips and tricks, though, because the cardinal rule of relational database development always applies. What is this cardinal rule?

NOTE

The cardinal rule of RDBMS development is "It Depends!" Most DBAs and SQL experts resist giving a straight or simple answer to a general question because no standard implementation exists. Every situation is different, and every organization is unique in some way.

Don't be discouraged when you ask the local expert which statement will perform better, and the answer is "It depends." The expert is just doing his or her job.

The key is to document each SQL change along with the reason for the change. Follow up by monitoring the effectiveness of every change to your SQL statements before moving them into a production environment.

This chapter is divided into three major sections. In the first section, you learn SQL guidelines for simple SQL statements. The second section covers guidelines for complex SQL statements such as joins and unions. The third section provides guidelines for the efficient use of the `INSERT`, `DELETE`, and `UPDATE` statements.

SQL Access Guidelines

The SQL access guidelines will help you develop efficient data retrieval SQL for DB2 applications. Test them to determine their usefulness and effectiveness in your environment.

Pretest All Embedded SQL

Before embedding SQL in an application program, you should test it using `SPUFI`, QMF, or whatever ad hoc query tool you have available. This way, you can reduce the amount of program testing by ensuring that all SQL code is syntactically correct and efficient. Only after the SQL statements have been thoroughly tested and debugged should they be placed in an application program.

Use `EXPLAIN`

Use the `EXPLAIN` command to gain further insight into the performance potential for each SQL statement in an application. When `EXPLAIN` is executed on an SQL statement or application plan, information about the access path chosen by the optimizer is provided. This information is inserted into a DB2 table called the `PLAN_TABLE`. By querying the `PLAN_TABLE`, an analyst can determine the potential efficiency of SQL queries. Part V, "DB2 Performance Tuning," provides a complete description of the EXPLAIN command and guidelines for interpreting its output.

Use EXPLAIN and analyze the results for each SQL statement before it is migrated to the production application. Following this procedure is important not only for SQL statements in application programs, but also for canned QMF queries, and any other, predictable, dynamic SQL queries. For application programs, EXPLAIN can be used with the EXPLAIN option of the BIND command. Specifying EXPLAIN(YES) when you use BIND on an application plan or package provides the access path information necessary to determine the efficiency of the statements in the program. For a QMF (or ad hoc) query, use EXPLAIN on it before allowing the statement to be used in production procedures.

The following is an example of running EXPLAIN for a SELECT statement:

```
EXPLAIN PLAN SET QUERYNO = 1 FOR
     SELECT   *
     FROM     DSN8510.DEPT
     WHERE    DEPT = 'D21';
```

EXPLAIN enables a programmer or DBA to analyze the chosen access path by studying the PLAN_TABLE.

Because EXPLAIN provides access path information based on the statistics stored in the DB2 Catalog, you should keep these statistics current and accurate. Sometimes you must "fudge" the DB2 Catalog statistics to produce production access paths in a test environment. (See the section "Influencing the Access Path" in Chapter 1 for more information.)

Use All PLAN_TABLE Columns Available

Each new release or version of DB2 adds new columns to the PLAN_TABLE. These new columns are used to report on new access paths and features. Sometimes shops fail to add the new PLAN_TABLE columns after a new release is installed. Be sure to verify that the PLAN_TABLE actually contains every column that is available for the current DB2 release being run. For more information on the PLAN_TABLE and the columns available for each DB2 release please refer to Chapter 18, "Using EXPLAIN."

Enable EXPLAIN for AUTO REBIND

If you're running under DB2 V3 or greater, EXPLAIN can be run for plans and packages that are automatically rebound. An AUTO REBIND occurs when an authorized user attempts to execute an invalid plan or package. Plans and packages are invalidated when an object that an access path in the plan or package is using is dropped. Prior to DB2 V3, the access path chosen during an automatic rebind could not be recorded.

EXPLAIN during AUTO REBIND can be enabled if you set an appropriate DSNZPARM. Be sure that a proper PLAN_TABLE exists before enabling this option.

Utilize Query Analysis Tools

To isolate potential performance problems in application plans or single SQL statements, utilize all available analysis tools, such as BMC Software's Patrol SQL-Explorer or PLATINUM *technology's* Plan Analyzer. These products analyze the SQL code, provide a clear, textual description of the access path selected by the DB2 optimizer, and recommend alternative methods of coding your queries.

Avoid SELECT *

As a general rule, a query should *never* ask DB2 for anything more than is required to satisfy the desired task. Each query should access only the columns needed for the function to be performed. Following this dictum results in maximum flexibility and efficiency.

The gain in flexibility is the result of decreased maintenance on application programs. Consider a table in which columns are modified, deleted, or added. Only programs that access the affected columns need to be changed. When a program uses SELECT *, however, every column in the table is accessed. The program must be modified when any of the columns change, even if the program doesn't use the changed columns. This use complicates the maintenance process.

For example, consider a program that contains the following statement:

```
EXEC SQL
     SELECT    *
     INTO      :DEPTREC
     FROM      DSN8510.DEPT
     WHERE     DEPT = :HV-DEPT
END-EXEC.
```

Suppose that the program is developed, tested, and migrated to the production environment. You then add a column to the DEPT table. The program then fails to execute the preceding statement because the DEPTREC layout does not contain the new column. (This program was compiled with the old DCLGEN.) The program must be recompiled with the new DCLGEN, a step that is not required when the program asks for only the columns it needs.

Additionally, by limiting your query to only those columns necessary

- The programmer does not need extra time to code for the extraneous columns.
- You avoid the DB2 overhead required to retrieve the extraneous columns.
- DB2 might be able to use an index-only access path that is unavailable for SELECT *.

Singleton SELECT Versus the Cursor

To return a single row, an application program can use a cursor or a singleton SELECT. A cursor requires an OPEN, FETCH, and CLOSE to retrieve one row, whereas a singleton SELECT requires only SELECT...INTO. Usually, the singleton SELECT outperforms the cursor.

When the selected row must be updated after it is retrieved, however, using a cursor with the FOR UPDATE OF clause is recommended over a singleton SELECT. The FOR UPDATE OF clause ensures the integrity of the data in the row because it causes DB2 to hold an X lock on the page containing the row to be updated. If you use a singleton SELECT, the row can be updated by someone else after the singleton SELECT but before the subsequent UPDATE, thereby causing the intermediate modification to be lost.

Use FOR FETCH ONLY

When a SELECT statement is used only for retrieval, code the FOR FETCH ONLY clause. This clause enables DB2 to use *block fetch*, which returns fetched rows more efficiently for distributed DB2 requests. Efficient row fetches are important for dynamic SQL in an application program or SPUFI.

QMF automatically appends FOR FETCH ONLY to SELECT statements. Static SQL embedded in an application program automatically uses block fetch if the BIND process determines it to be feasible.

Allowing block fetch is important in a distributed DB2 environment. If data is blocked, less overhead is required as data is passed over the communication lines.

NOTE

Version 4

As of DB2 V4, the FOR READ ONLY clause provides the same function as FOR FETCH ONLY, and it may be preferable because it is ODBC-compliant.

Avoid Using DISTINCT

The DISTINCT verb removes duplicate rows from an answer set. If duplicates will not cause a problem, do not code DISTINCT because it might add to overhead if it must invoke a sort to remove the duplicates.

Limit the Data Selected

Return the minimum number of columns and rows needed by your application program. Do not code generic queries (such as SELECT statements without a WHERE clause) that return more rows than necessary, and then filter the unnecessary rows with the application program. Doing so wastes disk I/O by retrieving useless data and wastes CPU and elapsed time returning the additional, unneeded rows to your program.

Allowing DB2 to use WHERE clauses to limit the data to be returned is almost always more efficient.

Code Predicates on Indexed Columns

DB2 usually performs more efficiently when it can satisfy a request using an existing index rather than no index. However, indexed access is not always the most efficient access method. For example, when you request most of the rows in a table or access by a non-clustered index, indexed access can result in a poorer performing query than non-indexed access. In fact, a scan can be more efficient (at times) when accessing as few as 25 percent of the total rows in a table.

You can find comprehensive guidelines for the efficient creation of DB2 indexes in Chapter 3.

Multicolumn Indexes

If a table has only multicolumn indexes, try to specify the high-level column in the WHERE clause of your query. This action results in an index scan with at least one matching column.

Consider Several Indexes Instead of a Multicolumn Index

Because DB2 can utilize multiple indexes in an access path for a single SQL statement, multiple indexes might be more efficient (from a global perspective) than a single multicolumn index. If access to the columns varies from query to query, multiple indexes might provide better overall performance for all your queries, at the expense of an individual query.

If you feel that multiple indexes might be of benefit for your specific situation, test their effectiveness first in a test environment by

- Dropping the multicolumn index
- Creating a single index for each of the columns in the multicolumn index
- Updating DB2 Catalog statistics to indicate production volume
- Running EXPLAIN on all the affected queries and analyzing the results

Use ORDER BY When the Sequence Is Important

You cannot guarantee the order of the rows returned from a SELECT statement without an ORDER BY clause. Due to the nature of the DB2 optimizer, the path by which the data is retrieved might change from execution to execution of an application program. For this reason, code the ORDER BY clause when the sequence of rows being returned is important.

Limit the Columns Specified in ORDER BY

When you use ORDER BY to sequence retrieved data, DB2 ensures that the data is sorted in order by the specified columns. Doing so usually involves the invocation of a sort (unless an appropriate index is available). The more columns that must be sorted, the less efficient the query. Therefore, use ORDER BY on only those columns that are absolutely necessary.

Use Equivalent Data Types

Use the same data types and lengths when comparing column values to host variables or literals. This way, you can eliminate the need for data conversion. For example, comparing a column defined as `CHAR(6)` to another column defined as `CHAR(6)` is more efficient than comparing a `CHAR(6)` column to a `CHAR(5)` column. When DB2 must convert data, available indexes are not used.

DB2 also does not use an index if the host variable or literal is longer than the column being compared, or if the host variable has a greater precision or a different data type than the column being compared. This situation adversely affects performance and should be avoided at all costs.

Use BETWEEN Instead of <= and >=

The `BETWEEN` predicate is usually more efficient than the combination of the *less than or equal to* predicate (<=) and the *greater than or equal to* predicate (>=) because the optimizer selects a more efficient access path for the `BETWEEN` predicate. In fact, in most cases DB2 converts <= and >= combinations into `BETWEEN` when it can. Performance reasons aside, one `BETWEEN` predicate is much easier to understand and maintain than multiple <= and >= predicates.

However, there is one particular instance where this guidelines does not apply—when comparing a host variable to two columns:

```
WHERE :HOST-VAR BETWEEN COLUMN1 AND COLUMN2
```

should be changed to

```
WHERE :HOST_VAR >= COLUMN1 and :HOST-VAR <= COLUMN2
```

The reason for this exception is that the `BETWEEN` formulation is a stage 2 predicate, whereas the preferred formulation is stage 1.

Use IN Instead of LIKE

Whenever feasible, use `IN` or `BETWEEN` instead of `LIKE` in the `WHERE` clause of a `SELECT`. If you know that only a certain number of occurrences exist, using `IN` with the specific list is more efficient than using `LIKE`. For example, use

```
IN ('VALUE1', 'VALUE2', 'VALUE3')
```

instead of

```
LIKE 'VALUE_'
```

The functionality of `LIKE` can be imitated using a range of values. For example, if you want a query to retrieve all employees with a last name beginning with *K*, you know that last names between *KAAAAAAAAAAA* and *KZZZZZZZZZZZ* also satisfy the request. In general, use

```
BETWEEN :VALUE_LO AND :VALUE_HI
```

instead of

```
LIKE 'VALUE_
```

Formulate LIKE Predicates with Care

Avoid using the LIKE predicate when the percentage sign (%) or the underscore (_) appears at the beginning of the comparison string because they prevent DB2 from using a matching index. The LIKE predicate can produce efficient results, however, when you use the percentage sign or underscore at the end or in the middle of the comparison string.

Not Okay	*Okay*
LIKE %NAME	LIKE NAME%
LIKE _NAME	LIKE NA_ME

DB2 does not use direct index lookup when a wildcard character is supplied as the first character of a LIKE predicate. DB2 can determine when a host variable contains a wildcard character as the first character of a LIKE predicate. The optimizer therefore does not assume that an index cannot be used; rather, it indicates that an index might be used. At runtime, DB2 determines whether the index will be used based on the value supplied to the host variable. When a wildcard character is specified for the first character of a LIKE predicate, DB2 uses a non-matching index scan or a tablespace scan to satisfy the search.

Avoid Using NOT (Except with EXISTS)

Version 4

Prior to DB2 V4, predicates using NOT were non-indexable and Stage 2. Predicates formed using NOT are evaluated at Stage 1 as of V4, but they are still non-indexable. Therefore, when possible, you should recode queries to avoid the use of NOT (<>). Take advantage of your understanding of the data being accessed. For example, if you know that no values are less than the value that you are testing for inequality, you could recode

```
COLUMN1  <>  value
```

as

```
COLUMN1  >=  value
```

See the section on complex SQL guidelines for guidance in the use of the EXISTS predicate.

Code the Most Restrictive Predicate First

When you code predicates in your SELECT statement, place the predicate that will eliminate the greatest number of rows first. For example, consider the following statement:

```
SELECT  EMPNO, FIRSTNME, LASTNAME
```

```
FROM     DSN8510.EMP
WHERE    WORKDEPT = 'D21'
AND      SEX = 'F';
```

Suppose that the WORKDEPT has 10 distinct values. (The SEX column obviously has only 2.) The predicate for the WORKDEPT column is coded first because it eliminates more rows than the predicate for the SEX column. The performance gain from predicate placement is usually minimal, but sometimes every little performance gain is significant.

This guideline is true only for like predicate types. In the preceding code, for example, both predicates are equality predicates. If the predicates were not the same, the guideline would not be applicable.

Use Predicates Wisely

By reducing the number of predicates on your SQL statements, you might be able to achieve better performance in two ways:

1. Reduced BIND time due to fewer options that must be examined by the DB2 optimizer.
2. Reduced execution time due to a smaller path length caused by the removal of redundant search criteria from the optimized access path. DB2 processes each predicate coded for the SQL statement. Removing predicates removes work, and less work equals less time to process the SQL.

However, if you remove predicates from SQL statements, you run the risk of changing the data access logic. So, remove predicates only when you're sure that their removal will not have an impact on the query results. For example, consider the following query:

```
SELECT   FIRST_NAME, LAST_NAME, GRADE_LEVEL
FROM     DSN8510.EMP
WHERE    JOB = 'DESIGNER'
AND      EDLEVEL >= 16;
```

This statement retrieves all rows for designers who are at an education level of 16 or above. But what if you know that the starting education level for all designers in an organization is 16? No one with a lower education level can be hired as a designer. In this case, the second predicate is redundant. Removing this predicate does not logically change the results, but it might enhance performance.

On the other hand, performance possibly can degrade when you remove predicates. As of DB2 V5, the optimizer analyzes correlation statistics when calculating filter factors. Examples of correlated columns include CITY and STATE (Chicago and Illinois are likely to occur together); FIRST_NAME and GENDER (Robert and male are likely to occur together).

Because the filter factor might change when a predicate is changed or removed, a different access path can be chosen. That access path might be more (or less) efficient than the one it replaces. The basic rule is to test the SQL both ways to determine which will perform better for each specific statement.

Truly "knowing your data," however, is imperative. For example, it is not sufficient to merely note that for current rows in the EMP table no designers are at an EDLEVEL below 16. This may just be a data coincidence. Do not base your knowledge of your data on the current state of the data, but on business requirements. You must truly *know* that a correlation between two columns (such as between JOB and EDLEVEL) actually exists before you modify your SQL to take advantage of this fact.

Be Careful with Arithmetic Precision

When you select columns using arithmetic expressions, be careful to ensure that the result of the expression has the correct precision. When an arithmetic expression operates on a column, DB2 determines the data type of the numbers in the expression and decides the correct data type for the result. Remember the following rules for performing arithmetic with DB2 columns:

- DB2 supports addition, subtraction, multiplication, and division.
- DATE, TIME, and TIMESTAMP columns can be operated on only by means of addition and subtraction. (See the section "Use Date and Time Arithmetic with Care" later in this chapter.)
- Floating-point numbers are displayed in scientific notation. Avoid using floating-point numbers because scientific notation is difficult for some users to comprehend. As of DB2 V2.3, DECIMAL columns can contain as many as 31 bytes of precision, which is adequate for most users.
- When an arithmetic expression operates on two numbers of different data types, DB2 returns the result using the data type with the highest precision. The only exception to this rule is that an expression involving two SMALLINT columns is returned as an INTEGER result.

The last rule may require additional clarification. When DB2 operates on two numbers, the result of the operation must be returned as a valid DB2 data type. Consult the following chart to determine the result data type for operations on any two numbers in DB2:

Statement	*Yields*
SMALLINT *operator* SMALLINT	INTEGER
SMALLINT *operator* INTEGER	INTEGER
SMALLINT *operator* DECIMAL	DECIMAL
SMALLINT *operator* FLOAT	FLOAT
INTEGER *operator* SMALLINT	INTEGER
INTEGER *operator* INTEGER	INTEGER
INTEGER *operator* DECIMAL	DECIMAL
INTEGER *operator* FLOAT	FLOAT

Statement	*Yields*
DECIMAL *operator* SMALLINT	DECIMAL
DECIMAL *operator* INTEGER	DECIMAL
DECIMAL *operator* DECIMAL	DECIMAL
DECIMAL *operator* FLOAT	FLOAT
FLOAT *operator* ANY DATA TYPE	FLOAT

For example, consider the following SELECT:

```
SELECT  EMPNO, EDLEVEL/2, SALARY/2
FROM    DSN8510.EMP
WHERE   EMPNO BETWEEN '000250' AND '000290';
```

This statement returns the following results:

```
EMPNO          COL1          COL2
------       --------      --------
000250          7          9590.00
000260          8          8625.00
000270          7         13690.00
000280          8         13125.00
000290          6          7670.00
```

Because EDLEVEL is an INTEGER and 2 is specified as an INTEGER, the result in COL1 is truncated and specified as an INTEGER. Because SALARY is a DECIMAL column and 2 is specified as an INTEGER, the result is a DECIMAL. If you must return a more precise number for COL1, consider specifying EDLEVEL/2.0. The result is a DECIMAL because 2.0 is specified as a DECIMAL.

Use Column Renaming with Arithmetic Expressions and Functions

Version 4

You can use the AS clause to give arithmetic expressions a column name, as follows:

```
SELECT  EMPNO, EDLEVEL/2 AS HALF_EDLEVEL, SALARY/2 AS HALF_SALARY
FROM    DSN8510.EMP
WHERE   EMPNO BETWEEN '000250' AND '000290';
```

If you give expressions a descriptive name, SQL becomes easier to understand and maintain. Likewise, when specifying functions in the SELECT list, use the AS clause to give the new column a name.

Decimal Precision and Scale

The precision of a decimal number is the total number of digits in the number (do not count the decimal point). For example, the number 983.201 has a precision of 6. The scale of a decimal number is equal to the number of digits to the right of the decimal point. In the previous example, the scale is 3.

Avoid Arithmetic Expressions in a Predicate

Version 5

An index is not used for a column when the column is in a predicate that includes arithmetic. You can perform calculations before the SQL statement and then use the result in the query. For example, prior to V5, you could recode this SQL statement

```
SELECT   PROJNO
FROM     DSN8510.PROJ
WHERE    PRSTDATE = :HV-DATE+10;
```

as this sequence of COBOL and SQL

```
ADD +10 TO HV-DATE.                        COBOL

SELECT   PROJNO                            SQL
FROM     DSN8510.PROJ
WHERE    PRSTDATE = :HV-DATE
```

As of DB2 V5, both statements are Stage 1, but only the second one is indexable.

Use Date and Time Arithmetic with Care

DB2 enables you to add and subtract DATE, TIME, and TIMESTAMP columns. In addition, you can add date and time durations to or subtract them from these columns.

Use date and time arithmetic with care. If users understand the capabilities and features of date and time arithmetic, they should have few problems implementing it. Keep the following rules in mind:

- When you issue date arithmetic statements using durations, do not try to establish a common conversion factor between durations of different types. For example, the date arithmetic statement

  ```
  1997/04/03 - 1 MONTH
  ```

  is *not* equivalent to statement

  ```
  1997/04/03 - 30 DAYS
  ```

  April has 30 days, so the normal response would be to subtract 30 days to subtract one month. The result of the first statement is 1997/03/03, but the result of the second statement is 1997/03/04. In general, use like durations (for example, use months or use days, but not both) when you issue date arithmetic.
- If one operand is a date, the other operand must be a date or a date duration. If one operand is a time, the other operand must be a time or a time duration. You cannot mix durations and data types with date and time arithmetic.
- If one operand is a timestamp, the other operand can be a time, a date, a time duration, or a date duration. The second operand cannot be a timestamp. You can mix date and time durations with timestamp data types.

- Date durations are expressed as a `DECIMAL(8,0)` number. The valid date durations are

DAY	DAYS
MONTH	MONTHS
YEAR	YEARS

- Time durations are expressed as a `DECIMAL(6,0)` number. The valid time durations are

HOUR	HOURS
MINUTE	MINUTES
SECOND	SECONDS
MICROSECOND	MICROSECONDS

Use Date Arithmetic to Determine the Day of the Week

Some application programs need to be able to determine the day of the week for a particular date. You can determine the day using DB2 date arithmetic, as follows:

```
DAYS(CURRENT DATE) - (DAYS(CURRENT DATE)/7) * 7
```

This expression returns an integer indicating the day of the week as shown in Table 2.1.

Table 2.1. Days of the week.

Integer	*Day of the Week*
0	Sunday
1	Monday
2	Tuesday
3	Wednesday
4	Thursday
5	Friday
6	Saturday

Specify the Number of Rows to Be Returned

When you code a cursor to fetch a predictable number of rows, consider specifying the number of rows to be retrieved in the `OPTIMIZE FOR n ROWS` clause of the `CURSOR`. This way, DB2 can select the optimal access path for the statement based on actual use.

Coding the `OPTIMIZE FOR n ROWS` clause of the `CURSOR` does not limit your program from fetching more than the specified number of rows. This statement can cause your program to be inefficient, however, when many more rows or many fewer rows than specified are retrieved.

Disable List Prefetch Using `OPTIMIZE FOR 1 ROW`

If a particular query experiences sub-optimal performance due to list prefetch, specifying `OPTIMIZE FOR 1 ROW` disables list prefetch. This capability might be of particular use in an online environment in which data is displayed to the end user a screen at a time.

Disable Index Access Using `OR 0 = 1`

During the tuning process, you can append `OR 0 = 1` to a predicate to eliminate index access. For example, consider a query against the `EMP` table on which two indexes exist: one on `EMPNO` and one on `WORKDEPT`.

```
SELECT   EMPNO, WORKDEPT, EDLEVEL, SALARY
FROM     DSN8510.EMP
WHERE    EMPNO BETWEEN '000020' AND '000350'
AND      (WORKDEPT > "A01" AND 0 = 1);
```

In this case, the `0 = 1` prohibits DB2 from choosing the `WORKDEPT` index, thus forcing DB2 to use either the index on `EMPNO` or a tablespace scan. Similar techniques include adding 0 to a numeric column or appending a null string to a character column to avoid indexed access.

Limit the Use of Scalar Functions

If you can avoid scalar functions in `WHERE` clauses without much trouble, do so. Use scalar functions, however, to offload work from the application to the database management system. Remember that an index is not used for columns to which scalar functions are applied. Scalar functions typically can be used in the `SELECT` list of SQL statements with no performance degradation.

Be Aware of Tablespace Partitioning Key Ranges

Version 4

When you access data in partitioned tablespaces, be aware of the values used for the partitioning scheme. Prior to V4, DB2 scanned the entire table in a tablespace scan of a partitioned table. As of DB2 V4, you can limit a tablespace scan to accessing a subset of the partitions if the predicates of the `WHERE` clause can be used to limit the key ranges that need to be scanned.

Specify Isolation Level for Individual SQL Statements

Version 4

As of DB2 V4, you can use the `WITH` clause to specify an explicit isolation level at the SQL statement level.

Four options are available:

- `WITH RR`: Repeatable Read
- `WITH RS`: Read Stability
- `WITH CS`: Cursor Stability
- `WITH UR`: Uncommitted Read (can be specified only if the result table is read-only)

Version 5

As of DB2 V5, the KEEP UPDATE LOCKS clause can be specified for RR and RS isolation levels. With KEEP UPDATE LOCKS, DB2 acquires X locks instead of U or S locks on all qualified rows or pages. Use this option to serialize updates when concurrency is not an issue.

Increase the Possibility of Stage 1 Processing

For SQL statements, you must consider at which stage the predicate is applied: Stage 1 or Stage 2. Stage 1 predicates were previously known as sargable predicates. *Sargable* is an IBM-defined term that stands for *s*earch *arg*u*able*. The term simply defines in which portion of DB2 a predicate can be satisfied.

The term *sargable* is ostensibly obsolete and has been replaced in the IBM literature by another term, *Stage 1 processing*. A predicate that can be satisfied by Stage 1 processing can be evaluated by the Data Manager portion of DB2, not the Relational Data System. The Data Manager component of DB2 is at a level closer to the data than the Relational Data System. You can find a more complete description of the components of DB2 in Chapter 13, "DB2 Behind the Scenes."

Because a Stage 1 predicate can be evaluated at an earlier Stage of data retrieval, you avoid the overhead of passing data from component to component of DB2. Try to use Stage 1 predicates rather than Stage 2 predicates because Stage 1 predicates are more efficient. The following list shows the predicates that can be satisfied by Stage 1 processing:

```
COLUMN_NAME operator value

COLUMN_NAME IS NULL

COLUMN_NAME BETWEEN val1 AND val2

COLUMN_NAME IN (list)

COLUMN_NAME LIKE pattern

COLUMN_NAME LIKE :host-variable

A.COLUMN_NAME1 operator B.COLUMN_NAME2

COLUMN_NAME operator (non-correlated subquery)

COLUMN_NAME operator (non-column expression)
```

Note that you can replace `operator` with =, <=, >=, <, >, or <>. Additionally, note that the seventh item in this list refers to the comparison of two columns from different tables. It is indicated by the A and B before the column names. If both columns were from the same table, the predicate would not be Stage 1. Additionally, a LIKE predicate ceases to be Stage 1 if the column is defined using a field procedure.

A non-column expression is any expression in which a column of a table is not specified. Examples of such expressions include

```
CURRENT TIMESTAMP - 10 DAYS

:HOST-VARIABLE + 20

FLOAT(8.5)
```

Stage 1 predicates combined with AND, combined with OR, or preceded by NOT are also Stage 1. All others are Stage 2.

However, you should not view use of Stage 1 predicates as a panacea. Adherence to Stage 1 is only one aspect of efficient query writing and does not guarantee the most effective way to code your query. Follow the rest of the advice in this chapter to create efficient SQL code.

CAUTION

This information is accurate as of DB2 V5. Stage 1 predicates tend to change with each release of DB2.

Increase the Possibility of Indexed Processing

A query that can use an index has more access path options, so it can be more efficient than a query that cannot use an index. The DB2 optimizer can use an index or indexes in a variety of ways to speed the retrieval of data from DB2 tables. For this reason, try to use indexable predicates rather than those that are not. The following list shows predicates that can be satisfied by using indexes:

```
COLUMN_NAME operator value
COLUMN_NAME IS NULL
COLUMN_NAME BETWEEN val1 AND val2
COLUMN_NAME IN (val1, val2, val3,...valn)
COLUMN_NAME LIKE pattern
COLUMN_NAME LIKE host-variable
A.COLUMN_NAME1 operator B.COLUMN_NAME2
COLUMN_NAME operator (non-correlated subquery)
COLUMN_NAME operator (non-column expression)
```

Note that you can replace *operator* with =, <=, >=, <, or >. Additionally, note that the seventh item in this list refers to the comparison of two columns from different tables. It is indicated by the A and B before the column names. If both columns were from the same table, the predicate would not be indexable.

Predicates formulated as shown combined with AND or OR are also indexable. However, note that predicates preceded by NOT are not indexable. Finally, DB2 considers predicates using LIKE with a host variable to be indexable unless the column has a field procedure defined on it or the host-variable begins with _ or %. Consider this example:

```
COLUMN_NAME LIKE host-variable
```

The preceding is indexable unless the *host-variable* begins with _ or %.

Using indexable predicates is not always the most efficient way to code your query. Indexability, like Stage 1 consideration, is only one aspect of efficient query writing. Follow the rest of the advice in this chapter to formulate efficient SQL code.

CAUTION

This information is accurate as of DB2 V5. Indexable predicates tend to change with each release of DB2.

Use SQL "Hints" to Trick the Optimizer

Version 5

Although non-column expressions are indexable as of DB2 V5, IBM has excepted certain expressions because they were used as tricks to fool the optimizer. The following "trick SQL" expressions are still non-indexable:

- Multiplication or division by 1
- Addition or subtraction of 0
- Concatenating an empty string

IBM did not include these expressions because these tricks have been deployed by DB2 developers to avoid indexed access since V1. A sample SQL statement using one of these tricks follows:

```
SELECT  EMPNO, WORKDEPT, EDLEVEL, SALARY
FROM    DSN8510.EMP
WHERE   EMPNO < (:HOST-VAR CONCAT "");
```

In this case, a tablespace scan is used because an empty string is concatenated to the host variable in the predicate and no other predicates are available for indexed access.

Complex SQL Guidelines

The preceding section provided guidelines for simple SQL SELECT statements. These statements retrieve rows from a single table only. Complex SQL can use a single SQL SELECT statement to retrieve rows from different tables. The four categories of complex SQL statements are

- Joins
- Subqueries
- Unions
- Grouping

UNION Versus UNION ALL

The UNION operator always results in a sort. When the UNION operator connects two SELECT statements, both SELECT statements are issued, the rows are sorted, and all duplicates are eliminated. If you want to avoid duplicates, use the UNION operator.

The UNION ALL operator, by contrast, does not invoke a sort. The SELECT statements connected by UNION ALL are executed, and all rows from the first SELECT statement are appended to all rows from the second SELECT statement. Duplicate rows might exist. Use UNION ALL when duplicate rows are required or, at least, are not a problem. Also use UNION ALL when you know that the SELECT statements will not return duplicates.

Use NOT EXISTS Instead of NOT IN

When you code a subquery using negation logic, use NOT EXISTS instead of NOT IN to increase the efficiency of your SQL statement. When you use NOT EXISTS, DB2 must verify only nonexistence. Doing so can reduce processing time significantly. With the NOT IN predicate, DB2 must materialize the complete results set.

Use a Constant for Existence Checking

When you use EXISTS to test for the existence of a particular row, specify a constant in the subquery SELECT list. The SELECT list of the subquery is unimportant because the statement checks for existence only, and does not actually return columns. For example, you can code SQL to list all employees who are responsible for at least one project, as follows:

```
SELECT  EMPNO
FROM    DSN8510.EMP    E
WHERE   EXISTS
         (SELECT  1
          FROM    DSN8510.PROJ    P
          WHERE   P.RESPEMP = E.EMPNO);
```

Be Aware of Predicate Transitive Closure Rules

Predicate transitive closure refers to the capability of the DB2 optimizer to use the rule of transitivity (if A=B and B=C, then A=C) to determine the most efficient access path for queries. The optimizer did not always have the capability to use the rule of transitivity.

Before DB2 V2.1, you produced a more efficient query by providing redundant information in the WHERE clause of a join statement, as in this example:

```
SELECT  A.COL1, A.COL2, B.COL1
FROM    TABLEA A, TABLEB B
WHERE   A.COL1 = B.COL1
AND     A.COL1 = :HOSTVAR;
```

This query can process more efficiently in pre-V2.1 releases of DB2 by coding a redundant predicate, as follows:

```
SELECT  A.COL1, A.COL2, B.COL1
FROM    TABLEA A, TABLEB B
WHERE   A.COL1 = B.COL1
AND     A.COL1 = :HOSTVAR
AND     B.COL1 = :HOSTVAR;
```

As of DB2 V2.1, the need to code redundant predicates for performance no longer exists for equijoins. As of DB2 V2.3, you no longer have to code redundant predicates for most types of joins, such as less-than joins or greater-than joins. However, predicate transitive closure is not applied with the `LIKE` predicate. Consider this example:

```
SELECT  A.COL1, A.COL2, B.COL1
FROM    TABLEA  A,
        TABLEB  B
WHERE   A.COL1 = B.COL1
AND     A.COL1 LIKE 'ABC%';
```

The preceding can be more efficiently coded as follows:

```
SELECT  A.COL1, A.COL2, B.COL1
FROM    TABLEA  A,
        TABLEB  B
WHERE   A.COL1 = B.COL1
AND     A.COL1 LIKE 'ABC%'
AND     B.COL1 LIKE 'ABC%';
```

Unless you're running a version of DB2 that does not support predicate transitive closure or using the `LIKE` clause as shown, do not code redundant predicates; doing so is unnecessary and might cause the query to be less efficient.

Use a Correlated Subselect to Determine "Top Ten"

In some situations, returning only a portion of the actual result set for a query is desirable. This situation most frequently manifests itself in the "Top Ten" problem (for example, returning the top-ten highest salaries in the company). Consider the following SQL:

```
SELECT SALARY, EMPNO, LASTNAME
FROM   DSN8510.EMP  E1
WHERE  10 > (SELECT COUNT(*)
             FROM   DSN8510.EMP E2
             WHERE  E1.SALARY < E2.SALARY);
```

The top-ten highest salaries are returned. You can alter the actual number by changing the literal value `10` to whatever number you want.

Minimize the Number of Rows in a Join

Joining many tables in one query can adversely affect performance. Although the maximum number of tables that can be joined in a single SQL statement is 15, the practical limit is usually fewer.

However, setting an artificial limit on the standard number of tables per join is not a wise course of action. In some situations, avoiding large, complex joins in an online environment may be necessary. However, the same statement might be completely acceptable in a batch job or ad hoc request.

The number of tables to be joined in any application should be based on the following:

- The total number of rows participating in the join
- The results you want to obtain from the query
- The level of performance you want
- The anticipated throughput of the application
- The type of application (OLTP versus OLAP or DSS)
- The environment in which the application will operate (online versus batch)
- The availability you want (for example, 24×7)

In general, however, always eliminate unnecessary tables from your join statement.

Consider Denormalizing to Reduce Joins

To minimize the need for joins, consider denormalization. Remember, however, that denormalization usually implies redundant data, dual updating, and extra DASD usage. Normalization optimizes data modification at the expense of data access; denormalization optimizes data access at the expense of data modification. You can find additional denormalization assistance in Chapter 3, "Data Definition Guidelines."

Reduce the Number of Rows to Be Joined

The number of rows participating in a join is the single most important determinant in predicting the response time of a join. To reduce join response time, reduce the number of rows to be joined in the join's predicates.

For example, when you try to determine which males in all departments reporting to department D01 make a salary of $35,000 or more, you can code the predicates for both SEX and SALARY as follows:

```
SELECT  E.LASTNAME, E.FIRSTNME
FROM    DSN8510.DEPT  D,
        DSN8510.EMP   E
WHERE   D.ADMRDEPT = 'D01'
AND     D.DEPTNO = E.WORKDEPT
AND     E.SEX = 'M'
AND     E.SALARY >= 35000.00;
```

If you fail to code either of the last two predicates, deciding instead to scan the results and pull out the information you need, more rows qualify for the join and the join is less efficient.

Join Using SQL Instead of Program Logic

Coding a join using SQL instead of COBOL or another high-level language is almost always more efficient. The DB2 optimizer has a vast array of tools in its arsenal to optimize the performance of SQL queries. Usually, a programmer will fail to consider the same number of possibilities as DB2.

If a specific SQL join is causing high overhead, consider the tuning options outlined in this chapter before deciding to implement the join using a program. To further emphasize the point, consider the results of a recent test. A three table join using `GROUP BY` and the `COUNT(*)` function similar to the one below was run:

```
SELECT   EMPNO, LASTNAME, COUNT(*)
FROM     DSN8510.EMP          E,
         DSN8510.EMPPROJACT   A,
         DSN8510.PROJ         P
WHERE    E.EMPNO = A.EMPNO
AND      P.PROJNAME IN ('PROJECT1', 'PROJECT7', 'PROJECT9')
AND      A.PROJNO = E.PROJNO
AND      A.EMPTIME > 40.0
GROUP BY EMPNO, PROJNAME
```

Additionally, an equivalent program was coded using three cursors (one for each join), internal sorting (using `Syncsort`, `DFSORT`, or a similar utility), and programmatic counting. Performance reports were run on both, and the SQL statement outperformed the equivalent application program by more than 800 percent in terms of elapsed time and more than 600 percent in terms of CPU time.

Use Joins Instead of Subqueries

A join can be more efficient than a correlated subquery or a subquery using `IN`. For example, this query joins two tables:

```
SELECT  EMPNO, LASTNAME
FROM    DSN8510.EMP,
        DSN8510.PROJ
WHERE   WORKDEPT = DEPTNO
AND     EMPNO = RESPEMP;
```

The preceding example is usually more efficient than the following query, which is formulated as a correlated subquery accessing the same two tables:

```
SELECT  EMPNO, LASTNAME
FROM    DSN8510.EMP X
WHERE   WORKDEPT =
        (SELECT  DEPTNO
         FROM    DSN8510.PROJ
         WHERE   RESPEMP = X.EMPNO);
```

The preceding two queries demonstrate how to turn a correlated subquery into a join. You can translate non-correlated subqueries into joins in the same manner. For example, the join

```
SELECT  EMPNO, LASTNAME
FROM    DSN8510.EMP
```

```
        DSN8510.DEPT
WHERE   WORKDEPT = DEPTNO
AND     DEPTNAME = 'PLANNING';
```

is usually more efficient than the subquery

```
SELECT  EMPNO, LASTNAME
FROM    DSN8510.EMP
WHERE   WORKDEPT IN
        (SELECT  DEPTNO
         FROM    DSN8510.DEPT
         WHERE   DEPTNAME = 'PLANNING');
```

Note that these two queries do not necessarily return the same results. If DEPTNO is not unique, the first SELECT statement could return more rows than the second SELECT statement, and some of the values for EMPNO could appear more than once in the results table.

Be aware, however, that with each new release of DB2, subqueries (both correlated and non-correlated) are becoming more and more efficient.

Join on Clustered Columns

When you join large tables, use clustered columns in the join criteria when possible. This way, you can reduce the need for intermediate sorts. Note that doing so might require clustering of the parent table by primary key and the child table by foreign key.

Join on Indexed Columns

The efficiency of your program improves when tables are joined based on indexed columns rather than on non-indexed ones. To increase the performance of joins, consider creating indexes specifically for the predicates being joined.

Use Caution When Specifying ORDER BY with a Join

When the results of a join must be sorted, limiting the ORDER BY to columns of a single table can cause DB2 to avoid a sort. Whenever you specify columns from multiple tables in the ORDER BY clause of a join statement, DB2 invokes a sort.

Avoid Cartesian Products

Never use a join statement without a predicate. A join without a predicate generates a results table in which every row from the first table is joined with every row from the other table: a Cartesian product. For example, joining—without a predicate—a 1,000 row table with another 1,000 row table results in a table with 1,000,000 rows. No additional information is provided by this join, so a lot of machine resources are wasted.

Provide Adequate Search Criteria

When possible, provide additional search criteria in the WHERE clause for every table in a join. These criteria are in addition to the join criteria, which are mandatory to avoid Cartesian products.

This information provides DB2 with the best opportunity for ranking the tables to be joined in the most efficient manner (that is, for reducing the size of intermediate results tables). In general, the more information you provide to DB2 for a query, the better the chances that the query will perform adequately.

Consider Using Explicit INNER JOINs

Instead of specifying joins by using a comma-delimited list of tables in the FROM clause, use INNER JOIN with the ON clause. Explicit INNER JOIN syntax might help when you're training new programmers in SQL because it provides a join keyword. Likewise, the join predicates must be isolated in the ON clause when you're using an explicit INNER JOIN. This way, reading, tuning, and maintaining the SQL code are easier.

Use Explicit OUTER JOINs

Avoid coding the old style of outer join requiring a simple SELECT, UNION, and correlated subselect after you have migrated to DB2 V4 and are sure that you will not fall back to a previous release. The new outer join syntax is easier to code, easier to maintain, and is more efficient to execute. An explicit OUTER JOIN uses one pass against the tables and as such usually outperforms an outer join using UNION or UNION ALL. Using explicit OUTER JOIN statements reduces the number of bugs and speed application development time due solely to the significant reduction in lines of code required. Furthermore, as IBM improves the optimizer over time, techniques designed to make outer joins more efficient will most likely focus only on the new, explicit outer join syntax and not on the old, complex SQL formulation.

Exception Reporting

You can use the bottom half of the old style of outer join to report just the exceptions when you don't need a full-blown outer join. Consider this example:

```
SELECT  D.DEPTNO, D.DEPTNAME, D.MGRNO, '* No Mgr Name *'
FROM    DSN8510.DEPT  D
WHERE   NOT EXISTS
        (SELECT  1
         FROM    DSN8510.EMP  E
         WHERE   D.MGRNO = E.EMPNO)
ORDER BY 1;
```

This SQL returns only the departments without a manager name.

Never Code a RIGHT OUTER JOIN

Favor coding LEFT OUTER JOIN over RIGHT OUTER JOIN. The choice is truly arbitrary, but the manner in which DB2 shows EXPLAIN information makes left outer joins easier to tune. A new, optional column has been added to the PLAN_TABLE to describe the type of outer join method being used by a particular SQL join statement. EXPLAIN populates the JOIN_TYPE column to describe the outer join method (FULL, RIGHT, or LEFT). The column contains the value F for a

FULL OUTER JOIN, L for a LEFT OUTER JOIN or RIGHT OUTER JOIN, or a blank for an INNER JOIN or no join. EXPLAIN always converts right outer joins to left outer joins. Therefore, deciphering the PLAN_TABLE data is more difficult for a RIGHT OUTER JOIN than for a LEFT OUTER JOIN.

Use COALESCE with FULL OUTER JOINs

Version 4

At times, you might need the COALESCE function to avoid nulls in the result columns of OUTER JOIN statements. The COALESCE function is a synonym for the VALUE function. To understand how COALESCE can be useful in an outer join, consider the following query:

```
SELECT   EMP.EMPNO, EMP.WORKDEPT, DEPT.DEPTNAME
FROM     EMP FULL OUTER JOIN DEPT
ON       EMP.WORKDEPT = DEPT.DEPTNO;
```

A portion of the results for this query looks like this:

EMPNO	WORKDEPT	DEPTNAME
200330	E21	SOFTWARE SUPPORT
200340	E21	SOFTWARE SUPPORT
------	---	DEVELOPMENT CENTER

Note that the department code for DEVELOPMENT CENTER is not displayed, even though you know by simple browsing of the DEPT table that the code is D01. The value is not returned because the query selects the WORKDEPT column from EMP, not the DEPTNO column from DEPT. You can rectify this situation by using the COALESCE function. The COALESCE function notifies DB2 to look for a value in both of the listed columns, one from each table in the outer join (in this case, EMP and DEPT). If a value is found in either table, it can be returned in the result set. Consider the following example:

```
SELECT   EMP.EMPNO,
         COALESCE(EMP.WORKDEPT, DEPT.DEPTNO) AS DEPTNUM,
         DEPT.DEPTNAME
FROM     EMP FULL OUTER JOIN DEPT
ON       EMP.WORKDEPT = DEPT.DEPTNO;
```

The results are changed as follows:

EMPNO	DEPTNUM	DEPTNAME
200330	E21	SOFTWARE SUPPORT
200340	E21	SOFTWARE SUPPORT
------	D01	DEVELOPMENT CENTER

In this case, the last row of the result set contains the correct department code. The COALESCE function determines that the department code is stored in the DEPT.DEPTNO column and returns that value instead of the null because there is no corresponding WORKDEPT number.

OUTER JOINs and Inline Views

Version 4

Be aware that you might need to combine inline views with the COALESCE function to return the appropriate results. Consider adding a local predicate to the preceding example:

```
SELECT  EMP.EMPNO,
        COALESCE(EMP.WORKDEPT, DEPT.DEPTNO) AS DEPTNUM,
        DEPT.DEPTNAME
FROM    EMP FULL OUTER JOIN DEPT
ON      EMP.WORKDEPT = DEPT.DEPTNO
WHERE   EMP.WORKDEPT = 'D01';
```

In this case, no rows are returned. The 'D01' department number is aligned with the "DEVELOPMENT CENTER" in the DEPT table as DEPTNO, not in the EMP table as WORKDEPT. The solution is to use an inline view as follows:

```
SELECT  EMPNO, DEPTNUM, DEPTNAME
FROM    (SELECT EMPNO,
                COALESCE(EMP.WORKDEPT, DEPT.DEPTNO) AS DEPTNUM,
                DEPT.DEPTNAME
         FROM   EMP FULL OUTER JOIN DEPT
         ON     EMP.WORKDEPT = DEPT.DEPTNO) AS OJ_EMP_DEPT
WHERE   DEPTNUM = 'D01';
```

This example finds the row for 'D01' because COALESCE is applied to the inline view before the local predicate is applied.

Optimize OUTER JOINs with Proper Predicate Placement

Version 4

Consider the following OUTER JOIN with a local predicate:

```
SELECT  EMP.EMPNO, EMP.LASTNAME, DEPT.DEPTNAME
FROM    EMP LEFT OUTER JOIN DEPT
ON      EMP.WORKDEPT = DEPT.DEPTNO
WHERE   EMP.SALARY > 50000.00;
```

The code looks correct and returns the appropriate rows. You may never encounter the inherent problem with this formulation in a test environment. However, when thousands or millions of rows are filtered out by additional predicates, this method of coding outer joins performs quite poorly.

In this case, the outer join is performed first, before any rows are filtered out. The result set in a production environment may comprise thousands or millions of rows without the local predicate. By applying the local predicate before the outer join takes place, however, the result set turns into just a few rows. To resolve this potential problem, use an inline view as follows:

```
SELECT  E.EMPNO, E.LASTNAME, DEPT.DEPTNAME
FROM    (SELECT EMPNO, LASTNAME
         FROM EMP
         WHERE SALARY > 50000.00) AS E
        LEFT OUTER JOIN DEPT
        ON E.WORKDEPT = DEPT.DEPTNO;
```

If you move the local predicate into the FROM clause as an inline view, the local predicate is evaluated before the outer join, thereby reducing the number of rows to be joined and enhancing performance. Of course, the resultant SQL is a bit more complex and difficult to code, explain, and maintain, but the performance gains can far outweigh these legitimate concerns.

If additional local predicates are required, you can specify additional inline views. If you want to return rows only for which a domestic resource has responsibility, you can change the sample query as shown:

```
SELECT   E.EMPNO, E.LASTNAME, DEPT.DEPTNAME
FROM     (SELECT EMPNO, LASTNAME
          FROM EMP
          WHERE SALARY > 50000.00) AS E
         LEFT OUTER JOIN
          (SELECT DEPTNO, DEPTNAME
           FROM DEPT
           WHERE MGRNO IS NOT NULL) AS D
         ON E.WORKDEPT = DEPT.DEPTNO;
```

Limit the Columns Grouped

When you use a GROUP BY clause to achieve data aggregation, specify only the columns that need to be grouped. Do not provide extraneous columns in the SELECT list and GROUP BY list. To accomplish data grouping, DB2 must sort the retrieved data before displaying it. The more columns that need to be sorted, the more work DB2 must do, and the poorer the performance of the SQL statement.

GROUP BY and ORDER BY Are Not Equivalent

Although the GROUP BY clause typically sorts data to aggregate, the results are not necessarily in order by the GROUP BY. If you want to ensure that the results are displayed in a specific order, you must use the ORDER BY clause. When you specify both GROUP BY and ORDER BY, and the ordering requirements are compatible, DB2 V5 can avoid the redundant sort.

Use Inline Views to Your Advantage

Version 4

Inline views, sometimes called *nested tables,* allow the FROM clause of a SELECT statement to contain another SELECT statement. You can write any table expression in the FROM clause, an area previously reserved for table, alias, and view names only.

Why would you want to use an inline view instead of simply creating an actual view prior to issuing the SELECT statement? The first potential benefit is that an inline view expression can be easier to understand. Instead of attempting to query the DB2 Catalog to extract the SQL definition of a view, the SQL is clearly displayed in the body of the SELECT statement. Second, as I've shown in previous guidelines, inline views can provide performance and functionality improvements when used with outer joins. Finally, inline views provide direct SQL support for certain complex queries that required a view prior to DB2 V4.

Inline views are useful, for example, when detail and aggregated information from a single table must be returned by a single query. A prime example is reporting on column length information from the DB2 Catalog. Consider a request to provide column details for each table, and on each row also report the maximum, minimum, and average column lengths for that table. The pre-DB2 V4 solution was to create a view. Consider the COL_LENGTH view based on SYSIBM.SYSCOLUMNS, as shown here:

```
CREATE VIEW COL_LENGTH
   (TABLE_NAME, MAX_LENGTH,
    MIN_LENGTH, AVG_LENGTH)
AS SELECT    TBNAME, MAX(LENGTH),
             MIN(LENGTH), AVG(LENGTH)
   FROM      SYSIBM.SYSCOLUMNS
   GROUP BY TBNAME
```

After the view is created, you can issue the following SELECT statement joining the view to the base table, thereby providing both detail and aggregate information on each report row:

```
SELECT    TBNAME, NAME, COLNO, LENGTH,
          MAX_LENGTH, MIN_LENGTH, AVG_LENGTH
FROM      SYSIBM.SYSCOLUMNS C,
          authid.COL_LENGTH V
WHERE     C.TBNAME = V.TABLE_NAME
ORDER BY 1, 3
```

The solution using inline views is to skip the view-creation step and simply execute the following SQL statement:

```
SELECT TBNAME, NAME, COLNO, LENGTH,
       MAX_LENGTH, MIN_LENGTH, AVG_LENGTH
FROM   SYSIBM.SYSCOLUMNS C,
       (SELECT TBNAME AS TABLE_NAME,
               MAX(LENGTH) AS MAX_LENGTH,
               MIN(LENGTH) AS MIN_LENGTH,
               AVG(LENGTH) AS AVG_LENGTH
        FROM   SYSIBM.SYSCOLUMNS
        GROUP BY TABLE_NAME) AS V
WHERE  C.TBNAME = V.TABLE_NAME
ORDER BY 1,3
```

The same result is returned in a single SQL statement, but without using a view. You must enclose inline view expressions in parentheses and must use a correlation name. You cannot refer to the correlation name for the inline view expression elsewhere in the same FROM clause, but you can use it outside the FROM clause (just like any other table or view name) as the qualifier of a column name.

Data Modification Guidelines

Under normal circumstances, you can modify data in a DB2 table in four ways:

- Using an SQL UPDATE statement
- Using an SQL INSERT statement

- Using an SQL DELETE statement
- Using the DB2 LOAD utility

This section provides tips for the efficient implementation of the first three methods. You can find guidelines for using the LOAD utility, as well as the other DB2 utilities, in Part VI, "DB2 Utilities and Commands."

Limit Updating Indexed Columns

When you update columns in indexes, a corresponding update is applied to all indexes in which the columns participate. Updating can have a substantial impact on performance due to the additional I/O overhead.

Use FOR UPDATE OF Correctly

Specify only those columns that actually will or can be updated in the FOR UPDATE OF column list of a cursor. DB2 does not use any index that contains columns listed in the FOR UPDATE OF clause.

Consider Using DELETE/INSERT Instead of FOR UPDATE OF

If all columns in a row are being updated, use DELETE on the old row and use INSERT on the new one rather than use the FOR UPDATE OF clause. This way, you give DB2 the opportunity to use an index. With the FOR UPDATE OF clause, DB2 would have to do a tablespace scan with an RR lock on the affected table.

Update Multiple Rows

You have two options for updating data using the SQL UPDATE verb:

- A cursor UPDATE using WHERE CURRENT OF
- A direct SQL UPDATE

If the data does not have to be retrieved by the application before the update, use the direct SQL UPDATE statement.

A cursor UPDATE with the WHERE CURRENT OF option performs worse than a direct UPDATE for two reasons. First, the rows to be updated must be retrieved from the cursor a row at a time. Each row is fetched and then updated. A direct UPDATE affects multiple rows with one statement. Second, when using a cursor, you must add the overhead of the OPEN and CLOSE statement.

Update Only Changed Columns

UPDATE statements should specify only columns in which the value will be modified. For example, if only the ACSTAFF column of the DSN8510.PROJACT table should be changed, do not code the following:

```
EXEC SQL
     FETCH C1
     INTO :HV-PROJNO, :HV-ACTNO, :HV-ACSTAFF,
          :HV-ACSTDATE, :HV-ACENDATE
END-EXEC.
MOVE 4.5 TO HV-ACSTAFF.
UPDATE DSN8510.PROJACT
       SET PROJNO   = :HV-PROJNO,
       SET ACTNO    = :HV-ACTNO,
       SET ACSTAFF  = :HV-ACSTAFF,
       SET ACSTDATE = :HV-ACSTDATE,
       SET ACENDATE = :HV-ACENDATE
WHERE CURRENT OF C1;
```

Although the host variables contain the same data currently stored in the table, you should avoid this type of coding. DB2 checks to see whether the data is different before performing the update. If none of the values are different than those already stored in the table, the update does not take place. Performance may suffer, though, because DB2 has to perform the value checking. You can avoid this situation by coding the UPDATE statement as follows:

```
UPDATE DSN8510.PROJACT
       SET ACSTAFF = :HV-ACSTAFF
WHERE CURRENT OF C1;
```

Disregard this guideline when the application you are developing requires you to code a complicated check algorithm that DB2 can perform automatically. Because of the complexity of the code needed to check for current values, implementing this type of processing is not always feasible. Nevertheless, try to avoid specifying useless updates of this type when issuing interactive SQL.

Consider Dropping Indexes Before Large Insertions

When you execute a large number of INSERTs for a single table, every index must be updated with the columns and the appropriate RIDs (row IDs) for each inserted row. For very large insertions, the indexes can become unorganized, causing poor performance. Dropping all indexes for the table, performing the INSERTs, and then re-creating the indexes might be more efficient. The trade-off to consider is the overhead of updating indexes versus the index recreation plus the rebinding of all application plans that used the indexes.

Exercise Caution When Issuing Ad Hoc DELETE Statements

Be extremely careful when issuing SQL DELETE statements outside the control of an application program. Remember that SQL acts on a set of data, not just one row. All rows that qualify based on the SQL WHERE clause are updated or deleted. For example, consider the following SQL statement:

```
DELETE
FROM DSN8510.DEPT;
```

This SQL statement, called a mass DELETE, effectively deletes every row from the DEPT table. Normally, this result is undesirable.

Exercise Caution When Issuing Ad Hoc UPDATE Statements

When issuing an ad hoc UPDATE, take care to specify an appropriate WHERE clause. Consider the following SQL statement:

```
UPDATE DSN8510.DEPT
SET DEPTNAME = 'NEW DEPARTMENT';
```

This SQL statement changes the value of the DEPTNAME column for every row in the table to the value 'NEW DEPARTMENT'. This result occurs because no WHERE clause is coded to limit the scope of the UPDATE. Requests of this nature are not usually desirable and should be avoided.

Mass DELETE Versus LOAD

Sometimes you need to empty a table. You can do so by issuing a mass DELETE or by loading an empty data set. A mass DELETE usually is more efficient when you're using segmented tablespaces. Loading an empty data set usually is more efficient when you're using simple or partitioned tablespaces.

Use INSERT and UPDATE to Add Long Columns

The maximum length of a string literal that can be inserted into DB2 is limited to 254 characters. This restriction poses a problem when you must insert a LONG VARCHAR column in an ad hoc environment.

To get around this limitation, issue an INSERT followed immediately by an UPDATE. For example, if you need to insert 260 bytes of data into a LONG VARCHAR column, begin by inserting the first 254 bytes as shown:

```
INSERT INTO your.table
COLUMNS     (LONG_COL,
             other columns)
VALUES      ('< first 254 bytes of LONG_COL >',
             other values);
```

Follow the INSERT with an UPDATE statement to add the rest of the data to the column, as in the following example:

```
UPDATE your.table
SET LONG_COL = LONG_COL || '< remaining 6 bytes of LONG_COL >',
WHERE KEY_COL = 'key value';
```

For this technique to be successful, a unique key column (or columns) must exist for the table. If each row cannot be uniquely identified, the UPDATE cannot be issued because it might update more data than you want.

List Columns for INSERT

When you are coding an INSERT statement in an application program, list the column names for each value you are inserting. Although you could merely align the values in the same order as the column names in the table, doing so leads only to confusion. Furthermore, if ALTER is used to add new columns to the table, every `INSERT` statement that does not explicitly list the columns being inserted will fail. The proper format is

```
INSERT INTO DSN8510.DEPT
        (DEPTNO,
         DEPTNAME,
         MGRNO,
         ADMRDEPT)
    VALUES
        ('077',
         'NEW DEPARTMENT',
         '123456',
         '123') ;
```

Summary

Manipulating data in DB2 tables using SQL can be a daunting task. Using the preceding guidelines will greatly ease this burden. Now that you understand how to access DB2 data efficiently, you're ready to learn how to define DB2 data structures properly. For more information on this subject, turn to Chapter 3.

3

Data Definition Guidelines

You must make many choices when implementing DB2 objects. The large number of alternatives can intimidate the beginning user. By following the data definition guidelines in this chapter, you can ensure that you make the proper physical design decisions. Rules are provided for selecting the appropriate DB2 DDL parameters, choosing the proper DB2 objects for your application, and implementing a properly designed physical database.

Naming Conventions

Before issuing DDL, standard names must be identified for all objects that will be created. As such, guidelines for DB2 naming conventions are discussed before DDL guidelines.

Develop and Enforce DB2 Naming Conventions

The first step in creating an optimal DB2 environment is the development of rigorous naming standards for all DB2 objects. This standard should be used with all other IT naming standards in your shop. Where possible, the DB2 naming conventions should be developed to peacefully coexist with your other standards, but not at the expense of impairing the DB2 environment. In all cases, naming standards should be approved by the corporate data administration department (if one exists).

Do not impose unnecessary restrictions on the names of objects accessed by end users. DB2 is supposed to be a user-friendly database management system. Strict, limiting naming conventions, if not developed logically, can be the antithesis of what you are striving to achieve with DB2.

For example, many shops impose an eight-character encoded table-naming convention on their environment. DB2 provides for 18-character table names, and there is no reason to restrict your table names to eight characters. There is even less reason for these names to be encoded. A reasonable table-naming convention is a two- or three-character application identifier prefix, followed by an underscore, and then a clear, user-friendly name.

For example, consider the customer name and address table in a customer maintenance system. The name of this table could be:

```
CMS_CUST_NAME_ADDR
```

The application identifier is CMS (for Customer Maintenance System), followed by an underscore and a clear table name, `CUST_NAME_ADDR`. If this table were named following an eight-character encoded name convention, it might appear as `TCMSNMAD`. This clearly is not a user-friendly name, and should be avoided.

In general, a standard naming convention should allow the use of all characters provided by DB2. (See Appendix G, "DB2 Limits," for a listing of DB2 size limitations for each type of object.) By using all available characters, the DB2 environment is easier to use and understand. All information pertaining to which indexes are defined for which tables, which tables are in which tablespaces, which tablespaces are in which databases, and so on can be found by querying the DB2 Catalog.

The only valid exception to using all available characters is when naming indexes. An index name can be 18 characters, but there are advantages to limiting it to eight characters. Indexes are unknown to most end users, so a limiting index name is not as great a blow to user friendliness as a limiting table name.

The problem with 18-character index names is the result of the strict data set naming convention required by DB2. This convention is

```
vcat.DSNDBx.dddddddd.ssssssss.I0001.Annn
```

where:

vcat	High-level qualifier, indicating an ICF catalog
x	C if VSAM cluster component D if VSAM data component
dddddddd	Database name
ssssssss	Tablespace name or index name
nnn	Partition number or the data set number

NOTE

A non-partitioned index can cover 32 2GB data sets. The first data set ends with 001, the second data set ends with 002, and so on.

If you use more than eight characters to name an index defined using a `STOGROUP`, or storage group, DB2 creates a unique, eight-character string to be used when defining the underlying data set for the index. If the index is created using native VSAM, the first eight characters of the name must be unique and must be used when defining the underlying VSAM data set. These two constraints can make the task of correlating indexes to data set names an administrative nightmare.

Establish Naming Conventions for All DB2 Objects

Be sure to create and publish naming standards for all DB2 objects. A comprehensive list of objects follows:

STOGROUP	Plan and Package
Database	Stored Procedure
Tablespace	Program
Table	DBRM
Referential Constraint	Check Constraint
View	Utility ID

Alias	Index
Synonym	Column
Collection	Version

You might also consider creating naming standards for other related objects such as FIELDPROCs, EDITPROCs, image copy data set names, PDS library names, and so on.

Sample DB2 naming standards follow. These standards are only suggestions. Your shop standards are likely to vary from these standards. Valid characters are all alphabetic characters, the underscore, and numbers.

DB2 Database Names

Format:	*Daaadddd*
aaa	application identifier
dddd	unique description

DB2 Tablespace Names

Format:	*Saaadddd*
aaa	application identifier
dddd	unique description

Table, View, Alias, and Synonym Names

Format:	aaa_dddddddddddddd
aaa	application identifier
dddddddddddddd	unique description up to 14 characters long

Temporary Table Names

Format:	TMP_dddddddddddddd
TMP	constant temporary indicator (consider an alternate shop standard if you already use TMP as an application identifier)
dddddddddddddd	unique description up to 14 characters long

DB2 Index Names

Format:	*Xaaadddd*
aaa	application identifier
dddd	unique description

STOGROUP Names

Format:	*Gaaadddd*
aaa	application identifier
dddd	unique description

Referential Constraint Names (Foreign Keys)

Format:	*Raaadddd*
aaa	application identifier
dddd	unique description

Check Constraint Names

Version 4

Format:	*Caaadddd*
aaa	application identifier
dddd	unique description (for example, first four characters of column name)

DB2 Column Names

Format:	up to 18 characters

DB2 column names should be as descriptive as possible to provide documentation, so try to use all 18 characters. When you use abbreviations to name a column in the 18-character limit, use the standard Data Management abbreviations. This ensures a consistent and effective database environment.

Columns that define the same attribute should be named the same. Additionally, the same name should never be used for different attributes. In other words, a column used as a primary key in one table should be named identically when used as a foreign key in other tables. The only valid exception is when the same attribute exists in one table multiple times. In this case, specify a substitute column name; you usually can use the attribute name with a descriptive suffix or prefix. For code supplied by vendors, you might have to make exceptions to this guideline of singular column names per attribute.

DB2 Plan Names

Format:	up to eight characters

The convention is that the name of the plan should be the same as the name of the application program to which it applies. If multiple program DBRMs (Database Request Modules) are bound to a single large plan, or if one plan is composed of many packages, the name should be assigned by the database administration department such that the name successfully identifies the application, is not an actual program name, and is unique in the DB2 subsystem.

DB2 Package Names

Format:	up to eight characters

Packages are named the same as the DBRM.

DBRM Names

Format:	up to eight characters

DBRMs generally are named the same as the program. If a single program is used to create multiple DBRMs, consult with the database administration department for an acceptable name.

Collection Names

Format:	aaa_dddddddd_eeeee
aaa	application identifier
eeeee	environment (BATCH, CAF, CICS, DLI, IMSDC, BMP, TSO, and so on)

Explicit Version Names

Format:	uuuuuuuu_date_tttt_s
uuuuuuuu	authid (of person performing precompile)
date	date of precompile (ISO format)
tttt	type of program (TEST, TEMP, PROD, QUAL, and so on)
s	sequence number (if required)

The explicit version name should be used when the programmer is to specify the version instead of having DB2 supply the version automatically at precompile time. An example of an explicit version name would be DBAPCSM_1994-01-01_TEMP_3, indicating that on New Year's Day user DBAPCSM precompiled this version as a temporary fix (at least) three times.

Automatic Version Names

The automatic version name must be permitted when DB2 is to assign the version name automatically at precompile time. In this case, the version name is a 26-byte ISO timestamp. For example, 1993-07-21-15.04.26.546405.

Utility ID

DB2 utility IDs should be unique for each utility to be executed. No two utilities can be run concurrently with the same ID.

The utility ID for all regularly scheduled DB2 utilities should be allowed to default to the name of the job. Because MVS does not permit two identically named jobs to execute at the same time, DB2 utility IDs will be forced to be unique.

DCLGEN Declare Members

Format:	oaaadddd	
o	object identifier:	
	T	table
	V	view
	A	alias
	S	synonym
aaa	application identifier	
dddd	unique description	

The unique description, *dddd*, should be the same as the tablespace to which the table has been defined. If more than one of any object type exists per tablespace, the database administration department should assign a unique name and provide that name to the appropriate application development staff.

Compliance

All DB2 object names should be assigned by the database administration department. It is also the database administration department's responsibility to enforce DB2 naming conventions.

Database, Tablespace, and Table Guidelines

When creating DB2 objects, an efficient environment can be created by heeding the following guidelines.

Define Useful Storage Groups

A storage group, known to DB2 as a STOGROUP, is an object used to identify a set of DASD volumes associated with an ICF catalog, or VCAT. Storage groups and user-defined VSAM are the two storage allocation options for DB2 data set definition.

Define more than one volume per storage group to allow for growth and to minimize out-of-space abend situations. A data set extend failure causes DB2 to check the STOGROUP volume entries and issue a VSAM `ALTER ADDVOLUMES` for the data set.

When defining multiple volumes to a storage group, DB2 keeps track of which volume was specified first in the list and tries to use that volume first. DB2 does not attempt to balance the load on the DASD volumes. Data set allocation is performed by IBM's Data Facility Product (DFP). The order in which the volumes are coded in the `CREATE STOGROUP` statement determines the order in which the volumes are used by DB2. When the first volume is full, or if for any reason

DFP determines that it cannot allocate a data set on that volume, DB2 (through DFP) moves to the next volume. You cannot retrieve this ordering information from the DB2 Catalog, though, so make sure you have documentation detailing the order in which the volumes were defined to the storage group.

If you would rather not administer multiple volume STOGROUPs, you must be prepared to handle abends resulting from a volume being out of space. Handling out-of-space conditions usually involves one of the following:

- Moving the data set to a volume with more space by altering the STOGROUP and then recovering or reorganizing the tablespace
- Adding a volume to the STOGROUP to accommodate additional data set extents

A good method of maintaining DB2 objects on multiple volumes is to define multiple STOGROUPs, each with a different volume as the first listed volume. For example, consider a new application assigned two volumes, called VOL1 and VOL2. Create two STOGROUPs as follows:

```
CREATE STOGROUP TESTSG1
   VOLUMES('VOL1', 'VOL2') VCAT appl ;
CREATE STOGROUP TESTSG2
   VOLUMES('VOL2', 'VOL1') VCAT appl ;
```

After creating these STOGROUPs, you can balance the load on the volumes by assigning some of the tablespaces to `TESTSG1` and some to `TESTSG2`. If one volume runs out of space, the other can serve as the backup.

The maximum number of volumes used by a storage group is 133 (even though DB2 allows more than 133 volumes to be defined to a storage group). It usually is difficult to monitor more than 3 or 4 volumes to a STOGROUP, however. All volumes in a storage group must be of the same type (for example, 3380, 3390, and so on).

Never Use SYSDEFLT

The default DB2 storage group is `SYSDEFLT`. `SYSDEFLT` is created when DB2 is installed, and is used when a storage group is not explicitly stated (and `VCAT` is not used) in a database, a tablespace, or an index `CREATE` statement. I recommend that you never use `SYSDEFLT`. Objects created using `SYSDEFLT` are hard to maintain and track. Additionally, creating many different DB2 objects from diverse applications on the same DASD volumes degrades performance and, eventually, no more space will remain on the volumes assigned to `SYSDEFLT`. If you grant the use of `SYSDEFLT` only to SYSADMs, you can limit its use.

User-Defined VSAM Data Set Definitions

When creating DB2 objects with the VCAT option instead of the STOGROUP option, you must create user-defined VSAM data sets explicitly using the VSAM Access Method Services utility, IDCAMS. You can use two types of VSAM data sets for representing DB2 tablespaces and index spaces: VSAM ESDS and VSAM LDS.

VSAM ESDS is an entry-sequenced data set, and VSAM LDS is a linear data set. A linear data set has a 4K CI size and does not contain the control information that entry-sequenced data sets normally contain. VSAM LDS and ESDS data sets are not used as plain VSAM data sets. DB2 uses the VSAM Media Manager to access these data sets. DB2 performs additional formatting of the VSAM data sets, causing them to operate differently than standard VSAM. Therefore, a direct VSAM read and write to a DB2 VSAM data set will fail.

Create DB2 data sets as VSAM linear data sets instead of as VSAM entry-sequenced data sets because DB2 can use LDS more efficiently.

An example of the IDCAMS data set definition specification follows:

```
DEFINE CLUSTER —
   (NAME (vcat.DSNDBC.dddddddd.ssssssss.I0001.Annn) —
    LINEAR —
    REUSE —
    VOLUMES (volume list)
    CYLINDER (primary   secondary) —
    SHAREOPTIONS (3 3) —
    ) —
DATA —
   (NAME (vcat.DSNDBD.dddddddd.ssssssss.I0001.Annn)) —
```

where:

vcat	high-level qualifier, indicating an ICF catalog
dddddddd	database name
ssssssss	tablespace name or index name
nnn	partition number or data set number

NOTE

Non-partitioned tablespaces and indexes can cover 32 2GB data sets. The first data set ends with 001, the second data set ends with 002, and so on.

volume list	listing of physical DASD devices
primary	primary space allocation quantity
secondary	secondary space allocation quantity

Alias and Synonym Definitions

Aliases can be accessed by users other than their creator, but synonyms can be accessed only by their creator. When a table is dropped, its synonyms are dropped but its aliases are retained. Aliases, which were new to DB2 as of V2.2, were added primarily for distributed processing. Remote tables add a location prefix to the table name. However, you can create an alias for a remote table, thereby giving it a shorter, local name because it no longer requires the location prefix.

The recommendation is to use synonyms for program development, use aliases for distributed applications, and use views for security and joining.

Database Definitions

Physically, a DB2 database is nothing more than a defined grouping of DB2 objects. One database per logical application system (or subsystem) is a good rule of thumb. A database contains no data, but acts as a high-level identifier for tracking other DB2 objects. The START and STOP commands can be issued at the database level, thereby affecting all objects grouped under that database.

Logically, a database should be used to group like tables. You can do this for all tables in an application system or for tables in a logical subsystem of a larger application. It makes sense to combine tables with similar functions and uses in a single database because it simplifies DB2 security and the starting and stopping of the application tablespaces and indexes.

As a general rule, though, place no more than three dozen tables in a single database. More tables than this usually are too difficult to administer and monitor. For applications that have multiple tables per tablespace, define no more than three dozen tablespaces to a single database.

When DDL is issued to drop or create objects in an existing database, the *database descriptor* (*DBD*) for the affected database must be modified. The DBD is a control structure used by DB2 to manage the objects under the control of a given database. For DB2 to modify the DBD, a lock must be taken. A DBD lock will cause contention, usually resulting in the failure of the DDL execution.

If the DDL is submitted when there is little or no activity, however, application users may be locked out while the DDL is being executed. An X lock will be taken on the DBD while the DDL executes. For very active databases, there may not be a dormant window in which a lock of this kind can be taken. This can cause undue stress on the system when new objects must be added—a good reason to limit the number of objects defined to a single database.

NOTE

An additional, though somewhat esoteric, consideration is the size of the DBD. A DBD contains a mapping of the tablespaces, tables, and indexes defined to a database. When a request for data is made, the DBD is loaded into an area of main storage called the EDM pool. The DBD should be small enough that it does not cause problems with EDM pool storage. Problems generally will not occur if your databases are not outrageously large and your EDM pool is well-defined. For a further discussion of DBDs and their effect on the EDM pool, see Chapters 15, "The Table-Based Infrastructure of DB2," and 21, "Tuning DB2's Components."

Specify Database Parameters

Specify a storage group and buffer pool for every database that you create. If you do not define a STOGROUP, the default DB2 storage group, SYSDEFLT, is assigned to the database. This is undesirable because the volumes assigned to SYSDEFLT become unmanageable if too many DB2 data sets are defined to them.

If you do not define a buffer pool, BP0 is used. Depending on shop standards, this may be desirable, but explicitly coding the buffer pool still is recommended to avoid confusion. A good rule is to explicitly code *every* pertinent parameter for every DB2 statement.

Never Use DSNDB04

The default DB2 database is DSNDB04. DSNDB04 is created during installation and is used when a database is not explicitly stated in a tablespace CREATE statement, or when a database and tablespace combination is not explicitly stated in a table CREATE statement. I recommend that you never use DSNDB04. Objects created in DSNDB04 are hard to maintain and track. To limit the use of DSNDB04, grant its use only to SYSADMs.

NOTE

An additional caveat usage of the default database, the REPAIR DROP DATABASE statement cannot be used on DSNDB04.

Be Aware of the Impact of Drops on DBDs

When an object is dropped, the related entry in the DBD is marked as logically deleted, but not physically deleted. Certain types of changes, such as removing a column, reordering columns, or changing a data type necessitate dropping and recreating tables. Each time the table is dropped and recreated, the DBD will grow. Very large DBDs can result in -904 SQLCODEs specifying the unavailable resource as the EDM Pool (resource 0600).

To reduce the size of the DBD, you must follow these steps:

1. REORG the tablespaces for tables which have been dropped and recreated. The log RBA recorded in SYSCOPY for this REORG will indicate to DB2 that the dropped tables are no longer in the tablespace.
2. Run MODIFY RECOVERY to remove the old image copy information for the dropped table. The preferred method with the least amount of down time is to run MODIFY RECOVERY DELETE AGE(*). This will shrink your DBD and delete all old SYSCOPY and SYSLGRNGX information.
3. Run an image copy for each tablespace to ensure recoverability.

Use Proper Tablespace Definitions

Explicitly define tablespaces. If a tablespace is not specified in the table creation statement, DB2 creates an implicit tablespace for new tables and sets all tablespace parameters to the default values. These values are unacceptable for most applications.

There are three types of DB2 tablespaces, each one useful in different circumstances:

- Simple tablespaces
- Segmented tablespaces
- Partitioned tablespaces

In general, use segmented tablespaces except as follows:

- Use partitioned tablespaces when you wish to encourage parallelism.
- Use partitioned tablespaces when the amount of data to be stored is very large (more than 1 million pages).
- Use partitioned tablespaces to reduce utility processing time and decrease contention.
- Use partitioned tablespaces to isolate specific data areas in dedicated data sets.
- Use partitioned tablespaces to improve data availability. If the data is partitioned by region, the partitions for the eastern, southern, and northern regions can be made available while the western region partition is being reorganized.
- Use partitioned tablespaces to improve recoverability. If the data is partitioned by region and an error impacts data for the eastern region only, then only the eastern partition needs to be recovered.
- Use a simple tablespace *only* when you need to mix data from different tables on one page.

The next three sections provide more in-depth guidelines for each of the tablespace types.

Using Simple Tablespaces

Simple tablespaces are found mostly in older DB2 applications (those developed before 1989). A simple tablespace can contain one or more tables, but in general only one table should be defined per simple tablespace. This is because a single page of a simple tablespace can contain rows from all the tables defined to the tablespace. Having multiple tables in a simple tablespace adversely affects concurrent data access, data availability, space management, and load utility processing. The LOAD utility with the REPLACE option obliterates all data in a tablespace, not just the data for the table being loaded. This usually is unacceptable for most application processing. Additionally, the compression ratio can be adversely impacted by storing multiple tables in a single tablespace.

Prior to DB2 V2.1, most DB2 tablespaces were defined as simple tablespaces because the only other option was a partitioned tablespace. Most applications developed on a version of DB2 after V1.3 use segmented tablespaces because of their enhanced performance and improved methods of handling multiple tables. Segmented tablespaces make simple tablespaces almost obsolete.

If an application must read rows from multiple tables in a predefined sequence, however, mixing the rows of these tables together in a single simple tablespace could prove beneficial. The rows should be mixed together on the page in a way that clusters the keys by which the rows will be accessed. This can be done by inserting the rows using a "round robin" approach, switching from table to table, as follows:

1. Create a tablespace as a simple tablespace; do not specify a `SEGSIZE` or `NUMPARTS` clause.
2. Create the two tables (for example, Table1 and Table2), assigning them both to the simple tablespace you just created.
3. Sort the input data set of values to be inserted into Table1 into key sequence order.
4. Sort the input data set of values to be inserted into Table2 into sequence by the foreign key that refers to the primary key of Table1.
5. Code a program that inserts a row into Table1, then inserts all corresponding foreign key rows into Table2.
6. Continue this pattern until all primary keys have been inserted.

When the application reads the data in this predefined sequence, the data from these two tables is clustered on the same (or a neighboring) page. Great care must be taken to ensure that the data is inserted in the proper sequence and that subsequent insertions do not alter the mix of data. Also, remember that mixing data rows from multiple tables on the same tablespace page adversely affects the performance of all queries, utilities, and applications that do not access the data in this manner. Be sure that the primary type of access to the data is by the predefined mixing sequence before implementing a simple tablespace in this manner.

Unless data-row mixing is being implemented, define no more than one table to each simple tablespace. Also, consider defining all your nonpartitioned tablespaces as segmented instead of simple.

Using Segmented Tablespaces

A segmented tablespace is the most efficient type of tablespace for most DB2 development efforts. A segmented tablespace provides most of the benefits of a simple tablespace, plus:

- Multiple tables can be defined to one segmented tablespace without the problems encountered when using simple tablespaces. Tables are stored in separate segments. Because data rows never are mixed on the same page, concurrent access to tables in the same segmented tablespace is not a problem.
- Segmented tablespaces handle free space more efficiently, which results in less overhead for inserts and for variable-length row updates.

- Mass delete processing is more efficient because only the space map—not the data itself—is updated. A mass delete of rows from a table in a simple tablespace causes every row to be physically read and deleted. The following is an example of a mass delete:

```
DELETE
FROM DSN8510.DEPT;
```

If DSN8510.DEPT is defined in a simple tablespace, all of its rows are read and deleted. If it is defined in a segmented tab

- Space can be reclaimed from dropped tables immediately. This reduces the need for reorganization.

Most of your application tablespaces should be segmented. All tablespaces that contain multiple tables (and do not need to mix data from multiple tables on a page) should be segmented. Even when you're defining one table for each tablespace, the performance advantage of the more efficient space utilization should compel you to use segmented tablespaces.

Choose the segment size carefully. Consider each of the following when selecting the segment size:

- SEGSIZE is defined as an integer representing the number of pages to be assigned to a segment. The size of a segment can be any multiple of 4, from 4 to 64, inclusive.
- DASD space is allocated based on the PRIQTY and SECQTY specifications for STOGROUP-defined tablespaces, or on the VSAM IDCAMS definition for user-defined VSAM tablespaces. However, this space can never be smaller than a full segment. The primary extent and all secondary extents are rounded to the next full segment before being allocated.
- Space cannot be allocated at less than a full track. Consult the "PRIQTY and SECQTY" section later in this chapter for additional information.
- When defining multiple tables in a segmented tablespace, keep tables of like size in the same tablespace. Do not combine large tables with small tables in a single segmented tablespace. Defining small tables in a tablespace with a large segment size could result in wasted DASD space.
- When a segmented tablespace contains multiple tables large enough to be processed using sequential prefetch, be sure to define the SEGSIZE according to the following chart. The segment size should be at least as large as the maximum number of pages that can be read by sequential prefetch. Otherwise, sequential prefetch could read pages that do not apply to the table being accessed, causing inefficient sequential prefetch processing.

Bufferpool Range	*Segment Size*
1 through 500	16
501 through 999	32
1000 and over	64

These numbers are valid as of DB2 V5, but may change for subsequent releases.

Using Partitioned Tablespaces

A partitioned tablespace is divided into components called *partitions.* Each partition resides in a separate physical data set. Partitioned tablespaces are designed to increase the availability of data in large tables.

Version 5

DB2 permits from 1 to 254 partitions per tablespace (from 1 to 64 partitions for non-LARGE tablespaces and those created prior to DB2 V5). As a general rule of thumb try to define tablespace partitions such that no one partition is more than 20 percent larger than the next largest partition. This provides even growth, which eases DASD monitoring and provides approximately even data access requirements and utility processing times across partitions. However, maintaining evenly distributed partitions may not be desirable when partitions are used to isolate data "hot spots."

For non-LARGE partitioned tablespaces, the number of partitions impacts the maximum size of the data set partition as follows:

Number of Partitions	*Maximum Data Set Size*
1 to 16	4 GB
17 to 32	2 GB
33 to 64	1 GB

Deciding to use a partitioned tablespace is not as simple as merely determining the size of the table. Application-level details, such as data contention, performance requirements, and the volume of updates to columns in the partitioning index must factor into the decision to use partitioned tablespaces.

Never attempt to avoid a partitioned tablespace by implementing several smaller tablespaces, each containing a subset of the total amount of data. When proceeding in this manner, the designer usually places separate tables, each with the same data characteristics, into each of the smaller tablespaces. This usually is a bad design decision because it introduces an uncontrolled and unneeded denormalization. (See the section in this chapter on "Denormalization" for more information.)

When data that logically belongs in one table is separated into multiple tables, SQL operations to access the data as a logical whole are made needlessly complex. One example of this complexity is the difficulty in enforcing unique keys across multiple tables. Although partitioned tablespaces can introduce additional complexities into your environment, these complexities never outweigh those introduced by mimicking partitioning with several smaller, identical tablespaces.

Before deciding to partition a tablespace, weigh the pros and cons. Consult the following lists of advantages and disadvantages before implementation:

Advantages of a partitioned tablespace:

- Each partition can be placed on a different DASD volume to increase access efficiency.
- Partitioned tablespaces are the only type of tablespace that can hold more than 64GB of data (the maximum size of simple and segmented tablespaces). As of DB2 V5, a partitioned tablespace can hold up to 1TB of data.
- Start and stop commands can be issued at the partition level. By stopping only specific partitions, the remaining partitions are available to be accessed, thereby promoting higher availability.
- Free space (PCTFREE and FREEPAGE) can be specified at the partition level, enabling the DBA to isolate data "hot spots" to a specific partition and tune accordingly.
- Query I/O, CPU, and Sysplex parallelism enable multiple engines to access different partitions in parallel, usually resulting in reduced elapsed time.
- Tablespace scans on partitioned tablespaces can skip partitions that are excluded based on the query predicates.
- The clustering index used for partitioning can be set up to decrease data contention. For example, if the tablespace will be partitioned by DEPT, each department (or range of compatible departments) could be placed in separate partitions. Each department is in a discrete physical data set, thereby reducing interdepartmental contention due to multiple departments coexisting on the same data page. Note that contention remains for data in non-partitioned indexes (although this contention has been significantly reduced by DB2 V4 and V5).
- DB2 creates a separate compression dictionary for each tablespace partition. Multiple dictionaries tend to cause better overall compression ratios. In addition, it is more likely that the partition-level compression dictionaries can be rebuilt more frequently than non-partitioned dictionaries. Frequent rebuilding of the compression dictionary can lead to a better overall compression ratio.
- The REORG, COPY, and RECOVER utilities can execute on tablespaces at the partition level. If these utilities are set to execute on partitions instead of on the entire tablespace, valuable time can be saved by processing only the partitions that need to be reorganized, copied, or recovered. Partition independence and resource serialization further increase the availability of partitions during utility processing.

Disadvantages of a partitioned tablespace:

- Only one table can be defined in a partitioned tablespace.
- The entire length of the key for the partitioning index cannot exceed 40 bytes.
- The columns of the partitioning index cannot be updated. To change a value in one of these columns, you must delete the row and then reinsert it with the new values.

- The range of key values for which data will be inserted into the table must be known and stable before you create the partitioning index. To define a partition, a range of values must be hard coded into the partitioning index definition. These ranges should distribute the data (more or less) evenly throughout the partitions. If you provide a stop-gap partition to catch all the values lower (or higher) than the defined range, monitor that partition to ensure that it does not grow dramatically or cause performance problems if it is smaller or larger than most other partitions.
- After you define the method of partitioning, you cannot change it easily. Individual partitions cannot be deleted or redefined. To drop the index that defines the partitioning, you must drop the table to which the index applies.

Reconsider Partitioning Tablespaces

To allow for query parallelism it is wise to reevaluate your basic notions regarding partitioning. The common "rule of thumb" regarding whether to create a partitioned tablespace instead of a segmented tablespace was to use partitioning only for larger tablespaces. This strategy is outdated.

Consider partitioning tablespaces that are accessed in a read-only manner by long running batch programs. Of course, very small tablespaces are rarely viable candidates for partitioning, even with DB2's advanced I/O, CPU, and Sysplex parallelism features. This is true because the smaller the amount of data to access, the more difficult it is to break it into pieces large enough such that concurrent, parallel processing will be helpful.

Place Partitions on Separate DASD Devices

Move each partition of the same partitioned tablespace to separate DASD volumes. Failure to do so will negatively affect the performance of query parallelism performed against those partitions. Disk drive head contention will occur because concurrent access is being performed on separate partitions that coexist on the same device.

Tablespace Parameters

Many parameters must be considered when creating a tablespace. Each of these parameters is discussed in this section.

LARGE

Version 5

The LARGE parameter is new as of DB2 Version 5 and is available for partitioned tablespaces only. When LARGE is specified approximately 1TB of data can be stored in the tablespace. A large tablespace can have up to 254 partitions, each containing up to 4GB. See Table 3.1 for definitions of storage abbreviations such as GB and TB.

Table 3.1. Storage abbreviations.

Abbrev.	*Term*	*Amount*
KB	Kilobyte	1,024 bytes
MB	Megabyte	1,024 KB
GB	Gigabyte	1,024 MB
TB	Terabyte	1,024 GB
PB	Petabyte	1,024 TB
EB	Exabyte	1,024 PB
ZB	Zettabyte	1,024 EB
YB	Yottabyte	1,024 ZB

When `LARGE` is not specified, the maximum storage amount is limited to 64GB, and the maximum number of partitions to 64.

CAUTION

If the `NUMPARTS` parameter is defined to be greater than 64, the tablespace will automatically be defined as a large tablespace even if the `LARGE` parameter is omitted.

Use LARGE Sparingly

Version 5

Although it may be tempting to define every tablespace as `LARGE`, space considerations and resource requirements need to be taken into account. `RID`s in a large tablespace are 5 bytes instead of 4 bytes. As such, index space usage will increase. Additionally, large tablespaces can use more datasets and increase resource consumption of utility processing. Therefore, a large tablespace should be used only under the following conditions:

- When more than 16 partitions are required and more than 1 GB must be stored per partition; or
- More than 64 partitions are required; or
- More than 64 GB of data must be stored in a single tablespace

LOCKSIZE

Version 4

The `LOCKSIZE` parameter indicates the type of locking DB2 performs for the given tablespace. The choices are

`ROW`	Row-level locking
`PAGE`	Page-level locking

TABLE	Table-level locking (for segmented tablespaces only)
TABLESPACE	Tablespace-level locking
ANY	Lets DB2 decide, starting with PAGE

In general, it is best to let DB2 handle the level of locking required. The recommended LOCKSIZE specification is therefore ANY, except in the following circumstances:

A read-only table defined in a single tablespace should be specified as LOCKSIZE TABLESPACE. There rarely is a reason to update the table, so page locks should be avoided.

A table that does not require shared access should be placed in a single tablespace specified as LOCKSIZE TABLESPACE. Shared access refers to multiple users (or jobs) accessing the table simultaneously.

A grouping of tables in a segmented tablespace used by a single user (for example, a QMF user) should be specified as LOCKSIZE TABLE. If only one user can access the tables, there is no reason to take page-level locks.

Favor specifying LOCKSIZE PAGE for production systems that cannot tolerate a lock escalation, but for which row locking would be overkill. When many accesses are made consistently to the same data, you must maximize concurrency. If lock escalation can occur (that is, a change from page locks to tablespace locks), concurrency is eliminated. If a particular production system always must support concurrent access, use LOCKSIZE PAGE and set the LOCKMAX parameter for the tablespace to 0.

Specify LOCKSIZE ROW only when concurrency is of paramount importance. When many users require concurrent access to data that has a high likelihood of existing on the same page, row locking may prove to be beneficial. In general, though, specify LOCKSIZE ROW only for those tablespaces where LOCKSIZE PAGE did not provide adequate concurrency. Row locking can cause performance problems because a row lock requires about the same amount of resources as a page lock. And, since there are usually multiple rows on a page, row locking will typically consume more resources. When LOCKSIZE ROW is used, all indexes defined on tables in the tablespace must be Type 2 indexes.

LOCKSIZE ANY is preferred in situations other than those just outlined because it allows DB2 to determine the optimal locking strategy based on actual access patterns. Locking begins with PAGE locks and escalates to TABLE or TABLESPACE locks when too many page locks are being held. The LOCKMAX parameter controls the number of locks that can be taken before escalation occurs. LOCKSIZE ANY generally provides an efficient locking pattern because it allows the DBMS to actively monitor and manage the locking strategy.

Use Row Locking with Care

Version 4

The resources required to acquire, maintain, and release a lock at the row level are a*bout the same as required for locking at the page level lock.* When row locking is used and a table or tablespace scan is required, DB2 will lock every row on every page accessed. The number of locks required to successfully accomplish a scan can have a detrimental impact on performance. If a table has 100 rows per page, a tablespace scan could possibly require nearly 100 times as many resources for row locks as it would for page locks.

Switch Locking Strategies Based Upon Processing

Some tables have different access patterns based upon the time of the day. For example, many applications are predominantly OLTP during work hours and predominantly batch during off hours. OLTP is usually characterized by short, indexed access to tables. Batch processing typically requires more intensive data access and table scans.

To take advantage of these situations, use the ALTER TABLESPACE statement to change the LOCKSIZE parameter to ROW for daylight processing. Before the nightly batch jobs and after online processing diminishes, alter the LOCKSIZE parameter back to ANY or PAGE.

By changing the locking strategy to conform to the type of processing, contention can be reduced thereby enhancing application performance.

LOCKMAX

The LOCKMAX parameter specifies the maximum number of page or row locks that any one process can hold at any one time for the tablespace. When the threshold is reached, the page or row locks are escalated to a table or tablespace lock.

Three options are available for setting the LOCKMAX parameter:

- The literal SYSTEM can be specified indicating that LOCKMAX should default to the system-wide value as specified in DSNZPARMS.
- The value 0 can be specified indicating that lock escalation should never occur for this tablespace.
- An integer value ranging from 1 to 2,147,483,647 can be specified indicating the actual number of row or page locks to tolerate before lock escalation.

Use Caution Before Disabling Lock Escalation

Specify LOCKMAX 0 only when you are absolutely sure of the impact it will have on your processing mix. A very high value for LOCKMAX can have a similar effect to LOCKMAX 0 with the added benefit of an escape if the number of locks becomes intolerable. Large batch jobs running against a tablespace specified as LOCKMAX 0 can severely constrain concurrent access if a large number of locks are held without an intelligent commit strategy. When volumes fluctuate (for example, monthly processing cycles), lock patterns can deviate from the norm, potentially causing concurrency problems.

USING

The method of storage allocation for the tablespace is defined with the USING parameter. You can specify either a STOGROUP name combined with a primary and secondary quantity for space allocation or a VCAT indicating the high-level ICF catalog identifier for user-defined VSAM data sets.

In most cases, you should create the majority of your tablespaces and indexes as STOGROUP-defined. This allows DB2 to do most of the work of creating and maintaining the underlying VSAM data sets, which contain the actual data.

Some DBAs believe that explicitly creating VSAM data sets for VCAT-defined tablespaces gives them more control over the physical allocation, placement, and movement of the VSAM data sets. Similar allocation, placement, and movement techniques, however, can be achieved using STOGROUPs if the STOGROUPs are properly created and maintained and the tablespaces are assigned to the STOGROUPs in a planned and orderly manner.

Another perceived advantage of VCAT-defined objects is the capability of recovering them if they inadvertently are dropped. The underlying, user-defined VSAM data sets for VCAT-defined objects are not deleted automatically when the corresponding object is dropped. You can recover the data for the tablespace using the DSN1COPY utility with the translate option. When you intentionally drop tablespaces, however, additional work is required to manually delete the data sets.

There is one large exception to this scenario: If a segmented tablespace is dropped erroneously, the data cannot be recovered regardless of whether it was VCAT- or STOGROUP-defined. When a table is dropped from a segmented tablespace, DB2 updates the space map for the tablespace to indicate that the data previously in the table has been deleted, and the corresponding space is available immediately for use by other tables. When a tablespace is dropped, DB2 implicitly drops all tables in that tablespace.

A DBA can attempt to recover from an inadvertent drop of a segmented tablespace, and will appear to be successful with one glaring problem: DB2 will indicate that there is no data in the tablespace after the recovery. As you can see, the so-called advantage of easy DSN1COPY recovery of dropped tables disappears for user-defined VSAM data sets when you use segmented tablespaces. This is crucial because more users are using segmented tablespaces to take advantage of their enhanced performance features and capability to handle multiple tables.

See Table 3.2 for a comparison of VCAT- and STOGROUP-defined data sets.

Table 3.2. VCAT definition versus STOGROUP definition.

	VCAT	*STOGROUP*
Need to know VSAM	Yes	No
User must physically create the underlying data sets	Yes	No
Can ALTER storage requirements using SQL	No	Yes
Can use AMS	Yes	No*
Confusing when data sets are defined on more than one DASD volume	No	Yes**
After dropping the table or the tablespace, the underlying data set is not deleted	Yes	No

*A tablespace initially created as a user-defined VSAM later can be altered to use STOGROUPs. A STOGROUP-defined tablespace can be altered to user-defined VSAM as well.

**Data in a segmented tablespace is unavailable after dropping the tablespace.

PRIQTY and SECQTY

If you are defining your tablespaces using the STOGROUP method, you must specify primary and secondary space allocations. The primary allocation is the amount of physical storage allocated when the tablespace is created. As the amount of data in the tablespace grows, secondary allocations of storage are taken. To accurately calculate the DASD space requirements, you must know the following:

- Number of columns in each row
- Data type for each column
- Nullability of each column
- Average size of variable columns
- Number of rows in the table
- Growth statistics
- Growth horizon
- Row compression statistics (if a compression routine is used)

The values specified for PRIQTY and SECQTY are in kilobytes. A DB2 page consists of 4K, so you should specify PRIQTY and SECQTY in multiples of four. Additionally, you should specify these quantities in terms of the type of DASD defined to the STOGROUP being used. For example, a tablespace with 4K pages defined on an IBM 3390 DASD device uses 48K for each physical track of storage. This corresponds to 12 pages. A data set cannot be allocated at less than a track, so it is wise to specify the primary and secondary allocations to at least a track boundary.

For an IBM 3390 DASD device, specify the primary and secondary quantities in multiples of 48. Here are the physical characteristics of the two most popular IBM DASD devices:

	Track	*Cylinder*	*Cylinders/Device*	*Bytes/Track*
3380 Device	40K	600K	885	47,476
3390 Device	48K	720K	1113	56,664

For segmented tablespaces, be sure to specify these quantities such that neither the primary nor the secondary allocation is less than a full segment. If you indicate a `SEGSIZE` of 12, for instance, do not specify less than four times the `SEGSIZE`, or 48K, for `PRIQTY` or `SECQTY`.

If you are allocating multiple tables to a single tablespace, calculate the `PRIQTY` and `SECQTY` separately for each table using the formulas in Table 3.3. When the calculations have been completed, add the totals for `PRIQTY` to get one large `PRIQTY` for the tablespace. Do the same for the `SECQTY` numbers. You might want to add approximately 10 percent to both `PRIQTY` and `SECQTY` when defining multiple tables to a simple tablespace. This additional space offsets the space wasted when rows of different lengths from different tables are combined on the same tablespace page. (See the section in this chapter called "Avoid Wasted Space" for more information.) Remember, however, that the practice of defining multiple tables to a single, simple tablespace is not encouraged.

Table 3.3. Lengths for DB2 data types.

Data Type	*Internal Length*	*COBOL WORKING STORAGE*	
`CHAR(n)`	n	01 identifier	PIC X(n)
`VARCHAR(n)`	max=n+2	01 identifier	
		49 identifier	PIC S9(4) COMP
		49 identifier	PIC X(n)
`LONG VARCHAR`	*	01 identifier	
		49 identifier	PIC S9(4) COMP
		49 identifier	PIC X(n)
`GRAPHIC(n)`	2sn	02 identifier	PIC G(n) DISPLAY-1
`VARGRAPHIC(n)`	(2sn)+2	01 identifier	
		49 identifier	PIC S9(4) COMP
		49 identifier	PIC G(n) DISPLAY-1
`LONG VARGRAPHIC`	*	01 identifier	
		49 identifier	PIC S9(4) COMP
		49 identifier	PIC G(n) DISPLAY-1
`SMALLINT`	2	01 identifier	PIC S9(4) COMP

continues

Table 3.3. continued

Data Type	*Internal Length*	*COBOL WORKING STORAGE*	
INTEGER	4	01 identifier	PIC S9(9) COMP
DECIMAL(p,s)	INTEGER (p/2)+1	01 identifier	PIC S9(p)V9(s) COMP-3
FLOAT(n) or REAL	8 (SINGLE PRECISION if n>21)	01 identifier	COMP-2
FLOAT(n) or FLOAT	4 (DOUBLE PRECISION if n<21)	01 identifier	COMP-1
DATE	4	01 identifier	PIC X(10)
TIME	3	01 identifier	PIC X(8)
TIMESTAMP	10	01 identifier	PIC X(26)

*See text following this table to calculate this length.

To calculate the internal length of a long character column, use these formulas:

Modified row size = (max row size)–(size of all other cols)–(nullable long char cols)

Internal length = 2 * INTEGER((INTEGER((modified row size)/(long cols in table))/2))

Next, calculate the number of rows per page and the total number of pages necessary. To do this, use the following formula:

Rows per page = (((page size) 22) * ((100 PCTFREE)/100)/row length)

Total pages = (number of rows) / (rows per page)

Finally, the PRIQTY is calculated as follows:

PRIQTY = total pages * 4

To accurately calculate the primary quantity for a table, you must make a series of calculations.

First, calculate the row length. To do this, add the length of each column, using Table 3.3 to determine each column's internal stored length. Remember to add one byte for each nullable column and two bytes for each variable column.

If the rows are compressed, determine the average compressed row size and use this for the following formulas.

To calculate SECQTY, you must estimate the growth statistics for the tablespace and the horizon over which this growth will occur.

For example, assume that you need to define the SECQTY for a tablespace that grows by 100 rows (growth statistics) over two months (growth horizon). If free space has been defined in the tablespace for 1,000 rows and you will reorganize this tablespace yearly (changing PRIQTY and SECQTY), you must provide for 200 rows in your SECQTY.

Divide the number of rows you want to provide for (in this case 200) by the number of rows per page. Round this number up to the next whole number divisible by 4 (to the track or cylinder boundary). Then specify this number as your SECQTY.

You may want to provide for secondary allocation in smaller chunks, not specifying the total number of rows in the initial SECQTY allocation. In the preceding example, you provided for 200 rows. By defining SECQTY large enough for 100 rows, you allocate three secondary extents before your yearly reorganization.

You may ask: why three? If each SECQTY can contain 100 rows and you must provide for 200 rows, shouldn't only two extents be allocated? No, there will be three. A secondary allocation is made when the amount of available space in the current extent reaches 50 percent of the next extent to be taken. So there are three allocations, but the third one is empty, or nearly empty.

As a general rule, avoid a large number of secondary extents. They decrease the efficiency of I/O, and I/O is the most critical bottleneck in most DB2 application systems.

Allocate Space on Cylinder Boundaries

Performance can be significantly affected based upon the choice of allocation unit. As an application inserts data into a table, DB2 will preformat space within the index and/or tablespace page set as necessary. This process will be more efficient if DB2 can preformat cylinders instead of tracks, because more space will be preformatted at once using cylinder allocation.

DB2 determines whether to use allocation units of tracks or cylinders based upon the value of PRIQTY and SECQTY. If either of these quantities is less than one cylinder, space for both primary and secondary will be allocated in tracks. For this reason, it is wise to specify both PRIQTY and SECQTY values of at least one cylinder for most tablespaces and indexes.

Allocating space in tracks is a valid option, however, under any of the following conditions:

- For small tablespaces and indexes that consume less than one cylinder of DASD
- For stable objects that are never updated SECQTY can be set to 0, causing DB2 to consider only PRIQTY when determining the allocation unit

Once again, avoid relying on default values. The default value for both PRIQTY and SECQTY is 3K, which will cause track allocation because it is less than one cylinder.

Free Space (PCTFREE and FREEPAGE)

The specification of free space in a tablespace or index can reduce the frequency of reorganization, reduce contention, and increase the efficiency of insertion. The PCTFREE parameter specifies what percentage of each page should remain available for future inserts. The FREEPAGE parameter indicates the specified number of pages after which a completely empty page is available.

Increasing free space decreases the number of rows per page and therefore decreases the efficiency of the bufferpool because fewer rows are retrieved per I/O. Increasing free space can improve concurrent processing, however, by reducing the number of rows on the same page. For example, consider a tablespace that contains a table clustered on the DEPARTMENT column. Each department must access and modify its data independent of other departments. By increasing free space, you decrease the occurrences of departments coexisting on tablespace pages because fewer rows exist per page.

Space can be used to keep areas of the tablespace available for the rows to be inserted. This results in a more efficient insert process, as well as more efficient access—with less unclustered data—after the rows have been inserted.

Understanding how insert activity affects DB2 data pages will aid in understanding how optimal free space specification can aid performance. When a row is inserted, DB2 will perform a space search algorithm to determine the optimal placement of the new row in the tablespace. This algorithm is different for segmented and non-segmented (simple and partitioned) tablespaces. For segmented tablespaces DB2 will:

- Identify the page to which the row should be inserted using the clustering index (if no clustering index exists, DB2 will search all segments for available space to insert the row).
- If space is available on that page, the row will be inserted; if space is not available, DB2 will search within the segment containing the target page for available space.
- If space is available in the segment, the row will be inserted; if space is not available, DB2 will search the last segment allocated in the tablespace for that specific table.
- If space is available, insert the row; otherwise DB2 will allocate a new segment.

For non-segmented tablespace DB2 searches for space as follows:

- Identify the page to which the row should be inserted using the clustering index.
- If space is available on that page, the row will be inserted; if space is not available, DB2 will search 16 contiguous pages before and after the target page.
- If space is available on any of those 32 pages, the row will be inserted; if space is not available, DB2 will scan from the beginning of the tablespace (or partition).
- If space is available, insert the row; otherwise DB2 will request a secondary extent.

For both segmented and non-segmented tablespaces, DB2 will bypass locked pages even if they contain sufficient free space to hold the row to be inserted.

If insert activity is skewed, with inserts clustered at certain locations in the tablespace, you may want to increase the free space to offset the space used for the heavily updated portions of the tablespaces. This increases the overall DASD usage but may provide better performance by decreasing the amount of unclustered data. Additionally, you could partition the tablespace such that the data area having the highest insert activity is isolated in its own partition. Free space could then be assigned by partition such that the insert "hot spot" has a higher PCTFREE and/or FREEPAGE specified. The other partitions could be assigned a lower free space.

If more than one table is assigned to a tablespace, calculate the free space for the table with the highest insert activity. This provides for more free space for tables with lower insert activity, but results in the best performance. Also, if the rows are compressed, calculate free space based on the average compressed row size.

When calculating free space, you must take into account that a certain amount of each page is wasted. DB2 uses 4K page sizes (of which 4,074 bytes are usable for data), and a maximum of 255 rows can be placed on one page. Consider a tablespace containing a single table with 122-byte rows. A single page can contain 33 rows. This leaves 48 bytes wasted per page, as follows:

4074 / 122 = 33.39

4074 - (122 * 33) = 48

Suppose that you want 10 percent free space in this tablespace. To specify that 10 percent of each page will be free space, you must factor the wasted space into the calculation. By specifying PCTFREE 10, 407 bytes are set aside as free space. However, 48 of those bytes can never be used, leaving 359 bytes free. Only two rows can fit in this space, whereas three would fit into 407 bytes. Factor the wasted space into your free-space calculations.

As a general rule, free space allocation depends on knowing the growth rate for the table, the frequency and impact of reorganization, and the concurrency needs of the application. Remember, PCTFREE is not the same as growth rate. Consider a tablespace that is allocated with a primary quantity of 7200K. If PCTFREE was set to 10, 720K is left free, with 6480K remaining for data storage. However, this provides a growth rate of 720/6480, or just over 11 percent, which is clearly a larger number than the PCTFREE specified. The general formula for converting growth rate to PCTFREE is:

PCTFREE = (growth rate) / (1 + growth rate)

To accommodate a 15 percent growth rate, only 13 percent (.15/1.15) of free space is necessary.

The other free space parameter is FREEPAGE. Specifying PCTFREE is sufficient for the free space needs of most tablespaces. If the tablespace is heavily updated, however, consider specifying FREEPAGE in conjunction with PCTFREE. See Table 3.4 for free space suggestions based on update frequency. Modify these numbers to include wasted space, as described previously.

Table 3.4. Free space allocation chart.

Type of Table Processing	FREEPAGE	PCTFREE
Read only	0	0
Less than 20 percent of table volume inserted between REORGs	0	10 to 20
20 to 60 percent of table volumes inserted between REORGs	0	20 to 30
Greater than 60 percent of table volumes inserted between REORGs	0 or (SEGSIZE-1)	20 to 30
Most inserts done in sequence by the clustering index	0	0 to 10
Tablespace with variable length rows being updated	0	10 to 20

BUFFERPOOL

DB2 provides 60 bufferpool options for tablespace and index objects. There are 50 4K bufferpools—BP0 through BP49—and 10 32K bufferpools—BP32K through BP32K9.

Data accessed from a DB2 table is first read from DASD, then moved into a bufferpool, and then returned to the requester. Data in the bufferpool can remain resident in memory, avoiding the expense of I/O for future queries that access the same data. There are many strategies for specifying bufferpools, and each is discussed fully in Part V, "DB2 Performance Tuning." For now, it's sufficient to mention the following rules:

- In general, many small to medium DB2 shops use a single bufferpool, namely BP0. For these types of shops, DB2 does a very capable job of managing I/O using a single, large BP0 containing most (or all) of a shop's tablespaces and indexes.
- As usage of DB2 grows, consider specifying additional bufferpools tuned for specific applications, tablespaces, indexes, or activities. The majority of mature DB2 shops fall into this category. Several bufferpool allocation and usage approaches are discussed in Part V.
- Avoid using BP32K for application tablespaces. If a tablespace is so large that it has pages requiring more than 4K, DB2 enforces the use of BP32K. DB2 arranges a tablespace assigned to the BP32K bufferpool as eight single 4K pages per 32K page. Therefore, every logical I/O to a 32K tablespace requires eight physical I/Os. To avoid using BP32K, denormalize tables if necessary. (See the section in this chapter on Denormalization for more information.)

The number of bufferpools in use at your shop depends on the DB2 workload and the amount of real and extended memory that can be assigned to the DB2 bufferpools. These topics are covered in greater detail in Part V.

BP32 and BP32K

Remember that BP32 and BP32K are two different sizes. BP32 is one of the fifty 4K bufferpools. BP32K is one of the ten 32K bufferpools. If you miss, or add, an erroneous "K" you may be using or allocating the wrong bufferpool.

TIP

Any bufferpool that contains a "K" in it is a 32K bufferpool. If the bufferpool does not contain a "K" it is a 4K bufferpool.

CLOSE YES or NO

Prior to DB2 V2.3, the CLOSE option specified whether the underlying VSAM data sets for the tablespace (or index space) should be closed each time the table was used. CLOSE YES indicated that the underlying data set was to be closed after use; CLOSE NO indicated the opposite. A performance gain was usually realized when you specified CLOSE NO. For tablespaces accessed infrequently (only once or twice daily), CLOSE YES might have been appropriate.

DB2 V2.3 introduced deferred close processing, sometimes referred to as *slow close.* Deferred close provided relief from the overhead associated with opening and closing data sets by closing the data sets only when the maximum number of open data sets is reached regardless of whether CLOSE YES or CLOSE NO was specified. However, DB2 V2.3 will also update SYSLGRNG every time the data set is not in use. This speeds the recovery because DB2 has a record of when updates could have occurred. But the constant SYSLGRNG updating can be a performance detriment during normal processing. Also, deferred close is a mixed blessing because DB2 V2.3 tablespaces that need to be closed after each access will remain open regardless of the CLOSE parameter specified.

DB2 V3 introduced a new open/close scenario referred to as *pseudo close.* Pseudo close offers the following features:

- A page set is not physically opened until it is first accessed, such as when an SQL statement or utility is executed against it.
- The VSAM open-for-update timestamp is not modified until data in the page set is updated. Previously, it was modified when the page set was first opened. This timestamp can be used by some types of software to determine when updated page set needs to be backed up. If an updated page set has not been modified for a specified number of DB2 checkpoints (DSNZPARM PCLOSEN) or a specified amount of time (DSNZPARM PCLOSET), then it is switched to a read-only state.

- Page sets specified as CLOSE NO are candidates for physical close when either the DDLIMIT or DSMAX limit has been reached
- SYSLGRNG records are updated for CLOSE YES data sets and are maintained by partition instead of at the data set level
- The performance problems associated updating SYSLGRNG are eliminated; SYSLGRNG entries will be written only when a data set (or partition) is converted to read only state, not every time the data set is not in use

TIP

In general, use CLOSE NO when running DB2 V2.2 and earlier; use CLOSE YES with caution for DB2 V2.3 because the overhead associated with updating SYSLGRNG every time data is accessed. Favor the use of CLOSE YES under DB2 V3 and greater, because the SYSLGRNG modification performance problems have been eliminated.

The maximum number of data sets that can be open in MVS at one time is 10,000.

ERASE YES or NO

The ERASE option specifies whether the physical DASD where the tablespace data set resides should be written over with binary zeroes when the table-space is dropped. Sensitive data that should never be accessed without proper authority should be set to ERASE YES. This ensures that the data in the table is erased when the table is dropped. Most tablespaces, however, should be specified as ERASE NO.

NUMPARTS and SEGSIZE

See the "Use Proper Tablespace Definitions" section earlier in this chapter for NUMPARTS and SEGSIZE recommendations. The NUMPARTS option is used only for partitioned tablespaces; SEGSIZE only for segmented tablespaces.

Defining Multiple Tables per Segmented Tablespace

A valuable and underutilized feature of DB2 is the capability to assign multiple tables to a single segmented tablespace. Doing so in the wrong situation, however, has several disadvantages. Consider the following advantages and disadvantages before proceeding with more than one table assigned to a segmented tablespace.

Advantages to defining multiple tables to a segmented tablespace include the following:

- There are fewer open data sets, causing less system overhead.
- There are fewer executions of the COPY, REORG, and RECOVER utilities per application system because these utilities are executed at the tablespace level.

- It is easier to group like tables for administrative tasks because the tables reside in the same physical tablespace.

Disadvantages to defining multiple tables to a segmented tablespace include the following:

- When only one table needs to be reorganized, all tables must be REORGed because they coexist in a single data set or group of data sets.
- If compression is used the compression ratio will be impacted by multiple tables instead of being optimized for the data patterns of a single table.
- The LOAD REPLACE utility will replace all data for all tables defined to the tablespace.
- There may be confusion about which tables are in which tablespaces, making monitoring and administration difficult.

In general, define each small to medium-size table (less than 1 million rows) to a single, segmented tablespace. Create a partitioned tablespace for each large table (more than 1 million rows). If you decide to group tables in a segmented tablespace, group only small tables (less than 32 pages). Provide a series of segmented tablespaces per application such that tables in the ranges defined in the following chart are grouped together. This will save space. Never group large tables (more than 32 pages) with other tables.

Number of Pages	*Tablespace Segment Size*
1 to 4	4
5 to 8	8
9 to 12	12
12 to 16	16
17 to 20	20
21 to 24	24
25 to 28	28
29 to 32	32

When the tablespace contains tables with the number of pages in the range on the left, assign to the tablespace the SEGSIZE indicated on the right.

Consider grouping tables related by referential integrity into a single, segmented tablespace. This is not always feasible because the size and access criteria of the tables may not lend themselves to multi-table segmented tablespaces. Grouping referentially related tables, however, simplifies your QUIESCE processing.

Compression

As of DB2 V3 data compression can be specified directly in a tablespace. Compression is indicated in the DDL by specifying COMPRESS YES for the tablespace. Likewise, it can be turned off in the DDL by specifying COMPRESS NO. When compression is specified, DB2 builds a static dictionary to control compression. It saves from 2 to 17 dictionary pages in the tablespace. These pages are stored after the header and first space map page.

DB2 compression provides two very clear benefits:

- Hardware-assisted compression
- It is provided free of charge with the base DB2 product

The hardware-assisted compression warrants further inspection. Hardware compression is available only to those users owning IBM's high-end CPU models (ES/9000 Model 511 or 711). This does not mean that DB2 compression features are only available to those with high-end CPUs. Hardware-assisted compression simply speeds up the compression and decompression of data—it is not a requirement for the inherent data compression features of DB2.

Overall, users who never looked at compression before it was provided with DB2 because of the cost of third party products should reevaluate their compression needs.

DDL Data Compression Versus Edit Procedures

DB2 data compression definitely should be used instead of the `DSN8HUFF` routine that is also supplied with DB2. But how does it compare to third party tools? Most third party vendors provide compression using `EDITPROC`s. However, these products are waning in popularity because of the excellent compression available to DB2 (as of V3) and the hardware-assist. Most users will find that DB2 can handle most of their compression requirements without needing a third party compression tool.

However, before completely refusing to evaluate third party solutions consider the following:

- IBM compression supplies only a single compression routine (based on the Ziv-Lempel algorithm) whereas several third party tools provide many different compression routines. This enables the user to better fit the algorithm to the composition of the data—using different compression algorithms for different types of data.
- The cost in time and effort to convert from prior compression methods to internal DB2 compression, although not significant, may not be cost justifiable when compared to other tasks facing your enterprise.
- Third party tool vendors are constantly enhancing their products to take better advantage of the operating system and the hardware environment. To ensure that you are getting the best "bang for your buck" in terms of data compression, it is wise to evaluate all of your options before settling on any given one.

CAUTION

For smaller tablespaces, it is possible that the dictionary used by DB2 for compression could use more space than compression saves. For this reason, avoid compressing smaller tablespaces.

General Data Compression Considerations

Why compress data? Consider an uncompressed table with a very large row size of 800 bytes. Therefore, five of this table's rows fit on a 4K page. If the compression routine achieves 30 percent compression, on average, the 800-byte row uses only 560 bytes, because 800–(800X.3) = 560. Now seven rows fit on a 4K page. Because I/O occurs at the page level, the cost of I/O is reduced because fewer pages must be read for tablespace scans, and the data is more likely to be in the bufferpool because more rows fit on a physical page.

This can be a significant reduction. Consider the following scenarios. A 10,000-row table with 800-byte rows requires 2,000 pages. Using a compression routine as outlined previously, the table would require only 1,429 pages. Another table also with 800-byte rows but now having 1 million rows would require 200,000 pages without a compression routine. Using the compression routine, you would reduce the pages to 142,858—a reduction of more than 50,000 pages.

Of course, there is always a trade-off: DASD savings for CPU cost of compressing and decompressing data. However, the cost should be minimal with hardware-assisted compression.

Encoding Scheme

Version 5

The `CCSID` parameter is used to specify the data encoding scheme to use for the tablespace: ASCII or EBCDIC. ASCII encoding is a new option for DB2 Version 5. The default is specified when DB2 is installed and is usually, but not always, EBCDIC. All data stored within a tablespace must use the same encoding scheme.

LOCKPART

Version 5

Specifying `LOCKPART YES` enables selective partition locking (SPL). With SPL individual partitions of a partitioned tablespace are locked only when accessed. SPL provides the following benefits:

- When SPL is enabled, applications accessing different partitions of a partitioned tablespace can enjoy greater concurrency.
- In a data sharing environment, DB2 and the IRLM can detect and optimize locking for situations in which no inter-subsystem activity exists by partition.

The default is `LOCKPART NO`, which indicates that locks are taken on the entire partitioned tablespace, not partition by partition.

MAXROWS

Version 5

The `MAXROWS` parameter indicates the maximum number of rows that can be stored on a tablespace page. The default is 255. Specify `MAXROWS` 255 unless there is a compelling reason to limit the number of rows per page, such as to limit contention for page locking.

Use MAXROWS 1 Instead of Using Dummy Columns

Version 5

A common design technique for older DB2 systems was to append dummy columns to DB2 tables to arbitrarily extend the row length. This was done to coerce DB2 into storing 1 row per page, effectively forcing a kludged type of row locking. However, this technique is invasive and undesirable because dummy columns will show up in DCLGENs and might not always be recognized as "dummies." DB2 V5 and later releases, the same effect can be accomplished by specifying `MAXROWS 1`.

General Tablespace Guidelines

For larger tablespaces (50K pages and more) that are very active, consider defining a single tablespace per database. This can reduce contention. To increase efficiency, assign very active tablespaces to volumes with low activity.

Table Definition Guidelines

In general, define one table for each entity for which you will be storing data. A table can be thought of as a grouping of attributes that identify a physical entity. The table name should conform to the entity name. For example, consider the sample table for employees, `DSN8510.EMP`. `EMP` is the name of the table that represents an entity known as "employee." An employee has many attributes, some of which are `EMPNO`, `FIRSTNME`, and `LASTNME`. These attributes are columns of the table.

When you create one table for each entity, the tables are easy to identify and use because they represent real-world "things."

Changing the Name of a Table

Version 5

New to DB2 V5 is the `RENAME` statement. `RENAME` enables DBAs to change the name of a DB2 table without dropping and re-creating the table. All table characteristics, data, and authorization is maintained.

Temporary Tables

Version 5

As of DB2 V5 temporary tables can be created to store intermediate SQL results. A temporary table exists only as long as the process that uses it. Temporary tables are created using the `CREATE GLOBAL TEMPORARY TABLE` statement. When created, the schema for the table is stored in `SYSIBM.SYSTABLES` just like any other table, but the `TYPE` column is set to 'G' to indicate a global temporary table.

A temporary table is instantiated when it is referenced in an `OPEN`, `SELECT INTO`, `INSERT`, or `DELETE` statement, not when it is created. Each application process that uses the temporary table creates a new instance of the table for its use. When using a temporary table, keep the following in mind:

- Because they are not persistent, locking, logging, and recovery do not apply to temporary tables.
- Indexes and constraints cannot be created on temporary tables.
- Null is the only default value permitted for columns of a temporary table.
- Temporary tables cannot be referenced by DB2 utilities.
- Temporary tables cannot be specified as the object of an `UPDATE` statement.
- When deleting from a temporary table, all rows must be deleted.
- Although views can be created on temporary tables, the `WITH CHECK OPTION` cannot be specified.

Temporary tables are most useful when a large result set must be returned from a stored procedure. Refer to Chapter 9, "Using DB2 Stored Procedures," for in-depth guidelines on using stored procedures.

Normalization

Normalization is the process of putting one fact in one appropriate place. This optimizes updates at the expense of retrievals. When a fact is stored in only one place, retrieving many different but related facts usually requires going to many different places. This tends to slow the retrieval process. Updating is quicker, however, because the fact you're updating exists in only one place.

Your DB2 tables should be based on a normalized logical data model. With a normalized data model, one fact is stored in one place, related facts about a single entity are stored together, and every column of each entity refers non-transitively to only the unique identifier for that entity.

Although an in-depth discussion of normalization is beyond the scope of this book, brief definitions of the first three normal forms follow.

- In *first normal form,* all entities must have a unique identifier, or key, that can be composed of one or more attributes. In addition, all attributes must be atomic and non-repeating. (*Atomic* means that the attribute must not be composed of multiple attributes. For example, `EMPNO` should not be composed of `SSN` and `FIRSTNAME` because these are separate attributes.)
- In *second normal form,* all attributes that are not part of the key must depend on the entire key for that entity.
- In *third normal form,* all attributes that are not part of the key must not depend on any other non-key attributes.

Denormalization

Speeding the retrieval of data from DB2 tables is a frequent requirement for DBAs and performance analysts. One way to accomplish this is to denormalize DB2 tables. The opposite of normalization, denormalization is the process of putting one fact in many places. This speeds data retrieval at the expense of data modification. This is not necessarily a bad decision, but should be undertaken only when a completely normalized design will not perform optimally. Consider these issues before denormalizing:

- Can the system achieve acceptable performance without denormalizing?
- Will denormalization render the database design unusable for ad hoc queries (that is, specialized expertise required to code queries against the denormalized design)?
- Will the performance of the system still be unacceptable after denormalizing?
- Will the system be less reliable due to denormalization?

If the answer to any of these questions is "yes," you should not denormalize your tables because the benefit will not exceed the cost. If, after considering these issues, you decide to denormalize, there are rules you should follow.

- If enough DASD is available, create the fully normalized tables and populate denormalized versions using the normalized tables. Access the denormalized tables in a read-only fashion. Create a controlled and scheduled population function to keep denormalized and normalized tables synchronized.
- If sufficient DASD does not exist, maintain denormalized tables programmatically. Be sure to update each denormalized table representing the same entity at the same time; alternatively, provide a rigorous schedule whereby table updates are synchronized. If you cannot avoid inconsistent data, inform all users of the implications.
- When updating any column that is replicated in many tables, update all copies simultaneously, or as close to simultaneously as possible given the physical constraints of your environment.
- If denormalized tables are ever out of sync with the normalized tables, be sure to inform users that batch reports and online queries may not show up-to-date information.
- Design the application so that it can be easily converted from denormalized tables to normalized tables.

There is only one reason to denormalize a relational design: performance. Several indicators help identify systems and tables that are candidates for denormalization. These indicators follow:

- Many critical queries and reports rely on data from more than one table. Often these requests must be processed in an online environment.
- Repeating groups must be processed in a group instead of individually.

- Many calculations must be applied to one or many columns before queries successfully can be answered.
- Tables must be accessed in different ways by different users during the same timeframe.
- Many large, primary keys are clumsy to query and use a large amount of DASD when carried as foreign key columns in related tables.
- Certain columns are queried a large percentage of the time. (Consider 60 percent or greater as a cautionary number flagging denormalization as an option.)

Many types of denormalized tables work around the problems caused by these indicators. Table 3.5 summarizes the types of denormalization, with a short description of when each type is useful. The sections that follow describe these denormalization types in greater detail.

Table 3.5. Types of denormalization.

Denormalization	*Use*
Prejoined Tables	When the cost of joining is prohibitive
Report Tables	When specialized critical reports are needed
Mirror Tables	When tables are required concurrently by two types of environments
Split Tables	When distinct groups use different parts of a table
Combined Tables	When one-to-one relationships exist
Redundant Data	To reduce the number of table joins required
Repeating Groups	To reduce I/O and (possibly) DASD
Derivable Data	To eliminate calculations and algorithms
Speed Tables	To support hierarchies

Denormalization: Prejoined Tables

If two or more tables need to be joined on a regular basis by an application, but the cost of the join is too prohibitive to support, consider creating tables of prejoined data. The prejoined tables should:

- Contain no redundant columns
- Contain only the columns necessary for the application to meet its processing needs
- Be created periodically using SQL to join the normalized tables

The cost of the join is incurred only once, when the prejoined tables are created. A prejoined table can be queried efficiently because every new query does not incur the overhead of the table join process.

Denormalization: Report Tables

Reports requiring special formatting or manipulation often are impossible to develop using SQL or QMF alone. If critical or highly visible reports of this nature must be viewed in an online environment, consider creating a table that represents the report. The table then can be queried using SQL or QMF.

Create the report using the appropriate mechanism in a batch environment. The report data then can be loaded into the report table in the appropriate sequence. The report table should:

- Contain one column for every column of the report
- Have a clustering index on the columns that provide the reporting sequence
- Not subvert relational tenets (for example, atomic data elements)

Report tables are ideal for storing the results of outer joins or other complex SQL statements. If an outer join is coded and then loaded into a table, you can retrieve the results of the outer join using a simple `SELECT` statement instead of using the `UNION` technique discussed in Chapter 1, "The Magic Words."

Denormalization: Mirror Tables

If an application system is very active, you may need to split processing into two (or more) distinct components. This requires the creation of duplicate, or *mirror,* tables.

Consider an application system that has heavy online traffic during the morning and early afternoon. The traffic consists of querying and updating data. Decision-support processing also is performed on the same application tables during the afternoon. The production work in the afternoon disrupts the decision-support processing, resulting in frequent timeouts and deadlocks.

These disruptions could be corrected by creating mirror tables: a foreground set of tables for the production traffic and a background set of tables for the decision-support reporting. To keep the application data-synchronized, you must establish a mechanism to migrate the foreground data periodically to the background tables. (One such mechanism is a batch job executing the `UNLOAD` sample program and the `LOAD` utility.) Migrate the information as often as necessary to ensure efficient and accurate decision-support processing.

Note that because the access needs of decision support and the production environment often are considerably different, different data definition decisions such as indexing and clustering may be chosen.

Denormalization: Split Tables

If separate pieces of one normalized table are accessed by different and distinct groups of users or applications, consider splitting the table into one denormalized table for each distinct processing group. Retain the original table if other applications access the entire table; in this scenario, the split tables should be handled as a special case of mirror table.

Tables can be split in two ways: vertically or horizontally. See Figure 3.1. A vertical split cuts a table column-wise, such that one group of columns is placed into a new table and the remaining columns are placed in another new table. Both of the split tables should retain the primary key columns. A horizontally split table is a row-wise split. To split a table horizontally, rows are classified into groups by key ranges. The rows from one key range are placed in one table, those from another key range are placed in a different table, and so on.

FIGURE 3.1.
Two methods of splitting tables.

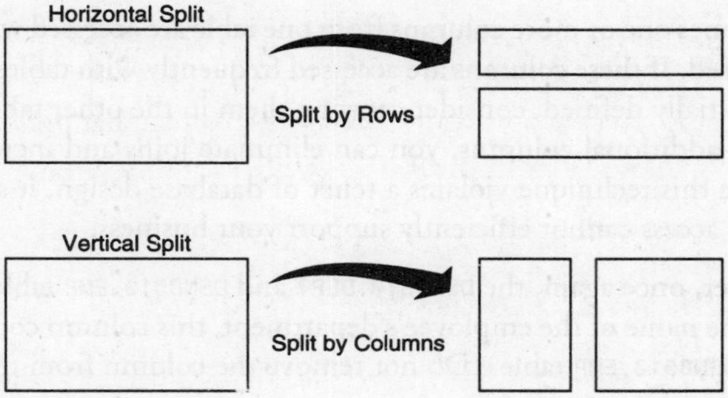

When splitting tables, designate one of the two tables as the parent table for referential integrity. If the original table still exists, it should be the parent table in all referential constraints. In this case, do not set up referential integrity for the split tables; they are derived from a referentially intact source.

When you split a table vertically, include one row per primary key in both tables to ease retrieval across tables. Do not eliminate rows from either of the two tables. Otherwise, updating and retrieving data from both tables is unnecessarily complicated.

When you split a table horizontally, try to split the rows between the new tables to avoid duplicating any one row in each new table. Simply stated, the operation of `UNION ALL`, when applied to the horizontally split tables, should not add more rows than those in the original, unsplit tables.

Denormalization: Combined Tables

If tables have a one-to-one relationship, consider combining them into a single table. Sometimes, one-to-many relationships can be combined into a single table, but the data update process is significantly complicated because of the increase in redundant data.

For example, consider combining the sample tables `DSN8510.DEPT` and `DSN8510.EMP` into a large table called `DSN8510.EMP_WITH_DEPT`. (See Appendix D, "DB2 Sample Tables," for a definition of the sample tables.) This new table would contain all the columns of both tables, except the `DEPTNO` column of `DSN8510.DEPT`. This column is excluded because it contains the same data as the `ADMRDEPT` column.

Each employee row therefore contains all the employee information, in addition to all the department information, for each employee. The department data is duplicated throughout the combined table because a department can employ many people. Tables of this sort should be considered prejoined tables, not combined tables, and treated accordingly. Only tables with one-to-one relationships should be considered combined tables.

Denormalization: Redundant Data

Sometimes one or more columns from one table are accessed whenever data from another table is accessed. If these columns are accessed frequently with tables other than those in which they were initially defined, consider carrying them in the other tables as redundant data. By carrying the additional columns, you can eliminate joins and increase the speed of data retrieval. Because this technique violates a tenet of database design, it should be attempted only if the normal access cannot efficiently support your business.

Consider, once again, the DSN8510.DEPT and DSN8510.EMP tables. If most employee queries require the name of the employee's department, this column could be carried as redundant data in the DSN8510.EMP table. (Do not remove the column from the DSN8510.DEPT table, though.)

Columns you want to carry as redundant data should have the following attributes:

- Only a few columns are necessary to support the redundancy
- The columns are stable, that is, updated infrequently
- The columns are used by many users or a few important users

Denormalization: Repeating Groups

When repeating groups are normalized, they are implemented as distinct rows instead of distinct columns. This usually results in higher DASD use and less efficient retrieval because there are more rows in the table and more rows must be read to satisfy queries that access the entire repeating group (or a subset of the repeating group).

Sometimes you can achieve significant performance gains when you denormalize the data by storing it in distinct columns. These gains, however, come at the expense of flexibility.

For example, consider an application that stores repeating group information in the following normalized table:

```
CREATE TABLE USER.PERIODIC_BALANCES
   (CUSTOMER_NO        CHAR(11)          NOT NULL,
    BALANCE_PERIOD     SMALLINT          NOT NULL,
    BALANCE            DECIMAL(15,2),

    PRIMARY KEY (CUSTOMER_NO, BALANCE_PERIOD)
   )
```

Available storage and DB2 requirements are the only limits to the number of balances per customer that you can store in this table. If you decided to string out the repeating group, BALANCE, into columns instead of rows, you must limit the number of balances to be carried in each row. The following is an example of stringing out repeating groups into columns after denormalization:

```
CREATE TABLE USER.PERIODIC_BALANCES
   (CUSTOMER_NO        CHAR(11)         NOT NULL,
    PERIOD1_BALANCE    DECIMAL(15,2),
    PERIOD2_BALANCE    DECIMAL(15,2),
    PERIOD3_BALANCE    DECIMAL(15,2),
    PERIOD4_BALANCE    DECIMAL(15,2),
    PERIOD5_BALANCE    DECIMAL(15,2),
    PERIOD6_BALANCE    DECIMAL(15,2),

    PRIMARY KEY (CUSTOMER_NO)
   )
IN SAMPLE.BALANCE;
```

In this example, only six balances can be stored for each customer. The number six is not important, but the limit on the number of values is important—it reduces the flexibility of data storage and should be avoided unless performance needs dictate otherwise.

Before you decide to implement repeating groups as columns instead of rows, be sure that the data:

- Rarely—preferably never—is aggregated, averaged, or compared in the row
- Occurs in a statistically well-behaved pattern
- Has a stable number of occurrences
- Usually is accessed collectively
- Has a predictable pattern of insertion and deletion

If any of the preceding criteria is not met, some SQL statements could be difficult to code—making the data less available due to inherently unsound data-modeling practices. This should be avoided because you usually denormalize data to make it more readily available.

Denormalization: Derivable Data

If the cost of deriving data with complicated formulas is prohibitive, consider storing the derived data instead of calculating it. When the underlying values that comprise the calculated value change, the stored derived data must be changed also; otherwise, inconsistent information could be reported.

Sometimes you cannot immediately update derived data elements when the columns on which they rely change. This can occur when the tables containing the derived elements are offline or are being operated on by a utility. In this situation, time the update of the derived data so that it occurs immediately after the table is available for update. Outdated derived data should never be made available for reporting and queries.

Denormalization: Hierarchies

A hierarchy is easy to support using a relational database such as DB2, but difficult to retrieve information from efficiently. For this reason, applications that rely on hierarchies often contain denormalized tables to speed data retrieval. Two examples of these types of systems are a Bill of Materials application and a Departmental Reporting system. A Bill of Materials application typically records information about parts assemblies, in which one part is composed of other parts. A Department Reporting system typically records the departmental structure of an organization, indicating which departments report to which other departments.

An effective way to denormalize a hierarchy is to create *speed tables.* Figure 3.1 depicts a department hierarchy for a given organization. The hierarchic tree is built so that the top node is the entire corporation. The other nodes represent departments at various levels in the corporation.

FIGURE 3.2.
A department hierarchy.

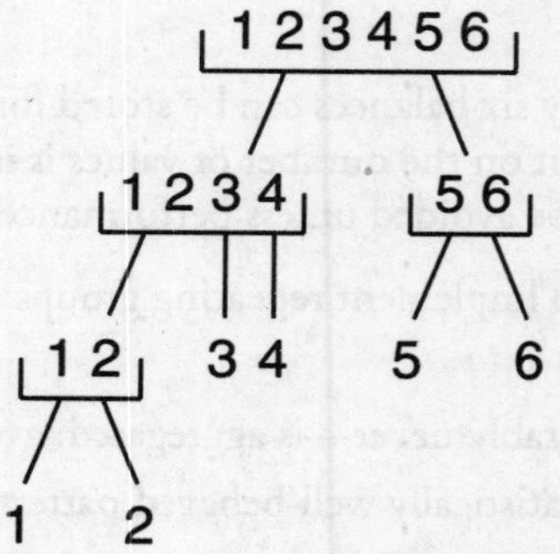

Department 123456 is the entire corporation. Departments 1234 and 56 report directly to 123456. Departments 12, 3, and 4 report directly to 1234 and indirectly to department 123456, and so on. This can be represented in a DB2 table as follows:

DEPTNO	PARENT_DEPPTNO	...other columns
123456	———	
1234	123456	
56	123456	
12	1234	
3	1234	
4	1234	
1	12	
2	12	
5	56	
6	56	

Department Table

This DB2 table is a classic relational implementation of a hierarchy. There are two department columns: one for the parent and one for the child. The table's data is an accurately normalized version of this hierarchy, containing everything represented in Figure 3.2. The complete hierarchy can be rebuilt with the proper data retrieval instructions.

Even though the implementation effectively records the entire hierarchy, a query to report all the departments under any other department is time consuming to code and inefficient to process. A sample query that returns all the departments reporting to the corporate node, 123456, is illustrated by this rather complex SQL statement:

```
SELECT   DEPTNO
FROM     DEPARTMENT
WHERE    PARENT_DEPTNO = '123456'
UNION
SELECT   DEPTNO
FROM     DEPARTMENT
WHERE    PARENT_DEPTNO IN
         (SELECT  DEPTNO
          FROM    DEPARTMENT
          WHERE   PARENT_DEPTNO = '123456')
UNION
SELECT   DEPTNO
FROM     DEPARTMENT
WHERE    PARENT_DEPTNO IN
         (SELECT  DEPTNO
          FROM    DEPARTMENT
WHERE    PARENT_DEPTNO IN
         (SELECT  DEPTNO
          FROM    DEPARTMENT
          WHERE   PARENT_DEPTNO = '123456');
```

This query can be built only if you know in advance the total number of possible levels the hierarchy can achieve. If there are *n* levels in the hierarchy, you need *n-1* UNIONs. The previous SQL statement assumes that only three levels are between the top and bottom of the department hierarchy. For every possible level of the hierarchy, you must add a more complex SELECT statement to the query in the form of a UNION. This implementation works, but is difficult to use and inefficient.

A faster way to query a hierarchy is to use a speed table. A speed table contains a row for every combination of the parent department and all its dependent departments, regardless of the level. Data is replicated in a speed table to increase the speed of data retrieval. The speed table for the hierarchy presented in Figure 3.2 is:

PARENT DEPTNO	CHILD DEPTNO	LEVEL	DETAIL	*...other columns*
123456	1234	1	N	
123456	56	1	N	
123456	12	2	N	
123456	1	3	Y	

PARENT DEPTNO	CHILD DEPTNO	LEVEL	DETAIL	...*other columns*
123456	2	3	Y	
123456	3	2	Y	
123456	4	2	Y	
123456	5	2	Y	
123456	6	2	Y	
1234	12	1	N	
1234	1	2	Y	
1234	2	2	Y	
1234	3	1	Y	
1234	4	1	Y	
3	3	1	Y	
4	4	1	Y	
12	1	1	Y	
12	2	1	Y	
1	1	1	Y	
2	2	1	Y	
56	5	1	Y	
56	6	1	Y	
5	5	1	Y	
6	6	1	Y	

Contrast this to the previous table, which recorded only the immediate children for each parent. The PARENT_DEPTNO column is the top of the hierarchy. The CHILD_DEPTNO column represents all the dependent nodes of the parent. The LEVEL column records the level in the hierarchy. The DETAIL column contains Y if the row represents a node at the bottom of the hierarchy, or N if the row represents a node that is not at the bottom. A speed table commonly contains other information needed by the application. Typical information includes the level in the hierarchy for the given node and, if the order within a level is important, the sequence of the nodes at the given level.

After the speed table has been built, you can write speed queries. The following are several informative queries. They would be inefficient if executed against the classical relational hierarchy, but are efficient when run against a speed table.

To retrieve all dependent departments for department 123456:

```
SELECT   CHILD_DEPTNO
FROM     DEPARTMENT_SPEED
WHERE    PARENT_DEPTNO = '123456';
```

To retrieve only the bottom-most, detail departments that report to department 123456:

```
SELECT   CHILD_DEPTNO
FROM     DEPARTMENT_SPEED
WHERE    PARENT_DEPTNO = '123456'
AND      DETAIL = 'Y';
```

To return the complete department hierarchy for department 123456:

```
SELECT   PARENT_DEPTNO, CHILD_DEPTNO, LEVEL
FROM     DEPARTMENT_SPEED
WHERE    PARENT_DEPTNO = '123456'
ORDER BY LEVEL;
```

A speed table commonly is built using a program written in COBOL or another high-level language. SQL alone usually is too inefficient to handle the creation of a speed table.

Denormalization to Avoid BP32K

Try to avoid using 32K bufferpools for application tablespaces because of the additional I/O that will be incurred. If a tablespace is so large as to have pages that require more than 4K, then DB2 will force the use of a 32K bufferpool. DB2 arranges a tablespace assigned to the BP32K bufferpool as 8 single 4K pages per 32K page. Every logical I/O to a 32K tablespace requires 8 physical I/Os. Use the vertical split technique to denormalize tables which would otherwise require 32K pages.

Periodically Test the Validity of Denormalization

The decision to denormalize never should be made lightly: Denormalization involves a lot of administrative dedication. This dedication takes the form of documenting denormalization decisions, ensuring valid data, scheduling migration, and keeping end users informed about the state of the tables. An additional category of administrative overhead is periodic analysis.

When an application has denormalized data, you should review the data and the environment periodically. Changes in hardware, software, and application requirements can alter the need for denormalization. To verify whether denormalization still is a valid decision, ask the following questions:

- Have the application-processing requirements changed such that the join criteria, the timing of reports, or the transaction throughput no longer require denormalized data?
- Did a new software release change performance considerations? For example, does the faster, microcode sorting of DB2 V2.3 eliminate the need for report tables clustered on sort keys? Or did the introduction of a new join method undo the need for prejoined tables?
- Did a new hardware release change performance considerations? For example, does the upgrade from an IBM 3090 180J to a 900 series machine reduce the amount of CPU consumption such that denormalization no longer is necessary?

In general, periodically test whether the extra cost related to processing with normalized tables justifies the benefit of denormalization. Monitor and reevaluate all denormalized applications by measuring the following criteria:

- I/O saved
- CPU saved
- Complexity of update programming
- Cost of returning to a normalized design

NOTE

To summarize, remember these basic rules:

- All things being equal, always favor a normalized design over a denormalized design.
- Normalization optimizes data modification at the expense of data access.
- Denormalization optimizes data access at the expense of data modification.

Row and Column Guidelines

As you create DB2 tables, you should be mindful of their composition (rows and columns) and how this affects performance. This section outlines several guidelines that ensure efficient row and column specification.

Use Compression to Increase Rows/Page Ratio

Version 5

Although the MAXROWS parameter is available as of DB2 V5, prior releases provided no explicit mechanism to specify the number of rows stored that can be stored on a single page. For releases of DB2 prior to Version 5, DB2 data compression can be used to alter the number of rows per page from 127 to 255 (the only two choices available). By altering compression on and off you can get 255 rows per page without compression. Simply issue the following set of SQL statements:

```
ALTER TABLESPACE tsname COMPRESS YES;
COMMIT;
ALTER TABLESPACE tsname COMPRESS NO;
COMMIT;
```

When the tablespace is altered to indicate COMPRESS YES, DB2 modifies the DBD to indicate that 255 rows can be stored per tablespace page. But, when the tablespace is altered back to COMPRESS NO status, DB2 does not change the DBD back. Be careful though, because if the database is ever dropped and recreated to perform maintenance you will need to reissue the preceding sequence of statements for all of the tablespaces that require 255 rows/page.

Avoid Wasted Space

If you do not use very large and very small row sizes, you can reduce the amount of space wasted by unusable bytes on the pages of a tablespace. Keep these rules in mind:

- A maximum of 255 rows can be stored on one tablespace page.
- A row length larger than 4056 will not fit on a 4K page; for rows of this size you must use a 32K page, which is much less efficient than a 4K page and therefore not recommended.
- For preV3 subsystems, a row length less than 31 bytes wastes space because only 127 rows can fit on a page, regardless of the size of the row.
- A row length of 2029 results in only one row per page because the second row will be too large to exist on the same page.

Determine row size carefully to avoid wasting space. If you can combine small tables or split large tables to avoid wasting a large amount of space, do so. It usually is impossible to avoid wasting some space, however.

Choose Meaningful Column Names

In many data processing shops, common names for data elements have been used for years. Sometimes these names seem arcane because they comply with physical constraints that have long since been overcome.

DB2 provides 18 characters for column names. You can enhance the usability of your applications if you use as many of these 18 characters as necessary to achieve easy-to-understand column names. For example, use `CUSTOMER_NAME` instead of `CNA0` for a customer name column. Do not use column names simply because people are accustomed to them.

This may be a tough sell in your organization, but it's well worth the effort. If you must support the older, non-descriptive names, consider creating tables with the fully descriptive names, then creating views of these tables with the old names. Eventually, people will convert to use the tables instead of the views.

Standardize Abbreviations

Every shop uses abbreviated data names. This isn't a bad practice—unless the specification of abbreviations is random, uncontrolled, or unplanned. Document and enforce strict abbreviation standards for data names in conjunction with your data-naming standards. For example, the `CUSTOMER_NAME` column mentioned in the previous section can be abbreviated in many ways (`CST_NME`, `CUST_NM`, `CUST_NAME`, and so on). Choose one standard abbreviation and stick to it.

Many shops use a list of tokens to create data abbreviation standards. This is fine as long as each token represents only one entity and each entity has only one abbreviation. For example:

Entity	*Standard Abbreviation*
CUSTOMER	CUST
NAME	NME

Sequence Columns to Achieve Optimal Performance

The sequencing of columns in a table is not important because the relational model states that columns must be non-positional. Columns and rows do not need to be sequenced for the retrieval commands to work on tables.

When you create a table, however, you must supply the columns in a particular order which becomes the order in which they physically are stored. The columns then can be retrieved in any order using the appropriate SQL SELECT statement.

When creating your tables, you will get better performance if you follow these rules for column sequencing:

- Place the primary key columns first to ease identification.
- Place frequently read columns next.
- Place infrequently read and infrequently updated columns next.
- Placc VARCHAR and VARGRAPHIC columns next.
- Place very frequently updated columns after variable columns. For varying length rows, DB2 logs updates from the point of the change to the end of the row. For fixed length rows (that is, no VARCHAR or VARGRAPHIC columns), frequently updated columns can be placed anywhere in the table because DB2 will log updates from the begin point of the change to the end point.
- Given the preceding constraints, try to sequence the columns in an order that makes sense to the users of the table.

Avoid Special Sequencing for Nullable Columns

Treat nullable columns the same as you would any other column. Some DBAs advise you to place nullable columns of the same data type after non-nullable columns. This is supposed to assist in administering the null columns, but in my opinion it does not. Sequencing nulls in this manner provides no clear benefit and should be avoided.

See the "DB2 Table Parameters" section later in this chapter for additional advice on nullable columns.

Define Columns Across Tables in the Same Way

When a column that defines the same attribute as another column is given a different column name, it is referred to by data administrators as a *column synonym.* In general, column synonyms should be avoided except in the situations detailed in this section.

Every attribute should be defined in one way, that is, with one distinct name and one distinct data type and length. The name should be different only if the same attribute needs to be represented as a column in one table more than once, or if the practical meaning of the attribute differs as a column from table to table. For example, suppose that a database contains a table that holds the colors of items. This column is called Color. The same database has a table with a Preferred Color column for customers. This is the same logical attribute, but its meaning changes based on the context. It is not clear to simply call the column Color in the Customer table, because it would imply that the customer is that color!

An attribute must be defined twice in self-referencing tables and in tables requiring multiple foreign key references to a single table. In these situations, create a standard prefixing or suffixing mechanism for the multiple columns. After you define the mechanism, stick to it. For example, the `DSN8510.DEPT` table in Appendix D, "DB2 Sample Tables," is a self-referencing table that does not follow these recommendations. The `ADMRDEPT` column represents the same attribute as the `DEPTNO` column, but the name is not consistent. A better name for the column would have been `ADMR_DEPTNO`. This adds the `ADMR` prefix to the attribute name, `DEPTNO`.

The practical meaning of columns that represent the same attribute may differ from table to table as well. In the sample tables, for example, the `MGRNO` column in the `DSN8510.DEPT` table represents the same attribute as the `EMPNO` column in the `DSN8510.EMP` table. The two columns can be named differently in this situation because the employee number in the `DEPT` table represents a manager, whereas the employee number in the `EMP` table represents any employee. (Perhaps the `MGRNO` column should have been named `MGR_EMPNO`.)

The sample tables provide another example of when this guideline should have been followed, but wasn't. Consider the same two tables: `DSN8510.DEPT` and `DSN8510.EMP`. Both contain the department number attribute. In the `DEPT` table, the column representing this attribute is `DEPTNO`, but in the `EMP` table, the column is `WORKDEPT`. This is confusing and should be avoided. In this instance, both should have been named `DEPTNO`.

Never use homonyms. A *homonym*, in DB2-column terminology, is a column that is spelled and pronounced the same as another column, but represents a different attribute.

Avoid Duplicate Rows

To conform to the relational model, every DB2 table should prohibit duplicate rows. Duplicate rows cause ambiguity and add no value.

If duplicates exist for an entity, either the entity has not been rigorously defined and normalized or a simple counter column can be added to the table. The counter column would contain a number indicating the number of duplicates for the given row.

Always Define a Primary Key

To assist in the unique identification of rows, define a primary (or unique) key for every DB2 table. The preferred way to define a primary key is with the `PRIMARY KEY` clause of the `CREATE TABLE` statement.

Sometimes the primary key for a table is too large to implement. The length of the primary key columns could be larger than DB2's maximum primary key length (254 bytes) or performance might suffer with the larger index. In these circumstances, define a surrogate key for the table.

Use Appropriate DB2 Data Types

Use the appropriate DB2 data type when defining table columns. (Recall the list of valid DB2 data types in Table 3.3.) Some people may advise you to avoid certain DB2 data types—this is unwise. Follow these rules:

- Use the DB2 `DATE` data type to represent all dates. Do not use a character or numeric representation of the date.
- Use the DB2 `TIME` data type to represent all times. Do not use a character or numeric representation of the time.
- Use the DB2 `TIMESTAMP` data type when the data and time are always needed together, but rarely needed alone. Do not use a character or numeric representation of the timestamp.
- Using `INTEGER` and `SMALLINT` data types is interchangeable with using the `DECIMAL` data type without scale. Specifying `DECIMAL` without scale sometimes is preferable to `INTEGER` and `SMALLINT` because it provides more control over the domain of the column. However, `DECIMAL` without scale might use additional DASD. For additional insight, see the trade-offs listed in the upcoming "Consider All Options when Defining Columns as `INTEGER`" section.
- If the data is only numeric, use a numeric-data type. If leading zeroes must be stored or reported, however, using the character data type is acceptable.
- Remember, DB2 uses the cardinality of a column to determine its filter factors used during access path selection. The specification of column data types can influence this access path selection.

There are more possible character (alphanumeric) values than there are numeric values for columns of equal length. For example, consider the following two columns:

```
COLUMN1    SMALLINT   NOT NULL
COLUMN2    CHAR(5)    NOT NULL
```

`COLUMN1` can contain values only in the range –32,768 to 32,767, for a total of 65,536 possible values. `COLUMN2`, however, can contain all the permutations and combinations of legal alphabetic characters, special characters, and numerals. So you can see how defining numeric data as a numeric-data type usually results in a more accurate access path selection by the DB2 optimizer; the specified domain is more accurate for filter factor calculations.

Analyze DATE and TIME Columns Versus TIMESTAMP Columns

When defining tables that require a date and time stamp, two solutions are available:

- Coding two columns, one as a DATE data type and the other as a TIME data type
- Coding one column specifying the TIMESTAMP data type

Each option has its benefits and drawbacks. Before choosing an approach, consider the following issues:

- With DATE and TIME you must use two columns. TIMESTAMP uses one column, thereby simplifying data access and modification.
- The combination of DATE and TIME columns requires 7 bytes of storage, while a TIMESTAMP column always requires 10 bytes of storage. Using the combination of DATE and TIME columns can save space.
- TIMESTAMP provides greater time accuracy, down to the microsecond level. TIME provides accuracy only to the second level. If precision is important, use TIMESTAMP, otherwise consider the combination of DATE and TIME.
- Date and time arithmetic can be easier to implement using TIMESTAMP data instead of a combination of DATE and TIME. Subtracting one TIMESTAMP from another results in a TIMESTAMP duration. To calculate a duration using DATE and TIME columns, two subtraction operations must occur: one for the DATE column and one for the TIME column.
- DB2 provides for the formatting of DATE and TIME columns via local DATE and TIME exits, the CHAR function, and the DATE and TIME precompiler options. These facilities are not available for TIMESTAMP columns. If the date and time information is to be extracted and displayed on a report or by an online application, the availability of these DB2-provided facilities for DATE and TIME columns should be considered when making your decision.

Consider Optimization When Choosing Data Type

The impact on optimization is another consideration when deciding whether to use a character or a numeric data type for a numeric column.

Consider, for example, a column that must store four-byte integers. This can be supported using a CHAR(4) data type or a SMALLINT data type. Often, the desire to use CHAR(4) is driven by the need to display leading zeroes on reports.

Data integrity will not be an issue assuming that all data is edit checked prior to insertion to the column (a big assumption). But even if edit checks are coded, DB2 is not aware of these and assumes that all combinations of characters are permitted. For access path determination on character columns, DB2 uses base 37 math. This assumes that usually one of the 26 alphabetic letters or the 10 numeric digits or a space will be used. This adds up to 37 possible characters. For a four-byte character column there are 37^4 or 1,874,161 possible values.

A SMALLINT column can range from -32,768 to 32,767 producing 65,536 possible small integer values. The drawback here is that negative or 5-digit product codes could be entered. However, if we adhere to our proper edit check assumption, the data integrity problems will be avoided here, as well.

DB2 will use the HIGH2KEY and LOW2KEY values to calculate filter factors. For character columns, the range between HIGH2KEY and LOW2KEY is larger than numeric columns because there are more total values. The filter factor will be larger for the numeric data type than for the character data type which may influence DB2 to choose a different access path. For this reason, favor the SMALLINT over the CHAR(4) definition.

Choose VARCHAR Columns Carefully

You can save DASD storage space by using variable columns instead of placing small amounts of data in a large fixed space. Each variable column carries a 2-byte overhead, however, for storing the length of the data. Additionally, variable columns tend to increase CPU usage and can cause the update process to become inefficient. When a variable column is updated with a larger value, the row becomes larger; if not enough space is available to store the row, it must be moved to another page. This makes the update and any subsequent retrieval slower.

Follow these rules when defining variable character columns:

- Avoid variable columns if a sufficient DASD is available to store the data using fixed columns.
- Do not define a variable columns if its maximum length is less than 30 bytes.
- Do not define a variable column if its maximum length is within 10 bytes of the average length of the column.
- Do not define a variable column when the data does not vary from row to row.
- Place variable columns at the end of the row, but before columns that are frequently updated.
- Consider redefining variable columns by placing multiple rows of fixed length columns in another table or by shortening the columns and placing the overflow in another table.

Monitor the Effectiveness of Variable Columns

Using views and SQL it is possible to query the DB2 Catalog to determine the effectiveness of using VARCHAR for a column instead of CHAR. Consider, for example, the PROJNAME column of the DSN8510.PROJ table. It is defined as VARCHAR(24).

To gauge whether VARCHAR is appropriate follow these steps:

1. Create a view that returns the length of the NAME column for every row, for example:

```
CREATE VIEW PROJNAME_LENGTH
          (COL_LGTH)
AS        SELECT LENGTH(PROJNAME)
          FROM   DSN8510.PROJ;
```

2. Then, issue the following query using SPUFI to produce a report detailing the LENGTH and number of occurrences for that length:

```
SELECT    COL_LGTH, COUNT(*)
FROM      PROJNAME_LENGTH
GROUP BY COL_LGTH
ORDER BY COL_LGTH;
```

This query will produce a report listing the lengths (in this case, from 1 to 24, excluding those lengths which do not occur) and the number of times that each length occurs in the table. These results can be analyzed to determine the range of lengths stored within the variable column.

If you are not concerned about this level of detail, the following query can be used instead to summarize the space characteristics of the variable column in question:

```
SELECT   24*COUNT(*),
         24,
         SUM(2+LENGTH(PROJNAME)),
         AVG(2+LENGTH(PROJNAME)),
         24*COUNT(*)-SUM(2+LENGTH(PROJNAME)),
         24-AVG(2+LENGTH(PROJNAME))
FROM     DSN8510.PROJ;
```

The constant 24 will need to be changed in the query to indicate the maximum length of the variable column as defined in the DDL. The individual columns returned by this report are defined in the following list:

Definition	*Calculation*
Space Used As CHAR(24)	24*COUNT(*)
Average Space Used As CHAR(24)	24
Space Used As VARCHAR(24)	SUM(2+LENGTH(PROJNAME))
Average Space Used As VARCHAR(24)	AVG(2+LENGTH(PROJNAME))
Total Space Saved	24*COUNT(*)-SUM(2+LENGTH(PROJNAME))
Average Space Saved	24-AVG(2+LENGTH(PROJNAME))

Use Odd DECIMAL Precision

Consider making the precision of all DECIMAL columns odd. This can provide an extra digit for the column being defined without using additional storage. For example, consider a column that must have a precision of 6 with a scale of 2. This would be defined as DECIMAL(6,2). By defining the column as DECIMAL(7,2) instead, numbers up to 99,999.99 can be stored instead of numbers up to 9,999.99. This can save future expansion efforts.

However, if you must ensure that the data in the column conforms to the specified domain (that is, even precision), specify even precision.

Consider All Options When Defining Columns as INTEGER

Use SMALLINT instead of INTEGER when the –32,768 to 32,767 range of values is appropriate. This data type usually is a good choice for sequencing type columns. The range of allowable values for the INTEGER data type is –2,147,483,648 to 2,147,483,647. These ranges may seem arbitrary, but are designed to store the maximum amount of information in the minimum amount of space. A SMALLINT column occupies 2 bytes, and an INTEGER column occupies only 4 bytes.

The alternative to SMALLINT and INTEGER data types is DECIMAL with a 0 scale. DECIMAL(5,0) supports the same range as SMALLINT, and DECIMAL(10,0) supports the same range as INTEGER. The DECIMAL equivalent of SMALLINT occupies 3 bytes of storage but permits values as large as 99,999 instead of only 32,767. The DECIMAL equivalent of INTEGER occupies 6 bytes but permits values as large as 9,999,999,999 instead of 2,147,483,647.

When deciding whether to use DECIMAL without scale to represent integer columns, another factor is control over the domain of acceptable values. The domain of SMALLINT and INTEGER columns is indicated by the range of allowable values for their respective data type. If you must ensure conformance to a domain, DECIMAL without scale provides the better control.

Suppose that you code a column called DAYS_ABSENT that indicates the number of days absent for employees in the DSN8510.EMP table. Suppose, too, that an employee cannot miss more than five days per year without being disciplined and that no one misses ten or more days. In this case, a single digit integer column could support the requirements for DAYS_ABSENT. A DECIMAL(1,0) column would occupy 2 bytes of physical storage and provide for values ranging from –9 to 9. By contrast, a SMALLINT column would occupy two bytes of physical storage and provide for values ranging from –32768 to 32,767. The DECIMAL(1,0) column, however, more closely matches the domain for the DAYS_ABSENT columns.

One final consideration: A decimal point is required with DECIMAL data, even when the data has no scale. For example, the integer 5 is 5. when expressed as a decimal. This can be confusing to programmers and users who are accustomed to dealing with integer data without a decimal point.

Consider all these factors when deciding whether to implement SMALLINT, INTEGER, or DECIMAL data types for integer columns.

DB2 Table Parameters

The preceding section concentrated on the rows and columns of a DB2 table. Other parameters also must be considered when creating DB2 tables. This section provides guidelines to assist you in your table creation endeavors.

Specify Appropriate Defaults

When a row is inserted or loaded into a table and no value is specified for a column but the column has a default specified, the column will be set to the value that has been identified in the column default specification. Two types of defaults are available: system-defined and user-defined.

Version 4

As of DB2 V4 each column can have a default value specifically tailored to it. These are known as user-defined defaults. Prior to V4, DB2 provided specific system-defined defaults for each data type. System-defined column default values are still used if an explicit default value is not specified and are outlined in Table 3.6. For existing rows, when a non-nullable column is added to a table, DATE, TIME, and TIMESTAMP data types default to the lowest possible value instead of the current value. DATE types will default to January 1, 0001; TIME types will default to 0:00:00; and timestamp types will default to a date of January 1, 0001 and a time of 0:00:00:00.

Table 3.6. System-defined column default values.

Data Type	*Default Value*
Numeric	Zero
Fixed-length string	Blanks
Varying-length string	String of length zero
Date	Current date
Time	Current time
Timestamp	Current timestamp

Four options are available for user-defined defaults: a constant value, USER, CURRENT SQLID, and NULL. When specifying a constant, the value must conform to the column on which it is defined. Specifying USER causes the column to default to the contents of the USER special register. When CURRENT SQLID is specified, the default value will be the SQL authid of the process performing the INSERT. NULL is self-explanatory.

In general, it is best to explicitly define the default value to be used for each column. If the system-defined default values are adequate for your application, it is fine to use them by not providing a value following the DEFAULT clause. Consider the following column definitions:

```
BONUS       DECIMAL(9,2)  DEFAULT 500.00,
COMM        DECIMAL(9,2)  NOT NULL WITH DEFAULT,
```

If a row is inserted without specifying BONUS and COMM, BONUS will default to 500.00 and COMM will default to zero.

Use Nulls with Care

A null is DB2's attempt to record missing or unknown information. When you assign a null to a column instance, it means that a value currently does not exist for the column. It's important to understand that a column assigned to null logically means one of two things: The column does not apply to this row, or the column applies to this row, but the information is not known at present.

For example, suppose that a table contains information on the hair color of employees. The HAIR_COLOR column is defined in the table as being capable of accepting nulls. Three new employees are added today: a man with black hair, a woman with unknown hair color, and a bald man. The woman with the unknown hair color and the bald man both could be assigned null HAIR_COLOR, but for different reasons. The hair column color for the woman would be null because she has hair but the color presently is unknown. The hair color column for the bald man would be null also, but this is because he has no hair and so hair color does not apply.

DB2 does not differentiate between nulls that signify unknown data and those that signify inapplicable data. This distinction must be made by the program logic of each application.

DB2 represents null in a special hidden column known as an *indicator variable*. An indicator variable is defined to DB2 for each column that can accept nulls. The indicator variable is transparent to an end user, but must be provided for when programming in a host language (such as COBOL or PL/I). Every column defined to a DB2 table must be designated as either allowing or disallowing nulls.

The default definition for columns in a DB2 table is to allow nulls. Nulls can be prohibited for a column by specifying the NOT NULL or NOT NULL WITH DEFAULT option in the CREATE TABLE statement.

Avoid nulls in columns that must participate in arithmetic logic (for example, DECIMAL money values). The AVG, COUNT DISTINCT, SUM, MAX, and MIN functions omit column occurrences set to null. The COUNT(*) function, however, does not omit columns set to null because it operates on rows. Thus, AVG is not equal to SUM/COUNT(*) when the average is being computed for a column that can contain nulls. If the COMM column is nullable, the result of the following query:

```
SELECT  AVG(COMM)
FROM    DSN8510.EMP;
```

is not the same as for this query:

```
SELECT  SUM(COMM)/COUNT(*)
FROM    DSN8510.EMP;
```

For this reason, avoid nulls in columns involved in math functions.

When DATE, TIME, and TIMESTAMP columns can be unknown, assign them as nullable. DB2 checks to ensure that only valid dates, times, and timestamps are placed in columns defined as such. If the column can be unknown, it must be defined to be nullable because the default for these columns is the current date, current time, and current timestamp (unless explicitly defined otherwise using the DEFAULT clause). Null, therefore, is the only available option for the recording of missing dates, times, and timestamps.

For every other column, determine whether nullability can be of benefit before allowing nulls. Consider these rules:

- When a nullable column participates in an ORDER BY or GROUP BY clause, the returned nulls are grouped at the high end of the sort order.
- Nulls are considered to be equal when duplicates are eliminated by SELECT DISTINCT or COUNT (DISTINCT *column*).
- A unique index considers nulls to be equivalent and disallows duplicate entries because of the existence of nulls, unless the WHERE NOT NULL clause is specified in the index.
- For comparison in a SELECT statement, two null columns are not considered equal. When a nullable column participates in a predicate in the WHERE or HAVING clause, the nulls that are encountered cause the comparison to evaluate to UNKNOWN.
- When a nullable column participates in a calculation, the result is null.
- Columns that participate in a primary key cannot be null.
- To test for the existence of nulls, use the special predicate IS NULL in the WHERE clause of the SELECT statement.
- You cannot simply state WHERE *column* = NULL. You must state WHERE *column* IS NULL.
- It is invalid to test if a column is < NULL, <= NULL, > NULL, or >= NULL. These are all meaningless because null is the absence of a value.
- You can assign a column to null using the = predicate in the SET clause of the UPDATE statement.

Examine these rules closely. ORDER BY, GROUP BY, DISTINCT, and unique indexes consider nulls to be equal and handle them accordingly. The SELECT statement, however, deems that the comparison of null columns is not equivalence, but unknown. This inconsistent handling of nulls is an anomaly that you must remember when using nulls. The following are several sample SQL queries and the effect nulls have on them.

```
SELECT   JOB, SUM(SALARY)
FROM     DSN8510.EMP
GROUP BY JOB;
```

This query returns the average salary for each type of job. All instances in which JOB is null will group at the bottom of the output.

```
SELECT   EMPNO, PROJNO, ACTNO, EMPTIME
         EMSTDATE, EMENDATE
FROM     DSN8510.EMPPROJACT
WHERE    EMSTDATE = EMENDATE;
```

This query retrieves all occurrences in which the project start date is equal to the project end date. This information is clearly erroneous, as anyone who has ever worked on a software development project can attest. The query does not return any rows in which either dates or both dates are null for two reasons: (1) two null columns are never equal for purposes of comparison, and (2) when either column of a comparison operator is null, the result is unknown.

```
UPDATE  DSN8510.DEPT
  SET   MGRNO = NULL
WHERE   MGRNO = '000010';
```

This query sets the `MGRNO` column to null wherever `MGRNO` is currently equal to `000010` in the `DEPT` table.

NOTE

Nulls sometimes are inappropriately referred to as null values. Using the term *value* to describe a null column is incorrect because the term *null* implies the lack of a value. The relational model has abandoned the idea of nulls in favor of a similar concept called marks. The two types of marks are an A-mark and an I-mark. An A-mark refers to information that is applicable but presently unknown, whereas an I-mark refers to inapplicable information (information that does not apply). If DB2 would implement marks rather than nulls, the problem of differentiating between inapplicable and unknown data would disappear.

Encoding Scheme

Version 5

The `CCSID` parameter can be used to specify ASCII or EBCDIC encoding at the table level as well as at the tablespace level. All data stored within a tablespace must use the same encoding scheme.

Use Drop Restriction

Version 4

To prohibit inadvertent table drops, use the `WITH RESTRICT ON DROP` clause of the `CREATE TABLE` statement. When `WITH RESTRICT ON DROP` is specified, drops cannot be issued for the table, its tablespace, and its database. To subsequently drop the table, it must first be altered to remove the `RESTRICT ON DROP` specification.

Use `LIKE` to Duplicate a Table's Schema

Use the `LIKE` clause to create a table with the same columns as another table. The following SQL creates a new table `OLD_PROJ` using the `PROJ` table as a template:

```
CREATE TABLE DSN8510.OLD_PROJ
LIKE DSN8510.PROJ;
```

The `LIKE` clause is particularly useful in the following instances

- When creating exception tables required by the `CHECK` utility
- When multiple instances of a similar table must be created
- When creating a `PLAN_TABLE`
- When creating the same table for multiple users

Use DB2 Referential Integrity

Referential integrity (RI) can be defined as a means of ensuring data integrity between tables related by primary and foreign keys. As of DB2 V5, foreign keys can refer to both primary keys and unique keys that are not explicitly defined as primary keys. The table with the primary key is called the *parent* table and the table with the foreign key is called the *dependent* table (or *child* table).

Referential constraints are defined using the `FOREIGN KEY` clause. A referential constraint consists of three components: a constraint name, the columns comprising the foreign key, and a references clause. The same constraint name can not be specified more than once for the same table. If a constraint name is not explicitly coded, DB2 will automatically create a unique name for the constraint derived from the name of the first column in the foreign key.

For example, consider the relationship between the `DSN8510.DEPT` and `DSN8510.EMP` tables. The diagram in Appendix D graphically depicts this relationship.

```
CREATE TABLE DSN8510.EMP
 (EMPNO              CHAR(6)          NOT NULL,
  FIRSTNME           VARCHAR(12)      NOT NULL,
  MIDINIT            CHAR(1)          NOT NULL,
  LASTNAME           VARCHAR(15)      NOT NULL,
  WORKDEPT           CHAR(3),
  PHONENO            CHAR(4) CONSTRAINT NUMBER CHECK
                     (PHONENO >= '0000' AND
                      PHONENO <= '9999'),
  HIREDATE           DATE,
  JOB                CHAR(8),
  EDLEVEL            SMALLINT,
  SEX                CHAR(1),
  BIRTHDATE          DATE,
  SALARY             DECIMAL(9,2),
  BONUS              DECIMAL(9,2),
  COMM               DECIMAL(9,2),
  PRIMARY KEY (EMPNO)
  FOREIGN KEY RED (WORKDEPT)
  REFERENCES DSN8510.DEPT ON DELETE SET NULL
 )
EDITPROC DSN8EAE1
IN DSN8D51A.DSN8S51E;

CREATE TABLE DSN8510.DEPT
 (DEPTNO             CHAR(3)          NOT NULL,
  DEPTNAME           VARCHAR(36)      NOT NULL,
  MGRNO              CHAR(6),
```

```
    ADMRDEPT            CHAR(3)           NOT NULL,
    LOCATION            CHAR(16),
    PRIMARY KEY (DEPTNO)
   )
  IN DSN8D51A.DSN8S51D;
  ALTER TABLE DSN8510.DEPT
    FOREIGN KEY RDD (ADMRDEPT)
      REFERENCES DSN8510.DEPT ON DELETE CASCADE;
  ALTER TABLE DSN8510.DEPT
    FOREIGN KEY RDE (MGRNO)
      REFERENCES DSN8510.EMP ON DELETE SET NULL;
```

The primary key of EMP is EMPNO; the primary key of DEPT is DEPTNO. Several foreign keys exist, but let's examine the foreign key that relates EMP to DEPT. The foreign key, named RDE, in the DEPT table relates the MGRNO column to a specific EMPNO in the EMP table. This referential constraint ensures that no MGRNO can exist in the DEPT table before the employee exists in the EMP table. The MGRNO must take on a value of EMPNO. Additionally, the foreign key value in DEPT cannot subsequently be updated to a value that is not a valid employee value in EMP, and the primary key of EMP cannot be deleted without the appropriate check for corresponding values in the DEPT foreign key column or columns.

To ensure that this integrity remains intact, DB2 has a series of rules for inserting, deleting, and updating:

- When inserting a row with a foreign key, DB2 checks the values of the foreign key columns against the values of the primary key columns in the parent table. If no matching primary key columns are found, the insert is disallowed. A new primary key can be inserted as long as it is unique.
- When updating foreign key values, DB2 performs the same checks as when it is inserting a row with a foreign key.
- Deleting a row with a foreign key is permitted. When deleting a row with a primary key, DB2 takes action as indicated in the DDL; it either restricts deletion, cascades deletes to foreign key rows, or sets all referenced foreign keys to null.

Three basic options can be specified when deleting a foreign key: RESTRICT, CASCADE, and SET NULL. RESTRICT disallows the deletion of the primary key row if any foreign keys relate to the row. CASCADE allows the deletion of the primary key row and also deletes the foreign key rows that relate to it. SET NULL allows the deletion of the primary key row and, instead of deleting all related foreign key rows, sets the foreign key columns to NULL. The processing needs of the application dictate which delete option should be specified in the table create statements.

NOTE

Version 5

DB2 V5 adds a fourth delete rule: NO ACTION. The behavior of NO ACTION is similar to RESTRICT. The only difference is between RESTRICT and NO ACTION is when the referential constraint is enforced.

- `RESTRICT` enforces the delete rule immediately
- `NO ACTION` enforces the delete rule at the end of the statement

When deleting multiple rows from a table with a self-referencing constraint `RESTRICT` would prohibit the `DELETE`, whereas `NO ACTION` can allow it to complete. To specify `ON DELETE NO ACTION` in a referential constraint, the `CURRENT RULES` special register must be set to STD, not DB2.

All of these options are valid and use nearly the same resources. If efficiency is your primary goal, the `RESTRICT` option usually uses fewer resources because data modification of dependent tables is not performed. If data modification is necessary, however, allowing DB2 to perform it is usually preferable to writing cascade or set null logic in a high-level language.

The general rule for implementing referential integrity is to use DB2's inherent features instead of coding RI with application code. DB2 usually has a more efficient means of implementing RI than the application. Also, why should a programmer code what already is available in the DBMS?

The exceptions to this rule are the subject of the rest of this section. DB2 does a referential integrity check for every row insertion. You can increase efficiency if your application does a single check of a row from the parent table and then makes multiple inserts to the child table.

Do not use DB2 RI on tables built from another system that already is referentially intact. If the tables are updated after being built or loaded from the external data source, consider building the RI into the application code where appropriate and ignoring the RI when building or updating the tables from the referentially intact source.

Do not use DB2 RI if tables are read only. If you need to scrub the data when loading, you still may want to use DB2 RI. If application code is used to load the tables, base your decision for implementing RI with DB2 DDL according to the other guidelines in this chapter.

If the application processing needs are such that the parent table is read before even one child is inserted, consider not implementing DB2 RI. In this case, DB2 would repeat the read process that the application must do anyway to satisfy its processing needs.

Define a primary (or unique) key to prohibit duplicate table rows. This should be done to ensure entity integrity regardless of whether dependent tables are related to the table being defined. Entity integrity ensures that each row in a table represents a single, real-world entity.

Avoid large referential sets. Try not to tie together all tables in a large system; otherwise, recovery, quiesce, and other utility processing will be difficult to develop and administer.

You should follow some general rules when deciding how to limit the scope of DB2-defined referential integrity:

- Limit referential structures to no more than three levels in any one direction. For example, consider the following structure:

  A → B → C ← D ← E ← F

  Consider breaking this structure into the following two structures and supporting the referential constraint from C ← D with application logic.

  A → B → C

  D ← E ← F

  This reduces the potential performance degradation caused by DB2's automatic RI checks. However, it also opens the door to data integrity problems caused by updates outside the scope of the application programs that enforce the integrity. Weigh the performance impact against the possible loss of integrity before deciding to bypass DB2-enforced RI.
- Try to control the number of cycles in a referential set. A cycle is a referential path that connects a table to itself. Table A is connected to itself in this sample cycle:

  A → B → C → A

  Furthermore, a table can not be delete-connected to itself in a cycle. A table is delete-connected to another table if it is a dependent of a table specified with a DELETE CASCADE rule.
- Whether RI is checked by DB2 or by an application program, overhead is incurred. Efficiency cannot be increased simply by moving RI from DB2 to the program. Be sure that the application program can achieve better performance than DB2 (by taking advantage of innate knowledge of the data that DB2 does not have) before eliminating DB2-enforced RI.
- If updates to tables are permitted in an uncontrolled environment (for example, QMF, SPUFI, or third-party table editors), implement DB2-enforced RI if data integrity is important. Otherwise, you cannot ensure that data is correct from a referential integrity standpoint.

Beware of Self-Referencing Constraints

A self-referencing constraint is one in which the parent table is also the dependent table. The sample table, DSN8510.PROJ contains a self-referencing constraint specifying that the MAJPROJ column must be a valid PROJNO.

Self-referencing constraints must be defined using the DELETE CASCADE rule. Exercise caution when deleting rows from these types of tables because a single delete could cause all of the table data to be completely wiped out!

Beware of RI Implementation Restrictions

Take the following restrictions into consideration when implementing RI on your DB2 tables:

- A self-referencing constraint must specify `DELETE CASCADE`
- A table cannot be delete-connected to itself
- Tables that are delete-connected to another table through multiple referential paths must employ the same `DELETE` rule and it must be either `CASCADE` or `RESTRICT`

Use Check Constraints

Version 4

Check constraints can be used to place specific data value restrictions on the contents of a column through the specification of an expression. The expression is explicitly defined in the table DDL and is formulated in much the same way that SQL `WHERE` clauses are formulated. Any attempt to modify the column data (for example, during `INSERT` or `UPDATE` processing) will cause the expression to be evaluated. If the modification conforms to the Boolean expression, the modification is permitted to continue. If not, the statement will fail with a constraint violation.

Check constraints consist of two components: a constraint name and a check condition. The same constraint name cannot be specified more than once for the same table. If a constraint name is not explicitly coded, DB2 will automatically create a unique name for the constraint derived from the name of the first column in the check condition.

The check condition defines the actual constraint logic. The check condition can be defined using any of the basic predicates (>, <, =, <>, <=, >=), as well as `BETWEEN`, `IN`, `LIKE`, and `NULL`. Furthermore, `AND` and `OR` can be used to string conditions together. However, please note the following restrictions:

- The entire length of the check condition can be no greater than 3,800 total bytes.
- The constraint can only refer to columns in the table in which it is created.
- Subselects, column functions, host variables, parameter markers, special registers, and columns defined with field procedures *cannot* be specified in a check constraint.
- The `NOT` logical operator *cannot* be used.
- The first operand *must be* the name of a column contained in the table. The second operand must be either another column name or a constant.
- If the second operand is a constant, it must be compatible with the data type of the first operand. If the second operand is a column, it must be the same data type as the first column specified.

The `EMP` table contains the following check constraint:

```
PHONENO  CHAR(4) CONSTRAINT NUMBER CHECK
                (PHONENO >= '0000' AND
                 PHONENO <= '9999'),
```

This constraint defines the valid range of values for the PHONENO column. The following are examples of check constraints which could be added to the EMP table:

```
CONSTRAINT CHECK_SALARY
CHECK (SALARY < 50000.00)

CONSTRAINT COMM_VS_SALARY
CHECK (SALARY > COMM)

CONSTRAINT COMM_BONUS
CHECK (COMM > 0 OR BONUS > 0)
```

The first check constraint ensures that no employee can earn a salary less than $50,000; the second constraint ensures that an employee's salary will always be greater than his or her commission; and the third constraint ensures that each employee will have either a commission or a bonus set up.

The primary benefit of check constraints is the ability to enforce business rules directly in each database without requiring additional application logic. Once defined, the business rule is physically implemented and cannot be bypassed. Check constraints also provide the following benefits:

- Because there is no additional programming required, DBAs can implement check constraints without involving the application programming staff.
- Check constraints provide better data integrity because a check constraint is always executed whenever the data is modified. Without a check constraint critical business rules could be bypassed during ad hoc data modification.
- Check constraints promote consistency. Because they are implemented once, in the table DDL, each constraint is always enforced. Constraints written in application logic, on the other hand, must be executed by each program that modifies the data to which the constraint applies. This can cause code duplication and inconsistent maintenance resulting in inaccurate business rule support.
- Typically check constraints coded in DDL will outperform the corresponding application code.

Beware of Semantics with Check Constraints

Version 4

DB2 performs no semantic checking on constraints and defaults. It will allow the DBA to define defaults that contradict check constraints. Furthermore, DB2 will allow the DBA to define check constraints that contradict one another. Care must be taken to avoid creating this type of problem. The following are examples of contradictory constraints:

```
CHECK (EMPNO > 10 AND EMPNO <9)
```

In this case, no value is both greater than 10 and less than 9, so nothing could ever be inserted. However, DB2 will allow this constraint to be defined.

```
EMP_TYPE    CHAR(8) DEFAULT 'NEW'
CHECK (EMP_TYPE IN ('TEMP', 'FULLTIME', 'CONTRACT'))
```

In this case, the default value is not one of the permitted EMP_TYPE values according to the defined constraint. No defaults would ever be inserted.

```
CHECK (EMPNO > 10)
CHECK (EMPNO >= 11)
```

In this case, the constraints are redundant. No logical harm is done, but both constraints will be checked, thereby impacting the performance of applications that modify the table in which the constraints exist.

Other potential semantic problems could occur:

- When the parent table indicates ON DELETE SET NULL but a rule is defined on the child table stating CHECK (COL1 IS NOT NULL)
- When two constraints are defined on the same column with contradictory conditions
- When the constraint requires that the column be NULL, but the column is defined as NOT NULL

Code Constraints at the Table Level

Version 4

Although single constraints (primary keys, unique keys, foreign keys, and check constraints) can be specified at the column level, avoid doing so. In terms of functionality, there is no difference between an integrity constraint defined at the table level and the same constraint defined at the column level. All constraints can be coded at the table level; only single column constraints can be coded at the column level. By coding all constraints at the table level, maintenance will be easier and clarity will be improved.

Code this (table level):

```
CREATE TABLE ORDER_ITEM
 (ORDERNO          CHAR(3)          NOT NULL,
  ITEMNO           CHAR(3)          NOT NULL,
  AMOUNT_ORD       DECIMAL(7,2)     NOT NULL,
  PRIMARY KEY (ORDERNO, ITEMNO)
  FOREIGN KEY ORD_ITM (ORDERNO)
    REFERENCES ORDER ON DELETE CASCADE
)
```

Instead of this (column level):

```
CREATE TABLE ORDER_ITEM
 (ORDERNO          CHAR(3)          NOT NULL
    REFERENCES ORDER ON DELETE CASCADE,
  ITEMNO           CHAR(3)          NOT NULL,
  AMOUNT_ORD       DECIMAL(7,2)     NOT NULL,
  PRIMARY KEY (ORDERNO, ITEMNO)
)
```

Consider Using Field Procedures

Field procedures are programs that transform data on insertion and convert the data to its original format on subsequent retrieval. You can use a FIELDPROC to transform character columns, as long as the columns are 254 bytes or less in length.

No FIELDPROCs are delivered with DB2, so they must be developed by the DB2 user. They are ideal for altering the sort sequence of values.

Consider Using Edit Procedures

An EDITPROC is functionally equivalent to a FIELDPROC, but it acts on an entire row instead of a column. Edit procedures are simply programs that transform data on insertion and convert the data to its original format on subsequent retrieval. Edit procedures are not supplied with DB2, so they must be developed by the user of DB2. They are ideal for implementing data compression routines.

Consider Using Validation Routine

A VALIDPROC receives a row and returns a value indicating whether LOAD, INSERT, UPDATE, or DELETE processing should proceed. A validation procedure is similar to an edit procedure but it cannot perform data transformation; it simply assesses the validity of the data.

A typical use for a VALIDPROC is to ensure valid domain values. For example, to enforce a Boolean domain, you could write a validation procedure to ensure that a certain portion of a row contains only T or F.

Consider DB2-Enforced Table Auditing

If you must audit user access to DB2 tables, you can specify an audit rule for your tables. Although the auditing features of DB2 are rudimentary, sometimes they are useful. DB2 has three table audit options: NONE, CHANGES, and ALL.

DB2 table auditing is done on a unit-of-work basis only. DB2 audits only the first table access of any particular type for each unit of work, not every table access. AUDIT CHANGES writes an audit trace record for the first insert, update, and delete made by each unit of work. AUDIT ALL writes an audit trace record for the first select, insert, update, and delete made by each unit of work. By specifying AUDIT NONE or by failing to code an audit parameter, table auditing is inactivated.

Before deciding to audit DB2 table access, consider that table auditing incurs overhead—each time a table is accessed in a new unit of work, an audit trace record is written. Additionally, even if auditing has been specified for a given table, no audit trace records are written unless the appropriate DB2 audit trace classes are activated. For AUDIT CHANGES, activate audit trace classes 1, 2, 3, 4, 7, and 8. For AUDIT ALL, activate audit trace classes 1 through 8.

In general, do not audit table access unless your application absolutely requires it.

Use Comments

Consider using the COMMENT ON statement to document the entities you create. As many as 254 characters of descriptive text can be applied to each column, table, and alias known to DB2.

The comment text is stored in a column named REMARKS in the SYSIBM.SYSTABLES and SYSIBM.SYSCOLUMNS tables of the DB2 Catalog.

If useful descriptions are maintained for all columns and tables, the DB2 Catalog can function as a crude data dictionary for DB2 objects. However, be aware that comments are stored in a VARCHAR column in each of the above tables.

CAUTION

When comments are specified, the overall size of the DB2 Catalog will expand and may grow to be larger than expected. Weigh the benefits of added documentation against the impact on the DB2 Catalog before automatically commented on all columns and tables.

Specify Labels

Where appropriate, designate a label for each column in the table using the LABEL ON statement. The maximum length for a column name is 18 characters, but a column label can have up to 30 characters. The label is stored in the DB2 Catalog in the SYSIBM.SYSCOLUMNS tables.

The column label provides a more descriptive name than the column name. QMF users can specify that they want to use labels rather than column names, thereby providing better report headings.

CAUTION

Once again, be aware that labels add to the overall size of the DB2 Catalog, specifically to the SYSIBM.SYSCOLUMNS table. However, labels will not cause the same amount of growth as comments because labels have a maximum size of 30 characters (as opposed to 254 for comments).

Index Guidelines

An *index* is a balanced B-tree structure that orders the values of columns in a table. When you index a table by one or more of its columns, you can access data directly and more efficiently because the index is ordered by the columns to be retrieved.

You also can create a DB2 index as a unique index. This forces the columns specified for the index to be unique within the table. If you try to insert or update these columns with nonunique values, an error code is displayed and the request fails.

Before creating any indexes, consider the following:

- Percentage of table access versus table update
- Performance requirements of accessing the table
- Performance requirements of modifying the table
- Frequency of INSERT, UPDATE, and DELETE operations
- Storage requirements
- Impact on recovery
- Impact of reorganization
- Impact on the LOAD utility

Remember that indexes are created to enhance performance. Keep the following in mind as you create indexes:

- Consider indexing on columns used in UNION, DISTINCT, GROUP BY, ORDER BY, and WHERE clauses.
- Limit the indexing of frequently updated columns.
- If indexing a table, explicitly create a clustering index. Failure to do so will result in DB2 clustering data by the first index created.
- Cluster on columns in GROUP BY, ORDER BY, and WHERE clauses.
- Choose the first column of multicolumn indexes wisely, based on the following hierarchy. First, choose columns that will be specified most frequently in SQL WHERE clauses (unless cardinality is very low). Second, choose columns that will be referenced most often in ORDER BY and GROUP BY clauses (once again, unless cardinality is very low). Third, choose columns with the highest cardinality.
- The biggest payback from an index comes from DB2's capability to locate and retrieve referenced data quickly. DB2's capability to do this is reduced when cardinality is low because multiple RIDs satisfy a given reference. Balance the cardinality of a column against the amount of time it is accessed, giving preference to data access over cardinality.
- There are no hard and fast rules for index creation. Experiment with different index combinations and gauge the efficiency of the results.

Version 5

- As of DB2 V5, it is not necessary to treat the creation of partitioned indexes any different than other indexes. In past releases, when partition independence was non-existent or limited, it was wise to restrict the number of indexes on a partitioned tablespace.
- Keep the number of columns in an index to a minimum. If only three columns are needed, index on only those three columns.

- Sometimes, however, it can be advantageous to include additional columns in an index to increase the chances of index-only access. (Index-only access is discussed further in Chapters 14 and 18.) For example, suppose that there is an index on the `DEPTNO` column of the `DSN8510.DEPT` table. The following query may use this index:

  ```
  SELECT   DEPTNAME
  FROM     DSN8510.DEPT
  WHERE    DEPTNO > 'D00';
  ```

  DB2 could use the index to access only those columns with a `DEPTNO` greater than `D00`, then access the data to return the `DEPT`.

- Avoid indexing on variable (`VARCHAR`, `VARGRAPHIC`) columns. DB2 expands the variable column to the maximum length specified for the column, thereby increasing overall DASD use.

Favor Type 2 Indexes Over Type 1 Indexes

Version 4

There are two types of indexes available to DB2: Type 1 and Type 2. Type 2 indexes were introduced with DB2 Version 4 and should be the standard index type implemented in your shop. Favor Type 2 over Type 1 indexes because they provide the following benefits:

- Eliminates index locking (the predominant cause of contention in most preV4 DB2 applications)
- Type 2 indexes do not use index subpages
- Type 2 indexes are the only type supported for ASCII-encoded tables
- Many newer DB2 features cannot be used unless Type 2 indexes are used; these features include row-level locking, data sharing, full partition independence, uncommitted reads, `UNIQUE WHERE NOT NULL`, and CPU and Sysplex parallelism

Furthermore, IBM is promoting Type 2 indexes as the standard and will most likely remove support for Type 1 indexes in a future release of DB2. As of DB2 V5, both Type 1 and Type 2 indexes are supported.

Create a Unique Index for Each Primary Key

Every primary key explicitly defined for a table must be associated with a corresponding unique index. If you do not create a unique index for a primary key, an incomplete key is defined for the table, making the table inaccessible.

Use `WHERE NOT NULL` to Allow Multiple Nulls in a `UNIQUE` Index

Version 4

Specify the `UNIQUE WHERE NOT NULL` clause to enable multiple nulls to exist in a unique index. This is useful when an index contains at least one nullable column, but all non-null entries must be unique. This option is only valid with Type 2 indexes.

Create Indexes for Foreign Keys

Unless an index already exists for access reasons or the table is too small to be indexed, create an index for each foreign key defined for a table. Because DB2's referential integrity feature accesses data defined as a foreign key "behind the scenes," it's a good idea to enhance the efficiency of this access by creating indexes.

Uniqueness Recommendations

You can enforce the uniqueness of a column or a group of columns by creating a unique index on those columns. You can have more than one unique index per table.

It usually is preferable to enforce the uniqueness of columns by creating unique indexes, thereby allowing the DBMS to do the work. The alternative is to code uniqueness logic in an application program to do the same work that DB2 does automatically. Remember: If security is liberal for application tables, ad hoc SQL users can modify table data without the application program, and thereby insert or update columns that should be unique to nonunique values.

When to Avoid Indexing

There are a few times when you should not define indexes. Avoid indexing when the table is very small, that is, less than 10 pages. Avoid indexing also when the table has heavy insert and delete activity but is relatively small, that is, less than 20 pages. A table also should not be indexed if it is accessed with a scan—in other words, if there is no conditional predicate access to the table.

When to Avoid Placing Columns in an Index

Sometimes you should not define indexes for columns. If the column is updated frequently and the table is less than 20 pages, do not place the column in an index.

Avoid defining an index for a column if an index on the column exists that would make the new index redundant. For example, if an index exists on `COL1`, `COL2` in `TABLE1`, an index on `COL1` is redundant. An index on `COL2` alone is not redundant because it is not the first column in the index.

When to Specify Extra Index Columns

When the column or columns to be indexed contain nonunique data, consider adding an extra column to increase the cardinality of the index. This reduces the index RID list and avoids chaining—an inefficient method of processing index entries. Uniqueness can be gauged by determining the cardinality for the columns in the index. The cardinality for the columns is nothing more than the number of distinct values stored in the columns. If this number is small (less than 10 percent of the total number of rows for the table), consider adding extra columns to the index. (A column's cardinality can be found in the DB2 Catalog using queries presented in Part IV, "DB2 Performance Monitoring.")

Indexing Large and Small Tables

For tables over 100 pages, define at least one index. If the table is larger (over 1,000 pages), try to limit the indexes to those that are absolutely necessary for adequate performance. When a large table has multiple indexes, update performance usually suffers. When large tables lack indexes, however, access efficiency usually suffers. This fragile balance must be monitored closely. In most situations, more indexes are better than fewer indexes because most applications are query intensive rather than update intensive.

In general, you should not index tables with 10 or fewer pages. But what about tables that are bigger than 10 pages—but not by much? For tables containing 10 to 50 pages, create appropriate indexes to satisfy uniqueness criteria or if the table frequently is joined to other tables. Create indexes also when the performance of queries that access the table suffers. Test the performance of the query after the index is created, though, to ensure that the index helps. When you index a small table, increased I/O (due to index accesses) may cause performance to suffer when compared to a complete scan of all the data in the table.

Index Overloading

Consider overloading an index when the row length of the table to be indexed is very short. A DB2 tablespace can fit only 255 rows in each page (127 for DB2 releases), but a DB2 index is not limited in the number of rows that each page can contain.

You can take advantage of this by overloading the index with columns. This is achieved by placing every column of a small table in an index. A better data-to-page ratio is achieved in the index than in the tablespace because more rows exist on each index leaf page. Scanning the leaf pages of the index requires fewer I/O operations than scanning the corresponding tablespace.

Multi-Index Access

DB2 can use more than one index to satisfy a data retrieval request. For example, consider two indexes on the DSN8510.DEPT table: one index for DEPTNO and another index for ADMRDEPT. If you executed the following query, DB2 could use both of these indexes to satisfy the request:

```
SELECT   DEPTNO, DEPTNAME, MGRNO
FROM     DSN8510.DEPT
WHERE    DEPTNO > 'D00'
AND      ADMRDEPT = 'D01';
```

If multi-index access is used, the index on DEPTNO is used to retrieve all departments with a DEPTNO greater than 'D00', and the index on ADMRDEPT is used to retrieve only rows containing 'D01'. Then these rows are intersected and the correct result is returned.

An alternative to the multi-index access just described is a single multicolumn index. If you create one index for the combination of columns ADMRDEPT, DEPTNO, DB2 could use this index, as well. When deciding whether to use multiple indexes or multicolumn indexes, consider the following guidelines:

- Multi-index access is usually less efficient than access by a single multicolumn index.
- Many multicolumn indexes require more DASD than multiple single-column indexes.
- Consider the access criteria for all applications that will be querying the table that must be indexed. If the indexing needs are light, a series of multicolumn indexes is usually the best solution. If the indexing needs are heavy and many combinations and permutations of columns are necessary to support the access criteria, multiple single-column indexes are usually the best solution.
- Sometimes one multicolumn index can fit the needs of many different access criteria. For example, suppose that the DSN8510.EMP table (see Appendix D) has three access needs, as follows:

  LASTNAME only

  LASTNAME and FIRSTNME

  LASTNAME, FIRSTNME, and BONUS

  One index on the concatenation of the LASTNAME, FIRSTNME, and BONUS columns would efficiently handle the access needs for this table. When only LASTNAME is required, only the first column of the index is used. When both LASTNAME and FIRSTNME are specified in a query, only the first two columns are used. Finally, if all three columns are specified in a query, the index uses all three columns.
- Consider the trade-off of DASD versus performance, and weigh the access criteria to determine the best indexing scenario for your implementation.

Specify Appropriate Index Parameters

The first general rule of thumb for index creation is to favor Type 2 over Type 1 indexes. Type 2 indexes avoid locking, are required for many of DB2's performance-oriented features, and are IBM's stated direction for DB2's indexing future.

The next wisest thing to do is to choose a useful clustering strategy. Clustering reduces I/O. The DB2 optimizer usually tries to use an index on a clustered column before using other indexes. Choose your clustering index wisely—in general, use the index accessed most often or accessed by the most critical SQL statements.

For a clustering index, you might want to try setting the number of subpages (for Type 1 indexes only) such that each subpage contains the same number of rows as the data pages of the tablespace. This can reduce locking of unrelated data. If the index is not clustered, do not attempt this, because the corresponding index subpages will contain different rows than the tablespace pages, and no gain in performance will be realized. Of course, the best approach is to convert Type 1 indexes to Type 2 indexes to avoid locking altogether.

Specify index free space the same as the tablespace free space. The same reason for the free space in the tablespace applies to the free space in the index. Remember that index "row" sizes are smaller than table row sizes, so plan accordingly when calculating free space. Also, as PCTFREE increases, the frequency of page splitting decreases and the efficiency of index updates increases.

When an index page is completely filled and a new entry must be inserted, DB2 splits the index leaf page involved in two, moving half the data to a new page. Splits can cause DB2 to lock at many levels of the index, possibly causing splits all the way back to the root page. This splitting, locking, and updating is inefficient and should be avoided by prudent use of free space and frequent index reorganizations. DB2 also uses a free page for splits if one is available within 64 pages of the original page being split. Use the suggestions in Table 3.7 as a rough guideline for specifying PCTFREE and FREEPAGE based on insert and update frequency.

Table 3.7. Index free space allocation chart.

Type of Index Processing	FREEPAGE	PCTFREE
Read only	0	0
Less than 20 percent of volume inserted or updated between REORGs	0	10 to 20
Twenty to 60 percent of volume inserted or updated between REORGs	63	20 to 30
Greater than 60 percent of volume inserted or updated between REORGs	15	20 to 30

For Type 1 indexes, increasing the number of subpages can decrease contention, but this may decrease the efficiency of access to the index data. Specify SUBPAGES 1 for frequently updated indexed columns. Better yet, avoid subpages altogether and use Type 2 indexes.

See the VCAT versus STOGROUP considerations presented in Table 3.2. The considerations for tablespace allocation apply also to index allocation.

Create Indexes Before Loading Tables

The LOAD utility update indexes efficiently. Usually, the LOAD utility is more efficient than building indexes for tables that already contain data. The data being loaded should be sorted into the order of the clustering index before execution.

Use Deferred Index Creation

The DEFER option on the CREATE INDEX statement allows the index to be created but not populated. The RECOVER INDEX utility can then be executed to populate the index. This will speed the index creation process because RECOVER INDEX usually populates index entries faster than CREATE INDEX.

Creating an stogroup-defined index with DEFER YES causes the underlying VSAM data set for the index to be allocated.

Additionally, the DB2 catalog is updated to record that the index exists. But, if the table being indexed currently contains data, DB2 will turn on the recover pending flag for the index space and issue a +610 SQLCODE. Subsequent execution of RECOVER INDEX will turn off the recover pending flag and populate the index.

Let DB2 Tell You What Indexes to Create

Consider using CREATE INDEX with the DEFER YES option to create many different indexes for new applications. The indexes will be recorded in the DB2 catalog, but will not be populated. Then, update the statistics in the DB2 catalog to indicate anticipated production volumes and run EXPLAIN on your performance-sensitive queries.

Use RECOVER INDEX to populate the indexes that were used and drop the indexes that were not used. In this way DB2 can help you choose which indexes will be useful.

Store Index and Tablespace Data Sets Separately

You should assign indexes to different STOGROUP s or different volumes than the tablespaces containing the tables to which the indexes apply. This reduces head contention and increases I/O efficiency.

Consider Separate Index Bufferpools

Consider placing critical indexes in a different bufferpool than your tablespaces. For more in-depth bufferpool consideration, see Chapter 18, "Using EXPLAIN."

PRIQTY and SECQTY

If you are defining indexes using the STOGROUP method, you must specify primary and secondary space allocations. The primary allocation is the amount of physical storage allocated when the index is created. As the amount of data in the index grows, secondary allocations of storage are taken. Use the guidelines specified for tablespace space allocations to guide your index space allocation efforts.

Explicitly Define Index Data Set Size

Use the PIECESIZE clause, new as of DB2 V5, to specify the largest data set size for a non-partitioned index—for example:

```
CREATE TYPE 2 UNIQUE INDEX DSN8510.XACT2
  ON DSN8510.ACT (ACTKWD ASC)
  USING STOGROUP DSN8G510
        PRIQTY 65536K
        SECQTY 8192K
        ERASE NO
  BUFFERPOOL BP0
  CLOSE NO
  PIECESIZE 256M;
```

This statement will limit the size of individual datasets for the XACT2 index (on DSN8510.ACT) to 256 megabytes.

CAUTION

Avoid setting the PIECESIZE too small. A new data set will be allocated each time the PIECESIZE threshold is reached. DB2 will increment the A001 component of the data set name each time. This makes the physical limit 999 data sets (A001 through A999). If PIECESIZE is set too small, the data set name can limit the size of the tablespace.

Miscellaneous DDL Guidelines

This section contains guidelines that are not easily categorized. They provide SQL guidance from an overall perspective of DB2 development.

Avoid Using DDL in an Application Program

Do not issue DDL from an application program. DDL statements should be planned by a database administrator and issued when they cause the least disruption to the production system.

When DROP, ALTER, and CREATE statements are used, DB2 must update its system catalog tables. These statements also place a lock on the database DBD being affected by the DDL. This can affect the overall performance of the DB2 system. When DDL is issued from an application program, DB2 object creation is difficult to control and schedule potentially causing lockout conditions in production systems.

Plan the Execution of DDL

Because of the potential impact on the application system (such as locking, new functionality, or new access paths), schedule the execution of DDL statements during off-peak hours.

Strive for Relational Purity

Learn and understand the relational model and let your design decisions be influenced by it. Assume that DB2 eventually will support all features of the relational model and plan accordingly. For example, if a procedural method can be used to implement outer joins, favor this method over the implementation of physical tables containing outer join data. This provides for an orderly migration to the features of the relational model as they become available in DB2.

Create Views with Care

Do not blindly create one view per base table. Many "experts" give this erroneous advice, but practice has proven that automatically creating views when tables are created provides little or no insulation against table changes. It usually creates more problems than it solves. See the next chapter for more information on views.

Favor Normalized Tables

Taking all the previous suggestions into account, avoid denormalization unless performance reasons dictate otherwise. Normalized tables, if they perform well, provide the optimal environment and should be favored over tables that are not normalized.

Summary

The selection you make as you define your DB2 object will have a definite impact on the performance of your DB2 applications. Make sure that you understand the DDL specifications and recommendations made in this chapter before implementing any DB2 database objects.

4

Miscellaneous Guidelines

This chapter provides SQL tips and techniques for the aspects of SQL not covered in the first three chapters. I've broken down these guidelines into three categories:

- DB2 security and authorization (DCL)
- View usage and implementation
- General SQL coding techniques

Authorization Guidelines

The proper application of DB2 security can have a significant impact on the usability and performance of DB2 programs. The capability to access and modify DB2 objects and resources is authorized with SQL `GRANT` statements and removed with SQL `REVOKE` statements. The complete security picture, however, is not this simple.

Many features of DB2 security can complicate security administration, such as

- The cascading effect of the DB2 `REVOKE` statement
- Secondary authorization IDs
- `PUBLIC` access
- Use of dynamic SQL

Guidelines for the proper implementation of DB2 security for each of these areas and more are addressed in this section on authorization guidelines.

Avoid Granting PUBLIC Access

Administering security can be a complex duty. Simply allowing blanket access to certain DB2 objects and resources often appears easier. The `PUBLIC` authority of DB2 gives the security administrator this option, but it is usually an unwise choice.

For example, when many shops install DB2, they grant `PUBLIC` access to the default database, DSNDB04. Inevitably, users assign tablespaces to this database. Because the tablespaces are in a default area, they are difficult to monitor and control. The area quickly becomes overused. The DBA unit is unaware of some tables that exist. If an error occurs, recovery might be impossible. Additionally, the only way to move a tablespace to a different database is by dropping the tablespace and redefining it, specifying another database name.

The only valid uses for `PUBLIC` access are for objects and resources that should be available to everyone who has access to the DB2 subsystem or if another security mechanism is in place. An example of the first use is granting the `BINDADD` privilege to `PUBLIC` in a test environment to allow all DB2 programmers to create DB2 application plans and packages. An example of the second use is granting `EXECUTE` authority for CICS transactions to `PUBLIC` and using CICS transaction security to control access. Other exceptions to avoiding `PUBLIC` access follow.

In some installations, the security is thought to be adequately provided by application programs, so PUBLIC access is implemented for objects. Implementing this access is unwise unless ad hoc access to these objects is forbidden. If ad hoc use is allowed, users have access to the data through SPUFI or QMF, and could corrupt the data. In general, you should grant PUBLIC access only as a last resort.

Grant SELECT Authority on SYSIBM.SYSDUMMY1 to PUBLIC

Version 5

Be sure to grant SELECT authority to PUBLIC for the SYSIBM.SYSDUMMY1 table. SYSIBM.SYSDUMMY1 contains a single row. It is designed to be used with SQL statements in which a table reference is needed but the table contents are unimportant.

Grant DISPLAY Authority to PUBLIC

Consider granting DISPLAY authority for each DB2 subsystem to PUBLIC. PUBLIC DISPLAY authority will not pose a security threat, but can improve productivity. Application developers can use DISPLAY to identify active programs and utilities impacting performance without requiring DBA assistance.

Do Not Repeat Security Grants

DB2 allows authorization to be granted multiple times to the same grantee for the same object or resource. As of DB2 V3, duplicate grants from the same grantor are not recorded in the DB2 Catalog. However, if the grants are from different grantors, duplicate authorizations still can occur. You should avoid duplicate authorizations because they cause confusion and clutter the DB2 Catalog with useless entries.

Duplicate authority is recorded in the DB2 Catalog most commonly when SQL GRANT statements have been coded in a common CLIST or a standard job. An example is a CLIST used by application programmers to BIND a plan and then GRANT execute authority to a list of users automatically. You should never provide this authority because it can lead to duplicate authorization entries in the DB2 Catalog.

Consolidate Security Grants

SELECT, INSERT, UPDATE, and DELETE authority should be granted using a single GRANT statement, rather than two to four separate statements. If one statement is used, one catalog row is created, instead of multiple rows (one for each GRANT statement that is issued).

Do Not Grant More Security Than Necessary

Secure your DB2 application environment. Using group-level authority (for example, SYSADM or SYSOPR) is tempting because coding and maintaining it is easier. Group authorities, however, often provide more security than is required. If system-development staff members are allowed to access and modify table data but are not allowed to create indexes and tables, do not grant them DBADM authority. Simply grant them the appropriate authority for the appropriate tables—in this case, SELECT, UPDATE, INSERT, and DELETE.

Plan DCL When Issuing DDL

Remember that when DB2 objects are dropped, the security for the objects is dropped, as well. If you plan to drop and re-create a database, for example, be prepared to re-create the security for the database and all subordinate objects (tablespaces and tables).

Remember also that when plans are freed, all security is removed for the freed plans. Take this fact into account before freeing plans that you might need later.

Use Group-Level Security and Secondary Authids

When possible, use group-level security (for example, DBADM and DBCTRL) and secondary authids to reduce administrative tasks. Do not use group-level security, however, if the group will provide unwanted authority to users.

An alternative authorization ID is provided when you use the secondary authid extension, a useful timesaving feature of DB2 security. Each primary authid can have secondary authids associated with it. You can create these associations by using an external security package such as RACF or a hard-coded table of IDs. You can then grant security to a secondary authid assigned to a functional group of users.

For example, if all users in the finance department have been assigned a secondary authid of FINANCE, you can provide them with blanket query access by granting the SELECT authority to FINANCE for all financial tables. No additional security at the primary authid level is necessary when personnel leave or are hired. This feature eases the administrative burden of security allocation.

Additionally, secondary authids can reduce the workload of the DBA staff by offloading authorization tasks to the corporate security group. Security administration groups typically can support adding and deleting authids from a RACF group, but are not usually capable of issuing appropriate DB2 DCL statements.

Create All DB2 Objects Using Secondary Authid

When objects are created, implicit authority is automatically granted to the object owner. By using secondary authids when creating DB2 objects, administrative burden can be reduced. This is important when DBAs do not have SYSADM authority or when the DBA staff changes. If a secondary authid is not used as the object owner, it may be necessary to drop and recreate entire object structures to revoke implicit authoritization.

Restrict SYSADM Authority

SYSADM is a powerful group authority that you should use sparingly. You should restrict its use to the corporate DBA function and the appropriate system programming support staff. End users, managers, and application development personnel should never need SYSADM authority. In general, no more than a half dozen technical support personnel should have SYSADM authority.

Use SYSCTRL for Additional Control

You can limit SYSADM authority even further by granting SYSCTRL instead of SYSADM to database administration and technical support personnel who play a backup role. SYSCTRL gives the same authority as SYSADM without access to data in application tables that were not created by the SYSCTRL user. End users, managers, and application development personnel should never be granted SYSCTRL authority.

SYSCTRL authority is one of the most misunderstood security features of DB2. It cannot be used to completely ensure that the SYSCTRL user will never have access to end-user data. A primary objective of the SYSCTRL authority is to enable a user—who has no general requirement to manipulate table data—to administer a DB2 environment. In essence, you can think of SYSCTRL as SYSADM without explicit DB2 data authority.

Basically, SYSCTRL authority implies that the user can exercise DBCTRL authority over tables in any database. However, CREATEDBA authority is also implicit under SYSCTRL. Therefore, the SYSCTRL user can create databases and obtain DBADM authority over them, thereby enabling the SYSCTRL user to access and modify the data in any table within that database.

To get around this problem, you should implement procedures or standards to ensure that the SYSCTRL user never creates databases. You must do so manually because there is no systematic way of prohibiting SYSCTRL from creating databases. Assign the database creation function to a SYSADM user. After the database is created by another user, the SYSCTRL user can administer the database without accessing the data. As long as the SYSCTRL user has not created the database in question and has not been granted any other authority (that is, SELECT, DBADM, and so on), he or she cannot access the data in user tables.

Use BINDAGENT for Package and Plan Administration

Use the BINDAGENT authority to permit the binding of plans and packages without the ability to execute them. BINDAGENT authority is sometimes called "assigning" authority. BINDAGENT authority enables one user to assign another user the capability of performing tasks (in this case, plan and package binding) on his or her behalf.

A centralized area in your organization should be responsible for binding production plans and packages. This area can be granted the BINDAGENT authority from all production plan and package owners. This approach is preferable to granting SYSADM or SYSCTRL because only bind operations are enabled when you grant BINDAGENT. BINDAGENT provides all the authority necessary to administer the bind function effectively.

Bind Plans from a Restricted Userid

You can acquire a greater level of control over the bind function by using a restricted userid for all production binding. This userid should have no logon capability so that the only access to the userid is through a batch job rather than online access. You can provide external security with RACF (or any other security tool) to prohibit the unauthorized use of this userid.

Batch jobs that bind the application plans and packages as necessary should be created. The restricted userid should have BINDAGENT authority to allow successful binding with the OWNER parameter. The batch jobs are then submitted with the restricted userid by the group in your organization responsible for binding. This solution permits multiple authorized individuals to submit batch binds from the same userid. This solution also can ease the administrative burden associated with plan and package ownership, the attrition of binding agent personnel, and plan monitoring.

This scenario might not be feasible if your data security standards prohibit restricted userids. Some data security shops think that restricted userids have a propensity to fall into unauthorized hands. If this situation cannot be prevented, restricted userids for binding might not be appropriate for your shop.

Do Not Issue DCL from Application Programs

Avoid issuing GRANT and REVOKE statements from an application program. Security is granted ideally by an agent who understands the authorization needs of the organization.

Although you can set up a parameter-driven program to administer security, you generally cannot automate the task completely. Also, your program must avoid granting duplicate privileges, which is allowed by DB2. Otherwise, many duplicate privileges could be granted for your system, impeding overall system performance.

Additionally, an application program that grants security must be executed by a user who has the appropriate security to issue the grants and the revokes coded in the application program. This could be a loophole in the security structure.

Finally, a program that issues REVOKE and GRANT statements can have a great impact on the overall scheme of your operating environment. Consider the following problems that can be caused by a program issuing DCL:

- The program tries to REVOKE a privilege from a user who is currently executing a transaction that would no longer be valid after the REVOKE.
- The program REVOKEs a privilege, causing numerous cascading REVOKEs that are difficult to trace after invocation. After the program is finished, the potential for many missing authorizations exists. This situation can wreak havoc on a production DB2 subsystem.

- What should the COMMIT and ROLLBACK structure of the program be? If the program abends, should all security be committed or rolled back and reapplied? The answer to these questions may not be immediately obvious in the absence of in-depth system documentation. It is better to avoid these types of questions by mandating that all DCL be issued by skilled technicians that understand the ramifications of each GRANT and REVOKE statement.

Be Careful When Granting Access to a Synonym

Avoid granting others access to a synonym. A synonym, by definition, can be used only by its creator. Granting access to a synonym grants access to the underlying base table for which the synonym was created.

For example, consider a synonym called USER1.DEPARTMENT for the DSN8510.DEPT table. If USER1 wants to grant USER2 the authority to query this synonym, USER1 could code the following:

```
GRANT SELECT
  ON TABLE USER1.DEPARTMENT
  TO USER2;
```

In this case, USER2 now has SELECT authority on the DSN8510.DEPT table, not on the synonym created by USER1. Because this situation can be confusing, you should avoid providing such access.

Be Aware of Automatic Security

When you create a DB2 object, DB2 automatically grants you full security to

- Use the object in any way
- Grant others the use of the object

If users need access to an object they did not create, they must get the creator, a SYSADM, a SYSCTRL, or someone else with the proper authority to grant them access. Additionally, the only way to change implicit authority is to drop the object and re-create it (and all dependent objects).

Be Aware of Package and Plan Security Differences

A user with the BIND privilege on a plan can free that plan, but a user with the BIND privilege on a package cannot free that package. To free a package, the user must meet one of the following conditions:

- Be the owner of the package
- Have SYSADM or SYSCTRL authority
- Have BINDAGENT privilege granted by the package owner

Avoid WITH GRANT OPTION

Be careful with the multilevel security of DB2. When a privilege is granted to a user using WITH GRANT OPTION, the user can also grant that privilege. This capability can create an administrative nightmare for DB2 security agents. Consider the following scenario:

1. SYSADM grants a privilege to USER1 with the grant option.
2. USER1 grants this privilege to USER2 without the grant option.
3. USER1 grants this privilege to USER3 with the grant option.
4. SYSADM grants this privilege to USER5 with the grant option.
5. USER5 grants this privilege to PUBLIC.
6. USER3 grants this privilege to USER9.
7. SYSADM revokes the privilege from USER1.

Who has this privilege now? When SYSADM revokes the privilege from USER1, DB2 cascades the revokes to all the users who were granted this privilege directly or indirectly by USER1. This effectively revokes the privilege from everybody except USER5. However, USER5 granted this privilege to PUBLIC, so everybody—including USER1—still has this privilege. WITH GRANT OPTION is the only privilege removed by the SYSADM revoke.

As a general rule, never allow the WITH GRANT OPTION in a production environment, and control and limit the availability of the WITH GRANT OPTION in a test environment. Consider purchasing an add-on security maintenance tool to monitor and minimize the effects of DB2's cascading revoke. Security tools are described further in Part VII, "The Ideal DB2 Environment."

Revoking a SYSADM

Use caution when revoking a SYSADM from the system. Simply revoking the SYSADM authority from a user can cause cascading revokes. To revoke a SYSADM without causing cascading revokes, follow this procedure:

1. Create a DSNZPARM member specifying the SYSADM userid to be revoked as an Install SYSADM. If both Install SYSADM parameters are currently being used, simply remove one of them and place the SYSADM userid to be revoked in its place. Removing an Install SYSADM does not cause cascading revokes.
2. Revoke the SYSADM authority from the user.
3. Modify the DSNZPARM member to remove the userid as an Install SYSADM. Replace the old Install SYSADM userid (if one was removed).

> **CAUTION**
>
> If, after you revoke SYSADM, the userid is still valid in the system, its associated user can revoke privileges that were previously granted when the user was a SYSADM. This user has this ability because the userid remains as the GRANTOR of the authority in the DB2 Catalog.

Avoid Explicit DELETE, UPDATE, and INSERT Authority

Consider not permitting users to have DELETE, UPDATE, and INSERT authority on production tables. You can enable users to modify data through application programs by granting them execute authority on an application plan that performs the desired type of updates. This way, you can effectively limit data modification to a controlled environment.

You should strictly control data modification because DB2 set-level processing can cause entire tables to be destroyed with a single SQL statement. Consider this example:

```
UPDATE DSN8510.DEPT
  SET DEPT = 'YYY';
```

This statement sets every department in the DEPT table to 'YYY', which is probably not required. If uncontrolled deletion, insertion, and modification are permitted, data almost certainly will be lost because of careless SQL modification statements.

Be Aware of Package and Plan Authorization Differences

Granting BIND PLAN authority to a userid implicitly grants the ability to free that plan. However, the same is not true of BIND PACKAGE authority. Only the package owner can free or drop a package.

Consider DCE Security

Version 5

DB2 V5 can use the Distributed Computing Environment (DCE) security services to authenticate remote users. Users can access any DCE-based server (including DB2 on OS/390) using a single DCE userid and password. DCE and DCE security are complex systems management topics for distributed, interconnected networks, and in-depth coverage is beyond the scope of this book.

Limit Alter Authority with the REFERENCES Privilege

Version 4

The REFERENCES privilege, available as of DB2 V4, grants a user authority to create or drop referential constraints in which the named table is the parent table. Grant the REFERENCES privilege to administrators needing to maintain RI but not needing general ALTER authority.

Consider Dynamic Authority

As of DB2 V4, authorization for dynamic SQL in application programs can be treated the same as static SQL. For more details, see Chapter 6, "Dynamic SQL Programming."

Use Stored Procedures to Implement Security

You can create stored procedures to provide specific, tailored security. You can do so by coding specific SQL statements within a stored procedure and granting specific access to that procedure. The users need not have authorization to the underlying tables accessed by the stored procedure. This approach allows you to hide complex authorization rules in the details of a stored procedure.

View Guidelines

DB2 enables you to create a virtual table known as a *view*. Often the dubious recommendation is made to create one view for each base table in a DB2 application system. The reasoning behind such a suggestion usually involves the desire to insulate application programs from database changes, which is supposedly achieved by writing all programs to access views instead of base tables. Although this idea sounds good, I explain why you should avoid indiscriminate view creation in the following sections.

All operations on a DB2 table result in another table. This is a requirement of the relational model. A view is a representation of data stored in one or more tables. It is defined using the select, project, and join operations.

A view is represented internally to DB2 by SQL statements, not by stored data. You therefore can define views using the same SQL statements that access data in base tables. The SQL comprising the view is executed only when the view is accessed. This allows the creation of logical tables that consist of a subset of columns from a base table or tables. When the data in the underlying base tables changes, the changes are reflected in any view that contains the base table. You also can create views based on multiple tables by using joins.

One of the most fertile grounds for disagreement between DB2 professionals is the appropriate use of views. Some analysts promote the liberal creation and use of views, whereas others preach a more conservative approach. Usually, their recommendations are based on notions of reducing a program's dependency on a DB2 object's data structure.

This section delineates the best philosophy for the creation and use of views based on my experience. By following each of the guidelines in this section, you can establish a sound framework for view creation and use in your organization.

The View Usage Rule

Create a view only when a specific, stated, and rational goal can be achieved by the view.

Each view must have a specific and logical use before it is created. (Do not simply create a view for each base table.) Views excel for the following seven basic uses:

- To provide row and column level security
- To ensure efficient access paths
- To ensure proper data derivation
- To mask complexity from the user
- To provide domain support
- To rename columns
- To provide solutions that cannot be accomplished without views

If you're creating a view that does not apply to one of these seven categories, you should re-examine your view requirements. Chances are, the use is not a good one.

Using Views to Implement Security

Views created to provide security on tables effectively create a logical table that is a subset of rows, columns, or both from the base table. By eliminating restricted columns from the column list and providing the proper predicates in the `WHERE` clause, you can create views to limit a user's access to portions of a table.

Using Views to Ensure Optimal Access

When you create a view for access, you can guarantee efficient access to the underlying base table by specifying indexed columns and proper join criteria. For efficient access, you can code views so that they specify columns indexed in the `WHERE` clause. Coding join logic into a view also increases the efficiency of access because the join is always performed properly. To code a proper join, use the `WHERE` clause to compare the columns from like domains.

Using Views for Data Derivation

Data derivation formulas can be coded into the `SELECT` list of a view, thereby ensuring that everyone is using the same calculation. Creating a view that contains a column named `TOTAL_SALARY` that is defined by selecting `SALARY + COMMISSION` is a good example of derived data in a view.

Using Views to Mask Complexity

Somewhat akin to coding appropriate access into views, coding complex SQL into views can mask the complexity from the user. Coding this way can be extremely useful when your shop employs novice DB2 users (whether they are programmers, analysts, managers, or typical end users).

Consider the following rather complex SQL that implements relational division:

```
SELECT DISTINCT PROJNO
FROM   DSN8510.PROJACT P1
WHERE  NOT EXISTS
       (SELECT  ACTNO
        FROM    DSN8510.ACT A
        WHERE   NOT EXISTS
                (SELECT PROJNO
                 FROM DSN8510.PROJACT P2
                 WHERE P1.PROJNO = P2.PROJNO
                 AND A.ACTNO = P2.ACTNO);
```

This query uses correlated subselects to return a list of all projects in the `PROJACT` table that require every activity listed in the `ACT` table. If you code this SQL into a view called `ALL_ACTIVITY_PROJ`, for example, the end user need only issue the following simple `SELECT` statement instead of the more complicated query:

```
SELECT  PROJNO
FROM    ALL_ACTIVTY_PROJ
```

Using Views to Support Domains

Most relational database management systems do not support *domains*, and DB2 is no exception. Domains are instrumental components of the relational model and, in fact, were in the original relational model published by Ted Codd in 1970—almost three decades ago! A domain basically identifies the valid range of values that a column can contain. Table check constraints can be used to create crude domains.

NOTE

Domains are more complex than this simple definition, of course. For example, the relational model states that only columns pooled from the same domain should be capable to be compared within a predicate (unless explicitly overridden).

You can implement some of the functionality of domains by using views and the `WITH CHECK OPTION` clause. The `WITH CHECK OPTION` clause ensures the update integrity of DB2 views. It guarantees that all data inserted or updated using the view adheres to the view specification. For example, consider the following view:

```
CREATE VIEW EMPLOYEE
  (EMP_NO, EMP_FIRST_NAME, EMP_MID_INIT,
   EMP_LAST_NAME, DEPT, JOB, SEX, SALARY)
AS
   SELECT  EMPNO, FIRSTNME, MIDINIT, LASTNAME,
           WORKDEPT, JOB, SEX, SALARY
   FROM    DSN8510.EMP
   WHERE   SEX IN ('M', 'F')
WITH CHECK OPTION;
```

The WITH CHECK OPTION clause, in this case, ensures that all updates made to this view can specify only the values 'M' or 'F' in the SEX column. Although this example is simplistic, you can easily extrapolate from this example where your organization can create views with predicates that specify code ranges using BETWEEN, patterns using LIKE, or a subselect against another table to identify the domain of a column.

Although you can create similar functionality by using check constraints, views can limit the columns and rows while providing data value checking. Consider the following example:

```
CREATE VIEW HIGH_PAID_EMP
      (EMP_NO, EMP_FIRST_NAME, EMP_MID_INIT,
       EMP_LAST_NAME, DEPT, JOB, SALARY)
    AS
      SELECT  EMPNO, FIRSTNME, MIDINIT, LASTNAME,
              WORKDEPT, JOB, SALARY
      FROM    DSN8510.EMP
      WHERE   SALARY > 75000.00
    WITH CHECK OPTION;
```

This view eliminates several columns (for example, PHONENO, HIREDATE, SEX, and so on) and multiple rows (where salary is less than or equal to $75,000). The view is updateable because all the columns not included in the view are nullable. However, only rows in which the salary conforms to the predicate can be modified. This combined functionality cannot be provided by check constraints alone.

Let me add these words of caution, however: When inserts or updates are performed using these types of views, DB2 evaluates the predicates to ensure that the data modification conforms to the predicates in the view. Be sure to perform adequate testing prior to implementing domains in this manner to safeguard against possible performance degradation.

You can specify the WITH CHECK OPTION clause for updateable views. This way, you can ensure that all data inserted or updated using the view adheres to the view specification. Consider the following view:

```
CREATE VIEW HIGH_PAID_EMP
  (EMPLOYEE_NO, FIRST_NAME, MIDDLE_INITIAL,
   LAST_NAME, DEPARTMENT, JOB, SEX, SALARY)
AS
   SELECT EMPNO, FIRSTNME, MIDINIT, LASTNAME,
   WORKDEPT, JOB, SEX, SALARY
   FROM   DSN8510.EMP
   WHERE  SALARY > 75000.00;
```

Without the WITH CHECK OPTION clause, you can use this view to add data about employees who make less than $75,000. Because this approach is probably not desirable, add WITH CHECK OPTION to the view to ensure that all added data is appropriate given the view definition.

As of DB2 V5, you can use WITH CHECK OPTION in two forms: Version 5

- WITH CASCADED CHECK OPTION specifies that all search conditions are checked for the view in which the clause exists and any views it accesses regardless of the check options specified.

- WITH LOCAL CHECK OPTION specifies that search conditions on underlying views are checked conditionally. If a check option exists in underlying views, it is checked; otherwise, it is not.

Prior to DB2 V5, the CASCADED and LOCAL keywords were not provided. The WITH CHECK OPTION clause provided the equivalent functionality of WITH LOCAL CHECK OPTION. To confuse matters, views created specifying WITH CHECK OPTION for DB2 V5 and higher will provide WITH CASCADED CHECK OPTION functionality. Therefore, the general rule of thumb is never to specify WITH CHECK OPTION as of V5; instead, you should specify either WITH CASCADED CHECK OPTION or WITH LOCAL CHECK OPTION.

Using Views to Rename Columns

You can rename columns in views. This capability is particularly useful if a table contains arcane or complicated column names. Sometimes, particularly for application packages purchased from third-party vendors, renaming columns using a view is useful to make the names more user-friendly. Good examples of such tables are the DB2 Catalog tables.

Consider the following view:

```
CREATE VIEW PLAN_DEPENDENCY
   (OBJECT_NAME, OBJECT_CREATOR, OBJECT_TYPE,
    PLAN_NAME, IBM_REQD)
AS
   SELECT BNAME, BCREATOR, BTYPE,
          DNAME, IBMREQD
   FROM   SYSIBM.SYSPLANDEP
```

Not only does this view rename the entity from SYSPLANDEP to the more easily understood name PLAN_DEPENDENCY, but it also renames each of the columns. Understanding PLAN_NAME as the name of the plan is easier than understanding DNAME. You can create views on each of the DB2 Catalog tables in this manner so that your programmers can better determine which columns contain the information that they require. Additionally, if you have other tables with clumsy table and/or column names, views can provide an elegant solution to renaming without your having to drop and re-create anything.

Version 4

As of DB2 V4, you can rename columns in queries by using the AS clause. However, the AS clause does not provide the same function as column renaming using views because you must still specify the original name of the column in the query.

Using Views When a Single SQL Statement Will Not Suffice

Prior to the introduction of inline views in DB2 V4, views were the only solution in some situations. Inline views have effectively eliminated the case in which you cannot code complex data access requests using SQL alone. Consider a scenario in which you want to report on detail information and summary information from a single table—for example, if you want to report on column length information from the DB2 Catalog. For each table, you want to provide all column details, and on each row, you also want to report the maximum, minimum, and average column lengths for that table. Additionally, you want to report the difference between the average column length and each individual column length.

Views provide one solution to this dilemma. Consider the `COL_LENGTH` view based on `SYSIBM.SYSCOLUMNS` shown here:

```
CREATE VIEW COL_LENGTH
   (TABLE_NAME, MAX_LENGTH, MIN_LENGTH, AVG_LENGTH)
AS
   SELECT    TBNAME, MAX(LENGTH),
             MIN(LENGTH), AVG(LENGTH)
   FROM      SYSIBM.SYSCOLUMNS
   GROUP BY TBNAME
```

After you create the view, you can issue the following `SELECT` statement joining the view to the base table, thereby providing both detail and aggregate information on each report row:

```
SELECT   TBNAME, NAME, COLNO, LENGTH,
         MAX_LENGTH, MIN_LENGTH, AVG_LENGTH,
         LENGTH - AVG_LENGTH
FROM     SYSIBM.SYSCOLUMNS  C,
         authid.COL_LENGTH  V
WHERE    C.TBNAME = V.TABLE_NAME
ORDER BY 1, 3
```

Version 4

However, with inline views, you can code an equivalent solution using one SQL statement, as follows:

```
SELECT   TBNAME, NAME, COLNO, LENGTH,
         MAX_LENGTH, MIN_LENGTH, AVG_LENGTH,
         LENGTH - AVG_LENGTH
FROM     SYSIBM.SYSCOLUMNS INNER JOIN
         (SELECT    TBNAME AS TABLE_NAME,
                    MAX(LENGTH) AS MAX_LENGTH,
                    MIN(LENGTH) AS MIN_LENGTH,
                    AVG(LENGTH) AS AVG_LENGTH
          FROM      SYSIBM.SYSCOLUMNS
          GROUP BY TABLE_NAME)
ON       TBNAME = TABLE_NAME
ORDER BY 1, 3
```

The one SQL statement solution is the preferred method because it is easier to understand, tune, and debug.

Reasons Not to Create One View Per Base Table

Often, the dubious recommendation is made to create one view for each base table in a DB2 application system. The reason behind such a suggestion usually involves the desire to insulate application programs from database changes. This insulation is purported to be achieved by mandating that all programs access views instead of base tables. Although this idea sounds good, you should avoid indiscriminate view creation.

The following is an example of a base table and the view that would be created for it. Here is the base table:

```
CREATE TABLE userid.BASE_TABLE
 (COLUMN1  CHAR(10)    NOT NULL,
  COLUMN2  DATE        NOT NULL WITH DEFAULT,
  COLUMN3  SMALLINT,
  COLUMN4  VARCHAR(50)
) IN DATABASE db_name;
```

And here is the base view:

```
CREATE VIEW userid.BASE_VIEW
 (COL1, COL2, COL3, COL4)
AS
  SELECT COLUMN1, COLUMN2, COLUMN3, COLUMN4
  FROM   userid.BASE_TABLE;
```

Because a base table view does not break any of the rules for view updateability, all SQL statements can be executed against it. The basic reasoning behind creating base table views is the erroneous belief that it provides increased data independence.

For every reason that can be given to create one view per base table, a better reason can be given to avoid doing so. This section details all the arguments for creating one view per base table and explains why the reasoning is not sound.

Adding Columns and the Impact on DB2 Programs

The first argument in favor of base table views is typically, "If I add a column to a table, I will not have to change any programs accessing that table." The reasoning behind this assertion is that you can write programs that are independent of the table columns. If a program retrieves data using `SELECT *` or `INSERT`s rows, no knowledge of new columns would be required if the column is added correctly.

The `SELECT *` statement returns all the columns in the table. If a column is added to a table after the program is coded, the program does not execute because the variable needed to store the newly retrieved column is not coded in the program. If the program uses a view, however, the program executes because the view has only the old columns, not including the new column just added.

If the program is coded to update views instead of base tables, the `INSERT` statement continues to work as well. However, the column added to the base table must allow default values. The default value can be either the null value or the DB2 default when a column is defined as `NOT NULL WITH DEFAULT`. The `INSERT` to the view continues to work even though the view does not contain the new column. The row is inserted, and the new column is assigned the appropriate default value.

It is not a good idea to use base table views to insulate programs from the impact of new columns. If you code your application programs properly, you do not have to make changes when a column is added. Proper program coding refers to coding all SQL statements with column names. If column names can be supplied in an SQL statement, the columns should always be explicitly specified in the SQL statement. This rule applies in particular to the `INSERT` and `SELECT` statement and is true whether you are using views or base tables.

The `SELECT *` statement should never be permitted in an application program. Every DB2 manual and text issues this warning—and with good reason. All DB2 objects can be dropped and re-created and/or altered. If a DB2 object upon which a program relies is modified, a `SELECT *` in that program ceases to function.

This caveat does not change because you're using views. Even views can be dropped and re-created. If the program uses `SELECT *` on a view and the view has changed, the program does not work until it is modified to reflect the changes made to the view.

Do not think that you will never modify a view. Some companies establish a policy of keeping views inline with their base tables. Doing so causes the view to change when the table changes. Others use views for security. As security changes, so do the views.

If you eliminate the `SELECT *` statement, you eliminate this reason for using views. An `INSERT` statement works against a base table the same as a base table view if the column names are provided in the `INSERT` statement. As long as you add the new column allowing a default value, the program continues to work.

Removing Columns and the Impact on DB2 Programs

When you remove a column from a DB2 table, you must drop and re-create the table without the column. You can re-create views that access the table being modified, substituting a constant value in place of the removed column. Application programs that access the views then return the constant rather than the column that was dropped.

It is not a good idea to use base table views to insulate programs from the impact of removing columns from a table. The thinking that if you remove a column from a table, you do not have to change the application program is untrue. If you remove the column from the base table, you must remove it from the view. If you do not remove it from the few and you add a constant to the view, the view can no longer be updated. Also, all queries and reports return a constant instead of the old column value, and the integrity of the system is jeopardized.

Users must be able to rely on the data in the database. If constants are returned on screens and reports, confusion will arise. Also, if the data (that is now a constant) is used in any calculations, these values are also unreliable. These unreliable calculation results could be generated and then inserted into the database, propagating bad data.

The removal of data from a database must be analyzed in the same manner as any change. Simply returning constants is not a solution and will cause more problems than it solves.

Splitting Tables and the Impact on DB2 Programs

Another popular argument in favor of using base table views centers on anticipating the need to split a DB2 table into two tables. The argument is that if you split a table into two tables, you can change the base table view and thereby avoid changing any program accessing the table. Sometimes one DB2 table must be split into two tables. This is usually done based on access requirements to increase the efficiency of retrieval. For example, consider a table with 10 columns. Fifty percent of the queries against the table access the first 6 columns. The remaining fifty percent of the queries access the other 4 columns and the key column. This table could be a candidate for splitting into two tables to improve access: one new table containing the first 6 columns and the second new table containing the remaining 4 columns and the key column.

If the programs use a view, you can recode the view to be a join of the two new tables. You do not have to change the programs to reflect the modification; only the view changes.

It is not a good idea to use base table views to insulate programs from the impact of splitting tables. If you must split a table into two tables, you must have a very good reason for doing so. As I indicated, this action is usually driven by performance considerations. To increase efficiency, you must change the underlying SQL to take advantage of the tables that have been split. Queries accessing columns in only one of the new tables must be modified to access only that table.

Using the logic given by the view supporters, no changes are made to programs. If no changes are made, performance suffers because of the view changes, though. The views are now joins instead of straight SELECTs. No SQL code changes. Every straight SELECT now creates a join, which is less efficient than a straight SELECT.

A change of this magnitude requires a thorough analysis of your application code. When table column definitions change, SQL changes and programs change; these changes cannot be avoided. A trained analyst or DBA must analyze the application's SQL, including SQL in application PLANs, QMF queries, and dynamic SQL. Queries that access columns from both of the new tables must be made into a join. You do not want to create indiscriminate joins, however. Queries that access columns from only one of the two tables must be recoded as a straight SELECT against that table to increase performance. Also, any programs that update the view must be changed. Remember, views that join tables cannot be updated.

If, after investigating, you determine that some queries require joining the two new tables, you can create a view to accommodate these queries. The view can even have the same name as the old table so that you can minimize program changes. The two new tables can be given new names. The view is created only when it is needed—a more reasonable approach to change management.

A change of this magnitude is rarely attempted after an application has been moved to production. This fact is usually not considered when the recommendation is made to use views.

Combining Tables and the Impact on DB2 Programs

Base table view proponents also advocate using views to insulate programs from the effects of combining two tables into a single table. This situation is the inverse of the preceding situation. If two tables are almost always joined, you can increase efficiency by creating a "prejoined" table. The overhead incurred by joining the two tables is avoided. Instead of a join, a straight SELECT can now be issued against the new table.

If the application programs use views in this instance, you can modify the views to subsets of the new combination table. In this way, you can avoid program changes.

Once again, base table views, do not provide the level of insulation desired. The two tables are combined because most queries must access both of the tables. If you simply combine the two tables into one table and change the views to subsets of the new prejoined table without changing the SQL, you degrade performance. The queries that were joins are still joins, but now they join the new views. Remember that the views are just subsets of one table now, so these queries join this one table to itself. This approach is usually less efficient than joining the two tables as they were previously defined.

Again, you must perform a great deal of analysis for a change of this magnitude. You must investigate all application SQL. If you determine that some queries access only one of the two old tables, you can define views with the same name as the old tables. You can give the new prejoined table a new name. This way, you can minimize program modification.

Additional Reasons for Base Table View

I can think of no valid reasoning to support this "feeling." Base table views do not provide a layer of protection between the application and the data. If one view is created for each base table, all types of SQL can be performed on the views. You can perform update and retrieval SQL in the same manner on the views as you can on the base tables.

The advice to create one view per base table is rooted in the fallacious assertion that applications can be ignorant of underlying changes to the database. Change impact analysis must be performed when tables are modified. Failure to do so results in a poorly performing application.

Miscellaneous View Guidelines

To ensure appropriate view usage, implement the following tips, techniques, and guidelines.

Follow the Synchronization Rule

Keep all views logically pure by synchronizing them with their underlying base tables.

When you make a change to a base table, you should analyze all views dependent on the base table to determine whether the change affects them. The view was created for a reason (see "The View Usage Rule" section earlier in this chapter) and should remain useful for that reason. You can accomplish this goal only by ensuring that subsequent changes pertinent to a specified use are made to all views that satisfy that use.

Consider a view that is based on the sample tables DSN8510.EMP and DSN8510.DEPT. The view is created to satisfy an access use; it provides information about departments, including the name of the department's manager. If you add a column specifying the employee's middle initial to the EMP table, you should add the column also to the EMP_DEPT view because it is pertinent to that view's use: to provide information about each department and each department's manager. You must drop and re-create the view.

The synchronization rule requires you to have strict procedures for change impact analysis. Every change to a base table should trigger the use of these procedures. You can create simple SQL queries to assist in the change impact analysis. These queries should pinpoint QMF queries, application plans, and dynamic SQL users that could be affected by specific changes. The following queries should assist your change impact analysis process.

To find all views dependent on the table to be changed, use the following:

```
SELECT   DCREATOR, DNAME
FROM     SYSIBM.SYSVIEWDEP
WHERE    BCREATOR = 'Table Creator'
AND      BNAME = 'Table Name';
```

To find all QMF queries that access the view, use the following:

```
SELECT   DISTINCT OWNER, NAME, TYPE
FROM     Q.OBJECT_DATA
WHERE    APPLDATA LIKE '%View Name%';
```

To find all plans dependent on the view, use the following:

```
SELECT   DNAME
FROM     SYSIBM.SYSPLANDEP
WHERE    BCREATOR = 'View Creator'
AND      BNAME = 'View Name';
```

To find all potential dynamic SQL users, use the following:

```
SELECT   GRANTEE
FROM     SYSIBM.SYSTABAUTH
WHERE    TCREATOR = 'View Creator'
AND      TTNAME = 'View Name';
```

Always execute these queries to determine what views might be affected by changes to base tables.

Be Aware of Non-Updateable Views

If you adhere to the preceding guidelines, most of your views will not be updateable. Views that join tables, use functions, use DISTINCT, or use GROUP BY and HAVING cannot be updated, deleted from, or inserted to. Views that contain derived data using arithmetic expressions, contain constants, or eliminate columns without default values cannot be inserted to. Keep this information in mind when you're creating and using views.

Specify Column Names

When you're creating views, DB2 provides the option of specifying new column names for the view or defaulting to the same column names as the underlying base table or tables. Explicitly specify view column names rather than allow them to default, even when you plan to use the same names as the underlying base tables. This approach provides more accurate documentation.

Be Aware of View Restrictions

Almost any SQL that can be issued natively can be coded into a view, except SQL that contains the `FOR UPDATE OF` clause, an `ORDER BY` specification, or the `UNION` operation.

Views can be accessed by SQL in the same way that tables are accessed by SQL. However, you must consider the rules about the types of views that can be updated. Table 4.1 lists the restrictions on view updating.

Table 4.1. Non-updateable view types.

View Type	*Restriction*
Views that join tables	Cannot delete, update, or insert
Views that use functions	Cannot delete, update, or insert
Views that use `DISTINCT`	Cannot delete, update, or insert
Views that use `GROUP BY` and `HAVING`	Cannot delete, update, or insert
Views that contain derived data using arithmetic expression	Cannot insert
Views that contain constants	Cannot insert
Views that eliminate columns without a default value	Cannot insert

Other SQL Guidelines

This final section on SQL guidelines contains advice for creating understandable and easily maintained SQL. When developing an application, you might be tempted to "let it be if it works." This advice is not good. You should strive for well-documented, structured code. The following miscellaneous guidelines will help you achieve that goal with your SQL statements.

Code SQL Statements in Block Style

You should code all SQL in block style. This standard should apply to all SQL code, whether embedded in a COBOL program, coded as a QMF query, or implemented using another tool. Use the following examples as standard templates for the SELECT, INSERT, UPDATE, and DELETE statements:

The following is the SELECT statement:

```
EXEC SQL
    SELECT    EMPNO, FIRSTNME, MIDINIT, LASTNAME
              WORKDEPT, PHONENO, EDLEVEL
    FROM      EMP
    WHERE     BONUS = 0
    OR        SALARY < 10000
    OR        (BONUS < 500
    AND       SALARY > 20000)
    OR        EMPNO IN ('000340', '000300', '000010')
    ORDER BY EMPNO, LASTNAME
END-EXEC.
```

The following is the INSERT statement:

```
EXEC SQL
    INSERT
    INTO DEPT
        (DEPTNO,
         DEPTNAME,
         MGRNO,
         ADMRDEPT
        )
    VALUES
        (:HOSTVAR-DEPTNO,
         :HOSTVAR-DEPTNAME,
         :HOSTVAR-MGRNO:NULLVAR-MGRNO,
         :HOSTVAR-ADMRDEPT
        )
END-EXEC.
```

The following is the DELETE statement:

```
EXEC SQL
    DELETE
    FROM     DEPT
    WHERE    DEPTNO = 'E21'
END-EXEC.
```

The following is the UPDATE statement:

```
EXEC SQL
    UPDATE EMP
    SET     JOB = 'MANAGER',
            EDLEVEL = :HOSTVAR-EDLEVEL,
            COMM = NULL,
            SALARY = :HOSTVAR-SALARY:NULLVAR-SALARY,
            BONUS = 1000
    WHERE   EMPNO = '000220'
END-EXEC.
```

These examples demonstrate the following rules:

- Code keywords such as SELECT, WHERE, FROM, and ORDER BY so that they are easily recognizable and begin at the far left of a new line.
- For SQL embedded in a host program, code the EXEC SQL and END-EXEC clauses on separate lines.
- Use parentheses where appropriate to clarify the intent of the SQL statement.
- Use indentation to show the levels in the WHERE clause.

Note that these examples are embedded SQL syntax because this shows more detail for coding in the block style. You can easily convert these examples to interactive SQL by removing the EXEC SQL, END_EXEC, and host variable references.

Comment All SQL Liberally

Comment ad hoc SQL statements using SQL comment syntax. Comment all embedded SQL statements using the syntax of the host language. Code all comments above the SQL statement. Specify the reason for the SQL and the predicted results.

Maintain Standard Libraries

Create standard libraries for BIND parameters, utility JCL, utility parameters, VSAM IDCAMS delete and define parameters for user-defined VSAM tablespaces, GRANT and REVOKE DCL, and DDL for all DB2 objects.

To maintain these libraries, ensure that all subsequent alterations to DDL are reflected in the DDL stored in the standard library. For example, if a table is altered to add a new column, be sure that the CREATE DDL table in the standard library is modified to also contain the new column. Because this task is time-consuming and error-prone, your shop should have an add-on utility from a secondary vendor that queries the DB2 Catalog and automatically creates DDL. Having this utility negates the need to store and maintain DDL in a standard library. For information on these (and other) types of add-on tools for DB2, consult Part VII.

Follow the Proliferation Avoidance Rule

Do not needlessly proliferate DB2 objects and security. Every DB2 object creation and authorization grant requires additional entries in the DB2 Catalog. Granting unneeded authority and creating needless tables, views, and synonyms causes catalog clutter—extraneous entries strewn about the DB2 Catalog tables. The larger the DB2 Catalog tables become, the less efficient your entire DB2 system will be.

The proliferation avoidance rule is based on common sense. Why create something that is not needed? It just takes up space that could be used for something that you do need.

Summary

SQL, although logically simple, is practically complex. The SQL tools, tips, and tricks presented in Part I can help you navigate the SQL seas. But what is that on the horizon? SQL alone often is insufficient for accessing your important production data. Application programs are required. Wonder how you can write them? You can find out in Part II, "DB2 Application Development."

II

DB2 Application Development

Part I, "SQL Tools, Tips, and Tricks," described the nature and features of SQL and introduced guidelines for its efficient and effective use. Part II provides information on the development of DB2 applications.

Chapter 5, "Using DB2 in an Application Program," the first chapter in this section, discusses the components of embedded static SQL programming and provides guidelines for the proper implementation of DB2 programs. Dynamic SQL is covered in-depth in Chapter 6, "Dynamic SQL Programming," complete with examples and coding guidelines.

Chapter 7, "Program Preparation," discusses the steps to take to prepare DB2 programs for execution. Chapter 8, "Alternative DB2 Application Development Methods," discusses guidelines for programming methods other than embedding SQL in a third-generation language.

Chapter 9, "Using DB2 Stored Procedures," presents how to implement efficient stored procedures. Finally, Chapter 10, "DB2 and the Internet," discusses how to connect DB2 databases to the Internet.

5

Using DB2 in an Application Program

DB2 application development consists of the construction of DB2 application programs. This statement begs the question: What is a DB2 application program? Let me begin to answer this question by reviewing standard application program development.

The development of an application system usually requires the use of a high-level language to encode the processing requirements of the application. A high-level language is any language that you can use to operate on data. You can break down high-level languages into the following categories:

- Database sublanguages, such as SQL
- 3GLs (third-generation languages), such as COBOL and FORTRAN, which are procedural
- 4GLs (fourth-generation languages), such as RAMIS and FOCUS, which are procedural but raise the level of abstraction a notch, often enabling non-MIS personnel to develop applications
- GUI-based programming languages, such as Visual Basic and PowerBuilder, which are used to build distributed, client/server applications.
- CASE (computer-aided software engineering) tools, which enable analysts to analyze and specify application models and parameters (upper CASE) and automatically generate application programs (lower CASE)
- Productivity tools, such as report writers and QMF, which are wonderful for developing portions of an application but usually not robust enough to be used for the development of a complete application

Sometimes you can develop a complete application system entirely with SQL, 4GLs, code generators, or productivity tools. However, these systems are rare (although code generation is gaining approval and support in many DP shops). Even though an application system can be coded without the use of a true programming language (3GL or GUI programming language), often a 3GL is still used because it generally outperforms the other application development tools just mentioned. This case is particularly true with code generators because the SQL that is generated is basic and not optimized for performance.

Back to the initial question: What is a DB2 application program? I consider a DB2 application program to be any program—developed using any of the preceding methods—that accesses data stored in DB2.

Most of the information in Part II of this book covers developing DB2 programs using third-generation languages, which constitute the bulk of DB2 applications. This is true for many reasons. Third-generation languages have been around longer than other application development tools and therefore have a larger installed base and a wider selection of professional programmers who understand them. Batch interfaces abound, but few online interfaces (CICS and IMS/DC) exist for most 4GLs and report writer tools.

Of course, GUI-based programming is on the rise, and many client/server applications are being developed to access DB2 data using these tools. The issues surrounding GUI-based DB2 programming are covered in Chapter 8, "Alternative DB2 Application Development Methods."

3GLs have proliferated for several other reasons. Their procedural nature eases the coding of complex logic structures (for example, IF-THEN-ELSE logic and looping). Other methods cannot usually meet complex reporting needs, such as the explosion of a hierarchy or side-by-side reporting of multiple, joined repeating groups. In addition, the performance of applications developed using alternative methods usually does not compare to the superb performance that you can achieve using 3GLs.

Embedded SQL Basics

To develop application programs that access DB2 tables, you must embed SQL statements in the program statements of the high-level language being used. Embedded DB2 SQL statements are supported in the following high-level languages:

ADA/370 V1.3
ADA Runtime Library 370 V1.3 with SQL MP for DB2
APL2 V2.2
APL2 Application Environment V2.2
Assembler H
IBM BASIC/MVS V1.2
IBM AD/Cycle C/370 V1.2
IBM C/370 Library V2.2
C/C++ for MVS/ESA V1.2
IBM COBOL for MVS V1.2
VS COBOL II and Library V1.4
VS FORTRAN V2.6
IBM Language Environment for MVS V1.5 (LE/370)
IBM PL/I for MVS V1.1.1
OS PL/I V2.3
IBM SAA AD/Cycle PROLOG/MVS V1

NOTE

IBM provides direct support for embedded SQL in the languages listed. Additionally, third party vendors offer support for a variety of other languages. For example, there are several suppliers of solutions enabling programs to issue SQL from a REXX EXEC.

These statements can be run in the following execution environments:

MVS batch using CAF

TSO batch

DL/I batch

CICS

IMS/DC (also known as IMS/TM)

IMS BMP

TSO (interactive)

RRSAF (Recovery Resource Manager Services Attachment Facility)

In this chapter, I focus on the rules for embedding SQL in COBOL application programs because COBOL is the most widely used language in the business data processing community. Much of the information is similar for the other languages. For language-specific information and syntax, consult the appropriate IBM manuals.

To embed SQL statements in an application program, you must follow strict rules. These rules have been established for a few reasons. One, they enable parsing programs (a DB2 precompiler) to identify embedded SQL statements easily in application code. Two, they ensure that the impedance mismatch between the non-procedural, set-level processing of SQL and the procedural, record-level processing of the high-level language has been taken into account. Three, these rules provide programs with the capability to change variables in the predicates of the embedded SQL at processing time. And four, they enable communication between the DB2 DBMS and the application program (for example, the reception of error and warning messages).

The capability to embed SQL statements in an application program allows high-level programming languages to access DB2 data. This capability provides the mechanism for the development of just about any type of DB2 application system.

All DB2 statements can be embedded in an application program. The list of SQL statements supported for embedding in an application program is presented in Table 5.1.

Table 5.1. Types of embedded SQL statements.

SQL Type	*SQL Statements*
DCL	GRANT and REVOKE
DDL	ALTER, CREATE, DROP, COMMENT ON, and LABEL ON
DML	DELETE, INSERT, SELECT, and UPDATE
Dynamic SQL	DESCRIBE, EXECUTE, EXECUTE IMMEDIATE, and PREPARE
Stored Procedures	CALL, ALLOCATE CURSOR, and ASSOCIATE LOCATORS

SQL Type	*SQL Statements*
Embedding control	CLOSE, DECLARE, FETCH, and OPEN
Transaction control	COMMIT and ROLLBACK
Package control	SET CURRENT PACKAGESET
General	EXPLAIN*, LOCK TABLE, and SET
Error handling	WHENEVER

* You can embed EXPLAIN only in TSO programs.

A DB2 program with embedded SQL statements is somewhat similar to an application program issuing reads and writes against a flat file or VSAM data set. The SQL statements are similar in function to file I/O. With a little basic understanding of embedded SQL rules and constructs, you, as an application programmer, can learn the methods necessary to embed SQL in a third-generation language, such as COBOL.

In the following sections, I discuss the techniques used to embed SQL statements in DB2 application programs.

Embedded SQL Guidelines

Table 5.2 outlines the differences between a DB2 program with embedded SQL statements and an application program accessing flat files. Flat files and DB2 tables, however, are not synonymous. The functionality of the two types of data storage objects are quite dissimilar.

Table 5.2. DB2 programming versus flat file programming.

DB2 Programming Considerations	*Flat File Programming Considerations*
No FD required for DB2 tables; DB2 tables must be declared	FD is required for each flat file to be processed by the program
No DD card needed in execution JCL for programs accessing DB2 tables	DD card required (unless the flat file is allocated dynamically)
DB2 tables need not be opened; instead, cursors are opened for each SQL statement*	Flat files must be opened before being processed
DB2 tables need not be closed; instead, cursors are closed for each SQL statement*	Flat files must be closed (if opened)

continues

Table 5.2. continued

DB2 Programming Considerations	*Flat File Programming Considerations*
Set-level processing	Record-level processing
Access to tables can be specified at the column (field element) level	Access to files based on reading a full record; all fields are always read or written
Success or failure of data is indicated by SQL return code	VSAM return code indicates success or failure
No more data indicated by +100 SQL return code	End of file is reported to the program
Cursors used to mimic record-level processing (see the section on cursors)	READ and WRITE statements are used to implement record-level processing

* DB2 opens and closes the VSAM data sets that house DB2 tablespaces "behind the scenes."

Delimit All SQL Statements

You must enclose all embedded SQL statements in an EXEC SQL block. This way, you can delimit the SQL statements so that the DB2 precompiler can efficiently parse the embedded SQL. The format of this block is

```
EXEC SQL
   put text of SQL statement here
END-EXEC.
```

For COBOL programs, you must code the EXEC SQL and END-EXEC delimiter clauses in your application program starting in column 12.

Explicitly Declare All DB2 Tables

Although you are not required to declare DB2 tables in your application program, doing so is good programming practice. Therefore, explicitly DECLARE all tables to be used by your application program. You should place the DECLARE TABLE statements in the WORKING-STORAGE section of your program, and they should be the first DB2-related variables defined in WORKING-STORAGE. This way, you can reduce the precompiler's work and make the table definitions easier to find in the program source code.

Additionally, standard DECLARE TABLE statements should be generated for every DB2 table. Create them with the DCLGEN command (covered in Chapter 7, "Program Preparation"), and then include them in your application program.

Comment Each SQL Statement

Make liberal use of comments to document the nature and purpose of each SQL statement embedded in your program. You should code all comments pertaining to embedded SQL in the comment syntax of the program's host language. Code COBOL comments as shown in the following example:

```
Column Numbers
        111
123456789012
      **
      ** Retrieve department name and manager from the
      ** DEPT table for a particular department number.
      **
          EXEC SQL
              SELECT    DEPTNAME, MGRNO
              INTO      :HOSTVAR-DEPTNAME,
                        :HOSTVAR-MGRNO
              FROM      DEPT
              WHERE     DEPTNO = :HOSTVAR-DEPTNO
          END-EXEC.
```

Include the SQLCA

You must include a structure called the SQLCA (SQL Communication Area) in each DB2 application program. You do so by coding the following statement in your WORKING-STORAGE section:

```
EXEC SQL
    INCLUDE SQLCA
END-EXEC.
```

The COBOL layout of the expanded SQLCA follows:

```
01  SQLCA.
    05  SQLCAID                 PIC X(8).
    05  SQLCABC                 PIC S9(9) COMPUTATIONAL.
    05  SQLCODE                 PIC S9(9) COMPUTATIONAL.
    05  SQLERRM.
        49  SQLERRML            PIC S9(4) COMPUTATIONAL.
        49  SQLERRMC            PIC X(70).
    05  SQLERRP                 PIC X(8).
     5  SQLERRD                 OCCURS 6 TIMES
                                PIC S9(9) COMPUTATIONAL.
    05  SQLWARN.
        10  SQLWARN0            PIC X(1).
        10  SQLWARN1            PIC X(1).
        10  SQLWARN2            PIC X(1).
        10  SQLWARN3            PIC X(1).
        10  SQLWARN4            PIC X(1).
        10  SQLWARN5            PIC X(1).
        10  SQLWARN6            PIC X(1).
        10  SQLWARN7            PIC X(1).
    05  SQLEXT.
        10  SQLWARN8            PIC X(1).
        10  SQLWARN9            PIC X(1).
        10  SQLWARNA            PIC X(1).
        10  SQLSTATE            PIC X(5).
```

The SQLCA is used to communicate information describing the success or failure of the execution of an embedded SQL statement. The following list defines each SQLCA field:

SQLCAID — Set to the constant value SQLCA to enable easy location of the SQLCA in a dump.

SQLCABC — Contains the value 136, the length of the SQLCA.

SQLCODE — Contains the return code passed by DB2 to the application program. The return code provides information about the execution of the last SQL statement. A value of zero indicates successful execution, a positive value indicates successful execution but with an exception, and a negative value indicates that the statement failed.

SQLERRM — This group-level field consists of a length and a message. SQLERRML contains the length of the message in SQLERRMC. The message contains additional information about any encountered error condition. Usually, only technical support personnel use this field for complex debugging situations, when the value of SQLCODE is not sufficient.

SQLERRP — Contains the name of the CSECT that detected the error reported by the SQLCODE. This information is not typically required by application programmers.

SQLERRD — This array contains six values used to diagnose error conditions. Only SQLERRD(3) and SQLERRD(5) are of use to most application programmers:

- SQLERRD(1) is the relational data system error code.
- SQLERRD(2) is the Data Manager error code.
- SQLERRD(3) is the number of rows inserted, deleted, or updated by the SQL statement.
- SQLERRD(4) is the estimate of resources required for the SQL statement (timerons).
- SQLERRD(5) is the column (position) of the syntax error for a dynamic SQL statement.
- SQLERRD(6) is the Buffer Manager error code.

SQLWARN0 — Contains W if any other SQLWARN field is set to W.

SQLWARN1 — Contains W if a character column is truncated when it is assigned to a host variable by the SQL statement.

SQLWARN2 — Contains W when a null-valued column is eliminated by built-in function processing.

SQLWARN3	Contains W when the number of columns retrieved does not match the number of fields in the host variable structure into which they are being selected.
SQLWARN4	Contains W when the SQL statement is an UPDATE or DELETE without a WHERE clause.
SQLWARN5	Contains W when an SQL statement that applies only to SQL/DS is issued.
SQLWARN6	Contains W when a DATE or TIMESTAMP conversion is performed during date arithmetic. For example, if 4 months are added to 1997-01-31, the result is 1997-04-31. Because April does not have 31 days, the results are converted to 1997-04-30.
SQLWARN7	Contains W when non-zero digits are dropped from the fractional part of a number used as the operand of a divide or multiply operation.
SQLWARN8	Contains W if a substitute character is used when a conversion routine cannot convert the character.
SQLWARN9	Contains W when COUNT DISTINCT processing ignores an arithmetic exception.
SQLWARNA	Contains W when any form of character conversion error is encountered.
SQLSTATE	Contains a return code indicating the status of the most recent SQL statement.

Check SQLCODE or SQLSTATE

SQLCODE contains the SQL return code, which indicates the success or failure of the last SQL statement executed. SQLSTATE is similar to SQLCODE but is consistent across DB2 (and ANSI-compliant SQL) platforms.

Code a COBOL IF statement immediately after every SQL statement to check the value of the SQLCODE. In general, gearing your application programs to check for SQLCODEs is easier because a simple condition can be employed to check for negative values.

If the SQLCODE returned by the SQLCA is less than zero, an SQL "error" was encountered. The term *error*, in this context, is confusing. A value less than zero could indicate a condition that is an error using SQL's terminology but is fine given the nature of your application. Thus, certain negative SQL codes are acceptable depending on their context.

For example, suppose that you try to insert a row into a table and receive an SQL code of -803, indicating a duplicate key value. (The row cannot be inserted because it violates the constraints of a unique index.) In this case, you might want to report the fact (and some details) and continue processing.

Check the SQLSTATE value, however, when you must check for a group of SQLCODEs associated with a single SQLSTATE or when your program runs on multiple platforms. SQLSTATE values consist of five characters: a two-character class code and a three-character subclass code. The class code indicates the type of error, and the subclass code details the explicit error within that error type. You can find a complete listing of SQLSTATEs, SQLSTATE class codes, and SQLCODEs in Appendix A, "DB2 SQLCODE and SQLSTATE Values."

Standardize Your Shop's Error Routine

Consider using a standardized error handling paragraph, one that can be used by all DB2 programs in your shop. The programs should load values to an error record that can be interpreted by the error handling paragraph. When a severe error is encountered, the programs invoke the error handling paragraph.

The error handling paragraph should do the following:

1. Call the DSNTIAR module, a program provided with DB2 that returns standard, textual error messages for SQLCODEs.
2. Display, print, or record the following information: the error record identifying the involved table, the paragraph, and pertinent host variables; the error text returned by DSNTIAR; and the current values in the SQLCA.
3. Issue a ROLLBACK. (This action is not absolutely required because an implicit rollback occurs if one is not requested.)
4. Call an ABEND module to generate a dump.

Your error handling paragraph can be as complex and precise as you want. Depending on the SQL code, different processing can occur; for example, you might not want to abend the program for every SQLCODE.

Listing 5.1 shows sample COBOL code with an error handling paragraph as just described. You can tailor this code to meet your needs.

Listing 5.1. COBOL error handling paragraph.

```
         .
         .
         .
WORKING-STORAGE SECTION.
         .
         .
         .
77  ERROR-TEXT-LENGTH            PIC S9(9)   COMP VALUE +960.
01  ERROR-RECORD.
    05  FILLER                   PIC X(11)   VALUE 'SQLCODE IS '.
    05  SQLCODE-DISP             PIC -999.
    05  FILLER                   PIC X(05)   VALUE SPACES.
    05  ERROR-TABLE              PIC X(18).
    05  ERROR-PARA               PIC X(30).
    05  ERROR-INFO               PIC X(40).
```

```
01  ERROR-MESSAGE.
    05  ERROR-MSG-LENGTH            PIC S9(9)   COMP VALUE +960.
    05  ERROR-MSG-TEXT              PIC X(120)  OCCURS 8 TIMES
                                                INDEXED BY ERROR-INDEX.
01  ERROR-ROLLBACK.
    05  FILLER              PIC X(20)   VALUE 'ROLLBACK SQLCODE IS '.
    05  SQLCODE-ROLLBACK            PIC -999.
        .
        .
PROCEDURE DIVISION.
        .
        .
1000-SAMPLE-PARAGRAPH.
    EXEC SQL
       SQL statement here
    END-EXEC.
    IF SQLCODE IS LESS THAN ZERO
       MOVE SQLCODE                     TO SQLCODE-DISP
       MOVE 'Table_Name'                TO ERR-TABLE
       MOVE '1000-SAMPLE-PARAGRAPH'     TO ERR-PARA
       MOVE 'Misc info, host variables, etc.'    TO ERR-INFO
       PERFORM 9999-SQL-ERROR
    ELSE
       Resume normal processing.
        .
        .
9990-SQL-ERROR.
    DISPLAY ERR-RECORD.
    CALL 'DSNTIAR' USING SQLCA,
                         ERROR-MESSAGE,
                         ERROR-TEXT-LENGTH.
    IF RETURN-CODE IS EQUAL TO ZERO
       PERFORM 9999-DISP-DSNTIAR-MSG
          VARYING ERROR-INDEX FROM 1 BY 1
          UNTIL ERROR-INDEX > 8
    ELSE
       DISPLAY 'DSNTIAR ERROR'
       CALL 'abend module'.
    DISPLAY 'SQLERRMC   ', SQLERRMC.
    DISPLAY 'SQLERRD1   ', SQLERRD(1).
    DISPLAY 'SQLERRD2   ', SQLERRD(2).
    DISPLAY 'SQLERRD3   ', SQLERRD(3)
    DISPLAY 'SQLERRD4   ', SQLERRD(4).
    DISPLAY 'SQLERRD5   ', SQLERRD(5).
    DISPLAY 'SQLERRD6   ', SQLERRD(6).
    DISPLAY 'SQLWARN0   ', SQLWARN0.
    DISPLAY 'SQLWARN1   ', SQLWARN1.
    DISPLAY 'SQLWARN2   ', SQLWARN2.
    DISPLAY 'SQLWARN3   ', SQLWARN3.
    DISPLAY 'SQLWARN4   ', SQLWARN4.
    DISPLAY 'SQLWARN5   ', SQLWARN5.
    DISPLAY 'SQLWARN6   ', SQLWARN6.
    DISPLAY 'SQLWARN7   ', SQLWARN7.
    DISPLAY 'SQLWARN8   ', SQLWARN8.
    DISPLAY 'SQLWARN9   ', SQLWARN9.
    DISPLAY 'SQLWARNA   ', SQLWARNA.
    EXEC SQL
       ROLLBACK
```

continues

Listing 5.1. continued

```
     END-EXEC.
     IF SQLCODE IS NOT EQUAL TO ZERO
          DISPLAY 'INVALID ROLLBACK'
          MOVE SQLCODE     TO SQLCODE-ROLLBACK
          DISPLAY ERROR-ROLLBACK.
     CALL 'abend module'.

9990-EXIT.
     EXIT.
9999-DISP-DSNTIAR-MSG.
     DISPLAY ERROR-MSG-TEXT(ERROR-INDEX).
9999-EXIT.
     EXIT.
```

When an error is encountered—in paragraph 1000, for example—an error message is formatted and an error paragraph is performed. The error paragraph displays the error message returned by DSNTIAR, dumps the contents of the SQLCA, and rolls back all updates, deletes, and inserts since the last COMMIT point.

NOTE

Use a formatted WORKING-STORAGE field to display the SQLCODE; otherwise, the value will be unreadable.

You can code the error handling paragraph in Listing 5.1 in a copy book that can then be included in each DB2 program. This way, you can standardize your shop's error processing and reduce the amount of code that each DB2 programmer must write.

Avoid Using WHENEVER

SQL has an error trapping statement called WHENEVER that you can embed in an application program. When the WHENEVER statement is processed, it applies to all subsequent SQL statements issued by the application program in which it is embedded. WHENEVER directs processing to continue or to branch to an error handling routine based on the SQLCODE returned for the statement. Several examples follow.

The following example indicates that processing will continue when an SQLCODE of +100 is encountered:

```
EXEC SQL
     WHENEVER NOT FOUND
          CONTINUE
END-EXEC.
```

When a warning is encountered, the second example of the WHENEVER statement causes the program to branch to a paragraph (in this case, ERROR-PARAGRAPH) to handle the warning:

```
EXEC SQL
    WHENEVER SQLWARNING
        GO TO ERROR-PARAGRAPH
END-EXEC.
```

When any negative SQLCODE is encountered, the next WHENEVER statement branches to a paragraph (once again, ERROR-PARAGRAPH) to handle errors:

```
EXEC SQL
    WHENEVER SQLERROR
        GO TO ERROR-PARAGRAPH
END-EXEC.
```

Each of the three types of the WHENEVER statement can use the GO TO or CONTINUE option, at the discretion of the programmer. These types of the WHENEVER statements trap three error conditions:

NOT FOUNDSQLCODE = +100

SQLWARNINGSQLCODE is positive but not +100 or SQLWARN0 = W

SQLERRORSQLCODE is negative

Avoid using the WHENEVER statement. It is almost always safer to code specific SQLCODE checks after each SQL statement and process accordingly. Additionally, you should avoid coding the GO TO verb as used by the WHENEVER statement.

Name DB2 Programs, Plans, Packages, and Variables Cautiously

Use caution when naming DB2 programs, plans, packages, and variables used in SQL statements. Do not use the following:

- The characters *DB2, SQL, DSN,* and *DSQ*
- SQL reserved words

You should avoid the listed character combinations for the following reasons. *DB2* is too generic and could be confused with a DB2 system component. Because SQLCA fields are prefixed with *SQL,* using these letters with another variable name can cause confusion with SQLCA fields. IBM uses the three-character prefix *DSN* to name DB2 system programs and *DSQ* to name QMF system programs.

If SQL reserved words are used for host variables (covered in the next section) and are not preceded by a colon, an error is returned. However, you should not use these words even if all host variables are preceded by a colon. Avoiding these words in your program, plan, and variable names reduces confusion and ambiguity. Table 5.3 lists all SQL reserved words.

Table 5.3. SQL reserved words.

ADD	ALL	ALTER
AND	ANY	AS
AUDIT	BETWEEN	BUFFERPOOL
BY	CALL	CAPTURE
CHAR	CHARACTER	CHECK
CLUSTER	COLLECTION	COLUMN
CONCAT	CONSTRAINT	COUNT
CURRENT	CURRENT_DATE	CURRENT_TIME
CURRENT_TIMESTAMP	CURSOR	DATABASE
DAY	DAYS	DEFAULT
DELETE	DESCRIPTOR	DISTINCT
DOUBLE	DROP	EDITPROC
END-EXEC	ERASE	ESCAPE
EXCEPT	EXECUTE	EXISTS
FIELDPROC	FOR	FROM
FULL	GO	GOTO
GRANT	GROUP	HAVING
HOUR	HOURS	IMMEDIATE
IN	INDEX	INNER
INOUT	INSERT	INTO
IS	JOIN	KEY
LEFT	LIKE	LOCKMAX
LOCKSIZE	MICROSECOND	MICROSECONDS
MINUTE	MINUTES	MONTH
MONTHS	NOT	NULL
NUMPARTS	OBID	OF
ON	OPTIMIZE	OR
ORDER	OUT	OUTER
PACKAGE	PART	PLAN
PRECISION	PRIQTY	PRIVILEGES
PROGRAM	REFERENCES	RIGHT
SECOND	SECONDS	SECQTY
SELECT	SET	SOME

STOGROUP	SUBPAGES	SYNONYM
TABLE	TABLESPACE	TO
UNION	UNIQUE	UPDATE
USER	USING	VALIDPROC
VALUES	VCAT	VIEW
VOLUMES	WHERE	WITH
YEAR	YEARS	

Additionally, IBM SQL reserves additional words. Using these words will not result in an error, but you should avoid their use to eliminate confusion. Additionally, these words are good candidates for future status as SQL reserved words when functionality is added to DB2. Table 5.4 lists all IBM SQL reserved words that are not also SQL reserved words. (Tables 5.3 and 5.4 collectively list all the IBM SQL database reserved words.)

Table 5.4. IBM SQL Reserved Words.

ACQUIRE	ALLOCATE	ASC
AUTHORIZATION	AVG	BIND
BINDADD	BIT	CASCADE
CCSID	COMMENT	COMMIT
CONNECT	CONTROL	CREATE
CREATETAB	DATA	DATE
DBA	DBADM	DBSPACE
DEC	DECIMAL	DESC
EXCLUSIVE	EXPLAIN	FETCH
FLOAT	FOREIGN	GRAPHIC
IDENTIFIED	INDICATOR	INT
INTEGER	INTERSECT	LABEL
LOCK	LONG	MAX
MIN	MIXED	MODE
NAMED	NHEADER	NUMERIC
ONLY	OPTION	ORDER
PAGE	PAGES	PCTFREE
PCTINDEX	PRIMARY	PRIVATE
PUBLIC	REAL	RELEASE

continues

Table 5.4. continued

RESET	RESOURCE	RESTRICT
REVOKE	ROLLBACK	ROW
ROWS	RUN	SBCS
SCHEDULE	SCHEMA	SHARE
SMALLINT	STATISTICS	STORPOOL
SUM	TIME	TIMESTAMP
TRANSLATE	VARCHAR	VARGRAPHIC
VARIABLE	WORK	

The guidelines in this section are applicable to every type of DB2 application program. Chapters 6 through 8 present guidelines for programming techniques used by specific types of DB2 application programs. Additionally, Chapter 9, "Using DB2 Stored Procedures," contains programming guidelines for each type of DB2 program environment.

Host Variables

When embedding SQL in an application program, you, as the programmer, rarely know every value that needs to be accessed by SQL predicates. Often you need to use variables to specify the values of predicates. For example, if a program will be reading a flat file or value input by a user from a terminal, you need a mechanism to place this value in an SQL statement as the program executes. This is the function of host variables.

A *host variable* is an area of storage allocated by the host language and referenced in an SQL statement. You define and name host variables using the syntax of the host language. For COBOL, you must define host variables in the `DATA DIVISION` of your program in the `WORKING-STORAGE` section or the `LINKAGE` section. Additionally, when you're using `INCLUDE`, you must delimit the host variable specifications by using `EXEC SQL` and `END-EXEC` (as previously discussed).

When you use host variables in SQL statements, prefix them with a colon (:). For example, a COBOL variable defined in the `DATA DIVISION` as

```
EXAMPLE-VARIABLE      PIC X(5)
```

should be referenced as follows when used in an embedded SQL statement:

```
:EXAMPLE-VARIABLE
```

When the same variable is referenced by the COBOL program outside the context of SQL, however, do not prefix the variable with a colon. If you do so, a compilation error results.

Host variables are the means of moving data from the program to DB2 and from DB2 to the program. Data can be read from a file, placed into host variables, and used to modify a DB2 table (through embedded SQL). For data retrieval, host variables are used to house the selected DB2 data. You also can use host variables to change predicate values in WHERE clauses. You can use host variables in the following ways:

- As output data areas in the INTO clause of the SELECT and FETCH statements
- As input data areas for the SET clause of the UPDATE statement
- As input data areas for the VALUES clause of the INSERT statement
- As search fields in the WHERE clause for SELECT, INSERT, UPDATE, and DELETE statements
- As literals in the SELECT list of a SELECT statement

Several examples of host variables used in SQL statements follow. In the first example, host variables are used in the SQL SELECT statement as literals in the SELECT list and as output data areas in the INTO clause:

```
EXEC SQL
    SELECT  EMPNO, :INCREASE-PCT,
            SALARY * :INCREASE-PCT
    INTO    :HOSTVAR-EMPNO,
            :HOSTVAR-INCRPCT,
            :HOSTVAR-SALARY
    FROM    EMP
    WHERE   EMPNO = '000110'
END-EXEC.
```

In the second example, host variables are used in the SET clause of the UPDATE statement and as a search field in the WHERE clause:

```
EXEC SQL
    UPDATE EMP
       SET SALARY = :HOSTVAR-SALARY
    WHERE  EMPNO = :HOSTVAR-EMPNO
END-EXEC.
```

The final example depicts host variables used in the VALUES clause of an SQL INSERT statement:

```
EXEC SQL
    INSERT INTO DEPT
    VALUES (:HOSTVAR-DEPTNO,
            :HOSTVAR-DEPTNAME,
            :HOSTVAR-MGRNO,
            :HOSTVAR-ADMRDEPT)
END-EXEC.
```

Host Structures

In addition to host variables, SQL statements can use host structures. Host structures enable SQL statements to specify a single structure for storing all retrieved columns. A host structure, then, is a COBOL group-level data area composed of host variables for all columns to be returned by a given SELECT statement.

The following is a host structure for the DSN8510.DEPT table:

```
01  DCLDEPT.
    10  DEPTNO               PIC X(3).
    10  DEPTNAME.
        49  DEPTNAME-LEN     PIC S9(4) USAGE COMP.
        49  DEPTNAME-TEXT    PIC X(36).
    10  MGRNO                PIC X(6).
    10  ADMRDEPT             PIC X(3).
    10  LOCATION             PIC X(16).
```

DCLDEPT is the host structure name in this example. You could write the following statement using this host structure:

```
EXEC SQL
    SELECT  DEPTNO, DEPTNAME, MGRNO, ADMRDEPT, LOCATION
    FROM    DEPT
    INTO    :DCLDEPT
    WHERE   DEPTNO = 'A00'
END-EXEC.
```

This statement populates the host variables for all columns defined under the DCLDEPT group-level data area.

Null Indicator Variables and Structures

Before you select or insert a column that can be set to null, it must have an indicator variable defined for it. You can use indicator variables also with the UPDATE statement to set columns to null. A third use for null indicators occurs when any column (defined as either nullable or not nullable) is retrieved using the built-in column functions AVG, MAX, MIN, and SUM. Finally, null indicators should be used in outer join statements for each column that can return a null result (even if the column is defined as not null).

If you fail to use an indicator variable, a -305 SQLCODE is returned when no rows meet the requirements of the predicates for the SQL statement containing the column function. For example, consider the following statement:

```
SELECT  MAX(SALARY)
FROM    DSN8510.EMP
WHERE   WORKDEPT = 'ZZZ';
```

Because no ZZZ department exists, the value of the maximum salary that is returned is null.

You should define null indicators in the WORKING-STORAGE section of your COBOL program as computational variables, with a picture clause specification of PIC S9(4). The null indicator variables for the DSN8510.EMP table look like this:

```
01  EMP-INDICATORS.
    10  WORKDEPT-IND    PIC S9(4) USAGE COMP.
    10  PHONENO-IND     PIC S9(4) USAGE COMP.
    10  HIREDATE-IND    PIC S9(4) USAGE COMP.
    10  JOB-IND         PIC S9(4) USAGE COMP.
    10  EDLEVEL-IND     PIC S9(4) USAGE COMP.
```

```
        10   SEX-IND          PIC S9(4) USAGE COMP.
        10   BIRTHDATE-IND    PIC S9(4) USAGE COMP.
        10   SALARY-IND       PIC S9(4) USAGE COMP.
        10   BONUS-IND        PIC S9(4) USAGE COMP.
        10   COMM-IND         PIC S9(4) USAGE COMP.
```

This structure contains the null indicators for all the nullable columns of the DSN8510.EMP table.

To associate null indicator variables with a particular host variable for a column, code the indicator variable immediately after the host variable, preceded by a colon. For example, to retrieve information regarding SALARY (a nullable column) from the DSN8510.EMP table, you can code the following embedded SQL statement:

```
EXEC SQL
    SELECT  EMPNO, SALARY
    INTO    :EMPNO,
            :SALARY:SALARY-IND
    FROM    EMP
    WHERE   EMPNO = '000100'
END-EXEC.
```

The null indicator variable is separate from both the column to which it pertains and the host variable for that column. To determine the value of any nullable column, a host variable and an indicator variable are required. The host variable contains the value of the column when it is not null. The indicator variable contains one of the following values to indicate a column's null status:

- A negative number indicates that the column has been set to null.
- The value -2 indicates that the column has been set to null as a result of a data conversion error.
- A positive or zero value indicates that the column is not null.
- If a column defined as a CHARACTER data type is truncated on retrieval because the host variable is not large enough, the indicator variable contains the original length of the truncated column.

You can use null indicator variables with corresponding host variables in the following situations:

- SET clause of the UPDATE statement
- VALUES clause of the INSERT statement
- INTO clause of the SELECT or FETCH statement

You can code null indicator structures in much the same way you code the host structures discussed previously. Null indicator structures enable host structures to be used when nullable columns are selected. A null indicator structure is defined as a null indicator variable with an OCCURS clause. The variable should occur once for each column in the corresponding host structure, as shown in the following section of code:

```
01   IDEPT PIC S9(4) USAGE COMP OCCURS 5 TIMES.
```

This null indicator structure defines the null indicators needed for retrieving rows from the DSN8510.DEPT table using a host structure. The DCLDEPT host structure has five columns, so the IDEPT null indicator structure occurs five times. When you're using a host structure for a table in which any column is nullable, one null indicator per column in the host structure is required.

You can use the host structure and null indicator structure together as follows:

```
EXEC SQL
    SELECT  DEPTNO, DEPTNAME, MGRNO, ADMRDEPT, LOCATION
    FROM    DEPT
    INTO    :DCLDEPT:DEPT-IND
    WHERE   DEPTNO = 'A00'
END-EXEC.
```

Based on the position in the null indicator structure, you can determine the null status of each column in the retrieved row. If the *n*th null indicator contains a negative value, the *n*th column is null. So, in this example, if DEPT-IND(3) is negative, MGRNO is null.

CAUTION

Always use a null indicator variable when referencing a nullable column. Failure to do so results in a -305 SQLCODE. If you fail to check the null status of the column being retrieved, your program may continue to execute, but the results will be questionable.

NOTE

You can avoid using null indicator variables by using the VALUE or COALESCE function. Both of these functions can be used to supply a value whenever DB2 would return a null. For example, VALUE(MANAGER_NAME,'*** No Manager Name ***') will return the actual value of MANAGER_NAME when the column is not null and the literal '*** No Manager Name ***' when the MANAGER_NAME column is null.

Host Variable Guidelines

Practice the following tips and techniques to ensure proper host variable usage.

Use Syntactically Valid Variable Names

Host variables can use any naming scheme that is valid for the definition of variables in the host language being used. For host variables defined using COBOL, underscores are not permitted. As a general rule, use hyphens instead of underscores.

Avoid Certain COBOL Clauses

COBOL host variable definitions cannot specify the `JUSTIFIED` or `BLANK WHEN ZERO` clauses.

You can specify the `OCCURS` clause only when you're defining a null indicator structure. Otherwise, you cannot use `OCCURS` for host variables.

Use Colons with Host Variables in SQL

You must use a colon with host variables when the host variable is an SQL reserved word or an indicator variable. The colon is optional when a host variable is used as follows:

- In the `INTO` clause of a `SELECT` statement
- In the `FROM` clause of a `PREPARE` statement
- In the `USING` clause of an `EXECUTE` or an `OPEN` statement
- In the `DESCRIPTOR` clause of an `EXECUTE`, a `FETCH`, or an `OPEN` statement
- In the `VALUES` clause of an `INSERT` statement
- Following `LIKE` in any `WHERE` clause
- Following `IN` in any `WHERE` clause
- Qualified by a host structure name

As a general rule, use a colon when referring to host variables in embedded SQL statements. This approach can reduce ambiguity and allows you to forget all the rules outlined in the preceding paragraph.

Avoid Host Structures

Favor individual host variables over host structures. Individual host variables are easier to understand, easier to support, and less likely to cause errors as a result of changes to tables.

Avoid Null Indicator Structures

Favor individual null indicator variables over null indicator structures. Individual null indicator variables can be named appropriately for each column to which they apply. Null indicator structures have a single common name and a subscript. Tying a subscripted variable name to a specific column can be tedious and error-prone.

For example, consider the host structure and its corresponding null indicator structure shown previously. The fact that `IDEPT(2)` is the null indicator variable for the `DEPTNAME` host variable is not obvious. If you had used separate null indicators for each nullable column, the null indicator for `DEPTNAME` could be called `DEPTNAME-IND`. With this naming convention, you can easily see that `DEPTNAME-IND` is the null indicator variable for `DEPTNAME`.

Version 4

Be forewarned that null indicator structures can be generated by `DCLGEN` (as of DB2 V4), whereas individual indicator variables must be explicitly coded by hand. Even so, individual null indicator variables are easier to use and therefore recommended over null indicator structures.

Define Host Variables Precisely

Define all your host variables correctly. Consult Appendix F, "Valid DB2 Data Types," for a complete list of valid DB2 data types and their corresponding COBOL definitions. Failure to define host variables correctly results in precompiler errors or poor performance due to access path selection based on non-equivalent data types, data conversions, and data truncation.

Use DCLGEN for Host Variable Generation

Use DCLGEN to generate host variables automatically for each column of each table to be accessed. DCLGEN ensures that the host variables are defined correctly.

Avoid DCLGEN for Null Indicator Generation

As I mentioned earlier, DCLGEN can optionally generate null indicator host structures. However, host structures are more difficult to use than individual null indicator variables and generally should be avoided.

Embedded SELECT Statements

The two types of embedded SQL SELECT statements are singleton SELECTs and cursor SELECTs. So far, all examples in the book have been singleton SELECTs.

Remember, SQL statements operate on a set of data and return a set of data. Host language programs, however, operate on data a row at a time. A singleton SELECT is simply an SQL SELECT statement that returns only one row. As such, it can be coded and embedded in a host language program with little effort: The singleton SELECT returns one row and the application program processes one row.

You code a singleton SELECT as follows:

```
EXEC SQL
    SELECT  DEPTNAME, MGRNO
    INTO    :HOSTVAR-DEPTNAME,
            :HOSTVAR-MGRNO
    FROM    DEPT
    WHERE   DEPTNO = 'A11'
END-EXEC.
```

The singleton SELECT statement differs from a normal SQL SELECT statement in that it must contain the INTO clause. In the INTO clause, you code the host variables that accept the data returned from the DB2 table by the SELECT statement.

Singleton SELECTs are usually quite efficient. Be sure, however, that the singleton SELECT returns only one row. If more than one row is retrieved, the first one is placed in the host variables defined by the INTO clause, and the SQLCODE is set to -811.

If your application program must process a SELECT statement that returns multiple rows, you must use a cursor, which is an object designed to handle multiple row results tables.

Programming with Cursors

Recall from Chapter 1, "The Magic Words," that an impedance mismatch occurs between SQL and the host language, such as COBOL. COBOL operates on data a row at a time; SQL operates on data a set at time. Without a proper vehicle for handling this impedance mismatch (such as arrays in APL2), using embedded SELECT statements would be impossible. IBM's solution is the structure known as a *symbolic cursor*, or simply *cursor*.

DB2 application programs use cursors to navigate through a set of rows returned by an embedded SQL SELECT statement. A cursor can be likened to a pointer. As the programmer, you declare a cursor and define an SQL statement for that cursor. After that, you can use the cursor in much the same manner as a sequential file. The cursor is opened, rows are fetched from the cursor one row at a time, and then the cursor is closed.

You can perform four distinct operations on cursors:

DECLARE	Defines the cursor, gives it a name unique to the program in which it is embedded, and assigns an SQL statement to the cursor name. The DECLARE statement does not execute the SQL statement; it merely defines the SQL statement.
OPEN	Readies the cursor for row retrieval. OPEN is an executable statement. It reads the SQL search fields, executes the SQL statement, and sometimes builds the results table. It does not assign values to host variables, though.
FETCH	Returns data from the results table one row at a time and assigns the values to specified host variables. If the results table is not built at cursor OPEN time, it is built FETCH by FETCH.
CLOSE	Releases all resources used by the cursor.

Whether the results table for the SQL statement is built at cursor OPEN time or as rows are fetched depends on the type of SQL statement and the access path. You will learn about access paths in Chapter 11, "The Doors to DB2."

When you're processing with cursors, an SQL statement can return zero, one, or many rows. The following list describes the cursor processing that occurs for the different number of retrieved rows:

One row	Use of the cursor is optional. A result set of one row occurs either because the SQL predicates provided specific qualifications to make the answer set distinct or because a unique index exists for a column or columns specified in the predicates of the WHERE clause.

Many rows	Cursor processing is mandatory. When multiple rows are returned by an SQL statement, a cursor must be coded. If multiple rows are returned by a SELECT statement not coded using a cursor, DB2 returns a -811 SQLCODE (the SQLSTATE value is 21000).
Zero rows	No rows exist for the specified conditions, or the specified conditions are improperly coded. When no rows are returned, the SQL return code is set to +100.

When cursors are used to process multiple rows, a FETCH statement is typically coded in a loop that reads and processes each row in succession. When no more rows are available to be fetched, the FETCH statement returns an SQLCODE of +100, indicating no more rows. For an example of cursor processing, consult Listing 5.2.

Listing 5.2. Cursor processing.

```
WORKING-STORAGE SECTION.
     .
     .
     .
    EXEC SQL
        DECLARE C1 CURSOR FOR
            SELECT   DEPTNO, DEPTNAME, MGRNO
            FROM     DEPT
            WHERE    ADMRDEPT = :ADMRDEPT
    END-EXEC.
     .
     .
     .
PROCEDURE DIVISION.
     .
     .
     .
    MOVE   'A00'      TO ADMRDEPT.
    EXEC SQL
        OPEN C1
    END-EXEC.

IF SQLCODE < 0
        PERFORM 9999-ERROR-PARAGRAPH.
    MOVE   'YES'    TO MORE-ROWS.
    PERFORM 200-PROCESS-DEPTS
        UNTIL MORE-ROWS = 'NO'.

    EXEC SQL
        CLOSE C1
    END-EXEC.
    GOBACK.
200-PROCESS-DEPTS.
     .
     .
     .
```

```
    EXEC SQL
        FETCH C1
        INTO :DEPTNO,
             :DEPTNAME,
             :MGRNO
    END-EXEC.
    IF SQLCODE < 0
        PERFORM 9999-ERROR-PARAGRAPH.

    IF SQLCODE = +100
        MOVE   'NO'       TO MORE-ROWS
    ELSE
          perform required processing.
```

In Listing 5.2, a cursor is declared for an SQL SELECT statement in WORKING-STORAGE. Values are moved to the host variables, and the cursor is opened. A loop fetches and processes information until no more rows are available; then the cursor is closed.

Using a Cursor for Data Modification

Often an application program must read data and then, based on its values, either update or delete the data. You use the UPDATE and DELETE SQL statements to modify and delete rows from DB2 tables. These statements, like the SELECT statement, operate on data a set at a time. How can you then first read the data before modifying it?

You do so by using a cursor and a special clause of the UPDATE and DELETE statements that can be used only by embedded SQL: WHERE CURRENT OF. You declare the cursor with a special FOR UPDATE OF clause.

Refer to Listing 5.3, which declares a cursor named C1 specifying the FOR UPDATE OF clause. The cursor is opened and a row is fetched. After examining the contents of the retrieved data, the program updates or deletes the row using the WHERE CURRENT OF C1 clause.

Listing 5.3. Updating with a cursor.

```
WORKING-STORAGE SECTION.
    EXEC SQL
        DECLARE C1 CURSOR FOR
            SELECT  DEPTNO, DEPTNAME, MGRNO
            FROM    DEPT
            WHERE   ADMRDEPT = :ADMRDEPT
            FOR UPDATE OF MGRNO
    END-EXEC.
PROCEDURE DIVISION.
          .
          .
          .
        MOVE   'A00'       TO ADMRDEPT.
```

continues

Listing 5.3. continued

```
          EXEC SQL
              OPEN C1
          END-EXEC.

          MOVE   'YES'      TO MORE-ROWS.

          PERFORM 200-MODIFY-DEPT-INFO
              UNTIL MORE-ROWS = 'NO'.

          EXEC SQL
              CLOSE C1
          END-EXEC.
          GOBACK.
      200-MODIFY-DEPT-INFO.
              .
              .
          EXEC SQL
              FETCH C1
              INTO  :DEPTNO,
                    :DEPTNAME,
                    :MGRNO
          END-EXEC.
          IF SQLCODE < 0
              PERFORM 9999-ERROR-PARAGRAPH.
          IF SQLCODE = +100
              MOVE  'NO'     TO MORE-ROWS
          ELSE
              EXEC SQL
                  UPDATE DEPT
                  SET MGRNO = '000060'
                  WHERE CURRENT OF C1
              END-EXEC.
```

These features enable you to perform row-by-row operations on DB2 tables, effectively mimicking sequential file processing.

Embedded SELECT and Cursor Coding Guidelines

Ensure efficient and accurate embedded SQL by following the subsequent guidelines.

Use Singleton SELECTs to Reduce Overhead

Try to use singleton SELECTs rather than cursors because the definition and processing of cursors adds overhead to a DB2 application program. However, be sure that the singleton SELECT returns only one row. This action is accomplished by selecting data only by the primary key column(s) or by columns defined in a unique index for that table.

If the program requires a SELECT statement that returns more than one row, you must use cursors.

If your program must issue a SELECT statement that returns more than one row but needs to process only the first row returned, consider coding a singleton SELECT instead of a cursor if performance is critical. Code the program to accept -811 as a successful SQL call and process the returned row. This technique is not recommended, however, because it may not work in subsequent releases of DB2.

Consider Cursor-Free Browsing

When a program needs to browse through the rows of a table based on a single column where a unique index exists, consider avoiding an cursor in favor of the following two SQL statements:

```
SELECT VALUE(MIN(SALARY),0)
INTO   :NEW-SAL-HVAR
FROM   EMP
WHERE  SALARY > :OLD-SAL-HVAR

SELECT EMPNO, LASTNAME, SALARY, BONUS
INTO   :HV-EMPNO, :HV-LASTNAME, :HV-SALARY, :HV-BONUS
FROM   EMP
WHERE  SALARY = :NEW-SAL-HVAR
```

The first time through the program, the host variable OLD-SAL-HVAR should be set to a value just lower than the lowest value that needs to be retrieved. By looping through the preceding two SQL statements, the program can avoid a cursor and browse the table rows until no more rows exist or the highest value is obtained. This technique can outperform a cursor in some situations.

Declare as Many Cursors as Needed

You can declare and open more than one cursor in any given program at any time. No limit is placed on the number of cursors permitted per application program.

Avoid Using Certain Cursors for Modification

You cannot use a cursor for updates or deletes if the DECLARE CURSOR statement includes any of the following:

- UNION clause
- DISTINCT clause
- GROUP BY clause
- ORDER BY clause
- Joins
- Subqueries
- Correlated subqueries
- Tables in read-only mode, ACCESS(RO)
- Tables in utility mode, ACCESS(UT)
- Read-only views

Place the DECLARE CURSOR Statement First

The DECLARE CURSOR statement must precede any other commands (such as OPEN, CLOSE, and FETCH) relating to the cursor because of the way the DB2 precompiler parses and extracts the SQL statements from the program.

The DECLARE CURSOR statement is not an executable statement and should not be coded in the PROCEDURE DIVISION of an application program. Although doing so does not cause a problem, it makes your program difficult to understand and could cause others to think that DECLARE is an executable statement.

You should place all cursor declarations in the WORKING-STORAGE section of the application program, immediately before PROCEDURE DIVISION. All host variable declarations must precede the DECLARE CURSOR statement in the application program.

Include Only the Columns Being Updated

When you're coding the FOR UPDATE OF clause of the DECLARE CURSOR statement, you should specify only the columns that will be updated. Coding more columns than is necessary can degrade performance.

In the FOR UPDATE OF clause of the DECLARE CURSOR statement, you must include all columns to be modified. Otherwise, subsequent UPDATE...WHERE CURRENT OF statements will not be allowed for those columns.

Always Use FOR UPDATE OF When Updating with a Cursor

Although doing so is not mandatory, you should code the FOR UPDATE OF clause of a DECLARE CURSOR statement used for deleting rows. This technique effectively locks the row before it is deleted so that no other process can access it. If rows earmarked for deletion are accessible by other programs and ad hoc users, the integrity of the data could be compromised.

Use WHERE CURRENT OF to Delete Single Rows Using a Cursor

Use the WHERE CURRENT OF clause on UPDATE and DELETE statements that are meant to modify only a single row. Failure to code the WHERE CURRENT OF clause results in the modification or deletion of every row in the table being processed.

Avoid the FOR UPDATE OF Clause on Non-Updatable Cursors

You cannot code the FOR UPDATE OF clause on cursors that access read-only data. These cursors contain SELECT statements that

- Access read-only views
- Join any tables
- Issue subqueries for two or more tables

- Access two or more tables using UNION
- Use built-in functions
- Use ORDER BY, GROUP BY, or HAVING
- Specify DISTINCT
- Specify literals or arithmetic expressions in the SELECT list

Open Cursors Before Fetching

Similar to a sequential file, a cursor must be opened before it can be fetched from or closed. You also cannot open a cursor twice without first closing it.

Initialize Host Variables

Initialize all host variables used by the cursor before opening the cursor. All host variables used in a cursor SELECT are evaluated when the cursor is opened, not when the cursor is declared or fetched from.

Use Care When Specifying Host Variables Used with FETCH

The FETCH statement retrieves data one row at a time only in a forward motion. In other words, rows that have already been retrieved cannot be retrieved again.

Synchronize the host variables fetched (or selected) with the SELECT list specified in the cursor declaration (or singleton SELECT). If the data type of the columns does not match the host variable, and the data cannot be converted, a compilation error results. This error can occur if host variables are transposed as follows:

```
EXEC SQL
    DECLARE C1 CURSOR
    SELECT  DEPTNO, ADMRDEPT
    FROM    DEPT
END-EXEC.
EXEC SQL
    FETCH C1
    INTO   :ADMRDEPT, :DEPTNO
END-EXEC.
```

The DEPTNO host variable is switched with the ADMRDEPT host variable in the FETCH statement. This switch does not cause a compilation error because both columns are the same data type and length, but it does cause data integrity problems.

Explicitly Close Cursors

When a DB2 program is finished, DB2 implicitly closes all cursors opened by the program. To increase performance, however, you should explicitly code the CLOSE statement for each cursor. The CLOSE statement can be executed only against previously OPENed cursors.

Use the WITH HOLD Clause to Retain Cursor Position

When a COMMIT is issued by the program, open cursors are closed unless the WITH HOLD option is coded for the cursor.

You can add the WITH HOLD parameter to a cursor as shown in the following example:

```
EXEC SQL
    DECLARE CSR1 CURSOR WITH HOLD FOR
        SELECT  EMPNO, LASTNAME
        FROM    EMP
        WHERE   SALARY > 30000
END-EXEC.
```

WITH HOLD prevents subsequent COMMITs from destroying the intermediate results table for the SELECT statement, thereby saving positioning within the cursor.

Open Cursors Only When Needed

Do not open a cursor until just before you need it. Close the cursor immediately after your program receives an SQLCODE of +100, which means that the program has finished processing the cursor. This way, you can reduce the consumption of system resources.

Modifying Data with Embedded SQL

Previously, I discussed the capability to update and delete single rows based on cursor positioning. You can also embed pure set-level processing UPDATE, DELETE, and INSERT SQL statements into a host language program.

Simply code the appropriate SQL statement, and delimit it with EXEC SQL and END-EXEC. The statement can contain host variables. When issued in the program, the statement is processed as though it were issued interactively. Consider this example:

```
EXEC SQL
    UPDATE EMP
        SET SALARY = SALARY * 1.05
        WHERE EMPNO = :EMPNO
END-EXEC.
EXEC SQL
    DELETE FROM PROJACT
    WHERE ACENDATE < CURRENT DATE
END-EXEC.
EXEC SQL
    INSERT INTO DEPT
        (DEPTNO,
         DEPTNAME,
         MGRNO,
         ADMRDEPT)
    VALUES
        (:DEPTNO,
         :DEPTNAME,
         :MGRNO,
         :ADMRDEPT)
END-EXEC.
```

These three SQL statements are examples of coding embedded data modification statements (UPDATE, DELETE, and INSERT) using host variables.

Embedded Modification SQL Guidelines

The following guidelines should be followed to ensure that optimal SQL data modification techniques are being deployed in your DB2 applications.

Favor Cursor-Controlled UPDATE and DELETE

Favor UPDATE and DELETE with a cursor specifying the FOR UPDATE OF clause over individual UPDATE and DELETE statements that use the set-level processing capabilities of SQL.

Set-level processing is preferable, however, when an OPEN, a FETCH, and a CLOSE are performed for each UPDATE or DELETE. Sometimes, performing these three actions cannot be avoided (for example, when applying transactions from a sequential input file).

Use FOR UPDATE OF to Ensure Data Integrity

If a program is coded to SELECT or FETCH a row and then, based on the row's contents, issue an UPDATE or DELETE, use a cursor with FOR UPDATE OF to ensure data integrity. The FOR UPDATE OF clause causes a lock to be taken on the data page when it is fetched, ensuring that no other process can modify the data before your program processes it. If the program simply SELECTs or FETCHs without the FOR UPDATE OF specification and then issues an SQL statement to modify the data, another process can modify the data in between, thereby invalidating your program's modification, overwriting your program's modification, or both.

CAUTION

When programming psuedo-conversation CICS transactions, FOR UPDATE OF is not sufficient to ensure integrity. A save and compare must be done prior to any update activity.

Specify a Primary Key in the WHERE Clause of UPDATE and DELETE Statements

Never issue independent, embedded, non-cursor controlled UPDATE and DELETE statements without specifying a primary key value or unique index column values in the WHERE clause unless you want to affect multiple rows. Without the unique WHERE clause specification, you might be unable to determine whether you have specified the correct row for modification. In addition, you could mistakenly update or delete multiple rows.

Use Set-at-a-Time INSERTs

If your program issues INSERT statements, try to use the statement's set-level processing capabilities. Using the set-level processing of INSERT is usually possible only when rows are being inserted into one table based on a SELECT from another table.

Use LOAD Rather than Multiple INSERTs

Favor the LOAD utility over an application program performing many insertions in a table. If the inserts are not dependent on coding constraints, format the input records to be loaded and use the LOAD utility. If the inserts are dependent on application code, consider writing an application program that writes a flat file that can subsequently be loaded using the LOAD utility. In general, LOAD outperforms a program issuing INSERTs by 50 to 75 percent.

Application Development Guidelines

The guidelines in this section aid you in coding more efficient DB2 application programs by

- Coding efficient embedded SQL
- Coding efficient host language constructs to process the embedded SQL
- Reducing concurrency
- Promoting the development of easily maintainable code

When you're designing a DB2 program, you can easily get caught up in programming for efficiency, thereby compromising the effectiveness of the program. Efficiency can be defined as "doing things right," whereas effectiveness can be defined as "doing the right thing."

Design embedded SQL programs to be as efficient as possible (following the guidelines in this book) without compromising the effectiveness of the program. Gauge program efficiency by the following criteria:

- CPU time
- Elapsed time
- Number and type of I/Os
- Lock wait time
- Transaction throughput

For a thorough discussion of DB2 performance monitoring and tuning, consult Parts IV, "DB2 Performance Monitoring," and V, "DB2 Performance Tuning." Gauge program effectiveness by the following criteria:

- User satisfaction
- Expected results versus actual results

- Integrity of the processed data
- Capability to meet prearranged service-level requirements

Code Modular DB2 Programs

You should design DB2 programs to be modular. One program should accomplish a single, well-defined task. If you need to execute multiple tasks, structure the programs so that tasks can be strung together by having the programs call one another. This approach is preferable to a single, large program that accomplishes many tasks for two reasons. One, single tasks in separate programs make the programs easier to understand and maintain. Two, if each task can be executed either alone or with other tasks, isolating the tasks in a program enables easier execution of any single task or list of tasks.

Consider Stored Procedures for Reusability

Version 4

When you're modularizing a DB2 application, do so with an eye toward reusability. Whenever a particular task must be performed across many programs, applications, or systems, consider developing a stored procedure. A stored procedure, after it is created, can be called from multiple applications. However, when you modify the code, you need to modify only the stored procedure code, not each individual program.

For more information on stored procedures, refer to Chapter 9.

Minimize the Size of DB2 Programs

Code DB2 programs to be as small as possible. Streamlining your application code to remove unnecessary statements results in better performance. This recommendation goes hand-in-hand with the preceding one.

Use Unqualified SQL

Use unqualified table, view, synonym, and alias names in application programs. This way, you can ease the process of moving programs, plans, and packages from the test environment to the production environment. If tables are explicitly qualified in an application program, and tables are qualified differently in test DB2 than they are in production DB2, programs must be modified before they are turned over to an operational production application.

When the program is bound, the tables are qualified by one of the following:

- If neither the `OWNER` nor `QUALIFIER` parameter is specified, tables are qualified by the userid of the binding agent.
- If only the `OWNER` is specified, tables are qualified by the token specified in the `OWNER` parameter.
- If a `QUALIFIER` is specified, all tables are qualified by the token specified to that parameter.

Avoid SELECT *

Never use `SELECT *` in an embedded SQL program. Request each column that needs to be accessed. Also, follow the SQL coding recommendations in Chapter 2, "Data Manipulation Guidelines."

Filter Data Using the SQL WHERE Clause

Favor the specification of DB2 predicates to filter rows from a desired results table instead of the selection of all rows and the use of program logic to filter those not needed. For example, coding the embedded `SELECT`

```
SELECT  EMPNO, LASTNAME, SALARY
FROM    EMP
WHERE   SALARY > 10000
```

is preferred to coding the same `SELECT` statement without the `WHERE` clause and following the `SELECT` statement with an `IF` statement:

```
IF SALARY < 10000
    NEXT SENTENCE
ELSE
    Process data.
```

The `WHERE` clause usually outperforms the host language `IF` statement because I/O is reduced.

Use SQL to Join Tables

To join tables, favor SQL over application logic, except when the data retrieved by the join must be updated. In this situation, consider coding multiple cursors to mimic the join process. Base the predicates of one cursor on the data retrieved from a fetch to the previous cursor.

Listing 5.4 presents pseudocode for retrieving data from a cursor declared with an SQL join statement.

Listing 5.4. Pseudocode for retrieving data from an SQL join.

```
EXEC SQL
    DECLARE JOINCSR CURSOR FOR
    SELECT  D.DEPTNO, D.DEPTNAME, E.EMPNO, E.SALARY
    FROM    DEPT    D,
            EMP     E
    WHERE   D.DEPTNO = E.WORKDEPT
END-EXEC.
EXEC SQL
    OPEN JOINCSR
END-EXEC.
Loop until no more rows returned or error
EXEC SQL
        FETCH JOINCSR
        INTO :DEPTNO, :DEPTNAME, :EMPNO, :SALARY
    END-EXEC
    Process retrieved data
end of loop
```

The criteria for joining tables are in the predicates of the SQL statement. Compare this method to the application join example in Listing 5.5. The pseudocode in this listing employs two cursors, each accessing a different table, to join the EMP table with the DEPT table using application logic.

Listing 5.5. Pseudocode for retrieving data from an application join.

```
EXEC SQL
    DECLARE DEPTCSR CURSOR FOR
    SELECT  DEPTNO, DEPTNAME
    FROM    DEPT
END-EXEC.
EXEC SQL
    DECLARE EMPCSR CURSOR FOR
    SELECT  EMPNO, SALARY
    FROM    EMP
    WHERE   WORKDEPT = :HV-WORKDEPT
END-EXEC.
EXEC SQL
    OPEN DEPTCSR
END-EXEC.
Loop until no more department rows or error
    EXEC SQL
        FETCH DEPTCSR
        INTO :DEPTNO, :DEPTNAME
    END-EXEC.
    MOVE DEPTNO TO HV-WORKDEPT.
    EXEC SQL
        OPEN EMPCSR
    END-EXEC.
    Loop until no more employee rows or error
        EXEC SQL
            FETCH EMPCSR
            INTO :EMPNO, :SALARY
        END-EXEC.
        Process retrieved data
    end of loop
end of loop
```

Joining tables by application logic requires additional code and is usually less efficient than an SQL join. When data will be updated in a cursor-controlled fashion, favor application joining over SQL joining because the results of an SQL join are not always updated directly. When you're updating the result rows of an application join, remember to code FOR UPDATE OF on each cursor, specifying every column that can be updated. When you're only reading the data without subsequent modification, remember to code FOR READ ONLY (or FOR FETCH ONLY) on the cursor.

Avoid Host Structures

Avoid selecting or fetching INTO a group-level host variable structure. Your program is more independent of table changes if you select or fetch into individual data elements. For example, code

```
EXEC SQL
    FETCH C1
    INTO :DEPTNO,
         :DEPTNAME:DEPTNAME-IND,
         :MGRNO:MGRNO-IND,
         :ADMDEPT:ADMRDEPT-IND
END-EXEC.
```

instead of

```
EXEC SQL
    FETCH C1
    INTO   :DCLDEPT:DEPT-IND
END-EXEC.
```

Although the second example appears easier to code, the first example is preferred. Using individual host variables instead of host structures makes programs easier to understand, easier to debug, and easier to maintain.

Use ORDER BY to Ensure Sequencing

Always use ORDER BY when your program must ensure the sequencing of returned rows. Otherwise, the rows are returned to your program in an unpredictable sequence.

Use FOR READ ONLY for Read-Only Access

Code all read-only SELECT statements—whether singleton SELECTs or using cursors—with the FOR READ ONLY (or FOR FETCH ONLY) cursor clause.

Explicitly Code Literals

When possible, code literals explicitly in the SQL statement rather than move the literals to host variables and then process the SQL statement using the host variables. This technique gives the DB2 optimization process the best opportunity for arriving at an optimal access path.

Version 5

Although DB2 V5 offers an option to re-optimize SQL statements on the fly, explicit literal coding still should be considered when feasible. It should not, however, be a forced standard.

Avoid Cursors If Possible

Whenever doing so is practical, avoid the use of a cursor. Cursors add overhead to an application program. You can avoid cursors, however, only when the program retrieves a single row from an application table or tables.

Code Cursors to Retrieve Multiple Rows

If you do not check for -811 SQLCODEs, always code a cursor for each SELECT statement that does not access tables either by the primary key or by columns specified in a unique index.

Specify Isolation Level by SQL Statement

Version 4

As of DB2 V4, each individual SQL statement can specify a different, appropriate isolation level. Although each DB2 plan and package has an isolation level, you can override it for individual SQL statements by using the WITH clause. You can specify the WITH clause for the following types of SQL statements:

- SELECT INTO
- DECLARE CURSOR
- INSERT
- Searched DELETE
- Searched UPDATE

Valid options are as follow:

- RR and RR KEEP UPDATE LOCKS (Repeatable Read)
- RS and RS KEEP UPDATE LOCKS (Read Stability)
- CS (Cursor Stability)
- UR (Uncommitted Read)

Version 5

The KEEP UPDATE LOCKS clause in new to DB2 V5. It indicates that DB2 is to acquire X locks instead of U or S locks on all qualifying rows or pages. Use KEEP UPDATE LOCKS sparingly. Although it can better serialize updates, it can reduce concurrency.

In Chapter 7, you can find additional guidance for each of the isolation levels.

Use the Sample Programs for Inspiration

IBM provides source code in several host languages for various sample application programs. This source code is in a PDS library named SYS1.DB2V5R1.DSNSAMP (or something similar) supplied with the DB2 system software. Samples of COBOL, PL/I, FORTRAN, Assembler, and C programs for TSO, CICS, and IMS are available in the aforementioned library.

Batch Programming Guidelines

When coding batch DB2 programs the following tips and tricks can be used to create effective and useful applications.

Favor Clustered Access

Whenever sequential access to table data is needed, process the table rows in clustered sequence.

Increase Parallel Processing

The architecture of IBM mainframes is such that multiple engines are available for processing. A batch program executing in a single, standard batch job can be processed by only a single engine. To maximize performance of CPU-bound programs, increase the parallelism of the program in one of two ways:

- Program Cloning: Clone the program and stratify the data access. Stratifying data access refers to dividing data access into logical subsets that can be processed independently.
- Query Parallelism: Utilize partitioned tablespaces and bind the application program specifying `DEGREE(ANY)` to indicate that DB2 should try to use query I/O, CPU, and Sysplex parallelism.

Using the first method, you, as the application developer, must physically create multiple clone programs. Each program clone must be functionally identical but will process a different subset of the data. For example, you could split a program that reads `DSN8510.EMP` to process employees into a series of programs that perform the same function, but each processes only a single department. The data can be stratified based on any consistent grouping of data that is comprehensive (all data to be processed is included) and non-overlapping (data in one subset does not occur in a different subset). For example, you can accomplish data stratification based on the following:

- Unique key ranges
- Tablespace partitions
- Functional groupings (for example, departments or companies)

Ensure that the data is stratified both programmatically and in the structure of the database. For example, if you're stratifying using partitioned tablespaces, ensure that each job operates only on data from a single partition. If data from multiple partitions can be accessed in concurrent jobs, timeout and deadlock problems might occur. Refer to Chapter 3, "Data Definition Guidelines," for DDL recommendations for increasing concurrency.

Also note that concurrency problems can still occur. When data from one subset physically coexists with data from another subset, lockout and timeout can take place for two reasons. One, DB2 locks at the page level. If data is stratified at any level other than the tablespace partition level, data from one subset can coexist on the same tablespace page as data from another subset.

Two, if an index (other than a partitioning index) is available, data from different subsets almost assuredly exists on the same index subpage. You can reduce this possibility by specifying a high subpage in the index DDL. (Of course, Type 1 indexes are the only type of index that can use subpages, but you should always favor Type 2 indexes over Type 1 indexes.) An alternative solution is to drop the index before processing and rebuild the index when finished. But this approach is not always feasible because a dropped index cannot be used (which may make other processes inefficient), and rebuilding a large index can be time consuming.

Using the second method, you can develop a single program. DB2 determines whether parallelism is of benefit. If you specify `DEGREE(ANY)`, DB2 formulates the appropriate degree of parallelism for each query in the program. The primary benefits accrued from allowing DB2 to specify parallelism are as follow:

- The avoidance of code duplication. Only one program is required. DB2 itself handles the parallel query execution.
- The ability of DB2 to determine the appropriate number of parallel engines per query (not per program).
- The ability of DB2 to change the degree of parallelism on the fly. If the resources are not available to process parallel queries, DB2 can automatically "turn off" parallelism at runtime.
- The ability of DB2 to enable Sysplex parallelism. With data sharing, when capacity requirements increase you can add extra engines. The cost to add additional engines is minimal and DB2 will automatically take advantage of additional engines.
- Finally, if the nature of the data changes such that a change to the degree of parallelism is warranted, all that is required is a new bind. DB2 automatically formulates the degree of parallelism at bind time.

However, potential problems arise when you're using query parallelism instead of program cloning:

- DB2 controls the number of parallel engines. The developer can exert no control. When program cloning is used, the number of parallel jobs is fixed and unchanging.
- One program can contain multiple queries, each with a different degree. Although this can be considered a benefit, it can also be confusing to novice programmers.
- DB2 I/O, CPU, and Sysplex parallelism are for read-only SQL. Updates, inserts, and deletes cannot be performed in parallel yet.
- Data stratification can be achieved only by tablespace partitioning. When a non-partitioned table is being joined to a table in a partitioned tablespace, DB2 may choose to automatically "partition" the non-partitioned table to enable more effective parallel processing.
- DB2 can "turn off" parallelism at runtime. Once again, though, this can be considered a benefit because DB2 is smart enough to disengage parallelism because of an overexerted system.

Both methods of achieving parallelism are viable as of DB2 V3 (for CPU parallelism, V4 is required; for Sysplex parallelism V5 is required). Whenever possible, favor DB2 parallelism over program cloning because it represents IBM's stated direction for achieving parallelism. Program cloning, although still useful for some applications, will become an obsolete method of data stratification as IBM improves DB2's parallel capabilities.

Use LOCK TABLE with Caution

As a general rule, use the `LOCK TABLE` command with caution. Discuss the implications of this command with your DBA staff before deciding to use it.

Issuing a `LOCK TABLE` statement locks all tables in the tablespace containing the table specified. It holds all locks until `COMMIT` or `DEALLOCATION`. This statement reduces concurrent access to all tables in the tablespace affected by the command.

The preceding rule notwithstanding, `LOCK TABLE` can significantly decrease an application program's processing time. If a significant number of page locks are taken during program execution, the addition of `LOCK TABLE` eliminates page locks, replacing them with table (or tablespace) locks. It thereby enhances performance by eliminating the overhead associated with page locks.

Balance the issuing of the `LOCK TABLE` command with the need for concurrent data access, the locking strategies in the DDL of the tablespaces, and the plans being run.

NOTE

You can use `LOCK TABLE` to explicitly limit concurrent access. For example, issuing a `LOCK TABLE` statement in a batch program can prevent online transactions from entering data before the batch cycle has completed.

Parameterize Lock Strategies

If a batch window exists wherein concurrent access is not required, but a high degree of concurrency is required after the batch window, consider coding batch programs with dynamic lock-switching capabilities. For example, if the batch window extends from 2:00 a.m. to 6:00 a.m., and a batch DB2 update program must run during that time, make the locking parameter-driven or system-clock-driven.

The program can read the system clock and determine whether it can complete before online processing begins at 6:00 a.m. This decision should be based on the average elapsed time required for the program to execute. If possible, the program should issue the `LOCK TABLE` statement. If this is not possible, the program should use the normal locking strategy as assigned by the tablespace DDL. A flexible locking strategy increases performance and reduces the program's impact on the online world.

An alternative method is to let the program accept the `TABLE` or `NORMAL` value as a parameter. If `TABLE` is specified as a parameter, the program issues `LOCK TABLE` statements. Otherwise, normal locking ensues. If `NORMAL` is specified, normal locking requires manual intervention and is not as easily implemented as the system time method.

Periodically `COMMIT` Work in Batch Update Programs

Favor issuing `COMMIT`s in all medium to large batch update programs. A `COMMIT` externalizes all updates that occurred in the program since the beginning of the program or the last `COMMIT`.

> **NOTE**
>
> `COMMIT` does not flush data from the DB2 bufferpool and physically apply the data to the table. It does, however, ensure that all modifications have been physically applied to the DB2 log, thereby ensuring data integrity and recoverability.

Any batch program that issues more than 500 updates is a candidate for `COMMIT` processing. Note that the number of updates issued by a program is not the most critical factor in determining whether `COMMIT`s will be useful. The most important factor is the amount of elapsed time required for the program to complete. The greater the amount of time needed, the more you should consider using `COMMIT`s (to reduce rollback time and reprocessing time in the event of program failure). You can safely assume, however, that the elapsed time increases as the number of updates increases.

Issuing `COMMIT`s in an application program is important for three reasons. First, if the program fails, all the updates are backed out to the last `COMMIT` point. This process could take twice the time it took to perform the updates in the first place if you are near the end of a program without `COMMIT`s that performs hundreds of updates.

Second, if you resubmit a failing program that issues no `COMMIT`s, the program redoes work unnecessarily.

Third, programs bound using the repeatable read page locking strategy or the `RELEASE(COMMIT)` tablespace locking strategy hold their respective page and tablespace locks until a `COMMIT` is issued. If no `COMMIT`s are issued during the program, locks are never released, thereby negatively affecting concurrent access.

Given these considerations for `COMMIT` processing, the following situations should compel you to code `COMMIT` logic in your batch programs:

- The update program must run in a small batch processing window.
- Concurrent batch or online access must occur during the time the batch update program is running.

NOTE

If the concurrent batch or online access uses ISOLATION(UR), COMMIT processing is irrelevant. However, most processing requires accurate data and as such does not use ISOLATION(UR).

If the preceding does not describe your situation, consider avoiding COMMITs. When update programs without COMMITs fail, you can generally restart them from the beginning because database changes have not been committed. Additionally, COMMITs require resources. By reducing or eliminating COMMITs, you can enhance performance (albeit at the expense of concurrency due to additional locks being held for a greater duration). Before you decide to avoid COMMIT processing, remember that all cataloged sequential files must be deleted, any updated VSAM files must be restored, and any IMS updates must be backed out before restarting the failing program. If the outlined situations change, you might need to retrofit your batch programs with COMMIT processing—a potentially painful process.

I recommend that you plan to issue COMMITs in every batch program. You can structure the logic so that the COMMIT processing is contingent on a parameter passed to the program. This approach enables an analyst to turn off COMMIT processing but ensures that all batch programs are prepared if COMMIT processing is required in the future.

Use Elapsed Time to Schedule COMMITs

Base the frequency of COMMITs on the information in Table 5.5 or on the elapsed time since the last COMMIT. Doing so provides a more consistent COMMIT frequency. If you insist on basing COMMIT processing on the number of rows processed instead of the elapsed time, estimate the elapsed time required to process a given number of rows and then correlate this time to Table 5.5 to determine the optimal COMMIT frequency.

Table 5.5. Recommendations for COMMIT frequency.

Application Requirement	COMMIT *Recommendations*
No concurrent access required and unlimited time for reprocessing in the event of an abend	Code program for COMMITs, but consider processing without COMMITs using a parameter)
No concurrency required but limited reprocessing time available	COMMIT in batch approximately every 15 minutes
Limited batch concurrency required; no concurrent online activity	COMMIT in batch every 1 to 5 minutes (more frequently to increase concurrency)
Online concurrency required	COMMIT in batch every 5 to 15 seconds

Choose Useful Units of Work

A *unit of work* is a portion of processing that achieves data integrity, is logically complete, and creates a point of recovery. Units of work are defined by the scope of the COMMITs issued by your program. (All data modification that occurs between COMMITs is considered to be in a unit of work.) Use care in choosing units of work for programs that issue INSERT, UPDATE, or DELETE statements.

Choosing a unit of work that provides data integrity is of paramount importance for programs that issue COMMITs. For example, consider an application program that modifies the project start and end dates in tables DSN8510.PROJACT and DSN8510.EMPPROJACT. The start and end DSN8510.PROJACT columns are

ACSTDATE	Estimated start date for the activity recorded in this row of the project activity table
ACENDATE	Estimated end date for the activity recorded in this row of the project activity table

The columns for DSN8510.EMPPROJACT are

EMSTDATE	Estimated start date when the employee will begin work on the activity recorded in this row of the employee project
EMENDATE	Estimated end date when the employee will have completed the activity recorded in this row of the employee project activity

The start and end dates in these two tables are logically related. A given activity for a project begins on a specified date and ends on a specified date. A given employee is assigned to work on each activity and is assigned also a start date and an end date for the activity.

Many employees can work on a single activity, but each employee can start and end his or her involvement with that activity at different times. The only stipulation is that the employees must begin and end their involvement within the start and end dates for that activity. Therein lies the relationship that ties these four columns together.

The unit of work for the program should be composed of the modifications to both tables. In other words, the program should not commit the changes to one table without committing the changes to the other table at the same time. If it does commit the changes to one but not the other, the implicit relationship between the dates in the two tables can be destroyed.

Consider the following situation. A project has a start date of 1997-12-01 and an end date of 1998-03-31. This information is recorded in the DSN8510.PROJACT table. Employees are assigned to work on activities in this project with start and end dates in the stated range. These dates are recorded in the DSN8510.EMPPROJACT table.

Later, you must modify the end date of the project to 1998-01-31. Consider the status of the data if the program updates the end date in the DSN8510.PROJACT table, commits the changes, and then abends. The data in the DSN8510.EMPPROJACT table has not been updated, so the end dates are not synchronized. An employee can still be assigned an activity with the old end date. For this reason, you should be sure to group related updates in the same unit of work.

Make Programs Restartable

In time-critical applications, DB2 batch programs that modify table data should be restartable if a system error occurs. To make a batch program restartable, you first create a DB2 table to control the checkpoint and restart processing for all DB2 update programs. A checkpoint is data written by an application program during its execution that identifies the status and extent of processing. This checkpoint is usually accomplished by storing the primary key of the table row being processed. The program must update the primary key as it processes before each COMMIT point. During restart processing, the primary key information is read, enabling the program to continue from where it left off.

The following DDL illustrates a DB2 table (and an associated index) that you can be used to support checkpoint and restart processing:

```
CREATE TABLE CHKPT_RSTRT
    (PROGRAM_NAME        CHAR(8)         NOT NULL,
     ITERATION           CHAR(4)         NOT NULL,
     COMMIT_FREQUENCY    SMALLINT        NOT NULL,
     NO_OF_COMMITS       SMALLINT        NOT NULL WITH DEFAULT,
     CHECKPOINT_TIME     TIMESTAMP       NOT NULL WITH DEFAULT,
     CHECKPOINT_AREA     CHAR(254)       NOT NULL WITH DEFAULT.
     PRIMARY KEY (PROGRAM_NAME, ITERATION)
    )
IN DATABASE.TBSPACE
;
CREATE UNIQUE INDEX XCHKPRST
    (PROGRAM_NAME, ITERATION)
     CLUSTER
     other parameters
;
```

When a batch program is restarted after an abend, it can continue where it left off if it follows certain steps. This is true because a checkpoint row was written indicating the last committed update, the time that the employee was processed, and the key of the processed employee table (ACTNO).

The following steps show you the coding necessary to make a program restartable:

1. Declare two cursors to SELECT rows to be updated in the PROJACT table. Code an ORDER BY for the columns of the unique index (PROJNO, ACTNO, and ACSTDATE). The first cursor should select the rows you want. It is used the first time the request is processed. For example,

```
    EXEC SQL DECLARE CSR1
        SELECT    PROJNO, ACTNO, ACSTDATE,
                  ACSTAFF, ACENDATE
```

```
       FROM      PROJACT
       ORDER BY PROJNO, ACTNO, ACSTDATE
   END-EXEC.
```

This statement reflects the needs of your application. The second cursor is for use after issuing COMMITs and for restart processing. It must reposition the cursor at the row following the last row processed. You can reposition the cursor by using WHERE clauses that reflect the ORDER BY on the primary key (or the unique column combination). For example,

```
   EXEC SQL DECLARE CSR2
       SELECT    PROJNO, ACTNO, ACSTDATE,
                 ACSTAFF, ACENDATE
       FROM      PROJACT
       WHERE     ((PROJNO = :CHKPT-PROJNO
       AND         ACTNO = :CHKPT-ACTNO
       AND         ACSTDATE > :CHKPT-ACSTDATE)
       OR         (PROJNO = :CHKPT-PROJNO
       AND         ACTNO > :CHKPT-ACTNO)
       OR         (PROJNO > :CHKPT-PROJNO))
       AND       PROJNO >= :CHKPT-PROJNO
       ORDER BY PROJNO, ACTNO, ACSTDATE
   END-EXEC.
```

This cursor begins processing at a point other than the beginning of the ORDER BY list. Although, technically you can use only the second cursor by coding low values for the host variables the first time through, doing so is not recommended. The first cursor usually provides better performance than the second, especially when the second cursor is artificially constrained by bogus host variable values. However, if you can determine (using EXPLAIN or other performance monitoring techniques) that the first cursor provides no appreciable performance gain over the second, use only one cursor.

2. SELECT the row from the CHKPT-RESTRT table for the program and iteration being processed. You can hard-code the program name into the program. Or, if the program can run parallel with itself, it should be able to accept as parameter-driven input an iteration token, used for identifying a particular batch run of the program.
3. If it is the first time through and CHECKPOINT_AREA contains data, the program is restarted. Move the appropriate values from the CHECKPOINT_AREA to the host variables used in the second cursor and OPEN it. If it is the first time through and the program is not restarted, OPEN the first PROJACT cursor.
4. FETCH a row from the opened cursor.
5. If the FETCH is successful, increment a WORKING-STORAGE variable that counts successful fetches.
6. Perform the UPDATE for the PROJACT row that was fetched.
7. If the fetch counter is equal to COMMIT_FREQUENCY, perform a commit paragraph. This paragraph should increment and update NO_OF_COMMITS and the CHECKPOINT_AREA column with the PROJNO, ACTNO, and ACSTDATE of the PROJACT row retrieved, and set CHECKPOINT_TIME to the current timestamp. It should then issue a COMMIT and reset the fetch counter to zero.

8. After a COMMIT, cursors are closed unless you specified the WITH HOLD option. If the WITH HOLD option is not used, the cursor must change after the first COMMIT is executed (unless only the second cursor shown previously is used). Remember, the first time through, the program can use the C1 cursor above; subsequently, it should always use C2.
9. When update processing is complete, reset the values of the columns in the CHKPT_RSTRT table to their original default values.

   If the CHKPT_RSTRT row for the program is reread after each COMMIT, you can modify the COMMIT_FREQUENCY column on the fly. If you determine that too few or too many checkpoints have been taken, based on the state of the data and the time elapsed and remaining, he or she can update the COMMIT_FREQUENCY (using QMF, SPUFI, or some other means) for that program only. Doing so dynamically changes the frequency at which the program COMMITs.

   Incurring the extra read usually causes little performance degradation because the page containing the row usually remains in the bufferpool because of its frequent access rate.

Following these nine steps enables you to restart your programs after a program failure. During processing, the CHKPT_RSTRT table is continually updated with current processing information. If the program abends, all updates—including updates to the CHKPT_RSTRT table—are rolled back to the last successful checkpoint. This way, the CHKPT_RSTRT table is synchronized with the updates made to the table. You can then restart the update program after you determine and correct the cause of the abend.

On restart, the CHKPT_RSTRT table is read, and the CHECKPOINT_AREA information is placed into a cursor that repositions the program to the data where the last update occurred.

Additional Notes on Restartability

If a restartable program uses the WITH HOLD option to prohibit cursor closing at COMMIT time, it can avoid the need to reposition the cursor constantly, thereby enabling more efficient processing. To be restartable, however, the program still requires a repositioning cursor so that it can bypass the work already completed.

When you specify the WITH HOLD option, the repositioning cursor is used only when the program is restarted, not during normal processing. Additional code and parameters are required to signal the program when to use the repositioning cursors.

Restartable programs using sequential input files can reposition the input files using one of two methods. The first way is to count the records read and place the counter in the CHKPT_RSTRT table. On restart, the table is read and multiple reads are issued (number of reads equals READ_COUNTER). Alternatively, for input files sorted by the checkpoint key, the program can use the information in the CHECKPOINT_AREA to read to the appropriate record.

Restartable programs writing sequential output files must handle each output file separately. Most sequential output files can have their disposition modified to MOD in the JCL, allowing the restarted program to continue writing to them. For the following types of output files, however, you must delete or modify output file records before restarting:

- Headers for report files with control break processing
- Output files with different record types
- Any output file requiring specialized application processing

Hold Cursors Rather Than Reposition

You also can use the concept of cursor repositioning for programs not coded to be restartable. If COMMITs are coded in a program that updates data using cursors, you have two options for repositioning cursors. You can use the WITH HOLD option of the cursor, or you can code two cursors, an initial cursor and a repositioning cursor, as shown in the previous example.

The best solution is to code the WITH HOLD clause for each cursor that needs to be accessed after a COMMIT. WITH HOLD prohibits the closing of the cursor by the COMMIT statement and maintains the position of the cursor. This option is available only with DB2 V2.3 or later.

Online Programming Guidelines

Utilize the following techniques to create efficient online DB2 applications.

Limit the Number of Pages Retrieved

To achieve subsecond transaction response time, try to limit the number of pages retrieved or modified. When subsecond response time is not required, the number of pages to be accessed can be increased until the service level agreement is not met. In general, try to avoid having an impact on more than 100 pages in online transactions.

Limit Online Joins

When you're joining rows, try to limit the number of rows returned by the transaction. There is a practical limit to the amount of data that a user can assimilate while sitting in front of a computer screen. Whenever possible, set a low limit on the number of rows returned (for example, approximately 125 rows, or 5 screens of data). For data intensive applications, adjust this total, as required, with the understanding that performance may suffer as additional data is accessed and returned to the screen.

Limit Online Sorts

To reduce online data sorting, try to avoid using GROUP BY, ORDER BY, DISTINCT, and UNION unless appropriate indexes are available.

Issue COMMITs Before Displaying

Always issue commits (CICS SYNCPOINT, TSO COMMIT, or IMS CHKP) before sending information to a terminal.

Modularize Transactions

When possible, design separate transactions for selecting, updating, inserting, and deleting rows. This way, you can minimize page locking and maximize modular program design.

Minimize Cascading DELETEs

Avoid online deletion of parent table rows involved in referential constraints specifying the CASCADE delete rule. When a row in the parent table is deleted, multiple deletes in dependent tables can occur. This result degrades online performance.

Be Aware of Overactive Data Areas

An *overactive* data area is a portion of a table or index that is accessed and updated considerably more than other tables (or portions thereof) in the online application. Be aware of overactive data areas.

Overactive data areas are characterized by the following features: a relatively small number of pages (usually 10 pages or fewer, and sometimes only 1 row), and a large volume of retrievals and updates (usually busy more than half the time that the online application is active).

Overactive data areas can be caused, for example, by using a table with one row (or a small number of rows) to assign sequential numbers for columns in other tables or files, or by using a table to store counters, totals, or averages of values stored in other tables or files. You also can cause overactive data areas when you use tables to implement domains that are volatile or heavily accessed by the online system. These situations cause many different programs to access and modify a small amount of data over and over. An inordinate number of resource unavailable and timeout abends can be caused by overactive data areas unless they are monitored and maintained.

Reduce the impact of overactive data areas by designing transactions with the following characteristics:

- Issue OPEN, FETCH, UPDATE, and CLOSE cursor statements (hereafter referred to as *update sequences*) as close to each other as possible.
- Invoke update sequences as rapidly as possible in the transaction; in other words, do not place unrelated operations in the series of instructions that update the overactive data area.
- Code as few intervening instructions as possible between the OPEN, FETCH, and CLOSE statements.

- Place the update sequence as close to the transaction commit point as possible (that is, near the end of the transaction code).
- Isolate the active range to a single partition (or several partitions). Assign the partitions to a dedicated buffer pool (perhaps with a related hiperspace) and to a device and controller that has excess capacity during peak periods.
- Use DDL to reduce the impact of overactive data areas and increase concurrent access. You can do so in three ways: for each table containing overactive data areas, you can convert Type 1 indexes to Type 2, increase the number of subpages for the Type 1 indexes on the tables, increase free space on the tablespace and indexes for the tables, and increase the `MAXROWS` tablespace parameter (or add a large column to the end of the row for each table thus reducing the number of rows per page).

Use TIMESTAMP for Sequencing

For columns, consider using `TIMESTAMP` data types instead of sequentially assigned numbers. You can generate timestamps automatically using the `CURRENT TIMESTAMP` special register (or the `NOT NULL WITH DEFAULT` option). A timestamp column has the same basic functionality as a sequentially assigned number, without the requirement of designing a table to assign sequential numbers. Remember, a table with a sequencing column can cause an overactive data area.

A column defined with the `TIMESTAMP` data type is marked by the date and time (down to the microsecond) that the row was inserted or updated. These numbers are serial unless updates occur across multiple time zones. Although duplicate timestamps can be generated if two transactions are entered at the same microsecond, this circumstance is rare. You can eliminate this possibility by coding a unique index on the column and checking for a `-803 SQLCODE` (duplicate index entry).

The only other drawback is the size of the timestamp data type. Although physically stored as only 10 bytes, the timestamp data is presented to the user as a 26-byte field. If users must remember the key, a timestamp usually does not suffice.

A common workaround for numbers that must be random is to use the microsecond portion of the timestamp as a random number generator to create keys automatically, without the need for a table to assign them. Note, though, that these numbers will not be sequenced by order of input.

Do Not INSERT into Empty Tables

Avoid inserting rows into empty tables in an online environment. Doing so causes multiple I/Os when you're updating indexes and causes index page splits. If you must insert rows into an empty table, consider one of the following options. You can format the table by prefilling it with index keys that can be updated online instead of inserted to. This way, you can reduce I/O and eliminate index page splitting because the index is not updated.

Another option is to partition the table so that inserts are grouped into separate partitions. This method does not reduce I/O, but it can limit page splitting because the index updates are spread across multiple index data sets instead of confined to just one.

Increase Concurrent Online Access

Limit deadlock and timeout situations by coding applications to increase their concurrency. One option is to code all transactions to access tables in the same order. For example, do not sequentially access departments in alphabetic order by DEPTNAME in one transaction, from highest to lowest DEPTNO in another, and from lowest to highest DEPTNO in yet another. Try to limit the sequential access to a table to a single method.

Another option is to update and delete using the WHERE CURRENT OF cursor option instead of using independent UPDATE and DELETE statements. A third option for increasing online throughput is to plan batch activity in online tables during inactive or off-peak periods.

Consider Saving Data Modification Statements Until the End of the Program

You can write an application program so that all modifications occur at the end of each unit of work instead of spreading them throughout the program. Because modifications do not actually occur until the end of the unit of work, the placement of the actual SQL modification statements is of no consequence to the eventual results of the program. If you place inserts, updates, and deletes at the end of the unit of work, the duration of locks held decreases. This technique can have a significant positive impact on concurrency and application performance.

Use OPTIMIZE FOR 1 ROW to Disable List Prefetch

Turning off list prefetch for online applications that display data on a page-by-page basis is often desirable. When you use list prefetch, DB2 acquires a list of RIDs from matching index entries, sorts the RIDs, and then accesses data pages using the RID list. The overhead associated with list prefetch usually causes performance degradation in an online, paging environment. OPTIMIZE FOR 1 ROW disables list prefetch and enhances performance.

Implement a Repositioning Cursor for Online Browsing

Use repositioning techniques, similar to those discussed for repositioning batch cursors, to permit online browsing and scrolling of retrieved rows by a primary key. Implement this cursor to reposition using a single column key:

```
EXEC SQL
    DECLARE SCROLL0 FOR
        SELECT    PROJNO, PROJNAME, MAJPROJ
        FROM      PROJ
        WHERE     PROJNO > :LAST-PROJNO
        ORDER BY PROJNO
END-EXEC.
```

You have two options for repositioning cursors when browsing data online. Both are efficient if indexes appear on columns in the predicates. Test both in your critical online applications to determine which performs better.

The first uses predicates tied together with AND:

```
EXEC SQL
    DECLARE SCROLL1 FOR
        SELECT   PROJNO, ACTNO, ACSTDATE,
                 ACSTAFF, ACENDATE
        FROM     PROJACT
        WHERE    (PROJNO = :LAST-PROJNO
        AND       ACTNO = :LAST-ACTNO
        AND       ACSTDATE > :LAST-ACSTDATE)
        OR       (PROJNO = :LAST-PROJNO
        AND       ACTNO > :LAST-ACTNO)
        OR       (PROJNO > :LAST-PROJNO)
        ORDER BY PROJNO, ACTNO, ACSTDATE
END-EXEC.
```

The second uses predicates tied together with OR:

```
EXEC SQL
    DECLARE SCROLL2 FOR
        SELECT    PROJNO, ACTNO, ACSTDATE,
                  ACSTAFF, ACENDATE
        ROM      PROJACT
        WHERE     (PROJNO >= :LAST-PROJNO)
        AND NOT   (PROJNO = :LAST-PROJNO AND ACTNO < :LAST-ACTNO)
        AND NOT   (PROJNO = :LAST-PROJNO AND ACTNO = :LAST-ACTNO
        AND        ACSTDATE <= :LAST-ACSTDATE)
        ORDER BY  PROJNO, ACTNO, ACSTDATE
END-EXEC.
```

The rows being browsed must have a primary key or unique index that can be used to control the scrolling and repositioning of the cursors. Otherwise, rows might be eliminated because the cursors cannot identify the last row accessed and displayed. If all occurrences of a set of columns are not displayed on a single screen, and more than one row has the same values, rows are lost when the cursor is repositioned after the last value (a duplicate) on the previous screen.

Summary

In this chapter, you delved into the murky waters of application programming using DB2. You learned the basics of embedded SQL and how to use cursors. Further, you explored techniques for effective data access and modification in both batch and online environments. It seems that smooth-sailing is ahead for your DB2 application development efforts. But the calm is short-lived. An approaching storm of dynamic SQL threatens to disturb the waters. To handle this storm, turn the page to Chapter 6, "Dynamic SQL Programming."

6

Dynamic SQL Programming

In Chapter 5, "Using DB2 in an Application Program," you learned about embedding static SQL into application programs to access DB2 tables. As you may recall from Chapter 1, "The Magic Words," though, you can embed another type of SQL in an application program: dynamic SQL.

Static SQL is hard-coded, and only the values of host variables in predicates can change. Dynamic SQL is characterized by its capability to change columns, tables, and predicates during a program's execution. This flexibility requires different techniques for embedding dynamic SQL in application programs.

Before you delve into the details of these techniques, you should know up front that the flexibility of dynamic SQL does not come without a price. In general, dynamic SQL is less efficient than static SQL. Read on to find out why.

Dynamic SQL Performance

The performance of dynamic SQL is one of the most widely debated DB2 issues. Some shops avoid it, and most of the ones that allow it place strict controls on its use. Completely avoiding dynamic SQL is unwise, but placing controls on its use is prudent. As new and faster versions of DB2 are released, some restrictions on dynamic SQL use should be eliminated.

You can find some good reasons for prohibiting dynamic SQL. You should avoid dynamic SQL when the dynamic SQL statements are just a series of static SQL statements in disguise. Consider an application that needs two or three predicates for one SELECT statement that is otherwise unchanged. Coding three static SELECT statements is more efficient than coding one dynamic SELECT with a changeable predicate. The static SQL takes more time to code but less time to execute. Another reason for avoiding dynamic SQL is that it almost always requires more overhead to process than equivalent static SQL.

Dynamic SQL incurs overhead because the cost of the dynamic bind, or PREPARE, must be added to the processing time of all dynamic SQL programs. However, this overhead may not be quite as costly as many people think it is. Running some queries using SPUFI with the DB2 Performance Trace turned on produced results for the cost of a PREPARE as shown in Table 6.1 (all times shown in seconds).

Table 6.1. Testing the overhead of PREPARE.

Measurement	*Test #1*	*Test #2*	*Test #3*	*Test #4*
Elapsed Time	0.2436	0.5633	0.8477	0.9326
TCB Time	0.04520	0.09391	0.13073	0.19333

The SQL statements that were prepared for each of the four tests are described here:

> Test #1: A simple `SELECT` of one column from one table with two predicates
>
> Test #2: A join of two tables selecting two columns using two predicates
>
> Test #3: A join of two tables selecting four columns using three predicates
>
> Test #4: A three table join selecting all columns

Of course, the times you get will vary based on your environment, the type of dynamic SQL you use, and the complexity of the statement being prepared. Complex SQL with many joins, unions, and subqueries takes longer to `PREPARE` than simple queries. However, factors such as the number of columns returned or the size of the table being accessed have little or no effect on the performance of the dynamic bind.

Before proceeding with a dynamic SQL project, you should perform some tests like this at your shop to determine the potential impact. To obtain this type of information, you need to start the DB2 Performance Trace using the CPU Trace Header [`TDATA(CPU)`] and run DB2PM SQL Trace Reports (or its equivalent with another performance monitoring tool).

Overhead issues notwithstanding, there are valid performance reasons for favoring dynamic SQL. For example, dynamic SQL can enable better use of indexes, choosing different indexes for different SQL formulations. Properly coded, dynamic SQL can use the column distribution statistics stored in the DB2 catalog, whereas static SQL is limited in how it can use these statistics. Use of the distribution statistics can cause DB2 to choose different access paths for the same query when different values are supplied to its predicates.

Version 5

The `REOPT(VARS)` bind parameter is available as of DB2 V5 to enable static SQL to make better use of non-uniform distribution statistics. When dynamic reoptimization is activated, a dynamic bind similar to what is performed for dynamic SQL is performed. For more information on reoptimization of static SQL, see Chapter 7, "Program Preparation."

Version 5

Additionally, DB2 V5 introduces the `KEEPDYNAMIC` bind option to enhance the performance of dynamic SQL. When a plan or package is bound specifying `KEEPDYNAMIC(YES)`, the prepared statement is maintained across `COMMIT` points. Prior to V5, only cursors using the `WITH HOLD` option kept the prepared statement after a `COMMIT`.

Dynamic SQL usually provides the most efficient development techniques for applications with changeable requirements (for example, numerous screen-driven queries).

In addition, dynamic SQL generally reduces the number of SQL statements coded in your application program, thereby reducing the size of the plan and increasing the efficient use of system memory. If you have a compelling reason to use dynamic SQL, ensure that the reason is sound and complies with the considerations listed in the following section.

Dynamic SQL Guidelines

The following tips, tricks, and guidelines should be followed to ensure that dynamic SQL is used in an optimal manner in your shop.

Favor Static SQL

Static SQL might be more efficient than dynamic SQL because dynamic SQL requires the execution of the `PREPARE` statement during program execution. Static SQL is prepared (bound) before execution.

Static SQL is sufficient for the programming needs of 90 percent of the applications you develop. If static SQL does not provide enough flexibility for the design of changeable SQL statements, consider using dynamic SQL. In many cases, the perceived need for dynamic SQL is merely the need for a series of static SQL statements in disguise.

You also should consider using dynamic SQL when it will boost performance because of limitations on the DB2 optimizer's capability to determine the values of host variables (prior to the DB2 V5 dynamic reoptimization bind option). In all other situations, favor the use of static SQL.

Use the Appropriate Class of Dynamic SQL

After you decide to use dynamic SQL rather than static SQL, be sure to code the correct class of dynamic SQL. Do not favor one class of dynamic SQL over another based solely on the difficulty of coding. Consider both the efficiency of the program and the difficulty of maintenance, as well as the difficulty of coding a dynamic SQL program. Performance is often the most important criterion. If a dynamic SQL program does not perform adequately, you should convert it to either static SQL or another class of dynamic SQL.

Favor non-select dynamic SQL over `EXECUTE IMMEDIATE` because the former gives the programmer additional flexibility in preparing SQL statements, which usually results in a more efficient program. Also, favor varying-list dynamic SQL over fixed-list dynamic SQL because the first gives the programmer greater control over which columns are accessed. Additionally, varying-list dynamic SQL gives the DB2 optimizer the greatest amount of freedom in selecting an efficient access path (for example, a greater opportunity for index-only access).

When you use varying-list dynamic SQL, overhead is incurred as the program determines the type of SQL statement and uses the `SQLDA` to identify the columns and their data types. Weigh the cost of this overhead against the opportunities for a better access path when you decide between fixed-list and varying-list dynamic SQL.

Do Not Fear Dynamic SQL

Dynamic SQL provides the DB2 programmer with a rich and useful set of features. The belief that dynamic SQL always should be avoided in favor of static SQL is slowly but surely evaporating. Dynamic SQL becomes more efficient with each successive release of DB2, thereby enticing users who have been frustrated in their attempts to mold dynamic SQL into the sometimes rigid confines of static SQL.

If you design dynamic SQL programs with care and do not abuse SQL's inherent functionality, you can achieve great results. Follow all the guidelines in this chapter closely. See Part V, "DB2 Performance Tuning," for a discussion of tuning and resource governing for dynamic SQL applications.

By this guideline, I do not mean to imply that you should use dynamic SQL where it is not merited. Simply apply common sense when deciding between static and dynamic SQL for your DB2 applications. Remember, any rule with a "never" in it (such as "*never* use dynamic SQL") is *usually* unwise!

Avoid Dynamic SQL for Specific Statements

Not every SQL statement can be executed as dynamic SQL. Most of these types of SQL statements provide for the execution of dynamic SQL or row-at-a-time processing. The following SQL statements cannot be executed dynamically:

```
CLOSE
DECLARE
DESCRIBE
EXECUTE
EXECUTE IMMEDIATE
FETCH
INCLUDE
OPEN
PREPARE
WHENEVER
```

Use Parameter Markers Instead of Host Variables

Dynamic SQL statements cannot contain host variables. They must use instead a device called a *parameter marker*. A parameter marker can be thought of as a dynamic host variable.

Consider Dynamic SQL When Accessing Non-Uniform Data

If you're accessing a table in which the data is not evenly distributed, dynamic SQL may perform better than static SQL. Distribution statistics are stored in the DB2 Catalog in two tables: SYSIBM.SYSCOLDISTSTAT and SYSIBM.SYSCOLDIST.

By default, RUNSTATS stores the 10 values that appear most frequently in the first column of an index along with the percentage that each value occurs in the column. As of DB2 V5, the RUNSTATS utility provides options for which distribution statistics can be collected for any number of values (and for any number of columns). Version 5

In some cases, the optimizer uses this information only for dynamic SQL. Static SQL still assumes even distribution unless the pertinent predicates use hard-coded values instead of host variables or dynamic reoptimization was specified at bind time using the `REOPT(VARS)` parameter.

Use Bind-Time Authorization Checking

Version 4

Prior to DB2 V4, users of dynamic SQL programs required explicit authorization to the underlying tables accessed by the program being executed. For complex programs, the task of granting authority multiple types (`INSERT`, `UPDATE`, `DELETE`, `INSERT`) of security for multiple tables to multiple users is time consuming, error prone, and difficult to administer.

The `DYNAMICRULES` parameter of the `BIND` command provides flexibility of authorization checking for dynamic SQL programs. Specifying `DYNAMICRULES(BIND)` causes DB2 to check for authorization at `BIND` time using the authority of the binding agent. Just like static SQL programs, no additional runtime authorization checking is required.

Specifying `DYNAMICRULES(RUN)` causes dynamic SQL programs to check for authorization at runtime (just like pre-V4 dynamic programs).

Consider Caching Prepared Statements

Version 5

As of DB2 V5, prepared dynamic SQL statements can be cached in memory. This feature enables programs to avoid redundant optimization and its associated overhead. Dynamic SQL caching must be enabled by the system administrator, and is either on or off at the subsystem level.

When dynamic SQL caching is enabled, dynamic `SELECT`, `INSERT`, `UPDATE`, and `DELETE` statements are eligible. The first `PREPARE` statement creates the dynamic plan and stores it in the EDM pool. If a `PREPARE` is requested for the same SQL statement, DB2 can reuse the cached statement. DB2 performs a character-by-character comparison of the SQL statement, rejecting reuse if any differences are found between what is cached and what is being requested for execution. Cached statements can be shared among threads, plans, and packages.

In general, for systems with heavy dynamic SQL use or where dynamic SQL programs issue the same statement multiple times, dynamic SQL caching can improve performance by reducing the overhead of multiple `PREPARE`s. However, dynamic SQL caching requires additional memory to increase the size of the EDM pool and can cause performance degradation for dynamic SQL that does not meet the preceding requirements because of the following:

- A cost is associated with caching an SQL statement. (DB2 must spend time moving the dynamic plan to the EDM pool.)
- If the SQL statements do not match, a cost is associated with the comparison that DB2 performs.
- EDM pool contention can occur when caching is enabled for environments in which dynamic SQL is used heavily.

The bottom line is that each shop must determine whether dynamic SQL caching will be beneficial given its current and planned mix of static and dynamic SQL. At any rate, the DBA group must communicate whether dynamic SQL caching is enabled to assist application developers in their decisions to use dynamic or static SQL.

Encourage Parallelism

Use the `SET CURRENT DEGREE = "ANY"` statement within dynamic SQL programs to encourage the use of query I/O, CPU, and Sysplex parallelism. When DB2 uses multiple, parallel engines to access data, the result can be enhanced performance.

Before you blindly place this statement in all dynamic SQL programs, however, be sure to analyze your environment to ensure that adequate resources are available to support parallelism. For example, ensure that adequate buffer space is available for multiple concurrent read engines.

Use Dynamic SQL to Access Dynamic Data

Dynamic SQL can prove beneficial for access to very active tables that fluctuate between many rows and few rows between plan rebinding. If you cannot increase the frequency of plan rebinding, you can use dynamic SQL to optimize queries based on current `RUNSTATS`.

Use the QMFCI

Another reason to use dynamic SQL is to allow programs to take advantage of the capabilities of QMF using the QMF Command Interface (QMFCI). Dynamic SQL is invoked when you use QMF to access DB2 data. The functionality provided by the QMFCI includes left and right scrolling and data formatting. The addition of these capabilities can offset any performance degradation that dynamic SQL might cause.

Be Wary of Poorly Designed Dynamic SQL

Online transaction-based systems require well-designed SQL to execute with subsecond response time. If you use dynamic SQL, the system is less likely to have well-designed SQL. If a program can change the SQL on the fly, the control required for online systems is relinquished and performance can suffer.

Do Not Avoid Varying-List `SELECT`

Often, application developers do not take the time to design a dynamic SQL application properly if it requires variable `SELECT`s. Usually, a varying-list `SELECT` is needed for proper performance, but a fixed-list `SELECT` is used to avoid using the `SQLDA` and pointer variables. This use limits the access path possibilities available to the optimizer and can degrade performance.

Be Aware of Dynamic SQL Tuning Difficulties

Dynamic SQL is more difficult to tune because it changes with each program execution. Dynamic SQL cannot be traced using the DB2 Catalog tables (SYSDBRM, SYSSTMT, SYSPLANREF, and SYSPLAN) because the SQL statements are not hard-coded into the program and therefore are not in the application plan.

Use the RLF

Proper administration of the Resource Limit Facility (RLF) is needed to control DB2 resources when dynamic SQL is executed. Thresholds for CPU use are coded in the RLF on an application-by-application basis. When the RLF threshold is reached, the application program does not ABEND. An SQL error code is issued when any statement exceeds the predetermined CPU usage. This environment requires additional support from a DBA standpoint for RLF administration and maintenance, as well as additional work from an application development standpoint for enhancing error-handling procedures.

Use Dynamic SQL for Tailoring Access

If you need to tailor access to DB2 tables based on user input from a screen or pick list, using dynamic SQL is the most efficient way to build your system. If you use static SQL, all possible rows must be returned, and the program must skip those not requested. This method incurs additional I/O and usually is less efficient than the corresponding dynamic SQL programs.

Consider the following: What if, for a certain query, 20 predicates are possible? The user of the program is permitted to choose up to 6 of these predicates for any given request. How many different static SQL statements do you need to code to satisfy these specifications?

First, determine the number of different ways that you can choose 6 predicates out of 20. To do so, you need to use combinatorial coefficients. So, if n is the number of different ways, then

```
n = (20 x 19 x 18 x 17 x 16 x 15) / (6 x 5 x 4 x 3 x 2 x 1)
n = (27,907,200) / (720)
n = 38,760
```

You get 38,760 separate static SELECTs, which is quite a large number, but it is still not sufficient to satisfy the request! The total number of different ways to choose 6 predicates out of 20 is 38,760 if the ordering of the predicates does not matter (which, for all intents and purposes, it does not). However, because the specifications clearly state that the user can choose *up to* 6, you have to modify the number. You therefore have to add in the following:

- The number of different ways of choosing 5 predicates out of 20
- The number of different ways of choosing 4 predicates out of 20
- The number of different ways of choosing 3 predicates out of 20
- The number of different ways of choosing 2 predicates out of 20
- The number of different ways of choosing 1 predicate out of 20

You can calculate this number as follows:

Ways to Choose 6 Predicates Out of 20

```
(20 x 19 x 18 x 17 x 16 x 15) / (6 x 5 x 4 x 3 x 2 x 1) = 38,760
```

Ways to Choose 5 Predicates Out of 20

```
(20 x 19 x 18 x 17 x 16) / (5 x 4 x 3 x 2 x 1) = 15,504
```

Ways to Choose 4 Predicates Out of 20

```
(20 x 19 x 18 x 17) / (4 x 3 x 2 x 1) = 4,845
```

Ways to Choose 3 Predicates Out of 20

```
(20 x 19 x 18) / (3 x 2 x 1) = 1,140
```

Ways to Choose 2 Predicates Out of 20

```
(20 x 19) / (2 x 1) = 190
```

Ways to Choose 1 Predicate Out of 20

```
20 / 1 = 20
```

Total Ways to Choose Up to 6 Predicates Out of 20

```
38,760 + 15,504 + 4,845 + 1,140 + 190 + 20 = 60,459
```

The grand total number of static SQL statements that must be coded comes actually to 60,459. In such a situation, in which over 60,000 SQL statements must be coded if static SQL must be used, you have one of two options:

- You can code for 40 days and 40 nights hoping to write 60,459 SQL statements successfully.
- You can compromise on the design and limit the users' flexibility.

Of course, the appropriate solution is to abandon static SQL and use dynamic SQL in this situation.

Use Dynamic SQL for Flexibility

Dynamic SQL programs sometimes respond more rapidly to business rules that change frequently. Because dynamic SQL is formulated as the program runs, the flexibility is greater than with static SQL programs. Users can react more quickly to changing business conditions by changing their selection criteria.

Avoid Dynamic SQL for Active Applications

Do not use dynamic SQL in systems with many users. The DBD (an internal DB2 control structure) is locked during the dynamic bind, and locks are taken on the DB2 Catalog. Both situations can cause related and unrelated applications to experience timeout and lockout problems.

Reasons You Should Know Dynamic SQL

You should understand what dynamic SQL is and what it can do for you for many reasons. As IBM improves the efficiency and functionality of dynamic SQL, more applications will use dynamic SQL. A working knowledge of dynamic SQL is necessary if you want to use DB2 fully and understand all its applications and utility programs. This section should make abundantly clear the fact that dynamic SQL is here to stay.

Dynamic SQL makes optimal use of the distribution statistics accumulated by `RUNSTATS`. Because the values are available when the optimizer determines the access path, it can arrive at a better solution for accessing the data. Static SQL, on the other hand, cannot use these statistics unless all predicate values are hard-coded or `REOPT(VARS)` is specified.

Distributed queries executed at the remote site using DB2 DUW private protocol use dynamic SQL. Some current distributed applications systems are based on this requirement.

QMF, `SPUFI`, and many other DB2 add-on tools for table editing and querying use dynamic SQL. Also, many fourth-generation language interfaces to DB2 support only dynamic SQL. Although the users of these tools are not required to know dynamic SQL, understanding its capabilities and drawbacks can help users develop efficient data access requests.

Using dynamic SQL is the only way to change SQL criteria such as complete predicates, columns in the `SELECT` list, and table names during the execution of a program. As long as application systems require these capabilities, dynamic SQL will be needed.

Dynamic SQL is optimized at runtime, and static SQL is optimized before execution. As a result, dynamic SQL may perform slower than static SQL. Sometimes, however, the additional overhead of runtime optimization is offset by the capability of dynamic SQL to change access path criteria based on current statistics during a program's execution.

The four classes of dynamic SQL are `EXECUTE IMMEDIATE`, non-`SELECT` dynamic SQL, fixed-list `SELECT`, and varying-list `SELECT`. The following sections cover each of these classes in depth.

EXECUTE IMMEDIATE

`EXECUTE IMMEDIATE` implicitly prepares and executes complete SQL statements coded in host variables.

Only a subset of SQL statements is available when you use the `EXECUTE IMMEDIATE` class of dynamic SQL. The most important SQL statement that is missing is the `SELECT` statement. Therefore, `EXECUTE IMMEDIATE` dynamic SQL cannot retrieve data from tables.

If you don't need to issue queries, you can write the SQL portion of your program in two steps. First, move the complete text for the statement to be executed into a host variable. Second, issue the `EXECUTE IMMEDIATE` statement specifying the host variable as an argument. The statement is prepared and executed automatically.

Listing 6.1 shows a simple use of EXECUTE IMMEDIATE that DELETEs rows from a table. The SQL statement is moved to a string variable and then executed.

Listing 6.1. A COBOL program using EXECUTE IMMEDIATE.

```
WORKING-STORAGE SECTION.
          .
          .
          .
     EXEC SQL
          INCLUDE SQLCA
     END-EXEC.
          .
          .
          .
     01   STRING-VARIABLE.
          49   STRING-VAR-LEN        PIC S9(4)    USAGE COMP.
          49   STRING-VAR-TXT        PIC X(100).
          .
          .
          .
PROCEDURE DIVISION.
          .
          .
          .
     MOVE +45 TO STRING-VAR-LEN.
     MOVE "DELETE FROM DSN8310.PROJ WHERE DEPTNO = 'A00'"
          TO STRING-VARIABLE.
     EXEC SQL
          EXECUTE IMMEDIATE :STRING-VARIABLE
     END-EXEC.
          .
          .
          .
```

You can replace the DELETE statement in Listing 6.1 with any of the following supported statements:

ALTER
COMMENT ON
COMMIT
CREATE
DELETE
DROP
EXPLAIN
GRANT
INSERT
LABEL ON
LOCK TABLE
REVOKE

```
ROLLBACK
SET
UPDATE
```

Despite the simplicity of the EXECUTE IMMEDIATE statement, it usually is not the best choice for application programs that issue dynamic SQL for two reasons. One, as I mentioned, EXECUTE IMMEDIATE does not support the SELECT statement. Two, performance can suffer when you use EXECUTE IMMEDIATE in a program that executes the same SQL statement many times.

After an EXECUTE IMMEDIATE is performed, the executable form of the SQL statement is destroyed. Thus, each time an EXECUTE IMMEDIATE statement is issued, it must be prepared again. This preparation is automatic and can involve a significant amount of overhead. A better choice is to code non-SELECT dynamic SQL using PREPARE and EXECUTE statements.

EXECUTE IMMEDIATE Guidelines

When developing dynamic SQL programs that use EXECUTE IMMEDIATE, observe the following guidelines.

Verify Dynamic SQL Syntax

Verify that the SQL statement to be executed with dynamic SQL uses the proper SQL syntax. This way, you can reduce the overhead incurred when improperly formatted SQL statements are rejected at execution time.

Use EXECUTE IMMEDIATE for Quick, One-Time Tasks

The EXECUTE IMMEDIATE class of dynamic SQL is useful for coding quick-and-dirty one-time processing or DBA utility-type programs. Consider using EXECUTE IMMEDIATE in the following types of programs:

- A DBA utility program that issues changeable GRANT and REVOKE statements
- A program that periodically generates DDL based on input parameters
- A parameter-driven modification program that corrects common data errors

Declare EXECUTE IMMEDIATE Host Variables Properly

The definition of the host variable used with EXECUTE IMMEDIATE must be in the correct format. Assembler, COBOL, and C programs must declare a varying-length string variable. FORTRAN programs must declare a fixed-list string variable. PL/I programs can declare either type of variable.

Non-SELECT Dynamic SQL

Non-SELECT dynamic SQL is the second of the four classes of dynamic SQL. You use it to explicitly prepare and execute SQL statements in an application program.

This class of dynamic SQL uses PREPARE and EXECUTE to issue SQL statements. As its name implies, non-SELECT dynamic SQL cannot issue the SELECT statement. Therefore, this class of dynamic SQL cannot query tables.

Listing 6.2 shows a simple use of non-SELECT dynamic SQL that DELETEs rows from a table.

Listing 6.2. A COBOL program using non-SELECT dynamic SQL.

```
WORKING-STORAGE SECTION.
         .
         .
         .
    EXEC SQL
        INCLUDE SQLCA
    END-EXEC.
         .
         .
         .
    01  STRING-VARIABLE.
        49  STRING-VAR-LEN       PIC S9(4)   USAGE COMP.
        49  STRING-VAR-TXT       PIC X(100).
         .
         .
         .
PROCEDURE DIVISION.
         .
         .
         .
    MOVE +45 TO STRING-VAR-LEN.
    MOVE "DELETE FROM DSN8310.PROJ WHERE DEPTNO = 'A00'"
         TO STRING-VARIABLE.
    EXEC SQL
        PREPARE STMT1 FROM :STRING-VARIABLE;
    END-EXEC.

    EXEC SQL
        EXECUTE STMT1;
    END-EXEC.
         .
         .
         .
```

As I noted before, you can replace the DELETE statement in this listing with any of the following supported statements:

```
ALTER
COMMENT ON
COMMIT
CREATE
DELETE
DROP
EXPLAIN
GRANT
INSERT
LABEL ON
LOCK TABLE
REVOKE
ROLLBACK
SET
UPDATE
```

Non-SELECT dynamic SQL can use a powerful feature of dynamic SQL called a *parameter marker*, which is a placeholder for host variables in a dynamic SQL statement. In Listing 6.3, a question mark is used as a parameter marker, replacing the 'A00' in the predicate. When the statement is executed, a value is moved to the host variable (:TVAL) and is coded as a parameter to the CURSOR with the USING clause. When this example is executed, the host variable value replaces the parameter marker.

Listing 6.3. Non-SELECT dynamic SQL using parameter markers.

```
WORKING-STORAGE SECTION.
        .
        .
        .
    EXEC SQL INCLUDE SQLCA END-EXEC.
        .
        .
        .
    01  STRING-VARIABLE.
        49  STRING-VAR-LEN        PIC S9(4)    USAGE COMP.
        49  STRING-VAR-TXT        PIC X(100).
        .
        .
        .
PROCEDURE DIVISION.
        .
        .
        .
    MOVE +40 TO STRING-VAR-LEN.
    MOVE "DELETE FROM DSN8310.PROJ WHERE DEPTNO = ?"
        TO STRING-VARIABLE.
```

```
EXEC SQL
    PREPARE STMT1 FROM :STRING-VARIABLE;
END-EXEC.
MOVE 'A00' TO TVAL.
EXEC SQL
    EXECUTE STMT1 USING :TVAL;
END-EXEC.
```

Non-SELECT dynamic SQL can provide huge performance benefits over EXECUTE IMMEDIATE. Consider a program that executes SQL statements based on an input file. A loop in the program reads a key value from the input file and issues a DELETE, INSERT, or UPDATE for the specified key. The EXECUTE IMMEDIATE class would incur the overhead of a PREPARE for each execution of each SQL statement inside the loop.

Using non-SELECT dynamic SQL, however, you can separate PREPARE and EXECUTE, isolating PREPARE outside the loop. The key value that provides the condition for the execution of the SQL statements can be substituted using a host variable and a parameter marker. If thousands of SQL statements must be executed, you can avoid having thousands of PREPAREs by using this technique. This method greatly reduces overhead and runtime and increases the efficient use of system resources.

Non-SELECT Dynamic SQL Guidelines

When developing non-SELECT dynamic SQL programs, heed the following guidelines.

Verify Dynamic SQL Syntax

Verify that the SQL statement to be executed with dynamic SQL uses the proper SQL syntax. This way, you can reduce the overhead incurred when improperly formatted SQL statements are rejected at execution time.

Use as Many Parameter Markers as Necessary

A prepared statement can contain more than one parameter marker. Use as many as necessary to ease development.

Issue Prepared Statements Multiple Times in a Unit of Work

After a statement is prepared, you can execute it many times in one unit of work without issuing another PREPARE. When you're using non-SELECT dynamic SQL, keep this guideline in mind and avoid the PREPARE verb as much as possible because of its significant overhead.

Know the Difference Between EXECUTE IMMEDIATE and Non-SELECT Dynamic SQL

You must understand the difference between EXECUTE IMMEDIATE and non-SELECT dynamic SQL before development. EXECUTE IMMEDIATE prepares the SQL statement each time it is executed, whereas non-SELECT dynamic SQL is prepared only when the program explicitly requests it. Using non-SELECT dynamic SQL can result in dramatic decreases in program execution time. For this reason, favor non-SELECT dynamic SQL over EXECUTE IMMEDIATE when issuing an SQL statement multiple times in a program loop.

Fixed-List SELECT

Until now, you have been unable to retrieve rows from DB2 tables using dynamic SQL. The next two classes of dynamic SQL provide this capability. The first and simplest is fixed-list SELECT.

You can use a fixed-list SELECT statement to explicitly prepare and execute SQL SELECT statements when the columns to be retrieved by the application program are known and unchanging. You need to do so to create the proper working-storage declaration for host variables in your program. If you do not know in advance the columns that will be accessed, you must use a varying-list SELECT statement.

Listing 6.4 shows a fixed-list SELECT statement. This example formulates a SELECT statement in the application program and moves it to a host variable. Next, a cursor is declared and the SELECT statement is prepared. The cursor then is opened and a loop to FETCH rows is invoked. When the program is finished, the cursor is closed.

Listing 6.4. Fixed-list SELECT dynamic SQL.

```
SQL to execute:
    SELECT   PROJNO, PROJNAME, RESPEMP
    FROM     DSN8310.PROJ
    WHERE    PROJNO   = ?
    AND      PRSTDATE = ?
    Move the "SQL to execute" to STRING-VARIABLE
    EXEC SQL DECLARE CSR2 CURSOR FOR FLSQL;
    EXEC SQL PREPARE FLSQL FROM :STRING-VARIABLE;
    EXEC SQL OPEN CSR2 USING :TVAL1, :TVAL2;
    Loop until no more rows to FETCH
    EXEC SQL
        FETCH CSR2 INTO :PROJNO, :PROJNAME, :RESPEMP;
    EXEC SQL CLOSE CSR2;
```

This example is simple because the SQL statement does not change. The benefit of dynamic SQL is its capability to modify the SQL statement. For example, you could move the SQL statement

```
SELECT  PROJNO, PROJNAME, RESPEMP
FROM    DSN8310.PROJ
WHERE   RESPEMP  = ?
AND     PRENDATE = ?
```

to the STRING-VARIABLE as shown in Listing 6.4 without modifying the OPEN or FETCH logic. Note that the second column of the predicate is different from the SQL statement as presented in Listing 6.4 (PRENDATE instead of PRSTDATE). Because both are the same data type (DATE), however, you can use TVAL2 for both if necessary. The host variables passed as parameters in the OPEN statement must have the same data type and length as the columns in the WHERE clause. If the data type and length of the columns in the WHERE clause change, the OPEN statement must be recoded with new USING parameters.

If parameter markers are not used in the SELECT statements, the markers could be eliminated and values could be substituted in the SQL statement to be executed. No parameters would be passed in the OPEN statement.

You can recode the OPEN statement also to pass parameters using an SQLDA (SQL Descriptor Area). The SQLDA would contain value descriptors and pointers to these values. You can recode the OPEN statement as follows:

```
EXEC-SQL
    OPEN CSR2 USING DESCRIPTOR :TVAL3;
END_EXEC.
```

DB2 uses the SQLDA to communicate information about dynamic SQL to an application program. The SQLDA sends information such as the type of the SQL statement being executed and the number and data type of columns being returned by a SELECT statement. It can be used by fixed-list SELECT and varying-list SELECT dynamic SQL. The following code illustrates the fields of the SQLDA:

```
*****************************************************************
***     SQLDA: SQL DESCRIPTOR AREA FOR COBOL II              ***
*****************************************************************
01   SQLDA.
     05 SQLDAID                     PIC X(8)    VALUE 'SQLDA'.
     05 SQLDABC                COMP PIC S9(8)   VALUE 13216.
     05 SQLN                   COMP PIC S9(4)   VALUE 750.
     05 SQLD                   COMP PIC S9(4)   VALUE 0.
     05 SQLVAR OCCURS 1 TO 750 TIMES DEPENDING ON SQLN.
        10 SQLTYPE             COMP PIC S9(4).
           88 SQLTYPE-FLOAT                     VALUE 480 481.
           88 SQLTYPE-DECIMAL                   VALUE 484 485.
           88 SQLTYPE-SMALLINT                  VALUE 500 501.
           88 SQLTYPE-INTEGER                   VALUE 496 497.
           88 SQLTYPE-DATE                      VALUE 384 385.
           88 SQLTYPE-TIME                      VALUE 388 389.
           88 SQLTYPE-TIMESTAMP                 VALUE 392 393.
           88 SQLTYPE-CHAR                      VALUE 452 453.
           88 SQLTYPE-VARCHAR                   VALUE 448 449.
           88 SQLTYPE-LONG-VARCHAR              VALUE 456 457.
           88 SQLTYPE-VAR-ONUL-CHAR             VALUE 460 461.
           88 SQLTYPE-GRAPHIC                   VALUE 468 469.
           88 SQLTYPE-VARGRAPH                  VALUE 464 465.
           88 SQLTYPE-LONG-VARGRAPH             VALUE 472 473.
```

```
        10 SQLLEN       COMP PIC S9(4).
        10 SQLDATA           POINTER.
        10 SQLIND            POINTER.
        10 SQLNAME.
           15 SQLNAMEL COMP PIC S9(4).
           15 SQLNAMEC COMP PIC X(30).
```

A description of the contents of the SQLDA fields is in the discussion of the next class of dynamic SQL, which relies heavily on the SQLDA.

Quite a bit of flexibility is offered by fixed-list SELECT dynamic SQL. Fixed-list dynamic SQL provides many of the same benefits for the SELECT statement as non-SELECT dynamic SQL provides for other SQL verbs. An SQL SELECT statement can be prepared once and then fetched from a loop. The columns to be retrieved must be static, however. If you need the additional flexibility of changing the columns to be accessed while executing, use a varying-list SELECT.

Fixed-List SELECT Guidelines

Follow the guidelines provided in this section when developing fixed-list SELECT dynamic SQL programs.

Use as Many Parameter Markers as Necessary

A prepared statement can contain more than one parameter marker. Use as many as necessary to ease development.

Issue Prepared Statements Multiple Times in a Unit of Work

After a statement is prepared, you can execute it many times in one unit of work without issuing another PREPARE.

Do Not Code the SQLDA in VS/COBOL

For fixed-list SELECT dynamic SQL, you cannot code the SQLDA in a VS/COBOL program.

Varying-List SELECT

Varying-list SELECT is the last class of dynamic SQL. You use it to explicitly prepare and execute SQL SELECT statements when you do not know in advance which columns will be retrieved by an application program.

Varying-list SELECT provides the most flexibility for dynamic SELECT statements. You can change tables, columns, and predicates on the fly.

WARNING

Because everything about the query can change during one invocation of the program, the number and type of host variables needed to store the retrieved rows cannot be known beforehand. The lack of knowledge regarding what is being retrieved adds considerable complexity to your application programs. (Note that FORTRAN and VS/COBOL programs cannot perform varying-list SELECT dynamic SQL statements.)

The SQLDA, as I mentioned, is the vehicle for communicating information about dynamic SQL between DB2 and the application program. It contains information about the type of SQL statement to be executed, the data type of each column accessed, and the address of each host variable needed to retrieve the columns. The SQLDA must be hard-coded into the COBOL II program's WORKING-STORAGE area, as shown here:

```
EXEC-SQL
   INCLUDE SQLDA
END_EXEC.
```

Table 6.2 defines each item in the SQLDA when it is used with varying-list SELECT.

Table 6.2. SQLDA data element definitions.

SQLDA *Field Name*	*Use in* DESCRIBE *or* PREPARE *Statement*
SQLDAID	Descriptive only; usually set to the literal "SQLDA" to aid in program debugging
SQLDABC	Length of the SQLDA
SQLN	Number of occurrences of SQLVAR available
SQLD	Number of occurrences of SQLVAR used
SQLTYPE	Data type and indicator of whether NULLs are allowed for the column
SQLLEN	External length of the column value
SQLDATA	Address of a host variable for a specific column
SQLIND	Address of NULL indicator variable for the preceding host variable
SQLNAME	Name or label of the column

The steps needed to code varying-list SELECT dynamic SQL to your application program vary according to the amount of information known about the SQL beforehand. Listing 6.5 details the steps necessary when you know that the statement to be executed is a SELECT statement.

The code differs from fixed-list SELECT in three ways: The PREPARE statement uses the SQLDA, the FETCH statement uses the SQLDA, and a step is added to store host variable addresses in the SQLDA.

Listing 6.5. Varying-list SELECT dynamic SQL.

```
SQL to execute: SELECT PROJNO, PROJNAME, RESPEMP
                FROM DSN8310.PROJ
                WHERE PROJNO = 'A00'
                AND PRSTDATE = '1988-10-10';
Move the "SQL to execute" to STRING-VARIABLE
EXEC SQL DECLARE CSR3 CURSOR FOR VLSQL;
EXEC SQL
    PREPARE VLSQL INTO SQLDA FROM :STRING-VARIABLE;
EXEC SQL OPEN CSR3;
Load storage addresses into the SQLDA
Loop until no more rows to FETCH
    EXEC SQL FETCH CSR3 USING DESCRIPTOR SQLDA;
EXEC SQL CLOSE CSR3;
```

When PREPARE is executed, DB2 returns information about the columns being returned by the SELECT statement. This information is in the SQLVAR group item of the SQLDA. Of particular interest is the SQLTYPE field. For each column to be returned, this field indicates the data type and whether NULLs are permitted. Note that in the SQLDA layout presented previously, all possible values for SQLTYPE are coded as 88-level COBOL structures. They can be used in the logic of your application program to test for specific data types. The valid values for SQLTYPE are shown in Table 6.3.

Table 6.3. Valid values for SQLTYPE.

SQLTYPE *Value* NULL *Allowed*	NULL *Not Allowed*	*Data Type*
384	385	DATE
388	389	TIME
392	393	TIMESTAMP
448	449	Small VARCHAR
452	453	Fixed CHAR
456	457	Long VARCHAR
460	461	VARCHAR optionally null-terminated
464	465	Small VARGRAPHIC
468	469	Fixed GRAPHIC
472	473	Long VARGRAPHIC

SQLTYPE *Value* NULL *Allowed*	NULL *Not Allowed*	*Data Type*
480	481	FLOAT
484	485	DECIMAL
496	497	INTEGER
500	501	SMALLINT

The first value listed is returned when NULLs are not permitted; the second is returned when NULLs are permitted. These two codes aid in the detection of the data type for each column. The application program issuing the dynamic SQL must interrogate the SQLDA, analyzing each occurrence of SQLVAR. This information is used to determine the address of a storage area of the proper size to accommodate each column returned. The address is stored in the SQLDATA field of the SQLDA. If the column can be NULL, the address of the NULL indicator is stored in the SQLIND field of the SQLDA. When this analysis is complete, data can be fetched using varying-list SELECT and the SQLDA information.

Note that the group item, SQLVAR, occurs 750 times. This number is the limit for the number of columns that can be returned by one SQL SELECT. If you're using DB2 V2.2 or older, the column limit is 300. You can modify the column limit number by changing the value of the SQLN field to a smaller number but not to a larger one. Coding a smaller number reduces the amount of storage required. If a greater number of columns is returned by the dynamic SELECT, the SQLVAR fields are not populated.

You can also code dynamic SQL without knowing anything about the statement to be executed. An example is a program that must read SQL statements from a terminal and execute them regardless of statement type. You can create this type of program by coding two SQLDAs: one full SQLDA and one minimal SQLDA (containing only the first 16 bytes of the full SQLDA) that PREPAREs the statement and determines whether it is a SELECT. If the statement is not a SELECT, you can simply EXECUTE the non-SELECT statement. If it is a SELECT, PREPARE it a second time with a full SQLDA and follow the steps in Listing 6.6.

Listing 6.6. Varying-list SELECT dynamic SQL with minimum SQLDA.

```
EXEC SQL INCLUDE SQLDA
EXEC SQL INCLUDE MINSQLDA
Read "SQL to execute" from external source
Move the "SQL to execute" to STRING-VARIABLE
EXEC SQL DECLARE CSR3 CURSOR FOR VLSQL;
EXEC SQL
    PREPARE VLSQL INTO MINSQLDA FROM :STRING-VARIABLE;
IF SQLD IN MINSQLDA = 0
    EXECUTE IMMEDIATE (SQL statement was not a SELECT)
    FINISHED.
```

continues

Listing 6.6. continued

```
EXEC SQL
    PREPARE VLSQL INTO SQLDA FROM :STRING-VARIABLE;
EXEC SQL OPEN CSR3;
Load storage addresses into the SQLDA
Loop until no more rows to FETCH
    EXEC SQL FETCH CSR3 USING DESCRIPTOR SQLDA;
EXEC SQL CLOSE CSR3;
```

In this section, I've provided a quick introduction to varying-list SELECT dynamic SQL. If you want to code parameter markers or need further information on acquiring storage or COBOL II pointer variables, consult the following IBM manuals:

VS COBOL II Application Programming Guide
DB2 Application Programming and SQL Guide
DB2 SQL Reference

Varying-List SELECT Guidelines

The following guidelines should be adhered to when developing varying-list SELECT dynamic SQL programs.

Use Varying-List SELECT with Care

Be sure that you understand the fundamental capabilities of varying-list SELECT dynamic SQL before trying to use it. You should understand completely the SQLDA, pointer variables, and how the language you're using implements pointers before proceeding.

Summary

Seriously consider using dynamic SQL under the following conditions:

- When the nature of the application program is truly changeable, not just a series of static SQL statements
- When the columns to be retrieved can vary from execution to execution
- When the predicates can vary from execution to execution
- When benefit can be accrued from interacting with other dynamic SQL applications—for example, using the QMF callable interface

7

Program Preparation

A DB2 application program must go through a process known as *program preparation* before it can run successfully. This chapter describes this procedure and its components. Accompanying guidelines for program preparation are provided, including the following:

- Choosing program preparation options to achieve optimum performance
- Plan and package management
- Preparing programs with minimum down time

Program Preparation Steps

Your first question might be "Just what is DB2 program preparation?" Quite simply, it is a series of code preprocessors that—when enacted in the proper sequence—create an executable load module and a DB2 application plan. The combination of the executable load module and the application plan is required before any DB2 program can be run, whether batch or online. CICS programs require an additional preprocessing step. This step is covered in Chapter 11, "The Doors to DB2."

Figure 7.1 shows DB2 program preparation graphically. This section outlines each program preparation step and its function.

FIGURE 7.1.
DB2 program preparation.

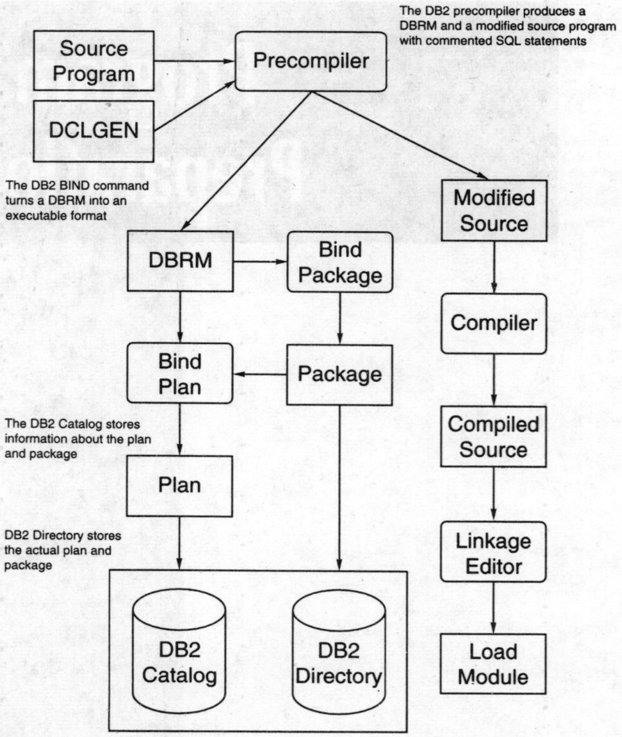

Issue the DCLGEN Command

Issue the DCLGEN command for a single table. On a table-by-table basis, DCLGEN produces a module that can be included in DB2 application programs. It reads the DB2 Catalog to determine the structure of the table and builds a COBOL copybook. The copybook contains a SQL DECLARE TABLE statement along with WORKING-STORAGE host variable definitions for each column in the table.

DCLGEN is not a required step because the DECLARE TABLE statement and corresponding host variables could be hard-coded in the application program. Skipping this step, however, is not recommended. Run the DCLGEN command for every table that will be embedded in a COBOL program. Then every program that accesses that table should be required to INCLUDE the generated copybook as the only means of declaring that table for embedded use. For the DEPTTABL copybook, use the following INCLUDE statement:

```
EXEC SQL
    INCLUDE DEPTTABL
END-EXEC.
```

DB2 must be running to invoke the DCLGEN command. See "Program Preparation Using DB2I," later in this chapter, and Chapter 29, "DB2 Commands," for more information on DCLGEN. A sample DCLGEN for the DSN8510.DEPT table follows:

```
***********************************************************
* DCLGEN TABLE(DSN8510.DEPT)                              *
*        LIBRARY(DBAPCSM.DB2.CNTL(DCLDEPT))               *
*        ACTION(REPLACE)                                  *
*        QUOTE                                            *
* ... IS THE DCLGEN COMMAND THAT MADE THE                 *
*     FOLLOWING STATEMENTS                                *
***********************************************************
EXEC SQL DECLARE DSN8510.DEPT TABLE
    ( DEPTNO       CHAR(3) NOT NULL,
      DEPTNAME     VARCHAR(36) NOT NULL,
      MGRNO        CHAR(6),
      ADMRDEPT     CHAR(3) NOT NULL,
      LOCATION     CHAR(16)
    ) END-EXEC.
*****************************************************
* COBOL DECLARATION FOR TABLE DSN8510.DEPT          *
*****************************************************
01  DCLDEPT.
    10  DEPTNO                PIC X(3).
    10  DEPTNAME.
        49  DEPTNAME-LEN      PIC S9(4) USAGE COMP.
        49  DEPTNAME-TEXT     PIC X(36).
    10  MGRNO                 PIC X(6).
    10  ADMRDEPT              PIC X(3).
    10  LOCATION              PIC X(16).
*****************************************************
* THE NUMBER OF COLUMNS DESCRIBED BY THIS           *
* DECLARATION IS 5                                  *
*****************************************************
```

As the example shows, the DCLGEN command produces a DECLARE TABLE statement and a COBOL field layout for DB2 host variables that can be used with the table.

NOTE

The DCLGEN command produces qualified table names in the DECLARE TABLE statement. You might need to edit these before embedding the DCLGEN output in an application program. Alternately, setting the current SQLID to the table owner will generate unqualified table names.

Version 4

DB2 V4 adds two features to the DCLGEN command: column prefixing and automatic creation of null indicator variables. Column prefixing, awkwardly enough, is specified using the COLSUFFIX(YES) parameter and the NAMES parameter. When these two options are specified, DCLGEN produces field names by appending the column name to the literal prefix specified by the NAMES parameter. If the previous DCLGEN were created specifying COLSUFFIX(YES) and NAMES(DPT), for example, the results would be as follows:

```
*************************************************************
* DCLGEN TABLE(DEPT)                                    *
*        LIBRARY(DBAPCSM.DB2.CNTL(DCLDEPT))             *
*        ACTION(REPLACE)                                 *
*        QUOTE                                           *
*        COLSUFFIX(YES) NAMES(DPT)                       *
* ... IS THE DCLGEN COMMAND THAT MADE THE               *
*     FOLLOWING STATEMENTS                               *
*************************************************************
EXEC SQL DECLARE DEPT TABLE
    ( DEPTNO         CHAR(3) NOT NULL,
      DEPTNAME       VARCHAR(36) NOT NULL,
      MGRNO          CHAR(6),
      ADMRDEPT       CHAR(3) NOT NULL,
      LOCATION       CHAR(16)
    ) END-EXEC.
*******************************************************
* COBOL DECLARATION FOR TABLE DEPT                  *
*******************************************************
01  DCLDEPT.
    10  DPT-DEPTNO                  PIC X(3).
    10  DPT-DEPTNAME.
        49  CPT-DEPTNAME-LEN        PIC S9(4) USAGE COMP.
        49  DPT-DEPTNAME-TEXT       PIC X(36).
    10  DPT-MGRNO                   PIC X(6).
    10  DPT-ADMRDEPT                PIC X(3).
    10  DPT-LOCATION                PIC X(16).
*******************************************************
* THE NUMBER OF COLUMNS DESCRIBED BY THIS           *
* DECLARATION IS 5                                  *
*******************************************************
```

You can create an array of null indicator variables by specifying `INDVAR(YES)`. However, use this feature with caution as null indicator arrays are more difficult to use than individual null indicator variables (for more details, refer to Chapter 6, "Dynamic SQL Programming").

Version 4

Precompile the Program

DB2 programs must be parsed and modified before normal compilation. The DB2 precompiler performs this task. When invoked, the precompiler performs the following functions:

- Searches for and expands DB2-related INCLUDE members
- Searches for SQL statements in the body of the program's source code
- Creates a modified version of the source program in which every SQL statement in the program is commented out and a `CALL` to the DB2 runtime interface module, along with applicable parameters, replaces each original SQL statement
- Extracts all SQL statements from the program and places them in a database request module (DBRM)
- Places a timestamp token in the modified source and the DBRM to ensure that these two items are inextricably tied
- Reports on the success or failure of the precompile process

The precompiler searches for SQL statements embedded in `EXEC SQL` and `END-EXEC` keywords. For this reason, every SQL statement, table declaration, or host variable in an `INCLUDE` copybook must be in an `EXEC SQL` block. DB2 does not need to be operational to precompile a DB2 program.

Issue the BIND Command

The `BIND` command is a type of compiler for SQL statements. In general, `BIND` reads SQL statements from DBRMs and produces a mechanism to access data as directed by the SQL statements being bound.

You can use two types of `BIND`s: `BIND PLAN` and `BIND PACKAGE`. `BIND PLAN` accepts as input one or more DBRMs produced from previous DB2 program precompilations, one or more packages produced from previous `BIND PACKAGE` commands, or a combination of DBRMs and package lists.

The output of the `BIND PLAN` command is an application plan containing executable logic representing optimized access paths to DB2 data. An application plan is executable only with a corresponding load module. Before you can run a DB2 program, regardless of environment, an application plan name must be specified.

The BIND PACKAGE command accepts as input a DBRM and produces a single package containing optimized access path logic. You then can bind packages into an application plan using the BIND PLAN command. A package is not executable and cannot be specified when a DB2 program is being run. You must bind a package into a plan before using it.

BIND performs many functions to create packages and plans that access the requested DB2 data, including the following:

- Reads the SQL statements in the DBRM and checks the syntax of those statements
- Checks that the DB2 tables and columns being accessed conform to the corresponding DB2 Catalog information
- Performs authorization validation (this task is optional)
- Optimizes the SQL statements into efficient access paths

The application packages and plans contain the access path specifications developed by the BIND command. The BIND command invokes the DB2 optimizer (discussed in depth in Chapter 11) to determine efficient access paths based on DB2 Catalog statistics (such as the availability of indexes, the organization of data, and the table size) and other pertinent information (such as number of processors, processor speed, and bufferpool specifications). The BIND command is performed in the Relational Data Services component of DB2.

Packages are available when using DB2 V2.3 or higher. A package can be bound for only a single DBRM. A package, therefore, is nothing more than optimized SQL from a single program. Although packages are discrete entities in the DB2 Catalog and Directory, they cannot be executed until they are bound into a plan. Plans are composed of either one or more DBRMs or one or more packages. Further discussion of plans and packages is deferred until later in this chapter.

The DB2 subsystem must be operational so that you can issue the BIND command. See "Program Preparation Using DB2I" and Chapter 29 for more information on the BIND command.

Compile the Program

The modified COBOL source data set produced by the DB2 precompiler must then be compiled. Use the standard VS/COBOL, COBOL II, or COBOL/370 compiler, depending on which version of COBOL you are using. DB2 does not need to be operational so that you can compile your program.

Link the Program

The compiled source then is link-edited to an executable load module. The appropriate DB2 host language interface module also must be included by the link edit step. This interface module is based on the environment (TSO, CICS, or IMS/TM) in which the program will execute.

If you have a call attach product or use an environment other than TSO, CICS, or IMS/TM, consult your shop standards to determine the appropriate language interface routine to include with your link edited program. The output of the link edit step is an executable load module, which then can be run with a plan containing the program's DBRM or package.

The link edit procedure does not require the services of DB2; therefore, the DB2 subsystem can be inactive when your program is being link edited.

Running a DB2 Program

After a program has been prepared as outlined in Figure 7.1, two separate, physical components have been produced: a DB2 plan and a link edited load module. Neither is executable without the other. The plan contains the access path specifications for the SQL statements in the program. The load module contains the executable machine instructions for the COBOL statements in the program.

If a load module is run outside the control of DB2, the program abends at the first SQL statement. Furthermore, a load module is forever tied to a specific DBRM—the DBRM produced by the same precompile that produced the modified source used in the link-edit process that produced the load module in question.

When you run an application program containing SQL statements, you must specify the name of the plan that will be used. The plan name must include the DBRM that was produced by the precompile process in the program preparation that created the load module being run. This is enforced by a timestamp token placed into both the DBRM and the modified source by the DB2 precompiler. At execution time, DB2 checks that the tokens indicate the compatibility of the plan and the load module. If they do not match, DB2 will not allow the SQL statements in the program to be run. A `-818` SQL code is returned for each SQL call attempted by the program.

DB2 programs can be executed in one of four ways:

- Batch TSO
- Call attach
- CICS
- IMS

Listing 7.1 provides the JCL to execute the program using TSO batch. For information about other methods, see Chapter 11.

Listing 7.1. Running a DB2 program in TSO batch.

```
//DB2JOBB  JOB (BATCH),'DB2 BATCH',MSGCLASS=X,CLASS=X,
//        NOTIFY=USER
//*
//***************************************************************
//*
//*          JCL TO RUN A DB2 PROGRAM IN BATCH
//*          USING THE TSO TERMINAL MONITOR PROGRAM
//*
//***************************************************************
//*
//JOBLIB      DD DSN=SYS1.DB2V510.DSNLOAD,DISP=SHR
//BATCHPRG    EXEC PGM=IKJEFT1B,DYNAMNBR=20
//SYSTSPRT    DD  SYSOUT=*
//SYSPRINT    DD  SYSOUT=*
//SYSUDUMP    DD  SYSOUT=*
//SYSTSIN     DD  *
  DSN SYSTEM(DSN)
  RUN PROGRAM(Place program name here)   -
  PLAN(Place plan name here)   -
  LIB('SYS1.DB2V510.RUNLIB.LOAD')
  END
/*
//
```

Preparing a DB2 Program

You can prepare a DB2 program in many ways. Following are the most common methods:

- Using the DB2I panels
- Using a standard DB2 program preparation procedure
- Using a DB2 program preparation CLIST or REXX EXEC
- Any combination of the preceding methods

Each shop has its own standards. Consult your shop standards for the supported method or methods of DB2 program preparation. This section discusses each of the preceding methods.

Program Preparation Using DB2I

DB2I, or DB2 Interactive, is an online, TSO/ISPF based interface to DB2 commands, DB2 administrative functions, and CLISTs provided with DB2. It is a panel-driven application that enables a user to prepare a DB2 program, among other things. DB2I is discussed further in Chapter 11.

You can use eight DB2I panels to assist with DB2 program preparation. The DB2I main menu, shown in Figure 7.2, appears when you select the DB2I option from the main menu.

NOTE

Some installations require the user to execute a preallocation `CLIST` before invoking DB2I. Consult your shop standards.

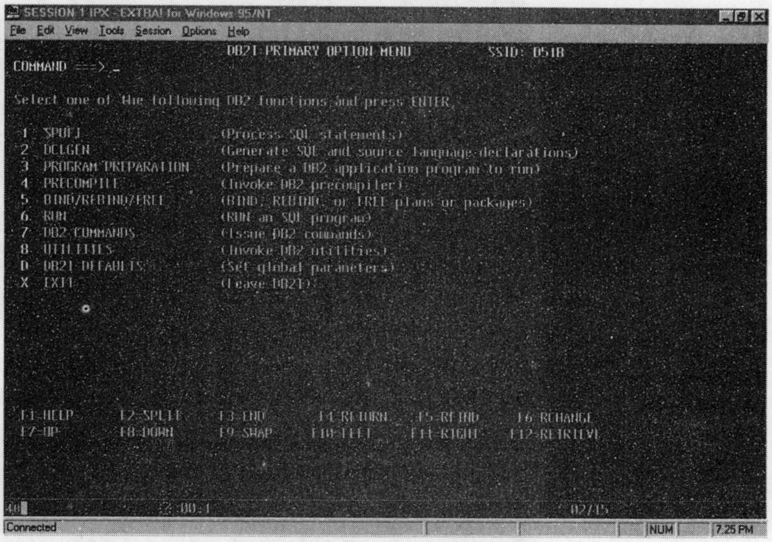

FIGURE 7.2.
The DB2I main menu.

Before proceeding to the main task of program preparation using DB2I, you first must ensure that the DB2I defaults have been properly set. Option D from the main menu displays the DB2I Defaults panel, which is shown in Figure 7.3. The default values usually are adequate. When you first enter DB2I, however, ensure that the correct DB2 subsystem name, application language, and delimiters are set.

After checking the DB2I Defaults panel, you need to create `DCLGEN` members for all tables that will be accessed in application programs. You should do this before writing any application code.

Choosing option 2 from the DB2I main menu displays the `DCLGEN` panel (see Figure 7.4). Specify the name of the table in option 1 and the name of the data set in which the DBRM will be placed in option 2. DB2 automatically creates the `DCLGEN` member, including `WORKING-STORAGE` fields and the `DECLARE TABLE` statement. `DCLGEN` will not allocate a new data set, so you must preallocate the data set specified in option 2 as a sequential data set with an LRECL of 80. Refer to the `DCLGEN` member (presented earlier in this chapter) for the `DSN8510.DEPT` table.

FIGURE 7.3.
The DB2I Defaults panel.

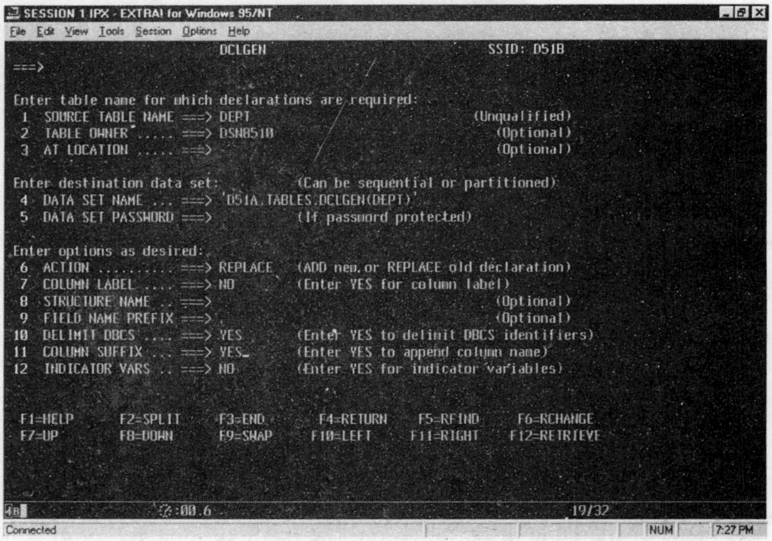

FIGURE 7.4.
The DB2I DCLGEN *panel.*

You use option 4 of DB2I to precompile DB2 application programs. Figure 7.5 shows the Precompile panel. To precompile a program, provide the following information in the specified locations on the Precompile panel:

- The name of the input data set containing the source code for the program you want to precompile

- The name of the DCLGEN library that contains the table declarations to be used by this program
- A DSNAME qualifier to be used by DB2I to build data set names for temporary work files required by the precompiler
- The name of the DBRM library that the precompiler will write to (this must be a partitioned data set with 80-byte records)

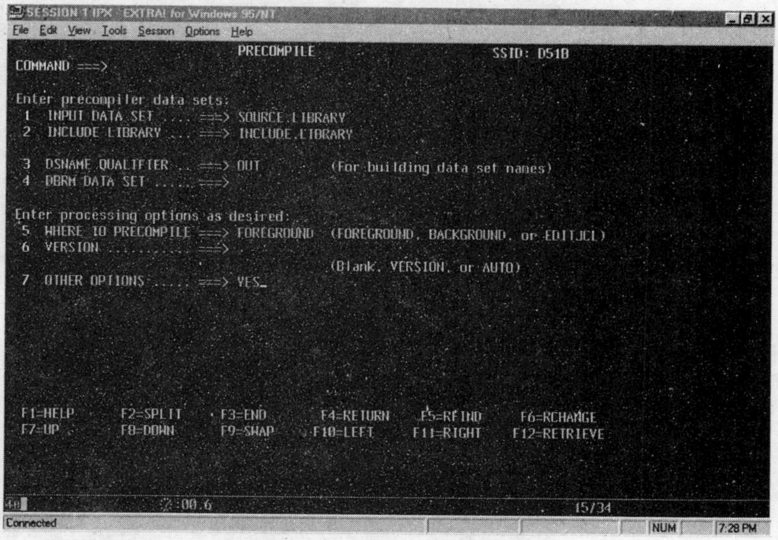

FIGURE 7.5.
The DB2I Precompile panel.

NOTE

You can run the precompiler in the foreground or the background.

You can bind, rebind, and free DB2 plans and packages using DB2I option 5. In this section, I discuss the BIND option because it is the only one needed for program preparation. (See Chapter 11 for a discussion of rebind and free.) As of DB2 V2.3, two bind panels are available: one for binding plans, as shown in Figure 7.6, and one for binding packages, as shown in Figure 7.7. The bind process creates plans or packages or both from one or more DBRMs. You should not attempt binding until the precompile successfully is completed.

You may have noticed that the compile and link edit steps are missing from the previous discussions of program preparation. DB2I option 3 takes you step-by-step through the entire DB2 program preparation procedure, displaying the previous panels (and an additional one). By entering the appropriate selections in the Program Preparation panel, shown in Figure 7.8, you can completely prepare and then run a source program.

FIGURE 7.6.
The DB2I Bind Plan panel.

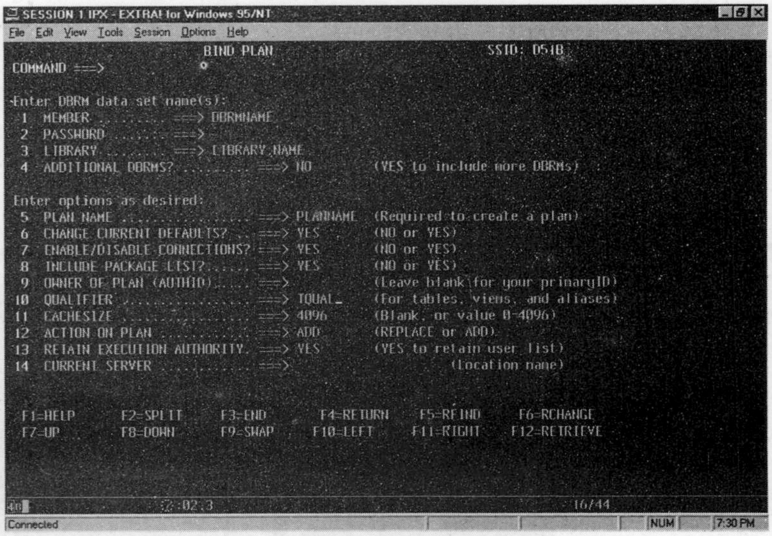

FIGURE 7.7.
The DB2I Bind Package panel.

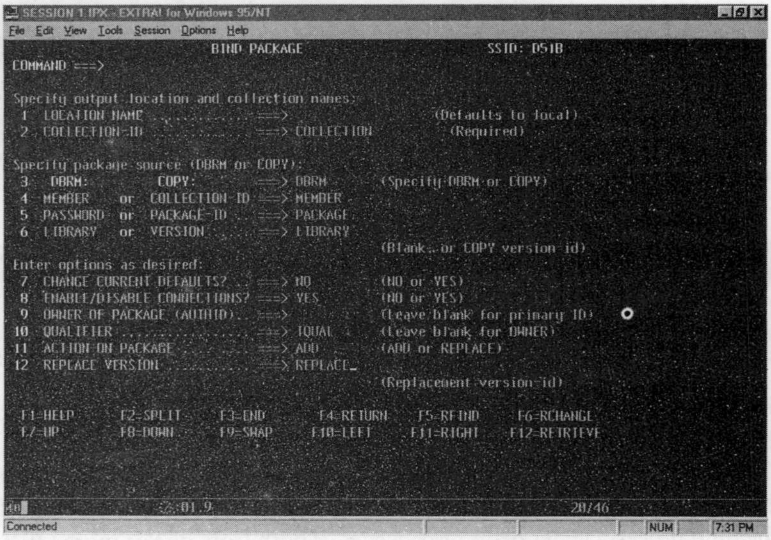

After you enter the necessary information in the Program Preparation panel, you are navigated through the Precompile panel (refer to Figure 7.5); a new panel for the specification of compilation, link edit, and run parameters (see Figure 7.9), and the Bind panels (refer to Figures 7.6 and 7.7).

FIGURE 7.8.
The DB2I Program Preparation panel.

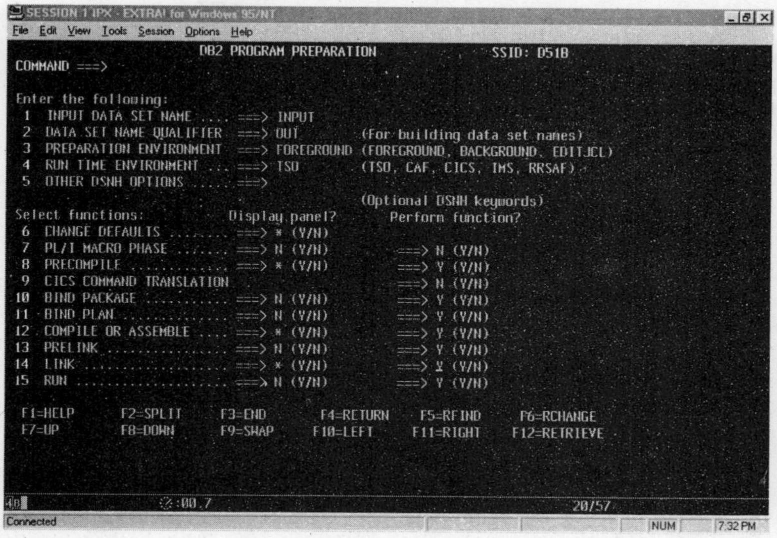

FIGURE 7.9.
The DB2I Compile, Prelink, Link, and Run panel.

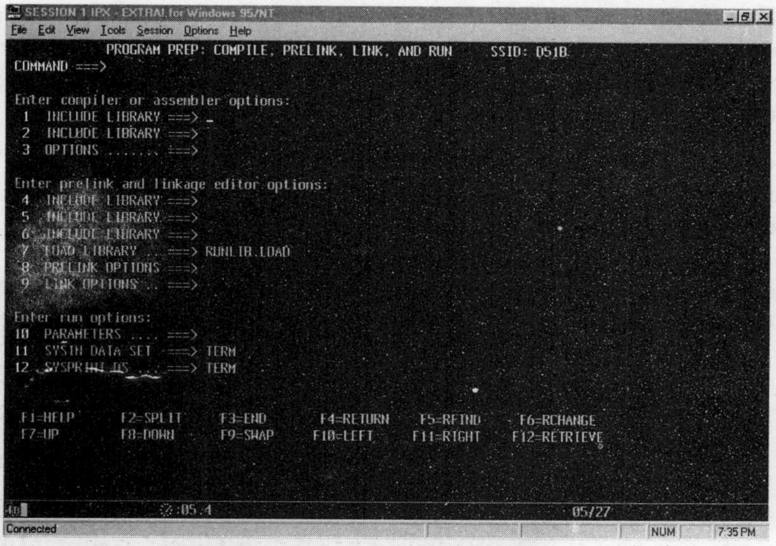

The panels are prefilled with the information provided in the Program Preparation panel. This probably is the easiest method of preparing a DB2 program. The following is a sample of the output generated by DB2I program preparation:

```
%DSNH  parameters
 SOURCE STATISTICS
    SOURCE LINES READ: 459
```

```
     NUMBER OF SYMBOLS: 77
     SYMBOL TABLE BYTES EXCLUDING ATTRIBUTES: 4928
THERE WERE 0 MESSAGES FOR THIS PROGRAM.
THERE WERE 0 MESSAGES SUPPRESSED BY THE FLAG OPTION.
101944 BYTES OF STORAGE WERE USED BY THE PRECOMPILER.
RETURN CODE IS 0
   DSNH740I ======= PRECOMPILER FINISHED, RC = 0 ======
            LISTING IN TEMP.PCLIST ====================
   DSNT252I - BIND OPTIONS FOR PLAN planname
          ACTION      ADD
          OWNER       authid
          VALIDATE    BIND
          ISOLATION   CS
          ACQUIRE     USE
          RELEASE     COMMIT
          EXPLAIN     YES
   DSNT253I - BIND OPTIONS FOR PLAN planname
          NODEFER     PREPARE
   DSNH740I ======= BIND FINISHED, RC = 0 =============
   DSNH740I ======= COB2 FINISHED, RC = 0 ======
            LISTING IN TEMP.LIST ====================
   DSNH740I ======= LINK FINISHED, RC = 0 ======
            LISTING IN TEMP.LINKLIST ====================
***
```

When you're using the DB2I Program Preparation option, the status of the program preparation appears onscreen. The italicized sections in the listing are replaced by the options you select when preparing your programs. Additionally, if you set any return codes to a non-zero number, you will encounter program preparation warnings or errors.

You can run DB2 programs using DB2I only if they are TSO programs. You also can simply run a DB2 program from DB2I option 6 (see Figure 7.10). Before you can run the program, however, you must first prepare it.

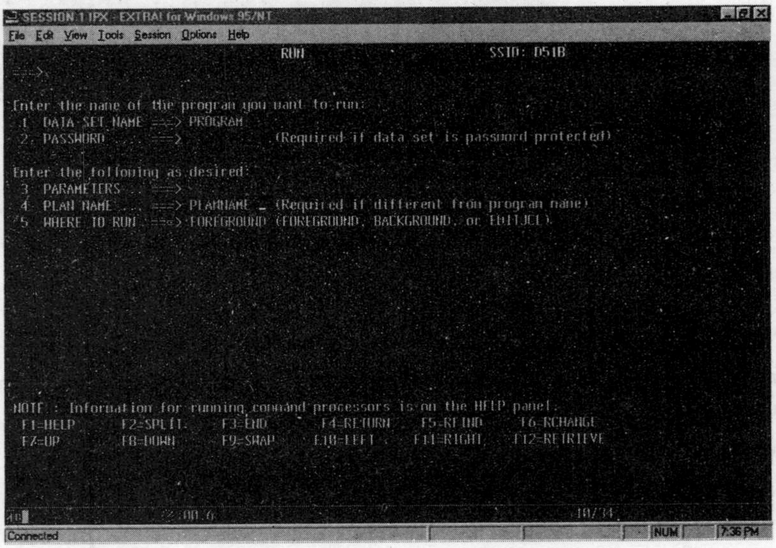

FIGURE 7.10.
The DB2I Run panel.

Program Preparation Using Batch Procedures

Some shops prefer to handle all DB2 program preparation with a batch job. The batch procedure handles all the steps required for DB2 program preparation, which results in an executable load module and plan.

Programmers often choose batch procedures to automate and standardize the specification of work data set names; compile, link, and bind parameters; and source, DBRM, and DCLGEN library names. A batch procedure invoked by common JCL with an override for the program name limits an application programmer's exposure to these miscellaneous program preparation factors. Listing 7.2 shows a common batch procedure. Note that the data set names and libraries for your shop will be different.

Listing 7.2. Sample program preparation procedure.

```
//COMPBAT PROC MBR='XXXXXXXX',          ** MEMBER NAME          **
//        FLEVEL='APPL.ID'               ** LIBRARY PREFIX       **
//        DB2='SYS1.DB2V510',            ** DB2 SYSTEM PREFIX    **
//        WORK='SYSDA',                  ** WORK FILES UNIT      **
//        SOURCE='APPL.ID.SOURCE',       ** SOURCE DATASET       **
//        SYSOUT='*'
//****************************************************************
//*       DB2 PRECOMPILE STEP FOR COBOL—BATCH
//****************************************************************
//DB2PC     EXEC  PGM=DSNHPC,
//          PARM='DATE(ISO),TIME(ISO),HOST(COB2),APOST'
//STEPLIB   DD DSN=&DB2..DSNLOAD,DISP=SHR
//SYSLIB    DD DSN=&FLEVEL..INCLUDE,DISP=SHR
//          DD DSN=&FLEVEL..DCLGENLB,DISP=SHR
//SYSCIN    DD DSN=&&SRCOUT,DISP=(NEW,PASS,DELETE),
//          UNIT=&WORK,
//          DCB=BLKSIZE=800,SPACE=(800,(800,500))
//SYSIN     DD DSN=&SOURCE(&MBR),DISP=SHR
//DBRMLIB   DD DSN=&FLEVEL..DBRMLIB(&MBR),DISP=SHR
//SYSPRINT DD SYSOUT=&SYSOUT
//SYSTERM   DD SYSOUT=&SYSOUT
//SYSUT1    DD SPACE=(800,(500,500)),UNIT=&WORK
//SYSUT2    DD SPACE=(800,(500,500)),UNIT=&WORK
//****************************************************************
//*     COBOL COMPILE
//****************************************************************
//COB       EXEC PGM=IGYCRCTL,
//          COND=(5,LT,DB2PC),
//          PARM=('NODYNAM,LIB,OBJECT,RENT,RES,APOST',
//          'DATA(24),XREF')
//STEPLIB   DD DSN=SYS1.COB2LIB,DISP=SHR
//SYSPRINT DD DSN=&&SPRNT,DISP=(MOD,PASS),UNIT=SYSDA,
//          SPACE=(TRK,(175,20)),DCB=BLKSIZE=16093
//SYSTERM   DD SYSOUT=&SYSOUT
//SYSUT1    DD UNIT=&WORK,SPACE=(CYL,(5,1))
//SYSUT2    DD UNIT=&WORK,SPACE=(CYL,(5,1))
//SYSUT3    DD UNIT=&WORK,SPACE=(CYL,(5,1))
//SYSUT4    DD UNIT=&WORK,SPACE=(CYL,(5,1))
```

continues

Listing 7.2. continued

```
//SYSUT5    DD UNIT=&WORK,SPACE=(CYL,(5,1))
//SYSUT6    DD UNIT=&WORK,SPACE=(CYL,(5,1))
//SYSUT7    DD UNIT=&WORK,SPACE=(CYL,(5,1))
//SYSLIN    DD DSN=&&OBJECT,DISP=(NEW,PASS,DELETE),
//             UNIT=&WORK,SPACE=(TRK,(25,10),RLSE),
//             DCB=(RECFM=FB,LRECL=80,BLKSIZE=2960)
//SYSLIB    DD DSN=&FLEVEL..COPYLIB,DISP=SHR
//SYSIN     DD DSN=&&SRCOUT,DISP=(OLD,DELETE,DELETE)
//****************************************************************
//*  PRINT THE SYSPRINT DATA SET IF THE RETURN CODE IS > 4
//****************************************************************
//GEN1      EXEC PGM=IEBGENER,COND=(5,GT,COB)
//SYSPRINT DD SYSOUT=*
//SYSUT3    DD UNIT=SYSDA,SPACE=(TRK,(10)),DISP=NEW
//SYSUT4    DD UNIT=SYSDA,SPACE=(TRK,(10)),DISP=NEW
//SYSIN     DD DUMMY
//SYSUT1    DD DSN=&&SPRNT,DISP=(OLD,PASS)
//SYSUT2    DD SYSOUT=*
//****************************************************************
//*      LINK EDIT THE BATCH PROGRAM FOR DB2
//****************************************************************
//LINKIT    EXEC PGM=HEWL,
//             COND=((5,LT,DB2PC),(5,LT,COB)),
//             PARM='LIST,XREF'
//SYSLIB    DD DSN=SYS1.COB2LIB,DISP=SHR
//          DD DSN=SYS1.COB2COMP,DISP=SHR
//          DD DSN=&DB2..DSNLOAD,DISP=SHR
//          DD DSN=&FLEVEL..BATCH.LOADLIB,DISP=SHR
//DB2LOAD   DD DSN=&DB2..DSNLOAD,DISP=SHR
//SYSLIN    DD DSN=&&OBJECT,DISP=(OLD,PASS)
//          DD DSN=&FLEVEL..LINKLIB(&MBR),DISP=SHR
//SYSLMOD   DD DSN=&FLEVEL..BATCH.LOADLIB(&MBR),DISP=SHR
//SYSPRINT DD SYSOUT=&SYSOUT
//SYSUT1    DD UNIT=&WORK,SPACE=(CYL,(1,2))
//****************************************************************
//*      BIND PLAN FOR THE MODULE
//****************************************************************
//BIND1     EXEC PGM=IKJEFT1B,DYNAMNBR=20,
//             COND=((5,LT,DB2PC),(5,LT,COB),(5,LT,LINKIT))
//STEPLIB   DD DSN=&DB2..DSNLOAD,DISP=SHR
//SYSTSPRT DD SYSOUT=*
//SYSPRINT DD SYSOUT=*
//SYSUDUMP DD SYSOUT=*
//DBRMLIB   DD DSN=&FLEVEL..DBRMLIB,DISP=SHR
//SYSTSIN   DD *
  DSN SYSTEM(DSN)
  BIND  PLAN(&MEMBER.)    MEMBER(&MEMBER.)  -
        ACTION(REPLACE)   RETAIN            -
        VALIDATE(BIND)    ACQUIRE(USE)      -
        RELEASE(COMMIT)   ISOLATION(CS)     -
        DEGREE(ANY)       EXPLAIN(YES)

  END
//
```

Program Preparation Using CLIST or REXX EXEC

Another common practice for some shops is to create a CLIST or REXX EXEC that can be invoked to prompt the user to enter program preparation options. The CLIST or EXEC reads the options as specified by the programmer and builds JCL to invoke program preparation using those parameters.

This method enables programmers to make quick changes to precompile, compile, and link edit parameters without requiring them to explicitly change parameters in JCL that they do not always fully understand. This method also can force specific options to be used, such as all binds must use ISOLATION(CS) or all links must use RMODE=31, by not allowing users to change them.

The CLIST or EXEC can use a standard procedure, as discussed in the preceding section, and automatically submit the job.

Program Preparation Using Multiple Methods

When you develop program preparation standards, the following goals should be paramount:

- Increase the understanding and usability of program preparation procedures
- Disable dangerous and undesired program preparation parameters
- Standardize the program preparation procedure
- Enable fast turnaround for programmers using the procedures

To accomplish the preceding goals, using a combination of the techniques described in this chapter is probably best. The only DB2 program preparation steps that require DB2 to be operational, for example, are DCLGEN and BIND. DCLGEN is not a factor because it normally is invoked outside the program preparation loop. The BIND command, however, usually is embedded in the procedure, CLIST, or REXX EXEC. If this is true, as shown in Listing 7.2, you could be inhibiting your program preparation process.

If DB2 is not operational, all program preparation jobs will fail in the bind step. Additionally, if your shop is configured with multiple CPUs, a job with a bind step must be run on the CPU containing the DB2 subsystem that will perform the bind. Without the bind step, the job is free to execute in any available machine because DB2 resources are not required.

I recommend the establishment of a common procedure to run all program preparation, except the bind step. You then should code CLIST or REXX EXEC to prompt only for the parameters your shop allows to be changed. It then will build JCL using the common procedure (without the bind step). CLIST or EXEC can ask whether a bind step should be added. This way, application programmers can precompile, compile, and link edit programs when DB2 is not operational, but gives them the option of binding when DB2 is operational. This can reduce the amount of down time because a single machine containing test DB2 will not become a bottleneck due to a vast number of compiles being submitted on a single CPU.

You can code a separate CLIST that enables programmers to bind after a successful execution of the precompile, compile, and link or whenever a bind is required. It should accept only certain bind parameters as input, thereby enforcing your shop's bind standards. Ideally, the CLIST should be able to bind the program in the foreground or the background using batch JCL.

Listings 7.3 and 7.4 are sample CLISTs to accomplish DB2 program preparation.

Listing 7.3. Precompile, compile, and link CLIST.

```
PROC 1 PLANNAME  JOB(BB)
/*    THIS CLIST ACCEPTS A PROGRAM NAME AS INPUT, PROMPTS
/*    FOR THE REQUIRED PROGRAM PREPARATION PARAMETERS,
/*    AND SUBMITS A BATCH JOB TO PREPARE THE PROGRAM
/*    FOR EXECUTION.
CONTROL PROMPT NOFLUSH END(DONE)
   K
   WRITE
ASKMSG:-
   WRITE
   WRITE        ENTER OUTPUT MESSAGE CLASS:
   WRITENR        =====>
   READ &MSG
   IF &MSG NE X AND &MSG NE A THEN DO-
      WRITE
      WRITE              INVALID MESSAGE CLASS ENTERED
      GOTO ASKMSG
   DONE
ASKSORC:-
   WRITE
   WRITE        ENTER NAME OF PROGRAM SOURCE LIBRARY TO USE:
   WRITE        (PRESS ENTER TO ACCEPT DEFAULT SOURCE LIBRARY)
   WRITENR        =====>
   READ &SORC
   IF &SORC =          THEN SET &SORCLB=&STR(DEFAULT.SORCLIB)
   ELSE                     SET &SORCLB=&SORC
ASKPREFX:-
   WRITE
   WRITE        ENTER THE PREFIX FOR YOUR APPLICATION LINK
   WRITE        AND DBRM LIBRARIES:
   WRITE        (PRESS ENTER TO ACCEPT DEFAULT PREFIX)
   WRITENR        =====>
   READ &PREF
   IF &PREF =          THEN SET &PREFX=&STR(DEFAULT.PREFIX)
   ELSE                     SET &PREFX=&PREF
BUILDJCL:-
   K
   WRITE             BUILDING PROGRAM PREPARATION JCL, PLEASE WAIT...
EDIT COMPLINK.CNTL NEW EMODE
10 //&SYSUID.&JOB JOB(job information),'PROG PREP &PROGNAME',
11 //      MSGLEVEL=(1,1),NOTIFY=&SYSUID.,MSGCLASS=&MSG,CLASS=X
15 //JOBLIB DD DSN=SYS1.DB2V2R3.LINKLIB,DISP=SHR
20 //PROGPREP    EXEC       COMPBAT,MBR=&PROGNAME.,FLEVEL=&PREFIX.,
22 //         SOURCE=&SORCLB.
24 /*
26 //
```

```
SUBM:-
   WRITE            PROGRAM, &PROGNAME WILL BE
   WRITE                  PRECOMPILED, COMPILED, AND LINKED
   WRITE                  FROM &SORCLB
   SUBMIT
   END NO
EXIT
```

Listing 7.4. Bind CLIST.

```
PROC 1 PLANNAME  JOB(BB)
/*     THIS CLIST ACCEPTS A PLANNAME AS INPUT, PROMPTS FOR   */
/*     THE REQUIRED BIND PARAMETERS, AND SUBMITS A BATCH    */
/*     JOB TO BIND THE PLAN                                 */
CONTROL PROMPT NOFLUSH END(DONE)
   K
   WRITE
ASKMSG:-
   WRITE
   WRITE       ENTER OUTPUT MESSAGE CLASS:
   WRITENR       =====>
   READ &MSG
   IF &MSG NE X AND &MSG NE A THEN DO-
      WRITE
      WRITE       INVALID MESSAGE CLASS ENTERED
      GOTO ASKMSG
   DONE
ASKLIB:-
   WRITE
   WRITE       ENTER NAME OF DBRM LIBRARY TO USE:
   WRITE       (PRESS ENTER TO ACCEPT DEFAULT DBRMLIB)
   WRITENR       =====>
   READ &LIB
   IF &LIB =         THEN SET &DLIB=&STR(DEFAULT.DBRMLIB)
   ELSE                    SET &DLIB=&LIB
ASKEXPL:-
   WRITE
   WRITE       DO YOU WANT TO DO AN EXPLAIN OF THIS PLAN (Y/N) ?
   WRITENR       =====>
   READ &EXP
   IF &EXP NE Y AND &EXP NE N THEN DO-
      WRITE
      WRITE       INVALID RESPONSE PLEASE ENTER ONLY Y OR N
      GOTO ASKEXPL
   DONE
   IF &EXP = N THEN SET &EXPL=&STR(NO)
   ELSE             SET &EXPL=&STR(YES)
ASKDBRM:-
   K
   WRITE
   WRITE       ENTER THE NAME OF ALL DBRMS TO BE BOUND INTO THIS
   WRITE       PLAN. BE SURE TO PLACE A COMMA BETWEEN EACH DBRM &
   WRITE       INCLUDE QUOTATION MARKS IF THERE IS MORE THAN ONE
   WRITE       DBRM. ( FOR EXAMPLE:: &STR(')DBRM1,DBRM2&STR(')  )
   WRITE       OR PRESS ENTER TO DEFAULT DBRM TO &PLANNAME
```

continues

Listing 7.4. continued

```
    WRITENR       =====>
    READ &DLIST
    IF &DLIST =         THEN SET &DBRM=&PLANNAME
    ELSE                     SET &DBRM=&LIST
BUILDJCL:-
    K
    WRITE      BUILDING BIND JCL, PLEASE WAIT...
EDIT BIND.CNTL NEW EMODE
10 //&SYSUID.&JOB JOB(job information),'BIND &PLANNAME',
11 //       MSGLEVEL=(1,1),NOTIFY=&SYSUID.,MSGCLASS=&MSG,CLASS=X
15 //JOBLIB DD DSN=SYS1.DB2V5R1.LINKLIB,DISP=SHR
20 //BIND       EXEC       PGM=IKJEFT1B,DYNAMBR=20
22 //SYSTSPRT      DD      SYSOUT=*
24 //SYSPRINT      DD      SYSOUT=*
26 //SYSABOUT   DD      SYSOUT=*
28 //SYSTSIN       DD       *
30 DSN SYSTEM(DSN)
32       BIND PLAN (&PLANNAME)        &STR(-)
34            MEMBER (&DBRM)          &STR(-)
36            LIBRARY (&DLIB)         &STR(-)
38            ACTION (REPLACE)        &STR(-)
40            VALIDATE (BIND)         &STR(-)
42            ISOLATION (CS)          &STR(-)
44            FLAG (I)                &STR(-)
46            ACQUIRE (USE)           &STR(-)
48            RELEASE (COMMIT)        &STR(-)
50            DEGREE (ANY)            &STR(-)
52            EXPLAIN (&EXPL)
54 END
56 /*
58 //
SUBM:-
    WRITE            &PLANNAME WILL BE BOUND
    WRITE                       USING &DBRM
    WRITE                       FROM &DLIB
    SUBMIT
    END NO
EXIT
```

What Is a DBRM?

Confusion often arises about the definition of a DBRM and its relationship to programs, plans, and packages. A *DBRM* is nothing more than a module containing SQL statements extracted from a source program by the DB2 precompiler. It is stored as a member of a partitioned data set. It is not stored in the DB2 Catalog or DB2 Directory.

Although a DB2 Catalog table named `SYSIBM.SYSDBRM` exists, it does not contain the DBRM. It also does not contain every DBRM created by the precompiler. It consists of information about DBRMs that have been bound into application plans and packages. If a DBRM is created and never bound, it is not referenced in this table.

When a DBRM is bound into a plan, all its SQL statements are placed into the SYSIBM.SYSSTMT DB2 Catalog table. When a DBRM is bound into a package, all its SQL statements are placed into the SYSIBM.SYSPACKSTMT table.

What Is a Plan?

A *plan* is an executable module containing the access path logic produced by the DB2 optimizer. It can be composed of one or more DBRMs and packages.

Plans are created by the BIND command. When a plan is bound, DB2 reads the following DB2 Catalog tables:

```
SYSIBM.SYSCOLDIST
SYSIBM.SYSCOLDISTSTATS
SYSIBM.SYSCOLSTATS
SYSIBM.SYSCOLUMNS
SYSIBM.SYSINDEXES
SYSIBM.SYSINDEXSTATS
SYSIBM.SYSPLAN
SYSIBM.SYSPLANAUTH
SYSIBM.SYSTABLES
SYSIBM.SYSTABLESPACE
SYSIBM.SYSTABSTATS
SYSIBM.SYSUSERAUTH
```

NOTE

The SYSIBM.SYSUSERAUTH table (the last one in the list) is read-only for BIND ADD.

Information about the plan is then stored in the following DB2 Catalog tables:

```
SYSIBM.SYSDBRM
SYSIBM.SYSPACKAUTH
SYSIBM.SYSPACKLIST
SYSIBM.SYSPLAN
SYSIBM.SYSPLANAUTH
SYSIBM.SYSPLANDEP
SYSIBM.SYSPLSYSTEM
SYSIBM.SYSSTMT
SYSIBM.SYSTABAUTH
```

Note that the DB2 Catalog stores only information about the plans. The executable form of the plan, called a *skeleton cursor table*, or SKCT, is stored in the DB2 Directory in the SYSIBM.SCT02 table. To learn more about the way that DB2 handles SKCTs at execution time, see Chapter 15, "The Table-Based Infrastrucutre of DB2."

What Is a Package?

A *package* is a single, bound DBRM with optimized access paths. Prior to DB2 V2.3, the only option available for binding was at the plan level. By using packages, the table access logic is "packaged" at a lower level of granularity, at the package or program level.

To execute a package, you first must include it in the package list of a plan. Packages are never directly executed—they are only indirectly executed when the plan in which they are contained executes. A plan can consist of one or more DBRMs, one or more packages, or a combination of packages and DBRMs.

To help differentiate between plans and packages, consider a grocery store analogy. Before going to the grocery store, you should prepare a shopping list. As you go through the aisles, when you find an item on your list, you place the item in your shopping cart. After your paying for the items at the check-out register, the clerk places your grocery items in a bag. You can think of the purchased items as DBRMs. The bag is the plan. You have multiple DBRMs (grocery items) in your plan (shopping bag).

In a package environment, rather than actually removing the items from the shelf, you would mark on your shopping list the location of each item in the store. Upon checking out, you would give the list to the clerk at the counter. The clerk then would place the list in the bag—not the actual items. The plan (bag) contains a list pointing to the physical location of the packages (grocery items) that are still on the shelf. This approach is a good way to compare and contrast the two different environments.

Package information is stored in its own DB2 Catalog tables. When a package is bound, DB2 reads the following DB2 Catalog tables:

```
SYSIBM.SYSCOLDIST
SYSIBM.SYSCOLDISTSTATS
SYSIBM.SYSCOLSTATS
SYSIBM.SYSCOLUMNS
SYSIBM.SYSINDEXES
SYSIBM.SYSINDEXSTATS
SYSIBM.SYSPACKAGE
SYSIBM.SYSPACKAUTH
SYSIBM.SYSTABLES
SYSIBM.SYSTABLESPACE
SYSIBM.SYSTABSTATS
SYSIBM.SYSUSERAUTH
```

NOTE

The SYSIBM.SYSUSERAUTH table (the last one in the list) is read only for BIND ADD.

Information about the package then is stored in the following DB2 Catalog tables:

```
SYSIBM.SYSPACKAGE
SYSIBM.SYSPACKAUTH
SYSIBM.SYSPACKDEP
SYSIBM.SYSPACKSTMT
SYSIBM.SYSPKSYSTEM
SYSIBM.SYSTABAUTH
```

The DB2 Catalog stores only information about the packages. The executable form of the package is stored as a skeleton package table in the DB2 Directory in the SYSIBM.SPT01 table.

A package also contains a location identifier, a collection identifier, and a package identifier. The location identifier specifies the site at which the package was bound. If your processing is local, you can forgo the specification of the location ID for packages.

The collection identifier represents a logical grouping of packages, and is covered in more detail in the next section of this chapter. The package identifier is the DBRM name bound into the package. This ties the package to the program to which it applies. A package is uniquely identified as follows when used in a statement to bind packages into a plan:

```
LOCATION.COLLECTION.PACKAGE
```

One final consideration when using packages is versioning. A package can have multiple versions, each with its own version identifier. The version identifier is carried as text in the DBRM, and is covered in more depth in the "Package Version Maintenance" section.

Package Benefits

Reduced bind time is the package benefit most often cited. When you are utilizing packages and the SQL within a program changes, only the package for that particular program needs to be rebound. If packages are not used when multiple DBRMs are bound into a plan and the SQL within one of those programs changes, the entire plan must be rebound. This wastes time because you must still rebind all the other DBRMs in that plan that did not change.

Another benefit of packages involves the granularity of bind parameters. With packages, you can specify your bind options at the program level because some of the bind parameters are now available to the BIND PACKAGE command, such as the isolation level and release parameters. By specifying different parameters for specific packages and including these packages into a plan, many combinations of isolation level and release are possible. You can, for example, create a single plan that provides an isolation level of cursor stability (CS) for one of its packages and an isolation level of repeatable read (RR) for another package. This combination of strategies is not possible in a plan-only environment.

The third benefit probably is the biggest benefit of all: versioning. Packages can be versioned, thus enabling you to have multiple versions of the same package existing at the same time in the DB2 Catalog. Simply by running the appropriate load module, DB2 chooses the correct package to execute. DB2 uses a package selection algorithm to execute the correct access path.

Packages also provide improved support for mirror tables. Because a package has a high level qualifier of collection, you can specify a collection for each of your mirror table environments. Suppose that you have an environment in which you have current and history data in separate tables. Using only plans, the following two options were available:

- You could write a program that specifically selected the appropriate high-level qualifier for each appropriate table, such as CURRENT or HISTORY, and hard-code that qualifier into your program.
- You could bind the program's DBRM into different plans, specifying a different owner for each.

In a package environment, you can use separate collections for each of these environments. This technique is discussed in detail in the "What Is a Collection?" and "BIND Guidelines" sections later in this chapter.

Additionally, packages provide for remote data access. If you are using DB2 remote unit of work, you can specify the location in which you want to bind the package. The DBRM will exist at the site from which you are issuing the BIND, but the package is created at the remote site indicated by the high-level qualifier of the package.

Package Administration Issues

Before deciding to implement packages, you will need to consider the potential administrative costs of packages. This section covers several areas of administrative concern surrounding package implementation.

Systematic Rebinding

A concern that might not be obvious immediately is the approach to systematic rebinding. Quite often, a production job is set up to rebind plans after executing a REORG and RUNSTATS. This setup ensures that access paths are optimal given the current state of the DB2 tablespaces and indexes. In an environment in which plans consist of multiple DBRMs, you can rebind a plan in a single job step. However, after migrating to an environment in which multiple packages exist per plan (rather than multiple DBRMs), you need to rebind each package individually. Remember that access paths exist at the package level, not at the plan level, so packages must be rebound. This results in multiple job steps: one per package. The administration of this environment will be more difficult because you will need to create and maintain additional job steps.

Package Version Maintenance

Another potential administrative headache is *package version maintenance.* Every time a DBRM with a different version identifier is bound to a package, a new version is created. This can cause many unused package versions to be retained. Additionally, when packages are freed, you must specify the location, collection, package, and version of each package you want to free.

If your shop allows many versions of packages to be created, a method is required to remove versions from the DB2 Catalog when their corresponding load modules no longer exist. Your shop, for example, may institute a policy that specifies the 5 most recent package versions are maintained in a production environment. The number 5 is not important; your shop may support 2, 12, or whatever is deemed appropriate. What *is* important is the notion that the number of versions be limited. Failure to do so causes your DB2 environment to be inundated with a very large DB2 Catalog. To administer versions, consider using a third-party tool to manage package versions as required.

Whenever the need arises to drop an old package from the system, you must know the version name associated with it. Consider the situation in which 100 versions exist and only 5 must be kept. To accomplish this, you must know the 95 version names you want to drop. If you created these versions using the VERSION(AUTO) option, you will need to remember versions named using a 26-byte timestamp. Without a tool, remembering these names is a difficult task.

Consider using DB2 Catalog queries to generate statements you can use to remove package versions. By using the information in the DB2 Catalog and the power of SQL, you can eliminate many of the tedious tasks associated with the freeing old package versions. The following SQL will generate the commands required to free all but the most recently created package version, as in the following:

```
SELECT   'FREE PACKAGE(' || COLLID || '.' ||
         NAME || '.(' || VERSION || '))'
FROM     SYSIBM.SYSPACKAGE A
WHERE    TIMESTAMP < (SELECT   MAX(TIMESTAMP)
                      FROM     SYSIBM.SYSPACKAGE B
                      WHERE    A.COLLID = B.COLLID
                      AND      A.NAME = B.NAME)
```

The result of this query is a series of FREE commands that can be submitted to DB2. Alternatively, you can modify the query to generate DROP statements that can be submitted to DB2 via SPUFI. You can add additional predicates to generate FREE commands for specific collections or packages.

Before executing the FREE commands, be sure that you really want to eliminate all package versions except for the most recent one. Additionally, inspect the generated FREE commands to ensure that they are syntactically correct. These statements may need to be modified prior to being executed. And, of course, after the package versions have been freed, you cannot use them again.

Production and Test in Same Subsystem

There may be some easing of the overall administrative burden by moving to packages. Consider shops that support both test and production application within the same DB2 subsystem. Although these types of shops are becoming increasingly rare, some still do exist and they may have valid reasons for the continuing coexistence of production and test with the same DB2 subsystem. In this case, converting to packages eases the administrative burden by enabling the application developer to specify production and test collections. An indicator, for example, can be embedded within the collection name specifying `PROD` or `TEST`. By binding packages into the appropriate collection, the production environment is effectively separated from the test environment.

Package Performance

Probably the biggest question that most shops have as they investigate moving to packages is "How will the packages perform in comparison to my current environment?" By following the advice, in this section you will understand how to make packages perform every bit as well as, if not better than, your current environment.

Usually, DB2 can retrieve the package quite easily because indexes exist on the DB2 Catalog tables that contain package information. Indexes on the `LOCATION`, `COLLID` (collection), `NAME` (package), and `CONTOKEN` columns make efficient package retrieval quite common.

Improper package list specification, however, *can* impact performance. Specifying the appropriate package list can shave critical sub-seconds from performance-critical applications. Follow these general rules of thumb when specifying your `PKLIST`:

- Make each plan package list as short as possible. Do not go to excessive lengths, however, to make the list contain only one or two packages. Make the `PKLIST` as short as possible, given the considerations and needs of your application.
- Place the most frequently used packages first in the package list.
- Consider specifying `collection.*` to minimize plan binding. If you bind multiple packages into a collection, you can include all those packages in the plan simply by binding the plan with `collection.*`. Any package that is added to that collection at a future point in time automatically is available to the plan.
- Avoid `*.*` because of the runtime authorization checking associated with it.

What Is a Collection?

A *collection* is a user-defined name from 1 to 18 characters that the programmer must specify for every package. A collection is not an actual, *physical* database object.

You can compare collections to databases. A DB2 database is not actually a *physical* object (ignoring, for the moment, the DBD). In much the same way that a database is a grouping of DB2 objects, a collection is a grouping of DB2 packages.

By specifying a different collection identifier for a package, the same DBRM can be bound into different packages. This capability permits program developers to use the same program DBRM for different packages, enabling easy access to tables that have the same structure (DDL) but different owners.

Assume, for example, that you have created copies of the DB2 sample tables and given them an authid of `DSNCLONE`. You now have a `DSN8510.DEPT` table and a `DSNCLONE.DEPT` table with the same physical construction (such as the same columns and keys). Likewise, assume that you have duplicated all the other sample tables. You then could write a single program, using unqualified embedded SQL, to access either the original or the cloned tables.

The trick is to use unqualified SQL. You could simply bind a program into one package with a collection identifier of `ORIG` and into another package with a collection identifier of `CLONE`. The bind for the package with the `ORIG` collection identifier specifies the `DSN8510` qualifier, and the bind for the `CLONE` collection package specifies the `DSNCLONE` qualifier. You would store both of these in the DB2 Catalog.

But how do you access these packages? Assume that both packages were generated from a DBRM named `SAMPPROG`. This would give you packages named `ORIG.SAMPPROG` and `CLONE.SAMPPROG`. You can bind both these packages into a plan called `SAMPPLAN`, for example, as in the following:

```
BIND  PLAN (SAMPPLAN)
      PKLIST(ORIG.SAMPPROG, CLONE.SAMPPROG)
```

The program then specifies which collection to use with the `SET CURRENT PACKAGESET` statement. By issuing the following statement, the plan is instructed to use the package identified by the value of the host variable (in this example, either `ORIG` or `CLONE`).

```
EXEC SQL
    SET CURRENT PACKAGESET = :HOST-VAR
END-EXEC.
```

Another use of packages is to identify and relate a series of programs to a given plan. You can bind a plan and specify a wildcard for the package identifier. This effectively ties to the plan all valid packages for the specified collection. Consider the following `BIND` statement, for example:

```
BIND  PLAN(SAMPLE)    PKLIST(ORIG.*)
```

All valid packages in the `ORIG` collection are bound to the `SAMPLE` plan. If new packages are bound specifying the `ORIG` collection identifier, they are included automatically in the `SAMPLE` plan; no bind or rebind is necessary.

Collection Size

Do not concern yourself with collection size. Bind as many packages into a single collection as you want. Remember, a collection is not a physical entity. It is merely a method of referencing packages.

Quite often people confuse collections with package lists. The size of a collection is irrelevant. The size of a package list is relevant—the smaller, the better.

Package List Size

You do not need to go to extraordinary means to limit the size of the package list as the performance gain realized due to smaller package lists usually is not significant. One test shows that the difference between accessing the first entry in a package list is only milliseconds faster than accessing the one hundredth entry in the package list.

A better reason to limit the size of the package list is to enhance maintainability. The fewer entries in the package list, the easier maintenance will be.

Versions

When using packages, you can keep multiple versions of a single package that refer to different versions of the corresponding application program. This way, the programmer can use a previous incarnation of a program without rebinding. Before the availability of packages, when programmers wanted to use an old version of a program, they were forced to rebind the program's plan using the correct DBRM. If the DBRM was unavailable, they had to repeat the entire program preparation process.

As of DB2 V2.3, you can specify a version as a parameter to the DB2 precompiler identifier up to 64 characters long. If so instructed, the precompiler can automatically generate a version identifier (which will be a timestamp). The version identifier is stored, much like the consistency token, in the DBRM and the link is generated from the precompile.

Other than the specification of the version at precompilation time, versioning is automatic and requires no programmer or operator intervention. Consider the following:

- When a package is bound into a plan, all versions of that package are bound into the plan.
- When a program is executed specifying that plan, DB2 checks the version identifier of the link that is running and finds the appropriate package version in the plan.
- If that version does not exist in the plan, the program will not run.
- To use a previous version of the program, simply restore and run the load module.

Versioning is a powerful feature of DB2 packages. You must take care, however, to administer the versions properly. Whenever a package is bound from a DBRM with a new version identifier, a new version of the package is created. As old versions of a package accumulate, you must periodically clean them up using the FREE command. Monitoring this accumulation is particularly important when the version identifier defaults to a timestamp because every new bind creates a new version.

Program Preparation Objects

The program preparation process is composed of many objects. Each of these objects is described as follows:

Source	Every program starts as a series of host language statements, known as the *application source*. The source gets run through the DB2 precompiler to have its SQL statements removed and placed in a DBRM.
Modified source	The DB2 precompiler creates the modified source module by stripping the source module of all its SQL statements. The modified source is passed to the host language compiler.
Load module	The linkage editor creates a load module using the output of the host language compiler. The load module contains the executable form of the host language statements and is executable in conjunction with an application plan.
DBRM	The DBRM is created by the DB2 precompiler from the SQL statements stripped from the program source code.
Plan	A plan is created by the BIND statement. It consists of the access paths required to execute the SQL statements for all DBRMs bound into the plan (either explicitly or as packages). The plan is executable in conjunction with the corresponding program load module.
Package	A package also is created by the BIND statement. It contains the access paths for a single DBRM.
Collection	A collection is an identifier used to control the creation of multiple packages from the same DBRM.
Version	A version is a token specified to the DB2 precompiler that enables multiple versions of the same collection and package to exist.

Program Preparation Guidelines

Although the chapter has discussed DB2 program preparation, few guidelines have been provided for its adequate implementation and administration. This section provides standard program preparation guidelines. The sections that follow provide guidelines for each program preparation component.

Be Aware of Default Names

If DB2 program preparation options are allowed to default, the following data set names are created:

`USERID.TEMP.PCLIST`	Precompiler listing
`USERID.TEMP.COBOL`	Modified COBOL source from the precompiler
`USERID.TEMP.LIST`	COBOL compiler listing
`USERID.TEMP.LINKLIST`	Linkage editor listing

Prepare DB2 Programs in the Background

Avoid running DB2 program preparation in the foreground. Background submission prevents your terminal from being tied up during program preparation. Additionally, if an error occurs during program preparation, a background job can be printed to document the error and assist in debugging.

Use the CICS Preprocessor

When preparing online DB2 application programs for the CICS environment, an additional program preparation step is required to preprocess CICS calls. Refer to Chapter 11 for additional information on CICS program preparation.

DCLGEN Guidelines

Follow these guidelines when issuing `DCLGEN` statements at your shop.

Use the Appropriate DCLGEN Library

Most shops allocate `DCLGEN` libraries. They are commonly either a partitioned data set or in the format specified by your shop's change management tool.

Control Who Creates DCLGEN Members

The DBA usually is responsible for creating `DCLGEN` members for each table. This establishes a point of control for managing change.

Avoid Modifying DCLGEN Members

Avoid modifying the code produced by the DCLGEN command. When the DECLARE TABLE code or WORKING-STORAGE variables are manually changed after DCLGEN creates them, the risk of syntax errors and incompatibilities increases.

Consider Prefixing DCLGEN Host Variables

Version 4

The DCLGEN command produces WORKING-STORAGE fields with the same names as the DB2 column names, except that underscores are converted to hyphens. Prior to DB2 V4, DCLGEN could not prefix each column automatically. It should be standard practice for shops to use DCLGEN with COLSUFFIX and NAMES to produce prefixed field names. When COLSUFFIX is not utilized, two tables having identical column names would have identical field names for each table.

Use Unqualified Table References

When you're using the DCLGEN command, set the current SQLID to the creator of the table to ensure that DCLGEN does not generate a qualified table name. Then, when specifying the DCLGEN options, provide an unqualified table name. This produces an unqualified DECLARE TABLE statement.

An alternative method can be used whereby a SYNONYM for every table is created for the DBA issuing the DCLGEN. The SYNONYM must be named the same as the table for which it has been created. The DBA should then specify the unqualified SYNONYM to DCLGEN. This produces an unqualified DECLARE TABLE statement.

Unfortunately, because DCLGEN does not provide the option of producing a qualified or unqualified DECLARE TABLE statement, DBAs must perform gyrations to unqualify their DECLARE TABLE statements.

Avoid Breaking DCLGEN Host Variables into Components

Although doing so is not generally recommended, you can modify the WORKING-STORAGE variables generated by DCLGEN to "break apart" columns into discrete components. Consider, for example, the following DCLGEN-created WORKING-STORAGE variables for the DSN8510.PROJACT table:

```
01  DCLPROJACT.
    10  PROJNO      PIC X(6).
    10  ACTNO       PIC S9(4)         USAGE COMP.
    10  ACSTAFF     PIC S999V99       USAGE COMP-3.
    10  ACSTDATE    PIC X(10).
    10  ACENDATE    PIC X(10).
```

The two date columns, ACSTDATE and ACENDATE, are composed of the year, the month, and the day. By changing the structure to "break apart" these columns, you could reference each component separately, as in the following example:

```
01  DCLPROJACT.
    10  PROJNO                        PIC X(6).
    10  ACTNO                         PIC S9(4)    USAGE COMP.
```

```
   10  ACSTAFF                 PIC S999V99 USAGE COMP-3.
   10  ACSTDATE.
       15  ACSTDATE-YEAR.
           20  ACSTDATE-CC     PIC X(2).
           20  ACSTDATE-YY     PIC X(2).
       15  ACSTDATE-FILLER1    PIC X.
       15  ACSTDATE-MONTH      PIC X(2).
       15  ACSTDATE-FILLER2    PIC X.
       15  ACSTDATE-DAY        PIC X(2).
   10  ACENDATE.
       15  ACENDATE-YEAR       PIC X(4).
       15  ACENDATE-FILLER1    PIC X.
       15  ACENDATE-MONTH      PIC X(2).
       15  ACENDATE-FILLER2    PIC X.
       15  ACENDATE-DAY        PIC X(2).
```

This approach is not favored because it is invasive to the generated DCLGEN code, which can result in errors, as mentioned previously. Instead, you should code structures that can be used to "break apart" these columns outside the DCLGEN, and then move the necessary columns to the structures outside the DCLGEN variables.

Avoid the Field Name PREFIX

Avoid the field name PREFIX option of DCLGEN. This option generates WORKING-STORAGE variables with a numeric suffix added to the PREFIX text. For example, if you ran DCLGEN for the DSN8510.PROJACT table and specified a PREFIX of COL, the following WORKING-STORAGE variable names would be generated:

```
01  DCLPROJACT.
    10  COL01       PIC X(6).
    10  COL02       PIC S9(4)     USAGE COMP.
    10  COL03       PIC S999V99   USAGE COMP-3.
    10  COL04       PIC X(10).
    10  COL05       PIC X(10).
```

Note how each column begins with the supplied prefix and ends with a number that steadily increases by 1. The COL01 column is used for the PROJNO column, COL02 for ACTNO, and so on. This type of DCLGEN should be avoided because the generated column names are difficult to trace to the appropriate WORKING-STORAGE variables.

Precompiler Guidelines

Follow these guidelines when precompiling DB2 programs.

Use the Appropriate DBRM Library

Most shops allocate DBRM libraries. These libraries must be set up as partitioned data sets with 80-byte records.

Retain DBRMs Only When Absolutely Necessary

Although the DBRM produced by the precompiler must be placed in a partitioned data set, DBRMs sometimes do not need to be retained. If the DBRM will be temporary due to the replication of program preparation during the testing process, it can be written to a temporary PDS. When the program is out of the testing phase, the DBRM can be written to a permanent PDS before it is migrated to production status.

Name the DBRM the Same as the Program

Ensure that the DBRM is named the same as the program from which it was created. This eases the administration of objects created and modified by the program preparation process.

Precompile Only When Required

Precompilation is not required by BASIC and APL2 programs that contain SQL statements. Refer to the appropriate BASIC and APL2 programming guides for additional information about these environments.

Use DEC31 to Impact Decimal Precision

DB2 supports decimal precision of either 15 or 31, depending upon the precompiler option. If decimal numbers with a precision greater 15 are to be utilized, you must specify the DEC31 precompiler option.

When you're using this option, examine the application program to verify that the host variables can accommodate 31-digit decimal precision.

Use LEVEL to Avoid Binding

LEVEL is a precompiler option that can be used when a program is modified but the SQL in the program has not changed. LEVEL is specified as a character string to be used by DB2 for consistency checking in place of the timestamp token. By precompiling a DBRM with the same level as before, a BIND can be avoided. You do not need to bind because SQL has not changed allowing DB2 to use the same access paths and the program to use the same package or plan as before.

Using LEVEL, a programmer can change his program without modifying the embedded SQL, and avoid worrying about having to bind. But care must be taken to ensure that the SQL is not changed. If the SQL is changed but a bind does not occur, unpredictable results can occur.

If LEVEL is used, DB2 will use the level as the consistency token and the default for version (if no version is specified).

Specify the Version with Care

Remember, you basically have two options for specifying the version name. Versions can be automatically defined by DB2 be specifying `VERSION(AUTO)` or explicitly named using the `VERSION(name)` precompile parameter. When versions are automatically assigned by DB2, a timestamp will be used.

If you explicitly name your versions, they will be more difficult to implement but easier to administer. The difficult part is providing a mechanism to ensure that programmers always specify an appropriate version when precompiling a program.

On the other hand, if you use automatic versioning, packages are easier to implement because DB2 is automatically naming the version for you, but much more difficult to administer. The administration difficulty occurs because the auto timestamp version is unwieldy to manually enter when package administration is necessary. Consider this when deciding how to name versions at your shop.

If your shop does not have an automated means of administering versions, consider explicitly specifying the version when precompiling a program.

BIND Guidelines

Using the following tips and techniques will ensure effective execution of the `BIND` statement and the creation of efficiently bound DB2 application programs.

Administer Initial Binds Centrally

A centralized administration group (DBA, bind agent, and so on) should be responsible for all initial binds of applications plans (`BIND ADD`). This provides a point of control for administering plan use and freeing old or unused plans when they are no longer required.

Keep Statistics Current for Binding

Before binding, ensure that the `RUNSTATS` utility has been executed recently for every table accessed by the plan or package to be bound. This allows the bind process to base access path selections on the most recent statistical information.

Avoid Default Parameters

Specify every bind parameter. Defaults are used for certain bind parameters when the `BIND` command is issued without specifying them. This could be dangerous because the default options are not always the best for performance and concurrency.

Group Like Programs into Collections

You should group like programs by binding them to packages and specifying the same collection identifier. If a customer application is composed of 12 DB2 programs, for example, bind each into a separate package with a collection identifier of `CUSTOMER`. This makes the administration of packages belonging to the same application easy.

Use Wildcard Package Lists

When multiple packages must exist in the same plan, favor using the wildcard capability of the `PKLIST` parameter of the `BIND PLAN` statement. To bind the 12-customer application packages (mentioned in the last guideline) to a single plan, for example, you could specify `PKLIST(CUSTOMER.*)`. Additionally, all new packages bound in the `CUSTOMER` collection are automatically added to that plan.

Specify Collections and Packages Carefully in the `PKLIST`

Avoiding the following scenario will eliminate confusion over which package is actually being used during program execution:

- Binding the same DBRM into different collections (such as `C1` and `C2`)
- Binding a plan with a package list specifying both collections (`C1.*,C2.*`), both packages (`C1.PACKAGE, C2.PACKAGE`), or a combination (`C1.*,C2.PACKAGE` or `C1.PACKAGE,C2.*`)
- Failing to specify `SET CURRENT PACKAGESET` in the application program

If the current package set is blank, the package is in any collection in the EDM pool, and the consistency tokens match, DB2 will return the package. It does not matter whether the package is from `C1` or `C2`. For this reason, specifying `SET CURRENT PACKAGESET` is imperative if you have a package bound into more than one collection in the `PKLIST` of the same plan. Although many think that DB2 uses packages in the order specified in the package list, this is only true if none of the packages are in the EDM pool when the plan executes. If a matching package is in the EDM pool and can be used, DB2 will use it and the program might execute an improper package.

Specify Explicit Consistency Tokens

Favor the specification of an explicit consistency token for package versioning over allowing it to default to a timestamp. If a new version with a new timestamp is created every time a package is bound, the DB2 Catalog quickly becomes cluttered with unused versions. Explicitly specifying a consistency token to control versions that must be saved is better. You could, for example, specify a release number such as `REL100`, and then increment the number to `REL101`, `REL102`, `REL200`, and so on, to indicate different versions of the software. In this manner, only one version, rather than many versions, of each release will exist.

Use the QUALIFIER Parameter

When binding packages, use the QUALIFIER parameter to specify an identifier to be used by the bind process to qualify all tables referenced by SQL statements in the DBRM being bound. The DSN8510.DEPT table, for example, is accessed if the following statement is embedded in a program bound to a package specifying a QUALIFIER of DSN8510:

```
EXEC SQL
    SELECT  DEPTNO, DEPTNAME
    INTO    :DEPTNO, :DEPTNAME
    FROM    DEPT
END-EXEC.
```

Users can specify a qualifier different from their userid if they have the necessary authority to issue the BIND command for the plan or package. The users do not need to be SYSADM or have a secondary authid, as is required with the OWNER parameter.

Optionally, the OWNER parameter can be used to qualify tables at BIND time. When specifying an OWNER, however, the binding agent must be either a SYSADM or set up with a secondary authid equal to the owner being specified.

Strategically Implement Multiple Qualified Tables

If a single plan needs to access tables with different qualifiers, consider one of the following two strategies. The first strategy is to create aliases or synonyms such that every table or view being accessed has the same qualifier. The second method is to separate the tables being accessed into logical processing groups by qualifier. Code a separate program to access each processing group. Then bind each program to a separate package, specifying the qualifier of the tables in that program. Finally, bind all the packages into a single plan.

Use One Program and Multiple Packages for Mirror Tables

When you use mirror tables, one program can access different tables. Suppose that you need an employee table for every month of the year. Each employee table is modeled after DSN8510.EMP but contains only the active employees for the month it supports. The following tables, for example, are differentiated by their qualifier:

```
JANUARY.EMP
FEBRUARY.EMP
MARCH.EMP
NOVEMBER.EMP
DECEMBER.EMP
```

Assume that you need 12 reports, each one providing a list of employees for a different month. One program can be coded to access a generic, unqualified EMP table. You then could bind the program to 12 separate packages (or plans), each specifying a different qualifier (JANUARY through DECEMBER). For more information on mirror tables, refer to Chapter 3, "Data Definition Guidelines."

Use the Correct ACTION Parameter

Specify the proper ACTION parameter for your bind. You can specify two types of actions: ADD or REPLACE. ADD indicates that the plan is new. REPLACE indicates that an old plan by the same name will be replaced. Specifying ACTION (REPLACE) for a new plan does not cause the bind to fail—it merely causes confusion.

Establish Acceptable BIND Plan Parameters

Favor the use of the following parameters when binding application plans:

```
ISOLATION (CS)
VALIDATE (BIND)
ACTION (REPLACE)
NODEFER (PREPARE)
FLAG (I)
ACQUIRE (USE)
RELEASE (COMMIT)
DEGREE (ANY)
CURRENTDATA (NO)
EXPLAIN (YES)
```

These BIND PLAN parameters usually produce the most efficient and effective DB2 plan. Reasons for choosing different options are discussed in other guidelines in this chapter.

Establish Acceptable BIND Package Parameters

Favor the use of the following parameters when binding packages:

```
ISOLATION (CS)
VALIDATE (BIND)
ACTION (REPLACE)
SQLERROR (NOPACKAGE)
FLAG (I)
RELEASE (COMMIT)
DEGREE (ANY)
CURRENTDATA (NO)
EXPLAIN (YES)
```

These BIND PACKAGE parameters usually produce the most efficient and effective DB2 package. Other guidelines in this chapter cover the occasions when you should choose another option.

Take Care When Specifying Isolation Level

The ISOLATION parameter of the BIND command specifies the isolation level of the package or plan. The isolation level determines the mode of page locking implemented by the program as it runs.

DB2 implements page and row locking at the program execution level, which means that all page or row locks are acquired as needed during the program run. Page or row locks are released when the program issues a COMMIT or ROLLBACK.

You can specify the following four isolation levels:

- Cursor stability (CS)
- Repeatable read (RR)
- Read stability (RS)
- Uncommitted read (UR)

They significantly affect how the program processes page locks.

Use Uncommitted Read with Caution

Anyone accustomed to application programming when access to a database is required understands the potential for concurrency problems. To ensure data integrity when one application program attempts to read data that is in the process of being changed by another, the DBMS must forbid access until the modification is complete. Most DBMS products, DB2 included, use a locking mechanism for all data items being changed. Therefore, when one task is updating data on a page, another task cannot access data (read or update) on that same page until the data modification is complete and committed.

Version 4

Programs that read DB2 data typically access numerous rows during their execution and are thus quite susceptible to concurrency problems. DB2 V4 provides read-through locks, also known as *dirty read* or *uncommitted read*, to help overcome concurrency problems. When you're using an uncommitted read, an application program can read data that has been changed but is not yet committed.

Dirty read capability is implemented at BIND time by specifying ISOLATION(UR). Application programs bound using the UR isolation level will read data without taking locks. This way, the application program can read data contained in the table as it is being manipulated. Consider the following sequence of events:

1. To change a specific value, at 9:00 a.m. a transaction containing the following SQL is executed:

   ```
   UPDATE     EMP
      SET FIRSTNME = "MICHELLE"
   WHERE      EMPNO = 10020;
   ```

   The transaction is a long-running one and continues to execute without issuing a COMMIT.

2. At 9:01 a.m., a second transaction attempts to SELECT the data that was changed, but not committed.

If the UR isolation level was specified for the second transaction, it would read the changed data even though it had yet to be committed. Obviously, if the program doesn't need to wait to take a lock and merely reads the data in whatever state it happens to be at that moment, the program will execute faster than if it had to wait for locks to be taken and resources to be freed before processing.

The implications of reading uncommitted data, however, must be carefully examined before being implemented. Several types of problems can occur. A dirty read can cause duplicate rows to be returned where none exist. Alternatively, a dirty read can cause no rows to be returned when one (or more) actually exists. Additionally, an ORDER BY clause does not guarantee that rows will be returned in order if the UR isolation level is used. Obviously, these problems must be taken into consideration before using the UR isolation level. The following rules apply to ISOLATION(UR):

- The UR isolation level applies to read-only operations: SELECT, SELECT INTO, and FETCH from a read-only result table.
- Any application plan or package bound with an isolation level of UR will use uncommitted read functionality for any read-only SQL. Operations contained in the same plan or package and are not read-only will use an isolation level of CS.
- The isolation level defined at the plan or package level during BIND or REBIND can be overridden as desired for each SQL statement in the program. You can use the WITH clause to specify the isolation level for any individual SQL statement, as in the following example:

  ```
  SELECT EMPNO, LASTNAME
  FROM EMP
  WITH UR;
  ```

  The WITH clause is used to allow an isolation level of RR, RS, CS, or UR to be used on a statement-by-statement basis. The UR isolation level can be used only with read-only SQL statements. This includes read-only cursors and SELECT INTO statements. The CS, RR, and RS isolation levels can be specified for SELECT, INSERT, UPDATE, and DELETE statements. The WITH clause, however, cannot be used with subselects.
- DB2 will not choose UR isolation with an access path that uses a Type 1 index. If the plan or package is rebound to change to UR isolation, DB2 will not consider any access paths that use a Type 1 index. If an acceptable Type 2 index cannot be found, DB2 will choose a table scan.

When is it appropriate to use UR isolation? The general rule of thumb is to avoid UR whenever the results must be 100 percent accurate. Following are examples of when this would be true:

- Calculations that must balance are being performed on the selected data.
- Data is being retrieved from one source to insert to or update another.
- Production, mission-critical work is being performed that cannot contain or cause data integrity problems.

In general, most current DB2 applications will not be candidates for dirty reads. In a few specific situations, however, the dirty read capability will be of major benefit. Consider the following cases in which the `UR` isolation level could prove to be useful:

- Access is required to a reference, code, or look-up table that basically is static in nature. Due to the non-volatile nature of the data, a dirty read would be no different than a normal read the majority of the time. In those cases when the code data is being modified, any application reading the data would incur minimum, if any, problems.
- Statistical processing must be performed on a large amount of data. Your company, for example, might want to determine the average age of female employees within a certain pay range. The impact of an uncommitted read on an average of multiple rows will be minimal because a single value changed will not greatly impact the result.
- Dirty reads can prove invaluable in a data warehousing environment that uses DB2 as the DBMS. A data warehouse is a time-sensitive, subject-oriented, store of business data that is used for online analytical processing. Other than periodic data propagation and/or replication, access to the data warehouse is read-only. Because the data is generally not changing, an uncommitted read is perfect in a read-only environment due to the fact that it can cause little damage. More data warehouse projects are being implemented in corporations worldwide and DB2 with dirty read capability is a very wise choice for data warehouse implementation.
- In those rare cases when a table, or set of tables, is used by a single user only, `UR` can make a lot of sense. If only one individual can be modifying the data, the application programs can be coded such that all (or most) reads are done using `UR` isolation level, and the data will still be accurate.
- Finally, if the data being accessed already is inconsistent, little harm can be done using a dirty read to access the information.

CAUTION

Although the dirty read capability can provide relief to concurrency problems and deliver faster performance in specific situations, it also can cause data integrity problems and inaccurate results. Be sure to understand the implications of the `UR` isolation level and the problems it can cause before diving headlong into implementing it in your production applications.

Avoid Repeatable Read `ISOLATION`

With repeatable read, or `RR`, all page locks are held until they are released by a `COMMIT`. Cursor stability, or `CS`, releases read-only page locks as soon as another page is accessed.

In most cases, you should specify CS to enable the greatest amount of application program concurrency. RR, however, is the default isolation level.

Use the RR page locking strategy only when an application program requires consistency in rows that may be accessed twice in one execution of the program, or when an application program requires data integrity that cannot be achieved with CS. Programs of this nature are rare.

For an example of the first reason to use RR page locking, consider a reporting program that scans a table to produce a detail report, and then scans it again to produce a summarized managerial report. If the program is bound using CS, the results of the first report might not match the results of the second.

Suppose that you are reporting the estimated completion dates for project activities. The first report lists every project and the estimated completion date. The second, managerial report lists only the projects with a completion date greater than one year.

The first report indicates that two activities are scheduled for more than one year. After the first report but before the second, however, an update occurs. A manager realizes that she underestimated the resources required for a project. She invokes a transaction (or uses QMF) to change the estimated completion date of one of her project's activities from 8 months to 14 months. The second report is produced by the same program, but reports 3 activities.

If the program has used an isolation level of RR rather than CS, an update between the production of the two reports would not have been allowed because the program would have maintained the locks it held from the generation of the first report.

For an example of the second reason to use RR page locking, consider a program that is looking for pertinent information about employees in the information center and software support departments who make more than $30,000 in base salary. The program opens a cursor based on the following SELECT statement:

```
SELECT   EMPNO, FIRSTNME, LASTNAME,
         WORKDEPT, SALARY
FROM     DSN8510.EMP
WHERE    WORKDEPT IN ('C01', 'E21')
AND      SALARY > 30000
```

The program then begins to fetch employee rows. Department 'C01' is the information center and department 'E21' is software support. Assume further, as would probably be the case, that the statement uses the DSN8510.XEMP2 index on the WORKDEPT column. An update program that implements employee modifications is running concurrently. The program, for example, handles transfers by moving employees from one department to another, and implements raises by increasing the salary.

Assume that Sally Kwan, one of your employees, has just been transferred from the information center to software support. Assume further that another information center employee, Heather Nicholls, received a 10 percent raise. Both these modifications will be implemented by the update program running concurrently with the report program.

If the report program were bound with an isolation level of `CS`, the second program could move Sally from `C01` to `E21` after she was reported to be in department `C01` but before the entire report was finished. Thus, she could be reported twice: once as an information center employee and again as a software support employee. Although this circumstance is rare, it can happen with programs that use cursor stability. If the program were bound instead with `RR`, this problem could not happen. The update program probably would not be allowed to run concurrently with a reporting program, however, because it would experience too many locking problems.

Now consider Heather's dilemma. The raise increases her salary 10 percent, from $28,420 to $31,262. Her salary now fits the parameters specified in the `WHERE` condition of the SQL statement. Will she be reported? It depends on whether the update occurs before or after the row has been retrieved by the index scan, which is clearly a tenuous situation. Once again, `RR` avoids this problem.

You might be wondering, "If `CS` has the potential to cause so many problems, why are you recommending its use? Why not trade the performance and concurrency gain of `CS` for the integrity of `RR`?" The answer is simple: The types of problems outlined are rare. The expense of using `RR`, however, is so great in terms of concurrency that the trade-off between the concurrency expense of `RR` and the efficiency of `CS` usually is not a sound one.

Consider Read Stability `ISOLATION` Over Repeatable Read

Version 4

The `RS` isolation level is similar in functionality to the `RR` isolation level. It indicates that a retrieved row or page is locked until the end of the unit of work. No other program can modify the data until the unit of work is complete, but other processes can insert values that might be read by your application if it accesses the row a second time.

Use read stability only when your program can handle retrieving a different set of rows each time a cursor or singleton `SELECT` is issued. If using read stability, be sure your application is not dependent on having the same number of rows returned each time.

Favor Acquiring Tablespace Locks When the Tablespace Is Used

In addition to a page locking strategy, every plan also has a tablespace locking strategy. This strategy is implemented by two bind parameters: `ACQUIRE` and `RELEASE`.

Remember that a page lock is acquired when the page is requested, and is released after a `COMMIT` or a `ROLLBACK`. Tablespace locking is different. DB2 uses a mixed tablespace locking strategy—the programmer specifies when to acquire and release tablespace locks by means of the `ACQUIRE` and `RELEASE` parameters. Tablespace locking is implemented only at the plan level; it is not implemented at the package level.

The options for the `ACQUIRE` parameter are `USE` and `ALLOCATE`. When you specify `USE`, tablespace locks are taken when the tablespace is accessed. With `ALLOCATE`, tablespace locks are taken when the plan is first allocated.

The options for RELEASE are COMMIT and DEALLOCATE. When you specify the COMMIT option, locks are released at commit or rollback time. When you specify DEALLOCATE, all locks are held until the plan finishes and is deallocated.

In general, use the following tablespace locking allocation strategy:

```
ACQUIRE (USE)
RELEASE (COMMIT)
```

This provides your program with the highest degree of concurrency.

When you have conditional table access in your program, consider using the following lock and resource allocation strategy:

```
ACQUIRE (USE)
RELEASE (DEALLOCATE)
```

With conditional table access, every invocation of the program does not cause that section of code to be executed. By specifying that locks will be acquired only when used, and released only when deallocated, you can increase the efficiency of a program because locks, once acquired, are held during the entire course of the program. This does reduce concurrency, however.

For a batch update program in which you know that you will access every table coded in your program, use the following lock and resource allocation strategy:

```
ACQUIRE (ALLOCATE)
RELEASE (DEALLOCATE)
```

All locks are acquired as soon as possible and are not released until they are absolutely not needed. This strategy, too, will reduce concurrency.

For high-volume transactions (one or more transactions per second throughput), use a CICS protected entry thread (RCT TYPE=ENTRY) with the following strategy:

```
ACQUIRE (ALLOCATE)
RELEASE (DEALLOCATE)
```

A high-volume transaction generally executes much faster if it is not bogged down with the accumulation of tablespace locks.

In all cases, you should obtain database administration approval before binding with parameters other than ACQUIRE (USE) and RELEASE (COMMIT).

Specify Validation at BIND Time

A validation strategy refers to the method of checking for the existence and validity of DB2 tables and DB2 access authorization. You can use two types of validation strategies: VALIDATE (BIND) or VALIDATE (RUN).

VALIDATE (BIND), the preferred option, validates at bind time. If a table is invalid or proper access authority has not been granted, the bind fails.

VALIDATE (RUN) validates DB2 table and security each time the plan is executed. This capability is useful if a table is changed or authority is granted after the bind is issued. It does, however, impose a potentially severe performance degradation because each SQL statement is validated each time it is executed.

Always specify VALIDATE (BIND) for production plans. Use VALIDATE (RUN) only in a testing environment.

Request All Error Information

Always specify FLAG (I), which causes the BIND command to return all information, warning, error, and completion messages. This option provides the greatest amount of information pertaining to the success or failure of the bind.

Specify an Appropriate CACHESIZE

The CACHESIZE parameter specifies the size of the authorization cache for a plan. The authorization cache is a portion of memory set aside for a plan to store valid authids that can execute the plan. By storing the authids in memory, the cost of I/O can be saved.

The cache can vary in size from 0 to 4,096 bytes in 256-byte increments. For a plan with a small number of users, specify the minimum size, 256. If the plan will have large number of users, then calculate the appropriate size as follows:

```
CACHESIZE = ( [number of concurrent users] * 8 ) + 32
```

Take the number returned by the formula and round up to the next 256 byte increment making sure not to exceed 4,096.

NOTE

The number 32 is added because the authid cache always uses 32 control bytes.

One final suggestion—if the plan is executed only infrequently, or has been granted to PUBLIC, do not cache authids. Specify a CACHESIZE of zero.

Version 5

As of DB2 V5, authorization can be cached for packages as well as plans. However, no CACHESIZE BIND parameter is available for packages. Instead, package caching must be enabled by the system administrator at the subsystem level.

Specify DEGREE(ANY) to Encourage Parallelism

When DEGREE(ANY) is specified, DB2 will attempt to execute queries using parallel engines whenever possible. Parallel queries are typically deployed against partitioned tablespaces, and can be used to access non-partitioned tablespaces when specified in a join with at least one partitioned tablespace.

At optimization time, DB2 can be directed to consider parallelism by specifying `DEGREE(ANY)` at `BIND` time for packages and plan. Following are the three types of parallelism:

- I/O—multiple read engines
- CPU—multiple processor and multiple read engines
- Sysplex—multiple data sharing subsystems

Parallelism can significantly enhance the performance of queries against partitioned tablespaces. By executing in parallel, elapsed time usually will decrease, even if CPU time does not. This results in an overall perceived performance gain because the same amount of work will be accomplished in less clock time.

Following are the types of queries that will benefit most from I/O parallelism:

- Access large amount of data, but return only a few rows
- Use column functions (`AVG`, `COUNT`, `MIN`, `MAX`, `SUM`)
- Access long rows

Version 4

CPU parallelism extends the capabilities of I/O parallelism and is new as of DB2 V4. When CPU parallelism is invoked, it is always used in conjunction with I/O parallelism. The reverse of this is not necessarily true. Most of the queries that benefit from I/O parallelism also will benefit from CPU parallelism because as the I/O bottlenecks are reduced, the CPU bottlenecks become more apparent.

Version 5

DB2 V5 extends the parallel capabilities of DB2 even further with Query Sysplex parallelism. When Sysplex parallelism is employed, DB2 can spread a single query across multiple central processors complexes within a data sharing group. For more information on data sharing and Sysplex parallelism, refer to Chapter 12, "Data Sharing."

Specify `NODEFER(PREPARE)`

Specify `NODEFER(PREPARE)`, rather than `DEFER(PREPARE)`, unless your program contains SQL statements that access DB2 tables at a remote location and are executed more than once during the program's invocation. In this case, specifying `DEFER(PREPARE)` can reduce the amount of message traffic by preparing each SQL statement only once at the remote location, when it is first accessed. Subsequent execution of the same statement in the same unit of recovery does not require an additional `PREPARE`.

Specify `SQLERROR(CONTINUE | NOPACKAGE)`

Two options for the `SQLERROR` parameter exist: `NOPACKAGE` and `CONTINUE`. `NOPACKAGE` is the recommended option when not operating in a distributed environment. By specifying `NOPACKAGE`, a package will not be created when an SQL error is encountered.

The other option is CONTINUE, which will create a package even if an error is encountered. Because SQL syntax varies from environment to environment, CONTINUE is a viable option when operating in a distributed environment. The package can be created, regardless of the error with the understanding that the SQL will function properly at the remote location.

Specify EXPLAIN(YES) for Production BINDs

At a minimum, all production BINDs should be performed with the EXPLAIN(YES) option. This allows the proper monitoring of the production access path selection made by DB2.

Use the ENABLE and DISABLE Parameters Effectively

You can use the ENABLE and DISABLE bind options to control the environment in which the plan or package being bound can be executed. ENABLE ensures that the plan or package operates in only the enabled environments. DISABLE permits execution of the plan or package by all subsystems except those explicitly disabled. ENABLE and DISABLE are mutually exclusive parameters (only one can be used per package or plan).

If a plan is bound specifying ENABLE(IMS), for example, only the IMS subsystem is permitted to execute the plan. If a plan is bound with the DISABLE(CICS) option, the CICS subsystem is not permitted to execute this plan.

Be careful when using ENABLE and DISABLE because they may function differently than one might originally think. ENABLE explicitly enables an environment for execution. The enabled environment, however, is the only environment that can execute the plan or package. So ENABLE limits the environments in which a package or plan can execute. By contrast, specifying DISABLE actually is more open because only one specific area is disabled, thereby implicitly enabling everything else. The bottom line is that ENABLE is more limiting than DISABLE.

Table 7.1 shows valid ENABLE and DISABLE specifications:

Table 7.1. Environments that can be enabled or disabled.

Specification	*Package or Plan Is Executed Only*
BATCH	As a batch job
DLIBATCH	As an IMS batch job
DB2CALL	With the Call Attach Facility
CICS	Online through CICS
IMS	Under the control of IMS
IMSBMP	As an IMS BMP (batch message processor)
IMSMPP	As an online IMS message processing program (that is, a transaction)
RRSAF	With the RRS Attachment Facility
REMOTE	As a remote program

Retain Security when Binding Existing Plans

Be sure to specify the RETAIN parameter for existing plans. RETAIN indicates that all bind and execute authority granted for this plan will be retained. If you fail to specify the RETAIN parameter, all authority for the plan is revoked.

Retain DBRMs Bound in Plans

Develop a consistent scheme for the maintenance and retention of DBRMs bound to application plans and packages. Ensure that DBRMs are copied to the appropriate library (test, education, production, and so on) before the binding of plans in the new environment. This applies to both new and modified programs.

Consider Dynamic Reoptimization

Version 5

When host variables or parameter markers are used in SQL statements in an application program, DB2 does not know the values that will be supplied at execution time. This lack of information causes DB2 to guess at the best access path using the information available at BIND time.

By specifying the BIND parameter REOPT(VARS), DB2 will reevaluate the access path at runtime when the host variable and parameter marker values are known. This should result in a better-formulated access path. Reoptimization, however, is not a panacea. Because DB2 must re-evaluate access paths at execution time, additional overhead will be consumed. This overhead can negate any performance gains achieved by the new access paths. Enabling reoptimization does not guarantee a different access path; it only allows DB2 to formulate the access path based on the runtime values used.

In general, reoptimization can be an easy-to-implement alternative to dynamic SQL. The overhead of reoptimization will be less than that associated with dynamic SQL because reoptimization does not require statement parsing, authorization checking, dependency checking, or table decomposition.

Do Not Blindly Enable Reoptimization for All Programs

Version 5

In general, consider specifying REOPT(VARS) in the following situations:

- Application programs in which multiple SQL statements utilize host variables (or parameter markers)
- SQL statements in which host variables (or parameter markers) are deployed against columns with very skewed distribution statistics
- Application programs in which dynamic SQL was considered, but avoided because of its complexity or overhead

Before implementing reoptimization, conduct performance tests to determine its effect on transaction performance.

Consider Isolating Reoptimized Statements

Version 5

The REOPT and NOREOPT parameters must be specified for an entire program when it is bound into a plan or package. Most programs commonly contain multiple SQL statements, not all of which will benefit from reoptimization.

Consider isolating specific SQL statements into a separate program, and binding it into a package. In this manner, individual SQL statements can be set for reoptimization without affecting the rest of the SQL in a program.

Keeping Prepared Statements Past COMMIT

Version 5

By specifying KEEPDYNAMIC(YES), dynamic SQL statements can be held past a COMMIT point. Specify KEEPDYNAMIC(YES) for dynamic SQL programs in DB2 subsystems in which the dynamic SQL prepare cache is enabled. This causes fewer dynamic binds and optimizes the performance of dynamic SQL programs.

Note that when KEEPDYNAMIC(YES) is specified, you also must use NOREOPT(VARS).

Linkage Editor Guidelines

The following guideline is useful to know when link-editing DB2 programs.

Link the Appropriate Language Interface Module

You must link the proper language interface module with the program's compiled module. The modules to use depend on the execution environment of the program being link-edited. Table 7.2 shows a list of modules required for different DB2 environments.

Table 7.2. Link-edit modules for DB2 programs.

Environment	*Language Interface*
TSO	DSNELI (for online ISPF and TSO batch)
CICS	DSNCLI
IMS/DC	DFSLI000
Call Attach	DSNALI
RRSAF	DSNRLI

Summary

You now should be able to code and prepare a DB2 application program using a standard 3GL. Some applications, however, do not rely solely on 3GL technology. Chapter 8, "Alternative DB2 Application Development Methods," discusses alternative ways of coding DB2 programs.

8

Alternative DB2 Application Development Methods

Part II has dealt primarily with DB2 application development using embedded SQL in a third-generation language such as COBOL. However, as I mentioned at the outset of Part II, you can use other methods to develop DB2 applications. With the growing popularity of client/server computing, these methods are gaining acceptance in the DP community.

In this chapter, I discuss the ramifications of using six alternative but perhaps complementary development methods to build DB2 applications: using stand-alone SQL, client/server programming languages, Call Level Interface and ODBC, fourth-generation languages, CASE tools, and report writers.

Developing Applications Using Only SQL

Although it is uncommon for an entire application to be developed with SQL alone, it is quite common for components of an application to be coded using only SQL. Pure SQL is a good choice for the quick development of code to satisfy simple application requirements. Examples include the following:

- Using the `UPDATE` statement to reset indicators in tables after batch processing
- Deleting every row from a table using a mass `DELETE` or deleting a predefined set of rows from a table after batch processing
- Creating simple, unformatted table listings
- Performing simple data entry controlled by a `CLIST` or REXX `EXEC`

SQL Application Guidelines

The following guidelines are helpful when developing an application using only SQL.

Use Native SQL Applications Sparingly

Although using native SQL in some circumstances is technically possible, avoid doing so unless the application truly can be developed without advanced formatting features or procedural logic. Achieving the level of professionalism required for most applications is difficult if you use SQL alone. For example, you cannot use SQL alone to format reports, loop through data a row at a time, or display a screen of data.

Enforce Integrity Using DB2 Features

If you develop a complete application or major portions of an application using only SQL, be sure to use the native features of DB2 to enforce the integrity of the application. For example, if data will be entered or modified using SQL alone, enforce user-defined integrity rules using check constraints or `VALIDPROC`s coded for each column and specified in the `CREATE TABLE` DDL.

Additionally, specify referential constraints for all relationships between tables and create unique indexes to enforce uniqueness requirements. This approach is the only way to provide integrity when a host language is not used.

Create Domain Tables

Mimic the use of domains when possible using domain tables or check constraints. Domain tables are two-column tables that contain all valid values (along with a description) for columns in other tables. Be sure to use referential integrity to tie these "domain" tables to the main tables. For example, you can create a "domain" table for the SEX column of the DSN8510.EMP table consisting of the following data:

SEX	DESCRIPTION
M	MALE
F	FEMALE

The primary key of this "domain" table is SEX. You specify the SEX column in the DSN8510.EMP as a foreign key referencing the domain table, thereby enforcing that only the values M or F can be placed in the foreign key column. This way, you can reduce the number of data entry errors.

Version 4

Check constraints provide an alternative approach to enforcing domain values. Instead of creating a new table coupled with referential constraints, you can add a single check constraint to the column to enforce the data content. Consider this example:

```
SEX               CHAR(1)
CONSTRAINT GENDER CHECK (SEX IN ("M", "F"))
```

Whether to choose domain tables or check constraints depends on the circumstances. Each is useful in different situations. Weigh the following benefits and drawbacks before choosing one method over the other:

- Check constraints are simply SQL predicates and cannot carry description columns (or any other columns), whereas domain tables can. Therefore, a domain table can be more self-documenting.
- Check constraints should outperform referential integrity because DB2 does not need to read data from multiple user tables to determine the validity of the data.
- Domain tables are easier to use when the domain is not static. Adding values to a check constraint requires DDL changes; adding values to a domain table requires a simple SQL INSERT.
- As the number of valid values increases, domain tables are easier to implement and maintain. The full text of a check constraint can contain no more than 3,800 bytes.

- When you're tying together domain tables using referential integrity, sometimes large referential sets are created. They can be difficult to administer and control. Large referential sets, however, may be preferable to program-enforced RI or, worse yet, allowing inaccurate data. When you're deciding whether to enforce RI for domain tables, balance performance and recoverability issues against possible data integrity violations. When large referential sets are created, consider breaking them up using check constraints for some of the simpler domains.

Follow SQL Coding Guidelines

When you're developing native SQL applications, follow the SQL coding guidelines presented in Chapter 2, "Data Manipulation Guidelines," to achieve optimal performance.

Using Client/Server Programming Languages

Distributed processing and client/server processing are quite widespread in the data processing community. Distributed processing describes the interaction of multiple computers working together to solve a business problem. Client/server processing is a specific type of distributed processing in which a client computer requests services from a server. The client is typically a personal computer with a graphical user interface (GUI). DB2 is a popular candidate as a database server.

The popularity of client/server development has an impact on the DB2 application development environment. Often, DB2 developers access DB2 using a client/server application development product that communicates to DB2 using a gateway product. Popular client/server programming languages include PowerBuilder, Visual Basic, Visual Age, and Delphi.

Connecting to DB2

IBM's Distributed Database Connection Services (DDCS) is available for Windows, OS/2, and several flavors of UNIX. You can use this gateway product to connect PC applications directly to DB2 for OS/390 and MVS. The Client Application Enabler (CAE) is also required and available on Windows, OS/2, and multiple UNIX variants. It enables remote clients to connect to DDCS (or DB2 Common Server).

The application (or ODBC driver) calls CAE, which in turn sends the request to the DDCS gateway. The DDCS gateway passes the call to DB2 for MVS in the form of a DRDA request, as illustrated in Figure 8.1. CAE and DDCS enable your applications or third-party products such as Microsoft Access and Lotus Approach running on the Windows platform to access DB2 for MVS directly.

FIGURE 8.1.
Using DDCS and CAE to connect to DB2.

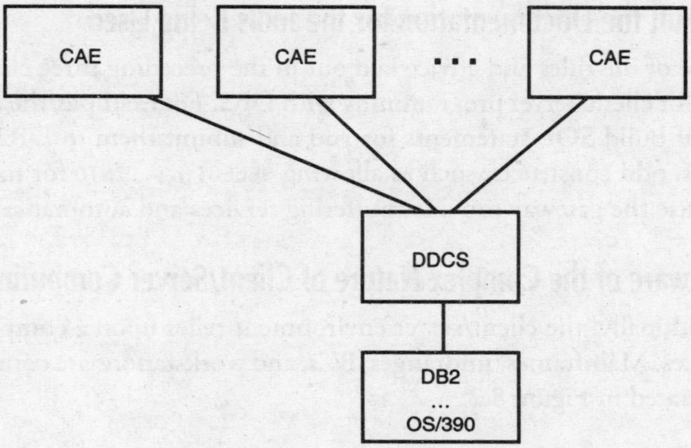

Client/Server Guidelines

Building client/server applications requires knowledge of multiple platforms and the network used to connect them. The following tips and tricks can be useful when building applications that span platforms.

Be Aware of SQL Anomalies

GUI-based client/server development tools may not offer SQL that is completely compatible with DB2 for MVS. As such, certain features discussed in the DB2 manuals (and this book) may not be available when you're using a client/server language.

Likewise, some client/server languages require a call level interface to SQL (such as ODBC). This requirement causes the application to use dynamic SQL with all the performance implications as discussed in Chapter 6, "Dynamic SQL Programming."

Bind and Block Properly for DDCS

When you're binding client packages accessing data in DB2 for MVS, you should use `BLOCKING ALL` to optimize data retrieval.

Configure DDCS for Connecting to DB2

Ensure that the block size between DDCS and the CAE (Client Application Enabler) is configured properly. Use the `RQRIOBLK` parameter to specify the maximum size of network I/O blocks. Use the default DRDA block size (32,767) if it does not cause paging when your application executes. If paging occurs, reduce `RQRIOBLK` until paging ceases. Paging typically causes significant application performance degradation. See Chapter 20, "Tuning DB2's Environment," for more information on paging and its impact on performance.

Consult the Documentation for the Tools Being Used

Some of the rules and advice laid out in the preceding three chapters of Part II may not hold true for client/server programming with DB2. For example, the client/server development tool might build SQL statements for you and submit them to DB2 through the gateway. Sometimes, odd constructs, such as allowing `SELECT ... INTO` for multiple rows can be permitted because the gateway provides buffering services and automatically handles building cursors.

Be Aware of the Complex Nature of Client/Server Computing

Additionally, the client/server environment relies upon a complex network of computing resources. Mainframes, midranges, PCs, and workstations are commonly networked together, as illustrated in Figure 8.2.

FIGURE 8.2.
A complex client/server environment.

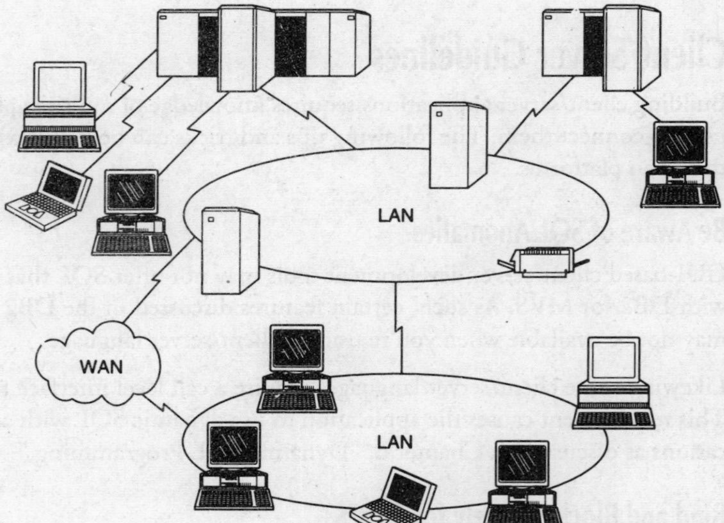

In a client/server environment, rely on the documentation that came with your application development tool and middleware product(s).

Use Stored Procedures

Version 4

Minimize network traffic by implementing stored procedures for frequently executed pieces of code. If you concentrate multiple SQL statements within a stored procedure, less data needs to be sent across the network. Network traffic is usually the single most important determinant of client/server application performance.

Consolidate SQL Requests When Possible

Consolidate related SQL statements into a single request to reduce the number of requests and responses transmitted across the network. For example, change

```
SELECT EMPNO, LASTNAME FROM EMP WHERE EMPNO < '001000';
SELECT EMPNO, LASTNAME FROM EMP WHERE EMPNO > '009000';
```

into

```
SELECT  EMPNO, LASTNAME
FROM    EMP
WHERE   EMPNO < '001000'
OR      EMPNO > '009000';
```

One SQL statement sends fewer requests across the network. You can use this technique on all SQL statements, not just SELECT statements.

Ensure FOR READ ONLY for Distributed Cursors

Be sure that the FOR READ ONLY (or FOR FETCH ONLY) is used on each DECLARE CURSOR statement. Failure to do so has a negative impact on performance by disabling efficient block fetching. The FOR READ ONLY clause is ODBC-compliant and therefore more appropriate in a complex client/server environment.

Consult Chapter 34, "DRDA," Chapter 35, "Distributed DB2," and Chapter 36, "Distribution Guidelines," for more information on the following topics:

- DB2 distributed database support
- The use of DB2 as a database server
- General distribution techniques and guidelines

Using Fourth-Generation Languages

Several fourth-generation languages (4GLs) are available at most DP shops. FOCUS, RAMIS, and NOMAD are examples of popular 4GLs. 4GLs, which operate at a higher level of abstraction than the standard 3GLs, can usually read, modify, process, and update data a set or a row at a time. For example, a 4GL can often issue a single command to list and display the contents of data stores. A 3GL program, in contrast, must read the data, test for the end of the file, move the data to an output format, and issue commands to control the display of a screen of data (for example, backward and forward scrolling, or counting the items per screen).

Consider using 4GLs for two reasons. First, a single 4GL statement usually corresponds to many 3GL statements. Because this capability provides a quicker programming cycle, production applications are online faster than traditional 3GL-developed applications. Second, 4GLs have a greatly reduced instruction set, which makes them easier to learn and master than 3GLs.

Be careful, though, because applications based on 4GLs rarely deliver the same level of performance as applications based on traditional languages. As with using pure SQL, writing entire applications using 4GL is uncommon but possible. More often, you will use 4GL to develop only certain components, such as

- Quick, one-time requests that are not run repeatedly in production.
- Specialized reports.
- Important portions of an application. (When critical components of an application are not delivered with the first release of the application, you can use a 4GL to deliver the most important portions of those components, thereby satisfying the users until you can fully develop the components using a traditional language.)

4GL Application Guidelines

Apply the following guidelines to optimize your DB2-based 4GL development efforts.

Avoid 4GLs When Performance Is Crucial

Avoid coding performance-oriented DB2 systems using fourth-generation languages. You can usually achieve a greater level of performance using traditional, third-generation languages.

Provide In-Depth 4GL Training

If you decide to use a 4GL, be sure that proper training is available. Although 4GLs can achieve similar results as 3GLs, they do not use the same techniques or methods. Developers unfamiliar with 4GLs usually do not produce the most efficient applications because of their tendency to use 3GL techniques or poorly developed 4GL techniques.

Avoid Proprietary Storage Formats

When you're using 4GLs, try to query data directly from DB2 tables instead of extracts. Extracting the data into the (sometimes proprietary) format of the 4GL can cause data consistency problems. By avoiding extracts, you ensure that the data queried using the 4GL is consistent with the data queried using conventional DB2 and SQL methods.

Extract Data as a Last Resort

Consider moving the data from DB2 tables to the 4GL format only if the performance of the 4GL program is unacceptable. (You should consider this approach only as a last resort.) If data will be extracted from DB2, you must run a regularly scheduled extraction procedure to keep the 4GL data current.

Use Embedded SQL If Possible

To retrieve DB2 data, try to use SQL embedded in the 4GL rather than use the language of the 4GL. The reasons for doing so follow:

- SQL is a universally accepted standard. Many 4GL products are on the market, and none is standard.
- Hiring SQL programmers who understand the SQL embedded in the 4GL is easier than hiring programmers who understand the syntax of the 4GL.
- Embedding SQL in a host language is a common and well-understood practice. Therefore, embedding SQL in a 4GL should, for the most part, correlate to embedding SQL in COBOL or another traditional language.

Join Tables Using SQL Instead of 4GL

If the 4GL provides a technique of relating or joining data from two physical data sources, shun using it when accessing data from DB2 tables. Instead, create a DB2 view that joins the required tables, and query that view using the 4GL. This approach almost always provides better performance. For example, I converted one application using a 4GL "join" into a 4GL query of a view that joined tables. The application reduced elapsed time by more than 250 percent after the conversion.

Understand the Strengths of 4GL

Use the strong points of the 4GL and DB2. You should use DB2 to control the integrity of the data, the modification of the data, and the access to the data. You should use the 4GL to generate reports, perform complex processes on the data after it has been retrieved, and mix non-DB2 data with DB2 data.

Using CASE

Computer-aided software engineering (CASE) is the name given to software that automates the software development process. CASE tools provide an integrated platform (or, more commonly, a series of non-integrated platforms) that can be used to drive the application development process from specification to the delivery of source code and an executable application system. The term *CASE*, however, has no universally accepted definition and can comprise anything from a diagramming tool to a data dictionary to a code generator. CASE tools usually are separated into two categories: upper CASE tools and lower CASE tools.

You use an upper CASE tool to develop system specifications and detail design. It generally provides a front-end diagramming tool as well as a back-end dictionary to control the components of the application design. CASE tools can also provide support for enforcing a system methodology, documenting the development process, and capturing design elements from current application systems.

Lower CASE tools support the physical coding of the application. Tools in this category include system and program testing tools, project management tools, and code generators. This section concentrates on the code generation portion of CASE. An application code generator usually reads application specifications input into the CASE tool in one or more of the following formats:

- A macro-level or English-like language that details the components of the application system at a pseudo-code level
- Data flow diagrams generated by another component of the CASE tool (or sometimes by a different CASE tool)
- Reverse-engineered program specifications or flowcharts

Based on the input, the code generator develops a program or series of programs to accomplish the specification of the application. IBM's Cross System Product (CSP) is an example of a code generator. The application programmer codes CSP instructions. The CSP instructions can be executed in 4GL fashion, or COBOL can be generated from the CSP. In addition, several other upper CASE tools generate CSP from program specifications.

Code-generating CASE tools try to provide the best portions of both the 3GL and 4GL worlds. They provide a quick application development environment because they raise the level of programming abstraction by accepting high-level designs or macro languages as input. They generally provide better performance than 4GLs because they can generate true, traditional 3GL source code.

Be careful when developing applications with this new method. Automatic code generation does not always produce the most efficient code. To produce efficient CASE-generated applications, follow the guidelines in the next section.

CASE Application Guidelines

The following guidelines are useful when using CASE tools to deploy DB2 applications.

Analyze Generated SQL Carefully

Code generators that develop embedded SQL programs usually produce functional SQL but do not always produce the most efficient SQL. Analyze the embedded SQL to verify that it conforms to the standards for efficient SQL outlined in Chapter 2.

Avoid Generalized I/O Routines

Sometimes a code generator produces source code that can be executed in multiple environments. This code often requires the use of an I/O routine to transform application requests for data into VSAM reads and writes, sequential file reads and writes, or database calls. When you use an I/O module, determining what SQL is accessing the DB2 tables is difficult. In addition, I/O routines usually use dynamic SQL instead of static SQL.

Favor code generators that produce true embedded SQL programs over products that use I/O routines. The programs are easier to debug, easier to maintain, and easier to tune.

Avoid Runtime Modules

Some code generators require the presence of a runtime module when the programs it generates are executed. Avoid these types of products because a runtime module adds overhead and decreases the efficiency of the generated application.

Favor Integrated CASE Tools

Choose a CASE tool that provides an integrated development platform instead of a wide array of disparate products to automate the system development life cycle (SDLC). When a CASE tool provides integration of the system development life cycle, you can save a lot of time because the tool automatically carries the application forward from stage to stage until it is finished. If the CASE tools are not integrated, time is wasted performing the following tasks:

- Converting the data from one phase to a format that can be read by the tool that supports the next phase.
- Verifying that the data in the tool that accepts data from another tool is accurate and conforms to the expected results based on the status of the data in the sending tool.
- Moving data from one tool to another. (Time is wasted installing and learning these tools, as well as debugging any problems that result from the migration process.)

To avoid these types of problems, choose a CASE tool that provides as many of the features listed in Table 8.1 as possible. Use this chart to evaluate and rank CASE tools to support the complete DB2 program development life cycle.

Table 8.1. CASE tool features checklist.

Features	*Supported (Y/N)?*	*Ranking*
	Supports the Business Strategy	
Enterprise data model capabilities		
Business data modeling		
Business decision matrices		
	Supports Prototyping	
Screen formatting		
Report formatting		
Rapidly developing executable modules		

continues

Table 8.1. continued

Features	*Supported (Y/N)?*	*Ranking*
	Supports Process Modeling	
Methodologies		
Linked to the data model		
Linked to the code generator		
Documentation		
	Supports Data Modeling	
Entity relationship diagramming		
Normalization		
Conceptual data model		
Supports subject areas		
Logical data model		
Physical data model		
Provides physical design recommendations		
Generates physical objects (such as tables or indexes)		
Linked to process model		
Documentation		
	Supports Diagramming	
Graphical interface		
Linked to process model		
Linked to data model		
Multiple diagramming techniques		
Documentation		
	Supports System Testing	
Administers test plan		
Creates test data		
User simulation		
Performance testing		
Stress testing		

Features	Supported (Y/N)?	Ranking
Supports System Testing		
Acceptance testing		
Documentation		
Supports EXPLAIN		
Supports Quality Assurance		
System failure administration		
Quality acceptance testing		
Documentation		
Supports Development		
Automatically generates SQL		
Supports override of automatic SQL		
Automates precompile and bind		
Supports plans		
Supports collections		
Supports packages		
Supports versioning		
Supports the Technical Environment		
Supports current hardware platforms		
Supports current software platforms (such as DBMS or languages)		
Supports distributed data		
Supports client/server processing		
Supports required printer(s)		
Interfaces with mainframes		
Interfaces with midranges		
Interfaces with PCs		
Interfaces with NCs		
LAN capability		
Web capability		

continues

Table 8.1. continued

Features	*Supported (Y/N)?*	*Ranking*
	Supports Input from Multiple Platforms	
Word processors		
Spreadsheets		
Databases		
HTML		
Other CASE tools		

Using Report Writers

Report writers are development tools you can use to generate professional reports from multiple data sources. You can consider a report writer as a specialized type of 4GL. Like 4GLs, they raise the level of abstraction by using fewer statements to produce reports than 3GLs do. They differ from true 4GLs in that they commonly are designed for one purpose: the generation of formatted reports.

For example, a report writer can often generate a report with a single command, whereas a 3GL must read data, format the data, program control breaks, format headers and footers, and then write the report record. IBM's Query Management Facility (QMF) and PLATINUM *technology's* Report Facility (PRF) are good examples of report writers for DB2.

PC-based report writers also are quite popular. They require a DDCS setup as discussed earlier. Examples of this type of tool include Seagate's Crystal Reports, Business Objects, and PLATINUM *technology's* Forest & Trees.

Report Writer Application Guidelines

When using report writers to build DB2 applications, be sure to consider the following guidelines.

Follow Previous Guidelines

The rules for fourth-generation languages also apply to report writers. Refer to the "4GL Application Guidelines" presented previously in this chapter.

Likewise, many popular report writers work in a client/server environment instead of completely on the mainframe. For example, the user interface runs on a PC but accesses data from DB2 tables on the mainframe. When you're using a report writer in a client/server environment, refer to the "Client/Server Guidelines" presented previously in this chapter for guidance.

Using the DB2 Call Level Interface and ODBC

Version 5

New as of DB2 V5 is another alternative development option, the Call Level Interface, or CLI. The CLI provides an alternative to embedded dynamic SQL. It is an application programming interface (API) that uses function calls to pass dynamic SQL statements as function arguments. DB2 CLI is based on the Microsoft Open Database Connectivity (ODBC) specification and the X/Open Call Level Interface specification.

NOTE

X/Open is an independent, worldwide open systems organization whose goal is to increase the portability of applications by combining existing and emerging standards. Microsoft's ODBC is based on the X/Open CLI specification and is the most popular CLI for relational database access.

The DB2 CLI is designed to be used by C and C++ programs instead of embedded SQL.

DB2 CLI applications differ from traditional DB2 programs using embedded, static SQL. When the CLI is used, a specific set of function calls is used at runtime to execute SQL statements and access database services. No precompilation is required. Contrast this system with a traditional, embedded SQL program that requires a precompiler to convert the SQL statements into executable code. The program is compiled, the SQL executables are bound to the data source, and only then can the program be executed.

Any statement that can be executed using dynamic SQL can be executed using the DB2 CLI. Because the DB2 CLI is based on open specifications such as ODBC, applications using the CLI are more portable than embedded SQL applications. Further, because a precompiler is not required, the code is not bound to the data source (in this case, DB2). This capability gives the application a degree of independence, allowing the code to connect directly to the appropriate data source at runtime without changing or preparing (precompiling/compiling/binding) the program.

Listing 8.1 shows a brief code example using DB2 CLI. Note the use of functions such as `SQLAllocStmt()` and `SQLExecDirect()` to issue SQL instead of explicitly embedded SQL statements.

Listing 8.1. Sample DB2 CLI code.

```
int
process_stmt(SQLHENV henv,
             SQLHDBC hdbc,
             SQLCHAR * sqlstr)
{
    SQLHSTMT        hsql;
```

continues

Listing 8.1. continued

```
        SQLRETURN       rc;
        /* allocate a statement handle */
        SQLAllocStmt(hdbc, &hsql);
        /* execute the SQL statement in "sqlstr"      */
        rc = SQLExecDirect(hsql, sqlstr, SQL_NTS);
        if (rc != SQL_SUCCESS)
            if (rc == SQL_NO_DATA_FOUND)
             {
              printf("\nThe SQL statement finished without an\n");
              printf("error but no data was found or modified\n");
              return (SQL_SUCCESS);
             } else
        /*  perform error checking routine */
```

DB2 CLI Guidelines

When building application programs using the DB2 CLI keep the following tips and techniques in mind.

Be Aware of the Minimum Requirements for Using CLI

The minimum requirements for a DB2 CLI application are the following:

- It must use C or C++—specifically, IBM C/C++ for MVS/ESA Version 3, Release 1, or higher.
- It must use the IBM Language Environment version 1, release 5, or higher for language runtime support.
- Each CLI program must be written and linked to execute `AMODE(31)` to indicate 31-bit addressing mode.

Increase Portability Using CLI and ASCII-Encoded Tables

When an application has a high probability of being ported to another environment, use the CLI and ASCII-encoded tables to improve open data access.

Be Aware of DB2 CLI and ODBC Differences

DB2 CLI is not 100 percent functionally equivalent to ODBC. The CLI contains most of ODBC version 2.0 as well as IBM extensions for DB2-specific features.

The DB2 CLI provides the following support:

- All ODBC level 1 functions
- All ODBC level 2 functions with the following four exceptions: `SQLBrowseConnect()`, `SQLDescribeParam()`, `SQLSetPos()`, and `SQLSetScrollOptions()`

- Some X/Open CLI functions
- Some DB2-specific functions (for example, SQLCA support)

Although use of the CLI eases portability of applications from DB2 to other ODBC-compliant DBMSs, you might need to make some modifications for the port to operate properly.

Use CLI to Reduce the Application Administration Burden

Using DB2 CLI can reduce the amount of application management and administration. Each DB2 CLI program does not need to be bound to each data source. Bind files provided with DB2 CLI need to be bound only once for all CLI applications.

However, use of the CLI requires dynamic SQL and C or C++ programming skills. Ensure that this trade-off is effective before switching to CLI programming for administrative reasons.

Understand That DRDA and CLI Are Complementary Techniques

Developers sometimes confuse CLI or ODBC with DRDA. DRDA is a remote connectivity architecture; CLI and ODBC are APIs for data manipulation in relational databases. You should view DRDA and CLI (as well as ODBC) as complementary to one another.

Consider Using Both Embedded SQL and CLI

An application can use both embedded SQL and CLI to its advantage. You can create a stored procedure using embedded, static SQL. The stored procedure can then be called from within a DB2 CLI application. After the stored procedure is created, any DB2 CLI or ODBC application can call it.

You also can write a mixed program that uses both DB2 CLI and embedded SQL. For example, you could write the bulk of the application using the DB2 CLI, but you could write critical components using embedded static SQL for performance or security reasons. Deploy your applications using this scenario only if static SQL stored procedures do not meet your application's needs. For more information on stored procedures, consult Chapter 9, "Using DB2 Stored Procedures."

Do Not Code Cursors with CLI

When you're using the DB2 CLI, explicit cursor declaration is not required. The CLI automatically creates cursors as needed, and the application can use the generated cursor in using fetches for multiple row `SELECT` statements as well as positioned `UPDATE` and `DELETE` statements.

Likewise, the `OPEN` statement is not required when you're using the CLI. When `SELECT` is executed, the CLI automatically opens the cursor.

Use Parameter Markers with CLI

Unlike embedded SQL, DB2 CLI allows the use of parameter markers when issuing the `SQLExecDirect()` function. The `SQLExecDirect()` function is the CLI equivalent of the `EXECUTE IMMEDIATE` statement.

Code `COMMIT` and `ROLLBACK` Using `SQLTransact()`

A `COMMIT` or `ROLLBACK` in DB2 CLI is issued via the `SQLTransact()` function call rather than by passing it as an SQL statement.

Check the Basic CLI Function Return Code

Each CLI function returns one of the following basic return codes:

- `SQL_SUCCESS`: The function completed successfully.
- `SQL_SUCCESS_WITH_INFO`: The function completed successfully, with a warning or other information.
- `SQL_NO_DATA_FOUND`: The function returned successfully, but no relevant data was found.
- `SQL_NEED_DATA`: The application tried to execute an SQL statement, but DB2 CLI lacks parameter data required.
- `SQL_ERROR`: The function failed.
- `SQL_INVALID_HANDLE`: The function failed because of an invalid input handle.

These return codes provide only rudimentary success or failure information. For detailed information, use the `SQLError()` function.

Use `SQLError()` to Check `SQLSTATE`

You can use the `SQLError()` function to obtain additional details that are not supplied by the basic CLI function return codes. Use `SQLError()` to check the success or failure of each call using the CLI when error diagnostic checking must be performed by the program.

The `SQLError()` function returns the following information:

- `SQLSTATE` code.
- The native DB2 error code. If the error or warning was detected by DB2 for MVS, this code is the `SQLCODE`; otherwise, it is set to `-99999`.
- The message text associated with the `SQLSTATE`.

The format and specification of most of the `SQLSTATE` values specified by the DB2 CLI are consistent with the values used by DB2 for OS/390, but some differences do exist. Refer to Table A.3 in Appendix A, "DB2 SQLCODE and SQLSTATE Values," for a listing of the DB2 CLI-specific `SQLSTATE` values.

Summary

In this chapter, you explored several non-traditional means of developing DB2 application programs. It is not always best to institute and enforce rigid development standards that do not take advantage of all the resources available to you. Contrast these alternative methods with the traditional DB2 application development environment as discussed in Chapters 5, 6, and 7. Are there applications at your shop that could benefit from techniques such as CLI, pure SQL, client/server technology, or 4GLs? If so, consider utilizing the techniques outlined in this chapter for future development efforts.

Now that you have examined traditional and nontraditional DB2 application development techniques, it is time to explore yet another way of writing DB2 programs—as stored procedures. Stored procedures differ from other DB2 programs and require different development and management techniques. Turn the page to begin learning about DB2 stored procedures.

9

Using DB2 Stored Procedures

In the past, DBMS products were designed to manage and store data in an optimal manner. Although these core capabilities are still required of modern DBMS products, the purview of the DBMS is no longer limited just to data. With the advent of client/server computing and active databases, procedural logic also is being stored and managed by the DBMS.

DB2 is maturing and gaining more functionality. The clear trend is that more and more procedural logic is being stored in the DBMS. One example of logic being stored in the DBMS is the exit routine. An exit routine, such as an `EDITPROC` or `VALIDPROC`, is usually coded in Assembler language. This code is then attached to a specific database object and is executed at a specified time, such as when data is inserted or modified. Exit routines have been available in DB2 for many years; typically, the DBA is responsible for coding and maintaining them. Exit routines, however, are primitive when compared with the procedural logic support provided by a modern RDBMS. The most popular RDBMS products support additional forms of database-administered procedural logic. Stored procedures are an example of this phenomenon.

What Is a Stored Procedure?

Stored procedures are specialized programs that are stored in the relational database management system instead of an external code library. You can think of stored procedures as similar to other database objects such as tables, views, and indexes because they are managed and controlled by the RDBMS. Depending on the particular implementation, stored procedures can also physically reside in the RDBMS. However, a stored procedure is not "physically" associated with any other object in the database. It can access and/or modify data in one or more tables. Basically, you can think of stored procedures as "programs" that "live" in the RDBMS.

A stored procedure must be directly and explicitly invoked before it can be executed. In other words, stored procedures are not event-driven. Contrast this concept with the concept of database triggers, which are event-driven and never explicitly called. Instead, triggers are automatically executed (sometimes referred to as "fired") by the RDBMS as the result of an action. Stored procedures are never automatically invoked.

DB2 provides stored procedure support as of V4 but does not yet provide trigger support.

The major motivating reason for stored procedure support is to move SQL code off the client and on the database server. Implementing stored procedures can result in less overhead than alternate development methods because one client request can invoke multiple SQL statements.

DB2's Stored Procedure Implementation

DB2 V4 provides support for stored procedures. However, DB2's implementation is quite different from the stored procedures available using other RDBMS products. For example, both Sybase SQL Server and Oracle enable you to code stored procedures using procedural extensions to SQL: Sybase provides Transact-SQL, and Oracle provides PL/SQL. DB2, on the other hand, enables you to write stored procedures using traditional programming languages. You can use any LE/370-supported language to code stored procedures. The supported languages are Assembler, C, C++, COBOL, OO COBOL, and PL/I.

DB2 stored procedures can issue both static and dynamic SQL statements with the exception of `CALL`, `COMMIT`, `ROLLBACK`, `CONNECT`, `SET CONNECTION`, and `RELEASE`. Additionally, a stored procedure can issue DB2 commands and IFI (Instrumentation Facility Interface) calls. Stored procedures can access flat files, VSAM files, and other files, as well as DB2 tables. Additionally, stored procedures can access resources in CICS, IMS, and other MVS address spaces, but no commit coordination exists between DB2 and the other resources.

Why Use Stored Procedures?

DB2 stored procedures have many potentially timesaving and useful applications. The major uses can be broken down into six categories: reusability, consistency, data integrity, maintenance, performance, and security, as described here.

Reusability: The predominant reason for using stored procedures is to promote code reusability. Instead of replicating code on multiple servers and in multiple programs, stored procedures allow code to reside in a single place—the database server. Stored procedures then can be called from client programs to access DB2 data. This approach is preferable to cannibalizing sections of program code for each new application system being developed. By developing a stored procedure, you can invoke the logic from multiple processes as needed, instead of rewriting it directly into each new process every time the code is required. When they are implemented wisely, stored procedures are useful for reducing the overall code maintenance effort. Because the stored procedure exists in one place, you can make changes quickly without propagating the change to multiple workstations.

Consistency: An additional benefit of stored procedures is increased consistency. If every user with the same requirements calls the same stored procedures, then the DBA can be assured that everyone is running the same code. If each individual user uses his or her own individual, separate code, no assurance can be given that the same logic is being used by everyone. In fact, you can be almost certain that inconsistencies will occur.

Maintenance: Stored procedures are particularly useful for reducing the overall code maintenance effort. Because the stored procedure exists in one place, you can make changes quickly without propagating the change to multiple workstations.

Data Integrity: Additionally, you can code stored procedures to support database integrity constraints. You can code column validation routines into stored procedures, which are called every time an attempt is made to modify the column data. Of course, these routines catch only planned changes that are issued through applications that use the stored procedure. Ad hoc changes are not checked; checking these changes requires triggers, which can call the stored procedure. (Of course, DB2 for MVS does not yet support triggers.)

Performance: Another common reason to employ stored procedures is to enhance performance. In a client/server environment, stored procedures can reduce network traffic because multiple SQL statements can be invoked with a single execution of a procedure instead of sending multiple requests across the communication lines. The diagram in Figure 9.1 depicts a call to a DB2 stored procedure. The passing of SQL and results occurs within the SPAS, instead of over the network as would be necessary without the stored procedure. Only two network requests are required: one to request that the stored procedure be run and one to pass the results back to the calling agent.

FIGURE 9.1.
Calling a stored procedure.

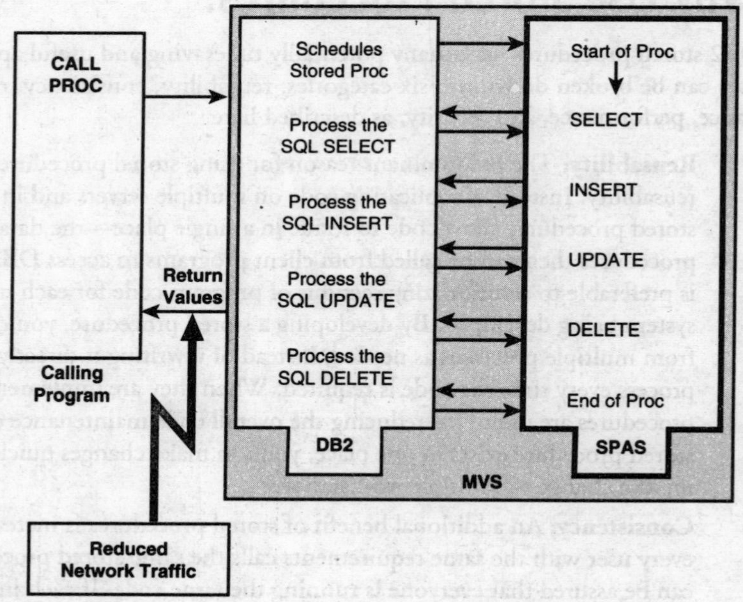

Security: You can use stored procedures to implement and simplify data security requirements. If a given group of users requires access to specific data items, you can develop a stored procedure that returns only those specific data items. You can then grant access to call the stored procedure to those users without giving them any additional authorization to the underlying objects accessed within the body of the stored procedure.

Stored procedures provide a myriad of other useful benefits including *flexibility* (stored procedures can issue both static and dynamic SQL statements and access DB2 and non-DB2 data), *ease of training* (DB2 stored procedures are written in traditional programming languages that application programmers already know), and *database protection* (stored procedures run in a separate address space from the database engine, thereby eliminating the possibility of users corrupting the DBMS installation).

Implementing DB2 Stored Procedures

Now that you understand what stored procedures are and why you would want to use them, you're ready to investigate how to implement stored procedures in DB2.

Developing a Stored Procedure

You can design and develop stored procedures in a similar manner to the way you develop any other application program. However, stored procedures have some special design requirements that you need to understand prior to developing them: using LE/370, coding parameters, returning result sets, and changing the program preparation procedure.

Using LE/370

You must develop stored procedures using an LE/370 language. LE/370 is mandatory for the use of stored procedures. LE/370 provides a common runtime environment for multiple, disparate programming languages. The runtime services available to LE/370 include error handling, storage management, and debugging. The benefit to DB2 is that the runtime services are the same for every programming language used to deploy stored procedures.

Because many stored procedures can run in a stored procedure address space, DB2 can avoid initializing, opening, and closing multiple runtime libraries for each new stored procedure. With LE/370, only one runtime library is required, it works with all LE/370 languages, and library initialization occurs only when the SPAS is started.

Coding Parameters

Parameters are essential to the effective use of stored procedures. Parameters allow data to be sent to and received from a stored procedure.

Each stored procedure has a parameter list associated with it. This list must be static and predefined to DB2 in the `SYSIBM.SYSPROCEDURES` table. The parameter list defines the data type, size, and disposition (output, input, or both) of each parameter. The complete process of registering stored procedures, including parameter lists, is outlined in the upcoming section "Registering Stored Procedures."

You must define the parameters to the stored procedure using the appropriate technique for the language you're using. For COBOL programs, you must define parameters in the `LINKAGE SECTION`. See Listing 9.1 for a sample stored procedure shell using COBOL.

Listing 9.1. COBOL stored procedure shell.

```
Must set up IDENTIFICATION and
    ENVIRONMENT DIVISIONS.

DATA DIVISION.
LINKAGE SECTION.
******************************************************
**        PARAMETERS DEFINED IN LINKAGE SECTION      **
******************************************************
01  IN-PARM          PIC X(20).
01  OUT-PARM         PIC X(30).

******************************************************
** INDICATOR VARIABLES USED ONLY IF PARMS CAN BE NULL **
******************************************************
01  NULL-INDVARS.
    05  INDVAR-1    PIC S9(4)  COMP.
    05  INDVAR-2    PIC S9(4)  COMP.

WORKING-STORAGE SECTION.

    Must declare all necessary variables.

******************************************************
**   PARAMETERS SPECIFIED TO THE PROCEDURE DIVISION   **
******************************************************
PROCEDURE DIVISION USING PARM-A, PARM-B, NULL-INDVARS.

MAIN-PARAGRAPH.
       .
       .
       .
    IF INDVAR-1 < 0
        if input parameter is null perform an error-routine
       .
       .
       .
    MOVE "SOME VALUE" TO OUT-PARM.
    MOVE ZERO TO INDVAR-2.
PROGRAM-END.
    GOBACK.
```

Be sure to test all input parameters that can be null. If the input parameter is null, you must code the program to handle that situation. Likewise, for output parameters that can be null, be sure to set the null indicator variable to zero if not null or -1 if null.

Additionally, be sure to set all input parameters to an appropriate value in the calling program prior to issuing the CALL to the stored procedure. The value of the stored procedure parameters is set at the time of the procedure CALL.

Returning Result Sets

Version 5

As of DB2 V5, a stored procedure can return multiple row result sets back to the calling program. If you enable result sets to be returned, stored procedures become more efficient and effective. Benefits include the following:

- Reduced network traffic, because an entire result set requires only a single network request
- Better application design, because stored procedures do not need to loop artificially through cursors to return data one row at a time
- Better flexibility, because more work can be done using stored procedures

Figure 9.2 shows the impact of result sets on stored procedure processing.

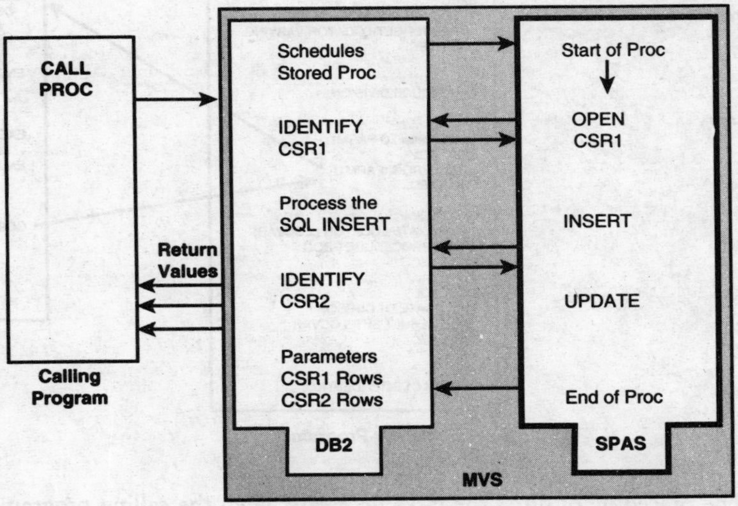

FIGURE 9.2.
A stored procedure returning result sets.

To implement stored procedures that return result sets, you must perform several steps. The first step is to ensure that the `RESULT_SETS` column for the stored procedure's row in `SYSPROCEDURES` is set to the appropriate value. `RESULT_SETS` specifies the maximum number of result sets that can be returned by the stored procedure. To enable the stored procedure to return result sets, you must set the column to a value greater than `0`.

The second step is to specify the `WITH RETURN` clause on each `OPEN` cursor statement for which result sets are to be returned. The cursors must not be closed by the stored procedure. When the stored procedure ends, the result sets are returned to the calling program.

The last step is coding the calling program to accept result sets from the stored procedure. See Figure 9.3 to view the interaction of a stored procedure with a calling program that accepts result sets. The first step is to declare a result set locator variable. Next, the calling program issues the `CALL` to execute the stored procedure. The stored procedure executes, opening a cursor that specifies the `WITH RETURN` clause. The stored procedure ends without closing the cursor, causing DB2 to return the result set automatically to the calling program. The calling program issues the `ASSOCIATE LOCATOR` statement to assign a value to the result set locator that was previously defined. The calling program then issues the `ALLOCATE CURSOR` statement to associate the query with the result set. Finally, the program can execute a loop to `FETCH` the rows of the result set.

FIGURE 9.3.
Coding to return a result set.

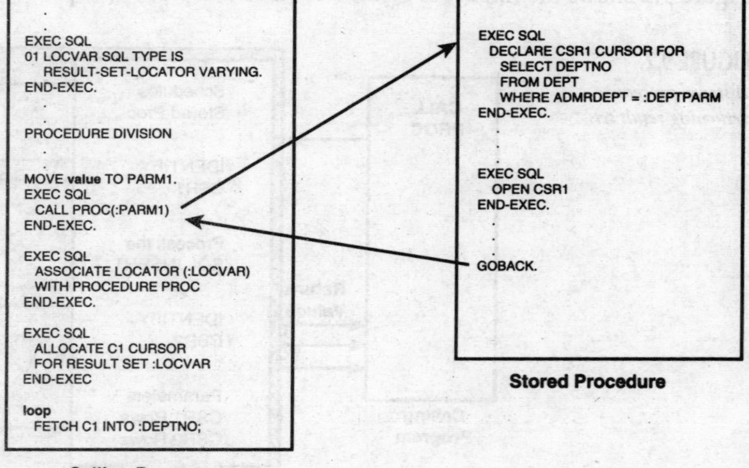

The preceding outlines the tasks necessary when the calling program knows what result sets can be returned by the stored procedure it is calling. However, special SQL statements—`DESCRIBE PROCEDURE` and `DESCRIBE CURSOR`—are available when the calling program does not know in advance the number of result sets that a stored procedure can return.

The `DESCRIBE PROCEDURE` statement returns the following information for a stored procedure that has already been called. The information, which is returned to the `SQLDA`, includes

- The number of result sets to be returned
- The result set locator value for each result set
- The name of the SQL cursor used by the stored procedure for each result set

The `DESCRIBE CURSOR` statement also returns information to the `SQLDA`, but it describe the columns accessed by the cursor.

Preparing Stored Procedure Programs

The program preparation process for stored procedures is essentially the same as for any program that accesses DB2. The program code must be precompiled, compiled, and then link-edited into an executable form. The DBRM must be bound into a package; no plan is required for the stored procedure.

When the program is link-edited, the LE/370 program library must be included. Likewise, the program for the stored procedure must link-edit either `DSNALI` (for CAF) or `DSNRLI` (for RRSAF), depending on which attachment facility is to be used.

No impact to the program preparation process is required for the calling program; you should use normal DB2 program preparation steps.

> **NOTE**
>
> A plan is still required for the calling program. Just the stored procedure (the called program) does not require a plan.

Registering Stored Procedures

After you code them, you must register stored procedures in the DB2 Catalog. This process is in sharp contrast to the manner in which other database objects are recorded in the DB2 Catalog. Typically, when an object is created, DB2 automatically stores the meta-data description of that object in the appropriate DB2 Catalog tables. For example, when a new table is created, DB2 automatically records the information in `SYSIBM.SYSTABLES`, `SYSIBM.SYSCOLUMNS`, and possibly `SYSIBM.SYSFIELDS`. Because stored procedures are not created within DB2, nor are they created using DDL, the database administrator must use SQL `INSERT` statements to populate a new DB2 Catalog table, `SYSIBM.SYSPROCEDURES`, with the meta-data for the stored procedure. See Table 9.1 for a description of this table.

Table 9.1. `SYSIBM.SYSPROCEDURES` columns.

Column Name	*Description*
`PROCEDURE`	Indicates the name of the stored procedure.
`AUTHID`	Indicates the authid of the user running the SQL application that issued the `CALL`. If blank, applies to all authids.
`LUNAME`	Specifies the `LUNAME` of the system that issued the `CALL`. If blank, applies to all systems.
`LOADMOD`	Indicates the MVS load module to use for this stored procedure.

continues

Table 9.1. continued

Column Name	*Description*
`LINKAGE`	Specifies the linkage convention used for passing parameters to the stored procedure: `N` `SIMPLE WITH NULLS` *blank* `SIMPLE` (input parameters cannot be null)
`COLLID`	Indicates the collection ID of the package for this stored procedure.
`LANGUAGE`	Lists the programming language used. Valid values are `ASSEMBLE`, `PL/I`, `COBOL`, or `C`.
`ASUTIME`	Specifies the number of service units permitted before an execution of the stored procedure is canceled.
`STAYRESIDENT`	Indicates whether the module is to remain in memory after the stored procedure finishes execution: `Y` Load module remains resident when stored procedure ends. *blank* Load module is removed from memory when stored procedure ends.
`IBMREQD`	Specifies `Y` if the row was supplied by IBM, or `N` if it was not.
`RUNOPTS`	Specifies the LE/370 runtime options to be used by this stored procedure.
`PARMLIST`	Lists the parameters expected by this stored procedure.
`RESULT_SETS`	Indicates the maximum number of query result sets that can be returned by this procedure.
`WLM_ENV`	Lists the name of the WLM environment used to run this procedure. A blank indicates that the procedure is to run in the DB2-established SPAS.
`PGM_TYPE`	Indicates whether the stored procedure is a main routine (`M`) or a subroutine (`S`).
`EXTERNAL_SECURITY`	Indicates whether a special RACF environment is needed to control access to non-SQL resources. Values are as follow: `N` Not required `Y` Required
`COMMIT_ON_RETURN`	Specifies whether work is to be committed upon successful completion of the stored procedure. Valid values are as follow: `N` Do not commit; continue UOW `Y` Commit null Same as `N`

Version 5

The RESULT_SETS, WLM_ENV, PGM_TYPE, EXTERNAL_SECURITY, and COMMIT_ON_RETURN columns are new to DB2 V5 to enable features such as returning multiple result sets and Workload Manager.

The following SQL provides an example of an INSERT to register a stored procedure:

```
INSERT INTO SYSIBM.SYSPROCEDURES
  (PROCEDURE, AUTHID, LUNAME, LOADMOD, LINKAGE,
   COLLID, LANGUAGE, ASUTIME, STAYRESIDENT,
   IBMREQD, RUNOPTS, PARMLIST, RESULT_SETS,
   WLM_ENV, PGM_TYPE, EXTERNAL_SECURITY,
   COMMIT_ON_RETURN)
 VALUES
  ('PROCNAME', ' ', ' ', 'LOADNAME', ' ',
   'COLL0001', 'COBOL', 0, 'Y',
   'N', ' ', 'NAME CHAR(20) INOUT', 1,
   ' ', 'M', 'N', 'N');
```

This SQL specifies a stored procedure written in COBOL and named PROCNAME with a load module named LOADNAME. It uses a package with a collection ID of COLL0001. Any location can execute this procedure. The program stays resident and uses the DB2 SPAS (not WLM), and no limit is set on the amount of time it can execute before being canceled. Furthermore, the stored procedure uses one input/output parameter, and the parameter cannot be null.

Configuring Parameter Lists

The parameters to be used by DB2 stored procedures must be predefined in the PARMLIST column of SYSPROCEDURES. You can define three types of parameters:

- IN: An input parameter
- OUT: An output parameter
- INOUT: A parameter that is used for both input and output

The type of the parameter must be predetermined and cannot be changed without modifying the registration in SYSPROCEDURES.

Consider, for example, a stored procedure with three parameters: an employee number, bonus, and total compensation. The stored procedure calculates the total compensation for a specified employee and returns it to the calling program. The bonus parameter is either set to 0 (in which case, no additional processing is performed) or to a percentage that the employee bonus is to be increased. If total compensation is greater than $100,000, the bonus percentage is cut in half. In this case, you could code the PARMLIST as follows:

```
EMPNO CHAR(6) INPUT, BONUS DEC(5,2) INOUT, COMPNSTN DEC(9,2)
```

This way, the stored procedure receives the employee number; receives, modifies, and then returns the bonus; and returns the total compensation.

An additional consideration when you're coding parameters for stored procedures is whether the parameters can be null. You use the `LINKAGE` column of `SYSPROCEDURES` to specify nullability. You have two choices:

- `SIMPLE WITH NULLS`: Nulls are allowed (`LINKAGE` is set to `N`).
- `SIMPLE`: Nulls are not allowed (`LINKAGE` is set to *blank*).

When nulls are permitted, the indicator variables must be passed to the stored procedure as an array, as shown in the example in Listing 9.1.

Managing Stored Procedures

After you register the stored procedure to DB2, you must start it by using a new DB2 command:

```
-START PROCEDURE(procedure name)
```

A stored procedure cannot be executed until it has first been started. Two additional administrative commands for stored procedures have been added:

```
-STOP PROCEDURE(procedure name) ACTION(REJECT | QUEUE)
```

The `STOP` command disables subsequent executions of the named stored procedure. You can specify the `ACTION` parameter to indicate whether future attempts to run the stored procedure will be entirely rejected or queued to be run when the stored procedure is started again.

```
-DISPLAY PROCEDURE(procedure name)
```

You can use the `DISPLAY` command to monitor the status of stored procedures. This command shows

- Whether the named procedure is currently started or stopped
- How many requests are currently executing
- The high water mark for concurrently running requests
- How many requests are currently queued
- The high water mark for concurrently running requests
- How many times a request has timed out

To run a stored procedure, you must explicitly issue a `CALL` statement. For example, the following statement calls a stored procedure named `SAMPLE`, sending a literal string as a parameter:

```
EXEC SQL
   CALL SAMPLE('ABC')
END-EXEC.
```

Executing a Stored Procedure

Stored procedures run in a separate DB2 address space known, appropriately enough, as the Stored Procedure Address Space (SPAS). IBM made a wise move in forcing stored procedures to run in their own address space because it eliminates the possibility of potentially bug-ridden stored procedure code "stepping on" the DB2 address spaces.

Version 5

As of DB2 V5, you can use multiple stored procedure address spaces. Doing so requires the use of the MVS Workload Manager (WLM). It allows stored procedures to be isolated in a particular address space based on the type of processing being performed. For example, OLTP stored procedures can be separated from data warehousing stored procedures. Using multiple SPAS, you can create an environment with multiple physical address spaces for stored procedures executing at the same dispatching priority as the calling program.

Using WLM to control multiple SPAS has the following benefits:

- It allows the creation of multiple environments to segregate stored procedures by processing type.
- It isolates stored procedures by address space. (If a stored procedure bug brings down one address space, others are still available.)
- It provides two-phase commit for non-SQL resources using RRSAF.
- It allows individual MVS dispatching priorities.
- It enables RACF control over access to non-SQL resources.

What Happens When a Stored Procedure Is Called

To execute a stored procedure, a program must issue the SQL `CALL` statement. When the `CALL` is issued, the name of the stored procedure and its list of parameters are sent to DB2. DB2 searches `SYSIBM.SYSPROCEDURES` for the appropriate row that defines the stored procedure to be executed. If the row is not found, the stored procedure does not run.

If the row is found, DB2 retrieves the pertinent information to allow the stored procedure to execute, including the actual load module. DB2 then finds a TCB to use for the stored procedure in the appropriate SPAS and indicates to the SPAS that the stored procedure is to be executed. The SPAS reuses the thread of the calling program to run the stored procedure. The stored procedure runs, assigns values to input/output and output parameters, and returns control to the calling program.

The calling program receives the input/output and output parameters and continues processing. The entire processing within the stored procedure is within the same unit of work as the `CALL` in the calling program. Locks acquired within the stored procedure continue to be held until released by the calling program (with a `COMMIT` or `ROLLBACK`).

Stored Procedure Guidelines

On the surface, stored procedures appear to be simple and highly effective new devices for enabling better application performance, enhancing database administration, and promoting code reusability. However, as with every DB2 feature, you can find good and bad ways to proceed with implementing stored procedures. Keep the following guidelines in mind as you develop stored procedures at your shop.

Do Not Nest Procedure Calls

When a procedure calls another procedure, the ensuing structure is called a *nested procedure.* DB2 does not currently permit one stored procedure to call another stored procedure. Nested procedures are difficult to test and modify. Furthermore, when one procedure calls another, the likelihood of reuse decreases because the complexity increases. Although DB2 currently does not support nested procedures, standardizing on this rule of thumb for all RDBMS stored procedure development is wise (and in case IBM changes this restriction in a future release).

Consider Using Subprograms

A stored procedure can call another program using the facilities of the programming language. The program being called cannot be a stored procedure, though. The use of subprograms enables better program reuse.

If you use subprograms, be sure to document their use within the stored procedure that calls the subprogram. The call statements used to execute the subprogram might be confused with the SQL `CALL` statement used to execute a stored procedure unless the program makes liberal use of comments.

Plan Stored Procedure Implementation

Design and implement only useful stored procedures. By *useful,* I mean only those stored procedures that support a business rule and are robust enough to perform a complete task without being too small to be trivial (a two-line procedure) or too large to be understood (a thousand-line procedure that performs every customer function known to the organization). To be useful, a stored procedure must

- Perform one task and perform it very well
- Correspond to a useful business function
- Be documented (including a description of the input, output, and the process)

Specify Atomic Parameters

Always specify parameters at an atomic level. In other words, every stored procedure parameter must be complete and non-divisible. For example, use

```
FNAME CHAR(20) IN, LNAME CHAR(30) IN
```

instead of

```
FULLNAME CHAR(50) IN
```

When you code parameters as non-atomic variable blocks, the stored procedure logic must parse the block. If changes occur to the data causing lengths or data type to change, procedures using atomic parameters are easier to modify and test.

Understand DB2's Limitations

Be sure to read and understand the limitations and requirements of DB2 stored procedures. For example, certain statements and commands cannot be issued from within a stored procedure. DB2 for MVS stored procedures cannot issue CALL, COMMIT, ROLLBACK, CONNECT, SET CONNECTION, and RELEASE; DB2 for Common Server stored procedures cannot issue CALL, CONNECT, SET CONNECT, RELEASE, CONNECT RESET, CREATE DATABASE, DROP DATABASE, BACKUP, RESTORE, and FORWARD RECOVERY.

Learn LE/370

You must write DB2 stored procedures using an LE/370 language. You therefore cannot use VS COBOL II to code stored procedures.

However, stored procedures can be called from any DB2-compatible programming language (even non-LE/370 languages).

Consider Using CODE/370

IBM offers CODE/370, an integrated toolset consisting of editing, compilation, and debugging tools. Without a tool such as CODE/370, testing and debugging DB2 stored procedures can be difficult. Both mainframe and workstation interfaces are available for CODE/370.

Use Stored Procedures for Internal DBA Tools

If your shop has technical DBAs who like to code their own administration tools performance monitoring applications, consider using stored procedures to issue DB2 commands and access trace records using IFI (Instrumentation Facility Interface). You can develop generalized procedures that are maintained by the DBA and accessed by multiple programs to start, stop, and display database objects or analyze IFCIDs and display performance details.

Use Appropriate Data Types for Parameters

Make sure that the calling program and the stored procedure use the same data type and length for each parameter. DB2 converts compatible data types, but by using the same data types and lengths, you can ensure efficient and effective execution.

Do Not Use Date and Time Parameters

DB2 does not permit you to use `DATE`, `TIME`, and `TIMESTAMP` data types as parameters. Instead, use the character equivalent of these data types when you need them as parameters.

Consider Using Output Parameters for the `SQLCA`

The `SQLCA` information for SQL statements executed in stored procedures is not returned to the calling program. Consider using output parameters to send `SQLCA` information to the calling program. This way, you can enable the calling program to determine the success or failure of SQL, as well as possibly providing error resolution information.

A separate output parameter is required for each SQL statement in the stored procedure (because the `SQLCA` of the stored procedure changes for each SQL statement execution).

Consider Using Global Temporary Tables

Version 5

Stored procedures can make excellent use of global temporary tables to store intermediate results. Consider the following uses:

- The stored procedure can `INSERT` data into a temporary table. A cursor can then be opened for the table with the results sent back to the calling program.
- Because stored procedures can access non-DB2 resources, data from IMS or IDMS can be accessed and stored in a temporary table. That data can then be accessed by the stored procedure using SQL, effectively enabling DB2 to IMS or IDMS joins.

Promote Reusability

As I mentioned earlier, the predominant reason for using stored procedures is to increase reusability. By reusing components—in this case, stored procedures—you can write applications more quickly using code that is already developed, tested, and working.

However noble the goal of reusable components, though, simply mandating the use of stored procedures does not ensure that goal. Documentation and management support (perhaps coercion) are necessary to ensure successful reuse. The basic maxim applies: "How can I reuse it if I don't know it exists or don't know what it does?"

Enable Distribution Using System-Directed Access

Stored procedures cannot issue a `CONNECT` statement. Therefore, application-directed remote access is unavailable to stored procedures. However, using three-part names (or aliases), stored procedures can implement system-directed remote access.

Make Stored Procedures Reentrant

Stored procedures perform better if they are prepared to be reentrant. When a stored procedure is reentrant, a single copy of the stored procedure is used by many clients. This use reduces the amount of virtual storage required for the stored procedure. You can use the RENT compiler option to make a COBOL stored procedure reentrant.

Make Stored Procedures Resident

Better use of system resources occurs if stored procedures are made reusable and remain resident in the SPAS. Specify Y in the STAYRESIDENT column of SYSIBM.SYSPROCEDURES, and avoid the NOREUS link-edit option. A program must be reentrant before it can be specified to stay resident. Therefore, the general recommendation is to make all stored procedures reentrant, reusable, and resident.

Specify Non-Blank COLLIDs

The collection ID of a stored procedure is specified in the SYSIBM.SYSPROCEDURES row that defines it. If COLLID is blank, the collection ID defaults to that of the package of the calling program. This result can be confusing. Explicitly specifying the collection ID is usually better when the stored procedure is registered.

The Procedural DBA

To implement and manage DB2 stored procedures effectively, a new type of DBA—a Procedural DBA—must be created. The creation of this new role will have an impact on the roles and responsibilities of the DBA and programming staff. However, effective implementation of a Procedural DBA function will result in an optimal environment for supporting stored procedures (and later, triggers, user-defined functions, and other types of DBMS-coupled application logic).

In this section, you will learn the requirements for the Procedural DBA.

The Classic Role of the DBA

Just about every database developer has his or her favorite curmudgeon DBA story. You know, those famous anecdotes that begin with "I have a problem..." and end with "...and then he told me to stop bothering him and read the manual." DBAs do not have a "warm and fuzzy" image. This image has more to do with the nature and scope of the job than anything else. The DBMS spans the enterprise, effectively placing the DBA on call for the applications of the entire organization.

To make matters worse, the role of the DBA has expanded over the years. In the pre-relational days, both database design and data access were complex. Programmers were required to explicitly code program logic to navigate through the database and access data. Typically, the pre-relational DBA was assigned the task of designing the hierarchic or network database design. This process usually consisted of both logical and physical database design, although it was not always recognized as such at the time. After the database was planned, designed, and implemented, and the DBA created backup and recovery jobs, little more than space management and reorganization were required. Keep in mind that I don't want to belittle these tasks. The pre-relational DBMS products such as IMS and IDMS required the DBA to run a complex series of utility programs to perform backup, recovery, and reorganization. These tasks consumed a large amount of time, energy, and effort.

As relational products displaced older DBMS products, the role of the DBA expanded. Of course, DBAs still designed databases, but increasingly these databases were generated from logical data models created by data administration staffs. The up-front effort in designing the physical database was reduced but not eliminated. Relational design still required physical implementation decisions such as indexing, denormalization, and partitioning schemes. Instead of merely concerning themselves with physical implementation and administration issues, however, DBAs found that they were becoming more intimately involved with procedural data access.

The nature of the RDBMS requires additional involvement during the design of data access routines. No longer were programmers navigating through the data; the RDBMS was. Optimizer technology embedded into the RDBMS was responsible for creating the access paths to the data. The optimization choices had to be reviewed by the DBA. Program and SQL design reviews became a vital component of the DBA's job. Furthermore, the DBA took on additional monitoring and tuning responsibilities. Backup, recovery, and reorganization were just a starting point. Now, DBAs used EXPLAIN, performance monitors, and SQL analysis tools to administer applications proactively.

Often, DBAs were not adequately trained in these areas. Programming is a distinctly different skill than creating well-designed relational databases. DBAs, more often than not, found that they had to be able to understand application logic and programming techniques to succeed.

The Role of the Procedural DBA

With the advent of stored procedures, the role of the DBA is expanding to encompass too many responsibilities for a single job function to perform the job capably. The solution is to split the DBA's job into two separate parts based on the database object to be supported: data objects or code objects like stored procedures.

The role of supporting stored procedures should fall to a group of professionals skilled in program development and procedural logic, as well as SQL and database administration. The Procedural DBA should be defined to support and manage stored procedures (and other server code objects) and other code-related DBA tasks, such as the following:

- DBMS Logic Support: Reviewing, supporting, debugging, tuning, and possibly even coding stored procedures, triggers, and user-defined functions. This task must include "on call" support.
- Application Program Design Reviews: Reviewing every application program completely before migrating the code to a production environment.

- Access Path Review and Analysis: Using EXPLAIN and other tools to determine the type of access chosen by DB2.
- SQL Debugging: Assisting developers with difficult SQL syntax and structures.
- Complex SQL Analysis and Rewrite: Tweaking SQL for optimal performance.

This role of the Procedural DBA is depicted graphically in Figure 9.4. The Procedural DBA should still report through the same management unit as the traditional DBA and not through the application programming staff. Reporting this way enables better skills sharing between the two distinct DBA types. Of course, a greater synergy is needed between the Procedural DBA and the application programmer/analyst. In fact, the typical job path for the Procedural DBA should come from the application programming ranks because the coding skill-base exists there.

FIGURE 9.4.
Procedural DBA tasks.

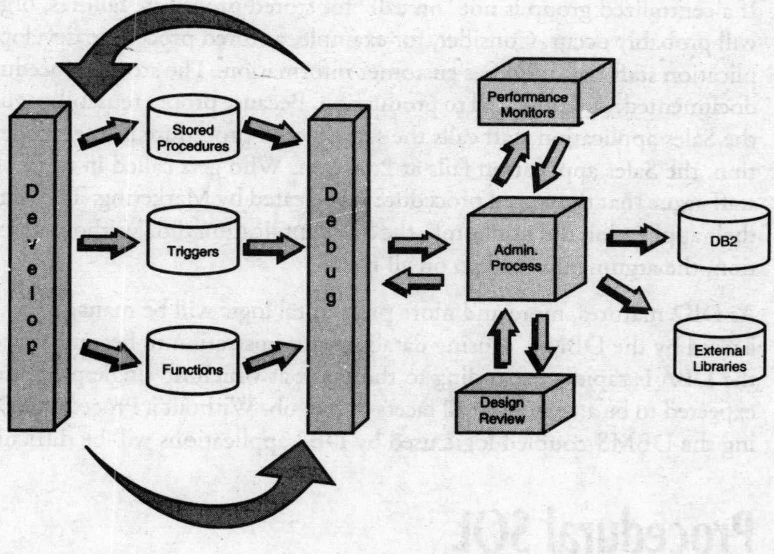

When the procedural tasks are off-loaded from the traditional, data-oriented DBAs, the DBAs will be free to concentrate on the actual physical design and implementation of databases. The result should be much better database design and performance.

The Politics of Procedures

After stored procedures are coded and made available to the DB2, applications and developers will begin to rely on them. Now that procedural logic is being managed by DB2, DBAs must grapple with the issues of quality, maintainability, and availability. How and when will these objects be tested? The impact of a failure is enterprise-wide, not relegated to a single application. This increases the visibility and criticality of these objects. Who is responsible if objects fail? The answer must be "a DBA."

Establishing a Procedural DBA function ensures that the political aspects of stored procedure creation, use, and support have been adequately determined and documented prior to implementation. Failure to do so will cause a multitude of questions that are not easy to answer without a centralized support group.

For example, who will code stored procedures, DBAs or application programmers? This decision can vary from shop to shop based on the size of the organization, the number of DBAs, and the commitment of the organization to stored procedures. A credible case can be made that the task should be a centralized function in order to promote reusability and documentation.

After the decision is made as to who develops the stored procedures, the next decision that needs to be made is who supports them. Stored procedure support must encompass design and code review, QA testing, documentation review, reusability testing, and "on call" support.

If a centralized group is not "on call" for stored procedure failures, organizational in-fighting will probably occur. Consider, for example, a stored procedure developed by a Marketing application staff that modifies customer information. The stored procedure is developed, tested, documented, and migrated to production. Because proper reusability guidelines were followed, the Sales application staff calls the same stored procedure in their code. Once it is in production, the Sales application fails at 2:00 a.m. Who gets called in to fix the problem? The Sales staff argue that the stored procedure was created by Marketing. The Marketing staff argue that their application did not bomb, the Sales application did. Without a centralized support function, the argument could go on all night.

As DB2 matures, more and more procedural logic will be managed by, stored in, and administered by the DBMS, causing database administration to become more complex. The role of the DBA is rapidly expanding to the point at which no single professional can be reasonably expected to be an expert in all facets of the job. Without a Procedural DBA function, supporting the DBMS-coupled logic used by DB2 applications will be difficult.

Procedural SQL

The major difference between DB2's stored procedure support and the other RDBMS vendors is the manner in which the stored procedure is coded. As I mentioned at the beginning of this chapter, other popular RDBMS products use procedural dialects of SQL for stored procedure creation. Oracle uses PL/SQL, Sybase uses Transact SQL, and Informix uses SPL. Each of these languages is proprietary, and they cannot interoperate with one another.

But what is procedural SQL? One of the biggest benefits derived from SQL (and relational technology in general) is the capability to operate on sets of data with a single line of code. By using a single SQL statement, you can retrieve, modify, or remove multiple rows. However, this capability also limits SQL's functionality. A procedural dialect of SQL eliminates this drawback through the addition of looping, branching, and flow of control statements. Procedural SQL has major implications on database design.

Procedural SQL will look familiar to anyone who has ever written any type of SQL or coded using any type of programming language. Typically, procedural SQL dialects contain constructs to support looping (`while`), exiting (`return`), branching (`goto`), conditional processing (`if...then...else`), blocking (`begin...end`), and variable definition and use.

The Benefits of Procedural SQL

The most useful procedural extension to SQL is the addition of procedural flow control statements. Flow control within procedural SQL is handled by typical programming constructs that you can mix with standard SQL statements. These typical constructs enable programmers to

- Embed SQL statements within a loop
- Group SQL statements together into executable blocks
- Test for specific conditions and perform one set of SQL statements when the condition is true, another set when the condition is false (`if ... else`)
- Suspend execution until a predefined condition occurs or a preset amount of time expires
- Perform unconditional branches to other areas of the procedural code

The addition of procedural commands to SQL provides a more flexible environment for application developers. Often, major components of an application can be delivered using nothing but SQL. You can code stored procedures and complex triggers using procedural SQL, thereby reducing the amount of host language (COBOL, C, PowerBuilder, and so on) programming required.

Additionally, when stored procedures can be written using just SQL, more users will be inclined to use these features. DB2 requires stored procedures to be written in a host language. This requirement may scare off many potential developers. Most DBAs I know avoid programming (especially in COBOL) like the plague.

In addition to SQL-only stored procedures, procedural SQL extensions also enable more complicated business requirements to be coded using nothing but SQL. For example, ANSI SQL provides no mechanism to examine each row of a result set during processing. Procedural SQL can accomplish this task quite handily using cursors and looping.

The Drawbacks of Procedural SQL

The biggest drawback to procedural SQL is that it is not currently in the ANSI SQL standard. DB2's stored procedure support is based on the ANSI SQL3 standard. Lack of ANSI support can result in each DBMS vendor supporting a different flavor of procedural SQL. If your shop has standardized on one particular DBMS or does not need to scale applications across multiple platforms, then you may not have this problem. But, then again, how many shops does this description actually describe? Probably not very many!

As the ANSI committee works on creating a standard version of SQL that includes procedural support, look for IBM to supply a procedural version of its SQL dialect based on the ANSI standard.

The bottom line is that scalability will suffer when applications are coded using non-standard extensions—like procedural SQL. Recoding applications that were designed to use stored procedures and triggers written using procedural SQL constructs is a non-trivial task. If an application needs to be scaled to a platform which uses a DBMS that does not support procedural SQL, a complete rewrite is exactly what must be done.

Performance drawbacks can be realized when using procedural SQL if the developer is not careful. For example, improper cursor specification can cause severe performance problems. This problem also can happen just as easily when cursors are used inside a host language. The problem is more inherent to application design than it is to procedural SQL.

The final drawback is that even procedural SQL dialects are not computationally complete. Most dialects of procedural SQL lack programming constructs to control the users' screens and mechanisms for data input/output (other than to relational tables).

DataBasic

IBM also provides an add-on stored procedure development product called DataBasic. DataBasic provides facilities for developing, testing, and maintaining stored procedures written for DB2 for AIX and DB2 for OS/2. (Support for DB2 for MVS is reportedly in development and will be provided in the future.) DataBasic provides a BASIC interpreter similar in functionality to Microsoft Visual Basic for the development of DB2 stored procedures. Using DataBasic, developers can create portable stored procedures in a visual programming environment.

Summary

Stored procedures are a powerful feature of DB2. They enable you to execute multiple data access statements with a single request. Additionally, they are controlled and managed by DB2, providing a consistent and reusable point of reference for frequently executed database code.

10

DB2 and the Internet

The data processing world is increasingly becoming an online world. This phenomenon is being driven by the Internet, a large, international network of interconnected computer systems.

HOW TO ACCESS THE INTERNET

All of the large, commercial online service providers such as Compuserve, America Online, and Microsoft Network offer access to the Internet. If you are accessing the Internet from home, you will probably access it from one of these servers.

However, most corporations provide Internet access directly via an ISP (Internet Service Provider). If this is the case, you will not have to set yourself up with an online service. The best way to find out whether your corporation has an ISP is to do some snooping. Ask your Help Desk, DBA, or manager whether your company is hooked up to the Internet. If so, all you will need is a TCP/IP connection and some basic software to begin surfing the net for DB2 nuggets!

The Internet Phenomenon

When discussing the Internet, most folks limit themselves to the World Wide Web. Howeyer, there are many components that make up the Internet. For purposes of this book, I will discuss the three primary components most useful to DB2 professionals: the World Wide Web, Usenet Newsgroups, and mailing lists.

The World Wide Web

The World Wide Web (WWW) uses a graphical interface and hypertext protocol to display information in a point and click environment. Using a Web browser (such as Netscape Navigator or Microsoft Internet Explorer), you can navigate through the Internet, accessing Web pages and FTP and gopher sites. A vast array of multimedia information (text, audio, video, and more) can be accessed using the WWW.

Having secured access to a Web browser, the first thing to do is to access a Web page. Web sites on the Internet provide a simple address that lets users access their site. That address, known as a URL (or Uniform Resource Locator), can be fed into a Web browser, thereby providing access to the site. The address is always preceded by the following:

```
http://
```

HTTP stands for HyperText Transfer Protocol, a communication protocol that understands that any document it retrieves contains information about future links referenced by the user. Of course, other Internet resources, such as gopher or FTP, can be accessed using a Web browser. For example, instead of typing `http`, the user can also specify the following:

`ftp://`	To access an FTP site
`file://`	To access a local (or networked) data file
`gopher://`	To access a gopher site
`mailto://`	To send mail
`news://`	To access Usenet Newsgroups

A Web page is a combination of text and graphics that provides hypertext links to other documents and services. The hypertext links are coded in the standard language known as HTML. An example showing my home page is depicted in Figure 10.1. The URL, `http://www.platinum.com/craigm`, is shown in the address box.

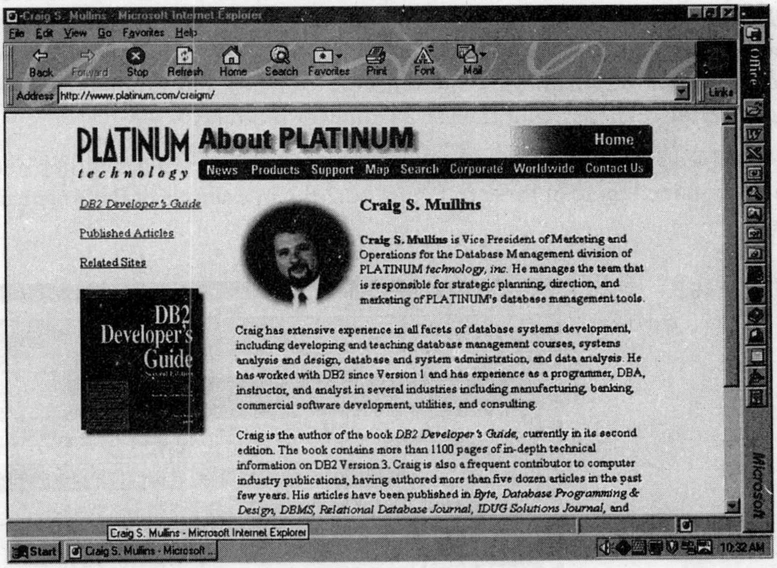

FIGURE 10.1.
The Craig S. Mullins page.
`(http://www.platinum.com/craigm)`

A page is the basic unit of every Web site. A Web page contains text, links, and images, but can also contain forms, frames, and tables.

Text on most WWW pages is formatted into multiple, layered headers and accompanying body text to help organize the information on the page. A link, sometimes referred to as a hyperlink, takes you to another page or to a graphic or other related file. Links can be textual or graphical. Textual links are underlined and in color. When you roll the cursor over a link it will change from an arrow into a pointing finger.

Forms are Web pages that have been organized using input boxes, pull-down lists, and radio buttons to enable easy data entry by users. Typically, forms are used to accept a user's demographic information or to enter credit card information when buying products over the Web.

Frames allow several windows to be shown on a single Web page. The most common usage is to display a Table of Contents in one frame while the user navigates through the Web site in another frame. Tables display information in formatted rows and columns.

After a Web page is accessed, hypertext links can be pointed to and clicked on leading the user through layers of information. The Web browser allows the user to navigate through pages and pages of useful information. The information can be printed, saved to disk, or simply browsed.

Usenet Newsgroups

A very fertile source of information on the Internet is found in various Usenet Newsgroups. Usenet, an abbreviation for User Network, is a large collection of discussion groups called newsgroups. Each newsgroup is a collection of articles pertaining to a single, predetermined topic. Newsgroup names usually reflect their focus. For example, `comp.databases.ibm-db2` contains discussions about the DB2 Family of products.

Using News Reader software, any Internet user can access a newsgroup and read the information contained therein. Refer to Figure 10.2 for an example of the America Online newsgroup reader.

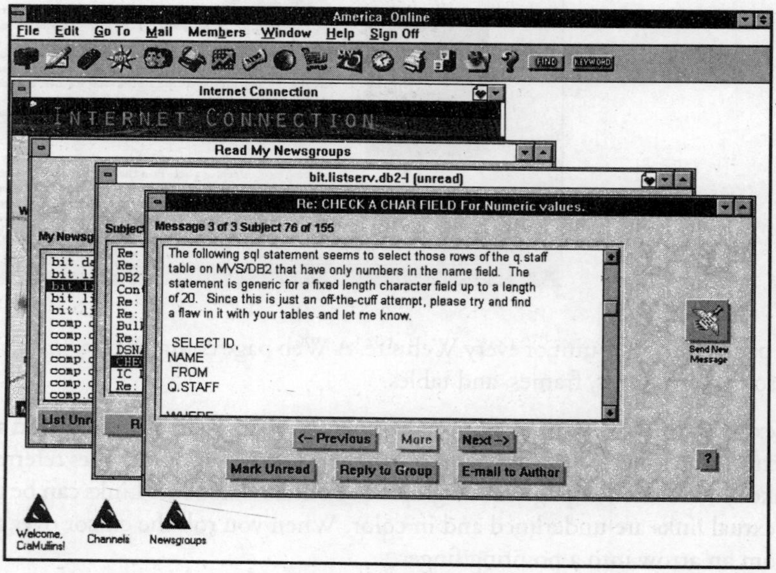

FIGURE 10.2.
A newsgroup reader.

Mailing Lists

Mailing lists are a sort of community bulletin board. You can think of mailing lists as equivalent to a mass mailing. There are around 40,000 mailing lists available on the Internet, and they operate using a list server. A *list server* is a program that automates the mailing list subscription requests and messages. The two most common list servers are Listserv and Majordomo. Listserv is also a common synonym for mailing list, but it is actually the name of a particular list server program.

Simply by subscribing to a mailing list, information is sent directly to your e-mail in-box. After subscribing to a mailing list, articles will begin to arrive in your e-mail box from a remote computer called a list server. The information that you will receive varies—from news releases, to announcements, to questions, to answers. This information is very similar to the information contained in a Compuserve forum, except that it comes directly to you via e-mail. Users can also respond to LISTSERV messages. Responses are sent back to the list server as e-mail, and the list server sends the response out to all other members of the mailing list.

To subscribe to a mailing list, simply send an e-mail to the appropriate subscription address requesting a subscription.

Using the Internet with DB2

There are two main reasons for DB2 professionals to use the Internet:

- To develop applications that allow for Web-based access to DB2 data
- To search for DB2 product, technical, and training information

Now take a look at ways of doing both of these.

Accessing DB2 Over the Internet

Allowing for Web-based access to valuable corporate data stored in relational databases makes this data more readily accessible to more people. Companies can obtain a competitive advantage by making their data available to employees over an intranet, or to customers and partners over an extranet.

NOTE

An *intranet* is a special Internet adaptation that can only be accessed by internal employees. Likewise, an *extranet* extends the accessibility in a secure manner only to authorized individuals.

IBM provides two options for accessing DB2 data over the Web: DB2 WWW and Net.Data.

Using the DB2 WWW Connection

DB2 WWW is an IBM product for connecting DB2 databases to the Web. Using a Web browser and DB2 WWW, companies can use the Internet as a front end to DB2 databases. Using DB2 WWW, data stored in DB2 tables is presented to users in the style of a Web page. This lets savvy Internet users quickly come up to speed at accessing DB2 data. DB2 WWW includes a procedural language to map between standard HTML and SQL, as well as a full-function graphing engine to return results to the Web browser in the form of mixed text and graphics.

DB2 WWW provides two-tier and three-tier client/server environments. In a two-tier environment, the database resides on the Internet server and client Web browsers access the data. For DB2 running on OS/390, this is applicable only if you use the mainframe as your Internet server. In a three-tier environment, the data can reside on both the local Internet server and a remote platform. This requires DDCS (Distributed Database Connection Services), CAE (Client Application Enabler), or DataJoiner. The three-tier setup is useful when your Internet server is a UNIX or Windows NT machine and you need to access DB2 data from the mainframe.

DB2 WWW uses a CGI runtime engine, which processes the input from HTML forms on the Web and sends SQL statements to a DB2 WWW application. This application consists of a macro file containing HTML input and report form definitions, SQL statements, and variable definitions. The application user sees only the Web page using the Web browser of his or her choice. To the end user, the application functions just like any other Web page. (See Figure 10.3.)

FIGURE 10.3.
How DB2 WWW works.

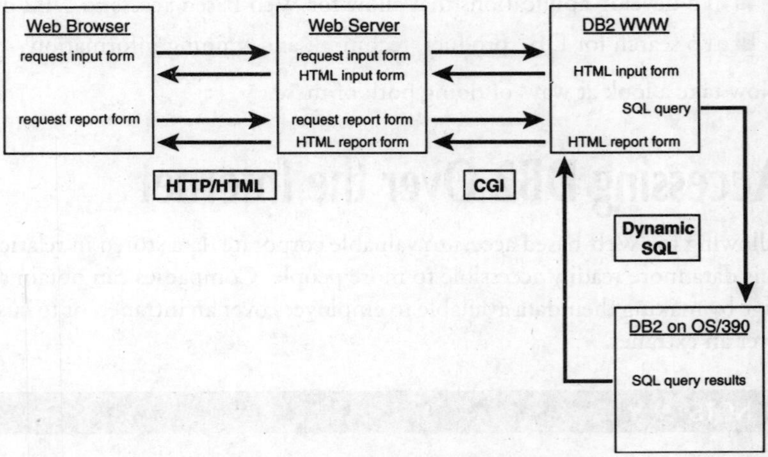

Because DB2 WWW applications use native HTML and SQL, developers do not need to learn complex new languages and syntax to connect DB2 databases to the Web. Furthermore, SQL `SELECT`, `INSERT`, `UPDATE`, and `DELETE` statements are supported for both data query and modification.

Net.Data

Net.Data, another IBM product, is an upwardly-compatible follow-on version of DB2 WWW. DB2 WWW applications are compatible with Net.Data (but not necessarily vice versa). Net.Data enhances the functionality of DB2 WWW in two ways.

The first is as a CGI application. In this case, it is invoked like DB2 WWW. The second is as an API application. In this case, the server calls Net.Data as a DLL (dynamic linked library) or shared library.

Net.Data supports Java by enabling calls to Java applets and JavaScripts for client-side processing. Using Java, you can create dynamic, complex Web-based applications. An additional benefit of Net.Data's support for JavaScripts is that data can be verified at the client's Web browser as it is entered, instead of on the server. This can enhance performance by reducing network traffic.

For additional server-side processing, your Web application can call scripts and functions written in SQL, Perl, REXX, or C/C++. Additionally, an API is available to extend Net.Data functionality.

Net.Data ships with DB2 V5.

Version 5

Internet Access Guidelines

When accessing DB2 data over the Internet, consider the following helpful tips and techniques.

Design Web Applications With the User in Mind

Be aware that the equipment on which you are developing your Web-based applications is probably more state-of-the-art than the equipment on which the application will be used. It is common for developers to have access to high resolution monitors and a lot of memory. Be sure to test the application on PC setups with less memory and on monitors of varying dot pitch and resolution.

Plan Your Security Requirements

When developing DB2 applications that are accessible using the Internet, be sure to plan adequate security into the application. DB2 WWW and Net.Data each provide authorization features that should be utilized to ensure that only authorized users are permitted access.

Consider Net.Data Live Connections

Before a query can be executed, the process must identify itself and connect to DB2. This can cause performance problems.

Net.Data can be used to establish a live connection by continuously running processes to perform the startup tasks. Once started, the process waits to execute subsequent requests.

> **NOTE**
>
> Live connections are required for API connections, but can be used for CGI connections, too.

Finding DB2 Information Using the Internet

The Internet (and other online services) provides a wealth of easily accessible information for the DB2 professional. The days of IBM-Link being the only place to turn for DB2 information are most decidedly over. Immediate access to volumes of information is readily available for the asking. Now examine some of the best places to look for DB2 information in cyberspace.

Internet Resources

A vast wealth of information is available through the Internet. However, it is rather difficult to learn what is available. The most useful Internet resources for DB2 professionals are Usenet Newsgroups, mailing lists, and access to the World Wide Web (WWW).

DB2-Related Usenet Newsgroups

There are newgroups available to satisfy just about every interest, and DB2 usage is no foreigner to Usenet. There are three primary newsgroups that DB2 users can access for DB2 news and information:

```
comp.databases
bit.listserv.db2-l
comp.databases.ibm-db2
```

Generic database information can be found on the `comp.databases` newsgroup. Some DB2 users post questions, comments, and information to this newsgroup because, for a long time, there was no newsgroup devoted to DB2. The only other option was to use the DB2 mailing list (discussed in the next section, "The DB2 Mailing List").

The `bit.listserv.db2-1 newsgroup` is very active with DB2 discussions and information. But, this newsgroup is a mirror copy of the DB2 mailing list. If you subscribe to the mailing list, the information in this newsgroup will not be new.

The third, and newest, newsgroup is `comp.databases.ibm-db2`. It was instituted in early 1995 to offload the DB2 traffic from the `comp.databases` newsgroup and to provide a dedicated newsgroup for DB2 users. However, the postings to this newsgroup predominantly pertain to the DB2 common server (as opposed to DB2 for OS/390). For a listing of other Usenet Newsgroups that may be of interest to DB2 users, see Table 10.1.

Table 10.1. Interesting Usenet Newsgroups.

Newsgroup Name	*Description*
`comp.client-server`	Information on client/server technology
`comp.compression.research`	Information on research in data compression techniques
`comp.databases`	Issues regarding databases and data management
`comp.databases.ibm-db2`	Information on IBM's DB2 Family of products
`comp.databases.informix`	Information on the Informix DBMS
`comp.databases.ingres`	Information on the CA-Ingres DBMS
`comp.databases.object`	Information on object-oriented database systems
`comp.databases.oracle.server`	Information on the ORACLE DBMS
`comp.databses.sybase`	Information on the SYBASE DBMS
`comp.databases.theory`	Discussions on database technology and theory
`comp.edu`	Computer science education
`comp.infosystems`	General discussion of information systems
`comp.misc`	General computer-related topics not covered elsewhere
`comp.os.os2.announce`	OS/2-related announcements
`comp.os.os2.apps`	Information on OS/2 applications
`comp.unix.admin`	UNIX administration discussions
`comp.unix.aix`	Information pertaining to IBM's version of UNIX, AIX
`comp.unix.questions`	Question and answer forum for UNIX novices
`bit.listserv.aix-1`	Information pertaining to AIX
`bit.listserv.appc-1`	Information pertaining to APPC
`bit.listserv.cics-1`	Information pertaining to CICS
`bit.listserv.candle-1`	Information on Candle Corporation products
`bit.listserv.dasig`	Database administration special interest group
`bit.listserv.db2-1`	Information pertaining to DB2
`bit.listserv.ibm-main`	IBM mainframe newsgroup
`bit.listserv.os2-1`	Information pertaining to OS/2
`bit.listserv.power-1`	Information pertaining to RS/6000 computers
`bit.listserv.sqlinfo`	Information pertaining to SQL/DS (DB2 for VSE and VM)

The DB2 Mailing List

The DB2 mailing list can be subscribed to by sending a message to the subscription address, `LISTSERV@AMERICAN.EDU`. The message should read as follows:

```
SUBSCRIBE DB2-L
```

After issuing the preceding command, the list server will send you a message asking you to confirm the subscription. Upon doing so, information will quickly begin flowing into your e-mail box (perhaps at a much quicker rate than you can reasonably digest). Literally, hundreds of messages may be sent to you every week.

To sign off of the newsgroup, send the following message to the same subscription address:

```
SIGNOFF DB2-L
```

In addition to a subscription address, mailing lists also have a posting address. This is the address to which mailing list posts must be sent. Never send subscription requests to the list's posting address. Correspondingly, never send a post to the subscription address.

The posting address for the DB2-L mailing list is `DB2-L@AMERICAN.EDU`. When a message is sent to this address, it will automatically be forwarded to everyone currently subscribed to the list.

DB2 Information on the Web

There are many Web pages providing useful DB2 information. Foremost, of course, is IBM's DB2 Family Web page. (See Figure 10.4.) From this page, you will be able to access release information, technical information, DB2 manuals online, and add-on product information.

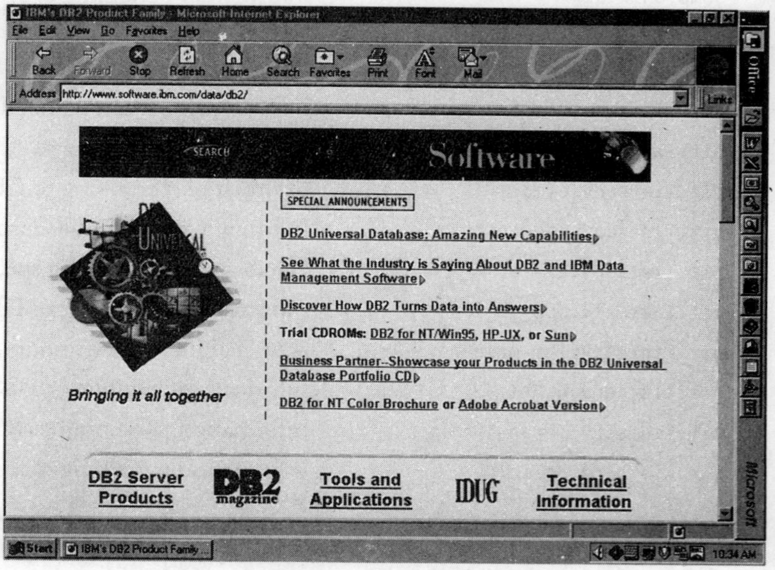

FIGURE 10.4.
The IBM DB2 Family page.
(`http://www.software.ibm.com/data/db2`)

Another useful IBM site is the Redbook site. IBM's International Technical Support Organization (ITSO) publishes many books on technical topics. The IBM ITSO Redbook site can be accessed at `http://www.redbooks.ibm.com/redbooks`. The Redbook site provides a searchable online catalog and the ability to order redbooks directly from IBM over the Web.

NOTE

A list of DB2-related redbooks is provided in Appendix E, "DB2 Manuals."

Three other Web sites that you should visit and bookmark are the Ron Raberd's DB2 reference site, Eric Loriaux's MVS site, and the JED-SP S/390 site. See Figures 10.5, 10.6, and 10.7. These sites contain pages of links to other related sites and are very useful.

FIGURE 10.5.
Ron Raberd's DB2 reference page.
(`http://www.webcom.com/~raberd/db2info.html`)

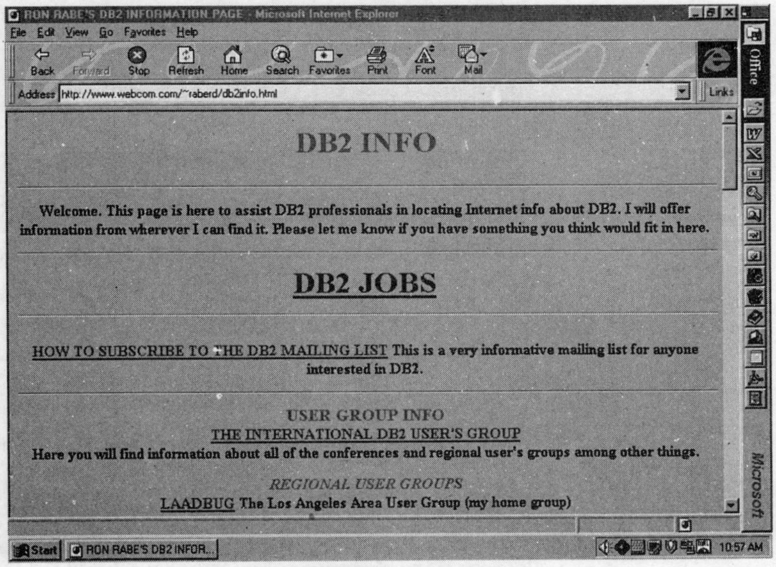

FIGURE 10.6.
Eric Loriaux's MVS site.
(`http://www.ping.be/~ping1475`)

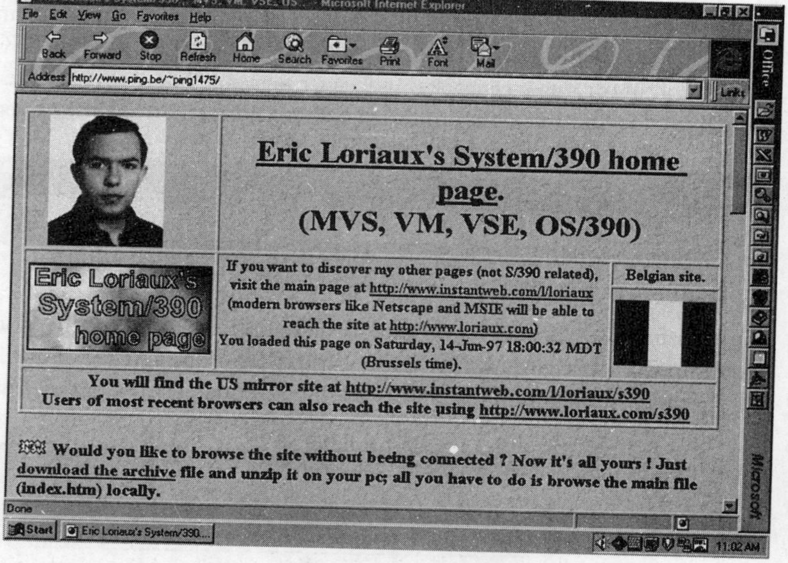

FIGURE 10.7.
The JED-SP S/390 home page.
(`http://www.jedsp.com/s390`)

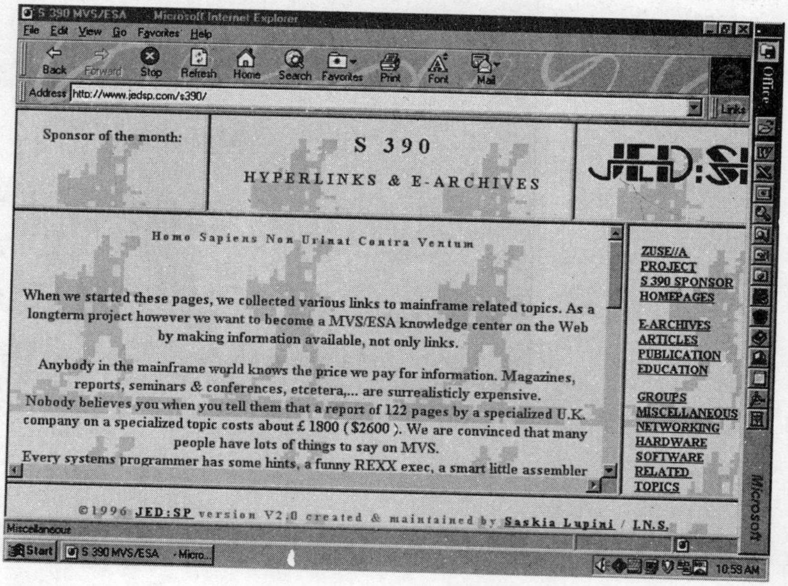

Many DB2 experts and consultants have their own Web sites that contain useful tips, tricks, and techniques, as well as their speaking schedules and copies of their presentations. One of the best of these sites is Richard Yevich's RYC, Inc. site. (See Figure 10.8.)

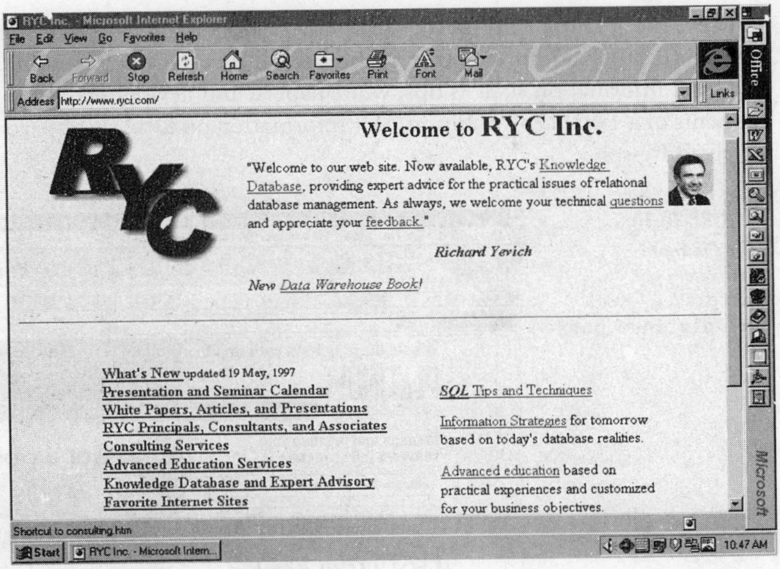

FIGURE 10.8.
The RYC, Inc. site.
(`http://www.ryci.com`)

Several of the many DB2 user groups also have Web sites. These sites contain many useful DB2 resources, such as meeting schedules, newsletters, DB2 tips, and presentations. The IDUG Web site (see Figure 10.9) is one that every DB2 professional should visit regularly. It contains information on upcoming conferences, as well as an online version of its DB2-related magazine, *IDUG Solutions Journal*.

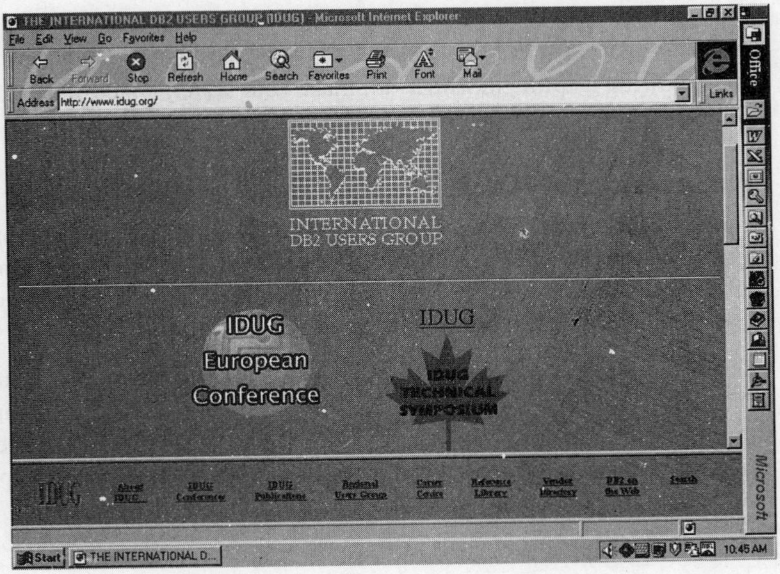

FIGURE 10.9.
The International DB2 User Group site.
(`http://www.idug.org`)

Finally, most of the third-party DB2 tool vendors also have Web sites. For an example, see Figure 10.10. In addition to information about their products, vendor sites often provide useful DB2 information such as tips, white papers, and newsletters. Refer to Chapter 32, "Components of a Total DB2 Solution," for information on DB2 third-party tool vendors and their Web addresses.

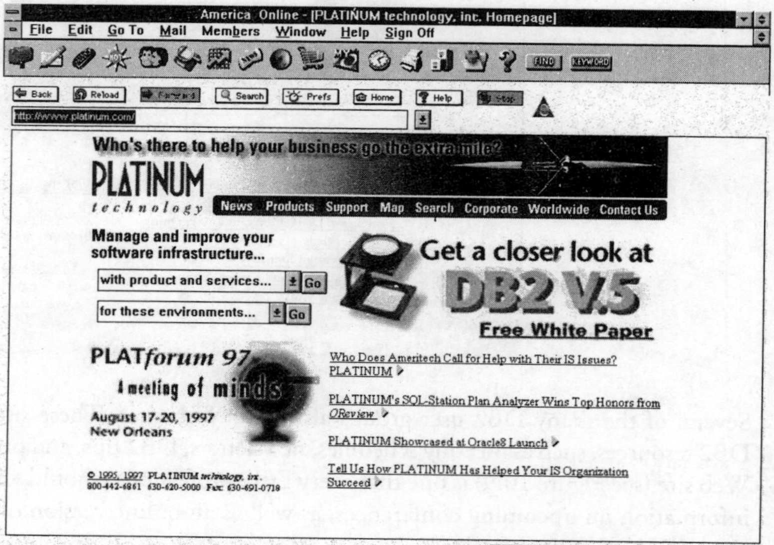

FIGURE 10.10.
The Platinum Technology site.
(`http://www.platinum.com`)

Internet Guidelines

The following helpful guidelines can make your search for DB2 information on the Internet easier and more rewarding.

Newsgroups Versus Mailing Lists

A newsgroup can only be viewed using News Reader software. You only need to point and click with most News Readers to view the contents of a newsgroup. A mailing list is an e-mail server. Notes are automatically forwarded to everyone on the distribution list. All you have to do is read your e-mail to access the information.

When a mailing list is mirrored to a newsgroup, use the newsgroup instead of the mailing list. Managing hundreds of e-mails from multiple mailing lists can be difficult. When the e-mail is mixed in with other e-mail messages in your in-box, it is difficult to keep up-to-date with the mailings. However, you can use a News Reader to read the newsgroup at your convenience. Interesting posts can be saved as text files.

Consider Digesting Mailing Lists

Many mailing lists offer the capability to accumulate messages and send them as one big e-mail. This is known as a digest. The benefit is that instead of receiving multiple daily messages from a mailing list, only one daily digest is sent.

To request digesting, simply send an e-mail to the subscription address requesting a digest. The digest request must be made after you have successfully subscribed to the mailing list.

For the DB2 mailing list, send the following message to the subscription address, `LISTSERV@AMERICAN.EDU`:

```
SET DB2-L DIGEST
```

The drawbacks to digests are that threads can be hard to follow, it is difficult to respond to messages, and they can become quite large.

Read the Archives

Contributions sent to the DB2 mailing list are automatically archived. You can get a list of the available archive files by sending the following command to `LISTSERV@AMERICAN.EDU`:

```
INDEX DB2-L
```

The files returned can be ordered using the following command:

```
GET DB2-L LOGxxxx
```

If Privacy Is an Issue, Conceal Your Identity

It is possible for others to determine that you are signed up to a DB2 mailing list by using the `review` command. This command sends the e-mail address and name of all subscribers to the requester. To block your name and address from appearing in this list, issue the following command:

```
SET DB2-L CONCEAL
```

Exercise Caution Before Using Information from the Internet

Because the Internet provides access to anyone with a computer and a modem, the information received can be less than reliable. It is quite common to post a question and receive multiple, conflicting answers (usually, the answers range from "yes," to "no," to "that question is not appropriate for this newsgroup").

Always use common sense before trying any posted tip, trick, or technique that seems dangerous. It probably is.

Avoid Cross-Posting

Cross-posting is the act of posting a single message to multiple newsgroups. Cross-posting is considered impolite and should be avoided. When a post is sent to multiple newsgroups, the cross-posted threads are difficult to read, usually off-topic, increase network traffic, and reduce the quality of the newsgroup discussions.

Know and Use Emoticons

Emoticons are drawings composed of text characters that are meant to look like a face expressing an emotion (hence the name emoticon). They are used on the Internet because it is difficult to convey emotions using text-based media like e-mail and newsgroups. The following are a few of the most popularly used emoticons:

`:)` a smile

`;)` a wink

Read the FAQs

FAQs (Frequently Asked Questions) are documents defining the focus of a newsgroup and answering the basic questions that most new users always ask. Be sure to read the FAQ for any newsgroup before posting to it. Unfortunately, the DB2 newsgroups do not have FAQs.

Use the searchable FAQ Web page (shown in Figure 10.11) to find Usenet FAQs.

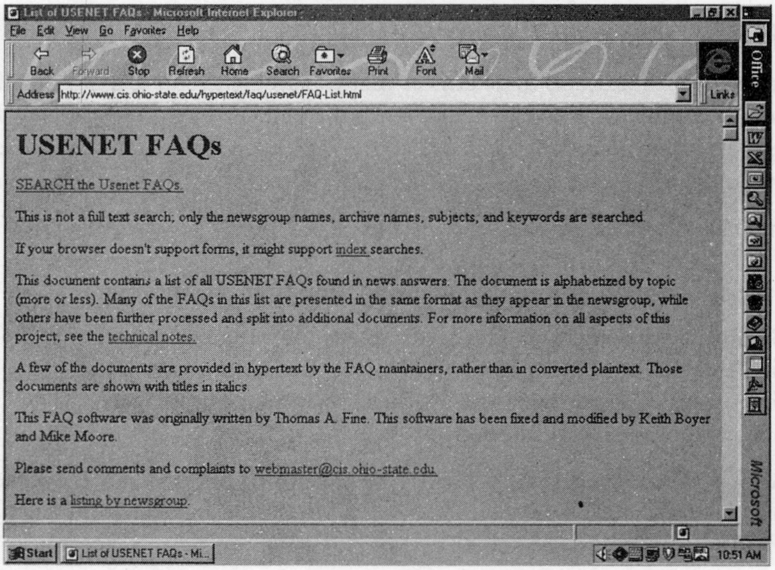

FIGURE 10.11.
Usenet FAQ Repository. (`http://www.cis.ohio-state.edu/hypertext/faq/usenet/FAQ-list.html`)

Avoid Flames

Flames are posts that are hostile, rude, or otherwise confrontational. Just as these things are not proper to do in person, they are improper on the Internet, as well. It is usually best to ignore flame messages.

Do Not Respond to Spams

The term *spam* is used to describe junk e-mails and postings that are off-topic, commercial, or otherwise violate good taste. When you receive a spam, just ignore it. Posting a long, nasty response to the spam back to the newsgroup or mailing list is just as inconsiderate as the original spam.

Basic Newsgroup Tips

Before reading and responding to Internet newsgroups, you should familiarize yourself with the Internet in general, and each newsgroup specifically. The following tips will ensure that you effectively utilize Internet newsgroups:

- Read the messages in the newsgroup for a period before posting. This will enable you to understand the dynamics of the newsgroup helping you to conform to its structure.
- Never post an off-topic message; be sure that it contains information pertinent to the newsgroup readers. Postings that are not relevant to the readers of the newsgroup are a waste of effort, time, and money.
- Always quote appropriate portions of messages to which you are responding. Do not quote the entire message if you are only responding to a portion of it.
- Even readers who might otherwise appreciate your message will be upset if it appears in the wrong group. Also, make sure that the subject of the message is accurate, descriptive, and specific to help readers decide whether to view it.
- Consider replying with an e-mail message if the response is not useful to the entire population of newsgroup readers.
- Keep messages as short and concise as possible.

Use The List of Lists

The List of Lists is a Web page that provides a searchable list of Internet mailing lists. It can be accessed at the following URL: `http://catalog.com/vivian/interest-group-search.html`. (See Figure 10.12.)

FIGURE 10.12.
The List of Lists.

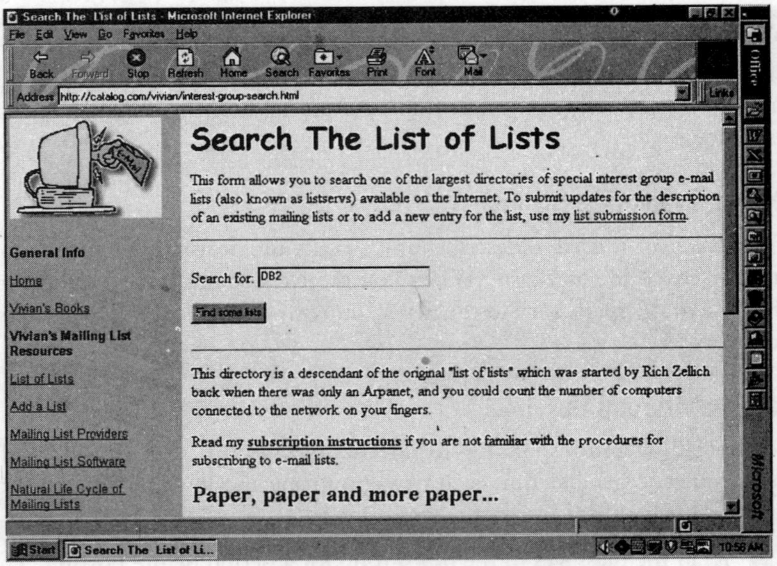

Other resources for mailing list information are

```
http://www.webcom.com/impulse/list.html
ftp://rtfm.mit.edu/pub/usenet-by-group/news.lists/
http://www.neosoft.com/internet/paml/
http://www.tile.net/tile/listserv/index.html
http://www.lsoft.com/
```

Additionally, you can subscribe to a mailing list for information about new and updated mailing lists. This is called the `new-list` and can be subscribed to by sending the following to `listserv@vm1.nodak.edu`:

```
subscribe new-list Craig Mullins
```

Substitute your name where I specified Craig Mullins.

Develop a List of Bookmarks

When you find a Web page that has useful information, use the bookmarking feature of your Web browser to record the URL for later use.

Use Search Engines on the Web

There is a wealth of information available over the WWW that will make the job of a database developer, database analyst, system programmer, or DBA much easier. However, finding all of it can be quite a task. Developing a list of bookmarks, while useful, can be difficult to create and even more difficult to maintain. Web sites are constantly moving, dying, and coming online.

It is impossible for a bookmark file (which is a static file containing links to other sites) to remain accurate for any length of time.

Instead of hunting and guessing for information resources, you can use a Web search engine, instead. There are quite a few search sites available, including Yahoo!, Excite, Lycos, and Alta Vista. These sites are designed to accept search keywords as input and return links to Web sites that contain information related to the keywords. With a search engine, the user types in a word or phrase (such as **database** or **DB2**). The response will be a listing of links to sites that match the search. The Alta Vista search engine is shown in Figure 10.13.

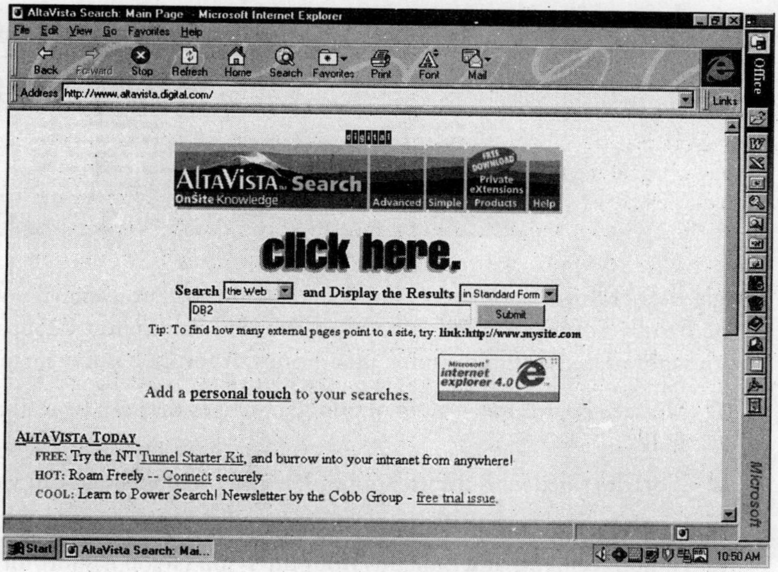

FIGURE 10.13.
The Alta Vista Search Engine.
`(http://www.altavista.digital.com)`

Use DejaNews

DejaNews is a search engine for Usenet newsgroups. It functions like a Web search engine, but provides indexed access to newsgroup postings. Use DejaNews to find relevant, older postings to newsgroups. The results of a DejaNews search are depicted in Figure 10.14.

CompuServe

The oldest and still one of the most popular online services is CompuServe. CompuServe offers a vast array of information that is not available directly on the Internet. CompuServe can be accessed in many different ways:

- Using a simple communications package (such as ProComm Plus or Kermit)
- Using the CompuServe Information Manager for Windows (WinCIM) or DOS
- Using CompuServe Navigator

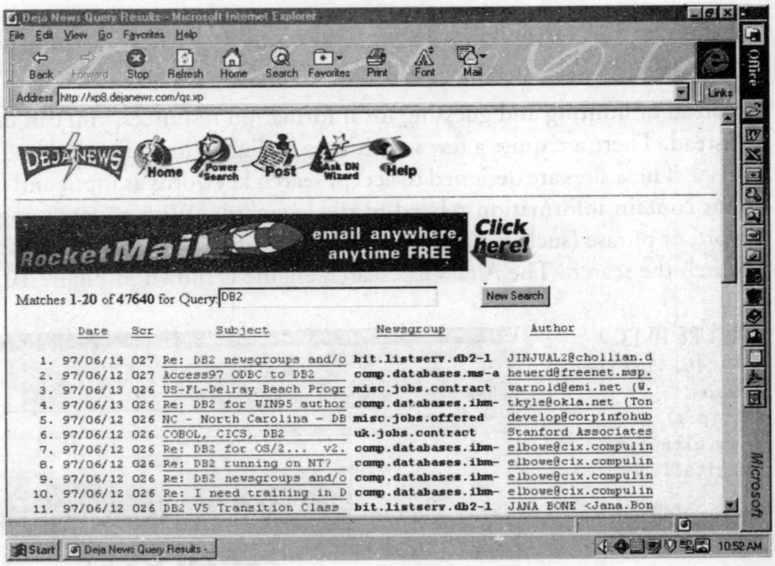

FIGURE 10.14.
The DejaNews search engine.
(`http://www.dejanews.com`)

Regardless of how you access CompuServe, as a DB2 professional you will want to find the DB2 Family Forum. Sometimes referred to as Special Interest Groups (or SIGs), forums can be thought of as electronic, online user groups. A forum has five main components:

- Message boards for posting of public messages that can be read and replied to immediately
- Libraries filled with information, files, and programs that can viewed and downloaded
- Conference rooms for immediate, online discussion sessions
- Announcements and bulletins from the sysop (sysop is short for "system operator;" the sysop is also known as a "forum administrator.")
- A member directory in which forum members can list their areas of expertise and interest

The DB2 Family Forum contains information about all of IBM's DB2 products. To access the DB2 Family Forum, simply type the command `GO IBMDB2` from any CompuServe prompt.

After you have accessed the DB2 Family Forum, be sure to check out the message board and the library sections. See Figure 10.15 for an example of the DB2 Family Forum message board. Messages in the message board can be read in threads. A thread is a series of postings and responses that usually read like a question-and-answer session. So, by following a thread, you will be able to immediately read any follow-up responses, comments, and answers for any posted message. There are quite often many interesting threads that provide a wealth of hands-on DB2 knowledge from actual users. DB2 experts from IBM, well-known industry consultants, and DBAs in the trenches regularly monitor and participate in this forum.

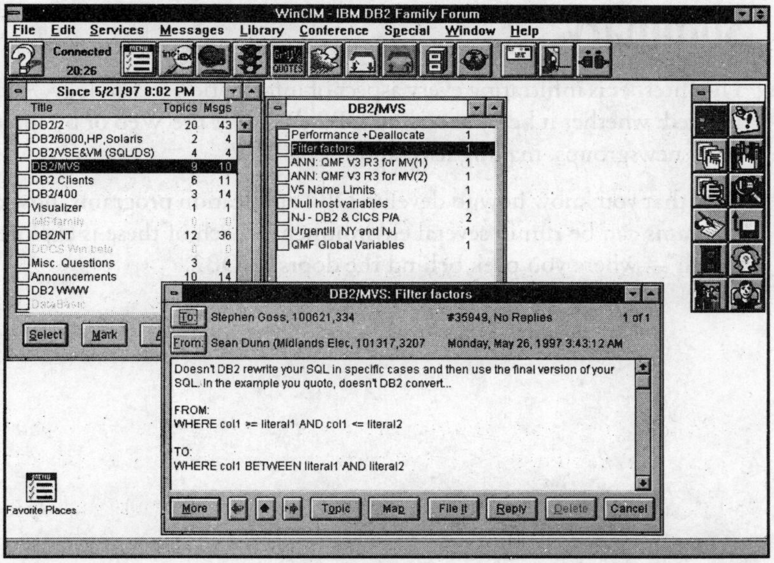

FIGURE 10.15.
DB2 Family Forum message board.

The library section is also of interest as it contains many useful nuggets of information. Recent downloadable files have included a SQL course, IBM white papers, DB2 tips and tricks from Platinum, and IBM product announcements. See Figure 10.16 for an example of a DB2 Family Forum library posting.

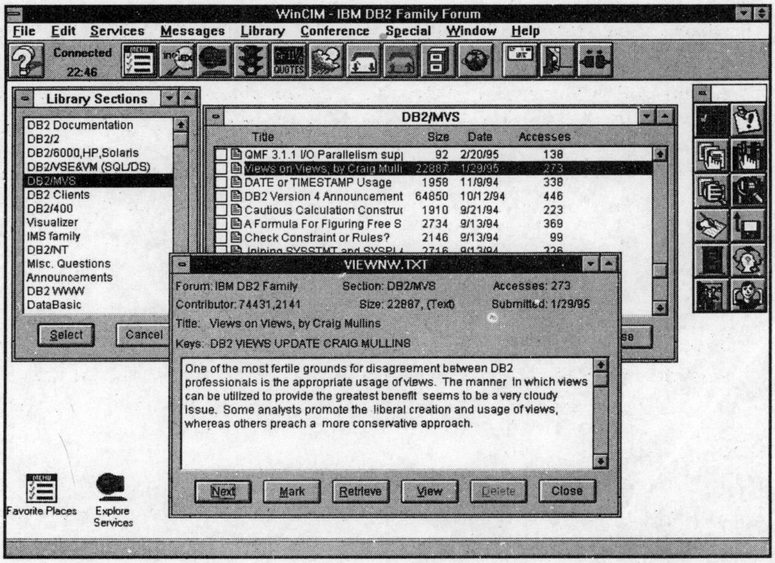

FIGURE 10.16.
DB2 Family Forum library.

Summary

The Internet is infiltrating every aspect of information technology. And DB2 is most definitely affected, whether it be by accessing DB2 data over the Web or by spreading DB2 information using newsgroups, mailing lists, and the WWW.

Now that you know how to develop DB2 application programs, how can you run them? DB2 programs can be run in several environments. Each of these is explored in Part III, "DB2 In-Depth"—where you peek behind the doors to DB2.

III

DB2 In-Depth

On the surface, DB2 looks simple. Pump in SQL, and DB2 throws back data. But for all the external simplicity of DB2, at its heart is a complex network of intricate code and communicating address spaces. How does all this stuff work?

Most people do not bother to find out. This is a pity. When programmers, analysts, and DBAs have the additional knowledge of the inner workings of DB2, application development is smoother, the code is more efficient, and problem resolution is faster.

So venture on, brave soul, and explore DB2 in-depth.

11

The Doors to DB2

You have learned how to embed SQL in application programs to access DB2 data, but you have yet to explore the possibilities when executing these programs. When accessing DB2 data, an application program is not limited to a specific technological platform. You can choose from the following environments when developing DB2 application systems (depending on their availability at your shop): TSO, CICS, IMS/VS, CAF, and RRSAF. You can think of each of these environments as a door that provides access to DB2 data. This chapter covers the advantages and disadvantages of each of these environments. First, I will discuss the basics of DB2 program execution that apply to all operating environments.

Each DB2 program must be connected to DB2 by an attachment facility, which is the mechanism by which an environment is connected to a DB2 subsystem. Additionally, a thread must be established for each embedded SQL program that is executing. A *thread* is a control structure used by DB2 to communicate with an application program. The thread is used to send requests to DB2, to send data from DB2 to the program, and to communicate (through the SQLCA) the status of each SQL statement after it is executed. Every program must communicate with DB2 by means of a thread. (See Figure 11.1.)

FIGURE 11.1.
All programs access DB2 using threads.

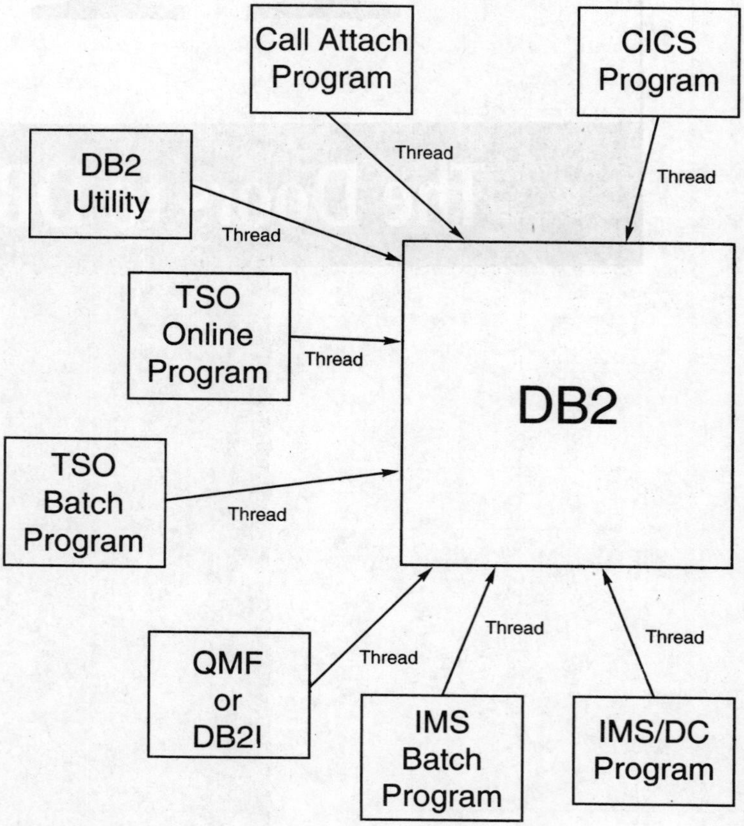

Now you can explore the process of invoking a DB2 application program. First, the program is initiated and the attachment facility appropriate for the environment in which the program is running is called. Next, security is checked (external MVS security, internal environment security, and DB2 security). Finally, upon execution of the first SQL statement in the program, a thread is created.

After the thread is established, DB2 loads the executable form of the appropriate plan from the DB2 Directory, where it is physically stored as a skeleton cursor table (SKCT). If the plan is composed of packages, DB2 loads the package table for the required packages into an area of memory reserved for DB2 program execution; this area is called the *Environmental Descriptor Management Pool*, or the EDM Pool. All DBDs required by the plan are also loaded into the EDM Pool from the DB2 Directory when the thread is established. Simply put, when a thread is created, DB2 performs the necessary housekeeping to ensure that the application program operates successfully.

Now that you have an overall picture of the way that an application program communicates with DB2, you can explore the processing environments. DB2 programs can be run in the foreground (also called *online*) or in the background (also called *batch*).

Online applications are characterized by interaction with an end user through a terminal. Most online applications display a screen that prompts the user for input, accept data from that screen, process the data, and display another screen until the user decides to end the session. Online programs are generally used to provide real-time update and query capabilities or to enter transactions for future batch processing.

Batch applications are characterized by their lack of user interactions. A batch program is typically submitted using JCL. It can accept parameters as input, but it does not rely on an end user being present during its execution. Batch programs are generally used to perform mass updates, to create reports, and to perform complex non-interactive processes.

Each environment provides different modes of operation, depending on whether the application is online or batch. For an overview of which environment supports which mode, consult Table 11.1.

Table 11.1. DB2 processing environments.

Environment	*Batch*	*Online*
TSO	Yes	Yes
CICS	No	Yes
IMS	Yes	Yes
CAF	Yes	Yes*
RRSAF	Yes	Yes

*Only when used with TSO

TSO (Time-Sharing Option)

TSO, or Time-Sharing Option, is one of the five basic environments from which DB2 data can be accessed. TSO enables users to interact with MVS using an online interface that is either screen- or panel-driven. The Interactive System Productivity Facility, or ISPF, provides the mechanism for communicating by panels, which is the common method for interaction between TSO applications and users. The TSO Attachment Facility provides access to DB2 resources in two ways:

- Online, in the TSO foreground, driven by application programs, CLISTs, or REXX EXECs coded to communicate with DB2 and TSO, possibly using ISPF panels
- In batch mode using the TSO Terminal Monitor Program, IKJEFT01 (or IKJEFT1B), to invoke the DSN command and run a DB2 application program

TSO is one of the three online environments supported by DB2, but unlike the other two, TSO is not transaction-driven. The TSO Attachment Facility operates by means of a communication channel that uses a single thread to direct DB2 calls. Each user can be logged on, in the foreground, to a single TSO address space at any time.

Each batch TSO job, however, initiates a different invocation of the TMP, enabling numerous batch TSO jobs submitted by the same user to run simultaneously. The batch jobs are independent of any foreground TSO activity. Thus, a single user, at any given time, can have one online TSO session communicating with DB2 and multiple batch TSO jobs communicating with DB2.

The TSO Attachment Facility is available for use by simply installing DB2. Communication between DB2 and TSO is accomplished with the DSN command processor, which is bundled with DB2. The DSN command processor enables users to issue DB2 commands in the TSO environment. One of these commands, the RUN command, executes DB2 application programs. (IBM bundles an online TSO application that can be used to access DB2 data: DB2 Interactive or DB2I. DB2I is discussed in greater depth later in this section.)

As you can see in Figure 11.2, the DSN command processor establishes the thread that enables TSO to communicate with DB2. An alternative method is to use the Call Attach Facility in TSO to communicate with DB2. The Call Attach Facility is discussed later in this chapter.

TSO/DB2 Parameters

DB2 is a parameter-driven subsystem. A series of parameters known as DSNZPARMs, or simply ZPARMs, is passed to DB2 when it is started. A complete discussion of the DSNZPARMs is supplied in Chapter 7, "Program Preparation." Because two of these parameters—IDFORE and IDBACK—apply directly to TSO, however, I will discuss them here.

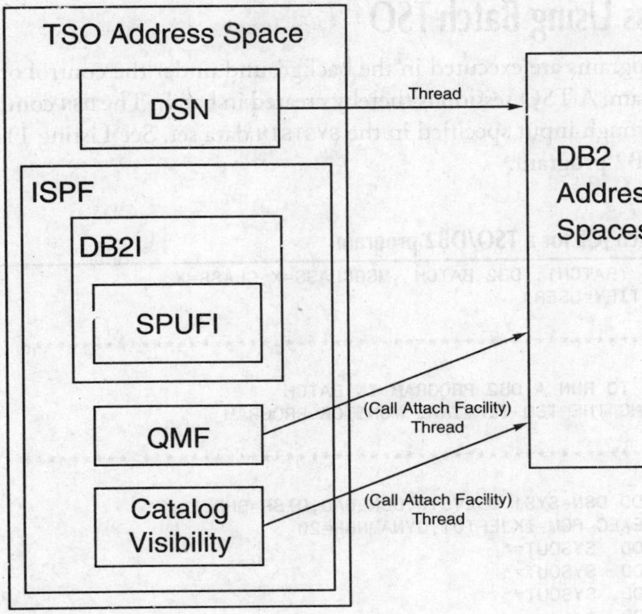

FIGURE 11.2.
Using the TSO Attach Facility.

`IDFORE` controls the number of users that can access DB2 simultaneously from the TSO foreground. The types of TSO foreground users include the following:

- DB2I
- QMF
- Users running the `DSN` command (through ISPF, `CLIST`s, REXX, and so on)
- Users running TSO/DB2 programs through the Call Attach Facility
- Users running any DB2 tool online in foreground TSO

DB2 limits the number of TSO foreground tasks to the number specified in the `IDFORE` parameter. When the limit is reached, any subsequent request for additional foreground TSO tasks is rejected.

`IDBACK` controls the number of concurrent DB2 batch connections. These connections, however, are not limited to TSO batch connections. They include the following:

- Batch DB2 jobs using the `DSN` command
- Batch DB2 jobs using the Call Attach Facility
- QMF batch jobs
- DB2 utilities

DB2 Access Using Batch TSO

DB2 batch programs are executed in the background under the control of the TSO terminal monitor program. A TSO session is thereby created in batch. The DSN command is invoked by this session through input specified in the SYSTSIN data set. See Listing 11.1 for JCL to run a batch TSO/DB2 program.

Listing 11.1. Batch JCL for a TSO/DB2 program.

```
//DB2JOBB JOB (BATCH),'DB2 BATCH',MSGCLASS=X,CLASS=X,
//          NOTIFY=USER
//*
//****************************************************************
//*
//*        JCL TO RUN A DB2 PROGRAM IN BATCH
//*        USING THE TSO TERMINAL MONITOR PROGRAM
//*
//****************************************************************
//*
//JOBLIB       DD DSN=SYS1.DB2V510.DSNLOAD,DISP=SHR
//BATCHPRG     EXEC PGM=IKJEFT01,DYNAMNBR=20
//SYSTSPRT     DD   SYSOUT=*
//SYSPRINT     DD   SYSOUT=*
//SYSUDUMP     DD   SYSOUT=*
//SYSTSIN      DD   *
  DSN SYSTEM(DB2P)
  RUN PROGRAM(PROG0001)  -
  PLAN(PLAN0001)  -
  LIB('APPL.LOAD.LIBRARY')
  END
/*
//
```

This JCL invokes TSO in batch, reads the SYSTSIN input, and invokes the DSN command processor for the DB2P subsystem. Next, it runs the program named PROG0001 using the plan PLAN0001. When the program is complete, the DSN session ends.

DB2 Access Using Foreground TSO

Another way to access DB2 data is through online, or foreground, TSO using the DSN command processor. You simply issue the following command from either ISPF option 6 or the TSO READY prompt:

```
DSN SYSTEM(xxxx)
```

Here, *xxxx* represents the DB2 subsystem name. This command places you under the control of DSN. A prompt labeled DSN appears, indicating that you are in the middle of a DSN session. You can issue any DSN subcommand, including the RUN subcommand. The DSN command processor and its associated subcommands are discussed more fully in Chapter 29, "DB2 Commands."

Suppose that you want to run a DB2 program called SAMPLE2 using the plan SAM2PLAN in foreground TSO. To do so, you can issue the following commands:

```
READY
  DSN SYSTEM(DB2T)
DSN
  RUN PROGRAM(SAMPLE2) PLAN(SAM2PLAN)
DSN
  END
READY
```

The boldface words are entered by the user. The other words are system prompts returned by TSO or the DSN command processor.

Rather than using the DSN command directly from a terminal, as just discussed, embedding the execution of a DB2 program in a CLIST or REXX EXEC is more common. A TSO user can invoke the CLIST or EXEC either directly by entering its name from ISPF option 6 or the TSO READY prompt, or as a selection from an ISPF panel. Figure 11.3 shows a common configuration for an online, TSO, ISPF-driven DB2 application.

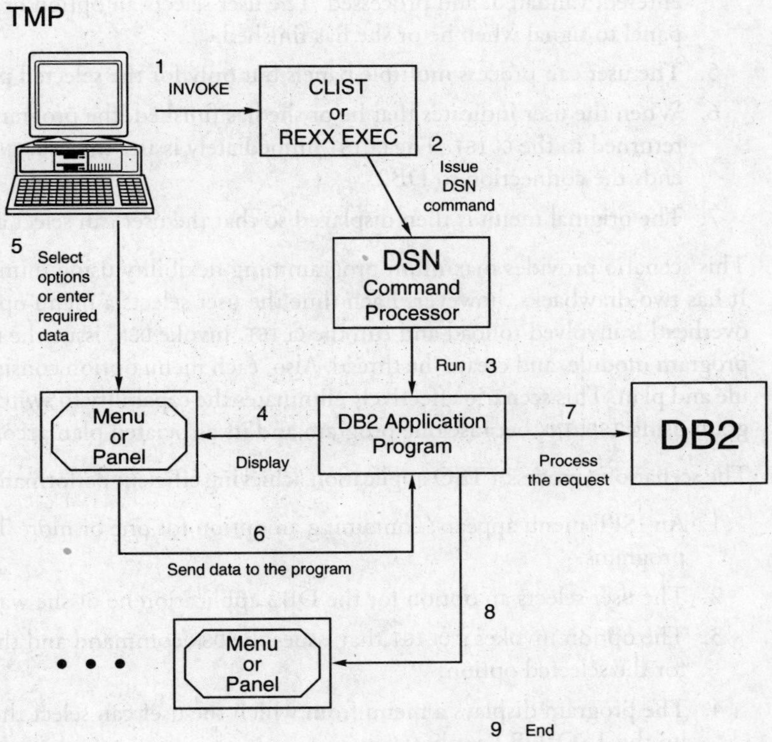

FIGURE 11.3.
A typical ISPF online DB2 application.

Online TSO/DB2 Design Techniques

Programmers can follow two basic scenarios for developing online TSO programs that access DB2 data. Each scenario provides a different level of runtime efficiency and support for application development. These two scenarios provide either fast application development or efficient performance.

Using the fast application development scenario enables programmers to make full use of the development tools provided by TSO and ISPF. The normal processing flow for this scenario is a seven-step process:

1. An ISPF menu appears, containing options for one or more TSO/DB2 application programs.
2. The user selects an option for the DB2 application he or she wants to execute.
3. The option invokes a `CLIST` that issues the `DSN` command and the `RUN` subcommand for the selected option.
4. The program displays a panel, engaging in a dialog with the user whereby data can be entered, validated, and processed. The user selects an option or function key on the panel to signal when he or she has finished.
5. The user can process multiple panels but only for the selected program.
6. When the user indicates that he or she has finished, the program ends and control is returned to the `CLIST`. The `CLIST` immediately issues the `DSN END` subcommand, which ends the connection to DB2.
7. The original menu is then displayed so that the user can select another option.

This scenario provides maximum programming flexibility using minimum system resources. It has two drawbacks, however. Each time the user selects a menu option, a large amount of overhead is involved to load and run the `CLIST`, invoke `DSN`, issue the `RUN` command, load the program module, and create the thread. Also, each menu option consists of a single load module and plan. This scenario effectively eliminates the capability to switch from program to program using `ISPLINK` because one program and its associated plan accomplish one task.

The scenario to process a TSO application achieving efficient performance is a nine-step process:

1. An ISPF menu appears, containing an option for one or more TSO/DB2 application programs.
2. The user selects an option for the DB2 application he or she wants to execute.
3. The option invokes a `CLIST` that issues the `DSN` command and the `RUN` subcommand for the selected option.
4. The program displays a menu from which the user can select the programs that make up the TSO/DB2 application.

5. When a menu option is chosen, the program calls another program. (All programs are linked into a single load module.)
6. The called program displays a panel, engaging in a dialog with the users whereby data can be entered, validated, and processed. The user selects an option or function key on the panel to signal when he or she has finished.
7. The user can process multiple panels in the program. You also can provide options to run other programs in the application based on user input or function keys.
8. When the user indicates that he or she has finished, the control program redisplays the menu. The user can then back out of the menu that causes the `CLIST` to issue the `DSN END` subcommand, ending the connection to DB2.
9. The original ISPF menu is then displayed so that the user can select another option.

When you develop applications using this scenario, overhead is reduced significantly. The `CLIST` is loaded and executed only once, `DSN` is invoked only once, the program modules are loaded only once, and a single thread is established once and used for the duration of the user's stay in the application.

This scenario has some drawbacks, however. The application can contain one potentially very large program load module. Each time a program is modified, the entire module must be link-edited again. This process uses a lot of CPU time. Also, application downtime is required because the application must wait for the link-edit process to complete. In addition, more virtual storage is required to store the program load module as it executes.

Additionally, you must take extra care when determining how to bind the application. For applications developed on releases of DB2 prior to V2.3, a single large plan consisting of every DBRM in the application was required. This scenario causes the same types of problems as a large program load module:

- Extra CPU time is used for a bind.
- Application downtime is increased while waiting for the bind.
- More virtual storage is required to hold the plan in the EDM Pool as the program runs.

The better application design option is for each program DBRM to be bound to a single package. All the packages are then included in the package list of a plan (either explicitly or using wildcards). This scenario reduces bind time, thereby decreasing CPU time and application downtime waiting for the bind to complete.

A final drawback to this scenario is that when the `DSN` command is used to run online TSO programs, the thread is created when the first SQL call is made. When the program is composed of many programs that call one another, a thread can be tied up for an inordinate amount of time.

When the application is invoked, the DSN command is issued, specifying the online application's load module and the composite plan. The thread created for this program's execution remains active until the program ends. One thread is used for each user of the TSO/DB2 application for the duration of its execution.

TSO is not a transaction-driven system. Users can enter a TSO application and leave a terminal inactive in the middle of the application, thus tying up a DB2 thread. That thread is not necessary when the user is thinking about what to do next or has walked away from the terminal.

An alternative solution is to use the Call Attach Facility to control the activation and deactivation of threads. This technique is addressed in the upcoming section on CAF.

DB2I and SPUFI

DB2I is a TSO-based DB2 application. It consists of a series of ISPF panels, programs, and CLISTs enabling rapid access to DB2 services and data. Using DB2I can increase the TSO DB2 developer's productivity. DB2I provides many features that can be exploited by the TSO user to query and administer DB2 data. To access DB2I, follow this sequence:

1. Log on to TSO as you normally would.
2. If the logon procedure does not automatically place you into ISPF, enter ISPF. The ISPF main menu appears.
3. Choose the DB2I option. This option most often is available directly from the main ISPF menu. However, DB2I could be on a different ISPF menu (for example, a System Services, Database Options, or User menu), or it could be accessible only through a CLIST. (Consult your shop standards, if necessary, to determine the correct method of accessing DB2I.) Each DB2I option is discussed in the following sections.

SPUFI Option

The first option in the DB2I main menu is SPUFI, or SQL Processor Using File Input. It reads SQL statements contained as text in a sequential file, processes those statements, and places you in an ISPF browse session to view the results. Figure 11.4 shows the SPUFI panel.

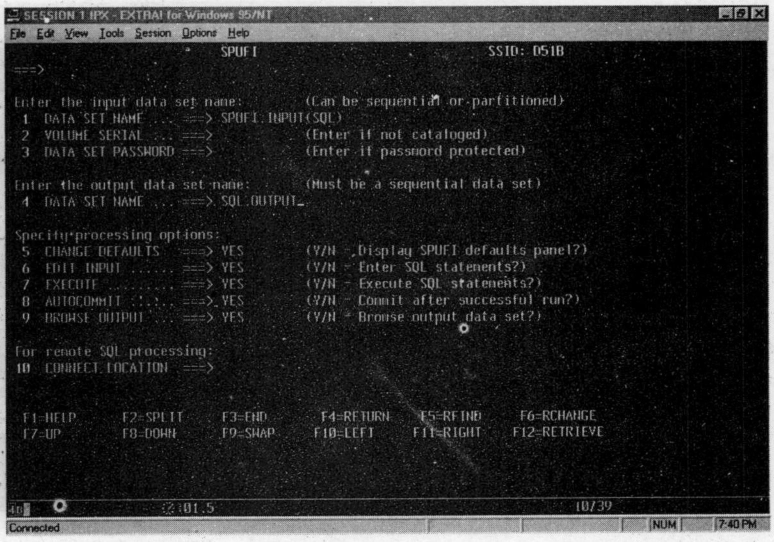

FIGURE 11.4.
The DB2I SPUFI panel.

By specifying an input and output data set and selecting the appropriate options, you can execute SQL statements in an online mode. The SPUFI options follow:

Change Defaults — When `Y` is specified , the SPUFI Defaults panel appears, as shown in Figure 11.5.

Edit Input — When `Y` is specified, SPUFI places you in an ISPF edit session for the input data set. This way, you can change the input SQL before its execution. Never specify `N` in this field. When you want to bypass editing your input file, place an asterisk (*) in this field; DB2I bypasses the edit step but resets the field to its previous value the next time SPUFI is invoked. If you use `N` and you forget to change the field back to `Y`, your next invocation of SPUFI executes SQL without allowing you to edit your SQL.

Execute — When `Y` is specified, the SQL in the input file is read and executed.

Autocommit — When `Y` is specified, a `COMMIT` is issued automatically after the successful execution of the SQL in the input file. When you specify `N`, SPUFI prompts you about whether a `COMMIT` should be issued. If the `COMMIT` is not issued, all changes are rolled back.

Browse Output — When `Y` is specified, SPUFI places you in an ISPF browse session for the output data set. You can view the results of the SQL that was executed.

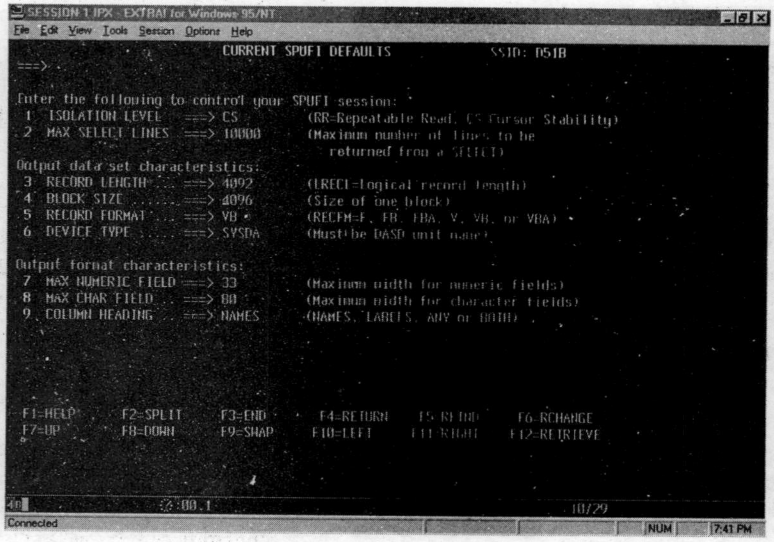

FIGURE 11.5.
The DB2I SPUFI Defaults panel.

Specifying Y for all these options except Change Defaults is common. Typically, defaults are changed only once—the first time someone uses SPUFI. ISPF saves the defaults entered from session to session. Use these options—as you see fit—to control your SPUFI executions.

The SPUFI input data set can contain multiple SQL statements, as long as they are separated by semicolons. For example, you could successfully code the following statements in a SPUFI input data set:

```
--
-- THIS SQL STATEMENT WILL SELECT ALL ROWS OF THE
-- SAMPLE TABLE, DSN8510.DEPT
 SELECT * FROM DSN8510.DEPT;
--
-- THIS SQL STATEMENT WILL SET THE SALARY FOR ALL EMPLOYEES
-- WITH THE LAST NAME OF 'KWAN' TO ZERO
 UPDATE DSN8510.EMP
 SET SALARY = 0
 WHERE LASTNAME = 'KWAN';
--
-- THIS SQL STATEMENT WILL ROLL BACK THE CHANGES MADE BY
-- THE PREVIOUS SQL STATEMENT
 ROLLBACK;
```

This sample input for the SPUFI processor contains three SQL statements. Each SQL statement is separated from the others by the semicolon that terminates each statement. Comments are preceded by two hyphens. When the SQL is executed and browsed, an output data set like the following appears:

```
---------+---------+---------+---------+---------+---------+-
-- THIS SQL STATEMENT WILL SELECT ALL ROWS OF THE
-- SAMPLE TABLE, DSN8510.DEPT
 SELECT * FROM DSN8510.DEPT;
---------+---------+---------+---------+---------+---------+-
DEPTNO  DEPTNAME                         MGRNO   ADMRDEPT
---------+---------+---------+---------+---------+---------+-
A00     SPIFFY COMPUTER SERVICE DIV.     000010  A00
B01     PLANNING                         000020  A00
C01     INFORMATION CENTER               000030  A00
D01     DEVELOPMENT CENTER               ------  A00
E01     SUPPORT SERVICES                 000050  A00
D11     MANUFACTURING SYSTEMS            000060  D01
D21     ADMINISTRATION SYSTEMS           000070  D01
E11     OPERATIONS                       000090  E01
E21     SOFTWARE SUPPORT                 000010  E01
DSNE610I NUMBER OF ROWS DISPLAYED IS 9
DSNE616I STATEMENT EXECUTION WAS SUCCESSFUL, SQLCODE IS 100
---------+---------+---------+---------+---------+---------+-
--
--THIS SQL STATEMENT WILL SET THE SALARY FOR ALL EMPLOYEES
--WITH THE LAST NAME OF 'KWAN' TO ZERO
 UPDATE DSN8510.EMP
 SET SALARY = 0
 WHERE LASTNAME = 'KWAN';
---------+---------+---------+---------+---------+---------+-
DSNE615I NUMBER OF ROWS AFFECTED IS 1
DSNE616I STATEMENT EXECUTION WAS SUCCESSFUL, SQLCODE IS 0
---------+---------+---------+---------+---------+---------+-
--
-- THIS SQL STATEMENT WILL ROLL BACK THE CHANGES MADE BY
-- THE PREVIOUS SQL STATEMENT
 ROLLBACK;
---------+---------+---------+---------+---------+---------+-
DSNE616I STATEMENT EXECUTION WAS SUCCESSFUL, SQLCODE IS 0
---------+---------+---------+---------+---------+---------+-
DSNE617I COMMIT PERFORMED, SQLCODE IS 0
DSNE616I STATEMENT EXECUTION WAS SUCCESSFUL, SQLCODE IS 0
---------+---------+---------+---------+---------+---------+-
DSNE601I SQL STATEMENTS ASSUMED TO BE BETWEEN COLUMNS 1 AND 72
DSNE620I NUMBER OF SQL STATEMENTS PROCESSED IS 3
DSNE621I NUMBER OF INPUT RECORDS READ IS 17
DSNE622I NUMBER OF OUTPUT RECORDS WRITTEN IS 48
```

The data set used for input of SQL must be allocated before invoking SPUFI. The data set can be empty and can be edited as part of the SPUFI session. It is recommended that each SPUFI user maintain a partitioned data set containing his or her SPUFI input. This way, users can keep and reference frequently used SQL statements. The SPUFI input data set should be defined as a fixed, blocked data set with an LRECL of 80. You can write SQL statements in all but the last 8 bytes of each input record; this area is reserved for sequence numbers.

You do not need to allocate the output data set before using SPUFI. If the output data set does not exist, SPUFI creates a virtual, blocked sequential data set with an LRECL of 4092.

Set the proper SPUFI defaults. (Refer to Figure 11.5.) You can set these defaults the first time you use SPUFI and then bypass them on subsequent SPUFI runs. Be sure to specify the following defaults:

Isolation Level	Always set this option to `CS`. If you require an Isolation Level of `RR`, you probably should be accessing the data programmatically rather than with SPUFI.
Max Select Lines	Set to an appropriate number. If you will be selecting from large tables that return more than 250 rows, the installation default value of `250` is insufficient. SPUFI stops returning rows after reaching the specified limit, and it issues a message indicating so.

The other default values are appropriate for most situations.

DCLGEN Option

The DCLGEN option in the DB2I main menu automatically produces a data set containing a `DECLARE TABLE` statement and valid `WORKING-STORAGE` host variables for a given DB2 table. You can include the data set in a COBOL program to enable embedded SQL access. See Chapter 7 for more details on DCLGEN.

Program Preparation Option

The Program Preparation option in the DB2I main menu prepares a program containing embedded SQL for execution. See Chapter 7 for more details on DB2 program preparation.

Precompile Option

Precompile is the fourth option on the DB2I main menu. In precompilation, a program containing embedded SQL is parsed to retrieve all SQL and replace it with calls to a runtime interface to DB2. See Chapter 7 for more details on precompiling a DB2 program.

Bind/Rebind/Free Option

When you select option 5 of the DB2I menu, the Bind/Rebind/Free menu shown in Figure 11.6 appears.

Option 1 on this menu provides the capability to bind a DB2 plan, and option 4 binds a package. These options are discussed fully in Chapter 7.

The second option is Rebind Plan. When you choose this option, the panel in Figure 11.7 appears. A plan can be rebound, thereby rechecking syntax, reestablishing access paths, and in general, redoing the bind. However, rebind does not enable you to add a DBRM to the plan.

In addition, if any of the rebind parameters are not specified, they default to the options specified at bind time, not to the traditional bind defaults. Rebind is particularly useful for determining new access paths after running the RUNSTATS utility.

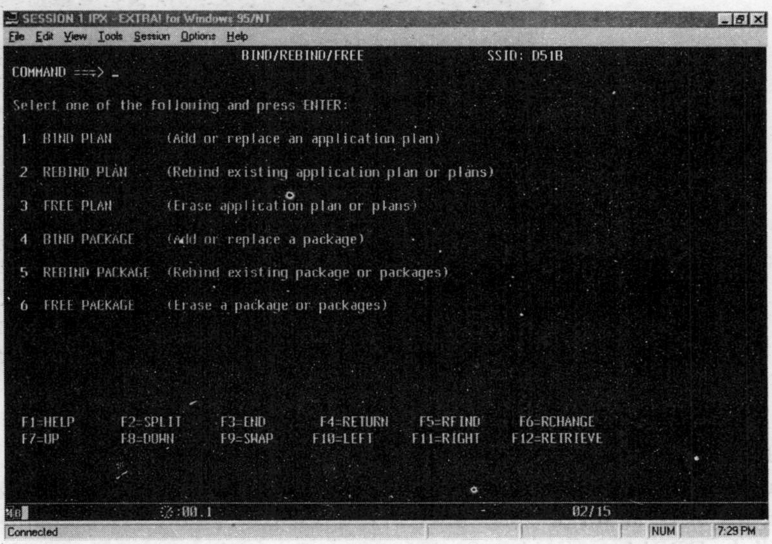

FIGURE 11.6.
The DB2I Bind/Rebind/Free menu.

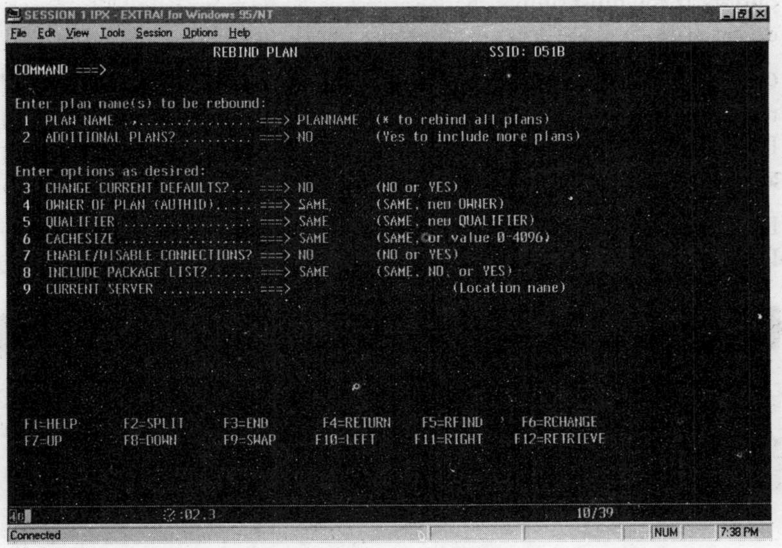

FIGURE 11.7.
The DB2I Rebind Plan panel.

Option 5 provides the capability to rebind a package. You rebind packages in much the same way you rebind plans. Figure 11.8 shows the Rebind Package panel.

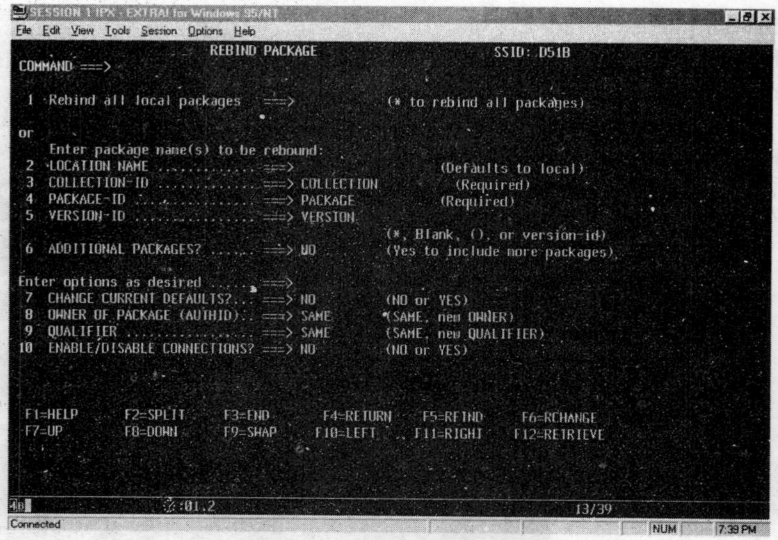

FIGURE 11.8.
The DB2I Rebind Package panel.

There is a significant amount of confusion about the difference between the `REBIND` command and the `BIND REPLACE` command. A `REBIND` simply *reevaluates access paths* for the DBRMs currently in a plan (or the single DBRM in a package). `BIND REPLACE`, on the other hand, *replaces* all the DBRMs in the plan. So, if you must use a different DBRM, `BIND REPLACE` is your only option. If you must simply change access path selections based on current statistics, `REBIND` will do the trick.

On the Bind/Rebind/Free menu, option 3, Free Plan, and option 6, Free Package, enable you to remove plans and packages from the system. Figure 11.9 shows the Free Plan panel, and Figure 11.10 shows the Free Package panel. You simply specify the names of the plans or packages to remove from the system, and they are *freed.*

Packages and plans you no longer use should be freed from the DB2 subsystem. Doing so frees DB2 Directory and DB2 Catalog pages for use by other packages and plans.

CAUTION

Never issue the `FREE (*)` command. This command drops every plan in the DB2 subsystem, which is probably not your intention. Additionally, a large amount of resources is used to execute this command.

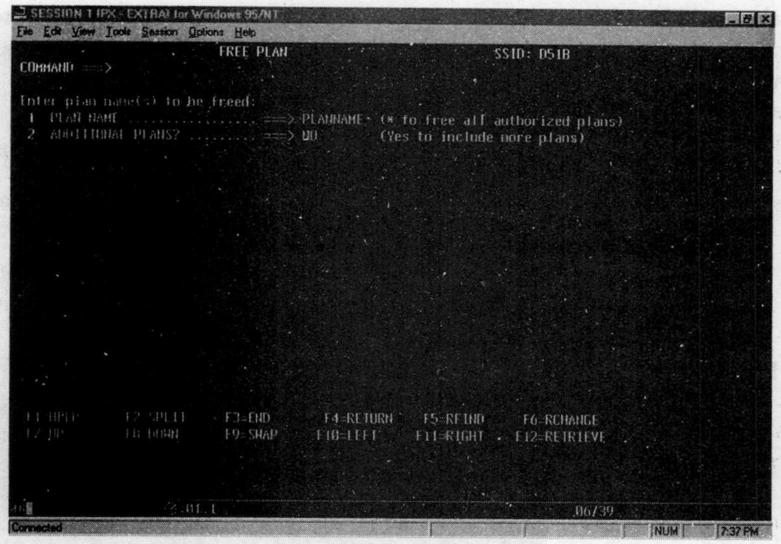

FIGURE 11.9.
The DB2I Free Plan panel.

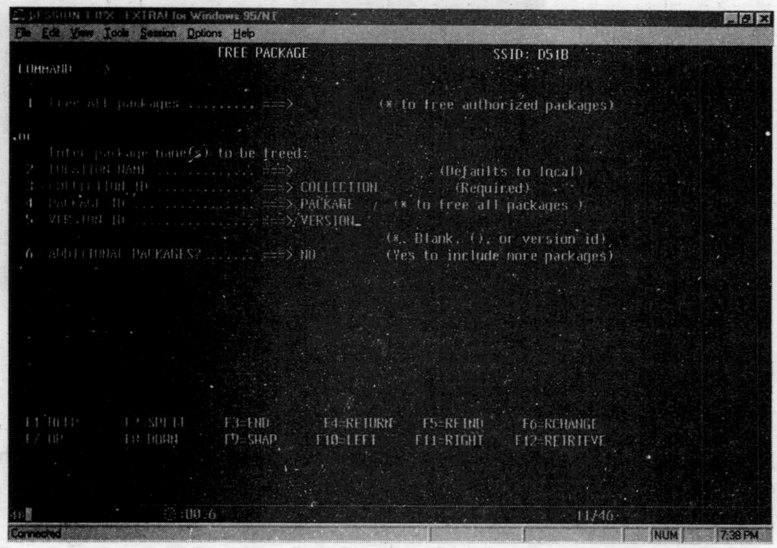

FIGURE 11.10.
The DB2I Free Package panel.

Run Option

The sixth DB2I option enables you to run a DB2 application program. The Run option is rarely used. More often, foreground DB2 programs are invoked by CLISTs, REXX EXECs, or ISPF panels, and background DB2 programs are invoked through preexisting batch JCL. When you select this option, the Run panel appears, as shown in Figure 11.11. You simply specify the load library data set (including the member name) for the program to be run, along with any necessary parameters, the appropriate plan name, and a `WHERE TO RUN` option. The three `WHERE TO RUN` options follow:

`FOREGROUND`	The program is run to completion, tying up the terminal from which the run was submitted for the duration of the program's run.
`BACKGROUND`	JCL is automatically built to run the program and is submitted in batch for processing.
`EDITJCL`	JCL is automatically built and displayed for you. You have the option of editing the JCL. You then can submit the JCL.

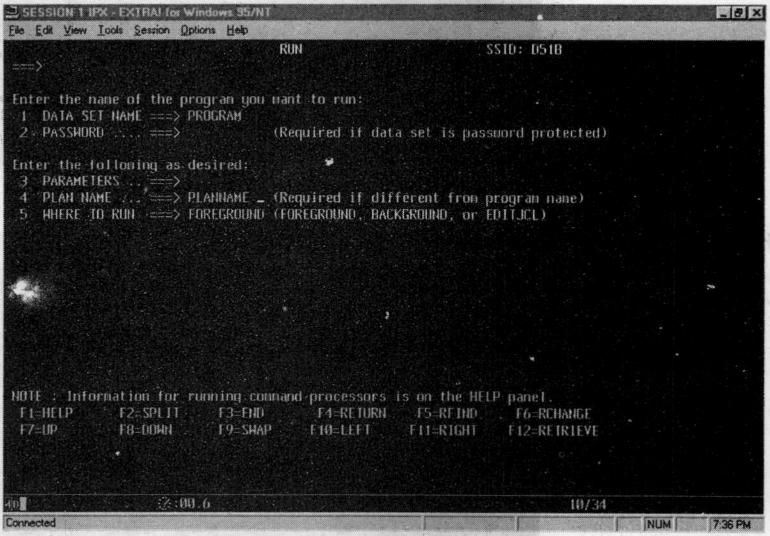

FIGURE 11.11.
The DB2I Run panel.

DB2 Commands Option

When you select DB2I option 7, DB2 Commands, the panel in Figure 11.12 appears, enabling you to submit DB2 commands using TSO. For example, the command shown in Figure 11.12 displays the status of the sample database, `DSN8D51A`. In-depth coverage of DB2 commands is included in Part VI, "DB2 Utilities and Commands."

Utilities Option

DB2I also provides panels that ease the administrative burdens of DB2 utility processing. Using option 8 of DB2I, the Utilities option, you can generate utility JCL, submit the utility JCL, display the status of utilities, and terminate utilities using a panel-driven interface. For a complete discussion of the DB2 utilities and the use of DB2I to control DB2 utility processing, consult Part VI.

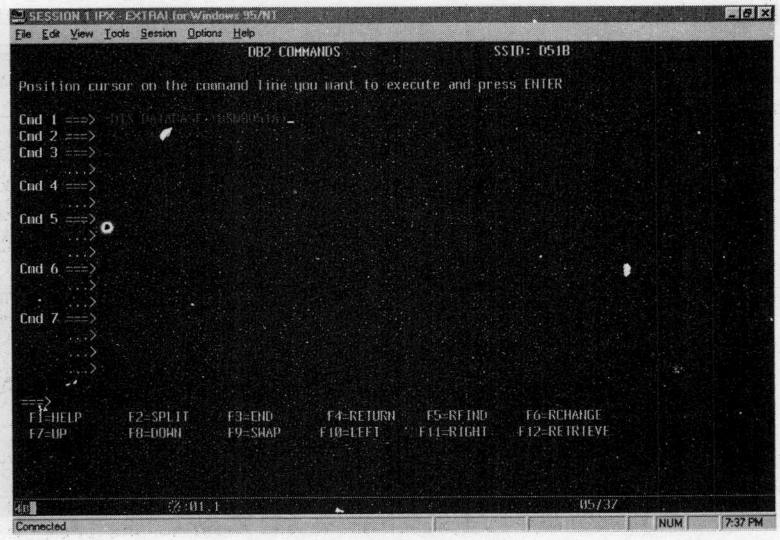

FIGURE 11.12.
The DB2I Commands panel.

DB2I Defaults Option

The Defaults panel, DB2I option D, lets you modify parameters that control the operation of DB2I. (See Figure 11.13.) Be sure that the proper DB2 subsystem is specified in the DB2 Name parameter. If your production DB2 subsystem runs on the same central electronic complex as your test DB2 subsystem, disaster can result if the name is not coded properly. Be sure also that you supply the proper language to be used for preparing DB2 programs in the Application Language parameter and a valid job card for your shop in the DB2I Job Statement parameter. A second default panel (such as the one shown in Figure 11.14) can be displayed for language defaults based on the Application Language chosen.

QMF

IBM's Query Management Facility, or QMF, is an interactive query tool used to produce formatted query output. QMF enables you to submit SQL queries dynamically, much like DB2I's SPUFI facility. QMF goes much further, however. Using a mechanism called a *QMF form*, you can format the results of your SQL queries into professional-looking reports.

To depict the basics of QMF, assume that you must produce a formatted report of all employees in the company. You invoke QMF, generally by choosing an option from the ISPF main menu. The QMF Home panel then appears, as shown in Figure 11.15. Notice the numbered options along the bottom portion of the screen. These numbers correspond to QMF functions that you can invoke by pressing the function key for the number indicated. For example, press F1 to request the first function, Help.

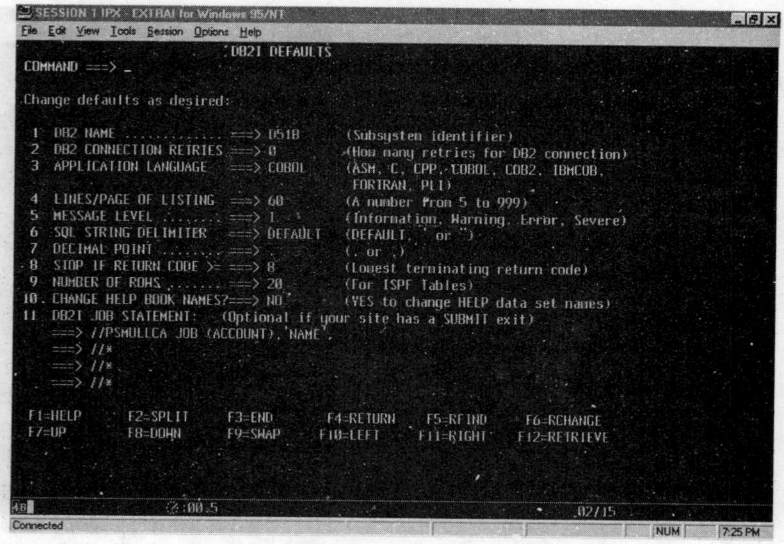

FIGURE 11.13.
The DB2I Defaults panel.

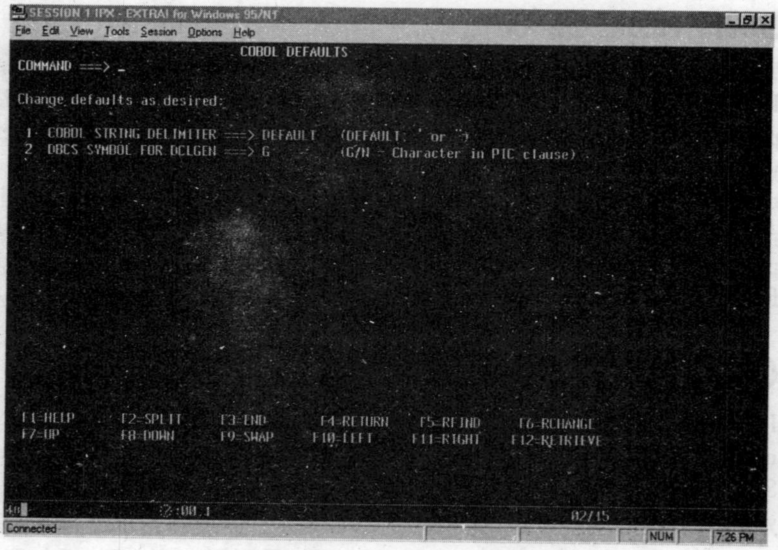

FIGURE 11.14.
The DB2I Defaults panel #2: COBOL defaults.

You can use three basic QMF objects to produce formatted reports of DB2 data: queries, forms, and procs. You begin by creating a query. Press F6 to navigate to the QMF Query panel, which is initially blank.

You will produce an employee report, so type the following statement at the COMMAND prompt:

```
COMMAND ===> DRAW SYSIBM.SYSPLAN
```

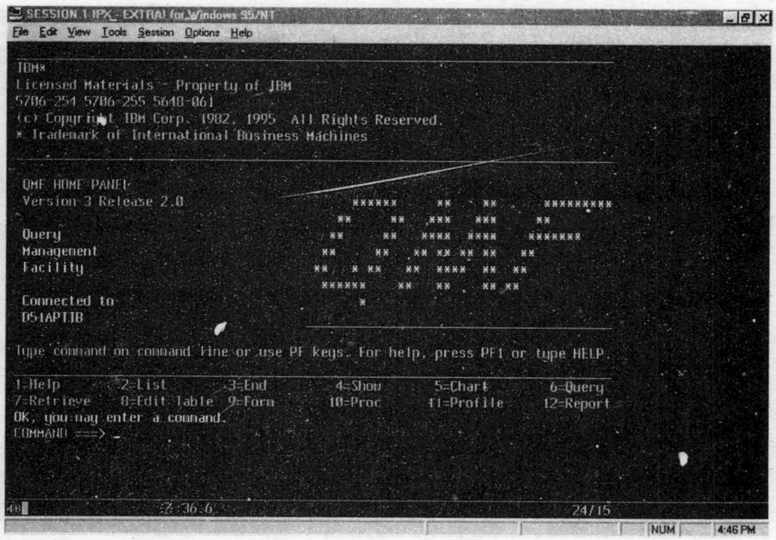

FIGURE 11.15.
The QMF Home panel.

The panel shown in Figure 11.16 then appears.

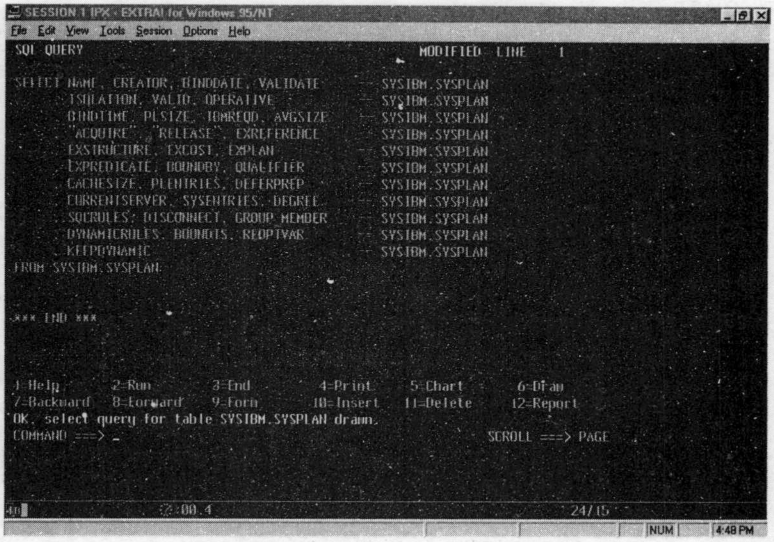

FIGURE 11.16.
The QMF Query panel.

To run this query, press F2. Doing so produces the report shown in Figure 11.17. You can print this report using F4 or format it using F9. When you press F9, the report form appears, as shown in Figure 11.18. A default form is generated for each query when it is run.

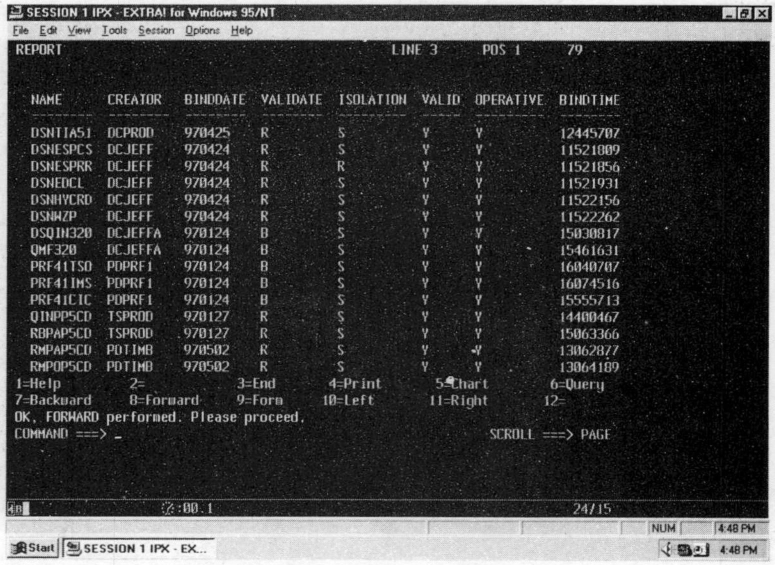

FIGURE 11.17.
The QMF Report panel.

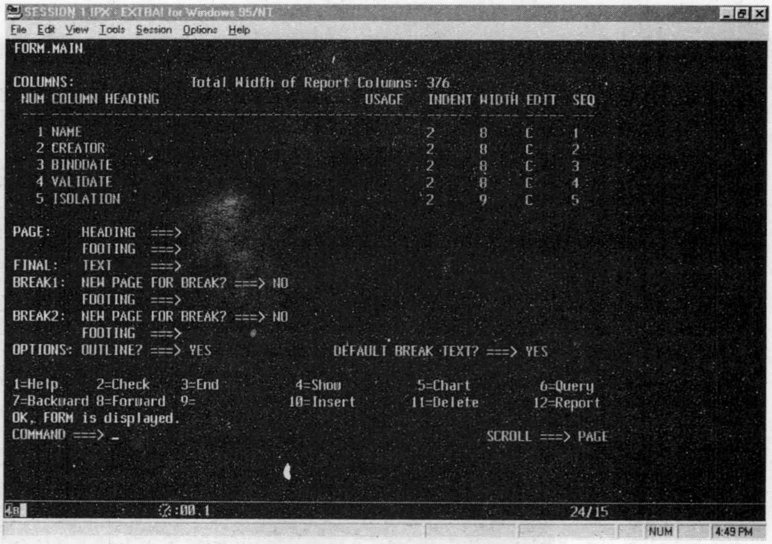

FIGURE 11.18.
The QMF Form panel.

You can use a QMF Form to produce a formatted report for the query output. QMF Forms enable you to perform the following:

- Code a different column heading
- Specify control breaks

- Code control-break heading and footing text
- Specify edit codes to transform column data (for example, suppress leading zeroes or display a currency symbol)
- Compute averages, percentages, standard deviations, and totals for specific columns
- Display summary results across a row, suppressing the supporting detail rows
- Omit columns in the query from the report

You can see how QMF gives you a great deal of power for creating quick, formatted reports from simple SQL queries.

The third QMF object, the QMF Proc, is another important feature of QMF. A QMF query can contain only one SQL statement. Contrast this capability with SPUFI, which can contain multiple SQL statements as long as they are separated by a semicolon.

To execute multiple SQL statements at one time, you use a QMF Proc. QMF Procs contain QMF commands that are tied together and executed serially. For example, see Figure 11.19. This QMF Proc runs one query, prints the results, and then runs another query and prints its results. You can string together as many run statements as necessary and store them as a QMF Proc.

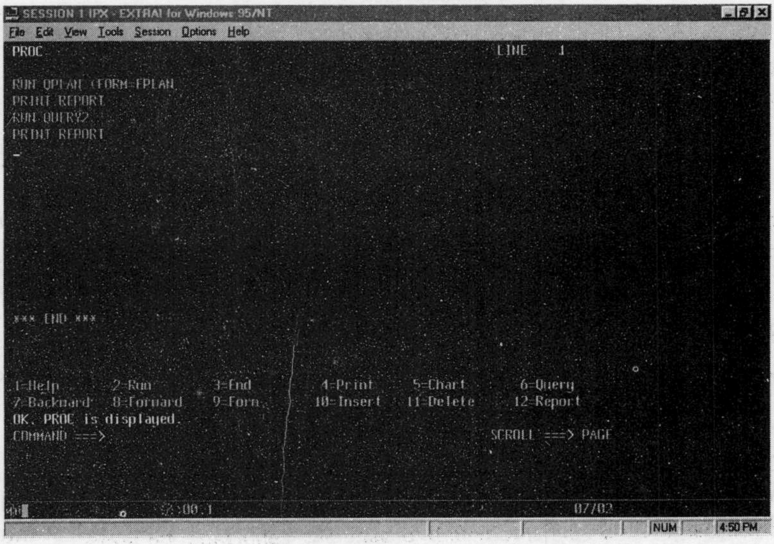

FIGURE 11.19.
The QMF Proc panel.

Using QMF is a quick way to produce high-quality professional reports. Following is a typical QMF user's session, shown also in Figure 11.20. If you type a single SQL statement and press a few function keys, an end-user report is generated.

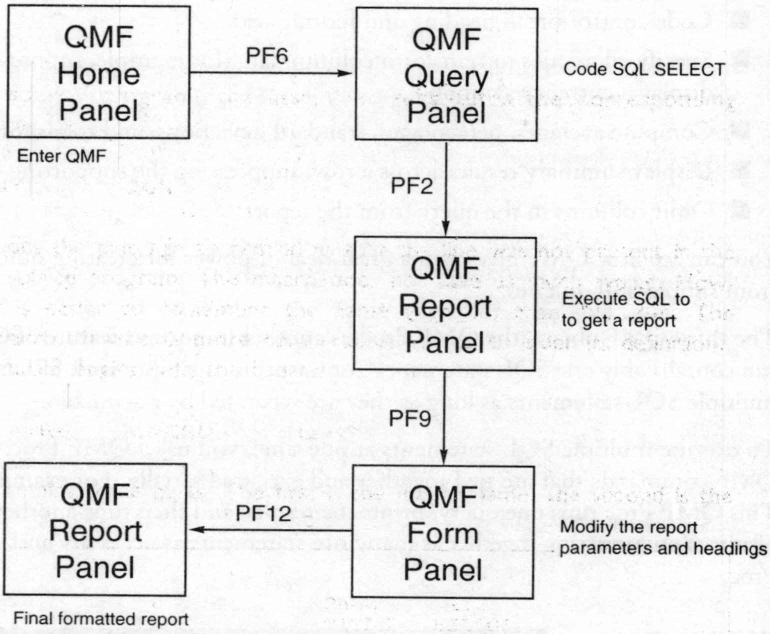

FIGURE 11.20.
A typical QMF session.

1. Enter QMF, and the QMF Home panel appears.
2. Press F6 to display the QMF Query panel. Code the SQL SELECT statement.
3. Press F2 to display the QMF Report panel. Execute the SQL statement to produce the report.
4. Press F9 to display the QMF Form panel. Modify the report parameters and headings as necessary.
5. Press F12 to display the QMF Report panel. Print the final formatted report.

Because this section provides only a quick introduction to QMF, you can consult the IBM QMF manuals listed in Appendix E, "DB2 Manuals," for additional guidance.

Other TSO-Based DB2 Tools

A host of vendor-supplied tools use TSO as their execution environment. In addition to QMF, IBM provides other tools with a TSO interface such as DB2-PM. Additionally, most of the third-party tools for DB2 database administration, analysis, and development are TSO-based. A comprehensive list of DB2 tool vendors and the types of tools available is provided in Chapter 32, "Components of a Total DB2 Solution."

TSO Guidelines

When utilizing DB2 in conjunction with TSO, the following guidelines should be used to ensure effective usage of DB2 and TSO.

Create MVS Performance Groups for DB2 Users

To ensure fast TSO response time, create separate MVS performance groups for TSO users who will access DB2 applications. TSO is generally associated with three periods, designated here as period1, period2, and period3. These periods dictate the amount of MVS resources assigned to a TSO user. Period1 provides more resources than period2, which in turn provides more resources than period3. As TSO users run DB2 applications, their address space is moved from an initial period to lower periods as resources are used. As the address space is moved lower, the TSO response time becomes slower.

For DB2 and QMF users, you can create TSO performance groups with higher levels of resources in period1 and period2. Also, you can prevent the lowering of their TSO sessions to period3. This way, you can provide an optimal environment for high-priority TSO/DB2 applications.

Integrate All Resources into the DB2 Unit of Work When Using TSO

When `COMMIT` processing is performed in online, TSO-based applications, DB2 controls the committing of its resources. The commit and recovery of any other resources, such as sequential input and output files, must be controlled through a program. This is in contrast to the other online environments, which control commit processing by commands native to the environment.

`COMMIT` processing in batch TSO/DB2 programs should follow the guidelines presented in Part II, "DB2 Application Development."

`COMMIT` Frequently in TSO/DB2 Applications

Online TSO/DB2 applications are subject to more frequent deadlocks and timeouts than DB2 applications using other transaction-oriented online environments. For this reason, you should commit more frequently in an online TSO/DB2 application than in DB2 applications running in other environments. Consider committing updates every row or two, rather than after a full screen. Committing might affect the efficiency of the application and should be handled on a program-by-program basis. Failure to commit frequently, however, can result in an unusable application because of lock contention.

Use ISPF Panels to Validate Screen Input

To perform validation checking, use the native functionality of ISPF rather than code validation routines. When ISPF performs the checking, the data is validated before it is processed by the application. This approach can reduce the overhead of loading the program and allocating the thread and other overhead related to program execution.

In addition, error checking is handled by the ISPF routines rather than by the application code. Code provided by the system is generally more error free than functionally equivalent application code. Finally, if you use the validation facilities of ISPF, you can greatly reduce the time it takes to develop TSO/DB2 applications.

Avoid TSO in Performance-Critical Applications

As a development platform for DB2-based applications, TSO is limited in its functionality and efficiency. You should follow these basic rules when deciding whether to use TSO as your online monitor. Do not choose TSO as the development platform for an online DB2-based application if you need subsecond response time or if more than 10 users will be accessing the application concurrently. However, you should choose TSO if you need an environment that speeds up the application development cycle. TSO provides a rich set of tools for developing and testing programs and ISPF screens.

Use ISPF Tables

Consider copying a DB2 table that must be browsed to an ISPF table at the beginning of the program and processing from the ISPF table instead of the DB2 table. This way, you can dramatically increase performance when an online TSO/DB2 program must continually reopen a cursor with an `ORDER BY` due to `COMMIT` processing. Instead, the ISPF table can be created from a cursor, sorted appropriately, and `COMMIT` processing will not cause the program to lose cursor positioning on the ISPF table.

However, you must consider the update implications of using an ISPF table when programming and executing programs using this technique. Updates made to the DB2 table by other users are not made to the ISPF table because it is a copy of the DB2 table for your program's use only. These updates can cause two problems.

One, updates made by other programs might be bypassed rather than processed by the program using the ISPF table. For example, if another program updates data and an ISPF table-driven program generates reports, the report might not contain the most current data.

Another potential problem is that the program using the ISPF table might make incorrect updates. For example, if the program reads the ISPF table and then updates the DB2 table, the following scenario could result:

Program 1	*Time*	*Program 2*
Copy EMP table	1	
to ISPF table	2	
	3	Update Emp 000010
	4	Commit
Read ISPF table	5	Update Emp 000020
Update Emp 000010	6	Commit
Read ISPF table	7	
Update Emp 000020	8	And so on

At time 1, Program 1 begins executing. It copies the EMP table to the ISPF table before Program 2 begins. At time 3, Program 2 begins executing, serially processing employees and adding 100 to each employee's bonus. After Program 1 copies the entire EMP table, it begins giving all employees in department B01 a 10 percent raise in their bonus.

You can see how the employees in department B01 will be disappointed when their bonus paycheck arrives. Program 2 adds 100, but Program 1, unaware of the additional 100, adds 10 percent to the old bonus amount. Consider employee 000020, who works in department B01. He starts with a bonus of $800. Program 2 adds 100, making his bonus $900. Then Program 1 processes employee 000020, setting his bonus to 800×1.10, or $880. Instead of a $990 bonus, he receives only $880.

Avoid Running Batch Programs in TSO Foreground

A DB2 program developed to run as a batch program (that is, with no user interaction while the program is running) can be run in the TSO foreground using the `DSN` command processor, but doing so is not recommended. Running a DB2 batch program in this manner needlessly ties up a user's TSO session and, more important, consumes a valuable foreground thread that could be used for true online processing. (Remember that the `IDFORE DSNZPARM` value limits the number of foreground threads available for use.)

Use IKJEFT1B

You must use the TSO Terminal Monitor Program to invoke the `DSN` command and run a DB2 application program in batch mode. The generic program name is `IKJEFT01`. However, system errors and user abends are not honored by `IKJEFT01`, making it difficult to perform error checking in subsequent JCL steps. To rectify this problem, you can use `IKJEFT1B` instead of `IKJEFT01`. `IKJEFT1B` passes non-zero return codes through to JES where they can be checked in the JCL job stream.

CICS (Customer Information Control System)

The second of the four "doors to DB2" is CICS (Customer Information Control System). CICS is a teleprocessing monitor that enables programmers to develop online, transaction-based programs. By means of BMS (Basic Mapping Support) and the data communications facilities of CICS, programs can display formatted data on screens and receive formatted data from users for further processing. A typical scenario for the execution of a CICS transaction follows:

1. The operator enters data on a terminal, including a transaction ID, and presses Enter. The data can simply be a transaction ID entered by the operator or a formatted BMS screen with the transaction ID.
2. CICS reads the data into the terminal I/O area, and a task is created.
3. CICS checks that the transaction ID is valid.
4. If the program for this transaction is not in main storage, the program is loaded.
5. The task is placed into the queue, waiting to be dispatched.
6. When the task is dispatched, the appropriate application program is run.
7. The program requests BMS to read data from the terminal.
8. BMS reads the data, and the program processes it.
9. The program requests BMS to display the data to a terminal.
10. BMS displays the data.
11. The task is terminated.

When DB2 data is accessed using CICS, multiple threads can be active simultaneously, giving multiple users concurrent access to a DB2 subsystem of a single CICS region. Contrast this functionality with the TSO environment, in which only one thread can be active for any given TSO address space.

A mechanism named the CICS Attach Facility connects CICS with DB2. Using the CICS Attach Facility, you can connect each CICS region to only one DB2 subsystem at a time. You can connect each DB2 subsystem, however, to more than one CICS region at one time, as you can see in Figure 11.21.

Before you delve too deeply into the specifics of the CICS Attach Facility, you should explore the basics of CICS further.

CICS Terminology and Operation

To fully understand the manner in which CICS controls the execution of an application program, you must first understand the relationships among tasks, transactions, and programs. These three terms define separate entities that function together, under the control of CICS, to create an online processing environment.

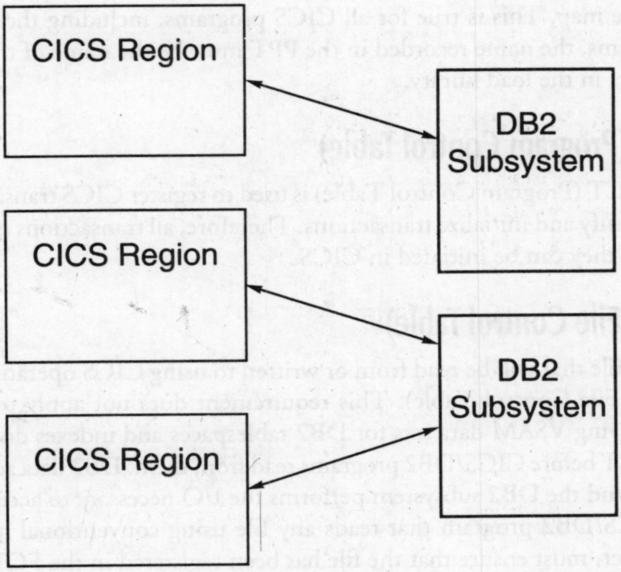

FIGURE 11.21.
CICS region to DB2 subsystem relationship.

A *task* is simply a unit of work scheduled by the operating system. CICS, a batch job, DB2, and TSO are examples of tasks. CICS, however, can schedule tasks under its control, much like the way an operating system schedules tasks. A *CICS task*, therefore, is a unit of work, composed of one or more programs, scheduled by CICS.

The purpose of a *transaction* is to initiate a task. A transaction is initiated by a 1- to 4-byte identifier that is defined to CICS through a control table. Generally, a one-to-one correspondence exists between CICS transactions and CICS tasks, but one transaction can initiate more than one task.

Finally, a *program* is an organized set of instructions that accomplishes an objective in a given unit of work. A CICS program can perform one or many CICS tasks.

CICS Tables

CICS uses tables, usually maintained by a systems programmer, to administer its online environment. These tables control the availability of CICS resources and direct CICS to operate in specific ways. Based on the values registered in these tables, CICS can be customized for each user site. The major tables that affect CICS/DB2 application programs are outlined in the subsections that follow.

PPT (Processing Program Table)

CICS programs and BMS maps must be registered in the PPT (Processing Program Table). If the program or map has not been recorded in the PPT, CICS cannot execute the program or use the map. This is true for all CICS programs, including those with embedded SQL. For programs, the name recorded in the PPT must be the name of the program load module as it appears in the load library.

PCT (Program Control Table)

The PCT (Program Control Table) is used to register CICS transactions. CICS reads this table to identify and initialize transactions. Therefore, all transactions must be registered in the PCT before they can be initiated in CICS.

FCT (File Control Table)

Every file that will be read from or written to using CICS operations must be registered in the FCT (File Control Table). This requirement does not apply to DB2 tables, however. The underlying VSAM data sets for DB2 tablespaces and indexes do not need to be registered in the FCT before CICS/DB2 programs read from them. DB2 data access is accomplished through SQL, and the DB2 subsystem performs the I/O necessary to access the data in DB2 data sets. A CICS/DB2 program that reads any file using conventional methods (that is, non-SQL), however, must ensure that the file has been registered in the FCT before accessing its data.

RCT (Resource Control Table)

When a DB2 program will be run under CICS, an additional table called the RCT (Resource Control Table) must be populated. The RCT applies only to CICS transactions that access DB2 data; it defines the manner in which DB2 resources will be used by CICS transactions. In particular, the RCT defines a plan for each transaction that can access DB2. Additionally, it defines parameters detailing the number and type of threads available for application plans and the DB2 command processor. You can find more details about RCT and its parameters in "The RCT Parameters" section, later in this chapter.

Other Tables

Other tables used by CICS control resource security, terminal definitions, logging and journaling, and the automatic invocation of program at CICS startup. A discussion of these tables is beyond the scope of this book.

CICS/DB2 Program Preparation

Another consideration when you're using CICS is the program preparation process. When CICS programs are prepared for execution, a step is added to the process to prepare the embedded CICS commands: the execution of the CICS command language translator. (See Figure 11.22.) You can think of the CICS command language translator as a precompiler for CICS commands. The CICS command language translator comments out the code embedded between `EXEC CICS` and `END-EXEC` and replaces it with standard COBOL `CALL` statements.

FIGURE 11.22.
CICS/DB2 program preparation.

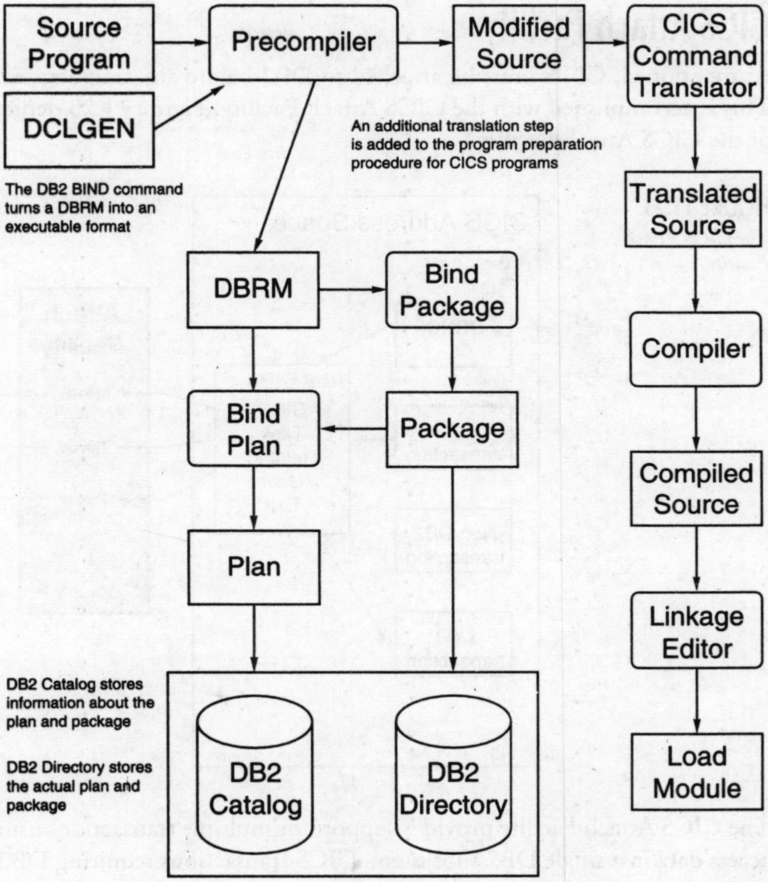

The rest of the program preparation procedure is essentially unchanged. One notable exception is that you must link the CICS language interface (`DSNCLI`), rather than the TSO language interface (`DSNELI`), to the load module.

When embedded CICS commands are encountered, the DB2 precompiler bypasses them, but the CICS command language translator returns warning messages. Thus, you might want to run the DB2 precompiler before running the CICS command language translator. Functionally, which precompiler is run first does not matter. Running the DB2 precompiler first, however, eliminates a host of unwanted messages and speeds up program preparation somewhat because the CICS command language translator needs to perform less work.

CICS Attach Facility

As mentioned, CICS must be attached to DB2 before any transaction can access DB2 data. This is accomplished with the CICS Attach Facility. Figure 11.23 depicts the basic operation of the CICS Attach Facility.

FIGURE 11.23.
The CICS Attach Facility.

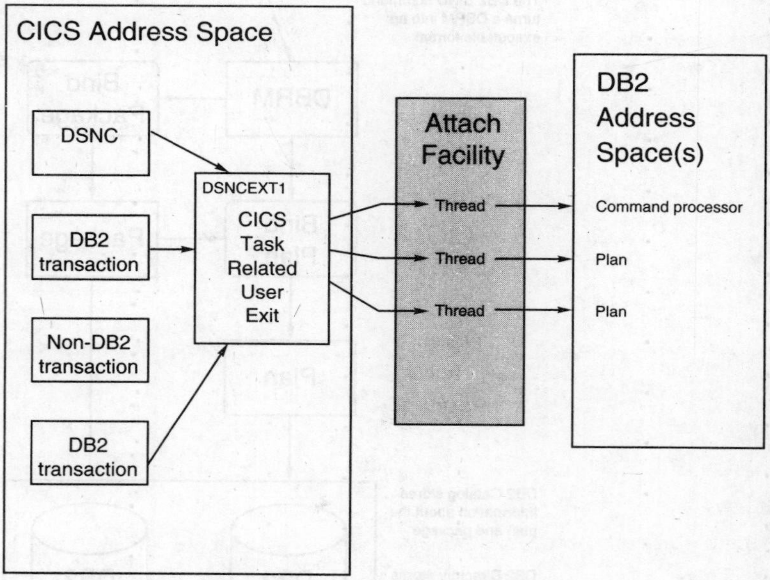

The CICS Attach Facility provides support for multiple transactions using multiple threads to access data in a single DB2 subsystem. CICS transactions requiring DB2 resources are routed to DB2 by `DSNCLI` each time an SQL statement is encountered. The routing is accomplished using the functionality of the CICS Task Related User Exit (TRUE). The TRUE formats the request for DB2 data and passes it to the CICS Attach Facility, which creates a new thread or reuses an existing one.

The following activities occur when a thread is created:

1. A DB2 sign-on is initiated, whereby the authorization ID identifying the user of the thread is established based on a parameter specified in the RCT.
2. A DB2 accounting record is written.
3. Authorization is checked for the user.
4. The executable form of the plan is loaded into memory as follows. The header portion of the SKCT is loaded into the EDM Pool, if it is not already there. This SKCT header is then copied to an executable form called a *cursor table*, which is also placed in the EDM Pool. (These terms are fully defined in Chapter 15, "The Table-Based Infrastructure of DB2.")

5. If VALIDATE(RUN) was specified at bind time for the plan, an incremental bind is performed. Avoid incremental binds by specifying VALIDATE(BIND).
6. If ACQUIRE(ALLOCATE) was specified at bind time for the plan, the following occurs. Locks are acquired for all tablespaces used by the plan, all DBDs are loaded into memory (EDM Pool) referenced by the plan, and all data sets to be used by the plan are opened, if they are not already open.

After the thread is created, the plan corresponding to the transaction being executed is allocated, and the SQL statement is processed. When the request for DB2 resources is satisfied, the data is passed back to the requesting CICS program through the TRUE. The thread is placed in an MVS-wait state until it is needed again. When the next SQL statement is encountered, the CICS program repeats the entire process except the thread creation because the thread has already been allocated and is waiting to be used.

When the CICS task is terminated or a CICS SYNCPOINT is issued, the thread is terminated and the following actions occur:

1. The CICS Attach Facility performs a two-phase commit, which synchronizes the updates and commits made to all defined CICS resources (for example, IMS databases, VSAM files, and sequential files) and DB2 tables. This process is described in more detail in the "Two-Phase Commit" section, later in this chapter.
2. A DB2 accounting record is written.
3. Tablespace locks are released.
4. The executable form of the plan is freed from the EDM Pool.
5. Memory used for working storage is freed.
6. If CLOSE(YES) was specified for tablespaces or indexes used by the thread, the underlying VSAM data sets are closed (provided no other resources are accessing them).

The CICS Attach Facility is started using the DSNC STRT command, indicating the RCT to use.

Types of Threads

As I mentioned, you use the RCT to define the attachment of CICS and DB2. The RCT also assigns a thread to each CICS/DB2 transaction. CICS transactions can use three types of threads to access DB2: command threads, entry threads, and pool threads.

Command threads can be used only by the DSNC command processor. If no command threads are available, pool threads are used.

Entry threads, also called dedicated threads, are associated with a single application plan. Multiple transactions can be assigned to an entry thread grouping defined in the RCT, but each transaction must use the same application plan. Subsequent CICS transactions that use the same application plan can reuse entry threads. This can result in decreased runtime because you avoid the cost of establishing the thread.

You can define entry threads to be either protected or unprotected. A protected thread remains available for a preset time, waiting for transactions that can reuse the thread to be run. An unprotected thread is terminated upon completion unless another transaction is already waiting to use it.

Finally, if an entry thread is not available for a transaction's use, it may be diverted to the pool, where it will utilize a pool thread. Any transaction specifically defined to the pool can use the *pool threads.* In addition, you can define any transaction to be divertable. A divertable transaction is one defined to an entry or command thread that, when no appropriate threads are available, will be diverted to use a pool thread. A pool thread is not reusable and is always terminated when the transaction using it is finished.

You define command, entry, and pool threads by specifying the appropriate parameters in the RCT. The following list summarizes the capabilities of the thread types:

COMD — Used solely for DSNC commands.

ENTRY — Used primarily for high-volume or high-priority transactions. Entry threads can be protected, reused, or diverted to the pool.

POOL — Used primarily for low-priority and low-volume transactions. Pool threads cannot be protected and cannot be diverted. Very limited thread reuse is available with pool threads (only when the first transaction in the queue requests the same plan as the one used by the thread being released—a rare occurrence indeed).

The RCT Parameters

The RCT defines the relationship environment between CICS transactions and DB2 plans. In essence, it defines the working environment for CICS/DB2 applications.

Each CICS region can have only one RCT active at any time. Typically, the CICS or DB2 systems programmer handles RCT changes, but application programmers, systems analysts, and DBAs should understand what is contained in the RCT. A sample RCT is shown in Listing 11.2.

Listing 11.2. A sample Resource Control Table (RCT).

```
*
*    DEFINE DEFAULTS IN INIT, A COMMAND MACRO, AND A POOL MACRO
*
     DSNCRCT TYPE=INIT,SUBID=DB2T,SUFFIX=1,SIGNID=XXXXXX,           X
           THRDMAX=22,TOKENI=YES

     DSNCRCT TYPE=COMD,THRDM=2,THRDA=1,THRDS=1,TWAIT=POOL

     DSNCRCT TYPE=POOL,THRDM=4,THRDA=4,PLAN=POOLPLAN
*
```

```
*     DEFINE AN ENTRY MACRO FOR PROTECTED THREADS
*
      DSNCRCT TYPE=ENTRY,TXID=TXN1,THRDM=4,THRDA=2,                    X
            THRDS=2,PLAN=TXN1PLAN,TWAIT=YES,AUTH=(TXID,*,*)
*
*     DEFINE AN ENTRY MACRO FOR HIGH-PRIORITY UNPROTECTED THREADS
*
      DSNCRCT TYPE=ENTRY,TXID=(TXN2,TXN3),THRDM=2,THRDA=2,             X
            THRDS=0,PLAN=MULTPLAN,TWAIT=POOL,AUTH=(TXID,*,*)
*
*     DEFINE AN ENTRY FOR LOW-PRIORITY UNPROTECTED THREADS
*
      DSNCRCT TYPE=ENTRY,TXID=TXN4,THRDM=1,THRDA=0,                    X
            THRDS=0,PLAN=TXN4PLAN,TWAIT=POOL,AUTH=(TXID,*,*)
*
*     DEFINE AN ENTRY MACRO FOR A MENUING SYSTEM BOUND TO A
*           SINGLE, LARGE PLAN
*
      DSNCRCT TYPE=ENTRY,TXID=(MENU,OPT1,OPT2,OPT3,OPT4),              X
            THRDM=4,THRDA=4,THRDS=3,PLAN=APPLPLAN,                     X
            TWAIT=POOL,AUTH=(SIGNID,*,*)
*
*     DEFINE AN ENTRY MACRO THAT WILL ABEND IF NO THREADS
*           ARE AVAILABLE (TWAIT=NO)
*
      DSNCRCT TYPE=ENTRY,TXID=SAMP,THRDM=1,THRDA=1,THRDS=1,            X
            PLAN=SAMPPLAN,TWAIT=NO,AUTH=(TXID,*,*)
*
*     DEFINE AN ENTRY THREAD FOR DYNAMIC PLAN SELECTION
*
      DSNCRCT TYPE=ENTRY,TXID=TXNS,THRDM=1,THRDA=1,                    X
            PLNEXIT=YES,PLNPGME=DSNCUEXT,AUTH=(CONSTANT,*,*)

      DSNCRCT TYPE=FINAL

      END
```

You can code five types of entries, known as macros, in the RCT. Each macro defines a portion of the CICS-DB2 attachment. The valid RCT `TYPE` entries follow:

`INIT`	Defines the basic parameters affecting the attachment of DB2 to CICS and the setup of defaults for threads
`COMD`	Defines the setup parameters for `DSNC` commands
`ENTRY`	Defines the dedicated threads
`POOL`	Defines the parameters for defining pool threads
`FINAL`	Specifies that no more RCT entries follow

Version 4

Consult Table 11.2 for the parameters that you can code for the RCT `INIT`, `COMD`, `POOL`, and `ENTRY` types of macros. No parameters are specified for the RCT `FINAL` macro. Three RCT parameters were added as of DB2 V4: `PLANI`, `PURGEC`, and `TXIDSO`. RCT `AUTH` values are outlined in Table 11.3.

Version 4

Table 11.2. RCT macro parameters.

		RCT INIT Macro Parameters	
Parameter	*Default*	*Valid Values*	*Description*
DPMODI	HIGH	HIGH, EQ, LOW	Specifies the default for the DPMODE parameter if it is not coded on subsequent ENTRY and POOL macros.
ERRDEST	(CSMT,*,*)	*Valid transient data destinations*	Specifies destinations for unsolicited messages.
PCTEROP	AEY9	AEY9, N906, N906D	Specifies the type of processing to occur following a create thread error.
PLANI	Entry PLAN or TXID	*Plan name*	Specifies the default name of any plan not using dynamic plan selection. If not specified, the plan name must be specified in each subsequent RCT ENTRY macro; otherwise, it will default to the transaction ID.
PLNPGMI	DSNCUEXT	---	Specifies the default value for the PLNPGME parameter if it is not coded on subsequent ENTRY and POOL macros for transactions using the dynamic plan selection.
PLNXTR1	193	1 to 200	Specifies the trace ID for the dynamic plan entry.
PLNXTR2	194	1 to 200	Specifies the trace ID for the dynamic plan exit.
PURGEC	(0,30)	(0,30) thru (59,59)	Specifies the purge cycle for a protected thread.

RCT INIT Macro Parameters			
Parameter	*Default*	*Valid Values*	*Description*
			The first value indicates minutes; the second indicates seconds.
ROLBI	YES	YES, NO	Specifies the default value for the ROLBE parameter if it is not coded on subsequent ENTRY and POOL macros.
SHDDEST	CSSL	*Valid transient data destinations*	Specifies a destination for the statistical report during CICS shutdown.
SIGNID	*Application name of CICS subsystem*	8-character string	Specifies the authorization ID used by the CICS Attach Facility when signing on to DB2.
SNAP	A	*Valid* SYSOUT *classes*	Specifies the SYSOUT class to be used by the CICS Attach Facility for snap dumps.
STRTWT	YES	YES, NO	Specifies action to be taken by the CICS Attach Facility during startup if DB2 is not operational. YES directs the CICS Attach Facility to wait for DB2 to come up and then attach. NO indicates that the CICS Attach Facility startup will fail.
SUBID	DSN	*4-character DB2 ID*	Specifies the DB2 subsystem to which this RCT will be attached.
SUFFIX	0	*1 byte*	Specifies an identifier for the RCT. It is the identifier *x*, as supplied in the DSNC STRT *x* command.

continues

Table 11.2. continued

RCT INIT Macro Parameters			
Parameter	*Default*	*Valid Values*	*Description*
THRDMAX	12	*Any integer greater than 4*	Specifies the absolute maximum number of threads that can be created by this Attach Facility.
TRACEID	192	*Any valid CICS trace ID*	Specifies a userid to be used by the CICS Attach Facility to be used for tracing.
TWAITI	YES	YES, NO, POOL	Specifies the default for the TWAIT parameter if it is not coded on subsequent ENTRY and POOL macros.
TOKENI	NO	YES, NO	Specifies the default for the TOKENE parameter if it is not coded on a subsequent ENTRY macro.
TXIDSO	YES	YES, NO	Specifies whether sign-ons are to be suppressed during thread reuse for pool threads and threads with multiple TXIDs.

RCT INIT Macro Parameters			
Parameter	*Default*	*Valid Values*	*Description*
AUTH	(USER, TERM,TXID)	*Character string*, GROUP, SIGNID, TERM, TXID, USER, USERID, * AUTH	Defines the authorization scheme to be used for the given transaction. As many as three values can be specified. The attachment facility tries to use them in the order specified from left to

RCT INIT Macro Parameters			
Parameter	*Default*	*Valid Values*	*Description*
			right. For the default values, it first tries to use the CICS sign-on ID, and then the CICS transaction ID. For a description of each AUTH value, see Table 11.3.
ROLBE	NO	YES, NO	Defines the action to be taken if this transaction will be the victim in the resolution of a deadlock. If YES is coded, a CICS SYNCPOINT ROLLBACK is issued and a -911 SQLCODE is returned to the program. If NO is coded, a CICS SYNCPOINT ROLLBACK is not issued and the SQLCODE is set to -913.
THRDA	1	*Positive integer or zero*	Defines the maximum number of threads that can be connected for the transaction, group of transactions, or pool. When the limit is reached, action is taken according to the values coded in the TWAIT parameter.
THRDM	1	*Positive integer or zero*	Defines the absolute maximum number of threads that can ever be connected for the transaction, group of transactions, or the pool.

continues

Table 11.2. continued

RCT INIT Macro Parameters			
Parameter	*Default*	*Valid Values*	*Description*
			This number must be equal to or greater than the value of THRDA. If it is greater than THRDA, you can issue the DSNC MODIFY TRANSACTION command to change the value of THRDA to a greater value but not a value greater than THRDM.
THRDS	1	*Positive integer or zero*	Specifies the number of protected threads. The value cannot exceed THRDA or 99, whichever is greater.
TWAIT	YES	YES, NO, POOL*	Specifies the action to be taken when a thread is required but the limit (THRDA) has been reached. YES indicates that the transaction should wait until a thread is available. NO causes the transaction to abend. POOL diverts the transaction to the pool, causing a pool thread to be used.
TXID	DSNC	DSNC	Specifies the transaction ID for DB2 command threads. It should always be set to DSNC.

RCT INIT Macro Parameters

Parameter	Default	Valid Values	Description
AUTH	(USER, TERM,TXID)	*Character string,* SIGNID, TERM, USERID, *	Defines the GROUP authorization scheme to be used for the giventransaction. You can specify as many as three values. The attachment facility tries to use them in the order specified from left to right. For the default values, it tries to use first the CICS sign-on ID, then the CICS terminal ID, and then the CICS transaction ID. For a description of each AUTH value, see Table 11.3.
DPMODE	HIGH	HIGH, EQ, LOW	Defines the dispatching priority limit that can be assigned to the task. This limit overrides the DPMODI parameter if it was coded on the INIT macro.
PLAN	TXID	*Plan name*	Defines the name of the plan to use for the transaction or transactions being defined. If it is not specified, the plan name defaults to the transaction ID.
PLNEXIT	NO	YES, NO	Indicates whether the dynamic plan selection will be used.

continues

Table 11.2. continued

RCT INIT Macro Parameters			
Parameter	*Default*	*Valid Values*	*Description*
PLNPGME	DSNCUEXT	*Program name*	Specifies the name of the exit program used to assign a plan name when the dynamic plan selection is used. This name overrides the PLNPGMI parameter if it was coded on the INIT macro.
ROLBE	YES	YES, NO	Defines the action to be taken if this transaction will be the victim in the resolution of a deadlock. If YES is coded, a CICS SYNCPOINT ROLLBACK is issued and a -911 SQLCODE is returned to the program. If NO is coded, a CICS SYNCPOINT ROLLBACK is not issued and the SQLCODE is set to -913.
TASKREQ	---	PA1-PA3, PF1-PF24, OPID, LPA, MSRE	This parameter is used when a transaction will be started by a 3270 function key.
THRDA	0	*Positive integer or zero*	Defines the maximum number of threads that can be connected for the transaction, group of transactions, or pool. When the limit is reached, action is taken according to the values coded in the TWAIT parameter.

RCT INIT Macro Parameters			
Parameter	*Default*	*Valid Values*	*Description*
THRDM	0	*Positive integer or zero*	Defines the absolute maximum number of threads that can ever be connected for the transaction, group of transactions, or the pool. This number must be equal to or greater than the value of THRDA. If it is greater than THRDA, you can issue the DSNC MODIFY TRANSACTION command to change the value of THRDA to a greater value but not a value greater than THRDM.
THRDS	0	*Positive integer or zero*	Specifies the number of protected threads. The value cannot exceed THRDA or 99, whichever is greater.
TWAIT	YES	YES, NO, POOL	Specifies the action to be taken when a thread is required but the limit (THRDA) has been reached. YES indicates that the transaction should wait until a thread is available. NO causes the transaction to abend. POOL diverts the transaction to the pool, causing a pool thread to be used.

continues

Table 11.2. continued

Parameter	Default	Valid Values	Description
		RCT INIT Macro Parameters	
TOKENE	NO	NO, YES	Specifies whether the CICS attachment facility will produce an accounting trace record for every transaction.
TXID	---	*Transaction ID or list of transaction IDs*	Specifies the transaction for this entry.
		RCT INIT Macro Parameters	
AUTH	(USER, TERM,TXID) SIGNID, TERM,	*Character string,* GROUP, TXID, USER, USERID, * AUTH	Defines the authorization scheme to be used for the given transaction. You can specify as many as three values. The attachment facility tries to use them in the order specified from left to right. For the default values, it tries to use first the CICS sign-on ID, then the CICS terminal ID, and then the CICS transaction ID. For a description of each value, see Table 11.3.
DPMODE	HIGH	HIGH, EQ, LOW	Defines the dispatching priority limit that can be assigned to the task. This limit overrides the DPMODI parameter if it was coded on the INIT macro.

RCT INIT Macro Parameters			
Parameter	*Default*	*Valid Values*	*Description*
PLAN	DEFAULT	*Plan name*	Defines the name of the plan to use for the transaction or transactions being defined. If it is not specified, the plan name defaults to the character string DEFAULT.
PLNEXIT	NO	YES, NO	Indicates whether the dynamic plan selection will be used.
PLNPGME	DSNCUEXT	*Program name*	Specifies the name of the exit program used to assign a plan name when the dynamic plan selection is used. This name overrides the PLNPGMI parameter if it was coded on the INIT macro.
ROLBE	YES	YES, NO	Defines the action to be taken if this transaction will be the victim in the resolution of a deadlock. If YES is coded, a CICS SYNCPOINT ROLLBACK is issued and a -911 SQLCODE is returned to the program. If NO is coded, a CICS SYNCPOINT ROLLBACK is not issued and the SQLCODE is set to -913.
TASKREQ	---	PA1-PA3, PF1-PF24, OPID, LPA, MSRE	This parameter is used when a transaction will be started by a 3270 function key.

continues

Table 11.2. continued

		RCT INIT Macro Parameters	
Parameter	*Default*	*Valid Values*	*Description*
THRDA	3	*Positive integer or zero*	Defines the maximum number of threads that can be connected for the transaction, group of transactions, or pool. When the limit is reached, action is taken according to the values coded in the TWAIT parameter.
THRDM	3	*Positive integer or zero*	Defines the absolute maximum number of threads that can ever be connected for the transaction, group of transactions, or the pool. This number must be the value of THRDA. If it is greater than THRDA, you can issue the DSNC MODIFY TRANSACTION command to change the value of THRDA to a greater value but not a value greater than THRDM.
THRDS	0	*Positive integer or zero*	Specifies the number of protected threads. The value cannot exceed THRDA or 99, whichever is greater.
TWAIT	YES	YES, NO	Specifies the action to be taken when a thread is required but the limit (THRDA) has been reached. YES indicates

RCT INIT Macro Parameters			
Parameter	*Default*	*Valid Values*	*Description*
			that the transaction should wait until a thread is available. NO causes the transaction to abend.
TXID	POOL	*Transaction ID or list of transaction IDs*	Specifies the transaction for this entry.

Table 11.3. RCT AUTH values.

AUTH *Value*	*Description*
Character string	The character string specified is used for the authorization ID.
GROUP	The RACF group ID is used for the authorization ID.
SIGNID	The SIGNID specified in the INIT RCT macro is used for the authorization ID.
TERM	The CICS terminal ID is used for the authorization ID.
TXID	The CICS transaction ID is used for the authorization ID.
USER	The CICS sign-on ID is used for the authorization ID.
USERID	This value is similar to the USER option but can be extended using DSN3@SGN to work with RACF to send a secondary authid.
*	Null. You can specify this value only for the second and third values. It Indicates that no additional authorization scheme will be used.

RCT Guidelines

The following guidelines provide helpful advice for generating efficient CICS RCTs.

Explicitly Code a COMD Entry

A command thread is generated regardless of whether it is specified in the RCT. Coding a COMD macro for command threads rather than using defaults, however, is a good idea. This way, you can track and change the parameters for command threads more easily.

Favor TWAIT=POOL Over TWAIT=NO

When you're coding the ENTRY macro, favor the use of TWAIT=POOL to avoid an excessive wait time or abends. Avoid the TWAIT=NO parameter because it increases the number of abends.

Code THRDM Greater Than THRDA

Code the THRDM parameter to be at least one greater than the THRDA parameter. This provides a buffer of at least one additional thread for tuning if additional entry threads are required.

Favor the Use of ROLBE=YES

Use ROLBE=YES to roll back changes automatically in the event of a deadlock or timeout. ROLBE=NO places the onus on the application program to decide whether to back out changes. ROLBE=YES can reduce the amount of coding needed in CICS programs.

Use DPMODE=EQ and DPMODE=HIGH

Use DPMODE=HIGH for only a few very high-priority transactions. Use DPMODE=EQ for most transactions. Avoid DPMODE=LOW unless someone you hate will be using transactions assigned to those threads.

Use TOKENE=YES

When CICS/DB2 threads are reused, accounting records are not cut unless the TOKENE=YES RCT parameter is coded on an ENTRY macro (or TOKENI=YES is coded on the INIT macro). Failure to specify TOKENE=YES might cause your performance monitor to report multiple transactions as a single transaction. This option is available only for DB2 V2.3 and higher.

Specifying TOKENE=YES also causes the CICS attachment facility to pass the CICS LU6.2 token to the DB2 accounting trace record. This capability is important because CICS produces accounting records at the transaction level, whereas DB2 produces accounting records at the thread level. If you include the token in the accounting records, DB2 and CICS accounting records can be easily correlated.

Use the Appropriate Thread Type

Table 11.4 suggests the types of threads to use for different transaction requirements. In general, transactions requiring high availability or throughput should have dedicated and protected threads. Low-volume or low-priority threads can be diverted to the pool.

Table 11.4. Thread specification by the type of transaction.

Transaction	*Thread to Use*	*Other Recommendations*
Very high volume High priority	ENTRY	THRDM > THRDA THRDA > 3 THRDS > 1 TWAIT = POOL (or YES) DPMODE = HIGH
Moderate to high volume High priority	ENTRY	THRDM > THRDA THRDA > 0 THRDS > 0 TWAIT = POOL
Low volume High priority	ENTRY	THRDM = 2 THRDA = 1 THRDS = 0 TWAIT = POOL DPMODE = HIGH
Low volume Moderate priority	ENTRY	THRDM = THRDA = 1 THRDS = 0 TWAIT = POOL
Low volume Low priority	ENTRY	THRDM = THRDA = THRDS = 0 TWAIT = POOL
Very low volume	POOL	THRDM > 3 THRDA > 2 TWAIT = YES

Avoid specifying transactions explicitly to the pool, but always define a pool macro.

Use DSNC

Use the `DSNC DISPLAY STATISTICS` command to monitor the CICS environment. You can find details on this command in Chapter 29.

Plan Management and Dynamic Plan Selection

In the CICS environment, multiple programs can be executed in a single task. For CICS, the task defines the unit of work. For DB2, the application plan defines the unit of work. The scope of the unit of work for these two environments must be synchronized for them to operate in harmony. DB2 provides this synchronization in two ways:

- You can bind all programs that can be initiated in a single CICS task to a single plan specified in the RCT for each transaction that can invoke any of the programs. An example was shown in Listing 11.2 for the menuing application.
- You can specify that dynamic plan selection is to be used. Listing 11.2 shows an example of this synchronization also.

Dynamic plan selection uses an exit routine, specified in the RCT by coding `PLNEXIT=YES` and `PLNPGME=exit-routine`. The exit routine determines the plan that should be used for the program being run. IBM supplies a sample exit routine called `DSNCUEXT` with DB2. This exit routine assigns the plan name to be the same as the program name. This approach is usually adequate, but you can code exit routines to assign plan names as your installation sees fit. Exit routines cannot contain SQL statements.

The first SQL statement executed after a CICS `SYNCPOINT` signals to DB2 that a new plan name needs to be selected. When you're using dynamic plan selection, your CICS programs must heed the following rules:

- Use the CICS `LINK` or `XCTL` command to call one program from another.
- Issue a CICS `SYNCPOINT` before the `LINK` or `XCTL`. Otherwise, the first SQL statement in the new program receives an `SQLCODE` of `-805`.
- Design your programs so that a complete application unit of work is completed in a single program. Failure to do so results in logical units of work that span physical units of work. Data integrity problems can result.

The second option for the synchronization of DB2 plans to CICS tasks is to create large plans consisting of the DBRMs or packages of all programs that can be called in a single CICS task. Prior to DB2 V2.3, this could not be achieved with packages, so all DBRMs had to be bound into a single plan. This approach had the following negative effects.

When a program changed, a new DBRM was created, which caused the large plan to be bound again. You could not use the `REBIND` command, and you had no way of simply adding or replacing a single DBRM. As the number of DBRMs added to a plan increased, the time to bind that plan increased. As the plan was being bound, execution of the CICS transactions using that plan was not permitted. Therefore, program changes effectively took the entire application offline. When dynamic plan selection or packages were used, however, only the programs being changed were unavailable.

A second negative effect was that as the plan's size increased, it used more virtual storage. Even though DB2 uses techniques to load only those portions of the plan needed to execute the SQL at hand, performance suffers somewhat as plans increase in size. When you use dynamic plan selection, however, plans are generally much smaller. When packages are used, the plan is broken into smaller pieces that the system can manage more easily.

The recommendation is to create plans using packages, not DBRMs. This technique should be easier to manage and more efficient than either large plans composed of DBRMs or dynamic plan selection. Packages, instead of DBRMs bound directly into plans, should be the standard for all DB2 shops. Yet, many shops still avoid packages because they avoid (or fear) change or simply have not had the time to convert older applications. So, if your installation is running a version of DB2 prior to V2.3 (or you have just stubbornly shunned packages), the recommendations change. Use dynamic plan selection for very large applications. Doing so decreases downtime due to program changes. For small applications (four or fewer programs), use a large plan composed of the DBRMs of each program.

Two-Phase Commit

As I already mentioned, changes made in a CICS program are committed by the CICS SYNCPOINT command. Likewise, you can invoke the SYNCPOINT ROLLBACK command to back out unwanted changes. You code these commands as follows:

```
EXEC CICS
    SYNCPOINT
END-EXEC.

EXEC CICS
    SYNCPOINT
    ROLLBACK
END-EXEC.
```

The SQL COMMIT and ROLLBACK verbs are not valid in CICS programs. An implicit commit is performed when a CICS transaction ends with the EXEC CICS RETURN command.

When a CICS SYNCPOINT is requested in a CICS/DB2 program, a two-phase commit is performed. The commit is done in two phases because CICS must commit changes made to resources under its jurisdiction (such as changes made to VSAM files), and DB2 must control the commit for changes made with SQL UPDATE, INSERT, and DELETE statements.

Figure 11.24 shows the two-phase commit process for CICS. CICS acts as the coordinator of the process, and DB2 acts as a participant. The first phase consists of CICS informing DB2 that a SYNCPOINT was requested. DB2 updates its log but retains all locks because the commit is not complete. When the log update is finished, DB2 informs CICS that it has completed phase 1. CICS then updates its log, retaining all locks.

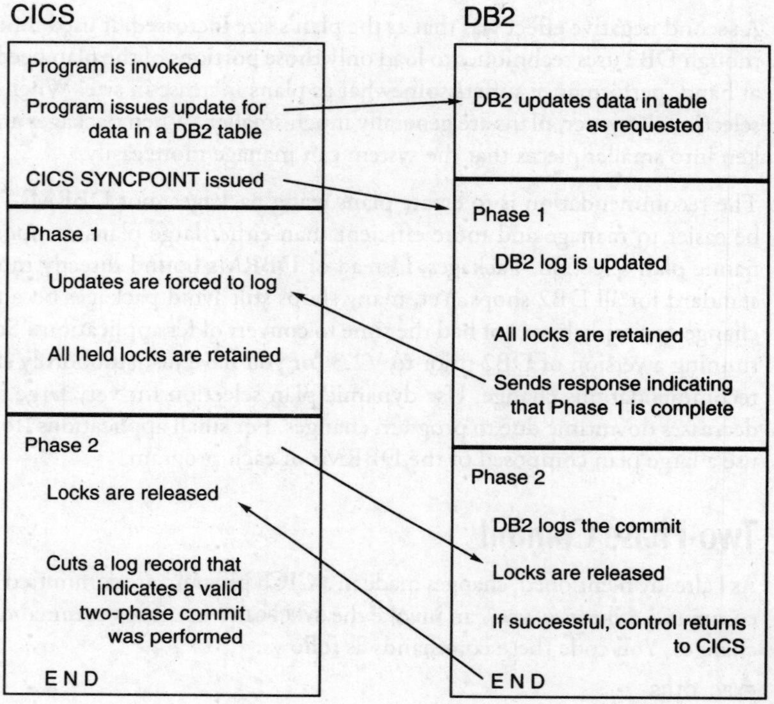

FIGURE 11.24.
The CICS two-phase commit process.

CICS signals DB2 to begin phase 2, in which DB2 logs the commit and releases its locks. If successful, DB2 sends control back to CICS so that CICS can release its locks and record the success of the `SYNCPOINT`.

The two-phase commit process virtually ensures the integrity of DB2 data modified by CICS transactions. If changes cannot be committed in either environment for any reason, they are rolled back in both. In a connection failure or a system crash, however, the commit status of some transactions may be in doubt. These transactions are referred to as *in-doubt threads*. After a system failure, when DB2 and CICS are started and the connection is reestablished, most in-doubt threads are resolved automatically. If any in-doubt threads exist, you can use the `RECOVER INDOUBT` command to commit or roll back the changes pending for these threads.

CICS Design Guidelines

When designing CICS transactions that access DB2 data, keep the following tips, tricks, and techniques in mind.

Bind CICS Plans for Performance

When you're binding plans for CICS transactions, follow these BIND guidelines:

High volume	ACQUIRE(ALLOCATE), RELEASE(DEALLOCATE)
All others	ACQUIRE(USE), RELEASE(COMMIT)

Binding high-volume transactions in this manner reduces overhead by ensuring that all resources are acquired before they are accessed. High-volume transactions should have no built-in conditional table access and should be as small as possible.

Decrease the Size of Your CICS Programs

The smaller the executable load module for a CICS program, the more efficient it will be. Therefore, CICS programmers should strive to reduce the size of their code. One way to do so is to increase the amount of reusable code. For example, modularize your program and use common modules rather than recode modules everywhere they are needed.

A second way to increase your reusable code is to use the COBOL REDEFINES clause to reduce the number of WORKING-STORAGE variables defined by the program. For example, consider a program requiring three text variables all used by different portions of the code. The first variable is 3 bytes long, the second is 8 bytes long, and another is 15 bytes long. Consider defining them as follows:

```
01   COMMON-VARS-1.
     05  THREE-BYTE-VAR       PIC X(3).
     05  FILLER               PIC X(12).

01   COMMON-VARS-2 REDEFINES COMMON-VARS-1.
     05  EIGHT-BYTE-VAR       PIC X(8).
     05  FILLER               PIC X(7).

01   COMMON-VARS-3 REDEFINES COMMON-VARS-1.
     05  FIFTEEN-BYTE-VAR     PIC X(15).
```

This way, you can save space. Before deciding to use this approach, however, you snould consider the following factors:

- The readability of the code is reduced when you use REDEFINES.
- The program cannot use redefined variables concurrently. Ensure that any variable redefined as another variable can never be used by the program at the same time as another variable assigned for the same redefined group.

Another way to increase reusable code is to use explicit constants in the program code to reduce the number of WORKING-STORAGE variables required. This approach can enhance performance, but it usually makes maintaining the program more difficult.

Avoid COBOL File Processing

Do not use the COBOL file processing verbs READ, WRITE, OPEN, and CLOSE to access non-DB2 data sets required by your CICS/DB2 programs. If you use these functions in a CICS program, an MVS wait results, causing severe performance degradation. Instead, use the corresponding CICS file processing services. See Table 11.5.

Table 11.5. CICS file processing commands.

	Random Access Commands
READ	Reads a specific record
WRITE	Writes a specific record
REWRITE	Updates a specific record
DELETE	Deletes a specific record
	Sequential Access Commands
STARTBR	Establishes sequential positioning in the file
READNEXT	Reads the next record sequentially
	Sequential Access Commands
READPREV	Reads the previous record sequentially
RESETBR	Resets positioning in the file
ENDBR	Ends sequential file access

Avoid Resource-Intensive COBOL Verbs

Avoid the following COBOL verbs and features in CICS programs because they use a large amount of system resources:

```
ACCEPT
DISPLAY
EXAMINE
EXHIBIT
SORT
TRACE
UNSTRING
VARIABLE MOVE
```

Use WORKING-STORAGE to Initialize Variables

To initialize variables, use the VALUES clause in WORKING-STORAGE rather than the MOVE and INITIALIZE statements.

Avoid Excessive PERFORMs and GOTOs

Design your programs to execute paragraphs sequentially as much as possible. The fewer PERFORMs and GOTOs you use, the better the program performance will be in CICS.

Avoid Conversational Programs

A conversational program receives data from a terminal, acts on the data, sends a response to the terminal, and waits for the terminal operator to respond. This process ties up a thread for the duration of the conversation.

Instead, use pseudoconversational techniques for your CICS/DB2 programs. *Pseudoconversational* programs appear to the operator as a continuous "conversation" consisting of requests and responses, but they are actually a series of separate tasks.

Favor Transfer Control Over Linking

Favor the use of the XCTL command over the LINK command to pass control from one program to another. LINK acquires extra storage, and XCTL does not.

Reduce the Overhead of Sequential Number Assignment

Consider using counters in main storage to assign sequential numbers. This way, you can reduce the overhead associated with other forms of assigning sequential numbers, such as reading a table containing the highest number. Remember that a rollback does not affect main storage. Therefore, rolling back a transaction can cause gaps in the numbering sequence.

Plan for Locking Problems

Plan for deadlocks and time-outs, and handle them accordingly in your program. If the RCT specifies ROLBE=YES, all changes are backed out automatically and a -911 SQLCODE is returned to your program. If ROLBE=NO is specified, -913 is passed to the SQLCODE and automatic backout does not occur. In this case, the application program must decide whether to issue a CICS SYNCPOINT ROLLBACK to back out the changes.

Synchronize Programs and RCT Entries

You must know the RCT parameters for your transaction before coding your program. Specifically, coding NO for the ROLBE or TWAIT parameters affects the program design significantly by adding a great deal of code to handle rollbacks and abends.

Use Protected Entry Threads for Performance

Minimize thread creation as much as possible by using protected entry threads for high-volume transactions and by using AUTH=(TXID,*,*) to encourage thread reuse.

Place SQL as Deep in the Program as Possible

Minimize thread use by placing all SQL statements as far as possible into the transaction. A thread is initiated when the first SQL call is encountered. The later in the execution that the SQL statement is encountered, the shorter the time during which the thread is used.

Avoid DDL

Never issue DDL from a CICS program. DDL execution is time intensive and acquires locks on the DB2 Catalog and DB2 Directory. Because CICS programs should be quick, they should avoid DDL.

Check the Availability of the Attach Facility

You must start the CICS Attach Facility for the appropriate DB2 subsystem before you execute CICS transactions that will run programs requiring access to DB2 data. If the CICS-to-DB2 connection is unavailable, the task abends with a CICS abend code of AEY9.

To avoid this type of abend, consider using the CICS HANDLE CONDITION command to check whether DB2 is available, as shown in Listing 11.3. This COBOL routine tests whether the CICS-to-DB2 connection has been started before issuing any SQL.

Listing 11.3. Checking for DB2 availability.

```
WORKING-STORAGE.
         .
         .
    77  WS-LGTH       PIC 9(8)  COMP.
    77  WS-PTR        PIC 9(4)  COMP.
         .
         .
         .

PROCEDURE DIVISION.
0000-MAINLINE.
         .
         .
         .
    EXEC CICS
```

```
        HANDLE CONDITION
        INVEXITREQ(9900-DB2-UNAVAILABLE)
   END-EXEC.

   EXEC CICS
        EXTRACT EXIT
        PROGRAM('DSNCEXT1')
        ENTRYNAME('DSNCSQL')
        GASET(WS-PTR)
        GALENGTH(WS-LGTH)
   END-EXEC.
        .
        .
9900-DB2-UNAVAILABLE.

   Inform the user that DB2 is unavailable

   Perform exception processing
```

Use Debugging Tools

Use CICS debugging facilities such as EDF to view CICS commands before and after their execution.

Implement Security Without Sacrificing Performance

While you're planning your security needs, keep performance in mind. If all security can be implemented with CICS transaction security, specify `AUTH=(TXID,*,*)` in the RCT for each transaction. In DB2, grant `EXECUTE` authority on the plan to the `TXID` name. This way, you can reduce the amount of authorization checking overhead.

IMS (Information Management System)

IMS is IBM's pre-relational database management system offering. It is based on the structuring of related data items in inverted trees or hierarchies. Although usually perceived as only a DBMS, IMS is a combination of two components:

- IMS/DB, the database management system
- IMS/TM, the transaction management environment or data communications component (previously known as IMS/DC, and still called by that name by many DBAs and systems programmers)

You can use these IMS components separately or together. Online access to IMS databases is achieved through IMS/TM or CICS. Access to IMS databases is provided also in a batch environment. When an IMS database is accessed through IMS/TM, it is said to be *online*; when it is accessed in batch, it is said to be *offline*. IMS/TM provides an online environment in which you can run application programs that communicate with a terminal, much like CICS. Like CICS, IMS/TM can be used by programs that access not only IMS databases but also DB2 tables.

IMS and CICS are alike in many respects, but they also have significant differences, outlined in the following paragraphs. For example, IMS uses a facility called MFS (Message Format Services) to format messages to terminals and printers; CICS uses BMS (Basic Mapping Support). IMS/TM controls its environment not through tables, but through a series of macros known as a SYSGEN. The SYSGEN defines the terminals, programs, transactions, and the general online environment for IMS/TM. Another difference is that all IMS programs require a program specification block (PSB), which defines the access to IMS/DB databases and IMS/TM resources. Along with IMS DBDs that define the structure of the IMS databases to be accessed, the PSBs are defined to control a program's scope of operation. An additional control block, the ACB (application control block), is used in the online world (and optionally in the batch environment) to combine the PSBs and DBDs into a single control block defining the control structure and scope of all IMS programs.

All IMS/TM activity is processed through a region. There are two types of regions. One control region manages IMS activity and processes commands. Application programs execute from dependent regions. As many as 255 dependent regions can exist for each IMS/TM subsystem. See Figure 11.25 for clarification.

FIGURE 11.25.
IMS/TM regions.

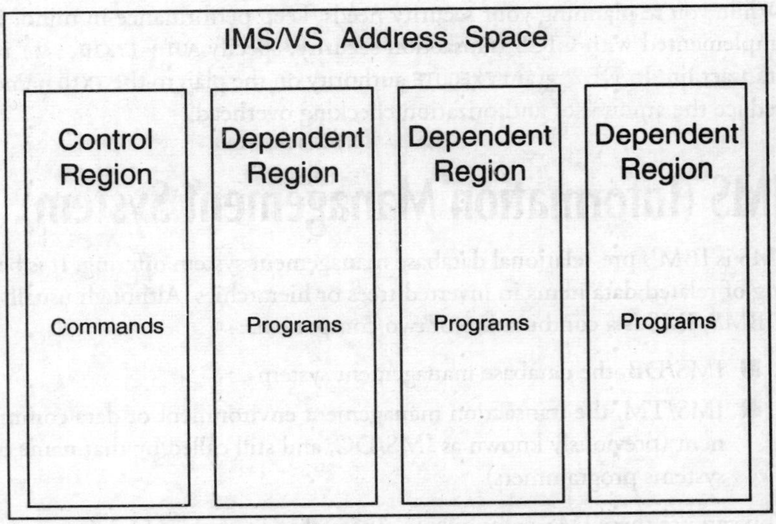

Types of IMS Programs

IMS programs are categorized, based on the environment in which they run and the types of databases they can access. The four types of IMS programs are batch programs, batch message processors, message processing programs, and fast path programs.

An *IMS batch program* is invoked by JCL and runs as an MVS batch job. IMS batch programs can access only offline IMS databases, unless IMS Data Base Recovery Control (DBRC) is used. When DB2 tables are accessed by IMS batch programs, they are commonly referred to as DL/I batch. DL/I (Data Language/I) is the language used to access data in IMS databases, just as SQL is the language used to access data in DB2 tables. Batch DL/I programs run independently of the IMS/TM environment.

The second type of IMS program is called a *batch message processor*, or BMP. BMPs are hybrid programs combining elements of both batch and online programs. A BMP runs under the jurisdiction of IMS/TM but is invoked by JES and operates as a batch program. All databases accessed by a BMP must be online to IMS/TM. The following are the two types of BMPs:

- Terminal-oriented BMPs can access the IMS message queue to send or receive messages from IMS/TM terminals.
- Batch-oriented BMPs do not access the message queue and cannot communicate with terminals.

True online IMS programs are called *message processing programs*, or MPPs. They are initiated by a transaction code, access online databases, and communicate with terminals through the message queue.

The final type of IMS program is a *fast path program*. Fast path programs are very high performance MPPs that access a special type of IMS database known as a fast path database.

The IMS Attach Facility

As with the other environments, a specialized attachment facility is provided with DB2 to enable IMS to access DB2 resources. The IMS Attach Facility, due to the nature of IMS, provides more flexibility in connecting to DB2 than the Attach Facilities for TSO or CICS.

In Figure 11.26, you can see that the following connections are supported using the IMS Attach Facility:

- One DB2 subsystem can connect to multiple IMS subsystems.
- One IMS subsystem can connect to multiple DB2 subsystems.
- One IMS region can connect to multiple DB2 subsystems.
- One IMS application program can access only one DB2 subsystem.

FIGURE 11.26.
The IMS Attach Facility.

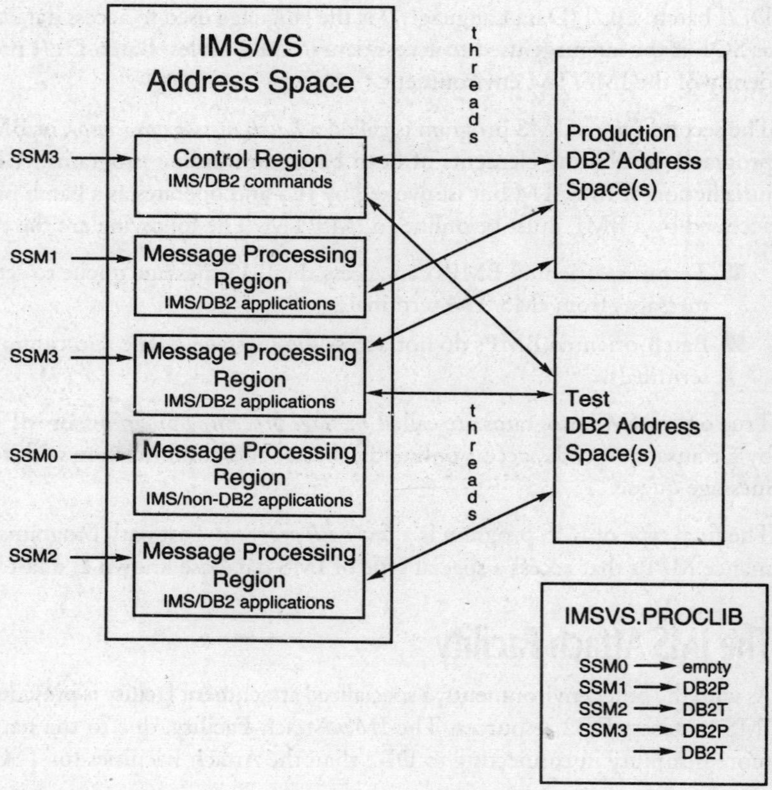

DB2 is connected to IMS by a subsystem member (SSM). The SSM defines the parameters of the IMS Attach Facility for both online and batch connections. The following list outlines the SSM parameters:

`SSN` The DB2 subsystem identifier (for example, DSN).

`LIT` The language interface token used to route SQL calls to the appropriate DB2 subsystem. Usually equal to SYS1.

`ESMT` The name of the DB2 initialization module, which must be set to `DSNMIN10`.

`RTT` The optional Resource Translation Table to be used. The `RTT` can be used to override IMS region options, such as the capability to specify a plan name different from the program name.

`ERR` The action IMS takes if the plan is not found or the DB2 subsystem is unavailable. The `ERR` options follow:

- `R` IMS returns control to the application program and sets the `SQLCODE` in the SQLCA to `-923`. `R` is the default.
- `Q` IMS causes an abend when operating in DL/1 batch. In an online environment, IMS `PSTOP`s the program and issues a `U3051` user abend code, backs out this transaction's activity to the last checkpoint, and requeues the input message.
- `A` IMS forces an abend with a `U3047` abend code. If executing in the online environment, the input message is deleted.

`CRC` The command recognition character to be used to identify a DB2 command in the IMS/TM environment using `/SSR`. `CRC` is not used in the DL/1 batch environment.

`CONNECTION` The connection name for a DL/1 batch program. This name must be unique for each concurrent batch IMS program that will access DB2. If a program is running with a given connection name, and another program with the same name tries to execute at the same time, the second program will fail. This parameter is invalid for the online attach.

`PLAN` The name of the plan to be used by the batch IMS/DB2 application program. This parameter is required only if the plan name is different from the program name. This parameter is invalid for the online attach.

`PROGRAM` The name of the program to be run. This parameter is invalid for the online attach.

Online Attach Considerations

Enabling the IMS Attach Facility for the online environment is the responsibility of a system programmer. IMS-to-DB2 connections are defined by changing the JCL used to invoke the IMS subsystem. The SSM is assigned to the JCL by a parameter on the `EXEC` card. The IMS `SYSGEN` procedure is unaffected by the addition of an IMS-to-DB2 connection.

To establish the connection between IMS/TM and DB2, you must perform the following steps:

1. Code an SSM line for each DB2 subsystem that must be connected to this IMS/TM region.
2. Place the SSM in the `IMSVS.PROCLIB` PDS defined to the IMS control region and specify the name in the SSM parameter of the `EXEC` statement. For example,

```
//IMS        EXEC       IMS . . . ,SSM=SSM1 . . .
//STEPLIB    DD         DSN=IMSVS.RESLIB,DISP=SHR
//           DD         DSN=SYS1.DB2V510.DSNLOAD,DISP=SHR
//           DD         DSN=SYS1.DB2V510.DSNEXIT,DISP=SHR
//PROCLIB    DD         DSN=IMSVS.PROCLIB,DISP=SHR
```

The SSM defined to the control region is the default for all dependent regions. If you do not want this default, code a separate SSM for each dependent region that has different IMS-to-DB2 connection needs, and follow the preceding steps for each of the dependent regions.

If more than one DB2 subsystem will be connected to a single region (control or dependent), the SSM for that region must contain a line for each of the DB2 subsystems. Then a second language interface module must be generated. The standard language interface module is `DFSLI000`; it uses SYS1 as its language interface token (LIT) in the SSM. You can create a second language interface module, `DFSLI002`, for example, by using SYS2 for its LIT.

You can generate the second language interface module using the `DFSLI` macro provided with IMS/VS. Consider this example:

```
DFSLI002   DFSLI   TYPE=DB2,LIT=SYS2
```

A program executing in any region connected to more than one DB2 subsystem accesses the appropriate DB2 subsystem based on which language interface module the program was link-edited with at program preparation time. In this example, the module would be either `DFSLI000` or `DFSLI002`.

`CONNECTION`, `PLAN`, and `PROGRAM` are batch parameters and, as such, are invalid when defining the SSM for IMS/TM. Sample online SSM definitions follow. The first is a simple SSM connecting the DB2P subsystem to IMS/TM:

```
DB2P,SYS1,DSNMIN10,,R,-
```

You use the second to connect two DB2 subsystems, DB2A and DB2B, to a single IMS/TM:

```
DB2A,SYS1,DSNMIN10,,R,-
DB2B,SYS2,DSNMIN10,,R,+
```

To access DB2A, `INCLUDE` the `DFSLI000` module (because it is associated with LIT SYS1) in the link-edit step for your programs. `DFSLI002`, on the other hand, is associated with LIT SYS2, so it is link-edited into programs that must access DB2B resources.

An online IMS/TM program (BMP, MPP, or fast path) must follow standard DB2 program preparation procedures (precompile, compile, link edit, and bind). However, a few special considerations apply:

- The appropriate language interface module (DFSLI000, DFSLI002, and so on) for the DB2 subsystem to be accessed must be link-edited into the load module.
- A PSB must be generated for the program to define the IMS databases and online resources that will be accessed by the program.
- The PSB (and all DBDs accessed by the program) must be included in the ACB for the online IMS/TM subsystem.
- The appropriate IMS SYSGEN macros must be coded for the transaction and program before it can be executed online.

The Resource Translation Table

You can define a resource translation table (RTT) using the DSNMAPN assembler macro. An RTT is necessary only when the plan name is not the same as the program name. Consider this example:

```
DSNMAPN      APN=PROGRAMX,PLAN=PLANX, . . .
```

This statement assigns the plan name, PLANX, to the program PROGRAMX. This macro must be linked to the DB2 load library with the name specified in the RTT parameter of the SSM being used.

IMS/TM Thread Use

Two types of threads are used by IMS/TM: command threads and transaction threads. The type of thread is contingent on the type of region it has been created for. Each region can have only one thread at any given time.

Threads emanating from IMS/TM are not created until they are needed, even though the IMS-to-DB2 connection has been established. The following process is for a command thread emanating from the control region:

1. After IMS/TM is brought up, the first DB2 command is issued from a terminal connected to IMS/TM using the /SSR IMS command.
2. IMS verifies that the user is permitted to issue the /SSR command.
3. IMS issues a SIGNON request using that user's userid, if available. If SIGNON security is not used, the LTERM is used (or, for a non-message-driven BMP, the PSB name is used).
4. IMS requests that DB2 create a thread.
5. When the thread has been created, the command is processed. Subsequent DB2 commands issued from IMS can reuse the thread. SIGNON is performed for these subsequent commands.

Additional processing is required for transaction threads. Transaction threads are created from a dependent region that was scheduled by the control region. The procedure for transaction thread creation and its use is shown in Figure 11 27.

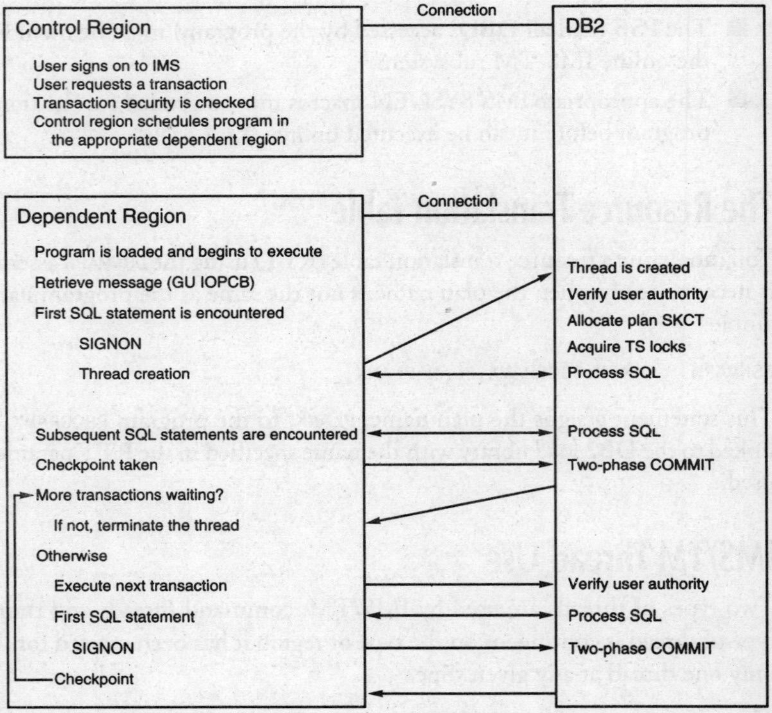
Control Region
User signs on to IMS
User requests a transaction
Transaction security is checked
Control region schedules program in the appropriate dependent region
Connection
DB2
Connection
Dependent Region
Program is loaded and begins to execute
Retrieve message (GU IOPCB)
First SQL statement is encountered
SIGNON
Thread creation
Subsequent SQL statements are encountered
Checkpoint taken
More transactions waiting?
If not, terminate the thread
Otherwise
Execute next transaction
First SQL statement
SIGNON
Checkpoint
Thread is created
Verify user authority
Allocate plan SKCT
Acquire TS locks
Process SQL
Process SQL
Two-phase COMMIT
Verify user authority
Process SQL
Two-phase COMMIT

FIGURE 11.27.
The IMS/DB2 transaction threads.

Two-Phase Commit

Recall that CICS programs commit changes by means of CICS commands and not the normal DB2 `COMMIT` statement. Likewise, changes made in IMS/TM programs are committed and rolled back by means of IMS commands. You code the IMS checkpoint command, which implements a `COMMIT`, as follows:

```
CALL    'CBLTDLI' USING NUM-OPS,
                        'CHKP',
                        IO-PCB,
                        CHKP-LENGTH,
                        CHKP-AREA.
```

You code the IMS rollback command as follows:

```
CALL    'CBLTDLI' USING NUM-OPS,
                        'ROLB',
                        IO-PCB,
                        CHKP-LENGTH,
                        CHKP-AREA.
```

The SQL verbs `COMMIT` and `ROLLBACK` are not valid in IMS/TM programs. An implicit commit is performed when a `GET UNIQUE` is issued to the message queue.

When a checkpoint is requested in an IMS/TM program, a two-phase commit is performed much like the two-phase commit discussed in the previous section on CICS. The commit is done in two phases to synchronize the updates made to IMS databases with those made to DB2 tables.

The two-phase commit process for IMS/TM programs is outlined in Figure 11.28. A component of IMS/TM called the *syncpoint coordinator* handles the coordination of commits.

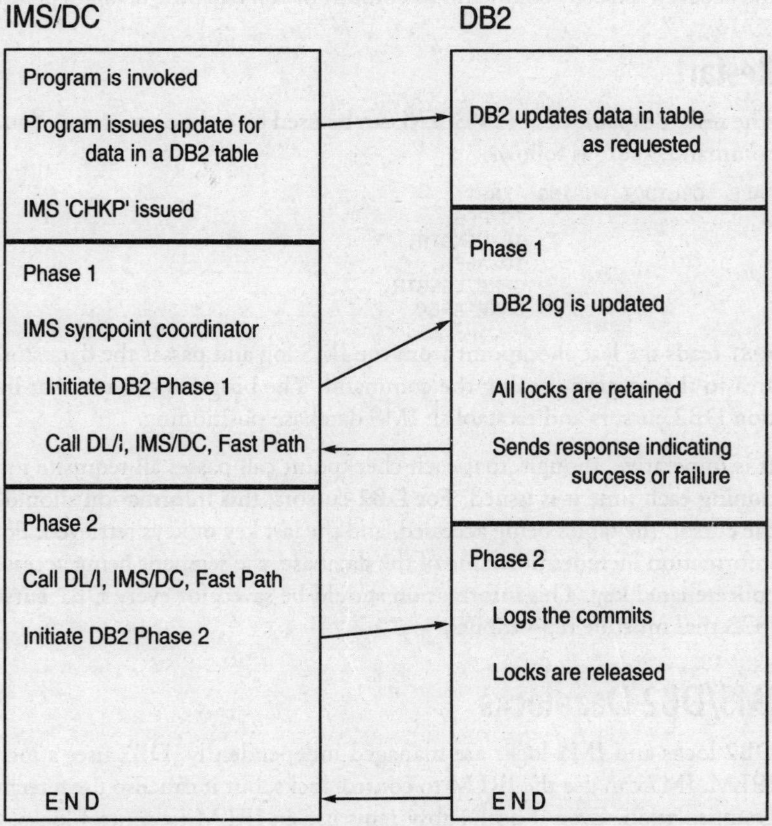

FIGURE 11.28.
The IMS/TM two-phase commit process.

Phase 1 of the commit process consists of IMS/TM informing each participant that a syncpoint has been reached and that each participant should prepare to commit. The participants can include DB2, DL/I, IMS/TM, and IMS Fast Path. Each participant performs the needed tasks to ensure that a commit is possible for that environment. DB2 updates its log, retains all locks, and informs the IMS syncpoint coordinator that phase 1 has been completed successfully.

If all other participants signal that the commit can proceed, phase 2 is initiated, whereby each participant is responsible for completing the commit. If any participant signals that phase 1 cannot be completed successfully, the entire unit of work is aborted and the updates are backed out. In phase 2, DB2 logs the commit and releases all locks.

The two-phase commit process virtually ensures the integrity of DB2 data modified by IMS/TM. If changes cannot be committed in either DB2 or IMS for any reason, they are rolled back in both. In a connection failure of a system crash, however, the commit status of some transactions may be in doubt. They are referred to as *in-doubt threads.* When DB2 and IMS/TM are started after a system failure, and the IMS-to-DB2 connection is reestablished, most in-doubt threads are resolved automatically. If any in-doubt threads remain, you can use the `RECOVER INDOUBT` command to commit or roll back the changes pending for these threads.

Restart

The restart capabilities of IMS/TM can be used by online programs. You code the IMS restart command, `XRST`, as follows:

```
CALL 'CBLTDLI' USING 'XRST',
                     IO-PCB,
                     IO-LENGTH,
                     IO-AREA,
                     CHKP-LENGTH,
                     CHKP-AREA.
```

`XRST` reads the last checkpoint from the IMS log and passes the data stored in the checkpoint area to the program issuing the command. The program can use that information to reposition DB2 cursors and reestablish IMS database positioning.

It is imperative, though, that each checkpoint call passes all requisite information for repositioning each time it is issued. For DB2 cursors, this information should include the name of the cursor, the tables being accessed, and the last key or keys retrieved. For IMS databases, this information includes the name of the database, the segment being accessed, and the complete concatenated key. This information should be saved for every DB2 cursor and IMS database PCB that must be repositioned.

IMS/DB2 Deadlocks

DB2 locks and IMS locks are managed independently. DB2 uses a lock manager called the IRLM. IMS can use the IRLM to control locks, but it can also use a technique known as program isolation. Even if both subsystems use an IRLM to control locks, IMS locks are issued independently from DB2 locks. As a result, a deadlock can occur. A complete description of deadlocks is included in Chapter 16, "Locking DB2 Data." An example of an IMS and DB2 deadlock is presented in the following processing sequence for two concurrently executing application programs:

Program 1	*Program 2*
Update IMS DBD1 Lock established	Update DB2 Table A Lock established

Program 1		*Program 2*
Intermediate processing		Intermediate processing
Update DB2 Table A		Update IMS DBD1
Lock (wait)	*Deadlock*	Lock (wait)

Program 1 requests a lock for DB2 resources that Program 2 holds, and Program 2 requests a lock for IMS resources that Program 1 holds. This deadlock must be resolved before either program can perform subsequent processing. One of the two programs must be targeted as the victim of the deadlock; in other words, it either abends or is timed out.

The deadlock situation is resolved differently depending on the program and the resource. When an MPP is the victim in a deadlock, it abends with a `U777` abend. When a batch-oriented BMP is the victim in a deadlock, the abend received depends on the type of resource that could not be locked:

- If only DL/I databases are affected, a `U777` abend results.
- If DL/I databases are affected in conjunction with fast path databases or DB2 tables, the PCB status field is set to `FD`.
- If fast path databases are involved, the PCB status field is set to `FD`.
- If DB2 tables are involved, the `SQLCODE` is set to `-911`.

IMS SYSGEN Guidelines

The following guidelines are useful when performing an IMS SYSGEN for DB2.

Promote Thread Use with PROCLIM

Specify the `PROCLIM` parameter of the `TRANSACT` macro to be greater than `1` to encourage thread reuse for IMS transactions that access DB2 tables. When multiple transactions are processed during the same PSB schedule, DB2 can reuse the thread, thereby reducing overhead by avoiding thread creation.

Use WFI and Fast Path Only for Critical Transactions

Threads are always reused by WFI (Wait For Input) transactions and Fast Path regions. The thread is not terminated unless the WFI or Fast Path region is stopped, so these regions tie up a thread indefinitely. For this reason, use WFI transactions and Fast Path regions for only high-volume, critical transactions. For low-volume transactions, use the `PROCLIM` parameter to control thread reuse.

Define the Transaction Mode Carefully

You can define a transaction to operate in one of two modes: `MODE=SNGL` or `MODE=MULTI`. `MODE=SNGL` transactions define a unit of work at the transaction level, whereas `MODE=MULTI` transactions string multiple transactions together into a unit of work. Single mode transactions cause a syncpoint when the transaction is completed. Multiple mode transactions do not reach a syncpoint until the program is terminated.

As the programmer, you must know the mode of the transaction before coding to implement CHKP processing effectively and to reestablish cursor and database positioning properly.

Use INQUIRY=YES for Read-Only Transactions

You can define read-only transactions by coding INQUIRY=YES for the TRANSACT macro. Transactions defined to be read-only cannot update IMS databases. When the transaction accesses DB2, it cannot modify data in DB2 tables. An attempt to issue the following SQL statements in a read-only transaction results in a -817 SQLCODE:

```
ALTER
CREATE
DELETE
DROP
GRANT
INSERT
REVOKE
UPDATE
```

DL/I Batch Interface

The DL/I batch interface enables batch IMS programs to access DB2 data. DL/I batch programs access DB2 data under the auspices of the IMS attach facility, which is defined by an SSM. When you're establishing an IMS-to-DB2 connection for a batch program, the JCL used to execute the batch program must contain the SSM parameters. It is assigned to the DDITV02 DD name, as shown in the following example:

```
//DDITV02   DD  *
DB2T,SYS1,DSNMIN10,,R,-,APPL01,,PGM01
/*
```

This SSM connects the PGM01 program to DB2T using a plan with the same name as the program. The program does not abend if DB2 is unavailable. Another SSM example follows:

```
//DDITV02   DD  *
DSN,SYS1,DSNMIN10,,A,-,APPL02,PLANNAME,PGM02
/*
```

This SSM uses plan PLANNAME to connect the PGM02 program to the DB2 subsystem named DSN. An abend is forced if DB2 is unavailable. If the DDITV02 DD name is missing or specified incorrectly, a connection is not made and the job abends.

Additionally, you can specify an output data set containing status and processing information by using the DDOTV02 DD name. If you do not specify the DDOTV02 DD name, processing continues without sending the status and processing information.

Sample JCL to run a DL/I batch program that accesses DB2 tables is shown in Listing 11.4. This JCL runs the `BTCHPROG` program using the `BTCHPLAN` plan. Notice that the JCL contains two steps. The first step runs the DL/I batch program, and the second step prints the contents of the `DDOTV02` data set. Printing the `DDOTV02` data set is a good idea because it can contain pertinent information for resolving any processing errors.

Listing 11.4. JCL to run a DL/I batch DB2 program.

```
//DB2JOBB  JOB (BATCH),'DL/I BATCH',MSGCLASS=X,CLASS=X,
//      NOTIFY=USER,REGION=4096K
//*
//****************************************************************
//*
//*        JCL TO RUN AN IMS/DB2 PROGRAM IN BATCH
//*
//*        PROGRAM NAME    :: BTCHPROG
//*        PLAN NAME       :: BTCHPLAN
//*        CONNECTION NAME :: DB2B0001
//*
//****************************************************************
//*
//JOBLIB     DD DSN=SYS1.DB2V510.DSNLOAD,DISP=SHR
//BATCHPRG   EXEC DLIBATCH,DBRC=Y,LOGT=SYSDA,COND=EVEN,
//           MSGCLASS='X',CLASS='X'
//G.STEPLIB  DD
//           DD
//           DD Add a DD for each DB2, COBOL, and program
//              load library
//G.IEFRDER  DD DSN=IMSLOG,DISP=(NEW,CATLG,CATLG),. . .
//G.STEPCAT  DD DSN=IMSCAT,DISP=SHR
//G.DDOTV02  DD DSN=&DDOTV02,DISP=(NEW,PASS,DELETE),
//           UNIT=SYSDA,DCB=(RECFM=VB,BLKSIZE=4096,LRECL=4092),
//           SPACE=(TRK,(1,1),RLSE)
//G.DDITV02  DD *
 DB2P,SYS1,DSNMIN10,,A,-,DB2B0001,BTCHPLAN,BTCHPROG
/*
//*
//****************************************************************
//*
//*        PRINT THE DDOTV02 DATASET IF THERE ARE PROBLEMS
//*
//****************************************************************
//*
//PRINTOUT   EXEC PGM=DFSERA10,COND=EVEN
//STEPLIB    DD DSN=IMS.RESLIB,DISP=SHR
//SYSPRINT   DD SYSOUT=X
//SYSUT1     DD DSN=&DDOTV02,DISP=(OLD,DELETE)
//SYSIN      DD *
CONTROL    CNTL   K=000,H=8000
OPTION     PRINT
/*
//
```

A DL/I batch program must follow standard DB2 program preparation procedures (precompile, compile, link-edit, and bind). However, a few special considerations apply:

- All DL/I batch programs must be link-edited using the `RMODE=24` and `AMODE=24` parameters.
- The `DFSLI000` language interface module must be link-edited to the load module.
- A PSB must be generated for the program to define the IMS databases to be accessed.

IMS/TM Design Guidelines

The following techniques should be applied when designing IMS transactions that access DB2 data.

Avoid DDL

Never issue DDL in an IMS/TM program. DDL execution is time intensive and acquires locks on the DB2 Catalog and the DB2 Directory. Because IMS/TM programs should be quick, they should avoid DDL.

Copy PCBs Before Each Checkpoint

Application programs should save the PCBs for all IMS databases before invoking an IMS `CHKP`. After the `CHKP`, copy the saved PCB back to the original to reestablish positioning in the IMS databases. Otherwise, the IMS database positioning is lost, much like DB2 cursor positioning is lost when a `COMMIT` is performed.

Be Aware of Cursor Closing Points

IMS closes all DB2 cursors in WFI and `MODE=SINGL` transactions when the program does a get unique (`GU`) to the message queue (`IOPCB`). Cursors also are closed when the program issues a `CHKP` call or when the program terminates.

Use a Scratch Pad Area

Use the SPA (Scratch Pad Area) to store temporary work and to implement pseudoconversational programs.

Use Fast Path for Sequential Number Assignment

Consider using IMS Fast Path database storage to assign sequential numbers. Accessing sequential numbers for assignment using Fast Path databases is more efficient than other conventional means (for example, reading a table containing the highest number).

Use Testing Tools

Use testing tools such as the Batch Terminal Simulator (BTS). The requirements for using BTS follow:

- The user must have MONITOR2 and TRACE authority.
- MONITOR Trace Class 1 must be activated for the plan being tested.
- The plan must be specified on the ./T control card.
- A new control card must be added as follows:

```
./P MBR=BTSCOM00 PA 000C14 PC=DB2T
```

Note that any valid DB2 subsystem ID can be substituted for DB2T.

Do Not Share IRLMs

The DBRC facility of IMS uses an IRLM to control locking when multiple jobs access shared databases. Never share a single IRLM between DB2 and IMS because doing so results in inefficient locking for both IMS and DB2. Also, a shared IRLM is difficult to monitor and tune. Specify a single IRLM for each DB2 subsystem and an IRLM for the IMS subsystem.

Consider IMS/ESA Quick Reschedule

For very active, critical transactions, use the quick reschedule feature of IMS/ESA (IMS V3.1). Quick reschedule creates a "hot region" for the execution of MPPs. When quick reschedule is implemented, the MPP region does not terminate when the PROCLIM count is reached if the message queue holds a qualifying transaction waiting to execute.

CAF (Call Attach Facility)

The next "door to DB2" is provided by the CAF, or Call Attach Facility. CAF differs from the previous attach mechanisms in that it does not provide teleprocessing services. CAF is used to manage connections between DB2 and batch and online TSO application programs, without the overhead of the TSO terminal monitor program.

CAF programs can be executed as one of the following:

- An MVS batch job
- A started task
- A TSO batch job
- An online TSO application

CAF is used to control a program's connection to DB2, as shown in Figure 11.30. The DB2 program communicates to DB2 through the CAF language interface, DSNALI. The primary benefit of using CAF is that the application can control the connection with CAF calls. Five CAF calls are used to control the connection:

CONNECT	Establishes a connection between the program's MVS address space and DB2
DISCONNECT	Eliminates the connection between the MVS address space and DB2

OPEN	Establishes a thread for the program to communicate with DB2
CLOSE	Terminates the thread
TRANSLATE	Provides the program with DB2 error message information, placing it in the SQLCA

Typically, a control program is created to handle the establishment and termination of the DB2 connection. It is the CAF module shown in Figure 11.29. Although this module is not required, it is recommended so that you can eliminate the repetitious coding of the tedious tasks associated with connecting, disconnecting, opening, and closing.

CAF programs must be link-edited with the CAF language interface module, DSNALI.

FIGURE 11.29.
The Call Attach Facility.

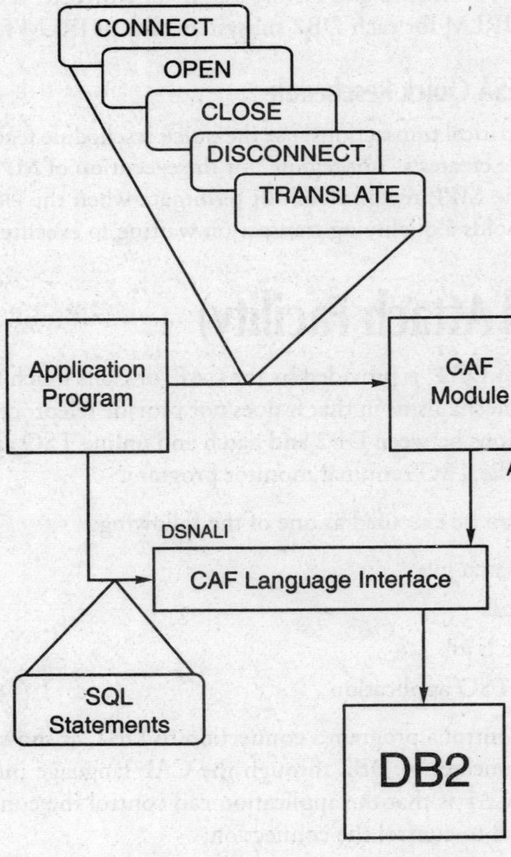

Thread Creation and Use

Two distinct methods for the creation of a CAF thread can be followed. In the first, shown in Figure 11.30, the application program explicitly requests a thread by using the CAF OPEN call.

The application uses the CLOSE call to explicitly terminate the thread. Explicit creation of CAF threads is particularly useful for online TSO CAF programs.

As I mentioned in the TSO section, an online TSO/DB2 program can tie up a thread for a long time when the DSN command is used to attach to DB2. When users of this type of application spend time thinking about their next action, or leave their terminal in the middle of the application, a program using the TSO attach consumes an active thread.

If the program instead used CAF to create a thread, each time the user presses Enter, the thread is terminated before the next screen appears. Although this use of DB2 resources is more effective because a thread is not consumed when no activity occurs, it is also less efficient because the overhead of thread termination and creation is added to each user action. Online TSO applications are not known for their speed, though, so fewer dormant threads in return for a slower response time might not be a bad trade-off.

The second method of thread creation is shown in Figure 11.31. This figure shows the implicit creation and termination of CAF threads. If the OPEN and CLOSE calls are not used, a thread is created when the first SQL statement is issued.

FIGURE 11.30.
Explicit CAF thread creation.

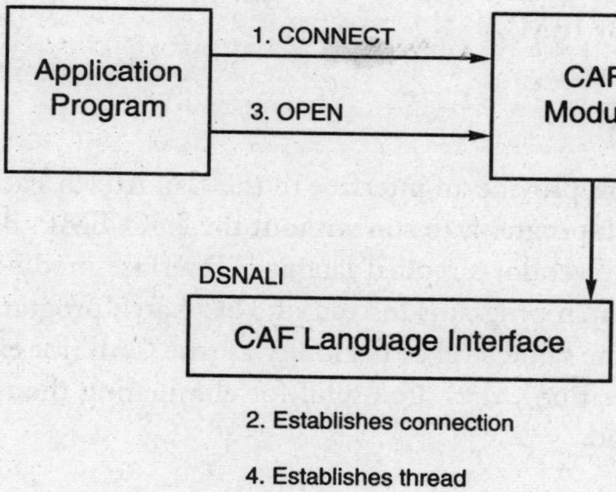

FIGURE 11.31.
Implicit CAF thread creation.

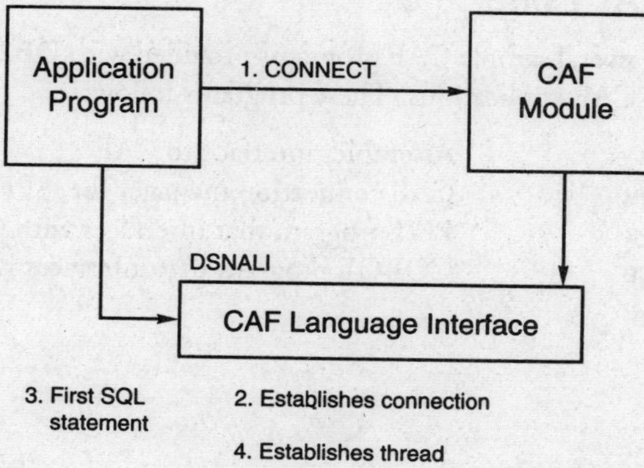

Benefits and Drawbacks of CAF

Before deciding to use CAF, you should consider all the ramifications of this decision. If used properly, CAF can enhance the performance and resource utilization of a DB2 application. If used improperly, CAF can cause problems.

One benefit of using CAF is that it provides explicit control of thread creation. In addition, CAF is more efficient than DSN because of the elimination of overhead required by the TSO TMP, IKJEFT01. Another benefit is that a program designed to use CAF can run when DB2 is down. It cannot access DB2 resources, but it can perform other tasks. This capability can be useful when the DB2 processing is optional, parameter driven, or contingent on other parts of the program.

CAF has its drawbacks too, though. For example, CAF requires more complex error handling procedures. DSN automatically formats error messages for connection failures, but CAF returns only a return code and a reason code. Another drawback is that DSN handles the connection automatically, but CAF requires the program to handle the connection. These drawbacks can be eliminated, however, if you modify the CAF interface module used at your site. Note that by modifying the CAF module your shop must support logic that otherwise is provided with DB2 (and supported by IBM).

Vendor Tools

Some vendor tools provide an interface to the Call Attach Facility. They are generally used to enable DB2 batch programs to run without the TSO TMP. By simply link-editing your DB2 program with the vendor-supplied language interface module, you can run DB2 batch programs as MVS batch programs instead of TSO batch programs. Although these tools do not usually provide the same level of flexibility as true CAF (for example, control over thread creation and termination), they are useful for eliminating the need for TSO in batch, thereby reducing overhead.

Sample CAF Code

You can use several sample CAF programs provided with DB2 as models for the development of your own CAF applications. These programs follow:

DSN8CA	Assembler interface to CAF
DSN8SPM	CAF connection manager for ISPF
DSN8SP3	PL/I program that interfaces with CAF
DSN8SC2	COBOL program that interfaces with CAF

RRSAF (Recoverable Resource Manager Services Attach Facility)

Version 5

RRSAF, or the Recoverable Resource Manager Services Attach Facility, is the final "door to DB2." RRSAF is a new attachment facility, available as of DB2 V5. RRSAF is similar in functionality to CAF but without the implicit connection capabilities. However, RRSAF provides the following additional capabilities and benefits:

- Applications can reuse DB2 threads for different userids (with `SIGNON` and `AUTH SIGNON`; requires RACF or a similar system authorization product).
- Applications (and stored procedures) can coordinate MVS-wide commitment of recoverable resources through OS/390. To qualify for participation in the MVS-wide commit, stored procedures must be executed in an MVS WLM-managed SPAS.
- DB2 threads can run under different TCBs.

As with CAF, RRSAF controls program connections to DB2. Seven functions are used to control the DB2 connections:

`SIGNON`	Specifies a userid (and optionally a secondary authid) for the connection
`AUTH SIGNON`	Specifies a userid (and optionally a secondary authid) for the connection and invokes the signon exit. The program must be APF authorized to execute this function.
`IDENTIFY`	Specifies that the program is a user of DB2 services.
`CREATE THREAD`	Establishes a connection between the program's MVS address space and DB2.
`TERMINATE THREAD`	Deallocates DB2 resources from the program.
`TERMINATE IDENTIFY`	Deallocates DB2 resources.
`TRANSLATE`	Provides the program with DB2 error message information, placing it in the SQLCA.

Consider using RRSAF as an alternative to CAF when the performance benefits of thread reuse are deemed necessary.

When you're preparing a program for RRSAF, you must link `DSNRLI` (the RRSAF interface) to the load module.

Comparison of the Environments

Now that you have learned about each environment in which DB2 programs can execute, you can begin to compare their features and capabilities. When choosing an operating environment for a DB2 application, you should ensure that it can support the data needs of the application. Typically, a corporation's data is spread across disparate processing platforms and data storage devices. Additionally, the data is stored in many different physical manifestations.

When you're choosing an environment for your application, consider the following:

- Do you have access to the environment that you want to use for a development platform? If not, can you obtain access?
- Can you access data key to your enterprise in the format in which it exists today, or will your choice of environment require that the data be duplicated and placed in a readable format?
- Are the programmers who will be working on the project knowledgeable in the chosen environment, or will extensive training be required?

Resource Availability

Table 11.6 presents resource availability categorized by each processing environment that has been discussed. You can use this table as a reference when deciding on a processing environment for your DB2 applications.

Table 11.6. A comparison of resource availability.

Resource	*CICS*	*TSO Online*	*TSO Batch*	*CAF*	*RRSAF*	*IMS MPP*	*IMS Fast Path*	*IMS BMP*	*DL/I Batch*
Flat file access	Yes	Yes	Yes	Yes	Yes	No	No	No*	Yes*
VSAM access	Yes	Yes	Yes	Yes	Yes	No	No**	No**	Yes**
Online IMS database	Yes	No	No	No	No	Yes	Yes	Yes	No
Offline IMS database	Yes	No	No	No	Yes	No	No	No	Yes
Invoked by JCL	No	No	Yes	Yes	Yes	No	No	Yes	Yes

Resource	*CICS*	*TSO Online*	*TSO Batch*	*CAF*	*RRSAF*	*IMS MPP*	*IMS Fast Path*	*IMS BMP*	*DL/I Batch*
Invoked by transaction	Yes	No	No	No	No	Yes	Yes	No	No
Invoked by CLIST or REXX EXEC	No	Yes	No	Yes	Yes	No	No	No	No
Invoked by ISPF	No	Yes	No	No	Yes	No	No	No	No

*IMS GSAM database

**IMS SHISAM database

You might find some of the entries in Table 11.6 confusing. The following explains these entries in more detail:

- *Yes* indicates that the processing environment listed across the top can access the resource defined along the left. Simply because the resource is accessible (as IBM delivers the products that support the environment), however, does not mean that you can use it in your shop. Some shops restrict and limit access, so consult your shop standards before proceeding with development plans based on Table 11.6.
- Flat file access is available using IMS calls when a GSAM (Generalized Sequential Access Method) database is defined for the flat file. IMS BMPs and batch programs can access flat files as GSAM databases. Access to flat files using pure OS/VS reads and writes is available only to IMS batch programs.
- All IMS programs can access VSAM KSDS data sets as a SHISAM (Simple Hierarchic Indexed Sequential Access Method) database. Again, IMS batch programs are the only type of IMS program that can access a VSAM file using VSAM data set commands.
- IMS online databases are those defined to the IMS control region and started for online access in IMS/TM. Conversely, an offline IMS database either is not defined under the IMS control region and is thus not accessible by IMS/TM, or it is stopped (sometimes referred to as DBRed) to IMS/TM.

Feasibility

After ensuring that what you want is possible, your next step is to ascertain whether it is feasible. An application is feasible in a specified environment if the response time and availability requirements of the application can be met satisfactorily by the environment. Typically, you should draw up a service-level agreement for each new application, developing a price-to-performance matrix. Consider this example:

> The online portion of the system must provide an average response time of *x* seconds, *y* percent of the time, for an average of *z* users. The cost per transaction is approximately *a*.

Use the information in Table 11.7 to determine which online environment is feasible for your project.

Table 11.7. Comparison of online development capabilities.

Characteristic	*TSO*	*CICS*	*IMS/TM*
Response time	Slow	Fast	Fast
Flexibility	High	Low	Low
Number of concurrent users	Fewer than 10	Many	Many
Overhead per user	Very high	Very low	Low
Program linking	Not easy	XCTL/LINK	Message switching
Online screen language	ISPF Dialog	BMS	MFS Manager
Screen development	Fast	Cumbersome	Cumbersome
Program development	Fast	Medium	Slow
Prototyping and testing tools	Many	Some	Few

As you ponder the choices of development environments for your DB2 applications, ask the following questions:

- What is the deadline for system development? What programming resources are available to meet this deadline? Do you have the requisite talent to develop the system in the optimal environment? If not, should you hire programmers or settle for a less than optimal solution?
- What are the performance requirements of the system? How many concurrent users will be using the system during peak processing time, and can the given environment support the workload?

Sometimes you have little or no choice. If a shop has only one environment, the decision is easy. If your shop has more than one environment, the right decision is never to confine yourself to only one environment. Each environment has its own strengths and weaknesses, and you should consider them in your application development solution.

When multiple environments are used to access DB2 data, they become inextricably wound in a critical mass. This situation can be difficult to administer and warrants consideration.

Batch Considerations

Although this chapter is primarily concerned with coverage of the online processing opportunities available to DB2, a quick discussion of the various batch processing options is in order. DB2 batch processing can be implemented using the following:

- DSN under TSO
- CAF or RRSAF
- Batch DL/I
- BMP under IMS/TM

In terms of performance, no significant differences exist among DSN, CAF, batch DL/I, and BMPs. However, if you need to squeeze every last bit of performance out of a batch application, consider these points:

- Because DSN uses TSO, you will have some additional overhead for TSO resources when compared to an equivalent CAF program.
- Because BMPs execute in an IMS control region, initialization will take longer than an equivalent DSN or CAF program.
- Commit processing tends to take longer for BMPs because they check for DB2 and IMS update activity.

Although performance differences are minimal, you will discover several coding implications:

- CAF and RRSAF programs require connection logic and error handling not required by DSN.
- IMS `SYNCPOINT` must be used in lieu of `COMMIT` for BMPs.
- DL/I batch programs require coding for the `DDITV02` data set.

The Critical Mass

Version 4

Prior to DB2 V4, when an application required DB2 access, the teleprocessing monitor (TSO, CICS, or IMS/TM) had to reside on the same MVS system as DB2. This situation created a critical mass, which is the set of subsystems tied by a single common attribute; they must access DB2 resources. For example, if a data-processing shop uses both CICS and IMS/TM to develop DB2 applications, the shop's critical mass would consist of the following:

- IMS/TM subsystem
- All CICS subsystems requiring DB2 access

- DB2 subsystem
- TSO subsystem if DB2I access is required

All of them must operate on the same CPU. Additionally, when an error occurs, they cannot be moved independently without losing DB2 access. A large shop could quickly use up the resources of its machine if all DB2 applications were developed on a single DB2 subsystem.

However, data sharing, new to DB2 V4, enables multiple DB2 subsystems to access the same data, which frees up resources, enables flexible configuration and management, expands capacity, and improves availability. Prior to data sharing, organizations had to slice applications into disparate, independently operating units in one of the following ways:

- You could develop IMS/TM applications on one DB2 subsystem, develop CICS applications on another, and develop TSO applications on yet another. This approach reduces the critical mass so that IMS/TM and CICS are not married together.
- Another method is to provide the separate DB2 subsystems with distributed access to DB2 data that must be shared.
- Yet another method is to choose a single teleprocessing environment for all DB2 applications.
- Last, by avoiding DB2I and QMF access, you can eliminate TSO from the critical mass. Instead, you submit SQL and DSN commands as batch invocations of TSO. Because this hampers ease of use and detracts from the overall user-friendliness of DB2, however, doing so is not recommended.

However, as of DB2 V4, the preferred method of avoiding the critical mass is to implement data sharing.

Summary

In this chapter, you learned how to develop DB2 applications for five different environments: TSO, CICS, IMS, CAF, and RRSAF. Each provide specific benefits, while also posing different types of challenges. Furthermore, you examined the online and batch characteristics of each environment, and how the environments can operate with each other. As more environments are used, the critical mass of subsystems and allied agents required for a specific DB2 subsystems increases. Data sharing helps to alleviate these concerns. Turn the page to Chapter 12, "Data Sharing," to explore the details and learn the secrets of data sharing.

12

Data Sharing

DB2 data sharing allows applications running on multiple DB2 subsystems to concurrently read and write to the same data sets. Simply stated, data sharing enables multiple DB2 subsystems to behave as one.

DB2 data sharing is optional; it need not be implemented. Check with your DBA or system administrator if you are not sure if data sharing is used in your organization.

Prior to DB2 V4, the only methods available for sharing DB2 data across subsystems were through distributed DB2 connections or using shared read only databases (using the ROSHARE option when creating databases). However, both of these options have drawbacks. The distributed option requires coding changes and the ROSHARE option supports read only access (and is being phased out by IBM).

Data Sharing Benefits

DB2 data sharing, though somewhat complex to implement and administer, provides many benefits. In the long run, most organizations will move to DB2 data sharing because of the many benefits outlined in this section.

The primary benefit of data sharing is to provide increased availability to data. DB2 data sharing provides a powerful technology for solving complex business problems in an optimal manner. Data is available for direct access across multiple DB2 subsystems. Furthermore applications can be run on multiple smaller, more competitively-priced microprocessor-based machines, thereby enhancing data availability and the price/performance ratio.

An additional benefit is expanded capacity. Capacity is increased because more processors are available to execute the DB2 application programs. Instead of a single DB2 subsystem on a single logical partition, multiple CPCs can be used to execute a program (or even a single query).

Each data sharing group may consist of multiple members, application programs are provided with enhanced data availability. One or more members of a group may fail without impacting application programs because the workload will be spread across the remaining DB2 members.

Data sharing increases the flexibility of configuring DB2. New members can be added to a data sharing group when it is necessary to increase the processing capacity of the group (for example, at month end or year end to handle additional processing). The individual members that were added to increase the processing capacity of the data sharing group are easily removed when it is determined that the additional capacity is no longer required.

Finally, larger organizations with multiple MVS machines, often devoted individual processors to groups of users. When an DB2 application was needed that spanned the organization, it was usually necessary to create a duplicate copy of the application for each DB2 on each system image used by the organization. With data sharing, a single data sharing group can be created for the entire organization (within the limit of 32 subsystems per group). This can alleviate the need to create multiple copies of an application.

Data Sharing Requirements

Data sharing consists of a complex combination of hardware and software. To share data, DB2 subsystems must belong to a predefined data sharing group. Each DB2 subsystem contained in the data sharing group is a member of that group. All members of the data sharing group access a common DB2 catalog and directory.

Each data sharing group is a MVS Cross-system Coupling Facility (XCF) group. XCF was introduced in MVS/SP 4.1 with the MVS Sysplex. A Sysplex is a set of MVS (or OS/390) systems that communicate and cooperate with one another. The group services provided by XCF enable DB2 data sharing groups to be defined. In addition, XCF enables the data sharing environment to track all members contained in the data sharing group. A site may have multiple MVS Sysplexes, each consisting of one or more MVS systems. Each individual Sysplex can consist of multiple data sharing groups.

DB2 data sharing requires a Sysplex environment that consists of the following:

- One or more central processor complexes (CPCs) that can attach to a coupling facility. A CPC is a collection of hardware consisting of main storage, one or more central processors, timers, and channels.
- At least one coupling facility. The coupling facility is the component that manages the shared resources of the connected CPCs. DB2 uses the coupling facility to provide data sharing groups with coordinated locking, bufferpools and communication. MVS V5 is required to install a DB2 coupling facility.
- At least one Sysplex timer. The Sysplex timer keeps the processor timestamps synchronized for all DB2's in the data sharing group.
- Connection to shared DASD. The user data, system catalog and directory data, and MVS catalog data must all reside on shared DASD.

NOTE

The DB2 logs and boot strap data sets (BSDS) belong to each DB2 member individually. However, they too must reside on shared DASD.

NOTE

It is recommended that your shop have a security facility that supports security in a sysplex environment before implementing DB2 data sharing. RACF Version 2 Release 1 provides this capability.

Refer to Figure 12.1 for an overview of a DB2 data sharing environment consisting of two DB2 subsystems connected using a coupling facility.

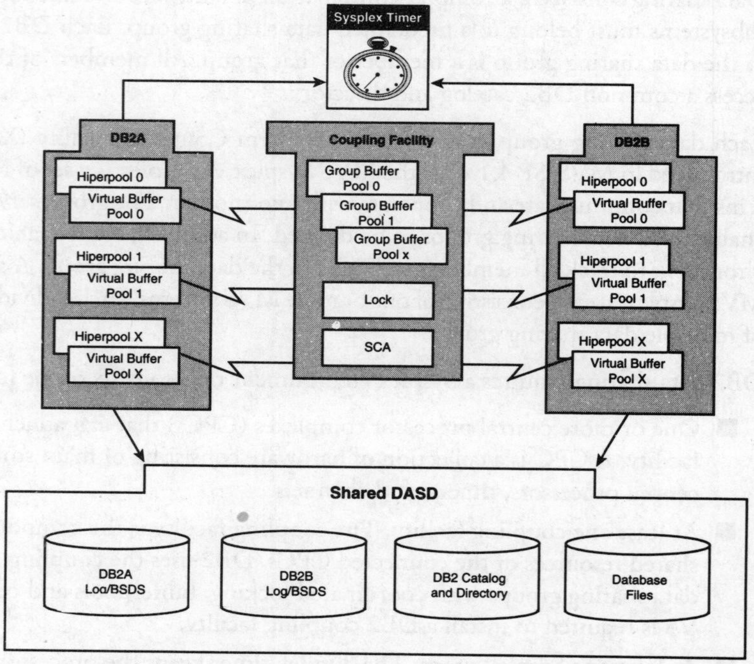

FIGURE 12.1.
A DB2 data sharing environment.

DB2 Data Sharing Groups

Data sharing groups may span multiple MVS systems. A data sharing group consists of individual DB2 subsystems, called members. Data sharing group members must belong to the same MVS Sysplex. Data sharing group members can only belong to one data sharing group.

Up to 32 DB2 subsystems can be members of a DB2 data sharing group. Each DB2 subsystem of the data sharing group can access all of the data in each of the subsystems as if it were local. Any DB2 object (tablespace, index, table, and so on), in any of the DB2 subsystems in the data sharing group, is available to all members of the group. This includes the shared DB2 catalog and directory.

Data sharing is done within the members of the data sharing group; a request can not span multiple groups.

Certain DB2 objects must be shared between members, whereas other objects are owned by members. See Table 12.1 for a breakdown of the shared versus non-shared objects.

Table 12.1. Shared and non-shared objects.

Shared Objects	*Non-Shared Objects*
DB2 Catalog	BSDS
DB2 Directory	Logs
Coupling Facility Structures	DSNDB07
Lock Structure	EDM Pool
Group Bufferpools	Local Bufferpools
Shared Communication Area	

Application Impact

No special programming is required for applications to access data in a DB2 data sharing environment. Each individual subsystem in the data sharing group uses the coupling facility to communicate with the other subsystems. The inter-system communication provided by DB2 data sharing provides a system image that resembles a single, stand-alone DB2 subsystem to the application.

No application programming changes are required. The only modifications that may need to be made to current application programs to run in a data sharing environment is to provide additional error checking for "data sharing" return codes.

There is a one to one relationship between MVS and data sharing transactions. The DB2 member where the transaction was initiated keeps all of the information related to that transaction that is needed to successfully execute it. Once a unit of work begins processing on a member, it is executed in its entirety on that member.

Impact on Attachment Interfaces

Likewise, DB2 data sharing has no impact on existing attachment interfaces. The DB2 subsystem name may still be used to attach to a particular DB2 subsystem. Application programs using the subsystem name will only be able to attach to those DB2 subsystems that reside on the same MVS system as they do.

TSO and CALL ATTACH support a new GROUP ATTACH name. This generic name is created during the group's originating member installation. The GROUP ATTACH name allows TSO and batch jobs to connect to any DB2 in the group. This eliminates the need to know the DB2 subsystem name on local MVS systems.

IMS and CICS transaction managers are unable to take advantage of the group attach name. They must remain sensitive to a specific DB2 subsystem to be able to resolve any in-doubt units of recovery.

Impact on DCL and DDL

Because all members of the data sharing group share a common catalog, security grants, table definitions, and program definitions only need to be executed once. DDL and DCL does not need to be rerun for each data sharing member.

Sysplex and Distributed Access

Distributed access requests, using both public and private DB2 protocols, can be made to a data sharing group. All members of the group have the same location name. This enables distributed requests to be made in a data sharing environment transparent to the application program.

Application Support

Even though the impact of data sharing on applications is minimal, the impact on application support is substantial. When DB2 subsystems are grouped together using data sharing, any application can access any database in any of the data sharing member subsystems. This can make debugging, supporting, and testing difficult.

Additionally, the software licensing impact of data sharing can also be quite problematic. Do not implement data sharing without first considering what supporting software is necessary. In a data sharing environment, software licenses that previously applied to a single machine only may have to be renegotiated for multiple machines (those in the Sysplex).

The DB2 Coupling Facility

DB2 uses the coupling facility to provide inter-member communications. The primary function of the coupling facility is to ensure data availability while maintaining data integrity across systems. This requires the coupling facility to provide core services to the data sharing group such as locking and caching of data. To do so, the CF requires three structures to synchronize the activities of the data sharing group members:

- **Lock structures** are required to control global locking across the data sharing group members. Global locks are required because multiple members can access the same data. As such, each member needs to know the state of the data before it can be modified. The lock structure propagates locks to all members of the data sharing group.
- The **list structure** enables communication across the sysplex environment.
- **Cache structures** provide common buffering for the systems in the sysplex. When a data page is updated by an individual data sharing member, a copy of that page is written to one of the global bufferpools. If other members need to refresh their copy of the data page in question, the copy is obtained from the coupling facility's global bufferpool instead of from DASD. This requires the members to check the appropriate coupling facility global bufferpool first, to determine whether the desired page needs to be read from DASD.

These structures ensure that data is synchronized between the members of the DB2 data sharing group.

Defining the Coupling Facility

A coupling facility is defined using Coupling Facility Resource Management (CFRM). CFRM is created by the IXCMIAPU utility. The CFRM is used to identify:

- Each individual coupling facility.
- Each structure within the individual coupling facilities.
- Space allocated to these structures.
- Ordered preferences and which coupling facility is used to store this ordered preference structure.
- An unordered exclusion list which defines the structures to keep separate from this structure.

Global Lock Management

Because data sharing group members can access any object from any member in the group, a global locking mechanism is required. This is done by the lock structure defined in the coupling facility. The lock structure is charged with managing inter-member locking. Without a global lock management process data integrity problems could occur when one member attempts to read (or change) data that is in the process of being changed by another member.

Data sharing groups utilize a global locking mechanism to preserve the integrity of the shared data. The global locking mechanism enables locks to be recognized between members.

For more details on the lock management process for data sharing environments, refer to Chapter 16, "Locking DB2 Data."

Global Inter-System Communication

The list structure component of the coupling facility contains status information used for inter-system communications. The list structure is also referred to as the Shared Communication Area, or SCA. The SCA maintains information about the state of databases, log files, and other details needed for DB2 recovery.

Global Data Buffering

Similar to the need for a global lock management technique, data sharing also requires global data buffering. Once again, this is so because a data sharing environment consists of multiple member DB2 subsystems. Each of those members has its own separate bufferpools and each member can access and change data in any database on any subsystem within the data sharing group.

In a data sharing environment, data pages may be found in:

- Local bufferpools
- Hiperpools
- Group bufferpools
- DASD (disk)

Updating and Reading Data

When data is modified, the changed data is stored in the bufferpool of the DB2 subsystem executing the transaction. The change is not immediately available to transactions that are executing in other members of the data sharing group. The coupling facility is used to provide all members of a data sharing group with a set of global buffer pools.

When modifications occur in a data sharing environment, DB2 must use force-at-commit processing. Force-at-commit writes pages changed by the transaction to the appropriate global bufferpools when a commit point is reached. Force-at-commit processing is new and used solely in a data sharing environment.

CAUTION

The changed page may be written prior to commit if local bufferpool write thresholds are reached.

NOTE

In a non-data sharing environment, DB2 does not write changed pages at a commit point. Instead, the buffer manager uses a deferred write algorithm which moves the expensive buffer write operations outside of the transaction path length.

During the write to the global bufferpool, the coupling facility notifies DB2 members that currently have the page cached in their local bufferpool to invalidate it so that the next access will cause the page to be read from the global bufferpool (or disk).

The read transaction tests the validity of all pages it finds in its local buffer pool. If the page is still valid, the read transaction accesses the page from its local bufferpool. If the page is marked invalid (due to a previous update by another member), the read transaction will refresh the changed page from the global bufferpool (or disk).

Defining Data Sharing Bufferpools

Data sharing members must use the same name for the global bufferpool as is used for the local bufferpool. For example, if BP5 is defined at the local subsystem level, BP5 must also be defined at the group bufferpool level. A group bufferpool must be defined for each associated local buffer pool. If a local bufferpool does not have a corresponding global bufferpool, resources utilizing the pool can only be used locally and can not be shared.

For more information on group bufferpool specification and tuning, see Chapter 21, "Tuning DB2's Components."

Data Sharing Naming Conventions

It is imperative that appropriate naming conventions are developed for data sharing constructs. This is important to enable effective management of the data sharing environment. Data sharing naming conventions fall into two categories:

- Group-level names for structures owned by the data sharing group. These names are shared by all members of the data sharing group. Group-level names that must be created include the following:

  DB2 group name—the name that is used to define the DB2 data sharing group to MVS. The group name can be no longer than characters and can be comprised of the characters A-Z, 0-9, $, #, and @. The group name must begin with an alphabetic character.

  Catalog alias—the name of the MVS catalog alias. This catalog alias can be up to 8 characters long. The DB2 group name should be used for the catalog alias name.

  IRLM group name—the name used to define the IRLM to the data sharing group

  Location name—each data sharing group has one DDF location name. This location is used by remote requests to indicate the data sharing group. This name can be up to 16 characters long.

  Generic LU name—this name allows remote requesters to configure their systems to treat the data sharing group as a single LU. The generic LU name can be up to 8 characters in length.

  Group attach name—a generic four-character name that is used by applications using TSO or CALL ATTACH. This enables the application to attach to any DB2 member that is contained in the data sharing group.

  Coupling facility structure names—names are required for the lock structure, SCA, and group bufferpools. These names are predefined by DB2 as shown in Table 12.2. In place of groupname, substitute the actual DB2 group name. For group bufferpools, the only difference is the prefix "G" added to the bufferpool name.

- Member-level names for structures owned by each DB2 data sharing member. Member-level names that must be created include:

  DB2 member name—the name that is used to identify the individual DB2 subsystem to MVS for inclusion into the data sharing group. Like the data sharing group name, this name can be no longer than 8 characters and can be comprised of the characters A-Z, 0-9, $, #, and @. The DB2 member name is used by DB2 to form its MVS cross-system coupling facility (XCF) member name.

  Subsystem name—the name can be up to four characters long and is used by all attachment interfaces.

  LU name—must be unique within the data sharing group and the network.

  Work file database name—each data sharing member must have its own work file database. The work file database in the non–data-sharing environment is known as DSNDB07. The work file database name can be up to 8 characters long.

  Command prefix—up to 8-character prefix used for DB2 command execution.

  IRLM subsystem name—defines the IRLM subsystem.

  IRLM procedure name—defines the IRLM startup procedure.

  ZPARM name—each member of a data sharing group has its own ZPARM load module.

Table 12.2. Coupling facility structure naming conventions.

Structure Type	*Naming Standard*
Lock Structure	*groupname*_LOCK1
SCA	*groupname*_SCA
Group Bufferpools	*groupname*_G*bufferpool*

Data Sharing Administration

One of the benefits of data sharing is that the entire environment can be administered from a single MVS console. The DB2 command prefix, which as of V4 can be eight characters long, is used to differentiate between the different members of a data sharing group.

NOTE

Individual data sharing group member names can be used as command prefixes.

In a sysplex environment administrative DB2 commands can be routed to any DB2 member from a single console. This eliminates the need to know the MVS system name to send DB2 commands. In addition, there is no need to use ROUTE DB2 commands in this environment (see Figure 12.2).

FIGURE 12.2.
Administering the DB2 data sharing environment.

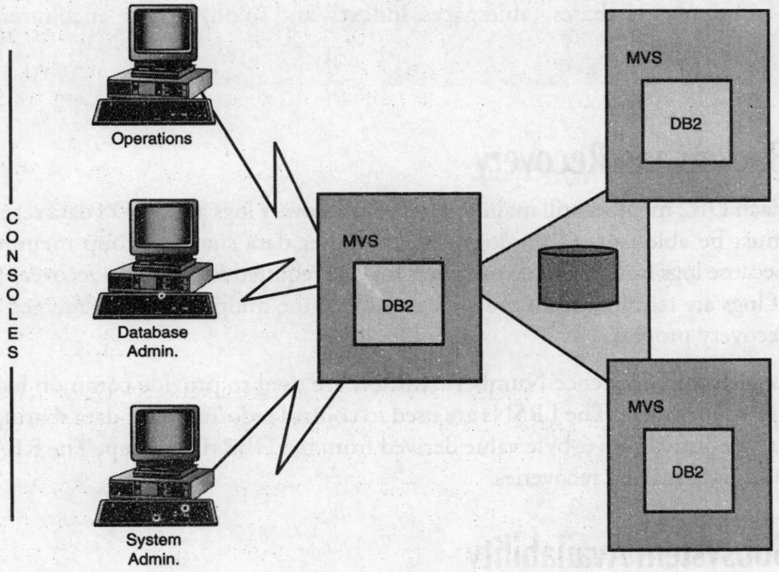

Data Sharing Group Creation

In order to enable data sharing, a common DB2 catalog is required. IBM does not provide an automated mechanism for merging data from multiple existing DB2 subsystems (RC/Merger, a third party tool, is available from PLATINUM technology). The process of merging systems is complex and should not be undertaken lightly. Merging subsystems is not solely a physical data movement problem but includes other administrative issues including the creation and enforcement of naming standards, DB2 security and authorization, backup and recovery, utility execution, data distribution, and on and on. Indeed, the decision to merge subsystems into a data sharing group will impact almost every aspect of database administration for the subsystems involved.

If you are still interested in merging pre-existing DB2 subsystems into a data sharing , an exhaustive 16-step process for merging data from individual DB2 subsystems is available in the IBM manual *Data Sharing: Planning and Administration* (SC26-3269-01).

CAUTION

Watch for duplicate object names when merging multiple DB2 catalogs into the shared DB2 catalog for the data sharing group. Because the objects were originally created in isolation from one another, it is likely that duplicate object names (for example, databases, tablespaces, indexes, and so on) may be encountered when catalogs are merged.

Backup and Recovery

Each DB2 member still maintains its own recovery logs and BSDS data sets. Each DB2 member must be able to read the logs of every other data sharing group member. This is required because logs from multiple members may be required to do media recovery for a single member. If logs are required from multiple members, the multiple logs are merged together during the recovery process.

Log Record Sequence Numbers (LRSN) are used to provide common log record sequencing across members. The LRSNs are used to control redo/undo for data sharing environments and are identified by a 6-byte value derived from the DB2 timestamp. The RBA is still used during non-data sharing recoveries.

Subsystem Availability

DB2 data sharing improves data availability by providing redundant failover capabilities. In the event of a DB2 data sharing group member failure, the remaining members are used to process the data requests. The workload is spread across the remaining DB2 members.

Uncommitted locks held by the failed member are retained. No member is permitted to obtain a lock that is not compatible with the retained locks. All other (non-locked) data is still accessible to the remaining DB2 members. Retained locks are purged during the restart process for the failed member.

The failed DB2 member can restart on the same or different MVS system.

Coupling Facility Recovery

Although unlikely, it is possible for the coupling facility to fail causing its structures to be lost. A dynamic rebuild of the coupling facility structures (lock, SCA) is executed during coupling facility recovery. However, if the dynamic rebuild fails, and the structures cannot be rebuilt on another coupling facility, all DB2 members contained in the data sharing group are brought down.

To recover from this scenario, a group restart is required. Group restart rebuilds the information that was lost from the SCA and/or lock structure using the logs of the DB2 group members. All of the logs for every data sharing group member must be available during the group restart process.

NOTE

Group restart does not necessarily mean that all DB2s in the group start up again, but information from all DB2s must be used to rebuild the lock structure or SCA.

Data Sharing Guidelines

When implementing data sharing in your shop, be sure to abide by the following guidelines.

Consider Multiple Coupling Facilities

To reduce the risk of downtime, deploy multiple coupling facilities. If one coupling facility fails, you can always switch to another "backup" coupling facility.

A recommended implementation is to have one coupling facility to house the group bufferpools and a second coupling facility for the SCA and lock structures.

Take Action to Help Prevent Coupling Facility Failures

To limit downtime due to coupling facility failure consider taking the following actions:

- Configure multiple coupling facilities.
- Reserve space in an alternate coupling facility in case the lock and SCA structures must be rebuilt.
- Use dedicated coupling facilities so that the MVS image is not lost during processor failure.
- Use uninterruptable power supplies for all dedicated coupling facilities.
- Configure more than one Sysplex timer.

Avoid Confusing Names for Data Sharing Groups

Avoid names that IBM uses for its XCF groups by avoiding the letters A-I as the first character of the group name (unless the first three characters are "DSN"). Additionally, avoid using "SYS" as the first three characters, and do not use the string "UNDESIG" as your group name.

Avoid Using DSNDB07 as a Work File Database Name

Each data sharing group member must have a work file database defined for it. Although one of the members of the data sharing group can use `DSNDB07`, this is not advisable. Instead, create a descriptive name, for each work file database, for example the string "WK" concatenated to the member name.

CAUTION

You cannot specify a name that begins with `DSNDB` unless the name is `DSNDB07`.

Be Aware of Sysplex Parallelism

Version 5

The biggest change to data sharing in DB2 V5 is Sysplex query parallelism. With sysplex parallelism, DB2 provides the ability to utilize the power of multiple DB2 subsystems on multiple CPCs to execute a single query. Refer to Chapter 14, "The Optimizer," for more information on all forms of query parallelism available with DB2.

Specify Lock Structure Size with Care

The size of the coupling facility's locking structure directly affects the number of false contentions (collisions) that occur. If the hash table is too small, the propensity for false collisions increases. Any contention, including false contention, requires additional asynchronous processing which negatively impacts performance.

Summary

In this chapter, you learned how to share data across multiple DB2 subsystems using the MVS Sysplex. Data sharing enables multiple DB2 subsystems to behave as one.

For additional information and guidelines on data sharing global locking refer to Chapter 16, "Locking DB2 Data." Additionally, tips and techniques for specifying and tuning bufferpools in a data sharing environment are contained in Chapter 21, "Tuning DB2's Components."

Now that we have examined how to share data, let's move on to examine the behind-the-scenes functionality of DB2.

13

DB2 Behind the Scenes

After reading the first twelve chapters of this book, you should have a sound understanding of the fundamental concepts of the DB2 database management system. You are familiar with the functionality and nature of SQL, and you understand the process of embedding SQL in an application program and preparing it for execution. Additionally, you learned many tips and techniques for achieving proper performance.

What is actually going on behind the scenes in DB2? When you create a table, how does DB2 create and store it? When you issue an SQL statement, what happens to it so that it returns your answer? Where are these application plans kept? What is going on "under the covers"? The remainder of Part III helps you answer these questions.

The Physical Storage of Data

The first segment of your journey behind the scenes of DB2 consists of learning the manner in which DB2 data is physically stored. Before you proceed, however, recall the types of DB2 objects: STOGROUPs, databases, tablespaces, tables, and indexes. See Figure 13.1. A database can be composed of many tablespaces, which in turn can contain one or more tables, which in turn can have indexes defined for them. In addition, databases, tablespaces, and indexes can all be assigned STOGROUPs.

Of these five objects, only three represent physical entities. STOGROUPs represent one or more physical DASD devices. Tablespaces and indexes relate to physical data sets. You should keep the following physical implementation guidelines in mind when you create DB2 objects:

- As many as 133 DASD volumes can be assigned to a single STOGROUP.
- A STOGROUP can turn over control to SMS.
- Usually only one VSAM data set is used for each non-partitioning index, simple tablespace, and segmented tablespace defined to DB2. Also, each data set can be no larger than 2 gigabytes. When the 2-gigabyte limit is reached, a new VSAM data set is allocated. You can use as many as 32 VSAM data sets.
- Multiple VSAM data sets are used for partitioned tablespaces and partitioning indexes. Only one data set can be used per partition. The maximum size of each data set used by a non-large partitioned tablespace is based on the number of defined partitions, as follows:

Partitions	*Maximum Size of VSAM Data Set*
2 through 16	4 gigabytes
17 through 32	2 gigabytes
33 through 64	1 gigabyte

- Large partitioned tablespaces can store up to approximately 1 terabyte of data. Instead of limiting the number of partitions to 64, a large partitioned tablespace can have up to 254 partitions, each storing up to 4 gigabytes of data.
- Data sets for partitioning indexes follow the same rules as those just outlined for partitioned tablespaces. All other indexes follow the rules for non-partitioned tablespaces.

FIGURE 13.1.
DB2 objects.

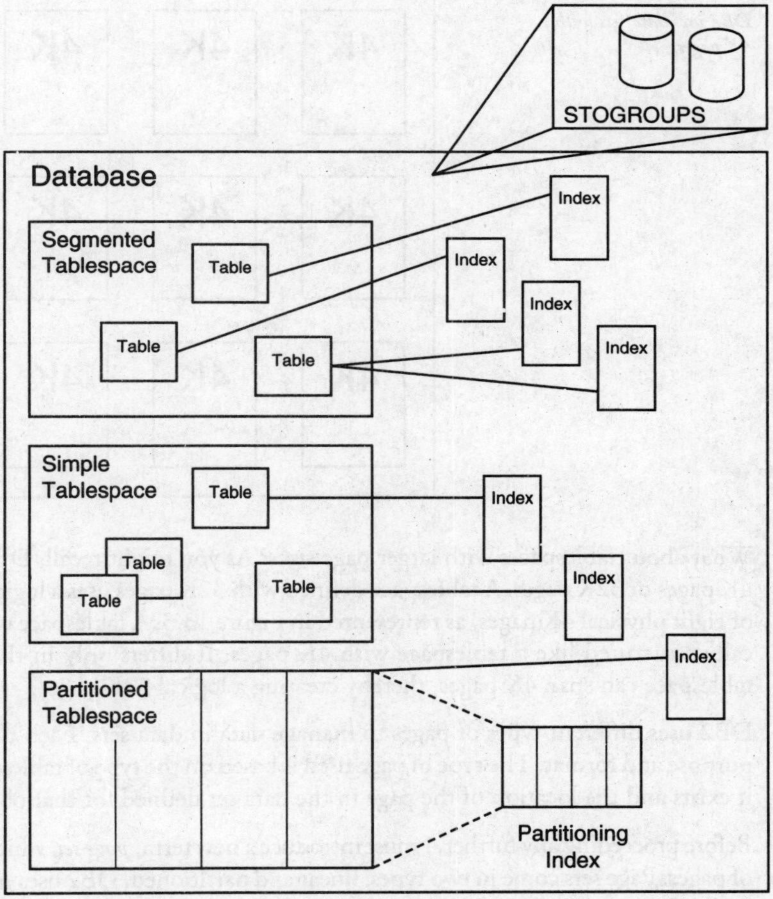

Data sets used by DB2 can be either VSAM entry-sequenced data sets (ESDS) or VSAM linear data sets (LDS). Linear data sets are more efficient because they do not contain the VSAM control interval information that an ESDS does. Additionally, an LDS has control intervals with a fixed length of 4,096 bytes. Also, future releases of DB2 will probably require linear data sets (but this is not the case as of DB2 V5).

Now that you know which data sets can be used, the next question is "How are these data sets structured?"

Every VSAM data set used to represent a DB2 tablespace or index is composed of pages. A page consists of 4,096 bytes, or 4K. You therefore can think of a data set used by DB2 tablespaces or indexes as shown in Figure 13.2.

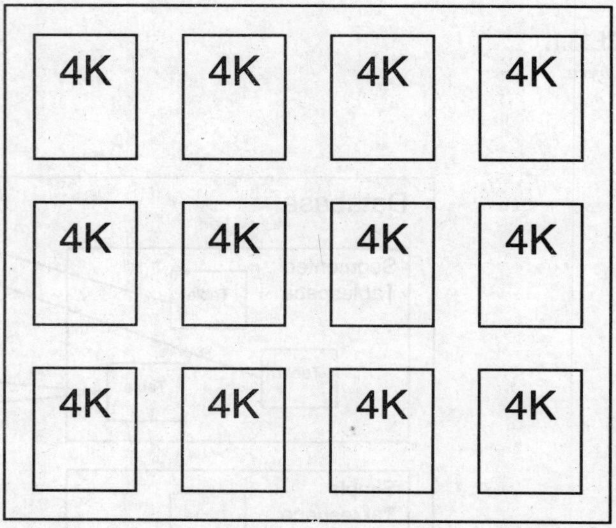

FIGURE 13.2.
DB2 uses data sets with 4K pages.

What about tablespaces with larger page sizes? As you might recall, DB2 tablespaces can have 4K pages or 32K pages. A tablespace defined with 32K pages uses a logical 32K page composed of eight physical 4K pages, as represented in Figure 13.3. A tablespace with 32K pages is physically structured like a tablespace with 4K pages. It differs only in that rows of a 32K page tablespace can span 4K pages, thereby creating a logical 32K page.

DB2 uses different types of pages to manage data in data sets. Each type of page has its own purpose and format. The type of page used is based on the type of tablespace or index for which it exists and the location of the page in the data set defined for that object.

Before proceeding any further, I must introduce a new term, *page set,* which is a physical grouping of pages. Page sets come in two types: linear and partitioned. DB2 uses *linear page sets* for simple tablespaces, segmented tablespaces, and indexes. DB2 uses *partitioned page sets* when it implements partitioned tablespaces.

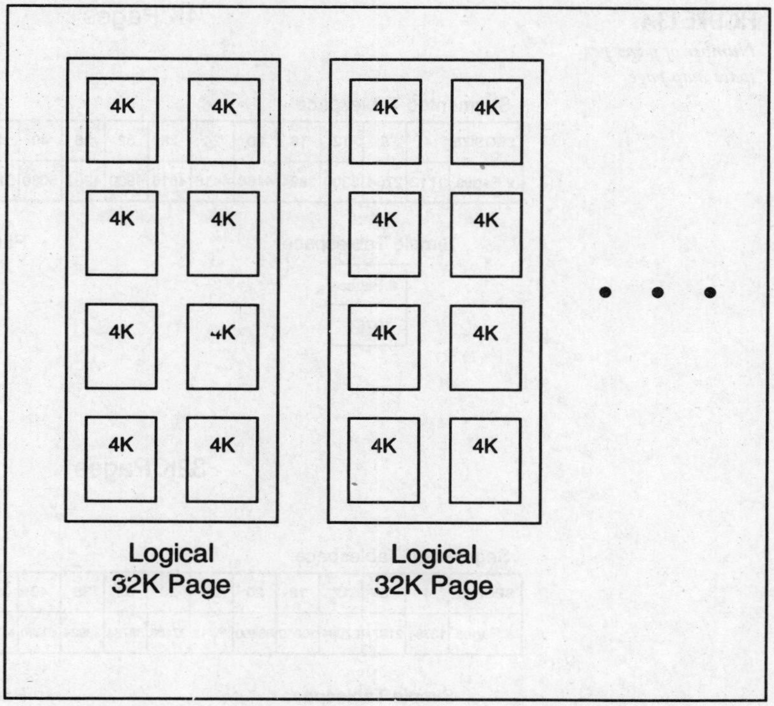

FIGURE 13.3.
32K pages are composed of eight 4K pages.

Each page set is composed of several types of pages. The *header page* contains control information used by DB2 to manage and maintain the tablespace. For example, the OBID and DBID (internal object and database identifiers used by DB2) of the tablespace and database are maintained here, as well as information on logging. Each linear page set has one header page; every partition of a partitioned page set has its own header page. The header page is the first page of a VSAM data set.

Space map pages contain information pertaining to the amount of free space available on pages in a page set. A space map page outlines the space available for a range of pages. See Figure 13.4 for the number of pages covered by a space map page based on the type of tablespace.

Data pages contain the user data for the tablespace or index page set. The layout of a data page depends on whether it is an index data page or a tablespace data page.

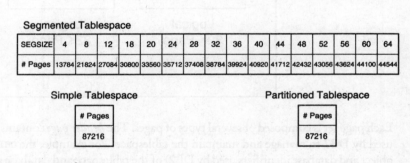

FIGURE 13.4.
Number of pages per space map page.

4K Pages

Segmented Tablespace

SEGSIZE	4	8	12	18	20	24	28	32	36	40	44	48	52	56	60	64
# Pages	1712	2704	3360	3824	4160	4416	4616	4800	4932	5080	5148	5232	5304	5376	5460	5504

Simple Tablespace

Pages
10764

Partitioned Tablespace

Pages
10764

32K Pages

Segmented Tablespace

SEGSIZE	4	8	12	18	20	24	28	32	36	40	44	48	52	56	60	64
# Pages	13784	21824	27084	30800	33560	35712	37408	38784	39924	40920	41712	42432	43056	43624	44100	44544

Simple Tablespace

Pages
87216

Partitioned Tablespace

Pages
87216

Tablespace Data Pages

Each tablespace data page is formatted as shown in Figure 13.5. Each page begins with a 20-byte header that records control information about the rest of the page. For example, the header contains the page set page number, pointers to free space in the page, and information pertaining to the validity and recoverability of the page.

At the very end of the page is a 1-byte trailer used as a consistency check token. DB2 checks the value in the trailer byte against a single bit in the page header to ensure that the data page is sound.

The next-to-last byte of each page contains a pointer to the next available ID map entry. The ID map is a series of contiguous 2-byte row pointers. One row pointer exists for every data row in the table. A maximum of 255 of these pointers can be defined per data page. The maximum number of rows per page is specified in each tablespace using the MAXROWS clause. Each row pointer identifies the location of a data row in the data page.

Each data page can contain one or more data rows. One data row exists for each row pointer, thereby enforcing a maximum of 255 data rows per data page. Each data row contains a 6-byte row header used to administer the status of the data row.

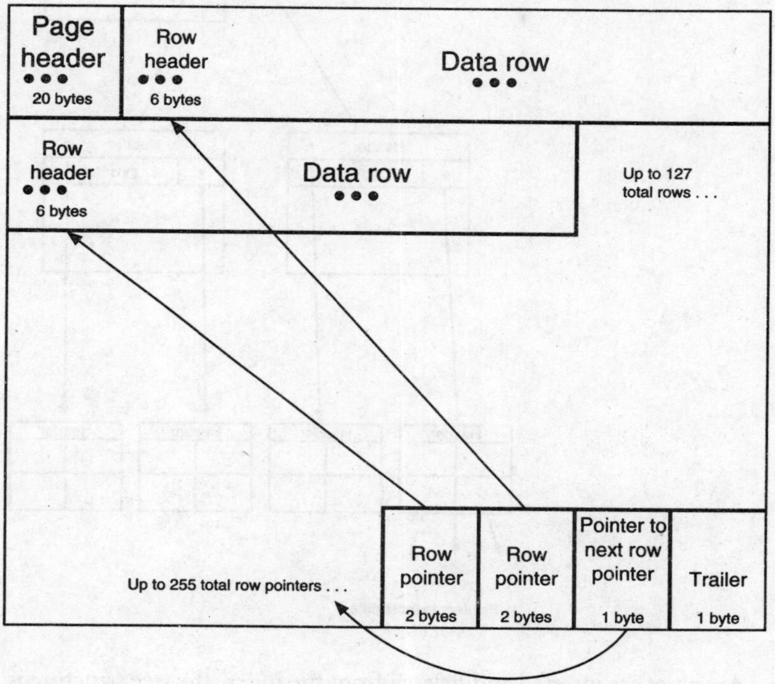

FIGURE 13.5.
Tablespace data page layout.

Index Data Pages

The data pages for a DB2 index are somewhat more complex than those for a DB2 tablespace. Before you delve into the specifics of the layout of index data pages, you should examine the basic structure of DB2 indexes.

A DB2 index is a modified *b-tree* (balanced tree) structure that orders data values for rapid retrieval. The values being indexed are stored in an inverted tree structure, as shown in Figure 13.6.

FIGURE 13.6.
DB2 index structure.

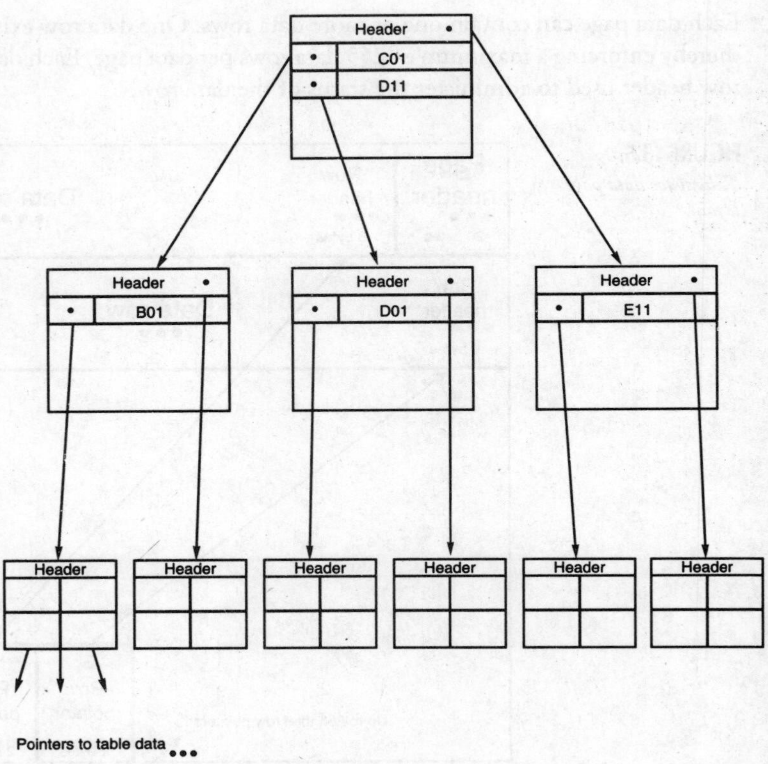

As values are inserted and deleted from the index, the tree structure is automatically balanced, realigning the hierarchy so that the path from top to bottom is uniform. This realignment minimizes the time required to access any given value by keeping the search paths as short as possible. To implement b-tree indexes, DB2 uses the following types of index data pages:

Space map pages	Space map pages determine what space is available in the index for DB2 to utilize.
Root page	Only one root page is available per index. The root page must exist at the highest level of the hierarchy for every index structure. It can be structured as either a leaf or a non-leaf page, depending on the number of entries in the index.
Non-leaf pages	Non-leaf pages are intermediate-level index pages in the b-tree hierarchy. Non-leaf pages need not exist. If they do exist, they contain pointers to other non-leaf pages or leaf pages. They never point to data rows.
Leaf pages	Leaf pages contain pointers to the data rows of a table. Leaf pages must always exist. In a single page index, the root page is a leaf page.

The pointers in the leaf pages of an index are called a *record ID*, or *RID*. Each RID is a combination of the tablespace page number and the row pointer for the data value, which together indicate the location of the data value.

NOTE

A RID is a record ID, not a row ID as is commonly assumed. A DB2 record is the combination of the record prefix and the row. Each record prefix is 6 bytes long. RIDs point to the record, not the row; therefore, a RID is a record ID. Don't let this information change the way you think. The data returned by your `SELECT` statements are still rows!

The level of a DB2 index indicates whether it contains non-leaf pages. The smallest DB2 index is a one-level index; the root page contains the pointers to the data rows. In this case, the root page is also a leaf page, and no non-leaf pages are available. This is true for Type 1 indexes only; no one-level Type 2 indexes exist. A two-level index does not contain non-leaf pages. The root page points directly to leaf pages, which in turn point to the rows containing the indexed data values.

A three-level index, such as the one shown in Figure 13.6, contains one level for the root page, another level for non-leaf pages, and a final level for leaf pages. The larger the number of levels for an index, the less efficient it will be. You can have any number of intermediate non-leaf page levels. Try not to have indexes with more than three levels because they are generally very inefficient.

DB2 uses two types of indexes: Type 1 and Type 2. The page layout and formatting of these two different types of indexes differ significantly.

Type 1 Index Data Pages

Version 4

Type 1 indexes are DB2's legacy index type. The indexes that have been available with DB2 since V1 have been known as Type 1 indexes since the introduction of DB2 V4, which added a new type of index (Type 2 indexes).

Type 1 non-leaf pages are physically formatted as shown in Figure 13.7. Each non-leaf page contains the following:

- A 12-byte index page header that houses consistency and recoverability information for the index.
- A 16-byte physical header that stores control information for the index page. For example, the physical header controls administrative housekeeping such as the type of page (leaf or non-leaf), the location of the page in the index structure, and the ordering and size of the indexed values.
- A 17-byte logical header that stores additional consistency and recoverability checking information, as well as administers free space.

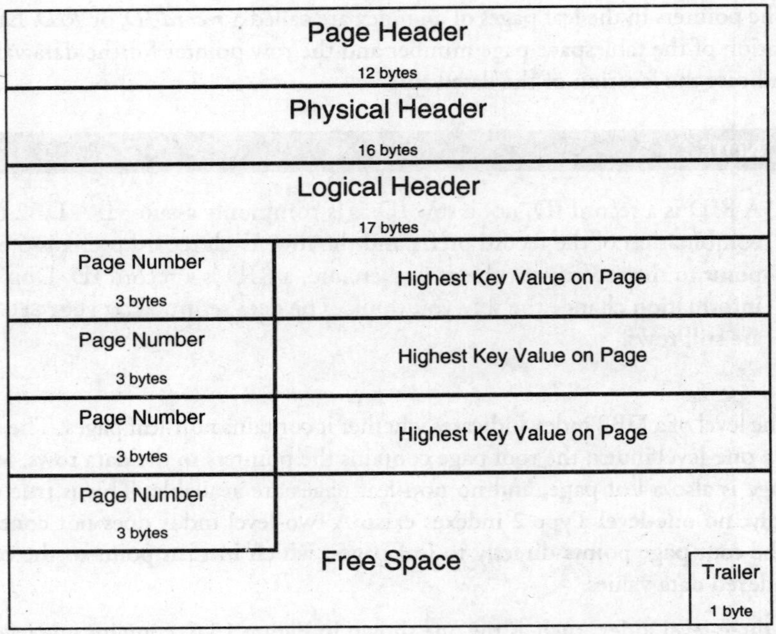

FIGURE 13.7.
Type 1 index non-leaf page layout.

The physical structure of a Type 1 index leaf page differs depending on the parameters specified when the index is created. Type 1 index pages can be broken down into smaller portions, known as *subpages.* A Type 1 index can be defined as having 1, 2, 4, 8, or 16 subpages. The physical structure of Type 1 index leaf pages depends on the number of subpages defined for the index.

See Figure 13.8 for the physical layout of a Type 1 index leaf page with a subpage specification of 1. The page header, physical header, and logical header are used for the same purposes as they are in non-leaf pages. The remainder of the page is used for index entries. Each index entry is composed of indexed values and RID pointers to the table data.

See Figure 13.9 for the physical layout of a Type 1 index leaf page with a subpage specification greater than 1. A subpage directory replaces the single logical header. This directory contains an array of pointers used to locate and administer the index subpages. Each subpage has its own logical header, allowing free space to exist on each subpage.

The final physical index structure to explore is the index entry. You can create both unique and non-unique indexes for each DB2 table. When the index key is of varying length, DB2 pads the columns to their maximum length, making the index keys a fixed length. A unique index contains entries, and each entry has a single RID. In a unique index, no two index entries can have the same value because the values being indexed are unique. See Figure 13.10.

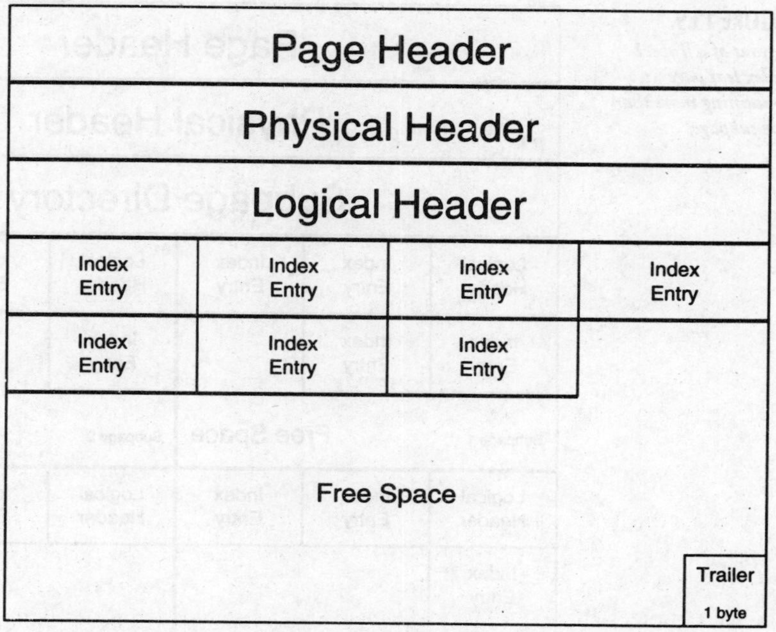

FIGURE 13.8.
Layout of a Type 1 index leaf page containing one subpage.

Version 4

As of DB2 V4, you can add the `WHERE NOT NULL` clause to a unique index causing multiple nulls to be stored. Therefore, an index specified as unique `WHERE NOT NULL` has multiple unique entries and possibly one non-unique entry for the nulls.

If the index can point to multiple table rows containing the same values, however, the index entry must support a RID list. In addition, a header is necessary to maintain the length of the RID list. This type of index entry is also shown in Figure 13.10.

Type 2 Index Data Pages

The Type 2 leaf page differs from the Type 1 leaf page in that entries are not stored contiguously in order on the page. Instead, a collated key map exists at the end of the Type 2 leaf page to order the entries. Type 2 index leaf pages are formatted as shown in Figure 13.11. When an entry is added to the index, the collated key map grows backward from the end of the page into the page. By traversing the key map within the page, DB2 can read entries in order by the index key. Additionally, Type 2 indexes have no subpages.

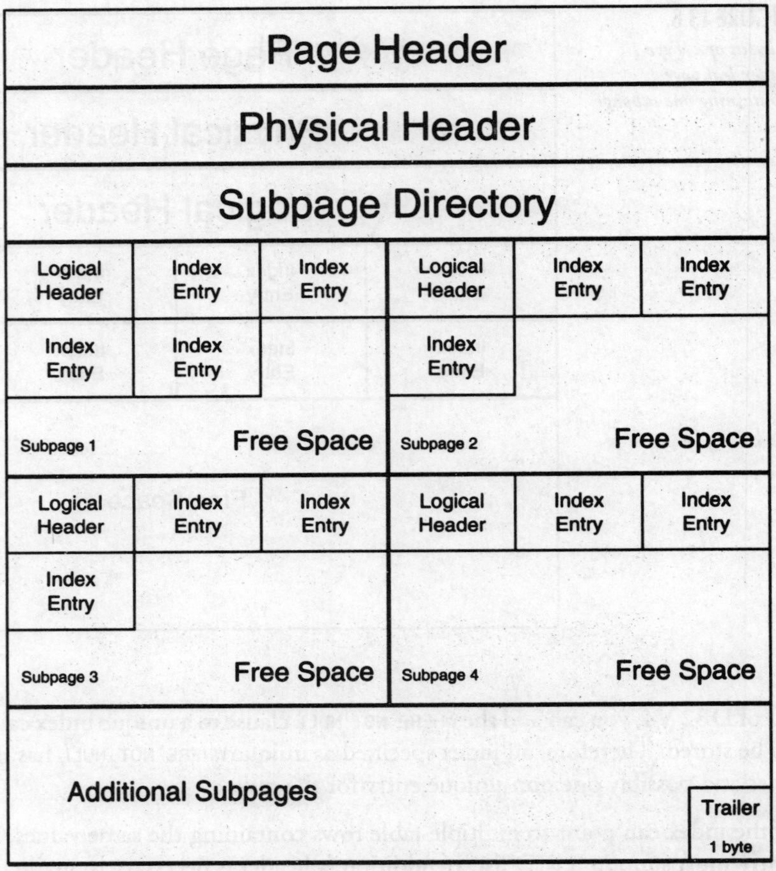

FIGURE 13.9.
Layout of a Type 1 index leaf page containing more than one subpage.

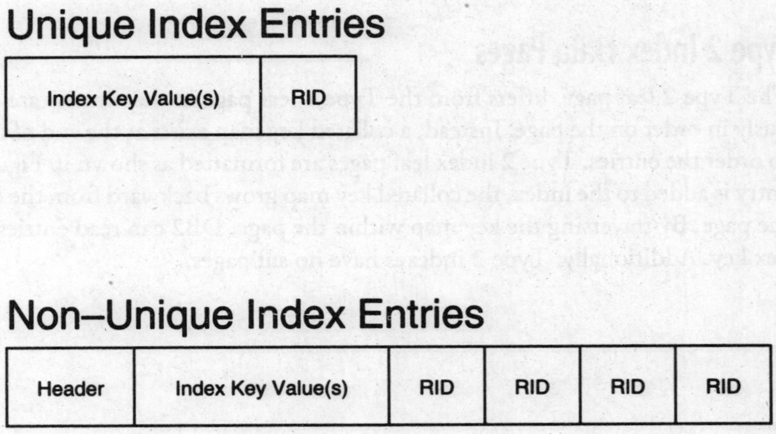

FIGURE 13.10.
Index entries.

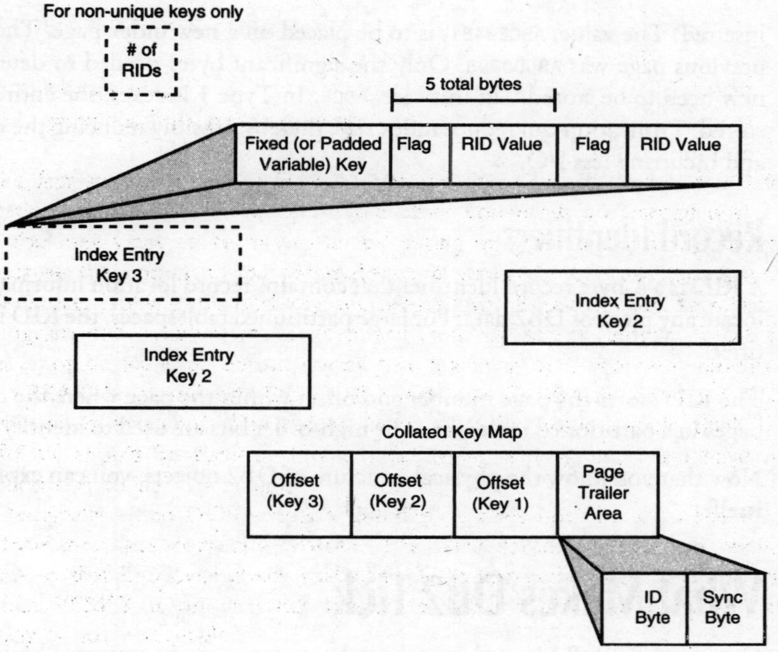

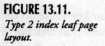

FIGURE 13.11.
Type 2 index leaf page layout.

Type 2 leaf page entries add a flag byte. The *flag byte* indicates the status of the RID. The first bit indicates whether the RID is pseudo-deleted. A *pseudo-delete* occurs when a RID has been marked for deletion. The second bit indicates that the RID is possibly uncommitted, and the third bit indicates that a RID hole follows. An array of RIDs is stored contiguously in ascending order to allow binary searching. For non-unique indexes, each index entry is preceded by a count of the number of RIDs.

NOTE

Type 2 indexes will need to be reorganized periodically to physically delete the pseudo-deleted RIDS. It is difficult to determine how many pseudo-deleted RIDs exist. Consider keeping a historical record of index size (using reports from the DB2 Catalog) for indexes that are larger than normal, and thus candidates for reorganization.

Type 2 non-leaf pages are similar in structure to Type 1 non-leaf pages. Each non-leaf page contains high keys with child page pointers. The last page pointer has no high key because it points to a child page that has entries greater than the highest high key in the parent.

Additionally, Type 2 index non-leaf pages deploy suffix truncation to reduce data storage needs and increase efficiency. Suffix truncation allows the non-leaf page to store only the most significant bytes of the key. For example, consider an index in which a new value is being inserted. The value, ABCE0481, is to be placed on a new index page. The last key value on the previous page was ABCD0398. Only the significant bytes needed to determine that this key is new need to be stored—in this case, ABCE. In Type 1 indexes, the entire length of each key is stored. Truncation can reduce index size, thereby possibly reducing the number of index levels and incurring less I/O.

Record Identifiers

A RID is a 4-byte record identifier that contains record location information. RIDs are used to locate any piece of DB2 data. For large partitioned tablespaces, the RID is a 5-byte record identifier.

The RID stores the page number and offset within the page where the data can be found. For pages in a partitioned tablespace, the high-order bits are used to identify the partition number.

Now that you know the physical structure of DB2 objects, you can explore the layout of DB2 itself.

What Makes DB2 Tick

Conceptually, DB2 is a relational database management system. Physically, DB2 is an amalgamation of address spaces and intersystem communication links that, when adequately tied together, provide the services of a relational database management system.

"What does all this information have to do with me?" you might wonder. Understanding the components of a piece of software helps you use that software more effectively. By understanding the physical layout of DB2, you can arrive at system solutions more quickly and develop SQL that performs better.

The information in this section is not very technical and does not delve into the bits and bytes of DB2. Instead, it presents the basic architecture of a DB2 subsystem and information about each component of that architecture.

Each DB2 subsystem consists of from three to five tasks started from the operator console, as shown in Figure 13.12. Each of these started tasks runs in a portion of the CPU called an *address space*. A description of these five address spaces follows.

The DBAS, or Database Services Address Space, provides the facility for the manipulation of DB2 data structures. The default name for this address space is DSNDBM1. (The address spaces may have been renamed at your shop.) This component of DB2 is responsible for the execution of SQL and the management of buffers, and it contains the core logic of the DBMS. The DBAS consists of three components, each of which performs specific tasks: the Relational Data System (RDS), the Data Manager (DM), and the Buffer Manager (BM). (See Figure 13.13.)

FIGURE 13.12.
The DB2 address spaces.

DBAS	SSAS	IRLM	DDF	SPAS
Database Functions	Logging	Locking	Distributed Requests	Stored Procedures
Buffering	Attachment coordination			
DSNDBM1	DSNMSTR	IRLMPROC	DSNDDF	

FIGURE 13.13.
The components of the Database Services Address Space.

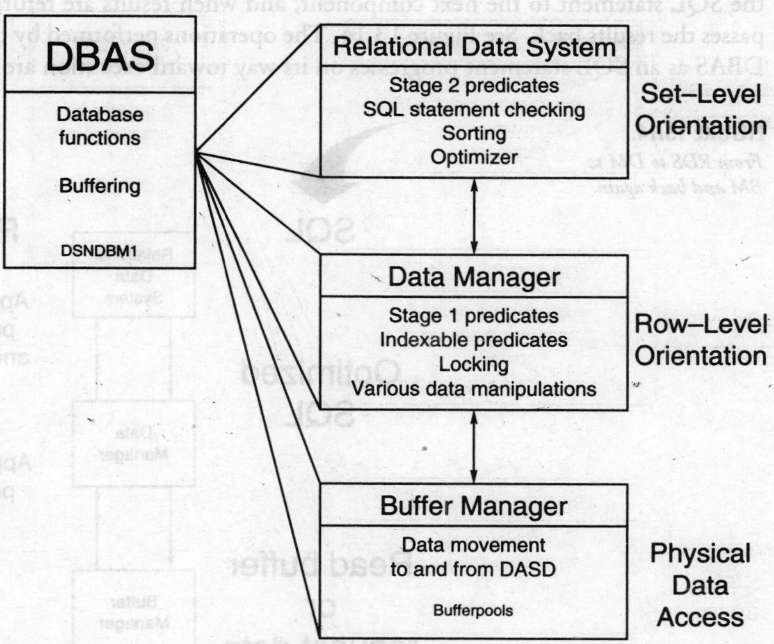

The SSAS, or System Services Address Space, coordinates the attachment of DB2 to other subsystems (CICS, IMS/TM, or TSO). SSAS is also responsible for all logging activities (physical logging, log archival, and BSDS). `DSNMSTR` is the default name for this address space. `DSNMSTR` is the started task which contains the DB2 log. The log should be monitored regularly for messages indicating the errors or problems with DB2.

The third address space required by DB2 is the IRLM, or Intersystem Resource Lock Manager. The IRLM is responsible for the management of all DB2 locks (including deadlock detection). The default name of this address space is `IRLMPROC`.

The next DB2 address space, DDF, or Distributed Data Facility, is optional. The DDF is required only when you want distributed database functionality. If your shop must enable remote DB2 subsystems to query data between one another, the DDF address space must be activated.

Version 4

The final address space (or series of address spaces) is devoted to the execution of stored procedures. These address spaces are known as the Stored Procedure Address Spaces, or SPAS.

Version 5

If you're running DB2 V4, only one SPAS is available. Under DB2 V5, however, if you're using the MVS WorkLoad Manager (WLM), you can define multiple SPAS.

These five address spaces contain the logic to handle all DB2 functionality effectively. As I mentioned previously, the DBAS is composed of three distinct elements. Each component passes the SQL statement to the next component, and when results are returned, each component passes the results back. See Figure 13.14. The operations performed by the components of the DBAS as an SQL statement progresses on its way toward execution are discussed next.

FIGURE 13.14.
From RDS to DM to BM and back again.

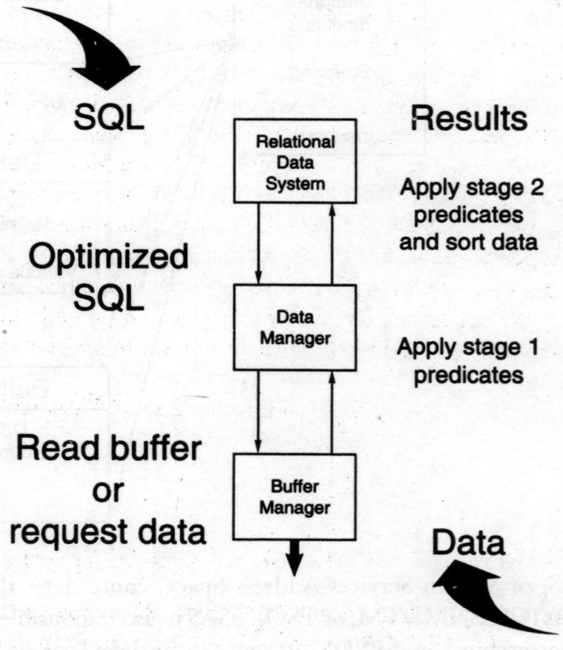

The RDS is the component that gives DB2 its set orientation. When an SQL statement requesting a set of columns and rows is passed to the RDS, the RDS determines the best mechanism for satisfying the request. Note that the RDS can parse an SQL statement and determine its needs. These needs, basically, can be any of the features supported by a relational database (such as selection, projection, or join).

When the RDS receives an SQL statement, it performs the following procedures:

- Checks authorization
- Resolves data element names into internal identifiers
- Checks the syntax of the SQL statement
- Optimizes the SQL statement and generates an access path

The RDS then passes the optimized SQL statement to the Data Manager (DM) for further processing. The function of the DM is to lower the level of data that is being operated on. In other words, the DM is the DB2 component that analyzes rows (either table rows or index rows) of data. The DM analyzes the request for data and then calls the Buffer Manager (BM) to satisfy the request.

The Buffer Manager accesses data for other DB2 components. It uses pools of memory set aside for the storage of frequently accessed data to create an efficient data access environment.

When a request is passed to the BM, it must determine whether the data is in the bufferpool. If the data is present, the BM accesses the data and sends it to the DM. If the data is not in the bufferpool, it calls the VSAM Media Manager, which reads the data and sends it back to the BM, which in turn sends the data back to the DM.

The DM receives the data passed to it by the BM and applies as many predicates as possible to reduce the answer set. Only Stage 1 predicates are applied in the DM. (These predicates are listed in Chapter 2, "Data Manipulation Guidelines.")

Finally, the RDS receives the data from the DM. All Stage 2 predicates are applied, the necessary sorting is performed, and the results are returned to the requester.

Now that you have learned about these components of DB2, you should be able to understand how this information can be helpful in developing a DB2 application. For example, consider Stage 1 and Stage 2 predicates. Now you can understand more easily that Stage 1 predicates are more efficient than Stage 2 predicates because you know that they are evaluated earlier in the process (in the DM instead of the RDS) and thereby avoid the overhead associated with the passing of additional data from one component to another.

Summary

This chapter presented you with a brief introduction inside DB2. You learned about the internal composition of DB2 objects and how data is stored. Additionally, you examined each of the address spaces that comprise a DB2 subsystem and learned the purpose of each. The next chapter leads you to an in-depth discussion of a portion of the RDS (which is a component of the DBAS): the DB2 Optimizer.

14

The Optimizer

The optimizer is the heart and soul of DB2. It analyzes an SQL statement and determines the most efficient access path available for satisfying the statement. It accomplishes this by parsing the SQL statement to determine which tables and columns must be accessed. It then queries statistics stored in the DB2 Catalog to determine the best method of accomplishing the tasks necessary to satisfy the SQL request

A summary of the DB2 Catalog information that can be used by the optimizer is provided in Table 14.1. The optimizer plugs this information into a series of complex formulas that it uses as it builds optimized access paths, as shown in Figure 14.1.

FIGURE 14.1.
The DB2 optimizer.

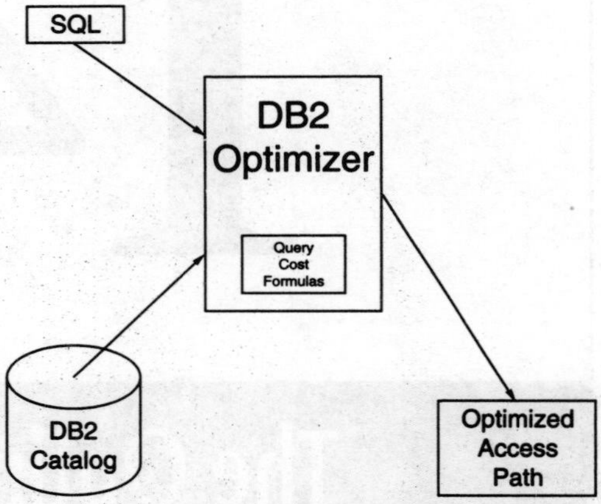

The optimizer is equivalent in function to an expert system. An expert system is a set of standard rules that when combined with situational data can return an expert opinion. For example, a medical expert system takes the set of rules determining which medication is useful for which illness, combines it with data describing the symptoms of ailments, and applies that knowledge base to a list of input symptoms. The DB2 optimizer renders expert opinions on data retrieval methods based on the situational data housed in the DB2 Catalog and a query input in an SQL format.

Table 14.1. Statistics analyzed during query optimization.

Type of Information	*DB2 Catalog Table*
Current status of the table	`SYSIBM.SYSTABLES`
	Number of rows
	Number of rows containing table data
	Percentage of rows that are compressed
	Number of pages
	Check whether the table uses an `EDITPROC`

Type of Information	*DB2 Catalog Table*
Current status of the tablespace	SYSIBM.SYSTABLESPACE
	Number of active pages
Current status of the index	SYSIBM.SYSINDEXES
	Check whether there is a usable index for this query and table
	Number of leaf pages used by the index
	Number of levels in index
	Number of discrete values for the entire index key
	Number of discrete values for the first column of the index key
	Check whether there is a clustering index; if so, check whether it is actually clustered
	Portion of any index that is clustered
Column information	SYSIBM.SYSCOLUMNS
	Number of discrete values for the column
	Range of values stored in the column
Distribution of values in columns	SYSIBM.SYSCOLDIST
	Percentage of data that is uniformly distributed
	Percentage of data that is not uniformly distributed

In this chapter, you discover the methods and strategies used by the optimizer as it creates optimized access paths for SQL statements.

Physical Data Independence

The notion of optimizing data access in the DBMS, a piece of system software, is one of the most powerful capabilities of DB2 (and other relational databases). Access to DB2 data is achieved by telling DB2 what to retrieve, not how to retrieve it. DB2's optimizer is the component that accomplishes this physical data independence.

Regardless of how the data is physically stored and manipulated, DB2 and SQL can still access that data. This separation of access criteria from physical storage characteristics is called *physical data independence.*

If indexes are removed, DB2 can still access the data (albeit less efficiently). If a column is added to the table being accessed, the data can still be manipulated by DB2 without changing the program code. This is all possible because the physical access paths to DB2 data are not coded by programmers in application programs, but are generated by DB2.

Compare this with older, legacy data manipulation mechanisms (VSAM, IMS, and flat files), in which the programmer must know the physical structure of the data. If there is an index, the programmer must code so that the index is used. If the index is removed, the program will not work unless changes are made. Not so with DB2 and SQL. All this flexibility is attributable to DB2's capability to optimize data manipulation requests automatically.

How the Optimizer Works

The optimizer performs complex calculations based on a host of information. To simplify the functionality of the optimizer, you can picture it as performing a four-step process:

1. Receive and verify the SQL statement.
2. Analyze the environment and optimize the method of satisfying the SQL statement.
3. Create machine-readable instructions to execute the optimized SQL.
4. Execute the instructions or store them for future execution.

The second step of this process is the most intriguing. How does the optimizer decide how to execute the vast array of SQL statements that can be sent its way?

The optimizer has many types of strategies for optimizing SQL. How does it choose which of these strategies to use in the optimized access paths? The details and logic used by the optimizer are not published by IBM, but the optimizer is a cost-based optimizer. This means that the optimizer will always attempt to formulate an access path for each query that reduces overall cost. To accomplish this, the DB2 optimizer evaluates and weighs four factors for each potential access path: the CPU cost, the I/O cost, the DB2 Catalog statistics, and the SQL statement.

CPU Cost

The optimizer tries to determine the cost of execution of each access path strategy for the query being optimized. Based on the serial number of the CPU, the optimizer estimates the CPU time required to accomplish the tasks associated with the access path it is analyzing. As it calculates this cost, it determines the costs involved in applying predicates, traversing pages (index and tablespace), and sorting.

I/O Cost

The optimizer estimates the cost of physically retrieving and writing the data. In so doing, the optimizer estimates the cost of I/O by using a series of formulas based on the following data: DB2 Catalog statistics, the size of the bufferpools, and the cost of work files used (sorting, intermediate results, and so on). These formulas result in a *filter factor*, which determines the relative I/O cost of the query. Filter factors are covered in more detail in the "Filter Factors" section, later in this chapter.

DB2 Catalog Statistics

Without the statistics stored in the DB2 Catalog, the optimizer would have a difficult time optimizing anything. These statistics provide the optimizer with information pertinent to the state of the tables that will be accessed by the SQL statement that is being optimized. The type of information available was summarized in Table 14.1. A complete listing of the DB2 Catalog statistics used by the optimizer is in Table 14.2. Partition-level statistics are used when determining the degree of parallelism for queries using I/O, CP, and Sysplex parallelism.

Table 14.2. DB2 Catalog columns analyzed by the optimizer.

Catalog Table	*Column*	*Description*
SYSIBM.SYSTABLES	CARD[4]	Number of rows for the table
	CARDF[5]	Number of rows for the table
	NPAGES	Number of pages used by the table
	EDPROC	Name of the EDITPROC exit routine, if any
	PCTROWCOMP	Percentage of active rows compressed for this table
SYSIBM.SYSTABLESPACE	NACTIVE	Number of allocated tablespace pages
SYSIBM.SYSCOLUMNS	LOW2KEY	Second lowest value for the column
	HIGH2KEY	Second highest value for the column
	COLCARD[4]	Number of distinct values for the column
	COLCARDF[5]	Number of distinct values for the column

continues

Table 14.2. continued

Catalog Table	*Column*	*Description*
SYSIBM.SYSINDEXES	CLUSTERRATIO	Percentage of rows in clustered order
	CLUSTERING	Whether CLUSTER YES was specified when the index was created
	FIRSTKEYCARD[4]	Number of distinct values for the first column of the index key
	FIRSTKEYCARDF[5]	Number of distinct values for the first column of the index key
	FULLKEYCARD[4]	Number of distinct values for the full index key
	FULLKEYCARDF[5]	Number of distinct values for the full index key
	NLEAF	Number of active leaf pages
	NLEVELS	Number of index b-tree levels
SYSIBM.SYSCOLDIST	TYPE[5]	Type of RUNSTATS gathered; frequent value or cardinality
	STATSTIME	Date and time RUNSTATS was run to produce this statistic
	COLVALUE	Non-uniform distribution column value
	FREQUENCY[4]	Percentage (multiplied by 100) of rows that contain the value indicated in the COLVALUE column
	FREQUENCYF[5]	Percentage (multiplied by 100) of rows that contain the value indicated in the COLVALUE column
SYSIBM.SYSCOLDISTSTATS	TYPE[5]	Type of RUNSTATS gathered; frequent value or cardinality
	CARDF[5]	Number of distinct values for the column group

Catalog Table	Column	Description
	COLGROUPCOLNO[5]	Specifies the columns associated with the statistics
	NUMCOLUMNS[5]	The number of columns associated with the statistics

[4] This column applies to DB2 V4 and earlier.

[5] This column applies to V5 and later.

Note that several column names have been changed for DB2 V5. The columns for V5 that have an *F* at the end of their names have been changed from `INTEGER` columns to `FLOAT` columns. This enables DB2 to store larger values in these columns. The largest value that can be stored in an `INTEGER` column is `2,147,483,647`. If the actual value for `CARD`, for example, is greater than this, DB2 is forced to store this largest value.

Version 5

In V5 and later, `RUNSTATS` can also keep track of correlated columns. *Correlated columns* have values that are related to one another. An example of a set of correlated columns is `CITY`, `STATE`, and `ZIP_CODE`. For example, the combination of `CHICAGO` for `CITY` and `IL` for `STATE` is much more likely to occur than `CHICAGO` and `AK`. As of V5, the `RUNSTATS` utility can keep track of these statistics.

Finally, the V5 `RUNSTATS` utility can generate more than 10 frequent values. Previous versions of DB2 were limited to just the top 10 most frequently occurring values for distribution statistics.

SQL Statement

The formulation of the SQL statement also enters into the access path decisions made by the optimizer. The complexity of the query, the number and type of predicates used (Stage 1 versus Stage 2), the usage of column and scalar functions, and the presence of ordering clauses (`ORDER BY`, `GROUP BY`, and `DISTINCT`) enter into the estimated cost that is calculated by the optimizer.

Filter Factors

Do you remember that Chapter 1, "The Magic Words," discussed filter factors? The optimizer calculates the filter factor for a query's predicates based on the number of rows that will be filtered out by the predicates.

The filter factor is a ratio that estimates I/O costs. The formulas used by the optimizer to calculate the filter factor are proprietary IBM information, but Table 14.3 provides a rough estimate. These formulas assume uniform data distribution, so they should be used only when determining the filter factor for static SQL queries or queries on tables having no distribution statistics stored in the DB2 Catalog. The filter factor for dynamic SQL queries is calculated using the distribution statistics, in SYSCOLDIST, if available.

Table 14.3. Filter factor formulas.

Predicate Type	*Formula*	*Default FF*
COL = value	1/FIRSTKEYCARDF [COL]	.04
COL = :host-var	1/FIRSTKEYCARDF [COL]	.04
COL <> value	1-(1/FIRSTKEYCARDF [COL])	.96
COL <> :host-var	1-(1/FIRSTKEYCARDF [COL])	.96
COL IN (list of values)	(list size)′(1/FIRSTKEYCARDF [COL])	.04′(list size)
COL NOT IN (list of values)	1-[(list size)′(1/FIRSTKEYCARDF [COL])]	1-[.04′(list size)]
COL IS NULL	1/FIRSTKEYCARDF [COL]	.04
COL IS NOT NULL	1-(1/FIRSTKEYCARDF [COL])	.96
COLA = COLB	smaller of 1/FIRSTKEYCARDF [COLA] 1/FIRSTKEYCARDF [COLB]	.04
COLA <> COLB	1-(smaller of 1/FIRSTKEYCARDF [COLA] 1/FIRSTKEYCARDF [COLB])	.96
COL < value	(LOW2KEY-value)/ (HIGH2KEY-LOW2KEY)	.33
COL <= value	(LOW2KEY-value)/ (HIGH2KEY-LOW2KEY)	.33
COL ¬> value	(LOW2KEY-value)/ (HIGH2KEY-LOW2KEY)	.33
COL > value	(HIGH2KEY-value)/ (HIGH2KEY-LOW2KEY)	.33
COL >= value	(HIGH2KEY-value)/ (HIGH2KEY-LOW2KEY)	.33
COL ¬< value	(HIGH2KEY-value)/ (HIGH2KEY-LOW2KEY)	.33
COL BETWEEN val1 AND val2	(val2-val1)/ (HIGH2KEY-LOW2KEY)	.01

Predicate Type	*Formula*	*Default FF*
COL LIKE 'char%'	(val2-val1)/ (HIGH2KEY-OW2KEY)	.01
COL LIKE '%char'	1	1
COL LIKE '_char'	1	1
COL op ANY (non-corr. sub)	- - -	.83
COL op ALL (non-corr. sub)	- - -	.16
COL IN (non-corr. sub)	FF(noncor. subquery)	.90
COL NOT IN (non-corr. sub)	1-FF(noncor. subquery)	.10
predicate1 AND predicate2	Multiply the filter factors of the two predicates, FF1'FF2	
predicate1 OR predicate2	Add filter factors and subtract the product, FF1+FF2-(FF1'FF2)	

For example, consider the following query:

```
SELECT   EMPNO, LASTNAME, SEX
FROM     DSN8510.EMP
WHERE    WORKDEPT = 'A00';
```

The column has an index called `DSN8510.XEMP2`. If this query were being optimized by DB2, the filter factor for the `WORKDEPT` predicate would be calculated to estimate the number of I/Os needed to satisfy this request.

Using the information in Table 14.3, you can see that the filter factor for this predicate is `1/FIRSTKEYCARDF`. So, if the value of the `FIRSTKEYCARDF` column in the `SYSIBM.SYSINDEXES` DB2 Catalog table is determined to be `9`, the filter factor for this query is 1/9, or .1111. In other words, DB2 assumes that approximately 11 percent of the rows from this table will satisfy this request.

You might be wondering how this information can help you. Well, with a bit of practical knowledge, you can begin to determine how your SQL statements will perform before executing them. If you remember nothing else about filter factors, remember this: *The lower the filter factor, the lower the cost, and, in general, the more efficient your query will be.*

Therefore, you can easily see that as you further qualify a query with additional predicates, you make it more efficient because the I/O requirements are reduced.

Access Path Strategies

As mentioned, the optimizer can choose from a wealth of solutions when selecting the optimal access path for an SQL statement. These solutions, called *strategies,* range from the simple method of using a series of sequential reads to the complex strategy of using multiple indexes to combine multiple tables. This section describes the features and functionality of these strategies.

Scans

Of the many decisions, perhaps the most important decision that must be made by the optimizer is whether an index will be used to satisfy the query. To determine this, the optimizer must first discover whether an index exists. Remember that you can query any column of any table known to DB2. An index does not have to be defined before SQL can be written to access that column. Therefore, it is important that the optimizer provide the capability to efficiently access non-indexed data.

An index is not used in three circumstances:

- When no indexes exist for the table and columns being accessed
- When Type 2 indexes are required for a specific feature (such as uncommitted read isolation), but only Type 1 indexes exist
- When the optimizer determines that the query can be executed more efficiently without using an index

In either of these two circumstances, the query is satisfied by sequentially reading the tablespace pages for the table being accessed.

Why would the optimizer determine that an index should not be used? Aren't indexes designed to make querying tables more efficient? The optimizer decides that an index should not be used for one of two reasons. The first reason is when the table being accessed has only a small number of rows. Using an index to query a small table can decrease performance because additional I/O is required. For example, consider a tablespace consisting of one page. Accessing this page without the index would require a single I/O. If you used an index, at least one additional I/O is required to read the index page, and more might be required if root pages, non-leaf pages, and leaf pages must be accessed.

The second reason for not using an index is that, for larger tables, the organization of the index could require additional I/O to satisfy the query. Factors affecting this are the full and first key cardinality of the index and the cluster ratio of the index.

When an index is not used to satisfy a query, the resulting access path uses a tablespace scan (see Figure 14.2). A tablespace scan performs page-by-page processing, reading every page of a tablespace (or table). Pages cannot be bypassed.

FIGURE 14.2.
A tablespace scan.

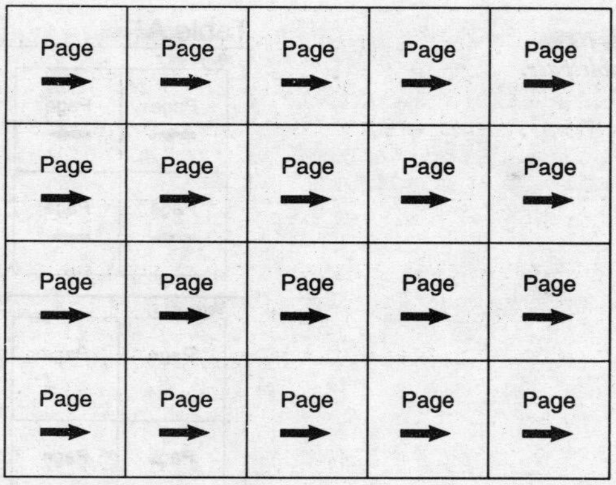

Following are the steps involved in a tablespace scan:

1. The RDS passes the request for a tablespace scan to the DM.
2. The DM asks the BM to read all the data pages of the accessed table, one by one. Tablespace scans usually invoke a fast type of bulk read known as *sequential prefetch.*
3. The BM determines whether the requested page is in the buffer and takes the appropriate action to retrieve the requested page and return it to the DM.
4. The DM scans the page and returns the selected columns to the RDS row by row. Predicates are applied by either the DM or the RDS, depending on whether the predicate is a Stage 1 or Stage 2 predicate.
5. The results are returned to the requesting agent.

It was mentioned that a tablespace scan reads every page of the tablespace (or table). If the optimizer indicates that a tablespace scan will occur, why do I bring up tables? There are two types of tablespace scans, and the type of tablespace scan requested depends on the type of tablespace being scanned.

A simple tablespace uses a tablespace scan as shown in Figure 14.2. Every page of the tablespace being scanned is read. This is true even if multiple tables are defined to the simple tablespace (which is one of the reasons to avoid multitable simple tablespaces).

When a segmented tablespace is scanned, a tablespace scan such as the one in Figure 14.3 is invoked. A segmented tablespace scan reads pages from only those segments used for the table being accessed. This could more appropriately be termed a *table scan.*

Version 4

Partitioned tablespace scans differ from simple and segmented tablespace scans because whole partitions can be skipped. DB2 can limit the partitions scanned to only those partitions that contain data relevant to the query. In order to do so, however, the query must specify a predicate that matches columns in the partitioning index.

FIGURE 14.3.
A segmented tablespace scan.

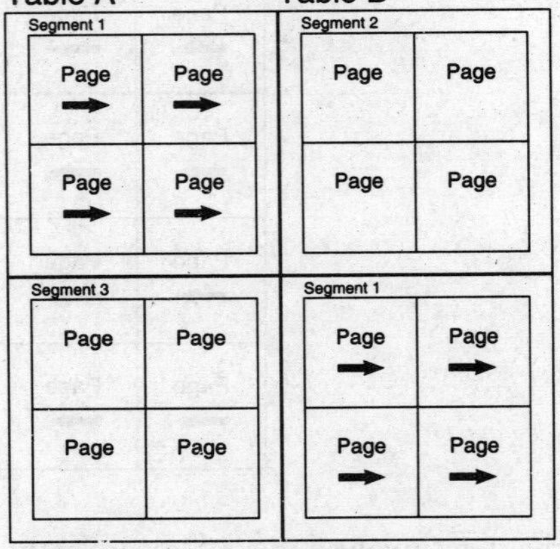

To understand how limited partition scans function, consider the following query in conjunction with Figure 14.4:

```
SELECT COL1, COLx
FROM T1
WHERE PART_KEY BETWEEN "H" AND "J"
AND    PART_KEY = "T";
```

FIGURE 14.4.
Partitioned tablespace scans.

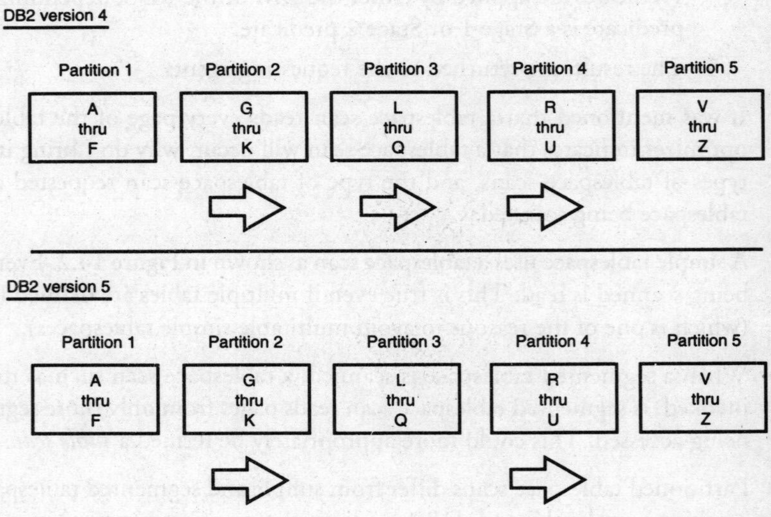

Table T1 is partitioned on the PART_KEY column C1. Note that there are five partitions in this tablespace as depicted in Figure 14.4. DB2 V4 understands that only partitions 2 through 4 contain data that will satisfy this request. (Data values containing H through J are in partition 2; T is in partition 4.) Therefore, DB2 can avoid scanning the data contained in partitions 1 and 5.

The V4 partitioned tablespace scan is still not as efficient as it can be. Note that partition 3 will be scanned in V4, even though it contains no data that can satisfy the query. DB2 V5 enables partition skipping within a scan. So given the same example as before, partitions 1, 3, and 5 can be skipped when running under DB2 V5.

Version 5

Limited partition scans can be combined with matching index scans when appropriate.

A limited partition scan can also be used for each table accessed in a join, as long as the access is sequential.

NOTE

When host variables or parameter markers are used in the first column of a multicolumn partitioning key, DB2 will not limit the partitions scanned. In these circumstances, DB2 doesn't know the qualified partition range at bind time.

Sequential Prefetch

Before discussing the various types of indexed data access, a discussion of sequential prefetch is in order. *Sequential prefetch* can be thought of as a read-ahead mechanism invoked to prefill DB2's buffers so that data is already in memory before it is requested. When sequential prefetch is requested, DB2 can be thought of as playing the role of a psychic, predicting that the extra pages being read will need to be accessed, because of the nature of the request.

The optimizer uses sequential prefetch when it determines that sequential processing is required. The sequential page processing of a tablespace scan is a good example of a process that can benefit from sequential prefetch. The optimizer requests sequential prefetch in one of three ways.

Static requests that the optimizer deems to be sequential cause the optimizer to request sequential prefetch at bind time. Sequential dynamic requests invoke sequential prefetch at execution time.

The third way in which the optimizer requests sequential prefetch is called sequential detection. *Sequential detection* can dynamically invoke sequential prefetch. Sequential detection "turns on" sequential prefetch for static requests that were not thought to be sequential at bind time but resulted in sequential data access during execution.

Sequential detection uses groupings of pages based on the size of the bufferpool to determine whether sequential prefetch should be requested. The size of the bufferpool is called the sequential detection indicator and is determined using the Normal Processing column of Table 14.4. The values in Table 14.4 apply to bufferpools with a 4K page size (BP0 through BP49). Call the sequential detection indicator *D*. Sequential detection will request prefetch when [(D/4)+1] out of (D/2) pages are accessed sequentially within a grouping of D pages.

Table 14.4. Sequential prefetch and detection values for 4K page bufferpools.

Bufferpool Size	*Number of Pages Read (Normal Processing)*	*Number of Pages Read (Utility Processing)*
0-223	8	16
224-999	16	32
1000+	32	64

For example, in an environment having 500 buffers, the sequential detection indicator would be 16. If 4 out of 8 pages accessed are sequential within a 16-page grouping, sequential detection invokes prefetch.

The sequential prefetch numbers are different for 32K page bufferpools. DB2 will prefetch fewer pages because they are larger (8 times larger than a 4K page). Table 14.5 shows the number of pages read by sequential prefetch when 32K page bufferpools are involved.

Table 14.5. Sequential prefetch values for 32K page bufferpools.

Bufferpool Size	*Number of Pages Read*
0-16	0 (prefetch disabled)
17-99	2
100+	4

Figure 14.5 shows the potential effect of sequential prefetch on a request. A normal DB2 I/O reads one page of data at a time. By contrast, a sequential prefetch I/O can read up to 32 pages at a time, which can have a dramatic effect on performance. Everything else being constant, sequential prefetch I/O can enhance efficiency by as much as 32 times over standard I/O.

The number of pages that can be requested in a single I/O by sequential prefetch depends on the number of pages allocated to the DB2 bufferpool, as shown in Tables 14.4 and 14.5.

As you plan your environment for the optimal use of sequential prefetch, keep a few of these final notes in mind. If sequential prefetch is requested by the optimizer, it is invoked immediately after the first single page I/O is performed. After this first I/O, DB2 kicks off two sequential prefetch I/Os—one for the pages that must be processed almost immediately and another for the second set of prefetched pages. This is done to reduce I/O wait time. Thereafter, each successive prefetch I/O is requested before all the currently prefetched pages have been processed. This scenario is shown in Figure 14.6.

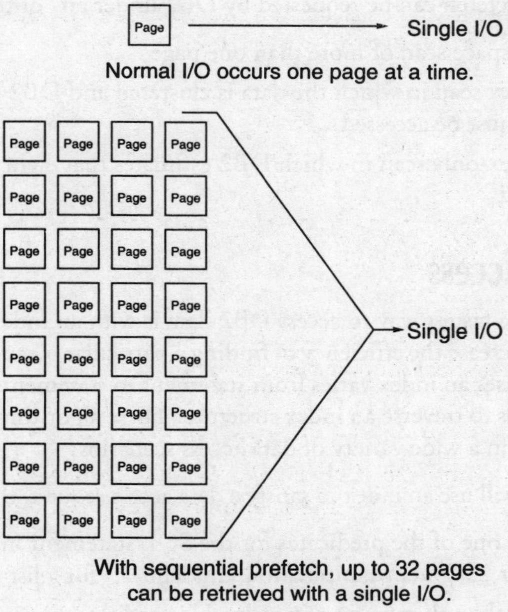

FIGURE 14.5.
Sequential prefetch.

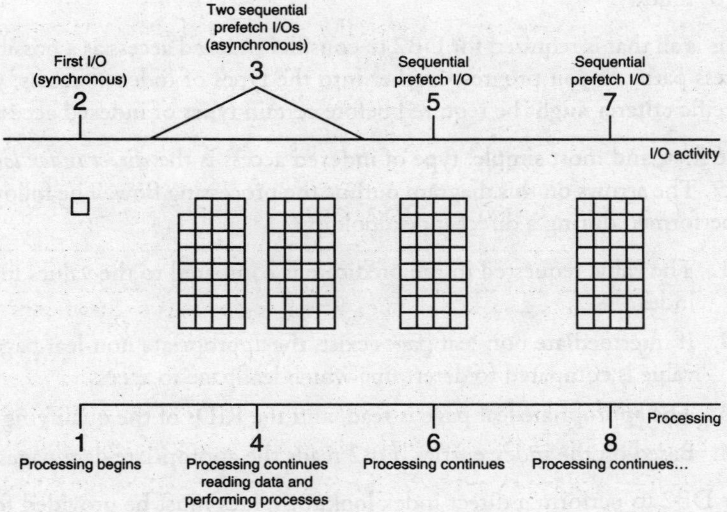

FIGURE 14.6.
Sequential prefetch processing.

Sequential prefetch is not the sole dominion of tablespace scans. Any process that relies on the sequential access of data pages (either index pages or tablespace pages) can benefit from sequential prefetch.

Sequential prefetch can be requested by DB2 under any of the following circumstances:

- A tablespace scan of more than one page
- An index scan in which the data is clustered and DB2 determines that eight or more pages must be accessed
- An index-only scan in which DB2 estimates that eight or more leaf pages must be accessed

Indexed Access

Generally, the fastest way to access DB2 data is with an index. Indexes are structured in such a way as to increase the efficiency of finding a particular piece of data. However, the manner in which DB2 uses an index varies from statement to statement. DB2 uses many different internal algorithms to traverse an index structure. These algorithms are designed to elicit optimum performance in a wide variety of data access scenarios.

Before DB2 will use an index to satisfy a data access request, the following criteria must be met:

- At least one of the predicates for the SQL statement must be indexable. Refer to Chapter 2, "Data Manipulation Guidelines," for a list of indexable predicates.
- One of the columns (in any indexable predicate) must exist as a column in an available index.

This is all that is required for DB2 to consider indexed access as a possible solution for a given access path. As you progress further into the types of indexed access, you will see that more specific criteria might be required before certain types of indexed access are permitted.

The first, and most simple, type of indexed access is the *direct index lookup,* shown in Figure 14.7. The arrows on this diagram outline the processing flow. The following sequence of steps is performed during a direct index lookup:

1. The value requested in the predicate is compared to the values in the root page of the index.
2. If intermediate non-leaf pages exist, the appropriate non-leaf page is read, and the value is compared to determine which leaf page to access.
3. The appropriate leaf page is read, and the RIDs of the qualifying rows are determined.
4. Based on the index entries, DB2 reads the appropriate data pages.

For DB2 to perform a direct index lookup, values must be provided for each column in the index. For example, consider an index on one of the sample tables, `DSN8510.XPROJAC1` on `DSN8510.PROJACT`. This index consists of three columns: `PROJNO`, `ACTNO`, and `ACSTDATE`. All three columns must appear in the SQL statement for a direct index lookup to occur. For example, consider the following:

```
SELECT    ACSTAFF, ACENDATE
FROM      DSN8510.PROJACT
WHERE     PROJNO = '000100'
AND       ACTNO = 1
AND       ACSTDATE = DATE('1991-12-31')
```

FIGURE 14.7.
Direct index lookup.

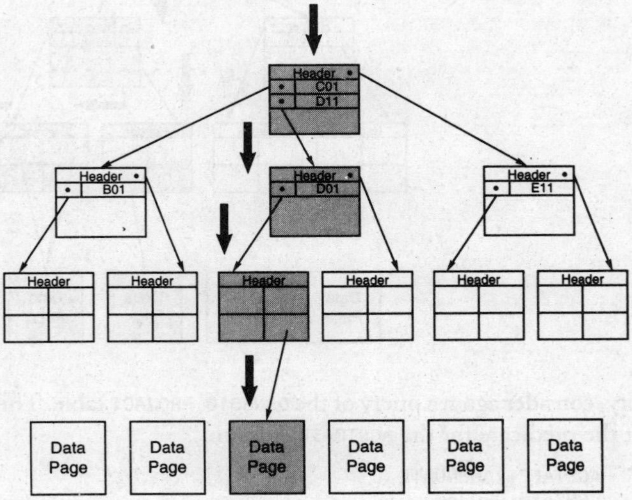

NOTE

Although the DATE function is not required in the above SQL statement, its use can reduce CPU time significantly.

If only one or two of these columns were specified as predicates, a direct index lookup could not occur because DB2 would not have a value for each column and could not match the full index key. Instead, an index scan could be chosen.

There are two types of index scans: *matching index scans* and *nonmatching index scans.* A matching index scan is sometimes called *absolute positioning*; a non-matching index scan is sometimes called *relative positioning.*

Remember the previous discussion of tablespace scans? Index scans are similar. When you invoke an index scan, the leaf pages of the index being used to facilitate access are read sequentially. Now I will examine these two types of index scans more closely.

A matching index scan begins at the root page of an index and works down to a leaf page in much the same manner as a direct index lookup does. However, because the complete key of the index is unavailable, DB2 must scan the leaf pages using the values that it does have, until all matching values have been retrieved. This is shown in Figure 14.8.

FIGURE 14.8.
A matching index scan.

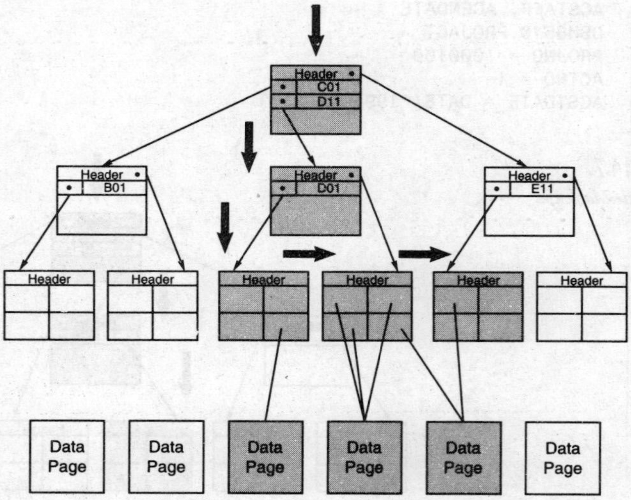

To clarify, consider again a query of the `DSN8510.PROJACT` table. This time, the query is recoded without the predicate for the `ACSTDATE` column:

```
SELECT   ACSTAFF, ACENDATE
FROM     DSN8510.PROJACT
WHERE    PROJNO = '000100'
AND      ACTNO = 1
```

The matching index scan locates the first leaf page with the appropriate value for `PROJNO` and `ACTNO` by traversing the index starting at the root. However, there can be multiple index entries with this combination of values and different `ACSTDATE` values. Therefore, leaf pages are sequentially scanned until no more valid `PROJNO`, `ACTNO`, and varying `ACSTDATE` combinations are encountered.

For a matching index scan to be requested, you must specify the high order column in the index key, which is `PROJNO` in the preceding example. This provides a starting point for DB2 to traverse the index structure from the root page to the appropriate leaf page.

What would happen, though, if you did not specify this high order column? Suppose that you alter the sample query such that a predicate for `PROJNO` is not specified:

```
SELECT   ACSTAFF, ACENDATE
FROM     DSN8510.PROJACT
WHERE    ACTNO = 1
AND      ACSTDATE = DATE('1991-12-31')
```

In this instance, a nonmatching index scan can be chosen. When a starting point cannot be determined because the first column in the key is unavailable, DB2 cannot use the index tree structure, but it can use the index leaf pages, as shown in Figure 14.9. A nonmatching index scan begins with the first leaf page in the index and sequentially scans subsequent leaf pages, applying the available predicates.

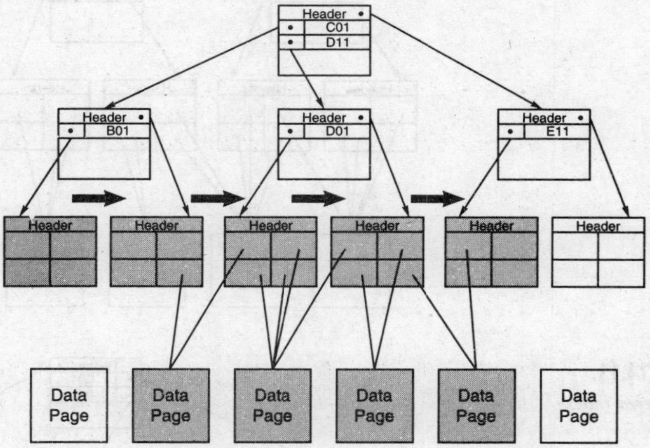

FIGURE 14.9.
A nonmatching index scan.

DB2 uses a nonmatching index scan instead of a tablespace scan for many reasons. A nonmatching index scan can be more efficient than a tablespace scan, especially if the data pages that must be accessed are in clustered order. As discussed in Chapter 2, you can create clustering indexes that dictate the order in which DB2 should attempt to store data. When data is clustered by a certain key, I/O can be reduced.

Of course, a nonmatching index scan can be done on a non-clustered index, also.

Compare the clustered index access shown in Figure 14.10 with the nonclustered index access in Figure 14.11. Clustered index access, as it proceeds from leaf page to leaf page, never requests a read for the same data page twice. It is evident from the figure that the same cannot be said for nonclustered index access.

Another time when a nonmatching index might be chosen is to maintain data in a particular order to satisfy an `ORDER BY` or `GROUP BY`. Finally, DB2 can avoid reading data pages completely if all the required data exists in the index. This feature is known as *index-only access* and is pictured in Figure 14.12.

Consider again the sample query. This time, it is recoded so that the only columns that must be accessed are `ACTNO` and `ACSTDATE` for predicate evaluation and `PROJNO`, which is returned in the select list:

```
SELECT    PROJNO
FROM      DSN8510.PROJACT
WHERE     ACTNO = 1
AND       ACSTDATE = DATE('1991-12-31')
```

FIGURE 14.10.
Clustered index access.

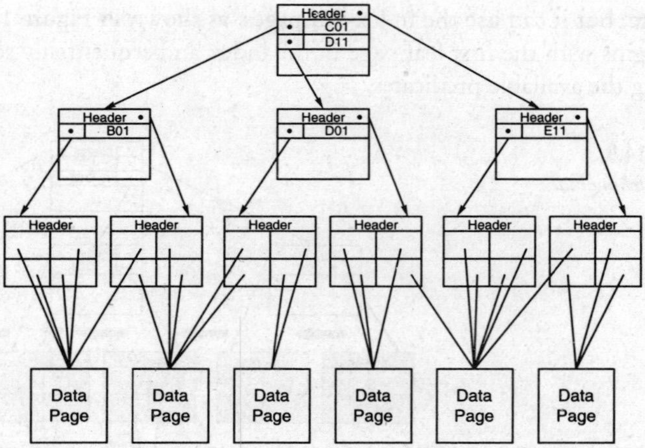

FIGURE 14.11.
Nonclustered index access.

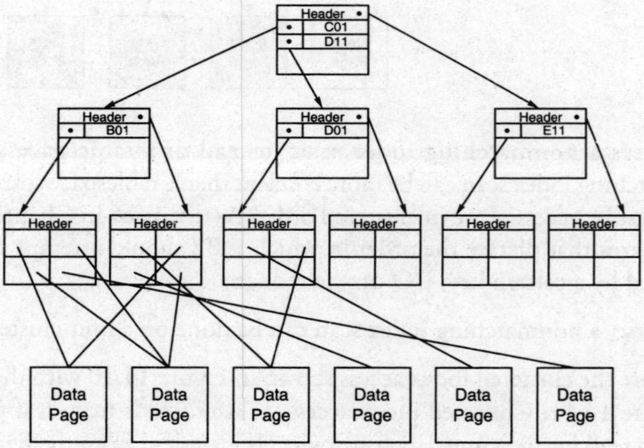

DB2 can satisfy this query by simply scanning the leaf pages of the index. It never accesses the tablespace data pages. A nonmatching index-only scan is usually much faster than a tablespace scan because index entries are generally smaller than the table rows that they point to.

DB2 can use three other methods to provide indexed access for optimized SQL. The first is *list prefetch.* As mentioned, accessing nonclustered data with an index can be inefficient. However, if DB2 determines beforehand that the degree of clustering is such that a high number of additional page I/Os might be requested, list prefetch can be requested to sort the access requests before requesting the data page I/Os (see Figure 14.13).

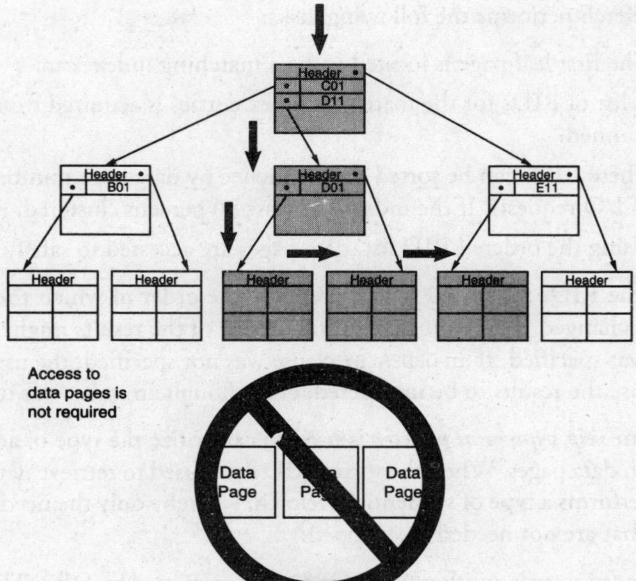

FIGURE 14.12.
Index-only access.

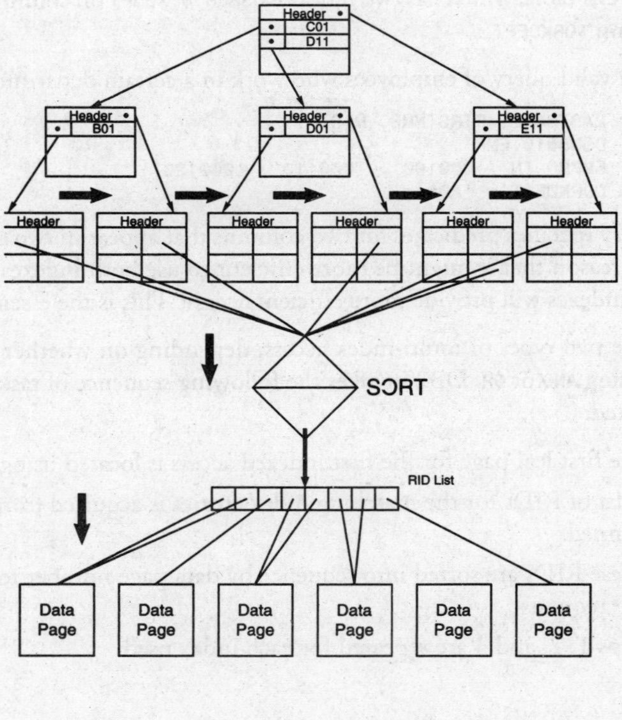

FIGURE 14.13.
List prefetch.

List prefetch performs the following tasks:

1. The first leaf page is located using a matching index scan.
2. A list of RIDs for the matching index entries is acquired from the leaf pages as they are scanned.
3. These RIDs can be sorted into sequence by data page number to reduce the number of I/O requests. If the index is at least 80 percent clustered, the sort is bypassed.
4. Using the ordered RID list, data pages are accessed to satisfy the request.

When the RIDs are sorted by list prefetch, the order in which they were retrieved from the index is changed. Therefore, an additional sort of the results might be required if an ORDER BY clause was specified. If an ORDER BY clause was not specified, the use of list prefetch will probably cause the results to be unordered, even though an index was used.

The term *skip sequential prefetch* is used to categorize the type of access that list prefetch performs on data pages. When the sorted RID list is used to retrieve data pages, list prefetch effectively performs a type of sequential prefetch, whereby only the needed data pages are accessed. Those that are not needed are skipped.

Multi-index access is another type of indexed access used by DB2. The idea behind multi-index access is to use more than one index for a single access path. For example, consider the DSN8510.EMP table, which has two indexes: DSN8510.XEMP1 on column EMPNO and DSN8510.XEMP2 on column WORKDEPT.

Here is a valid query of employees who work in a certain department:

```
SELECT   LASTNAME, FIRSTNME, MIDINIT
FROM     DSN8510.EMP
WHERE    EMPNO IN ('000100', '000110', '000120')
AND      WORKDEPT = 'A00';
```

This query specifies predicates for two columns that appear in two separate indexes. Doesn't it stand to reason that it might be more efficient to use both indexes than to estimate which of the two indexes will provide more efficient access? This is the essence of multi-index access.

There are two types of multi-index access, depending on whether the predicates are tied together using AND or OR. DB2 invokes the following sequence of tasks when multi-index access is requested:

1. The first leaf page for the first indexed access is located using a matching index scan.
2. A list of RIDs for the matching index entries is acquired from the leaf pages as they are scanned.
3. These RIDs are sorted into sequence by data page number to reduce the number of I/O requests.
4. Steps 1, 2, and 3 are repeated for each index used.

5. If the SQL statement being processed concatenated its predicates using the AND connector (such as in the sample query), the RID lists are intersected as shown in Figure 14.14. RID intersection is the process of combining multiple RID lists by keeping only the RIDs that exist in both RID lists.

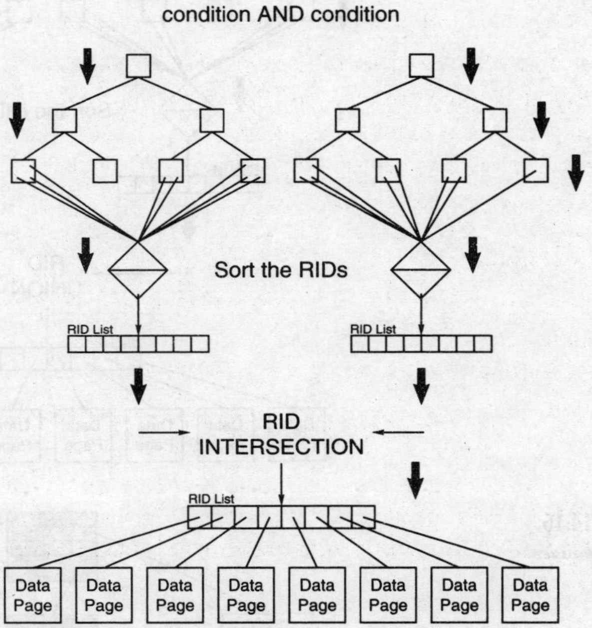

FIGURE 14.14.
Multi-index access (AND).

6. If the SQL statement being processed concatenated its predicates using the OR connector (such as the following query), the RID lists are combined using a UNION, as shown in Figure 14.15.

```
SELECT    LASTNAME, FIRSTNME, MIDINIT
FROM      DSN8510.EMP
WHERE     EMPNO IN ('000100', '000110', '000120')
OR        WORKDEPT = 'A00';
```

RID UNION is the process of combining multiple RID lists by appending all the RIDs into a single list and eliminating duplicates.

7. Using the final, combined RID list, data pages are accessed to satisfy the request. As with list prefetch, skip sequential prefetch is used to access these pages.

The final type of indexed access is *index lookaside*. Although index lookaside is technically not an access path but a technique employed by DB2, it is still appropriate to discuss it in the context of indexed access. Index lookaside optimizes the manner in which index pages can be accessed (see Figure 14.16).

FIGURE 14.15.
Multi-index access (OR).

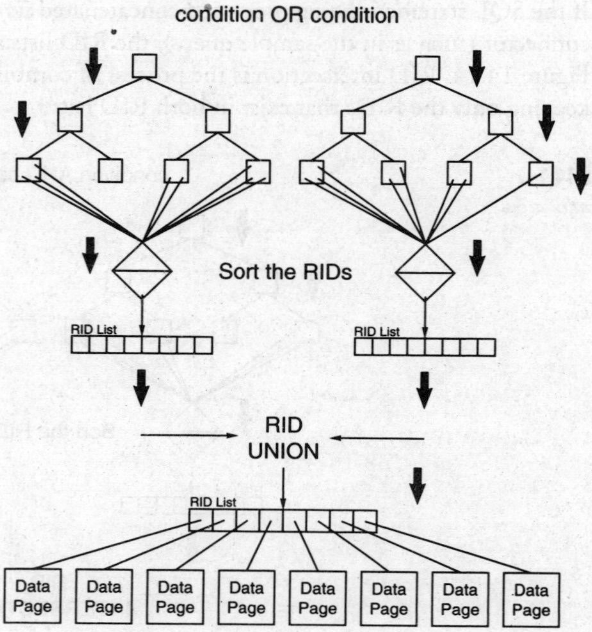

FIGURE 14.16.
Index lookaside.

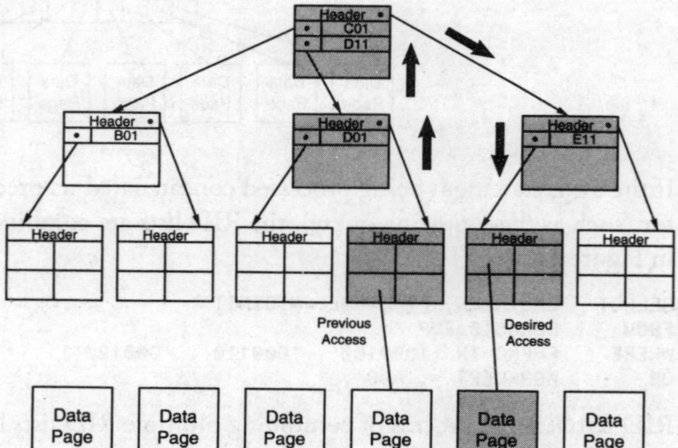

Normally, DB2 traverses the b-tree structure of the index to locate an index entry. This can involve significant overhead as DB2 checks the root and intermediate non-leaf index pages. When using index lookaside, the path length required to find a particular leaf page can be reduced. The index lookaside technique begins only after an initial index access has taken place. Using index lookaside, DB2 checks for the RID of the desired row first on the current leaf page and next on the immediately higher non-leaf page. If unsuccessful, DB2 then reverts to a standard index lookup.

By checking the current leaf page and the immediately higher non-leaf page, DB2 increases its chances of locating the desired RID sooner and adds only a minimal amount of overhead (because the ranges of values covered by the leaf and non-leaf pages are stored in cache memory upon first execution of the SELECT).

Query Parallelism

Another technique that can be applied by the optimizer is *query parallelism.* There are three types of query parallelism that DB2 can perform:

- Query I/O parallelism (as of DB2 V3)
- Query CP parallelism (as of DB2 V4)
- Query Sysplex parallelism (as of DB2 V5)

After the initial access path has been determined by the optimizer, an additional step can occur to determine whether parallelism is appropriate. The initial access path (pre-parallelism) is referred to as the *sequential plan.*

In general, when DB2 plans to use sequential prefetch for a single table or multiple tables against data in a partitioned tablespace, query parallelism can be invoked to activate multiple parallel tasks to access the data. A separate subtask MVS SRB is initiated for each parallel task.

Query I/O parallelism enables concurrent I/O streams to be initiated for a single query, as shown in Figure 14.17. This can significantly enhance the performance of I/O bound queries against partitioned tablespaces. Breaking the data access for the query into concurrent I/O streams executed in parallel should reduce the overall elapsed time for the query. With query I/O parallelism, DB2 is limited to operating on a single processor for each query.

FIGURE 14.17.
Query I/O parallelism.

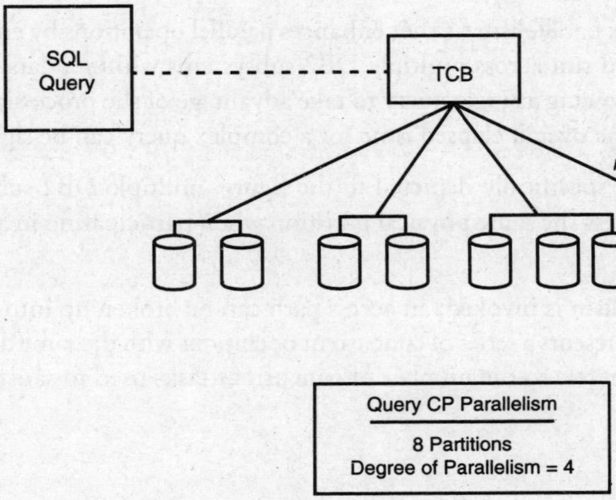

Version 4

Query CP parallelism enables multitasking of I/O streams and CPU processing within a query (see Figure 14.18). CP parallelism always uses I/O parallelism; it cannot be invoked separately. In query CP parallelism, a large query is decomposed into multiple smaller queries that can be executed concurrently with one another on multiple processors. Query CP parallelism should further reduce the elapsed time for a query.

FIGURE 14.18.
Query CP parallelism.

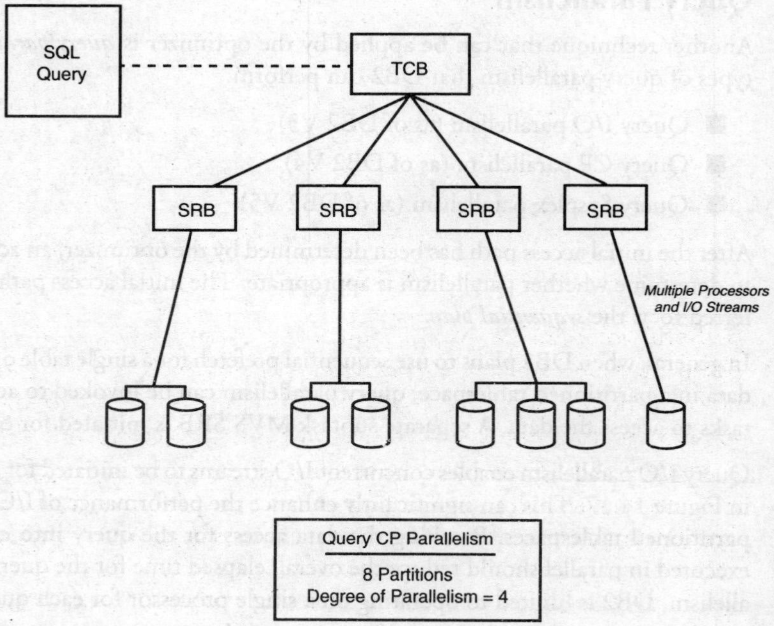

Version 5

Query Sysplex parallelism further enhances parallel operations by enabling a single query to be broken up and run across multiple DB2 subsystems within a data-sharing group (see Figure 14.19). By allowing a single query to take advantage of the processing power of multiple DB2 subsystems, the overall elapsed time for a complex query can be significantly decreased.

Although not specifically depicted in the figure, multiple DB2 subsystems in a data-sharing group can access the same physical partition when participating in a query Sysplex parallelism operation.

When parallelism is invoked, an access path can be broken up into parallel groups. Each parallel group represents a series of concurrent operations with the same degree of parallelism. *Degree of parallelism* refers to the number of concurrent tasks used to satisfy the query.

FIGURE 14.19.
Query Sysplex parallelism.

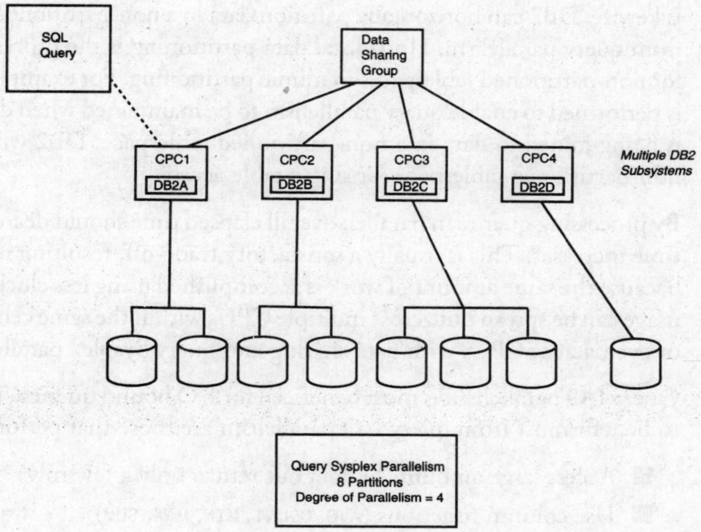

Figures 14.17, 14.18, and 14.19 show a tablespace scan accessing a partitioned tablespace with a degree of parallelism of 4. The degree of parallelism is determined by the optimizer based upon the estimated CPU and I/O cost using partition-level statistics stored in the following DB2 catalog tables:

- `SYSCOLDISTSTATS` contains partition-level, non-uniform distribution statistics for the key columns of each partitioned index.
- `SYSCOLSTATS` contains general partition-level statistics (such as value ranges and cardinality) for each column identified to `RUNSTATS`.
- `SYSTABSTATS` contains partition-level statistics (such as cardinality, compression information, and active pages) for each tablespace partition.
- `SYSINDEXSTATS` contains partition-level statistics (such as cardinality, cluster ratio, and index levels) for each index partition.

The degree of parallelism can be downgraded at runtime if host variables indicate that only a portion of the data is to be accessed or if sufficient bufferpool space is not available.

It is particularly important to note that DB2 might choose not to issue one parallel task per partition. Determination of the degree of parallelism is based upon the information in the DB2 Catalog, the number of partitions for the accessed tablespaces, system resources, and the nature of the query. Each parallel task can access the following:

- An entire partition
- A portion of a single partition
- Multiple partitions
- Portions of multiple partitions

Likewise, DB2 can horizontally partition data in a non-partitioned tablespace in order to benefit from query parallelism. Horizontal data partitioning is the process of creating range predicates for non-partitioned tablespaces to mimic partitioning. For example, horizontal data partitioning is performed to enable query parallelism to be maintained when data in a partitioned tablespace is being joined to data in a non-partitioned tablespace. DB2 will not horizontally partition a non-partitioned tablespace for single table access.

By processing queries in parallel, overall elapsed time should decrease significantly, even if CPU time increases. This is usually a satisfactory trade-off, resulting in an overall performance gain because the same amount of work is accomplished using less clock time. Additionally, the CPU usage can be spread out across multiple CPUs within the same central processor complex (CPC) or even across CPCs with data sharing and query Sysplex parallelism.

Query I/O parallelism is most beneficial for I/O bound queries. The types of queries that stand to benefit most from query I/O parallelism are those that perform the following functions:

- Access large amounts of data but return only a few rows
- Use column functions (`AVG`, `COUNT`, `MIN`, `MAX`, `SUM`)
- Access long rows

Query CP parallelism is most beneficial for scans of large partitioned tablespaces, and query Sysplex parallelism is most beneficial for complex queries that require a lot of processing power.

Query Sysplex Parallelism Terms and Issues

The DB2 subsystem that originates the SQL query is referred to as the *parallelism coordinator*. A member that assists in the processing of a parallel query is called a *parallelism assistant*. Data must be returned to the parallelism coordinator from each parallelism assistant. This is accomplished in one of two ways. When work files are required (for example, for sorting), the parallelism coordinator can access the data directly from the work files. Otherwise, the cross-system coupling facility is used to return the data to the parallelism coordinator.

Restrictions on Query Parallelism Usage

Note the following query parallelism restrictions:

- For all types of query parallelism, a limited partition scan can be invoked for queries against a single table only.
- Query CP parallelism and query Sysplex parallelism require Type 2 indexes.
- Query Sysplex parallelism cannot be used with multiple index access, list prefetch, or queries using RR and RS isolation levels.
- For cursors defined using the `WITH HOLD` clause, the only type of parallelism that can be deployed is query I/O parallelism.

- Parallelism is for queries only; as such, only SELECT statements can benefit from parallelism. Furthermore, the SELECT statement must not be in an updateable or ambiguous cursor.
- The CURRENTDATA(NO) bind parameter must be specified for parallelism to be invoked.
- Parallelism cannot be used with multicolumn merge scan joins, type-N hybrid joins, outer joins, index access for an IN list, materialized views, or materialized nested table expressions, and it cannot be used across UNION query blocks, when accessing a temporary table, or when EXISTS is specified.

NOTE

A type-N hybrid join retrieves the inner table RIDs using a clustered index (when SORTN_JOIN="N" in the PLAN_TABLE).

Join Methods

The optimizer has a series of methods to enable DB2 to join tables. When more than one DB2 table is referenced in the FROM clause of a single SQL SELECT statement, a request is being made to join tables. Based on the join criteria, a series of instructions must be carried out to combine the data from the tables.

How does DB2 do this? Multitable queries are broken down into several access paths. The DB2 optimizer selects two of the tables and creates an optimized access path for accomplishing that join. When that join is satisfied, the results are joined to another table. This process continues until all specified tables have been joined.

When joining tables, the access path defines how each single table will be accessed and also how it will be joined with the next table. Thus, each access path chooses not only an access path strategy (for example, a tablespace scan versus indexed access) but also a join algorithm. The join algorithm, or join method, defines the basic procedure for combining the tables. DB2 has three methods for joining tables:

- Nested loop join
- Merge scan join
- Hybrid join

Each method operates differently from the others but achieves the same results. However, the choice of join method has an important effect on the performance of the join. Each join method used by DB2 is engineered such that, given a set of statistics, optimum performance can be achieved. Therefore, you should understand the different join methods and the factors that cause them to be chosen.

How do these join methods operate? A basic series of steps is common to each join method. In general, the first decision to be made is which table should be processed first. This table is referred to as the *outer table*. After this decision is made, a series of operations are performed on the outer table to prepare it for joining. Rows from that table are then combined to the second table, called the *inner table*. A series of operations are also performed on the inner table either before the join occurs, as the join occurs, or both. This general join procedure is depicted in Figure 14.20.

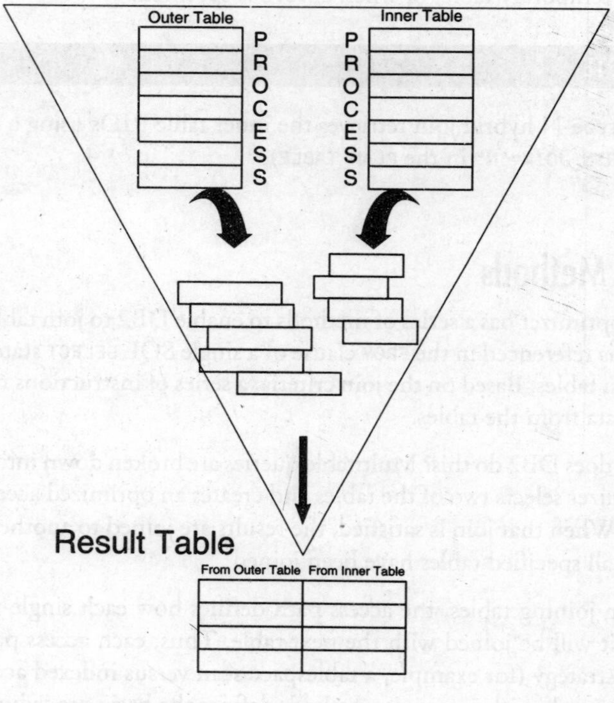

FIGURE 14.20.
Generalized join process.

Although all joins are composed of similar steps, each of DB2's three join methods are strikingly dissimilar when you get beyond the generalities.

The optimizer understands the advantages and disadvantages of each method and how the use of that method can affect performance. Based on the current statistics in the DB2 Catalog, the optimizer understands also which tables are best for the inner table and the outer table.

Nested Loop Join

The most common type of join method is the *nested loop join*, which is shown in Figure 14.21. A qualifying row is identified in the outer table, and then the inner table is scanned searching for a match. (A *qualifying row* is one in which the predicates for columns in the table match.)

When the inner table scan is complete, another qualifying row in the outer table is identified. The inner table is scanned for a match again, and so on. The repeated scanning of the inner table is usually accomplished with an index so as not to incur undue I/O costs.

FIGURE 14.21.
Nested loop join.

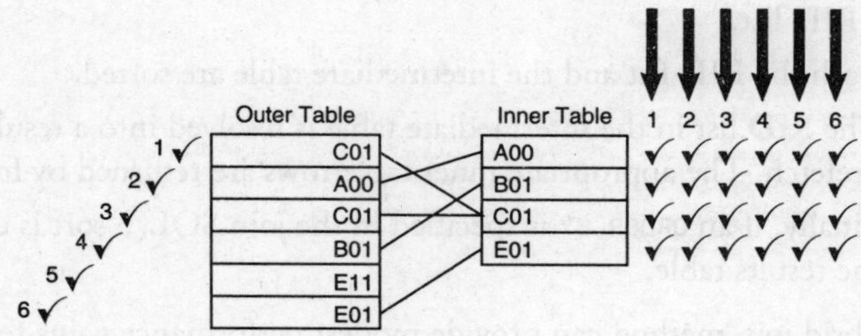

Merge Scan Join

The second type of join method that can be used by DB2 is the *merge scan join*. In a merge scan join, the tables to be joined are ordered by the keys. This ordering can be the result of either a sort or indexed access (see Figure 14.22). After ensuring that both the outer and inner tables are properly sequenced, each table is read sequentially, and the join columns are matched. Neither table is read more than once during a merge scan join.

FIGURE 14.22.
Merge scan join.

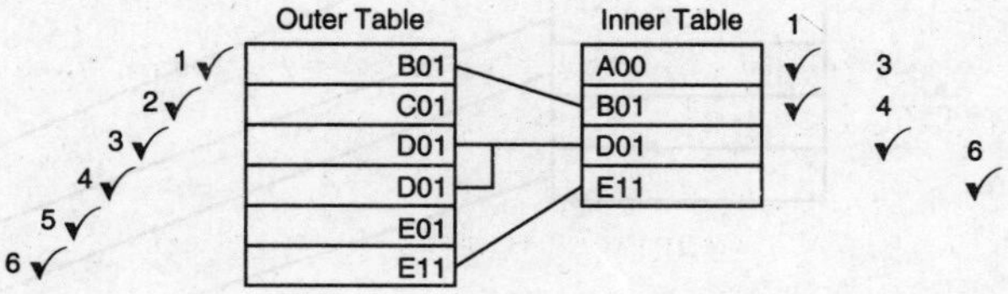

Hybrid Join

The third type of join, the hybrid join, was introduced in DB2 V2.3. The *hybrid join* is a mixture of the other join methods and list prefetch. Figure 14.23 shows the processing flow used by the hybrid join.

The hybrid join works as follows:

1. Using either indexed access or a sort, qualifying outer table rows are accessed in order by the join columns of the inner table.
2. As the outer table rows are accessed in sequence, they are compared to an appropriate index on the inner table. In a hybrid join, there must be an index on the join columns of the inner table.

3. The index entry RIDs from the qualifying inner table are combined with the required columns of the outer table, forming an intermediate table. This intermediate table then consists of the selected outer table columns and the RIDs of the matching rows from the index on the inner table. The RIDs are also placed in the RID pool, forming a RID list.
4. Both the RID list and the intermediate table are sorted.
5. The RID list in the intermediate table is resolved into a results table using list prefetch. The appropriate inner table rows are returned by following the RIDs.
6. Finally, if an `ORDER BY` is specified in the join SQL, a sort is usually required to order the results table.

The hybrid join method can provide modest performance gains for applications that process medium-sized table joins. However, most shops have few access paths that use this type of join.

FIGURE 14.23.
A hybrid join.

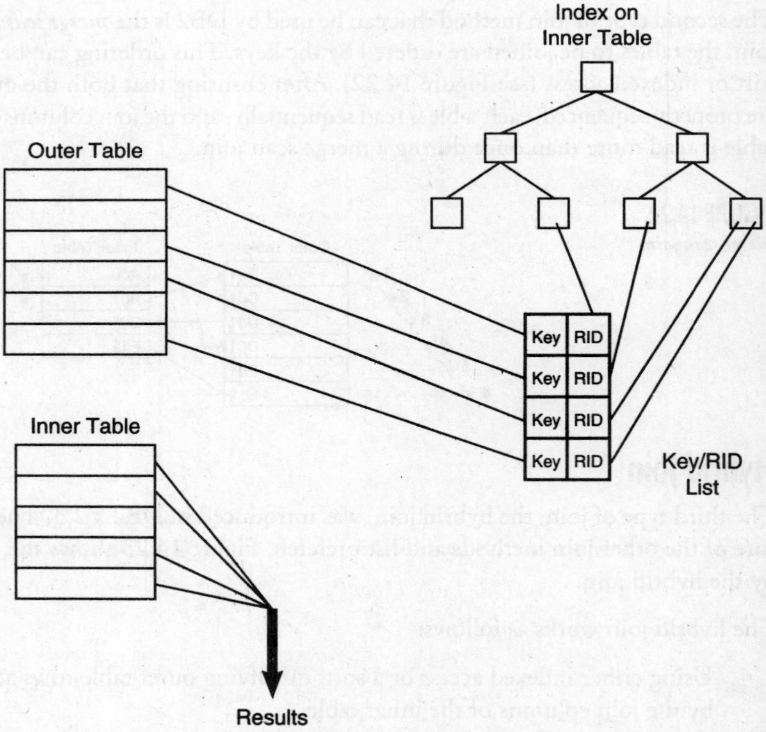

NOTE

Any of the three join methods can be used for both inner and outer joins.

Join Method Comparison

You might be wondering which join method DB2 uses in a given circumstance. Although there is no foolproof method to determine which method is used, there are some guidelines:

- Merge scan joins are usually chosen when an appropriate index is unavailable on one of the tables. This involves sorting and can use a high amount of overhead.
- Nested loop joins are very effective when an index exists on the inner table, thereby reducing the overhead of the repeated table scan.
- The smaller of the two tables being joined is usually chosen as the outer table in a nested loop join. This reduces the impact of the repeated inner table scan.
- The hybrid join is chosen only if an index exists on the inner table.
- Query parallelism can be combined with any of the join methods, enabling joins to be processed in parallel.

Many shops are biased toward the nested loop join, feeling that nested loop joins almost always outperform merge scan joins. However, the performance of the merge scan join has been significantly enhanced over the life of DB2. As of DB2 V3 and later, merge scan joins are a viable, production-quality join method.

See Figure 14.24 for an estimate of the performance of the join methods as a function of the number of qualifying rows being joined.

FIGURE 14.24.
Relative join performance.

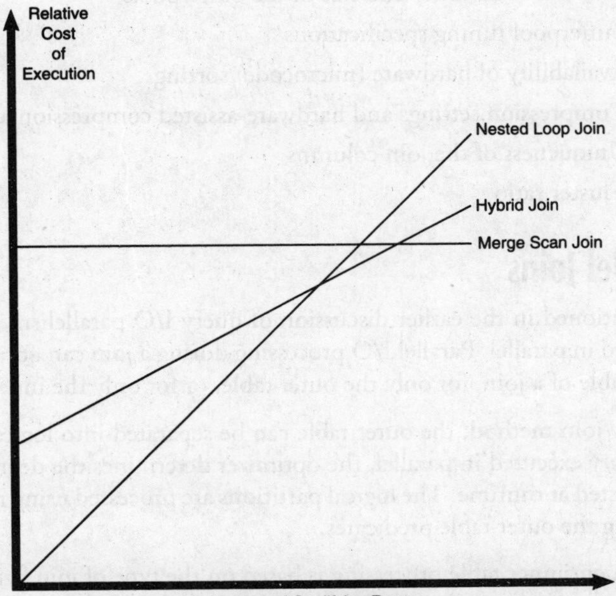

In general, the guidelines are as follows:

- The nested loop join is preferred in terms of execution cost when a small number of rows qualify for the join.
- The nested loop join is preferred whenever the `OPTIMIZE FOR n ROWS` clause is used, regardless of the number of qualifying rows.
- As the number of qualifying rows increases, the merge scan join becomes the preferred method.
- Finally, for a small number of cases with a medium number of rows, the hybrid join is the best performer.

These generalizations are purposefully vague. The exact number of qualifying rows for these cut-offs depends on many influencing factors. These factors include, but are not limited to, the following:

- Database design
- Type of CPU
- Type of DASD device
- Use of DASD cache
- Version of DB2
- Data-sharing environment
- Amount of memory and size of the bufferpools
- Bufferpool tuning specifications
- Availability of hardware (microcode) sorting
- Compression settings and hardware-assisted compression availability
- Uniqueness of the join columns
- Cluster ratio

Parallel Joins

As mentioned in the earlier discussion of query I/O parallelism, it is possible for joins to be executed in parallel. Parallel I/O processing during a join can occur for both the outer and the inner table of a join, for only the outer table, or for only the inner table.

For any join method, the outer table can be separated into logical partitions. As is true with any query executed in parallel, the optimizer determines the degree of parallelism, which can be adjusted at runtime. The logical partitions are processed using multiple parallel I/O streams applying the outer table predicates.

Subsequent inner table processing is based on the type of join being performed.

Nested Loop Join and Parallelism

To perform a nested loop join in parallel, the key ranges for the inner table logical partitions might need to be adjusted to match the logical partitioning of the outer table. This ensures that the number of logical partitions is equivalent for the outer and inner tables. Likewise, if the outer table was not processed using parallelism, the filtered outer table rows will need to be logically partitioned to match the inner table partitioning. In both cases, the logical partitioning is accomplished using the ESA sort assist. It is possible, however, that the outer table rows need not be sorted. In this case, the ESA sort assist will simply adjust the outer table key range to match the partitioning key range of the inner table.

Additionally, if the inner table is not partitioned, it can be horizontally partitioned to enable parallelism to continue. Alternatively, the inner table can be passed to the ESA sort assist, causing sort output to be partitioned to match outer table sort output.

Multiple parallel I/O streams are then used to join the filtered outer table rows to the inner table using the nested loop procedure described previously. The rows are returned in random order unless an additional sort is required for `ORDER BY`, `GROUP BY`, or `DISTINCT`.

Merge Scan Join and Parallelism

To enable parallel merge scan joining, outer table rows are passed into the ESA sort assist, causing the sort output to be repartitioned to match the logical partitioning of the inner table. The outer table access could have been either parallel or non-parallel. A single column merge scan join is then executed using multiple parallel I/O streams. (Query I/O parallelism cannot sort all of the join columns for merge scan join.)

If the inner table is not partitioned, it can be horizontally partitioned to enable parallelism to continue.

The rows are returned in random order unless an additional sort is required for `ORDER BY`, `GROUP BY`, or `DISTINCT`.

Hybrid Join and Parallelism

Hybrid join processing with query I/O parallelism also passes outer table rows to the ESA sort assist to logically repartition the output to match the logical partitioning of the inner table.

After the outer table results are repartitioned to match the logical partitioning of the inner table, hybrid join processing is executed using parallel I/O streams. The rows are returned in page number order unless an additional sort is required for `ORDER BY`, `GROUP BY`, or `DISTINCT`.

For parallelism to be invoked on the inner table, a highly clustered index must exist on the join columns. If such an index does not exist, the sort of the RID list and intermediate table will prevent parallel access to the inner table.

Parallel Join Notes

In any case, remember that during join processing, parallel access can occur as follows:

- On just the inner table
- On just the outer table
- On both the inner and outer tables
- On neither the inner or outer tables

Query parallelism is designed to enable DB2 to multitask when accessing data in partitioned tablespaces. When joining a partitioned table to a non-partitioned table, DB2 might choose to logically partition the non-partitioned table to enable parallel access to continue across the join.

Other Operations Performed by the Optimizer

So far, you have learned about sequential access methods, indexed access methods, and join methods. The optimizer can perform other operations as well. For example, using a feature known as *predicate transitive closure,* the optimizer can make a performance decision to satisfy a query using a predicate that isn't even coded in the SQL statement being optimized. Consider the following SQL statements:

```
SELECT  D.DEPTNAME, E.LASTNAME
FROM    DSN8510.DEPT   D,
        DSN8510.EMP    E
WHERE   D.DEPTNO = E.WORKDEPT
AND     D.DEPTNO = 'A00'
```

and

```
SELECT  D.DEPTNAME, E.LASTNAME
FROM    DSN8510.DEPT     D,
        DSN8510.EMP      E
WHERE   D.DEPTNO = E.WORKDEPT
AND     E.WORKDEPT = 'A00'
```

These two statements are functionally equivalent. Because `DEPTNO` and `WORKDEPT` are always equal, you could specify either column in the second predicate. The query is usually more efficient, however, if the predicate is applied to the larger of the two tables (in this case, `DSN8510.DEPT`), thereby reducing the number of qualifying rows.

With predicate transitive closure, the programmer doesn't have to worry about this factor. DB2 considers the access path for both columns regardless of which is coded in the predicate. Therefore, DB2 can optimize a query based on predicates that are not even coded by the programmer.

Predicate transitive closure is not performed on every type of predicate. As of DB2 V5, the `IN` and `LIKE` predicates are excluded from predicate transitive closure. The DB2 optimizer is currently not capable of determining when predicate transitive closure could be useful for the `IN` and `LIKE` predicates.

The DB2 optimizer is responsible also for generating optimized access paths for subqueries. Remember from Chapter 1 that there are two types of subqueries: non-correlated and correlated. The type of subquery determines the type of access path that DB2 chooses.

The access path for a non-correlated subquery always processes the subselect first. This type of processing is called *inside-out subquery access.* The table in the subselect is the inner table and is processed first. The table in the outer SELECT is the outer table and is processed last, hence the name inside-out processing. Consider the following subquery:

```
SELECT   LASTNAME
FROM     DSN8510.EMP
WHERE    WORKDEPT IN
         (SELECT  DEPTNO
          FROM    DSN8510.DEPT
          WHERE   DEPTNAME = 'OPERATIONS');
```

The access path formulated by the optimizer for a non-correlated subquery is shown in Figure 14.25.

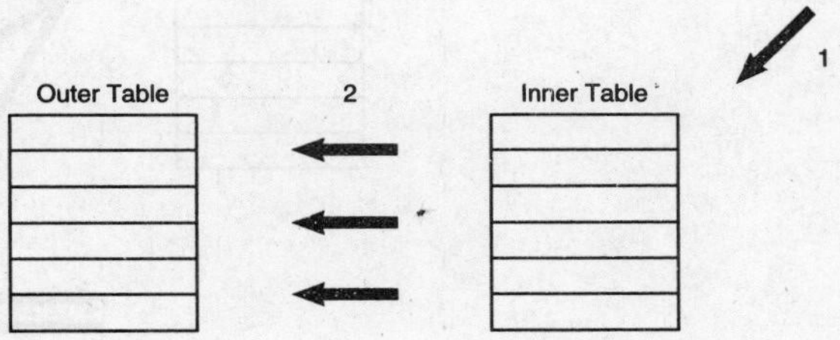

FIGURE 14.25.
A non-correlated subquery.

The access path for a non-correlated subquery consists of the following steps:

1. Access the inner table, the one in the subselect (DSN8510.DEPT), using either a tablespace scan or an index.
2. Sort the results and remove all duplicates.
3. Place the results in an intermediate table.
4. Access the outer table, comparing all qualifying rows to those in the intermediate results table for a match.

A correlated subquery, on the other hand, is performed using *outside-in-outside subquery access.* Consider the following correlated subquery:

```
SELECT   LASTNAME, SALARY
FROM     DSN8510.EMP   E
WHERE    EXISTS
          (SELECT  PROJNO
           FROM    DSN8510.EMPPROJACT   P
           WHERE   P.EMPNO = E.EMPNO);
```

The access path formulated by the optimizer for this correlated subquery consists of the following steps:

1. Access the outer table, which is the DSN8510.EMP table, using either a tablespace scan or indexed access.
2. For each qualifying outer table row, evaluate the subquery for the inner table.
3. Pass the results of the inner table subquery to the outer SELECT one row at a time. (In this case, the row is not returned because of the EXISTS predicate; instead, a flag is set to true or false.)
4. Evaluate the outer query predicate using the inner query results (row by row). This causes a round-robin type of access such as that shown in Figure 14.26.

FIGURE 14.26.
A correlated subquery.

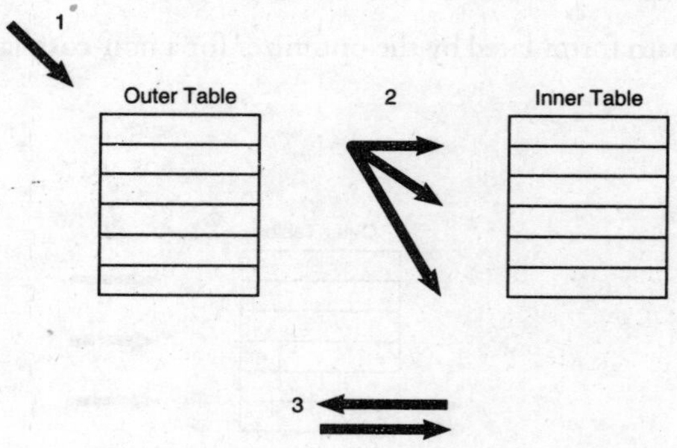

Some further notes on subqueries follow. In general, the subselect portion of a correlated subquery is reevaluated for each qualifying outer row. However, if the subquery returns a single value, it can be saved in an intermediate work area such that it need not be reevaluated for every qualifying outer table row. An example of a correlated subquery where this is possible follows:

```
SELECT   LASTNAME
FROM     DSN8510.EMP E1
WHERE    SALARY <
         (SELECT  AVG(SALARY)
          FROM    DSN8510.EMP  E2
          WHERE   E1.WORKDEPT = E2.WORKDEPT)
```

One average salary value is returned for each department. Thus, only a single inner table evaluation is required for each department, instead of a continual reevaluation for each qualifying outer table row.

Although subqueries are often the most obvious way to access data from multiple tables, they might not be the most efficient. A good rule of thumb is to recode subqueries as joins, whenever possible. The DB2 optimizer generally has greater flexibility in choosing efficient access paths for joins than it does for subqueries. For example, the following query

```
SELECT   LASTNAME, SALARY
FROM     DSN8510.EMP
WHERE    WORKDEPT IN
         (SELECT DEPTNO
          FROM   DSN8510.DEPT
          WHERE  ADMRDEPT = 'A00')
```

can be recoded as a join:

```
SELECT   E.LASTNAME, E.SALARY
FROM     DSN8510.EMP     E,
         DSN8510.DEPT    D
WHERE    E.WORKDEPT = D.DEPTNO
AND      D.ADMRDEPT = 'A00'
```

One final type of operation that can be performed by the optimizer is the optimization of queries based on views. DB2 employs one of two methods when accessing data in views: view merge or view materialization.

View merge is the more efficient of the two methods. Using this technique, DB2 will merge the SQL in the view DDL with the SQL accessing the view. The merged SQL is then used to formulate an access path against the base tables in the views.

View materialization is chosen when DB2 determines that it is not possible to merge the SQL in the view DDL with the SQL accessing the view. Instead of combining the two SQL statements into a single statement, view materialization creates an intermediate work table using the view SQL and then executes the SELECT from the view against the temporary table. Consult Table 14.6 to determine when view materialization is required.

Table 14.6. When does view materialization occur?

SELECT *from View*	DISTINCT	GROUP BY	*Column Function*	*Column Function w/*DISTINCT
		SELECT in DDL		
Join	MAT	MAT	MAT	MAT
DISTINCT	MAT	MER	MER	MAT
GROUP BY	MAT	MAT	MAT	MAT
Column Function	MAT	MAT	MAT	MAT
Column Function w/DISTINCT	MAT	MAT	MAT	MAT
SELECT subset of View Cols	MAT	MER	MER	MER

If the SELECT from the view contains any of the components listed in the left column, combined with the view DDL containing any of the components listed along the top, analyze the column entry in the table. MAT represents view materialization; MER represents view merge. If the view SELECT/view DDL combination does not appear in the table, view merge will be used.

Summary

The optimizer combines access path strategies to form an efficient access path. However, not all the strategies are compatible, as shown in Table 14.7. As you can plainly see, the optimizer must follow a mountain of rules as it performs its optimization.

Here are some further notes on Table 14.7:

- Each access path is composed of at least one strategy and possibly many. A *Yes* in any block in the matrix indicates that the two strategies can be used together in a single access path; a *No* indicates incompatibility.
- For the join methods, the matrix entries apply to any one portion of the join (that is, the access path for either the inner table or the outer table).
- Sequential detection is always invoked in conjunction with sequential prefetch.
- Index-only access must be used in conjunction with one of the index access path strategies.
- For the hybrid join method, the inner table is always accessed with an index using a form of list prefetch; the outer table can be accessed using any access method deemed by the optimizer to be most efficient.

You have covered a large number of topics under the heading of the DB2 optimizer. This should drive home the point that the optimizer is a complex piece of software. Although we know quite a bit about what the optimizer can do, we know little about how it decides what to do. This is not surprising. IBM has invested a great amount of time, money, and effort in DB2 and has also staked a large portion of its future on DB2's success. IBM wouldn't want to publish the internals of the optimizer, thus enabling competitors to copy its functionality.

The optimizer and the access paths it chooses are the most complex parts of DB2. Even though the subject is complex, an understanding of the optimizer is crucial for every user. This chapter fulfills this requirement. But where does the DB2 optimizer get the information to formulate efficient access paths? Where else—from the DB2 Catalog, the subject of the next chapter.

Table 14.7. Access path strategy compatibility matrix.

	Simple Tablespace Scan	*Partitioned Tablespace Scan*	*Segmented Tablespace Scan*	*Sequential Prefetch/ Detection*	*Query Parallelism*	*Direct Index Lookup*	*Matching Index Scan*
Simple Tablespace Scan	- - -	No	No	Yes	Yes	No	No
Partitioned Tablespace Scan	No	- - -	Yes	Yes	Yes	No	No
Segmented Tablespace Scan	No	No	- - -	Yes	Yes	No	No
Sequential Prefetch/ Detection	Yes	Yes	Yes	- - -	Yes	No	Yes
Query Parallelism	No	Yes	No	Yes	- - -	No	Yes
Direct Index Lookup	No	No	No	No	No	- - -	Yes
Matching Index Scan	No	No	No	Yes	Yes	Yes	- - -
Nonmatching Index Scan	No	No	No	Yes	Yes	No	No
Index Lookaside	No	No	No	No	No	No	Yes

continues

Table 14.7. continued

	Simple Tablespace Scan	*Partitioned Tablespace Scan*	*Segmented Tablespace Scan*	*Sequential Prefetch/ Detection*	*Query Parallelism*	*Direct Index Lookup*	*Matching Index Scan*
Multi-Index Access	No	No	No	Yes	No	No	Yes
Index-Only Access	No	No	No	Yes	Yes	Yes	Yes
List Prefetch	No	No	No	No	No	No	Yes
Nested Loop Join	Yes	Yes	Yes	Yes	Yes	Yes	Yes
Merge Scan Join	Yes	Yes	Yes	Yes	Yes	Yes	Yes
Hybrid Join	Yes	Yes	Yes	Yes	Yes	Yes	Yes

	Non-Matching Index Scan	*Index Lookaside*	*Multi-Index Access*	*Index-Only Access*	*List Prefetch*	*Nested Loop Join*	*Merge Scan*	*Hybrid Join*
Simple Tablespace Scan	No	No	No	No	No	Yes	Yes	Yes
Partitioned Tablespace Scan	No	No	No	No	No	Yes	Yes	Yes
Segmented Tablespace Scan	No	No	No	No	No	Yes	Yes	Yes
Sequential Prefetch/ Detection	Yes	No	No	Yes	No	Yes	Yes	Yes
Query Parallelism	Yes	No	No	Yes	No	Yes	Yes	Yes
Direct Index Lookup	No	No	No	Yes	No	Yes	Yes	Yes
Matching Index Scan	No	Yes	Yes	Yes	Yes	Yes	Yes	Yes
Nonmatching Index Scan	- - -	Yes	No	Yes	No	Yes	Yes	Yes
Index Lookaside	Yes	- - -	No	Yes	No	Yes	Yes	Yes

continues

Table 14.7. continued

	Non-Matching Index Scan	Index Lookaside	Multi-Index Access	Index-Only Access	List Prefetch	Nested Loop Join	Merge Scan	Hybrid Join
Multi-Index Access	No	No	---	No	Yes	Yes	Yes	Yes
Index-Only Access	Yes	Yes	No	---	No	Yes	Yes	Yes
List Prefetch	No	No	Yes	No	---	Yes	Yes	Yes
Nested Loop Join	Yes	Yes	Yes	Yes	Yes	---	---	---
Merge Scan Join	Yes	Yes	Yes	Yes	Yes	---	---	---
Hybrid Join	Yes	Yes	Yes	Yes	Yes	---	---	---

15

The Table-Based Infrastructure of DB2

Appropriately enough for a relational database, DB2 has a set of tables that functions as a repository for all DB2 objects. These tables define the infrastructure of DB2, enabling simple detection of and access to DB2 objects. Two sets of tables store all the data related to DB2 objects: the DB2 Catalog and the DB2 Directory.

The DB2 Catalog

The entire DBMS relies on the system catalog, or the DB2 Catalog. If the DB2 optimizer is the heart and soul of DB2, the DB2 Catalog is its brain. The knowledge base of every object known to DB2 is stored in the DB2 Catalog.

What Is the DB2 Catalog?

See Table 15.1 for a short description of each table in the DB2 Catalog. For a more complete description, see Appendix B, "The DB2 Catalog Tables."

Table 15.1. Tables in the DB2 Catalog.

Table	*Contents*
IPNAMES	To set up distributed TCP/IP connections
LOCATIONS	Contains distributed location information for every accessible remote server
LULIST	Contains the list of LUNAMEs for a given distributed location (when multiple LUNAMEs are associated with a single location)
LUMODES	Information on distributed conversation limits
LUNAMES	Contains information for every SNA client or server that communicates with the DB2 subsystem
MODESELECT	Information assigning mode names to conversations supporting outgoing SQL requests
SYSCHECKDEP	Column references for CHECK constraints
SYSCHECKS	CHECK constraint specifications
SYSCOLAUTH	The UPDATE privileges held by DB2 users on table or view columns
SYSCOLDIST	The nonuniform distribution statistics for the 10 most frequently occurring values in a column
SYSCOLDISTSTATS	The nonuniform distribution statistics for the 10 most frequently occurring values for the first key column in a partitioned index

Table	Contents
SYSCOLSTATS	The partition statistics for selected columns
SYSCOLUMNS	Information about every column of every DB2 table and view
SYSCOPY	Information on the execution of DB2 utilities required by DB2 recovery
SYSDATABASE	Information about every DB2 database
SYSDBAUTH	Database privileges held by DB2 users
SYSDBRM	DBRM information only for DBRMs bound into DB2 plans
SYSDUMMY1	Contains no information; this table is for use in SQL statements requiring a table reference without regard to data content
SYSFIELDS	Information on field procedures implemented for DB2 tables
SYSFOREIGNKEYS	Information about all columns participating in foreign keys
SYSINDEXES	Information about every DB2 index
SYSINDEXPART	Information about the physical structure and storage of every DB2 index
SYSINDEXSTATS	Partitioned index statistics by partition
SYSKEYS	Information about every column of every DB2 index
SYSLINKS	Information about the links between DB2 Catalog tables
SYSPACKAGE	Information about every package known to DB2
SYSPACKAUTH	Package privileges held by DB2 users
SYSPACKDEP	A cross-reference of DB2 objects required for DB2 packages
SYSPACKLIST	The package list for plans bound specifying packages
SYSPACKSTMT	All SQL statements contained in each DB2 package
SYSPKSYSTEM	The systems (such as CICS, IMS, or batch) enabled for DB2 packages
SYSPLAN	Information about every plan known to DB2
SYSPLANAUTH	Plan privileges held by DB2 users
SYSPLANDEP	A cross-reference of DB2 objects required by DB2 plans
SYSPLSYSTEM	The systems (such as CICS, IMS, or batch) enabled for DB2 plans
SYSPROCEDURES	The stored procedures available to the DB2 subsystem
SYSRELS	The referential integrity information for every relationship defined to DB2

continues

Table 15.1. continued

Table	*Contents*
SYSRESAUTH	Resource privileges held by DB2 users
SYSSTMT	All SQL statements contained in each DB2 plan bound from a DBRM
SYSSTOGROUP	Information about every DB2 storage group
SYSSTRINGS	Character conversion information
SYSSYNONYMS	Information about every DB2 synonym
SYSTABAUTH	Table privileges held by DB2 users
SYSTABLEPART	Information about the physical structure and storage of every DB2 tablespace
SYSTABLES	Information about every DB2 table
SYSTABLESPACE	Information about every DB2 tablespace
SYSTABSTATS	Partitioned tablespace statistics by partition
SYSUSERAUTH	System privileges held by DB2 users
SYSVIEWDEP	A cross-reference of DB2 objects required by DB2 views
SYSVIEWS	The SQL CREATE VIEW statement for every DB2 view
SYSVLTREE	A portion of the internal representation of complex or long views
SYSVOLUMES	A cross-reference of DASD volumes assigned to DB2 storage groups
SYSVTREE	The first 4,000 bytes of the internal representation of the view; the remaining portion of longer or complex views is stored in SYSVLTREE
USERNAMES	Outbound and inbound ID translation information

NOTE

Version 4

Three tables were added to the DB2 Catalog for DB2 V4—one to house stored procedure information (SYSIBM.SYSPROCEDURES) and two to store information on table check constraints (SYSIBM.SYSCHECKS and SYSIBM.SYSCHECKDEP).

NOTE

Version 5

Eight tables were added to the DB2 Catalog for DB2 V5. Prior to DB2 V5, six of those tables were stored in the Communication Database, also known as the CDB. The CDB was used to describe the connections of a local DB2 subsystem to other systems. The CDB tables were housed in a separate database—DSNDDF. As of V5, the tables were renamed and moved into the DB2 Catalog. The CDB tables that have been renamed and rolled into the DB2 Catalog since DB2 V5 are as follows:

Old CDB Table Name	*V5 DB2 Catalog Table Name*
SYSIBM.SYSLOCATIONS	SYSIBM.LOCATIONS
SYSIBM.SYSLULIST	SYSIBM.LULIST
SYSIBM.SYSLUMODES	SYSIBM.LUMODES
SYSIBM.SYSLUNAMES	SYSIBM.LUNAMES
SYSIBM.SYSMODESELECT	SYSIBM.MODESELECT
SYSIBM.SYSUSERNAMES	SYSIBM.USERNAMES

The two other tables added to the DB2 Catalog for DB2 V5 are `SYSIBM.IPNAMES` and `SYSIBM.SYSDUMMY1`.

The DB2 Catalog is composed of 12 tablespaces and 54 tables all in a single database, `DSNDB06`. Each DB2 Catalog table maintains data about an aspect of the DB2 environment. In that respect, the DB2 Catalog functions as a data dictionary for DB2, supporting and maintaining data about the DB2 environment. (A *data dictionary* maintains meta-data, or data about data.) The DB2 Catalog records all the information required by DB2 for the following functional areas:

Objects	STOGROUPS, databases, tablespaces, partitions, tables, columns, views, synonyms, aliases, indexes, index keys, foreign keys, relationships, plans, packages, and DBRMs
Security	Database privileges, plan privileges, system privileges, table privileges, view privileges, and use privileges
Utility	Image copy data sets, `REORG` executions, `LOAD` executions, and object organization efficiency information
Distribution	How DB2 subsystems are connected for data distribution and DRDA usage
Environmental	Links and relationships between the DB2 Catalog tables and other control information

How does the DB2 Catalog support data about these areas? For the most part, the tables of the DB2 Catalog cannot be modified using standard SQL data manipulation language statements. You cannot use INSERT statements, DELETE statements, or UPDATE statements (with a few exceptions) to modify these tables. Instead, the DB2 Catalog operates as a semiactive, integrated, and nonsubvertible data dictionary. The definitions of these three adjectives follow.

First, the DB2 Catalog is said to be *semiactive.* An active dictionary is built, maintained, and used as the result of the creation of the objects defined to the dictionary. In other words, as the user is utilizing the intrinsic functions of the DBMS, meta-data is being accumulated and populated in the active data dictionary.

The DB2 Catalog, therefore, is active in the sense that when standard DB2 SQL is issued, the DB2 Catalog is either updated or accessed. All the information in the DB2 Catalog, however, is not completely up-to-date, and some of the tables must be proactively populated (such as SYSIBM.SYSPROCEDURES).

You can see where the DB2 Catalog operates as an active data dictionary. Remember that the three types of SQL are DDL, DCL, and DML. When DDL is issued to create DB2 objects such as databases, tablespaces, and tables, the pertinent descriptive information is stored in the DB2 Catalog.

Figure 15.1 shows the effects of DDL on the DB2 Catalog. When a CREATE, DROP, or ALTER statement is issued, information is recorded or updated in the DB2 Catalog. The same is true for security SQL data control language statements. The GRANT and REVOKE statements cause information to be added or removed from DB2 Catalog tables (see Figure 15.2). Data manipulation language SQL statements use the DB2 Catalog to ensure that the statements accurately reference the DB2 objects being manipulated (such as column names and data types).

Why then is the DB2 Catalog classified as only semiactive rather than completely active? The DB2 Catalog houses important information about the physical organization of DB2 objects. For example, the following information is maintained in the DB2 Catalog:

- The number of rows in a given DB2 table or a given DB2 tablespace
- The number of distinct values in a given DB2 index
- The physical order of the rows in the table for a set of keys

This information is populated by means of the DB2 RUNSTATS utility. A truly active data dictionary would update this information as data is populated in the application tablespaces, tables, and indexes. This was deemed to be too costly, and rightly so. Therefore, the DB2 Catalog is only semiactive.

The DB2 Catalog is also described as being *integrated.* The DB2 Catalog and the DB2 DBMS are inherently bound together, neither having purpose or function without the other. The DB2 Catalog without DB2 defines nothing; DB2 without the DB2 Catalog has nothing defined that it can operate on.

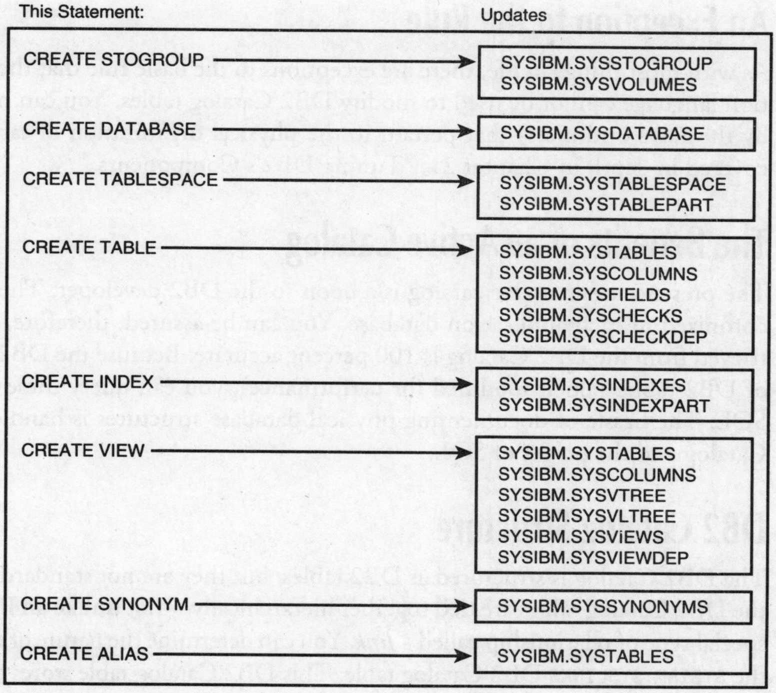

FIGURE 15.1.
The effect of DDL on the DB2 Catalog.

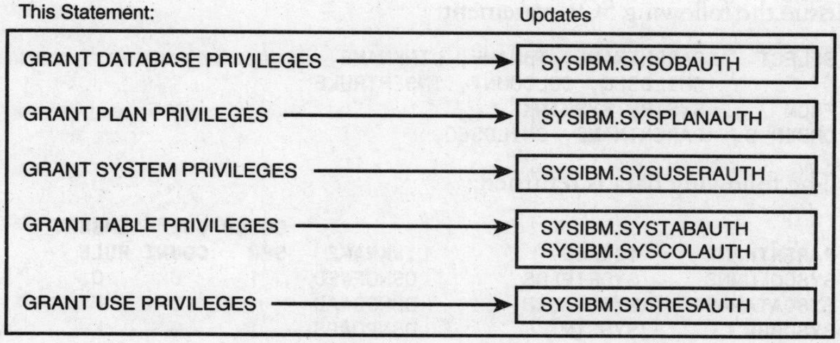

FIGURE 15.2.
The effect of DCL on the DB2 Catalog.

The final adjective used to classify the DB2 Catalog is *nonsubvertible.* This simply means that the DB2 Catalog is updated as DB2 is used by standard DB2 features; the DB2 Catalog cannot be updated behind DB2's back. Suppose that you created a table with 20 columns. You cannot subsequently update the DB2 Catalog to indicate that the table has 15 columns instead of 20 without using standard DB2 data definition language SQL statements to drop and re-create the table.

An Exception to the Rule

As with most things in life, there are exceptions to the basic rule that the SQL data manipulation language cannot be used to modify DB2 Catalog tables. You can modify columns (used by the DB2 optimizer) that pertain to the physical organization of table data. This topic is covered in depth in Chapter 21, "Tuning DB2's Components."

The Benefits of an Active Catalog

The presence of an active catalog is a boon to the DB2 developer. The DB2 Catalog is synchronized to each application database. You can be assured, therefore, that the metadata retrieved from the DB2 Catalog is 100 percent accurate. Because the DB2 Catalog is composed of DB2 tables (albeit modified for performance), you can query these tables using standard SQL. The hassle of documenting physical database structures is handled by the active DB2 Catalog and the power of SQL.

DB2 Catalog Structure

The DB2 Catalog is structured as DB2 tables, but they are not standard DB2 tables. Many of the DB2 Catalog tables are tied together hierarchically—not unlike an IMS database—using a special type of relationship called a *link*. You can determine the nature of these links by querying the SYSIBM.SYSLINKS DB2 Catalog table. This DB2 Catalog table stores the pertinent information defining the relationships between other DB2 Catalog tables. To view this information, issue the following SQL statement:

```
SELECT    PARENTNAME, TBNAME, LINKNAME,
          CHILDSEQ, COLCOUNT, INSERTRULE
FROM      SYSIBM.SYSLINKS
ORDER BY  PARENTNAME, CHILDSEQ
```

The following data is returned:

PARENTNAME	TBNAME	LINKNAME	CHILD SEQ	COL COUNT	INSERT RULE
SYSCOLUMNS	SYSFIELDS	DSNDF#FD	1	0	O
SYSDATABASE	SYSDBAUTH	DSNDD#AD	1	0	F
SYSDBRM	SYSSTMT	DSNPD#PS	1	0	L
SYSINDEXES	SYSINDEXPART	DSNDC#DR	1	1	U
SYSINDEXES	SYSKEYS	DSNDX#DK	2	1	U
SYSPLAN	SYSDBRM	DSNPP#PD	1	1	U
SYSPLAN	SYSPLANAUTH	DSNPP#AP	2	0	F
SYSPLAN	SYSPLANDEP	DSNPP#PU	3	0	F
SYSRELS	SYSLINKS	DSNDR#DL	1	0	O
SYSRELS	SYSFOREIGNKEYS	DSNDR#DF	2	1	U
SYSSTOGROUP	SYSVOLUMES	DSNSS#SV	1	0	L
SYSTABAUTH	SYSCOLAUTH	DSNAT#AF	1	0	F
SYSTABLES	SYSCOLUMNS	DSNDT#DF	1	1	U
SYSTABLES	SYSRELS	DSNDT#DR	2	1	U
SYSTABLES	SYSINDEXES	DSNDT#DX	3	0	F
SYSTABLES	SYSTABAUTH	DSNDT#AT	4	0	F

```
SYSTABLES        SYSSYNONYMS    DSNDT#DY   5   0   F
SYSTABLESPACE    SYSTABLEPART   DSNDS#DP   1   1   U
SYSTABLESPACE    SYSTABLES      DSNDS#DT   2   0   F
SYSVTREE         SYSVLTREE      DSNVT#VL   1   0   L
SYSVTREE         SYSVIEWS       DSNVT#VW   2   1   U
SYSVTREE         SYSVIEWDEP     DSNVT#VU   3   0   F
```

This information can be used to construct the physical composition of the DB2 Catalog links. To accomplish this, keep the following rules in mind:

- The PARENTNAME is the name of the superior table in the hierarchy. The TBNAME is the name of the subordinate table, or child table, in the hierarchy.
- The CHILDSEQ and COLCOUNT columns refer to the clustering and ordering of the data in the relationship.
- The INSERTRULE column determines the order in which data is inserted into the relationship. This concept is similar to the insert rule for IMS databases. Valid insert rules are shown in Table 15.2.

Table 15.2. DB2 Catalog link insert rules.

Insert Rule	*Meaning*	*Description*
F	FIRST	Inserts new values as the first data value in the relationship
L	LAST	Inserts new values as the last data value in the relationship
O	ONE	Permits only one data value for the relationship
U	UNIQUE	Does not allow duplicate data values for the relationship

The newer DB2 Catalog tables do not use links; they use proper referential constraints. You can see this by browsing the previous output and noting the lack of V2.3 and V3 DB2 Catalog tables.

Hierarchical diagrams of the DB2 Catalog depicting links and relationships are shown in Figures 15.3 through 15.5.

The specifics of what information is stored in what portion of the DB2 Catalog are contained in Appendix B. Consult this appendix for the answers to the following questions:

- Which tablespaces contain which DB2 Catalog tables?
- Which columns are in which DB2 Catalog tables?
- Which information is contained in which columns?
- Which indexes exist on which DB2 Catalog tables?

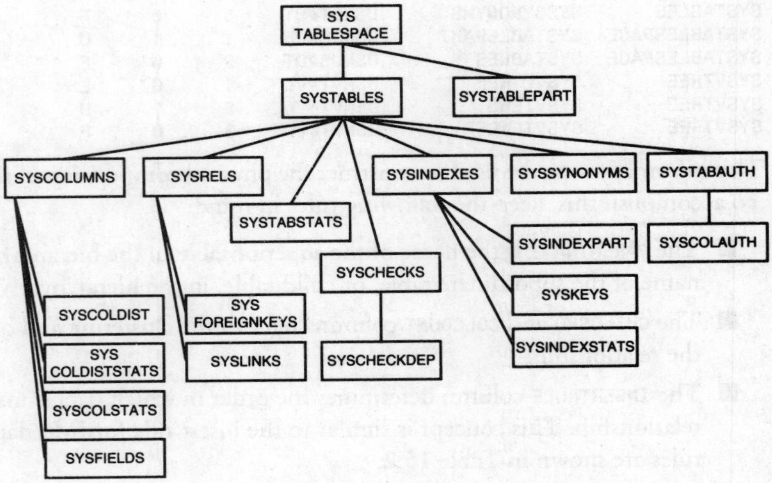

FIGURE 15.3.
The DB2 Catalog tablespaces, tables, and indexes.

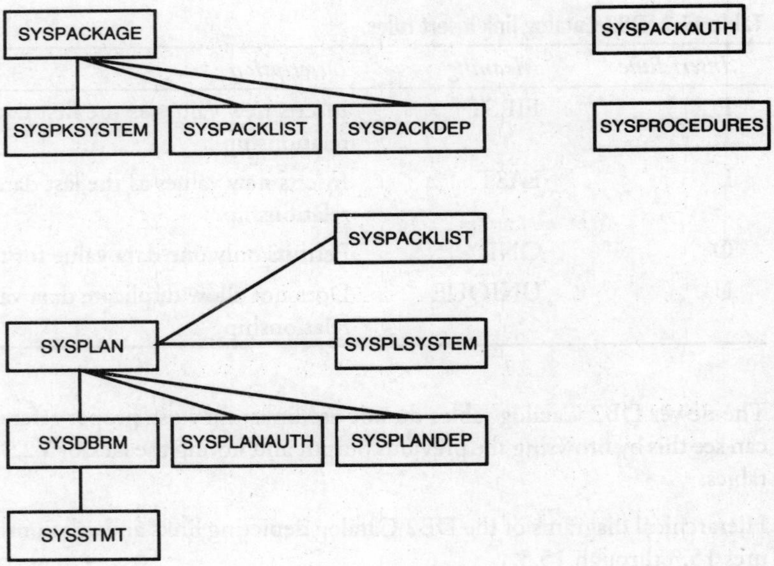

FIGURE 15.4.
The DB2 Catalog plans and packages.

As you query the DB2 Catalog, remember that DB2 indexes are used only by SQL queries against the DB2 Catalog, never by internal DB2 operations. For example, when the `BIND` command queries the DB2 Catalog for syntax checking and access path selection, only the internal DB2 Catalog links are used.

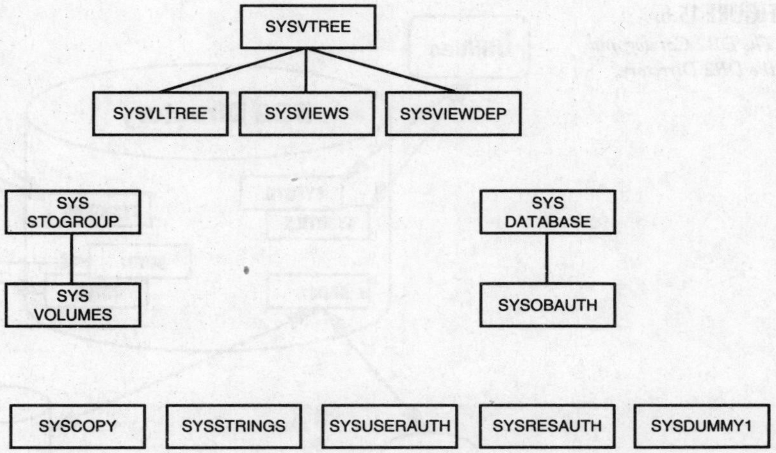

FIGURE 15.5.
The DB2 Catalog views, STOGROUPs, and databases.

The DB2 Directory

Many DB2 application developers are unaware that DB2 uses a second dictionary-like structure in addition to the DB2 Catalog. This is the DB2 Directory. Used for storing detailed, technical information about aspects of DB2's operation, the DB2 Directory is for DB2's internal use only.

The DB2 Directory is composed of five "tables." These "tables," however, are not true DB2 tables because they are not addressable using SQL. From here on, they are referred to as structures instead of tables. These structures control DB2 housekeeping tasks and house complex control structures used by DB2. See Figure 15.6 for a summation of the relationships between the DB2 Catalog, the DB2 Directory, and DB2 operations. A quick rundown of the information stored in the DB2 Directory is in the following sections.

SCT02

The `SCT02` structure holds the skeleton cursor tables (SKCTs) for DB2 application plans. These skeleton cursor tables contain the instructions for implementing the access path logic determined by the DB2 optimizer.

The `BIND PLAN` command causes skeleton cursor tables to be created in the `SCT02` structure. Executing the `FREE PLAN` command causes the appropriate skeleton cursor tables to be removed from `SCT02`. When a DB2 program is run, DB2 loads the skeleton cursor table into an area of memory called the EDM Pool to enable execution of the SQL embedded in the application program.

FIGURE 15.6.
The DB2 Catalog and the DB2 Directory.

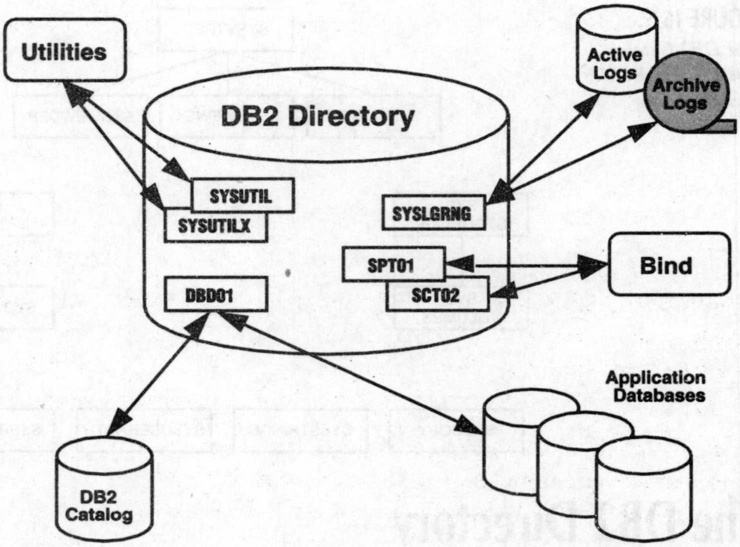

SPT01

Similar to the skeleton cursor tables are skeleton package tables which are housed in the `SPT01` DB2 Directory structure. The skeleton package tables contain the access path information for DB2 packages.

The `BIND PACKAGE` command causes skeleton package tables to be created in the `SPT01` structure. Executing the `FREE PACKAGE` command causes the appropriate skeleton package tables to be removed from the DB2 Directory. When running a DB2 program that is based on a plan with a package list, DB2 loads both the skeleton cursor table for the plan and the skeleton package tables for the packages into memory to enable execution of the SQL embedded in the application program.

DBD01

Database descriptors, or DBDs, are stored in the `DBD01` DB2 Directory structure. A DBD is an internal description of all the DB2 objects that were defined subordinate to a database. DB2 uses the DBD as an efficient representation of the information stored in the DB2 Catalog for these objects. Instead of accessing the DB2 Catalog for DB2 object information, DB2 accesses the DBD housed in the DB2 Directory because it is more efficient to do so.

The DBD in the DB2 Directory can become out of sync with the physical DB2 objects that it represents, but this is unlikely. If this does happen, you will encounter many odd and unexplainable abends. The situation can be corrected using the `REPAIR DBD` utility, which is covered in Chapter 25, "Backup and Recovery Utilities." Furthermore, the `REPAIR DBD TEST DATABASE` utility can be run to detect when a DBD is out of sync with the actual physical objects.

SYSUTILX

DB2 monitors the execution of all online DB2 utilities. Information about the status of all started DB2 utilities is maintained in the SYSUTILX DB2 Directory structure. As each utility progresses, the step and its status are recorded. Utility restart is controlled through the information stored in SYSUTILX.

Note that this structure maintains information only for started DB2 utilities. Each utility step consumes a separate row, or record, in SYSUTILX. When the utility finishes normally or is terminated, all information about that utility is purged from SYSUTILX.

SYSLGRNGX

The RBA ranges from the DB2 logs are recorded on SYSLGRNGX for tablespace updates. When recovery is requested, DB2 can efficiently locate the required logs and quickly identify the portion of those logs needed for recovery.

NOTE

As of DB2 V4, SYSLGRNGX replaces SYSLGRNG in the DB2 Directory. This was done to extend the log range information stored in this table.

Version 4

QMF Administrative Tables

Although technically QMF is not part of DB2, it is an integral part of the DB2 architecture in most corporations. This book does not delve into the mechanics of QMF, except when you can gain an insight into a DB2 feature. The QMF Administrative Tables are mentioned in this chapter for insight into the mechanics of QMF as it relates to DB2 performance.

You can think of the QMF Administrative Tables as a DB2 Catalog for QMF—or the QMF Catalog, if you will. They administer QMF housekeeping data, house control structures and data, and maintain QMF object security. DB2 database administrators should remember the following:

- The QMF Administrative Tables contain control data integral to the operation of QMF. If QMF is relied on for production work, these tables should be protected like any other DB2 tables.
- Because QMF Administrative Tables are DB2 tables, you can access and modify them using SQL. In a pinch, quick changes can be made to QMF objects by DBA (with the appropriate DB2 security).

- Monitor the space used by the QMF Administrative Tables and, whenever necessary, expand the primary space allocation and REORG to remove secondary extents.
- As the number of QMF users grows and the volume of queries, forms, and procedures created by these users expands, the size of the QMF Administrative Tables grows. This can degrade the performance of QMF. You should periodically execute the RUNSTATS utility for all of the QMF Administrative Tables and rebind the QMF plan (for example, called QMF310 or QMF311 for QMF V3.1) to optimize the performance of QMF.

See Appendix C, "The QMF Administrative Tables," for a breakdown of the data housed in the QMF Administrative Tables.

Summary

The haze is lifting. Slowly but surely, the confusion surrounding the internal structure of DB2 is being replaced by understanding. You know how DB2 data is accessed, where DB2 structural data is stored, and how DB2 runs. But what happens when many people try to access the same data? How does DB2 provide for the concurrent updating of data? To find out, forge ahead to the next chapter.

16

Locking DB2 Data

DB2 automatically guarantees the integrity of data by enforcing several locking strategies. These strategies permit multiple users from multiple environments to access and modify data concurrently.

DB2 combines the following strategies to implement an overall locking strategy:

- Table and tablespace locking
- IRLM page and row locking
- Internal page and row latching
- Claims and drains to achieve partition independence
- Checking commit log sequence numbers (CLSN) and PUNC bits to achieve lock avoidance
- Global locking through the coupling facility in a data sharing environment

What exactly is locking? How does DB2 utilize these strategies to lock pages and guarantee data integrity? Why does DB2 have to lock data before it can process it? What is the difference between a lock and a latch? How can DB2 provide data integrity while operating on separate partitions concurrently? Finally, how can DB2 avoid locks and still guarantee data integrity?

These questions are answered in this chapter. In addition, this chapter provides practical information on lock compatibilities that can aid you in program development and scheduling.

How DB2 Manages Locking

Anyone accustomed to application programming when access to a database is required understands the potential for concurrency problems. When one application program tries to read data that is in the process of being changed by another, the DBMS must forbid access until the modification is complete in order to ensure data integrity. Most DBMS products, DB2 included, use a locking mechanism for all data items being changed. Therefore, when one task is updating data on a page, another task cannot access data (read or update) on that same page until the data modification is complete and committed.

When multiple users can access and update the same data at the same time, a locking mechanism is required. This mechanism must be capable of differentiating between stable data and uncertain data. *Stable data* has been successfully committed and is not involved in an update in a current unit of work. *Uncertain data* is currently involved in an operation that could modify its contents. Consider the example in Listing 16.1.

Listing 16.1. A typical processing scenario.

```
Program #1                    Timeline     Program #2
.                             T1           .
.                                          .
.                                          .
.                                          .
SQL statement                 T2           .
accessing EMPNO '000010'                   .
.                                          .
.                                          .
SQL statement                 T3           .
updating '000010'                          .
.                                          .
.                                          .
.                             T4           SQL statement
                                           accessing EMPNO '000010'
.                                          .
.                                          .
Commit                        T5           .
.                                          .
.                                          .
.                                          .
.                             T6           SQL statement updating '000010'
.                                          .
.                                          .
.                             T7           Commit
```

If program #1 updates a piece of data on page 1, you must ensure that program #2 cannot access the data until program #1 commits the unit of work. Otherwise, a loss of integrity could result. Without a locking mechanism, the following sequence of events would be possible:

1. Program #1 retrieves a row from `DSN8510.EMP` for `EMPNO '000010'`.
2. Program #1 issues an update statement to change that employee's salary to `55000`.
3. Program #2 retrieves the `DSN8510.EMP` row for `EMPNO '000010'`. Because the change was not committed, the old value for the salary, `52750`, is retrieved.
4. Program #1 commits the change, causing the salary to be `55000`.
5. Program #2 changes a value in a different column and commits the change.
6. The value for salary is now back to `52750`, negating the change made by program #1.

A DBMS can avoid this situation by using a locking mechanism. DB2 supports locking at four levels, or *granularities*: tablespace-level locking, table-level locking, page-level locking, and, as of DB2 V4, row-level locking.

More precisely, DB2 locks are enacted on data as shown in Figure 16.1.

These two charts are hierarchical. Locks can be taken at any level in the locking hierarchy without taking a lock at the lower level. However, locks cannot be taken at the lower levels without a compatible higher-level lock also being taken. For example, you can take a tablespace lock without taking any other lock, but you cannot take a page lock without first securing a tablespace-level lock (and a table lock as well if the page is part of a table in a segmented tablespace containing more than one table).

FIGURE 16.1.
The DB2 locking hierarchy.

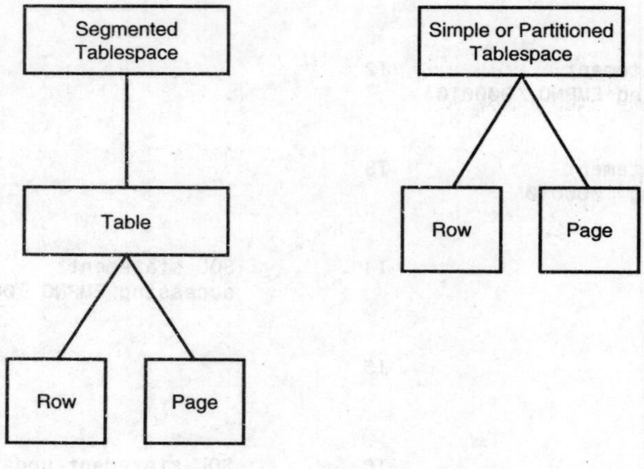

Version 4

Additionally, as illustrated in the diagrams in Figure 16.1, a page lock does not have to be taken before a row lock is taken. Your locking strategy requires an "either/or" type of choice by tablespace: either row locking or page locking. An in-depth discussion on the merits of both follows later in this chapter. Both page locks and row locks escalate to a table level and then to a tablespace level for segmented tables or straight to a tablespace level for simple or partitioned tablespaces. A table or tablespace cannot have both page locks and row locks held against it at the same time.

Many modes of locking are supported by DB2, but they can be divided into two types:

- Locks to enable the reading of data
- Locks to enable the updating of data

This overview is too simplistic; DB2 uses varieties of these two types to indicate the type of locking required. They are covered in more depth later in this chapter.

Locks Versus Latches

A true lock is handled by DB2 using the IRLM. However, whenever doing so is practical, DB2 tries to *lock* pages without going to the IRLM. This type of lock is called a *latch*.

True locks are always set in the IRLM. Latches, by contrast, are set internally by DB2, without going to the IRLM.

When a latch is taken instead of a lock, it is handled by internal DB2 code; so the cross-memory service calls to the IRLM are eliminated. Also, a latch requires about one-third the number of instructions as a lock. Therefore, latches are more efficient than locks because they avoid the overhead associated with calling an external address space.

Latches are used when a resource serialization situation is required for a short time. Prior to DB2 V3, latches were generally used to lock only DB2 index pages and internal DB2 resources. When you're running V3 or later, DB2 uses latching more frequently. This use includes data page latches.

Both latches and locks guarantee data integrity. In subsequent sections, when I use the term *lock* generically, I am referring to both locks and latches.

Lock Duration

Before you learn about the various types of locks that can be acquired by DB2, you should understand *lock duration*, which refers to the length of time that a lock is maintained.

The duration of a lock is based on the bind options chosen for the program requesting locks. Locks can be acquired either immediately when the plan is requested to be run or iteratively as needed during the execution of the program. Locks can be released when the plan is terminated or when they are no longer required for a unit of work.

The bind parameters affecting DB2 locking are covered in detail in Chapter 13, "DB2 Behind the Scenes." They are repeated in the following sections as a reminder.

Bind Parameters Affecting Tablespace Locks

`ACQUIRE(ALLOCATE)` versus `ACQUIRE(USE)`: The `ALLOCATE` option specifies that locks will be acquired when the plan is allocated, which normally occurs when the first SQL statement is issued. The `USE` option indicates that locks will be acquired only as they are required, SQL statement by SQL statement.

`RELEASE(DEALLOCATE)` versus `RELEASE(COMMIT)`: When you specify `DEALLOCATE` for a plan, locks are not released until the plan is terminated. When you specify `COMMIT`, tablespace locks are released when a `COMMIT` is encountered.

Bind Parameters Affecting Page and Row Locks

`ISOLATION` level (`RR` versus `CS` versus `UR`): `RR` holds page and row locks until a `COMMIT` point, whereas `CS` acquires and releases page locks as pages are read and processed. `UR` avoids locking altogether. Regardless of the `ISOLATION` level chosen, all page locks are released when a `COMMIT` is encountered.

Implementing Dirty Reads Using `ISOLATION(UR)`

Version 4

Programs that read DB2 data typically access numerous rows during their execution and are thus quite susceptible to concurrency problems. DB2, as of version 4, provides read-through locks, also known as "dirty reads" or "uncommitted reads," to help overcome concurrency problems. When using uncommitted reads, an application program can read data that has been changed but is not yet committed.

Dirty read capability is implemented using the UR isolation level (UR stands for uncommitted read). When an application program uses the UR isolation level, it reads data without taking locks. This way, the application program can read data contained in the table as it is being manipulated.

How does "dirty read" impact data availability and integrity? Consider the following sequence of events:

1. At 9:00 a.m., a transaction is executed containing the following SQL to change a specific value:

   ```
   UPDATE DSN8510.EMP
       SET FIRST_NAME = "MICHELLE"
   WHERE EMPNO = "10020";
   ```

   The transaction, which is a long-running one, continues to execute without issuing a COMMIT.

2. At 9:01 a.m., a second transaction attempts to SELECT the data that was changed but not committed.

If the UR isolation level were specified for the second transaction, it would read the changed data even though it had yet to be committed. Obviously, if the program does not wait to take a lock and merely reads the data in whatever state it happens to be at that moment, the program will execute faster than if it has to wait for locks to be taken and resources to be freed before processing.

However, you must carefully examine the implications of reading uncommitted data before implementing such a plan. Several types of "problems" can occur. A dirty read can cause duplicate rows to be returned where none exist. Also, a dirty read can cause no rows to be returned when one (or more) actually exists. Additionally, an ORDER BY clause does not guarantee that rows will be returned in order if the UR isolation level is used. Obviously, you must take these "problems" into consideration before using the UR isolation level. Guidelines for when, and when not, to choose UR are given later in this chapter.

UR Isolation Requirements

The UR isolation level applies to read-only operations: SELECT, SELECT INTO, and FETCH from a read-only result table. Any application plan or package bound with an isolation level of UR uses uncommitted read functionality for read-only SQL. Operations that are contained in the same plan or package that are not read-only use an isolation level of CS.

You can override the isolation level that is defined at the plan or package level during BIND or REBIND as you want for each SQL statement in the program by using the WITH clause, as shown in the following SQL:

```
SELECT EMPNO, LAST_NAME
FROM   DSN8510.EMP
WITH UR;
```

The WITH clause allows an isolation level to be specified at the statement level in an application program. However, the restriction that the UR isolation level can be used with read-only SQL statements only still applies.

The UR isolation level is incompatible with Type 1 indexes. If the plan or package is rebound to change to UR isolation, DB2 does not consider any access paths that use a Type 1 index. If an acceptable Type 2 index cannot be found, DB2 chooses a tablespace scan.

When to Use Dirty Reads

When is using UR isolation appropriate? The general rule of thumb is to avoid UR whenever the results must be 100 percent accurate. Examples would be when

- Calculations that must balance are performed on the selected data
- Data is retrieved from one source to insert to or update another
- Production, mission-critical work that cannot contain or cause data-integrity problems is performed

In general, most current DB2 applications are not candidates for dirty reads. However, in a few specific situations, the dirty read capability is of major benefit. Consider the following cases in which the UR isolation level could prove to be useful:

- Access is required to a reference, code, or lookup table that is basically static in nature. Due to the non-volatile nature of the data, a dirty read would be no different than a normal read the majority of the time. In the cases in which the code data is being modified, any application reading the data would incur minimum, if any, problems.
- Statistical processing must be performed on a large amount of data. For example, your company may want to determine the average age of female employees within a certain pay range. The impact of an uncommitted read on an average of multiple rows is minimal because a single value changed does not have a great impact on the result.
- Dirty reads can prove invaluable in a data warehousing environment that uses DB2 as the DBMS. A data warehouse is a time-sensitive, subject-oriented store of business data that is used for online analytical processing. Other than periodic data propagation and/or replication, access to the data warehouse is read only. An uncommitted read is perfect in a read-only environment because it can cause little damage because the data is generally not changing. More and more data warehouse projects are being implemented in corporations worldwide, and DB2 with dirty read capability is a wise choice for data warehouse implementation.
- In the rare cases in which a table, or set of tables, is used by a single user only, UR can make a lot of sense. If only one individual can modify the data, the application

programs can be coded so that all (or most) reads are done using `UR` isolation level, and the data will still be accurate.

- In pseudo-conversational transactions, use the save and compare technique. A program using the save and compare technique saves data for later comparison to ensure that the data was not changed by other concurrent transactions.

  Consider the following sequence of events: transaction 1 changes customer A on page 100. A page lock will be taken on all rows on page 100. Transaction 2 requests customer C, which is on page 100. Transaction 2 must wait for transaction 1 to finish. This wait is not necessary. Even if these transactions are trying to get the same row, the save then compare technique would catch this.

- Finally, if the data being accessed is already inconsistent, little harm can be done by using a dirty read to access the information.

Tablespace Locks

A tablespace lock is acquired when a DB2 table or index is accessed. Note that I said *accessed,* not *updated.* The tablespace is locked even when simple read-only access is occurring.

Refer to Table 16.1 for a listing of the types of tablespace locks that can be acquired during the execution of an SQL statement. Every tablespace lock implies two types of access: the access acquired by the lock requester and the access allowed to other subsequent, concurrent processes.

Table 16.1. Tablespace locks.

Lock	*Meaning*	*Access Acquired*	*Access Allowed to Others*
S	SHARE	Read only	Read only
U	UPDATE	Read with intent to update	Read only
X	EXCLUSIVE	Update	No access
IS	INTENT SHARE	Read only	Update
IX	INTENT EXCLUSIVE	Update	Update
SIX	SHARE/INTENT EXCLUSIVE	Read or Update	Read only

The type of tablespace lock used by DB2 during processing is contingent on several factors, including the tablespace `LOCKSIZE` specified in the DDL, the bind parameters chosen for the plan being run, and the type of processing requested. Table 16.2 provides a synopsis of the initial tablespace locks acquired under certain conditions.

Table 16.2. How tablespace locks are acquired.

Type of Processing	LOCKSIZE	*Isolation*	*Initial Lock Acquired*
MODIFY	ANY	CS	IX
MODIFY	PAGE/ROW	CS	IX
MODIFY	TABLESPACE	CS	X
MODIFY	ANY	RR	X
MODIFY	PAGE/ROW	RR	X
MODIFY	TABLESPACE	RR	X
SELECT	ANY	CS	IS
SELECT	PAGE/ROW	CS	IS
SELECT	TABLESPACE	CS	S
SELECT	ANY	RR	S
SELECT	PAGE/ROW	RR	S
SELECT	TABLESPACE	RR	S

A tablespace U-lock indicates intent to update, but an update has not occurred. This is caused by using a cursor with the FOR UPDATE OF clause. A U-lock is non-exclusive because it can be taken while tasks have S-locks on the same tablespace. More information on tablespace lock compatibility follows in Table 16.3.

An additional consideration is that tablespace locks are usually taken in combination with table and page locks, but they can be used on their own. When you specify the LOCKSIZE TABLESPACE DDL parameter, tablespace locks alone are used as the locking mechanism for the data in that tablespace. This way, concurrent access is limited and concurrent update processing is eliminated.

Similar in function to the LOCKSIZE DDL parameter is the LOCK TABLE statement. The LOCK TABLE statement requests an immediate lock on the specified table. The LOCK TABLE statement has two forms—one to request a share lock and one to request an exclusive lock.

```
LOCK TABLE table_name IN SHARE MODE;
LOCK TABLE table_name IN EXCLUSIVE MODE;
```

CAUTION

The LOCK TABLE statement locks all tables in a simple tablespace even though only one table is specified.

A locking scheme is not effective unless multiple processes can secure different types of locks on the same resource concurrently. With DB2 locking, some types of tablespace locks can be acquired concurrently by discrete processes. Two locks that can be acquired concurrently on the same resource are said to be compatible with one another.

Refer to Table 16.3 for a breakdown of DB2 tablespace lock compatibility. A *Yes* in the matrix indicates that the two locks are compatible and can be acquired by distinct processes on the same tablespace concurrently. A *No* indicates that the two locks are incompatible. In general, two locks cannot be taken concurrently if they allow concurrent processes to negatively affect the integrity of data in the tablespace.

Table 16.3. Tablespace lock compatibility matrix.

Locks for PGM2	*Locks for PGM1*					
	S	U	X	IS	IX	SIX
S	Yes	Yes	No	Yes	No	No
U	Yes	No	No	Yes	No	No
X	No	No	No	No	No	No
IS	Yes	Yes	No	Yes	Yes	Yes
IX	No	No	No	Yes	Yes	No
SIX	No	No	No	Yes	No	No

Table Locks

You can use table locks only when segmented tablespaces are involved in the process. Table locks are always associated with a corresponding tablespace lock.

The same types of locks are used for table locks as are used for tablespace locks. S, U, X, IS, IX, and SIX table locks can be acquired by DB2 processes when data in segmented tablespaces is accessed. Table 16.1 describes the options available to DB2 for table locking. The compatibility chart in Table 16.3 applies to table locks as well as tablespace locks.

For a table lock to be acquired, an IS-lock must first be acquired on the segmented tablespace in which the table exists. The type of table lock to be taken depends on the LOCKSIZE specified in the DDL, the bind parameters chosen for the plan being run, and the type of processing requested. Table 16.4 is a modified version of Table 16.2, showing the initial types of tablespaces and table locks acquired given a certain set of conditions. Table locks are never acquired when the LOCKSIZE TABLESPACE parameter is used.

Table 16.4. How table locks are acquired.

Type of Processing	LOCKSIZE	*Isolation*	*Tablespace Lock Acquired*	*Table Lock Acquired*
MODIFY	ANY	CS	IS	IX
MODIFY	PAGE	CS	IS	IX
MODIFY	TABLE	CS	IS	X
MODIFY	ANY	RR	IS	X
MODIFY	PAGE	RR	IS	X
MODIFY	TABLE	RR	IS	X
SELECT	ANY	CS	IS	IS
SELECT	PAGE	CS	IS	IS
SELECT	TABLE	CS	IS	S
SELECT	ANY	RR	IS	S
SELECT	PAGE	RR	IS	S
SELECT	TABLE	RR	IS	S

Page Locks

The types of page locks that DB2 can take are outlined in Table 16.5. S-locks allow data to be read concurrently but not modified. With an X-lock, data on a page can be modified (with INSERT, UPDATE, or DELETE), but concurrent access is not allowed. U-locks enable X-locks to be queued, whereas S-locks exist on data that must be modified.

Table 16.5. Page locks.

Lock	*Meaning*	*Access Acquired*	*Access Allowed to Others*
S	SHARE	Read only	Read only
U	UPDATE	Read with intent to update	Read only
X	EXCLUSIVE	Update	No access

As with tablespace locks, concurrent page locks can be acquired but only with compatible page locks. The compatibility matrix for page locks is shown in Table 16.6.

Table 16.6. Page lock compatibility matrix.

Locks for PGM2	*Locks for PGM1*		
	S	U	X
S	Yes	Yes	No
U	Yes	No	No
X	No	No	No

When are these page locks taken? Page locks can be acquired only under the following conditions:

- The DDL for the object requesting a lock specifies `LOCKSIZE PAGE` or `LOCKSIZE ANY`.
- If `LOCKSIZE ANY` was specified, the `NUMLKTS` threshold or the tablespace `LOCKMAX` specification must not have been bypassed. You learn more about these topics later in this section.
- If `ISOLATION(RR)` was used when the plan was bound, the optimizer might decide not to use page locking.

If all these factors are met, page locking progresses as outlined in Table 16.7. The type of processing in the left column causes the indicated page lock to be acquired for the scope of pages identified in the right column. A page lock is held until it is released as specified by the `ISOLATION` level of the plan requesting the particular lock.

NOTE

Page locks can be promoted from one type of lock to another based on the type of processing that is occurring. A program can `FETCH` a row using a cursor with the `FOR UPDATE OF` clause, causing a `U`-lock to be acquired on that row's page. Later, the program can modify that row, causing the `U`-lock to be promoted to an `X`-lock.

Table 16.7. How page locks are acquired.

Type of Processing	*Page Lock Acquired*	*Pages Affected*
`SELECT/FETCH`	S	Page by page as they are fetched
`OPEN CURSOR` for `SELECT`	S	All pages affected
`SELECT/FETCH FOR UPDATE OF`	U	Page by page as they are fetched
`UPDATE`	X	Page by page
`INSERT`	X	Page by page
`DELETE`	X	Page by page

Row Locks

Version 4

The smallest piece of DB2 data that you can lock is the individual row. The types of row locks that DB2 can take are similar to the types of page locks that it can take. Refer to Table 16.8. S-locks allow data to be read concurrently but not modified. With an X-lock, you can modify data in that row (using INSERT, UPDATE, or DELETE), but concurrent access is not allowed. U-locks enable X-locks to be queued, whereas S-locks exist on data that must be modified.

Table 16.8. Row locks.

Lock	*Meaning*	*Access Acquired*	*Access Allowed to Others*
S	SHARE	Read only	Read only
U	UPDATE	Read with intent to update	Read only
X	EXCLUSIVE	Update	No access

Once again, concurrent row locks can be acquired but only with compatible row locks. Table 16.9 shows the compatibility matrix for row locks.

Table 16.9. Row lock compatibility matrix.

Locks for PGM2	*Locks for PGM1*		
	S	U	X
S	Yes	Yes	No
U	Yes	No	No
X	No	No	No

When are these row locks taken? Row locks can be acquired when the DDL for the object requesting a lock specifies LOCKSIZE ROW. (Although it is theoretically possible for LOCKSIZE ANY to choose row locks, in practice I have yet to see this happen as of DB2 V5.) Row locking progresses as outlined in Table 16.10. The type of processing in the left column causes the indicated row lock to be acquired for the scope of rows identified in the right column. A row lock is held until it is released as specified by the ISOLATION level of the plan requesting the particular lock.

NOTE

Row locks can be promoted from one type of lock to another based on the type of processing that is occurring. A program can FETCH a row using a cursor with the FOR UPDATE OF clause, causing a U-lock to be acquired on that row. Later, the program can modify that row, causing the U-lock to be promoted to an X-lock.

Table 16.10. How row locks are acquired.

Type of Processing	*Row Lock Acquired*	*Rows Affected*
`SELECT/FETCH`	S	Row by row as they are fetched
`OPEN CURSOR for SELECT`	S	All rows affected
`SELECT/FETCH FOR UPDATE OF`	U	Row by row as they are fetched
`UPDATE`	X	Row by row
`INSERT`	X	Row by row
`DELETE`	X	Row by row

Page Locks Versus Row Locks

The answer to the question of whether to use page locks or row locks is, of course, "It depends!" The nature of your specific data and applications determine whether page or row locks are most applicable.

The resources required to acquire, maintain, and release a row lock are just about the same as the resources required for a page lock. Therefore, the number of rows per page must be factored into the row-versus-page locking decision. The more rows per page, the more resources will be consumed. For example, a tablespace with a single table that houses 25 rows per page can consume as much as 25 more resources for locking if row locks are chosen over page locks. However, contention can be reduced by locking a row at a time instead of a page at a time. Of course, this estimate is very rough, and other factors (such as lock avoidance) can reduce the number of locks acquired, and thereby reduce the overhead associated with row locking. However, row locking almost always consumes more resources than page locking. Likewise, if two applications running concurrently access the same data in different orders, row locking might actually decrease concurrent data access.

You must therefore ask these questions:

- What is the nature of the applications that access the objects in question? Of course, the answer to this question differs not only from organization to organization, but also from application to application within the same organization.
- Which is more important, reducing the resources required to execute an application or increasing data availability? The answer to this question is, of course, "It depends!"

As a general rule of thumb, favor specifying `LOCKSIZE ANY` and let DB2 decide for you. Also, if you're experiencing contention on tablespace that is currently using `LOCKSIZE PAGE`, consider changing to `LOCKSIZE ROW` and gauging the impact on performance, resource consumption, and concurrent data access.

Deadlocks and Timeouts

When a lock is requested, a series of operations is performed to ensure that the requested lock can be acquired. (See Figure 16.2.) Two conditions can cause the lock acquisition request to fail: a deadlock or a timeout.

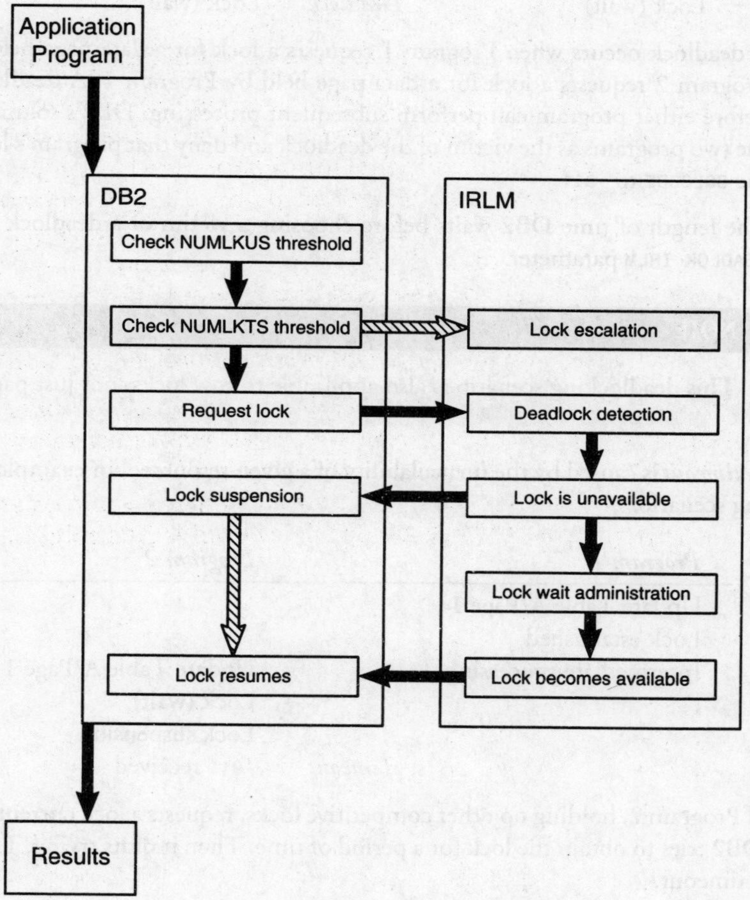

FIGURE 16.2.
Processing a lock request.

A *deadlock* occurs when two separate processes compete for resources held by one another. DB2 performs deadlock detection for both locks and latches. For example, consider the following processing sequence for two concurrently executing application programs:

Program 1		*Program 2*
Update Table B/Page 1		Update Table A/Page 1
Lock established		Lock established
Intermediate processing		Intermediate processing
Update Table A/Page 1		Update Table B/Page 1
Lock (wait)	*Deadlock*	Lock (wait)

A deadlock occurs when Program 1 requests a lock for a data page held by Program 2, and Program 2 requests a lock for a data page held by Program 1. A deadlock must be resolved before either program can perform subsequent processing. DB2's solution is to target one of the two programs as the victim of the deadlock and deny that program's lock request by setting the `SQLCODE` to `-911`.

The length of time DB2 waits before choosing a victim of a deadlock is determined by the `DEADLOK IRLM` parameter.

NOTE

This deadlocking scenario is also applicable to row locks, not just page locks.

A *timeout* is caused by the unavailability of a given resource. For example, consider the following scenario:

Program 1		*Program 2*
Update Table A/Page 1		
Lock established		
Intermediate processing		Update Table A/Page 1
.		Lock (wait)
.		Lock suspension
.	*Timeout*	`-911` received

If Program 2, holding no other competitive locks, requests a lock currently held by Program 1, DB2 tries to obtain the lock for a period of time. Then it quits trying. This example illustrates a timeout.

The length of time a user waits for an unavailable resource before being *timed out* is determined by the `IRLMRWT DSNZPARM` parameter.

NOTE

This timeout scenario is also applicable to row locks, not just page locks.

Partition Independence

As of DB2 V3, resource serialization has been augmented to include claims and drains in addition to transaction locking. The claim and drain process enables DB2 to perform concurrent operations on multiple partitions of the same tablespace.

Claims and drains provide a new "locking" mechanism to control concurrency for resources between SQL statements, utilities, and commands. Do not confuse the issue: DB2 continues to use transaction locking (pre-V3 locking), as well as claims and drains.

As with transaction locks, claims and drains can time out while waiting for a resource.

Claims

DB2 uses a *claim* to register that a resource is being accessed. The following resources can be claimed:

- Simple tablespaces
- Segmented tablespaces
- A single data partition of a partitioned tablespace
- A non-partitioned index space
- A single index partition of a partitioned index

Think of claims as usage indicators. A process stakes a claim on a resource, telling DB2, in effect, "Hey, I'm using this!"

Claims prevent drains from acquiring a resource. A claim is acquired when a resource is first accessed. This is true regardless of the `ACQUIRE` parameter specified (`USE` or `ALLOCATE`). Claims are released at commit time, except for cursors declared using the `WITH HOLD` clause or when the claimer is a utility.

Multiple agents can claim a single resource. Claims on objects are acquired by the following:

- SQL statements (`SELECT`, `INSERT`, `UPDATE`, `DELETE`)
- DB2 restart on `INDOUBT` objects
- Some utilities (for example, `COPY SHRLEVEL CHANGE`, `RUNSTATS SHRLEVEL CHANGE`, and `REPORT`)

Every claim has a *claim class* associated with it. The claim class is based on the type of access being requested, as follows:

- A `CS` claim is acquired when data is read from a package or plan bound specifying `ISOLATION(CS)`.
- An `RR` claim is acquired when data is read from a package or plan bound specifying `ISOLATION(RR)`.
- A write claim is acquired when data is deleted, inserted, or updated.

Drains

Like claims, *drains* also are acquired when a resource is first accessed. A drain acquires a resource by quiescing claims against that resource. Drains can be requested by commands and utilities.

Multiple drainers can access a single resource. However, a process that drains all claim classes cannot drain an object concurrently with any other process.

To more fully understand the concept of draining, think back to the last time that you went to a movie theater. Before anyone is permitted into the movie, the prior attendees must first be cleared out. In essence, this example illustrates the concept of draining. DB2 drains make sure that all other users of a resource are cleared out before allowing any subsequent access.

The following resources can be drained:

- Simple tablespaces
- Segmented tablespaces
- A single data partition of a partitioned tablespace
- A non-partitioned index space
- A single index partition of a partitioned index

A drain places drain locks on a resource. A drain lock is acquired for each claim class that must be released. Drain locks prohibit processes from attempting to drain the same object at the same time.

The process of quiescing a claim class and prohibiting new claims from being acquired for the resource is called *draining*. Draining allows DB2 utilities and commands to acquire partial or full control of a specific object with a minimal impact on concurrent access.

Three types of drain locks can be acquired:

- A cursor stability drain lock
- A repeatable read drain lock
- A write drain lock

A drain requires either partial control of a resource, in which case a write drain lock is taken, or complete control of a resource, accomplished by placing a CS drain lock, an RR drain lock, and a write drain lock on an object.

You can think of drains as the mechanism for telling new claimers, "Hey, you can't use this in that way!" The specific action being prevented by the drain is based on the claim class being drained. Draining write claims enables concurrent access to the resource, but the resource cannot be modified. Draining read (CS and/or RR) and write claims prevents any and all concurrent access.

Drain locks are released when the utility or command completes. When the resource has been drained of all appropriate claim classes, the drainer acquires sole access to the resource.

Claim and Drain Lock Compatibility

As with transaction locks, concurrent claims and drains can be taken, but only if they are compatible with one another. Table 16.11 shows which drains are compatible with existing claims.

Table 16.11. Claim/drain compatibility matrix.

Existing Claim for PGM2	*Drain required by PGM1*		
	Write	CS	RR
Write	No	No	No
RR	Yes	No	No
CS	Yes	No	No

Table 16.12 shows which drains are compatible with existing drains.

Table 16.12. Drain/drain compatibility matrix.

Existing Drain for PGM2	*Drain required by PGM1*		
	Write	CS	RR
Write	Yes	No	No
RR	No	No	No
CS	No	No	No

When Is Transaction Locking Used?

You use transaction locks to serialize access to a resource between multiple claimers, such as two SQL statements or an SQL statement and a utility that takes claims, such as RUNSTATS SHRLEVEL(CHANGE).

When Are Claims and Drains Used?

Claims and drains serialize access between a claimer and a drainer. For example, an INSERT statement is a claimer that must be dealt with by the LOAD utility, which is a drainer.

Drain locks are used to control concurrency when both a command and a utility try to access the same resource.

Lock Avoidance

Lock avoidance is a mechanism employed by DB2 V3 (and above) to access data without locking while maintaining data integrity. It prohibits access to uncommitted data and serializes access to pages. Lock avoidance improves performance by reducing the overall volume of lock requests.

In general, DB2 avoids locking data pages if it can determine that the data to be accessed is committed and that no semantics are violated by not acquiring the lock. DB2 avoids locks by examining the log to verify the committed state of the data.

When determining if lock avoidance techniques will be practical, DB2 first scans the page to be accessed to determine whether any rows qualify. If none qualify, a lock is not required.

For each data page to be accessed, the RBA of the last page update (stored in the data page header) is compared with the log RBA for the oldest active unit of recovery. This RBA is called the Commit Log Sequence Number, or CLSN. If the CLSN is greater than the last page update RBA, the data on the page has been committed and the page lock can be avoided.

Additionally, a new bit is stored in the record header for each row on the page. The bit is called the Possibly UNCommitted, or PUNC, bit. The PUNC bit indicates whether update activity has been performed on the row. For each qualifying row on the page, the PUNC bit is checked to see whether it is off. This indicates that the row has not been updated since the last time the bit was turned off. Therefore, locking can be avoided.

NOTE

IBM provides no method to determine whether the PUNC bit is on or off for each row. Therefore, you should ensure that any table that can be modified should be reorganized on a regularly scheduled basis.

If neither CLSN or PUNC bit testing indicates that a lock can be avoided, DB2 acquires the requisite lock.

In addition to enhancing performance, lock avoidance increases data availability. Data that in previous releases would have been considered locked, and therefore unavailable, is now considered accessible.

When Lock Avoidance Can Occur

Lock avoidance *can be used only for data pages*, not for type 1 index pages. (Type 2 indexes are never locked.) Further, DB2 Catalog and DB2 Directory access does not use lock avoidance techniques.

You can avoid locks under the following circumstances:

- For any pages accessed by read-only or ambiguous queries bound with ISOLATION(CS) and CURRENTDATA NO
- For any unqualified rows accessed by queries bound with ISOLATION(CS) or ISOLATION(RS)
- When DB2 system-managed referential integrity checks for dependent rows caused by either the primary key being updated, or the parent row being deleted and the DELETE RESTRICT rule is in effect
- For both COPY and RUNSTATS when SHRLEVEL(CHANGE) is specified

Data Sharing Global Lock Management

Version 4

Because data sharing group members can access any object from any member in the group, a global locking mechanism is required. It is handled by the lock structure defined in the coupling facility. The lock structure is charged with managing inter-member locking. Without a global lock management process, data integrity problems could occur when one member attempts to read (or change) data that is in the process of being changed by another member.

Data sharing groups utilize a global locking mechanism to preserve the integrity of the shared data. The global locking mechanism allows locks to be recognized between members.

Global Locking

All members of a data sharing group must be aware of locks that are held or requested by the other members. The DB2 data sharing group utilizes the coupling facility to establish and administer global locks.

The IRLM performs locking within each member DB2 subsystem. Additionally, the IRLM communicates with the coupling facility to establish global locks. Each member of the data sharing group communicates lock requests to the coupling facility's lock structure. The manner in which a transaction takes locks during execution does not change. The only difference is that, instead of being local locks, the locks being taken are global in nature.

DB2 data sharing does not use message passing to perform global locking. The members DB2 IRLMs use the coupling facility to do global locking. Contention can be identified quickly without having to suspend the tasks to send messages around to the other DB2 members contained in the data sharing group. The following list outlines the events that occur when transactions from different DB2 members try to access the same piece of data:

1. TXN1 requests a lock that is handled by the local IRLM.

2. The local IRLM passes the request to the coupling facility global lock structures to ensure that no other members have incompatible locks. No incompatible locks are found, so the lock is taken.
3. TXN2 requests a lock that is handled by its local IRLM. The lock is for the same data held by TXN1 executing in a different DB2 subsystem.
4. Once again, the local IRLM passes the request to the coupling facility global lock structures to check for lock compatibility. In this case, an incompatible lock is found, so the lock request cannot be granted. The task is suspended.
5. Eventually, TXN1 executes a `COMMIT`, which releases all local and global locks.
6. TXN2 now can successfully execute the lock and continue processing.

Lock Structures

The coupling facility contains several lock structures that are used for global locking purposes. The lock lists contain names of modified resources. This information is used to notify members of the data sharing group that the various resources have been changed.

Additionally, a hash table is used to identify compatible and incompatible lock modes. If the same hash value is used for the same resource name from different systems (with incompatible lock modes), lock contention will occur. If the same hash value is used for different resource names (called a *hashing collision*), false contention will occur. Any contention requires additional asynchronous processing to occur.

Hierarchical Locking

DB2 data sharing introduces the concept of explicit hierarchical locking to reduce global locking overhead (which increases global locking performance). Explicit hierarchical locking allows data sharing to differentiate between global and local locks. When no inter-DB2 interest occurs in a resource, the local IRLM can grant locks locally on the resources that are lower in the hierarchy. This feature allows the local DB2 to obtain local locks on pages or rows for that tablespace without notifying the coupling facility. In a data sharing environment, locks on the top parents are always propagated to the coupling facility lock structures. (These structures are detailed on the previous page.) In addition, the local DB2 propagates locks on children, depending on the compatibility of the maximum lock held on a tablespace that also has other members of the DB2 data sharing group requesting locks on it.

P-Locks Versus L-Locks

DB2 data sharing introduces two new lock identifiers: P-locks and L-locks.

P-Locks

P-locks preserve inter-DB2 coherency of buffered pages. P-locks are owned by the member DB2 subsystem and are used for physical resources such as page sets. These physical resources can be either data objects or index objects. P-locks are held for the length of time the pages are locally cached in the local buffer pool. As such, data can be cached beyond a transaction commit point.

P-locks are negotiable. If multiple DB2 members hold incompatible P-locks, the IRLMs try to downgrade lock compatibility. P-locks are never timed out. Because P-locks are not owned by transactions, they cannot be deadlocked. The sole job of a P-lock is to ensure inter-DB2 coherency. P-locks notify the data sharing group that a member of that group is performing work on that resource. This way, the coupling facility can become involved and begin treating the resources globally.

L-Locks

L-locks are used for both intra- and inter-DB2 concurrency between transactions. L-locks can either be local or global in scope. L-locks are owned by transactions and are held for COMMIT or allocation duration. L-locks are not negotiable and, as such, must wait for incompatible L-locks held by other DB2 members to be released before they can be taken. Suspended L-locks can be timed out by the IRLM.

DB2 Locking Guidelines

Locking is a complex subject, and it can take much time and effort to understand and master its intricacies. Do not be frustrated if these concepts escape you after an initial reading of this chapter. Instead, refer to the following guidelines to assist you in designing your application's locking needs. Let this information settle for a while and then reread the chapter.

Be Aware of the Effect of Referential Integrity on Locking

When tablespace locks are acquired because of the processing of referential constraints, all locking specifications, except the ACQUIRE bind parameter, are obeyed. Locks acquired because of referential integrity always acquire locks when needed, acting as though ACQUIRE(USE) were specified, regardless of the ACQUIRE parameter.

Establish Acceptable BIND Plan Parameters

This information is covered in more detail in Chapter 7, "Program Preparation," but it is repeated here because it affects DB2 locking. Favor the use of the following parameters when binding application plans because they usually produce the most efficient and effective DB2 plan. In particular, the ISOLATION, ACQUIRE, and RELEASE parameters specified in the following list create an efficient plan in terms of enabling a large degree of concurrent processing.

Favor the use of the following parameters when binding application plans:

```
ISOLATION (CS)
VALIDATE (BIND)
ACTION (REPLACE)
NODEFER (PREPARE)
FLAG (I)
ACQUIRE (USE)
RELEASE (COMMIT)
DEGREE (ANY)
CURRENTDATA (NO)
EXPLAIN (YES)
```

These `BIND PLAN` parameters usually produce the most efficient and effective DB2 plan.

Establish Acceptable BIND Package Parameters

The `ISOLATION` parameter is the most important in terms of locking for DB2 packages. The following list of parameters should be favored when binding packages:

```
ISOLATION (CS)
VALIDATE (BIND)
ACTION (REPLACE)
SQLERROR (NOPACKAGE)
FLAG (I)
RELEASE (COMMIT)
DEGREE (ANY)
CURRENTDATA (NO)
EXPLAIN (YES)
```

Usually, these `BIND PACKAGE` parameters produce the most efficient and effective DB2 package. Other guidelines in this chapter cover the occasions when you should choose another option.

Be Aware of Lock Promotion

When binding a plan with an `ISOLATION` level of `RR`, the optimizer sometimes decides that tablespace locks will perform better than page locks. As such, the optimizer promotes the locking level to tablespace locking, regardless of the `LOCKSIZE` specified in the DDL. This process is called *lock promotion.*

Be Aware of Lock Escalation

When you set the `LOCKSIZE` bind parameter to `ANY`, DB2 processing begins with page-level locking. As processing continues and locks are acquired, however, DB2 might decide that too many page (or row) locks have been acquired, causing inefficient processing. The lock count includes locks for data pages, plus type-1 index pages and subpages.

In this scenario, DB2 escalates the level of locking from page (or row) locks to table or tablespace locks—a procedure called *lock escalation.* The threshold governing when lock escalation occurs is set in one of two ways:

- The DSNZPARM start-up parameters for DB2
- The LOCKMAX parameter of the CREATE or ALTER TABLESPACE statement (which is stored in the MAXROWS column of SYSIBM.SYSTABLESPACE)

Lock escalation applies only to objects defined with LOCKSIZE ANY in the DDL. A table lock can never be escalated to a tablespace lock. Tablespace locks are the highest level of locking and, therefore, cannot be escalated.

User Lock Escalation

If a single user accumulates more page locks than are allowed by the DB2 subsystem (as set in DSNZPARMs), the program is informed via a -904 SQLCODE. The program can either issue a ROLLBACK and produce a message indicating that the program should be modified to COMMIT more frequently or, alternately, escalate the locking strategy itself by explicitly issuing a LOCK TABLE statement within the code.

Prior to implementing the second approach, refer to the upcoming guideline, "Use LOCK TABLE with Caution," for further clarification on the ramifications of using LOCK TABLE.

Use DSNZPARM Parameters to Control Lock Escalation

The two DSNZPARM parameters used to govern DB2 locking are NUMLKTS and NUMLKUS. NUMLKTS defines the threshold for the number of page locks that can be concurrently held for any one tablespace by any single DB2 application (thread). When the threshold is reached, DB2 escalates all page locks for objects defined as LOCKSIZE ANY according to the following rules:

- All page locks held for data in segmented tablespaces are escalated to table locks.
- All page locks held for data in simple or partitioned tablespaces are escalated to tablespace locks.

NUMLKUS defines the threshold for the total number of page locks across all tablespaces that can be concurrently held by a single DB2 application. When any given application attempts to acquire a lock that would cause the application to surpass the NUMLKUS threshold, the application receives a resource unavailable message (SQLCODE of -904).

Use LOCKSIZE ANY

In general, letting DB2 handle the level of locking required is best. The recommended LOCKSIZE specification is therefore ANY, unless a compelling reason can be given to use another LOCKSIZE. Refer to Chapter 3, "Data Definition Guidelines," for possible reasons.

Use LOCKMAX to Control Lock Escalation by Tablespace

Version 4

The LOCKMAX parameter specifies the maximum number of page or row locks that any one process can hold at any one time for the tablespace. When the threshold is reached, the page or row locks are escalated to a table or tablespace lock. The LOCKMAX parameter is similar to the NUMLKTS parameter, but for a single tablespace only.

Set IRLM Parameters to Optimize Locking

When the IRLM is installed, you must code a series of parameters that affect the performance of DB2 locking. In particular, you should define the IRLM so that it effectively utilizes memory to avoid locking performance problems. The IRLM parameters are detailed in Table 16.13.

Table 16.13. Recommended IRLM parameters.

Parameter	*Recommended Value*	*Reason*
SCOPE	LOCAL	The IRLM should be local.
DEADLOK	(15,4)	Every 15 seconds, the IRLM goes into a deadlock detection cycle.
PC	NO	Cross-memory services are not used when requesting IRLM functions; instead, the locks are stored in ECSA and therefore are directly addressable.
ITRACE	NO	Never turn on the IRLM trace because it uses a vast amount of resources.

Use LOCK TABLE with Caution

Use the LOCK TABLE statement to control the efficiency of locking in programs that will issue many page lock requests. The LOCK TABLE statement is coded as a standard SQL statement and can be embedded in an application program.

There are two types of LOCK TABLE requests. The LOCK TABLE...IN SHARE MODE command acquires an S-lock on the table specified in the statement. This locking strategy effectively eliminates the possibility of concurrent modification programs running while the LOCK TABLE is in effect. *Note:* The S-lock is obtained on the tablespace for tables contained in non-segmented tablespaces.

The LOCK TABLE...IN EXCLUSIVE MODE command acquires an X-lock on the table specified in the statement. All concurrent processing is suspended until the X-lock is released. *Note:* The X-lock is obtained on the tablespace for tables contained in non-segmented tablespaces.

The table locks acquired as a result of the LOCK TABLE statement are held until the next COMMIT point unless ACQUIRE(DEALLOCATE) was specified for the plan issuing the LOCK TABLE statement. In that situation, the lock is held until the program terminates.

Encourage Lock Avoidance

To encourage DB2 to avoid locks, try the following:

- Whenever practical, specify ISOLATION(CS) and CURRENTDATA NO when binding packages and plans.
- Avoid ambiguous cursors by specifying FOR READ ONLY or FOR FETCH ONLY when a cursor is not to be used for updating.

Be Aware of Concurrent Access with Partition Independence

Partition independence allows more jobs to be run concurrently. This capability can strain system resources. You should monitor CPU usage and I/O when taking advantage of partition independence to submit concurrent jobs that would have needed to be serialized with previous versions.

Use Type 2 Indexes

Using Type 2 indexes instead of Type 1 indexes decreases contention because locks are not taken on Type 1 indexes. Using Type 2 indexes instead of Type 1 indexes is almost always best.

Increase Subpages for Type 1 Indexes to Reduce Contention

If you're still using Type 1 indexes, use the SUBPAGES parameter to influence contention. When index lock contention is a problem (such as when many timeouts and deadlocks are encountered), increase the number of index SUBPAGES specified for the indexes causing the lock problems.

Use Caution When Specifying WITH HOLD

Using the CURSOR WITH HOLD clause causes locks and claims to be held across commits. This capability can increase the number of timeouts and affect availability. Before coding the WITH HOLD clause on a cursor, be sure that the benefit gained by doing so is not negated by reduced availability.

Access Tables in the Same Order

Design all application programs to access tables in the same order. Doing so reduces the likelihood of deadlocks. Consider the following:

Program 1	*Program 2*
Lock on DEPT	Lock on EMP
Request Lock on EMP	Request Lock on DEPT

In this scenario, a deadlock occurs. However, if both programs accessed DEPT, followed by EMP, the deadlock situation could be avoided.

Design Application Programs with Locking in Mind

Minimize the effect of locking through proper application program design. Limit the number of rows that are accessed by coding predicates to filter unwanted rows. Doing so reduces the number of locks on pages containing rows that are accessed but not required, thereby reducing timeouts and deadlocks.

Also, you should design update programs so that the update is as close to the commit point as possible. Doing so reduces the time that locks are held during a unit of work, which also reduces timeouts and deadlocks.

Keep Similar Things Together

Place tables for the same application into the same database. Each application process should use as few databases as possible.

Furthermore, each application process that creates private tables should have a dedicated private database in which to create the tables. Do not use a database that is in use for other, production database objects.

CAUTION

As with all advice, remember the cardinal rule of DB2: It depends! There are legitimate reasons for storing similar things separately. For example, as databases grow in size and activity increases, it might make sense to reduce the database size by storing fewer tablespaces per database.

Cluster Data

Use clustering to encourage DB2 to maintain data that is accessed together on the same page. If you use page locking, fewer locks are required to access multiple rows if the rows are clustered on the same page or pages.

Choose Segmented Over Simple Tablespaces for Locking Efficiency

Both simple and segmented tablespaces can contain more than one table. A lock on a simple tablespace locks all the data in every table because rows from different tables can be intermingled on the same page. In a segmented tablespace, rows from different tables are contained in different pages. Locking a page does not lock data from more than one table. Additionally, for segmented tablespaces only, DB2 can acquire a lock on a single table.

Consider Increasing Free Space

If you increase free space, fewer rows are stored on a single page. Therefore, fewer rows are locked by a single page lock. This approach can decrease contention. However, it consumes additional DASD, and it can also decrease the performance of tablespace scans.

Consider Decreasing Number of Rows Per Page

Version 5

The `MAXROWS` option of the `CREATE TABLESPACE` statement is new as of DB2 V5. It can be used to decrease the number of rows stored on a tablespace page. The fewer rows per page, the less intrusive page locking will be because fewer rows will be impacted by a page lock.

Other DB2 Components

You are near the end of your excursion behind the scenes of DB2. Before you finish, however, you should know about two other DB2 components that operate behind the scenes: the Boot Strap Data Set (BSDS) and DB2 logging.

The BSDS is a VSAM KSDS data set utilized by DB2 to control and administer the DB2 log data sets. It is an integral component of DB2, controlling the log data sets and managing an inventory of those logs. The BSDS is also used to record the image copy backups taken for the `SYSIBM.SYSCOPY` DB2 Catalog table. Because `SYSIBM.SYSCOPY` records all other DB2 image copies, another location must be used to record image copies of the `SYSIBM.SYSCOPY` table.

DB2 logs every modification made to every piece of DB2 data. Log records are written for every `INSERT`, `UPDATE`, and `DELETE` SQL statement that is successfully executed and committed. DB2 logs each updated row from the first byte updated to the end of the row. These log records are written to the active logs. DB2 usually has two active log data sets to safeguard against physical DASD errors. The active logs must reside on DASD. (They cannot reside on tape.) The active log data sets are managed by DB2 using the BSDS.

As the active logs are filled, DB2 invokes a process called *log offloading* to move the log information offline to archive log data sets. This process reduces the chances of the active logs filling up during DB2 processing, which would stifle the DB2 environment. DB2 can access archive logs to evoke tablespace recovery. The BSDS manages and administers the archive logs.

The Big Picture

Now that you have seen what is happening in DB2 behind the scenes, I will tie all this information together with a single picture. Figure 16.3 contains all the DB2 components that operate together to achieve an effective and useful relational database management system.

FIGURE 16.3.
DB2: The big picture.

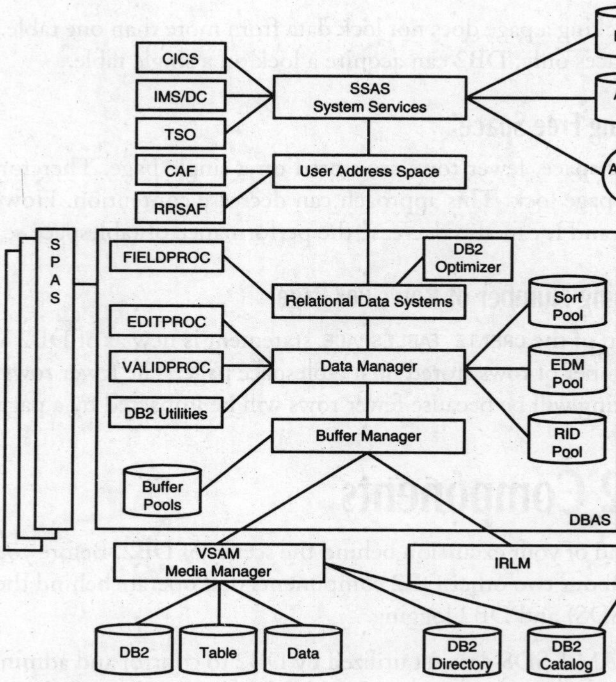

Summary

In this chapter, you learned how DB2 can guarantee the accuracy of its data by enacting data locks. Locking is a complex subject with many intricate details that can be difficult to understand. There are numerous types of locks, accompanied by a vast array of locking terms and strategies to learn. You should consider reading this chapter several times to master all of the nuances of DB2 locking.

After you are comfortable with DB2 locking, turn the page to begin your journey into the world of DB2 performance monitoring.

IV

DB2 Performance Monitoring

After you have established a DB2 environment and installed application systems that access that environment, it is imperative that the environment be monitored regularly to ensure optimal performance. The job of monitoring DB2 performance usually is performed by a database administrator, performance analyst, or system administrator.

Many factors contribute to the performance level achieved by DB2 applications. Unless an orderly and consistent approach to DB2 performance monitoring is implemented, an effective approach to tuning cannot be achieved and the performance of DB2 applications might fluctuate wildly from execution to execution.

Let's examine the traits of DB2 that make performance monitoring a crucial component of the DB2 environment. DB2 is an MVS subsystem composed of many intricate pieces. Each of these pieces is responsible for different performance-critical operations. In Chapters 10 and 11, you learned that DB2 itself is composed of several distinct address spaces that communicate with one another. You learned also about the features of the optimizer. Without a way to measure the relative performance of each of these pieces, it is impossible to gauge factors affecting the overall performance of DB2 applications, programs, and SQL statements.

In addition, DB2 applications regularly communicate with other MVS subsystems, which also require routine performance monitoring. The capability to monitor MVS batch, CICS, IMS/DC, and TSO address spaces as well as other DB2 address spaces using distributed database capabilities is critical. Many factors influence not only the performance of DB2, but also the performance of these other MVS subsystems. It is important, therefore, to implement and follow a regular schedule of monitoring the performance of all the interacting components of the DB2 environment.

Part IV presents a methodical approach to the evaluation of DB2 performance. This section discusses the many elements that make up DB2 performance monitoring, including DB2 traces, IBM's DB2 performance monitor, and other DB2 and allied agent performance monitors. Remember, though, that this section covers the *monitoring* of DB2 performance. Methods of pinpointing potential performance problems are examined, but guidelines for correcting them are not covered until Part V, "DB2 Performance Tuning."

Defining DB2 Performance

You must have a firm definition of DB2 performance before you learn ways to monitor it. You can think of DB2 performance using the familiar concepts of supply and demand. Users demand information from DB2. DB2 supplies information to those requesting it. The rate at which DB2 supplies the demand for information can be termed DB2 performance.

Five factors influence DB2's performance: workload, throughput, resources, optimization, and contention.

- The *workload* that is requested of DB2 defines the demand. It is a combination of online transactions, batch jobs, and system commands directed through the system at any given time. Workload can fluctuate drastically from day to day, hour to hour, and even minute to minute. Sometimes workload can be predicted (such as heavy month-end processing of payroll, or very light access after 5:30 p.m., when most users have left for the day), but other times it is unpredictable. The overall workload has a major impact on DB2 performance.
- *Throughput* defines the overall capability of the computer to process data. It is a composite of I/O speed, CPU speed, and the efficiency of the operating system.
- The hardware and software tools at the disposal of the system are known as the *resources* of the system. Examples of system resources include memory (such as that allocated to bufferpools or address spaces), DASD, cache controllers, and microcode.
- The fourth defining element of DB2 performance is *optimization.* All types of systems can be optimized, but DB2 is unique in that optimization is (for the most part) accomplished internal to DB2.
- When the demand (workload) for a particular resource is high, *contention* can result. Contention is the condition in which two or more components of the workload are attempting to use a single resource in a conflicting way (for example, dual updates to the same data page). As contention increases, throughput decreases.

NOTE

DB2 performance can be defined as the optimization of resource use to increase throughput and minimize contention, enabling the largest possible workload to be processed.

How do we measure the performance of DB2? There are many methods, ranging from waiting for a user to complain to writing a customized performance monitor for your shop. Neither of these approaches is recommended, however. The first does not provide an optimal environment for the user, and the second does not provide an optimal environment for the systems professional. Instead, to monitor all aspects of your DB2 environment, you should use the capabilities of DB2 in conjunction with software tools provided by IBM and other vendors.

Types of DB2 Performance Monitoring

There are many types of DB2 performance monitoring. It is wise to implement procedures for all different types of DB2 performance monitoring. If you do not monitor using all available methods, your environment has an exposure that might cause performance degradation that cannot be quickly diagnosed and corrected.

DB2 performance monitoring can be broken down into the following eight categories:

- DB2 traces and reporting
- Sampling DB2 control blocks
- Sampling application address spaces during program execution
- MVS-allied agent monitoring
- Distributed network monitoring
- Access path evaluation
- DB2 Catalog reporting
- Monitoring DB2 console messages

In the ensuing chapters, each of these performance monitoring categories is covered in-depth, complete with strategies for supporting them in your environment.

17

Traditional DB2 Performance Monitoring

The first part of any DB2 performance monitoring strategy should be to provide a comprehensive approach to the monitoring of the DB2 subsystems operating at your shop. This approach involves monitoring not only the threads accessing DB2, but also the DB2 address spaces. You can accomplish this task in three ways:

- Batch reports run against DB2 trace records. While DB2 is running, you can activate traces that accumulate information, which can be used to monitor both the performance of the DB2 subsystem and the applications being run.
- Online access to DB2 trace information and DB2 control blocks. This type of monitoring also can provide information on DB2 and its subordinate applications.
- Sampling DB2 application programs as they run and analyzing which portions of the code use the most resources.

I will examine these monitoring methods later in this chapter, but first I will outline some performance monitoring basics. When you're implementing a performance monitoring methodology, keep these basic caveats in mind:

- Do not overdo monitoring and tracing. DB2 performance monitoring uses a tremendous amount of resources. Sometimes the associated overhead is worthwhile because the monitoring (problem determination or exception notification) can help alleviate or avoid a problem. However, absorbing a large CPU overhead for monitoring a DB2 subsystem that is already performing within the desired scope of acceptance is not worthwhile.
- Plan and implement two types of monitoring strategies at your shop: ongoing performance monitoring to ferret out exceptions and procedures for monitoring exceptions after they have been observed.
- Do not try to drive a nail with a bulldozer. Use the correct tool for the job, based on the type of problem you're monitoring. You would be unwise to turn on a trace that causes 200 percent CPU overhead to solve a production problem that could be solved just as easily by other types of monitoring (using EXPLAIN or DB2 Catalog reports, for example).
- Tuning should not consume your every waking moment. Establish your DB2 performance tuning goals in advance, and stop when they have been achieved. Too often, tuning goes beyond the point at which reasonable gains can be realized for the amount of effort exerted. (For example, if your goal is to achieve a five-second response time for a TSO application, stop when you have achieved that goal.)

DB2 Traces

The first type of performance monitoring I discuss here is monitoring based on reading trace information. You can think of a DB2 trace as a window into the performance characteristics of aspects of the DB2 workload. DB2 traces record diagnostic information describing particular events. As DB2 operates, it writes trace information that can be read and analyzed to obtain performance information.

DB2 provides six types of traces, and each describes information about the DB2 environment. These six types of traces are outlined in Table 17.1.

Table 17.1. DB2 trace types.

Trace	*Started By*	*Description*
Accounting	DSNZPARM or -START TRACE	Records performance information about the execution of DB2 application programs
Audit	DSNZPARM or -START TRACE	Provides information about DB2 DDL, security, utilities, and data modification
Global	DSNZPARM or -START TRACE	Provides information for the servicing of DB2
Monitor	DSNZPARM or -START TRACE	Records data useful for online monitoring of the DB2 subsystem and DB2 application programs
Performance	-START TRACE	Collects detailed data about DB2 events, enabling database and performance analysts to pinpoint the causes of performance problems
Statistics	DSNZPARM or -START TRACE	Records information regarding the DB2 subsystem's use of resources

Note that you start DB2 traces in two ways: by specifying the appropriate DSNZPARMs at DB2 startup or by using the -START TRACE command to initiate specific traces when DB2 is already running.

Each trace is broken down further into classes, each of which provides information about aspects of that trace. Classes are composed of IFCIDs. An IFCID (sometimes pronounced *if-kid*) defines a record that represents a trace event. IFCIDs are the single smallest unit of tracing that can be invoked by DB2. All these DB2 trace types are discussed in the following sections.

Accounting Trace

The accounting trace is probably the single most important trace for judging the performance of DB2 application programs. Using the accounting trace records, DB2 writes data pertaining to the following:

- CPU and elapsed time of the program
- EDM pool use
- Locks and latches requested for the program
- Number of get page requests, by bufferpool, issued by the program
- Number of synchronous writes
- Type of SQL issued by the program
- Number of COMMITs and ABORTs issued by the program
- Program's use of sequential prefetch and other DB2 performance features

Estimated overhead: DB2 accounting class 1 adds approximately 3 percent CPU overhead. DB2 accounting classes 1, 2, and 3 together add approximately 5 percent CPU overhead. You cannot run class 2 or 3 without also running class 1.

Accounting trace classes 7 and 8 provide performance trace information at the package level. Enabling this level of tracing can cause significant overhead.

Audit Trace

The audit trace is useful for installations that must meticulously track specific types of DB2 events. Not every shop needs the audit trace. However, those wanting to audit by authid, specific table accesses, and other DB2 events will find the audit trace invaluable. Eight categories of audit information are provided:

- All instances in which an authorization failure occurs—for example, if USER1 attempts to SELECT information from a table for which he or she has not been granted the appropriate authority
- All executions of the DB2 data control language GRANT and REVOKE statements
- Every DDL statement issued for specific tables created by specifying AUDIT CHANGES or AUDIT ALL
- The first DELETE, INSERT, or UPDATE for an audited table
- The first SELECT for only the tables created specifying AUDIT ALL
- DML statements encountered by DB2 when binding
- All authid changes resulting from execution of the SET CURRENT SQLID statement
- All execution of DB2 utilities

This type of data is often required of critical DB2 applications housing sensitive data, such as payroll or billing applications.

Estimated overhead: Approximately 5 percent CPU overhead per transaction is added when all audit trace classes are started. See the "Tracing Guidelines" section later in this chapter for additional information on audit trace overhead.

Global Trace

Global trace information is used to service DB2. A global trace records information regarding entries and exits from internal DB2 modules as well as other information about DB2 internals. It is not accessible through tools that monitor DB2 performance. Most sites will never need to use the DB2 global trace. You should avoid it unless an IBM representative requests that your shop initiate it.

CAUTION

IBM states that the global trace can add 100 percent CPU overhead to your DB2 subsystem.

Monitor Trace

An amalgamation of useful performance monitoring information is recorded by the DB2 monitor trace. Most of the information is also provided by other types of DB2 traces. The primary reason for the existence of the monitor trace type is to enable you to write application programs that provide online monitoring of DB2 performance.

Information provided by the monitor trace includes the following:

- DB2 statistics trace information
- DB2 accounting trace information
- Information about current SQL statements

Estimated overhead: The overhead that results from the monitor trace depends on how it is used at your site. If, as recommended, class 1 is always active, and classes 2 and 3 are started and stopped as required, the overhead is minimal (approximately 2 to 5 percent, depending on the activity of the DB2 system and the number of times that the other classes are started and stopped). However, if your installation makes use of the reserved classes (30 through 32) or additional classes (as some vendors do), your site will incur additional overhead.

Performance Trace

The DB2 performance trace records an abundance of information about all types of DB2 events. You should use it only after you have exhausted all other avenues of monitoring and tuning because it consumes a great deal of system resources.

When a difficult problem persists, the performance trace can provide valuable information, including the following:

- Text of the SQL statement
- Complete trace of the execution of SQL statements, including details of all events (cursor creation and manipulation, actual reads and writes, fetches, and so on) associated with the execution of the SQL statement
- All index accesses
- All data access due to referential constraints

Estimated overhead: When all DB2 performance trace classes are active, as much as 100 percent CPU overhead can be incurred by each program being traced. The actual overhead might be greater if the system has a large amount of activity. Furthermore, due to the large number of trace records cut by the DB2 performance trace, system-wide (DB2 and non-DB2) performance might suffer because of possible SMF or GTF contention. The overhead when using only classes 1, 2, and 3, however, ranges from 20 to 30 percent rather than 100 percent.

Statistics Trace

Information pertaining to the entire DB2 subsystem is recorded in statistics trace records. This information is particularly useful for measuring the activity and response of DB2 as a whole. Information on the utilization and status of the bufferpools, DB2 locking, DB2 logging, and DB2 storage is accumulated.

Estimated overhead: An average of 2 percent CPU overhead per transaction.

Trace Destinations

When a trace is started, DB2 formats records containing the requested information. After the information is prepared, it must be externalized. DB2 traces can be written to six destinations:

GTF	(Generalized Trace Facility) is a component of MVS and is used for storing large volumes of trace data.
RES	RES is a wraparound table residing in memory.
SMF	SMF (System Management Facility) is a source of data collection used by MVS to accumulate information and measurements. This destination is the most common for DB2 traces.
SRV	SRV is a routine used primarily by IBM support personnel for servicing DB2.
OP*n*	OP*n* (where n is a value from 1 to 8) is an output buffer area used by the Instrumentation Facility Interface (IFI).
OPX	OPX is a generic output buffer. When used as a destination, OPX signals DB2 to assign the next available OP*n* buffer (OP1 to OP8).

The Instrumentation Facility Interface, which is a DB2 trace interface, enables DB2 programs to read, write, and create DB2 trace records and issue DB2 commands. Many online DB2 performance monitors are based on the IFI.

Consult Table 17.2 for a synopsis of the available and recommended destinations for each DB2 trace type. Y indicates that the specified trace destination is valid for the given type of trace; N indicates that it is not.

Table 17.2. DB2 trace destinations.

Type of Trace	*GTF*	*RES*	*SMF*	*SRV*	*OPn*	*OPX*	*Recommended Destination*
Statistics	Y	N	Default	Y	Y	Y	SMF
Accounting	Y	N	Default	Y	Y	Y	SMF
Audit	Y	N	Default	Y	Y	Y	SMF
Performance	Y	N	Default	Y	Y	Y	GTF
Monitor	Y	N	Y	Y	Y	D	OP*n*
Global	Y	Default	Y	Y	Y	Y	SRV

Tracing Guidelines

Consider abiding by the following guidelines to implement an effective DB2 tracing strategy at your shop.

Collect Basic Statistics

At a minimum, begin the DB2 accounting classes 1 and 2 and statistics class 1 traces at DB2 start-up time. This way, you can ensure that basic statistics are accumulated for the DB2 subsystem and every DB2 plan executed. These traces require little overhead. If you do not start these traces, you cannot use traces to monitor DB2 performance (the method used by DB2-PM).

Consider starting accounting class 3 at DB2 start-up time as well. It tracks DB2 wait time and is useful for tracking I/O and tracking problems external to DB2.

Note that accounting classes 2 and 3 cannot be activated unless accounting class 1 is active.

Use Accounting Trace Classes 7 and 8 with Caution

Accounting classes 7 and 8 cause DB2 to write trace records at the package level. Although monitoring DB2 programs at the package level may seem to be appropriate, do so with caution to avoid undue performance degradation.

If package level performance monitoring is absolutely essential for certain applications, consider starting these trace classes for only those plans. This way, you can produce the requisite information with as little overhead as possible.

Use the Audit Trace Wisely

If your shop has tables created with the AUDIT parameter, start all audit trace classes.

If your shop has no audited tables, use the DSNZPARMs at DB2 startup to start only audit classes 1, 2, and 7 to audit authorization failures, DCL, and utility execution. Except for these types of processing, audit classes 1, 2, and 7 add no additional overhead. Because most transactions do not result in authorization failures or issue GRANTs, REVOKEs, or utilities, running these trace classes is cost effective.

Let Your Performance Monitor Start Traces

Do not start the monitor trace using DSNZPARMs unless online performance monitors in your shop explicitly require you to do so. It is best to start only monitor trace class 1 and to use a performance monitor that starts and stops the other monitor classes as required.

Avoid starting the monitor trace through the use of the -START TRACE command under DB2. When this command is entered manually in this manner, a great degree of coordination is required to start and stop the monitor trace according to the requirements of your online monitor.

Use Caution When Running Performance Traces

Use the performance trace with great care. Performance traces must be explicitly started with the -START TRACE command. Starting the performance trace only for the plan (or plans) you want to monitor by using the PLAN( ) parameter of the -START TRACE command is wise. Here's an example:

```
-START TRACE(PERFM) CLASS(1,2,3) PLAN(PLANNAME) DEST(GTF)
```

Failure to start the trace at the plan level can result in the trace being started for all plans, which causes undue overhead on all DB2 plans that execute while the trace is active.

Avoid Performance Trace Class 7

Never use performance trace class 7 unless directed by IBM. Lock detail trace records are written when performance trace class 7 is activated. They can cause as much as a 100 percent increase in CPU overhead per program being traced.

Avoid Global Trace

Avoid the global trace unless directed to use it by a member of your IBM support staff. This trace should be used only for servicing DB2.

Use IFCIDs

Consider avoiding the trace classes altogether, and start traces specifying only the IFCIDs needed. This way, you can reduce the overhead associated with tracing by recording only the trace events that are needed. You can do so by using the `-START TRACE` command, as follows:

```
-START TRACE(PERFM) CLASS(1) IFCID(1,2,42,43,107,153)
```

This command starts only IFCIDs 1, 2, 42, 43, 107, and 153.

Because this task can be tedious, if you decide to trace only at the IFCID level, use a performance monitor that starts these IFCID-level traces based on menu choices. For example, if you choose to trace the elapsed time of DB2 utility jobs, the monitor or tool would have a menu option for this, initiating the correct IFCID traces (for example, IFCIDs 023 through 025). For more information on the Instrumentation Facility Interface and IFCIDs, consult the *DB2 Administration Guide*.

DB2-PM

IBM's DB2-PM is the most widely used batch performance monitor for DB2. Although DB2-PM also provides an online component, it is not as widely used (though it has been significantly improved since its initial release). I discuss the online portion of DB2-PM briefly in the next section. In this section, I concentrate solely on the batch performance monitoring characteristics of DB2-PM.

DB2-PM permits performance analysts to review formatted trace records to assist in evaluating the performance of not only the DB2 subsystem, but also DB2 applications. (See Figure 17.1.) As the DB2 subsystem executes, trace records are written to either GTF or SMF. Which trace records are written depends on which DB2 traces are active. The trace information is then funneled to DB2-PM, which creates requested reports and graphs.

DB2-PM can generate many categories of performance reports, known as *report sets*. A brief description of each report set follows:

Accounting	Summarizes the utilization of DB2 resources such as CPU and elapsed time, SQL use, buffer use, and locking.
Audit	Tracks the access of DB2 resources. Provides information on authorization failures, `GRANT`s and `REVOKE`s, access to auditable tables, `SET SQLID` executions, and utility execution.
I/O Activity	Summarizes DB2 reads and writes to the bufferpool, EDM pool, active and archive logs, and the BSDS.
Locking	Reports the level of lock suspension and contention in the DB2 subsystem.
Record Trace	Displays DB2 trace records from the input source.

SQL Trace	Reports on detailed activity associated with each SQL statement.
Statistics	Summarizes the statistics for an entire DB2 subsystem. Useful for obtaining a synopsis of DB2 activity.
Summary	Reports on the activity performed by DB2-PM to produce the requested reports.
System Parameters	Creates a report detailing the values assigned by DSNZPARMs.
Transit time	Produces a report detailing the average elapsed time for DB2 units of work by component.

Many types and styles of reports can be generated within each set. The following sections describe each DB2-PM report set.

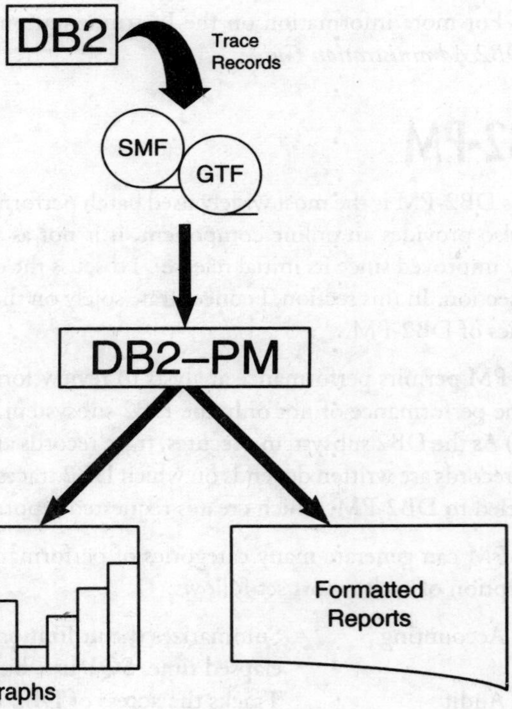

FIGURE 17.1.
DB2-PM operation.

Accounting Report Set

The DB2-PM accounting report set provides information on the performance of DB2 applications. Two basic layouts are provided for accounting reports: short and long.

The accounting reports provide the following type of information about the performance of DB2 applications:

- The start and stop time for each program
- The number of commits and aborts encountered
- The type of SQL statements used and how often each type was issued
- The number of buffer manager requests
- Use of locks
- Amount of CPU resources consumed
- Asynchronous and synchronous I/O wait time
- Lock and latch wait time
- RID pool processing
- Distributed processing
- Resource limit facility (RLF) statistics

For an example of the type of information provided on a short accounting report, refer to the accounting report excerpt shown in Listing 17.1. This report provides a host of summarized performance data for each plan, broken down by DBRM.

Listing 17.1. DB2-PM accounting report—short.

```
LOCATION: CHICAGO                         DB2 PERFORMANCE MONITOR (V3)                      PAGE: 1-1
SUBSYSTEM: DB2P                              ACCOUNTING REPORT - SHORT                  DB2 VERSION: V5
INTERVAL FROM: 07/02/97 18:35:14.13                                            REQUESTED FROM: NOT SPECIFIED
         TO: 07/02/97 18:38:13.42         ORDER: PLANNAME                                    TO: NOT SPECIFIED
        #OCCURS #ROLLBK SELECTS INSERTS UPDATES DELETES CLASS1 EL.TIME CLASS2 EL.TIME GETPAGES SYN.READ LOCK SUS
PLANNAME #DISTRS #COMMIT FETCHES   OPENS  CLOSES PREPARE CLASS1 TCBTIME CLASS2 TCBTIME BUF.UPDT TOT.PREF #LOCKOUT
-------- ------- ------- ------- ------- ------- ------- -------------- -------------- -------- -------- --------
PRG00000      19       0    8.24    2.39    3.33    2.49       2.938984       2.879021    81.29    12.29     0.49
               0      27    2.35    2.35    2.35    0.00       0.019870       0.017809    30.42     0.59        0

 -------------------------------------------------------------------------------------------------
 | PROGRAM NAME      TYPE      #OCCUR  SQLSTMT  CL7 ELAP.TIME  CL7 TCB.TIME  CL8 SUSP.TIME  CL8 SUSP |
 | PRG00100          DBRM          10    12.00       3.298190      0.015465       3.198018      9.71 |
 | PRG00150          DBRM           2     8.00       1.981201      0.017810       1.980012      8.92 |
 | PRG00192          DBRM           7     7.00       2.010191      0.189153       1.702439      9.28 |
 -------------------------------------------------------------------------------------------------
```

Each plan is reported in two rows. Refer to the first row of the report, the one for `PRG00000`. Two rows of numbers belong to this plan. The first row corresponds to the first row of the header. For example, this row shows 19 occurrences of this plan (`#OCCUR`), 0 rollback requests (`#ROLLBK`), 8.24 `SELECTS`, and 2.39 `INSERTS`. The second row corresponds to the second row of the report header. For example, it has no distributed requests, 27 `COMMITS`, and 2.35 `FETCHES`.

The second component of this report details each of the packages and/or DBRMs for the plan. For each package or DBRM, DB2-PM reports the number of occurrences and SQL statements, along with elapsed, TCB, and suspension times and total number of suspensions. This information is provided only if Accounting trace classes 7 and 8 are specified.

The report shown was generated by requesting DB2-PM to sort the output by PLANNAME only. The following sort options are available:

- CONNECT: Connection ID
- CONNTYPE: Connection type
- CORRNAME: Correlation name
- CORRNMBR: Correlation number
- ORIGAUTH: Original authorization ID
- PLANNAME: Plan name
- PRIMAUTH/AUTHID: Primary authorization ID/authorization ID
- REQLOC: Requesting location

Likewise, you can combine these options together, such as PRIMAUTH-PLANNAME-REQLOC. This combination would cause a report to be generated containing a row for each unique combination of primary authorization ID, plan name, and requesting location.

The short accounting report is useful for monitoring the overall performance of your DB2 applications. Using this report, you can perform the following functions:

- Determine how many times a plan was executed during a specific time frame. The #OCCURS column specifies this information.
- With the appropriate request, determine how many times a given user executed a given plan.
- Investigate basic performance statistics, such as elapsed and CPU time, at the DBRM or package level.
- Spot-check plans for average SQL activity. If you know the basic operations performed by your plans, you can use the short accounting report to determine whether the SQL being issued by your plans corresponds to your expectations. For example, you can determine whether update plans are actually updating. Columns 3 through 6 of this report contain basic SQL information. Remember, however, that this information is averaged. For example, plan PRG00000 issued 2.39 inserts on average, but the plan was executed 19 times. Obviously, the same number of inserts does not occur each time the plan is executed.
- Determine dynamic SQL activity. By checking for PREPARE activity, you can determine which plans are issuing dynamic SQL.
- Obtain an overall reflection of response time. The Class 1 and Class 2 Elapsed and TCB Time columns report the overall average elapsed and CPU time for the given plan. Class 1 is the overall application time; Class 2 is the time spent in DB2. If these numbers are very large or outside the normal expected response time range, further investigation might be warranted.

- Review average I/O characteristics. The average number of GETPAGEs corresponds to requests for data from DB2. SYN.READ corresponds to a non-sequential prefetch direct read. You can skim these numbers quickly to obtain an overall idea of the efficiency of reading DB2 data.
- Monitor other information such as lock suspensions (LOCK SUS) and timeouts and deadlocks (#LOCKOUT) using this report to determine whether contention problems exist.

At the end of the short accounting report, a synopsis of the plans on the report is presented. The plans are sorted in order by TCB time spent in DB2 and wait time spent in DB2. This synopsis is useful when you're analyzing which plan takes the longest time to execute.

If the short accounting report signals that potential problems exist, a long accounting report can be requested. This report provides much more detail for each entry on the short accounting report. The long accounting report documents performance information in great depth and is one of the most useful tools for performance analysis.

The long accounting report is composed of eight distinct sections:

Part 1	CPU and elapsed time information, broken down by class, at the plan level
Part 2	Overall highlights for the particular plan
Part 3	In-depth SQL activity for the plan
Part 4	Detailed locking statistics for the plan
Part 5	Program status information for the plan
Part 6	Miscellaneous plan information, including RID processing, I/O parallelism information, and Data Capture processing
Part 7	In-depth bufferpool (virtual pool and hiperpool) usage statistics
Part 8	DBRM and Package detail information

You should use the long accounting report to further analyze the performance of particular plans. The detail on this report can appear intimidating at first, but reading it is simple after you get used to it.

The first step after producing this report is to scan it quickly for obvious problems. In the following sections, you will examine each of the individual components of this report in more detail.

Long Accounting Report: CPU and Elapsed Time

The CPU and Elapsed Time portion of the long accounting report contains a breakdown of the amount of time the plan took to execute. Elapsed time, CPU time, I/O time, and locking time are displayed in great detail. See Listing 17.2.

Listing 17.2. Accounting report—long (Part 1).

```
AVERAGE          APPL (CLASS 1) DB2 (CLASS 2) IFI (CLASS 5) CLASS 3 SUSP      AVERAGE TIME AV.EVENT
------------     --------------  ------------ ------------- --------------    ------------ --------
ELAPSED TIME          1.092617      0.670903            N/P LOCK/LATCH            0.008687     1.00
TCB TIME              0.852081      0.556737            N/P SYNCHRON. I/O         0.000000     0.00
SRB TIME              0.000023      0.000005            N/A OTHER READ I/O        0.000000     0.00
NOT ACCOUNT.               N/A      0.110078            N/A OTHER WRTE I/O        0.000000     0.00
DB2 ENT/EXIT               N/A       9123.00            N/A SER.TASK SWTCH        0.000000     0.00
                                                            ARC.LOG(QUIES)        0.000000     0.00
DCAPT.DESCR.               N/A           N/A            N/P ARC.LOG READ          0.000000     0.00
LOG EXTRACT.               N/A           N/A            N/P DRAIN LOCK            0.000000     0.00
                                                            CLAIM RELEASE         0.000000     0.00
NOT NULL                    17            17              0 PAGE LATCH            0.000000     0.00
                                                            TOTAL CLASS 3         0.008687     1.00
                                                            NOT NULL                     8
```

When you're analyzing this section, first compare the application times (Class 1) to the DB2 times (Class 2). If a huge discrepancy exists between these numbers, the problem may be outside the realm of DB2 (for example, VSAM opens and closes, application loops, or waiting for synchronous I/O).

Class 3 information reports wait time. Of particular interest is the amount of time spent waiting for I/O. If the average SYNCHRON. I/O wait time is high, investigate the application for reasons that would cause additional reads, such as the following:

- Was the program recently modified to perform more SELECT statements?
- Was the plan recently rebound, causing a different access path to be chosen?
- Was query I/O parallelism recently "turned on" for this plan using DEGREE(ANY)?
- Was additional data added to the tables accessed by this plan?

If no additional data is being read, investigate other reasons such as insufficient buffers, insufficient EDM pool storage, or disk contention.

Turning your attention to locking, if LOCK/LATCH suspension time is higher than expected, review the lock detail shown in Part 4 of the long accounting report.

Long Accounting Report: Highlights

After you peruse the execution times, a quick analysis of the highlights portion of the report is useful. It contains some basic details about the nature of the application that will be useful for subsequent performance analysis. See Listing 17.3.

Listing 17.3. Accounting report—long (Part 2).

```
HIGHLIGHTS
--------------------------
#OCCURENCES       :    18
#ALLIEDS          :
```

```
#ALLIEDS DISTRIB:     0
#DBATS          :
#DBATS DISTRIB. :     0
#NO PACKAGE DATA:     0
#NORMAL TERMINAT:    17
#ABNORMAL TERMIN:     1
#INCREMENT. BIND:     0
#COMMITS        :    17
#ROLLBACKS      :     1
UPDATE/COMMIT   :  0.00
```

You should review the following highlight fields:

- To determine the number of times a plan was executed during the reported time frame, review the total number of occurrences (`#OCCURENCES`).
- If the number of commits is not higher than the number of normal terminations, the program did not perform more than one commit per execution. You might need to review the program to ensure that a proper commit strategy is in place. This situation is not necessarily bad, but it warrants further investigation.
- Analyze the number of normal and abnormal terminations for each plan. Further investigation may be warranted if a particular plan has an inordinate number of aborts.
- If the value for `#INCREMENT. BIND` is not `0`, the plan is being automatically rebound before it is executed. This situation is referred to as an incremental bind. Either the plan is marked as invalid because an index was removed (or because of some other DDL change), causing an automatic rebind, or the plan was bound with `VALIDATE(RUN)`. To optimize performance, avoid these situations when possible.

Long Accounting Report: SQL Activity

An understanding of the type of SQL being issued by the application is essential during performance analysis. The long accounting report provides a comprehensive summary of the SQL issued, grouped into DML, DCL, and DDL sections. See Listing 17.4.

Listing 17.4. Accounting report—long (Part 3).

```
SQL DML    AVERAGE  TOTAL  SQL DCL            TOTAL SQL DDL     CREATE DROP ALTER
--------- -------- ------  ------------------ ----- ----------- ------ ---- -----
SELECT        1.00     17  LOCK TABLE             0 TABLE            0    0     0
INSERT        0.00      0  GRANT                  0 INDEX            0    0     0
UPDATE        0.00      0  REVOKE                 0 TABLESPACE       0    0     0
DELETE        0.00      0  SET CURR.SQLID         0 DATABASE         0    0     0
                           SET HOST VAR           0 STOGROUP         0    0     0
DESCRIBE      0.00      0  SET CURR.DEGREE        0 SYNONYM          0    0     0
DESC.TBL      0.00      0                           VIEW             0    0     0
PREPARE       0.00      0  CONNECT TYPE 1         0 ALIAS            0    0     0
OPEN          3.00     51  CONNECT TYPE 2         0 PACKAGE          0    0     0
```

continues

Listing 17.4. continued

```
FETCH        4553.00  77401  SET CONNECTION            0
CLOSE           3.00     51  RELEASE                   0 TOTAL          0    0    0

DML-ALL      4559.00  77503  DCL-ALL                   0 COMMENT ON     0
                                                         LABEL ON       0
```

Scan the DML section of the report to verify the type of processing that is occurring. You can quickly uncover a problem if the application is thought to be read-only but INSERT, UPDATE, and/or DELETE activity is not 0. Likewise, if DESCRIBE, DESC.TBL, and/or PREPARE are not 0, the application is performing dynamic SQL statements and should be analyzed accordingly.

Additionally, DDL is not generally permitted in application programs. When you spot unplanned DDL activity within an application program, you should consider it a problem.

I can say the same about DCL GRANT and REVOKE statements. They are not generally coded in application programs, either. However, LOCK TABLE, SET, and CONNECT are valid and useful statements that will show up from time to time. When they do, ensure that they are valid uses, as follows:

- LOCK TABLE should be used with caution because it takes a lock on the entire table (or tablespace) instead of page locking. It reduces concurrency but can improve performance.
- SET CURR.DEGREE is specified for dynamic SQL query I/O parallelism.
- CONNECT indicates distributed activity.

Long Accounting Report: Locking Activity

The locking activity component of the long accounting report is useful for isolating the average and total number of locks, timeouts, deadlocks, lock escalations, and lock/latch suspensions. See Listing 17.5.

Listing 17.5. Accounting report—long (Part 4).

```
LOCKING             AVERAGE    TOTAL
---------------     --------   -----
TIMEOUTS               0.06        1
DEADLOCKS              0.00        0
ESCAL.(SHARED)         0.00        0
ESCAL.(EXCLUS)         0.00        0
MAX LOCKS HELD         0.41        3
LOCK REQUEST           8.00      136
UNLOCK REQUEST         1.00       17
QUERY REQUEST          0.00        0
CHANGE REQUEST         0.00        0
OTHER REQUEST          0.00        0
LOCK SUSPENS.          0.00        0
```

```
LATCH SUSPENS.       0.06       1
OTHER SUSPENS.       0.00       0
TOTAL SUSPENS.       0.06       1

DRAIN/CLAIM        AVERAGE   TOTAL
--------------     -------   -----
DRAIN REQUESTS       0.00       0
DRAIN FAILED         0.00       0
CLAIM REQUESTS       3.00      51
CLAIM FAILED         0.00       0
```

Additionally, average and total claims and drains are detailed in this section.

Consider the following general rules of thumb for locking analysis:

- If the value for `MAX LOCKS HELD` is very high, it may be beneficial to consider issuing `LOCK TABLE`.
- If the value for `TIMEOUTS` is very high, consider either reevaluating the type of access being performed by the application or changing the `DSNZPARM` value for the length of time to wait for a resource timeout. Factors that could increase the number of timeouts include different programs accessing the same tables in a different order, inappropriate locking strategies (`RR` versus `CS`), and heavy concurrent ad hoc access.
- If `ESCAL.(SHARED)` and `ESCAL.(EXCLUS)` are not `0`, lock escalation is occurring. The plan therefore causes page locks to escalate to tablespace locks (for those tablespaces defined as `LOCKSIZE ANY`). This situation could cause lock contention for other plans requiring these tablespaces.
- If the value for `TOTAL SUSPENS.` is high (over 10,000), there is probably a great deal of contention for the data that your plan requires. This situation usually indicates that index subpages should be increased or page locking specified instead of `ANY`.

Long Accounting Report: Program Status

If a large number of abnormal terminations were reported in the long accounting report highlights section, analysis of the program status section may be appropriate. See Listing 17.6.

Listing 17.6. Accounting report—long (Part 5).

```
NORMAL TERM.       AVERAGE TOTAL  ABNORMAL TERM.        TOTAL IN DOUBT          TOTAL
---------------    ------- -----  ------------------    ----- -------------     -----
NEW USER              0.94    17  APPL.PROGR. ABEND         1 APPL.PGM ABEND        0
DEALLOCATION          0.00     0  END OF MEMORY             0 END OF MEMORY         0
APPL.PROGR. END       0.00     0  RESOL.IN DOUBT            0 END OF TASK           0
IFC MON.READ          0.00     0  CANCEL FORCE              0 CANCEL FORCE          0
RESIGNON              0.00     0
DBAT INACTIVE         0.00     0
```

Long Accounting Report: Miscellaneous Information

The miscellaneous information reported in this section of the long accounting report can be crucial in performance analysis. See Listing 17.7. Three independent components are reported in this section:

- RID list processing
- I/O parallelism
- Data capture

Listing 17.7. Accounting report—long (Part 6).

```
RID LIST            AVERAGE TOTAL I/O PARALLELISM    TOTAL DATA CAPTURE    AVERAGE TOTAL
------------------- ------- ----- ------------------ ----- --------------- ------- -----
USED                   0.00     0 MAXIMUM DEGREE         0 IFI CALLS MADE  N/P     N/P
FAIL-NO STORAGE        0.00     0 GROUPS EXECUTED        0 REC. CAPTURED   N/P     N/P
FAIL-LIMIT EXC.        0.00     0 PLANNED DEGREE         0 LOG REC. READ   N/P     N/P
                                  REDUCED DEGREE         0 ROWS RETURNED   N/P     N/P
                                  SEQ - CURSOR           0 RECORDS RETURN  N/P     N/P
                                  SEQ - NO ESA SORT      0 DATA.DESC.RET.  N/P     N/P
                                  SEQ - NO BUFFER        0 TABLES RETURN   N/P     N/P
                                                           DESCRIBES       N/P     N/P
```

If any access path in the application program requires either list prefetch or a hybrid join, analysis of the `RID LIST` performance statistics is essential. Of particular importance is the `FAIL-NO STORAGE` value. Whenever this value is not zero (`0`), you should take immediate action either to increase the size of the RID pool or tweak the access path to eliminate RID list processing.

Careful analysis of the I/O parallelism section is appropriate whenever you're analyzing performance statistics for a plan or package bound with `DEGREE(ANY)`:

- When `REDUCED DEGREE` is not zero (`0`), insufficient resources were available to execute the application with the optimal number of read engines. You might need to evaluate the overall mix of applications in the system at the same time. Reducing concurrent activity may release resources that the program can use to run with the planned number of parallel read engines.
- When any of the `SEQ` categories is not zero (`0`), DB2 reverted to a sequential plan. Therefore, I/O parallelism was "turned off." You might need to analyze the program and the environment to determine why query I/O parallelism was disabled.

Long Accounting Report: Bufferpool Information

The bufferpool information is probably the most important portion of the long accounting report. A poorly tuned bufferpool environment can greatly affect the performance of a DB2 subsystem. Analysis of this section of the report (see Listing 17.8) provides a performance analyst with a better understanding of how the program utilizes available buffers.

Listing 17.8. Accounting report—long (Part 7).

```
BP0                    AVERAGE     TOTAL   BP10                   AVERAGE     TOTAL
--------------------  --------  --------   --------------------  --------  --------
EXPANSIONS                 N/A       N/A   EXPANSIONS                 N/A       N/A
GETPAGES                 85.47      1453   GETPAGES                219.00      3723
BUFFER UPDATES           86.00      1462   BUFFER UPDATES            0.00         0
SYNCHRONOUS WRITE         0.00         0   SYNCHRONOUS WRITE         0.00         0
SYNCHRONOUS READ          0.18         3   SYNCHRONOUS READ          0.00         0
SEQUENTIAL PREFETCH       0.00         0   SEQUENTIAL PREFETCH       7.00       119
LIST PREFETCH             0.00         0   LIST PREFETCH             0.00         0
DYNAMIC PREFETCH          1.00        17   DYNAMIC PREFETCH          0.00         0
PAGES READ ASYNCHR.       8.00       136   PAGES READ ASYNCHR.       0.00         0
HPOOL WRITES              0.00         0   HPOOL WRITES              0.00         0
HPOOL WRITES-FAILED       0.00         0   HPOOL WRITES-FAILED       0.00         0
PAGES READ-HPOOL          0.00         0   PAGES READ-HPOOL          0.00         0
HPOOL READS               0.00         0   HPOOL READS               0.00         0
HPOOL READS FAILED        0.00         0   HPOOL READS FAILED        0.00         0
TOT4K                  AVERAGE     TOTAL
--------------------  --------  --------
EXPANSIONS                 N/A       N/A
GETPAGES                304.47      5176
BUFFER UPDATES           86.00      1462
SYNCHRONOUS WRITE         0.00         0
SYNCHRONOUS READ          0.18         3
SEQUENTIAL PREFETCH       7.00       119
LIST PREFETCH             0.00         0
DYNAMIC PREFETCH          1.00        17
PAGES READ ASYNCHR.       8.00       136
HPOOL WRITES              0.00         0
HPOOL WRITES-FAILED       0.00         0
PAGES READ-HPOOL          0.00         0
HPOOL READS               0.00         0
HPOOL READS FAILED        0.00         0
```

The first step is to get a feeling for the overall type of I/O requested for this plan. You should answer the following questions:

- How many bufferpools were accessed? Were more (or fewer) bufferpools used than expected?
- Were any 32K bufferpools accessed? Should they have been? Use of 32K bufferpools can greatly affect the performance by increasing I/O costs.
- Did the program read pages from an associated hiperpool?
- Was sequential prefetch used? Based on your knowledge of the program, should it have been? Was dynamic prefetch enabled?
- Was list prefetch invoked? If so, be sure to analyze the RID List Processing in the Miscellaneous Information section of this report (discussed in the preceding section).
- How many pages were requested (GETPAGES)? The number of GETPAGES is a good indicator of the amount of work being done by the program.

- Were any synchronous writes performed? A synchronous write is sometimes called a non-deferred write. Synchronous writes occur immediately on request. Most DB2 writes are deferred, which means that they are made in the bufferpool and recorded in the log but not physically externalized to DASD until later. Synchronous writes usually indicate that the bufferpool is overutilized.

All the aforementioned information is broken down by bufferpool.

Your next task in analyzing this report is to calculate the average read efficiency. Read efficiency can be defined as the average number of pages that DB2 can request without incurring additional I/O. This information gives you an idea of how well the SQL in this plan has used the available bufferpools. Use the following formula to calculate read efficiency:

```
(Total GETPAGEs) / [(SEQUENTIAL PREFETCH) + (DYNAMIC PREFETCH) + (SYNCHRONOUS READ)]
```

Using the example, the read efficiency for the plan would be

```
5176 / [119 + 17 + 3] = 5176 / 139 = 37.23
```

For this plan, then, DB2 can request an average of 37 pages before incurring a physical I/O request. This number is quite good. It should be expected also because of the high number of sequential prefetch requests. Remember, sequential prefetch reads 32 pages with a single I/O.

In general, read efficiency should be in the following ranges:

- For online transactions with significant random access, the read efficiency can be in a range of 1.5 through 3 and still provide good I/O utilization.
- For transactions that open cursors and fetch numerous rows, the read efficiency should be higher, possibly approaching 10. However, it is not abnormal for most online transactions to have a low read efficiency.
- For batch programs, shoot for a read efficiency in excess of 10. The actual read efficiency each program can achieve is highly dependent on the functionality required for that program. Programs with a large amount of sequential access should have a much higher read efficiency than those processing randomly.
- When programs have very few SQL statements, or SQL statements returning a single row, read efficiency is generally low. Because few SQL statements are issued, the potential for using buffered input is reduced.
- For any program in which sequential prefetch is anticipated, the read efficiency should approach 32.

The read efficiency also can be calculated by bufferpool to determine its effectiveness for the plan in question. Remember, though, when read efficiency is calculated using the information from an accounting report, it is for a single plan only. You can ascertain the overall effectiveness of each bufferpool by calculating read efficiency based on information from a DB2-PM statistics report or from the `-DISPLAY BUFFERPOOL` command.

Long Accounting Report: Package/DBRM Information

The final component of the long accounting report is detailed information for each package and DBRM in the plan. See Listing 17.9. To obtain this information, you must start the appropriate accounting traces (class 7 and class 8).

Listing 17.9. Accounting report—long (Part 8).

```
PRG00100            VALUE     PRG00100              TIMES     PRG00100              AVERAGE TIME  AVG.EV  TIME/EVENT
------------------  --------  ------------------  ---------  ------------------  ------------  ------  ----------
TYPE                DBRM      ELAP-CL7 TIME-AVG   0.670800  LOCK/LATCH              0.009924    1.00    0.009924
                              TCB                 0.556637  SYNCHRONOUS I/O         0.000000    0.00         N/C
LOCATION            N/A       WAITING             0.114162  OTHER READ I/O          0.000000    0.00         N/C
COLLECTION ID       N/A       SUSPENSION-CL8      0.009924  OTHER WRITE I/O         0.000000    0.00         N/C
PROGRAM NAME        PRG00100  NOT ACCOUNTED       0.110076  SERV.TASK SWITCH        0.000000    0.00         N/C
                                                            ARCH.LOG(QUIESCE)       0.000000    0.00         N/C
OCCURENCES          17        AVG.DB2 ENTRY/EXIT   9122.00  ARCHIVE LOG READ        0.000000    0.00         N/C
SQL STMT - AVERAGE  4559.0    DB2 ENTRY/EXIT        155074  DRAIN LOCK              0.000000    0.00         N/C
SQL STMT - TOTAL    77503                                   CLAIM RELEASE           0.000000    0.00         N/C
                              NOT NULL (CL7)            17  PAGE LATCH              0.000000    0.00         N/C
                                                            TOTAL CL8 SUSPENS.      0.009924    1.00    0.009924
                                                            NOT NULL (CL8)                 7
PRG00101            VALUE     PRG00101              TIMES     PRG00101              AVERAGE TIME  AVG.EV  TIME/EVENT
------------------  --------  ------------------  ---------  ------------------  ------------  ------  ----------
TYPE                DBRM      ELAP-CL7 TIME-AVG   0.781030  LOCK/LATCH              0.006902    1.00    0.006902
                              TCB                 0.461371  SYNCHRONOUS I/O         0.000000    0.00         N/C
LOCATION            N/A       WAITING             0.101390  OTHER READ I/O          0.000000    0.00         N/C
COLLECTION ID       N/A       SUSPENSION-CL8      0.010430  OTHER WRITE I/O         0.000000    0.00         N/C
PROGRAM NAME        PRG00101  NOT ACCOUNTED       0.102061  SERV.TASK SWITCH        0.000000    0.00         N/C
                                                            ARCH.LOG(QUIESCE)       0.000000    0.00         N/C
OCCURENCES          17        AVG.DB2 ENTRY/EXIT   4573.00  ARCHIVE LOG READ        0.000000    0.00         N/C
SQL STMT - AVERAGE  392.0     DB2 ENTRY/EXIT         77741  DRAIN LOCK              0.000000    0.00         N/C
SQL STMT - TOTAL    6664                                    CLAIM RELEASE           0.000000    0.00         N/C
                              NOT NULL (CL7)            17  PAGE LATCH              0.000000    0.00         N/C
                                                            TOTAL CL8 SUSPENS.      0.006902    1.00    0.006902
                                                            NOT NULL (CL8)                 7
```

This level of detail might be necessary for plans composed of multiple DBRMs and/or packages. For example, if a locking problem is identified, determining which DBRM (or package) is experiencing the problem may be difficult if you don't have the appropriate level of detail.

Accounting Trace Reports

The accounting report set also contains two additional reports: the Short and Long Accounting Trace reports. These reports produce similar information, but for a single execution of a plan. By contrast, the short and long accounting reports provide performance information averaged for all executions of a plan by a given user.

Audit Report Set

The DB2-PM audit report set shows DB2 auditing information. Although this data is generally not performance-oriented, you can use it to monitor usage characteristics of a DB2 subsystem. The Audit Summary report, shown in Listing 17.10, is a synopsis of the eight audit trace categories (as outlined previously in this chapter).

Listing 17.10. DB2-PM Audit Summary report.

```
   LOCATION: CHICAGO     DB2 PERFORMANCE MONITOR (V4)                      PAGE: 1-1
      GROUP: DB2G1P      AUDIT REPORT - SUMMARY                 REQUESTED FROM: NOT SPECIFIED
     MEMBER: DB2P                                                          TO: NOT SPECIFIED
  SUBSYSTEM: DB2P        ORDER: PRIMAUTH-PLANNAME                  ACTUAL FROM: 05/17/97 07:28:39.17
DB2 VERSION: V4          SCOPE: MEMBER                                     TO: 05/17/97 11:31:12.25

                             AUTH    GRANT/ DDL    DML READ DML WRITE DML     AUTHID UTILITY
PRIMAUTH PLANNAME TOTAL FAILURE REVOKE ACCESS ACCESS   ACCESS    AT BIND CHANGE ACCESS
-------- -------- ----- ------- ------ ------ -------- --------- ------- ------ -------
AUTHID2
         DSNTEP2      4       0      0      0        0         0       4      0       0
         DSNUTIL      4       0      0      0        0         0       0      0       4
         TXN00001    12       1      0      1        2         2       0      0       0
         TXN00012    10       0      0      0        2         5       0     10       0
*TOTAL*              30       1      0      1        4         7       4     10       4
AUTHID5
         DSNTEP2      4       0      0      0        0         0       4      0       0
         TXN00030    16       2      1      8        2         2       0      2       0
*TOTAL*              20       2      1      8        2         2       4      2       4

*GRAND TOTAL*        50       3      1      9        6         9       8     12       8
END OF REPORT
```

If you require further audit detail, DB2-PM also provides an Audit Detail report and an Audit Trace report. The Audit Detail report breaks each category into a separate report, showing the resource accessed, the date and the time of the access, and other pertinent information. The Audit Trace report displays each audit trace record in timestamp order.

The Explain Report Set

The explain report set describes the DB2 access path of selected SQL statements. DB2 uses the EXPLAIN command and information from the DB2 Catalog to produce a description of the access path chosen. Combining information from the PLAN_TABLE and the DB2 Catalog is the primary purpose of the DB2-PM explain report set. To execute reports in the explain report set, you must have access to DB2. This requirement differs from most of the other DB2-PM reports.

I/O Activity Report Set

The I/O activity report set is somewhat misnamed. It does not report on the I/O activity of DB2 applications. Instead, it is relegated to reporting on the I/O activity of DB2 bufferpools, the EDM pool, and the log manager. An example of the information provided on the I/O Activity Summary report is shown in Listing 17.11.

Listing 17.11. DB2-PM I/O Activity Summary report.

```
                                               AET
BUFFER POOL                           TOTALS SSSS.THT
---------------------------------- -------- --------
TOTAL I/O REQUESTS                      262    0.014
TOTAL READ I/O REQUESTS                 247    0.012
NON-PREFETCH READS                      171
PREFETCH REQUESTS
UNSUCCESSFUL                              1
SUCCESSFUL                               75
PAGES READ                              N/C
PAGES READ / SUCC READ                  N/C
TOTAL WRITE REQUESTS                     68    0.164
SYNCH WRITES                              1    0.021
PAGES WRITTEN PER WRITE                 1.0
ASYNCH WRITES                            67    0.164
PAGES WRITTEN PER WRITE                 2.3
                                  CT/PT/DBD  LOADS    AET    AVG LEN
EDM POOL                          REFERENCES FROM DASD SSSS.THT (BYTES)
--------------------------------- ---------- --------- -------- --------
CURSOR TABLE - HEADER                      1         1    0.000   2049.0
CURSOR TABLE - DIRECTORY                   0         0      N/C      0.0
CURSOR TABLE - RDS SECTION                 4         4    0.000    634.0
-- TOTAL PLANS --                           5         5    0.000   5474.0
-- TOTAL PLANS --                           5         5    0.000   5474.0
PACKAGE TABLE - HEADER                     2         2    0.003   1208.0
PACKAGE TABLE - DIRECTORY                  2         2    0.001    156.0
PACKAGE TABLE - RDS SECTION                6         6    0.001    747.7
-- TOTAL PACKAGES --                       10        10    0.002    719.6
-- TOTAL PACKAGES --                       10        10    0.002    719.6
DATABASE DESCRIPTORS                       1         1    0.000   4012.0
DATABASE DESCRIPTORS                       1         1    0.000   4012.0
                                               AET
ACTIVE LOG                            TOTALS SSSS.THT
---------------------------------- -------- --------
TOTAL WAITS                              22    0.015
READ REQUESTS                             0      N/C
WRITE REQUESTS                           22    0.015
CONT. CI / WRITE                        1.6
OTHER WAITS                               0      N/C
ALLOCATE                                  0      N/C
DEALLOCATE                                0      N/C
ARCHIVE UNAVAILABLE                       0      N/C
BUFFERS UNAVAILABLE                       0      N/C
DATASET UNAVAILABLE                       0      N/C
OPEN                                      0      N/C
CLOSE                                     0      N/C
```

continues

Listing 17.11. continued

```
                                         AET
ARCHIVE LOG/BSDS             TOTALS  SSSS.THT
---------------------------  --------  --------
ARCHIVE WAITS                     0       N/C
ARCHIVE READ REQ                  0       N/C
DASD READ                         0
TAPE READ                         0
ARCHIVE WRITE REQ                 0       N/C
BLOCK / WRITE                   N/C
BSDS READ REQ                     2     0.089
BSDS WRITE REQ                    2     0.044
```

As with the other report sets, the I/O activity report set provides detail reports that show the I/O activity for each of these resources.

Locking Report Set

The locking report set provides reports that disclose lock contention and suspensions in the DB2 subsystem. These reports can be helpful when you're analyzing locking-related problems.

For example, if a Long Accounting report indicated a high number of timeouts or deadlocks, a Lock Contention Summary report, such as the one shown in Listing 17.12, could be produced. This report provides information on who was involved in the contention and what resource was unavailable because of the lock.

Listing 17.12. DB2-PM Lock Contention Summary report.

```
LOCK CONTENTION SUMMARY
LOCATION: CHICAGO                                        BY PRIMAUTH/PLANNAME
------ TASK HOLDING RESOURCE ------ ----                  TASK WAITING ON RESOURCE ----
PRIMAUTH PLANNAME         PRIMAUTH PLANNAME         DATABASE OBJECT    TIMEOUTS DEADLOCK
-------- --------         -------- --------         -------- --------  -------- --------
AUTHID01 DSNESPRR         AUTHID02 TXN00001         DSN8D23A DSN8S23D         1        0
```

You can use the Lock Suspension Summary, shown in Listing 17.13, when an accounting report indicates a high number of lock suspensions. This report details the cause of each suspension and whether it was subsequently resumed or resulted in a timeout or deadlock.

Listing 17.13. DB2-PM Lock Suspension Summary report.

```
LOCATION: CHICAGO              DB2 PERFORMANCE MONITOR (V3)                      PAGE:1-1
SUBSYSTEM: DB2P               LOCKING REPORT - SUSPENSION                DB2 VERSION: V5
INTERVAL FROM: 8/27/97 12:02:15.34     SUMMARY               REQUESTED FROM: NOT SPECIFIED 1
            TO: 8/28/97 00:15:54.50                                        TO: NOT SPECIFIED
                               ORDER - PRIMAUTH-PLANNAME
PRIMAUTH          -- REASON -- ---------------- REASON FOR RESUME ---------------
```

```
PLANNAME TYPE OF RESOURCE RESOURCE TOTAL    FOR SUSPEND---NORMAL---TIMEOUT/CANCEL---DEADLOCK---
         REQUEST TYPE     NAME     SUSPENDS LR LC OTHR NMBR AET NMBR        AET NMBR      AET
-------- ------- -------- -------- -------- -- -- ---- ---- ------------ ------------ ---------
AUTHID01
DSNESPCS LOCK    INDEX    DSN8D51A XDEPT1   1  1  0    0    0   N/C      1  51.309011 0    N/C
         QUERY   INDEX    DSN8D51A XDEPT1   1  0  0    1    1   0.005078 0  N/C       0    N/C
***** SUM FOR DSNESPCS       *****          2  1  0    1    1   0.005078 1  51.309011 0    N/C
LOCKING REPORT COMPLETE
```

The locking report set provides detail reports that show the lock contentions and suspensions, ordered by the time each lock event occurred.

Record Trace Report Set

The record trace report set provides not reports per se, but a dump of the trace records fed to it as input. The record trace reports are not molded into a report format as are the other DB2-PM reports. They simply display DB2 trace records in a readable format.

The three record trace reports are the Record Trace Summary report, the Sort Record Trace report, and the Long Record Trace report. The Record Trace Summary report lists an overview of the DB2 trace records, without all the supporting detail. The Sort Record Trace report provides a listing of most of the DB2 trace records you need to see, along with supporting detail. Several serviceability trace records are not displayed. The Long Record Trace report lists all DB2 trace records.

The record trace reports are useful for determining what type of trace data is available for an input source data set. If another DB2-PM execution (to produce, for example, an accounting detail report) is unsuccessful or does not produce the data you want, you can run a record trace to ensure that the input data set contains the needed trace records to produce the requested report.

Note that the record trace reports might produce a large amount of output. You can specify which types of DB2 trace records should be displayed. If you're looking for a particular type of trace record, be sure to reduce your output by specifying the data for which you're looking.

SQL Trace Report Set

To monitor the performance of data manipulation language statements, you can use the SQL trace report set. These reports are necessary only when a program has encountered a performance problem. The SQL trace breaks down each SQL statement into the events that must occur to satisfy the request. This information includes preparation, aborts, commits, the beginning and ending of each type of SQL statement, cursor opens and closes, accesses due to referential integrity, I/O events, thread creation and termination, and all types of indexed accesses.

You will find four types of SQL trace reports. The SQL Trace Summary report provides a synopsis of each type of SQL statement and the performance characteristics of that statement.

The second type of SQL trace report is the SQL Short Trace report. It lists the performance characteristics of each SQL statement, including the beginning and end of each statement and the work accomplished in between. It does not provide I/O activity, locking, and sorting information.

The SQL Long Trace report provides the same information as the SQL Short Trace report but includes I/O activity, locking, and sorting information.

Finally, the SQL DML report extends the SQL Trace Summary report, providing data for each SQL statement, not just for each SQL statement type.

The SQL Short and Long Trace reports can be extremely long reports that are cumbersome to read. Therefore, producing these reports only when a performance problem must be corrected is usually wise. In addition, the SQL trace reports require the DB2 performance trace to be active. This trace carries a large amount of overhead. Before you request this report, you would be wise to "eyeball" the offending program for glaring errors (such as looping or Cartesian products) and to tinker with the SQL to see whether you can improve performance.

Also, after you produce these reports, you should have more than one experienced analyst read them. I have seen SQL trace reports that were six feet long. Be prepared for a lot of work to ferret out the needed information from these reports.

Statistics Report Set

The second most popular DB2-PM report set (next to the accounting report set) is the statistics report set. Statistics reports provide performance information about the DB2 subsystem. The data on these reports can help you detect areas of concern when you're monitoring DB2 performance. Usually, these reports point you in the direction of a problem; additional DB2-PM reports are required to fully analyze the complete scope of the performance problem.

Listing 17.14, an example of the DB2-PM Statistics Short report, shows a summary of all DB2 activity for the DB2 subsystem during the specified time.

Listing 17.14. DB2-PM Statistics Short report.

```
  LOCATION: CHICAGO                     DB2 PERFORMANCE MONITOR (V4)                  PAGE: 1-1
     GROUP: DB2G1P                      STATISTICS REPORT - SHORT          REQUESTED FROM: NOT SPECIFIED
    MEMBER: DB2P                                                                       TO: NOT SPECIFIED
 SUBSYSTEM: DB2P                                                            INTERVAL FROM: 07/10/97 12:32:09.73
DB2 VERSION: V4                                SCOPE: MEMBER                           TO: 07/10/97 12:56:42.51

---- HIGHLIGHTS -----------------------------------------------------------------------------------------------
INTERVAL START: 07/10/97 12:32:09.73 INTERVAL ELAPSED: 24:32.77260 INCREMENTAL BINDS: 0.00       DBAT QUEUED: N/P
INTERVAL END:   07/10/97 12:56:42.51  OUTAGE ELAPSED: 0.000000   AUTH SUCC.W/OUT CATALOG: 2.00 DB2 COMMAND: 3.00
SAMPLING START: 07/10/97 12:32:09.73   TOTAL THREADS: 1.00     BUFF.UPDT/PAGES WRITTEN: 2.52       TOTAL API: 0.00
SAMPLING END  : 07/10/97 12:56:42.51   TOTAL COMMITS: 4.00     PAGES WRITTEN/WRITE I/O: 1.17          MEMBER: N/A
```

```
CPU TIMES                           TCB TIME SRB TIME TOTAL TIME  OPEN/CLOSE ACTIVITY          QUANTITY
----------------------------------- -------- -------- ----------  ---------------------------  --------
SYSTEM SERVICES ADDRESS SPACE       0.213783 0.097449 0.311232    OPEN DATASETS - HWM             29.00
DATABASE SERVICES ADDRESS SPACE     0.292474 0.155593 0.448066    OPEN DATASETS                   29.00
IRLM                                0.002940 0.447174 0.450114    IN USE DATA SETS                19.00
DDF ADDRESS SPACE                   N/P      N/P      N/P         SUCCESSFUL LOGICAL REOPEN        6.00
NON-CPU TIME                        N/A      N/A      24:31.563191

SQL DML QUANTITY SQL DCL      QUANTITY SQL DDL   QUANTITY LOCKING ACTIVITY QUANTITY DATA SHARING LOCKS QUANTITY
------- -------- ------------ -------- -------- --------- ------------------------- -------------------------
SELECT      4.00 LOCK TABLE       0.00 CREATES       0.00 DEADLOCKS            0.00 LOCK REQ.(P-LOCK)    48.00
INSERT     16.00 GRANT            0.00 DROPS         0.00 TIMEOUTS             0.00 UNLOCK REQ.(P-LCK)    0.00
UPDATE     12.00 REVOKE           0.00 ALTERS        0.00 SUSPENSIONS-LOCK     2.00 CHANGE REQ.(P-LCK)    9.00
DELETE      0.00 SET HOST VAR.    0.00 COMMENT ON    0.00 SUSPENSIONS-OTHR     0.00 SYNC.XES - LOCK     186.00
PREPARE     0.00 SET SQLID        0.00 LABEL ON      0.00 LOCK REQUESTS      351.00 SYNC.XES - CHANGE    13.00
DESCRIBE    0.00 SET DEGREE       0.00 TOTAL         0.00 UNLOCK REQUEST     178.00 SYNC.XES - UNLOCK   154.00
DESC.TBL    0.00 SET RULES        0.00                    LOCK ESCALAT(SH)     0.00 ASYN.XES-RESOURCES    0.00
OPEN       16.00 CONNECT TYPE 1   0.00                    LOCK ESCALAT(EX)     0.00 TOTAL SUSPENDS       30.00
CLOSE       8.00 CONNECT TYPE 2   0.00                    DRAIN REQUESTS       0.00 P-LCK/NFY ENG.UNAV    0.00
FETCH      20.00 RELEASE          0.00                    CLAIM REQUESTS      96.00 INCOM.RETAINED LCK    0.00
TOTAL      76.00 SET CONNECTION   0.00                                              PSET/PART NEGOTIAT   16.00
                 TOTAL            0.00                                              PAGE NEGOTIATION      0.00
RID LIST              QUANTITY STORED PROCEDURES QUANTITY QUERY PARALLELISM QUANTITY PLAN/PACKAGE PROC. QUANTITY
--------------------- -------- ----------------- -------- -------------------------- ---------------------------
MAX BLOCKS ALLOCATED      0.00 CALL STATEMENTS       0.00 MAX DEGREE            0.00 PLAN ALLOC-ATTEMPTS     1.00
CURRENT BLKS ALLOC.       0.00 PROCEDURE ABENDS      0.00 GROUPS EXECUTED       0.00 PLAN ALLOC-SUCCESS      1.00
FAILED-NO STORAGE         0.00 CALL TIMEOUTS         0.00 PLANNED DEGREE        0.00 PACK ALLOC-ATTEMPTS     0.00
FAILED-RDS LIMIT          0.00 CALL REJECTED         0.00 REDUCED-NO BUFFER     0.00 PACK ALLOC-SUCCESS      0.00
FAILED-DM LIMIT           0.00                            FALL TO SEQUENTIAL    0.00 AUTOBIND ATTEMPTS       0.00
FAILED-PROCESS LIMIT      0.00                                                       AUTOBIND SUCCESSFUL     0.00

SUBSYSTEM SERVICES               QUANTITY  LOG ACTIVITY                     QUANTITY  EDM POOL                  QUANTITY
-------------------------------  --------  -------------------------------- --------  ------------------------- --------
IDENTIFY                             0.00  READS SATISFIED-OUTPUT BUFFER        0.00  PAGES IN EDM POOL           225.00
CREATE THREAD                        1.00  READS SATISFIED-ACTIVE LOG           0.00  FREE PAGES IN FREE CHAIN    196.00
SIGNON                               4.00  READS SATISFIED-ARCHIVE LOG          0.00  FAILS DUE TO POOL FULL        0.00
TERMINATE                            0.00  READ DELAYED-UNAVAILABLE RESOURCE    0.00  PAGES USED FOR CT             8.00
ROLLBACK                             0.00  READ DELAYED-ARCH.ALLOC. LIMIT        N/A  PAGES USED FOR PT             0.00
COMMIT PHASE 1                       4.00  WRITE-NOWAIT                        76.00  PAGES USED FOR DBD           12.00
COMMIT PHASE 2                       4.00  WRITE OUTPUT LOG BUFFERS             8.00  PAGES USED FOR SKCT           9.00
READ ONLY COMMIT                     0.00  BSDS ACCESS REQUESTS                 2.00  PAGES USED FOR SKPT           0.00
UNITS OF RECOVERY GONE INDOUBT       0.00  UNAVAILABLE OUTPUT LOG BUFFER        0.00  REQUESTS FOR CT SECTIONS     10.00
UNITS OF RECOVERY INDOUBT RESOLV     0.00  CONTROL INTERVAL CREATED-ACTIVE      3.00  CT NOT IN EDM POOL           10.00
SYNCHS (SINGLE PHASE COMMIT)         0.00  ARCHIVE LOG READ ALLOCATION          0.00  REQUESTS FOR PT SECTIONS      0.00
QUEUED AT CREATE THREAD              0.00  ARCHIVE LOG WRITE ALLOCAT.           0.00  PT NOT IN EDM POOL            0.00
SYSTEM EVENT CHECKPOINT              0.00                                             REQUESTS FOR DBD SECTIONS     3.00
                                                                                      DBD NOT IN EDM POOL           0.00

   LOCATION: CHICAGO        DB2 PERFORMANCE MONITOR (V4)               PAGE: 1-2
      GROUP: DB2G1P           STATISTICS REPORT - SHORT      REQUESTED FROM: NOT SPECIFIED
     MEMBER: DB2P                                                        TO: NOT SPECIFIED
  SUBSYSTEM: DB2P                                             INTERVAL FROM: 07/10/97 12:32:09.73
 DB2 VERSION: V4                  SCOPE: MEMBER                          TO: 07/10/97 12:56:42.51
```

continues

Listing 17.14. continued

```
---- HIGHLIGHTS ----------------------------------------------------------------------------------------------------------
INTERVAL START: 07/10/97 12:32:09.73 INTERVAL ELAPSED: 24:32.77260 INCREMENTAL BINDS        : 0.00 DBAT QUEUED: N/P
INTERVAL END  : 07/10/97 12:56:42.51 OUTAGE ELAPSED  :    0.000000 AUTH SUCC.W/OUT CATALOG: 2.00 DB2 COMMAND:3.00
SAMPLING START: 07/10/97 12:32:09.73 TOTAL THREADS   :        1.00 BUFF.UPDT/PAGES WRITTEN: 2.52 TOTAL API  :0.00
SAMPLING END  : 07/10/97 12:56:42.51 TOTAL COMMITS   :        4.00 PAGES WRITTEN/WRITE I/O: 1.17 MEMBER     : N/A

BP0   GENERAL          QUANTITY  BP2   GENERAL          QUANTITY  TOT4K  GENERAL          QUANTITY
-------------------    --------  -------------------    --------  -------------------     --------
EXPANSIONS                  N/A  EXPANSIONS                  N/A  EXPANSIONS                   N/A
GETPAGES-SEQ&RANDOM     2302.00  GETPAGES-SEQ&RANDOM       72.00  GETPAGES-SEQ&RANDOM      2375.00
GETPAGES-SEQ.ONLY          0.00  GETPAGES-SEQ.ONLY          0.00  GETPAGES-SEQ.ONLY           0.00
SYNC.READ-SEQ&RANDOM      12.00  SYNC.READ-SEQ&RANDOM      27.00  SYNC.READ-SEQ&RANDOM       39.00
SYNC.READ-SEQ.ONLY         0.00  SYNC.READ-SEQ.ONLY         0.00  SYNC.READ-SEQ.ONLY          0.00
SEQ.PREFETCH REQ          10.00  SEQ.PREFETCH REQ           0.00  SEQ.PREFETCH REQ           10.00
SEQ.PREFETCH READS        10.00  SEQ.PREFETCH READS         0.00  SEQ.PREFETCH READS         10.00
PAGES READ-SEQ.PREF.     159.00  PAGES READ-SEQ.PREF.       0.00  PAGES READ-SEQ.PREF.      159.00
LST.PREFETCH REQUEST       0.00  LST.PREFETCH REQUEST       0.00  LST.PREFETCH REQUEST        0.00
LST.PREFETCH READS         0.00  LST.PREFETCH READS         0.00  LST.PREFETCH READS          0.00
PAGES READ-LST.PREF.       0.00  PAGES READ-LST.PREF.       0.00  PAGES READ-LST.PREF.        0.00
DYN.PREFETCH REQUEST       0.00  DYN.PREFETCH REQUEST       0.00  DYN.PREFETCH REQUEST        0.00
DYN.PREFETCH READS         0.00  DYN.PREFETCH READS         0.00  DYN.PREFETCH READS          0.00
PAGES READ-DYN.PREF.       0.00  PAGES READ-DYN.PREF.       0.00  PAGES READ-DYN.PREF.        0.00
BUFFER UPDATES            37.00  BUFFER UPDATES            16.00  BUFFER UPDATES             53.00
SYNCHRONOUS WRITES         0.00  SYNCHRONOUS WRITES         0.00  SYNCHRONOUS WRITES          0.00
ASYNCHRONOUS WRITES       15.00  ASYNCHRONOUS WRITES        3.00  ASYNCHRONOUS WRITES        18.00
DATA SET OPENS            10.00  DATA SET OPENS             8.00  DATA SET OPENS             18.00
HDW THRESHOLD              0.00  HDW THRESHOLD              0.00  HDW THRESHOLD               0.00
VDW THRESHOLD              0.00  VDW THRESHOLD              0.00  VDW THRESHOLD               0.00
DM THRESHOLD               0.00  DM THRESHOLD               0.00  DM THRESHOLD                0.00

GROUP BP0              QUANTITY  GROUP BP2              QUANTITY  GROUP TOT4K             QUANTITY
-------------------    --------  -------------------    --------  -------------------     --------
SYN.READ(XI)-RETURN      422.00  SYN.READ(XI)-RETURN        9.00  SYN.READ(XI)-RETURN       431.00
SYN.READ(XI)-R/W INT       0.00  SYN.READ(XI)-R/W INT       0.00  SYN.READ(XI)-R/W INT        0.00
SYN.READ(XI)-NO R/W        0.00  SYN.READ(XI)-NO R/W        0.00  SYN.READ(XI)-NO R/W         0.00
SYN.READ(NF)-RETURN        0.00  SYN.READ(NF)-RETURN        0.00  SYN.READ(NF)-RETURN         0.00
SYN.READ(NF)-R/W INT       1.00  SYN.READ(NF)-R/W INT       0.00  SYN.READ(NF)-R/W INT        1.00
SYN.READ(NF)-NO R/W        0.00  SYN.READ(NF)-NO R/W        0.00  SYN.READ(NF)-NO R/W         0.00
ASYN.READ-RETURNED         0.00  ASYN.READ-RETURNED         0.00  ASYN.READ-RETURNED          0.00
ASYN.READ-R/W INT.         0.00  ASYN.READ-R/W INT.         0.00  ASYN.READ-R/W INT.          0.00
ASYN.READ-NO R/W INT       0.00  ASYN.READ-NO R/W INT       0.00  ASYN.READ-NO R/W INT        0.00
CLEAN PAGES SYN.WRTN       0.00  CLEAN PAGES SYN.WRTN       0.00  CLEAN PAGES SYN.WRTN        0.00
CHANGED PGS SYN.WRTN      20.00  CHANGED PGS SYN.WRTN       9.00  CHANGED PGS SYN.WRTN       29.00
CLEAN PAGES ASYN.WRT       0.00  CLEAN PAGES ASYN.WRT       0.00  CLEAN PAGES ASYN.WRT        0.00
CHANGED PGS ASYN.WRT      12.00  CHANGED PGS ASYN.WRT       3.00  CHANGED PGS ASYN.WRT       15.00
REG.PG LIST (RPL) RQ       0.00  REG.PG LIST (RPL) RQ       0.00  REG.PG LIST (RPL) RQ        0.00
CLEAN PGS READ RPL         0.00  CLEAN PGS READ RPL         0.00  CLEAN PGS READ RPL          0.00
CHANGED PGS READ RPL       0.00  CHANGED PGS READ RPL       0.00  CHANGED PGS READ RPL        0.00
PAGES CASTOUT             18.00  PAGES CASTOUT              3.00  PAGES CASTOUT              21.00
CASTOUT CLASS THRESH       0.00  CASTOUT CLASS THRESH       0.00  CASTOUT CLASS THRESH        0.00
GROUP BP CAST.THRESH       0.00  GROUP BP CAST.THRESH       0.00  GROUP BP CAST.THRESH        0.00
CASTOUT ENG.UNAVAIL.       0.00  CASTOUT ENG.UNAVAIL.       0.00  CASTOUT ENG.UNAVAIL.        0.00
WRITE ENG.UNAVAIL.         0.00  WRITE ENG.UNAVAIL.         0.00  WRITE ENG.UNAVAIL.          0.00
READ FAILED-NO STOR.       0.00  READ FAILED-NO STOR.       0.00  READ FAILED-NO STOR.        0.00
WRITE FAILED-NO STOR       0.00  WRITE FAILED-NO STOR       0.00  WRITE FAILED-NO STOR        0.00
OTHER REQUESTS            43.00  OTHER REQUESTS            17.00  OTHER REQUESTS             60.00
```

You can use this report to monitor a DB2 subsystem at a glance. Pertinent system-wide statistics are provided for bufferpool management, log management, locking, and EDM pool utilization.

The Statistics Short report is useful for monitoring the DB2 bufferpools, specifically regarding I/O activity and bufferpool utilization. One statistic of interest is the DATA SET OPENS number, which indicates the number of times a VSAM open was requested for a DB2 tablespace or index. In the example, the number for BP0 is 10; for BP2, it is 8. A large number of data set opens could indicate that an object was defined with CLOSE YES. This may not be a problem, however, because the number is relatively low (in this example) and objects are also opened when they are first requested.

You should analyze the other bufferpool report items to get an idea of the overall efficiency of the bufferpool. For example, you can calculate the overall efficiency of the bufferpool using this calculation:

```
GETPAGE REQUESTS
-----------------------------------------------------------------
 (PREFETCH READ I/O OPERATIONS) + (TOTAL READ I/O OPERATIONS)
```

In the example, the bufferpool read efficiency for BP0 is

```
2302 / [12 + 10] = 104.63
```

This number is good. It is typically smaller for transaction-oriented environments and larger for batch-oriented environments. Also, this number is larger if you have large bufferpools. Other factors affecting read efficiency are the length of the sample, the amount of time since the last recycle of DB2, and the mix of concurrent applications.

In addition, the following bufferpool report numbers should be zero (0):

Bufferpool Expansions
Synchronous Writes
HDW Threshold
VDW Threshold
DM Threshold
Work File Not Created—No Buffer

If these numbers are not zero, the bufferpools have not been specified adequately. See Chapter 21, "Tuning DB2's Components," for advice on setting up your bufferpools.

Version 4

Information on group bufferpools for data sharing environments follows the local bufferpool information.

The statistics reports also can assist you in monitoring log management. You can determine the types of processing during this time frame from viewing the *Log Activity* section. If *Reads Satisfied from Active Log* or *Reads Satisfied from Archive Log* is greater than zero, a recover utility was run during this time frame. You can glean additional recovery information from the *Subsystem Service* portion of the report.

Also, ensure that the *Unavailable Output Log Buffers* is zero. If it is not, you should specify additional log buffers in your DSNZPARM start-up parameters.

Another aspect of DB2 system-wide performance that the DB2 statistics report helps to monitor is locking. This report is particularly useful for monitoring the number of suspensions, deadlocks, and timeouts in proportion to the total number of locks requested. Use the following calculation:

```
LOCK REQUESTS
-------------------------------------------
SUSPENSIONS-LOCK + SUSPENSIONS-OTHER + DEADLOCKS + TIMEOUTS)
```

This calculation provides you with a ratio of troublesome locks to successful locks, as shown here:

```
351 / (2 + 0 + 0 + 0) = 175.5
```

The larger this number, the less lock contention your system is experiencing. Data sharing lock requests (P-locks) are also displayed on the DB2 Statistics report.

EDM pool utilization is the final system-wide performance indicator that you can monitor using the DB2 Statistics Short report. To calculate the efficiency of the EDM pool, use the following formula:

```
(REQ FOR CT SECTIONS) + (REQUESTS FOR DBD)
-------------------------------------------
 (LOAD CT SECT FROM DASD) + (LOAD DBD FROM DASD)
```

Using the example, here's the calculation:

```
(151 + 432) / (70 + 0) = 8.32
```

Therefore, on average, 8.32 cursor tables and DBDs were requested before DB2 had to read one from DASD. This number should be as high as possible to avoid delays due to reading objects from the DB2 Directory.

In addition to the Statistics Summary report, a Statistics Detail report provides multiple pages of detail supporting the summary information. Also, the Short and Long Statistics Trace reports are useful for analyzing DB2 resource use in-depth.

Summary Report Set

The summary report set is used to provide a summarization of DB2-PM events. Three summary reports are provided every time DB2-PM is run.

The Job Summary Log details the traces that were started and stopped during the time frame that was reported. Additionally, a summary of the requested DB2-PM reports is provided. The Message Log contains any DB2-PM error messages. Finally, the Trace Record Distribution report provides a synopsis of the types of DB2 trace records and the number of times they were encountered in this job.

These reports are not useful for evaluating DB2 performance. They are used solely to support DB2-PM processing.

System Parameters Report Set

The DB2-PM System Parameters report provides a formatted listing of the DSNZPARM parameters specified when DB2 was started. This two-page report shows information such as the following:

- Install SYSADM IDs and Install SYSOPR IDs
- EDM Pool Size
- Bufferpool Sizes and Information
- IRLM Information (IRLM Name, IRLMRWT, Auto Start)
- User Information (CTHREAD, IDFORE, IDBACK)
- Automatic Trace Start Information
- Lock Escalation
- Log Information (Number of Archive Logs, Archive Copy Prefixes, Checkpoint Frequency)
- Data Definition Control Support
- Distributed Database Information (DDF)
- Stored Procedure Information (SPAS)
- DFHSM Usage
- Other System Parameters

The System Parameters report can be produced automatically in conjunction with any other DB2-PM reports. It is produced only if a -START TRACE command was issued during the time frame for the requested report. This report is useful for determining the parameters in use for the DB2 subsystem.

Transit Time Report Set

The final report set is the transit time report set. A transit report differs from other types of reports in that it provides performance information for all events that occur between a create thread and a terminate thread. A transit can be several plan executions due to thread reuse.

The Transit Time Summary report, shown in Listing 17.15, breaks down transit information into its components. For example, the transit for the DSNUTIL plan is broken down into the time for each separate phase of the REORG.

Listing 17.15. DB2-PM Transit Time Summary report.

```
INTERVAL FROM 8/27/97 12:24:35.63              DB2 PERFORMANCE MONITOR (V2 R1 M1)      DB2 ID:   DB2T    PAGE 1
         TO   8/28/97 00:05:43.02
                                             TRANSIT TIME SUMMARY                REQUESTED FROM   NOT SPECIFIED
                                                                                            TO    NOT SPECIFIED

                                             BY PRIMAUTH/PLANNAME
                  ------------- AVERAGE  ELAPSED TIMES -----            TOTAL                 DETAIL
                 #TRANSITS, #CREATE CREATE  COMMIT,                ---- WORKLOAD ----- ----- WORKLOAD -----
                   TOTAL    THREAD, THREAD,  TERM.    DB2,      TRANSIT
PRIMAUTH PLANNAME TRANSIT AET #COMMIT SIGNON THREAD  UNATTRIB.   TYPE   # OCCUR    AET      TYPE     #OCCUR  AET
                  MMM:SS.THT            SSS.THT SSS.THT MMM:SS.THT                  MMM:SS.THT
-------- -------- -------- ---------- ------- ------- ---------- ------- ------- ---------- ----------------------
AUTHID02 DSNUTIL          1         1   0.001   0.091      8.702 UTILITY       1      8.702 PHASE  TYPE #ITEMS  PHS ET
                      9.552         4   0.000   0.019      0.809 REORG         1            UNLOAD  R       18  0.527
                                                                                            RELOAD  R        9  3.980
                                                                                            SORT    I       18  4.102
                                                                                            BUILD   I       18  0.893
```

Different levels of detail are provided by the three other types of transit time reports: Transit Time Detail report, Short Transit Time Trace report, and Long Transit Time Trace report.

Transit time reports are useful for determining the performance of DB2 utility phases and SQL activity. Like the SQL trace reports, they may contain a large amount of information and should be used only when specific performance problems are encountered.

Using DB2-PM

Before you can run DB2-PM, you must have trace records produced by DB2 to feed into DB2-PM. Each DB2-PM report set requires certain traces to be started. For a synopsis of which traces to start for which information, see Table 17.3. Note that DB2-PM will not fail if you request a report for which no information or insufficient information is available. The report that DB2-PM generates, however, will be empty or incomplete.

Table 17.3. Traces to initiate for each DB2-PM report type.

Report Type	*Recommended Traces*	*Information Provided*
Accounting (General)	Accounting Class 1	General accounting information
	Accounting Class 2	In DB2 times
	Accounting Class 3	Suspension times, out of DB2 times, system events
Accounting Long	Accounting Class 1	General accounting information
	Accounting Class 2	In DB2 times

Report Type	*Recommended Traces*	*Information Provided*
	Accounting Class 3	Suspension times, out of DB2 times, system events
	Accounting Class 4	Installation-defined
	Accounting Class 5	Time spent processing IFI requests
	Accounting Class 7	Entry or exit from DB2 event signaling for package and DBRM accounting
	Accounting Class 8	Package wait time
Audit	Audit Class 1	Authorization failures
	Audit Class 2	DCL
	Audit Class 3	DDL
	Audit Class 4	DML: First SELECT of audited table
	Audit Class 5	DML: First UPDATE for audited tables
	Audit Class 6	Bind
	Audit Class 7	SET CURRENT SQLID
	Audit Class 8	Utility executions
	Audit Class 9	User-defined
I/O Activity	Performance Class 4	Bufferpool and EDM pool statistics
	Performance Class 5	Logging and BSDS statistics
Locking	Performance Class 6	Lock suspensions, lock resumes, and lock contention information
Record Trace	No traces specifically required	Formatted dump of all DB2 trace records in the given input data set
SQL Trace	Accounting Class 1	General accounting information
	Accounting Class 2	In DB2 times
	Performance Class 2	Aborts, commits, and thread-related data
	Performance Class 3	Sort, AMS, plan, cursor, static SQL, and dynamic SQL statistics
	Performance Class 4	Physical reads and writes
	Performance Class 6	Lock suspensions, lock resumes, and lock contention information

continues

Table 17.3. continued

Report Type	*Recommended Traces*	*Information Provided*
	Performance Class 8	Index access and sequential scan data
	Performance Class 13	EDITPROC and VALIDPROC access
Statistics	Statistics Class 1	System and database services statistics
	Statistics Class 2	Installation-defined
	Statistics Class 3	Deadlock information
	Statistics Class 4	DB2 exception condition
Summary	No traces specifically required	Basic summary of the steps taken by DB2-PM to produce other reports
System Parameters	At least one type of trace	Installation parameters (DSNZPARMs)
Transit Time	Performance Class 1	Background events
	Performance Class 2	Aborts, commits, and thread-related data
	Performance Class 3	Sort, AMS, plans, cursor, static SQL, and dynamic SQL statistics
	Performance Class 4	Physical reads and writes
	Performance Class 6	Lock suspensions, lock resumes, and lock contention information
	Performance Class 10	Optimizer and bind statistics
	Performance Class 13	EDITPROC and VALIDPROC access

Be sure to start the appropriate traces as outlined in Table 17.3 before running DB2-PM. To run a report indicated in the left column, you should start the recommended traces to get useful information from DB2-PM. If a particular trace is not started, the DB2-PM report still prints, but you do not get all the information the report can provide. Failure to start all these traces may result in some report values being left blank or listed as N/C.

You should develop standards for the production of DB2-PM reports to monitor the performance of DB2 and its applications at your shop. Use the chart in Table 17.4 as a guideline for establishing a regular DB2-PM reporting cycle. You can modify and augment this table based on your shop's DB2 performance monitoring requirements and standards.

Table 17.4. DB2-PM monitoring reference.

Resource to Monitor	*DB2-PM Report*	*Frequency*
DB2 Subsystem Performance	Statistics Summary	Weekly
	Statistics Detail	As needed
	I/O Activity Summary	Monthly
	I/O Bufferpool Activity Detail	As needed
	I/O EDM Pool Activity Detail	As needed
	I/O Log Manager Activity Detail	As needed
	System Parameters	When DB2 is recycled
	Audit Summary	Weekly
DB2 Application Performance	Accounting Short	Daily
	Accounting Long	As needed
	Audited DML Access	Weekly
	Lock Contention	As needed
	Lock Suspension	As needed
Exception	Transit Time report solving	Problem monitoring
	SQL Trace	Problem solving
	Record Trace	DB2 or DB2-PM problem solving
	Summary report	DB2-PM problem solving
	Lock Contention	Problem solving
	Lock Suspension	Problem solving
Security	Audit Authorization Failures	Weekly
	Audit Authorization Control	Weekly
	Audit Authorization Change	Weekly
	Audited DDL Access	Weekly
	Audited DML Access	Weekly
	Audit Utility Access	Weekly

Some performance monitoring software from other vendors can provide the same batch reporting functionality as DB2-PM. Because DB2-PM is not as mature an online performance monitor as other products, you might want to reconsider whether you need DB2-PM. Before you decide to avoid DB2-PM in favor of the batch performance monitoring provided by another tool, consider the following:

- When performance problems that require IBM intervention persist, IBM often requests that you run a performance trace and generate DB2-PM reports for the trace. To be sure that IBM will accept reports generated by the third-party tool, compare the output from the vendor tool to the output from DB2-PM. If the reports are almost identical, you usually will not have a problem. To be absolutely sure, ask your IBM support center.
- DB2-PM is an industry standard for batch performance monitoring. Taking classes on performance monitoring is easier when the monitoring is based on DB2-PM reports. Classes offered by IBM (and others) on DB2 performance usually use DB2-PM reports as examples. As such, having access to DB2-PM is helpful for students. Additionally, if you need to add staff, DB2-PM trained personnel are easier to find.
- DB2-PM is updated for new releases of DB2 more quickly than third-party monitoring tools because IBM is closer than anyone else to the code of DB2. If you need to migrate to new versions of DB2 rapidly, DB2-PM may be the only monitor positioned for the new release at the same time as your shop.

Online DB2 Performance Monitors

In addition to a batch performance monitor such as DB2-PM, DB2 shops must also have an online performance monitor, which is simply a tool that provides real-time reporting on DB2 performance statistics as DB2 operates. In contrast, a batch performance monitor reads previously generated trace records from an input data set.

Traditional VTAM Performance Monitors

The most common way to provide online performance monitoring capabilities is by online access to DB2 trace information in the `MONITOR` trace class. These tools are accessed directly through VTAM in the same way that CICS or TSO are accessed through VTAM. You generally specify OPX or OP*n* for the destination of the `MONITOR` trace. This way, you can place the trace records into a buffer that can be read using the IFI.

Some online DB2 performance monitors also provide direct access to DB2 performance data by reading the control blocks of the DB2 and application address spaces. This type of monitoring provides a "window" to up-to-the-minute performance statistics while DB2 is running. This information is important if quick reaction to performance problems is required.

Most online DB2 performance monitors provide a menu-driven interface accessible from TSO or VTAM. It enables online performance monitors to start and stop traces as needed based on the menu options chosen by the user. Consequently, you can reduce overhead and diminish the learning curve involved in understanding DB2 traces and their correspondence to performance reports.

Following are some typical uses of online performance monitors. Many online performance monitors can establish effective exception-based monitoring. When specified performance thresholds are reached, triggers can offer notification and take action. For example, you could set a trigger when the number of lock suspensions for the `TXN00002` plan is reached; when the trigger is activated, a message is sent to the console and a batch report is generated to provide accounting detail information for the plan. You can set any number of triggers for many thresholds. Following are suggestions for setting thresholds:

- When a bufferpool threshold is reached (`PREFETCH DISABLED`, `DEFERRED WRITE THRESHOLD`, or `DM CRITICAL THRESHOLD`).
- For critical transactions, when predefined performance objectives are not met. For example, if `TXN00001` requires subsecond response time, set a trigger to notify a DBA when the transaction receives a class 1 accounting elapsed time exceeding 1 second by more than 25 percent.
- Many types of thresholds can be established. Most online monitors support this capability. As such, you can customize the thresholds for the needs of your DB2 environment.

Online performance monitors can produce real-time `EXPLAIN`s for long-running SQL statements. If an SQL statement is taking a significant amount of time to process, an analyst can display the SQL statement as it executes and dynamically issue an `EXPLAIN` for the statement. Even as the statement executes, an understanding of why it is taking so long to run can be achieved.

NOTE

A complete discussion of the `EXPLAIN` statement is provided in the next chapter.

Online performance monitors can also reduce the burden of monitoring more than one DB2 subsystem. Multiple DB2 subsystems can be tied to a single online performance monitor to enable monitoring of distributed capabilities, multiple production DB2s, or test and production DB2 subsystems, all from a single session.

Some online performance monitors provide historical trending. These monitors track performance statistics and store them in DB2 tables or in VSAM files with a timestamp. They also provide the capability to query these stores of performance data to assist in the following:

- Analyzing recent history. Most SQL statements execute quickly, making difficult the job of capturing and displaying information about the SQL statement as it executes. However, you might not want to wait until the SMF data is available to run a batch report. Quick access to recent past-performance data in these external data stores provides a type of online monitoring that is as close to real time as is usually needed.
- Determining performance trends, such as a transaction steadily increasing in its CPU consumption or elapsed time.
- Performing capacity planning based on a snapshot of the recent performance of DB2 applications.

Some monitors also run when DB2 is down to provide access to the historical data accumulated by the monitor.

A final benefit of online DB2 performance monitors is their capability to interface with other MVS monitors for IMS/TM, CICS, MVS, or VTAM. This way, an analyst gets a view of the entire spectrum of system performance. Understanding and analyzing the data from each of these monitors, however, requires a different skill. Quite often, one person cannot master all these monitors.

Agent-Based Performance Management

The leading database performance monitoring software is increasingly becoming agent-based. An agent-based performance management tool requires portions to be installed on both the server and the client. The server component constantly monitors and polls for predefined events; the client component provides console operations that accept alerts triggered by the server. In a DB2 environment, the MVS or OS/390 machine is the server; the client is typically a PC running Windows 95 or Windows NT.

Agent-based technology provides several advantages over traditional monitoring technology. An agent is continually operating and autonomous. It can communicate with end users and other agents to create a proactive performance management environment. Agents do not require constant user interaction to operate; they are self-contained and independently executing. Likewise, a good agent-based performance management solution does not require a permanent link to the initiating event. The agent therefore continues to operate even if the console is shut down.

Agent-based performance management tools became popular in the UNIX environment with the advent of client/server application development. Examples of popular agent-based monitors include BMC Software's Patrol and PLATINUM *technology*'s DBVision. Both BMC and PLATINUM are currently offering versions of their agent-based tools for DB2 on the mainframe.

Online Performance Monitoring Summary

Some vendors sell monitors in all these areas, providing a sort of seamless interface that can simplify movement from one type of monitoring to another. For example, if a DB2 monitor reports that a CICS transaction is experiencing a performance problem, being able to switch to a CICS monitor to further explore the situation would be beneficial.

In Chapter 32, "Components of a Total DB2 Solution," I discuss online performance monitors for DB2 further and list several vendors that supply them. You also can write your own DB2 performance monitor using the Instrumentation Facility Interface (IFI) provided with DB2. However, you should not undertake this task unless you are a skilled system programmer willing to retool your home-grown monitor for every new release of DB2.

Viewing DB2 Console Messages

Another way to monitor DB2 performance is to view the DB2 console messages for the active `DSNMSTR` address space. You can obtain a wealth of statistics from this log.

To view DB2 console messages, you must be able to view the `DSNMSTR` region either as it executes or, for an inactive DB2 subsystem, from the spool. Most shops have a tool for displaying the outlist of jobs that are executing or have completed but remain on the queue. An example of such a tool is IBM's SDF.

Using your outlist display tool, select the `DSNMSTR` job. (This job may have been renamed at your shop to something such as `DB2TMSTR` or `DB2MSTR`.) View the JES message log, which contains DB2 messages that are helpful in determining problems.

Information in the DB2 message log can help you monitor many situations. Several examples follow.

When you first view the console messages, a screen similar to Figure 17.2 is displayed. In the DB2 start-up messages, look for the `DSNZ002I` message code. It shows you the `DSNZPARM` load module name that supplied DB2 with its start-up parameters. From this first part of the DB2 console log, you also can determine the following:

- The time DB2 was started (in the example, 18:01:52)
- The name of the Boot Strap Data Set (BSDS) and associated information
- The name of the active log data sets and associated log RBA information

Sometimes, when DB2 performs a log offload, the overall performance of the DB2 subsystem suffers. This outcome can be the result of the physical placement of log data sets and DASD contention as DB2 copies data from the active logs to archive log tapes and switches active logs.

FIGURE 17.2.
DB2 console messages.

```
BROWSE - DB2TMSTR(J4730): JESMSGLG ------------------ LINE 00000000 COL 001 080
COMMAND ===>                                                    SCROLL ===> CSR
******************************** TOP OF DATA *********************************
IAT6140 JOB ORIGIN FROM GROUP=ANYLOCAL, DSP=SR , DEVICE=STC      , 000
18:01:52 IAT4401  LOCATE FOR STEP=IEFPROC  DD=BSDS1     DSN=DB2T.BSDS01
18:01:52 IAT4402 STORCLAS=CRITGS, MGMTCLAS=DBASE
18:01:52 IAT4401  LOCATE FOR STEP=IEFPROC  DD=BSDS2     DSN=DB2T.BSDS02
18:01:52 IAT4402 STORCLAS=CRITGS, MGMTCLAS=DBASE
18:01:52  IEF403I DB2TMSTR - STARTED - TIME=18.01.52
18:01:53  DSNZ002I - SUBSYS DB2T SYSTEM PARAMETERS LOAD MODULE NAME IS DSNZPARM
18:01:55  DSNY001I - SUBSYSTEM STARTING
18:01:55  IEC161I 056-084,DB2TMSTR,DB2TMSTR,BSDS1,,,DB2T.BSDS01,
18:01:55  IEC161I DB2T.BSDS01.DATA,CATALOG.DB2T.VDB2001
18:01:56  IEC161I 056-084,DB2TMSTR,DB2TMSTR,BSDS1,,,DB2T.BSDS01,
18:01:56  IEC161I DB2T.BSDS01.INDEX,CATALOG.DB2T.VDB2001
18:01:56  IEC161I 062-086,DB2TMSTR,DB2TMSTR,BSDS1,,,DB2T.BSDS01,
18:01:56  IEC161I DB2T.BSDS01.DATA,CATALOG.DB2T.VDB2001
18:01:56  IEC161I 056-084,DB2TMSTR,DB2TMSTR,BSDS2,,,DB2T.BSDS02,
18:01:56  IEC161I DB2T.BSDS02.DATA,CATALOG.DB2T.VDB2001
18:01:56  IEC161I 056-084,DB2TMSTR,DB2TMSTR,BSDS2,,,DB2T.BSDS02,
18:01:56  IEC161I DB2T.BSDS02.INDEX,CATALOG.DB2T.VDB2001
18:01:56  IEC161I 062-086,DB2TMSTR,DB2TMSTR,BSDS2,,,DB2T.BSDS02,
18:01:56  IEC161I DB2T.BSDS02.DATA,CATALOG.DB2T.VDB2001
18:01:57  DSNJ127I - SYSTEM TIMESTAMP FOR BSDS= 91.324 17:51:41.70
18:02:03  DSNJ001I - DSNJW007 CURRENT COPY 1 ACTIVE LOG DATA
18:02:03  SET IS DSNAME=DB2T.LOGCOPY1.DS02,
18:02:03  STARTRBA=00047449F000,ENDRBA=000474C19FFF
18:02:03  DSNJ001I - DSNJW007 CURRENT COPY 2 ACTIVE LOG DATA
18:02:03  SET IS DSNAME=DB2T.LOGCOPY2.DS02,
18:02:03  STARTRBA=00047449F000,ENDRBA=000474C19FFF
18:02:04  S DB2TDBM1
18:02:23  DSNR001I - RESTART INITIATED
```

In Figure 17.3, find the DB2 message `DSNJ002I`, which indicates the time an active log data set is full (10:25:21 in the example). The `DSNJ139I` message is issued when the log offload has completed successfully (10:26:47 in the example). This efficient log offload required a little more than one minute to complete. If users complain about poor performance that can be tracked back to log offload periods, investigate the DASD placement of your active logs. Specify multiple active logs, and place each active log data set on a separate DASD device. As an additional consideration, think about caching the DASD devices used for DB2 active logs.

Resource unavailable messages are also in this message log. You can find them by searching for `DSNT501I` messages. For example, refer to the portion of the log displayed in Figure 17.4. It shows a resource unavailable message occurring at 18:17:26. From this message, you can determine who received the unavailable resource message (correlation ID), what was unavailable, and why. In this case, a tablespace was unavailable for reason code `00C900A3`, which is a check pending situation. (As you can see by scanning further messages in the log, the check pending situation is cleared up approximately four minutes later.)

Another area that requires monitoring is locking contention. When a high degree of lock contention occurs in a DB2 subsystem, you get many timeout and deadlock messages. Message code `DSNT375I` is issued when a deadlock occurs, and `DSNT376I` is issued for every timeout. Figure 17.5 shows two examples of timeouts due to lock contention. You can determine who is timing out, who holds the lock that causes the timeout, and what resource has been locked so that access is unavailable. In the example, the `DSNDB01.DBD01` DB2 Directory database is locked, probably due to the concurrent execution of DDL by the indicated correlation ID.

FIGURE 17.3.
Log offloading.

```
BROWSE - DB2TMSTR(J4730): JESMSGLG ----------------- LINE 00001363 COL 001 080
COMMAND ===>                                                  SCROLL ===> CSR
10:25:21  DSNJ002I - FULL ACTIVE LOG DATA SET
10:25:21  DSNAME=DB2T.LOGCOPY2.DS03, STARTRBA=000474C1A000, ENDRBA=000476F41FFF
10:25:21  DSNJ001I - DSNJW307 CURRENT COPY 2 ACTIVE LOG DATA
10:25:21  SET IS DSNAME=DB2T.LOGCOPY2.DS01,
10:25:21  STARTRBA=000476F42000,ENDRBA=000479269FFF
10:25:22 IAT5200 JOB DB2TMSTR (JOB04730) IN SETUP ON MAIN=SYS2
10:25:22 IAT5210 JOB SYS00484 (JOB04730) SYS2     MOUNT C SCRTCH ON AB8  ,SL,RI
10:25:22 *IAT5210 JOB DB2TMSTR (JOB04730) SYS2     MOUNT C SCRTCH ON AB8  ,SL,R
10:25:29  IEC705I TAPE ON AB8,036855,SL,NOCOMP,DB2TMSTR,DB2TMSTR
10:25:31 IAT5200 JOB DB2TMSTR (JOB04730) IN SETUP ON MAIN=SYS2
10:25:31 IAT5210 JOB SYS00485 (JOB04730) SYS2     MOUNT C SCRTCH ON AB9  ,SL,RI
10:25:31 *IAT5210 JOB DB2TMSTR (JOB04730) SYS2     MOUNT C SCRTCH ON AB9  ,SL,R
10:25:52  IEC705I TAPE ON AB9,050403,SL,NOCOMP,DB2TMSTR,DB2TMSTR
10:26:37  IEF234E R AB8,036855,PVT,DB2TMSTR,DB2TMSTR
10:26:37  DSNJ003I - FULL ARCHIVE LOG VOLUME
10:26:37  DSNAME=DB2T.ARCHLOG1.A0000522, STARTRBA=000474C1A000,
10:26:37  ENDRBA=000476F41FFF, UNIT=TAPE, COPY1VOL=036855, VOLSPAN=00,
10:26:37  CATLG=YES
10:26:46  IEF234E R AB9,050403,PVT,DB2TMSTR,DB2TMSTR
10:26:47  DSNJ003I - FULL ARCHIVE LOG VOLUME
10:26:47  DSNAME=DB2T.ARCHLOG2.A0000522, STARTRBA=000474C1A000,
10:26:47  ENDRBA=000476F41FFF, UNIT=TAPE, COPY2VOL=050403, VOLSPAN=00,
10:26:47  CATLG=YES
10:26:47  DSNJ139I - LOG OFFLOAD TASK ENDED
10:34:28  DSN3201I - ABNORMAL EOT IN PROGRESS FOR USER=CON9DJB
10:34:28  CONNECTION-ID=DB2CALL CORRELATION-ID=CON9DJBZ....
10:43:54  DSN3201I - ABNORMAL EOT IN PROGRESS FOR USER=CON9SXB
10:43:54  CONNECTION-ID=DB2CALL CORRELATION-ID=CON9SXB ....
10:48:43  DSN3201I - ABNORMAL EOT IN PROGRESS FOR USER=CON9DMB
10:48:43  CONNECTION-ID=DB2CALL CORRELATION-ID=CON9DMB ....
```

FIGURE 17.4.
Resource unavailable.

```
BROWSE - DB2TMSTR(J4730): JESMSGLG ----------------- LINE 00003944 COL 001 080
COMMAND ===>                                                  SCROLL ===> CSR
18:17:26  DSNT501I - DSNIPSFI RESOURCE UNAVAILABLE
18:17:26            CORRELATION-ID=CON9JPW ....
18:17:26            CONNECTION-ID=DB2CALL
18:17:26            LUW-ID=*
18:17:26            REASON 00C900A3
18:17:26            TYPE 00000200
18:17:26            NAME DCSCDB02.CSSTSSCR
18:21:12  DSNU973I - DSNUGCKP - TABLESPACE DCSCDB02.CSSTSSCR IS
18:21:12  NOT CHECK PENDING
18:21:12                  CORRELATION ID=CON9JPWL....
18:21:12                  CONNECTION ID=UTILITY                   LUW ID=*
18:21:16  DSNU971I - DSNUGCKP - TABLESPACE DCSCDB02.CSSTSSCR IS
18:21:16  CHECK PENDING
18:21:16                  CORRELATION ID=CON9JPWL....
18:21:16                  CONNECTION ID=UTILITY
18:21:16                  LUW ID=*
18:21:27  DSNU973I - DSNUGCKP - TABLESPACE DCSCDB02.CSSTSSCR IS
18:21:27  NOT CHECK PENDING
18:21:27                  CORRELATION ID=CON9JPWL....
18:21:27                  CONNECTION ID=UTILITY                   LUW ID=*
19:21:25  DSNJ002I - FULL ACTIVE LOG DATA SET
19:21:25  DSNAME=DB2T.LOGCOPY1.DS01, STARTRBA=00047D8BA000, ENDRBA=00047FBE1FFF
19:21:25  DSNJ001I - DSNJW307 CURRENT COPY 1 ACTIVE LOG DATA
19:21:25  SET IS DSNAME=DB2T.LOGCOPY1.DS02,
19:21:25  STARTRBA=00047FBE2000,ENDRBA=000481F09FFF
19:21:25  DSNJ002I - FULL ACTIVE LOG DATA SET
19:21:25  DSNAME=DB2T.LOGCOPY2.DS01, STARTRBA=00047D8BA000, ENDRBA=00047FBE1FFF
19:21:25  DSNJ001I - DSNJW307 CURRENT COPY 2 ACTIVE LOG DATA
19:21:25  SET IS DSNAME=DB2T.LOGCOPY2.DS02,
19:21:25  STARTRBA=00047FBE2000,ENDRBA=000481F09FFF
```

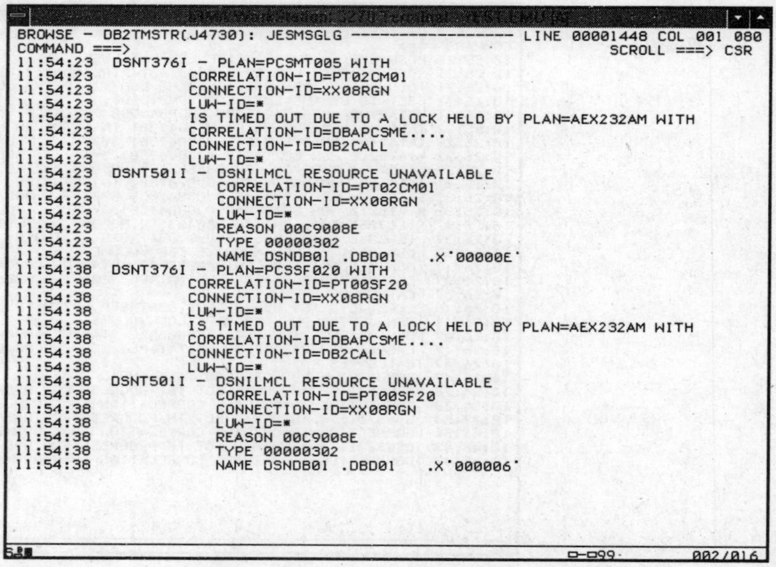

```
BROWSE - DB2TMSTR(J4730): JESMSGLG ---------------- LINE 00001448 COL 001 080
COMMAND ===>                                                 SCROLL ===> CSR
11:54:23  DSNT376I - PLAN=PCSMT005 WITH
11:54:23            CORRELATION-ID=PT02CM01
11:54:23            CONNECTION-ID=XX08RGN
11:54:23            LUW-ID=*
11:54:23            IS TIMED OUT DUE TO A LOCK HELD BY PLAN=AEX232AM WITH
11:54:23            CORRELATION-ID=DBAPCSME....
11:54:23            CONNECTION-ID=DB2CALL
11:54:23            LUW-ID=*
11:54:23  DSNT501I - DSNILMCL RESOURCE UNAVAILABLE
11:54:23               CORRELATION-ID=PT02CM01
11:54:23               CONNECTION-ID=XX08RGN
11:54:23               LUW-ID=*
11:54:23               REASON 00C9008E
11:54:23               TYPE 00000302
11:54:23               NAME DSNDB01 .DBD01     .X'00000E'
11:54:38  DSNT376I - PLAN=PCSSF020 WITH
11:54:38            CORRELATION-ID=PT00SF20
11:54:38            CONNECTION-ID=XX08RGN
11:54:38            LUW-ID=*
11:54:38            IS TIMED OUT DUE TO A LOCK HELD BY PLAN=AEX232AM WITH
11:54:38            CORRELATION-ID=DBAPCSME....
11:54:38            CONNECTION-ID=DB2CALL
11:54:38            LUW-ID=*
11:54:38  DSNT501I - DSNILMCL RESOURCE UNAVAILABLE
11:54:38               CORRELATION-ID=PT00SF20
11:54:38               CONNECTION-ID=XX08RGN
11:54:38               LUW-ID=*
11:54:38               REASON 00C9008E
11:54:38               TYPE 00000302
11:54:38               NAME DSNDB01 .DBD01     .X'000006'
```

FIGURE 17.5.
Locking contention and timeouts.

The final monitoring advice in this section concentrates on two internal plans used by DB2: `BCT` (Basic Cursor Table) and `BINDCT`. DB2 uses the `BCT` plan to issue commands. For example, assume that you issue a `-STOP DATABASE` command, but the database cannot be stopped immediately because someone is holding a lock on the DBD. The database is placed in stop pending (`STOPP`) status, and DB2 continues issuing the command using the `BCT` plan until it is successful.

In Figure 17.6, the `BCT` plan is timed out at 14:58:26 and then again at 14:59:41. This timeout occurred because an attempt was made to issue `-STOP DATABASE` while another job was issuing DDL for objects in the database. The `BCT` plan tries to stop the database repeatedly until it succeeds.

DB2 uses the `BINDCT` plan to bind packages and plans. If users have problems binding, the cause of the problem can be determined by looking in the log for occurrences of `BINDCT`. In the example in Figure 17.7, the bind failed because someone was using a vendor tool that held a lock on the DB2 Catalog. Because the `BIND` command must update the DB2 Catalog with plan information, the concurrent lock on the catalog caused the `BIND` to fail.

The situations covered here are a few of the most common monitoring uses for the DB2 console message log. Look for corroborating evidence in this log when you're trying to resolve or track down the cause of a DB2 problem.

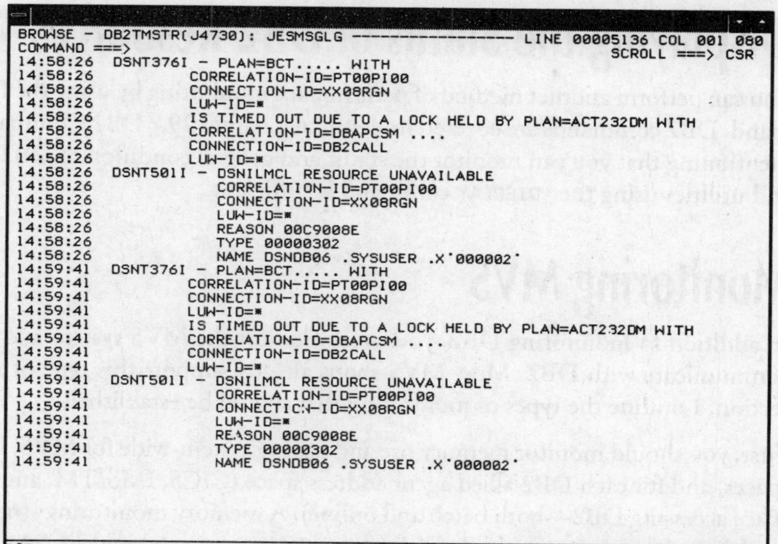

```
BROWSE - DB2TMSTR(J4730): JESMSGLG ------------------ LINE 00005136 COL 001 080
COMMAND ===>                                                  SCROLL ===> CSR
14:58:26  DSNT376I - PLAN=BCT..... WITH
14:58:26            CORRELATION-ID=PT00PI00
14:58:26            CONNECTION-ID=XX08RGN
14:58:26            LUW-ID=*
14:58:26            IS TIMED OUT DUE TO A LOCK HELD BY PLAN=ACT232DM WITH
14:58:26            CORRELATION-ID=DBAPCSM ....
14:58:26            CONNECTION-ID=DB2CALL
14:58:26            LUW-ID=*
14:58:26  DSNT501I - DSNILMCL RESOURCE UNAVAILABLE
14:58:26               CORRELATION-ID=PT00PI00
14:58:26               CONNECTION-ID=XX08RGN
14:58:26               LUW-ID=*
14:58:26               REASON 00C9008E
14:58:26               TYPE 00000302
14:58:26               NAME DSNDB06 .SYSUSER .X'000002'
14:59:41  DSNT376I - PLAN=BCT..... WITH
14:59:41            CORRELATION-ID=PT00PI00
14:59:41            CONNECTION-ID=XX08RGN
14:59:41            LUW-ID=*
14:59:41            IS TIMED OUT DUE TO A LOCK HELD BY PLAN=ACT232DM WITH
14:59:41            CORRELATION-ID=DBAPCSM ....
14:59:41            CONNECTION-ID=DB2CALL
14:59:41            LUW-ID=*
14:59:41  DSNT501I - DSNILMCL RESOURCE UNAVAILABLE
14:59:41               CORRELATION-ID=PT00PI00
14:59:41               CONNECTION-ID=XX08RGN
14:59:41               LUW-ID=*
14:59:41               REASON 00C9008E
14:59:41               TYPE 00000302
14:59:41               NAME DSNDB06 .SYSUSER .X'000002'
                                                                     002/015
```

FIGURE 17.6.
The BCT *plan.*

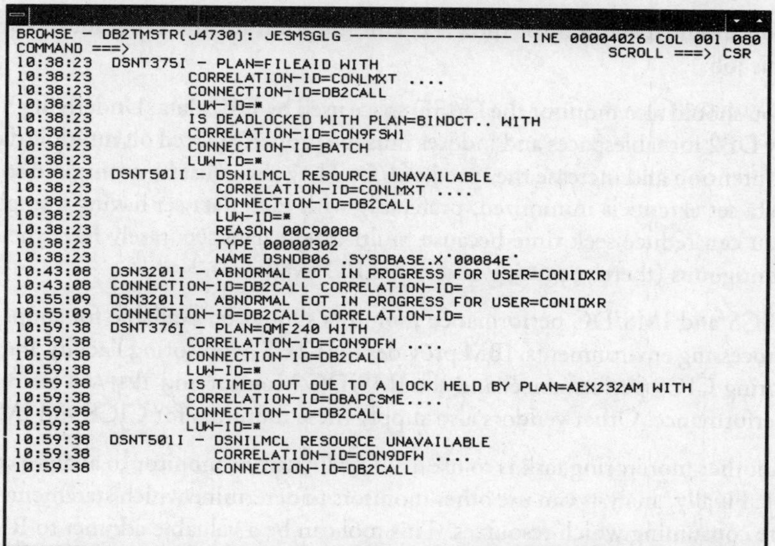

```
BROWSE - DB2TMSTR(J4730): JESMSGLG ------------------ LINE 00004026 COL 001 080
COMMAND ===>                                                  SCROLL ===> CSR
10:38:23  DSNT375I - PLAN=FILEAID WITH
10:38:23            CORRELATION-ID=CONLMXT ....
10:38:23            CONNECTION-ID=DB2CALL
10:38:23            LUW-ID=*
10:38:23            IS DEADLOCKED WITH PLAN=BINDCT.. WITH
10:38:23            CORRELATION-ID=CON9FSW1
10:38:23            CONNECTION-ID=BATCH
10:38:23            LUW-ID=*
10:38:23  DSNT501I - DSNILMCL RESOURCE UNAVAILABLE
10:38:23               CORRELATION-ID=CONLMXT ....
10:38:23               CONNECTION-ID=DB2CALL
10:38:23               LUW-ID=*
10:38:23               REASON 00C90088
10:38:23               TYPE 00000302
10:38:23               NAME DSNDB06 .SYSDBASE.X'00084E'
10:43:08  DSN3201I - ABNORMAL EOT IN PROGRESS FOR USER=CONIDXR
10:43:08  CONNECTION-ID=DB2CALL CORRELATION-ID=
10:55:09  DSN3201I - ABNORMAL EOT IN PROGRESS FOR USER=CONIDXR
10:55:09  CONNECTION-ID=DB2CALL CORRELATION-ID=
10:59:38  DSNT376I - PLAN=QMF240 WITH
10:59:38            CORRELATION-ID=CON9DFW ....
10:59:38            CONNECTION-ID=DB2CALL
10:59:38            LUW-ID=*
10:59:38            IS TIMED OUT DUE TO A LOCK HELD BY PLAN=AEX232AM WITH
10:59:38            CORRELATION-ID=DBAPCSME....
10:59:38            CONNECTION-ID=DB2CALL
10:59:38            LUW-ID=*
10:59:38  DSNT501I - DSNILMCL RESOURCE UNAVAILABLE
10:59:38               CORRELATION-ID=CON9DFW ....
10:59:38               CONNECTION-ID=DB2CALL
                                                                     002/015
```

FIGURE 17.7.
The BINCDT *plan.*

Displaying the Status of DB2 Resources

You can perform another method of performance monitoring by using the DB2 -DISPLAY command. DB2 commands are covered in-depth in Chapter 29, "DB2 Commands." At this point, mentioning that you can monitor the status and general condition of DB2 databases, threads, and utilities using the -DISPLAY command is sufficient.

Monitoring MVS

In addition to monitoring DB2, you must monitor the MVS system and its subsystems that communicate with DB2. Most MVS shops already support this type of monitoring. In this section, I outline the types of monitoring that should be established.

First, you should monitor memory use and paging system-wide for MVS, for the DB2 address spaces, and for each DB2 allied agent address space (CICS, IMS/TM, and every TSO address space accessing DB2—both batch and online). A memory monitoring strategy should include guidelines for monitoring both CSA (common storage area) and ECSA (expanded common storage area). You can do so by using IBM's RMF (Resource Measurement Facility).

You should also monitor the CPU consumption for the DB2 address spaces. RMF can do this job.

You should also monitor the DASD space used by DB2 data. Underlying VSAM data sets used by DB2 for tablespaces and indexes must be properly placed on multiple data sets to avoid disk contention and increase the speed of I/O. They also must be monitored so that the number of data set extents is minimized, preferably with each data set having a single extent. This way, you can reduce seek time because multi-extent data sets rarely have their extents physically contiguous (thereby causing additional I/O overhead).

CICS and IMS/DC performance monitors should be available for shops that use these teleprocessing environments. IBM provides the CICS Monitoring Facility and CICSPARS for monitoring CICS performance, and the IMS/DC Monitor and IMSPARS for monitoring IMS/DC performance. Other vendors also supply these monitors for CICS and IMS/DC.

Another monitoring task is to use a VTAM network monitor to analyze communication traffic. Finally, analysts can use other monitors to determine which statements in a single program are consuming which resources. This tool can be a valuable adjunct to RMF.

Summary

In this chapter, you learned the basics of monitoring DB2 subsystems for performance information. You learned about the DB2 traces that contain valuable performance data as well as methods of accessing and reporting on this information. But monitoring the DB2 subsystem is only one component of an overall performance management strategy. The next step is to use `EXPLAIN` to delve into the access paths used by DB2 to execute SQL statement. Turn the page to begin examining the use of `EXPLAIN`.

18

Using EXPLAIN

You can use the EXPLAIN feature to detail the access paths chosen by the DB2 optimizer for SQL statements. EXPLAIN should be a key component of your performance monitoring strategy. The information provided by EXPLAIN is invaluable for determining the following:

- The work DB2 does "behind the scenes" to satisfy a single SQL statement
- Whether DB2 uses available indexes and, if indexes are used, how DB2 uses them
- The order in which DB2 tables are accessed to satisfy join criteria
- Whether a sort is required for the SQL statement
- Intentional tablespace locking requirements for a statement
- Whether DB2 uses query parallelism to satisfy an SQL statement
- The performance of an SQL statement based on the access paths chosen

How EXPLAIN Works

To see how EXPLAIN works, refer to Figure 18.1. A single SQL statement, or a series of SQL statements in a package or plan, can be the subject of an EXPLAIN. When EXPLAIN is requested, the SQL statements are passed through the DB2 optimizer, and the access paths that DB2 chooses are externalized, in coded format, into a PLAN_TABLE. A PLAN_TABLE is nothing more than a standard DB2 table that must be defined with predetermined columns, data types, and lengths.

FIGURE 18.1.
How EXPLAIN *works.*

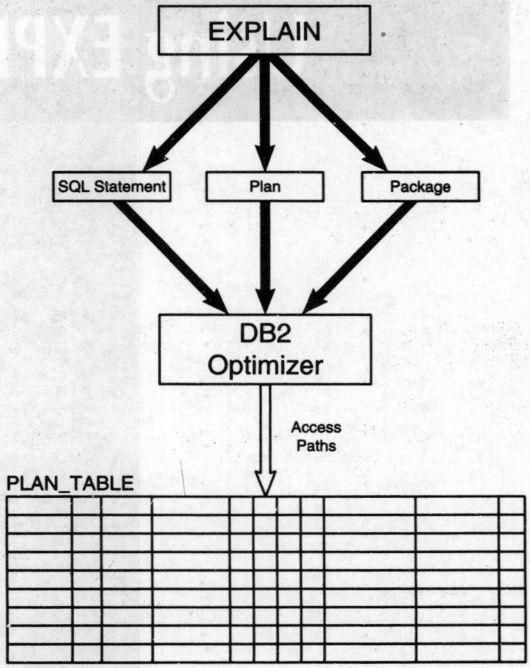

You can use the following DDL to create a PLAN_TABLE:

```
CREATE TABLE userid.PLAN_TABLE
(
 QUERYNO           INTEGER        NOT NULL,
 QBLOCKNO          SMALLINT       NOT NULL,
 APPLNAME          CHAR(8)        NOT NULL,
 PROGNAME          CHAR(8)        NOT NULL,
 PLANNO            SMALLINT       NOT NULL,
 METHOD            SMALLINT       NOT NULL,
 CREATOR           CHAR(8)        NOT NULL,
 TNAME             CHAR(18)       NOT NULL,
 TABNO             SMALLINT       NOT NULL,
 ACCESSTYPE        CHAR(2)        NOT NULL,
 MATCHCOLS         SMALLINT       NOT NULL,
 ACCESSCREATOR     CHAR(8)        NOT NULL,
 ACCESSNAME        CHAR(18)       NOT NULL,
 INDEXONLY         CHAR(1)        NOT NULL,
 SORTN_UNIQ        CHAR(1)        NOT NULL,
 SORTN_JOIN        CHAR(1)        NOT NULL,
 SORTN_ORDERBY     CHAR(1)        NOT NULL,
 SORTN_GROUPBY     CHAR(1)        NOT NULL,
 SORTC_UNIQ        CHAR(1)        NOT NULL,
 SORTC_JOIN        CHAR(1)        NOT NULL,
 SORTC_ORDERBY     CHAR(1)        NOT NULL,
 SORTC_GROUPBY     CHAR(1)        NOT NULL,
 TSLOCKMODE        CHAR(3)        NOT NULL,
 TIMESTAMP         CHAR(16)       NOT NULL,
 REMARKS           VARCHAR(254)   NOT NULL,                (25 column format)
 PREFETCH          CHAR(1)        NOT NULL WITH DEFAULT,
 COLUMN_FN_EVAL    CHAR(1)        NOT NULL WITH DEFAULT,
 MIXOPSEQ          SMALLINT       NOT NULL WITH DEFAULT,   (28 column format)
 VERSION           VARCHAR(64)    NOT NULL WITH DEFAULT,
 COLLID            CHAR(18)       NOT NULL WITH DEFAULT,   (30 column format)
 ACCESS_DEGREE     SMALLINT,
 ACCESS_PGROUP_ID  SMALLINT,
 JOIN_DEGREE       SMALLINT,
 JOIN_PGROUP_ID    SMALLINT,                               (34 column format)
 SORTC_PGROUP_ID   SMALLINT,
 SORTN_PGROUP_ID   SMALLINT,
 PARALLELISM_MODE  CHAR(1),
 MERGE_JOIN_COLS   SMALLINT,
 CORRELATION_NAME  CHAR(18),
 PAGE_RANGE        CHAR(1)        NOT NULL,
 JOIN_TYPE         CHAR(1)        NOT NULL,
 GROUP_MEMBER      CHAR(8)        NOT NULL,
 IBM_SERVICE_DATA  VARCHAR(254)   NOT NULL,                (43 column format)
 WHEN_OPTIMIZE     CHAR(1)        NOT NULL,
 QBLOCK_TYPE       CHAR(6)        NOT NULL,
 BIND_TIME         TIMESTAMP      NOT NULL                 (46 column format)
) IN database.tablespace;
```

Note that the PLAN_TABLE is created in the default database (DSNDB04) and STOGROUP (SYSDEFLT) in a DB2-generated tablespace, unless a database and a tablespace are created for the PLAN_TABLE and they are referenced in the IN clause of the CREATE TABLE statement.

The following six PLAN_TABLE formats are actually supported by DB2 V5:

- The 25-column format, which includes all columns through REMARKS (pre-DB2 V2.2)
- The 28-column format, which includes all columns through MIXOPSEQ (DB2 V2.2)
- The 30-column format, which includes all columns through COLLID (DB2 V2.3)
- The 34-column format, which includes all columns through JOIN_PGROUP_ID (DB2 V3)
- The 34-column format, which includes all columns through IBM_SERVICE_DATA (DB2 V4)
- The complete 46-column format, which includes all columns (DB2 V5). The general recommendation is to always use the complete 46-column format. The other formats exist to provide support for PLAN_TABLEs built under older versions of DB2 that did not support all the current columns.

If a PLAN_TABLE already exists, you can use the LIKE clause of CREATE TABLE to create PLAN_TABLEs for individual users based on a master PLAN_TABLE. Having a PLAN_TABLE for the following users is a good idea:

- Every DB2 application programmer. This way, they can analyze and evaluate the access paths chosen for the SQL embedded in their application programs.
- Every individual owner of every production DB2 plan. This way, an EXPLAIN can be run on production DB2 packages and plans.
- Every DBA and system programmer. This way, they can analyze access paths for ad hoc and dynamic SQL statements.

To EXPLAIN a single SQL statement, precede the SQL statement with the EXPLAIN command as follows:

```
EXPLAIN ALL SET QUERYNO = integer FOR
SQL statement ;
```

It can be executed in the same way as any other SQL statement. QUERYNO, which you can set to any integer, is used for identification in the PLAN_TABLE. For example, the following EXPLAIN statement populates the PLAN_TABLE with the access paths chosen for the indicated sample table query:

```
EXPLAIN ALL SET QUERYNO = 1 FOR
SELECT    FIRSTNME, MIDINIT, LASTNAME
FROM      DSN8510.EMP
WHERE     EMPNO = '000240';
```

The other method of issuing an EXPLAIN is as a part of the BIND command. If you indicate EXPLAIN(YES) when binding a package or a plan, DB2 externalizes the access paths chosen for all SQL statements in that DBRM (or DBRMs) to the PLAN_TABLE.

Querying the PLAN_TABLE

After you issue the EXPLAIN command on your SQL statements, the next logical step is to inspect the results. Because EXPLAIN places the access path information in a DB2 table, you can use an SQL query to retrieve this information, as follows:

```
SELECT    QUERYNO, QBLOCKNO, QBLOCK_TYPE, APPLNAME, PROGNAME, PLANNO,
          METHOD, CREATOR, TNAME, TABNO, ACCESSTYPE, JOIN_TYPE,
          MATCHCOLS, ACCESSNAME, INDEXONLY, SORTN_PGROUP_ID,
          SORTN_UNIQ, SORTN_JOIN, SORTN_ORDERBY, SORTN_GROUPBY,
          SORTC_PGROUP_ID, SORTC_UNIQ, SORTC_JOIN,
          SORTC_ORDERBY, SORTC_GROUPBY, TSLOCKMODE,
          TIMESTAMP, PREFETCH, COLUMN_FN_EVAL, MIXOPSEQ,
          COLLID, VERSION, ACCESS_DEGREE, ACCESS_PGROUP_ID,
          JOIN_DEGREE, JOIN_PGROUP_ID, PARALLELISM_MODE,
          MERGE_JOIN_COLS, CORRELATION_NAME, PAGE_RANGE,
          GROUP_MEMBER, WHEN_OPTIMIZE, BIND_TIME
FROM      ownerid.PLAN_TABLE
ORDER BY  APPLNAME, COLLID, VERSION, PROGNAME,
          TIMESTAMP DESC, QUERYNO, QBLOCKNO, PLANNO
```

NOTE

The following columns were new as of DB2 V4. They cannot be accessed prior to DB2 V4. These columns are not populated for EXPLAIN statistics accumulated prior to V4: SORTC_PGROUP_ID, SORTN_PGROUP_ID, PARALLELISM_MODE, MERGE_JOIN_COLS, CORRELATION_NAME, PAGE_RANGE, JOIN_TYPE, GROUP_MEMBER, and IBM_SERVICE_DATA.

Version 4

NOTE

The following columns were new as of DB2 V5. They cannot be accessed prior to DB2 V5. These columns are not populated for EXPLAIN statistics accumulated prior to V5: WHEN_OPTIMIZE, QBLOCK_TYPE, and BIND_TIME.

Version 5

A common method of retrieving access path data from the PLAN_TABLE is to use QMF or a GUI-based query tool to format the results of a simple SELECT statement. This way, you can organize and display the results of the query in a consistent and manageable fashion.

It is crucial that the TIMESTAMP column be in descending order. Because EXPLAINs are executed as a result of the BIND command, access path data is added to the PLAN_TABLE with a different timestamp. The old data is not purged from the PLAN_TABLE each time an EXPLAIN is performed. If you specify the descending sort option on the TIMESTAMP column, you can ensure that the EXPLAIN data in the report is sorted in order from the most recent to the oldest access path for each SQL statement in the PLAN_TABLE. Sorting this way is important if the PLAN_TABLEs you are working with are not purged.

If you want to retrieve information placed in the PLAN_TABLE for a single SQL statement, you can issue the following query:

```
SELECT   QUERYNO, QBLOCKNO, QBLOCK_TYPE, PLANNO, METHOD, TNAME,
         ACCESSTYPE, JOIN_TYPE, MATCHCOLS, ACCESSNAME,
         INDEXONLY, SORTN_PGROUP_ID, SORTN_UNIQ, SORTN_JOIN,
         SORTN_ORDERBY, SORTN_GROUPBY, SORTC_PGROUP_ID,
         SORTC_UNIQ, SORTC_JOIN, SORTC_ORDERBY, SORTC_GROUPBY,
         TSLOCKMODE, PREFETCH, COLUMN_FN_EVAL, MIXOPSEQ,
         ACCESS_DEGREE, ACCESS_PGROUP_ID, JOIN_DEGREE,
         JOIN_PGROUP_ID, PARALLELISM_MODE, MERGE_JOIN_COLS,
         CORRELATION_NAME, PAGE_RANGE, GROUP_MEMBER,
         WHEN_OPTIMIZE, BIND_TIME
FROM     ownerid.PLAN_TABLE
ORDER BY QUERYNO, QBLOCKNO, PLANNO
```

The preceding eliminates from the query the package and plan information, as well as the name of the table creator. Throughout the remainder of this chapter, I present PLAN_TABLE information for several types of SQL statements. Variants of this query are used to show the PLAN_TABLE data for each EXPLAIN statement.

The PLAN_TABLE Columns

Now that you have some basic PLAN_TABLE queries to assist you with DB2 performance monitoring, you can begin to EXPLAIN your application's SQL statements and analyze their access paths. But remember, because the access path information in the PLAN_TABLE is encoded, you must have a type of decoder to understand this information. This information is provided in Table 18.1. A description of every column of the PLAN_TABLE is provided, along with the report heading used by the QMF form as shown previously.

The first column in Table 18.1 shows the name of the column in the PLAN_TABLE, and the second column defines the data in the columns.

Table 18.1. PLAN_TABLE columns.

PLAN_TABLE *Column*	*Description*
QUERYNO	Indicates an integer value assigned by the user issuing the EXPLAIN, or by DB2. Enables the user to differentiate between EXPLAIN statements.
QBLOCKNO	Indicates an integer value enabling the identification of subselects or a union in a given SQL statement. The first subselect is numbered 1; the second, 2; and so on.
APPLNAME	Contains the plan name for rows inserted as a result of running BIND PLAN specifying EXPLAIN(YES). Contains the package name for rows inserted as a result of running BIND PACKAGE with EXPLAIN(YES). Otherwise, contains blanks for rows inserted as a result of dynamic EXPLAIN statements.

PLAN_TABLE *Column*	*Description*
PROGNAME	Contains the name of the program in which the SQL statement is embedded. If a dynamic EXPLAIN is issued from QMF, this column contains DSQIESQL.
PLANNO	Contains an integer value indicating the step of the plan in which QBLOCKNO is processed (that is, the order in which plan steps are undertaken).
METHOD	Contains an integer value identifying the access method used for the given step: 0 First table accessed (can also indicate an outer table or a continuation of the previous table accessed) 1 Nested loop join 2 Merge scan join 3 Independent sort; Sort happens as a result of ORDER BY, GROUP BY, SELECT DISTINCT, a quantified predicate, or an IN predicate 4 Hybrid join
CREATOR	Indicates the creator of the table identified by TNAME or is blank when METHOD equals 3.
TNAME	Indicates the name of the table being accessed or is blank when METHOD equals 3.
TABNO	Contains an integer value assigned to table references to differentiate between multiple references to the same table in the same SQL statement.
ACCESSTYPE	Indicates the method of accessing the table: I Indexed access I1 One-fetch index scan R Tablespace scan N Index access with an IN predicate M Multiple index scan MX Specification of the index name for multiple index access MI Multiple index access by RID intersection

continues

Table 18.1. continued

PLAN_TABLE *Column*	*Description*
	MU — Multiple index access by RID union
	blank — Row applies to QBLOCKNO 1 of an INSERT or DELETE statement or an UPDATE statement using a cursor with the WHERE CURRENT OF clause specified
MATCHCOLS	Contains an integer value with the number of index columns used in an index scan when ACCESSTYPE is I, I1, N, or MX. Otherwise, contains 0.
ACCESSCREATOR	Indicates the creator of the index when ACCESSTYPE is I, I1, N, or MX. Otherwise, it is blank.
ACCESSNAME	Indicates the name of the index used when ACCESSTYPE is I, I1, N, or MX. Otherwise, it is blank.
INDEXONLY	A value of Y indicates that access to the index is sufficient to satisfy the query. N indicates that access to the tablespace is also required.
SORTN_UNIQ	A value of Y indicates that a sort must be performed on the new table to remove duplicates.
SORTN_JOIN	A value of Y indicates that a sort must be performed on the new table to accomplish a merge scan join. Or a sort is performed on the RID list and intermediate table of a hybrid join.
SORTN_ORDERBY	A value of Y indicates that a sort must be performed on the new table to order rows.
SORTN_GROUPBY	A value of Y indicates that a sort must be performed on the new table to group rows.
SORTC_UNIQ	A value of Y indicates that a sort must be performed on the composite table to remove duplicates.
SORTC_JOIN	A value of Y indicates that a sort must be performed on the composite table to accomplish a join (any type).
SORTC_ORDERBY	A value of Y indicates that a sort must be performed on the composite table to order rows.
SORTC_GROUP	A value of Y indicates that a sort must be performed on the composite table to group rows.

PLAN_TABLE *Column*	*Description*	
TSLOCKMODE	Contains the lock level applied to the new table, its tablespace, or partitions. If the isolation level can be determined at BIND time, the values can be as follow:	
	IS	Intent share lock
	IX	Intent exclusive lock
	S	Share lock
	U	Update lock
	X	Exclusive lock
	SIX	Share with intent exclusive lock
	N	No lock (UR isolation level)
	If the isolation level cannot be determined at BIND time, the lock mode values can be as follow:	
	NS	For UR, no lock; for CS, RS, or RR, an S-lock
	NIS	For UR, no lock; for CS, RS, or RR, an IS-lock
	NSS	For UR, no lock; for CS or RS, an IS-lock; for RR, an S-lock
	SS	For UR, CS, or RS, an IS-lock; for RR, an S-lock
TIMESTAMP	Indicates the date and time the EXPLAIN for this row was issued. This internal representation of a date and time is not in DB2 timestamp format.	
REMARKS	Contains a 254-byte character string for commenting EXPLAIN results.	
PREFETCH	Contains an indicator of which type of prefetch will be used:	
	S	Sequential prefetch can be used
	L	List prefetch can be used
	blank	Prefetch is not used initially, or prefetch use is unknown
COLUMN_FN_EVAL	Indicates when the column function is evaluated:	
	R	Data retrieval time
	S	Sort time
	blank	Unknown (runtime division)
MIXOPSEQ	Contains a small integer value indicating the sequence of the multiple index operation.	

continues

Table 18.1. continued

PLAN_TABLE *Column*	*Description*
VERSION	Contains the version identifier for the package.
COLLID	Contains the collection ID for the package.
ACCESS_DEGREE	Indicates the number of parallel tasks utilized by the query. For statements containing host variables, this column is set to 0. (Although this column is set at bind time, it can be redetermined at execution time.)
ACCESS_PGROUP_ID	Contains a sequential number identifying the parallel group accessing the new table. (Although this column is set at bind time, it can be redetermined at execution time.)
JOIN_DEGREE	Indicates the number of parallel tasks used in joining the composite table with the new table. For statements containing host variables, this column is set to 0. (Although this column is set at bind time, it can be redetermined at execution time.)
JOIN_PGROUP_ID	A sequential number identifying the parallel group joining the composite table to the new table. (Although this column is set at bind time, it can be redetermined at execution time.)
SORTC_PGROUP_ID	Contains the parallel group identifier for the parallel sort of the composite table.
SORTN_PGROUP_ID	Contains the parallel group identifier for the parallel sort of the new table.
PARALLELISM_MODE	Indicates the type of parallelism, that is used at bind time: I Query I/O parallelism C Query CPU parallelism X Query Sysplex parallelism *blank* No parallelism, or mode will be determined at runtime
MERGE_JOIN_COLS	Indicates the number of columns joined during a merge scan join (METHOD = 2).
CORRELATION_NAME	Indicates the correlation name for the table or view specified in the statement. Blank if no correlation name. A correlation name is an alternate name for a table, view, or inline view. It can be specified in the FROM clause of a query and in the first clause of an UPDATE or DELETE statement. For example, D is the correlation name in the following clause: FROM DSN8510.DEPT D

PLAN_TABLE *Column*	*Description*	
PAGE_RANGE	Indicates whether the table qualifies for page range tablespace scans in which only a subset of the available partitions are scanned:	
	Y	Yes
	blank	No
JOIN_TYPE	Indicates the type of join being implemented:	
	F	Full outer join
	L	Left outer join (or a converted right outer join)
	blank	Inner join (or no join)
GROUP_MEMBER	Indicates the member name of the DB2 that executed EXPLAIN. The column is blank if the DB2 subsystem was not in a data sharing environment when EXPLAIN was executed.	
IBM_SERVICE_DATA	For IBM use only.	
WHEN_OPTIMIZE	Specifies when the access path was determined:	
	blank	At BIND time
	B	At BIND time, but will be reoptimized at runtime [bound with REOPT(VARS)]
	R	At runtime [bound with REOPT(VARS)]
QBLOCK_TYPE	Indicates the type of SQL operation performed for the query block:	
	SELECT	SELECT
	SELUPD	SELECT with FOR UPDATE OF
	INSERT	INSERT
	UPDATE	UPDATE
	UPDCUR	UPDATE WHERE CURRENT OF CURSOR
	DELETE	DELETE
	DELCUR	DELETE WHERE CURRENT OF CURSOR
	CORSUB	Correlated subquery
	NCOSUB	Non-correlated subquery
BIND_TIME	Indicates the time the plan or package for the statement or query block was bound.	

Recall from Chapter 13, "DB2 Behind the Scenes," the access strategies that DB2 can choose in determining the access path for a query. Understanding how these access path strategies relate to the PLAN_TABLE columns is useful. The following sections provide a synopsis of the strategies and how to recognize them based on particular PLAN_TABLE columns.

The specific type of operation to which the PLAN_TABLE row applies is recorded in the QBLOCK_TYPE column. It is new as of DB2 V5.

Tablespace scans are indicated by ACCESSTYPE being set to R. For a partitioned tablespace scan in which specific partitions can be skipped, ACCESSTYPE is set to R and PAGE_RANGE is set to Y. Index scans are indicated by ACCESSTYPE being set to any other value except a space.

When PREFETCH is set to S, sequential prefetch can be used; when it is set to L, list prefetch can be used. Even if the PREFETCH column is not set to L or S, however, prefetch can still be used at execution time. Whether sequential detection is used cannot be determined from the PLAN_TABLE because it is specified for use only at execution time.

If an index is used to access data, it is identified by creator and name in the ACCESSCREATOR and ACCESSNAME columns. A direct index lookup *cannot* be determined from the PLAN_TABLE *alone*. In general, a direct index lookup is indicated when the MATCHCOLS column equals the same number of columns in the index and the index is unique. For a non-unique index, this same PLAN_TABLE row can indicate a matching index scan. This additional information must be retrieved from the DB2 Catalog.

A non-matching index scan is indicated when the MATCHCOLS=0. The INDEXONLY column is set to Y for index-only access, or to [ ] when the tablespace data pages must be accessed in addition to the index information. Finally, multiple-index access can be determined by the existence of M, MX, MI, or MU in the ACCESSTYPE column.

Clustered and non-clustered index access cannot be determined using the PLAN_TABLE. Also, index lookaside is generally available when DB2 indexes are used.

A parallel query is indicated by values in ACCESS_DEGREE indicating the number of parallel streams to be invoked. It is the number of parallel tasks that BIND deems optimal. The degree can be decreased at runtime. The type of parallelism (I/O, CPU, or Sysplex) is recorded in the PARALLELISM_MODE column. Parallel tasks are grouped into parallel groups as indicated by the value(s) in ACCESS_PGROUP_ID. JOIN_DEGREE and JOIN_PGROUP_ID are populated when tables are joined in parallel.

For the different join methods, the METHOD column is set to 1 for a nested loop join, 2 for a merge scan join, or 4 for a hybrid join.

Now that you know what to look for, you can examine some sample access paths.

Sample Access Paths

The primary objective of EXPLAIN is to provide a means by which an analyst can "see" the access paths chosen by DB2. This section provides some EXPLAIN examples showing the SQL statement, rows from a PLAN_TABLE that were the result of an EXPLAIN being run for that SQL statement, and an analysis of the output. Based on the results of the EXPLAIN, you might decide that a better access path is available for that SQL statement. This process involves tuning, which is discussed in Part V. This section concentrates solely on showing the EXPLAIN results for different types of accesses.

PLAN_TABLE rows for various types of accesses follow. You can use them as a guide to recognizing access path strategies in the PLAN_TABLE. Italicized column data is unique to the access path strategy being demonstrated. (For example, in the first row shown, the *R* in the TYP column is italicized, indicating that a tablespace scan is used.)

Tablespace Scan

QUERY NUMBER	QRY BLK	PLANNO QBLK STEP	METH	TABLE NAME	TYP	MCOL	INDEX	IXO	SORT NNNN UJOG / SORT CCCC UJOG	LOCK MODE	PF	COL FN EVAL	MULT IDX SEQ
1	1	1	0	PROJ	*R*	0		N	NNNN NNNN	IS			0

Partitioned Tablespace Scan

QUERY NUMBER	QRY BLK	PLANNO QBLK STEP	METH	TABLE NAME	TYP	MCOL	INDEX	IXO	SORT NNNN UJOG / SORT CCCC UJOG	LOCK MODE	PF	COL FN EVAL	MULT IDX SEQ	PAGE RANGE
2	1	1	0	EMP	*R*	0		N	NNNN NNNN	IS			0	*Y*

Sequential Prefetch

QUERY NUMBER	QRY BLK	PLANNO QBLK STEP	METH	TABLE NAME	TYP	MCOL	INDEX	IXO	SORT NNNN UJOG / SORT CCCC UJOG	LOCK MODE	PF	COL FN EVAL	MULT IDX SEQ
3	1	1	0	EMP	R	0		N	NNNN NNNN	IS	*S*		0

Index Lookup

QUERY NUMBER	QRY BLK	PLANNO QBLK STEP	METH	TABLE NAME	TYP	MCOL	INDEX	IXO	SORT NNNN UJOG / SORT CCCC UJOG	LOCK MODE	PF	COL FN EVAL	MULT IDX SEQ
4	1	1	0	EMP	*I*	*1*	XEMP1	N	NNNN NNNN	IS			0

Index Scan

QUERY NUMBER	QRY BLK	PLANNO QBLK STEP	METH	TABLE NAME	TYP	MCOL	INDEX	IXO	SORT NNNN UJOG / SORT CCCC UJOG	LOCK MODE	PF	COL FN EVAL	MULT IDX SEQ
5	1	1	0	EMP	*I*	*0*	XEMP1	N	NNNN NNNN	IS			0

List Prefetch

QUERY NUMBER	QRY BLK	PLANNO QBLK STEP	METH	TABLE NAME	TYP	MCOL	INDEX	IXO	SORT NNNN UJOG / SORT CCCC UJOG	LOCK MODE	PF	COL FN EVAL	MULT IDX SEQ
6	1	1	0	EMP	I	0	XEMP1	N	NNNN NNNN	IS	*L*		0

Multi-Index Access (RID Union)

QUERY NUMBER	QRY BLK	*PLANNO* QBLK STEP	METH	TABLE NAME	TYP	MCOL	INDEX	IXO	SORT NNNN UJOG	SORT CCCC UJOG	LOCK MODE	PF	COL FN EVAL	MULT IDX SEQ
7	1	1	0	DEPT	M	0		N	NNNN	NNNN	IS	L		0
7	1	1	0	DEPT	MX	0	XDEPT1	Y	NNNN	NNNN	IS	S		1
7	1	1	0	DEPT	MX	0	XDEPT2	Y	NNNN	NNNN	IS	S		2
7	1	1	0	DEPT	*MU*	0		N	NNNN	NNNN	IS			3

Multi-Index Access (RID Union)

QUERY NUMBER	QRY BLK	*PLANNO* QBLK STEP	METH	TABLE NAME	TYP	MCOL	INDEX	IXO	SORT NNNN UJOG	SORT CCCC UJOG	LOCK MODE	PF	COL FN EVAL	MULT IDX SEQ
8	1	1	0	DEPT	M	0		N	NNNN	NNNN	IS	L		0
8	1	1	0	DEPT	MX	0	XDEPT1	Y	NNNN	NNNN	IS	S		1
8	1	1	0	DEPT	MX	0	XDEPT2	Y	NNNN	NNNN	IS	S		2
8	1	1	0	DEPT	*MI*	0		N	NNNN	NNNN	IS			3

Index Only Access

QUERY NUMBER	QRY BLK	*PLANNO* QBLK STEP	METH	TABLE NAME	TYP	MCOL	INDEX	IXO	SORT NNNN UJOG	SORT CCCC UJOG	LOCK MODE	PF	COL FN EVAL	MULT IDX SEQ
9	1	1	0	PROJACT	*I*	0	XPROJAC1	*Y*	NNNN	NNNN	IS			0

Index Access (When IN Predicate is Used)

QUERY NUMBER	QRY BLK	*PLANNO* QBLK STEP	METH	TABLE NAME	TYP	MCOL	INDEX	IXO	SORT NNNN UJOG	SORT CCCC UJOG	LOCK MODE	PF	COL FN EVAL	MULT IDX SEQ
10	1	1	0	PROJACT	*N*	0	XPROJAC1	N	NNNN	NNNN	IS			0

Sorting: ORDER BY Specified in a Query (and sort is required)

QUERY NUMBER	QRY BLK	*PLANNO* QBLK STEP	METH	TABLE NAME	TYP	MCOL	INDEX	IXO	SORT NNNN UJOG	SORT CCCC UJOG	LOCK MODE	PF	COL FN EVAL	MULT IDX SEQ
11	1	1	0	DEPT	R	0		N	NNNN	NNNN	IS	S		0
11	1	2	3	DEPT		0		N	NNNN	NN*Y*N				

Sorting: GROUP BY Specified in a Query (and sort is required)

QUERY NUMBER	QRY BLK	*PLANNO* QBLK STEP	METH	TABLE NAME	TYP	MCOL	INDEX	IXO	SORT NNNN UJOG	SORT CCCC UJOG	LOCK MODE	PF	COL FN EVAL	MULT IDX SEQ
12	1	1	0	DEPT	R	0		N	NNNN	NNNN	IS			0
12	1	2	3	DEPT		0		N	NNNN	NNN*Y*				

Merge Scan Join

QUERY NUMBER	QRY BLK	*PLANNO* QBLK STEP	METH	TABLE NAME	TYP	MCOL	INDEX	IXO	SORT NNNN UJOG	SORT CCCC UJOG	LOCK MODE	PF	COL FN EVAL	MULT IDX SEQ
13	1	1	0	DEPT	R	0		N	NNNN	NNNN	IS	S		0
13	1	2	*2*	EMP	R	0		N	N*Y*NN	N*Y*NN	IS			

Nested Loop Join

QUERY NUMBER	QRY BLK	*PLANNO* QBLK STEP	METH	TABLE NAME	TYP	MCOL	INDEX	IXO	SORT NNNN UJOG	SORT CCCC UJOG	LOCK MODE	PF	COL FN EVAL	MULT IDX SEQ
14	1	1	0	DEPT	I	0	XDEPT1	N	NNNN	NNNN	IS			0
14	1	2	*1*	EMP	I	1	XEMP1	N	NNNN	NNNN	IS			

Hybrid Join (Access via Clustered Index)

QUERY NUMBER	QRY BLK	PLANNO QBLK STEP	METH	TABLE NAME	TYP	MCOL	INDEX	IXO	SORT NNNN UJOG	SORT CCCC UJOG	LOCK MODE	PF	COL FN EVAL	MULT IDX SEQ
15	1	1	0	DEPT	I	1	XDEPT1	N	NNNN	NNNN	IS			0
15	1	2	4	EMP	I	1	XEMP1	N	NNNN	NNNN	IS	L		

Hybrid Join (Access via Non-Clustered Index)

QUERY NUMBER	QRY BLK	PLANNO QBLK STEP	METH	TABLE NAME	TYP	MCOL	INDEX	IXO	SORT NNNN UJOG	SORT CCCC UJOG	LOCK MODE	PF	COL FN EVAL	MULT IDX SEQ
16	1	1	0	DEPT	I	1	XDEPT2	N	NYNN	NNNN	IS			0
16	1	2	4	EMP	I	1	XEMP1	N	NNNN	NNNN	IS	L		

Union

QUERY NUMBER	QRY BLK	PLANNO QBLK STEP	METH	TABLE NAME	TYP	MCOL	INDEX	IXO	SORT NNNN UJOG	SORT CCCC UJOG	LOCK MODE	PF	COL FN EVAL	MULT IDX SEQ
17	1	1	0	DEPT	I	1	XDEPT1	N	NNNN	NNNN	IS			0
17	2	1	0	DEPT	R	0		N	NNNN	NNNN	IS	S		
17	2	2	3			0		N	NNNN	YNNN				

SELECT With Column Function

QUERY NUMBER	QRY BLK	PLANNO QBLK STEP	METH	TABLE NAME	TYP	MCOL	INDEX	IXO	SORT NNNN UJOG	SORT CCCC UJOG	LOCK MODE	PF	COL FN EVAL	MULT IDX SEQ
18	1	1	0	EMP	R	0		N	NNNN	NNNN	IS	S	R	0

SELECT Using an Index With MAX / MIN

QUERY NUMBER	QRY BLK	PLANNO QBLK STEP	METH	TABLE NAME	TYP	MCOL	INDEX	IXO	SORT NNNN UJOG	SORT CCCC UJOG	LOCK MODE	PF	COL FN EVAL	MULT IDX SEQ
19	1	1	0	DEPT	I1	1	XDEPT1	Y	NNNN	NNNN	IS		R	0

SELECT From Partitioned Tablespace Showing I/O Parallelism

QRY NBR	QRY BLK	PLANNO QBLK STEP	METH	TABLE NAME	TYP	MCOL	IDX	IXO	SORT NNNN UJOG	SORT CCCC UJOG	LOCK MODE	PF	ACCESS DEGREE	ACCESS PGROUP ID	PAR MODE
20	1	1	0	DEPT_P	R	0		N	NNNN	NNNN	S	S	4	1	

SELECT From Partitioned Tablespace Showing CPU Parallelism

QRY NBR	QRY BLK	PLANNO QBLK STEP	METH	TABLE NAME	TYP	MCOL	INDX	IXO	SORT NNNN UJOG	SORT CCCC UJOG	LOCK MODE	PF	ACCESS DEGREE	ACCESS PGROUP ID	PAR MODE
21	1	1	0	DEPT_P	R	0		N	NNNN	NNNN	S	S	4	1	

Joining and I/O Parallelism

QRY NBR	QRY BLK	PLANNO QBLK STEP	METH	TABLE NAME	TYP	SORT NNNN UJOG	SORT CCCC UJOG	LOCK MODE	PF	ACCESS DEGREE	ACCESS PGROUP ID	JOIN DEGREE	JOIN PGROUP ID	PAR MODE
22	1	1	0	TAB1	R	NNNN	NNNN	S	S	8	1			1
22	1	2	2	TAB2	R	NNYN	NNYN	S	S	4	2	2	3	1

Left Outer Join (or a converted Right Outer Join)

QUERY NUMBER	QRY BLK	PLANNO QBLK STEP	METH	TABLE NAME	TYP	MCOL	INDEX	IXO	SORT NNNN UJOG	SORT CCCC UJOG	LOCK MODE	PF	COL FN EVAL	JOIN TYPE
23	1	1	0	DEPT	I	0	XDEPT1	N	NNNN	NNNN	IS			
23	1	2	*1*	EMP	I	1	XEMP1	N	NNNN	NNNN	IS			*L*

Full Outer Join

QUERY NUMBER	QRY BLK	PLANNO QBLK STEP	METH	TABLE NAME	TYP	MCOL	INDEX	IXO	SORT NNNN UJOG	SORT CCCC UJOG	LOCK MODE	PF	COL FN EVAL	JOIN TYPE
24	1	1	0	DEPT	I	0	XDEPT1	N	NNNN	NNNN	IS			
24	1	2	*1*	EMP	I	1	XEMP1	N	NNNN	NNNN	IS			*F*

Relational Division

QUERY NUMBER	QRY BLK	PLANNO QBLK STEP	METH	TABLE NAME	TYP	MCOL	INDEX	IXO	SORT NNNN UJOG	SORT CCCC UJOG	LOCK MODE	PF	COL FN EVAL
25	1	1	0	PROJACT	R	0		N	NNNN	NNNN	IS	S	
25	2	1	0	ACT	R	0		N	NNNN	NNNN	IS	S	
25	3	1	0	PROJACT	I	2	XPROJACT1	Y	NNNN	NNNN	IS		

EXPLAIN Guidelines

Implement the following guidelines to effectively EXPLAIN and optimize the SQL statements used in your DB2 applications.

Influence the Optimizer to Obtain Efficient Access Paths

You can influence the optimizer to choose different access paths in a variety of ways. Methods for accomplishing this task are outlined in Part V.

Populate the PLAN_TABLE in Production

Bind production packages and plans using EXPLAIN(YES). This way, you can create a trail of access paths that can be examined when a performance problem occurs.

Educate All DB2 Technicians in the Use of EXPLAIN

Train all technical DB2 users in the use of EXPLAIN. Although not everyone will be able to analyze the results in depth, all programmers, analysts, and systems programmers should understand, at a minimum, how to issue EXPLAIN for plans, packages, and single SQL statements, the meaning of each column in the PLAN_TABLE, and how to identify whether an index was used for a query.

Identify Modifications with Care

Prior to DB2 V5, identifying INSERT, UPDATE, and DELETE statements in a PLAN_TABLE is sometimes difficult. INSERT statements have a blank in the ACCESSTYPE column because no specific access path strategies can be chosen for an INSERT. Because UPDATE and DELETE statements, on the other hand, can use access path strategies, identifying them can be difficult. When the statement is embedded in a program, it can be traced back to the program using the QUERYNO column. When it is placed in the PLAN_TABLE as the result of an independent EXPLAIN, be sure to record which QUERYNO applies to which query.

Version 5

DB2 V5 provides the QBLOCK_TYPE column in the PLAN_TABLE. This column contains a description of the type of statement that was analyzed for each specific query block. Be sure to review this column when you analyze PLAN_TABLE rows for DB2 V5 and subsequent releases.

Use REMARKS for Documentation

Use the REMARKS column in the PLAN_TABLE to record historical information in the PLAN_TABLE for specific access paths. One recommendation is to record in the REMARKS column the SQL statement that was EXPLAINed to produce the given PLAN_TABLE rows. Another recommendation is to record identifying comments. For example, if the rows represent the access path for a given query after an index was added, set the REMARKS column to something like ADDED INDEX *INDEXNAME*.

Keep RUNSTATS Accurate

The EXPLAIN results are only as good as the statistics in the DB2 Catalog. Ensure that RUNSTATS has been run before issuing any EXPLAIN commands. If RUNSTATS has not been run, verify that the DB2 Catalog statistics are still appropriate before running EXPLAIN.

Be Aware of Missing Pieces

Keep in mind that to analyze SQL performance properly, you will require more than just the EXPLAIN results in the PLAN_TABLE. Proper performance analysis requires the following:

- A listing of the actual SQL statement
- A listing of the actual DDL (or the DB2 Catalog information) for the objects being accessed and/or modified
- The actual filter factors used when creating the access path
- The high-level code (3GL/4GL) in which the SQL statement is embedded
- The actual DB2 Catalog statistics that were in place at the time the EXPLAIN was performed

- The DB2 release level and maintenance level at the time the EXPLAIN was run
- Knowledge of the bind parameters used for the plan(s) and/or package(s) in which the SQL statement is embedded
- Knowledge of the DB2 subsystem(s) in which the SQL statement will be executed (including settings for bufferpools, hiperpools, EDM Pool, locking parameters, and so on)
- Knowledge of the hardware environment where the SQL is being run (including type of mainframe, number and type of processors, amount of memory, and so on)
- Knowledge of concurrent activity in the system when the SQL statement was (or will be) executed

CAUTION

For data sharing environments, the PLAN_TABLE does not indicate which subsystem was used to BIND the plan. This shortcoming is important if the subsystems within a data sharing environment are assigned to different machines or are assigned different resources.

This additional information can be used, along with the PLAN_TABLE output, to estimate the performance of any given SQL statement.

Several other pieces of information are missing from the PLAN_TABLE, thus making the task of performance estimation significantly more difficult. The first missing EXPLAIN component is that the PLAN_TABLE does not show access paths for referentially accessed tables. For example, the following statement accesses not only the DEPT table but also the EMP table and the PROJ table because they are tied to DEPT by referential constraints:

```
DELETE
FROM    DSN8510.EMP
WHERE   EMPNO = '000100';
```

EXPLAIN should record the fact that these tables are accessed because of the RI defined on the EMP table, but it does not. (This information should also be recorded in the DB2 Catalog in the SYSIBM.SYSPLANDEP table, but it is not there either.) The only way to determine the extent of referentially accessed data is with a performance monitoring tool.

When indexes are accessed as the result of a DELETE or UPDATE statement, EXPLAIN fails to record this information. RID sorts invoked (or not invoked) by list PREFETCH also are not reported by EXPLAIN.

Runtime modifications to the access path determined at bind time are not recorded in the PLAN_TABLE. For example, simply by examining the PLAN_TABLE, you cannot determine whether sequential detection will be invoked or whether the degree of parallelism will be reduced at runtime.

Additionally, EXPLAIN cannot provide information about the high-level language in which it is embedded. An efficient access path could be chosen for an SQL statement that is embedded improperly in an application program. Examples of inefficient SQL embedding follow:

- The SQL statement is executed more than once unnecessarily.
- A singleton SELECT is embedded in a loop and executed repeatedly when fetching from a cursor is more efficient.
- Cursor OPENs and CLOSEs are not evaluated as to their efficiency; a program might perform many opens and closes on a single cursor unnecessarily, and EXPLAIN will not record this fact.

EXPLAIN does not provide information on the order in which predicates are applied. For example, consider the following statement:

```
SELECT   DEPTNO, DEPTNAME
FROM     DSN8510.DEPT
WHERE    MGRNO > '000030'
AND      ADMRDEPT = 'A00';
```

Which predicate does DB2 apply first?

```
MGRNO > '000030'
```

or

```
ADMRDEPT = 'A00'
```

EXPLAIN does not provide this data.

Delete Unneeded PLAN_TABLE Rows

Periodically purge rows from your PLAN_TABLEs to remove obsolete access path information. However, you might want to retain more than the most recent EXPLAIN data to maintain a history of access path selection decisions made by DB2 for a given SQL statement. Move these "history" rows to another table defined the same as the PLAN_TABLE but not used by EXPLAIN. This way, you can ensure that the PLAN_TABLEs used by EXPLAIN are as small as possible, thus increasing the efficiency of EXPLAIN processing.

Consider PLAN_TABLE Indexes

Create indexes for very large PLAN_TABLEs. Consider indexing on columns frequently appearing in predicates or ORDER BY clauses. Of course, these indexes should be Type 2 indexes to accrue all the benefits not available to Type 1 indexes.

Run RUNSTATS on All PLAN_TABLEs

Always run RUNSTATS on the PLAN_TABLE tablespace. PLAN_TABLEs are frequently updated and queried. As such, DB2 needs current statistics to create optimal access paths for these queries against the PLAN_TABLEs. Furthermore, the statistics accumulated by RUNSTATS can help to determine if a REORG of the PLAN_TABLE tablespace is required.

NOTE

For PLAN_TABLEs that will grow to be very large, consider enabling compression to reduce the amount of disk space required for EXPLAIN data.

Strive for the Most Efficient Access Path

As you analyze PLAN_TABLE results, remember that some access paths are more efficient than others. Only three types of access paths can be chosen: direct index lookup, index scan, or tablespace scan. However, these three types of accesses can be combined with other DB2 performance features (refer to Chapter 14, "The Optimizer"). A basic hierarchy of efficient access paths from most efficient (those incurring the least I/O) to least efficient (those incurring the most I/O) follows:

Index-only direct index lookup
Direct index lookup with data access
Index-only matching index scan
Index-only non-matching index scan
Matching clustered index access
Matching non-clustered index access
Non-matching clustered index access
Non-matching non-clustered index access
Partitioned tablespace scan skipping multiple partitions (partition scan)
Segmented tablespace scan (table scan)
Simple tablespace scan

This list represents only general cases in which a limited number of rows are to be retrieved. The hierarchy should be viewed in reverse order when most of the rows of a table are being accessed. For example, a tablespace scan can outperform indexed access if as little as 25 percent of the rows of the table are accessed to satisfy the query. Likewise, a tablespace scan almost always outperforms indexed access for small tables (fewer than 10 pages), regardless of the number of rows to be accessed. Although keeping the preceding hierarchy in mind when evaluating EXPLAIN results is a good idea, each SQL statement should be analyzed independently to determine the optimal access paths.

When determining which path is most efficient, the answer always comes down to the number of rows required to be read and the number of rows that qualify.

In general, the optimizer does a great job for this complete task. The exceptional cases, however, will compel you to become an EXPLAIN/access path expert so that you can tune the troublesome queries.

Use Tools to Assist in EXPLAIN Analysis

Several products that augment the functionality of the EXPLAIN command are available. Examples include PLATINUM *technology*'s Plan Analyzer and Candle Corporation's DB/Explain. Refer to Chapter 32, "Components of a Total DB2 Solution," for a discussion of SQL access path analysis products.

Summary

In this chapter, you learned how to use the EXPLAIN statement to gather information on the SQL statement access paths chosen by DB2. By carefully collecting and analyzing PLAN_TABLE data, you can tweak SQL statements and your environment to optimize DB2 performance.

But you also learned that EXPLAIN does not tell the whole story. Much of the additional information needed to tune DB2 performance is contained in the DB2 Catalog. The next chapter covers how monitor DB2 objects using the DB2 Catalog.

19

DB2 Object Monitoring Using the DB2 Catalog

To maintain efficient production DB2-based systems, you must periodically monitor the DB2 objects that make up those systems. This type of monitoring is an essential component of post-implementation duties because the production environment is dynamic. Fluctuations in business activity, errors in the logical or physical design, or lack of communication can cause a system to perform inadequately. An effective strategy for monitoring DB2 objects in the production environment will catch and forestall problems before they affect performance.

Additionally, if you have a DB2 Catalog monitoring strategy in place, reacting to performance problems becomes simpler. This chapter describes basic categories of DB2 Catalog queries, along with SQL statements querying specific DB2 Catalog information. I present queries in the following categories:

- Navigational queries, which help you maneuver through the sea of DB2 objects in your DB2 subsystems
- Physical analysis queries, which depict the physical state of your application tablespaces and indexes
- Queries that aid programmers (and other analysts) in identifying the components of DB2 packages and plans
- Application efficiency queries, which combine DB2 Catalog statistics with the `PLAN_TABLE` output from `EXPLAIN` to identify problem queries quickly
- Authorization queries, which identify the authority implemented for each type of DB2 security
- Partition statistics queries, which aid the analysis of partitioned tablespaces for parallel access

You can implement these queries using SPUFI or QMF. You should set them up to run as a batch job; otherwise, your terminal will be needlessly tied up executing them. You also would be wise to schedule these queries regularly and then save the output on paper, on microfiche, or in a report storage facility with an online query facility.

Each category contains several DB2 Catalog queries you can use for performance monitoring. Each query is accompanied by an analysis that highlights problems that can be trapped by reviewing the output results of the query.

In implementing this DB2 Catalog monitoring strategy, I have made the following assumptions:

- All application plans are bound with the `EXPLAIN(YES)` option.
- Each application has its own `PLAN_TABLE` for the storage of the `EXPLAIN` results.
- Scheduled production `STOSPACE` and `RUNSTATS` jobs are executed on a regular basis to ensure that the statistical information in the DB2 Catalog is current; otherwise, the queries might provide inaccurate information.
- Plans are rebound when `RUNSTATS` has been executed so that all access paths are based on current statistical information. If you have not done so, you should have a valid,

documented reason. When the access paths for your packages and plans are not based on current DB2 Catalog statistics, tuning SQL using the DB2 Catalog queries presented in this chapter is difficult.

Having a report of each PLAN_TABLE for each application is also useful. This way, you can check the DB2 Catalog information against the optimizer access path selection information. You can obtain these reports by using the following query (which was shown also in the preceding chapter):

```
SELECT    QUERYNO, QBLOCKNO, QBLOCK_TYPE, PLANNO, METHOD, TNAME,
          ACCESSTYPE, JOIN_TYPE, MATCHCOLS, ACCESSNAME,
          INDEXONLY, SORTN_PGROUP_ID, SORTN_UNIQ, SORTN_JOIN,
          SORTN_ORDERBY, SORTN_GROUPBY, SORTC_PGROUP_ID,
          SORTC_UNIQ, SORTC_JOIN, SORTC_ORDERBY, SORTC_GROUPBY,
          TSLOCKMODE, PREFETCH, COLUMN_FN_EVAL, MIXOPSEQ,
          ACCESS_DEGREE, ACCESS_PGROUP_ID, JOIN_DEGREE,
          JOIN_PGROUP_ID, PARALLELISM_MODE, MERGE_JOIN_COLS,
          CORRELATION_NAME, PAGE_RANGE, GROUP_MEMBER,
          WHEN_OPTIMIZE, BIND_TIME
FROM      ownerid.PLAN_TABLE
ORDER BY QUERYNO, QBLOCKNO, PLANNO
```

NOTE

The following columns were new as of DB2 V4. They cannot be accessed prior to DB2 V4. These columns are not populated for EXPLAIN statistics accumulated prior to V4: SORTC_PGROUP_ID, SORTN_PGROUP_ID, PARALLELISM_MODE, MERGE_JOIN_COLS, CORRELATION_NAME, PAGE_RANGE, JOIN_TYPE, GROUP_MEMBER, and IBM_SERVICE_DATA.

Version 4

NOTE

The following columns were new as of DB2 V5. They cannot be accessed prior to DB2 V5. These columns are not populated for EXPLAIN statistics accumulated prior to V5: WHEN_OPTIMIZE, QBLOCK_TYPE, and BIND_TIME.

Version 5

Navigational Queries

To perform database and system administration functions for DB2, often you must quickly locate and identify objects and their dependencies. Suppose that a DBA must analyze a poorly performing query. The DBA has the query and a report of the EXPLAIN for the query, but no listing of available indexes and candidate columns for creating indexes. Or what if a query accessing a view is performing poorly? An analyst must find the composition of the view and the tables (or views) on which it is based. The navigational queries identified in this section provide object listing capabilities and more.

The first navigational query provides a listing of the tables in your DB2 subsystem by database, tablespace, and creator:

```
SELECT   T.DBNAME, T.TSNAME, T.CREATOR, T.NAME, T.CREATEDTS,
         T.ALTEREDTS, C.COLNO, C.NAME, C.COLTYPE, C.LENGTH,
         C.SCALE, C.NULLS, C.DEFAULT, C.COLCARD,
         HEX(C.HIGH2KEY), HEX(C.LOW2KEY), C.FLDPROC
FROM     SYSIBM.SYSCOLUMNS    C,
         SYSIBM.SYSTABLES     T
WHERE    T.CREATOR = C.TBCREATOR
AND      T.NAME = C.TBNAME
AND      T.TYPE =  'T'
ORDER BY T.DBNAME, T.TSNAME, T.CREATOR, T.NAME, C.COLNO
```

This query is good for identifying the composition of your DB2 tables, down to the data type and length of the columns.

Another useful navigational query presents an index listing:

```
SELECT   T.DBNAME, T.TSNAME, T.CREATOR, T.NAME, I.CREATOR,
         I.NAME, I.INDEXTYPE, I.UNIQUERULE, I.CLUSTERING,
         I.CLUSTERED, I.CREATEDTS, I.ALTEREDTS, I.PIECESIZE,
         K.COLSEQ, K.COLNAME, K.ORDERING
FROM     SYSIBM.SYSKEYS       K,
         SYSIBM.SYSTABLES     T,
         SYSIBM.SYSINDEXES    I
WHERE    (I.TBCREATOR = T.CREATOR   AND  I.TBNAME = T.NAME)
AND      (K.IXCREATOR = I.CREATOR   AND  K.IXNAME = I.NAME)
ORDER BY 1, 2, 3, 4, 5, 6
```

This query lists all indexes in your DB2 subsystem by database, tablespace, table creator, and table. It is similar to the table listing query and can be used to identify the columns that make up each index.

By viewing the output from these two queries, you can ascertain the hierarchy of DB2 objects (indexes in tables in tablespaces in databases). Additionally, these queries report the time the table or index was initially created and the time each was last altered. This information can be useful in an emergency situation when you need to determine what has been changed.

The output from these queries is superb for navigation. The DBA can easily get lost in a flood of production objects. By periodically running these queries and saving the output, a DBA can have a current profile of the environment in each DB2 subsystem that must be monitored.

Large installations might have thousands of tables and indexes, making the reports generated by these queries unwieldy. If these queries produce too much information to be easily digested for one report, consider adding a `WHERE` clause to query only the objects you're interested in at the time. For example, add the following clause to report on information contained in specific databases only:

```
WHERE T.DBNAME IN ('DATABAS1', 'DATABAS2', DATABAS9')
```

Eliminating the sample databases (DSN8D51A, DSN8D51P), the DB2 Catalog database (DSNDB06), and any extraneous databases (such as QMF and databases for third-party products) is usually desirable. However, doing so is optional; you may want to monitor everything known to DB2.

Although the primary purpose of these two queries is navigation, they also can aid in problem determination and performance tuning. For example, note the following query:

```
SELECT   A.COL1, A.COL2, B.COL3
FROM     TABLE1 A, TABLE2 B
WHERE    A.COL1 = B.COL4;
```

If this query is not performing properly, you would want to know the column types and lengths for COL1 in TABLE1 and COL4 in TABLE2. The type and length for both columns should be the same. If they are not, you can deduce that DB2 is performing a data conversion to make the comparison, which affects performance.

If the data type and length are the same, you would want to see what indexes (if any) are defined on these columns and then analyze the EXPLAIN output. Other significant data might be the uniqueness of each index, whether the index is clustered (these items influence the optimizer's choice of access path), and the number of tables in a tablespace (they can cause performance degradation for non-segmented tablespaces). You can obtain all this information from these reports.

Another useful navigational report is the view listing query:

```
SELECT   CREATOR, NAME, SEQNO, CHECK, TEXT
FROM     SYSIBM.SYSVIEWS
ORDER BY CREATOR, NAME, SEQNO
```

The output from this query identifies all views known to DB2 along with the SQL text used to create the view. This information is useful when you're monitoring how SQL performs when it accesses DB2 views.

NOTE

This report may have multiple rows per view.

Monitoring the aliases and synonyms defined for DB2 tables also is desirable. The next query provides a listing of all aliases known to the DB2 subsystem:

```
SELECT   CREATOR, NAME, TBCREATOR, TBNAME, CREATEDBY
FROM     SYSIBM.SYSTABLES
WHERE    TYPE = 'A'
ORDER BY CREATOR, NAME
```

This one provides a listing of all synonyms:

```
SELECT   CREATOR, NAME, TBCREATOR, TBNAME, CREATEDBY
FROM     SYSIBM.SYSSYNONYMS
ORDER BY CREATOR, NAME
```

By scanning the names returned by the table, view, alias, and synonym listing queries, you can reference the complete repository of objects that can be specified in the FROM clause of SQL SELECT statements. One additional table-related query reports on the temporary tables defined to DB2:

Version 5

```
SELECT   CREATOR, NAME, TBCREATOR, TBNAME, CREATEDBY
FROM     SYSIBM.SYSTABLES
WHERE    TYPE = 'T'
ORDER BY CREATOR, NAME
```

Temporary tables are used to house temporary results in application programs that are required only for the life of the program but can benefit from being accessed using SQL.

When referential integrity is implemented for a DB2 application, DBAs, programmers, and analysts must have quick access to the referential constraints defined for the tables of the application. This information is usually in the form of a logical data model depicting the relationships between the tables. However, this information is not sufficient because physical design decisions could have overridden the logical model. Although these design decisions should be documented, having ready access to the physical implementation of the referential integrity defined to your system is wise. This query provides a listing of referential constraints by dependent table:

```
SELECT   F.CREATOR, F.TBNAME, R.REFTBCREATOR, R.REFTBNAME,
         F.RELNAME, R.DELETERULE, F.COLSEQ, F.COLNAME
FROM     SYSIBM.SYSFOREIGNKEYS     F,
         SYSIBM.SYSRELS            R
WHERE    F.CREATOR = R.CREATOR
AND      F.TBNAME = R.TBNAME
AND      F.RELNAME = R.RELNAME
ORDER BY F.CREATOR, F.TBNAME, R.REFTBCREATOR, R.REFTBNAME
```

This one provides a listing of all referential constraints by parent table:

```
SELECT   R.REFTBCREATOR, R.REFTBNAME, F.CREATOR, F.TBNAME,
         F.RELNAME, R.DELETERULE, F.COLSEQ, F.COLNAME
FROM     SYSIBM.SYSFOREIGNKEYS     F,
         SYSIBM.SYSRELS            R
WHERE    F.CREATOR = R.CREATOR
AND      F.TBNAME = R.TBNAME
AND      F.RELNAME = R.RELNAME
ORDER BY R.REFTBCREATOR, R.REFTBNAME, F.CREATOR, F.TBNAME
```

These two queries provide the same information in two useful formats: the first by dependent (or child) table and the second by parent table. For a refresher on these referential integrity terms, see Figure 19.1.

The output from both of these referential integrity queries is useful when you're searching for relationships between tables—both forward from the parent table and backward from the dependent table. This query returns all the information that defines each referential constraint, including the following:

- The creator and name of the parent and dependent tables that make up the referential constraint
- The constraint name
- The DELETE RULE for each referential constraint
- The columns that make up the foreign key

FIGURE 19.1.
Referential integrity terms.

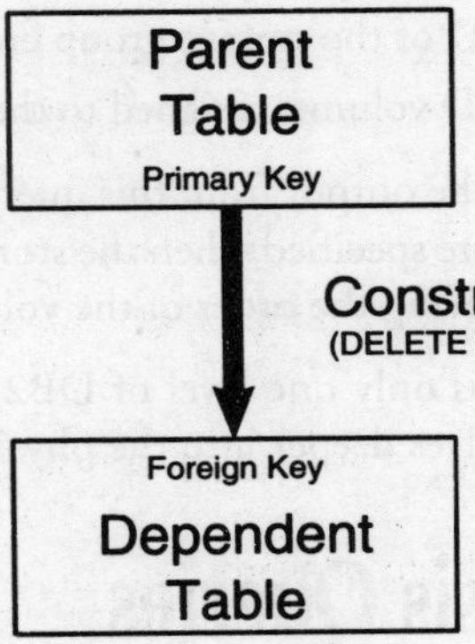

This information is useful for programmers and analysts writing data modification programs. The referential constraints affect both the functions that modify data in tables participating in referential constraints and the SQLCODEs returned to the program. DBAs need this information, with the index listing data described previously, to ensure that adequate indexes are defined for all foreign keys.

Knowing all the check constraints used in the DB2 subsystem is also useful. The following query displays all the check constraints and lists the columns to which each check constraint applies:

```
SELECT    TBOWNER, TBNAME, CHECKNAME, COLNAME
FROM      SYSIBM.SYSCHECKDEP
ORDER BY TBOWNER, TBNAME, CHECKNAME
```

To find the actual text of each check constraint, you can issue the following SQL:

```
SELECT    TBOWNER, TBNAME, CHECKNAME, TIMESTAMP,
          CHECKCONDITION
FROM      SYSIBM.SYSCHECKS
ORDER BY TBOWNER, TBNAME, CHECKNAME
```

Finally, here is the STOGROUP listing query:

```
SELECT    A.NAME, A.VCATNAME, A.VPASSWORD, A.SPACE,
          A.SPCDATE, A.CREATEDBY, B.VOLID
FROM      SYSIBM.SYSSTOGROUP  A,
          SYSIBM.SYSVOLUMES   B
WHERE     A.NAME = B.SGNAME
ORDER BY A.NAME
```

This query shows each storage group defined to your DB2 subsystem, along with pertinent information about the STOGROUP, such as

- The associated VCAT, used as the high-level qualifier for all data sets created for objects assigned to this storage group
- The password, if any
- The total space used by objects assigned to this STOGROUP
- The authorization ID of the storage group creator
- The IDs of the DASD volumes assigned to the STOGROUP or * if SMS is being used

Use caution in reviewing the output from this query because the volumes are not returned in the order in which they were specified when the storage group was created. DB2 does not provide the capability of retrieving the order of the volumes in the STOGROUP.

Navigational monitoring is only one level of DB2 performance monitoring using the DB2 Catalog. The next level delves deeper into the physical characteristics of DB2 objects.

Physical Analysis Queries

Sometimes you must trace a performance problem in a DB2 query to the physical level. Characteristics at the physical level are determined when DB2 objects are defined and can be modified by SQL ALTER statements or the statistics that reflect the state of the data in the physical objects. This section concentrates on tablespaces and indexes; these objects require a physical data set.

You have many options for creating a DB2 object. If poor choices are made, performance is affected. You can find an analysis of the proper DDL choices in Chapter 3, "Data Definition Guidelines." You can use the physical statistics queries to monitor these options.

The physical tablespace statistics query provides a listing of all tablespaces in each database and lists the physical definitions and aggregate statistics detail for each tablespace:

```
SELECT   T.DBNAME, T.NAME, T.IMPLICIT, T.LOCKMAX, T.LOCKRULE,
         T.ERASERULE, T.CLOSERULE, T.PARTITIONS, T.TYPE, T.SEGSIZE,
         T.NTABLES, T.NACTIVE, T.PGSIZE, T.MAXROWS, T.ENCODING_SCHEME,
         P.CARDF, P.FARINDREF, P.NEARINDREF, P.PERCACTIVE, P.PERCDROP,
         P.COMPRESS, P.PAGESAVE, P.FREEPAGE, P.PCTFREE, P.STORNAME,
         P.VCATNAME, P.STATSTIME, P.PARTITION, P.GBPCACHE
FROM     SYSIBM.SYSTABLESPACE    T,
         SYSIBM.SYSTABLEPART     P
WHERE    T.NAME = P.TSNAME
AND      T.DBNAME = P.DBNAME
ORDER BY T.DBNAME, T.NAME, P.PARTITION
```

Having reported on physical tablespace statistics, the next step is to analyze physical index statistics. The physical index statistics query provides a report of all indexes grouped by owner, along with the physical definitions and aggregate statistics supporting each index:

```
SELECT    I.CREATOR, I.NAME, I.INDEXTYPE, I.UNIQUERULE, I.CLUSTERING,
          I.CLUSTERED, I.CLUSTERRATIO, I.FIRSTKEYCARDF,
          I.FULLKEYCARDF, I.NLEAF, I.NLEVELS, I.PGSIZE,
          4096/I.PGSIZE, I.ERASERULE, I.CLOSERULE, P.CARDF,
          P.FAROFFPOSF, P.LEAFDIST, P.NEAROFFPOSF, P.FREEPAGE,
          P.PCTFREE, P.STORNAME, P.VCATNAME, P.STATSTIME, P.PARTITION
FROM      SYSIBM.SYSINDEXES    I,
          SYSIBM.SYSINDEXPART  P
WHERE     I.NAME = P.IXNAME
AND       I.CREATOR = P.IXCREATOR
ORDER BY I.CREATOR, I.NAME, P.PARTITION
```

These reports are invaluable tools for diagnosing performance problems when they happen. Frequently, you also can use them to catch problems before they occur.

Both of these queries show the CLOSE RULE associated with the tablespace or index. For applications using versions of DB2 prior to V2.3, monitor this rule for both tablespaces and indexes. A CLOSE RULE of Y indicates that the system performs a VSAM open and close every time an object is accessed. The performance of any query that accesses an object defined this way is impeded. A CLOSE RULE of N performs the VSAM open only the first time the object is accessed. It then remains open until DB2 is shut down. This process enhances the performance of queries accessing these objects. Although it adds the overhead associated with keeping a data set open, the overhead is minimal and better than a slow running query.

You must review each tablespace and index to determine the CLOSE RULE for it. Objects accessed infrequently or only once per day do not need to remain open. As a basic rule, you should define tablespaces as CLOSE NO unless you have a good reason to define them otherwise. When a query causes performance problems, examine the CLOSE RULE for each tablespace and index involved in the query.

If you're using DB2 V3 or later releases, monitoring CLOSE RULE is not as important because DB2 now performs a pseudo-close, reducing the impact of the implicit, behind-the-scenes data set opening and closing. Thus, you should modify most tablespaces and indexes to use CLOSE YES to take advantage of DB2's improved data set OPEN and CLOSE management techniques.

The physical analysis queries are also useful in determining the frequency of reorganization. Monitor the following information:

```
PERCDROP
NEAROFFPOS
FAROFFPOS
NEARINDREF
FARINDREF
LEAFDIST
CLUSTERRATIO
```

NOTE

NEAROFFPOS, FAROFFPOS, and CLUSTERRATIO apply to clustering indexes only.

NOTE

For DB2 V5 and later releases, use NEAROFFPOSF and FAROFFPOSF instead. They are floating-point numbers as opposed to integers. The integer columns are no longer used as of DB2 V5.

The PERCDROP column for tablespaces indicates the percentage of space occupied by rows from dropped tables. Non-segmented tablespaces cannot reclaim this space until they are reorganized.

The PAGESAVE column for tablespaces indicates the percentage of pages saved (per partition) by using ESA compression.

Both the tablespace and index queries display the STATSTIME column. It is crucial because STATSTIME provides a timestamp indicating when RUNSTATS was run to produce the statistical information being reported.

Far-off and near-off pages indicate the degree of tablespace or index disorganization. For non-segmented tablespaces, a page is *near off* if the difference between the page and the next one is between 2 and 15 pages inclusive. For segmented tablespaces, a page is considered near off the present page if the difference between the two pages is between 2 and the SEGSIZE×2. A page is *far off* if the difference is 16 or greater. NEAROFFPOS for an index indicates the number of times a different near-off page must be accessed when accessing all the tablespace rows in indexed order. The definition of FAROFFPOS is the same except that far-off page is substituted for near-off page.

NOTE

For segmented tablespaces only: After a REORG, the NEAROFFPOS can be greater than 0 if there are multiple space map pages.

The NEARINDREF and FARINDREF columns for a tablespace indicate the number of rows that have been relocated either near (2 to 15 pages) or far away (16 or more pages) from their original location. This relocation can occur as the result of updates to variable length rows (that is, rows with VARCHAR columns, tables with EDITPROCs, or compressed rows).

LEAFDIST helps determine the relative efficiency of each index. LEAFDIST indicates the average number of pages between successive index leaf pages. The more intervening pages, the less efficient the index will be.

Finally, you can use CLUSTERRATIO to determine the overall condition of the index as it corresponds to the physical order of the tablespace data. The more clustered an index is, the greater its conformance to the order of the rows as they are physically aligned in the tablespace. A cluster ratio of 100 percent indicates that the index and the tablespace ordering matches exactly. As the cluster ratio diminishes, access that uses the index becomes less efficient.

NOTE

CLUSTERRATIO for partitioned indexes can be found in SYSIBM.SYSINDEXSTATS. This CLUSTERRATIO is at the partition level and can help to determine if only a subset of the partitions must be reorganized.

Table 19.1 is a guide to using this information to determine how frequently tablespaces and indexes should be reorganized. A + indicates that you should REORG more frequently as the value in that column gets larger. A – indicates that you should REORG more frequently as the value gets smaller. As the number of + or – increases, the need to REORG becomes more urgent. For example, as PCT DROPPED gets larger, the need to REORG is very urgent, as indicated by five plus signs.

Table 19.1. Reorganization indicators.

Column	*Object*	*Impact*
PERCDROP	Tablespace	+++++
NEAROFFPOSF	Tablespace	+
FAROFFPOSF	Tablespace	++++
NEARINDREF	Index	+
FARINDREF	Index	++++
LEAFDIST	Index	+++
CLUSTERRATIO	Index	–––––

You also can use the physical analysis queries to learn at a glance the physical characteristics of your tablespaces and indexes. For example, these queries return the following:

- Tablespace and index information about partitioning, page size, erase rule, close rule, cardinality, and storage group or VCAT specification
- Information about tablespace lock rules, segment size, and whether the tablespace was created implicitly (without explicit DDL)
- Index-specific statistics such as uniqueness and clustering information

Note that the index query returns both the index subpage size (PGSIZE) and the page size divided into 4096, which is the subpage number specified in the DDL. For example, if SUBPAGES 4 was specified when the index was created, PGSIZE is 1024 (4096/4=1024). Both PGSIZE and SUBPAGES are useful in monitoring the physical characteristics of Type 1 indexes. This information is useful for Type 1indexes only; Type 2 indexes always have a page size of 4096.

Analyzing the tablespace and index space use also is useful. By monitoring PERCACTIVE, FREEPAGE, and PCTFREE and using a data set allocation report or a LISTCAT output, you can review and modify space utilization. Generally, when PERCACTIVE is low, you should redefine the tablespace or index with a smaller PRIQTY, a smaller SECQTY, or both. Free space can be changed as well. In any event, you must monitor these reports with the data set statistics. Also remember that changes to space characteristics do not take effect unless the tablespace being altered is reorganized and the index is reorganized or recovered.

Following are notes on using LISTCAT with DB2 data sets. LISTCAT reads the ICF catalog and displays pertinent values for data sets. The values returned by LISTCAT are generally useful for determining the overall status of a data set. However, when the data set is a VSAM data set used by DB2 for tablespaces or indexes, only some fields in the ICF catalog are accurate. They are as follows:

High used RBA
Number of extents
High allocated RBA
Size of each extent
DFP indicators
Volumes for each extent

CAUTION

If the V5 PREFORMAT option is used, the high used RBA value can be misleading.

You can analyze DB2 tablespace and index DASD use further with the following queries.

You can monitor tablespace DASD use by analyzing the results of this query:

```
SELECT    T.DBNAME, T.NAME, T.PARTITIONS, T.NTABLES,
          T.NACTIVE, T.SPACE, (100*T.NACTIVE*T.PGSIZE)/T.SPACE,
          P.PARTITION, P.PQTY, P.SQTY, P.STORTYPE, P.STORNAME,
          P.VCATNAME
FROM      SYSIBM.SYSTABLESPACE    T,
          SYSIBM.SYSTABLEPART     P
WHERE     T.DBNAME = P.DBNAME
AND       T.NAME = P.TSNAME
ORDER BY 1, 2, 3, 4, 5, 6, 7, 8
```

NOTE

For partitioned tablespaces, consider joining to the `SYSIBM.SYSTABSTATS` table to get the statistics by partition.

You can monitor index DASD use by analyzing the results of the following query:

```
SELECT    I.CREATOR, I.NAME, I.INDEXTYPE, I.INDEXSPACE, I.SPACE,
          I.PGSIZE, 4096/I.PGSIZE, P.PARTITION, P.PQTY, P.SQTY,
          P.STORTYPE, P.STORNAME, P.VCATNAME
FROM      SYSIBM.SYSINDEXES    I,
          SYSIBM.SYSINDEXPART  P
WHERE     I.NAME = P.IXNAME
AND       I.CREATOR = P.IXCREATOR
ORDER BY 1, 2, 3, 4, 5, 6, 7
```

These queries return information about only the particular object's DASD space use. The index DASD use query simply repeats the information from the previous physical index statistics query, presenting only DASD space use information. The tablespace DASD query adds a calculation column:

```
[(100*T.NACTIVE*T.PGSIZE)/T.SPACE]
```

CAUTION

Several factors can cause the previous queries to be inaccurate. The `SPACE` values are only collected for STOGROUP-defined objects that have not been archived by SMS. Furthermore, if the V5 `PREFORMAT` option is used, the space information might be misleading.

This calculation shows the percentage of the tablespace being utilized. This number should be monitored to determine a tablespace's DASD requirements. If this number remains below 75 percent for an extended time, and little growth is expected, decrease the space and reorganize the tablespace, or use `DSN1COPY` to migrate rows to a smaller data set. If the number is 100 percent or close to it, and growth is expected, increase the space.

The final physical statistics query presented here is the column value occurrence query. Three versions are shown. The first is viable for DB2 V5 and greater:

```
SELECT    T.DBNAME, T.TSNAME, D.TBOWNER, D.TBNAME,
          D.NAME, D.FREQUENCYF, D.COLVALUE, D.STATSTIME
FROM      SYSIBM.SYSCOLDIST    D,
          SYSIBM.SYSTABLES     T
WHERE     D.TBOWNER = T.CREATOR
AND       D.TBNAME = T.NAME
AND       D.TYPE = 'F'
ORDER BY T.DBNAME, T.TSNAME, D.TBOWNER, D.TBNAME, D.NAME
```

Because DB2 V5 enables non-uniform distribution statistics to be collected for groups of multiple columns, the information in the NAME column is the first column in the grouping of columns in the "key." Also, FREQUENCY changed to FREQUENCYF (an integer column changed to a floating-point column). The second query is viable for DB2 V3 and V4 only:

```
SELECT   T.DBNAME, T.TSNAME, D.TBOWNER, D.TBNAME,
         D.NAME, D.FREQUENCY, D.COLVALUE, D.STATSTIME
FROM     SYSIBM.SYSCOLDIST   D,
         SYSIBM.SYSTABLES    T
WHERE    D.TBOWNER = T.CREATOR
AND      D.TBNAME = T.NAME
ORDER BY T.DBNAME, T.TSNAME, D.TBOWNER, D.TBNAME, D.NAME
```

Prior to DB2 V3, non-uniform distribution statistics were stored in SYSFIELDS instead of SYSCOLDIST. This change necessitates a second column value occurrence query to be used only by shops running DB2 V2.3 and earlier:

```
SELECT   T.DBNAME, T.TSNAME, F.TBCREATOR, F.TBNAME,
         F.NAME, F.EXITPARML, F.EXITPARM
FROM     SYSIBM.SYSFIELDS    F,
         SYSIBM.SYSTABLES    T
WHERE    F.TBCREATOR = T.CREATOR
AND      F.TBNAME = T.NAME
AND      F.FLDPROC = '       '
ORDER BY T.DBNAME, T.TSNAME, F.TBCREATOR, F.TBNAME, F.NAME
```

CAUTION

If SYSIBM.SYSFIELDS was never purged after moving to DB2 V3 (or later), old non-uniform distribution statistics are probably still stored in SYSFIELDS, but not used. These artifacts can be misleading if misconstrued to be current. Further, the additional storage required to maintain the statistics might cause performance problems by preventing SYSDBASE from being reduced in size as much as possible.

These queries display the non-uniform distribution statistics stored in the DB2 Catalog for specific columns of each table. The output is arranged in order by database, tablespace, table creator, and table name. The output includes as many as 10 of the most frequently occurring values for table columns that are the first column of the index key.

The data shows the column value along with the percentage of times (multiplied by 100) it occurs for that column. This information is useful for tuning dynamic SQL queries. DB2 can choose a different access path for the same SQL statement when predicates contain literals for columns with distribution statistics. The optimizer uses this occurrence information to calculate filter factors. The higher the number of occurrences, the fewer rows the optimizer assumes it can filter out. Column values that appear in this report therefore could require SQL tuning. Additionally, you can use the MODIFY utility to remove these rows. Refer to Chapter 27, "Catalog Manipulation Utilities," for more information on the MODIFY utility.

After this level of performance analysis has been exhausted, you must broaden the scope of your tuning effort. Doing so involves analyzing SQL statements in application programs and possibly building new indexes or changing SQL in application queries.

Partition Statistics Queries

Partition-level statistics are accumulated by RUNSTATS to enable the optimizer to make query parallelism decisions.

SYSIBM.SYSCOLDISTSTATS contains partition-level, non-uniform distribution statistics. RUNSTATS collects values for the key columns of each partitioned index. You can use the following query in conjunction with the column value occurrence query presented earlier:

```
SELECT   T.DBNAME, T.TSNAME, D.PARTITION, D.TBOWNER,
         D.TBNAME, D.NAME, D.FREQUENCYF, D.COLVALUE,
         D.STATSTIME
FROM     SYSIBM.SYSCOLDISTSTATS   D,
         SYSIBM.SYSTABLES         T
WHERE    D.TBOWNER = T.CREATOR
AND      D.TBNAME = T.NAME
AND      D.TYPE = 'F'
ORDER BY T.DBNAME, T.TSNAME, D.PARTITION,
         D.TBOWNER, D.TBNAME, D.NAME
```

NOTE

Once again, DB2 V5 allows non-uniform distribution statistics to be collected for groups of multiple columns. Therefore, the information in the NAME column is the first column in the grouping of columns in the "key." Also, FREQUENCY changed to FREQUENCYF (an integer column changed to a floating point column).

Be sure to label the results of the queries in this section as partition-level statistics so that they are not confused with the equivalent non-partitioned reports I discussed in previous sections.

The results of the queries in the previous section depicted all tablespaces and indexes, whether partitioned or not. Additional statistics are maintained at the partition level for partitioned tablespaces and indexes. Partition-level physical statistics queries can be issued to retrieve these statistics.

The following query provides a report of partitioned tablespaces only, by database, listing the partition-level statistics for each tablespace partition:

```
SELECT   P.DBNAME, S.NAME, S.PARTITION, S.NACTIVE, S.CARD,
         S.PCTPAGES, S.PCTROWCOMP, S.STATSTIME
FROM     SYSIBM.SYSTABLEPART      P,
         SYSIBM.SYSTABSTATS       S
WHERE    P.PARTITION = S.PARTITION
AND      P.DBNAME = S.DBNAME
AND      P.TSNAME = S.TSNAME
ORDER BY P.DBNAME, S.NAME, S.PARTITION
```

You can issue a partition-level physical index statistics query to retrieve partition statistics for partitioning indexes. The following query provides a report of partitioned indexes only, listing the partition-level statistics for each partition:

```
SELECT    OWNER, NAME, PARTITION, CLUSTERRATIO, FIRSTKEYCARD,
          FULLKEYCARD, NLEAF, NLEVELS, KEYCOUNT, STATSTIME
FROM      SYSIBM.SYSINDEXSTATS
ORDER BY OWNER, NAME, PARTITION
```

You can analyze the results of the tablespace and index partition-level statistics reports to help you determine whether query parallelism could enhance performance of queries accessing these partitioned tablespaces.

Programmer's Aid Queries

Often, you must determine which plans and packages are in a DB2 subsystem. The following programmer's aid queries help you keep this information accurate. Plans can contain DBRMs, packages, or both. The following query lists the plans that contain DBRMs and the DBRMs they contain:

```
SELECT    P.NAME, P.CREATOR, P.BOUNDTS, P.ISOLATION,
          P.VALID, P.OPERATIVE, P.ACQUIRE, P.RELEASE, P.EXPLAN,
          P.GROUPMEMBER, P.DYNAMICRULES, P.REOPTVAR, P.KEEPDYNAMIC
          D.NAME, D.PDSNAME, D.PRECOMPTS, D.HOSTLANG
FROM      SYSIBM.SYSPLAN P,
          SYSIBM.SYSDBRM D
WHERE     P.NAME = D.PLNAME
ORDER BY P.NAME, D.NAME, D.PRECOMPDATE, D.PRECOMPTIME
```

NOTE

Version 5

For SYSIBM.SYSPLAN, you can substitute the BOUNDTS column for BINDDATE and BINDTIME as of DB2 V5. Also, PRECOMPTS replaces PRECOMPTIME and PRECOMPDATE in SYSIBM.SYSDBRM.

The next programmer's aid query lists all plans that contain packages and the packages they contain. Remember that packages are composed of a single DBRM.

```
SELECT    P.NAME, P.CREATOR, P.BINDDATE, P.BINDTIME,
          P.ISOLATION, P.VALID, P.OPERATIVE, P.ACQUIRE,
          P.RELEASE, P.EXPLAN, K.COLLID, K.NAME, K.TIMESTAMP
FROM      SYSIBM.SYSPLAN        P,
          SYSIBM.SYSPACKLIST    K
WHERE     P.NAME = K.PLANNAME
ORDER BY P.NAME, K.COLLID, K.NAME, K.TIMESTAMP
```

You can use the following query to track the DBRM libraries and packages. It details DBRM information for all packages. Although the DBRM name and the package name are equivalent, and a one-to-one correlation exists between packages and DBRMs, monitoring the DBRM information for each package is useful.

```
SELECT   COLLID, NAME, CREATOR, QUALIFIER, TIMESTAMP,
         BINDTIME, ISOLATION, VALID, OPERATIVE, RELEASE,
         EXPLAIN, PCTIMESTAMP, PDSNAME, VERSION
         GROUPMEMBER, DEFERPREPARE, DYNAMICRULES, REOPTVAR, KEEPDYNAMIC
FROM     SYSIBM.SYSPACKAGE
ORDER BY COLLID, NAME, VERSION
```

You can use the output from these three queries to track the composition and disposition of all DB2 plans and packages. For example, you can determine whether a plan or package is valid and operative. Invalid and inoperative plans require rebinding (and possible program changes) before execution. You can check on the parameters used to bind the plan or package, such as the isolation level specified (for example, `CS` versus `RR` versus `UR`) or whether reoptimization is available for dynamic SQL (`REOPTVARS`). You also can monitor the bind parameters. Ensure that they are specified as outlined in Chapter 7, "Program Preparation." Finally, you can trace `-818 SQLCODE`s by checking `PRECOMPTS` (or `PRECOMPTIME` and `PRECOMPDATE`) against the date and time stored for the appropriate program load module.

Another query that may be useful is to determine which plan and packages have SQL statements that use explicit, statement-level dirty reads (isolation `UR`). You can use the following queries to find these plans and packages.

Use this query to find plans containing SQL using the `WITH 'UR'` clause:

```
SELECT   DISTINCT S.PLNAME
FROM     SYSIBM.SYSPLAN      P,
         SYSIBM.SYSSTMT      S
WHERE    P.NAME = S.PLNAME
AND      S.ISOLATION = 'U'
ORDER BY S.PLNAME;
```

Use this query to find packages containing SQL using the `WITH 'UR'` clause:

```
SELECT   DISTINCT P.COLLID, P.NAME, P.VERSION
FROM     SYSIBM.SYSPACKAGE  P,
         SYSIBM.SYSPACKSTMT S
WHERE    P.LOCATION = S.LOCATION
AND      P.COLLID = S.COLLID
AND      P.NAME = S.NAME
AND      P.VERSION = S.VERSION
AND      S.ISOLATION = 'U'
ORDER BY P.COLLID, P.NAME, P.VERSION;
```

Three other queries are useful as programmer's aids. The plan dependency query follows:

```
SELECT   D.DNAME, P.CREATOR, P.QUALIFIER, P.VALID, P.ISOLATION,
         P.ACQUIRE, P.RELEASE, P.EXPLAN, P.PLSIZE, D.BCREATOR,
         D.BNAME, D.BTYPE
FROM     SYSIBM.SYSPLANDEP   D,
         SYSIBM.SYSPLAN      P
WHERE    P.NAME = D.DNAME
ORDER BY D.DNAME, D.BTYPE, D.BCREATOR, D.BNAME
```

Likewise, the package dependency query can be quite useful:

```
SELECT   P.COLLID, D.DNAME, P.CONTOKEN, P.CREATOR,
         P.QUALIFIER, P.VALID, P.ISOLATION, P.RELEASE,
         P.EXPLAIN, P.PKSIZE, D.BQUALIFIER, D.BNAME, D.BTYPE
FROM     SYSIBM.SYSPACKDEP    D,
         SYSIBM.SYSPACKAGE    P
WHERE    P.NAME = D.DNAME
AND      P.COLLID = D.DCOLLID
AND      P.CONTOKEN = D.CONTOKEN
ORDER BY P.COLLID, D.DNAME, P.CONTOKEN, D.BTYPE, D.BCREATOR,
         D.BNAME
```

These queries detail the DB2 objects used by every DB2 plan and package. When database changes are needed, you can analyze the output from these queries to determine which packages and plans might be affected by structural changes.

Finally, programmers may need to know what stored procedures are available and how they are defined. The following stored procedure programmer's aid query provides this type of information:

```
SELECT   PROCEDURE, LANGUAGE, PGM_TYPE, LOADMOD,
         COLLID, LINKAGE, AUTHID, LUNAME, ASUTIME,
         COMMIT_ON_RETURN, STAYRESIDENT, RUNOPTS,
         PARMLIST, RESULT_SETS, WLM_ENV, EXTERNAL_SECURITY
FROM     SYSIBM.SYSPROCEDURES
```

NOTE

Version 5

The preceding query executes under DB2 V5. To run it under DB2 V4, you can remove the following columns from the `SELECT` list: `RESULT_SETS`, `WLM_ENV`, `PGM_TYPE`, `EXTERNAL SECURITY`, and `COMMIT_ON_RETURN`.

The next section takes this form of DB2 performance monitoring to the next level, incorporating DB2 Catalog monitoring with `EXPLAIN`.

Application Efficiency Queries

The application efficiency queries combine the best of `EXPLAIN` monitoring with the best of DB2 Catalog monitoring. The reports produced by these queries show many potential performance problems. By combining the DB2 Catalog information with the output from `EXPLAIN`, you can identify a series of "problem queries."

These problem queries are grouped into two categories: tablespace scans and index scans. DB2 scans data sets to satisfy queries using tablespace scans and index scans. A tablespace scan reads every page in the tablespace and does not use an index. An index scan might or might not read every index subpage.

The tablespace scan query follows:

```
SELECT   E.APPLNAME, E.PROGNAME, E.QUERYNO, E.TNAME,
         T.NPAGES, E.TIMESTAMP, S.SEQNO, S.TEXT
FROM     ownerid.PLAN_TABLE  E,
         SYSIBM.SYSTABLES    T,
         SYSIBM.SYSSTMT      S
WHERE    ACCESSTYPE = 'R'
AND      (T.NPAGES > 50 OR T.NPAGES < 0)
AND      T.NAME = E.TNAME
AND      T.CREATOR = E.CREATOR
AND      S.NAME = E.PROGNAME
AND      S.PLNAME = E.APPLNAME
AND      S.STMTNO = E.QUERYNO
ORDER BY E.APPLNAME, E.PROGNAME, E.TIMESTAMP DESC,
         E.QUERYNO, S.SEQNO
```

The following is the index scan query:

```
SELECT   E.APPLNAME, E.PROGNAME, E.QUERYNO, I.NAME, I.NLEAF,
         I.COLCOUNT, E.MATCHCOLS, E.INDEXONLY, E.TIMESTAMP,
         S.SEQNO, S.TEXT,
FROM     ownerid.PLAN_TABLE  E,
         SYSIBM.SYSINDEXES   I,
         SYSIBM.SYSSTMT      S
WHERE    E.ACCESSTYPE = 'I'
AND      N.LEAF > 100
AND      E.MATCHCOLS < I.COLCOUNT
AND      I.NAME = E.ACCESSNAME
AND      I.CREATOR = E.ACCESSCREATOR
AND      S.NAME = E.PROGNAME
AND      S.PLNAME = E.APPLNAME
AND      S.STMTNO = E.QUERYNO
ORDER BY E.APPLNAME, E.PROGNAME, E.TIMESTAMP DESC,
         E.QUERYNO, S.SEQNO
```

Because these queries usually take a long time to run, they should not be executed in parallel with heavy production DB2 processing or during the online DB2 transaction window. To ensure that the scan queries operate efficiently, make sure that the PLAN_TABLE used in each query does not contain extraneous data. Strive to maintain only the most recent EXPLAIN data from production BIND jobs in the table. Also, keep EXPLAIN information only for plans that must be monitored. Executing RUNSTATS on your PLAN_TABLEs also can increase the performance of these queries.

The tablespace scan report lists queries that scan more than 50 pages and queries that access tables without current RUNSTATS information. If the NO OF PAGES is -1 for any table, RUNSTATS has not been run. A RUNSTATS job should be executed as soon as possible, followed by a rebind of any plan that uses this table. Everything else on this report should be monitored closely. For tables just over the 50-page threshold, the effect on performance is uncertain. As the number of scanned pages increases, so does the potential for performance problems.

The 50-page cutoff is arbitrary; you might want to redefine it as you gauge the usefulness of the information returned. If you monitor only large tables, you might want to increase this number to 100 (or larger). This number varies according to your shop's definition of a "large table." If you have a small bufferpool (fewer than 1,000 buffers), you might want to reduce this number.

For tables with 20 or more pages, try to create indexes to satisfy the predicates in your query. (Creating an index for every predicate, however, is not always possible.) DB2 references recommend that indexes be considered when the number of pages in a tablespace reaches 5, 6, or 15. I have found 20 pages to be a good number in practice.

The index scan query reports on all SQL statements that scan more than 100 index leaf pages on which a match on the columns in the query is not a complete match on all index columns. As the number of `MATCHING COLUMNS` increases, performance problems decrease. The worst case is zero `MATCHING COLUMNS`, but even this number might be acceptable for an index-only scan.

You might need to be modify the 100-page cutoff value for the index scan query too. You might want to use the same number as the one chosen for the tablespace scan report.

Although every query listed in these reports is not necessarily a problem query, you should closely monitor each one. Corrective actions for poorly performing queries are outlined in Part V, "DB2 Performance Tuning."

Authorization Queries

You can implement five types of security in DB2: database security, plan and package security, system-level authorization, security on tables and views, and resource privileges:

Database security Controls database-level privileges. Anyone holding a database privilege can perform actions on all dependent database objects.

Plan and package Dictates whether users can copy security packages and bind or execute plans and packages.

System-level Indicates system-wide authority, *authorization* such as global authority to create new objects, authority to trace, and the capability to hold specific system-wide authorities, such as `SYSADM`, `SYSCTRL`, and `SYSOPR`.

Security on tables Indicates whether the data in the tables and views and views can be accessed or updated. This authorization is granted at the table, view, or column level.

Resource privileges Indicates whether users can use DB2 resources such as bufferpools, tablespaces, and storage groups.

You can execute the following queries to ascertain the authority granted for each of these types of security. Note that two forms of each query are provided; the authorization information can be returned either in DB2 object (or DB2 resource) order or by the user who possesses the authority.

Database authority query:

```
SELECT    NAME, GRANTEE, GRANTOR, GRANTEDTS, GRANTEETYPE,
          CREATETABAUTH, CREATETSAUTH, DBADMAUTH,
          DBCTRLAUTH, DBMAINTAUTH, DISPLAYDBAUTH,
          DROPAUTH, IMAGCOPYAUTH, LOADAUTH, REORGAUTH,
          RECOVERDBAUTH, REPAIRAUTH, STARTDBAUTH,
          STATSAUTH, STOPAUTH, AUTHHOWGOT
FROM      SYSIBM.SYSDBAUTH
ORDER BY NAME, GRANTEE, GRANTOR
```

Table authority query:

```
SELECT    TCREATOR, TTNAME, SCREATOR, STNAME, GRANTEE, GRANTOR,
          GRANTEETYPE, UPDATECOLS, ALTERAUTH, DELETEAUTH, GRANTEDTS,
          INDEXAUTH, INSERTAUTH, SELECTAUTH, UPDATEAUTH,
          REFCOLS, REFERENCESAUTH, AUTHHOWGOT
FROM      SYSIBM.SYSTABAUTH
ORDER BY TCREATOR, TTNAME, GRANTEE, GRANTOR
```

Column authority query:

```
SELECT    CREATOR, TNAME, COLNAME, PRIVILEGE, GRANTEE, GRANTOR,
          GRANTEETYPE, TIMESTAMP, DATEGRANTED, TIMEGRANTED
FROM      SYSIBM.SYSCOLAUTH
ORDER BY CREATOR, TNAME, COLNAME, GRANTEE
```

Resource authority query:

```
SELECT    QUALIFIER, NAME, OBTYPE, GRANTEE, GRANTOR,
          GRANTEDTS, USEAUTH, AUTHHOWGOT
FROM      SYSIBM.SYSRESAUTH
ORDER BY GRANTEE, QUALIFIER, NAME, GRANTOR
```

User authority query:

```
SELECT    GRANTEE, GRANTOR, GRANTEDTS, ALTERBPAUTH,
          BINDADDAUTH, BSDSAUTH, CREATETMTABAUTH,
          CREATEDBAAUTH, CREATEDBCAUTH, CREATESGAUTH,
          CREATEALIASAUTH, DISPLAYAUTH, RECOVERAUTH,
          STOPALLAUTH, STOSPACEAUTH, SYSADMAUTH, SYSCTRLAUTH,
          SYSOPRAUTH, BINDAGENTAUTH, ARCHIVEAUTH,
          TRACEAUTH, MON1AUTH, MON2AUTH, AUTHHOWGOT
FROM      SYSIBM.SYSUSERAUTH
ORDER BY GRANTEE, GRANTOR
```

Plan authority query:

```
SELECT    NAME, GRANTEE, GRANTOR, GRANTEDTS,
          GRANTEETYPE,BINDAUTH, EXECUTEAUTH, AUTHHOWGOT,
FROM      SYSIBM.SYSPLANAUTH
ORDER BY NAME, GRANTEE, GRANTOR
```

Package authority query:

```
SELECT    COLLID, NAME, GRANTEE, GRANTOR, CONTOKEN,
          TIMESTAMP, GRANTEETYPE, AUTHHOWGOT,
          BINDAUTH, COPYAUTH, EXECUTEAUTH
FROM      SYSIBM.SYSPACKAUTH
ORDER BY COLLID, NAME, GRANTEE, GRANTOR
```

Version 5

NOTE

For DB2 V5, the GRANTEDTS column has been added to SYSCOLAUTH, SYSDBAUTH, SYSPLANAUTH, SYSRESAUTH, SYSUSERAUTH, and SYSTABAUTH. This column is used in place of the TIMEGRANTED and DATEGRANTED columns. To make these queries operable for DB2 V4 and prior releases, you can replace GRANTEDTS with TIMEGRANTED and DATEGRANTED for each query.

Security is not often associated with performance monitoring, but it can help you determine the following items. If certain types of authority are granted to many users, and security checking becomes inefficient, you might want to grant the authority to PUBLIC. This way, you can reduce the number of entries in the DB2 Catalog, thereby reducing the strain on the DB2 subsystem. Don't grant PUBLIC access, however, if audit regulations or data sensitivity is an issue.

In addition, monitoring who can access data can help you determine the potential effect on workload. As the number of users who can access a piece of data increases, the potential for workload and capacity problems increases.

DB2 Catalog Query Guidelines

Heed the following advice when implementing DB2 Catalog queries to obtain information about your DB2 environment.

Use Queries as a Starting Point

The queries in this chapter are only suggestions. If you want to change the sort order or alter the columns being queried, you can use the queries in this chapter as templates. For example, to determine the table authority granted to users, you can modify the sort order of the table authority query, as shown in the following SQL statement:

```
SELECT    TCREATOR, TTNAME, SCREATOR, STNAME, GRANTEE, GRANTOR,
          GRANTEETYPE, UPDATECOLS, ALTERAUTH, DELETEAUTH, GRANTEDTS
          INDEXAUTH, INSERTAUTH, SELECTAUTH, UPDATEAUTH,
          REFCOLS, REFERENCESAUTH, AUTHHOWGOT
FROM      SYSIBM.SYSTABAUTH
ORDER BY GRANTEE, TCREATOR, TTNAME, GRANTOR
```

The reports in this chapter are suggestions that have worked well for me. Changing them to suit your needs is easy because of the ad hoc nature of SQL.

Use QMF to Create Formatted Reports

The queries in this chapter were developed using QMF. You can run them weekly using a batch QMF job. Using the batch job is easier than submitting the queries weekly from QMF or through SPUFI. Simply build batch QMF JCL, incorporate all these queries and forms into a proc, and then run the proc.

You can create QMF forms for each query to present the output in a pleasing format. You can change control breaks, different headings for columns, and the spacing between columns. A sample QMF form for the table listing query is presented in Listing 19.1. To create a form for any of the queries in this chapter in QMF, simply type and execute the query. Press F9 to display the form panel and then modify the form.

Listing 19.1. Sample QMF form for the table listing query.

```
FORM.COLUMNS
Total Width of Report Columns: 189
NUM  COLUMN HEADING USAGE    INDENT   WIDTH   EDIT   SEQ
1    _DATABASE      BREAK1   1        8       C      1
2    TABLE_SPACE    BREAK2   1        8       C      2
3    TABLE_CREATOR  BREAK3   1        8       C      3
4    _TABLE         BREAK3   1        18      C      4
5    CREATEDTS               1        26      TSI    5
6    ALTEREDTS               1        26      TSI    6
7    COL_NO                  1        3       L      7
8    COLUMN_NAME             1        18      C      8
9    COLUMN_TYPE             1        8       C      9
10   COLUMN_LENGTH           1        6       L      10
11   SCALE                   1        6       L      11
12   NU_LL                   1        2       C      12
13   DF_LT                   1        2       C      13
14   COL_CARD                1        8       L      14
15   HIGH2_KEY               1        8       C      15
16   LOW2_KEY                1        8       C      16
17   FLD_PROC                1        4       C      17
```

Become Familiar with the Data in the DB2 Catalog

You can produce many reports from the DB2 Catalog to aid in performance monitoring. This chapter details some of them. As you become more familiar with the DB2 Catalog and the needs of your application, you can formulate additional queries geared to the needs of your organization.

Summary

DB2 has a reputation of being easy for users to understand; they specify *what* data to retrieve, not *how* to retrieve it. The layer of complexity removed for the users, however, had to be relegated elsewhere: to the code of DB2.

DB2 also has a reputation as a large resource consumer. This reputation is largely because of DB2's complexity. Because DB2 performance analysts must understand and monitor this complexity, they require an array of performance monitoring tools and techniques. Part IV outlines the majority of these tools. (See Chapter 32, "Components of a Total DB2 Solution," for information on third-party performance monitoring tools.)

To review, an effective monitoring strategy includes the following:

- Scheduled batch performance monitor jobs to report on the recent performance of DB2 applications and the DB2 subsystem
- An online monitor that executes when DB2 executes to enable quick monitoring of performance problems as they occur
- Online monitors for all teleprocessing environments in which DB2 transactions execute (for example, CICS, IMS/TM, or TSO)
- Regular monitoring of MVS for memory use and VTAM for network use
- Scheduled reports from the DB2 Catalog
- Access to the DB2 `DSNMSTR` address space to review console messages
- Use of the DB2 `-DISPLAY` command to view databases, threads, and utility execution

Part V delves into tuning the performance of DB2.

V

DB2 Performance Tuning

Now that you understand how to monitor the DB2 environment, you must develop a plan to analyze the performance data you have accumulated and *tune* DB2 to boost performance. As you will see in this chapter, diverse tuning strategies are involved in making DB2 perform optimally.

It is not sufficient to merely monitor and tune DB2 alone. A comprehensive DB2 tuning program involves monitoring and tuning the following five areas:

- The MVS system
- The DB2 subsystem
- The teleprocessing environments
- DB2 database design
- DB2 application program design

Some areas require more DB2 tuning attention than others. The DB2 performance tuning pie, although split into five pieces, is not split into five *equal* pieces. Figure V.1 shows the percentage of tuning available for each area. Each percentage represents a comparative number encompassing the estimated number of incidences in the environment requiring tuning.

FIGURE V.1.
The DB2 performance tuning pie.

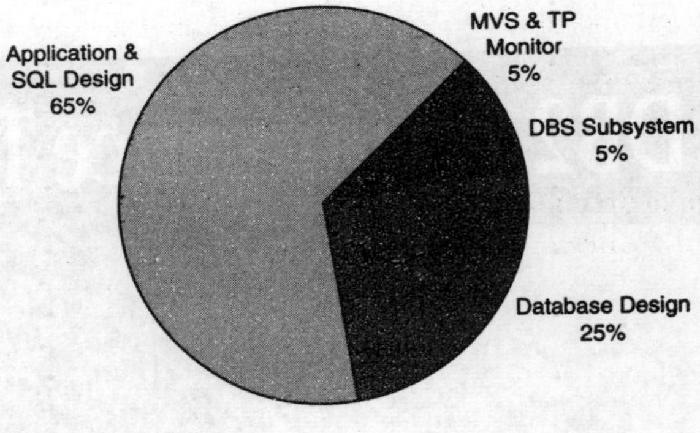

For example, the MVS system constitutes a small portion of the tuning pie. This does not mean that there are few tuning options for MVS. Instead, it means that the number of times a DB2 performance problem is due to an MVS factor is minimal.

As the size of the piece of pie increases, the opportunities for DB2 performance tuning generally increase. But note that these numbers are estimates. Your tuning experiences might vary, but if they vary significantly, be sure that you are concentrating your tuning efforts wisely. The 80-20 rule applies here: 80 percent of performance gains accrue from 20 percent of your tuning efforts, as shown in Figure V.2. In other words, do not expend undue energy "tuning the life" out of an area if you expect only small gains. Instead, distribute your tuning efforts across each area. Concentrate on problem areas or areas in which you expect large performance gains.

FIGURE V.2.
The 80-20 rule.

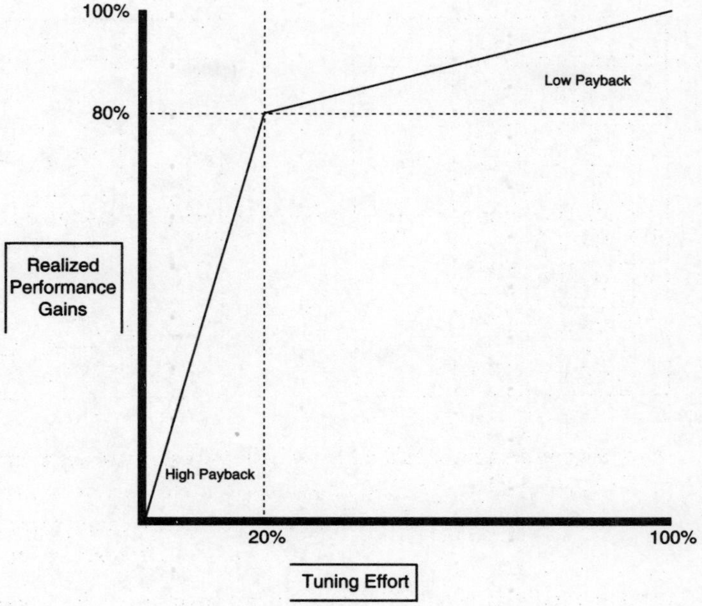

Return your attention to Figure V.1, and you can see that the majority of DB2 performance problems result from improper application design, such as inefficient SQL, redundant SQL, or poor BIND options. The second most prominent area for tuning is in the application's relational database design. Was it based on relational techniques or converted from a nonrelational platform? Is it normalized, overnormalized, or undernormalized? Can it support the application requirements? The final three areas—the MVS, teleprocessing, and DB2 subsystems—should make up a small portion of your tuning efforts.

Remember, though, that you must monitor and tune each area that affects DB2 performance. Simply because there are fewer MVS tuning opportunities, for example, does not mean that the impact of a poorly tuned MVS subsystem is less substantial than a poorly tuned DB2 application program. Quite to the contrary! If MVS is not tuned to enable optimal DB2 performance, no amount of application tuning will ever result in proper performance. Implement a tuning strategy that encompasses all aspects of DB2 performance.

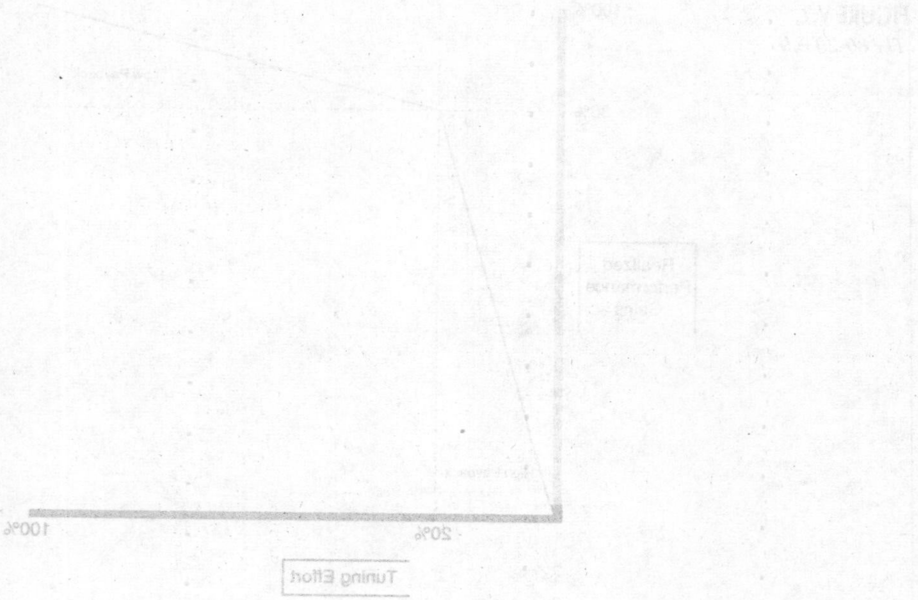

Return your attention to Figure V.1, and you can see that the majority of DB2 performance problems result from improper application design, such as inefficient SQL, redundant SQL, or poor BIND options. The second most prominent area for tuning is in the application's relational database design. Was it based on relational techniques or converted from a nonrelational platform? Is it normalized, overnormalized, or undernormalized? Can it support the application requirements? The final three areas—the MVS, teleprocessing, and DB2 subsystems—should make up a small portion of your tuning efforts.

Remember, though, that you must monitor and tune each area that affects DB2 performance. Simply because there are fewer MVS tuning opportunities, for example, does not mean that the impact of a poorly tuned MVS subsystem is less substantial than a poorly tuned DB2 application program. Quite to the contrary! If MVS is not tuned to enable optimal DB2 performance, no amount of application tuning will ever result in proper performance. Implement a tuning strategy that encompasses all aspects of DB2 performance.

20

Tuning DB2's Environment

System tuning for DB2 performance can be applied outside DB2—to the environment in which DB2 operates—or inside DB2—to the components of DB2 or under DB2's control. This chapter concentrates on the tuning of DB2's environment.

Tuning the MVS Environment

MVS tuning is a complex task best accomplished by extensively trained technicians. All DB2 users, however, should understand the basics of MVS resource exploitation and the avenues for tuning it. MVS tuning, as it affects DB2 performance, can be broken down into four areas:

- Memory use
- CPU use
- I/O use
- Operating system environment parameters

Now turn your attention to each of these four areas. The sections that follow offer various tuning guidelines and strategies along the way.

Tuning Memory Use

How does DB2 utilize available memory? Before answering this question, you need a basic understanding of what memory is and how it is used by MVS. *Memory* is the working storage available for programs and the data the programs use as they operate.

Storage is often used as a synonym for memory. MVS stands for Multiple Virtual Storage, which refers to MVS's capability to manage virtual memory. To manage virtual memory, the operating system uses a large pool of memory, known as *virtual storage*, to "back up" *real storage*. (Real storage is also called central storage. Virtual storage is also called expanded storage.)

Real storage is addressable. Programs and their data must be placed in real storage before they can run. Virtual memory management is the reason that multiple address spaces can execute concurrently, regardless of the physical memory they eventually use. This way, the system can process more jobs than can be held in real storage; information is swapped back and forth between virtual storage and real storage, a process known as *paging*.

You'll discover two types of paging. The first, moving data between virtual and real storage, is inexpensive in terms of resource consumption and occurs regularly. As more real storage is requested, a second type of paging can result. This type of paging consists of moving portions of memory to DASD temporarily. This type is expensive and should be avoided.

TUNING STRATEGY

Use storage isolation to fence the DB2 address spaces. Doing so prevents DB2 from paging to DASD. Storage isolation must be implemented by MVS systems programmers.

MVS virtual storage can be broken down further in two ways:

- Common area versus private area
- Above the line versus below the line

The *common area* is the portion of virtual storage addressable from any address space. The *private area* stores data that is addressable by only an individual address space. A common area and private area exist both above and below the line. But what does that mean?

Above and below the line refers to an imaginary line in virtual storage at the 16-megabyte level. Memory above the line is often called *extended storage.* In earlier versions of MVS, 16 megabytes was the upper limit for virtual and real storage addressability. New releases of MVS add addressability above the 16-megabyte line.

The constraints imposed by the addressing schemes of older systems, however, can cause dense packing of applications into memory below the line. Systems that use memory above the line provide more efficient memory management, as well as relief for systems requiring memory use below the line.

How does DB2 fit into this memory structure? Refer to Figure 20.1. DB2 manages memory efficiently, making use of extended storage when possible. A well-tuned DB2 subsystem requires less than 2 megabytes of virtual storage below the line. What causes DB2 to use virtual storage above the line? Take a closer look at some of the factors influencing DB2's use of memory.

Bufferpools

DB2 provides 60 virtual bufferpools and optional hiperpools for maintaining recently accessed table and index pages in virtual storage. The Buffer Manager component of DB2 manages I/O and the use of buffers to reduce the cost of I/O. If the Buffer Manager can satisfy a `GETPAGE` request from memory in the bufferpool rather than from DASD, performance can increase significantly.

DB2 uses 50 bufferpools for 4K pages (named BP0 through BP49) and 10 bufferpools for 32K pages (named BP32K and BP32K1 through BP32K9). The size of the bufferpools is specified in pages.

Tuning DB2 bufferpools is a critical piece of overall DB2 subsystem tuning. Strategies for effective bufferpool tuning are presented in Chapter 21, "Tuning DB2's Components," in the section on DB2 subsystem tuning.

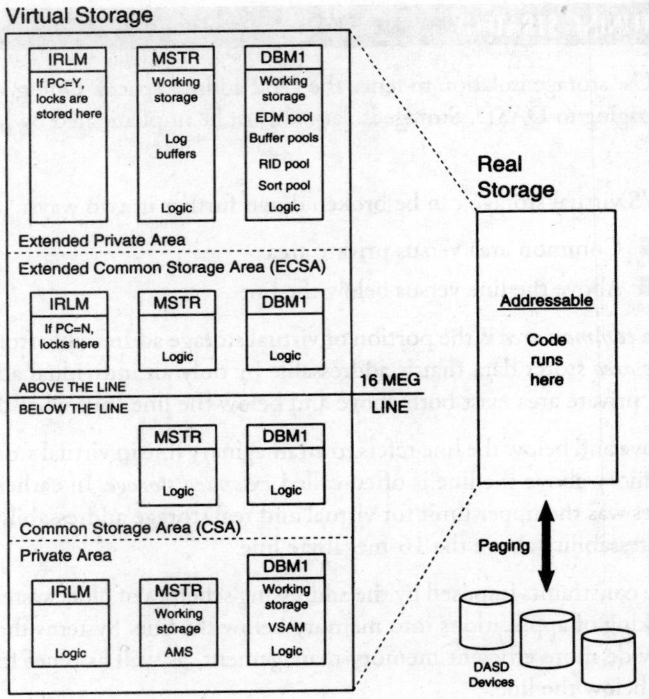

FIGURE 20.1.
DB2 memory use.

In addition to the bufferpools, DB2 creates a RID pool and a sort pool. RIDs processed during the execution of list prefetch are stored in the RID pool. Remember that hybrid joins and multiple-index access paths use list prefetch. The RID pool should be increased as your application's use of list prefetch increases.

The sort pool, sometimes called a *sort work area,* is used when DB2 invokes a sort. Before I discuss the sort pool, examine the DB2 sorting process, which is shown in Figure 20.2. The RDS (Relational Data Services) component of DB2 uses a tournament sort technique to perform internal DB2 sorting.

The tournament sort works as follows:

- Rows to be sorted are passed through a tree structure like the one in Figure 20.2. A row enters the tree at the bottom. It is compared to rows already in the tree, and the lowest values (for ascending sequence) or the highest values (for descending sequence) are moved up the tree.
- When a row emerges from the top of the tree, it is usually placed in an ordered set of rows in memory. Sometimes, however, a value emerges from the top of the tree but does not fit into the current ordered set because it is out of range.
- When a row does not fit into the current ordered set, the complete ordered set of rows is written to a logical work file. This ordered set is then called a *run.*

- Logical work files are located in the bufferpool. As logical work files grow, sometimes they are written to physical work files. DB2 uses the DSNDB07 database to store physical work files.
- After all the rows have passed through the tree, the accumulated runs are merged, forming a sorted results set. This set is returned to the requester, completely sorted.

FIGURE 20.2.
How DB2 sorts.

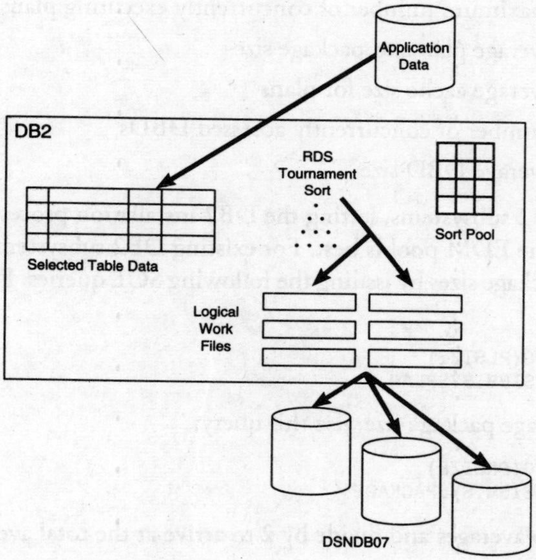

How, then, does the sort pool affect RDS sorting? As the sort pool becomes larger, so does the tree used for the tournament sort. As the tree becomes larger, fewer runs are produced. As fewer runs are produced, less data must be merged and the likelihood of using DSNDB07 diminishes. The result is a more efficient sort process.

The size of the RID and sort pools can be explicitly specified using DSNZPARMs for DB2 V3 and later releases. In prior releases, the size of these pools was based on the bufferpool specifications. If the RID and sort pools are not explicitly specified, they default to values using the pre-V3 formula. This formula adds the total size of the BP0, BP1, BP2, and BP32K bufferpools together and allocates the RID and sort pools as a percentage of this total. The percentage is defined as follows:

	Size	*Minimum*	*Maximum*
RID Pool	50%	0	250,000 pages
Sort Pool	10%	60 pages	16,000 pages

Explicitly specifying the RID and sort pool sizes is better than allowing them to default.

EDM Pool

The EDM pool is used to maintain DBDs, plan cursor tables, and package tables needed by executing SQL statements. The size of the EDM pool is specified in the DSNZPARMs and must be determined before starting DB2. To estimate the size of the EDM pool, you must have the following information:

- The maximum number of concurrently executing plans and packages
- The average plan and package size
- The average cache size for plans
- The number of concurrently accessed DBDs
- The average DBD size

For new DB2 subsystems, letting the DB2 installation process use default values to calculate the size of the EDM pool is best. For existing DB2 subsystems, you can arrive at the average plan and package sizes by issuing the following SQL queries. For the average plan size, use this query:

```
SELECT   AVG(PLSIZE)
FROM     SYSIBM.SYSPLAN
```

For the average package size, use this query:

```
SELECT   AVG(PKSIZE)
FROM     SYSIBM.SYSPACKAGE
```

Add the two averages and divide by 2 to arrive at the total average plan and package size.

TUNING STRATEGY

Binding with the ACQUIRE(USE) option results in smaller plan sizes than binding with ACQUIRE(ALLOCATE). Additional code is stored with the plan for ACQUIRE(ALLOCATE). To reduce the amount of storage used by plans and packages in the EDM pool, specify ACQUIRE(USE) at bind time. However, plan size should never be the determining factor for the specification of the ACQUIRE parameter. Instead, follow the guidelines presented in Chapter 7, "Program Preparation."

Another factor influencing the overall size of plans is the authorization cache. You can associate an authid cache for each plan by setting the size in the CACHESIZE parameter of the BIND command.

TUNING STRATEGY

Binding with the `CACHESIZE(0)` option also results in smaller plan sizes. However, the caching of authids enhances performance. So, once again, plan size should not be the determining factor in setting `CACHESIZE` either. The default cache size is 1024K, which is probably overkill for many shops. Use the formula specified in Chapter 7 to calculate an appropriate `CACHESIZE` for each plan—instead of relying on the default.

NOTE

Authids are not checked for plans that can be executed by `PUBLIC`. Avoid specifying a `CACHESIZE` for these plans.

For the average size of the plan authorization ID cache, use the following query:

```
SELECT   AVG(CACHESIZE)
FROM     SYSIBM.SYSPLAN
```

Version 5

Package authorization caching, introduced with DB2 V5, is a system-wide option. Caching is either enabled or disabled for the entire subsystem and a global cache is used. Therefore, package authorization caching does not have an impact on package size.

To arrive at the average DBD size, you must know the average number of columns per table and the average number of tables per database. A general formula for calculating the average DBD size follows:

```
average DBD size = [(average # of tables per database) x 1K]
                 + [(average # of columns per table) x .5K]
```

You can use the following queries to arrive at the average number of tables per database and the average number of columns per table. First, issue this query to determine the total number of databases defined for your DB2 subsystem:

```
SELECT   COUNT(*)
FROM     SYSIBM.SYSDATABASE
```

Then, to determine the average number of tables per database, issue the following query, substituting the result of the preceding query for `?`:

```
SELECT   COUNT(*) / ?
FROM     SYSIBM.SYSTABLES
WHERE    TYPE = 'T'
```

If the result of the first query is `12`, for example, this query would become

```
SELECT   COUNT(*) / 12
FROM     SYSIBM.SYSTABLES
WHERE    TYPE = 'T'
```

You can use the following queries to arrive at the average number of columns per table. First, issue the following query to determine the total number of tables defined for your DB2 subsystem:

```
SELECT   COUNT(*)
FROM     SYSIBM.SYSTABLES
WHERE    TYPE = 'T'
```

Next, to determine the average number of columns per table, issue the following query, again substituting the result of the preceding query for ?:

```
SELECT   COUNT(*) / ?
FROM     SYSIBM.SYSCOLUMNS
WHERE    TYPE = 'T'
```

To arrive at the average number of concurrent plans, packages, and DBDs, you would be wise to accumulate a series of DB2 accounting statistics for your peak processing time. Use these figures to estimate the number of concurrent plans.

Determining the average number of concurrent packages is not easy. You must completely understand your particular DB2 implementation to be successful at determining this number. Asking the following questions can help:

- How many plans use packages instead of simply DBRMs? Issue the following two queries to determine this information:

```
SELECT   COUNT(DISTINCT PLANNAME)
FROM     SYSIBM.SYSPACKLIST

SELECT   COUNT(*)
FROM     SYSIBM.SYSPLAN
WHERE    OPERATIVE = "Y"
AND      VALID IN("Y","A")
```

- On average, how many versions of a package are permitted to remain in the DB2 Catalog? How many are used?

To determine the average number of concurrent DBDs, you must understand each application's database use. If an application that typically uses three databases is much more active than another that uses 12 databases, you must factor this information into your EDM pool sizing strategy. Obtaining this information can be difficult, so you might need to estimate. A general calculation for the EDM pool size follows:

```
EDM Pool Size = [(((#CPP) + (#TPP/4)) x PP-AVG) +
                 (((#CPP) + (#TPP/4)) x C-AVG)  +
                 ((#DBD) x DBD-AVG) + 50K] x 1.25
```

Value	*Description*
#CPP	Number of concurrent plans and packages
#TPP	Total number of plans and packages
#DBD	Total number of concurrently used databases
PP-AVG	Average size of all plans and packages
C-AVG	Average authorization cache size
DBD-AVG	Average authorization cache size

The systems programmer calculates the size of the EDM pool during DB2 installation based on estimates of the values discussed in this section. The installation CLIST for DB2 contains the preceding algorithm. The calculation used by the DB2 installation process is only as good as the information supplied to it. The default values are adequate for most medium-sized shops. As DB2 use expands, however, the EDM pool should expand proportionally.

TUNING STRATEGY

Overestimate the size of the EDM pool. Having EDM pool memory available as the number of DB2 plans, packages, and databases increases is better than reacting to a problem after it occurs. Periodically monitor the number of plans, packages, and databases in conjunction with usage statistics, and increase the EDM pool as your DB2 use increases.

DB2 Working Storage

DB2 working storage is memory (both above and below the line) used by DB2 as a temporary work area. IBM recommends that you set aside 40K of memory per concurrent DB2 user for working storage, but this number is too small. The best way to estimate the working storage size for DB2 is to separate the number of concurrent DB2 users into users of dynamic SQL and users of static SQL. Dynamic SQL uses more working storage (but less of the EDM pool) than static SQL. Figure on approximately 25K per static SQL user and 75K per dynamic SQL user. Additionally, DB2 itself uses 600K. Therefore, you can estimate DB2 working storage usage by using the following:

```
(concurrent static SQL users x 25K) +
(concurrent dynamic SQL users x 75K) + 600K
```

TUNING STRATEGY

You cannot explicitly tune the amount of memory used by concurrent static and dynamic SQL. Implicit control over the number of users can be established by the `DSNZPARM` values specified for `IDFORE`, `IDBACK`, and `CTHREAD`.

DB2 Code

The DB2 code itself requires approximately 4,300K of storage. This value is inflexible.

IRLM

Locks are maintained in memory by the IRLM. This capability enables DB2 to process a lock request quickly and efficiently without a physical read. The IRLM uses approximately 250 bytes per lock.

TUNING STRATEGY

If the IRLM start-up parameters specify `PC=Y`, the locks are stored in the private address space for the IRLM. `PC=N` stores the locks in expanded memory, so this specification is more efficient than `PC=Y`.

Open Data Sets

Each open VSAM data set requires approximately 1.8K for the VSAM control block that is created. This memory use is minimal, given the performance benefit gained by DB2 applications when VSAM data sets need not be opened and closed. Refer to Chapter 3, "Data Definition Guidelines," for a discussion of the `CLOSE` parameter for DB2 tablespaces and indexes and its effect on performance.

TUNING STRATEGY

Use segmented tablespaces with multiple tables to reduce the amount of memory used by open data sets. When each table is assigned to a unique tablespace, DB2 must manage more open data sets—one for each tablespace and table combination. As the number of tables in a tablespace increases, DB2 must manage fewer open data sets. (All considerations for multitable tablespaces, as outlined in Chapter 3, still apply.)

TUNING STRATEGY

The memory cost per open data set, approximately 1.8K, is small in comparison to the performance gains associated with leaving the data sets open to avoid VSAM open and close operations. Favor using `CLOSE YES` for most of your tablespaces and indexes when using DB2 V3 or later. Doing so leaves data sets open until the maximum number of open data sets is reached. At this point, the least recently used data sets are closed. For tablespaces and indexes used by DB2 V2.2 and prior, use `CLOSE NO`. For DB2 V2.3, analyze the cost of `SYSLGRNG` updating versus the memory utilized by open data sets. For DB2 V2.3, updates to tablespaces only (not indexes) cause `SYSLGRNG` updates.

Total Memory Requirements

By adding the memory requirements, as specified in the preceding sections, for the EDM pool, bufferpools, RID pool, sort pool, working storage, open data sets, and IRLM for each DB2 subsystem, you can estimate the memory resources required for DB2. If insufficient memory is available, consider limiting the availability of DB2 until more memory can be procured.

TUNING STRATEGY

DB2 uses virtual and real storage. DB2's performance increases as you assign more memory. If you intend to have very large DB2 applications, do not be stingy with memory.

Tuning CPU Use

Tuning CPU use is a factor in reducing DB2 resource consumption and providing an efficient environment. The major factors affecting CPU cost are as follow:

- Amount and type of I/O
- Number of GETPAGE requests
- Number of columns selected in the SQL statement
- Number of predicates applied per SQL statement

The following paragraphs offer additional information about each of these factors, including suggested tuning strategies.

By reducing physical I/O requests, you decrease CPU consumption. Similarly, the use of sequential prefetch can decrease CPU cost because more data is returned per physical I/O.

TUNING STRATEGY

Encourage the use of sequential prefetch when every (or almost every) row in a table will be accessed. You can do so by coding SELECT statements without predicates, by coding SELECT statements with minimal predicates on columns that are not indexed, or sometimes, by specifying a large number in the OPTIMIZE clause (for example, OPTIMIZE FOR 1000000 ROWS). Because the OPTIMIZE FOR [] ROWS clause was meant to reduce the estimated number of rows to be retrieved (not to increase that number), this trick does not always work.

Each GETPAGE request causes the Data Manager to request a page from the Buffer Manager, which causes additional CPU use.

TUNING STRATEGY

If possible, serialize data requests in static applications so that requests for the same piece of data are not duplicated. If a program requires the same data more than once, the processes that act on that data can be enacted contiguously, requiring a single I/O instead of multiple I/Os. For example, if an employee's department number is required in three separate parts of a transaction, select the information once and save it for the other two times.

As the number of selected columns increases, DB2 must do more work to manipulate these columns, thereby using excess CPU.

TUNING STRATEGY

Code each `SELECT` statement (even ad hoc SQL) to return only columns that are absolutely needed.

As your number of predicates increases, DB2 must do more work to evaluate the predicates and ensure that the data returned satisfies the requirements of the predicates.

TUNING STRATEGY

Avoid coding redundant predicates. Use your knowledge of the application data in coding SQL. For example, if you know that employees must have an `EDLEVEL` of `14` or higher to hold the title of `MANAGER`, use this knowledge when you're writing SQL statements. The `EDLEVEL` predicate in the following query should not be coded because it is redundant, given the preceding qualification:

```
SELECT   EMPNO, LASTNAME
FROM     DSN8510.EMP
WHERE    JOB = 'MANAGER'
AND      EDLEVEL >= 14;
```

Document the removal of redundant predicates in case policy changes. For example, if managers can have an education level of `10`, the `EDLEVEL` predicate is no longer redundant and must be added to the query again. Because tracking this information can be difficult, you should avoid removing predicates that are currently redundant but that might not always be so.

Tuning I/O

I/O is probably the single most critical factor in the overall performance of your DB2 subsystem and applications. This factor is due to the physical nature of I/O: It is limited by hardware speed. The mechanical functionality of a storage device is slower and more prone to breakdown than the rapid, chip-based technologies of CPU and memory. For this reason, paying attention to the details of tuning the I/O characteristics of your environment is wise.

What is I/O? Simply stated, I/O is a transfer of data by the CPU from one medium to another. *I* stands for input, or the process of receiving data from a physical storage medium. *O* stands for output, which is the process of moving data to a physical storage device. In every case, an I/O involves moving data from one area to another.

In the strictest sense of the term, an I/O can be a movement of data from the bufferpool to a working storage area used by your program. This type, however, is a trivial I/O with a lower cost than an I/O requiring disk access, which is the type of I/O you must minimize and tune.

The best way to minimize the cost of I/O is to use very large bufferpools. This way, you can increase the possibility that any requested page is already in memory, thereby tuning I/O by sometimes eliminating it. In general, I/O decreases as the size of the bufferpools increases. This method, however, has drawbacks. Bufferpools should be backed up with real and virtual memory, but your shop might not have extra memory to give DB2. Also, DB2 basically takes whatever memory you give it and still could use more.

Even with large bufferpools, data must be read from DASD at some point to place the data in the bufferpools. Tuning I/O, therefore, is wise.

The number of all reads and writes makes up the I/O workload incurred for any single resource. The cost of I/O, therefore, is affected by the DASD device, the number of pages retrieved per I/O, and the type of write operation.

The characteristics of the DASD device that contains the data being read include the speed of the device, the number of data sets on the device, the proximity of the device to the device controller, and concurrent access to the device.

The second factor affecting I/O cost is the number of pages retrieved per I/O. As I indicated in the preceding section, sequential prefetch can increase the number of pages read per I/O. Sequential prefetch also functions as a read-ahead engine. Reads are performed in the background, before they are needed and while other useful work is being accomplished. This way, I/O wait time can be significantly reduced.

Refer to the following average response times. (Note that all times are approximate.) A single page being read by sequential prefetch can be two to four times more efficient than a single page read by synchronous I/O.

Device	*Sequential Prefetch*	*Sequential Prefetch (per page)*	*Synchronous Read*
3380	80ms	2.5ms	25ms
3390	40ms	1.5ms	10ms

The third factor in I/O cost is the type of write operation: asynchronous versus synchronous. DB2 can not only read data in the background but also write data in the background. In most cases, DB2 does not physically externalize a data modification to DASD immediately following the successful completion of the SQL DELETE, INSERT, or UPDATE statement. Instead, the modification is externalized to the log. Only when the modified page is removed from DB2's buffers is it written to DASD. This process is called an asynchronous, or deferred, write. Synchronous writes, on the other hand, are immediately written to DASD. DB2 tries to avoid them, and it should. If you ensure that sufficient buffers are available, synchronous writes can be avoided almost entirely.

Several types of I/O must be tuned. They can be categorized in the following five groups:

Application I/O
Internal I/O
Sort I/O
Log I/O
Paging I/O

In the sections that follow, you will examine each of these types of I/O.

Application I/O

Application I/O is incurred to retrieve and update application data. As DB2 applications execute, they read and modify data stored in DB2 tables. This process requires I/O.

You can apply the following strategies to tune all five types of I/O covered here, not just application I/O. They are of primary importance, however, for application I/O.

TUNING STRATEGY

Tune I/O by increasing the size of the bufferpools. With larger bufferpools, application data can remain in the bufferpool longer. When data is in the bufferpool, it can be accessed quickly by the application without issuing a physical I/O.

TUNING STRATEGY

Tune I/O speed by using the fastest disk drives available. For example, replace older 3380 devices with newer, faster 3390 devices. Most applications require multiple I/Os as they execute. For each I/O, you can save from 15ms to 40ms. The performance gains can be tremendous for applications requiring thousands (or even millions) of I/Os.

TUNING STRATEGY

(For non-SMS users only): Use proper data set placement strategies to reduce DASD contention. To do so, follow these basic rules:

- Never place a table's indexes on the same DASD device as the tablespace used for the table.
- Analyze the access pattern for each application. When tables are frequently accessed together, consider placing them on separate devices to minimize contention.
- Limit shared DASD. Putting multiple, heavily accessed data sets from different applications on the same device is unwise. Cross-application contention can occur, causing head movement, undue contention, and I/O waits. Be cautious not only of high-use DB2 tables sharing a single volume, but also of mixing DB2 tables with highly accessed VSAM, QSAM, and other data sets.
- Place the most heavily accessed tablespaces and indexes closest to the DASD controller unit. The closer a DASD device is on the string to the actual controller, the higher its priority will be. The performance gain from this placement is minimal (especially for 3390 devices), but consider this option when you must squeeze out every last bit of performance.
- Avoid having tablespace and index data sets in multiple extents. When the data set consists of more than a single extent, excess head movement can result, reducing the efficiency of I/O.
- Use the `PIECESIZE` parameter (new as of DB2 V5) to explicitly distribute non-partitioned tablespaces and indexes over multiple devices.
- Favor allocation of data sets in cylinders.

Another factor impacting the efficiency of accessing DB2 application data is partitioning. When data is partitioned, it is more likely that DB2 can utilize query parallelism to read data.

TUNING STRATEGY

Consider partitioning simple and segmented tablespaces to take advantage of DB2's parallel I/O capabilities.

Internal I/O

DB2 requires internal I/Os as it operates. Different types of data must be read and updated by DB2 as applications, utilities, and commands execute. This type of I/O occurs during the following:

- Recording utility execution information in the DB2 Directory
- Updating the DB2 Catalog as a result of DCL, DDL, or utility executions
- Reading the DB2 Catalog and DB2 Directory when certain DB2 commands (for example, `-DISPLAY DATABASE`) are issued
- Retrieving skeleton cursor tables, skeleton plan tables, and DBDs from the DB2 Directory to enable programs to execute
- Retrieving data from the DB2 Catalog during `BIND`, `REBIND`, and dynamic SQL use
- Miscellaneous DB2 Catalog I/O for plans marked as `VALIDATE(RUN)` and for other runtime needs
- Reading the Resource Limit Specification Table

TUNING STRATEGY

Limit activities that incur internal I/O during heavy DB2 application activity. This way, you can reduce the possibility of application timeouts due to the unavailability of internal DB2 resources resulting from contention.

TUNING STRATEGY

To enhance the performance of I/O to the DB2 Catalog, consider placing the DB2 Catalog in a solid-state device that uses memory chips rather than mechanical DASD. Although solid-state devices are often expensive, they can reduce I/O cost significantly. A power outage, however, can cause the DB2 Catalog to be unavailable or damaged. For many shops, this risk might be too great to take. You can find additional tuning strategies for the DB2 Catalog and DB2 Directory in Chapter 21.

Sort I/O

Sorting can cause an I/O burden on the DB2 subsystem. To sort very large sets of rows, DB2 sometimes uses physical work files in the `DSNDB07` database to store intermediate sort results. `DSNDB07` consists of tablespaces stored on DASD. The use of disk-based work files for sorting can dramatically affect performance.

TUNING STRATEGY

Consider placing DSNDB07 on a solid-state device when applications in your DB2 subsystem require large sorts of many rows or the sorting of a moderate number of very large rows.

TUNING STRATEGY

As I mentioned, you can reduce sort I/Os by increasing the size of bufferpools not used for DB2 objects. Additional memory, as much as 10 percent of each bufferpool, is allocated to the sort pool. This additional memory allocation increases the RDS sort pool and reduces the possibility of I/Os to DSNDB07.

TUNING STRATEGY

Tune DSNDB07 because you will probably use it eventually. Be sure that multiple tablespaces are defined for DSNDB07 and that they are placed on separate DASD devices. Furthermore, ensure that the underlying VSAM data sets for the DSNDB07 tablespaces are not extents.

TUNING STRATEGY

If the cost of sorting is causing a bottleneck at your shop, ensure that you are using the following sorting enhancements:

- The microcode sort feature can improve the cost of sorting by as much as 50 percent. Microcode is very efficient software embedded in the architecture of the operating system. The microcode sort can be used only by DB2 V2.3 and higher and only when DB2 is run on one of the following CPU models: ES/9000 Model 190 and above, ES/3090-9000T, and ES/3090 Models 180J, 200J, 280J, and above.
- Provide for unlimited logical work files based on the size of the bufferpool. This capability can significantly reduce I/O because more sort data can be contained in memory rather than written out to DSNDB07. *Note:* Before DB2 V2.3, only 255 logical work files could be specified.
- Each logical work file page can contain 255 rows rather than DB2's standard 127 rows per page. Because many sorts are on only a few columns, more rows can now fit on a page, reducing buffer use and requiring fewer I/Os to DSNDB07.

Log I/O

Log I/O occurs when changes are made to DB2 data. Log records are written to DB2's active log data sets for each row that is updated, deleted, or inserted. Every modification (with the exception of `REORG LOG NO` and `LOAD LOG NO`) is logged by DB2 to enable data recovery. In addition, when you run the `RECOVER` utility to restore or recover DB2 tablespaces, an active log data set (and sometimes multiple archive log data sets) must be read.

For these reasons, optimal placement of DB2 log data sets on DASD is critical.

TUNING STRATEGY

Place log data sets on 3390 DASD volumes with the DASD fast write feature. DASD fast write is a caching technique that significantly enhances the speed of I/O for DB2 log data sets.

The two types of DB2 log data sets are active logs and archive logs. As the active log data sets are filled, DB2 invokes a process called *log offloading* to move information from the active logs to the archive logs. Log offloading can have a severe impact on the throughput of a DB2 subsystem.

TUNING STRATEGY

Never place more than one active log data set on the same DASD volume. Otherwise, the overall performance of DB2 will be impaired significantly during the log offloading process.

Optimal utilization of tapes and tape drives is critical for an efficient DB2 log offloading process. Recall from Chapter 16, "Locking DB2 Data," that log offloading is the process of writing entries from the active log to the archive log.

NOTE

Consider making the active log the same size as a full cartridge. When the log is offloaded, it will utilize a full cartridge, resulting in fewer wasted tapes.

Paging I/O

Paging I/Os occur when memory is overutilized and pages of storage are relocated temporarily to DASD. When needed, they will be read from DASD back into main storage. This process causes very high overhead.

TUNING STRATEGY

Avoid paging by fencing the DB2 address spaces as suggested in the section titled "Tuning Memory Use" at the beginning of this chapter.

TUNING STRATEGY

Increase the amount of real and virtual storage for your CPU. When you increase the amount of memory, paging is less frequent.

In addition to the tuning of I/O at the data set level, you must monitor and tune I/O at the DASD device level. The overall performance of I/O depends on the efficiency of each DASD volume to which DB2 data sets have been allocated.

TUNING STRATEGY

Consistently monitor each DASD volume to ensure that contention is minimal. You can do so with a third-party tool designed to report on the usage characteristics of DASD devices. In general, if device contention for any DASD volume is greater than 30 percent, an I/O problem exists. Each shop should analyze its DASD usage patterns, reducing contention as much as possible given the shop's budgetary constraints. When contention is high, however, consider moving some data sets on the device to other, less active volumes.

Some DASD devices offer hardware caching as an option for all data sets stored on the device. In these cases, the actual disk drive can be used to cache data reads. These features are not usually effective for reading DB2 data.

TUNING STRATEGY

Avoid caching for DASD volumes containing DB2 application tablespace and index data sets. The benefits of caching are greatly reduced for most DB2 application processing because of the efficient, asynchronous manner in which DB2 can read data (using sequential prefetch) and write data (using deferred write).

Tuning Various MVS Parameters and Options

Because MVS is a complex operating system, it can be difficult to comprehend. In this section, I discuss—in easy-to-understand language—some environmental tuning options for MVS.

The MVS environment is driven by the Systems Resource Manager (SRM). The SRM functions are based on parameters coded by systems programmers in the `SYS1.PARMLIB` library. Three members of this data set are responsible for defining most performance-oriented parameters for MVS: `OPT`, `IPS`, and `ICS`. You can tune the items discussed in this chapter by modifying these members. However, I do not discuss how to set these parameters in this book.

You should not take this type of tuning lightly. MVS tuning is complex, and a change made to benefit DB2 might affect another MVS subsystem. All DB2 personnel in your shop (including management, database administration, and DB2, IMS, CICS, and MVS systems programming) should discuss these types of tuning options before implementing them. Only a trained systems programmer should make these types of changes.

The first item to consider is whether a job is swappable. A *swappable* job can be temporarily swapped out of the system by MVS. When a job is swapped out, it is not processed. It therefore is not using CPU, cannot request I/O, and generally is dormant until it is swapped back into the system. Almost all of your jobs should be swappable so that MVS can perform as it was designed—maximizing the number of jobs that can be processed concurrently with a minimum of resources.

Because the DB2 address spaces, however, are non-swappable, DB2 itself is never swapped out. Therefore, a DB2 application program requesting DB2 functions never has to wait for DB2 because it has been swapped out. The following list outlines which components of your overall environment can be swappable:

DB2	Non-swappable
CICS	Swappable or non-swappable
IMS	Non-swappable
TSO	Swappable
QMF	Swappable
Application	Swappable

TUNING STRATEGY

When a CICS subsystem is being used to access DB2, it should be defined as non-swappable to decrease the response time (and thereby increase the performance) of the DB2/CICS transactions.

Usually, an application address space is swapped out so that MVS can maintain even control over the processing environment. MVS might determine that a job should be swapped out for the following reasons:

- Too many jobs are running concurrently for all of them to be swapped in simultaneously. The maximum number of address spaces that can be simultaneously swapped in is controlled by the SRM based on parameters and the workload.
- Another job needs to execute.
- A shortage of memory.
- Terminal wait. A TSO user might be staring at the screen, thinking about what to do next. Online TSO application programs do not need to be swapped in until the user takes another action.

The *dispatching priority* of an address space is a means of controlling the rate at which the address space can consume resources. A higher dispatching priority for an address space translates into faster performance because resources are more readily available to jobs with higher dispatching priorities. Controlling the dispatching priorities of jobs is an important tuning technique.

Normally, SRM controls the dispatching priority. Systems programmers assign the dispatching priority of different address spaces. To ensure optimal DB2 performance, arrange the dispatching priorities of your DB2-related address spaces as shown in Figure 20.3. Batch application address spaces are generally dispatched below TSO (Long). Some critical batch jobs could be dispatched higher than TSO (Long).

FIGURE 20.3.
Dispatching priority hierarchy.

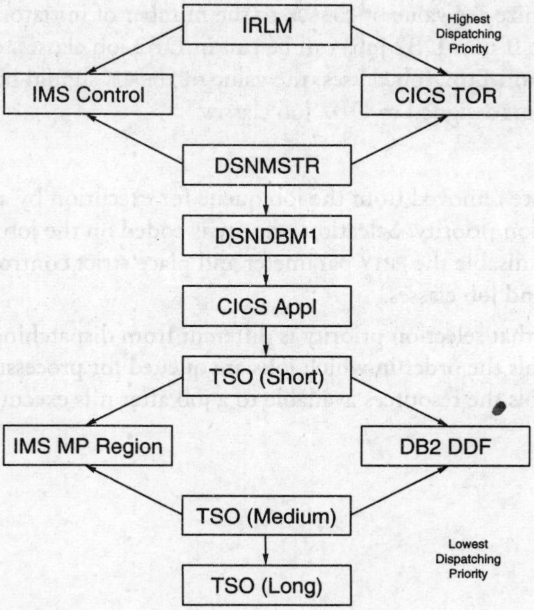

TUNING STRATEGY

Increasing the dispatching priority of batch DB2 application jobs that are critical or long-running increases their performance. However, this increase is at the expense of other jobs running with lower dispatching priorities. Tinkering with the dispatching priorities of application jobs is not a good practice unless it is an emergency. The dispatching priority of an address space can be changed on the fly, but only by authorized personnel.

When you're planning for a high amount of batch activity, ensure that an adequate number of *initiators* is available for the batch jobs. Initiators are essentially servers, under the control of JES, that process jobs as they are queued. In determining whether initiators are available, take the following into account:

- An initiator is assigned to a job class or classes, specified on the job card of your batch JCL. If an initiator is not assigned to the job class that your DB2 jobs will be using, that initiator will not be used.
- The number of initiators available for DB2 job classes dictates the number of DB2 batch jobs that can run concurrently from an MVS perspective. The `IDBACK DSNZPARM` parameter determines the number of background DB2 jobs that can be run concurrently from a DB2 perspective.

TUNING STRATEGY

Synchronize the value of `IDBACK` to the number of initiators for the DB2 job classes at your site. If non-DB2 jobs can be run in DB2 job classes, or if the initiator is available also for non-DB2 job classes, the value of `IDBACK` should be less than the total number of initiators assigned to DB2 job classes.

- Jobs are removed from the job queue for execution by an initiator in order of their selection priority. Selection priority is coded on the job card of your JCL (`PRTY`). Most shops disable the `PRTY` parameter and place strict controls on the selection priority of jobs and job classes.

  Note that selection priority is different from dispatching priority. *Selection priority* controls the order in which jobs are queued for processing. *Dispatching priority* controls the resources available to a job after it is executing.

TUNING STRATEGY

Where initiators are at a premium (for example, fewer initiators than concurrent jobs), ensure that the DB2 jobs with the highest priority are assigned a higher selection priority than other DB2 jobs. This way, you can ensure that DB2 jobs are processed in order from most critical to least critical by the system.

MVS tuning is an important facet of DB2 tuning. After the MVS environment has been tuned properly, it should operate smoothly with little intervention (from DB2's perspective). Getting to the optimal MVS environment, however, can be an arduous task.

Tuning MVS is only one component of DB2 environment tuning. Tuning the teleprocessing environment, discussed next, is vital in achieving proper online performance.

Tuning the Teleprocessing Environment

Tuning your teleprocessing environment is essential to ensure that your online transactions are running in an optimal fashion. DB2 can use any of the three teleprocessors supplied by IBM: CICS, IMS/TM (IMS/DC), and TSO. The tuning advice is different for each.

In this section, I do not provide in-depth tuning advice for your teleprocessing environments. An entire book could be devoted to the tuning of CICS, IMS/TM, and TSO. Your shop should ensure that the requisite level of tuning expertise is available. However, you should keep several basic online tuning strategies in mind. The following guidelines are applicable for each teleprocessing environment supported by DB2.

Limit Time on the Transaction Queue

Tune to limit the time that transactions spend on the input queue and the output queue. This way, you can decrease overhead and increase response time.

Design Online Programs for Performance

Ensure that all the program design techniques presented in Chapter 11, "The Doors to DB2," are utilized.

Store Frequently Used Data in Memory

Place into memory as many heavily used resources as possible. For example, consider using MVS/ESA data spaces for CICS tables.

Make Critical Programs Resident

Consider making programs for heavily accessed transactions resident to reduce the I/O associated with loading the program. A resident program remains in memory after the first execution, thereby eliminating the overhead of loading it each time it is accessed.

Buffer All Non-DB2 Data Sets

Ensure that all access to non-DB2 data sets (such as VSAM or IMS) is buffered properly using the techniques available for the teleprocessing environment.

Summary

In this chapter, you learned many techniques for tuning the DB2 environment to optimize performance. There are many different components that impact the overall DB2 environment and must be tuned. You examined how to tune MVS features, including memory, CPU, I/O, and system parameters. Additionally, the allied agents that access DB2 must be tuned as well.

Now that you understand how to tune the DB2 environment, move on to the next chapter where you will explore the many facets of tuning the DB2 subsystem itself.

21

Tuning DB2's Components

After ensuring that the MVS and teleprocessing environments are tuned properly, you can turn your attention to tuning elements integral to DB2. This chapter discusses the three main DB2 components that can be tuned: the DB2 subsystem, the database design, and the application code.

Tuning the DB2 Subsystem

Another level of DB2 tuning is the DB2 subsystem level. This type of tuning is generally performed by a DB2 systems programmer or database administrator. Several techniques can be used to tune DB2 itself. These techniques can be broken down into three basic categories:

- DB2 Catalog tuning techniques
- Tuning DB2 system parameters
- Tuning the IRLM

Each of these tuning methods is covered in the following sections.

Tuning the DB2 Catalog

One of the major factors influencing overall DB2 subsystem performance is the physical condition of the DB2 Catalog and DB2 Directory tablespaces. These tablespaces are not like regular DB2 tablespaces. Prior to DB2 V4, you could not REORG the DB2 Catalog and DB2 Directory tablespaces.

TUNING STRATEGY

Ensure that the DB2 Catalog data sets are not in multiple extents. When a data set spans more than one extent, overhead accrues due to the additional I/O needed to move from extent to extent. To increase the size of DB2 Catalog data sets, you must invoke a DB2 Catalog recovery. This procedure is documented in Chapter 6 of the *DB2 Administration Guide.*

Version 4

Institute procedures to analyze the organization of the DB2 Catalog and DB2 Directory tablespaces and indexes. Beginning with DB2 V4, you can reorganize inefficient objects in the DB2 Catalog and DB2 Directory. In-depth information on reorganizing the DB2 Catalog is provided in Chapter 26, "Data Organization Utilities."

Regardless of the release of DB2 you are running, it is possible to issue the RECOVER INDEX utility on the DB2 Catalog indexes, thereby reorganizing them. Periodically recover these indexes when DB2 use grows. Refer to Appendix B, "The DB2 Catalog Tables," for a listing of the DB2 Catalog tables and indexes.

DB2 does not make use of indexes when it accesses the DB2 Catalog for internal use. For example, binding, DDL execution, and authorization checking do not use DB2 indexes. These indexes are used only by users issuing queries against DB2 Catalog tables. Whether these indexes are used or not is based on the optimization of the DB2 Catalog queries and whether the DB2 optimizer deems that they are beneficial. Instead, DB2 traverses pointers, or links, maintained in the DB2 Catalog. These pointers make internal access to the DB2 Catalog very efficient.

TUNING STRATEGY

Execute RUNSTATS on the DB2 Catalog tablespaces and indexes. Without current statistics, DB2 cannot optimize DB2 Catalog queries. Additionally, RUNSTATS provides statistics enabling DBAs to determine when to reorganize the DB2 Catalog tablespaces.

Although it is difficult to directly influence the efficiency of internal access to the DB2 Catalog and DB2 Directory, certain measures can be taken to eliminate obstructions to performance. For instance, follow proper data set placement procedures to reduce DASD head contention.

TUNING STRATEGY

Do not place other data sets on the volumes occupied by the DB2 Catalog and DB2 Directory data sets. Place the DB2 Catalog data sets on different volumes than the DB2 Directory data sets. Place DB2 Catalog tablespaces on different volumes than the indexes on the DB2 Catalog.

TUNING STRATEGY

If you have additional DASD, consider separating the DB2 Catalog tablespaces by function, on distinct volumes.

On volume #1, place SYSPLAN, which is the tablespace used by application programs for binding plans.

On volume #2, place SYSPKAGE, which is the tablespace used by application programs for binding packages. Keep these tablespaces on separate volumes. Because plans can be composed of multiple packages, DB2 may read from SYSPKAGE and write to SYSPLAN when binding plans. Failure to separate these two tablespaces can result in head contention.

On volume #3, place SYSCOPY, which is the tablespace used by utilities. This enhances the performance of DB2 utilities.

On volume #4, place the remaining DB2 Catalog tablespaces: SYSDDF, SYSDBASE, SYSDBAUT, SYSGPAUT, SYSGROUP, SYSSTATS, SYSSTR, SYSUSER, and SYSVIEWS. These tablespaces can usually coexist safely on a single volume because they are rarely accessed in a way that causes head contention.

The DB2 Catalog is central to most facets of DB2 processing. It records the existence of every object used by DB2. As such, it is often queried by DBAs, programmers, and ad hoc users. Large queries against the DB2 Catalog can cause performance degradation.

TUNING STRATEGY

Consider isolating the DB2 Catalog tablespaces and indexes in a single bufferpool. This bufferpool must be BP0. To isolate the system catalog objects in BP0, ensure that all other objects are created in other bufferpools (BP1 through BP49, BP32K through BP32K9).

TUNING STRATEGY

Version 4

Consider monitoring the SQL access to DB2 Catalog tables and creating additional Type 2 indexes on tables that are heavily accessed by non-indexed columns. The ability to add indexes to DB2 Catalog tables was introduced with DB2 V4. Additionally, consider converting existing DB2 Catalog indexes from Type 1 to Type 2.

Additionally, many DB2 add-on tools access the DB2 Catalog as they execute, which can result in a bottleneck. Because the DB2 Catalog provides a centralized repository of information on all objects defined to DB2, it is natural for programmers, analysts, and managers to request access to the DB2 Catalog tables for queries. This can cause contention and reduce performance.

TUNING STRATEGY

Consider making a shadow copy of the DB2 Catalog for programmer queries and use by vendor tools. This reduces DB2 Catalog contention. If most external access to the DB2 Catalog is redirected to a shadow copy, internal access is much quicker. The shadow DB2 Catalog tables should never be allowed to get too outdated. Consider updating them weekly.

To implement this strategy, you must plan a period of inactivity during which the DB2 Catalog can be successfully copied to the shadow tables. Consider using `ISOLATION(UR)` when unloading the DB2 Catalog rows for movement to the shadow copy. For assistance with implementing this strategy, follow the guidelines presented in Chapter 3, "Data Definition Guidelines," for denormalizing with shadow tables.

TUNING STRATEGY

If you don't use a shadow copy of the DB2 Catalog, consider limiting access to the DB2 Catalog by allowing queries only through views. You can create views so that users or applications can see only their own data. Additionally, views joining several DB2 Catalog tables can be created to ensure that DB2 Catalog tables are joined in the most efficient manner.

Finally, remember that when DB2 objects are created, DB2 must read and update several DB2 Catalog tables. This results in many locks on DB2 Catalog pages as the objects are being built. To reduce contention and the resultant timeouts and deadlocks, schedule all DDL during off-peak processing periods (for example, in the early morning after the batch cycle but before the first online use).

TUNING STRATEGY

Consider priming the DB2 Catalog with objects for each new authorization ID that will be used as a creator. This avoids what some people refer to as the "first-time effect." Whenever initial inserts are performed for an authorization ID, additional overhead is involved in updating indexes and pointers. So, for each new authorization ID, consider creating a dummy database, tablespace, table, index, synonym, view, package, and plan. As is the case with all DDL, you should do this only at an off-peak time. These objects need never be used and can be dropped or freed after actual DB2 objects have been created for the authorization ID. This is less of a concern for a test DB2 subsystem where performance is a less critical issue.

DSNZPARMs

The makeup of the DB2 environment is driven by a series of system parameters specified when DB2 is started. These system parameters are commonly referred to as DSNZPARMs, or ZPARMs for short.

The DSNZPARMs define the settings for many performance-related items. Several of the ZPARMs influence overall system performance.

NOTE

Prior to DB2 V3, bufferpool specifications were coded into the ZPARMs. As of DB2 V3, they can be set using the DB2 command ALTER BUFFERPOOL.

Traces

Traces can be started automatically based on DSNZPARM specifications. Most shops use this feature to ensure that certain DB2 trace information is always available to track performance problems. The DSNZPARM options for automatically starting traces are AUDITST, TRACSTR, SMFACCT, SMFSTAT, and MON.

TUNING STRATEGY

Ensure that every trace that is automatically started is necessary. Recall from Chapter 17, "Traditional DB2 Performance Monitoring," that traces add overhead. Stopping traces reduces overhead, thereby increasing performance.

Locking

Lock escalation thresholds are set by the following DSNZPARM options of the system parameters:

NUMLKTS	Maximum number of page locks for a single tablespace before escalating them to a tablespace lock
NUMLKUS	Maximum number of page locks held by a single user on all tablespaces before escalating all of that user's locks to a tablespace lock

TUNING STRATEGY

To increase concurrency, set the NUMLKTS and NUMLKUS thresholds high to minimize lock escalation. Otherwise, the default values are usually adequate (NUMLKTS=1000 and NUMLKUS=5000).

Version 4

Lock escalation can also be controlled on a tablespace by tablespace basis using the LOCKMAX parameter. Information on the LOCKMAX parameter can be found in Chapter 3, "Data Definition Guidelines." When specified, the LOCKMAX parameter overrides NUMLKTS.

Logging

The parameters that define DB2's logging features are also specified in the DSNZPARMs. Options can be used to affect the frequency of writing log buffers and the size of the log buffers. The DSNZPARM options that affect DB2 logging are WRTHRSH, INBUFF, and OUTBUFF.

TUNING STRATEGY

For moderate-to-large DB2 subsystems, increase the size of WRTHRSH to decrease the frequency of physical I/Os being issued to write log information to the log data sets. The default value is 20, which indicates that 20 buffers must be filled before starting to write to the logs. This number can vary from 1 to 256, but I have found that 60 balances performance against recovery. The larger this number, the more likely that DB2 data will be lost if DB2 terminates abnormally. IBM recommends WRTHRSH be set within the range of 32 to 64 (even though the default is 20).

TUNING STRATEGY

Most shops simply use the default log output buffer size of 400K. This is adequate for small shops (those with only one or two small, noncritical DB2 applications). The maximum value for OUTBUFF is 4,000K. Shops with large, critical DB2 applications should probably specify a very large OUTBUFF—up to the maximum of 4,000K if sufficient memory is available. This increases overall performance because more logging activity is performed in memory.

Timeouts

The amount of time to wait for an unavailable resource to become available before timing out is controlled by the DSNZPARM value, IRLMRWT. When one user has a lock on a DB2 resource that another user needs, DB2 waits for the time specified by IRLMRWT and then issues a -911 or -913 SQLCODE.

TUNING STRATEGY

IRLMRWT controls the amount of time to wait before timing out both foreground and background tasks. Therefore, you must balance a reasonable amount of time for a batch job to wait versus a reasonable amount of time for an online transaction to wait. If this value is too high, transactions wait too long for unavailable resources before timing out. If this value is too low, batch jobs abend with timeouts more frequently. The default value of 60 seconds is a good compromise.

TUNING STRATEGY

Sometimes it is impossible to find a compromise value for IRLMRWT. Online transactions wait too long to time out, or batch jobs time out too frequently. If this is the case, consider starting DB2 in the morning for online activity with a modest IRLMRWT value (45 or 60 seconds) and starting it again in the evening for batch jobs with a larger IRLMRWT value (90 to 120 seconds). In this scenario, DB2 must go down and come back up during the day. (This might be impossible for shops running 24 hours a day, 7 days a week.)

Additionally, the UTIMOUT parameter can be used to indicate the number of resource timeout cycles that a utility will wait for a drain lock before timing out.

TUNING STRATEGY

The value of UTIMOUT is based on the value of IRLMRWT. If UTIMOUT is set to 6 (which is the default), a utility will wait six times as long as an SQL statement before timing out.

Active Users

The number of active users can be controlled by the DSNZPARM settings, including the following:

CTHREAD	Controls the absolute number of maximum DB2 threads that can be running concurrently
IDFORE	Sets the maximum number of TSO users that can be connected to DB2 simultaneously
IDBACK	Controls the number of background batch jobs accessing DB2
MAXDBAT	Specifies the maximum number of concurrent distributed threads that can be active at one time

TUNING STRATEGY

Use the CTHREAD parameter to ensure that no more than the maximum number of DB2 users planned for can access DB2 at a single time. Failure to keep this number synchronized with other DB2 resources can cause performance degradation. For example, if your bufferpools and EDM pool are tuned to be optimal for 30 users, never allow CTHREAD to exceed 30 until you have reexamined these other areas. The same is true for IDFORE to control TSO use, IDBACK to control the proliferation of batch DB2 jobs, and MAXDBAT to control distributed DB2 jobs.

EDM Pool

The size of the EDM pool is specified in the DSNZPARM value named EDMPOOL. The use of the EDM pool and its requirements are described in Chapter 20, in the section titled "Tuning Memory Use."

Drowning in a Bufferpool of Tears

The single most critical system-related factor influencing DB2 performance is the setup of sufficient bufferpools. A bufferpool acts as a cache between DB2 and the physical DASD devices on which the data resides. After data has been read, the DB2 Buffer Manager places the page into a bufferpool page stored in memory. Bufferpools, therefore, reduce the impact of I/O on the system by enabling DB2 to read and write data to memory locations synchronously, while performing time-intensive physical I/O asynchronously.

Through judicious management of the bufferpools, DB2 can keep the most recently used pages of data in memory so that they can be reused without incurring additional I/O. A page of data can remain in the bufferpool for quite some time, as long as it is being accessed frequently. Figure 21.1 shows pages of data being read into the bufferpool and reused by multiple programs before finally being written back to DASD. Processing is more efficient as physical I/Os decrease and bufferpool I/Os increase.

FIGURE 21.1.
DB2 bufferpool processing.

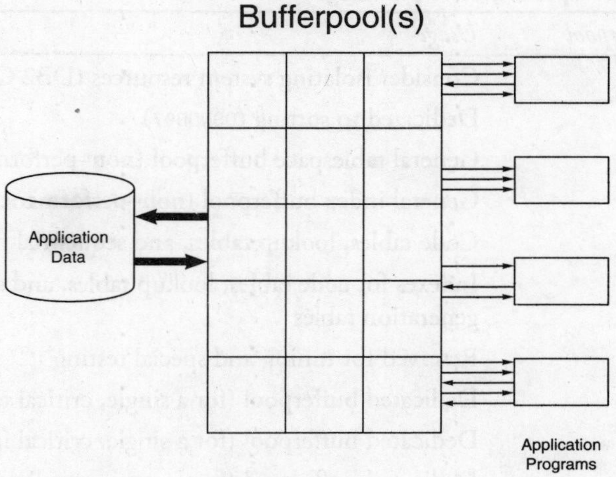

How does the bufferpool work? DB2 performs all I/O-related operations under the control of its Buffer Manager component. As pages are read, they are placed into 4K pages in the bufferpool using a hashing algorithm based on an identifier for the data set and the number of the page in the data set. When data is subsequently requested, DB2 can check the bufferpool quickly using hashing techniques. This provides efficient data retrieval. Additionally, DB2 data modification operations write to the bufferpool, which is more efficient than writing directly to DASD.

How does DB2 keep track of what data is updated in the bufferpool? This is accomplished by attaching a state to each bufferpool page: available or not available. An available buffer page meets the following two criteria:

- The page does not contain data updated by an SQL statement, which means that the page must be externalized to DASD before another page can take its place.
- The page does not contain data currently being used by a DB2 application.

An unavailable page is one that does not meet both of the criteria because it has either been updated and not yet written to DASD, or it is currently in use. When a page is available, it is said to be available for stealing. *Stealing* is the process whereby DB2 replaces the current data in a buffer page with a different page of data. (The least recently used available buffer page is stolen first.)

Prior to DB2 V3, only four bufferpools were provided to manage DB2 data. DB2 V3 and later releases provide 60 bufferpools to monitor, tune, and tweak.

Although every shop's usage of bufferpools differs, some basic ideas can be used to separate different types of processing into disparate bufferpools. Consult Table 21.1 for one possible bufferpool usage scenario. This is just one possible scenario and is not a general recommendation for bufferpool allocation.

Table 21.1. A possible bufferpool usage scenario.

Bufferpool	*Usage*
BP0	Consider isolating system resources (DB2 Catalog, RLST, and so on)
BP1	Dedicated to sorting (DSNDB07)
BP2	General tablespace bufferpool (non–performance-critical)
BP3	General index bufferpool (non–performance-critical)
BP4	Code tables, lookup tables, and sequential number generation tables
BP5	Indexes for code tables, lookup tables, and sequential number generation tables
BP6	Reserved for tuning and special testing
BP7	Dedicated bufferpool (for a single, critical tablespace)
BP8	Dedicated bufferpool (for a single, critical index)
BP9	Dedicated bufferpool (for an entire application)
BP10-BP49	Additional dedicated bufferpools (per tablespace, index, partition, application, or any combination thereof)
BP32Ks	At least one BP32K for large joins; more if 32K tablespaces are permitted

I will examine several aspects of this scenario. The first bufferpool, BP0, can be reserved for system data sets such as the DB2 Catalog, QMF control tables, and Resource Limit Specification tables. By isolating these resources into a separate bufferpool, system data pages will not contend for the same bufferpool space as application data pages.

Likewise, a single bufferpool (for example, BP1) can be set aside for sorting. If your environment requires many large sorts that use physical work files, isolating DSNDB07 (the sort work database) in its own bufferpool may be beneficial. This is accomplished by assigning all `DSNDB07` tablespaces to the targeted bufferpool (BP1).

Another technique for the allocation of bufferpools is to use separate bufferpools for indexes and tablespaces. This can be accomplished by creating tablespaces in one bufferpool (for example, BP2) and indexes in another (for example, BP3). The idea behind this strategy is to enable DB2 to maintain more frequently accessed data by type of object. For instance, if indexes are isolated in their own bufferpool, large sequential prefetch requests do not cause index pages to be flushed, because the sequential prefetch is occurring in a different bufferpool. Thus, index pages usually remain in memory longer, which increases performance for indexed access.

Tables providing specialized functions can also be isolated. This is depicted by BP4 and BP5. Because these tables are very frequently accessed, they are often the cause of I/O bottlenecks that negatively impact performance. Creating the tablespaces for these tables in a specialized bufferpool can allow the entire table to remain in memory, vastly improving online performance. Additionally, the isolation of specialized tables into their own bufferpools enables pinpoint tuning for these frequently accessed tables (and indexes). General-purpose tables (and their associated indexes) accessed by multiple programs are good candidates for this type of strategy. Following are some examples:

- Tables used to control the assignment of sequential numbers.
- Lookup tables and code tables used by multiple applications.
- Tables and indexes used to control application-based security.
- Indexes with heavy index-only access. Isolating these indexes in their own bufferpool may enable the leaf pages to remain in memory.

Regardless of the number of bufferpools that your shop intends to utilize, you should always reserve one of the 4K bufferpools for tuning and testing (BP6, in the example). By reserving a bufferpool for tuning, you can `ALTER` problem objects to use the tuning bufferpool and run performance monitor reports to isolate I/O to the problem objects. The reports can be analyzed to assist in tuning.

It is usually a wise idea to use multiple bufferpools for different types of processing. This should minimize bufferpool page contention. In the example, BP7 through BP49 are used for dedicated processing. For example, you may want to isolate one heavily accessed tablespace and/or index in its own bufferpool to ensure that no other processing will steal its buffer pages. Likewise, you may want to use a bufferpool per application—isolating all of that application's objects into its own bufferpool(s).

The DB2 bufferpools have a huge impact on performance. There are several schools of thought on how best to implement DB2 bufferpools. For example, you may want to consider using separate bufferpools to do the following:

- Separate sequential access from random access
- Separate ad hoc from production
- Isolate QMF tablespaces used for the SAVE DATA command
- Isolate tablespaces and indexes used by third-party tools

One Large Bufferpool?

The general recommendation from IBM in years past was to use only BP0, specifying one large bufferpool for all DB2 page sets. This strategy turns over to DB2 the entire control for bufferpool management. Because DB2 uses efficient buffer-handling techniques, good performance can be achieved using a single large bufferpool.

Some small DB2 systems can get by with specifying one large bufferpool, using BP0 and letting DB2 do the bufferpool management. I recommend that you begin with this strategy (unless you have experience with larger implementations or a good handle on the application access criteria) and then experiment with specialized bufferpool strategies as you optimize the performance of specific types of processing.

However, the days when most shops employed the single bufferpool strategy are over. As the amount of data stored in DB2 databases increases, specialized types of tuning are necessary to optimize data access. This usually results in the implementation of multiple bufferpools. Why else would IBM provide 60 of them?

Notes on Multiple Bufferpool Use

The following guidelines are helpful when allocating multiple bufferpools at your shop.

Ensure That Sufficient Memory Is Available

Before implementing multiple bufferpools, be sure that your environment has the memory to back up the bufferpools. The specification of large bufferpools without sufficient memory to back them up can cause paging. Paging to DASD is extremely nasty and should be avoided at all costs.

Document Bufferpool Assignments

Be sure to keep track of which DB2 objects are assigned to which bufferpool. Failure to do so can result in confusion. Of course, DB2 Catalog queries can be used for obtaining this information.

Modify Bufferpools to Reflect Processing Requirements

Defining multiple bufferpools so that they are used optimally throughout the day is difficult. For example, suppose that DSNDB07 is assigned to its own bufferpool. Because sorting activity is generally much higher during the batch window than during the day, buffers assigned to DSNDB07 can go unused during the transaction processing window.

Another example is when you assign tables used heavily in the online world to their own bufferpool. Online transaction processing usually subsides (or stops entirely) when nightly batch jobs are running. Online tables might be accessed sparingly in batch, if at all. This causes the buffers assigned for those online tables to go unused during batch processing.

Unless you are using one large BP0, it is difficult to use resources optimally during the entire processing day. Ask yourself if the performance gained by the use of multiple bufferpools offsets the potential for wasted resources. Quite often, the answer is a resounding "Yes."

As of V3, DB2 provides the capability to dynamically modify the size of bufferpools using the ALTER BUFFERPOOL command. Consider using ALTER BUFFERPOOL to change bufferpool sizes to reflect the type of processing being performed. For example, to optimize the DSNDB07 scenario mentioned previously, try the following:

- Prior to batch processing, issue the following command: `-ALTER BUFFERPOOL BP1 VPSIZE(`*max amount*`)`
- After batch processing, issue the following command: `-ALTER BUFFERPOOL BP1 VPSIZE(`*min amount*`)`

The execution of these commands can be automated so that the appropriate bufferpool allocations are automatically invoked at the appropriate time.

Bufferpool Parameters

For DB2 V2.3 and earlier releases, the only bufferpool tuning available was changing the minimum and maximum sizes of an entire bufferpool. DB2 V3 eliminated minimum and maximum sizes. For V3 and later releases only a single size can be specified for each bufferpool.

DB2 provides many bufferpool tuning options that can be set using the ALTER BUFFERPOOL command. These options are described in the following paragraphs.

The first parameter, VPSIZE, is arguably the most important. It defines the size of the individual virtual pool. The value can range from 0 to 400,000 for 4K bufferpools and from 0 to 50,000 for 32K bufferpools. The minimum size of BP0 is 56 because the DB2 Catalog tablespaces and indexes are required to use BP0. The capability to dynamically alter the size of a virtual pool enables DBAs to expand and contract virtual pool sizes without stopping DB2. Altering VPSIZE causes the virtual pool to be dynamically resized. If VPSIZE is altered to zero, DB2 issues a quiesce and when all activity is complete, the virtual pool is deleted.

The sequential steal threshold can be tuned using VPSEQT. VPSEQT is expressed as a percentage of the virtual pool size (VPSIZE). This number is the percentage of the virtual pool that can be monopolized by sequential processing, such as sequential prefetch. When this threshold is reached, sequential prefetch will be disabled. All subsequent reads will be performed one page at a time until the number of pages available drops below the specified threshold. The value of VPSEQT can range from 0 to 100, and the default is 80.

TUNING STRATEGY

If the sequential steal threshold is reached often, consider either increasing the VPSEQT percentage or increasing the size of the associated bufferpool. When sequential prefetch is disabled, performance degradation will ensue.

Additionally, the sequential steal threshold for parallel operations can be explicitly set using VPPSEQT. This parallel sequential steal threshold is expressed as a percentage of the nonparallel sequential steal threshold (VPSEQT). The value of VPPSEQT can range from 0 to 100, and the default is 50.

TUNING STRATEGY

Consider isolating data sets that are very frequently accessed sequentially into a bufferpool with VPPSEQT equal to 100. This enables the entire bufferpool to be monopolized by sequential access.

TUNING STRATEGY

By setting VPPSEQT to 0, you can ensure that parallel I/O will not be available for this virtual pool. *I am not necessarily recommending this, just pointing it out.* If you want to ensure that I/O parallelism is not used for a particular bufferpool, setting VPPSEQT to 0 will do the trick.

Version 5

The assisting parallel sequential threshold can be explicitly set using VPXPSEQT. This threshold sets the percentage of the parallel sequential threshold that is available to assist another parallel group member to process a query. The VPXPSEQT sequential threshold is expressed as a percentage of the parallel sequential steal threshold (VPPSEQT). The value of VPXPSEQT can range from 0 to 100, and the default is 0.

To understand the relationship that exists among the previously discussed four "VP" bufferpool parameters, see Figure 21.2. This diagram depicts the bufferpool specification that would be generated by the following command:

```
-ALTER BUFFERPOOL BP1 VPSIZE(2000) VPSEQT(80) VPPSEQT(50) VPXPSEQT(25)
```

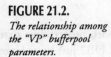

FIGURE 21.2.
The relationship among the "VP" bufferpool parameters.

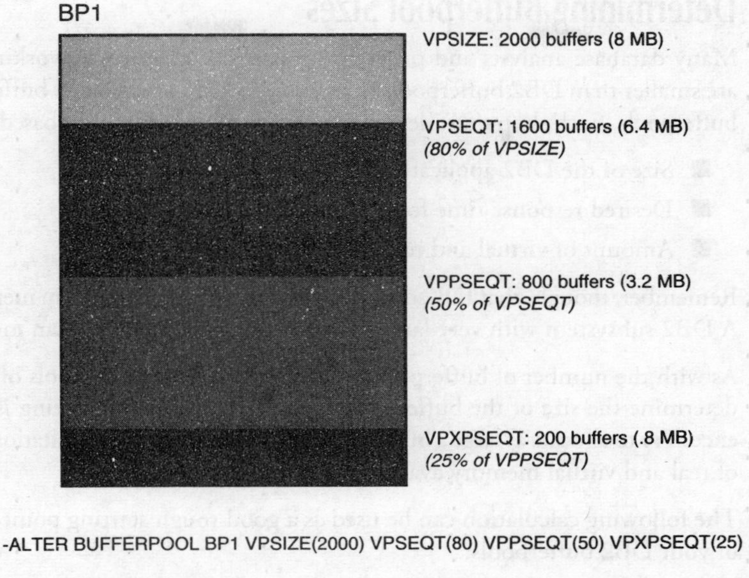

DWQT can be used to specify the deferred write threshold. This threshold is expressed as a percentage of the virtual pool size (VPSIZE). It specifies when deferred writes will begin to occur. When the percentage of unavailable pages exceeds the DWQT value, pages will be written to DASD immediately (not deferred, as normal) until the number of available pages reaches 10 percent of (DWQT×VPSIZE). The value of DWQT can range from 0 to 100, and the default is 50.

TUNING STRATEGY

Reaching the deferred write threshold does not constitute a problem; it is simply the way that DB2 operates.

Additionally, VDWQT can be used to set the deferred write threshold per data set. VDWQT is expressed as a percentage of the virtual pool size (VPSIZE). When the percentage of pages containing updated data for a single data set exceeds this threshold, immediate writes will begin to occur. The value of VDWQT can range from 0 to 90 and the default is 10. This value should *always* be less than DWQT.

The sequential steal threshold (80 percent) and the deferred write thresholds (50 and 10 percent) were automatic and unchangeable for DB2 V2.3 and earlier.

Determining Bufferpool Sizes

Many database analysts and programmers are accustomed to working with bufferpools that are smaller than DB2 bufferpools (for example, IMS and VSAM buffers). DB2 just loves large bufferpools. Each shop must determine the size of its bufferpools based on the following factors:

- Size of the DB2 applications that must be processed
- Desired response time for DB2 applications
- Amount of virtual and real storage available

Remember, though, that DB2 does not allocate bufferpool pages in memory until it needs them. A DB2 subsystem with very large bufferpools might not use them most of the time.

As with the number of bufferpools to use, there are several schools of thought on how best to determine the size of the bufferpool. I think that bufferpool sizing is more an art than a science. Try to allocate as large a bufferpool as possible within the limitations defined by the amount of real and virtual memory available.

The following calculation can be used as a good rough starting point for determining the size of your DB2 bufferpools:

```
[number of concurrent users x 80] + [(desired number of transactions per second) x
(average GETPAGEs per transaction)] + [(Total # of leaf pages for all indexes) x
.70]
```

The resulting number represents the number of 4K pages to allocate for all your bufferpools. If you are using only BP0, the entire amount can be coded for that bufferpool. If you are using multiple bufferpools, a percentage of this number must be apportioned to each bufferpool you are using.

This formula is useful for estimating a bufferpool that balances the following:

- Workload
- Throughput
- Size of the DB2 subsystem

Workload is factored in by the average `GETPAGEs` per transaction and the number of concurrent users. As workload (in terms of both number of users and amount of resources consumed) increases, so does the number of users and the average `GETPAGEs` per transaction.

Throughput is determined by the desired number of transactions per second. The bufferpool number is greater as you increase the desired number of transactions per second. Larger bufferpools are useful in helping to force more work through DB2.

The size of the DB2 subsystem is represented by the number of index leaf pages. As the number of DB2 applications grows, the number of indexes defined for them grows also, thereby increasing the number of index leaf pages as DB2 use expands.

Recommendations for determining some of these values follow. Use the value of CTHREAD to determine the number of concurrent users. If you are sure that your system rarely reaches this maximum, you can reduce your estimate for concurrent users.

To estimate the number of transactions per second, use values from service-level agreement contracts for your applications. If service-level agreements are unavailable, estimate this value based on your experience and DB2-PM accounting summary reports.

To get an idea of overall workload and processing spikes (such as month-end processing), produce accounting summary reports for peak activity periods (for example, the most active two-hour period) across several days and during at least five weeks. Then arrive at an average for total transactions processed during that period by adding the # OCCUR from the GRAND TOTAL line of each report and dividing by the total number of reports you created. This number is, roughly, the average number of transactions processed during the peak period. Divide this number by 7200 (the number of seconds in two hours) for the average number of transactions per second. Then double this number because the workload is probably not evenly distributed throughout the course of the two hours. Also, never use a number that is less than 10 transactions per second.

You can approximate the average number of GETPAGEs per transaction with the accounting summary or accounting detail reports (such as those provided by DB2-PM). Add all GETPAGEs for all transactions reported, then divide this number by the total number of transactions reported. Base this estimate on transactions only—including batch programs would cause a large overestimate. Online transactions are generally optimized to read a small amount of data, whereas batch jobs can read millions of pages.

To determine the number of leaf pages for the indexes in your DB2 subsystem, issue the following query:

```
SELECT    SUM(NLEAF)
FROM      SYSIBM.SYSINDEXES;
```

DB2 Bufferpool Guidelines

You can use the following guidelines to ensure an effective DB2 bufferpool specification at your shop.

Be Aware of Bufferpool Thresholds

Be aware of the following overall effects of the bufferpool thresholds:

Data Manager Threshold	This is referred to as a critical bufferpool. When 95 percent of a bufferpool's pages are unavailable, the Buffer Manager does a GETPAGE and a release of the page for every accessed row. This is very inefficient and should be avoided at all costs.

Immediate Write Threshold	When 97.5 percent of a bufferpool's pages are unavailable, deferred write is disabled. All writes are performed synchronously until the percentage of unavailable pages is below 97.5 percent.

TUNING STRATEGY

Increase the size of your bufferpools when these bufferpool thresholds are reached:

Data Manager threshold: 95%
Immediate Write threshold: 97.5%

It is best to avoid reaching these thresholds because they degrade performance. (The immediate write threshold degrades performance the most.)

Be Generous with Your Bufferpool Allocations

A bufferpool that is too large is always better than a bufferpool that is too small. However, do not make the bufferpool so large that it requires paging to DASD.

Monitor BP0 Carefully

The DB2 Catalog and DB2 Directory are assigned to BP0. This cannot be changed. Therefore, even if other bufferpools are used for most of your application tablespaces and indexes, pay close attention to BP0. A poorly performing DB2 Catalog or DB2 Directory can severely hamper system-wide performance.

Allocate BP32K

Specify a 32K bufferpool—even if you have no tablespaces in your system with 32K pages—to ensure that joins requiring more than 4K can operate. If BP32K is not defined, at least with a minimal number of pages, joins referencing columns that add up to 4097 or greater will fail.

The default size of BP32K is 12 pages, which is a good number to start with if you allow large joins. Some shops avoid allocating BP32K to ensure that large joins are not attempted. Avoiding BP32K allocation is also an option, depending on your shop standards. Remember, 32K-page I/O is much less efficient than 4K-page I/O.

Be Aware of the 32K Bufferpool Names

One caution regarding the bufferpool enhancements for DB2 V3: Remember that BP32 and BP32K are two different bufferpools. BP32 is one of the 50 4K bufferpools available with DB2 V3. BP32K is one of the 10 32K bufferpools. If you miss or add an erroneous *K*, you may wind up using or allocating the wrong bufferpool.

Consider Reserving a Bufferpool for Tuning

Even if you do not utilize multiple bufferpools, consider using unused bufferpools for performance monitoring and tuning. When a performance problem is identified, tablespaces or indexes suspected of causing the problem can be altered to use the tuning bufferpool. Then you can turn on traces and rerun the application causing the performance problem. When monitoring the performance of the application, I/O, GETPAGEs, and the usage characteristics of the bufferpool can be monitored separately from the other bufferpools.

Hiperpools

Hiperpools can be considered extensions to the regular bufferpools, which are also referred to as virtual pools. Working in conjunction with the virtual pools, hiperpools provide a second level of data caching. When old information is targeted to be discarded from (or, moved out of) the bufferpool, it will be moved to the hiperpool instead (if a hiperpool has been defined for that bufferpool).

Only clean pages will be moved to the hiperpool, though. Clean pages are those in which the data that was modified has already been written back to DASD. No data with pending modifications will ever reside in a hiperpool.

Each of the 60 virtual pools can optionally have a hiperpool associated with it. There is a one-to-one relationship between virtual pools and hiperpools. A virtual pool can have one and only one hiperpool associated with it, but it also can have none. A hiperpool must have one and only one virtual pool associated with it.

Hiperpools are page addressable, so before data can be accessed by an application, it must be moved from the hiperpool to the virtual pool (which is byte addressable). Hiperpools are backed by expanded storage only, whereas virtual pools are backed by central storage, expanded storage, and possibly DASD if paging occurs. Keeping this information in mind, consider using hiperpools instead of specifying extremely large virtual pools without a hiperpool.

When you specify a virtual pool without a hiperpool, you are letting MVS allocate the bufferpool storage required in both central and expanded memory.

TUNING STRATEGY

If possible, specify a virtual pool that will completely fit in central storage and a hiperpool associated with that virtual pool. The DB2 Buffer Manager will handle the movement from expanded to central storage and should be more efficient than simply implementing a single large virtual pool. Of course, you will need to monitor the system to ensure that the virtual pool is utilizing central storage in an optimally efficient manner.

To utilize hiperpools, you must be using at least MVS/ESA 4.3 on an ES/9000 Model 511 or 711 series processor (or higher model) with ADMF (Asynchronous Data Mover Facility).

CAUTION

The total of all hiperpools defined cannot exceed 8 gigabytes.

Hiperpool Parameters

The `ALTER BUFFERPOOL` command can be used to tune hiperpool options as well as virtual pool options. The hiperpool parameter options are described in the following paragraphs.

The first option, `CASTOUT`, indicates whether hiperpool pages are stealable by MVS. The value can be either `YES` or `NO`. Specifying `YES` enables MVS to discard data in the hiperpool if an expanded storage shortage is encountered. A value of `NO` prohibits MVS from discarding hiperpool data unless one of the following occurs:

- The hiperpool is deleted
- MVS hiperspace maintenance occurs
- Hiperspace storage is explicitly released

Just as `VPSIZE` controls the size of virtual pools, `HPSIZE` is used to specify the size of each individual hiperpool. When the size of a hiperpool is altered, it immediately expands or contracts as specified. The value can range from 0 to 2,097,152 for 4K bufferpools and from 0 to 262,144 for 32K bufferpools. The total of all hiperpools defined cannot exceed 8 gigabytes.

Sequential steal thresholds also can be specified for hiperpools, using the `HPSEQT` parameter. `HPSEQT` is expressed as a percentage of the hiperpool size (`HPSIZE`). It specifies the percentage of the hiperpool that can be monopolized by sequential processing, such as sequential prefetch. The value of `HPSEQT` can range from 0 to 100, and the default is 80.

TUNING STRATEGY

If you know that the majority of your sequential prefetch requests will never be accessed again, you may want to tune your hiperpools to avoid sequential data. Do this by specifying `HPSEQT=0`. This ensures that only randomly accessed data will be moved to the hiperpool.

There are no deferred write thresholds for hiperpools because only clean data is stored in the hiperpool. Therefore, pages never need to be written from the hiperpool to DASD.

Data Sharing Group Bufferpools

Version 4

If data sharing is implemented, group bufferpools are required. A group bufferpool must be defined for each bufferpool defined to each data sharing member. Data is cached from the local bufferpools to the group bufferpools during the processing of a data sharing request.

A page set is said to be GBP-dependent when two or more data sharing group members have concurrent read/write interest in it. The page set is marked as GBP-dependent during the update process and changed pages are written to the group bufferpool. GBP-dependent marking also affects DB2 Catalog and Directory page sets of the shared DB2 catalog. For GBP-dependent page sets, all changed pages are first written to the group bufferpool.

Changed data pages are written to the coupling facility at `COMMIT` for GBP-dependent page sets. This enables committed data to be immediately available to the other DB2 data sharing group members.

The following describes a few typical operations and how a page is passed among the local and group bufferpools. The following scenario is based on a data sharing environment with two member subsystems (DB2A and DB2B):

- An application in DB2A updates a column. The DB2A subsystem checks the coupling facility to determine if it should read the page from the global bufferpools or directly from disk. If DB2A determines that the page is not cached globally, it will read the page(s) from shared DASD and store the page(s) in its local bufferpool—for example, BP6.
- An application in DB2B wants to update the same page. A global lock (P-Lock, discussed in Chapter 16, "Locking DB2 Data") is taken indicating to the member that the page is shared. DB2A is notified and writes the changed data page to global bufferpool GBP6.
- DB2B retrieves the page from the global bufferpools and puts it in its own BP6.
- DB2B updates the data page and moves it back to the global bufferpool. The coupling facility invalidates the page contained in the local bufferpool for DB2A.
- If DB2A needs to re-read the data page, it will determine that the page has been marked invalid. Therefore, the page is retrieved from global bufferpool GBP6.

The GBPCACHE Parameter

Version 4

The `GBPCACHE` clause can be specified on the `CREATE` and `ALTER` statement for tablespaces and indexes. `GBPCACHE` is used to indicate how the global bufferpool is to be used for a particular tablespace or index. There are two options for `GBPCACHE`: `CHANGED` and `ALL`.

If `CHANGED` is specified, and the tablespace or index has no inter-DB2 read/write interest, the group bufferpool will not be used. When an inter-DB2 read/write interest exists, only changed pages are written to the group bufferpool.

If GBPCACHE is set to ALL, changed pages are written to the group bufferpool. Clean pages are written to the group bufferpool as they are read from the shared disk.

The Castout Process

Changed data is moved from a group bufferpool to disk by means of a castout process. The group bufferpool castout process reads the pages contained in the GBP and writes them to the owning DB2's local buffer, as well as to the physical DASD devices. This process is depicted in Figure 21.3. The castout process moves data from a group bufferpool to DASD through one of the data sharing group members. This is required because there is no direct connection from a coupling facility to DASD.

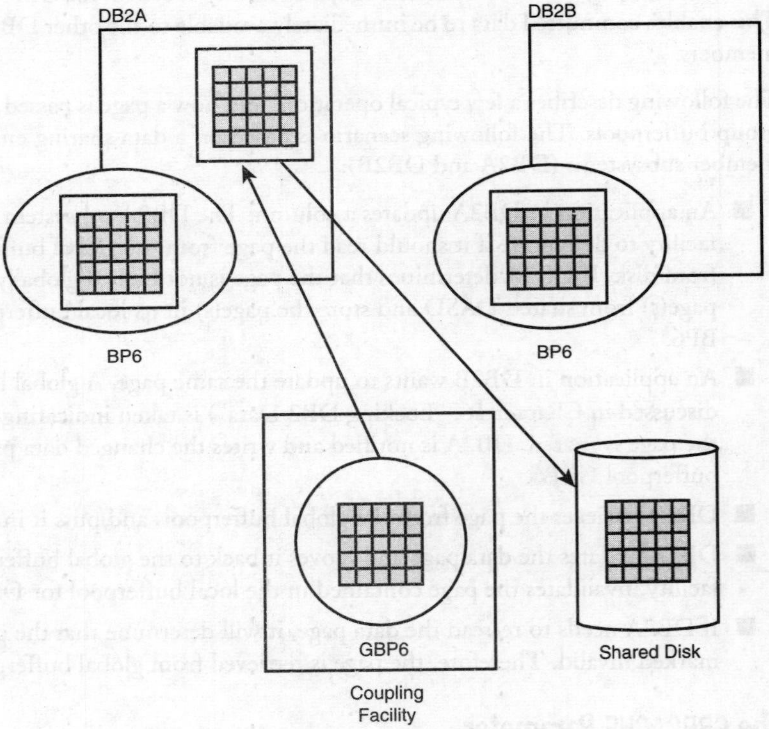

FIGURE 21.3.
The castout process.

The coupling facility is still able to update pages during the castout process. The castout process is triggered by:

- The changed page threshold for a page set is reached.
- The total changed page threshold for the group bufferpool is reached.
- The group bufferpool checkpoint is reached.

NOTE

Because the coupling facility may contain data that is more recent than what is contained on the DASD devices, DB2 employs coupling facility recovery mechanisms to recover the data in case of coupling facility failure.

Data Sharing Bufferpool Guidelines

Consider the following guidelines when specifying bufferpools for data sharing.

Select Group Bufferpool Thresholds with Care

The castout process can have a negative impact on data sharing performance. Keep castout process execution to a minimum by carefully considering the thresholds that are related to each group bufferpool. You can control the castout process by changing the two group bufferpool thresholds:

- The group bufferpool castout threshold determines the total number of changed pages that can exist in the group bufferpool before castout occurs. DB2 casts out a sufficient amount of data to ensure that the number of changed pages is below the threshold. The group bufferpool castout threshold is specified as a percentage of the total number of pages in the group bufferpool. The default value is 50, which specified castout is initiated when the group bufferpool is 50 percent full of changed pages.
- The class castout threshold also is used to control when data is cast out of a group bufferpool. DB2 internally maps modified data pages belonging to the same tablespace, index, or partition to the same castout class queues. A castout class queue is an internal mechanism used by DB2 to control the castout process for groups of page sets. When DB2 writes modified pages to the group bufferpool, it determines how many modified pages are in a particular class castout queue. When the number of modified pages for a castout class queue exceeds the threshold, DB2 casts out data pages from that queue. The castout class threshold is specified as a percentage of the total number of changed pages in the group bufferpool for a given castout class. The default for the class castout is 10, indicating that castout is initiated when 10 percent of the group bufferpool contains modified pages for the class.

Do Not Underestimate the Size of the Cache Structure

The size of the group bufferpool structure has a major influence on the frequency of castout process execution. This can negatively affect performance.

The total cache structure size affects performance similar to the way that VPSIZE affects the performance of non-group bufferpools (virtual pools). In addition, the less memory allocated to the group bufferpool, the more frequent the castout process.

The number of directory entries also affects performance. A directory entry contains control information for one page regardless of the number of places that page is cached. There is a one-to-one correspondence between cached physical data pages and directory entries. If a page is in the group bufferpool and in the virtual bufferpools of two members, there is only one directory entry for the page. Each directory entry is 208 bytes for 4K pages and 264 bytes for 32K pages. A directory entry is used by the coupling facility to determine where to send cross-invalidation signals when a page of data is changed or when that directory entry must be reused. The higher the write-to-read ratio, the more directory entries are needed.

The final impact on performance is the number of data entries. Data entries are the actual places where the data page resides. The greater the number of distinct pages that are cached, the more directory entries are needed.

Use Partitioned Tablespace

Design for parallel processing by using partitioned tablespaces for data that is accessed in a data sharing environment. This encourages the use of sysplex query parallelism. DB2 performs effective parallel processing only when data is partitioned.

IRLM Tuning Options

Until now, I have considered tuning options for the DB2 database address space and system services address space. You also can tune the IRLM address space.

When the IRLM is started, several parameters can be specified in the JCL for the IRLM. These options can have a significant effect on DB2 performance.

`DEADLOK`	Indicates when the IRLM executes a deadlock detection cycle. The IRLM must check for deadlocks frequently to avoid long waits for resources that will never be made available.
`ITRACE`	Indicates whether an IRLM trace will be started.
`PC`	Indicates where IRLM locks will be stored in memory.

TUNING STRATEGY

A good value for the `DEADLOK` parameter is 15 seconds. However, this parameter should be evenly divisible into the `IRLMRWT DSNZPARM` value to ensure synchronization between IRLM deadlock detection and DB2 timeout waits.

TUNING STRATEGY

Never issue an IRLM trace for an IRLM used by DB2. Specify `ITRACE=NO`. The IRLM trace rapidly degrades performance and does not provide much useful information.

TUNING STRATEGY

Specify PC=NO. This guarantees that cross memory services are not used for DB2 locking. Instead, locks are stored in ECSA and are directly addressable.

Tuning the Database Design

The design of DB2 objects also can be tuned for performance. If changes to DB2 tables, columns, keys, or referential constraints are required, however, the application logic usually must be changed also. Retrofitting application code after it has been coded and tested is not simple.

Several tuning opportunities do not affect application code. When multiple tablespaces are assigned to a DB2 database, locking of the DBD in the DB2 Directory occurs when DDL (ALTER, CREATE, or DROP) is issued for an object in that database. This effectively freezes all access to objects defined to that database.

TUNING STRATEGY

When a high degree of object alteration, creation, and removal occurs in a DB2 database, avoid placing critical production tables in the tablespaces in that database. If they are already in that database, consider moving them to a separate database. This does not involve any application programming changes, but DB2 utility parameters that access tablespaces (such as DBNAME.TSNAME) might need to be changed.

Also, if performance is severely degraded, consider denormalization. Several techniques for denormalizing DB2 tables are discussed in Chapter 3.

Be sure to specify proper performance-oriented parameters for all DB2 objects. For an in-depth discussion of these, refer to Chapter 3. A synopsis of these parameters is provided in Table 21.2.

Table 21.2. Coding DDL for performance.

DB2 Object	*Performance-Oriented DDL Options*
Database	Limit DDL against production databases
Tablespace	In general, use segmented tablespaces
	Partition tablespaces with very large tables
	Partition tablespaces to take advantage of parallelism
	Segment tablespaces for mass delete efficiency
	Use simple tablespaces to intermix rows from multiple tables

continues

Table 21.2. continued

DB2 Object	*Performance-Oriented DDL Options*
	Specify CLOSE YES (for DB2 V3 and greater)
	Specify CLOSE NO (for DB2 V2.2 and prior)
	Specify LOCKSIZE ANY to let DB2 handle locking
	Specify LOCKSIZE PAGE to enforce page-level locking and eliminate lock escalation
	Specify LOCKSIZE ROW to enforce row-level locking
	Specify LOCKSIZE TABLESPACE for read-only tables
	Specify free space to tune inserts and delay page splits
Table	In general, specify one table per tablespace
	Do not specify an audit parameter unless it is absolutely necessary for the application
	Avoid FIELDPROCs, EDITPROCs, and VALIDPROCs unless they are absolutely necessary for the application
	Specify WITH RESTRICT ON DROP to inadvertent drops
	Use DB2 referential integrity instead of application referential integrity
	Use check constraints instead of application logic to enforce column data values
View	Do not use one view per base table
	Use views to enforce security
	Use views to enforce join criteria
Alias	Use aliases as globally accessible synonyms
Index	Create indexes for critical SQL predicates
	Index to avoid sorts
	Specify CLOSE YES (for DB2 V3 and greater)
	Specify CLOSE NO (for DB2 V2.2 and prior)
	Use Type 2 indexes to avoid index locks
	Use Type 2 indexes because Type 1 indexes will be phased out over time
	Specify free space to tune inserts
	Cluster the most frequently used index
	Increase subpages to reduce contention (Type 1 only)
	Decrease subpages to enhance read-only processing (Type 1 only)

Tuning the Application

As was evident from the DB2 performance tuning pie, tuning the application design provides the single greatest benefit to overall DB2 performance. You can use several methods to accomplish this, each of which is covered in this section. Before proceeding, however, I will review the access paths, particularly the information about filter factors.

Analyzing Access Paths

To determine the actual "behind the scenes" operations being performed by DB2 for each SQL statement, you must analyze the access path chosen for the statement by the DB2 optimizer. An access path, as discussed in Chapter 14, "The Optimizer," is the method DB2 chooses to carry out the data manipulation requested in SQL statements. The DB2 EXPLAIN statement places information about the access paths in a PLAN_TABLE, which can be inspected by a technical analyst. You can use the information in Chapter 14 in conjunction with the access path data to create a complete picture of the operations being performed for each SQL statement.

Is DB2 on its own when making its access path determinations? The ideal answer to this question would be "Yes." It would be wonderful if DB2 always had all the information it needed, required no external input, and never chose the wrong access path. However, you do not yet live in this ideal world. DB2 sometimes chooses an inefficient access path over another, more efficient one for the following reasons:

- The statistics might be outdated if RUNSTATS was never run or not run recently. This causes the access paths to be chosen based on incorrect assumptions about the current environment.
- Certain physical parameters are not yet taken into account by the optimizer when it determines access paths. Some examples are differences between physical storage devices (the model of DASD device, or faster devices), the number of data set extents, and COBOL (or other 3GL) code.
- Concurrent processes (scheduling) are not considered by the optimizer.
- The DB2 optimizer is prone to problems associated with every application program; it is fallible. (However, given its complexity, its success rate is admirable.)

For these reasons, you may decide to artificially influence the optimizer's decision process. Techniques for accomplishing this are addressed in the next section.

Before I move on, I will survey the factors addressed by the DB2 optimizer. The optimizer will take the size of the bufferpools into account when determining access paths. As the size of the bufferpools increases, DB2 assumes that read efficiency increases also.

The optimizer also takes into account the type of CPU being used during access path selection. DB2 chooses different access techniques based on the perceived performance of the processor.

This is important to remember when modeling SQL in a test DB2 subsystem using production statistics. If the production DB2 subsystem has a different number of buffers or if it runs on a different CPU, the optimizer might choose a different access path in the production environment than it did in the test environment, even if the SQL and the DB2 Catalog statistics are identical.

To get around this, the following measures can be taken:

- When evaluating access paths for SQL statements using production statistics, be sure that the test DB2 subsystem is using the same CPU or a different CPU of the same type. This may be difficult for larger shops with several DB2 subsystems running on various machines, all configured differently.
- Specify that test DB2 bufferpools be the same as the production bufferpools to ensure that access paths do not change as a result of different bufferpool sizes. However, setting test bufferpools as high as production bufferpools can waste memory resources, and setting production bufferpools as low as test bufferpools can degrade performance.

The wisest action is simply not trying to avoid access path discrepancies between DB2 subsystems. Running DB2 subsystems with artificial constraints such as those just outlined is counterproductive to optimizing DB2 performance. Just remember that a test access path determined using production statistics does not guarantee that the production access path is identical. Besides, it is wise to continuously monitor the production access paths for all SQL statements, because they can change when plans or packages are bound or rebound.

TUNING STRATEGY

Analyze *all* production DB2 access paths. Some shops analyze only the access paths for static SQL embedded in application programs, but this is inadequate. Develop a plan for analyzing all components of DB2 programs, including the following:

- The structure of the application program to ensure that proper coding techniques are used. Also be sure that otherwise efficient-looking SQL embedded in a program loop does not occur without a proper reason.
- All SQL, whether static or dynamic, embedded in application programs. This includes SQL in online transactions, batch programs, client/server programs, report writers, 4GLs, CASE tools, and decision support systems.
- All regularly executed or critical ad hoc, dynamic SQL. This includes, but is not necessarily limited to, SQL executed by `SPUFI`, `QMF`, `DSNTIAD`, `DSNTIAUL`, or `DSNTEP2`, SQL generated by any application system on the fly, SQL generated or submitted using vendor tools, data warehouse queries, and SQL shipped from remote sites, including remote mainframes, minis, and PC workstations.
- Every SQL statement in the DB2 program must be followed by a check of the `SQLCODE` or `SQLSTATE`.

Influencing the Optimizer

There are several methods of tuning the system to change access paths or influence access path selection. This section describes several observations on changing the access paths selected by DB2.

The optimizer is one of the most intricate pieces of software on the market. It does an admirable job of optimizing SQL requests. To achieve this level of success, the optimizer contains a great deal of performance-specific expertise. For example, the optimizer estimates both elapsed times and CPU times when choosing an access path. When an SQL statement is rebound, the optimizer might choose a new access path that increases CPU time but decreases elapsed time. Most shops choose to enhance elapsed time at the expense of additional CPU use because elapsed time has a measurable effect on user productivity. In other words, it is good to trade off CPU cycles for user satisfaction, and the DB2 optimizer attempts to accomplish this.

However, the optimizer is not infallible. Sometimes the application analyst understands the nature of the data better than DB2 (at the present time). You can influence the optimizer into choosing an access path that you know is a better one but the optimizer thinks is a worse one. As the functionality and complexity of the optimizer is enhanced from release to release of DB2, the need to trick the optimizer in this way should diminish.

There are four ways to influence the optimizer's access path decisions:

- Standard, DB2-based methods
- Tweaking SQL statements
- Specifying the `OPTIMIZE FOR n ROWS` clause
- Updating DB2 Catalog statistics

The next section discusses each of these methods.

Standard Methods

Of all the methods for influencing the DB2 optimizer, standard DB2 methods are the only mandatory ones. Try all the standard methods covered in this section before attempting one of the other methods. There are several reasons for this.

The standard methods place the burden for generating optimal access paths on the shoulders of DB2, which is where it usually belongs. They also use IBM-supported techniques available for every version and release of DB2. Finally, these methods generally provide the greatest gain for the smallest effort.

There are three standard methods for tuning DB2 access paths. The first method is ensuring that accurate statistics are available using the `RUNSTATS` utility and the `BIND` or `REBIND` command. `RUNSTATS`, which is discussed in detail in Chapter 27, "Catalog Manipulation Utilities," populates the DB2 Catalog with statistics that indicate the state of your DB2 objects, including the following:

- Their organization
- The cardinality of tablespaces, tables, columns, and indexes
- The column range

All of these factors are considered by the optimizer when it chooses what it deems to be the optimal access path for a given SQL statement.

TUNING STRATEGY

Execute RUNSTATS at least once for every tablespace, table, column, and index known to your DB2 subsystem. Schedule regular RUNSTATS executions for all DB2 objects that are not read-only. This keeps the DB2 Catalog information current, enabling proper access path selection.

The second standard method for tuning DB2 access paths is ensuring that the DB2 objects are properly organized. Disorganized objects, if properly reorganized, might be chosen for an access path. An object is disorganized when data modification statements executed against the object cause data to be stored in a non-optimal fashion, such as nonclustered data or data that exists on a different page than its RID, thereby spanning more than one physical page. To organize these objects more efficiently, run the REORG utility, followed by RUNSTATS and REBIND. In-depth coverage of the REORG utility and guidelines for its use are in Chapter 26, "Data Organization Utilities."

TUNING STRATEGY

Use the DB2 Catalog queries in Chapter 19, "DB2 Object Monitoring Using the DB2 Catalog," to determine when your DB2 tablespaces and indexes need to be reorganized:

- Reorganize a tablespace when the CLUSTERRATIO of its clustering index falls below 95 percent. (Schedule this so that it does not affect system performance and availability.)
- Reorganize any index (or index partition) when LEAFDIST is greater than 200. If the value of FREEPAGE for the index is not 0, reorganize only when LEAFDIST is greater than 300. Of course, you should not blindly reorganize indexes when they reach these thresholds. You should weigh the observed performance degradation against the cost of running the index reorganization jobs before reorganizing your application's indexes.
- Reorganize all DB2 tablespaces and indexes when their data set is in more than two physical extents. Before reorganizing, ensure that space allocations have been modified to cause all data to be stored in one extent.

> You may want to reorganize more frequently than indicated here by creating scheduled REORG jobs for heavily accessed or critical DB2 tablespaces and indexes. This limits performance problems due to disorganized DB2 objects and reduces the number of reorganizations that must be manually scheduled or submitted by a DBA or performance analyst.

The third standard method for tuning DB2 access paths is to encourage parallelism. Consider changing simple and segmented tablespaces to partitioned tablespaces to encourage I/O, CPU, and Sysplex parallelism. Furthermore, it may be advantageous to repartition already partitioned tablespaces to better align ranges of values, thereby promoting better parallel access.

The fourth and final standard method for tuning DB2 access paths is ensuring that there are proper indexes by creating new indexes or dropping unnecessary and unused indexes. DB2 relies on indexes to achieve optimum performance.

Analyze the predicates in your SQL statements to determine whether there is an index that DB2 can use. Indexes can be used efficiently by DB2 if the first column of the index key is specified in an indexable predicate in the SQL statement. Refer to Chapter 2, "Data Manipulation Guidelines," for a discussion of indexable and nonindexable predicates. If no index meets these requirements, consider creating one. As you index more columns referenced in predicates, performance generally increases.

Dropping unused indexes is another critical part of application tuning. Every table INSERT and DELETE incurs I/O to every index defined for that table. Every UPDATE of indexed columns incurs I/O to every index defined for that column. If an index is not being used, drop it. This reduces the I/O incurred for data modification SQL statements, reduces RUNSTATS resource requirements, and speeds REORG and RECOVER processing.

Tweaking the SQL Statement

If you do not want to change the DB2 Catalog statistics but the standard methods outlined in the preceding section are not helpful, you might consider tweaking the offending SQL statement. *Tweaking* is the process of changing a statement in a nonintuitive fashion, without altering its functionality.

One method of tweaking SQL to influence DB2's access path selection is to code redundant predicates. Recall from Chapter 14 that when DB2 calculates the filter factor for an SQL statement, it multiplies the filter factors for all predicates connected with AND.

TUNING STRATEGY

You can lower the filter factor of a query by adding redundant predicates as follows:

Change this statement	*To this*
`SELECT LASTNAME`	`SELECT LASTNAME`
`FROM DSN8510.EMP`	`FROM DSN8510.EMP`
`WHERE WORKDEPT = :VAR`	`WHERE WORKDEPT = :VAR`
	`AND WORKDEPT = :VAR`
	`AND WORKDEPT = :VAR`

The two predicates added to the end are redundant and do not affect SQL statement functionally. However, DB2 calculates a lower filter factor, which increases the possibility that an index on the WORKDEPT column will be chosen. The lower filter factor also increases the possibility that the table will be chosen as the outer table, if the redundant predicates are used for a join.

TUNING STRATEGY

When redundant predicates are added to enhance performance, as outlined in the preceding strategy, be sure to document the reasons for the extra predicates. Failure to do so may cause a maintenance programmer to assume that the redundant predicates are an error and thus remove them.

Another option for getting a small amount of performance out of an SQL statement is to change the physical order of the predicates in your SQL code. DB2 evaluates predicates first by predicate type, then according to the order in which it encounters the predicates. The four types of SQL predicates are listed in the order that DB2 processes them:

Equality, in which a column is tested for equivalence to another column, a variable, or a literal

Ranges, in which a column is tested against a range of values (for example, greater than, less than, or BETWEEN)

IN, where a column is tested for equivalence against a list of values

Stage 2 predicates

TUNING STRATEGY

Place the most restrictive predicates at the beginning of your predicate list. For example, consider the following query:

```
SELECT   LASTNAME
FROM     DSN8510.EMP
WHERE    WORKDEPT = 'A00'
AND      SEX = 'M'
```

The first predicate has a lower filter factor than the second because there are fewer workers in department `A00` than there are males in the entire company. This does not increase performance by much, but it can shave a little off a query's processing time.

Before deciding to tweak SQL statements to achieve different access paths, remember that you are changing SQL code in a nonintuitive fashion. For each modification you make to increase performance, document the reasons in the program, the data dictionary, and the system documentation. Otherwise, the tweaked SQL could be maintained after it is no longer required, or modified when it is required for performance.

Also remember that the changes could enhance performance for one release of DB2 but result in no gain or decreased efficiency in subsequent releases. Reexamine your SQL for each new version and release of DB2.

OPTIMIZE FOR *n* ROWS

The final method of influencing access path selection is to specify `OPTIMIZE FOR n ROWS` for a cursor `SELECT` statement. This clause enables programmers to specify the estimated maximum number of rows that will be retrieved.

By indicating that a different number of rows will be returned than DB2 anticipates, you can influence access path selection. For example, consider the following statement:

```
EXEC SQL
    DECLARE OPT_CUR FOR
        SELECT   WORKDEPT, EMPNO, SALARY
        FROM     DSN8510.EMP
        WHERE    WORKDEPT IN ('A00', 'D11')
        OPTIMIZE FOR 5 ROWS
END-EXEC.
```

The number of rows to be returned has been set to 5, even though this query could return more than 5 rows. DB2 formulates an access path optimized for 5 rows. More rows can be retrieved, but performance could suffer if you greatly exceed the estimated maximum.

This type of tuning is preferable to both updating the DB2 Catalog statistics and tweaking the SQL statement. It provides more information to DB2's optimization process, thereby giving DB2 the opportunity to establish a better access path. The crucial point, though, is that DB2 is doing the optimization; no manual updates or artificial SQL constructs are required.

TUNING STRATEGY

When coding online transactions in which 25 rows (for example) are displayed on the screen, use the `OPTIMIZE FOR n ROWS` clause, setting *n* equal to 25.

TUNING STRATEGY

When using the `OPTIMIZE FOR n ROWS` clause, make *n* as accurate as possible. An accurate estimate gives DB2 the best opportunity to achieve optimum performance for the statement and also helps document the purpose of the SQL statement. Using an accurate value for *n* also positions your application to take advantage of future enhancements to the `OPTIMIZE FOR n ROWS` clause.

NOTE

When using `OPTIMIZE FOR n ROWS` to disable list prefetch, always set the value of *n* to 1. This technique works well to ensure that list prefetch will not be used.

CAUTION

Version 4

As of V4, DB2 will use the value of *n* for the block size of a distributed network request. The smaller the value of *n*, the fewer rows sent across the network for each block. The only exception is that when *n*=1, DB2 will set the block size to 16.

Changing DB2 Catalog Statistics

When the standard methods of influencing DB2's access path selection are not satisfactory, you can resort to updating the statistics in the DB2 Catalog. Only certain DB2 Catalog statistics can be modified using SQL `UPDATE`, `INSERT`, and `DELETE` statements instead of the normal method using `RUNSTATS`. This SQL modification of the DB2 Catalog can be performed only by a SYSADM.

Table 21.3 lists the DB2 Catalog statistics that affect access path selection and specifies whether they can be modified. Remember, for parallel queries, the sequential access path is generated and only then is the parallel access strategy generated. You can use this table to determine which DB2 Catalog columns can be updated by SQL statements and which are used by the optimizer during sequential and parallel access path determination.

Table 21.3. DB2 Catalog statistics used during optimization.

DB2 Catalog Table	*Column*	*Update?*	*Used by the Optimizer?*	*Description*
SYSCOLDIST	FREQUENCYF	A	Y	Percentage (×100) that the value in COLVALUE is in the column
	COLVALUE	A	Y	Nonuniform distribution column value
	STATSTIME	A	Y	Indicates the time RUNSTATS was run to generate these statistics
SYSCOLDISTSTATS	PARTITION	A	P	The partition to which this statistic applies
	FREQUENCYF	A	P	Percentage (×100) that the value in COLVALUE is in the column
	COLVALUE	A	P	Nonuniform distribution column value
	STATSTIME	A	P	Indicates the time RUNSTATS was run to generate these statistics
SYSCOLSTATS	PARTITION	■	P	The partition to which this statistic applies
	LOWKEY	Y	P	Lowest value for the column
	LOW2KEY	Y	P	Second lowest value for the column
	HIGHKEY	Y	P	Highest value for the column
	HIGH2KEY	Y	P	Second highest value for the column

continues

Table 21.3. continued

DB2 Catalog Table	*Column*	*Update?*	*Used by the Optimizer?*	*Description*
	COLCARD	Y	P	Number of distinct values for the column
	STATSTIME	Y	P	Indicates the time RUNSTATS was run to generate these statistics
SYSCOLUMNS	LOW2KEY	Y	Y	Second lowest value for the column
	HIGH2KEY	Y	Y	Second highest value for the column
	COLCARDF	Y	Y	Number of distinct values for the column
	FOREIGNKEY	Y	■	Indicates whether column contains BIT DATA
	STATSTIME	Y	Y	Indicates the time RUNSTATS was run to generate these statistics
SYSINDEXES	CLUSTERRATIO	Y	Y	Percentage of rows in clustered order
	CLUSTERED	■	■	Indicates whether the tablespace is clustered
	FIRSTKEYCARDF	Y	Y	Number of distinct values for the first column of the index key
	FULLKEYCARDF	Y	Y	Number of distinct values for the full index key
	NLEAF	Y	Y	Number of active leaf pages
	NLEVELS	Y	Y	Number of index b-tree levels

DB2 Catalog Table	Column	Update?	Used by the Optimizer?	Description
	STATSTIME	Y	Y	Indicates the time RUNSTATS was run to generate these statistics
SYSINDEXSTATS	PARTITION	A	P	The partition to which this statistic applies
	CLUSTERRATIO	Y	P	Percentage of rows in clustered order
	FIRSTKEYCARD	Y	P	Number of distinct values for the first column of the index key
	FULLKEYCARD	Y	P	Number of distinct values for the full index key
	NLEAF	Y	P	Number of active leaf pages
	NLEVELS	Y	P	Number of index b-tree levels
	STATSTIME	Y	P	Indicates the time RUNSTATS was run to generate these statistics
SYSTABLES	CARD	Y	Y	Number of rows for a table
	NPAGES	Y	Y	Number of pages used by the table
	PCTPAGES	Y	Y	Percentage of tablespace pages that contains rows for this table
	PCTROWCOMP	Y	Y	Percentage (×100) of rows compressed

continues

Table 21.3. continued

DB2 Catalog Table	Column	Update?	Used by the Optimizer?	Description
	STATSTIME	Y	Y	Indicates the time RUNSTATS was run to generate these statistics
SYSTABLESPACE	NACTIVE	Y	Y	Number of allocated tablespace pages
	STATSTIME	Y	Y	Indicates the time RUNSTATS was run to generate these statistics
SYSTABSTATS	PARTITION	■	P	The partition to which this statistic applies
	CARD	Y	P	Number of rows for the partition
	NPAGES	Y	P	Number of pages used by the partition
	PCTPAGES	Y	P	Percentage of tablespace pages that contains rows for this partition
	PCTROWCOMP	Y	P	Percentage (×100) of rows compressed
	STATSTIME	Y	P	Indicates the time RUNSTATS was run to generate these statistics

Legend:
A = Insert, Update, and Delete
■ = No
P = Used for parallel path generation only
Y = Yes

The two predominant reasons for changing DB2 Catalog statistics to influence the access path selection are to influence DB2 to use an index and to influence DB2 to change the order in which tables are joined. In each case, the tuning methods require that you "play around" with the DB2 Catalog statistics to create a lower filter factor. You should keep in mind five rules when doing so.

Rule 1: As first key cardinality (FIRSTKEYCARD or FIRSTKEYCARDF) increases, the filter factor decreases. As the filter factor decreases, DB2 is more inclined to use an index to satisfy the SQL statement.

Rule 2: As an index becomes more clustered, you increase the probability that DB2 will use it. To enhance the probability of an unclustered index being used, increase its cluster ratio (CLUSTERRATIO) to a value between 96 and 100, preferably 100.

TUNING STRATEGY

To influence DB2 to use an index, adjust the COLCARD, FIRSTKEYCARD, and FULLKEYCARD columns to an artificially high value. As cardinality increases, the filter factor decreases. As the filter factor decreases, the chance that DB2 will use an available index becomes greater. DB2 assumes that a low filter factor means that only a few rows are being returned, causing indexed access to be more efficient. Adjusting COLCARD, FIRSTKEYCARD, and FULLKEYCARD is also useful for getting DB2 to choose an unclustered index because DB2 is more reluctant to use an unclustered index with higher filter factors. You also can change the value of CLUSTERRATIO to 100 to remove DB2's reluctance to use unclustered indexes from the access path selection puzzle.

Rule 3: DB2's choice for inner and outer tables is a delicate trade-off. Because the inner table is accessed many times for each qualifying outer table row, it should be as small as possible to reduce the time needed to scan multiple rows for each outer table row. The more inner table rows, the longer the scan. But the outer table should also be as small as possible to reduce the overhead of opening and closing the internal cursor on the inner table.

It is impossible to choose the smallest table as both the inner table and the outer table. When two tables are joined, one must be chosen as the inner table, and the other must be chosen as the outer table. My experience has shown that as the size of a table grows, the DB2 optimizer favors using it as the outer table in a nested loop join. Therefore, changing the cardinality (CARD) of the table that you want as the outer table to an artificially high value can influence DB2 to choose that table as the outer table.

Rule 4: As column cardinality (COLCARD or COLCARDF) decreases, DB2 favors the use of the nested loop join over the merge scan join. Decrease COLCARD to favor the nested loop join.

Rule 5: HIGH2KEY and LOW2KEY can be altered to more accurately reflect the overall range of values stored in a column. This is particularly useful for influencing access path selection for data with a skewed distribution.

The combination of HIGH2KEY and LOW2KEY provides a range of probable values accessed for a particular column. The absolute highest and lowest values are discarded to create a more realistic range. For certain types of predicates, DB2 uses the following formula when calculating filter factor:

```
Filter factor = (Value-LOW2KEY) / (HIGH2KEY-LOW2KEY)
```

Because HIGH2KEY and LOW2KEY can affect the size of the filter factor, the range of values that they provide can significantly affect access path selection.

TUNING STRATEGY

For troublesome queries, check whether the distribution of data in the columns accessed is skewed. If you query SYSIBM.SYSCOLDIST (or SYSIBM.SYSFIELDS for DB2 V2.3), as discussed in Chapter 19, the 10 most frequently occurring values are shown for indexed columns. To be absolutely accurate, however, obtain a count for each column value, not just the top 10:

```
SELECT     COL, COUNT(*)
FROM       your.table
GROUP BY   COL
ORDER BY   COL
```

This query produces an ordered listing of column values. You can use this list to determine the distribution of values. If a few values occur much more frequently than the other values, the data is not evenly distributed. In this circumstance, consider using dynamic SQL or hard coding predicate values instead of using host variables. This enables DB2 to use the DB2 Catalog nonuniform distribution statistics when calculating filter factors.

TUNING STRATEGY

Referring to the results of the query in the preceding tuning strategy, if a few values are at the beginning or end of the report, consider changing LOW2KEY and HIGH2KEY to different values. DB2 uses LOW2KEY and HIGH2KEY when calculating filter factors. So, even though the valid domain of small integers is –32768 to +32767, the valid range for access path selection is defined by LOW2KEY and HIGH2KEY, which may set the range to +45 to +1249, for example. As the range of values decreases, the filter factor decreases because there are fewer potential values in the range of values.

TUNING STRATEGY

If neither dynamic SQL nor hard-coded predicates are practical, change HIGH2KEY to a lower value and LOW2KEY to a higher value to reduce the range of possible values, thereby lowering the filter factor. Alternatively, or additionally, you can increase COLCARD, FIRSTKEYCARD, and FULLKEYCARD.

Remember that modifying DB2 Catalog statistics is not trivial. Simply making the changes indicated in this section might be insufficient to resolve your performance problems because of DB2's knowledge of the DB2 Catalog statistics. Some statistical values have implicit relationships. When one value changes, DB2 assumes that the others have changed also. These relationships follow:

- When you change COLCARD for a column in an index, be sure to also change the FIRSTKEYCARD of any index in which the column participates as the first column of the index key, and the FULLKEYCARD of any index in which the column participates.
- Provide a value to both HIGH2KEY and LOW2KEY when you change cardinality information. When COLCARD is not –1, DB2 assumes that statistics are available. DB2 factors these high and low key values into its access path selection decision. Failure to provide both a HIGH2KEY and a LOW2KEY can result in the calculation of inaccurate filter factors and the selection of inappropriate access paths.

Before deciding to update DB2 Catalog statistics to force DB2 to choose different access paths, heed the following warnings. First, never change the DB2 Catalog statistics without documenting the following:

- Why the statistics will be modified
- How the modifications will be made and how frequently the changes must be run
- The current values for each statistic and the values they will be changed to

Be aware that when you change DB2 Catalog statistics, you are robbing from Peter to pay Paul. In other words, your changes might enhance the performance of one query at the expense of the performance of another query.

DB2 maintenance (PTFs, new releases, and new versions) might change the access path selection logic in the DB2 optimizer. As a result of applying maintenance, binding or rebinding static and dynamic SQL operations could result in different access paths, thereby invalidating your hard work. In other words, IBM might get around to correcting the problem that you solved using trickery in the logic of DB2.

Choosing the correct values for the statistics and keeping the statistics accurate can be an intimidating task. Do not undertake this endeavor lightly. Plan to spend many hours changing statistics, rebinding plans, changing statistics again, rebinding again, and so on.

The situation that caused the need to tinker with the statistics in the DB2 Catalog could change. For example, the properties of the data could vary as your application ages. Distribution, table and column cardinality, and the range of values stored could change. If the statistics are not changing because they have been artificially set outside the jurisdiction of RUNSTATS, these changes in the data cannot be considered by the DB2 optimizer, and an inefficient access path could be used indefinitely.

TUNING STRATEGY

When DB2 Catalog statistics have been changed to influence access path selection, periodically execute RUNSTATS and rebind to determine if the artificial statistics are still required. If they are, simply reissue the DB2 Catalog UPDATE statements. If not, eliminate this artificial constraint from your environment. Failure to implement this strategy eventually results in inefficient access paths in your environment (as DB2 and your applications mature).

Only a SYSADM can update the DB2 Catalog. SYSADMs have a great amount of authority, so it is generally a good idea to limit the number of SYSADMs in your shop. When the DB2 Catalog needs to be altered, an undue burden is placed on the SYSADMs.

When the DB2 Catalog has been updated using SQL, all subsequent RUNSTATS executions must be followed by a series of SQL statements to reapply the updates to the DB2 Catalog.

TUNING STRATEGY

If possible, give a single production userid SYSADM authority for modifying DB2 Catalog statistics. This userid has the following requirements:

- Should not have online TSO logon capabilities because only batch jobs need to be run using it
- Should be under the same strict controls placed on production jobs at your site
- Should be used to run only DB2 Catalog update jobs

A DBA or some other knowledgeable user can then create UPDATE statements to change the DB2 Catalog statistics as desired. A batch job running under the authid for the production SYSADM can then run the UPDATE statements in production. Because the SYSADM userid has no logon capabilities, the possibility for abuse is limited to the controls placed on the production environment (such as who can update production job streams, who can submit them, or what review process is in place).

Miscellaneous Guidelines

The following miscellaneous guidelines provide you with useful general tips for improving DB2 performance.

Limit Ordering to Avoid Scanning

The optimizer is more likely to choose an index scan when ordering is important (ORDER BY, GROUP BY, or DISTINCT) and the index is clustered by the columns to be sorted.

Maximize Buffers and Minimize Data Access

If the inner table fits in 2 percent of the bufferpool, the nested loop join is favored. Therefore, to increase the chances of nested loop joins, increase the size of the bufferpool (or decrease the size of the inner table, if possible).

Consider Deleting Nonuniform Distribution Statistics

To decrease wild fluctuations in the performance of dynamic SQL statements, consider removing the nonuniform distribution statistics (NUDS) from the DB2 Catalog. Although dynamic SQL makes the best use of these statistics, the overall performance of applications that heavily use dynamic SQL can suffer. The optimizer might choose a different access path for the same dynamic SQL statement, depending on the values supplied to the predicates. In theory, this should be the desired goal. In practice, however, the results might be unexpected.

For example, consider the following dynamic SQL statement:

```
SELECT    EMPNO, LASTNAME
FROM      DSN8510.EMP
WHERE     WORKDEPT = ?
```

The access path might change depending on the value of WORKDEPT because the optimizer calculates different filter factors for each value, based on the distribution statistics. As the number of occurrences stored in SYSIBM.SYSFIELDS increases, the filter factor decreases. This makes DB2 think that fewer rows will be returned, which increases the chance that an index will be used and affects the choice of inner and outer tables for joins.

For DB2 V2.3, these statistics are stored in the SYSIBM.SYSFIELDS table and can be removed using MODIFY STATISTICS. For DB2 V3 and later releases, these statistics are stored in the SYSIBM.SYSCOLDIST and SYSIBM.SYSCOLDISTSTATS tables and can be removed using SQL DELETE statements.

This suggested guideline does not mean that you should always delete the NUDS. My advice is quite to the contrary. When using dynamic SQL, allow DB2 the chance to use these statistics. Delete these statistics only when performance is unacceptable. (They can always be repopulated later with RUNSTATS.)

Consider Collecting More Than Just the Top Ten NUDS

Version 5

If non-uniform distribution impacts more than just the top ten most frequently occurring values, you should consider using the `FREQVAL` option of `RUNSTATS` to capture more than 10 values. Capture only as many as will prove to be useful for optimizing queries against the non-uniformly distributed data.

DB2 Referential Integrity Use

Referential integrity (RI) is the implementation of constraints between tables so that values from one table control the values in another. Recall that a referential constraint between a parent table and a dependent table is defined by a relationship between the columns of the tables. The parent table's primary key columns control the values permissible in the dependent table's foreign key columns. For example, in the sample table, `DSN8510.EMP`, the `WORKDEPT` column (the foreign key) must reference a valid department as defined in the `DSN8510.DEPT` table's `DEPTNO` column (the primary key).

DB2 provides two options for implementing RI. DB2-enforced referential integrity is specified by DDL options. All modifications, whether embedded in an application program or ad hoc, must comply to the referential constraints.

Application-enforced referential integrity is coded in an application program. Every program that can update referentially constrained tables must contain logic to enforce the referential integrity. This type of RI is not applicable to ad hoc updates.

With DB2-enforced RI, CPU use is reduced because the Data Manager component of DB2 performs DB2-enforced RI checking, whereas the RDS component of DB2 performs application-enforced RI checking. Additionally, rows accessed for RI checking when using application-enforced RI must be passed back to the application from DB2. DB2-enforced RI does not require this passing of data, further reducing CPU time.

In addition, DB2-enforced RI uses an index (if one is available) when enforcing the referential constraint. In application-enforced RI, index use is based on the SQL used by each program to enforce the constraint.

TUNING STRATEGY

DB2-enforced referential integrity is generally more efficient than application-enforced RI. When you build new applications, use DB2-enforced referential integrity and consider retrofitting older applications that require performance tuning.

TUNING STRATEGY

If no ad hoc updating is permitted, consider using application-based RI:

- If an application program can be written so that a single check is made for a row from the parent table, multiple inserts to the child table are performed.
- If the application processing needs are such that the parent table is read before inserting the child (even one child), DB2 just repeats the read process that the application must do anyway.

TUNING STRATEGY

Do not implement DB2-enforced or application-enforced RI in the following cases:

- If DB2 tables are built from another system that is already referentially intact
- If application tables are accessed as read-only

General Application Tuning

This chapter has concentrated on some of the more complex methods of tuning your DB2 applications. A wealth of less complex information about building efficient SQL is also available. For this type of general SQL coding advice, and guidelines for coding efficient, performance-oriented SQL (DCL, DDL, and DML), refer to Chapters 2 through 4.

The Causes of DB2 Performance Problems

All performance problems are caused by change. Change can take many forms, including the following:

- Physical changes to the environment, such as a new CPU, new DASD devices, or different tape drives.
- Changes to system software, such as a new release of a product (for example, QMF, CICS, or GDDM), the alteration of a product (for example, the addition of more or fewer CICS regions or an IMS SYSGEN), or a new product (for example, implementation of DFHSM). Also included is the installation of a new release or version of DB2, which can result in changes in access paths and the utilization of features new to DB2.
- Changes to the DB2 engine from maintenance releases, which can change the optimizer.

- Change in system capacity. More or fewer jobs could be executing concurrently when the performance problem occurs.
- Environment changes, such as the implementation of client/server programs or the adoption of data sharing.
- Database changes. This involves changes to any DB2 object, and ranges from adding a new column or an index to dropping and re-creating an object.
- Changes to the application development methodology, such as usage of check constraints instead of application logic or the use of stored procedures.
- Changes to application code.

Performance problems are not caused by magic. Something tangible changes, creating a performance problem in the application. The challenge of tuning is to find the source of the change, gauge its impact, and formulate a solution.

See Figure 21.4. This hierarchy shows the order of magnitude by which each type of resource can affect DB2 performance. The resource with the highest potential for affecting performance is at the top. This does not mean that the bulk of your problems will be at the highest level. Recall the performance tuning pie presented at the beginning of Part V. Although MVS packs the largest wallop in terms of its potential for degrading performance when improperly tuned, it consists of only approximately 5 percent of the tuning opportunity.

FIGURE 21.4.
The tuning hierarchy in terms of impact.

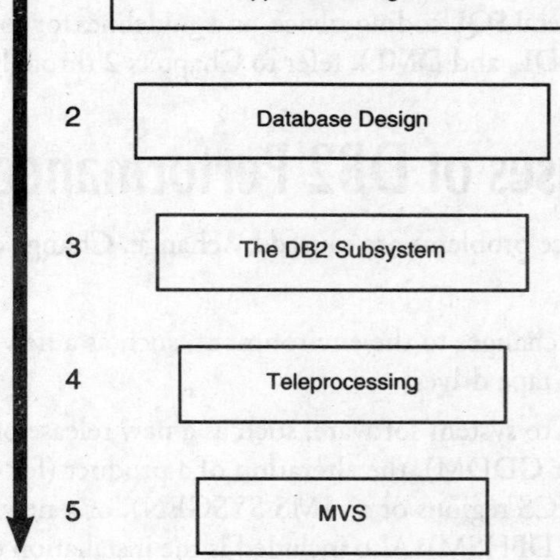

Although the majority of your problems will be application-oriented, you must explore the tuning opportunities presented in the other environments when application tuning has little effect.

The following is a quick reference of the possible tuning options for each environment.

To tune MVS:

Change the dispatching priority.
Modify swappability.
Add memory.
Upgrade CPU.
Implement data sharing.
Use an active performance monitor (enables tuning on the fly).

To tune the teleprocessing environments:

Change the system generation parameters.
Tune the program definition (PSBs and PPT entries).
Modify the Attachment Facility parameters.
Add or change table entries.
Use an active performance monitor (enables tuning on the fly).

To tune the DB2 subsystem:

Modify DSNZPARMs to increase log buffers, increase or decrease the number of concurrent users, change lock escalation, and so on.
Issue ALTER BUFFERPOOL commands to change bufferpool sizes, increase or decrease bufferpool thresholds, and modify associated hiperpools.
Tune the DB2 Catalog, including dropping and freeing objects, executing MODIFY, reorganizing DB2 Catalog tablespaces and indexes, recovering the DB2 Catalog indexes, converting DB2 Catalog indexes to Type 2, adding indexes to the DB2 Catalog, changing data set placement, moving the DB2 Catalog to a faster DASD device, and implementing data set shadowing.
Perform DSNDB07 tuning.
Use a tool to change DSNZPARMs on the fly.

To tune the DB2 database design:

Modify the logical and physical model.
Modify and issue DDL.
Execute ALTER statements.
Ensure that proper parameters are specified.
Implement table changes.
Partition simple and segmented tablespaces.
Spread non-partitioned objects over multiple devices using PIECESIZE.
Add indexes.
Use Type 2 indexes.

To tune the DB2 database design:
`REORG` tablespaces.
`REORG` or `RECOVER` indexes.
Consider or reconsider data compression.
Denormalize the database design.

To tune shared data:
Denormalize the database design.
Add redundant tables.

To tune programs:
Perform SQL tuning.
Tune the high-level language (such as COBOL or 4GL).
Use a program restructuring tool.
Run `RUNSTATS`.
Execute `EXPLAIN`, modify your code, and `REBIND`.
Use the `OPTIMIZE FOR` *n* `ROWS` clause.
Consider activating query parallelism.
Change locking strategies.
Change the DB2 Catalog statistics and `REBIND`.
Use a testing tool to provide what if testing and tuning.
Use a tool to sample the application's address space as it executes.

It is important not to confuse the issue, so I will present another tuning hierarchy. Figure 21.5 outlines the order in which DB2 problems should be investigated. Start at the top and work your way down. Only when you have tried all avenues of tuning at one level should you move to the next.

TUNING STRATEGY

Implement at your shop a standard that incorporates tuning hierarchies similar to the ones shown in Figures 21.4 and 21.5.

Document your tuning standard, stating that each component of the DB2 tuning hierarchies should be considered when DB2 performance problems are encountered. Include in the document all the tools that can be used. If possible, get managerial agreement from all areas involved to reduce the friction that can occur when diverse groups attempt to resolve a DB2 tuning problem.

FIGURE 21.5.
The tuning hierarchy in terms of cause.

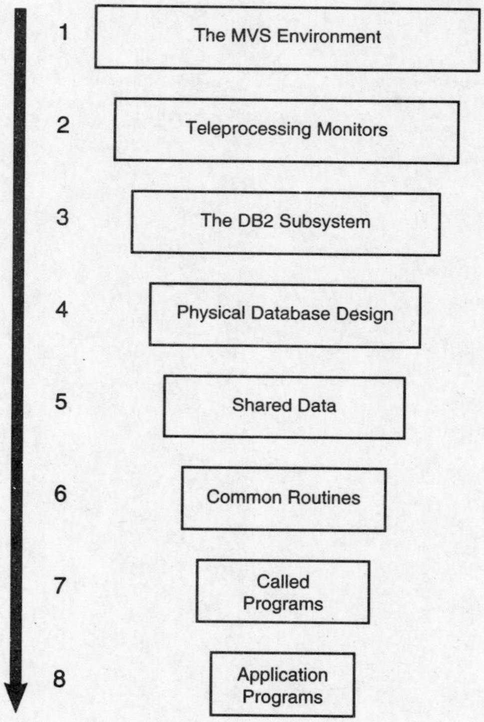

Summary

DB2 subsystem tuning is a major component of ensuring the overall efficiency of DB2 applications. You learned about the many tuning options available to tune DB2 including DSNZPARM parameters, DB2 Catalog statistics, database design issues, and SQL coding techniques. Now that you understand how to tune DB2 internals, move to the next chapter where you will learn how to implement controls to govern the execution of DB2 applications.

22

DB2 Resource Governing

In addition to performance monitoring and tuning, actively controlling certain types of SQL can be beneficial. For example, consider a critical decision support query that retrieves hundreds, thousands, or even millions of rows from DB2 tables. If the query is well-planned, the designer will have a good idea of the amount of time necessary to satisfy the request.

As time goes on, however, the performance of the query could degrade for many reasons, such as unorganized indexes and tablespaces, additional rows being returned, or outdated RUNSTATS. This degradation could affect the entire system because S-locks are being held and DB2 resources are being monopolized. It would be desirable, therefore, to disallow access on a prespecified basis when performance falls outside an acceptable range.

The Resource Limit Facility

The DB2 Resource Limit Facility (RLF) is a governor that limits specific DB2 resources that can be consumed by dynamic SQL. The RLF limits the CPU consumed by dynamic SQL issued by plan name, terminating the requests that exceed the limit and returning a -905 SQLCODE to the requesting program. The RLF also limits dynamic SQL issued by collection name. This effectively limits the dynamic SQL capabilities of all plans and packages of a collection.

Also, the RLF can control when the BIND command can be issued. The RLF establishes a means whereby particular plans, packages, or entire collections are unavailable for binding, even to those authorized to issue the BIND command. In addition to checking for BIND authority, DB2 checks the RLF specifications before allowing a bind.

The RLF is designed to govern performance based on rows in a table known as a Resource Limit Specification Table (RLST). To define the RLST, use this DDL:

```
CREATE DATABASE DSNRLST;

CREATE TABLESPACE DSNRLSxx
IN DSNRLST;

CREATE TABLE authid.DSNRLSTxx
(AUTHID         CHAR(8)    NOT NULL WITH DEFAULT,
 PLANNAME       CHAR(8)    NOT NULL WITH DEFAULT,
 ASUTIME        INTEGER,
 LUNAME         CHAR(8)    NOT NULL WITH DEFAULT,
 RLFFUNC        CHAR(1)    NOT NULL WITH DEFAULT,
 RLFBIND        CHAR(7)    NOT NULL WITH DEFAULT,
 RLFCOLLN       CHAR(18)   NOT NULL WITH DEFAULT
 RLFPKG         CHAR(8)    NOT NULL WITH DEFAULT
 )
IN DSNRLST.DNSRLSxx;

CREATE UNIQUE INDEX authid.DSNARLxx
ON authid.DSNRLSTxx
  (AUTHID, PLANNAME, LUNAME)
CLUSTER CLOSE NO;
```

Following is a definition of each column in the RLST:

AUTHID	Identifies the primary authorization ID of the user to whom the limit set by this row applies. If blank, this row applies to all primary authorization IDs at the location specified by the LUNAME column.
PLANNAME	Specifies the plan name for which the limit set by this row applies. If blank, this row applies to all plan names at the location specified by the LUNAME column. PLANNAME is valid only when RLFFUNC is blank. If RLFFUNC contains a value, the column must be blank or the entire row is ignored.
ASUTIME	Specifies the maximum number of CPU service units permitted for any single dynamic SQL statement. If NULL, this row does not apply a limit. If less than or equal to 0, this row indicates that dynamic SQL is not permitted.
LUNAME	The logical unit name of the site where the request originated. If blank, this row applies to the local site. If PUBLIC, this row applies to all sites.
RLFFUNC	Indicates the type of resource this row is limiting: *blank* = row governs dynamic SQL by plan name 1 = row governs BIND for plans or packages in collections 2 = row governs dynamic SQL by collection and package names If any other values are in this column, the row is ignored.
RLFBIND	Indicates whether the BIND command is permitted. The value[ ] indicates that BIND is not allowed; any other value means that the BIND command is allowed. Valid only when RLFFUNC equals 1.
RLFCOLLN	Specifies the name of the collection to which this RLF row applies. If blank, this row applies to all packages at the location specified by the LUNAME column. RLFCOLLN is valid only when RLFFUNC equals 2. If RLFFUNC does not equal 2, the column must be blank or the entire row is ignored.
RLFPKG	Specifies the package name for which the limit set by this row applies. If blank, this row applies to all packages at the location specified by the LUNAME column. RLFPKG is valid only when RLFFUNC equals 2. If RLFFUNC does not equal 2, the column must be blank or the entire row is ignored.

TUNING STRATEGY

Regulate the impact of dynamic SQL using the RLF. Dynamic SQL is used by SPUFI, QMF, and many vendor-supplied tools. Limit these types of tools to reduce the possibility of runaway ad hoc queries that hog system resources.

You can create multiple RLSTs, with each controlling resources in a different manner. Some reasons for doing this are as follows:

- To control the same resources in different RLSTs with different limits.
- To control different resources in different RLSTs.
- To eliminate resource control for a plan or package from a certain RLST, thereby removing the limit.
- To control one type of limiting separately from another type—for example, to control binds in one RLST, plans and packages in another, and users in another. However, this is impractical because only one RLST can be active at any given time.

The RLF is started using the `START RLIMIT` command, which is discussed in Chapter 29, "DB2 Commands." Using this command, a DBA can specify which RLST should be activated for resource limiting.

TUNING STRATEGY

Use several RLSTs to control dynamic SQL access differently during different periods. For example, consider a plan containing dynamic SQL statements that consumes 10 CPU seconds normally but consumes 20 CPU seconds during month-end processing. You can define two RLSTs—one with a limit of 10 and another with a limit of 20. The first RLST is active most of the time, but the DBA can switch the RLF to use the second RLST during month-end processing. This ensures that both normal and month-end processing are controlled adequately.

The QMF Governor

Because QMF uses dynamic SQL, the RLF can be used to govern QMF resource use. To control the usage of QMF, a row would be inserted specifying the following:

- A blank `AUTHID` (so the limit applies to all users)
- The QMF plan name in the `PLANNAME` column (for QMF V3.1, this is usually QMF310 or QMF311)
- The resource limit in `ASUTIME`

If necessary, multiple rows could be inserted with varying resource limits for different authids.

However, the QMF Governor can govern QMF use independently from DB2 and SQL use. The QMF Governor provides the capability to prompt users or to cancel threads based on excessive resource use. Resource use is either a CPU time limit or a limit based on the number of rows retrieved by a single query.

The operation of the QMF Governor is controlled by rows inserted into a QMF control table named `Q.RESOURCE_TABLE`. DDL to create this table is shown in the following SQL statement:

```
CREATE TABLE Q.RESOURCE_TABLE
(RESOURCE_GROUP       CHAR(16)   NOT NULL ,
 RESOURCE_OPTION      CHAR(16)   NOT NULL ,
 INTVAL               INTEGER,
 FLOATVAL             FLOAT,
 CHARVAL              VARCHAR(80)
)
IN DSQDBCTL.DSQTSGOV ;
```

Values inserted into the first three columns of this table control QMF resource governing. The last two columns, `FLOATVAL` and `CHARVAL`, are not used by the IBM-supplied QMF Governor.

The following list shows the values that can be supplied for the `RESOURCE_OPTION` column, indicating the types of QMF governing available:

`SCOPE` Sets the overall QMF resource governing environment. If a row has `RESOURCE_OPTION` set to `SCOPE`, and the row contains a value of 0 in the `INTVAL` column, governing is enabled. Any other value disables the QMF Governor.

`TIMEPROMPT` Sets the amount of CPU time that can be incurred before prompting users to cancel or continue. If `INTVAL` is 0, less than 0, or null, prompting does not occur.

`TIMELIMIT` Sets the amount of CPU time that can be incurred before canceling. This is an unconditional cancellation, without a prompt. The `INTVAL` specified for `TIMELIMIT` should always be greater than the corresponding `TIMEPROMPT` value. If `INTVAL` is 0, less than 0, or null, cancellation does not occur.

`TIMECHECK` Sets the amount of time that must elapse before performing CPU time checks as specified by `TIMEPROMPT` and `TIMELIMIT`. If `INTVAL` is 0, less than 0, or null, time checking does not occur, regardless of the `TIMEPROMPT` and `TIMELIMIT` settings.

`ROWPROMPT` Sets the maximum number of rows that can be retrieved before prompting the user to cancel or continue. If `INTVAL` is 0, less than 0, or null, prompting does not occur.

`ROWLIMIT` Sets the maximum number of rows that can be retrieved before canceling. This is an unconditional cancellation, without a prompt. The `INTVAL` specified for `TIMELIMIT` should always be greater than the corresponding `TIMEPROMPT` value. If `INTVAL` is 0, less than 0, or null, cancellation does not occur.

When the QMF Governor is set to prompt when reaching a particular threshold, the users are told the amount of CPU time consumed and the number of rows retrieved. This prompt looks like the following:

```
DSQUE00 QMF governor prompt:
Command has run for nnnnnn seconds of CPU times
and fetched mmmmmm rows of data.

==> To continue QMF command press the "ENTER" key.
==> To cancel QMF command type "CANCEL" then press the "ENTER" key.
==> To turn off prompting type "NOPROMPT" then press the "ENTER" key.
```

Users have the choice to continue or cancel their request. Users can request also that additional prompting be disabled. If the request is continued and prompting is not disabled, subsequent prompts are displayed as the limits are reached. Additionally, the QMF Governor might cancel a request if additional limits are met.

TUNING STRATEGY

Use the QMF Governor at least to prompt users when thresholds are bypassed. This enables users to police their own requests. At a minimum, also set a high system-wide cancellation time in case users choose the `NOPROMPT` option. You can set this with the QMF Governor or the RLF for the QMF plan.

The QMF *F* Parameter

In addition to the governor, QMF provides a feature that is a cross between resource limitation and performance tuning. You can use this feature, called the *F* parameter, or FPARM, to control the number of rows fetched before displaying a QMF report. This is useful when a large number of rows is fetched but only the first few need to be displayed.

Figure 22.1 shows how the FPARM works. Assume that the FPARM has been set to 100. When the QMF query is initiated, up to the first 100 rows are fetched. If more than 100 rows are in the answer set, the thread remains active. When the user pages down, QMF displays additional rows but does not fetch any more rows until row 101 has been requested. This process keeps repeating, in blocks of 100 rows (or however many rows *F* has been set to). If the user specifies M (for max) and presses F8 (for page down), all remaining rows are fetched, and the active thread is terminated.

Consider the following points. The thread is not terminated until all rows have been retrieved successfully or the user keys in the `RESET DATA` command. When the *F* parameter is set too low, this can cause additional overhead due to additional active plans.

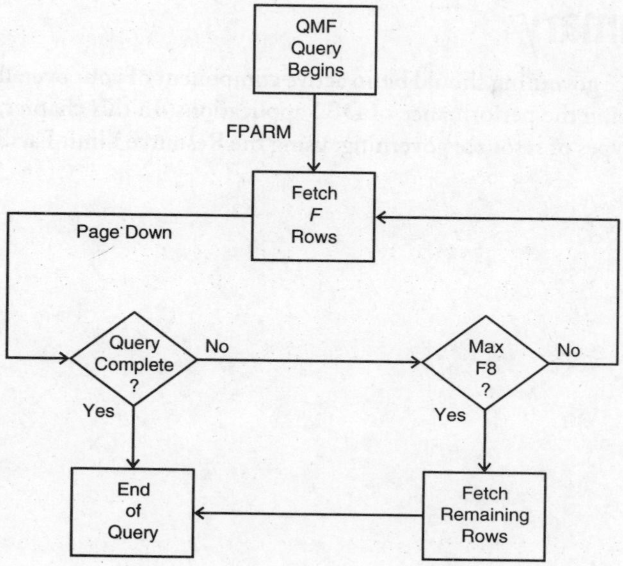

FIGURE 22.1.
The QMF F *parameter.*

Also, the FPARM has little effect on some types of queries. For example, a query with a large answer set requiring sorting consumes a significant amount of CPU time before any fetching is performed. Be sure to set the RLF or the QMF Governor to control CPU use for these types of queries.

TUNING STRATEGY

Reduce QMF I/O requirements by setting the FPARM to 50. This is approximately double the number of rows that can fit on one QMF report page online. Therefore, users can page back and forth between the first two pages of data without incurring additional I/O. Users frequently issue a QMF query, look at the first page of data, and move to the next query, without looking at every page. An FPARM of 50 optimizes the performance of these types of queries.

Depending on the profile of your QMF users and their propensity to look at multiple pages, you can adjust the FPARM accordingly. Use the following formula to calculate the FPARM:

FPARM = [number of rows per online report page * approximate number of pages viewed per user] + [number of rows per online report page]

For example, if QMF users tend to look at five pages of data, the FPARM could be set to (25 * 5) + 25, which equals 150.

Summary

Resource governing should be an active component of your overall strategy for controlling and optimizing the performance of DB2 applications. In this chapter, you learned about two different types of resource governing: using the Resource Limit Facility and the QMF Governor.

VI

DB2 Utilities and Commands

DB2 has a comprehensive collection of utility programs to help you organize and administer DB2 databases. You can use these utilities, for example, to ensure the proper physical data structure, to back up and recover application data, and to gather current statistical information about DB2 databases. A host of commands is also available to enable you to actively monitor and support the DB2 database structure and DB2 access from multiple environments.

Part VI introduces you to these utility programs and the operator commands provided with DB2. And, as you have seen throughout this book, guideline sections are included. Guidelines for each utility and command as well as general utility usage guidelines are presented. Other useful features of Part VI are the description of DB2 pending states and DB2 contingency planning guidelines.

23

An Introduction to DB2 Utilities

DB2 utility programs are divided into four broad categories:

- Online utilities
- Offline utilities
- Service aids
- Sample programs

Each of these categories is defined in Part VI. A complete description of every utility that makes up each category is also provided. Sample JCL listings are provided for each utility. The job names, data set names, space allocations, and volumes used in the JCL are only examples. The database and tablespace names are from the DB2 sample tables used throughout this book. These names should be changed to reflect the needs of your application.

The online utilities are referred to as *online* because they execute under the control of DB2. They are run using the `DSNUTILB` program, which is supplied with DB2. `DSNUTILB` uses the Call Attach facility to run as an independent batch program.

Online utilities operate using control card input. `DSNUTILB` reads the control card input and then executes the proper utility based on the input. The first word in the control card is the name of the utility to be processed, followed by the other parameters required for the utility.

In this chapter, all the sample JCL for the online utilities uses `DSNUPROC`, a generic utility procedure supplied with DB2.

Recall from Chapter 11, "The Doors to DB2," that online DB2 utilities can be controlled by DB2I option 8. The DB2I utility panels are shown in Figures 23.1 and 23.2. JCL to execute DB2 utilities can be generated by these DB2I panels.

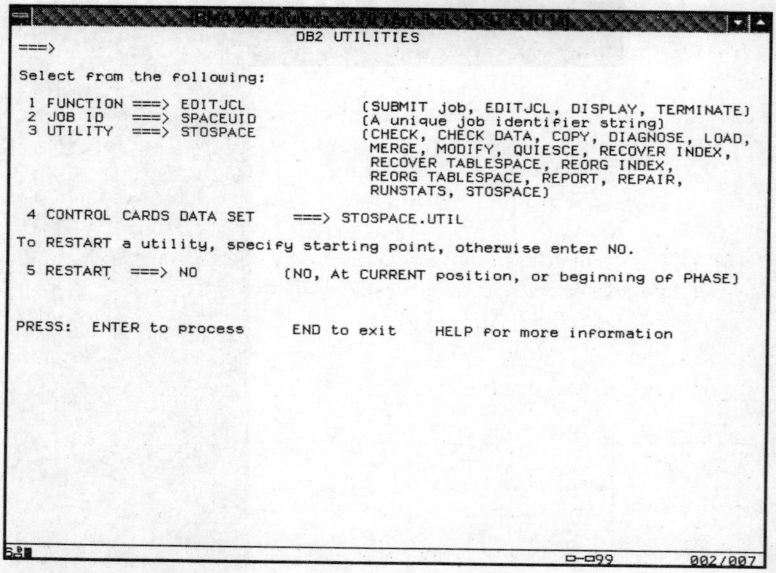

```
                              DB2 UTILITIES
===>

Select from the following:

 1 FUNCTION ===> EDITJCL              (SUBMIT job, EDITJCL, DISPLAY, TERMINATE)
 2 JOB ID   ===> SPACEUID             (A unique job identifier string)
 3 UTILITY  ===> STOSPACE             (CHECK, CHECK DATA, COPY, DIAGNOSE, LOAD,
                                       MERGE, MODIFY, QUIESCE, RECOVER INDEX,
                                       RECOVER TABLESPACE, REORG INDEX,
                                       REORG TABLESPACE, REPORT, REPAIR,
                                       RUNSTATS, STOSPACE)

 4 CONTROL CARDS DATA SET     ===> STOSPACE.UTIL

To RESTART a utility, specify starting point, otherwise enter NO.

 5 RESTART  ===> NO         (NO, At CURRENT position, or beginning of PHASE)


PRESS:  ENTER to process     END to exit     HELP for more information
```

FIGURE 23.1.
DB2I utility JCL generation panel 1.

The first panel, shown in Figure 23.1, is set to generate JCL for the STOSPACE utility. The second panel, shown in Figure 23.2, provides additional information used by certain DB2 utilities. If the first panel were set to generate JCL for the COPY, LOAD, or REORG utilities, the second panel would prompt the user to enter data set names required for those utilities.

The DB2I utility JCL generation panels provide four basic options:

SUBMIT	JCL is automatically built to execute the requested DB2 utility, and it is submitted in batch for processing.
EDITJCL	JCL is automatically built and displayed for the user. The user can edit the JCL, if desired, and then submit the JCL.
DISPLAY	The status of a utility identified by JOB ID is displayed online.
TERMINATE	A utility identified by JOB ID is terminated. This cancels a running utility or removes an inactive utility from the DB2 subsystem, thereby disabling future restartability for the utility.

FIGURE 23.2.
DB2I utility JCL generation panel 2.

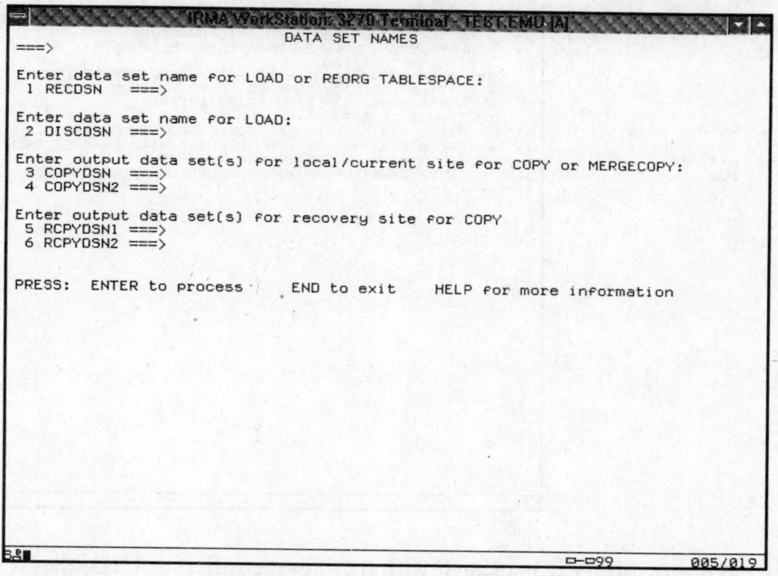

The DISPLAY and TERMINATE options are merely menu-driven implementations of the DB2 –DISPLAY and –TERMINATE commands. The SUBMIT and EDITJCL options provide automated DB2 utility JCL generation and submission. The DB2I utility program provides only rudimentary DB2 utility JCL, however. It works as follows:

1. The user specifies either SUBMIT or EDITJCL and a JOB ID that uniquely identifies a utility.

2. The user specifies one of the supported utilities (refer to Figure 23.1).
3. The user then specifies on the panel the data set containing the utility control cards to be used. The data set must be preallocated.
4. As directed by the panel, the user supplies additional data set names, depending on the selected utility.
5. JCL is generated for the requested utility.

The DB2I utility generator displays the output messages shown in Figure 23.3 when Enter is pressed and the request is processed.

The JCL generated by DB2I for the `STOSPACE` utility is shown in Figure 23.4. Generating JCL for a utility each time it is required, however, can be cumbersome. Many users create a partitioned data set containing sample utility JCL that they can modify as needed. The examples in Part VI can be used as templates for the creation of DB2 utility JCL for use in your shop.

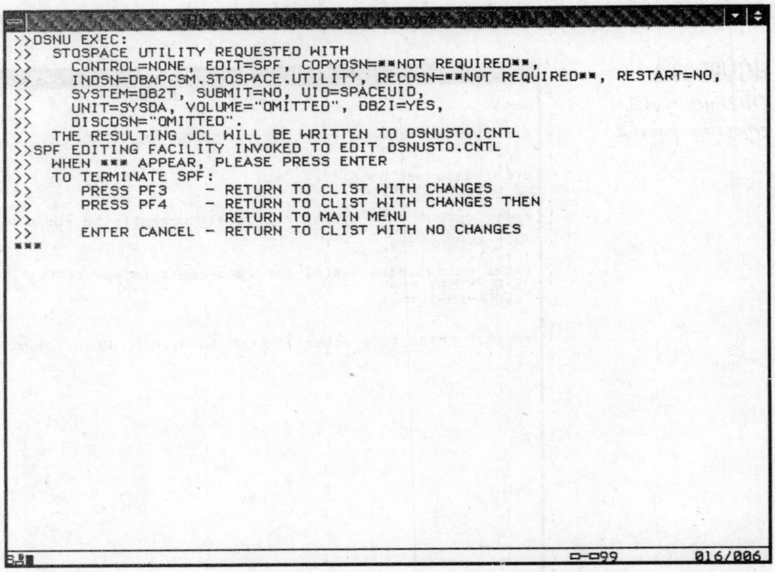
>>DSNU EXEC:
>> STOSPACE UTILITY REQUESTED WITH
>> CONTROL=NONE, EDIT=SPF, COPYDSN=**NOT REQUIRED**,
>> INDSN=DBAPCSM.STOSPACE.UTILITY, RECDSN=**NOT REQUIRED**, RESTART=NO,
>> SYSTEM=DB2T, SUBMIT=NO, UID=SPACEUID,
>> UNIT=SYSDA, VOLUME="OMITTED", DB2I=YES,
>> DISCDSN="OMITTED".
>> THE RESULTING JCL WILL BE WRITTEN TO DSNUSTO.CNTL
>>SPF EDITING FACILITY INVOKED TO EDIT DSNUSTO.CNTL
>> WHEN *** APPEAR, PLEASE PRESS ENTER
>> TO TERMINATE SPF:
>> PRESS PF3 - RETURN TO CLIST WITH CHANGES
>> PRESS PF4 - RETURN TO CLIST WITH CHANGES THEN
>> RETURN TO MAIN MENU
>> ENTER CANCEL - RETURN TO CLIST WITH NO CHANGES
***
016/006

FIGURE 23.3.
DB2I JCL generation output messages.

Each online utility is associated with a utility identifier, or UID, that is passed to `DSNUTILB` as a parameter to uniquely identify the utility to DB2. Two utilities with the same UID cannot execute concurrently.

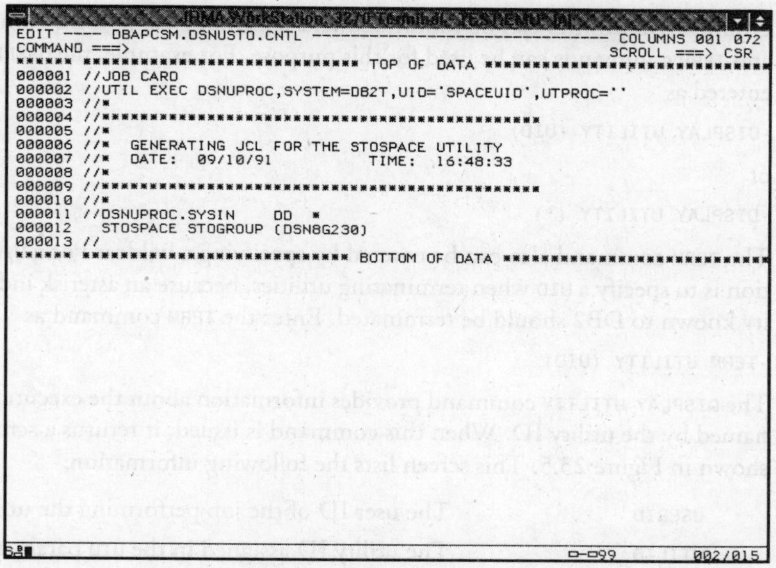

```
IRMA WorkStation, 3270 Terminal, TESTEMU [A]
EDIT ---- DBAPCSM.DSNUSTO.CNTL ----------------------------- COLUMNS 001 072
COMMAND ===>                                                  SCROLL ===> CSR
****** ***************************** TOP OF DATA ******************************
000001 //JOB CARD
000002 //UTIL EXEC DSNUPROC,SYSTEM=DB2T,UID='SPACEUID',UTPROC=''
000003 //*
000004 //*************************************************
000005 //*
000006 //*  GENERATING JCL FOR THE STOSPACE UTILITY
000007 //*  DATE:  09/10/91              TIME:  16:48:33
000008 //*
000009 //*************************************************
000010 //*
000011 //DSNUPROC.SYSIN    DD  *
000012     STOSPACE STOGROUP (DSN8G230)
000013 //
****** **************************** BOTTOM OF DATA ****************************
                                                              002/015
```

FIGURE 23.4.
Generated JCL for the STOSPACE *utility.*

The DSNUPROC procedure requires the specification of override parameters to function properly. These parameters should be coded as follows:

LIB	The DB2 link library assigned to your DB2 system. This can be obtained from the database administrator or the system programmer responsible for DB2.
SYSTEM	The DB2 system containing the objects on which the utility will be run.
UID	Identifies the utility to the DB2 system. If this value is blank, the UID defaults to the job name. This enables an analyst or DBA to quickly identify the job associated with a utility. Also, because two identically named MVS jobs cannot run concurrently, two utilities with the same UID cannot run concurrently. This minimizes the possibility of incorrectly restarting or rerunning an abending job.
UTPROC	This value initially should be blank (that is, UTPROC=''). This parameter is assigned a value only during restart. A value of 'RESTART(PHASE)' restarts the utility at the beginning of the last executed phase. A value of 'RESTART' restarts the utility at the last or current commit point. The type of restart, PHASE or COMMIT, must be determined by analyzing the type of utility and the abend.

Online DB2 utilities can be monitored and controlled using DB2 commands. The DISPLAY and TERM commands can be used for this purpose. For example, the DISPLAY command can be entered as

```
-DISPLAY UTILITY (UID)
```

or

```
-DISPLAY UTILITY (*)
```

The TERM command also can be entered by specifying a wildcard or a UID. The recommendation is to specify a UID when terminating utilities, because an asterisk indicates that every utility known to DB2 should be terminated. Enter the TERM command as

```
-TERM UTILITY (UID)
```

The DISPLAY UTILITY command provides information about the execution status of the utility named by the utility ID. When this command is issued, it returns a screen similar to the one shown in Figure 23.5. This screen lists the following information:

USERID	The user ID of the job performing the utility.
UTILID	The utility ID assigned in the UID parameter on the EXEC card. If the UID parameter is not provided, UTILID is the same name as the jobname.
STATEMENT	The number of the control card containing the utility statement that is being processed (if more than one utility control card is supplied as input to the utility step).
UTILITY	The type of utility that is being executed. For example, if a reorganization is run, UTILITY contains REORG.
PHASE	The phase of the utility being executed. The phases for each utility are discussed in Part VI.
COUNT	A count of the number of records (pages or rows, depending on the utility and phase being monitored) processed by the phase. Count also may be the number of index entries being processed. Count isn't always kept by every utility phase, however.
STATUS	The status of the utility. ACTIVE indicates that the utility is currently active and should not be terminated. If terminated, the utility will abend. STOPPED means that the utility is currently stopped and should be restarted or terminated, depending on the state of the job and the procedures in place for restarting or rerunning.

The TERM command terminates the execution of a DB2 utility. Think carefully before terminating a utility. After a utility is terminated, it cannot be restarted. Instead, it must be rerun, which involves reprocessing.

Five types of online DB2 utilities are provided:

- Data consistency utilities
- Backup and recovery utilities
- Data organization utilities
- Catalog manipulation utilities
- Miscellaneous utilities

FIGURE 23.5.
Output from the `—DISPLAY UTILITY (*)` *command.*

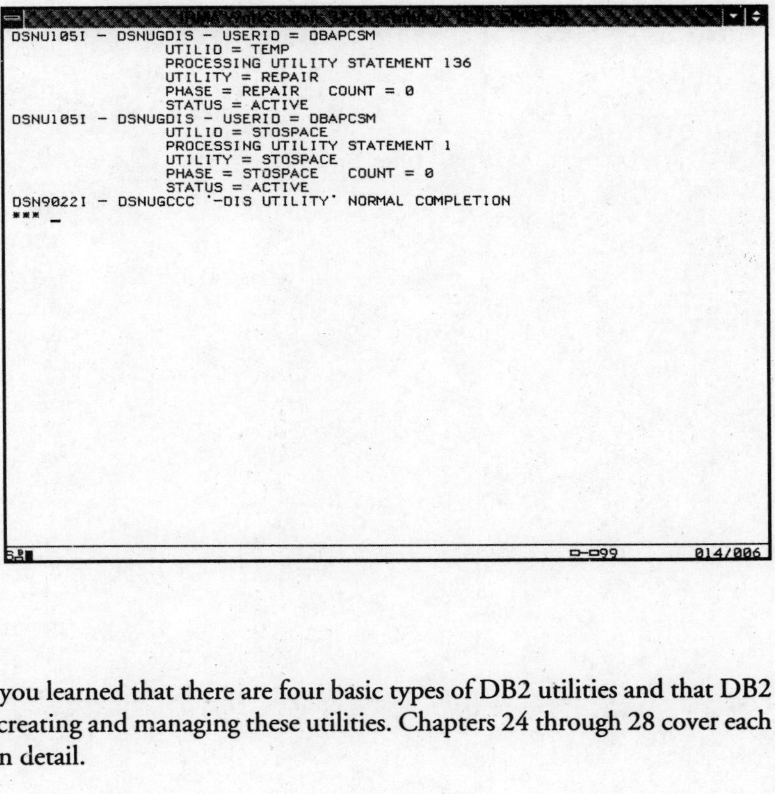

DSNU105I - DSNUGDIS - USERID = DBAPCSM
UTILID = TEMP
PROCESSING UTILITY STATEMENT 136
UTILITY = REPAIR
PHASE = REPAIR COUNT = 0
STATUS = ACTIVE
DSNU105I - DSNUGDIS - USERID = DBAPCSM
UTILID = STOSPACE
PROCESSING UTILITY STATEMENT 1
UTILITY = STOSPACE
PHASE = STOSPACE COUNT = 0
STATUS = ACTIVE
DSN9022I - DSNUGCCC '-DIS UTILITY' NORMAL COMPLETION
***
014/006

Summary

In this brief chapter, you learned that there are four basic types of DB2 utilities and that DB2 provides features for creating and managing these utilities. Chapters 24 through 28 cover each of the DB2 utilities in detail.

24

Data Consistency Utilities

Often, the consistency of data in a DB2 database must be monitored and controlled. In the scope of DB2 databases, *consistency* encompasses four things:

- The consistency of reference from index entries to corresponding table rows
- The consistency of data values in referential structures
- The consistency of data values conforming to check constraints
- The general consistency of DB2 data sets and data

Recall from previous chapters that a DB2 index is composed of column key values and RID pointers to rows in the DB2 table containing these values. Because the table and index information are in different physical data sets, the information in the index could become invalid. If the index key values or pointers become inconsistent, you would want to be able to pinpoint and correct the inconsistencies. This is the first type of consistency.

The second type of consistency refers to the referential integrity feature of DB2. When a primary-key-to-foreign-key relationship is defined between DB2 tables, a referential structure is created. Every foreign key in the dependent table must either match a primary key value in the parent table or be null. If, due to other utility processing, the referential integrity rules are violated, you must be able to view and possibly correct the violations.

Version 4

The third type of consistency refers to ensuring that data values conform to specific values (or ranges of values). This is implemented using check constraints. A check constraint uses expressions to place specific data value restrictions on the contents of a column. The expression is explicitly defined in the table DDL and is formulated in much the same way that SQL WHERE clauses are formulated. Every data value stored in a column with a check constraint should conform to the predefined check constraint expression.

General consistency is the final type of consistency. If portions of DB2 tablespace and index data sets contain invalid, inconsistent, or incorrect data because of hardware or software errors, you want to be able to correct the erroneous information.

The data consistency utilities are used to monitor, control, and administer these three types of data consistency errors. There are three data consistency utilities (CHECK, REPAIR, and REPORT) with a total of five functions. This chapter describes all of them.

The CHECK Utility

The CHECK utility checks the integrity of DB2 data structures. It has three purposes. The first is to check referential integrity between two tables, displaying and potentially resolving referential constraint violations. The second purpose of the CHECK utility is to ensure that data values conform to the check constraints specified for the table. The third and final purpose is to check DB2 indexes for consistency. This consists of comparing the key values of indexed columns to their corresponding table values, as well as evaluating RIDs in the tables and indexes being checked.

The CHECK DATA Option

The CHECK DATA utility is used to verify the accuracy and integrity of data in DB2 tables.

Referential Integrity Checking

One function of the CHECK DATA option of the CHECK utility checks the status of referential constraints. It is used to validate foreign key values in the rows of a dependent table against primary key values in its associated parent table. For example, consider a referential constraint defined in the DB2 sample tables. The DSN8510.DEPT table has a foreign key, RDE, defined on the column MGRNO. It references the primary key of DSN8510.EMP, which is the EMPNO column. The CHECK DATA utility can be used to verify that all occurrences of MGRNO in the DSN8510.DEPT sample table refer to a valid EMPNO in the DSN8510.EMP sample table.

CHECK DATA can run against a single tablespace, multiple tablespaces, or a single partition of a partitioned tablespace.

CHECK DATA can delete invalid rows and copy them to an exception table. The CHECK DATA utility resets the check pending status if constraint violations are not encountered or if the utility was run with the DELETE YES option.

The JCL in Listing 24.1 can be used to check data in the DB2 sample tables that contain referential constraints.

Listing 24.1. CHECK DATA JCL.

```
//DB2JOBU  JOB (UTILITY),'DB2 CHECK DATA',MSGCLASS=X,CLASS=X,
//   NOTIFY=USER
//*
//****************************************************************
//*
//*            DB2 CHECK DATA UTILITY
//*
//****************************************************************
//*
//UTIL EXEC DSNUPROC,SYSTEM=DSN,UID='CHEKDATA',UTPROC=''
//*
//*  UTILITY WORK DATASETS
//*
//DSNUPROC.SORTWK01 DD UNIT=SYSDA,SPACE=(CYL,(5,1))
//DSNUPROC.SORTWK02 DD UNIT=SYSDA,SPACE=(CYL,(5,1))
//DSNUPROC.SORTOUT DD DSN=&&SORTOUT,
//       UNIT=SYSDA,SPACE=(CYL,(5,1))
//DSNUPROC.SYSERR DD DSN=&&SYSERR,
//       UNIT=SYSDA,SPACE=(CYL,(1,1))
//DSNUPROC.SYSUT1 DD DSN=&&SYSUT1,
//       UNIT=SYSDA,SPACE=(CYL,(5,1))
//DSNUPROC.UTPRINT DD SYSOUT=X
//*
//*  UTILITY INPUT CONTROL STATEMENTS
```

continues

Listing 24.1. continued

```
//*        This CHECK DATA statement checks DSN8510.DEPT for
//*        referential constraint violations, deletes all
//*        offending rows, and places them into the exception
//*        table, DSN8510.DEPT_EXCPTN.
//*
//DSNUPROC.SYSIN    DD  *
   CHECK DATA TABLESPACE DSN8D51A.DSN8S51D
   FOR EXCEPTION IN DSN8510.DEPT
         USE DSN8510.DEPT_EXCPTN
   SCOPE ALL    DELETE YES
/*
//
```

NOTE

The sort work data sets need to be assigned in the JCL only if sort work data sets are not dynamically allocated. Additionally, you should consider explicitly defining sort work data sets when checking very large tables.

Check Constraint Checking

The second function of the CHECK DATA option of the CHECK utility checks the status of check constraints. It is used to validate column values against check constraints defined on those columns. For example, consider a check constraint defined on the SALARY column of the DSN8510.EMP table, as follows:

```
CONSTRAINT CHECK_SALARY
CHECK (SALARY < 50000.00)
```

All values of the SALARY column must be less than 50000.00 or they are in violation of the check constraint. The CHECK DATA utility can be used to verify that all occurrences of SALARY in the DSN8510.EMP sample table actually contain a valid SALARY conforming to the check constraint.

The columns of a table can contain values that violate the check constraint in the following two circumstances:

1. When a table that already contains data is altered to add a check constraint, enforcement of the constraint depends upon the value of the DB2 CURRENT RULES special register. If the value of the CURRENT RULES register is DB2, check constraint enforcement is deferred during table alteration and the table is placed in a check pending state. If the value of the CURRENT RULES register is STD, check constraint enforcement is immediate. If no rows violate the constraint, the alteration proceeds normally. If existing rows do violate the constraint, the table is placed in a check pending state.
2. When the LOAD utility is executed specifying the ENFORCE NO clause.

The syntax and JCL specification for checking check constraints is the same as is used for checking referential constraints.

CHECK DATA Phases

UTILINIT	Sets up and initializes the CHECK DATA utility.
SCANTAB	Extracts keys by index or tablespace scan and places them in the SYSUT1 DD.
SORT	Sorts the foreign keys using the SORTOUT DD (if the foreign keys were not extracted using an index).
CHECKDAT	Compares the extracted foreign keys to the index entries for the corresponding primary key. This phase also issues error messages for invalid foreign keys.
REPORTCK	Copies the invalid rows to the specified exception table and then deletes them from the source table if the DELETE YES option was chosen.
UTILTERM	Performs the final utility cleanup.

Estimating CHECK DATA Work Data Set Sizes

The CHECK DATA utility requires the use of work data sets to accomplish referential constraint checking. The following formulas can help you estimate the sizes of the work data sets required by the CHECK DATA utility. These calculations provide estimated data set sizes. More complex and precise calculations are in the *DB2 Utility Reference* manual. The formulas presented here, however, produce generally satisfactory results.

```
SYSUT1 = (size of the largest foreign key + 13)
➥x (total number of rows in the table to be checked)
➥x (total number of foreign keys defined for the table)
```

NOTE

If any number is 0, substitute 1.

```
SORTOUT = (size of SYSUT1)
SORTWKxx = (size of SORTOUT) x 2
SYSERR = (number of estimated referential constraint violations) x 60
```

NOTE

Allocate at least one cylinder to the SYSERR data set.

After calculating the estimated size, in bytes, for each work data set, convert the number into cylinders, rounding up to the next whole cylinder. Allocating work data sets in cylinder increments enhances the utility's performance.

CHECK DATA Locking Considerations

The CHECK DATA utility can run concurrently with the following utilities:

- DIAGNOSE
- MERGECOPY
- MODIFY
- REPORT
- STOSPACE

CHECK DATA, when run specifying DELETE NO, will drain write claim classes for the tablespace and indexes being processed. When DELETE YES is specified, all claim classes are drained for the tablespace and indexes impacted.

When CHECK DATA is run against an individual partition, DB2 also drains the write claim class for the logical partition of the Type 2 indexes impacted if DELETE NO is specified. If DELETE YES is specified, then DB2 drains all claim classes for the logical partition of the Type 2 indexes being acted upon. Regardless of the other options specified, if the FOR EXCEPTION option is specified, the tablespace containing the exception table (and any indexes) will have all claim classes drained.

CHECK DATA Guidelines

Before you execute the CHECK DATA utility, be sure to consider the following guidelines.

Use CHECK DATA to Ensure Data Integrity

Favor the use of the CHECK DATA utility to reset the check pending status on DB2 tablespaces. CHECK DATA is the only way to verify, in an automated fashion and on demand, that DB2 table data is referentially intact and that the data conforms to all check constraints. The alternate methods of resetting the check pending status are as follows:

- Running the REPAIR utility, specifying SET NOCHECKPEND for the appropriate tablespaces
- Issuing the START DATABASE command, specifying ACCESS(FORCE)

Neither option ensures data integrity.

Another valid way to reset the check pending status is with the LOAD utility, specifying the ENFORCE CONSTRAINTS option. However, this requires a sequential data set suitable for loading, and this type of data set is not readily available for most application tablespaces. Even if a load data set is available, the data it contains might be out of date, and thus of little benefit.

Use SCOPE PENDING

Specify the SCOPE PENDING option when executing the CHECK DATA utility to reduce the amount of work the utility must perform. With the SCOPE PENDING option, CHECK DATA checks only the rows that need to be checked for all tables in the specified tablespace. This means that only data in check pending is checked. If the tablespace is not in check pending, the CHECK DATA utility issues a message and terminates processing. This is the most efficient way to execute the CHECK DATA utility because it minimizes runtime by avoiding unnecessary work. The alternative is to specify SCOPE ALL, which checks all dependent tables in the specified tablespaces.

Run CHECK DATA When Data Integrity Is Questionable

Execute CHECK DATA after the following:

- Loading a table without specifying the ENFORCE CONSTRAINTS option.
- A check constraint is added to a table, and data within an existing row of that table violates the constraint.
- A table is altered to add a check constraint and the CURRENT RULES special register contains DB2.
- When row violations are encountered by the CHECK DATA utility using the DELETE NO option.
- The partial recovery of tablespaces in a referential set.

Both situations result in DB2 placing the loaded or recovered tablespaces into a check pending status. The CHECK DATA utility is necessary to ensure referentially sound data and to remove the check pending status, permitting future data access.

Bypass CHECK DATA Only When Data Integrity Is Verifiable

After a full recovery of all tablespaces in a referential set, you might want to bypass the execution of the CHECK DATA utility. Depending on the order in which the recovery took place, some tablespaces are placed in a check pending status. If you have followed the COPY guidelines presented in this book, however, the full recovery of a tablespace set is referentially sound. In this case, the REPAIR utility specifying the SET NOCHECKPEND option can be used instead of CHECK DATA, because CHECK DATA would be a waste of time.

Define Exception Tables for Tables That Require CHECK DATA

An exception table stores the rows that violate the referential constraint being checked. An exception table should be identical to the table being checked but with the addition of two columns: one column identifies the RID of the offending row, and the other identifies a TIMESTAMP that indicates when the CHECK DATA utility was run.

These two columns can have any name as long as it isn't the same name as another column in the table. The names used in the following example are recommended because they clearly identify the column's use. To avoid ambiguity, use the same column names for all exception tables. The exception table can be created using the following DDL statements:

```
CREATE TABLE
  DSN8510.DEPT_EXCPTN
  LIKE DSN8510.DEPT;

ALTER TABLE
  DSN8510.DEPT_EXCPTN
  ADD  RID         CHAR(4);

ALTER TABLE
  DSN8510.DEPT_EXCPTN
  ADD  CHECK_TS    TIMESTAMP;
```

The exception table does not need to be empty when the CHECK DATA utility is run because the TIMESTAMP column identifies which execution of CHECK DATA inserted the offending rows.

Do not create a unique index for any exception table. A unique index could cause the CHECK DATA utility to fail because of the insertion of non-unique key values. Non-unique indexes should not pose a problem.

Place the exception tables in a segmented tablespace. You also can place multiple exception tables in a single segmented tablespace.

Use DELETE YES for Optimum Automation

Rows that violate the referential constraint can be deleted from the table being checked if the DELETE YES parameter was specified. This is often the preferred method of executing the CHECK DATA utility in a production environment because the elimination of constraint violations is automated. If the deleted rows are needed, they can be retrieved from the exception table.

If DELETE NO is specified instead of DELETE YES, the CHECK DATA utility does not reset the check pending flag, but the rows in violation of the constraint are identified for future action.

A problem can occur, however, when you run the CHECK DATA utility with the DELETE YES option. When a row is deleted from the dependent table, it could cause cascading deletes to one or more dependent tables. This may result in valid data being deleted if the violation is caused by a missing primary key in a parent table. For this reason, you might want to avoid the DELETE YES option. At any rate, exercise caution when checking data with DELETE YES.

Be Aware of Inconsistent Indexes

If rows that appear to be valid are deleted, ensure that the indexes defined for the dependen and parent tables are valid. If data in either index is invalid, the CHECK DATA utility might indi cate referential constraint violations, even though there are none. Indexes can be checked fo validity using the CHECK INDEX utility (discussed in the next section).

Also, ensure that the parent table contains all expected data. If rows are missing because of improper deletions or partial loads, CHECK DATA will delete the foreign key rows as well (if DELETE YES was specified).

Consider Checking at the Partition Level

CHECK DATA can be executed at the partition level. Choosing to check at the partition level provides the following benefits:

- Pinpoint integrity checking can be performed. If the user has a good idea which partition has a data integrity problem, CHECK DATA can be run on that partition only.
- A regularly scheduled CHECK DATA pattern can be established, whereby a single partition is checked daily (or weekly). This establishes a data-integrity checking process that eventually checks the entire table, but not so frequently as to cause availability problems.

Rerun CHECK DATA After an Abend

The CHECK DATA utility cannot be restarted. If it abends during execution, determine the cause of the abend, terminate the utility, and rerun it. Common causes for CHECK DATA abends are lockout conditions due to concurrent data access and changes to the table being checked (for example, new columns), without corresponding changes to the exception table.

The CHECK INDEX Option

The CHECK INDEX option of the CHECK utility checks for the consistency of index data and its corresponding table data. This option identifies and reports RID pointer errors for missing index keys and index key mismatches. CHECK INDEX does not correct invalid index entries; it merely identifies them for future correction.

CHECK INDEX can run against an entire index or a single index partition. CHECK INDEX can identify three problems:

- No corresponding row in the table for a given index entry.
- No index entry for a valid table row.
- The data in the indexed columns for the table does not match the corresponding index key for a given matching RID.

To correct these errors, the user can execute the RECOVER INDEX utility to rebuild the index based on the current table data. When mismatch-type errors occur, however, a data analyst who is experienced with the application that contains the problem table or index should research the cause of the anomaly. The predominant causes of invalid indexes are the uncontrolled use of the DSN1COPY utility and the partial recovery of application tables or indexes.

The JCL to execute the CHECK INDEX utility is shown in Listing 24.2.

Listing 24.2. CHECK INDEX JCL.

```
//DB2JOBU  JOB (UTILITY),'DB2 CHECK INDEX',MSGCLASS=X,CLASS=X,
//    NOTIFY=USER
//*
//****************************************************************
//*
//*              DB2 CHECK INDEX UTILITY
//*
//****************************************************************
//*
//UTIL EXEC DSNUPROC,SYSTEM=DSN,UID='CHEKINDX',UTPROC=''
//*
//*  UTILITY WORK DATASETS
//*
//DSNUPROC.SORTWK01 DD UNIT=SYSDA,SPACE=(CYL,(2,1))
//DSNUPROC.SORTWK02 DD UNIT=SYSDA,SPACE=(CYL,(2,1))
//DSNUPROC.SYSUT1 DD DSN=&&SYSUT1,
//        UNIT=SYSDA,SPACE=(CYL,(2,1)),DCB=BUFNO=20
//DSNUPROC.UTPRINT DD SYSOUT=X
//*
//*  UTILITY INPUT CONTROL STATEMENTS
//*        The first CHECK INDEX statement checks all indexes
//*        for the named tablespace.
//*        The next two CHECK INDEX statements check only the
//*        specifically named indexes.
//*
//DSNUPROC.SYSIN    DD  *
    CHECK INDEX(ALL) TABLESPACE DSN8D51A.DSN8S51D
    CHECK INDEX NAME (DSN8510.XACT1)
    CHECK INDEX NAME (DSN8510.XACT2)
/*
//
```

CHECK INDEX Phases

UTILINIT	Sets up and initializes the CHECK INDEX utility
UNLOAD	Unloads index entries to the SYSUT1 DD
SORT	Sorts the unloaded index entries using SORTOUT DD
CHECKIDX	Scans the table to validate the sorted index entries against the table data
UTILTERM	Performs the final utility cleanup

Estimating CHECK INDEX Work Data Set Sizes

The CHECK INDEX utility requires work data sets to accomplish index checking. The following formulas help you estimate the sizes for the work data sets required by the CHECK INDEX utility. These calculations provide estimated sizes only. More complex and precise calculations can be found in the *DB2 Utility Guide and Reference* manual, but these formulas should produce comparable results:

```
SYSUT1 = (size of the largest index + 13) x (total number of rows in largest index
➥to be checked)
SORTWKxx = (size of SYSUT1) x 2
```

After calculating the estimated size, in bytes, for each work data set, convert the number into cylinders, rounding up to the next whole cylinder. Allocating work data sets in cylinder increments enhances the utility's performance. This is true for all utilities.

CHECK INDEX Locking Considerations

The CHECK INDEX utility can run concurrently with all utilities except the following:

- CHECK DATA
- LOAD
- RECOVER
- REORG INDEX
- REORG UNLOAD CONTINUE
- REORG UNLOAD PAUSE
- REPAIR REPLACE
- REPAIR DELETE

CHECK INDEX will drain write claim classes for both the index or index partition (including a logical partition of a Type 2 index) and the tablespace being processed.

CHECK INDEX Guidelines

The following tips and techniques will prove useful when you implement the CHECK INDEX utility at your shop.

Run CHECK INDEX Only When Needed

Inconsistencies in DB2 indexes are rare in adequately controlled and administered environments. For this reason, do not regularly schedule the execution of the CHECK INDEX utility for the production indexes in your shop. It usually wastes processing time and increases an application's batch window.

The CHECK INDEX utility should be run only when inconsistent data is observed or when an uncontrolled environment allows (or permits) the liberal use of DSN1COPY or partial recovery.

NOTE

Consider running CHECK INDEX for an entire DB2 subsystem prior to a migration. If a corrupt index exists, you can correct it prior to the migration.

Use CHECK INDEX After Potentially Dangerous Operations

Execute CHECK INDEX after a conditional restart or a partial application recovery.

Use CHECK INDEX on the DB2 Catalog When Necessary

CHECK INDEX can be used to check DB2 Catalog and DB2 Directory indexes.

Check Indexes at the Partition Level When Possible

CHECK INDEX can be run at the partition level (unless you are using a release of DB2 prior to V3). Pinpoint integrity checking can be performed if the user knows which index partition has corrupted entries. Running CHECK INDEX on that partition only can save processing time.

Rerun CHECK INDEX After an Abend

The CHECK INDEX utility cannot be restarted. If it abends during execution, determine the cause of the abend, terminate the utility, and rerun. The most common cause for CHECK INDEX failure is a timeout because the index is locked out by another user.

Buffer CHECK INDEX Work Data Sets Appropriately

Ensure that adequate data set buffering is specified for the work data sets. The BUFNO parameter can be used on the DCB information of JCL DD statements to change buffering. The BUFNO parameter creates read and write buffers in main storage for this data set, thereby enhancing the performance of the utility.

In DB2 V3, the DCB=BUFNO default was 8. For DB2 V4 and later, the DCB=BUFNO default is 20.

Ensure that sufficient memory (real or expanded) is available, however, before increasing the BUFNO specification for your CHECK INDEX work data sets.

The REPAIR Utility

The REPAIR utility is designed to modify DB2 data and associated data structures when there is an error or problem. It has three distinct uses. The first is to test DBD definitions in the DB2 Directory and to synchronize DB2 Catalog database information with the DB2 Directory DBD definition. The second use is to physically change specific locations in a data set using a zap. The third and final type of REPAIR is to reset pending flags that are erroneously set or unnecessary.

REPAIR Phases

The REPAIR utility has three phases, regardless of which type of REPAIR is run. These phases are as follows:

UTILINIT	Sets up and initializes the REPAIR utility
REPAIR	Locates and repairs the data or resets the appropriate pending flag
UTILTERM	Performs the final utility cleanup

The REPAIR DBD Option

The REPAIR utility can be used to test, maintain, and modify DB2 database information. DB2 maintains database information in the DB2 Catalog SYSIBM.SYSDATABASE table. An object known as a DBD is also maintained in the DB2 Directory in the SYSIBM.DBD01 "table." You can use the REPAIR option with the DBD specification to perform the following functions:

- Test the definition of a DB2 database by comparing information in the DB2 Catalog to information in the DB2 Directory.
- Diagnose database synchronization problems and report differences between the DB2 Catalog information and the DBD stored in the DB2 Directory.
- Rebuild a DBD definition in the DB2 Directory based on the information in the DB2 Catalog.
- Drop an invalid database (if the SQL DROP statement cannot be used because of database inconsistencies). REPAIR DBD can remove the DBD from the DB2 Directory and delete all corresponding rows from the appropriate DB2 Catalog tables.

Listing 24.3 contains sample JCL to REPAIR the DBD for the DSN8D51A sample database.

Listing 24.3. REPAIR DBD JCL.

```
//DB2JOBU  JOB (UTILITY),'DB2 REPAIR DBD',MSGCLASS=X,CLASS=X,
//   NOTIFY=USER
//*
//****************************************************************
//*
//*          DB2 REPAIR UTILITY   : : DBD REPAIR
//*
//****************************************************************
//*
//UTIL EXEC DSNUPROC,SYSTEM=DSN,UID='REPRDBD',UTPROC=''
//*
//*  UTILITY INPUT CONTROL STATEMENTS
//*        The first REPAIR statement builds a DBD based on
//*        the DB2 Catalog and compares it to the corresponding
//*        DBD in the DB2 Directory.
```

continues

Listing 24.3. continued

```
//*       The second REPAIR statement reports inconsistencies,
//*       if any exist.
//*
//DSNUPROC.SYSIN    DD  *
    REPAIR DBD TEST DATABASE DSN8D51A

    REPAIR DBD DIAGNOSE DATABASE DSN8D51A OUTDDN SYSREC
/*
//
```

REPAIR DBD Guidelines

The following guidelines provide useful techniques for running the REPAIR DBD utility.

Log All Repairs

Run the REPAIR utility with the LOG YES option. This ensures that all data changes are logged to DB2 and are therefore recoverable.

Consult IBM Before Using DROP or REBUILD

Do not issue the REPAIR DBD utility with the DROP or REBUILD option without consulting your IBM Support Center. These options can be dangerous if used improperly.

Use TEST and DIAGNOSE for Error Resolution

When databases, or their subordinate objects, exhibit peculiar behavior, consider executing REPAIR DBD with the TEST option. If this run returns a condition code other than 0, run REPAIR DBD with the DIAGNOSE option and consult your IBM Support Center for additional guidance. You should also consider implementing a regularly scheduled REPAIR DBD run to test consistently check for problems.

The REPAIR LOCATE Option

The LOCATE option of the REPAIR utility zaps DB2 data. The term *zap* refers to the physical modification of data at specific address locations. This form of the REPAIR utility can be used to perform the following functions:

- Delete an entire row from a tablespace
- Replace data at specific locations in a tablespace or index
- Reset broken tablespace page bits

The REPAIR LOCATE utility functions similarly to the IBM AMASPZAP utility. By specifying page locations and offsets, specific RIDs, or key data, you can use the REPAIR utility to alter the data stored at the specified location. Although it generally is not recommended and is not easy, the REPAIR LOCATE utility can sometimes be of considerable help in resolving errors difficult to correct by normal means (that is, using SQL).

The sample JCL provided in Listing 24.4 depicts the REPAIR JCL necessary to modify the data on the third page of the fourth partition at offset 50 for the sample tablespace DSN8D51A.DSN8S51E.

Listing 24.4. REPAIR LOCATE JCL.

```
//DB2JOBU  JOB (UTILITY),'DB2 REPAIR LOCATE',MSGCLASS=X,CLASS=X,
//   NOTIFY=USER
//*
//****************************************************************
//*
//*         DB2 REPAIR UTILITY   : : LOCATE AND MODIFY DATA
//*
//****************************************************************
//*
//UTIL EXEC DSNUPROC,SYSTEM=DSN,UID='REPRLOCT',UTPROC=''
//*
//*  UTILITY INPUT CONTROL STATEMENTS
//*       The REPAIR statement modifies the data on the third
//*       page at offset X'0080' from the value 'SP' to the
//*       value 'ST'.  This update happens only if that location
//*       contains 'SP'.  Additionally, the two characters are
//*       dumped to ensure that the modification is correct.
//*
//DSNUPROC.SYSIN    DD  *
    REPAIR OBJECT
        LOCATE TABLESPACE DSN8D51A.DSN8S51D PAGE X'03'
               VERIFY OFFSET X'0080' DATA 'SP'
               REPLACE OFFSET X'0080' DATA 'ST'
               DUMP OFFSET X'0080' LENGTH 2
/*
//
```

REPAIR LOCATE Locking Considerations

The REPAIR LOCATE utility with the DUMP option takes an S-lock on the tablespace and an index, if available, during the REPAIR phase. The REPAIR LOCATE utility with the REPLACE option takes a SIX-lock on the tablespace and any related indexes during the REPAIR phase.

REPAIR LOCATE Guidelines

Follow the guidelines suggested in this section when implementing and executing the REPAIR LOCATE utility.

Log All Repairs

Run the REPAIR utility with the LOG YES option. This ensures that all data changes are logged to DB2 and are therefore recoverable.

Ensure That Adequate Recovery Is Available

Create a backup copy of any tablespace to be operated on by the REPAIR utility when the intent is to modify data. To make a backup, use the COPY utility or the DSN1COPY service aid utility.

Avoid SVC Dumps When Using REPAIR

When determining the location and values of data to be repaired, use a dump produced only by one of the following methods:

- REPAIR with the DUMP option
- DSN1COPY service aid utility
- DSN1PRNT service aid utility

Do not use an SVC dump, because the information contained therein might not accurately depict the DB2 data as it exists on DASD.

Use VERIFY with REPLACE

When replacing data in a DB2 tablespace, code the VERIFY option, which ensures that the value of the data being changed is as expected. If the value does not match the VERIFY specification, subsequent REPLACE specifications will not occur. This provides the highest degree of safety when executing the REPAIR utility, and also maintains data integrity.

Use REPAIR LOCATE with Caution

REPAIR LOCATE should be used only by a knowledgeable systems programmer or DBA. Familiarity with the MVS utility program AMASPZAP is helpful.

Do Not Use REPAIR on the DB2 Catalog and DB2 Directory

REPAIR LOCATE can be used to modify the DB2 Catalog and DB2 Directory data sets. However, these data sets have a special format and should be modified with great care. It is recommended that REPAIR never be run on these data sets. If you do not heed this warning, be sure to consult the *DB2 Diagnosis Guide and Reference* for the physical format of these data sets before proceeding.

Repair the "Broken" Page Bit When Necessary

Sometimes DB2 erroneously sets the "broken" page bit. If you determine that the page is correct after examining the contents using dumps and the REPAIR utility, you can invoke REPAIR

LOCATE with the RESET option to reset the "broken" page bit. However, be absolutely sure that the page in question is accurate before modifying this bit.

Grant REPAIR Authority Judiciously

Remember that REPAIR authority must be granted before anyone can execute the REPAIR utility. However, it is common for many shops to grant REPAIR authority to beginning users or production jobs in order to reset pending flags. Because the REPAIR authority cannot be broken down into which option is needed (that is, DBD, LOCATE, or SET), blanket authority to execute any type of REPAIR is given when REPAIR authority is granted. This could be dangerous if an uneducated user stumbles across the ability to zap DB2 tablespace data.

Remember that REPAIR authority is implicit in the group-level DBCTRL, DBADM, SYSCTRL, and SYSADM authorities.

The REPAIR SET Option

When the REPAIR utility is executed with the SET option, it can be used to reset copy pending, check pending, and recover pending flags. As of DB2 V3, these flags can be set at the partition level, as well as at the tablespace level. In general, these flags are maintained by DB2 to indicate the status of tablespaces and indexes. When DB2 turns on a flag for a tablespace or index, it indicates that the object is in an indeterminate state.

When the copy pending flag is set, it indicates that the COPY utility must be used to back up the tablespace or partition to ensure adequate recoverability. Copy pending status is set when unlogged changes have been made to DB2 tablespaces, or when a reference to a full image copy is no longer available in the DB2 Catalog.

The check pending flag indicates that the CHECK DATA utility should be run because data has been inserted into a table containing a referential constraint without ensuring that the data conforms to the referential integrity.

The recover pending flag indicates that the tablespace or the index must be recovered because a utility operating on that object has ended abnormally, possibly causing inconsistent or corrupted data.

Sometimes, however, these flags are set by DB2 but the corresponding utility does not need to be run because of other application factors. In this case, the REPAIR SET utility can be run to reset the appropriate pending flag.

Listing 24.5 shows JCL that can be used to reset check pending, copy pending, and recover pending restrictions for the sample tablespaces. It also contains a REPAIR statement to reset the recover pending status for an index on one of the sample tables.

Listing 24.5. REPAIR SET JCL.

```
//DB2JOBU  JOB (UTILITY),'DB2 REPAIR SET',MSGCLASS=X,CLASS=X,
//   NOTIFY=USER
//*
//****************************************************************
//*
//*      DB2 REPAIR UTILITY  : : RESET PENDING FLAGS
//*
//****************************************************************
//*
//UTIL EXEC DSNUPROC,SYSTEM=DSN,UID='REPRSETP',UTPROC=''
//*
//*  UTILITY INPUT CONTROL STATEMENTS
//*    1. The first REPAIR statement resets the copy pending
//*       status for the named tablespace.
//*    2. The second REPAIR statement resets the check pending
//*       status for two tablespaces.
//*    3. The third REPAIR statement resets the recover pending
//*       status for the named tablespace.
//*    4. The fourth and final REPAIR statement resets the
//*       copy pending status for the named index.
//*
//DSNUPROC.SYSIN    DD  *
   REPAIR SET TABLESPACE DSN8D51A.DSN8S51E  NOCOPYPEND
   REPAIR SET TABLESPACE DSN8D51A.DSN8S51E  NOCHECKPEND
          SET TABLESPACE DSN8D51A.DSN8S51C  NOCHECKPEND
   REPAIR SET TABLESPACE DSN8D51A.DSN8S51R  NORCVRPEND
   REPAIR SET INDEX      DSN8510.XPROJAC1   NORCVRPEND
/*
//
```

REPAIR SET Guidelines

Use the following guidelines when deciding how to utilize REPAIR SET.

Favor the COPY Utility over REPAIR SET NOCOPYPEND

To reset the copy pending flag, it is almost always better to run the COPY utility to take a full image copy rather than use REPAIR. Situations contrary to this advice follow:

- Data loaded from a stable source does not need to be copied if the source is maintained. (The data can always be reloaded.) If the data is loaded with the LOG NO option, run REPAIR to reset the check pending condition rather than create an image copy that will never be used.
- When the MODIFY RECOVERY utility is run—deleting the last image copy for a tablespace—DB2 sets the copy pending flag. If the image copy data set deleted from the SYSIBM.SYSCOPY table is still available, however, recovery to that image copy can be accomplished using the DSN1COPY service aid. This requires manual intervention to recover a tablespace and is not recommended.

- Test data with a short life span often does not need to be copied because it can be easily re-created. If the copy pending restriction is set for a table of this nature, it is usually quicker to run REPAIR than to create an image copy.

Favor the CHECK DATA Utility over REPAIR SET NOCHECKPEND

To reset the check pending flag, it is almost always better to run the CHECK DATA utility to enforce referential constraints rather than use REPAIR. Situations contrary to this advice follow:

- If referential constraint violations are checked by an application program later in a job stream, the REPAIR utility can be run to reset the copy pending restriction. This allows the subsequent deletion of referential constraint violations by the application program. However, the DB2 CHECK DATA utility generally is infallible, and application programs are not, so this scenario should be avoided unless you are retrofitting referential integrity into a system that already exists without it.
- If check pending has been set for a tablespace containing a table that will have data loaded into it using the LOAD utility (with the REPLACE and ENFORCE CONSTRAINTS options) before data will be accessed, the CHECK DATA utility can be bypassed because the LOAD utility enforces the referential constraints.

Favor the RECOVER Utility over REPAIR SET NORCVRPEND

To reset the recover pending flag, it is almost always better to run the RECOVER utility to recover a DB2 tablespace or index to a time or state rather than use REPAIR.

There is only one situation contrary to this advice. When the LOAD utility abnormally terminates, the recover pending flag is set, and running LOAD REPLACE rather than RECOVER is appropriate. It is never advisable to set the recover pending flag using REPAIR unless the data is not critical and can be lost without dire consequences.

Use LEVELID to Use a Down-Level Data Set

Version 4

The LEVELID parameter sets the level identifier of the named tablespace or partition to a new identifier.

You cannot use LEVELID with an open tablespace or partition, a tablespace or partition with outstanding indoubt log records, or pages in the logical page list (LPL).

CAUTION

Actions impacting a down-level data set might cause data integrity and accuracy problems. Use this option at your own risk as IBM will take no responsibility for data problems resulting from the use of down-level data sets.

The REPORT Utility

Two types of reports can be generated with the REPORT utility. The first is a tablespace set report showing the names of all tablespaces and tables tied together by referential integrity. This type of report is described in the next section. The second type deals with recovery and is discussed in Chapter 25, "Backup and Recover Utilities."

The REPORT TABLESPACESET Option

The REPORT TABLESPACESET utility generates a report detailing all tables and tablespaces in a referential tablespace set. As you can see in the sample JCL in Listing 24.6, the input to the utility is a single tablespace. The output is a report of all related tablespaces and tables.

Listing 24.6. REPORT TABLESPACESET JCL.

```
//DB2JOBU  JOB  (UTILITY),'DB2 REPORT TS',MSGCLASS=X,
//    NOTIFY=DB2JOBU,USER=DB2JOBU
//*
//****************************************************************
//*
//*              DB2 REPORT TABLESPACESET UTILITY
//*
//****************************************************************
//*
//UTIL EXEC DSNUPROC,SYSTEM=DSN,UID='REPORTTS',UTPROC=''
//*
//*   UTILITY INPUT CONTROL STATEMENTS
//*      The REPORT statement generates a report of all objects
//*      referentially tied to the named tablespace
//*
//DSNUPROC.SYSIN    DD  *
    REPORT TABLESPACESET TABLESPACE DSN8D51A.DSN8S51D
/*
//
```

REPORT TABLESPACESET Guidelines

Use the following tips and techniques when running the REPORT TABLESPACESET utility.

Use REPORT TABLESPACESET Reports for Documentation

The REPORT TABLESPACESET utility is particularly useful for monitoring DB2 objects that are referentially related. DB2 Catalog reports such as those described in Chapter 19, "DB2 Object Monitoring Using the DB2 Catalog," are also useful but are difficult to structure so that a complete tablespace set is returned given a tablespace anywhere in the set.

Rerun the REPORT Utility After Resolving Abends

Run the REPORT TABLESPACESET utility for every tablespace added to the production DB2 subystem. Additionally, if referential constraints are added to current application tables, run the REPORT TABLESPACESET utility on their corresponding tablespaces immediately after their implementation. Store these reports as documentation for reference.

Periodically run the REPORT TABLESPACESET utility for tablespaces that DB2 Catalog queries dentify as containing tables defined with referential constraints. Ensure that the QUIESCE utility, when executed against these tablespaces, is coded to quiesce *all* tablespaces identified by the report—as well as any other tablespace that is logically related to any tablespace in the ablespace set (such as programmatic referential integrity).

f the REPORT utility abends, terminate the utility, if necessary, and rerun it.

The DIAGNOSE Utility

The DIAGNOSE utility is an online utility that can be used to diagnose problems, especially problems with other DB2 utilities. Sample JCL is provided in Listing 24.7.

isting 24.7. DIAGNOSE JCL.

```
/DB2JOBU  JOB  (UTILITY),'DB2 DIAGNOSE',MSGCLASS=X,CLASS=X,
/         NOTIFY=USER
/*
/****************************************************************
/*
/*                      DB2 DIAGNOSE UTILITY
/*
/****************************************************************
/*
/UTIL EXEC DSNUPROC,SYSTEM=DSN,UID='DIAGNOSE',UTPROC=''
/*
/*  Display all records in the SYSIBM.SYSUTIL DB2 Directory table
/*
/DSNUPROC.SYSIN    DD  *
   DIAGNOSE DISPLAY SYSUTILX
*
/
```

The DIAGNOSE utility can be used to force dumps for utility abends and format SYSIBM.SYSUTILX nformation for printing. It should be used only under instructions and supervision from an BM Support Center.

Summary

The utilities in this chapter help you keep the data in your DB2 tables consistent. But what if a hardware error occurs? Or an abend? The next chapter prepares you for these situations by discussing utilities that back up and recover your data.

25

Backup and Recovery Utilities

The backup and recovery utilities supplied with DB2 are wonderfully complex. They remo much of the burden of database recovery from the DBA or analyst and place it where it b longs: squarely on the shoulders of the DBMS.

Ten forms of backup and recovery are provided by six DB2 utilities. The nine forms (and tl associated DB2 utility for each) are as follows:

- Backup of all tablespace data (COPY utility)
- Incremental backup of tablespace data (COPY utility)
- Analyze a tablespace to determine if a full or incremental backup is required (COPY utility)
- Merging of incremental copies (MERGECOPY utility)
- Full recovery of tablespace data based on the image copy and the log data (RECOVER utility)
- Restoration of a tablespace to an image copy or point in time, referred to hereafter as partial recovery (RECOVER utility)
- Re-creation of DB2 indexes from tablespace data (RECOVER utility)
- Recording of a point of consistency for a tablespace or a set of tablespaces (QUIESCE utility)
- Repair of damaged data (REPAIR utility)
- Reporting of currently available recovery data (REPORT RECOVERY utility)

The COPY Utility

The COPY utility is used to create an image copy backup data set for a complete tablespace o single partition of a tablespace. It can be executed so that a full image copy or an incremen image copy is created. A *full image copy* is a complete copy of all the data stored in the tablespa or tablespace partition being copied. An *incremental image copy* is a copy of only the tablespa pages that have been modified due to inserts, updates, or deletes since the last full or increme tal image copy.

The COPY utility utilizes the SYSIBM.SYSCOPY table to maintain a catalog of tablespace ima copies. Every successful execution of the COPY utility places in this table at least one new ro that indicates the status of the image copy. Information stored in the table includes the ima copy data set name, the date and time of the COPY, the log RBA at the time of the copy, and t volume serial numbers for uncataloged image copy data sets. This information is read by t RECOVER utility to enable automated tablespace recovery.

The JCL in Listing 25.1 depicts a full image copy; the JCL in Listing 25.2 is an incremental image copy. The full image copy takes dual copies, whereas the incremental takes only a single image copy data set.

Listing 25.1. Image copy JCL.

```
//DB2JOBU JOB (UTILITY),'FULL IMAGE COPY',CLASS=X,MSGCLASS=X,
//        NOTIFY=USER
//*
//****************************************************************
//*
//*       DB2 COPY UTILITY::FULL COPY
//*
//****************************************************************
//*
//COPY EXEC DSNUPROC,SYSTEM=DSN,UID='FULLCOPY',UTPROC=''
//*
//DSNUPROC.COPY1 DD DSN=CAT.FULLCOPY.SEQ.DATASET1(+1),
//      DISP=(MOD,CATLG),DCB=(SYS1.MODEL,BUFNO=20),
//      SPACE=(CYL,(5,2),RLSE),UNIT=3390
//DSNUPROC.COPY2 DD DSN=CAT.FULLCOPY.SEQ.DATASET2(+1),
//      DISP=(MOD,CATLG),DCB=(SYS1.MODEL,BUFNO=20),
//      SPACE=(CYL,(5,2),RLSE),UNIT=3390
//DSNUPROC.SYSIN    DD  *
  COPY TABLESPACE DSN8D51A.DSN8S51D
      COPYDDN (COPY1, COPY2)
      SHRLEVEL REFERENCE
      DSNUM ALL    FULL YES
/*
//
```

Listing 25.2. Incremental image copy JCL.

```
//DB2JOBU JOB (UTILITY),'INCREMENTAL COPY',CLASS=X,MSGCLASS=X,
//        NOTIFY=USER
//*
//****************************************************************
//*
//*       DB2 COPY UTILITY :: INCREMENTAL COPY
//*
//****************************************************************
//*
//COPY EXEC DSNUPROC,SYSTEM=DSN,UID='INCRCOPY',UTPROC=''
//*
//DSNUPROC.SYSCOPY DD DSN=CAT.INCRCOPY.SEQ.DATASET(+1),
//      DISP=(MOD,CATLG),DCB=(SYS1.MODEL,BUFNO=20),
//      SPACE=(CYL,(2,2),RLSE),UNIT=3380
//DSNUPROC.SYSIN    DD  *
  COPY TABLESPACE DSN8D51A.DSN8S51D SHRLEVEL REFERENCE
      DSNUM ALL    FULL NO
/*
//
```

COPY Phases

The COPY utility has three phases:

UTILINIT	Sets up and initializes the COPY utility.
COPY	Copies the tablespace data to the sequential file specified in the SYSCOPY DD statement.
UTILTERM	Performs the final utility cleanup.

Calculating SYSCOPY Data Set Size

To create a valid image copy, the COPY utility requires that the SYSCOPY data set be allocated. The following formula calculates the proper size for this data set:

```
SYSCOPY = (number of formatted pages) x 4096
```

NOTE

For segmented tablespaces, empty formatted pages are not copied. This will reduce the size of the backup data set.

If the tablespace being copied uses 32K pages, multiply the result of the preceding calculation by 8. The total number of pages used by a tablespace can be retrieved from the VSAM LISTCAT command or from the DB2 Catalog as specified in the NACTIVE column in SYSIBM.SYSTABLESPACE. If you use the DB2 Catalog method, ensure that the statistics are current by running the RUNSTATS utility (discussed in Chapter 27, "Catalog Manipulation Utilities").

After calculating the estimated size in bytes for this data set, convert the number to cylinders, rounding up to the next whole cylinder. Allocating data sets used by DB2 utilities in cylinder increments enhances the utility's performance.

COPY Locking Considerations

Copies running against the different partitions of the same tablespace can run concurrently. Many other utilities can run concurrently with COPY, as well. The COPY utility (whether SHRLEVEL REFERENCE or SHRLEVEL CHANGE) can run concurrently with the following utilities (each accessing the same object):

- CHECK INDEX
- DIAGNOSE
- MODIFY STATISTICS
- RECOVER INDEX

- REORG INDEX
- REORG UNLOAD ONLY
- REPAIR LOCATE (DUMP or VERIFY)
- REPORT
- RUNSTATS
- STOSPACE

Furthermore, the COPY utility can run concurrently with REPAIR LOCATE INDEX (PAGE REPLACE) and QUIESCE, but only when run specifying SHRLEVEL REFERENCE.

The COPY utility with the SHRLEVEL REFERENCE option drains the write claim class. This enables concurrent SQL read access. When SHRLEVEL CHANGE is specified, the COPY utility will claim the read claim class. Concurrent read and write access is permitted with one exception. A DELETE with no WHERE clause is not permitted on a table in a segmented tablespace while COPY SHRLEVEL CHANGE is running.

COPY Guidelines

You can use the following tips and techniques to ensure that the COPY utility is used effectively at your organization.

Increase Performance Using Inline Copies

Version 5

As of DB2 V5, the LOAD and REORG utilities can take inline image copies during regular utility processing. By taking advantage of this capability, overall performance is enhanced because fewer scans of the data are required to produce the image copy data sets.

Balance the Use of Incremental and Full Image Copies

For most application tablespaces, favor the creation of full image copies over incremental image copies. The time saved by incremental copying is often minimal, but the additional work to recover using incremental copies is usually burdensome.

To reduce the batch processing window, use incremental image copies for very large tablespaces that incur only a small number of modifications between image copy runs. However, base the decision to use incremental image copies rather than full image copies on the percentage of tablespace pages that have been modified, not on the number of rows that have been modified. The image copy utility reports on the percentage of pages modified, so you can monitor this number. Consider using incremental image copies if this number is consistently small (for example, less than 20 percent).

You should consider incremental copying as the tablespace becomes larger and the batch window becomes smaller.

Take Full Image Copies to Encourage Sequential Prefetch

Remember that DB2 utilities requiring sequential data access use sequential prefetch, thereby enhancing utility performance. Thus, full image copies are often quicker than incremental image copies. A full image copy sequentially reads every page to create the image copy. An incremental image copy must check page bits to determine whether data has changed, then access only the changed pages.

When incremental image copying does not use sequential prefetch, full image copying can be more efficient. Extra time is used because of the additional MERGECOPY step and the inefficient processing (that is, nonsequential prefetch). Compare the performance of incremental and full image copies before deciding to use incremental image copies.

Take Full Image Copies for Active and Smaller Tablespaces

Take full image copies for tablespaces in which 40 percent or more of the pages are modified between executions of the COPY utility.

Always take full image copies of tablespaces that contain less than 50,000 pages.

Specify SHRLEVEL REFERENCE to Reduce Recovery Time

COPY specifying SHRLEVEL REFERENCE rather than SHRLEVEL CHANGE. This reduces the time for tablespace recovery. See the section titled "RECOVER TABLESPACE Guidelines" later in this chapter.

Running COPY with SHRLEVEL CHANGE can cause uncommitted data to be recorded on the copy. For this reason, recovering to a SHRLEVEL CHANGE copy using the TOCOPY option is not recommended.

An additional reason to avoid SHRLEVEL CHANGE is the impact on the performance of the COPY utility. Because other users can access the tablespace being copied, the performance of the COPY could degrade because of concurrent access. Note, however, that SHRLEVEL REFERENCE has only a performance advantage—not an integrity advantage—over SHRLEVEL CHANGE.

Code JCL Changes to Make COPY Restartable

To make the COPY utility restartable, specify the SYSCOPY DD statement as DISP=(MOD,CATLG,CATLG). When restarting the COPY utility, change the data set disposition to DISP=(MOD,KEEP,KEEP).

Create a Consistent Recovery Point

QUIESCE all tablespaces in the tablespace set before copying. Do this even when some tablespaces do not need to be copied so you can provide a consistent point of recovery for all referentially tied tablespaces. Create a batch job stream that accomplishes the following steps:

1. START all tablespaces in the tablespace set using ACCESS(UT) or ACCESS(RO). Starting the tablespaces in RO mode enables concurrent read access while the COPY is running.
2. QUIESCE all tablespaces in the tablespace set.
3. Execute the COPY utility for all tablespaces to be copied.
4. START all tablespaces in the tablespace set using ACCESS(RW).

NOTE

The consistent backup created by this series of steps is ideal for populating a test environment (using DSN1COPY).

Consider Creating DASD Image Copies

When possible, use DASD rather than tape for the image copy SYSCOPY data sets that will remain at the local site for recovery. This speeds the COPY process; DASD is faster than tape, and you eliminate the time it takes the operator (or the automated robot tape loader) to load a new tape on the tape drive.

Buffer the SYSCOPY Data Set Appropriately

For large image copies set the BUFNO parameter in the JCL for the SYSCOPY DD statement to a number greater than 20. The BUFNO parameter creates read and write buffers in main storage for the data set, thereby enhancing the performance of the COPY utility. The default for BUFNO is 8 for DB2 V3 and 20 for DB2 V4.

Ensure that sufficient memory (real or expanded) is available, however, before increasing the BUFNO specification for your SYSCOPY data sets.

Favor Dual Image Copies

Take dual image copies for every tablespace being copied to eliminate the possibility of an invalid image copy due to an I/O error or damaged tape. As of DB2 V2.3, the COPY utility can do this automatically. Prior to DB2 V2.3, only a single image copy can be taken by a single invocation of the COPY utility. To create dual image copies with an older release of DB2, you have two choices:

- Run the COPY utility again, and incur all the expense associated with it
- Copy the image copy data set to an uncataloged data set of the same name using IEBGENER or another utility that copies entire data sets

Prepare for disasters by sending additional image copies off-site. As of DB2 V2.3, the COPY utility can enable this automatically. Prior to DB2 V2.3, the COPY utility can take only a local copy.

To create remote image copies using a prior release of DB2, you must either run the COPY utility again and incur all the expense associated with it, or copy the image copy to an uncataloged data set of the same name using IEBGENER or another utility that copies entire data sets. The only practical solution, however, is to use IEBGENER, because the COPY utility stores the image copy data set name in the SYSIBM.SYSCOPY table and can automatically recall it for RECOVER processing. If the tape has been shipped to a remote site, though, the RECOVER utility will fail without operator intervention. Additional contingency planning details are provided in Chapter 31, "DB2 Contingency Planning."

Compress Image Copies

To conserve tapes, consider compressing image copies. Use the silo compression if it's available. Additionally, many shops have third-party tools to compress data on tape cartridges.

If your shop does not compress cartridges by default, add the following parameter to the DCB specification for the SYSCOPY DD:

```
DCB=TRTCH=COMP
```

Consider Using DFSMS to Make Backup Copies

As of DB2, V3 DFSMS can be utilized in the backup and recovery strategy for DB2 tablespaces. V3 provides the capability to recover from backup copies of DB2 data sets taken using the concurrent copy feature of DFSMS. To take viable copies using DB2 V3 and DFSMS, use the following strategy:

1. START all tablespaces to be backed up in read-only mode; ACCESS(RO).
2. QUIESCE the objects specifying the WRITE(YES) parameter.
3. Use DFSMS to copy the data sets for the tablespaces in question.
4. START the tablespaces in RW mode.

DB2 does not keep track of these copies in the DB2 Catalog.

Version 4

As of DB2 V4, DFSMS can be invoked under the control of DB2 using the COPY utility. This greatly enhances the ability to utilize DFSMS within a DB2 backup and recovery plan. DFSMS is invoked by specifying the CONCURRENT parameter on the COPY utility. The image copy data sets created by the COPY utility and DFSMS are stored in the DB2 Catalog (SYSIBM.SYSCOPY) with an ICTYPE of F and an STYPE of C.

NOTE

An output data set for DFSMS messages is required to be specified to the DSSPRINT DD card when CONCURRENT copy is specified and the SYSPRINT DD card is defined to a data set.

CAUTION

You cannot use SHRLEVEL CHANGE with CONCURRENT COPY for tablespaces having a 32K page size.

Use CHANGELIMIT to Help with Copies

Version 5

The CHANGELIMIT parameter can be specified on the COPY utility. When CHANGELIMIT is specified, COPY analyzes the number of changed pages since the last copy.

CHANGELIMIT accepts one or two integers (from 1 to 100) as input. Each integer is a percentage. The first indicates the threshold for taking an incremental image copy; the second for taking a full image copy. So, for example, specifying CHANGELIMIT (10,20) would indicate that an incremental image copy is to be taken when 10 percent or more of the pages have changed; a full image copy is to be taken when 20 percent or more of the pages have changed.

When CHANGELIMIT is specified with COPY, return codes are set as indicated in Table 25.1.

Table 25.1. COPY / CHANGELIMIT return codes.

Return Code	*Description*
1	The percentage of changed pages is greater than the low CHANGELIMIT value, but less than the high CHANGELIMIT value; incremental copy is recommended or taken
2	The percentage of changed pages is greater than the high CHANGELIMIT value; full image copy is recommended or taken
3	Neither percentage is met; no image copy is recommended or taken
8	The COPY step failed

The information obtained can be used for two purposes:

- If REPORTONLY is specified, a report of the number of changed pages is produced. Further action can be taken after reviewing the report or checking the return code in the JCL.
- Without the REPORTONLY parameter, the COPY utility automatically decides whether or not to take an image copy—if it does take an image copy, the COPY utility determines whether the image is to be incremental or full.

The MERGECOPY Utility

The MERGECOPY utility combines multiple incremental image copy data sets into a new full or incremental image copy data set. See Listing 25.3 for sample JCL. The first control card depicts the merging of image copy data sets for the DSN8D51A.DSN8S51D tablespace into a full image copy. The second control card shows statements that create a new incremental image copy data set for the DSN8D51A.DSN8S51E tablespace.

Listing 25.3. MERGECOPY JCL.

```
//DB2JOBU JOB (UTILITY), 'MERGECOPY',CLASS=X,MSGCLASS=X,NOTIFY=USER
//*
//****************************************************************
//*
//*        DB2 MERGECOPY UTILITY
//*
//****************************************************************
//*
//COPY EXEC DSNUPROC,SYSTEM=DSN,UID='MERGCOPY',UTPROC=''
//*
//* UTILITY WORK DATASETS
//*
//DSNUPROC.SYSUT1 DD DSN=CAT.SYSUT1,DISP=(MOD,CATLG,CATLG),
//        UNIT=SYSDA,SPACE=(CYL,(10,1)),DCB=BUFNO=20
//DSNUPROC.SYSCOPY1 DD DSN=CAT.FULLCOPY.SEQ.DATASETD(+1),
//        DISP=(MOD,CATLG),DCB=(SYS1.MODEL, BUFNO=20),
//        SPACE=(CYL,(5,1),RLSE),UNIT=TAPE
//DSNUPROC.SYSCOPY2 DD DSN=CAT.INCRCOPY.SEQ.DATASETE(+1),
//        DISP=(MOD,CATLG),DCB=(SYS1.MODEL, BUFNO=20),
//        SPACE=(CYL,(2,1),RLSE),UNIT=TAPE
//*
//*  UTILITY INPUT CONTROL STATEMENTS
//*       The first MERGECOPY statement creates a new full
//*       image copy for the DSN8D51A.
//*       The second statement creates a new incremental copy
//*       for the named tablespace.
//*
//DSNUPROC.SYSIN    DD  *
   MERGECOPY TABLESPACE DSN8D51A.DSN8S51D
             DSNUM ALL    NEWCOPY YES
             COPYDDN SYSCOPY1
   MERGECOPY TABLESPACE DSN8D51A.DSN8S51E
             DSNUM ALL    NEWCOPY NO
             COPYDDN SYSCOPY2
/*
//
```

MERGECOPY Phases

UTILINIT Sets up and initializes the MERGECOPY utility.

MERGE Merges the full and incremental image copy data sets for the indicated tablespace using the SYSUT1 DD data set for temporary work space (if necessary), then places the final merged copy in the data set specified by the SYSCOPY DD statement.

UTILTERM Performs the final utility cleanup.

Estimating SYSUT1 and SYSCOPY Data Set Sizes

The MERGECOPY utility sometimes requires the use of the SYSUT1 work data set to merge image copies. If it is impossible to simultaneously allocate all the data sets to be merged, SYSUT1 is used to hold intermediate output from the merge. If enough tape drives are not available (to allocate the incremental copy data sets) when MERGECOPY runs, be sure to allocate a SYSUT1 data set.

The SYSCOPY data set holds the final merged image copy data and must be specified. The space required for this data set is the same as would be required for the SYSCOPY data set for the COPY utility. A merged image copy and a full image copy should be functionally equivalent and therefore should consume the same amount of space.

The following formula should be used to calculate an estimated size for this data set. This calculation is only an estimate. More complex and precise calculations are in the *DB2 Utility Guide and Reference* manual, but this formula should produce comparable results.

```
SYSUT1 = (size of the largest data set to be merged) x 1.5
SYSCOPY = (number of formatted pages) x 4096
```

If the tablespace being merged uses 32K pages, multiply the result of the SYSCOPY calculation by 8. The total number of pages used by a tablespace can be retrieved from either the VSAM LISTCAT command or the DB2 Catalog as specified in the NACTIVE column of SYSIBM.SYSTABLESPACE. If you are using the DB2 Catalog method, ensure that the statistics are current by running the RUNSTATS utility.

After calculating the estimated size for the data sets, convert the number into cylinders, rounding up to the next whole cylinder. Allocating work data sets in cylinder increments enhances the utility's performance.

Concurrency

Concurrent read and write activity can occur during execution of the MERGECOPY utility. The MERGECOPY utility can run concurrently with any utility except the following:

- COPY
- MERGECOPY
- MODIFY RECOVERY
- RECOVER

MERGECOPY Guidelines

When running MERGECOPY, consider abiding by the following guidelines.

Merge Incremental Copies as Soon as Possible

Directly after the execution of an incremental COPY, run the MERGECOPY utility to create a new full image copy. In this way, the resources to create a new full image copy are used at a non-critical time. If you decide to avoid the creation of full image copies until there is an error, valuable time can be consumed by processing that could have taken place at a less critical time.

Use MERGECOPY to Create Full Image Copies

Specify NEWCOPY YES to produce a new full image copy. NEWCOPY NO can be used to produce a new incremental copy. Favor the creation of new full image copies rather than incremental copies because less work must be performed to correct an error if full tablespace image copies exist.

Specify the SYSUT1 Data Set

Always specify a data set for SYSUT1 to avoid rerunning MERGECOPY. If SYSUT1 is not specified, the MERGECOPY job might be unable to allocate all the data sets needed for the merge, thereby requiring that MERGECOPY be run again. This must continue until all incremental copies have been merged into a new image copy data set, either full or incremental.

If SYSUT1 is not specified, the output of the MERGECOPY utility indicates whether another merge must be run. MERGECOPY produces a message indicating the number of existing data sets and the number of merged data sets. If these numbers are not equal, rerun the MERGECOPY utility. Again, this can be avoided by specifying a SYSUT1 data set.

Buffer the SYSCOPY Data Set Appropriately

For large image copies, set the BUFNO parameter in the JCL for the SYSCOPY DD statements to a number greater than 20. The BUFNO parameter creates read and write buffers in main storage for the data set, thereby enhancing the performance of the COPY utility. The default for BUFNO is 8 for DB2 V3 and 20 for DB2 V4.

sure that sufficient memory (real or expanded) is available, however, before increasing the 'NO specification for your SYSCOPY data sets.

nsider Buffering the SYSUT1 Data Set

nsider specifying a larger BUFNO for the SYSUT1 data set if you expect many incremental im- copies to be required. Remember that BUFNO=8 is the DB2 V3 default and BUFNO=20 is the 32 V4 (and later) default.

ne QUIESCE Utility

e QUIESCE utility is used to record a point of consistency for related application or system lespaces. QUIESCE ensures that all tablespaces in the scope of the QUIESCE are referentially act. It does this by externalizing all data modifications to DASD and recording log RBAs in SYSIBM.SYSCOPY DB2 Catalog table, indicating a point of consistency for future recovery. the sections titled "The RECOVER Utility" and "The RECOVER TABLESPACE Utility" later in s chapter for further information on recovering DB2 tablespaces.

nple JCL for the QUIESCE utility is in Listing 25.4. This will quiesce all the tablespaces for DB2 sample tables.

ing 25.4. QUIESCE JCL.

```
B2JOBU  JOB (UTILITY),'QUIESCE',CLASS=X,MSGCLASS=X,NOTIFY=USER
*
*****************************************************************
*
*      DB2 QUIESCE UTILITY
*
*      Step 1:  STARTUT:  Start all tablespaces in the
*               tablespace set in utility-only mode.
*      Step 2:  QUIESCE:  Quiesce all tablespaces in the
*               tablespace set.
*      Step 3:  STARTRW:  Start all tablespaces in the
*               tablespace set in read/write mode.
*
*****************************************************************
*
STARTUT EXEC PGM=IKJEFT01,DYNAMNBR=20
STEPLIB DD DSN=DSN510.DSNLOAD,DISP=SHR
SYSPRINT DD SYSOUT=*
SYSTSPRT DD SYSOUT=*
SYSOUT   DD SYSOUT=*
SYSUDUMP DD SYSOUT=*
SYSTSIN  DD *
 SYSTEM (DSN)
ART DATABASE (DSN8D51A) ACCESS (UT)
)
```

continues

Listing 25.4. continued

```
//QUIESCE EXEC DSNUPROC,SYSTEM=DSN,UID='QUIESCTS',UTPROC='',
//             COND=(0,NE,STARTUT)
//DSNUPROC.SYSIN     DD  *
    QUIESCE TABLESPACE DSN8D51A.DSN8S51C
            TABLESPACE DSN8D51A.DSN8S51D
            TABLESPACE DSN8D51A.DSN8S51E
            TABLESPACE DSN8D51A.DSN8S51R
            TABLESPACE DSN8D51A.ACT
            TABLESPACE DSN8D51A.PROJ
            TABLESPACE DSN8D51A.PROJACT
            TABLESPACE DSN8D51A.EMPPROJA WRITE YES
/*
//STARTRW EXEC PGM=IKJEFT01,DYNAMNBR=20,COND=EVEN
//STEPLIB DD DSN=DSN510.DSNLOAD,DISP=SHR
//*
//SYSPRINT DD SYSOUT=*
//SYSTSPRT DD SYSOUT=*
//SYSOUT   DD SYSOUT=*
//SYSUDUMP DD SYSOUT=*
//SYSTSIN  DD *
DSN SYSTEM (DSN)
-START DATABASE (DSN8D51A) ACCESS (RW)
END
/*
//
```

QUIESCE Phases

The QUIESCE utility has three phases:

UTILINIT	Sets up and initializes the QUIESCE utility
QUIESCE	Determines the point of consistency and updates the DB2 Catalog
UTILTERM	Performs the final utility cleanup

QUIESCE Locking Considerations

The following utilities can run concurrently with QUIESCE:

- CHECK INDEX
- COPY SHRLEVEL REFERENCE
- DIAGNOSE
- MERGECOPY
- MODIFY
- REORG UNLOAD ONLY
- REPAIR LOCATE (DUMP or VERIFY)

- REPORT
- RUNSTATS
- STOSPACE

The QUIESCE utility will drain all write claim classes. If WRITE YES is specified, QUIESCE will also drain all write claim classes on an associated partitioning index (or partition) and any nonpartitioned indexes. Concurrent read access is permitted during a QUIESCE.

QUIESCE Guidelines

Implement the following guidelines to ensure effective usage of the QUIESCE utility as you shop.

Run QUIESCE Before COPY

QUIESCE all tablespaces in a tablespace set before copying them. When QUIESCE will be run for a tablespace in a tablespace set, QUIESCE every tablespace in the tablespace set to ensure data consistency and referential integrity. Of course, if the COPY PENDING flag is on, QUIESCE will fail.

Specify the WRITE Option

Be sure to specify whether changed pages in the bufferpool are to be externalized to DASD. Specifying WRITE YES will cause pages in the bufferpool to be written; specifying WRITE NO will not. The default is WRITE YES.

QUIESCE the System Databases Before Copying

QUIESCE all DSNDB01 and DSNDB06 tablespaces before copying the DB2 Catalog. Before quiescing these tablespaces, consider placing the databases into utility-only mode using the DB2 START command.

Only an Install SYSADM can QUIESCE the DB2 Directory and DB2 Catalog.

Use QUIESCE to Create Interim Points of Recovery

QUIESCE can be used to set up recovery points between regularly scheduled image copies. However, QUIESCE does not replace the need for image copies.

QUIESCE Tablespaces Related by Application RI

Even when tablespaces are not tied together using DB2-defined referential integrity but are related by application code, use the QUIESCE utility to ensure the integrity of the data in the tables. This establishes a point of consistency for tablespaces that are related but not controlled by the DBMS.

The QUIESCE utility cannot be run on a tablespace that has a copy pending, check pending, or recovery pending status.

Consider Quiescing Online Tablespaces While Activity Is Low

Run QUIESCE as frequently as possible for tablespaces containing tables modified online. This enables the recovery of the tablespaces to a point after the last full image copy if there is an error. Do not run the QUIESCE utility during very active periods, however, because it requires a share lock on all the tablespaces that it processes. This means that tablespaces being processed by QUIESCE cannot be modified until the QUIESCE utility completes.

As a general rule, consider quiescing all online systems at least once a day during the least active processing period.

Code Multiple Tablespaces per QUIESCE

When quiescing multiple tablespaces, code the utility control cards with multiple tablespaces assigned to one QUIESCE keyword. For example, code this

```
QUIESCE TABLESPACE  DSN8D51A.DSN8S51C
        TABLESPACE  DSN8D51A.DSN8S51D
        TABLESPACE  DSN8D51A.DSN8S51E
```

instead of

```
QUIESCE TABLESPACE  DSN8D51A.DSN8S51C
QUIESCE TABLESPACE  DSN8D51A.DSN8S51D
QUIESCE TABLESPACE  DSN8D51A.DSN8S51E
```

By coding the control cards the first way, you ensure that the quiesce point for all the tablespaces is consistent. If the control cards are coded as shown in the second example, the QUIESCE utility is invoked three times, resulting in a different point of consistency for each tablespace. If you follow the guidelines for starting all tablespaces in utility-only mode before running QUIESCE, either QUIESCE option will work. However, getting into the habit of coding the control cards as shown in the first example prevents errors if the start does not finish successfully before the QUIESCE begins to execute.

If the list of tablespaces on which the QUIESCE utility is being executed exceeds 1165, it will be terminated with a return code of 8. To QUIESCE groups of more than 1165 tablespaces follow this procedure:

1. Stop all the tablespaces before quiescing.
2. Break the tablespaces into groups of no more than 1165 tablespaces each.
3. Quiesce each group with a single QUIESCE statement. These QUIESCEs can be run in parallel to decrease the overall elapsed time.
4. Start all the tablespaces only after all QUIESCE statements have finished.

Consider Using QUIESCE at the Partition Level

The QUIESCE utility can be requested at the partition level. When it makes sense within your environment, consider using this ability to fine tune your backup and recovery strategy.

The RECOVER Utility

The recovery of DB2 data is an automated process rigorously controlled by the database management system. Figure 25.1 shows the flow of normal DB2 recovery. The standard unit of recovery for DB2 is the tablespace. The DB2 COPY utility is used to create an image copy backup of the tablespace data sets. All DB2 image copy data set information is recorded in the DB2 Catalog in the SYSIBM.SYSCOPY table. It is not necessary to keep track of the image copy data sets externally because DB2 manages this information independent of the application code.

FIGURE 25.1.
DB2 recovery.

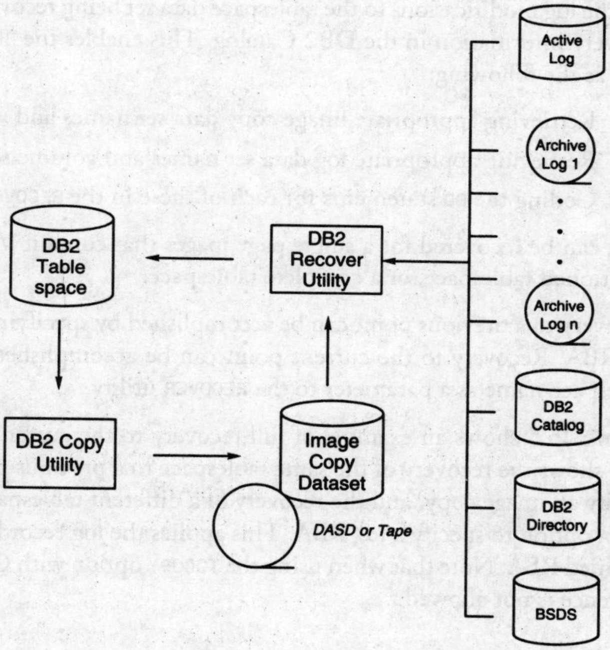

DB2 is also responsible for keeping a log of all changes made to tablespaces. With a few exceptions, all updates are recorded in the DB2 *active log*. When an active log is full, DB2 creates an *archive log*. Many archive logs are created during normal DB2 application processing. All this information is stored in the DB2 Directory's SYSIBM.SYSLGRNG table and the Boot Strap Data Set (BSDS). Refer to Chapter 15, "The Table-Based Infrastructure of DB2," for a complete description of the internal DB2 tables and data sets.

The DB2 RECOVER utility reads all control information pertaining to data recovery and applies the recorded changes contained in the copies and logs, as instructed by the DBMS and the RECOVER utility control parameters.

Basically, the RECOVER utility is used to restore DB2 tablespaces and indexes to a specific point in time. You can run two forms of the RECOVER utility: RECOVER TABLESPACE and RECOVER INDEX. Both are discussed in the following sections.

The RECOVER TABLESPACE Utility

The RECOVER TABLESPACE utility restores tablespaces to a current or previous state. It first reads the DB2 Catalog to determine the availability of full and incremental image copies, then reads the DB2 logs to determine interim modifications. The utility then applies the image copies and the log modifications to the tablespace data set being recovered. The DBMS maintains the recovery information in the DB2 Catalog. This enables the RECOVER utility to automate tasks such as the following:

- Retrieving appropriate image copy data set names and volume serial numbers
- Retrieving appropriate log data set names and volume serial numbers
- Coding the DD statements for each of these in the RECOVER JCL

Data can be recovered for a single page, pages that contain I/O errors, a single partition of a partitioned tablespace, or a complete tablespace.

Recovery to a previous point can be accomplished by specifying a full image copy or a specific log RBA. Recovery to the current point can be accomplished by simply specifying only the tablespace name as a parameter to the RECOVER utility.

Listing 25.5 shows an example of full recovery to the current point for a tablespace. Listing 25.6 shows the recovery of the same tablespace to a previous point using the TOCOPY option to specify an image copy, and the recovery of a different tablespace to a previous point using the TORBA option to specify a log RBA. This applies the log records only up to, not including, the specified RBA. Note that when using the TOCOPY option with GDG datasets, the relative GDG reference is not allowed.

Listing 25.5. JCL for full recovery.

```
//DB2JOBU JOB (UTILITY),'FULL RECOVERY',CLASS=X,MSGCLASS=X,
//NOTIFY=USER
//*
//****************************************************************
//*
//*       DB2 RECOVER UTILITY  ::  FULL RECOVERY
//*
//****************************************************************
//*
//RCVR EXEC DSNUPROC,SYSTEM=DSN,UID='FULLRECV',UTPROC=''
//*
//*  UTILITY INPUT CONTROL STATEMENTS
//*     1. The first RECOVER statement recovers the
//*        DSN8D51A.DSN8S51C tablespace to the current point
//*        in time.
```

```
//*     2. The second RECOVER statement recovers all indexes
//*        in the tablespace.
//*
//DSNUPROC.SYSIN    DD  *
    RECOVER TABLESPACE DSN8D51A.DSN8S51C DSNUM ALL
    RECOVER INDEX(ALL) TABLESPACE DSN8D51A.DSN8S51C
/*
//
```

Listing 25.6. JCL for partial recovery.

```
//DB2JOBU JOB (UTILITY),'PRTL RECOVERY',CLASS=X,MSGCLASS=X,
//          NOTIFY=USER
//*
//****************************************************************
//*
//*         DB2 RECOVER UTILITY  ::  PARTIAL RECOVERY
//*
//****************************************************************
//*
//RCVR EXEC DSNUPROC,SYSTEM=DSN,UID='PRTLRECV',UTPROC=''
//*
//*  UTILITY INPUT CONTROL STATEMENTS
//*    1. The first RECOVER statement recovers the
//*       DSN8D51A.DSN8S51D tablespace to the named
//*       image copy data set.
//*    2. The second RECOVER statement recovers the
//*       DSN8D51A.DSN8S51C tablespace to the specified
//*       log RBA.
//*
//DSNUPROC.SYSIN    DD  *
   RECOVER TABLESPACE DSN8D51A.DSN8S51D
           TOCOPY CAT.FULLCOPY.DATASETD.G0001V00
   RECOVER TABLESPACE DSN8D51A.DSN8S51C
           TORBA X'0000EF2C66F4'
/*
//
```

RECOVER TABLESPACE Phases

The RECOVER TABLESPACE utility has four phases:

UTILINIT	Sets up and initializes the RECOVER utility
RESTORE	Locates and merges all appropriate image copy data sets, after which the tablespace is restored to the given point using the merged image copy data
LOGAPPLY	Locates outstanding modifications for the tablespace being recovered and applies them to that tablespace
UTILTERM	Performs the final utility cleanup

The RESTORE phase is bypassed if the LOGAPPLY option is specified.

RECOVER TABLESPACE Locking Considerations

The RECOVER utility can run concurrently with the following utilities:

- DIAGNOSE
- MODIFY STATISTICS
- REPORT
- STOSPACE

Additionally, unless RECOVER TOCOPY or TORBA is specified, RECOVER can run concurrently wi REORG INDEX, REPAIR LOCATE INDEX, and RUNSTATS INDEX.

The RECOVER utility drains all claim classes for the tablespace or partition being recovered, r gardless of the options specified. However, if the ERROR-RANGE option is specified, the locki level is downgraded to a write claim during the UTILINIT phase.

If either the TORBA or TOCOPY option is specified, RECOVER will drain all claim classes for the i dex or index partition, as well.

RECOVER TABLESPACE Guidelines

Be sure to implement the following guidelines when you are recovering tablespaces.

Do Not Specify Work Data Sets

The RECOVER TABLESPACE utility does not require work data sets to recover DB2 tablespace

For High Performance, Avoid Recovery Using SHRLEVEL CHANGE Image Copies

If RECOVER TABLESPACE is used for a tablespace in which an image copy data set was created wi the SHRLEVEL CHANGE specification, the performance of the RECOVER utility degrades. The l RBA stored for an image copy taken with SHRLEVEL CHANGE is at an earlier portion of the l because the tablespace can be modified during the execution of the COPY utility. Therefore, t RECOVER utility reads the log RBA recorded with the image copy in the SYSIBM.SYSCOPY tal and scans the active and archive logs for changes starting with that RBA. Performance c degrade because more log records are read.

Recover SHRLEVEL CHANGE Copies Appropriately

Image copies taken using SHRLEVEL CHANGE must be recovered to the current point in time or a specific point in time using TORBA (not TOCOPY). If a SHRLEVEL CHANGE image copy is recover using the TOCOPY option, it will be in an indeterminate stage.

Be Aware of Underlying VSAM Data Set Deletions

The underlying VSAM data sets for STOGROUP-defined tablespaces are deleted and defined by the RECOVER TABLESPACE utility. If the tablespace has been user-defined, the corresponding VSAM data set is not deleted.

Recover Multiple Tablespaces with a Single RECOVER

When multiple tablespaces must be recovered, code the utility control cards with multiple tablespaces assigned to one RECOVER keyword. For example, code this

```
RECOVER TABLESPACE  DSN8D51A.DSN8S51C
        TABLESPACE  DSN8D51A.DSN8S51D
        TABLESPACE  DSN8D51A.DSN8S51E
```

instead of

```
RECOVER TABLESPACE  DSN8D51A.DSN8S51C
RECOVER TABLESPACE  DSN8D51A.DSN8S51D
RECOVER TABLESPACE  DSN8D51A.DSN8S51E
```

Coding the control cards the first way ensures that the archive and active logs are read only once. If the control cards are coded as shown in the second example, the RECOVER TABLESPACE utility runs three times, causing the archive and active logs to be read separately for each invocation of the utility. This reduces CPU time, elapsed time, and time spent waiting for an operator to load the archive tapes.

Explicitly Allocate Image Copy Data Sets

DB2 dynamically allocates image copy and log data sets during the execution of the RECOVER utility to minimize an analyst's work during recovery. However, the image copy input to the RECOVER utility can be specified explicitly in the JCL by simply coding a DD statement for each full and incremental image copy to be used. The DD statement can use any name not already used by the RECOVER JCL. DB2 will not dynamically allocate an image copy data set if it finds a DD statement with a matching data set name specified in the RECOVER JCL.

If image copy data sets are explicitly allocated as just described, the UNIT=AFF parameter can be coded to single-thread the image copy input to the RECOVER utility.

Use DB2's Capability to Fall Back to Previous Image Copies

Current point-in-time recovery attempts to allocate the most recent full image copy for processing. If an error is encountered for that image copy, the RECOVER utility uses the previous full image copy.

If a tape image copy data set is unavailable, the operator can reply NO to the tape mount message to cause DB2 to use a previous image copy.

Take Incremental Image Copies to Reduce Log Reading

If incremental image copies exist, the RECOVER TABLESPACE utility attempts to use them to reduce the number of log data sets and records that must be processed to accomplish the recovery.

Remember to Recover Indexes

Execute the RECOVER INDEX utility for all tablespaces recovered using the partial recovery options TOCOPY or TORBA. Failure to do so results in invalid indexes.

Do Not Specify Relative Generation Numbers for GDG Image Copies

The TOCOPY option of the RECOVER TABLESPACE utility is used to explicitly name an image copy data set to which the named tablespace will be recovered. If the image copy data set is a GDG, the fully qualified data set name must be specified, including the absolute generation and version number. Relative generation number specification is not supported by the RECOVER utility.

Specify a Valid Image Copy Data Set

When the TOCOPY option is used, the image copy data set specified must be recorded in the SYSIBM.SYSCOPY table. If it is not, the recovery fails.

Recover Tablespaces at the Same Level as the Available Image Copies

Recovery must be processed according to the type of image copy available. For example, if image copies were taken for a partitioned tablespace at the DSNUM level, RECOVER TABLESPACE must operate at the DSNUM level.

Recover Only Complete Units of Work

Avoid recovering tablespaces to an RBA other than an RBA recorded in the SYSIBM.SYSCOPY table as a result of the QUIESCE utility. Recovery to an RBA other than a quiesce point RBA may cause recovery to the middle of a unit of work, resulting in inconsistent data.

Recover Only Consistent Image Copies

Avoid using the TOCOPY option to recover tablespaces to an image copy created with SHRLEVEL CHANGE. Doing so can cause data integrity problems because the image copy may reflect partial unit of work changes. Because the tablespace might have been modified during the execution of the COPY utility, the image copy without the corresponding log changes represents data in an inconsistent state.

Use RECOVER with DFSMS Copies

DB2 provides the capability to recover from backup copies of DB2 data sets taken using the concurrent copy feature of DFSMS. Follow these steps to accomplish this:

1. STOP all tablespaces to be recovered.
2. START the objects in utility mode or read-only mode; ACCESS(UT) or ACCESS(RO).
3. Use DFSMS to restore the data sets for the tablespaces in question.
4. Use RECOVER with the LOGAPPLY option to apply only log records and not RESTORE from an image copy.
5. START the tablespaces in RW mode.

Restart the RECOVER Utility as Needed

RECOVER TABLESPACE is a restartable utility. No special consideration is necessary because work data sets are not required when recovering a tablespace alone. The utility can be restarted by changing the DSNUTILB JCL parameter to UTPROC=RESTART.

Follow the Procedures in the IBM Manual When Recovering System Tablespaces

The DB2 Catalog and DB2 Directory tablespaces can be recovered using the RECOVER TABLESPACE utility, but the recovery must be performed in a specific order. Consult the *DB2 Database Administration Guide* for details.

The RECOVER INDEX Utility

The RECOVER INDEX utility can be used to re-create indexes from current data. Indexes are always recovered from actual table data, not from image copy and log data. RECOVER INDEX scans the table on which the index is based and regenerates the index based on the current data. JCL to run the RECOVER INDEX utility is provided in Listing 25.7.

Listing 25.7. RECOVER INDEX JCL.

```
//DB2JOBU  JOB (UTILITY),'DB2 RECVR INDEX',MSGCLASS=X,CLASS=X,
//         NOTIFY=USER
//*
//****************************************************************
//*
//*        DB2 RECOVER INDEX UTILITY
//*
//****************************************************************
//*
//UTIL EXEC DSNUPROC,SYSTEM=DSN,UID='RCVRINDX',UTPROC=''
//*
//*  UTILITY WORK DATASETS
//*
//DSNUPROC.SORTWK01 DDUNIT=SYSDA,SPACE=(CYL,(2,1))
//DSNUPROC.SORTWK02 DDUNIT=SYSDA,SPACE=(CYL,(2,1))
//DSNUPROC.SYSUT1 DD DSN=&&SYSUT1,
//      UNIT=SYSDA,SPACE=(CYL,(2,1)),DCB=BUFNO=20
//DSNUPROC.UTPRINT DD SYSOUT=X
//*
```

continues

Listing 25.7. continued

```
//*  UTILITY INPUT CONTROL STATEMENTS
//*     1. The first RECOVER INDEX statement rebuilds the
//*        DSN8510.XPROJ2 index.
//*     2. The second RECOVER INDEX statement rebuilds only
//*        the third partition of the DSN8510.XEMP1
//*        partitioning index.
//*     3. The third and final RECOVER INDEX statement
//*        rebuilds all indexes on all tables in the
//*        DSN8D51A.DSN8S51C tablespace.
//*
//DSNUPROC.SYSIN     DD  *
   RECOVER INDEX (DSN8510.XPROJ2)
   RECOVER INDEX (DSN8510.XEMP1) DSNUM 3
   RECOVER INDEX (ALL) TABLESPACE DSN8D51A.DSN8S51C
/*
//
```

NOTE

The sort work data sets need to be assigned in the JCL only if sort work data sets are not dynamic allocated. Additionally, you should consider explicitly defining sort work data sets when recovering very large indexes.

RECOVER INDEX Phases

There are five phases of the RECOVER INDEX utility:

- UTILINIT — Sets up and initializes the RECOVER utility.
- UNLOAD — Unloads data from the appropriate table and places it in the data set assigned to the SYSUT1 DD statement.
- SORT — Sorts the index data using the data sets assigned to the DD statements: SORTOUT and SORTWK*xx* (or to the dynamically assigned sort work data sets).
- BUILD — Builds indexes and checks for duplicate key errors. Unique indexes with duplicate key errors are not recovered successfully.
- UTILTERM — Performs the final utility cleanup.

Estimating RECOVER INDEX Work Data Set Sizes

The RECOVER INDEX utility requires work data sets to recover DB2 indexes. The following formulas can help you calculate estimated sizes for these work data sets. More complex and precise calculations are in the *DB2 Utility Guide and Reference* manual, but these formulas should produce comparable results.

```
SYSUT1 = (size of the largest index key + 13) x (total number of rows in the
➥associated table for the index) x (number of indexes on the table)
SORTWKxx = (size of SYSUT1) x 2
```

NOTE

If any of these numbers is 0, substitute 1.

After calculating the estimated size in bytes for each work data set, convert the number into cylinders, rounding up to the next whole cylinder. Allocating work data sets in cylinder increments enhances the utility's performance.

RECOVER INDEX Locking Considerations

Index recovery can run concurrently with the following utilities:

- COPY SHRLEVEL REFERENCE
- DIAGNOSE
- MERGECOPY
- MODIFY
- REORG UNLOAD ONLY (without a clustered index)
- REPAIR LOCATE by RID or TABLESPACE (DUMP or VERIFY)
- REPORT
- RUNSTATS TABLESPACE
- STOSPACE

The RECOVER INDEX utility drains all claim classes for the index being recovered and drains the write claim class for the associated tablespace.

If RECOVER INDEX is being specified for an individual partition, the utility drains all claim classes for the index partition, a nonpartitioned Type 1 index, and the logical partition of a Type 2 index. The read claim class is drained for nonpartitioned Type 2 indexes. Also, it will drain write claim classes for the associated tablespace partition.

RECOVER INDEX Guidelines

The following guidelines can be applied to ensure effective usage of the RECOVER INDEX utility.

Avoid SYSUT1 If Possible

Version 4

As of DB2 V4, the SYSUT1 data set is no longer required to recover indexes. By removing SYSUT1 from the JCL, the RECOVER will perform faster. However, if SYSUT1 is not included, the RECOVER INDEX utility is not restartable in the UNLOAD phase.

Precede RECOVER INDEX with CHECK INDEX for Large Indexes

Execute the CHECK INDEX utility for large indexes before running RECOVER INDEX. If CHECK INDEX indicates that the index is invalid, RECOVER INDEX should be run. If CHECK INDEX indicates that the index is valid, however, you can save valuable processing time because CHECK INDEX is significantly faster than RECOVER INDEX.

Be Aware of Underlying VSAM Data Set Deletions

The underlying VSAM data sets for STOGROUP-defined indexes are deleted and defined by the RECOVER INDEX utility. If the index has been user-defined, the corresponding VSAM data set is not deleted.

Reorganize System Indexes Using RECOVER INDEX

Although the DB2 Catalog and DB2 Directory tablespaces and indexes cannot be reorganized, their indexes can be recovered. This effectively reorganizes these indexes.

Rerun RECOVER INDEX When Necessary

RECOVER INDEX is not restartable unless the SYSUT1 data set is specified and cataloged. If the RECOVER INDEX abends, terminate the utility, correct the cause of the abend, and rerun the utility. Typical causes for RECOVER INDEX abends include the unavailability of the applicable tablespace and VSAM data set allocation failures.

The REPAIR Utility

The REPAIR utility, discussed in Chapter 24, "Data Consistency Utilities," also can be an integral part of data recovery. REPAIR can be used to assist with a recovery if, based on the order and type of recovery attempted, it can be determined that pending flags can be reset with the REPAIR utility rather than another corresponding utility. This may speed recovery when time is critical.

Additionally, if data is damaged or invalid, the REPAIR utility can be used to modify the data.

The REPORT RECOVERY Utility

The REPORT RECOVERY utility is the second type of REPORT utility provided by DB2. It can be used to generate a report on tablespace recovery information. The report contains information from the DB2 Directory, the DB2 Catalog, and the BSDS. The input to the utility is either a tablespace or a single partition of a partitioned tablespace. REPORT RECOVERY has several options, including the following:

- Providing tablespace recovery information to the last recoverable point, which is the last execution of a full image copy, LOAD REPLACE LOG YES, or REORG LOG YES

- Providing all recovery information for a tablespace, not just information to the last recoverable point
- Providing a list of volume serial numbers for the image copy data sets and archive log data sets needed for recovery

The output of REPORT RECOVERY is a report of all related DB2 recovery information for the tablespaces and tables, including image copy information, log RBA information, and archive log information needed to recover the requested tablespace.

The sample JCL in Listing 25.8 produces a report up to the last recoverable point for the sample tablespace DSN8D51A.DSN8S51C.

Listing 25.8. REPORT RECOVERY JCL.

```
//DB2JOBU  JOB  (UTILITY),'DB2 REPRT RCVRY',MSGCLASS=X,CLASS=X,
//          NOTIFY=USER
//*
//****************************************************************
//*
//*         DB2 REPORT RECOVERY UTILITY
//*
//****************************************************************
//*
//UTIL EXEC DSNUPROC,SYSTEM=DB2T,UID='REPORTRC',UTPROC=''
//DSNUPROC.SYSIN    DD  *
    REPORT RECOVERY TABLESPACE DSN8D51A.DSN8S51E
/*
//
```

REPORT RECOVERY Locking Considerations

The REPORT utility is compatible with all other utilities. It functions like any other process that reads DB2 data.

REPORT RECOVERY Guidelines

The REPORT RECOVERY utility can be used to determine which data sets will be needed by the RECOVERY utility before recovering a tablespace. This can be useful when you must determine whether the requisite data sets are still cataloged or available.

Summary

In this chapter, you learned how to plan for and implement DB2 backup and recovery. You examined the utilities required to accomplish backup and recovery: COPY, MERGECOPY, RECOVER, QUIESCE, REPAIR, and REPORT RECOVERY. Turn the page to the next chapter to discover which utilities to use to efficiently organize DB2 data.

26

Data Organization Utilities

The data organization utilities affect the physical data sets of the DB2 objects for which they are run. Rows of data and their sequence are affected by these utilities. The data organization utilities are LOAD and REORG. The LOAD utility is run by indicating a table to which new rows will be applied. REORG is run at the tablespace or index level, moving data to optimal locations in the data set.

The LOAD Utility

The LOAD utility is used to accomplish bulk inserts to DB2 tables. It can add rows to a table, retaining the current data, or it can replace existing rows with the new data.

Table Loading Philosophies

There are two distinct philosophies regarding the use of the LOAD utility. The first and generally recommended philosophy takes more time to implement but is easier to support. It requires the reservation of sufficient DASD to catalog the LOAD work data sets in case the LOAD job abends.

The work data sets for the LOAD job are allocated for the DDNAMEs SORTOUT, SYSUT1, SYSERR, and SYSMAP with DISP = (MOD,DELETE,CATLG). This enables the data sets to be allocated as new for the initial running of the REORG job. If the job abends, it catalogs the data sets in case they can be used in a restart. After the step completes successfully, the data sets are deleted. The space for these data sets must be planned and available before the LOAD job runs.

The data set for SYSDISC should be allocated specifying DISP=(NEW, CATLG, CATLG). If there are discards, the LOAD utility returns an RC=4, and it does not abend. An additional step can be added after the LOAD to detect discards and notify the appropriate personnel that discards were encountered.

By creating your LOAD job with this philosophy, you can restart an abending LOAD job with little effort after the cause of the abend has been corrected. See Listing 26.1. You simply specify one of the RESTART options in the UTPROC parameter for DSNUTILB.

Listing 26.1. LOAD JCL (restartable).

```
//DB2JOBU  JOB (UTILITY),'DB2 LOAD',MSGCLASS=X,CLASS=X,
//         NOTIFY=USER
//*
//****************************************************************
//*
//*           DB2 LOAD UTILITY (RESTARTABLE)
//*
//****************************************************************
//*
//UTIL EXEC DSNUPROC,SYSTEM=DSN,UID='LOADDATA',UTPROC=''
//*
```

```
//*  UTILITY WORK DATASETS
//*
//DSNUPROC.SORTWK01 DDUNIT=SYSDA,SPACE=(CYL,(2,1))
//DSNUPROC.SORTWK02 DDUNIT=SYSDA,SPACE=(CYL,(2,1))
//DSNUPROC.SORTOUT DD DSN=CAT.SORTOUT,DISP=(MOD,CATLG,CATLG),
//        UNIT=SYSDA,SPACE=(CYL,(2,1))
//DSNUPROC.SYSMAP DD DSN=CAT.SYSUT1,DISP=(MOD,DELETE,CATLG),
//        UNIT=SYSDA,SPACE=(CYL,(2,1)),DCB=BUFNO=20
//DSNUPROC.SYSUT1 DD DSN=CAT.SYSUT1,DISP=(MOD,DELETE,CATLG),
//        UNIT=SYSDA,SPACE=(CYL,(2,1)),DCB=BUFNO=20
//DSNUPROC.SYSDISC DD DSN=CAT.SYSDISC,DISP=(MOD,DELETE,CATLG),
//        UNIT=SYSDA,SPACE=(CYL,(1,1))
//DSNUPROC.SYSERR DD DSN=CAT.SYSERR,DISP=(MOD,DELETE,CATLG),
//        UNIT=SYSDA,SPACE=(CYL,(1,1))
//DSNUPROC.SYSREC00 DD DSN=CAT.LOAD.INPUT.DATASETA,DISP=SHR,DCB=BUFNO=20
//DSNUPROC.UTPRINT DD SYSOUT=X
//*
//*  UTILITY INPUT CONTROL STATEMENTS
//*       The LOAD statement reloads the DSN8510.ACT table
//*
//DSNUPROC.SYSIN    DD  *
  LOAD DATA REPLACE INDDN SYSREC00 LOG NO
  INTO TABLE DSN8510.ACT
     (ACTNO         POSITION ( 1 )  SMALLINT,
      ACTKWD        POSITION ( 3 )  CHAR ( 6 ),
      ACTDESC       POSITION ( 9 )  CHAR ( 20 )
)
/*
//
```

NOTE

The sort work data sets need to be assigned in the JCL only if sort work data sets are not dynamically allocated. Additionally, you should consider explicitly defining sort work data sets when loading very large tables.

The second philosophy is easier to implement but more difficult to support. No additional DASD is required because all LOAD work data sets are temporary. Therefore, all interim work data sets are lost when the job abends. See Listing 26.2 for sample JCL.

Listing 26.2. LOAD JCL (nonrestartable).

```
//DB2JOBU  JOB (UTILITY),'DB2 LOAD',MSGCLASS=X,CLASS=X,
//   NOTIFY=USER,REGION=3M
//*
//****************************************************************
//*
//*          DB2 LOAD UTILITY (NON-RESTARTABLE)
//*
//****************************************************************
```

continues

Listing 26.2. continued

```
//*
//UTIL EXEC DSNUPROC,SYSTEM=DSN,UID='LOADDATA',UTPROC=''
//*
//*  UTILITY WORK DATASETS
//*
//DSNUPROC.SORTWK01 DD DSN=&&SORTWK01,
//        UNIT=SYSDA,SPACE=(CYL,(2,1))
//DSNUPROC.SORTWK02 DD DSN=&&SORTWK02,
//        UNIT=SYSDA,SPACE=(CYL,(2,1))
//DSNUPROC.SORTOUT DD DSN=&&SORTOUT,
//        UNIT=SYSDA,SPACE=(CYL,(2,1))
//DSNUPROC.SYSMAP DD DSN=CAT.SYSUT1,DISP=(MOD,CATLG,CATLG),
//        UNIT=SYSDA,SPACE=(CYL,(2,1))
//DSNUPROC.SYSUT1 DD DSN=&&SYSUT1,DCB=BUFNO=10
//        UNIT=SYSDA,SPACE=(CYL,(2,1))
//DSNUPROC.SYSDISC DD DSN=CAT.SYSDISC,DISP=(MOD,CATLG,CATLG),
//        UNIT=SYSDA,SPACE=(CYL,(1,1))
//DSNUPROC.SYSERR DD DSN=&&SYSERR,
//        UNIT=SYSDA,SPACE=(CYL,(1,1))
//DSNUPROC.SYSREC00 DD DSN=CAT.LOAD.INPUT.DATASETD,DISP=SHR,DCB=BUFNO=10
//DSNUPROC.UTPRINT DD SYSOUT=X
//*
//*  UTILITY INPUT CONTROL STATEMENTS
//*       The LOAD statement adds the data in SYSREC00 to
//*       the DSN8510.DEPT table.
//*
//DSNUPROC.SYSIN    DD  *
  LOAD DATA RESUME(YES) ENFORCE CONSTRAINTS LOG NO
  INDDN SYSREC00 INTO TABLE DSN8510.DEPT
      (DEPTNO         POSITION(    1)
                      CHAR(        3),
       DEPTNAME       POSITION(    4)
                      VARCHAR,
       MGRNO          POSITION(   42)
                      CHAR(        6)  NULLIF(    48)='?',
       ADMRDEPT       POSITION(   49)
                      CHAR(        3)
)
/*
//
```

To restart this LOAD job, you must determine in which phase the job abended. If the job abends in any phase of a LOAD REPLACE, you can simply terminate the utility and rerun. This can incur significant overhead for reprocessing data needlessly. If the first philosophy is used, reprocessing is usually avoided.

For a LOAD RESUME(YES), however, if the job abends in any phase other than UTILINIT, you must restore the tablespace for the table being loaded to a previous point in time. This can be accomplished by running the RECOVER TOCOPY utility or by running a full RECOVER if the LOG NO option of the LOAD utility was specified. After restoring the tablespace (and possibly its associated indexes), you must correct the cause of the abend, terminate the utility, and then rerun the job. As you can see, this method is significantly more difficult to restart than the first method.

Try to use the first philosophy rather than the second. This makes recovery from error situations as smooth and painless as possible.

Estimating LOAD Work Data Set Sizes

The LOAD utility requires work data sets to load data into DB2 tables. The following formulas can help you calculate estimated sizes for these work data sets. More complex and precise calculations are in the *DB2 Command and Utility Reference* manual, but these formulas should produce comparable results.

```
SORTOUT = (size of the largest index key or foreign key + 12)
      ➥x(total number of rows in the table to be loaded)
      ➥x(total number of indexes defined for the table)
      ➥x(total number of foreign keys in the table) x 1.2
```

NOTE

If any number in the SORTOUT calculation is 0, substitute 1.

The multiplier 1.2 is factored into the calculation to provide a "fudge factor." If you are absolutely sure of your numbers, the calculation can be made more precise by eliminating the additional multiplication of 1.2.

```
SYSUT1 = (size of the largest index key or foreign key + 12)
      ➥x (total number of rows to be loaded to the table)
      ➥x (total number of indexes defined for the table)
      ➥x (total number of foreign keys in the table) x 1.2

SORTWKxx = (size of SYSUT1) x 2

 SYSERR = ((number of estimated unique index errors)
        ➥+ (number of estimated data conversion errors)
        ➥+ (number of estimated referential constraint violations)) x 80
```

NOTE

Always allocate the SYSERR data set to be at least one cylinder.

```
SYSMAP = (total number of rows to be loaded to the table) x 16
```

NOTE

The SYSMAP data set is required if either of the following is true:

- Discard processing is requested.
- The tablespace is segmented or partitioned.

```
SYSDISC = Allocate the SYSDISC data set to be the same size as the data set
       ➥containing the rows to be loaded by the LOAD utility
```

NOTE

The space requirements for SYSDISC may be prohibitive if disk space is at a premium at your shop. Instead of allocating the SYSDISC data set as large as the data being loaded, consider using a small primary quantity and a larger secondary quantity—for example:

```
SPACE=(CYL,(0,50),RLSE)
```

NOTE

Although the SYSDISC data set is optional, specifying it is highly recommended in order to trap records that cannot be loaded.

After calculating the estimated size in bytes for each work data set, convert the number into cylinders, rounding up to the next whole cylinder. Allocating work data sets in cylinder increments enhances the utility's performance.

LOAD Phases

There are nine possible phases of the LOAD utility:

UTILINIT	Sets up and initializes the LOAD utility.
RELOAD	Reads the sequential data set specified as input and loads the data to the specified table. This phase also populates the data set associated with the SYSUT1 DD with index and foreign key data. The compression

	dictionary is rebuilt in this step for COMPRESS YES tablespaces. The copy pending flag is reset at the end of this phase if an inline copy is produced (unless the SORTKEYS parameter is specified).
SORT	Sorts the index and foreign key data using the data sets assigned to the SORTOUT and SORTWKxx DD statements.
BUILD	Builds indexes and identifies duplicate keys, placing the error information in SYSERR. The recovery pending flag is reset for all nonunique indexes. The copy pending flag is reset at the end of this phase if an inline copy is produced unless the SORTKEYS parameter is specified.
INDEXVAL	Reads the SYSERR data set to correct unique index violations. The recovery pending flag is reset for all unique indexes.
ENFORCE	Checks foreign keys for conformance to referential constraints and stores the error information in SYSERR. Resets check pending flag for tablespace.
DISCARD	Reads the SYSERR information to correct referential constraint violations and places the erroneous records in the SYSDISC data set.
REPORT	Sends reports of unique index violations and referential constraint violations to SYSPRINT.
UTILTERM	Performs the final utility cleanup.

Creating an Inline Copy During the LOAD

Version 5

As of DB2 V5 it is possible to create a full image copy data set during the execution of the LOAD utility. This is referred to as an inline COPY. The image copy will be a SHRLEVEL REFERENCE copy.

There are two major benefits of taking an inline copy. The first is that a second pass of the data is not required to create a DB2 image copy. The second is that the tablespace into which the data is being loaded will not be placed into a copy pending state when inline copy is specified, even if the LOG NO option is specified.

To create an inline copy, use the COPYDDN and RECOVERYDDN keywords. You can specify up to two primary and two secondary copies.

LOAD Rerun/Restart Procedures

The LOAD utility can be restarted. The restart or rerun procedure is determined by the abending phase of the LOAD step. There are two ways to determine the phase in which the abend occurred.

The first method is to issue the DISPLAY UTILITY command to determine which utilities are currently active, stopped, or terminating in the DB2 system. The format of the command is

```
—DISPLAY UTILITY(*)
```

The second method to determine the abending phase is to view the SYSPRINT DD statement of the LOAD step. This method is not as desirable as the first, but it is the only method you can use when the DB2 system is down. At the completion of each phase, DB2 prints a line stating that the phase has completed. You can assume that the phase immediately following the last phase reported complete in the SYSPRINT DD statement is the phase that was executing when the abend occurred.

After determining the phase of the LOAD utility at the time of the abend, follow the steps outlined here to restart or rerun the load. In the following procedures, it is assumed that your LOAD utility processing is generally restartable.

If the abend occurred in the UTILINIT phase:

1. Determine the cause of the abend. An abend in this step is usually caused by another utility executing with the same UID or a utility that is incompatible with another utility currently executing.
2. Resolve the cause of the abend. An abend in this phase is probably due to improper job scheduling. Issue the DISPLAY UTILITY command to determine which utilities are currently in process for the DB2 system. Resolve the scheduling problem by allowing conflicting utilities to complete before proceeding to step 3.

   Another possible cause is insufficient sort space. If the SORTWKxx data sets are dynamically added, try to resolve the problem using the following methods:

   - Use the SORTDEVT clause to dynamically create the SORTWKxx data sets some place else.
   - Clean the work packs by deleting or moving extraneous files.
   - Explicitly allocate the appropriate sort work data sets in the JCL.
3. Restart the job at the LOAD step.

If the abend occurred in the RELOAD phase:

1. Determine the cause of the abend. An abend in this step is usually caused by insufficient space allocated to the SYSUT1 DD statement. Another cause is that the VSAM data set associated with the tablespace has run out of available DASD space.
2. Resolve the cause of the abend.
   a. If the problem is an out-of-space abend (B37) on the SYSUT1 DD statement, the data set associated with that DD statement will have been cataloged. Allocate a new data set with additional space, copy the SYSUT1 data set to the new data set, delete the original SYSUT1 data set, and rename the new data set to the same name as the original SYSUT1 data set.
   b. If the problem is an out-of-space abend on the VSAM data set containing the tablespace being reloaded, contact the DBA or DASD support unit. This situation can be corrected by adding another volume to the STOGROUP be

used; using IDCAMS to redefine the VSAM data set, move the VSAM data set, or both; or altering the primary space allocation quantity for the index, the secondary space allocation quantity for the index, or both.

3. Restart the job at the LOAD step with a temporary JCL change to alter the UTPROC parameter to RESTART.

If the abend occurred in the SORT phase:

1. Determine the cause of the abend. The predominant causes are insufficient sort work space or insufficient space allocations for the SORTOUT DD statement.
2. Resolve the cause of the abend. If the problem is insufficient space on the sort work or SORTOUT DD statements, simply increase the allocations and proceed to step 3.
3. Restart the job at the LOAD step with a temporary change to alter the UTPROC parameter to RESTART(PHASE).

If the abend occurred in the BUILD phase:

1. Determine the cause for the abend. An abend in this step is usually caused by insufficient space allocated to the SYSERR DD statement. Another cause is that the VSAM data set associated with the index space has run out of available DASD space.
2. Resolve the cause of the abend:
   a. If the problem is an out-of-space abend (B37) on the SYSERR DD statement, the data set associated with the DD statement will have been cataloged. Allocate a new data set with additional space, copy the SYSERR data set to the new data set, delete the original SYSERR data set, and rename the new data set to the same name as the original SYSERR data set.
   b. If the problem is an out-of-space abend on the VSAM data set containing the index space being reloaded, contact the DBA or DASD support unit. This situation can be corrected by adding another volume to the STOGROUP being used; using IDCAMS to redefine the VSAM data set, move the VSAM data set, or both; or altering the primary space allocation quantity for the index, the secondary space allocation quantity for the index, or both.
3. a. If LOAD was run using the REPLACE option, restart the job at the LOAD step with a temporary change to alter the UTPROC parameter to RESTART(PHASE).
   b. If LOAD was run using the RESUME YES option, the LOAD is not restartable. Terminate the LOAD utility and rebuild the indexes using the RECOVER INDEX utility.

NOTE

When the SORTKEYS parameter is used and the LOAD utility terminates during the RELOAD, SORT, or BUILD phases, then both RESTART and RESTART(PHASE) restart from the beginning of the RELOAD phase.

If the abend occurred in the INDEXVAL phase:

1. Determine the cause of the abend. Abends in this phase are rare. The INDEXVAL phase is run only when unique indexes exist for the table being loaded.
2. Resolve the cause of the abend.
3. Restart the job at the LOAD step with a temporary JCL change to alter the UTPROC parameter to RESTART(PHASE).

If the abend occurred in the ENFORCE phase:

1. Determine the cause for the abend. An abend in this step is usually caused by insufficient space allocated to the SYSERR DD statement. The ENFORCE phase is optional and is not always run.
2. Resolve the cause of the abend. If the problem is an out-of-space abend (B37) on the SYSERR DD statement, the data set associated with that DD statement will have been cataloged. Allocate a new data set with additional space, copy the SYSERR data set to the new data set, delete the original SYSERR data set, and rename the new data set to the same name as the original SYSERR data set.
3. Restart the job at the LOAD step with a temporary change to alter the UTPROC parameter to RESTART.

If the abend occurred in the DISCARD phase:

1. Determine the cause for the abend. An abend in this step is usually caused by insufficient space allocated to the SYSDISC DD statement. The DISCARD phase is optional and is not always run.
2. Resolve the cause of abend. If the problem is an out-of-space abend (B37) on the SYSDISC DD statement, the data set associated with that DD statement will have been cataloged. Allocate a new data set with additional space, copy the SYSDISC data set to the new data set, delete the original SYSDISC data set, and rename the new data set to the same name as the original SYSDISC data set.
3. Restart the job at the LOAD step with a temporary change to alter the UTPROC parameter to RESTART.

If the abend occurred in the REPORT phase:

1. Determine the cause for the abend. Abends in the REPORT phase are rare. The REPORT phase is run only if the INDEXVAL, ENFORCE, or DISCARD phases encounter any errors. Sometimes the cause for an abend in this phase is insufficient space allocated to the sort work data sets because the report is sorted by error type and input sequence.
2. Resolve the cause of the abend. If the problem was caused by insufficient space on the sort work or SORTOUT DD statements, simply increase the allocations and proceed to step 3.
3. Restart the job at the LOAD step with a temporary change to alter the UTPROC parameter to RESTART(PHASE).

If the abend occurred in the UTILTERM phase:

1. An abend in this phase is unlikely because all the work required for the load has been completed. A problem at this phase means that DB2 cannot terminate the utility.
2. Terminate the DB2 utility by issuing the TERM UTILITY command. The format of the command is

   -TERM UTILITY(*UID*)

   where *UID* is obtained from the -DISPLAY UTILITY (*) command.
3. If the LOAD utility work data sets associated with this job were cataloged as a result of the abend, uncatalog them and force the job's completion.

LOAD Locking Considerations

The LOAD utility can run concurrently with the following utilities (each accessing the same object):

- DIAGNOSE
- MODIFY STATISTICS
- REPORT
- STOSPACE

The LOAD utility will drain all claim classes for the tablespace or partition being loaded and any associated indexes, index partitions, and logical index partitions. Furthermore, if the ENFORCE option is specified, LOAD will drain the write claim class for the primary key index.

Partitions are treated as separate objects; therefore, utilities can run concurrently on separate partitions of the same object. However, if a type 1 nonpartitioning index exists on the tablespace, contention will occur. For nonpartitioning type 2 indexes, a partition load will drain only the logical partition. Additionally, the page set recovery pending flag is not set.

LOAD Guidelines

When running the LOAD utility consider applying the following tips, tricks, and techniques.

Consider Using SORTKEYS

Version 5

When index keys are not already in sorted order and indexes exist on the table into which data is being loaded, consider using the SORTKEYS keyword. When SORTKEYS is specified, index keys are sorted in memory, rather than being written to work files. This can improve performance by the following:

- Eliminating the expensive I/O operations to disk
- Reducing the space requirements for the SYSUT1 and SORTOUT data sets
- Reducing elapsed time from the start of the reload phase to the end of the build phase

An estimate of the number of keys to be sorted can be supplied. This is optional, but recommended because the extracted keys will be written to a work data set, minimizing the efficiency gains of using the SORTKEYS parameter. To estimate the number of keys to sort, use the following calculation:

```
Number of Keys = (Total number of rows to be loaded) x
                 [(number of indexes on the table) +
                  (number of foreign keys {unless index exists for the FK}) +
                  ((number of foreign keys participating in multiple
                    relationships) x (number of relationships - 1))
                 ]
```

NOTE

If more than one table is being loaded, the preceding calculation must be repeated for each table—the sum of the results is used.

Serialize Loads for Tables in the Same Database

The LOAD utility is sensitive to concurrent processing. Plan to serialize LOAD jobs for tables in the same database rather than run them concurrently. Concurrently submitted LOAD jobs tend to cause timeout conditions or languish in the UTILINIT phase until the RELOAD phase of other concurrent LOAD jobs is finished.

NOTE

Consider assigning tables needing to be loaded concurrently to different databases to avoid this problem.

Use LOAD to Append or Replace Rows

You can use LOAD to replace data in a table by specifying the REPLACE option. LOAD also can append new data to a table, leaving current data intact, by specifying the RESUME(YES) option. Choose the appropriate option based on your data loading needs.

Use LOAD to Perform Mass Deletes

Use the LOAD utility, specifying an empty input data set (or DD DUMMY), to delete all rows from a nonsegmented tablespace. This is called a *mass delete*. LOAD is usually more efficient than DELETE SQL without a WHERE clause. Specifying the LOG NO option to avoid logging data changes will further enhance the performance of the mass delete. Note, however, the following considerations:

- If multiple tables are assigned to a simple tablespace, the LOAD utility deletes all rows for all tables in that tablespace.
- Consider loading a DUMMY data set even for segmented tablespaces if a large amount of data must be deleted. Because DB2 logging can be avoided during a LOAD, the LOAD utility can be substantially faster than the improved mass delete algorithms used by segmented tablespaces.

Use Fixed Blocked Input

To enhance the performance of the LOAD utility, use a fixed blocked input data set rather than a variable blocked data set.

Buffer the Work Data Sets Appropriately

For large loads, set the BUFNO parameter in the JCL for the SYSUT1 DD statement to a number greater than 20. A BUFNO of approximately 20 is recommended for medium-sized indexes, and a BUFNO between 50 and 100 is recommended for larger tables. The BUFNO parameter creates read and write buffers in main storage for the data set, thereby enhancing the performance of the LOAD utility. The default for BUFNO is 8 for DB2 V3 and 20 for DB2 V4.

Ensure that sufficient memory (real or expanded) is available, however, before increasing the BUFNO specification for your SYSCOPY data sets.

Enforce RI During Table Loading When Possible

Favor using the ENFORCE option of the LOAD utility to enforce referential constraints instead of running CHECK DATA after the LOAD completes. It is usually more efficient to process the loaded data once, as it is loaded, than to process the data twice, once to load it and once to check it. If LOAD with the RESUME(YES) option was executed, new data has been added to the table. However, if ENFORCE was not specified and a subsequent CHECK DATA is run, CHECK DATA will check the entire table, not just the new data.

Ensure That LOAD Input Data Sets Are in Key Sequence

Always sort the LOAD input data set into sequence by the columns designated in the clustering index. Otherwise, the LOAD utility does not load data in clustering order, and the tablespace and indexes will be inefficiently organized.

REORG After Loading Only When the Input Is Not Sorted

If data is not loaded in clustering sequence, consider following the LOAD with a tablespace reorganization. This can be performed all the time, which is not recommended, or based on the value of CLUSTER RATIO stored in the DB2 Catalog for the tablespace and its clustering index. If CLUSTER RATIO is not 100 percent for a newly loaded table, the REORG utility should be used to cluster and organize the application data.

NOTE

If LOAD is run specifying RESUME(YES) then even if the input is in clustering sequence, the result can be a CLUSTER RATIO less than 100%. It is best to avoid sorting the input in this case, run the load, and then run the REORG utility to cluster and organize the data.

Favor the Use of LOG NO

Use the LOG NO option unless the table to be loaded is very small. This avoids the overhead of logging the loaded data and speeds load processing. If data is loaded without being logged, however, follow the LOAD utility with a full image copy.

Specify KEEPDICTIONARY for Performance

The LOAD utility will rebuild the compression dictionary for tablespaces defined with the COMPRESS YES parameter. Specifying the KEEPDICTIONARY parameter causes the LOAD utility to bypass dictionary rebuilding. The LOAD REPLACE option must be specified in order to build the compression dictionary.

This will improve the overall performance of the LOAD utility because the CPU cycles used to build the dictionary can be avoided. However, this option should be utilized only when you are sure that the same basic type of data is being loaded into the table. If the type of data differs substantially, allowing the LOAD utility to rebuild the compression dictionary will provide for more optimal data compression.

NOTE

Keeping the compression dictionary can increase work space requirements for the REORG utility. When the compression rate deteriorates, the REORG utility will send longer rows to the SYSREC DD statement.

Avoid Nullable Columns for Frequently Loaded Tables

Loading tables with nullable columns can degrade the LOAD utility's performance. If a table will be loaded frequently (daily, for example), consider reducing or eliminating the number of nullable columns defined to the table to increase the performance of the LOAD utility. This is not always practical or desirable because many program changes may be required to change columns from nullable to NOT NULL or to NOT NULL WITH DEFAULT. Additionally, nullable columns might make more sense than default values given the specification of the application.

Avoid Decimal Columns for Frequently Loaded Tables

Avoid DECIMAL columns for tables that are loaded frequently. Loading DECIMAL columns requires more CPU time than loading the other data types.

Avoid Data Conversion

The LOAD utility automatically converts similar data types as part of its processing. However, try to avoid data conversion, because the LOAD utility requires additional CPU time to process these conversions.

The following data conversions are performed automatically by the LOAD utility:

Original Data Type	*Converted Data Type*
SMALLINT	INTEGER
	DECIMAL
	FLOAT
INTEGER	SMALLINT
	DECIMAL
	FLOAT
DECIMAL	SMALLINT
	INTEGER
	FLOAT
FLOAT	SMALLINT
	INTEGER
	DECIMAL
CHAR	VARCHAR
	LONG VARCHAR
VARCHAR	CHAR
	LONG VARCHAR
GRAPHIC	VARGRAPHIC
	LONG VARGRAPHIC
VARGRAPHIC	GRAPHIC
	LONG VARGRAPHIC
TIMESTAMP EXT	DATE
	TIME
	TIMESTAMP

Reduce CPU Use by Explicitly Coding All LOAD Parameters

Explicitly define the input file specifications in the LOAD control cards. Do this even when the data set to be loaded conforms to all the default lengths specified in Table 26.1. This reduces the LOAD utility's CPU use.

Table 26.1. Default LOAD lengths.

Column Data Type	*Default Length*
SMALLINT	2
INTEGER	4
DECIMAL	Column's precision
REAL	4
DOUBLE PRECISION	8
DATE	10
TIME	8
TIMESTAMP	26
CHAR	Column's length
VARCHAR	Column's maximum length
GRAPHIC	Double the column's length
VARGRAPHIC	Double the column's maximum length

If the input file specifications are not explicitly identified, the LOAD utility assumes that the input data set is formatted with the defaults specified in Table 26.1.

NOTE

You can use the DSNTIAUL sample program to build LOAD control cards with explicit definitions.

Create All Indexes Before Loading

It is usually more efficient to define all indexes before using the LOAD utility. The LOAD utility uses an efficient algorithm to build DB2 indexes.

If indexes must be created after the data has been loaded, create the indexes with the DEFER YES option and build them later using the RECOVER INDEX utility.

Favor LOAD over INSERT

To insert initial data into a DB2 table, favor the use of the LOAD utility with the REPLACE option over an application program coded to process INSERTs. LOAD should be favored even if the application normally processes INSERTs as part of its design. The initial loading of DB2 table data usually involves the insertion of many more rows than does typical application processing. For the initial population of table data, the LOAD utility is generally more efficient and less error-prone than a corresponding application program, and also maintains free space.

Consider using the LOAD utility with the RESUME(YES) option to process a large volume of table insertions. LOAD is usually more efficient and less error-prone than a corresponding application program that issues a large number of INSERTs.

Do Not Load Tables in a Multitable Simple Tablespace

Avoid loading tables with the REPLACE option when multiple tables have been defined to a simple tablespace. The LOAD utility with the REPLACE option deletes all rows in all tables in the simple tablespace, which is not usually the desired result.

Execute RUNSTATS After Loading

Execute the RUNSTATS utility immediately after loading a DB2 table. This is necessary in order to maintain current table statistics for access path determination. Of course, access paths for static SQL will not change unless all packages and plans accessing the table are rebound. Any dynamic SQL statements will immediately take advantage of the new statistics.

Consider Loading by Partition

Concurrent loading of multiple partitions of a single tablespace can be achieved using partition independence. This technique is useful for reducing the overall elapsed time of loading a table in a partitioned tablespace.

The existence of Type 1 nonpartitioning indexes mitigates the usefulness of this technique.

Use Data Contingency Options as Required

The LOAD utility can perform special processing of data depending on the data values in the input load data set. Data contingency processing parameters indicate a field defined in the LOAD parameters or a beginning and ending location of data items to be checked. The data contingency processing parameters follow:

NULLIF — Sets column values to null if a particular character string is found at a particular location—for example:

```
NULLIF (22) = '?'
```

DEFAULTIF — Sets column values to a predefined default value if a particular character string is found at a particular location—for example:

```
DEFAULTIF FIELD = 'DEFLT'
```

`WHEN` Limits the loaded data to specific records in the load input data set—for example:

```
LOAD DATA REPLACE
INTO DSN8510.DEPT
WHEN (1 : 3) = 'A00'
```

`CONTINUEIF` Used when there are record types in the input load data set. Specifies that loading will continue, logically concatenating the next record to the previous input record—for example:

```
LOAD DATA
INTO DSN8510.EMP
CONTINUEIF (10 : 10) = 'X'
```

Separate Work Data Sets

Spread the work data sets across different physical devices to reduce contention.

The REORG Utility

The REORG utility can be used to reorganize DB2 tablespaces and indexes, thereby improving the efficiency of access to those objects. Reorganization is required periodically to ensure that the data is situated in an optimal fashion for subsequent access. Reorganization reclusters data, resets free space to the amount specified in the CREATE DDL, and deletes and redefines the underlying VSAM data sets for STOGROUP-defined objects.

Proper planning and scheduling of the REORG utility is a complex subject. Many factors influence the requirements for executing the REORG utility. The following topics highlight the necessary decisions for implementing an efficient REORG policy in your DB2 environment.

Recommended Reorganization Standards

You should develop rigorous standards for the REORG utility because it is the most significant aid in achieving optimal DB2 performance. The standard will influence the input to the REORG utility, the REORG job streams, and the rerun and restart procedures for REORG utilities.

As with the LOAD utility, there are two philosophies for implementing the REORG utility. Individual databases, tablespaces, and applications can mix and match philosophies. One philosophy, however, should be chosen for every non-read-only tablespace and index in every DB2 application. Failure to follow a standard reorganization philosophy and schedule will result in poorly performing DB2 applications. The REORG philosophy must be recorded and maintained for each tablespace and index created.

The philosophies presented here strike a balance between programmer productivity, ease of use and comprehension by operations and control staff, and the effective use of DB2 resources.

Reorganization Philosophies

Two REORG philosophies can be adopted by DB2-based application systems. The first, which is generally the recommended philosophy, is more time-consuming to implement but easier to support. It requires that sufficient DASD be reserved to catalog the REORG work data sets if the REORG job abends.

The three work data sets for the REORG job are allocated for the SYSREC, SYSUT1, and SORTOUT DDNAMEs with DISP = (MOD,DELETE,CATLG). This specification enables the data sets to be allocated as new for the initial running of the REORG job. If the job abends, however, it will catalog the data sets for use in a possible restart. After the step completes successfully, the data sets are deleted. The space for these data sets must be planned and available before the REORG job is executed.

The sample REORG JCL in Listing 26.3 follows this philosophy. By creating your REORG job according to this philosophy, you can restart an abending REORG job with little effort after the cause of the abend has been corrected. You simply specify one of the RESTART options in the UTPROC parameter for DSNUTILB.

Listing 26.3. REORG JCL (restartable).

```
//DB2JOBU  JOB (UTILITY),'DB2 REORG',MSGCLASS=X,CLASS=X,
//          NOTIFY=USER
//*
//****************************************************************
//*
//*             DB2 REORG UTILITY (RESTARTABLE)
//*
//****************************************************************
//*
//UTIL EXEC DSNUPROC,SYSTEM=DSN,UID='REORGTS',UTPROC=''
//*
//*  UTILITY WORK DATASETS
//*
//DSNUPROC.SORTWK01 DDUNIT=SYSDA,SPACE=(CYL,(2,1))
//DSNUPROC.SORTWK02 DDUNIT=SYSDA,SPACE=(CYL,(2,1))
//DSNUPROC.SORTOUT DD DSN=CAT.SORTOUT,DISP=(MOD,DELETE,CATLG),
//         UNIT=SYSDA,SPACE=(CYL,(2,1))
//DSNUPROC.SYSUT1 DD DSN=CAT.SYSUT1,DISP=(MOD,DELETE,CATLG),
//         UNIT=SYSDA,SPACE=(CYL,(2,1)),DCB=BUFNO=20
//DSNUPROC.SYSREC DD DSN=OUTPUT.DATASETD,DISP=(MOD,CATLG,CATLG),
//         UNIT=SYSDA,SPACE=(CYL,(15,5)),DCB=BUFNO=20
//DSNUPROC.SYSPRINT DD SYSOUT=*
//DSNUPROC.UTPRINT DD SYSOUT=*
//*
//*  UTILITY INPUT CONTROL STATEMENTS
//*      The REORG statement reorganizes the second partition
//*      of DSN8D51A.DSN8S51E.
//*
//DSNUPROC.SYSIN     DD   *
  REORG TABLESPACE DSN8D51A.DSN8S51E PART 2/*
//
```

The second philosophy is easier to implement but more difficult to support. No additional DASD is required because all REORG work data sets are defined as temporary. Therefore, upon abnormal completion, all interim work data sets are lost. See Listing 26.4 for a sample JCL.

Listing 26.4. REORG JCL (nonrestartable).

```
//DB2JOBU  JOB (UTILITY),'DB2 REORG',MSGCLASS=X,CLASS=X,
//      NOTIFY=USER,REGION=4096K
//*
//****************************************************************
//*
//*           DB2 REORG UTILITY (NON-RESTARTABLE)
//*
//****************************************************************
//*
//UTIL EXEC DSNUPROC,SYSTEM=DSN,UID='REORGTS',UTPROC=''
//*
//*  UTILITY WORK DATASETS
//*
//DSNUPROC.SORTWK01 DDUNIT=SYSDA,SPACE=(CYL,(2,1))
//DSNUPROC.SORTWK02 DDUNIT=SYSDA,SPACE=(CYL,(2,1))
//DSNUPROC.SORTOUT DD DSN=&&SORTOUT,
//        UNIT=SYSDA,SPACE=(CYL,(2,1))
//DSNUPROC.SYSUT1 DD DSN=&&SYSUT1,
//        UNIT=SYSDA,SPACE=(CYL,(2,1)),DCB=BUFNO=20
//DSNUPROC.SYSREC DD DSN=&&SYSREC,
//        UNIT=SYSDA,SPACE=(CYL,(15,5)),DCB=BUFNO=20
//DSNUPROC.SYSPRINT DD SYSOUT=*
//DSNUPROC.UTPRINT DD SYSOUT=*
//*
//*  UTILITY INPUT CONTROL STATEMENTS
//*    1. The first REORG statement reorganizes the
//*       named tablespace.
//*    2. The second REORG statement reorganizes the
//*       named index.
//*
//DSNUPROC.SYSIN    DD  *
REORG TABLESPACE DSN8D51A.DSN8S51D
REORG INDEX (DSN8510.XACT1)
/*
//
```

To restart this REORG job, you must determine in which phase the job abended. If it abended in any phase other than the UTILINIT phase or UNLOAD phase, you must restore the tablespace being reorganized to a previous point. You can do this by running either the RECOVER TOCOPY utility or a simple RECOVER (if the LOG NO option of the REORG utility was specified).

After restoring the tablespace (and possibly its associated indexes), you must correct the cause of the abend, terminate the utility, and rerun the job. As you can see, this method is significantly more difficult to restart.

Try to use the first philosophy rather than the second. The first reorganization philosophy makes recovery from errors as smooth and painless as possible.

Reorganization Frequency

The frequency of reorganization is different for every DB2 application. Sometimes the reorganization frequency is different for tablespaces and indexes in the same application because different data requires different reorganization schedules. These schedules depend on the following factors:

- Frequency of modification activity (insertions, updates, and deletions)
- Application transaction volume
- Amount of free space allocated when the tablespace or index was created

The scheduling of reorganizations should be determined by the Database Administrator, taking into account the input of the application development team as well as end-user requirements. The following information must be obtained for each DB2 table to determine the proper scheduling of tablespace and index reorganizations:

- The data availability requirement to enable effective REORG scheduling
- The insertion and deletion frequency for each table and tablespace
- The number of rows per table
- An indication of uneven distribution of data values in a table
- The frequency and volume of updates to critical columns in that table. (*Critical columns* are defined as columns in the clustering index, columns containing variable data, any column used in SQL predicates, or any column that is sorted or grouped.)

Most of this information can be obtained from the DB2 Catalog if the application already exists. For new application tablespaces and indexes, this information must be based on application specifications, user requirements, and estimates culled from any existing non-DB2 systems.

Further information on determining the frequency of reorganization is provided in Parts IV and V.

Reorganization Job Stream

The total reorganization schedule should include a RUNSTATS job or step, two COPY jobs or steps for each tablespace being reorganized, and a REBIND job or step for all plans using tables in any of the tablespaces being reorganized.

The RUNSTATS job is required in order to record the current tablespace and index statistics to the DB2 Catalog. This provides the DB2 optimizer with current data to use in determining optimal access paths.

An image copy should always be taken immediately before any tablespace REORG is run. This ensures that the data is recoverable, because the REORG utility alters the physical positioning of application data. The second COPY job is required after the REORG if it was performed with the LOG NO option.

Version 5

The second COPY job or step can be eliminated with DB2 V5 if an inline COPY is performed during the REORG. Similar to the inline COPY feature of LOAD, a SHRLEVEL REFERENCE full image copy can be performed as a part of the REORG. To create an inline copy, use the COPYDDN and RECOVERYDDN keywords. You can specify up to two primary and two secondary copies. When a REORG job runs with the LOG NO option, DB2 turns on the copy pending flag for each tablespace specified in the REORG (unless inline copy is used). The LOG NO parameter tells DB2 not to log the changes. This minimizes the performance impact of the reorganization on the DB2 system and enables your REORG job to finish faster.

When the LOG NO parameter is specified, you *must* take an image copy of the tablespace after the REORG has completed and before it can be updated. It is good practice to back up your tablespaces after a reorganization anyway. A REBIND job for all production plans should be included to enable DB2 to create new access paths based on the current statistics provided by the RUNSTATS job.

If all the tablespaces for an application are being reorganized, each utility should be in a separate job—one REORG job, one RUNSTATS job, one COPY job, and one REBIND job. These common jobs can be used independently of the REORG job. If isolated tablespaces in an application are being reorganized, it might be acceptable to perform the REORG, RUNSTATS, COPY, and REBIND as separate steps in a single job. Follow your shop guidelines for job creation standards.

Estimating REORG Work Data Set Sizes

The REORG utility requires the use of work data sets to reorganize tablespaces and indexes. The following formulas help you estimate the sizes for these work data sets. More complex and precise calculations are in the *DB2 Utility Guide and Reference* manual, but these formulas should produce comparable results.

```
SYSREC = (number of pages in tablespace) x 4096 x 1.10
```

NOTE

If the tablespace being reorganized uses 32K pages, multiply the SYSREC number by 8. The total number of pages used by a tablespace can be retrieved from either the VSAM LISTCAT command or the DB2 Catalog, as specified in the NACTIVE column of SYSIBM.SYSTABLESPACE. If you use the DB2 Catalog method, ensure that the statistics are current by running the RUNSTATS utility (discussed in Chapter 27, "Catalog Manipulation Utilities").

An additional 10 percent of space is specified because of the expansion of variable columns and the reformatting performed by the REORG UNLOAD phase.

```
SORTOUT = (size of the largest index key + 12)
    ➥x (largest number of rows to be loaded to a single table)
    ➥x (total number of nonclustering indexes defined for each table) x 1.2
```

NOTE

If any number in the SORTOUT calculation is 0, substitute 1.

The multiplier 1.2 is factored into the calculation to provide a "fudge factor." If you are absolutely sure of your numbers, the calculation can be made more precise by eliminating the additional multiplication of 1.2.

```
SYSUT1 = (size of the largest index key + 12)
    ➥x (largest number of rows to be loaded to a single table)
    ➥x (total number of nonclustering indexes defined for each table) x 1.2
```

NOTE

If any number in the SYSUT1 calculation is 0, substitute 1.

The multiplier 1.2 is factored into the calculation to provide a "fudge factor." If you are absolutely sure of your numbers, the calculation can be made more precise by eliminating the additional multiplication of 1.2.

```
SORTWKxx = (size of SYSUT1) x 2
```

NOTE

If any number in the SORTWKxx calculation is 0, substitute 1.

After calculating the estimated size in bytes for each work data set, convert the number into cylinders, rounding up to the next whole cylinder. Allocating work data sets in cylinder increments enhances the utility's performance.

REORG Phases

UTILINIT	Sets up and initializes the REORG utility.
UNLOAD	Unloads the data into a sequential data set (SYSREC). If a clustering index exists and either SORTDATA or SHRLEVEL CHANGE is specified, the data is sorted. The compression dictionary is rebuilt in this step for COMPRESS YES tablespaces.

`RELOAD`	Reads the records from the sequential data set (`SYSREC`), loads them to the tablespace, and extracts index keys (`SYSUT1`). Creates a full image copy if `COPYDDN`, `RECOVERYDDN`, `SHRLEVEL REFERENCE`, or `SHRLEVEL CHANGE` are specified. If `SORTKEYS` is specified, the index keys are sorted by a subtask. This phase is not performed for `REORG`.
`INDEX.SORT`	Sorts the key entries before updating indexes, if any exist. `SYSUT1` is the input to the sort, and `SORTOUT` is the output of the sort. This phase can be skipped if there is only one key per table, if the data is reloaded in key order, or if the data is reloaded grouped by table. If `SORTKEYS` is used, passes sorted keys in memory to the `BUILD` phase.
`BUILD`	Updates any indexes to reflect the new location of records.
`LOG`	Only for `SHRLEVEL CHANGE`: processes the log iteratively to append changes to the image copies.
`SWITCH`	Switches access to a shadow copy of the tablespace or partition being reorganized (online `REORG`) with `SHRLEVEL REFERENCE` or `CHANGE`.
`BUILD2`	Corrects nonpartitioning indexes when reorganizing a partition using `SHRLEVEL REFERENCE` or `CHANGE`.
`UTILTERM`	Performs the final utility cleanup.

REORG Rerun/Restart Procedures

The `REORG` restart procedure depends on the phase that the reorganization utility was running when the abend occurred. There are two ways to determine the phase in which the abend occurred.

The first method is to issue the `DISPLAY UTILITY` command to determine which utilities are currently active, stopped, or terminating in the DB2 system. The format of the command is

```
—DISPLAY UTILITY(*)
```

The second way to determine the abending phase is to view the `SYSPRINT DD` statement of the `REORG` step. This method is not as desirable as the first, but it is the only method you can use when the DB2 system is down. At the completion of each phase, DB2 prints a line stating that the phase has finished. You can assume that the phase immediately following the last phase reported complete in the `SYSPRINT DD` statement is the phase that was executing when the abend occurred.

After determining the phase of the `REORG` utility at the time of the abend, follow the steps outlined here to restart or rerun the reorganization. In the following procedures, it is assumed that your `REORG` processing is restartable.

If the abend occurred in the UTILINIT phase:

1. Determine the cause of the abend. An abend in this step is usually caused by another utility executing with the same UID or a utility that is incompatible with another utility currently executing.
2. Resolve the cause of abend. An abend in this phase is probably due to improper job scheduling. Issue the DISPLAY UTILITY command to determine which utilities are currently in process for the DB2 system. Resolve the scheduling problem by allowing conflicting utilities to complete before proceeding to step 3.
3. Restart the job at the REORG step.

If the abend occurred in the UNLOAD phase:

1. Determine the cause of the abend. An abend in this step is usually caused by insufficient space allocated to the SYSREC DD statement.
2. Resolve the cause of the abend. If the problem is an out-of-space abend (B37) on the SYSREC DD statement, the data set associated with that DD statement will have been cataloged. Allocate a new data set with additional space, copy the SYSREC data set to the new data set, delete the original SYSREC data set, and rename the new data set to the same name as the original SYSREC data set.
3. Restart the job at the REORG step with a temporary change to alter the UTPROC parameter to RESTART. This restarts the utility at the point of the last commit.

If the abend occurred in the RELOAD phase:

1. Determine the cause of the abend. An abend in this phase is usually a Resource Unavailable abend due to another user allocating the tablespace or the VSAM data set associated with the tablespace running out of space. Note the SHRLEVEL specified for the REORG.

   When an abend occurs in this phase, the tablespace will be in recover pending and copy pending status. Associated indexes will be in recover pending status.
2. Resolve the cause of the abend.
   a. If the problem is a time-out due to another job or user accessing the tablespace to be reloaded, determine the conflicting job or user access and wait for it to complete processing before proceeding to step 3.
   b. If the problem is an out-of-space abend on the VSAM data set containing the tablespace being reloaded, contact the DBA or DASD support unit. This situation can be corrected by adding another volume to the STOGROUP being used; by using IDCAMS to redefine the VSAM data set, move the VSAM data set, or both; or by altering the primary space allocation quantity for the index, the secondary space allocation quantity for the index, or both.

3. a. If the abend was not due to an error in the data set for the SYSREC DD statement, restart the job at the REORG step with a temporary change to alter the UTPROC parameter to RESTART.

   b. If the abend was caused by an error in the data set for the SYSREC DD statement, first terminate the utility by issuing the –TERM UTILITY(*UID*) command. Then recover the tablespace by executing the Recover tablespace utility. Next, re-create a temporary copy of the control cards used as input to the REORG step. Omit the control cards for all utilities executed in the step before the abend. This bypasses the work accomplished before the abend. The first card in the new data set should be the utility that was executing at the time of the abend. Finally, restart the job at the REORG step using the modified control cards.

   c. For SHRLEVEL NONE, the tablespace and indexes are left in recovery pending status. Once the tablespace is recovered, the REORG job can be rerun. For SHRLEVEL REFERENCE or CHANGE, the data records are reloaded into shadow copies so the original objects are not impacted. The job can be rerun.

If the abend occurred in the SORT phase:

1. Determine the cause of the abend. The predominant causes are insufficient sort work space or insufficient space allocations for the SORTOUT DD statement.
   When an abend occurs in this phase, the tablespace will be in copy pending status. Associated indexes will be in recover pending status.
2. Resolve the cause of the abend. If the problem is insufficient space on either the sort work or SORTOUT DD statements, simply increase the allocations and proceed to step 3.
3. Restart the job at the REORG step with a temporary change to alter the UTPROC parameter to RESTART(PHASE).

If the abend occurred in the BUILD phase:

1. Determine the cause for the abend. An abend in this step is usually the result of the VSAM data set associated with the indexspace running out of space.

   When an abend occurs in this phase, the tablespace will be in copy pending status.
2. Resolve the cause of abend. If the problem is an out-of-space abend on the VSAM data set containing the indexspace being reloaded, contact the DBA or DASD support unit. This situation can be corrected by adding another volume to the STOGROUP being used—by using IDCAMS to redefine the VSAM data set, move the VSAM data set, or both—or by altering the primary space allocation quantity for the index, the secondary space allocation quantity for the index, or both.
3. Restart the job at the REORG step with a temporary change to alter the UTPROC parameter to RESTART(PHASE).

For abends in the SORT, BUILD, or LOG phases, the SHRLEVEL option can impact the response:

1. For SHRLEVEL NONE, indexes that were not built will be in recovery pending status. Run REORG with the SORTDATA option or RECOVER INDEX to rebuild these indexes.

   For SHRLEVEL REFERENCE or CHANGE, the records are reloaded into shadow objects, so the original objects have not been affected by REORG. The job can be rerun.

If the abend occurred in the SWITCH phase:

1. All data sets that were renamed to their shadow counterparts are renamed back. This leaves the objects in their original state. The job can be rerun. If there is a problem in renaming to the original data sets, then the objects are placed in recovery pending status. The tablespace can then be recovered using the image copy created by REORG. The indexes must also be recovered.

If the abend occurred in the BUILD2 phase:

1. The logical partition is left in recovery pending status. Run RECOVER INDEX for the logical partition to complete the REORG.

If the abend occurred in the UTILTERM phase:

1. An abend in this phase is unlikely because all the work required for the reorganization has been completed. A problem at this phase means that DB2 cannot terminate the utility.

   The tablespace will be in copy pending status.
2. Terminate the DB2 utility by issuing the TERM UTILITY command. The format of the command is

   –TERM UTILITY(*UID*)

   where *UID* is obtained from the –DISPLAY UTILITY (*) command.
3. If data sets associated with the SYSREC, SYSUT1, and SORTOUT DD statements were cataloged as a result of the abend, uncatalog them and force the job to complete.

REORG and the SHRLEVEL Parameter

Version 5

As of DB2 V5, the SHRLEVEL parameter has been added to the REORG utility. Similar to the functionality of SHRLEVEL in other DB2 utilities, the SHRLEVEL parameter controls the level of concurrent data access permitted during a REORG. There are three SHRLEVEL options for REORG: NONE, REFERENCE, and CHANGE.

SHRLEVEL NONE indicates that concurrent data reading is permitted while data is being unloaded, but no access is permitted during the RELOAD phase. This is the default and is the manner in which REORG is executed for all versions of DB2 prior to V5.

SHRLEVEL REFERENCE indicates that concurrent read access is permitted during both the UNLOAD and RELOAD phases of the REORG.

SHRLEVEL CHANGE indicates concurrent read and write access is available throughout most of the reorganization.

Both SHRLEVEL REFERENCE and SHRLEVEL CHANGE require a shadow copy of the object being reorganized.

Using SHRLEVEL CHANGE to Achieve Online REORG

Version 5

Data availability can be greatly enhanced through the use of SHRLEVEL CHANGE when reorganizing tablespaces. This option, known as Online REORG, is new as of DB2 V5. When using online REORG, full read and write access is available to the data during most phases of the REORG utility. This is achieved by modifying the way in which REORG operates (see Figure 26.1). Online REORG takes the following steps:

1. Data is unloaded from the tablespace, partition, or index during which read and write access is available.
2. Data is reloaded into a shadow copy of the data store being reorganized. Read and write access is still available to the original tablespace, partition, or index.
3. The log entries recording the changes made to the original data set while the shadow reload was occurring are applied to the shadow. Read and usually write access is still available to the original tablespace, partition, or index. This step is performed iteratively based upon the conditions specified in MAXRO, DEADLINE, DELAY, and LONGLOG.
4. The original and the copy are swapped so that future access is to the newly reorganized version of the data. Data is unavailable until the swap is accomplished.
5. Read and write access to the data is enabled again.

Online REORG should not be used all of the time because there are drawbacks to its use. First and foremost is the need to have excess disk space to store the shadow copy. The shadow copy typically consumes at least as much space as the object being reorganized. More space may be required because REORG reclaims free space.

Because of the need to apply changes from the log, online REORG is most effectively used when transaction throughput is low and most transactions are of short duration. Furthermore, avoid scheduling REORG with SHRLEVEL CHANGE when low-tolerance applications are executing.

FIGURE 26.1.
Online REORG *processing.*

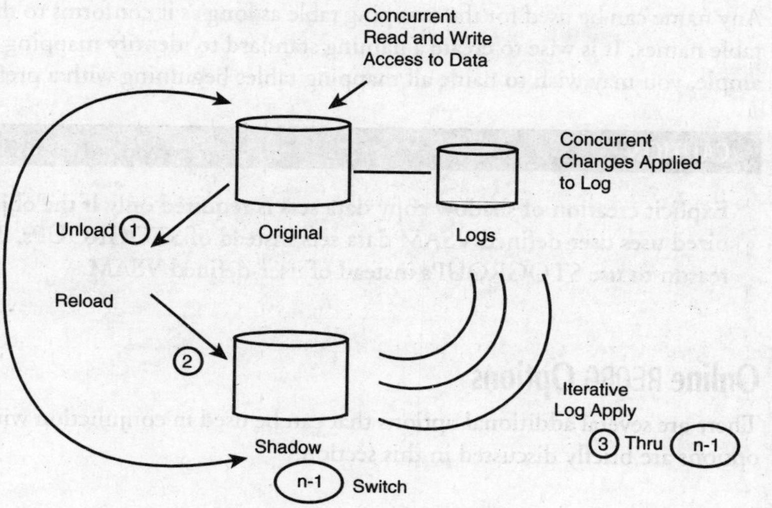

The Mapping Table

A mapping table must be specified whenever a SHRLEVEL CHANGE reorganization is run. The mapping table is used by REORG to map between the RIDs of records in the original copy and the like RIDs in the shadow copy. The mapping table must use the following definition as a template:

```
CREATE TABLE table-name
    (TYPE          CHAR(1) NOT NULL,
     SOURCE_RID    CHAR(5) NOT NULL,
     TARGET_XRID   CHAR(9) NOT NULL WITH DEFAULT,
     LRSN          CHAR(6) NOT NULL
    );
```

Additionally, an index must be created for the mapping table using the following template:

```
CREATE TYPE 2 UNIQUE INDEX index-name
   ON TABLE table-name
   (SOURCE_RID ASC,
    TYPE,
    TARGET_XRID,
    LRSN
   );
```

Create the table in a segmented tablespace explicitly set aside for the use of the mapping table. Multiple mapping tables can be created in the segmented tablespace if concurrent online REORGs are required to be run. One mapping table is required per online REORG execution. Although a single mapping table can be reused for multiple REORGs, they can not be concurrent REORGs.

Any name can be used for the mapping table as long as it conforms to the DB2 restrictions on table names. It is wise to create a naming standard to identify mapping tables as such. For example, you may wish to name all mapping tables beginning with a prefix of MAP_.

CAUTION

Explicit creation of shadow copy data sets is required only if the object being reorganized uses user-defined VSAM data sets instead of STOGROUPs. This is yet another reason to use STOGROUPs instead of user-defined VSAM.

Online REORG Options

There are several additional options that can be used in conjunction with online REORG. These options are briefly discussed in this section.

MAXRO

The MAXRO option is an integer that specified the amount of time for the last iteration of log processing for the online REORG. DB2 continues to iteratively apply log records until it determines that the next iteration will take less than the indicated MAXRO value. Of course, the actual execution time for the last iteration may actually exceed the MAXRO value.

Specifying a small positive MAXRO value reduces the length of the period of read-only access, but it might increase the elapsed time for REORG to complete. If you specify a huge positive value, the second iteration of log processing is probably the last iteration.

NOTE

The ALTER UTILITY command can be used to change the value of MAXRO during the execution of an online REORG.

The MAXRO parameter can also be set to DEFER instead of an integer value. The DEFER option indicates that log processing iterations can continue indefinitely. If DEFER is specified, the online REORG will not start the final log processing iteration until the MAXRO value is modified using the ALTER UTIL command.

When DEFER is specified and DB2 determines that the time for the current iteration and the estimated time for the next iteration are both less than five seconds, DB2 will send a message to the console (DSNU362I) indicating that a pause will be inserted before the next log iteration.

When running an online REORG specifying DEFER, the operator should scan for DSNU362I messages to determine when to issue an ALTER UTIL command to change the MAXRO value.

The DEFER parameter should always be used in conjunction with LONGLOG CONTINUE.

LONGLOG

The LONGLOG parameter designates how DB2 will react if the number of records that the next log processing iteration is not lower than the number that the previous iterations processed. If this occurs, the REORG log processing may never catch up to the write activity of the concurrently executing transactions and programs.

If LONGLOG CONTINUE is specified, DB2 will continue processing the REORG until the time on the JOB statement expires. When MAXRO DEFER is used in conjunction with LONGLOG CONTINUE, the online REORG continues with read/write access still permitted to the original tablespace, partition, or index. When the switch to the shadow copy is required, an operator or DBA must issue the ALTER UTIL command with a large integer MAXRO value. CONTINUE is the default LONGLOG value.

If LONGLOG TERM is specified, DB2 terminates reorganization after the delay specified by the DELAY parameter (discussed in the next section).

If LONGLOG DRAIN is specified, DB2 drains the write claim class after the delay specified by the DELAY parameter, thereby forcing the final log processing iteration to happen.

DELAY

The DELAY parameter is used in conjunction with the LONGLOG parameter. It indicates the minimum amount of time before the TERM or DRAIN activity is performed.

DEADLINE

The DEADLINE parameter provides a mechanism for shutting off an online REORG. If DB2 determines that the switch phase will not finish by the deadline, DB2 terminates the REORG.

If DEADLINE NONE is specified, then there is no deadline and the REORG can continue indefinitely. This is the default option.

If DEADLINE *timestamp* is specified, the REORG must finish before the specified date and time deadline. This indicates that the switch phase of the log processing must be finished by the timestamp provided.

CAUTION

The timestamp provided to the DEADLINE parameter must be in the future. The REORG will not commence if the date/time combination has already passed.

REORG TABLESPACE Locking Considerations

The REORG TABLESPACE utility, regardless of the execution options specified, can run concurrently with the following utilities (each accessing the same object):

- DIAGNOSE
- REPORT

When REORG TABLESPACE is run specifying SHRLEVEL NONE and UNLOAD ONLY, the following additional utilities can be run concurrently:

- CHECK INDEX
- COPY
- QUIESCE
- RECOVER INDEX (only when a clustering index does not exist)
- REORG INDEX (only when a clustering index does not exist)
- REORG SHRLEVEL NONE UNLOAD ONLY
- REPAIR DUMP or VERIFY
- REPAIR LOCATE INDEX PAGE REPLACE (only when a clustering index does not exist)
- RUNSTATS
- STOSPACE

The REORG TABLESPACE utility when run specifying UNLOAD ONLY will drain all write claim classes for the tablespace or partition being reorganized. Additionally, if a clustering index exists, the REORG utility will drain all write claim classes for the index or partition.

SHRLEVEL NONE

When REORG TABLESPACE SHRLEVEL NONE is executed with the UNLOAD CONTINUE or UNLOAD PAUSE options, the following locking activity occurs:

- Write claim classes are drained for the tablespace or tablespace partition and the associated index or index partition during the UNLOAD phase.
- All claim classes are drained for the tablespace or tablespace partition and the associated index or index partition during the RELOAD phase.
- Write claim classes are drained for the logical partition of a nonpartitioned Type 2 index during the RELOAD phase.
- For a REORG of a single partition, all claim classes are drained for the logical partition of a non partitioned Type 2 index during the RELOAD phase.

If a nonpartitioning index exists on the tablespace, concurrent utilities operating on the same partition might fail due to contention problems unless the index is a Type 2 index.

SHRLEVEL REFERENCE

When REORG TABLESPACE SHRLEVEL REFERENCE is executed with the UNLOAD CONTINUE or UNLOAD PAUSE options, the following locking activity occurs:

- Write claim classes are drained for the tablespace or tablespace partition and the associated partitioning index and nonpartitioned index during the UNLOAD phase.
- All claim classes are drained for the tablespace or tablespace partition and the associated partitioning index and nonpartitioned Type 1 indexes during the SWITCH phase.
- Write claim classes are drained for the logical partition of a nonpartitioned Type 2 index during the SWITCH phase.
- Write claim classes are drained for the tablespace or tablespace partition and the associated partitioning index and nonpartitioned Type 1 indexes during the UNLOAD phase.
- All claim classes are drained for the logical partition of a nonpartitioned Type 2 index during the UNLOAD phase.
- All claim classes are drained for the tablespace or tablespace partition and the associated partitioning index and nonpartitioned Type 1 indexes during the SWITCH phase of a single partition REORG.
- For a REORG of a single partition, the repeatable read class is drained for a nonpartitioned Type 2 index during the SWITCH phase.

SHRLEVEL CHANGE

When REORG TABLESPACE SHRLEVEL CHANGE is executed with the UNLOAD CONTINUE or UNLOAD PAUSE options, the following locking activity occurs:

- The read claim class is claimed for the tablespace and associated indexes during the UNLOAD phase.
- The write claim class is drained for the tablespace and associated indexes during the LOG phase.
- All claim classes are drained for the tablespace and associated indexes during the SWITCH phase.

REORG INDEX Locking Considerations

The REORG INDEX utility is compatible with the following utilities:

- COPY
- DIAGNOSE

- MERGECOPY
- MODIFY RECOVERY
- RECOVER TABLESPACE (no options)
- RECOVER TABLESPACE ERROR RANGE
- REORG SHRLEVEL NONE UNLOAD ONLY (only when a clustering index does not exist)
- REPAIR LOCATE RID (DUMP, VERIFY, or REPLACE)
- REPAIR LOCATE TABLESPACE PAGE REPLACE
- REPORT
- RUNSTATS TABLESPACE
- STOSPACE

SHRLEVEL NONE

When REORG INDEX SHRLEVEL NONE is executed, the write claim class is drained for the index or index partition during the UNLOAD phase and all claim classes are drained during both the SORT and BUILD phase. Remember, the SORT phase can be skipped.

SHRLEVEL REFERENCE

When REORG INDEX SHRLEVEL REFERENCE is executed, the write claim class is drained for the index or index partition during the UNLOAD phase—all claim classes are drained during the SWITCH phase.

SHRLEVEL CHANGE

When REORG INDEX SHRLEVEL CHANGE is executed, the read claim class is claimed for the index or index partition during the UNLOAD phase. Additionally, the write claim class is drained during the last iteration of the log processing—all claim classes are drained during the SWITCH phase.

REORG Guidelines

By adhering to the following guidelines, you will ensure efficient and effective reorganization of DB2 tablespaces.

Ensure That Adequate Recovery Is Available

Take an image copy of every tablespace to be reorganized before executing the REORG utility. All image copies taken before the reorganization are marked as invalid for current point-in-time recovery by the REORG utility. These image copies can be used only with the TORBA or TOCOPY options of the RECOVER utility.

Take an image copy of every tablespace reorganized after using the LOG NO option of the REORG utility. All tablespaces reorganized with the LOG NO option are placed into copy pending status.

Analyze Clustering Before Reorganizing

Consider the CLUSTER RATIO of a tablespace before reorganizing. If the tablespace to be reorganized is not clustered, specify the SORTDATA parameter. The SORTDATA option causes the data to be unloaded according to its physical sequence in the tablespace. The data is then sorted in sequence by the clustering index columns.

If the SORTDATA parameter is not specified, the tablespace data is unloaded using the clustering index, which is highly efficient when the tablespace is clustered. If the tablespace is not clustered, however, unloading by the clustering index causes REORG to scan the tablespace data in an inefficient manner. Refer to Chapter 19, "DB2 Object Monitoring Using the DB2 Catalog," for DB2 Catalog queries to obtain CLUSTER RATIO.

DB2 does not consider a default clustering index to be clustering for the purposes of unloading for a REORG. Only an explicitly created clustering index, if available, will be used.

If the CLUSTER RATIO for a tablespace is less than 90 percent, consider using the SORTDATA option. When data is less than 90 percent clustered, unloading physically and sorting is usually more efficient than scanning data. Furthermore, the DBA statistics NEAROFFPOS and FAROFFPOS can be used to judge whether to use the SORTDATA option.

Monitor the results of the REORG utility with and without the SORTDATA option, however, to gauge its effectiveness with different application tablespaces.

NOTE

Use of the SORTDATA option can increase the sort work requirements of the REORG utility, especially for tables with long rows and few indexes.

Consider Unloading and Loading Instead of REORG

The SORTDATA parameter is available for DB2 V2.3 and greater. If you are using an earlier release of DB2, consider avoiding the REORG utility for large, highly unclustered tables. Instead, you can execute the following steps:

1. Use DSNTIAUL to unload the data. You can specify a LOCK TABLE statement as part of the input to DSNTIAUL to effectively block concurrent data modification.
2. Use DFSORT to sort the data into sequence by the columns of the clustering index.
3. Use the DB2 LOAD utility with the REPLACE and ENFORCE CONSTRAINTS options to reload the data.

This has the same effect as a REORG.

Follow General Reorganization Rules

As a general rule, reorganize indexes when the LEAFDIST value is large or the number of levels is greater than four. Reorganize tablespaces when the CLUSTER RATIO drops below 95 percent or when FARINDREF is large. Reorganizing a large tablespace as soon as the CLUSTER RATIO is not 100 percent could produce significant performance gains.

Consider Using SORTKEYS

Version 5

REORG provides a SORTKEYS parameter similar to the SORTKEYS parameter of LOAD. When more than multiple indexes exist and need to be created, consider using the SORTKEYS keyword. When SORTKEYS is specified, index keys are sorted in parallel with the RELOAD and BUILD phases, thereby improving performance.

An estimate of the number of keys to be sorted can be supplied. To estimate the number of keys to sort, use the following calculation:

```
Number of Keys = (Total number of rows in the table) x
                 [(number of indexes on the table) +
                  (number of foreign keys)]
```

Consider Using NOSYSREC

Version 5

The NOSYSREC option can be used so that the REORG process does not require unload data set. This can enhance performance because intermediate disk I/O is eliminated. In order to use the NOSYSREC option, neither the UNLOAD PAUSE nor the UNLOAD ONLY options can be used. Furthermore, you must specify SORTDATA, and SHRLEVEL REFERENCE or SHRLEVEL CHANGE.

However, the NOSYSREC option affects the restartability of the REORG utility. For a SHRLEVEL REFERENCE tablespace REORG, if an error occurs during the RELOAD phase, you must restart at the UNLOAD phase, effectively unloading all of the data again. This is so because the previously unloaded data has not been saved to disk. Likewise, for a REORG TABLESPACE SHRLEVEL NONE, if an error occurs during the RELOAD phase, a RECOVER TABLESPACE is required. Therefore, it is wise to create an image copy prior to running REORG SHRLEVEL NONE with the NOSYSREC option.

Buffer REORG Work Data Sets

Ensure that adequate buffering is specified for the work data set by explicitly coding a larger BUFNO parameter in the REORG utility JCL for the SYSUT1 and SYSREC DD statements. The BUFNO parameter creates read and write buffers in main storage for the data set, thereby enhancing the utility's performance. A BUFNO of approximately 20 is recommended for medium-sized tablespaces, and a BUFNO between 50 and 100 is recommended for larger tablespaces. However, ensure that sufficient memory (real or expanded) is available before increasing the BUFNO specification for your REORG work data sets.

Specify KEEPDICTIONARY for Performance

The REORG utility will rebuild the compression dictionary for tablespaces defined with the COMPRESS YES parameter. Specifying the KEEPDICTIONARY parameter causes the REORG utility to bypass dictionary rebuilding.

This can improve the overall performance of the REORG utility because the CPU cycles used to build the dictionary can be avoided. However, as the compression ratio deteriorates, the LRECL of the SYSREC data set will get longer. Do not utilize the KEEPDICTIONARY option if the type of data in the table has changed significantly since the last time the dictionary was built. Remember, the dictionary is built at LOAD or REORG time only. If the type of data being stored has changed significantly, allowing the REORG utility to rebuild the compression dictionary will provide for more optimal data compression.

Be Aware of VARCHAR Overhead

The REORG utility unloads VARCHAR columns by padding them with spaces to their maximum length. This reduces the efficiency of reorganizing.

Be Aware of VSAM DELETE and DEFINE Activity

The underlying VSAM data sets for STOGROUP-defined tablespaces and indexes are deleted and defined by the REORG utility. If the tablespace or index data set has been user-defined, the corresponding VSAM data set is not deleted.

Consider Concurrently Reorganizing Partitions

It is possible to execute the REORG utility concurrently on separate partitions of a single partitioned tablespace. By reorganizing partitions concurrently, the overall elapsed time to complete the REORG should be substantially lower than a single REORG of the entire partitioned tablespace. However, the overall CPU usage will probably increase. This is usually a satisfactory trade-off however, as elapsed time impacts overall data availability.

Use REORG to Move STOGROUP-Defined Data Sets

The REORG utility can be used to reallocate and move STOGROUP-defined data sets. By altering STOGROUP, PRIQTY, or SECQTY and then reorganizing the tablespace or index, data set level modification can be implemented.

Execute RUNSTATS After Reorganizing

Execute the RUNSTATS utility immediately after reorganizing a DB2 table. This is necessary to maintain current table statistics for access path determination. Plans and packages must be rebound if access paths are to be determined using the updated statistics. Any dynamic SQL statements will immediately take advantage of the new statistics.

Consider Reorganizing Indexes More Frequently Than Tablespaces

The cost of reorganizing an index is small compared to the cost of reorganizing a tablespace. Sometimes, simply executing REORG INDEX on a tablespace's indexes can enhance system performance. Reorganizing an index will not impact clustering, but it will do the following:

- Possibly impact the number of index levels.
- Reorganize and optimize the index page layout, removing inefficiencies introduced due to page splits.
- Reset the LEAFDIST value to 0.
- Reset free space.

Consider Design Changes to Reduce REORG Frequency

You can reduce the frequency of REORG by adding more free space (PCTFREE, FREEPAGE), updating in place to preformatted tables (all possible rows), avoiding VARCHAR, and reorganizing indexes more frequently.

Reorganizing the DB2 Catalog

Version 4

Prior to DB2 V4, it was not possible to reorganize the tablespaces in the DB2 Catalog and DB2 Directory because of the internal hashing and link structures built into these databases. Of the many new features added to DB2 V4, one of the most eagerly awaited by database administrators is the ability to expediently reorganize the DB2 Catalog and DB2 Directory in a systematic manner.

The DB2 Catalog is the central repository for DB2 object and user meta-data. DB2 is constantly referring to that meta data as it processes applications and queries. The physical condition of the tablespaces and indexes that comprise the DB2 Catalog is therefore a major component in overall DB2 subsystem performance.

Likewise, the DB2 directory contains internal control structures such as DBDs and skeleton cursor tables that can be accessed only by DB2 itself. The information in the DB2 directory is critical for database access, utility processing, plan and package execution, and logging. Efficient access to this information is quite critical.

Prior to DB2 V4, reorganization of the DB2 Catalog and DB2 Directory using the REORG utility was not possible. The only option for any type of "reorganization" activity was to run the RECOVER INDEX utility on DB2 Catalog indexes. This rebuilt the indexes, but had no impact on the underlying data housed in the actual physical tablespace. As of DB2 V4, it is permitted to execute the REORG utility on tablespaces and indexes in the DB2 Catalog database (DSNDB06) and on specific tablespaces (SCT02, SPT01, and DBD01) in the DB2 Directory database (DSNDB01).

Vhen Should the DB2 Catalog and Directory Be Reorganized?

'o determine when to reorganize the system catalog, DBAs can use most of the same basic ndicators used to determine whether application tablespaces should be reorganized. Although always has been a wise course of action to execute RUNSTATS on the DB2 Catalog tablespaces, becomes even more important now that these tablespaces can be reorganized. These statiscs can be analyzed to determine when a REORG should be run. When RUNSTATS is run for a atalog tablespace, the statistics about that system catalog tablespace are gathered and then stored ne DB2 Catalog tables themselves. Table 26.2 provides a basic guide to help determine when reorganize system catalog tablespaces and indexes.

able 26.2. DB2 Catalog reorganization indicators.

Column	*Catalog Table*	*Object*	*Impact*
NEAROFFPOSF	SYSIBM.SYSINDEXPART	TABLESPACE	+
FAROFFPOSF	SYSIBM.SYSINDEXPART	TABLESPACE	++++
CLUSTERRATIO	SYSIBM.SYSINDEXES	INDEX	-----
NEARINDREF	SYSIBM.SYSTABLEPART	INDEX	+
FARINDREF	SYSIBM.SYSTABLEPART	INDEX	++++
LEAFDIST	SYSIBM.SYSINDEXPART	INDEX	+++

'his table is similar to the one in Chapter 19 that details reorganization indicators for applicaion tablespaces and indexes (as opposed to system catalog tablespaces and indexes). The colmn and table name where the statistic can be found is given in the first two columns of the hart. The third column indicates whether the statistic is applicable for a tablespace or an inlex. The fourth column gives an indication of the impact of the statistic. A plus (+) sign indiates that you should REORG more frequently as the value in that column gets larger. A minus -) sign indicates that you should REORG more frequently as the value gets smaller. As the numer of "+" or "-" signs increases, the need to REORG becomes more urgent. For example, as AROFFPOSF gets larger, the need to REORG is very urgent, as indicated by the four plus (+) signs.

'or the SYSDBASE, SYSVIEWS, and SYSPLAN catalog tablespaces, the value for the FAROFFPOSF and IEAROFFPOSF columns of SYSINDEXPART can be higher than for other tablespaces before they need o be reorganized. In addition to the guidelines in Table 26.2, consider catalog and directory eorganization in the following situations:

- To reclaim space and size tablespaces appropriately when DB2 Catalog and Directory data sets are not using a significant portion of their allocated disk space (PRIQTY).
- When it is necessary to move the DB2 Catalog and Directory to a different device.
- When the DB2 Catalog and Directory data sets contain a large number of secondary extents.

Synchronizing System Catalog Reorganization

It is a more difficult prospect to determine when the DB2 Directory tablespaces should be reorganized. The RUNSTATS utility does not maintain statistics for these "tablespaces" like it can for the DB2 Catalog. However, it is possible to base the reorganization of the DB2 Directory tablespaces on the reorganization schedule of the DB2 Catalog tablespaces. In fact, in certain situations, it is imperative that specific DB2 Directory tablespaces are reorganized when a "companion" DB2 Catalog tablespace is reorganized. The chart contained in Table 26.3 provides information on keeping the DB2 Catalog and DB2 Directory tablespaces "in sync."

Table 26.3. DB2 Directory reorganization indicators.

When You REORG...	*Be Sure to Also* REORG...
DSNDB06.SYSDBASE	DSNDB01.DBD01
DSNDB06.SYSPLAN	DSNDB01.SCT02
DSNDB06.SYSPKAGE	DSNDB01.SPT01

These tablespaces are logically related. DB2 requires that you reorganize them at the same time to keep them synchronized.

DB2 Catalog Reorganization Details

There are 12 system catalog tablespaces and six directory tablespaces (see Tables 26.4 and 26.5). DB2 has different rules for different sets of these tablespaces. There are three groupings of tablespaces:

- Cannot be reorganized at all
- Can be reorganized using normal REORG procedures
- Can be reorganized using special REORG procedures

Table 26.4. DB2 Catalog tablespaces (DSNDB06).

Tablespace	*Definition*
SYSCOPY	Contains image copy information (one table)
SYSDBASE	Contains database object information (14 tables)
SYSDBAUT	Contains database and database authority information (two tables)
SYSDDF	Contains information about distributed DB2 connections (seven tables)
SYSGPAUT	Contains resource authority information (one table)

Tablespace	*Definition*
SYSGROUP	Contains storage group information (two tables)
SYSPLAN	Contains plan information (five tables)
SYSPKAGE	Contains package and stored procedure information (eight tables)
SYSSTATS	Contains optimization statistics (five tables)
SYSSTR	Contains translation and check constraint information (four tables)
SYSUSER	Contains user authority information (one table)
SYSVIEWS	Contains view information (four tables)

Table 26.5. DB2 Directory tablespaces (DSNDB01).

Tablespace	*Definition*
DBD01	Contains database descriptor information (one table)
SCT01	Contains skeleton cursor table information (one table)
SPT02	Contains skeleton package table information (one table)
SYSLGRNGX	Contains recovery log range information (one table)
SYSUTILX	Contains utility processing information (one table)

There are only two tablespaces in the first grouping of tablespaces that cannot be reorganized at all: DSNDB01.SYSUTILX and DSNDB01.SYSLGRNGX. Do not attempt to reorganize these tablespaces as DB2 will not permit it.

The second grouping of tablespaces are those that the REORG utility processes as it would any other tablespace:

- DSNSB06.SYSCOPY
- DSNDB06.SYSDDF
- DSNSB06.SYSGPAUT
- DSNSB06.SYSPKAGE
- DSNSB06.SYSSTATS
- DSNSB06.SYSSTR
- DSNSB06.SYSUSER
- DSNSB01.SCT02
- DSNSB01.SPT01

The third, and final grouping of tablespaces, must be processed differently than other tablespaces:

- DSNDB06.SYSDBASE
- DSNDB06.SYSDBAUT
- DSNDB06.SYSGROUP
- DSNDB06.SYSPLAN
- DSNDB06.SYSVIEWS
- DSNDB01.DBD01

These six tablespaces require special "handling and care." Because they have a different internal configuration than most other tablespaces, a different calculation is required for the size of the unload data set (SYSREC) used during the REORG utility. These tablespaces contain internal links. Links are internal pointers that tie the information in their tables together hierarchically. A link can be thought of as a type of parent-child relationship that, due to these links, the BUILD and SORT phases of the REORG utility are not executed.

The WORKDDN, SORTDATA, SORTDEVT, SORTNUM options are ignored when reorganizing these tablespaces. Also, the REORG utility cannot be restarted from the last checkpoint when used against these six tablespaces. Instead, it must be restarted from the beginning of the phase. Finally, as mentioned before, a different set of steps must be executed during reorganization for these tablespaces.

Steps to REORG the Six "Special" Tablespaces

The following steps should be used when reorganizing the six "special" tablespaces:

1. Calculate the size of unload data set (SYSREC).

   The SYSREC data set for the "special" tablespaces has a different format than the other tablespaces. This causes a special calculation to be required to determine its size. The equation to use is

   ```
   DATA SET SIZE IN BYTES = (28 + LONGROW) * NUMROWS
   ```

   NUMROWS is the number of rows to be contained in the data set and LONGROW is the length of the longest in the tablespace. The value for LONGROW can be determined by running the following SQL statement:

   ```
   SELECT   MAX(RECLENGTH)
   FROM     SYSIBM.SYSTABLES
   WHERE    DBNAME = 'DSNDB06'
   AND      TSNAME = 'name of tablespace to REORG'
   AND      CREATOR = 'SYSIBM';
   ```

2. Ensure that incompatible operations are not executing.
3. Start database DSNDB01 and DSNDB06 for read only access.
4. Run QUIESCE and DSN1CHKR utilities.
5. Take a full image copy of entire DB2 Catalog and Directory tablespaces.

6. Start DSNDB01 and DSNDB06 for utility access.
7. Execute REORG utility.
8. Take a full image copy of entire DB2 Catalog and Directory tablespaces.
9. Start tablespace and associated indexes for read/write access.

NOTE

It is important to take a full image copy before and after reorganizing any DB2 Catalog or Directory tablespace.

Steps to REORG Regular Tablespaces

The following steps should be used when reorganizing the remaining, "regular" system catalog and directory tablespaces:

1. Calculate the size of unload data set (SYSREC) using the normal calculation:
   `DATA SET SIZE IN BYTES = LONGROW * NUMROWS`
   In this case it is unnecessary to add the additional 28 bytes to the length of the longest row. This is because these system catalog tablespaces do not utilize links.
2. Ensure that incompatible operations are not concurrently executing (see the next section for an explanation of incompatible operations).
3. Start the tablespace and its associated indexes for read-only access.
4. Run CHECK INDEX on all indexes associated with the tablespace that is being reorganized.
5. Take a full image copy of the entire DB2 Catalog and Directory tablespaces.
6. Start the tablespace and its associated indexes for utility access.
7. Execute the REORG utility.
8. Take a full image copy of the entire DB2 Catalog and Directory tablespaces.
9. Start the tablespace and any associated indexes for read/write access.

These steps should be familiar to you because they closely follow the steps executed during the reorganization of an application data tablespace. There are several additional required steps added as precautions because of the critical nature of the DB2 Catalog and Directory.

NOTE

It is important to take a full image copy before and after reorganizing any DB2 Catalog or Directory tablespace.

Catalog Reorganization Restrictions

In addition to the procedures outlined previously, there are several restrictions on the manner in which the REORG TABLESPACE utility can be used with system catalog tablespaces. First, recall that the SYSUTILX and SYSLGRNGX tablespaces in the DB2 Directory cannot be reorganized.

When reorganizing the DB2 Catalog (DSNDB06) and DB2 Directory (DSNDB01) tablespaces, the following options cannot be used:

- The UNLOAD ONLY option is not permitted.
- Online REORG is not permitted for catalog and directory tablespaces with links.
- The LOG YES option is not permitted as image copies are explicitly required following a catalog and/or directory reorganization.

Also, the reorganization of two specific tablespaces are treated differently than any other in the manner in which the are tracked by DB2. Generally, DB2 records the reorganization of any tablespace in the SYSIBM.SYSCOPY system catalog table. However, DB2 records the reorganization of the DSNSB06.SYSCOPY and DSNDB01.DBD01 tablespaces in the log instead.

Finally, in many 24×7 environments, it may be necessary to reorganize the system catalog and dictionary while it is being accessed. However, because of the central nature of the system catalog and directory to the operation of DB2, the following restrictions apply to concurrent activity during catalog reorganization:

- ALTER, DROP, and CREATE statements cannot be executed during the reorganization of any DB2 catalog or DB2 directory tablespace with the exception of SYSIBM.SYSSTR and SYSIBM.SYSCOPY.
- The BIND and FREE commands cannot be issued when the following tablespaces are being reorganized: SYSIBM.SYSDBAUT, SYSIBM.SYSDBASE, SYSIBM.SYSGPAUT, SYSIBM.SYSPKAGE, SYSIBM.SYSPLAN, SYSIBM.SYSSTATS, SYSIBM.SYSUSER, and SYSIBM.SYSVIEWS.
- No DB2 utility can be running while SYSIBM.SYSCOPY, SYSIBM.SYSDBASE, SYSIBM.SYSDBAUT, SYSIBM.SYSSTATS, and/or SYSIBM.SYSUSER are being reorganized.
- No plan or package may be executed during the reorganization of SYSIBM.SYSPLAN and SYSIBM.SYSPKAGE.
- The GRANT and REVOKE statements cannot be issued when REORG is being run on SYSIBM.SYSDBASE, SYSIBM.SYSDBAUT, SYSIBM.SYSGPAUT, SYSIBM.SYSPKAGE, SYSIBM.SYSPLAN, and/or SYSIBM.SYSUSER.

The ability to reorganize the DB2 Catalog and Directory tablespaces provides the DBA with a potent tool for his or her system-tuning arsenal.

Summary

This chapter discussed ways to ensure the proper organization of your data. Data organization is essential for optimal performance. But after the data is properly organized, it is important to inform DB2 of that fact. The next chapter discusses how to do that and how to keep the system databases running efficiently.

27

Catalog Manipulation Utilities

The DB2 Catalog and the DB2 Directory are essential to the continuing performance of your DB2 subsystem. This chapter discusses several utilities that can help you keep these system databases in an optimal state.

The CATMAINT Utility

The CATMAINT utility is used when migrating from one version or release of DB2 to another. It changes the structure of the DB2 Catalog by altering and creating DB2 tables and indexes using the special links and hashes in the DB2 Catalog database. The CATMAINT utility modifies the DB2 Catalog objects in place.

An execution of CATMAINT cannot be partially successful; all the catalog changes are made when the job is successful, or none are made when the job fails.

CATMAINT can be executed by INSTALL SYSADM specified in the DSNZPARMs.

CATMAINT Guidelines

The guideline presented next should be followed when you are considering CATMAINT usage.

Use CATMAINT Only as Directed

The CATMAINT utility should be used only when migrating to a new release of DB2, and then only as directed by IBM in the DB2 release migration procedures.

The MODIFY Utility

The MODIFY utility is used to delete rows from DB2 Catalog and DB2 Directory tables. MODIFY is the clean-up utility. When information in the DB2 Catalog or DB2 Directory is no longer relevant or desirable, MODIFY can be used to delete the unwanted rows.

There are two components of the MODIFY utility:

- MODIFY RECOVERY deletes rows related to data recovery from both the DB2 Catalog and DB2 Directory.
- MODIFY STATISTICS deletes the nonuniform statistics that the RUNSTATS utility stored in the SYSIBM.SYSFIELDS DB2 Catalog table for DB2 V3 and prior releases.

NOTE

Before migrating from V3 to a later release of DB2, consider using the MODIFY STATISTICS utility to perform a mass delete of the useless non-uniform distribution statistics in SYSIBM.SYSFIELDS.

MODIFY Phases

The MODIFY utility uses three phases, regardless of whether recovery or statistical information is being deleted:

UTILINIT	Sets up and initializes the MODIFY utility
MODIFY	Deletes rows for either SYSIBM.SYSCOPY or SYSIBM.SYSFIELDS, depending on the option chosen by the DB2 Catalog
UTILTERM	Performs the final utility cleanup

The MODIFY RECOVERY Utility

The RECOVERY option of the MODIFY utility removes recovery information from SYSIBM.SYSCOPY and SYSIBM.SYSLGRNGX. Recovery information can be removed in two ways. You can delete rows that are older than a specified number of days, or before specified data.

The JCL to execute the MODIFY utility with the RECOVERY option is provided in Listing 27.1. Both the DELETE AGE and DELETE DATE options are shown.

Listing 27.1. MODIFY RECOVERY JCL.

```
//DB2JOBU  JOB (UTILITY),'DB2 MOD RCV',MSGCLASS=X,CLASS=X,
//         NOTIFY=USER
//*
//****************************************************************
//*
//*        DB2 MODIFY RECOVERY UTILITY
//*
//****************************************************************
//*
//UTIL EXEC DSNUPROC,SYSTEM=DSN,UID='MODIRECV',UTPROC=''
//*
//*  UTILITY INPUT CONTROL STATEMENTS
//*    1. The first statement deletes all SYSCOPY information
//*       older than 80 days for the named tablespace.
//*    2. The second statement deletes all SYSCOPY information
//*       with a date before December 31, 1992 for the named
//*       tablespace.
//*
//DSNUPROC.SYSIN    DD  *
  MODIFY RECOVERY TABLESPACE DSN8D51A.DSN8S51E AGE (80)
  MODIFY RECOVERY TABLESPACE DSN8D51A.DSN8S51D DATE (921231)
/*
//
```

MODIFY RECOVERY Locking Considerations

The MODIFY RECOVERY utility can run concurrently on the same object with all utilities *except* the following:

- COPY
- LOAD
- MERGECOPY
- MODIFY RECOVERY
- RECOVER
- REORG

The MODIFY RECOVERY utility will drain write claim classes for the tablespace or partition being operated upon.

MODIFY RECOVERY Guidelines

When running MODIFY RECOVERY you should consider using the following tips and techniques

Run MODIFY RECOVERY Regularly

The MODIFY RECOVERY utility should be run monthly to eliminate old recovery information stored in SYSIBM.SYSCOPY and SYSIBM.SYSLGRNGX. Running this utility more frequently is usually difficult to administer. Running it less frequently causes the recovery tables to grow, affecting the performance of the DB2 CHECK, COPY, LOAD, MERGECOPY, RECOVER, and REORG utilities. Access to other DB2 Catalog tables on the same DASD volumes as these tables also may be degraded.

CAUTION

The MODIFY RECOVERY utility places an X lock on the SYSCOPY tablespace. As such, run MODIFY RECOVERY when there is little or no concurrent SYSCOPY activity.

The definition of *old recovery information* must be defined on an application-by-applicatio basis. Usually, DB2 applications run the COPY utility for all tablespaces at a consistent tim Sometimes, however, the definition of what should be deleted must be made on a tablespac by-tablespace basis. One way to define "old recovery information" is anything that is older th the oldest archive log.

Ensure That Two Full Copies Are Always Available

As a general rule, leave at least two full image copy data sets for each tablespace in the SYSIBM.SYSCOPY table. In this way, DB2 can use a previous image copy if the most recent one is damaged or unavailable. Additionally, if the full image copy data sets are SHRLEVEL CHANGE, ensure that the log is older than the oldest image copy. If the log does not predate the oldest image, the image copy is not very useful.

Synchronize MODIFY RECOVERY Execution with the Deletion of Log and Copy Data Sets

The MODIFY RECOVERY utility deletes rows from only the SYSIBM.SYSCOPY and SYSIBM.SYSLGRNGX tables. It does not physically delete the image copy data sets corresponding to the deleted SYSIBM.SYSCOPY rows, nor does it physically delete the log data sets associated with the deleted SYSIBM.SYSLGRNGX log ranges. To delete these data sets, run separate jobs—at the same time that MODIFY RECOVERY is run—using IEFBR14 or IDCAMS. Alternately, assign an expiration date to the log data sets.

Be Aware of Copy Pending Ramifications

If MODIFY RECOVERY deletes recovery information for a tablespace such that full recovery cannot be accomplished, the tablespace is placed in copy pending status.

Be Aware of the Nonstandard DATE Format

For DB2 V3 and earlier releases, be careful when specifying the DATE option of the MODIFY RECOVERY utility. The data is in the format YYMMDD, rather than the standard DB2 date format. If you want October 16, 1997, for example, you must specify it as 971016 rather than as 1997-10-16.

Version 5

DB2 V5 accepts the century as input to the DATE clause (DB2 V4 will do this with a PTF). However, the date must be specified using a non-standard date format, as follows:

```
MODIFY RECOVERY TABLESPACE DSN8D51A.DSN8S51D DATE (19921231)
```

The MODIFY STATISTICS Utility

The RUNSTATS utility collects nonuniform distribution statistics (NUDS) and stores them in SYSCOLDIST and SYSCOLDISTSTATS. (Prior to DB2 V3 they were stored in SYSFIELDS.)

The MODIFY STATISTICS utility can be used to remove nonuniform distribution statistics from SYSFIELDS. Sample JCL for the MODIFY utility with the STATISTICS option is in Listing 27.2.

SYSCOLDIST and SYSCOLDISTSTATS can be directly modified using SQL UPDATE, INSERT, and DELETE statements. As such, MODIFY STATISTICS is not useful for DB2 V3 and later releases.

Listing 27.2. MODIFY STATISTICS JCL.

```
//DB2JOBU  JOB (UTILITY),'DB2 MOD STAT',MSGCLASS=X,CLASS=X,
//         NOTIFY=USER
//*
//****************************************************************
//*
//*           DB2 MODIFY STATISTICS UTILITY
//*
//****************************************************************
//*
//UTIL EXEC DSNUPROC,SYSTEM=DSN,UID='MODISTAT',UTPROC=''
//*
//*  UTILITY INPUT CONTROL STATEMENTS
//*      The MODIFY statement deletes all SYSFIELDS information
//*      for the EMPNO column of the DSN8310.EMP table.
//*
//DSNUPROC.SYSIN    DD  *
    MODIFY STATISTICS
           TABLE (DSN8310.EMP)   COLUMN (EMPNO)
           DELETE NONUNIFORM
/*
//
```

MODIFY Guidelines

Consider deploying the following techniques when executing the MODIFY utility.

Remedy Pending States Before Running MODIFY

The MODIFY utility cannot be run for a tablespace that is in recover or check pending status. This applies to both the MODIFY RECOVERY utility and the MODIFY STATISTICS utility.

The RUNSTATS Utility

The RUNSTATS utility collects statistical information for DB2 tables, tablespaces, partitions, indexes, and columns. It can place this information into DB2 Catalog tables or simply produce a report of the statistical information. The statistics in these tables are used for two primary reasons: to provide organizational information for DBAs and to be used as input to the DB2 optimizer during the BIND process to determine optimal access paths for SQL queries. The statistical information can also be queried using SQL. Several sample DB2 Catalog queries were presented in Chapter 19, "DB2 Object Monitoring Using the DB2 Catalog." The diagram in Figure 27.1 details the functionality of the RUNSTATS utility.

You can use the RUNSTATS utility to

- Produce a statistics report without updating the DB2 Catalog tables
- Update the DB2 Catalog with only DB2 optimizer statistics

- Update the DB2 Catalog with only DBA monitoring statistics
- Update the DB2 Catalog with all the statistics that have been gathered

This flexibility can be useful when you want to determine the effect of RUNSTATS on specific SQL queries—without updating the current usable statistics. Also, if the statistics used by the DB2 optimizer have been modified, RUNSTATS can still be run to gather the DBA monitoring statistics.

FIGURE 27.1.
The RUNSTATS *utility.*

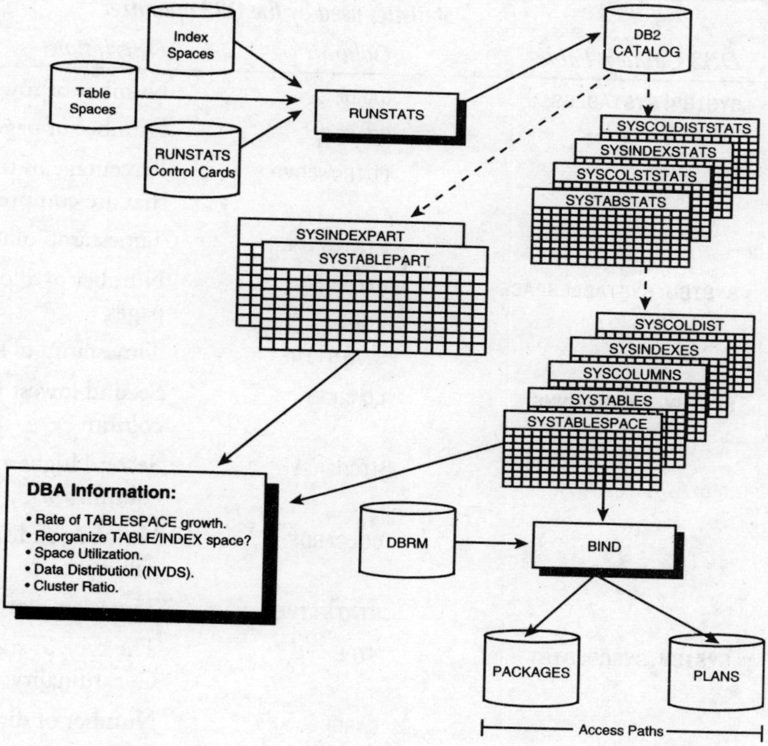

Consult Table 27.1 for a breakdown of the types of statistics gathered by RUNSTATS. The information in this table is accurate as of DB2 V5. For DB2 V4 and previous releases, some of the columns will appear with different names. For example, some columns now end in "F," such as CARDF and FREQUENCYF; whereas in previous releases there was no "F" suffix. The new columns ending in "F" signify that the column is stored as a FLOAT data type; in past releases the columns were stored as integers. These changes were made to accommodate large partitioned tablespaces.

Version 5

NOTE

After migrating to DB2 V5 from an earlier release, be sure to execute RUNSTATS to populate the new columns that end in "F".

Table 27.1. Statistics gathered by RUNSTATS.

	Statistics used by the DB2 optimizer	
DB2 Catalog Table	*Column*	*Description*
SYSIBM.SYSTABLES	CARDF	Number of rows for a table
	NPAGES	Number of pages used by the table
	PCTROWCOMP	Percentage of total active rows that are compressed for this table
	STATSTIME	Timestamp of RUNSTATS execution
SYSIBM.SYSTABLESPACE	NACTIVE	Number of allocated tablespace pages
	STATSTIME	Timestamp of RUNSTATS execution
SYSIBM.SYSCOLUMNS	LOW2KEY	Second lowest value for the column
	HIGH2KEY	Second highest value for the column
	COLCARDF	Number of distinct values for the column
	STATSTIME	Timestamp of RUNSTATS execution
SYSIBM.SYSCOLDIST	TYPE	The type of stats collected: C=cardinality; F=frequent value
	CARDF	Number of distinct values for the column group.
	COLVALUE	Nonuniform distribution column value
	FREQUENCYF	Percentage (× 100) that the value in EXITPARM exists in the column
	STATSTIME	Timestamp of RUNSTATS execution
	NUMCOLUMNS	Number of columns associated with the statistics
	COLGROUPCOLNO	Identifies the set of columns associated with the statistics

Statistics used by the DB2 optimizer

DB2 Catalog Table	*Column*	*Description*
SYSIBM.SYSINDEXES	CLUSTERED	Whether or not the table is clustered
	CLUSTERRATIO	Percentage of rows in clustered order
	CLUSTERING	Whether CLUSTER was specified when the index was created
	FIRSTKEYCARDF	Number of distinct values for the first column of the index key
	FULLKEYCARDF	Number of distinct values for the full index key
	NLEAF	Number of active leaf pages
	NLEVELS	Number of index b-tree levels
	STATSTIME	Timestamp of RUNSTATS execution

Statistics used by DB2 for Query Parallelism

DB2 Catalog Table	*Column*	*Description*
SYSIBM.SYSCOLDISTSTATS	TYPE	The type of stats collected: C=cardinality; F=frequent value
	CARDF	Number of distinct values for the column group.
	PARTITION	Partition number
	COLVALUE	Nonuniform distribution column value
	FREQUENCYF	Percentage (×100) that the value in EXITPARM exists in the column
	STATSTIME	Timestamp of RUNSTATS execution
	NUMCOLUMNS	Number of columns associated with the statistics
	COLGROUPCOLNO	Identifies the set of columns associated with the statistics
SYSIBM.SYSCOLSTATS	PARTITION	Partition number
	LOW2KEY	Second lowest value for the column
	LOWKEY	Lowest value for the column

continues

Table 27.1. continued

DB2 Catalog Table	Column	Description
Statistics used by DB2 for Query Parallelism		
	HIGH2KEY	Second highest value for the column
	HIGHKEY	Highest value for the column
	COLCARD	Number of distinct values for the column
	STATSTIME	Timestamp of RUNSTATS execution
SYSIBM.SYSINDEXSTATS	PARTITION	Partition number
	CLUSTERRATIO	Percentage of rows in clustered order
	FIRSTKEYCARD	Number of distinct values for the first column of the index key
	FULLKEYCARD	Number of distinct values for the full index key
	NLEAF	Number of active leaf pages
	NLEVELS	Number of index b-tree levels
	STATSTIME	Timestamp of RUNSTATS execution
SYSIBM.SYSTABSTATS	PARTITION	Partition number
	CARD	Number of rows for a table
	NACTIVE	Number of allocated tablespace pages
	NPAGES	Number of pages used by the table
	PCTPAGES	Percentage of tablespace pages that contain rows for this table
	PCTROWCOMP	Percentage of total active rows that are compressed for this table
	STATSTIME	Timestamp of RUNSTATS execution
Statistics used by the DBAs for DB2 subsystem monitoring		
DB2 Catalog Table	*Column*	*Description*
SYSIBM.SYSTABLEPART	CARD	Number of rows in the tablespace
	NEARINDREF	Number of rows between 2 and 16 pages from their original page
	FARINDREF	Number of rows more than 16 pages from their original page

Statistics used by the DBAs for DB2 subsystem monitoring		
DB2 Catalog Table	*Column*	*Description*
	PAGESAVE	Percentage of pages saved due to data compression
	PERCACTIVE	Percentage of space that contains table rows in this tablespace
	PERCDROP	Percentage of space used by rows from dropped tables
SYSIBM.SYSINDEXPART	CARDF	Number of rows referenced by the index
	LEAFDIST	Average distance between successive pages multiplied by 100
	NEAROFFPOSF	Number of times you must access a near-off page when accessing all rows in indexed order
	FAROFFPOSF	Number of times you must access a far-off page when accessing all rows in indexed order

There are two forms of the RUNSTATS utility. The first form operates at the tablespace level and optionally at the table, index, and column levels. Listing 27.3 shows RUNSTATS JCL executing the RUNSTATS utility twice: once for the DSN8510.DEPT tablespace and all its indexes and a second time for the DSN8510.EMP table and some of its columns.

Listing 27.3. RUNSTATS TABLESPACE JCL.

```
//DB2JOBU  JOB (UTILITY),'DB2 RUNSTATS',MSGCLASS=X,CLASS=X,
//         NOTIFY=USER
//*
//****************************************************************
//*
//*                DB2 RUNSTATS TABLESPACE UTILITY
//*
//****************************************************************
//*
//UTIL EXEC DSNUPROC,SYSTEM=DSN,UID='STATSTS',UTPROC=''
//*
//*  UTILITY INPUT CONTROL STATEMENTS
//*     1. The first statement accumulates statistics for the
//*        given tablespace based on the named index columns.
//*     2. The second statement accumulates statistics only for
//*        the named table and columns in the named tablespace.
//*
//DSNUPROC.SYSIN    DD  *
```

continues

Listing 27.3. continued

```
    RUNSTATS TABLESPACE DSN8D51A.DSN8S51D
         INDEX (ALL)        SHRLEVEL REFERENCE
    RUNSTATS TABLESPACE DSN8D51A.DSN8S51E
         TABLE (DSN8510.EMO)
         COLUMN (FIRSTNME,MIDINIT,LASTNAME,SALARY,BONUS,COMM)
         SHRLEVEL REFERENCE
/*
//
```

The other form operates only at the index level. Listing 27.4 demonstrates JCL to execute RUNSTATS for a specific DB2 index.

Listing 27.4. RUNSTATS INDEX JCL.

```
//DB2JOBU  JOB (UTILITY),'DB2 RUNS IX',MSGCLASS=X,CLASS=X,
//         NOTIFY=USER
//*
//****************************************************************
//*
//*           DB2 RUNSTATS INDEX UTILITY
//*
//****************************************************************
//*
//UTIL EXEC DSNUPROC,SYSTEM=DSN,UID='STATSIX',UTPROC=''
//*
//*   UTILITY INPUT CONTROL STATEMENTS
//*      The RUNSTATS statement accumulates statistics for the
//*      given index.
//*
//DSNUPROC.SYSIN    DD   *
    RUNSTATS INDEX (DSN8510.XEMPPROJACT2)
/*
//
```

RUNSTATS Phases

The RUNSTATS utility has three phases:

UTILINIT	Sets up and initializes the RUNSTATS utility
RUNSTATS	Samples the tablespace data, the index data, or both, and then updates the DB2 Catalog tables with the statistical information
UTILTERM	Performs the final utility cleanup

RUNSTATS Locking Considerations

The RUNSTATS utility, regardless of whether it is being run to collect TABLESPACE statistics or INDEX statistics, can operate concurrently with the following utilities:

- CHECK INDEX
- COPY
- DIAGNOSE
- MERGECOPY
- MODIFY
- QUIESCE
- REORG UNLOAD ONLY
- REPAIR (DUMP or MODIFY)
- REPORT
- RUNSTATS
- STOSPACE

Furthermore, RUNSTATS TABLESPACE can operate concurrently with RECOVER INDEX, REORG INDEX, and REPAIR LOCATE INDEX PAGE REPLACE.

RUNSTATS INDEX can be run concurrently with the following:

- RECOVER TABLESPACE (no options)
- RECOVER ERROR RANGE
- REPAIR LOCATE KEY or RID (DELETE or REPLACE), only if SHRLEVEL CHANGE is specified
- REPAIR LOCATE TABLESPACE PAGE REPLACE

When the RUNSTATS utility is executed with the SHRLEVEL REFERENCE option, it drains write claim classes to the tablespace, tablespace partition, index, or index partition. If SHRLEVEL CHANGE is specified, the RUNSTATS utility will claim the read claim class for the object being operated upon, however, no locking occurs if the object is a Type 2 index.

RUNSTATS Guidelines

Use the following tips and techniques to implement effective RUNSTATS jobs at your shop.

Execute RUNSTATS During Off-Peak Hours

RUNSTATS can cause DB2 Catalog contention problems for a DB2 subsystem because it can update the following DB2 Catalog tables:

```
SYSIBM.SYSCOLDIST
SYSIBM.SYSCOLDISTSTATS
SYSIBM.SYSCOLSTATS
SYSIBM.SYSCOLUMNS
SYSIBM.SYSINDEXES
SYSIBM.SYSINDEXPART
```

SYSIBM.SYSINDEXSTATS
SYSIBM.SYSTABLES
SYSIBM.SYSTABLEPART
SYSIBM.SYSTABLESPACE
SYSIBM.SYSTABSTATS
SYSIBM.SYSFIELDS (DB2 V2.2 and V2.3 only)

Execute RUNSTATS during an off-peak period to avoid performance degradation.

Execute RUNSTATS Multiple Times for Long Column Lists

A limit of 10 columns can be specified per RUNSTATS execution. If you must gather statistics on more than 10 columns, issue multiple executions of the RUNSTATS utility, specifying as many as 10 columns per run.

Be Aware of DB2's Notion of Clustering

Although the calculation of CLUSTER RATIO has not been published by IBM, DB2 does not weigh duplicate values in the same way as unique values. For example, consider a table with a SMALLINT column that contains the following values in the physical sequence indicated:

1
3
4
95 occurrences of 7
6
9

This would seem to be 99 percent clustered because 6 is the only value out of sequence. This is not the case, however, because of the complex algorithm DB2 uses for factoring duplicates into the CLUSTER RATIO.

Execute RUNSTATS After Significant Data Changes

Run the RUNSTATS utility liberally. The cost of RUNSTATS usually is negligible for small- to medium-size tablespaces. Moreover, the payback in optimized dynamic SQL, and static SQL when plans are re-bound using valid statistics, can be significant.

Always schedule the running of the RUNSTATS utility for dynamic production data. This gives DB2 the most accurate volume data on which to base its access path selections. Discuss the frequency of production RUNSTATS jobs with your database administration unit.

For volatile tables, consider running the RUNSTATS utility at least monthly.

Favor Using SHRLEVEL REFERENCE

To ensure the accuracy of the statistics gathered by RUNSTATS, favor the use of the SHRLEVEL REFERENCE option. For tablespaces that must be online 24 hours a day, however, execute RUNSTATS with the SHRLEVEL CHANGE option during off-peak processing periods.

Use Good Judgment When Scheduling RUNSTATS

Although it may seem best to execute RUNSTATS to record each and every modification to DB2 table data, it is probably overkill. Not every data modification will affect performance. Deciding which will and which won't, however, is an arduous task requiring good judgment. Before running RUNSTATS, analyze the type of data in the tablespace, the scope of the change, and the number of changes. The overhead of running the RUNSTATS utility and the data availability needs of the application could make it impossible to run the utility as frequently as you want.

It is good practice to execute RUNSTATS in the following situations:

- When new data is loaded into a table
- When a new column is added to a table and is at least partially populated
- When a new index is created
- When a tablespace or index is reorganized
- When a large number of data modifications have been applied to a particular table (updates, deletions, and/or insertions)
- After recovering a tablespace or index

Do Not Avoid RUNSTATS Even When Changing Statistics Using SQL

The DB2 optimizer is not perfect. Sometimes, the RUNSTATS information stored in the DB2 Catalog must be altered. This should be a last resort.

Also, do not forgo the execution of RUNSTATS after modifying the DB2 Catalog statistics. At the least, RUNSTATS should be run to report on the current statistics, without updating the DB2 Catalog. However, this will make all the DB2 Catalog statistics for the tablespace outdated, not just the ones that need to be static. Therefore, consider running RUNSTATS to update the DB2 Catalog, regardless of whether the statistics have been modified, but follow the RUNSTATS job with a SQL UPDATE, INSERT, or DELETE statement to make the changes.

Consider Collecting Partition-Level Statistics

RUNSTATS can be executed by partition, thereby collecting statistics for a tablespace one partition at a time. Employ this technique to collect statistics (over time) while increasing data availability. Additionally, consider collecting RUNSTATS more frequently for volatile partitions, and less frequently for other partitions.

Consider Sampling

Version 5

The SAMPLE parameter, new as of DB2 V5, enables the RUNSTATS utility to use sampling methods to collect statistics instead of scanning every row in the tablespace, tables, and indexes specified. When sampling is specified, the overall resource consumption, CPU time, and elapsed time required by RUNSTATS can be substantially reduced. However, the accuracy of the collected statistics is impacted because only a subset of the rows are read to estimate statistics such as cardinality, high key value, and low key value.

In general, consider sampling only when RUNSTATS takes too much time to execute within the structure of your environment. Additionally, specify as high a sampling percentage as possible because the more data that is sampled, the more accurate the statistics are. For example

```
RUNSTATS TABLESPACE DSN8D51A.DSN8S51D
    TABLE (ALL)     SAMPLE 50
```

This statement causes RUNSTATS to use a sampling rate of 50 percent for the specified tablespace and tables.

Consider Collecting Frequent Value Statistics

Version 5

As of DB2 V5, the KEYCARD and FREQVAL parameters can be used with RUNSTATS. DB2 typically views any two columns as independent from one another. However, frequent value statistics enable DB2 to capture information about correlated columns. Columns are considered to be correlated with one another when their values are related in some manner. Consider, for example, CITY and STATE columns. If the CITY column is set to "CHICAGO" it is much more common for the STATE to be set to "IL" than any other state. However, without frequent value statistics, DB2 would consider Chicago, FL, to be just as common as Chicago, IL.

With a multi-column index for CITY and STATE, the RUNSTATS utility can be used to collect frequent value statistics to "learn" about the correlation between the two columns. For example, consider the following RUNSTATS specification for DSN8510.XEMPPROJACT1 (a unique index on PROJNO, ACTNO, EMSTDATE, and EMPNO):

```
RUNSTATS INDEX DSN8510.XEMPPROJACT1
    KEYCARD
    FREQVAL NUMCOLS 2 COUNT 15
```

This statement causes the cardinality values to be collected for the concatenation of the first and second columns of the index (in this case, PROJNO and ACTNO). The top 15 most frequently occurring values will be collected. These statistics are most useful for queries against columns that are actually correlated in some manner where a matching index scan is used for the columns indicated.

The STOSPACE Utility

The STOSPACE utility is executed on a STOGROUP or list of STOGROUPs. It populates the DB2 Catalog with tablespace and index data set DASD usage statistics. These statistics are culled from the appropriate ICF Catalog as indicated in the STOGROUP for which the STOSPACE utility is being executed. All space usage statistics stored in the DB2 Catalog are specified in terms of kilobytes (1024 bytes).

JCL to execute the STOSPACE utility for all storage groups known to the DB2 system is in Listing 27.5. The * in the JCL can be replaced with either a single STOGROUP name or a list of STOGROUP names separated by commas.

Listing 27.5. STOSPACE JCL.

```
//DB2JOBU  JOB (UTILITY),'DB2 STOSPACE',MSGCLASS=X,CLASS=X,
//         NOTIFY=USER
//*
//****************************************************************
//*
//*                    DB2 STOSPACE UTILITY
//*
//****************************************************************
//*
//UTIL EXEC DSNUPROC,SYSTEM=DSN,UID='STOSPACE',UTPROC=''
//DSNUPROC.SYSIN    DD  *
   STOSPACE STOGROUP (*)
/*
//
```

STOSPACE Phases

The STOSPACE utility has three phases:

UTILINIT	Sets up and initializes the STOSPACE utility.
STOSPACE	Analyzes the VSAM catalog for each tablespace and index in the indicated STOGROUPs. Space utilization statistics are gathered, and the DB2 Catalog is updated.
UTILTERM	Performs the final utility cleanup.

STOSPACE Locking Considerations

The STOSPACE utility can be run concurrently with all utilities.

STOSPACE Guidelines

When running the STOSPACE utility, use the following guidelines to ensure effective storage management.

Run STOSPACE Regularly

The STOSPACE utility should be run weekly for STOGROUPs to which highly active tablespaces and indexes are assigned. It should be executed at least monthly for *all* STOGROUPs defined to the DB2 system.

Be Aware of DB2 Catalog Updates Caused by STOSPACE

The STOSPACE utility updates the following DB2 Catalog tables and columns:

Table	*Column*
SYSIBM.SYSSTOGROUP	SPACE and SPCDATE
SYSIBM.SYSINDEXES	SPACE
SYSIBM.SYSINDEXPART	SPACE
SYSIBM.SYSTABLESPACE	SPACE
SYSIBM.SYSTABLEPART	SPACE

If the SPACE column in the SYSIBM.SYSSTOGROUP table is 0 after running the STOSPACE utility, consider dropping the STOGROUP, because no objects are currently defined for it. You can issue the following query to determine this:

```
SELECT   NAME, SPACE
FROM     SYSIBM.SYSSTOGROUP
WHERE    SPACE = 0
ORDER BY NAME
```

Be careful, however, if your shop uses DFHSM to automatically migrate inactive data sets to tape. Issue the following query to be sure that no objects have been defined to the STOGROUPs with a SPACE value of 0:

```
SELECT *
FROM   SYSIBM.SYSSTOGROUP ST
WHERE  NOT EXISTS
       (SELECT 1
        FROM    SYSIBM.SYSINDEXPART IP
        WHERE   ST.NAME = IP.STORNAME)
AND    NOT EXISTS
       (SELECT 1
        FROM    SYSIBM.SYSTABLEPART TP
        WHERE   ST.NAME = TP.STORNAME)
```

If no objects are returned by this query, the STOGROUPs previously identified probably can be dropped. There is one more problem, however. If a STOGROUP used as the default storage group for an active database is dropped, future tablespace and index DDL must explicitly specify a STOGROUP rather than rely on the default STOGROUP for the database. This is not usually a problem because the recommendation is to explicitly specify every parameter when creating DB2 objects. You can use the following query to determine whether a STOGROUP is used as the default STOGROUP for a database:

```
SELECT    NAME
FROM      SYSIBM.SYSDATABASE
WHERE     STGROUP = 'STOGROUP';
```

Monitor DASD Usage

Run the DB2 DASD usage queries (presented in Chapter 19) after successfully running the STOSPACE utility. This helps you monitor DASD used by DB2 objects.

Now that you have your DB2 Catalog in order, look at several other types of DB2 "utilities" in Chapter 28, "Miscellaneous Utilities."

Summary

In this chapter, you explored methods of manipulating the DB2 Catalog and the DB2 Directory using DB2 utilities. The utilities covered in this chapter—CATMAINT, MODIFY, and RUNSTATS—are essential to ensure an optimal DB2 subsystem.

28

Miscellaneous Utilities

In the previous two chapters, you looked at the DB2 online utilities. Several other DB2 utilit programs are outside this category. (As might be expected, if there are online utilities, there ar also offline utilities.) DB2 also provides service aids and sample programs that have propertie and objectives similar to true DB2 utilities. This chapter discusses each of these remaining type of utilities.

The Offline Utilities

The offline utilities can be executed when DB2 is not active. Most DB2 service aid utilities ca be executed also when DB2 is inactive, but IBM does not consider them to be offline utilities (The service aids are covered in the next section.)

Two offline utilities are used to administer the DB2 logs. These utilities should be used onl by technical support personnel who understand the intricacies of DB2 logging. As such, onl the DB2 systems programmer or DBA who installs and maintains the DB2 system should us these utilities. A brief introduction to these utilities, however, should increase your overa understanding of DB2 logging.

The Change Log Inventory Utility (DSNJU003)

DSNJU003, better known as the Change Log Inventory utility, modifies the bootstrap data se (BSDS). Its primary function is to add or delete active and archive logs for the DB2 subsysten Sample JCL to add an archive log data set is provided in Listing 28.1.

Listing 28.1. DSNJU003 JCL (change log inventory).

```
//DB2JOBU  JOB (UTILITY),'DSNJU003',MSGCLASS=X,CLASS=X,
//          NOTIFY=USER
//*
//****************************************************************
//*        DB2 CHANGE LOG INVENTORY
//****************************************************************
//*
//DSNJU003 EXEC PGM=DSNJU003
//SYSUT1   DD  DSN=DB2CAT.BSDS01,DISP=OLD
//SYSUT2   DD  DSN=DB2CAT.BSDS02,DISP=OLD
//SYSIN     DD  *
NEWLOG DSNAME=DB2CAT.FIRST.COPY,COPY1
NEWLOG DSNAME=DB2CAT.SECOND.COPY,COPY2
/*
//
```

The Print Log Map Utility (DSNJU004)

DSNJU004, or the Print Log Map utility, is used to display the status of the logs in the BSD Sample JCL is provided in Listing 28.2.

Listing 28.2. DSNJU004 JCL (print log map).

```
//DB2JOBU  JOB (UTILITY),'DSNJU004',MSGCLASS=X,CLASS=X,
//          NOTIFY=USER
//*
//****************************************************************
//*        DB2 PRINT LOG MAP
//****************************************************************
//*
//DSNJU004 EXEC PGM=DSNJU004
//SYSUT1   DD  DSN=DB2CAT.BSDS01,DISP=SHR
//SYSPRINT DD SYSOUT=*
//
```

Log Utility Guideline

Use the following tip when running DSNJU004.

Use DSNJU004 for Documentation

Run DSNJU004, the Print Log Map utility, before and after running the change log utility. You can use the output of DSNJU004 to document the log change being implemented.

The DB2 Log Preformat Utility (DSNJLOGF)

Version 5

DSNJLOGF, the DB2 Log Preformat utility, preformats DB2 active log data sets. The execution of this utility is not mandatory for new active log data sets. However, if DSNJLOGF has not been run prior to the first write activity for the log, DB2 will preformat the log at that time, incurring a delay. Sample JCL is provided in Listing 28.3.

Listing 28.3. DSNJLOGF JCL.

```
//DB2JOBU  JOB (UTILITY),'DSNJLOGF',MSGCLASS=X,CLASS=X,
//          NOTIFY=USER
//*
//****************************************************************
//*        DB2 LOG PREFORMAT
//****************************************************************
//*
//*  Preformat the DB2 active log data sets
//*
//PREF11 EXEC PGM=DSNJLOGF
//SYSPRINT DD SYSOUT=*
//SYSUDUMP DD SYSOUT=*
//SYSUT1   DD  DSN=DSN510.LOGCOPY1.DS01,DISP=SHR
//*
//PREF12 EXEC PGM=DSNJLOGF
//SYSPRINT DD SYSOUT=*
//SYSUDUMP DD SYSOUT=*
```

continues

Listing 28.3. continued

```
//SYSUT1   DD   DSN=DSN510.LOGCOPY1.DS02,DISP=SHR
//*
//PREF21 EXEC PGM=DSNJLOGF
//SYSPRINT DD SYSOUT=*
//SYSUDUMP DD SYSOUT=*
//SYSUT1   DD   DSN=DSN510.LOGCOPY2.DS01,DISP=SHR
//*
//PREF22 EXEC PGM=DSNJLOGF
//SYSPRINT DD SYSOUT=*
//SYSUDUMP DD SYSOUT=*
//SYSUT1   DD   DSN=DSN510.LOGCOPY2.DS02,DISP=SHR
//
```

DSNJLOGF Guideline

Use the following guideline when running DSNJLOGF.

Use DSNJLOGF

Execute the DSNJLOGF utility instead of allowing DB2 to preformat the active log data set during processing. This will eliminate delays due to log data set preformatting.

Service Aids

The DB2 service aids are batch utilities that perform DB2 administrative activities outside the control of the DB2 subsystem (with the exception of DSN1SDMP). This can be useful if an error makes the DB2 system inactive. For example, the service aids can copy DB2 data sets and print formatted dumps of their contents without DB2 being active. Every DB2 specialist should have a working knowledge of the service aid utilities. The service aids are

DSN1CHKR	DB2 Catalog and DB2 Directory Integrity Verification utility
DSN1COMP	Data Compression Analysis utility
DSN1COPY	Offline Tablespace Copy utility
DSN1SDMP	Dump and Trace utility
DSN1LOGP	Recovery Log Extractor utility
DSN1PRNT	Formatted Tablespace Dump utility

The Catalog Integrity Verification Utility (DSN1CHKR)

DSN1CHKR, the Catalog Integrity Verification utility, verifies the integrity of the DB2 Catalog and DB2 Directory. Sample JCL is provided in Listing 28.4.

Listing 28.4. DSN1CHKR JCL.

```
//DB2JOBU  JOB (UTILITY),'DSN1CHKR',MSGCLASS=X,CLASS=X,
//         NOTIFY=USER
//*
//****************************************************************
//*        DB2 CATALOG CHECK SERVICE AID
//****************************************************************
//*
//*  Verifies the integrity of the SYSPLAN tablespace
//*
//CHECK EXEC PGM=DSN1CHKR,PARM='FORMAT'
//SYSUT1  DD  DSN=DB2CAT.DSNDBC.DSNDB06.SYSPLAN.I0001.A001,DISP=SHR
//SYSPRINT DD SYSOUT=*
//
```

> **CAUTION**
>
> The SYSUTILX and SYSLGRNGX tables are not checkable using DSN1CHKR. This is true even though the predecessors to these tables were checkable (SYSUTIL prior to V3 and SYSLGRNG prior to V4).

DSN1CHKR Guideline

Review the following techniques when using DSN1CHKR to verify the integrity of DB2 Catalog tablespaces.

Schedule DSN1CHKR Runs Regularly

Execute the DSN1CHKR utility for the DB2 Catalog and DB2 Directory weekly to catch problems early, before they affect production processing.

Consider Starting the DB2 Catalog in Read-Only Mode

For the results of DSN1CHKR to be 100 percent accurate, DB2 must be down or the tablespaces being checked must be started in read-only mode (or stopped). To minimize the outage, consider copying the tablespaces to be checked to VSAM files. The VSAM files can be checked instead of the actual DB2 Catalog tablespaces. It should take less time to copy the files to VSAM than to check the actual tablespace data sets.

Take Additional DB2 Catalog Verification Steps

In addition to running DSN1CHKR, consider the following steps to ensure DB2 Catalog integrity:

- Run DSN1COPY with the check option against all DB2 Catalog indexes and tablespaces.
- Run the Check Index utility against all catalog indexes.

The Compression Analyzer (DSN1COMP)

The Compression Analyzer service aid, also known as DSN1COMP, can be used to approximate the results of DB2 V3 ESA data compression. DSN1COMP can be run on a tablespace data set, a sequential data set containing a DB2 tablespace or partition, a full image copy data set, or an incremental image copy data set. It will provide the following statistics:

- Space used with compression
- Space used without compression
- Percentage of bytes saved by using compression
- Total pages required with compression
- Total pages required without compression
- Percentage of pages saved by using compression
- Number of dictionary entries
- Number of dictionary pages required
- Average size of a compressed row

CAUTION

DSN1COMP cannot be run against compressed objects. Because the compression dictionary can age, it can be difficult to determine when to replace the dictionary because DSN1COMP cannot be used for this purpose.

Sample DSN1COMP JCL is provided in Listing 28.5. This job reads the VSAM data set for the DSN8D51A.DSN8S51D tablespace specified in the SYSUT1 DD statement and analyzes the data producing estimated compression statistics.

Listing 28.5. DSN1COMP JCL.

```
//DB2JOBU  JOB (UTILITY),'DB2 DSN1COMP',MSGCLASS=X,CLASS=X,
//         NOTIFY=USER
//*
//****************************************************************
//*
//*        DB2 DSN1COMP SERVICE AID UTILITY
//*
//****************************************************************
//*
//JOBLIB DD DSN=DSN510.DSNLOAD,DISP=SHR
//DSN1COPY EXEC PGM=DSN1COMP,PARM='ROWLIMIT(20000)'
//SYSPRINT DD  SYSOUT=*
//SYSUDUMP DD  SYSOUT=*
//SYSUT1 DD DSN=DB2CAT.DSNDBC.DSN8D51A.DSN8S51D.I0001.A001,DISP=OLD,AMP=
➥('BUFND=181')
//
```

There are numerous parameters that can be supplied to the DSN1COMP utility. The following are the most commonly used parameters:

- FREEPAGE—Indicates the frequency of inserting a completely blank page when calculating the percentage of pages saved. The default is 0. You should specify the same value used for FREEPAGE in the CREATE TABLESPACE DDL for the tablespace being analyzed.
- PCTFREE—Specifies the percentage of each page to leave free when calculating the percentage of pages saved. The default is 5. Once again, you should specify the same value used for PCTFREE in the CREATE TABLESPACE DDL for the tablespace being analyzed.
- FULLCOPY—Indicates that a full image copy is being used as input. If the tablespace is partitioned, you should also use the NUMPARTS parameter.
- INCRCOPY—Indicates that an incremental image copy is used as input. Once again, for partitioned tablespaces, you should also specify the NUMPARTS parameter.
- REORG—Indicates that the estimate should be based on the compression savings achieveable by the REORG utility. If REORG is not specified, the estimate is the savings that the LOAD utility would achieve.
- ROWLIMIT—Specifies the maximum number of rows to evaluate in order to provide the compression estimate. You should use this option to limit the elapsed and processor time required by DSN1COMP.

DSN1COMP Guideline

To ensure effective compression planning, consider the following guideline as you execute the DSN1COMP utility.

Utilize DSN1COMP to Plan for Compression

Execute the DSN1COMP utility for tablespaces that are candidates for compression. The statistics provided by this utility can be analyzed to determine whether compression will be cost-effective.

In general, contrast the percentage of pages saved when using compression against the anticipated increase in CPU time to determine whether compression is desirable. The CPU increase should be negligible when DB2 is using hardware compression.

The Offline Tablespace Copy Service Aid (DSN1COPY)

The Offline Tablespace Copy service aid, better known as DSN1COPY, has a multitude of uses. For example, it can be used to copy data sets or check the validity of tablespace and index pages. Another use is to translate DB2 object identifiers for the migration of objects between DB2 subsystems or to recover data from accidentally dropped objects. DSN1COPY also can print hexadecimal dumps of DB2 tablespace and index data sets.

Its first function, however, is to copy data sets. DSN1COPY can be used to copy VSAM data sets to sequential data sets, and vice versa. It also can copy VSAM data sets to other VSAM data sets and can copy sequential data sets to other sequential data sets. As such, DSN1COPY can be used to

- Create a sequential data set copy of a DB2 tablespace or index data set.
- Create a sequential data set copy of another sequential data set copy produced by DSN1COPY.
- Create a sequential data set copy of an image copy data set produced using the DB2 COPY utility, except for segmented tablespaces. (The DB2 COPY utility skips empty pages in DB2 V2.3 and above, thereby rendering the image copy data set incompatible with DSN1COPY.)
- Restore a DB2 tablespace or index using a sequential data set produced by DSN1COPY.
- Restore a DB2 tablespace using a full image copy data set produced using the DB2 COPY utility.
- Move DB2 data sets from one disk pack to another to replace DASD (such as migrating from 3380s to 3390s).
- Move a DB2 tablespace or indexspace from a smaller data set to a larger data set to eliminate extents. Or, move a DB2 tablespace or indexspace from a larger data set to a smaller data set to eliminate wasted space.

CAUTION

If you change the allocation size of a DB2 data set using DSN1COPY, be sure also to change the PRIQTY and SECQTY values for the object to reflect the change in the DB2 Catalog.

DSN1COPY runs as an MVS batch job, so it can run as an offline utility when the DB2 subsystem is inactive. It can run also when the DB2 subsystem is active, but the objects it operates on should be stopped to ensure that DSN1COPY creates valid output. DSN1COPY does not check to see whether an object is stopped before carrying out its task. DSN1COPY does not communicate with DB2.

CAUTION

DSN1COPY performs a page by page copy. Therefore, you cannot use DSN1COPY to alter the structure of DB2 data sets. For example, you cannot copy a partitioned tablespace into a simple tablespace.

Sample DSN1COPY JCL is provided in Listing 28.6. This job reads the VSAM data set for the DSN8D51A.DSN8S51D tablespace specified in the SYSUT1 DD statement and then copies it to the sequential data set specified in the SYSUT2 DD statement.

Listing 28.6. DSN1COPY JCL.

```
//DB2JOBU  JOB (UTILITY),'DB2 DSN1COPY',MSGCLASS=X,CLASS=X,
//            NOTIFY=USER
//*
//****************************************************************
//*
//*         DB2 DSN1COPY SERVICE AID UTILITY
//*
//****************************************************************
//*
//JOBLIB DD DSN=DSN510.DSNLOAD,DISP=SHR
//STOPDB EXEC PGM=IKJEFT01,DYNAMNBR=20
//STEPLIB DD DSN=DSN510.DSNLOAD,DISP=SHR
//SYSPRINT DD SYSOUT=*
//SYSTSPRT DD SYSOUT=*
//SYSOUT   DD SYSOUT=*
//SYSUDUMP DD SYSOUT=*
//SYSTSIN  DD *
DSN SYSTEM (DSN)
-STOP DATABASE (DSN8D51A) SPACENAM(DSN8S51D)
END
/*
//DSN1COPY EXEC PGM=DSN1COPY,PARM='CHECK'
//SYSPRINT DD  SYSOUT=*
//SYSUDUMP DD  SYSOUT=*
//SYSUT1 DD DSN=DB2CAT.DSNDBC.DSN8D51A.DSN8S51D.I0001.A001,DISP=OLD,AMP=
➥('BUFND=181')
//SYSUT2 DD DSN=OUTPUT.SEQ.DATASET,DISP=OLD,DCB=BUFNO=20
/*
//STARTRW EXEC PGM=IKJEFT01,DYNAMNBR=20,COND=EVEN
//STEPLIB DD DSN=DSN510.DSNLOAD,DISP=SHR
//*
//SYSPRINT DD SYSOUT=*
//SYSTSPRT DD SYSOUT=*
//SYSOUT   DD SYSOUT=*
//SYSUDUMP DD SYSOUT=*
//SYSTSIN  DD *
DSN SYSTEM (DSN)
-START DATABASE (DSN8D51A) SPACENAM(DSN8S51D)
END
/*
//
```

One of the best features of the DSN1COPY utility is its capability to modify the internal object identifier stored in DB2 tablespace and index data sets, as well as in data sets produced by DSN1COPY and the DB2 COPY utility. When you specify the OBIDXLAT option, DSN1COPY reads a data set specified by the SYSXLAT DD statement. This data set lists source and target DBIDs, PSIDs or ISOBIDs, and OBIDs.

Each record in the SYSXLAT file must contain a pair of integers separated by a comma. The first integer is the source ID and the second integer is the target ID. The first record in the SYSXLAT file contains the source and target DBIDs. The second record contains the source and target PSIDs or ISOBIDs for indexes. All subsequent records in the SYSXLAT data set are OBIDs for tables.

Version 4

Only the first two records are required for a Type 1 index; for a Type 2 index, the SYSXLAT data set must contain the table OBID in addition to the DBID and ISOBID.

CAUTION

The DSN1COPY utility can only translate up to 500 record OBIDs at a time.

For example, assume that you accidentally dropped the DSN8D51A database after the JCL in Listing 28.6 was run. Because this database uses STOGROUP-defined objects, all the data has been lost. However, after re-creating the database, tablespaces, tables, and other objects for DSN8D51A, you can restore the DSN8S51D tablespace using DSN1COPY with the OBIDXLAT option. Consider the sample JCL using this option as shown in Listing 28.7. It is operating on the sequential data set produced in Listing 28.6, copying it back to the data set for the DSN8D51A.DSN8S51D tablespace. This job translates the DBID for database DSN8D51A from 283 to 201, the PSID for the DSN8S51D tablespace from 0002 to 0003, and the OBID for the DSN8510.DEPT table from 0020 to 0008.

Listing 28.7. DSN1COPY JCL (using the OBIDXLAT option).

```
//DB2JOBU  JOB (UTILITY),'DB2 DSN1COPY',MSGCLASS=X,CLASS=X,
//         NOTIFY=USER
//*
//****************************************************************
//*
//*        DB2 DSN1COPY SERVICE AID UTILITY
//*
//****************************************************************
//*
//JOBLIB DD DSN=DSN510.DSNLOAD,DISP=SHR
//DSN1COPY EXEC PGM=DSN1COPY,PARM='OBIDXLAT'
//SYSPRINT DD  SYSOUT=*
//SYSUDUMP DD  SYSOUT=*
//SYSUT1 DD DSN=DB2CAT.DSNDBC.DSN8D51A.DSN8S51D.I0001.A001,DISP=OLD,AMP=
➥('BVCND=81')
//SYSUT2 DD DSN=DB2CATP.DSNDBC.DSN8D51A.DSN8S51D.I0001.A001,DISP=OLD,AMP=
➥('BUFND=181')
//*
//*  The SYSXLAT input will ::
//*     Translate the DBID 283 (sending) into 201 on
//*     the receiving end.
//*     Translate the OBID 2 (sending) into 3 on the
//*     receiving end.
```

```
//*         Translate the PSID 20 (sending) into 8 on the
//*         receiving end.
//*
//SYSXLAT DD *
283  201
2    3
20   8
/*
//
```

The object identifiers for the old objects can be found in two ways. First, you can scan old DBID/PSID/OBID reports. Second, you can use DSN1PRNT to list the first three pages of the copy data set. The object identifiers are shown in the formatted listing produced for those pages. Obtain the new object identifiers using the DB2 Catalog reports listed in Chapter 19, "DB2 Object Monitoring Using the DB2 Catalog."

DSN1COPY Guidelines

When planning your DSN1COPY jobs, be sure to consult the following tips and guidelines.

Issue the Stop Command Before Running DSN1COPY

Never run the DSN1COPY utility for a DB2 object until it has been explicitly stopped for all access in the appropriate DB2 subsystem. This advice can be ignored if DB2 is not active.

Use DSN1PRNT Instead of DSN1COPY for Hex Dumps

Although DSN1COPY can be used to obtain a hex dump of a DB2 data set, favor the use of DSN1PRNT because it produces a listing that is formatted, and thus easier to use.

Estimate the Size of SYSUT2 Based on 4K Pages

When the SYSUT2 data set is a sequential data set, estimate its size using the following formula:

```
(Number of pages) ´ 4096
```

Specify the space parameter in cylinders by rounding this number up to the next whole cylinder. If the object being copied uses 32K pages, multiply this number by eight and remember to specify the 32K option of DSN1COPY.

The total number of pages used by a tablespace can be retrieved from the VSAM LISTCAT command or the DB2 Catalog as specified in the NACTIVE column of SYSIBM.SYSTABLESPACE. If you are using the DB2 Catalog method, ensure that the statistics are current by running the RUNSTATS utility.

Do Not Use DSN1COPY on Log Data Sets

Avoid using the DSN1COPY utility on DB2 log data sets because certain options can invalidate the log data.

The DB2 Dump and Trace Program (DSN1SDMP)

DSN1SDMP is the IFC selective dump utility. Although technically defined by IBM to be a service aid utility, DSN1SDMP is actually a DB2 application program. It must be run under the TSO terminal monitor program, IKJEFT01. DSN1SDMP, unlike the other service aids, can be run only when DB2 is operational.

Using the Instrumentation Facility Interface, DSN1SDMP can write DB2 trace records to a sequential data set named in the SDMPTRAC DD statement. It can also force system dumps for DB2 utilities or when specific DB2 events occur. For shops without a DB2 performance monitor, DSN1SDMP can come in handy in trying to resolve system problems. Sample JCL is shown in Listing 28.8.

Listing 28.8. DSN1SDMP JCL.

```
//DB2JOBU  JOB  (UTILITY),'DSN1SDMP',MSGCLASS=X,CLASS=X,
//         NOTIFY=USER
//*
//****************************************************************
//*
//*        DB2 FORCE DUMP UTILITY  : :
//*           CONSULT IBM BEFORE RUNNING
//*
//****************************************************************
//*
//JOBLIB DD DSN=DSN510.DSNLOAD,DISP=SHR
//DUMPER EXEC PGM=IKJEFT01,DYNAMNBR=20
//SYSTSPRT DD  SYSOUT=*
//SYSPRINT DD  SYSOUT=*
//SYSUDUMP DD  SYSOUT=*
//SDMPPRNT DD SYSOUT=*
//SDMPTRAC DD DSN=CAT.TRACE.SEQ.DATASET,
//         DISP=(MOD,CATLG,CATLG),SPACE=(8192,(100,100)),UNIT=SYSDA,
//         DCB=(DSORG=PS,RECFM=VB,LRECL=8188,BLKSIZE=8192)
//SYSTSIN  DD  *
DSN SYSTEM(DSN)
RUN PROGRAM(DSN1SDMP)  PLAN(DSN1SDMP)
LIB('DSN510.RUNLIB.LOAD')
END
/*
//SDMPDD  *
CONSULT IBM BEFORE USING
IBM SUPPORT CENTER WILL PROVIDE OPTIONS
/*
//
```

DSN1SDMP Data Sets

SDMPIN	Input parameters to the DSN1SDMP utility
SDMPPRNT	DSN1SDMP output messages

SYSABEND	System dump if DSN1SDMP abends
SDMPTRAC	Output trace records

DSN1SDMP Guidelines

You can use the following guidelines as a blueprint for effective DSN1SDMP usage.

Use DSN1SDMP Only as Directed

DSN1SDMP should be used only under instructions from the IBM Support Center.

Be Sure That the User Has the Authority to Run DSN1SDMP

To execute the DSN1SDMP service aid, the requester must have the requisite authority to start and stop the DB2 traces, as well as the MONITOR1 or MONITOR2 privilege.

The Recovery Log Extractor (DSN1LOGP)

DSN1LOGP, otherwise known as the Recovery Log Extractor, produces a formatted listing of a specific DB2 recovery log. When a log is operated on by DSN1LOGP, an active DB2 subsystem must not be currently processing the log.

DSN1LOGP produces a detailed or a summary report. The detailed report displays entire log records. The summary report condenses the log records, displaying only the information necessary to request a partial recovery. As such, the detailed report is rarely used. Sample JCL is shown in Listing 28.9.

Listing 28.9. DSN1LOGP JCL.

```
//DB2JOBU  JOB (UTILITY),'DSN1LOGP',MSGCLASS=X,CLASS=X,
//          NOTIFY=USER
//*
//*****************************************************************
//*
//*        DB2 RECOVERY LOG EXTRACTOR
//*
//*****************************************************************
//*
//DSN1LOGP PGM=DSN1LOGP
//SYSPRINT DD SYSOUT=*
//SYSABEND DD SYSOUT=*
//SYSSUMRY DD SYSOUT=*
//BSDS DD DSN=DB2CAT.BSDS01,DISP=SHR
//SYSIN DD *
RBASTART(E300F4)
RBAEND(F40000)
SUMMARY(YES)
/*
//
```

DSN1LOGP Guidelines

The following techniques can be used to produce effective log extract reports using the DSN1LOGP service aid.

Do Not Run DSN1LOGP on the Active Log

DSN1LOGP cannot be run on the active log that DB2 is currently using for logging. It can be run on the other active logs as well as on the archive logs. Given this caveat, DSN1LOGP can be run while DB2 is operational.

Use the DSN1LOGP Output to Assist in Recovery

You can use the output report produced by the DSN1LOGP service aid utility to determine an appropriate log RBA for partial recovery by the RECOVER TORBA utility. This method should be used only when an appropriate log RBA is available in the SYSIBM.SYSCOPY table as the result of running the QUIESCE utility.

The DB2 Data Set Dump Creator (DSN1PRNT)

The program name for the DB2 Data Set Dump Creator is DSN1PRNT. It can be used to print hexadecimal and formatted dumps of DB2 tablespace, indexspace, and image copy data sets. It is useful for searching for values and dumping only the pages containing the specified value. Sample JCL is in Listing 28.10.

Listing 28.10. DSN1PRNT JCL.

```
//DB2JOBU  JOB (UTILITY),'DSN1PRNT',MSGCLASS=X,CLASS=X,
//           NOTIFY=USER
//*
//****************************************************************
//*
//*        DB2 DATA SET DUMP SERVICE AID
//*
//****************************************************************
//*
//DSN1PRNT PGM=DSN1PRNT,PARM='PRINT,FORMAT'
//SYSPRINT DD SYSOUT=*
//SYSUT1 DD DSN=DB2CAT.DSNDBC.DSN8D51A.DSN8S51D.I0001.A001,DISP=SHR,AMP=
➥('BUFND=181')
//
```

DSN1PRNT Guidelines

Consider the following guidelines when using DNS1PRNT to dump DB2 data sets.

Analyze Problems Using DSN1PRNT Output

Use DSN1PRNT to track down data problems and page errors. By scanning the dump of a DB2 data set, you can view the format of the page and the data on the page.

Be Aware of Potential Errors

If DSN1PRNT encounters an error on a page of a DB2 data set, an error message is printed. If you specified the FORMAT option, the output is not formatted. All pages without errors are formatted.

Use DSN1PRNT for All DB2 Data Set Dumps

Favor the use of DSN1PRNT over other data set dump utilities (such as DSN1COPY) because of the formatting feature of DSN1PRNT.

Run DSN1PRNT Only for Stopped DB2 Objects

When running DSN1PRNT when DB2 is active, be sure that the data set being dumped has been stopped. This ensures that the data being dumped is accurate and unchanging.

Be Aware of 32K Page Data Sets

If the object being dumped uses 32K pages, remember to specify the 32K option of DSN1PRNT.

Sample Programs

The sample programs are DB2 application programs supplied by IBM with DB2. They are normal DB2 application programs that require precompilation, compilation, linking, and binding, as described in Chapter 7, "Program Preparation." These programs run using the TSO Terminal Monitor Program, IKJEFT01, as described in Chapter 11, "The Doors to DB2." Therefore, you must provide a DB2 system name, a program name, a DB2 load library name, and a plan name for each sample program execution.

You must verify the load library and plan names associated with these programs at your site with your DBA or system administrator. The JCL examples in the following sections specify the default load library, and plan names are the same as the sample program names.

The Dynamic SQL Processor (DSNTEP2)

DSNTEP2 is a PL/I application program that can be used to issue DB2 dynamic SQL statements. The sample JCL in Listing 28.11 demonstrates the capability of this program to issue DCL, DDL, and DML dynamically.

Listing 28.11. DSNTEP2 JCL.

```
//DB2JOBU  JOB (UTILITY),'DB2 SAMPLE SQL',MSGCLASS=X,CLASS=X,
//          NOTIFY=USER
//*
//****************************************************************
//*
//*        DB2 SAMPLE SQL PROGRAM
//*
//****************************************************************
//*
//JOBLIB DD DSN=DSN510.DSNLOAD,DISP=SHR
//BATCHSQL EXEC PGM=IKJEFT01,DYNAMNBR=20
//SYSTSPRT DD  SYSOUT=*
//SYSPRINT DD  SYSOUT=*
//SYSUDUMP DD  SYSOUT=*
//SYSTSIN  DD  *
DSN SYSTEM(DSN)
RUN PROGRAM(DSNTEP2)  PLAN(DSNTEP23)  -
LIB('DSN510.RUNLIB.LOAD')
END
/*
//SYSIN    DD  *
SELECT * FROM SYSIBM.SYSTABLES ;

UPDATE DSN8510.DEPT
SET DEPTNAME = 'CHANGED NAME'
WHERE DEPTNO = 'D01' ;

INSERT INTO DSN8510.ACT
VALUES (129, 'XXXXXX', 'SAMPLE ACCT') ;

DELETE FROM DSN8510.EMP
WHERE SALARY < 1000 ;

CREATE DATABASE TESTNAME
BUFFERPOOL BP12
STOGROUP DSN8G510 ;

GRANT DBADM ON TESTNAME TO USERA ;

/*
//
```

Because DSNTEP2 is an application program, it must be compiled, linked, and bound before it can be used. Additionally, because the source code is provided in PL/I, it can be modified easily by a knowledgeable PL/I programmer.

DSNTEP2 can process almost every SQL statement that can be executed dynamically. DSNTEP2 accepts

- The GRANT and REVOKE DCL statements
- The ALTER, COMMENT ON, CREATE, and DROP DDL statements

- The DELETE, INSERT, SELECT, and UPDATE DML statements
- The COMMIT, ROLLBACK, EXEC SQL, EXPLAIN, and LOCK statements

The only important statement that DSNTEP2 does not support is the LABEL ON DDL statement. DSNTEP2 can be modified easily to support this statement.

DSNTEP2 Guidelines

The following tips and techniques should be utilized when executing SQL statements using DSNTEP2.

Code DSNTEP2 Input in the First 72 Bytes of the Input Data Set

DSNTEP2 reads SQL statements from an input data set with 80-byte records. The SQL statements must be coded in the first 72 bytes of each input record. SQL statements can span multiple input records and are terminated by a semicolon (;). Semicolons are not permitted in the text of the SQL statement.

Be Aware of DSNTEP2 Error Handling

Each SQL statement is automatically committed by DSNTEP2. When DSNTEP2 encounters an SQL error, it continues processing the next SQL statement in the input data set. When 10 SQL errors have been encountered, DSNTEP2 ends. If any SQL errors occurred during the execution of DSNTEP2, a return code of 8 is received.

Do Not Rerun Committed Work

To rerun DSNTEP2, remember that all SQL statements that completed with a 0 SQL code were committed. These statements should not be rerun. All SQL statements completed with a negative SQL code must be corrected and reprocessed.

Liberally Comment DSNTEP2 Input

Comments can be passed to DSNTEP2 in the SQL statements using two hyphens in columns 1 and 2 or a single asterisk in column 1.

Use DSNTEP2 to Batch Large Streams of SQL

Use DSNTEP2 to simulate SPUFI in a batch environment. This can be useful because it enables the execution of dynamic SQL statements from an input data set without monopolizing a TSO terminal as SPUFI does. This can have a significant effect when issuing multiple DDL statements to create DB2 objects.

The Dynamic SQL Update Program (DSNTIAD)

DSNTIAD is an assembler application program that can issue the same DB2 dynamic SQL statements as DSNTEP2, with the exception of the SELECT statement. For this reason, it almost always is preferable for applications programmers to use DSNTEP2 rather than DSNTIAD. If your shop does not have the PL/I compiler, however, DSNTIAD must be used. Because DSNTIAD is a sample program, its source code can be modified to accept SELECT statements. This task is complex and should not be undertaken by a beginning programmer.

Additionally, DSNTIAD supports the LABEL ON statement, whereas DSNTEP2 does not. Also note that DSNTIAD can be a little more efficient than DSNTEP2 because it is written in assembler. Sample DSNTIAD JCL is provided in Listing 28.12.

Listing 28.12. DSNTIAD JCL.

```
//DB2JOBU  JOB (UTILITY),'DB2 SAMPLE UPD',MSGCLASS=X,CLASS=X,
//          NOTIFY=USER
//*
//****************************************************************
//*
//*        DB2 SAMPLE SQL UPDATE PROGRAM
//*
//****************************************************************
//*
//JOBLIB DD DSN=DSN510.DSNLOAD,DISP=SHR
//BATUPSQL EXEC PGM=IKJEFT01,DYNAMNBR=20
//SYSTSPRT DD  SYSOUT=*
//SYSPRINT DD  SYSOUT=*
//SYSUDUMP DD  SYSOUT=*
//SYSTSIN  DD  *
DSN SYSTEM(DSN)
RUN PROGRAM(DSNTIAD)  PLAN(DSNTIAD3)
LIB('DSN510.RUNLIB.LOAD')
END
/*
//SYSIN    DD  *
UPDATE DSN8510.DEPT
SET DEPTNAME = 'CHANGED NAME'
WHERE DEPTNO = 'D01' ;

INSERT INTO DSN8510.ACT
VALUES (129, 'XXXXXX', 'SAMPLE ACCT') ;

DELETE FROM DSN8510.EMP
WHERE SALARY < 1000 ;

CREATE DATABASE TESTNAME
BUFFERPOOL BP12
STOGROUP DSN8G510 ;

GRANT DBADM ON TESTNAME TO USERA ;
/*
//
```

DSNTIAD Guidelines

Use the following guidelines to ensure the effective execution of SQL using DSNTIAD.

Use DSNTIAD for DDL

Consider using DSNTIAD rather than DSNTEP2 to submit batch DDL.

Control DSNTIAD Execution Authority

Consider giving only DBAs and systems programmers the authority to execute DSNTIAD. Allow everyone to execute DSNTEP2 because it provides support for the SELECT statement.

Do Not Comment DSNTIAD Input

Unlike DSNTEP2, DSNTIAD does not accept comments embedded in SQL statements.

Be Aware of DSNTIAD Error Handling

Each SQL statement is automatically committed by DSNTIAD. When an SQL error is encountered, DSNTIAD continues processing the next SQL statement in the input data set. When 10 SQL errors have been encountered, DSNTIAD ends. If any SQL errors occur during the execution of DSNTIAD, a return code of 8 is received.

Do Not Rerun Committed Work

When rerunning DSNTIAD, remember that all SQL statements that completed with a 0 SQL code were committed. All SQL statements that completed with a negative SQL code need to be corrected and reprocessed.

The Unload Utility (DSNTIAUL)

The only option for creating a readable sequential unload data set for DB2 tables (without writing an application program) is the DSNTIAUL sample program. The UNLOAD phase of the REORG utility unloads DB2 data from a tablespace, but the data can be processed only by the RELOAD phase of the REORG utility because it is not in a readable format.

DSNTIAUL is a DB2 application program written in assembler. It can unload the data from one or more DB2 tables or views into a sequential data set. The LOAD utility then can use this data set. Additionally, DSNTIAUL can produce the requisite control cards for the LOAD utility to load the sequential data set back into the specific DB2 table. Consider the JCL provided in Listing 28.13.

Listing 28.13. DSNTIAUL JCL.

```
//DB2JOBU  JOB (UTILITY),'DB2 SAMPLE UNLD',MSGCLASS=X,CLASS=X,
//         NOTIFY=USER
//*
//****************************************************************
//*
//*        DB2 SAMPLE UNLOAD PROGRAM
//*
//****************************************************************
//*
//JOBLIB DD DSN=DSN510.DSNLOAD,DISP=SHR
//UNLOAD  EXEC PGM=IKJEFT01,DYNAMNBR=20,COND=(4,LT)
//SYSTSPRT DD SYSOUT=*
//SYSTSIN  DD *
DSN SYSTEM(DSN)
RUN  PROGRAM(DSNTIAUL) PLAN(DSNTIAU5) -
LIB('DSN510.RUNLIB.LOAD')
/*
//SYSPRINT DD SYSOUT=*
//SYSUDUMP DD SYSOUT=*
//SYSREC00 DD DSN=DEPT.UNLOAD.DATASET,DISP=(,CATLG,DELETE),
//            UNIT=SYSDA,SPACE=(CYL,(1,1)),DCB=BUFNO=20
//SYSPUNCH DD DSN=DEPT.RELOAD.UTILITY.INPUT,DISP=(,CATLG,DELETE),
//            UNIT=SYSDA,SPACE=(TRK,(1,1),RLSE)
//SYSIN    DD *
DSN8510.DEPT
/*
//
```

After running the JCL in Listing 28.13, the DSN8510.DEPT table is unloaded into the SYSREC00 data set. The SYSPUNCH data set contains the generated LOAD control cards. The generated LOAD control cards look like this:

```
LOAD DATA INDDN SYSREC00 LOG NO INTO TABLE
     DSN8510.DEPT
 (
  DEPTNO        POSITION(       1        )
  CHAR(              3) ,
  DEPTNAME      POSITION(       4        )
  VARCHAR                       ,
  MGRNO         POSITION(      42        )
  CHAR(              6)
             NULLIF(       48)='?',
  ADMRDEPT      POSITION(      49        )
  CHAR(              3)
 )
```

Because DSNTIAUL is an application program, it must be precompiled, assembled, and bound into an application plan before it can be used.

DSNTIAUL Guidelines

When unloading data from DB2 tables using DSNTIAUL, keep the following techniques in mind.

Use DSNTIAUL to Create Unloaded Flat Files

Use DSNTIAUL to produce sequential data sets containing DB2 data from one or more tables. Running DSNTIAUL is significantly easier than coding an application program to extract the desired data.

Use WHERE and ORDER BY with DSNTIAUL

DSNTIAUL can accept WHERE clauses and ORDER BY clauses to limit the data to be unloaded and sort the unloaded data, respectively. However, the combination of the table name and its associated WHERE and ORDER BY clauses cannot exceed 72 total characters.

Use DSNTIAUL to Unload from a View

DSNTIAUL can unload data from DB2 views. When data from multiple tables must be unloaded into a single data set, create a view that joins the two tables and use DSNTIAUL to unload the data from that view.

Use the 'SQL' Parameter

Complete SELECT statements can be specified in SYSIN. This is accomplished by specifying PARMS('SQL') in the SYSTSIN data set. When PARMS('SQL') is specified, the 72-byte restriction is lifted. The largest SQL statement that can be specified is 32,765 bytes.

Keep Your SYSREC Data Sets Synchronized

Unloaded data is placed into a data set associated with the SYSRECxx DD statement. When multiple tables will be unloaded to multiple data sets using DSNTIAUL, be careful when you specify the SYSRECxx data sets. SYSREC00 refers to the first unload utility card, SYSREC01 refers to the second, and so on. Because SYSREC00 is the first DD statement, the number associated with the SYSRECxx DD statement is 1 less than the corresponding input statement being processed.

Unload No More than 100 Tables with a Single DSNTIAUL Execution

No more than 100 input control cards can be successfully processed by a single execution of the DSNTIAUL utility.

Consider Using LOCK TABLE with DSNTIAUL

The LOCK TABLE statement can be used with DSNTIAUL to create a consistent unload file. By issuing the LOCK TABLE statement, you ensure that no modifications are made to the table during the timeframe of the unload execution.

Consider Using DSNTIAUL for Data Movement and Storage

You can deploy the DSNTIAUL program for many useful purposes. Any activity that requires bulk movement of data from a DB2 table is ideal for DSNTIAUL. Consider the following uses:

- To migrate data from one DB2 subsystem to another
- To save data when the structure of a table must be changed by dropping and re-creating it
- To copy data before a table structure change is made (because old image copy data sets cannot be applied after a structure change)
- To create a comma-delimited file (other DBMSs can accept a delimited file as input to a load or restore process)

Summary

In this chapter, you learned about the three types of nontraditional DB2 utility programs: offline utilities, service aids, and sample programs. Each of these programs provide utility-like functionality. Every DB2 developer will, at some point, need to use one of the programs.

Now that you have mastered DB2 utilities, turn the page and learn about DB2 commands and how they can be used to control the DB2 environment.

29

DB2 Commands

DB2 commands are operator-issued requests that administer DB2 resources and environments. There are six categories of DB2 commands, which are delineated by the environment from which they are issued. These are

- DB2 environment commands
- DSN commands
- IMS commands
- CICS commands
- TSO commands
- IRLM commands

Each of these categories is discussed in this chapter.

DB2 Environment Commands

DB2 environment commands usually are issued either through the DB2I ISPF panels or by batch TSO under the control of the `DSN` command. However, they can be issued from an MVS console, from IMS/TM using the specialized command `/SSR`, or from CICS using the specialized CICS command `DSNC`. The DB2 environment commands can be used to monitor and control DB2 databases, resources, and processing. There are three types of environment commands:

- Information-gathering commands
- Administrative commands
- Environment control commands

All DB2 environment commands have a common structure, as follows:

```
cp command operand
```

The `cp` is the command prefix assigned when DB2 is installed. The command prefix identifies a single DB2 susbsystem, targeting the command as a DB2 command for a specific DB2 subsystem. The command prefix is built from a combination of the subsystem recognition character concatenated to the DB2 subsystem name. Prior to DB2 V4, only the single character subsystem recognition character was available to identify subsystems. The multi-character command prefix enables more meaningful names to be used. A subsystem recognition character is assigned when DB2 is installed. The default recognition character is a hyphen, but it can be changed by each installation depending on the environment from which the command is issued. The following characters can be used as subsystem recognition characters:

```
¢       +       ;       ?
.       ¦       -       :
<       !       /       #
(       $       ,       @
*       )       %       "
'       =
```

Version 4

A sample DB2 command might be

```
-DB2A DISPLAY DATABASE(DSNDB07)
```

The command specifies that the `DSNDB07` database in the `DB2A` subsystem is to be displayed.

The *command* portion of the environment command is the DB2 command verb. The *operand* is the combination of optional and required keywords and values necessary to successfully issue the command.

Figure 29.1 shows a DB2 environment command, `-DISPLAY DATABASE`, issued through option 7 of the DB2I panel. The response to that command is shown in Figure 29.2. Listing 29.1 is the JCL needed to issue the same command in a batch job.

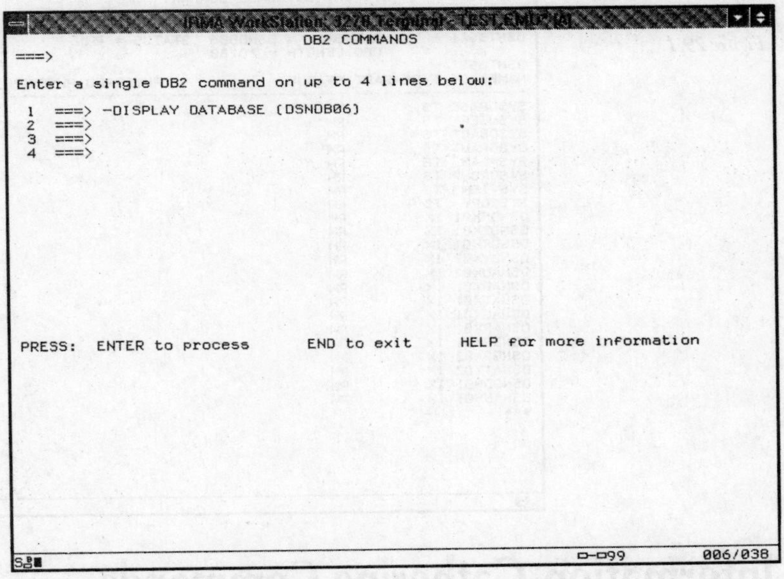

FIGURE 29.1.
Issuing a DB2 command through DB2I.

Listing 29.1. JCL to issue a DB2 command in batch.

```
//DB2JOBC  JOB (COMMAND),'DB2 COMMAND SQL',MSGCLASS=X,CLASS=X,
//         NOTIFY=USER
//*
//****************************************************************
//*
//*        JCL TO ISSUE DB2 COMMAND
//*
//****************************************************************
//*
//JOBLIB DD DSN=DSN510.DSNLOAD,DISP=SHR
//BATCHCOM EXEC PGM=IKJEFT01,DYNAMNBR=20
//SYSTSPRT DD  SYSOUT=*
//SYSPRINT DD  SYSOUT=*
```

continues

Listing 29.1. continued

```
//SYSUDUMP DD  SYSOUT=*
//SYSTSIN  DD  *
  DSN SYSTEM(DSN)
  - DISPLAY DATABASE (DSNDB06)
  END
/*
//
```

The three types of DB2 environment commands are presented in the following sections.

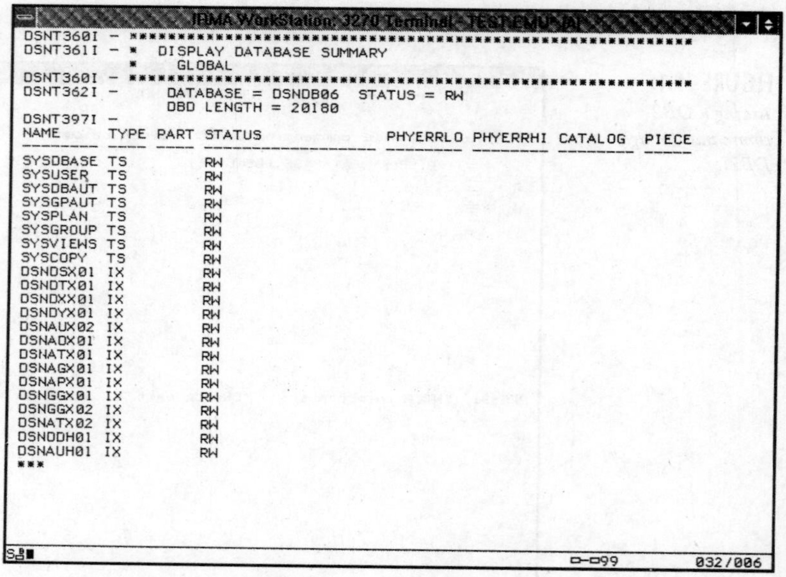
IRMA WorkStation: 3270 Terminal - TESTEMU [A]
DSNT360I - ***
DSNT361I - * DISPLAY DATABASE SUMMARY
* GLOBAL
DSNT360I - ***
DSNT362I - DATABASE = DSNDB06 STATUS = RW
DBD LENGTH = 20180
DSNT397I -
NAME TYPE PART STATUS PHYERRLO PHYERRHI CATALOG PIECE
SYSDBASE TS RW
SYSUSER TS RW
SYSDBAUT TS RW
SYSGPAUT TS RW
SYSPLAN TS RW
SYSGROUP TS RW
SYSVIEWS TS RW
SYSCOPY TS RW
DSNDSX01 IX RW
DSNDTX01 IX RW
DSNDXX01 IX RW
DSNDYX01 IX RW
DSNAUX02 IX RW
DSNADX01 IX RW
DSNATX01 IX RW
DSNAGX01 IX RW
DSNAPX01 IX RW
DSNGGX01 IX RW
DSNGGX02 IX RW
DSNATX02 IX RW
DSNDDH01 IX RW
DSNAUH01 IX RW
***
99
032/006

FIGURE 29.2.
Response to the DB2 command issued in Figure 29.1.

Information-Gathering Commands

The information-gathering DB2 environment commands can be used to monitor DB2 objects and resources. They can return the status of DB2 databases, threads, utilities, and traces, as well as monitor the Resource Limit Facility and distributed data locations.

The `DISPLAY` command is used for information gathering. A description of each of the 12 forms of the `DISPLAY` command follows:

`- DISPLAY ARCHIVE`	Display input archive log information.
`- DISPLAY BUFFERPOOL`	Displays the current status of active and/or inactive bufferpools.
`- DISPLAY DATABASE`	Displays the status and pending information for DB2 databases, tablespaces, and indexes.

`-DISPLAY DATABASE LOCKS`	Displays the locks for the DB2 databases, tablespaces, and indexes (including transaction locks and drain locks). An option for the command, `CLAIMS`, shows claims that are being held on a resource.
`-DISPLAY GROUP`	Displays information about the data sharing group.
`-DISPLAY GROUPBUFFERPOOL`	Displays information about the status of DB2 group bufferpools.
`-DISPLAY LOCATION`	Displays information for distributed threads.
`-DISPLAY PROCEDURE`	Displays information about stored procedures.
`-DISPLAY RLIMIT`	Displays the status of the Resource Limit Facility, including the ID of the active RLST (Resource Limit Specification Table).
`-DISPLAY THREAD`	Displays active and in-doubt connections to DB2 for a specified connection or all connections.
`-DISPLAY TRACE`	Displays a list of active trace types and classes along with the specified destinations for each; consult Chapter 17, "Traditional DB2 Performance Monitoring," for a discussion of DB2 trace types and classes.
`-DISPLAY UTILITY`	Displays the status of all active, stopped, or terminating utilities.

Information-Gathering Command Guidelines

Use the following guidelines when issuing commands to gather information about DB2 and its environment.

Use the `LIMIT` Option to Increase the Amount of Displayed Information

Use the `LIMIT` parameter of the `DISPLAY DATABASE` command to view database object lists greater than 50 lines long. The default number of lines returned by the `DISPLAY` command is 50, but the `LIMIT` parameter can be used to set the maximum number of lines returned to any numeric value. Because 50 lines of output usually is not sufficient to view all objects in a medium-size database, the recommendation is to specify the `LIMIT` parameter as follows:

```
-DISPLAY DATABASE(DSND851A) LIMIT(300)
```

To indicate no limit, you can replace the numeric limit with an asterisk (*).

Use `DISPLAY BUFFERPOOL` to Monitor DB2 Bufferpools

Use the `DISPLAY BUFFERPOOL` command to display allocation information for each bufferpool. Refer to the example in Listing 29.2 for details of the information provided by `DISPLAY BUFFERPOOL`.

Listing 29.2. Results of DISPLAY BUFFERPOOL.

```
-DISPLAY BUFFERPOOL (BP0)

DSNB401I < BUFFERPOOL NAME BP0, BUFFERPOOL ID 0, USE COUNT 90
DSNB402I < VIRTUAL BUFFERPOOL SIZE = 2000 BUFFERS
                ALLOCATED         =     2000   TO BE DELETED    =       0
                IN USE/UPDATED    =       12
DSNB403I < HIPERPOOL SIZE = 100000 BUFFERS, CASTOUT = YES
            ALLOCATED        =    100000   TO BE DELETED    =       0
            BACKED BY ES     =     91402
DSNB404I < THRESHOLDS -
            VP SEQUENTIAL              = 80   HP SEQUENTIAL          = 80
            DEFERRED WRITE             = 50   VERTICAL DEFERRED WRT = 10
            IOP SEQUENTIAL             = 50
DSNB405I < HIPERSPACE NAMES - @001SSOP
DSN9022I < DSNB1CMD '-DISPLAY BUFFERPOOL' NORMAL COMPLETION
```

Use the DETAIL Parameter for Bufferpool Tuning Information

To produce reports detailing bufferpool usage, specify the DETAIL parameter. Using DETAIL(INTERVAL) produces bufferpool usage information since the last execution of DISPLAY BUFFERPOOL using DETAIL(INTERVAL). To report on bufferpool usage as of the time it was activated, specify DETAIL(*).

Listing 29.3 depicts the type of information provided by the DETAIL option of DISPLAY BUFFERPOOL.

Listing 29.3. Results of DISPLAY BUFFERPOOL.

```
-DISPLAY BUFFERPOOL (BP0), DETAIL(INTERVAL)

DSNB401I < BUFFERPOOL NAME BP0, BUFFERPOOL ID 0, USE COUNT 90
DSNB402I < VIRTUAL BUFFERPOOL SIZE = 2000 BUFFERS
            ALLOCATED        =      2000   TO BE DELETED    =       0
            IN USE/UPDATED   =        12
DSNB403I < HIPERPOOL SIZE = 100000 BUFFERS, CASTOUT = YES
            ALLOCATED        =    100000   TO BE DELETED    =       0
            BACKED BY ES     =     91402
DSNB404I < THRESHOLDS -
            VP SEQUENTIAL              = 80   HP SEQUENTIAL          = 80
            DEFERRED WRITE             = 50   VERTICAL DEFERRED WRT = 10
            IOP SEQUENTIAL             = 50
DSNB405I < HIPERSPACE NAMES - @001SSOP
DSNB409I < INCREMENTAL STATISITCS SINCE 05:43:22 DEC 23, 1993
DSNB411I < RANDOM GETPAGE      =      230 SYNC READ I/O ( R) =    180
            SEQ.   GETPAGE     =      610 SYNC READ I/O ( S) =     20
            DMTH HIT           =        0
DSNB412I < SEQUENTIAL PREFETCH -
            REQUESTS           =        124    PREFETCH I/O   =     10
            PAGES READ         =         69
```

```
DSNB413I < LIST PREFETCH -
                REQUESTS              =       0    PREFETCH I/O    =     0
                PAGES READ            =       0
DSNB414I < DYNAMIC PREFETCH -
                REQUESTS              =       0    PREFETCH I/O    =     0
                PAGES READ            =       0
DSNB415I < PREFETCH DISABLED -
                NO BUFFER             =       0    NO READ ENGINE  =     0
DSNB420I < SYSPAGE UPDATES    =       0  SYS PAGES WRITTEN =     0
                ASYNC WRITE I/O       =       0  SYNC WRITE I/O   =     0
DSNB421I < DWT HIT            =       0  VERTICAL DWT HIT  =     0
                NO WRITE ENGINE       =       0
DSNB430I < HIPERPOOL ACTIVITY (NOT USING ASYNCHRONOUS
                DATA MOVER FACILITY) -
                        SYNC HP READS    =     100    SYNC HP WRITES   =   120
                        ASYNC HP READS   =       0    ASYNC HP WRITES  =     0
                        READ FAILURES    =       0    WRITE FAILURES   =     0
DSNB431I < HIPERPOOL ACTIVITY (USING ASYNCHRONOUS
                DATA MOVER FACILITY) -
                        HP READS         =     231    HP WRITES        =   263
                        READ FAILURES    =       0    WRITE FAILURES   =     0
DSNB440I < I/O PARALLEL ACTIVITY -
                        PARALL REQUEST   =       2    DEGRADED PARALL  =     0
DSN9022I < DSNB1CMD '-DISPLAY BUFFERPOOL' NORMAL COMPLETION
```

This report can be used to augment bufferpool tuning. Suggested action items are as follows:

- Monitor the read efficiency of each bufferpool using the following formula, as presented in Chapter 14. The higher the number, the better.

```
(Total GETPAGEs) /        [     (SEQUENTIAL PREFETCH) +
          (DYNAMIC PREFETCH) +
          (SYNCHRONOUS READ)
]
```

- If I/O is consistently high, consider tuning the bufferpool to handle the additional workload. For example, you could add virtual pool pages or hiperpool pages.

Use the LIST and LSTATS Parameters for Additional Detail

For additional bufferpool information, the LIST and LSTATS parameters can be specified:

LIST — Lists the open tablespaces and indexes within the specified bufferpool(s).

LSTATS — Lists statistics for the tablespaces and indexes reported by LIST. Statistical information is reset each time DISPLAY with LSTATS is issued, so the statistics are as of the last time LSTATS was issued.

Use DISPLAY DATABASE to Monitor DB2 Objects

Use the DISPLAY DATABASE command to monitor the status of tablespaces and indexes. The possible status values follow. When a status other than RO or RW is encountered, the object is in an indeterminate state or is being processed by a DB2 utility.

CHKP	The CHECK PENDING status has been set for this tablespace or partition.
COPY	The COPY PENDING flag has been set for this tablespace or partition.
DEFER	Deferred restart is required for the object.
GRECP	The tablespace, tablespace partition, index, index partition, or logical index partition is in the group bufferpool RECOVER PENDING state.
INDBT	In-doubt processing is required for the object.
LPL	The tablespace, tablespace partition, index, index partition, or logical index partition has logical page errors.
OPENF	The tablespace, tablespace partition, index, index partition, or logical index partition had an open data set failure.
PSRCP	Indicates PAGE SET RECOVER PENDING state for an index (non-partitioning indexes).
RECP	The RECOVER PENDING flag has been set for this tablespace, tablespace partition, index, index partition, or logical index partition.
REST	Restart processing has been initiated for the tablespace, tablespace partition, index, index partition, or logical index partition.
RO	The tablespace, tablespace partition, index, index partition, or logical index partition has been started for read-only processing.
RW	The tablespace, tablespace partition, index, index partition, or logical index partition has been started for read and write processing.
STOP	The tablespace, tablespace partition, index, index partition, or logical index partition has been stopped.
STOPE	The tablespace or index is stopped because of an invalid log RBA or LRSN in one of its pages.
STOPP	A stop is pending for the tablespace, tablespace partition, index, index partition, or logical index partition.
UT	The tablespace, tablespace partition, index, index partition, or logical index partition has been started for the execution of utilities only.
UTRO	The tablespace, tablespace partition, index, index partition, or logical index partition has been started for RW processing, but only RO processing is enabled because a utility is in progress for that object.

UTRW The tablespace, tablespace partition, index, index partition, or logical index partition has been started for RW processing, and a utility is in progress for that object.

UTUT The tablespace, tablespace partition, index, index partition, or logical index partition has been started for RW processing, but only UT processing is enabled because a utility is in progress for that object.

Use DISPLAY DATABASE to View Restricted Objects

By specifying the RESTRICT option on the DISPLAY DATABASE command, only restricted DB2 objects are listed. A database is considered restricted if it is in one of the following states:

- Stopped
- Started for RO or UT processing

A tablespace or index is considered restricted if it is in one of the following states:

- Stopped
- Started for RO or UT processing
- Being processed by a stopped or active utility
- In a pending state (CHKP, COPY, RECP, or GRECP)
- Contains an LPL or page error range

Use the RESTRICT option to ascertain whether any objects require action to restore them to a usable state.

Use DISPLAY DATABASE to View Objects Being Used

By specifying the ACTIVE option of the DISPLAY DATABASE command, only tablespaces and indexes that have been allocated for use by an application are listed. Use the ACTIVE option to determine the currently allocated objects.

Use DISPLAY DATABASE to Determine Database Usage

The USE option of the DISPLAY DATABASE command displays information on how the database is being used. It returns information on the applications and subsystems to which the database is allocated, the connection IDs, correlation IDs, and authorization IDs for all applications allocated to the displayed tablespaces and the LUWID and location of remote threads accessing the database.

Use DISPLAY DATABASE to View Locking Information

Two options of the DISPLAY DATABASE command, LOCKS and CLAIMERS, can be used to view locking details for the database and its associated tablespaces. The LOCKS clause displays the applications and subsystems having locks held, waited on, or retained for the specified database as well as the transaction locks for all tablespaces, tables, index spaces and tablespace partitions being displayed. It will also show drain locks held by running jobs.

The CLAIMERS clause displays the claims on all tablespaces, index spaces, and tablespace partitions whose status is displayed. If the CLAIMERS clause is specified, it overrides both the LOCKS and USE clauses.

Use DISPLAY DATABASE to View the Logical Page List

Version 4

Pages that are logically in error are written to a special list known as the logical page list (LPL). A logical page error is one that can be corrected without redefining physical devices—for example, an error caused by a connection problem. The LPL clause can be specified on the DISPLAY DATABASE command to view the logical page errors for the database, tablespace, or partition. Logical page errors can be cleared by starting or recovering the object in question.

> **NOTE**
>
> If starting the object with the LPL error does not work, DB2 will upgrade the failure to a physical failure. If this occurs, the object must be recovered.

Use Wildcards to View Multiple Databases

DISPLAY DATABASE can use the asterisk as a wildcard specifier in the operand portion of the command. Consider the following command:

```
-DISPLAY DATABASE (DSN8*)
```

This command lists only the databases that contain the DSN8 characters as the first four characters in their name—the sample database.

Use DISPLAY PROCEDURE to Monitor Stored Procedure Statistics

Version 4

The display command can be used to monitor the status of stored procedures. This command will show:

- Whether the named procedure is currently started or stopped
- How many requests are currently executing
- The high water mark for concurrently running requests
- How many requests are currently queued
- The high water mark for concurrently running requests
- How many times a request has timed-out

Use DISPLAY UTILITY to Monitor DB2 Utilities

The DISPLAY UTILITY command can be used to monitor the progress of an active utility. By monitoring the current phase of the utility and matching this information with the utility phase information, you can determine the relative progress of the utility as it processes.

For example, if the DISPLAY UTILITY command indicates that the current phase of a LOAD utility is the REPORT phase, you know that there is only one more phase and that seven phases have been processed.

> **NOTE**
>
> The IBM service aid and sample programs will not appear in the DISPLAY UTILITY output.

> **NOTE**
>
> Most third-party utilities do not show up when -DIS UTIL is issued if they run outside the scope of DB2. Use the display tool provided by the third-party vendor instead.

Use DISPLAY UTILITY to Gauge a Utility's Progress

For the DB2 COPY, REORG, and RUNSTATS utilities, the DISPLAY UTILITY also can be used to monitor the progress of particular phases. The COUNT specified for each phase lists the number of pages that have been loaded, unloaded, copied, or read.

The REORG utility in Figure 29.3 is in the RELOAD phase and has processed 11 records. COUNT = *nnn* indicates that *nnn* pages have been unloaded by the REORG utility in the UNLOAD phase. By comparing this number to the number of pages for the tablespace as found in the NACTIVE column of SYSIBM.SYSTABLESPACE, you can track the progress of the following phases:

Utility	*Phase*
COPY	COPY
REORG	UNLOAD, RELOAD
RUNSTATS	RUNSTATS

> **NOTE**
>
> You also can check the progress of the CHECK, LOAD, RECOVER, and MERGE utilities using -DIS UTIL. The number of rows, index entries, or pages that have been processed is displayed.

FIGURE 29.3.
`DISPLAY UTILITY` *output.*

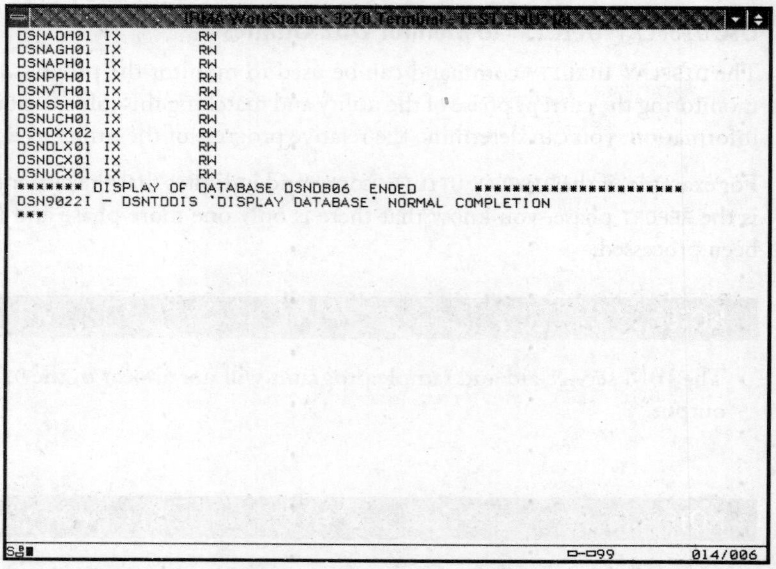

Centralize `DISPLAY` Capability

A centralized area in your organization should have the capability to issue all the information-gathering commands online to effectively administer the DB2 subsystem. This centralized area should be staffed such that support is available when DB2 applications, queries, or utilities are being processed.

Be Wary of the Dynamic Nature of Displayed Information

The information returned by the `DISPLAY` command is dynamic. As the information is displayed, it may also be changing, making the displayed information inaccurate. Therefore, do not rely solely on information issued by the `DISPLAY` command unless it can be verified from another source or by multiple executions of the same `DISPLAY` command. Other sources for verification include online performance monitors and calling end users. Usually, a combination of sources should be consulted before taking any action based on information returned from the `DISPLAY` command.

Administrative Commands

Administrative commands are provided to assist the user with the active administration, resource specification, and environment modification of DB2 subsystems. Each command modifies an environmental aspect of the DB2 subsystem. The administrative commands are as follows:

`-ALTER BUFFERPOOL`	Used to alter bufferpool size, thresholds, and `CASTOUT` attributes for active and inactive bufferpools.
`-ALTER GROUPBUFFERPOOL`	Used to alter the attributed of group bufferpools.
`-ALTER UTILITY`	Can change the value of some parameters for the `REORG` utility.
`-ARCHIVE LOG`	Forces a DB2 log archival.
`-CANCEL THREAD`	Cancels a local or distributed DB2 thread.
`-MODIFY TRACE`	Changes the specifications for active DB2 traces.
`-RECOVER BSDS`	Re-establishes a valid Boot Strap Data Set after an I/O error on the BSDS data set.
`-RECOVER INDOUBT`	Recovers in-doubt threads that cannot be recovered automatically by DB2 or the appropriate transaction manager.
`-RESET GENERICLU`	Purges information stored by `VTAM` in the coupling facility.
`-RESET INDOUBT`	Purges information from the "in doubt" thread report (generated by the `-DISPLAY THREAD` command).
`-SET ARCHIVE`	Used to set the parameters for log archiving.
`-START DATABASE`	Starts a stopped database, tablespace, tablespace partition, index, or index partition or changes the status of these objects to `RW`, `RO`, or `UT`.
`-START PROCEDURE`	Starts a stored procedure enabling subsequent execution using the `CALL` statement.
`-START RLIMIT`	Starts the Resource Limit Facility with a specific Resource Limit Specification Table (RLST).
`-START TRACE`	Activates DB2 traces, classes, and `IFCID`s; specifies limiting constraints for plans and authids; specifies the output destination for the activated trace records.
`-STOP DATABASE`	Stops a database, a tablespace, or an index and closes the underlying `VSAM` data sets associated with the stopped object. As of DB2 V3, partitions can be stopped individually.
`-STOP PROCEDURE`	Stops a stored procedure disabling subsequent execution.
`-STOP RLIMIT`	Stops the Resource Limit Facility.
`-STOP TRACE`	Stops the specified DB2 traces and classes.
`-TERM UTILITY`	Terminates the execution of an active or a stopped DB2 utility, releases all the resources that are being utilized by the utility, and cleans up the DB2 Directory.

Administrative Command Guidelines

When you issue administrative commands, you are actually changing the DB2 environment. Administrative commands should be used with caution. Review the following guidelines before utilizing administrative commands.

Educate the Users of Administrative Commands

All administrative commands should be issued only by an experienced analyst who knows the DB2 commands and their effect on the DB2 subsystem and its components. This should be accomplished by administering strict DB2 security controls.

Use `ALTER BUFFERPOOL` to Dynamically Manage Bufferpools

As of DB2 V3, the `ALTER BUFFERPOOL` command can be used to dynamically change the size and characteristics of a bufferpool. The following parameters can be used to change the bufferpool using `ALTER BUFFERPOOL`:

`VPSIZE`	Size of the virtual bufferpool
`HPSIZE`	Size of the associated hiperpool
`VPSEQT`	Virtual pool sequential steal threshold
`HPSEQT`	Hiperpool sequential steal threshold
`VPPSEQT`	Virtual pool parallel sequential steal threshold
`VPXPSEQT`	Virtual pool assisting parallel sequential steal threshold
`DWQT`	Virtual pool deferred write threshold
`VDWQT`	Virtual pool vertical deferred write threshold (by data set)
`CASTOUT`	Hiperpool dirty page discard

Use `ALTER UTILITY` to Impact `REORG` Processing

Version 5

The `ALTER UTILITY` command can be used to change the value of the `DEADLINE`, `MAXRO`, `LONGLOG`, and `DELAY` parameters for `REORG` utilities running `SHRLEVEL REFERENCE` or `SHRLEVEL CHANGE`. Refer to Chapter 26, "Data Organization Utilities," for more information on the functionality of these parameters.

Use `ARCHIVE LOG` to Synchronize Disaster Recovery Plans with DB2

Issue the `ARCHIVE LOG` command to synchronize DB2 log archival and copying with application and DB2 Catalog image copies sent to a remote site for disaster recovery. See Chapter 31, "DB2 Contingency Planning," for further guidance.

Use `ARCHIVE LOG` to Synchronize New Logs with Shift Changes

Sometimes a new active DB2 log should begin at the commencement of each new operational shift. This can be accomplished with the `ARCHIVE LOG` command.

Use RECOVER INDOUBT with Caution

The RECOVER INDOUBT command can abort or commit changes made by in-doubt threads. Be cautious before committing in-doubt threads. Most DB2 programs are coded to process updates in commit scopes defined as a unit of work.

The unit of work, as described in Chapter 5, "Using DB2 in an Application Program," is coded as much as possible to maintain data integrity between related tables. If the RECOVER INDOUBT command commits changes for a partial unit of work, the affected tables may not be in a consistent state. If database-enforced referential integrity is *always* used, this is not a concern because the database forces the tables to be in a consistent state. However, very few applications require that every referential constraint be explicitly defined and enforced by DB2.

Avoid Using ACCESS(FORCE)

Issuing the START DATABASE command with the ACCESS(FORCE) option is not recommended because it may cause tablespaces or indexes to be in an inconsistent state. ACCESS(FORCE) forces all pending flags (check, copy, and recover) to be reset for the specified object. Never use ACCESS(FORCE) unless you are absolutely sure that the data is in a consistent state for the specified object (for example, after restoring objects using the DSN1COPY service aid utility).

To be safe, never use ACCESS(FORCE). Instead, use the appropriate utility to reset the exception flags.

Ensure That DASD Is Online Before Stopping Databases

The DASD volume for the underlying VSAM data sets for the object that will be started by the START DATABASE command do not need to be online when the START command is issued. Because the STOP DATABASE command closes the underlying VSAM data sets, however, the corresponding volume for that object must be online when the STOP command is issued.

Start and Stop at the Partition Level

The START and STOP commands can be executed for partitioned tablespaces and indexes at the partition level. This functionality enhances availability by enabling users to stop only portions of an application (tablespace or index).

Be Aware of the Time Constraints of the STOP Command

The STOP command can be used to close VSAM data sets and cause buffer pages associated with the closed data set to be flushed and forced to DASD. The VSAM close operation may take a while before it is complete, though. The buffers may not be flushed completely to DASD immediately after the STOP DATABASE command completes. Subsequent processing must consider this fact.

Explicitly Start Objects Stopped with the SPACENAM Parameter

When a tablespace or index is explicitly stopped using the `SPACENAM` parameter of the `STOP DATABASE` command, it must be explicitly started again before it can be accessed. Starting at the database level will not affect the status of explicitly stopped tablespaces or indexes.

Use START PROCEDURE Before Calling

Version 4

The `START PROCEDURE` command must be issued for each DB2 stored procedure prior to any application calling the stored procedure. Failure to start a stored procedure before trying to execute it with the `CALL` statement results in the `CALL` statement failing.

Use the ACTION Clause When Stopping Stored Procedures

Version 4

The stop command disables subsequent executions of the named stored procedure. The `ACTION` clause can be specified to indicate whether future attempts to run the stored procedure will be entirely rejected `[ACTION(REJECT)]` or queued `[ACTION(QUEUE)]` to be run when the stored procedure is started again.

Use START RLIMIT to Vary Resource Limits

`START RLIMIT` can use different resource limit specification tables (RLST) with different limits. By specifying the `ID` parameter, a specific RLST is chosen. For example:

```
-START RLIMIT ID=02
```

starts the `RLF` using the `SYSIBM.DSNRLS02` table. This enables different limits to be specified for

- Different times of the day
- Batch and online processing
- Heavy and light ad hoc processing

Use START TRACE to Specify Trace Destinations

When issuing the `START TRACE` command, each type of trace can specify different destinations for the trace output. The following lists destinations for each type of trace:

Trace Destination	*Trace Types*
GTF	ACCTG, AUDIT, GLOBAL, MONITOR, PERFM, STAT
OP*n*	ACCTG, AUDIT, GLOBAL, MONITOR, PERFM, STAT
OPX	ACCTG, AUDIT, GLOBAL, MONITOR, PERFM, STAT
RES	GLOBAL
SMF	ACCTG, AUDIT, GLOBAL, MONITOR, PERFM, STAT
SRV	ACCTG, AUDIT, GLOBAL, MONITOR, PERFM, STAT

Use START TRACE to Specify Constraints

When you issue the START TRACE command, each type of trace can place optional constraints on the data to be collected. The following lists constraints for each type of trace:

Constraint Type	*Trace Types*
AUTHID	ACCTG, AUDIT, GLOBAL, MONITOR, PERFM
CLASS	ACCTG, AUDIT, GLOBAL, MONITOR, PERFM, STAT
PLAN	ACCTG, AUDIT, GLOBAL, MONITOR, PERFM
RMID	GLOBAL, MONITOR, PERFM

Use No More Than Six Active Traces

Although as many as 32 traces can be active at one time, you should limit the number of active traces to 6 to avoid performance degradation. Add this recommendation to the trace guidelines presented in Chapter 17, "Traditional DB2 Performance Monitoring," to establish the proper controls for issuing DB2 traces.

Be Aware of the Authority Required to Terminate Utilities

To terminate utilities, the issuer of the TERM UTILITY command must meet *one* of the following requirements. The issuer must

- Be the user who initially submitted the utility
- Have SYSADM, SYSCTRL, or SYSOPR authority

If your operational support staff must have the ability to terminate utilities that they did not originally submit, they should be granted SYSOPR authority. However, SYSOPR authority permits the user to START DB2 and STOP DB2, which is not generally acceptable because the uncontrolled issuing of these commands can wreak havoc on a production system. There is no viable alternative to SYSOPR authority, though, because explicit TERM UTILITY authority is unavailable.

Avoid Using Wildcards When Terminating Utilities

When terminating utilities, explicitly specify the UID to be terminated, rather than use the -TERMINATE UTILITY command to terminate all utilities invoked by your ID. When you explicitly specify what should be terminated, you avoid inadvertently terminating an active utility. After a utility is terminated, it can never be restarted. The utility must be rerun from the beginning and may require data recovery before rerunning.

Environment Control Commands

The environment control commands affect the status of the DB2 subsystem and the Distributed Data Facility. These commands commonly are issued only by the DB2 systems programmer, systems administrator, or DBA. A brief description of the environment control commands follows:

- START DB2	Initializes and establishes the DB2 subsystem
- START DDF	Starts the Distributed Data Facility
- STOP DB2	Stops the DB2 subsystem
- STOP DDF	Stops the Distributed Data Facility

Environment Control Command Guidelines

Before issuing environment control commands, be sure to review the following guidelines.

Control the Use of Environment Control Commands

Secure the environment control commands so that they are issued only by technically astute administrative areas.

Verify the Completion of START DB2 and STOP DB2

Make sure that the START DB2 command successfully completes by ensuring that access to DB2 is available using DB2I. Another way to verify that the START DB2 command was successful is to make certain that the started tasks for DB2 are active. The default names for these tasks are

DSNMSTR	DB2 Master Region
DSNDBM1	DB2 Database Region
IRLMPROC	DB2 IRLM

Your installation probably has renamed these address spaces, but the names are probably similar.

Be sure that the STOP DB2 command successfully completes by ensuring that the started tasks for the subsystem being stopped are no longer active.

Verify the Completion of START DDF and STOP DDF

The status of the START DDF and STOP DDF commands can be checked by monitoring the status of the DDF address space. (The default name of the DDF address space is DSNDDF.)

Use MODE(FORCE) Sparingly

Exercise caution before stopping the DB2 subsystem with the MODE(FORCE) parameter. The FORCE option terminates all active programs and utilities. As such, in-doubt units of recovery may result by forcing DB2 to stop in this manner. The MODE(QUIESCE) option allows all active programs and utilities to complete before DB2 is stopped.

When DB2 is stopped with `MODE(FORCE)` or `MODE(QUIESCE)`, only currently executing programs are affected. No new programs or utilities are permitted to run.

DSN Commands

DSN commands are actually subcommands of the DSN command processor. DSN is a control program that enables users to issue DB2 environment commands, plan management commands, and commands to develop and run application programs. DSN commands can be run in TSO foreground, either directly or indirectly, or in TSO background. An example of issuing the DSN command processor indirectly in foreground is through DB2I. (The DB2I panels accomplish most of their functions by issuing DSN commands.) DSN commands can be issued in the background with the `IKJEFT01` terminal monitor program.

There are nine DSN commands:

`DSN` A command processor that enables the user to issue DB2 environment commands from a TSO session or in a batch job. For example:

```
DSN SYSTEM (DSN)
     - DISPLAY THREAD (*)
END
```

The DSN command processor must be invoked before any DSN command that follows can be issued.

`ABEND` Used to request and obtain a dump when problems are suspected with another DSN subcommand. Use this DSN command under the guidance of the IBM Support Center.

`BIND` Builds an application plan or package from one or more database request modules.

`DCLGEN` Produces the SQL `DECLARE TABLE` specification and a working storage data declaration section for VS/COBOL, COBOL II, PL/I, or C.

`END` Terminates the DSN session and returns the user to TSO.

`FREE` Deletes application plans and packages.

`REBIND` Rebuilds an application plan or package when SQL statements in a program's DBRM have not been changed. `REBIND` also can modify the `BIND` parameters.

`RUN` Executes an application program. The program can contain SQL statements, but this is not required.

`SPUFI` Executes the SPUFI program. This subcommand can be issued only when processing under ISPF; it cannot be submitted in a batch job.

DSN Command Guidelines

Deploy the following guidelines to ensure effective usage of the DSN command processor.

Use DB2I, Online TSO, or a Batch Job to Invoke DSN

The DSN command processor can be invoked in three ways: from the DB2I panels, online by entering DSN (which enables the user to enter subcommands at the DSN prompt), or in batch, specifying subcommands in the SYSTSIN data set.

In general, it is safest to invoke the DSN commands from the DB2I panels. Some DSN commands such as RUN and BIND, however, may need to be processed in a batch job that invokes the DSN command under the auspices of IKJEFT01. Batch TSO is the only method IBM supplies with DB2 for running a batch DB2 program.

Refer to Chapter 11, "The Doors to DB2," for examples of issuing DSN commands through the DB2I panels.

Use END to Terminate a DSN Command Session

A DSN session is terminated by issuing the END subcommand, by issuing a new DSN command, or by pressing the attention key (PA1) twice in succession.

Use the TEST Option to Trace DSN Problems

If a subcommand or function of the DSN command appears to be functioning improperly, the TEST option can be used to trace DSN commands.

IMS Commands

The IMS commands affect the operation of DB2 and IMS/TM. IMS commands must be issued from a valid terminal connected to IMS/TM, and the issuer must have the appropriate IMS authority. Consult the IMS manuals in the following list for additional information on IMS commands:

SC26-8013, IMS/ESA Administration Guide: System
SC26-8014, IMS/ESA Administration Guide: Transaction Manager
SC26-8028, IMS/ESA Messages and Codes
SC26-8029, IMS/ESA Operations Guide
SC26-8030, IMS/ESA Operator's Reference
SC26-8032, IMS/ESA Sample Operating Procedures
SC26-8042, IME/ESA Summary of Operator Commands
GG24-3203, IMS/VS A Planning Guide for DB2

The following IMS commands pertain to DB2:

/CHANGE	Resets in-doubt units of recovery
/DISPLAY	Displays outstanding units of recovery or the status of the connection between IMS/TM and the DB2 subsystem
/SSR	Enables the user to issue DB2 environment commands from an IMS/TM terminal, for example: `/SSR -DISPLAY THREAD (*)`
/START	Enables the connection between IMS/TM and an active DB2 subsystem
/STOP	Disables the connection between IMS/TM and an active DB2 subsystem
/TRACE	Enables and disables IMS tracing

IMS Command Guidelines

The following techniques are useful when issuing IMS commands that impact DB2.

Control the Use of Critical IMS Commands

The /CHANGE, /START, and /STOP commands should be secured commands. Because these commands can damage IMS/TM transactions that are being processed, they should be avoided during peak processing times. A centralized authority consisting of only systems programmers and DBAs should administer and invoke these commands.

Use /START and /STOP to Refresh the IMS-to-DB2 Connection

The /START and /STOP commands can be used to refresh the IMS to DB2 subsystem connection without bringing down IMS/TM.

Use /TRACE with Caution

The /TRACE command should be issued only by a qualified analyst who understands the ramifications of IMS tracing. This is usually best left to the IMS DBA or systems programmer.

CICS Commands

The CICS commands affect the operation of DB2 and CICS. CICS commands must be issued from a valid terminal connected to CICS, and the issuer must have the appropriate CICS authority. Consult the CICS manuals in the following list for additional information on CICS commands:

SC33-1163, CICS/ESA Installation Guide
SC33-1167, CICS/ESA Operations and Utilities
SC33-1177, CICS/ESA Messages and Codes

SC33-1176, CICS/ESA Problem Determination Guide
SC33-1164, CICS/ESA System Definition Guide
GG24-3202, CICS-DB2 Interface Guide

All CICS commands that pertain to DB2 are prefixed with DSNC. DSNC is a CICS transaction that enables the execution of DB2 commands from a CICS terminal.

The following CICS commands pertain to DB2:

DSNC	Enables the user to issue DB2 environment commands from a CICS terminal. For example: `DSNC -DISPLAY THREAD(*)` DSNC is also a required prefix for all CICS commands related to DB2.
DSNC DISCONNECT	Enables the user to disconnect DB2 threads.
DSNC DISPLAY	Displays RCT and statistical information for CICS transactions that access DB2 data. If more than one page of information is displayed by this command, use the following syntax to page through the information. At the top of the CICS screen, enter P/x, where x is a number indicating which page to display. P/1 displays page 1, P/2 displays page 2, and so on.
DSNC MODIFY	Enables the modification of RCT values online.
DSNC STOP	Disables the CICS attachment to DB2.
DSNC STRT	Enables the CICS attachment to DB2.

CICS Command Guidelines

The following techniques are useful when issuing CICS commands that impact DB2.

Control the Use of Critical CICS Commands

The DSNC DISCONNECT, DSNC MODIFY, DSNC STRT, and DSNC STOP commands should be secured commands. Because these commands can damage CICS transactions that are being processed, they should be avoided during peak processing times. A centralized authority consisting of only systems programmers and DBAs should administer and invoke these commands.

Use DSNC DISPLAY STATISTICS to Monitor DB2 Transaction Information

Use the DSNC DISPLAY STATISTICS command to obtain statistics for DB2 transactions. The information provided by this command is an accumulation of statistical counters because the CICS attachment to DB2 is activated with the DSNC STRT command. Directly after the DB2 subsystem is attached to CICS, all of these numbers are 0; this should be taken into account in analyzing these statistics. For example, these counters are significantly smaller if the attachment is stopped and started daily instead of once a month.

Sample `DSNC DISPLAY` output is provided in Figure 29.4. The following list defines each of the columns listed by the `DSNC DISPLAY` command.

`TRAN`
: Transaction name associated with this `RCT` entry. If the entry defines a group, the first transaction in the group is listed.

`PLAN`
: Plan name associated with this `RCT` entry. `DSNC` does not have a transaction associated with it, so `PLAN` is blank. A string of asterisks indicates that dynamic plan allocation was specified for this `RCT` entry.

`CALLS`
: Number of SQL executions issued by transactions associated with this `RCT` entry.

`COMMITS`
: Number of `COMMIT`s executed by transactions associated with this `RCT` entry.

`ABORTS`
: Number of aborts, including both abends and rollbacks, encountered by transactions associated with this `RCT` entry.

`AUTHS`
: Number of sign-ons for transactions associated with this `RCT` entry. A sign-on occurs only when a new thread is created or when an existing thread is reused with a new authid or a different plan.

`W/P`
: Number of times any transaction associated with this `RCT` entry was diverted to the pool or had to wait for an available thread.

`HIGH`
: High-water mark for the number of threads needed by any transaction associated with this `RCT` entry.

FIGURE 29.4.
`DSNC DISPLAY STATISTICS` *output.*

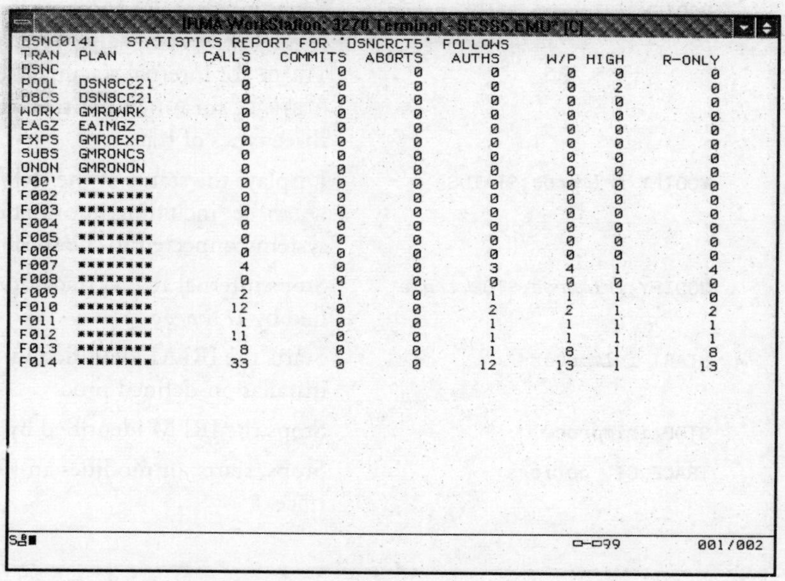

```
DSNC014I   STATISTICS REPORT FOR 'DSNCRCT5' FOLLOWS
TRAN  PLAN          CALLS   COMMITS  ABORTS    AUTHS      W/P HIGH    R-ONLY
DSNC                    0         0       0        0        0    0         0
POOL  DSN8CC21          0         0       0        0        0    2         0
D8CS  DSN8CC21          0         0       0        0        0    0         0
WORK  GMROWRK           0         0       0        0        0    0         0
EAGZ  EAIMGZ            0         0       0        0        0    0         0
EXPS  GMROEXP           0         0       0        0        0    0         0
SUBS  GMRONCS           0         0       0        0        0    0         0
ONON  GMRONON           0         0       0        0        0    0         0
F00'  ********          0         0       0        0        0    0         0
F002  ********          0         0       0        0        0    0         0
F003  ********          0         0       0        0        0    0         0
F004  ********          0         0       0        0        0    0         0
F005  ********          0         0       0        0        0    0         0
F006  ********          0         0       0        0        0    0         0
F007  ********          4         0       0        3        4    1         4
F008  ********          0         0       0        0        0    0         0
F009  ********          2         1       0        1        1    1         0
F010  ********         12         0       0        2        2    1         2
F011  ********          1         0       0        1        1    1         1
F012  ********         11         0       0        1        1    1         1
F013  ********          8         0       0        1        8    1         8
F014  ********         33         0       0       12       13    1        13
```

TSO Commands

The DB2 TSO commands are CLISTs that can be used to help compile and run DB2 programs or build utility JCL. The TSO commands are issued from a TSO session, either online using ISPF panels or in batch using the IKJEFT01 program. There are two TSO commands:

DSNH	Can be used to precompile, translate, compile, link, bind, and run DB2 application programs written in VS/COBOL, COBOL II, assembler H, assembler, FORTRAN, PL/I, or C
DSNU	Can be used to generate JCL for any online DB2 utility

IRLM Commands

The IRLM commands affect the operation of the IRLM defined to a DB2 subsystem. IRLM commands must originate from an MVS console, and the issuer must have the appropriate security.

The following IRLM commands pertain to DB2:

MODIFY *irlmproc*,ABEND	Terminates the IRLM identified by *irlmproc* abnormally, regardless of whether any IMS/VS subsystems are controlled by the specified IRLM. Compare this command with the MODIFY *irlmproc*,STOP *trace* command.
MODIFY *irlmproc*,START *trace*	Starts internal IRLM traces for the IRLM identified by *irlmproc*. Valid trace specifications are ITRACE for internal tracing, GTRACE for GTF tracing, PTBTRACE for PTB buffer tracing, or TRACE to start all three types of traces.
MODIFY *irlmproc*,STATUS	Displays the status of the IRLM identified by *irlmproc*, including information for each subsystem connected to the specified IRLM.
MODIFY *irlmproc*,STOP *trace*	Stops internal IRLM traces for the IRLM identified by *irlmproc*.
START *irlmproc*	Starts the IRLM identified by *irlmproc* using an installation-defined proc.
STOP *irlmproc*	Stops the IRLM identified by *irlmproc*.
TRACE CT, *options*	Stops, starts, or modifies an IRLM diagnostic trace.

IRLM Command Guidelines

The following guidelines offer practical advice for using commands that impact the DB2 IRLM.

Stop the IRLM to Stop DB2

The quickest way to bring down a DB2 subsystem is to issue the `STOP` *`irlmproc`* command from an MVS console. When the `-STOP DB2` command does not terminate the DB2 subsystem quickly enough, consider stopping that DB2 subsystem's IRLM.

Use the `STATUS` Parameter to Monitor the IRLM

Use the `STATUS` option of the `MODIFY` *`irlmproc`* command to periodically monitor the effectiveness of the IRLM.

Summary

In this chapter, you learned how to issue DB2 commands to administer DB2 resources and environments. You examined the six types of DB2 commands learning the best way to implement and use each. The six categories of DB2 commands covered are as follows:

- DB2 environment commands
- DSN commands
- IMS commands
- CICS commands
- TSO commands
- IRLM commands

30

DB2 Utility and Command Guidelines

Now you know about each of the DB2 utilities and commands. The specific definitions and usage guidelines presented in the first few chapters of Part VI, "DB2 Utilities and Commands," are certainly helpful, but some general considerations should be discussed. This chapter presents general guidelines for the effective use of DB2 utilities and commands, and it also discusses the pending states.

This chapter presents general advice. Whereas previous chapters presented specific guidelines for each utility, command, or group of utilities or commands, this chapter covers topics that span more than one utility or command.

Utility Guidelines

The following topics provide useful guidance for the development and usage of DB2 utilities.

DB2 Online Utility Return Codes

When an online utility runs, a return code is provided indicating the status of the utility execution. If the utility runs to normal completion, the return code is set to 0.

A return code of 4 indicates that the utility completed running, but with warnings. Review the utility output to determine whether some type of reprocessing is required. A warning often indicates a condition that requires no additional consideration.

A return code of 8 means that the utility did not complete successfully. Determine the cause and execute the utility again.

A return code of 12 is an authorization error, which means that the user is not authorized to execute the utility. Either grant the user the proper authority or have an authorized user execute the utility.

DB2 Utility Work Data Sets

Many DB2 online utilities require the allocation of work data sets to complete the task at hand. These work data sets were presented in the first chapters in Part VI. Because a central reference often is handy, the required and optional work data sets for the DB2 online utilities are presented together in Table 30.1. The data sets used by DB2 utilities are listed along the top of the table. The utilities that use these data sets are listed along the left side of the table. Consult the legend to determine the necessity of coding these data sets in the JCL.

Table 30.1. Required utility data sets.

	SORTOUT	SORTWKXX	SYSCOPY	SYSDISC	SYSERR	SYSMAP	SYSREC	SYSUT1	UTPRNT	SYSIN	SYSPRINT
`CHECK DATA`	R	R			R			R		R	R
`COPY`			R							R	R
`LOAD`	X/C	R		O	O	O	R	R	R	R	R
`MERGECOPY`			R					O		R	R
`RECOVER INDEX`		R						O	R	R	R
`REORG INDEX` (unique, Type 1)								R		R	R
`REORG INDEX` (unique, Type 2)								R			
`REORG INDEX` (non-unique, Type 1)	R	R						R	R	R	R
`REORG INDEX` (non-unique, Type 2)								R			
`REORG`	X	R					R	R	R	R	R

O = Optional (based on utility parameters)
R = Required
X = Required if indexes exist
C = Required if referential constraints exist and the `ENFORCE CONSTRAINTS` option is used

DB2 Utility Catalog Contention

DB2 utilities read and update DB2 Catalog and DB2 Directory tables. This can cause contention when multiple utilities are run concurrently. Table 30.2 lists the DB2 Catalog tables that are either updated or read by the online DB2 utilities. In addition, DB2 utilities update the `SYSIBM.SYSUTILX` DB2 Directory table.

DB2 utilities also use claim and drain processing instead of transaction locks to reduce contention and increase availability.

Table 30.2. Utility contention.

Utility	*Updates*	*Reads*
CHECK	SYSIBM.SYSCOPY	SYSIBM.SYSCHECKDEP SYSIBM.SYSCHECKS SYSIBM.SYSCOLUMNS SYSIBM.SYSINDEXES SYSIBM.SYSINDEXPART SYSIBM.SYSTABLES SYSIBM.SYSTABLEPART SYSIBM.SYSTABLESPACE
COPY	SYSIBM.SYSCOPY	SYSIBM.SYSCOLUMNS SYSIBM.SYSINDEXES SYSIBM.SYSINDEXPART SYSIBM.SYSTABLES SYSIBM.SYSTABLEPART SYSIBM.SYSTABLESPACE
LOAD	SYSIBM.SYSCOPY	SYSIBM.SYSTABLES
MERGECOPY	SYSIBM.SYSCOPY	
MODIFY		
RECOVERY	SYSIBM.SYSCOPY	
RECOVER	SYSIBM.SYSCOPY	SYSIBM.SYSCOLUMNS SYSIBM.SYSINDEXES SYSIBM.SYSINDEXPART SYSIBM.SYSTABLES SYSIBM.SYSTABLEPART SYSIBM.SYSTABLESPACE
QUIESCE	SYSIBM.SYSCOPY	
REORG	SYSIBM.SYSCOPY	SYSIBM.SYSCOLUMNS SYSIBM.SYSINDEXES SYSIBM.SYSINDEXPART SYSIBM.SYSTABLES SYSIBM.SYSTABLEPART SYSIBM.SYSTABLESPACE
REPAIR SET		
NOCHCKPEND	SYSIBM.SYSTABLES SYSIBM.SYSTABLEPART	
NORCVRPEND	DB2 Directory	
NOCOPYPEND	DB2 Directory	

Utility	*Updates*	*Reads*
RUNSTATS	SYSIBM.SYSCOLDIST	Objects being analyzed
	SYSIBM.SYSCOLDISTSTATS	
	SYSIBM.SYSCOLSTATS	
	SYSIBM.SYSCOLUMNS	
	SYSIBM.SYSINDEXES	
	SYSIBM.SYSINDEXPART	
	SYSIBM.SYSINDEXSTATS	
	SYSIBM.SYSTABLES	
	SYSIBM.SYSTABLEPART	
	SYSIBM.SYSTABLESPACE	
	SYSIBM.SYSTABSTATS	
STOSPACE	SYSIBM.SYSINDEXES	
	SYSIBM.SYSTABLESPACE	
	SYSIBM.SYSSTOGROUP	
	SYSIBM.SYSTABLEPART	
	SYSIBM.SYSINDEXPART	

Partition Level Operation

DB2 online utilities can operate at the tablespace partition level. The following utilities can be issued for a single partition or for all the partitions of a tablespace:

COPY, MERGECOPY, RECOVER, and REPORT BACKUP and RECOVERY utilities
LOAD and REORG data organization utilities
MODIFY catalog manipulation utility

Coding Utility Control Cards

All DB2 utility control card input must be contained in 80-character record images. The utility statements must be confined to columns 1 through 72. All input in columns 73 through 80 is ignored by DB2.

Automatically Generate Utility Control Cards

Consider using DB2 Catalog queries to generate utility control card input. By creating standard queries for each utility, you improve the accuracy of the utility input syntax. For example, the following query automatically generates input to the RECOVER utility to invoke full tablespace recovery for all tablespaces in a given database:

```
SELECT   'RECOVER TABLESPACE ' || DBNAME ||
         '.' || NAME || 'DSNUM ALL'
FROM     SYSIBM.SYSTABLESPACE
WHERE    DBNAME = 'DSN8D51A';
```

This query generates RECOVER TABLESPACE control cards for every tablespace in the sample database. You can formulate queries to automatically create control card input for most of the online utilities.

Specify the BUFNO JCL Parameter

Various guidelines in Part VI recommend specific BUFNO JCL parameter settings for different utility work data sets. Each installation defines a default number of buffers adequate for the data sets used by most batch jobs. The DB2 utilities, however, can benefit by increasing the work data set buffers. Therefore, if sufficient memory is available to increase the buffering of DB2 utility work data sets, always do so.

Allocate Sufficient Sort Work Space for DFSORT

The CHECK INDEX, LOAD, RECOVER INDEX, and REORG utilities require an external sort routine. DB2 uses an IBM-supplied sort utility named DFSORT. You can use the SORTDEVT and SORTNUM parameters of these utilities to allow the system to allocate the sort work area dynamically. This way, the sort work specification never needs to be adjusted or sized—the system manages the required size.

CAUTION

For very large tablespaces requiring a large amount of sort work space, consider explicit allocation of sort work data sets because the system might not be able to allocate large amounts of space during the utility execution.

The SORTDEVT parameter is used to specify the device type for temporary data sets to be dynamically allocated by DFSORT. The SORTNUM parameter specifies the number of temporary data sets to be dynamically allocated by the sort program. If you use SORTDEVT and omit SORTNUM, DFSORT will determine how many data sets to allocate on its own.

NOTE

No sort work space is required when reorganizing Type 2 indexes. Additionally, REORG does not require sort work space for unique, Type 1 indexes.

No sort work space is required when loading a table with no indexes or a single index, when the data to be loaded is in order by the index key.

If SORTDEVT and SORTNUM are not used, you must explicitly specify sort work data sets in the utility JCL. The SORTWKxx DD statement defines the characteristics and location of the intermediate storage data sets used by DFSORT. Multiple data sets can be allocated for the temporary sort work space required by DFSORT. Specify each sort work data set to a different SORTWKxx DD statement. The xx is a two-digit indicator ranging from 00 to 99. In general, begin with 00 and work your way up. No more than 32 SORTWKxx data sets will be used by DFSORT.

All the data sets allocated to the SORTWKxx DD statements must be allocated on the same media type. Although DFSORT permits the allocation of work data sets to a tape unit, avoid doing this for DB2 utilities because it causes severe performance degradation. Additionally, the SORTWKxx DD statements must be allocated on the same type of unit (for example, one SORTWKxx data set cannot be allocated to a 3390 device if the others are allocated to 3380 devices).

Specify the SPACE allocation for the SORTWKxx data sets in cylinder increments. If you don't, DFSORT will reallocate the data sets in cylinder increments anyway.

For performance, specifying one or two large SORTWKxx data sets is preferable to specifying multiple smaller data sets. For more information on DFSORT, consult the *IBM DFSORT Application Programming Guide* (SC33-4035).

When Loading or Reorganizing, Specify LOG NO

To reduce the overhead associated with the LOAD and REORG job, use LOG NO. DB2 logs every modification to DB2 data, except when the LOAD and REORG utilities run with the LOG NO option. When you use LOG NO, however, an image copy must be taken after the successful completion of the LOAD or REORG job.

Back Up Data Using the COPY Utility or DFSMS

To back up data, use the COPY utility rather than DSN1COPY. DSN1COPY operates "behind DB2's back." If you always use the COPY utility, DB2 will have an accurate record of all backup data sets. DFSMS is also a valid copy mechanism.

CAUTION

DSN1COPY, DSN1PRNT, and DSN1COMP cannot be used on a concurrent copy.

RECOVER INDEX Versus CREATE INDEX

For very large existing tables, it is quicker to use the RECOVER INDEX utility to build an index than to simply issue a CREATE INDEX statement. RECOVER INDEX is more efficient because it uses an external sort. However, the RECOVER INDEX utility is designed to rebuild indexes, not initially build them as part of a CREATE statement.

The CREATE INDEX DDL provides the option to defer index population by specifying DEFER YES. This causes an index to be built as an empty shell. After the index is created, it will be put into recover pending status. The RECOVER INDEX utility can then be executed to populate the index. This process is usually much more efficient for indexes on very large tables.

The Pending States

DB2 weaves an intricate web of checks and balances to ensure the integrity of the data housed in its tables. DB2 ensures that image copies, recovers, and referential integrity checks are performed as needed, based on an application's job stream.

For example, if data is loaded into a table with DB2 logging turned off, no further updates can be made to that table until an image copy is made or the table is reloaded with changes logged. If DB2 did not enforce this, valuable application data could be lost because of hardware or software failures. DB2 controls the integrity of its data through the use of *pending flags*.

A tablespace is in a pending state when the check pending, copy pending, or recover pending flag is set for that tablespace.

Why Pending States Occur

A tablespace's check pending flag is set when

- A check constraint is added to a table and data within an existing row of that table violates the constraint.
- A table is altered to add a check constraint and the CURRENT RULES special register contains 'DB2'.
- A tablespace with a table or tables containing referential constraints is partialiy recovered (that is, RECOVER TORBA or RECOVER TOCOPY is run).
- The CHECK DATA utility is run for a table in the tablespace specifying DELETE NO and referential constraint or check constraint violations are encountered.
- The LOAD utility is run for a table in the tablespace specifying the ENFORCE NO option and either RI or check constraints exist for any table in the tablespace.
- A table in the tablespace is altered to add a new foreign key.
- Any table in a referential set is dropped.
- Any database or tablespace containing tables in a referential set is dropped.

A tablespace's copy pending flag is set when

- The REORG utility is run for the tablespace specifying LOG NO or the LOAD utility is run for a table in the tablespace specifying LOG NO.
- A tablespace with a table or tables containing referential constraints is partially recovered (that is, RECOVER TORBA or RECOVER TOCOPY is run).
- The MODIFY utility is run deleting the last full image copy data set from the SYSIBM.SYSCOPY table.

A tablespace's recover pending flag is set when

- A RECOVER or REORG utility is run for the tablespace abends.
- A LOAD utility is run for tables in the tablespace abends.

An index's recover pending flag is set when

- A tablespace with a table or tables containing referential constraints is partially recovered (that is, RECOVER TORBA or RECOVER TOCOPY is run).
- Abends occur in the RECOVER, REORG, or LOAD utility.
- The index is created specifying DEFER YES.

How to Correct Pending States

The check pending flag for the tablespace can be reset by

- Running the CHECK DATA utility for the tables in the tablespace specifying DELETE NO if no constraint violations are encountered.
- Running the CHECK DATA utility for the tables in the tablespace specifying DELETE YES.
- Running the LOAD utility specifying the ENFORCE CONSTRAINTS option.
- Altering tables in the tablespace to drop foreign keys and check constraints.
- Running the REPAIR utility specifying SET NOCHECKPEND for the tablespace or issuing the START command for the tablespace with the ACCESS(FORCE) parameter. Neither option corrects the problem flagged by the pending state; they merely reset the pending flag.

The copy pending flag for the tablespace can be reset by

- Running the REORG utility with the LOG YES option or running the utility with both the REPLACE and LOG YES options.
- Running the COPY utility specifying both the SHRLEVEL REFERENCE and the FULL YES options.
- Running the REPAIR utility specifying SET NOCOPYPEND for the tablespace or issuing the START command for the tablespace with the ACCESS(FORCE) parameter. Neither option corrects the problem flagged by the pending state; they merely reset the pending flag.

The recover pending flag for the tablespace can be reset by

- Running the LOAD utility with the REPLACE option.
- Running a full recovery for the tablespace.
- Running the REPAIR utility specifying SET NORCVRPEND for the tablespace or issuing the START command for the tablespace with the ACCESS(FORCE) parameter. Neither option corrects the problem flagged by the pending state; they merely reset the pending flag.

The recover pending flag for the index can be reset by

- Running the RECOVER INDEX utility for the index.
- Running the REPAIR utility specifying SET NORCVRPEND for the index or issuing the START command for the index with the ACCESS(FORCE) parameter. Neither option corrects the problem flagged by the pending state; they merely reset the pending flag.

Summary

Although you now have a comprehensive understanding of DB2 utilities and commands, one more issue must be discussed in the framework of utilities and commands: DB2 disaster recovery. The next chapter covers various contingency planning scenarios, incorporating DB2 utilities and commands into those scenarios.

31

DB2 Contingency Planning

Contingency planning for disaster recovery is a complex task in the best of situations. Unfortunately, the best of situations does not exist in a DB2 environment. This chapter defines the limitations of DB2 in the framework of disaster recovery and suggests solutions to the problems that these limitations create. This chapter pertains to the recovery of DB2 application data, not to the recovery of the DB2 subsystem (and related data).

Suggestions, cautions, requirements, and techniques are provided to help you create a disaster recovery plan for your DB2 applications.

What Is a Disaster?

It is quite natural for organizations to begin developing a disaster recovery plan before stepping back to analyze the question "What is a disaster?" Without a firm understanding of what type of disasters can occur, it is quite probable that the plan will be incomplete. A good place to start is to define the term *disaster*. The Oxford American dictionary defines a disaster as a "sudden great misfortune." It helps to expand on this, though. My definition follows:

> A *disaster* is any event that has a small chance of transpiring, a high level of uncertainty, and a potentially devastating outcome.

Most of us have witnessed (at least on the news) a disaster situation. Tornadoes, hurricanes, earthquakes, and fires are prime examples of natural disasters. Disasters can also be man-made, such as electric failure, bursting pipes, and war. However, relatively few of us have actually lived through a disaster of the proportion shown on television. But many of us have had our basements flooded or been in an automobile accident. A disaster does not have to have global consequences in order for it to be a disaster to you.

Although disasters by their very definition are unpredictable and unlikely, a disaster is something that you must plan for. Every company should have a comprehensive and tested disaster plan that details how to resume business operations in the event of a disaster. Companies with disaster plans will provide a higher degree of customer satisfaction and, in the long run, will be more successful than companies with no plan. Disaster recovery for DB2 should be an integral component of your overall business recovery plan. But to what degree should the disaster planning be taken? Before your company can ascertain the appropriate level of recoverability, you must analyze the risks and determine the objectives.

Determining and Managing Risk

A disaster recovery plan is developed to minimize the costs resulting from losses of, or damages to, the resources or capabilities of your IT facilities. The success of any DB2 disaster recovery plan depends on how well you ascertain the risks involved. First, you must recognize potential disaster situations and understand the consequences of each. How these disasters affect your business is the bottom line reason for contingency planning in the first place. If your shop is on the coast, for example, tornadoes, floods, and hurricanes are more likely than earthquakes (unless you are in California).

Each DB2 application must undergo an analysis period whereby the impact of losing the application is evaluated. This can only be accomplished with the input of those individuals who will be affected—the end users.

Risk can be broken up into three categories: financial loss, business service interruption, and legal responsibilities. Within each category, there are varying degrees of risk. Each application has a different impact on the company's bottom line the longer it is unavailable. Consider a bank, for example. Having the demand deposit application unavailable will cause a greater loss than having the human resources application unavailable.

Similarly, varying degrees of business service interruption and legal responsibilities also will exist. Most applications will be impacted by each of the three risk areas, and each application should be analyzed to determine the level of risk associated with it. The disaster recovery plan needs to factor each of these categories into the mix to determine which applications are most critical.

When developing your disaster recovery plan, remember that business needs are the motivating force behind your planning. It is prudent, therefore, to separate your systems into critical and non-critical applications based on business needs. The definition of a system as critical must be made by the area responsible for the business function that the system supports. It is a good idea to rank your applications into classes to determine which applications have the biggest impact if they are not available.

Class 1	Super Critical Application. This class of application must be supported with current data and is one of the most important to support immediately. It must be recovered in the first group of applications to be recovered at the disaster site. This group should be limited to 5 or fewer applications to ensure that only the most critical applications are processed first.
Class 2	Business Critical Application. This class of application is important but falls outside the top 5 applications in terms of impact to the business. It must be available at the remote site within the first 2 to 3 days. Typically, it requires current data.
Class 3	Moderately Critical Application. This class of application must be available if the disaster lasts longer than one week. However, its impact to the business is less critical, allowing it to wait for all Class 1 and 2 applications to be recovered first. Its data requirements vary from current, to daily, to possibly weekly.

Class 4	Required Application. This application needs to be supported at the remote site, but it is not critical. Data can be from the last available backup.
Class 5	Non-critical Application. This application need not be supported in the event of a disaster.

Develop disaster recovery plans first for the critical applications. These support the functions that are absolutely necessary should your company experience a disaster. Based upon these rankings, the appropriate backup strategy can be employed for the tablespaces in each DB2 application.

Disaster Recovery Requirements

I have described the reasons why a disaster recovery plan is needed, but what should the goals of this disaster recovery plan be? One part of that plan must deal with the recovery of DB2 data. Most disaster recovery plans are composed of four goals:

- Avoid the loss of data
- Avoid the reprocessing of transactions
- Avoid causing inconsistent data
- Limit the time needed to restart critical application processing

These goals often conflict. For example, how can critical applications be online quickly when they usually consist of large databases? How can the loss of data be avoided when thousands of transactions update DB2 tables every second? Each decision in the plan requires a trade-off to be made.

After you target applications for disaster planning, you then should decide on a disaster recovery strategy. This chapter details three strategies for DB2 disaster recovery planning—the sledgehammer, the scalpel, and DSN1COPY. Each has its strengths and weaknesses. You can choose one strategy or mix and match strategies based on the recovery requirements of each application.

Disaster Strikes

The situation is grim. There has been a devastating fire at your data processing shop. All computer hardware, software, and data at your site has been destroyed. Are you adequately prepared to recover your DB2 data at a remote processing site?

In this section, it is assumed that your data processing shop has planned for remote processing in the event of a disaster. In addition, it is assumed that the operating system software and environment have been recovered successfully. Given these caveats, let's continue with our discussion of DB2 disaster planning.

DB2 disaster recovery happens in two steps: the recovery of the DB2 subsystem and the recovery of the application data. The primary concern of the DBA should be the recovery of the operational data. To accomplish this, however, you must recover your DB2 subsystem first. Therefore, your initial concern should be developing a comprehensive plan for recovering your DB2 subsystem. IBM's *DB2 Administration Guide* covers this topic in depth.

DB2 Recovery Basics

To fully understand DB2 disaster recovery, you must first review basic DB2 recovery procedures and techniques. The standard tools of DB2 recovery are the image copy backup, the DB2 log tapes, and internal DB2 tables and data sets. Refer to Chapter 25, "Backup and Recovery Utilities," (and Figure 25.1) for a discussion of DB2 recovery basics.

The `RECOVER` utility is invoked to restore the tablespace data. DB2 uses all the information it stores in active and archive logs, the DB2 Catalog, the DB2 Directory, and the BSDS to recover tablespace data with a minimum of user input. The only input the `RECOVER` utility requires is the name of the tablespace to be recovered. DB2 does the rest. The reduction of user input in a recovery situation lessens the possibility of errors during a potentially hectic and confusing time. The automation of the recovery process, however, is just the circumstance that can complicate offsite DB2 disaster recovery planning.

Strategy #1: The Sledgehammer

This first strategy is referred to as *the sledgehammer* because it is a basic approach to application backup and recovery. This strategy should be considered for non–24-hour applications, noncritical applications, and nonvolatile applications. It is easy to implement and consists of the following steps:

1. Stop the DB2 subsystem to ensure stable application data. This establishes a system-wide point of consistency.
2. Copy all tablespaces using a utility to dump complete DASD volumes. Utilities such as FDR, from Innovation Data Processing, and DFSMS, from IBM, work well.
3. When all DASD volumes containing DB2 data have been successfully copied, restart the DB2 subsystem.
4. Copy the backup tapes and send them offsite.
5. Recovery at the remote site is then performed a complete DASD volume at a time.

There are some problems with this strategy, however. For example, many shops require DB2 to be available 24 hours a day, so stopping the DB2 subsystem is not an option.

As an alternative to stopping the DB2 subsystem, each application could have a regularly scheduled job to stop only the application. The job would need to quiesce the application tablespaces, the DB2 Catalog (`DSNDB06`), and the DB2 Directory (`DSNDB01`) and then stop each application tablespace. Note that only an Install System Administrator (SYSADM) can quiesce the DB2 Catalog and DB2 Directory. The complete volume backup could be performed at this point, and, when complete, the application tablespaces could be restarted.

An additional problem arises when DB2 data sets are strewn across numerous DASD volumes. If the backup process copies data a complete volume at a time, many non-DB2 data sets that are not required for DB2 recovery will be copied. Most tools that perform complete DASD volume copies can also copy specific data sets, but this complicates the backup process by requiring the user to maintain a list of DB2 data sets as well as a list of DB2 volumes for backing up.

If DFSMS, commonly referred to as *system managed storage*, is used to automate the placement of DB2 tablespace and index data sets, the location of these data sets is controlled by DFSMS and is dynamic. Therefore, the DB2 tablespace or index data set being backed up will not consistently remain on the same DASD volume. This further complicates the DASD volume backup strategy.

The sledgehammer strategy is effective for shops willing to trade 24-hour processing capabilities for ease of disaster recovery preparation. But this strategy is not the optimal solution for most DB2 installations because most shops are unwilling to make this trade-off. Shutting down DB2 effectively prohibits the execution of every application that uses DB2 tables. This is usually impossible. Even running the QUIESCE utility affects other applications by forcing a point of consistency on the DB2 Catalog and the DB2 Directory. If you want to avoid these points of contention, choose another strategy.

DFSMS Concurrent Copy

DB2 V3 added functionality for recovering from backups produced using DFSMS (Data Facility Storage Management Subsystem). The DFSMS concurrent copy function can copy a data set concurrently with other access. To restore the data sets, you can manually apply the DFSMS copies, and then you can use the RECOVER utility for point-in-time recovery in conjunction with the DB2 log. However, DB2 did not keep track of the DFSMS copies under DB2 V3.

Version 4

DB2 V4 comes with the ability to invoke a DFSMS concurrent copy directly from the DB2 COPY utility. A DFSMS concurrent copy is recorded in the DB2 Catalog SYSIBM.SYSCOPY table with ICTYPE of F and STYPE of C. Likewise, DB2 can automatically restore DFSMS copies using the RECOVER utility. When RECOVER is invoked and a DFSMS copy needs to be part of the recovery, DB2 will invoke the DFDSS RESTORE command to apply the DFSMS concurrent copy. Of course, the copy can be applied outside the scope of the DB2 RECOVER utility if so desired.

Strategy #2: The Scalpel

The second strategy uses native DB2 functionality to prepare for disaster recovery. This strategy is called *the scalpel* because it is precise and accurate. It involves the following steps:

1. Produce two or more image copy backups, at least one of which must be on tape.
2. Send the tape image copy backup to the remote site. You should do this as soon as possible after the tape has been created to avoid having the tape damaged in a subsequent disaster.
3. Do not back up indexes.
4. Produce a daily report (using `DSNTEP2` or QMF) from the `SYSIBM.SYSCOPY` table and send a copy of the report to the remote site. A sample query that accomplishes this follows:

```
SELECT    DBNAME, TSNAME, DSNUM, TIMESTAMP, ICTYPE,
          DSNAME, FILESEQNO, SHRLEVEL, DSVOLSER
FROM      SYSIBM.SYSCOPY
ORDER BY DBNAME, TSNAME, DSNUM, TIMESTAMP
```

   A QMF form that can be used with the query is provided in Listing 31.1. The automated running of this query can be accomplished with relative ease by setting up a batch QMF job and sending `SYSOUT` to a tape data set that can be sent offsite.

Listing 31.1. QMF form to be used with the SYSCOPY query.

```
Total Width of Report Columns: 150

NUM  COLUMN HEADING      USAGE    INDENT   WIDTH   EDIT   SEQ
 1   DATABASE            BREAK1   1          8     C      1
 2   TABLE_SPACE         BREAK2   1          8     C      2
 3   DS_NUM              BREAK3   1          3     L      3
 4   TIMESTAMP                    1         26     C      4
 5   IC_TYPE                      1          4     C      5
 6   DATASET NAME                 1         44     C      6
 7   FIL_SEQ_NO                   1          3     C      7
 8   SHR_LVL                      1          3     C      8
 9   VOL SERIAL LIST              1         42     C      9
```

This report details all the information available for DB2 to use for recovery. Be sure to synchronize the running of this report with the running of the DB2 Catalog backup sent offsite to ensure that the corresponding offsite DB2 Catalog image copy conforms to the data in this report.

Use Table 31.1 to interpret the value of the `ICTYPE` column in this report. `ICTYPE` refers to the type of recovery information recorded in the `SYSIBM.SYSCOPY` table.

Table 31.1. SYSIBM.SYSCOPY ICTYPES.

Type	*Description*
F	Full image copy
I	Incremental image copy
P	Partial recovery point (RECOVER TOCOPY or RECOVER TORBA)
Q	QUIESCE (point of consistency RBA)
R	LOAD REPLACE (LOG YES)
S	LOAD REPLACE (LOG NO)
T	TERM UTILITY command
W	REORG (LOG NO)
X	REORG (LOG YES)
Y	LOAD (LOG NO)
Z	LOAD (LOG YES)

5. Use DSNJU004 to produce a BSDS log map report and send a copy of the report to the remote site.
6. Recovery at the remote site is performed a tablespace at a time. Use RECOVER INDEX to rebuild all indexes. Run CHECK DATA to resolve any constraint violations.
7. For this method of disaster recovery preparation to succeed, the DB2 system data sets must be backed up and sent offsite. Be sure to create offsite backups of the DB2 Catalog, the BSDS, the DB2 Directory, and the archive logs at least daily for volatile systems and at least weekly for all systems, regardless of their volatility.

The scalpel method differs from the sledgehammer in many ways, but perhaps the most im portant way is its reliance on DB2. Only application data recorded in the DB2 Catalog, th DB2 Directory, and the BSDS can be recovered. For this reason, the scalpel method relies heavil on the capability to recover the DB2 subsystem. Application data is as current as the last backu of the DB2 subsystem—one of the headaches caused by the automation of the DB2 recover process.

Consider, for example, an application that sends three image copy backups to a remote si daily. One backup is sent offsite in the morning to allow for post-batch recovery, another sent offsite in the afternoon to allow recovery of all morning transactions, and a third is se offsite in the evening to allow recovery of all pre-batch transactions.

However, if only one DB2 Catalog copy is sent offsite daily, for example, after the morni copy but before the afternoon copy, remote recovery can proceed only to the morning co plus any archive logs sent offsite.

or this reaso.., try to synchronize your application image copies with your DB2 Catalog back-ps. Additionally, as mentioned, ensure that the reports at the remote site reflect the status of ne DB2 Catalog image copies. Otherwise, you will end up with greater confusion during the isaster recovery scenario, increased data loss, and unusable image copies at your remote site.

'he amount of data lost in an offsite recovery depends not only on the synchronization of pplication tablespace backups with DB2 Catalog backups but also on the timeliness of the ackup of archive logs and the synchronization of the DB2 Catalog backup with the logs. When ne DB2 Catalog is backed up to be sent offsite, issue the `ARCHIVE LOG` command as part of the opy job. Send to the remote site a copy of the archived log that was produced along with the)B2 Catalog image copies.

NOTE

This synchronization of DB2 Catalog and archive logs can be accomplished with only DB2 V2.3 or later.

dditionally, keep at least three image copy backup tapes at your remote site. This provides a .tisfactory number of backups if one or more of your image copy tapes is damaged. DB2 au-matically falls back to previous image copy backups when a tape is damaged. Changes are pplied from the archive logs to re-create the data lost by falling back to the previous image opy.

ote also that updates recorded on the DB2 active logs at the time of the disaster are lost. ecovery can be performed through only the last archive log available at the remote site.

he final consideration for the scalpel method is the creation of the underlying tablespace and dexspace data sets at the remote site. If you are using native VSAM, you must use `AMS` to eate the data sets before recovering each tablespace and its related indexes. If you are using TOGROUPs for your production data sets, simply ensure that the STOGROUPs have been tered to point to valid DASD volumes at the remote site. The `RECOVER` utility creates the un-rlying VSAM data sets for you.

trategy #3: DSN1COPY

he third strategy, using `DSN1COPY`, generally is not recommended because it operates behind e back of DB2 and therefore sacrifices the rigorous control provided by DB2 backup and covery procedures. Implementing disaster recovery in this manner can be beneficial, how-er, for a limited number of non-critical applications.

This strategy is close to the sledgehammer approach but a little more complicated. Follow these steps for each DSN1COPY that must be executed:

1. Use the START command with the MODE(RO) option to place all the tablespaces to be backed up in read only mode.
2. Issue QUIESCE WRITE(YES) for all the tablespaces that will be backed up using DSN1COPY.
3. Execute the DSN1COPY utility for each tablespace being copied.
4. Start all the tablespaces in read-write mode using the START command using the MODE(RW) option.

Recovery at the remote site must be performed using DSN1COPY because these backup data sets are not recorded in the DB2 Catalog. Therefore, each tablespace and indexspace data set must be created using AMS before the DSN1COPY can be executed to restore the application data.

This complex and potentially error-prone process should be avoided. If your application data is very stable, however, you might want to avoid recording backups in the DB2 Catalog to simplify your DB2 Catalog maintenance procedures. The MODIFY utility must be executed periodically to clean up the SYSIBM.SYSCOPY table and the SYSIBM.SYSLGRNGX table. MODIFY is run specifying a tablespace and a date range that deletes all image copy and log information for the tablespace for that date range. Each application must supply the appropriate date range for image copy deletion.

If your date range is unknown, unstable, or random, you might want to avoid using the DB2 Catalog for recovery altogether. You could simply create four DSN1COPY backups every time your (stable) application data changes. Retaining two onsite and sending two offsite should suffice. Remember, this method should be used only for stable data and is not recommended. The most desirable method is to use the DB2 COPY and RECOVER utilities and to execute the MODIFY utility on a tablespace-by-tablespace basis for each application.

Non-Critical Applications

Non-critical (Class 4 and possibly Class 5) applications should be considered only after complete disaster recovery procedures have been implemented for the critical applications. If you follow the procedures outlined in this chapter, you will have an exemplary disaster recovery plan for all your applications.

Sometimes, however, simple DSN1COPY data sets for each tablespace in the non-critical application suffice for offsite recovery. These should be taken when DB2 is not operational (or the application has been stopped). Because the application is non-critical, the DSN1COPY might need to be performed less frequently. This decision must be made on an application-by-application basis.

For some non-critical (pure Class 5) applications, the decision might be made not to develop disaster recovery procedures. This decision is valid only when the system can be lost completely. Obviously, application systems of this type are rare.

DB2 Environmental Considerations

Sometimes recovery is targeted to be performed at an alternative site that is already running DB2. This is not advisable. During a disaster, your whole machine will be lost. In addition to DB2, MVS, JES, and TSO, all other system software must be recovered. Your disaster recovery plan will become needlessly complex if you plan to recover to an existing system. Reconfiguring software that is already operational usually is more difficult than bringing everything up from scratch.

If you insist on a plan to recover to a DB2 subsystem that already exists, remember the following. All databases, tablespaces, tables, and indexes must be created at the remote site. This could be performed either at the time of the disaster (which is complex and error-prone) or before the disaster (which is easy but consumes resources). With either option, all DB2 objects must exist before the image copy data sets can be restored. This can be accomplished only by using the `DSN1COPY` service aid with the `OBIDXLAT` option.

You should maintain a comprehensive report that lists the `DBID` for each database, the `PSID` for each tablespace, and the `OBID` for each table in both DB2 subsystems. (`DBID`s, `PSID`s, and `OBID`s identify each object to DB2 and are stored in the DB2 Catalog.) A query to produce this report follows:

```
SELECT     S.DBNAME, S.DBID, S.NAME, S.PSID,
           T.CREATOR, T.NAME, T.OBID
FROM       SYSIBM.SYSTABLESPACE     S,
           SYSIBM.SYSTABLES         T
WHERE      S.DBNAME = T.DBNAME
AND        S.NAME   = T.TSNAME
AND        T.TYPE   = 'T'
ORDER BY S.DBNAME, S.DBID, S.NAME, S.PSID, T.CREATOR, T.NAME
```

A QMF form to create a formatted report using this query is presented in Listing 31.2. The report generated by this query should be sent to the remote site to assist with disaster recovery. The information can be used as a reference when using `DSN1COPY` with the `OBIDXLAT` option. This is the only way to accomplish recovery to a different DB2 subsystem.

Listing 31.2. QMF form to be used with the DBID/PSID/OBID query.

```
Total Width of Report Columns: 61

NUM  COLUMN HEADING      USAGE     INDENT   WIDTH   EDIT   SEQ
 1   DATABASE            BREAK1    1        8       C      1
 2   DBID                BREAK1    1        4       L      2
 3   TABLE_SPACE         BREAK2    1        8       C      3
```

continues

Listing 31.2. continued

```
4   PSID              BREAK2      1      4     L    4
5   TABLE_CREATOR                 1      8     C    5
6   TABLE_NAME                    1     18     C    6
7   OBID                          1      4     L    7
```

Data set management techniques also must be considered. If you allocate VSAM data sets for all production tablespaces and indexes, you must use AMS to create the underlying data sets before recovery at the remote site. If you use STOGROUPs, though, the data sets are allocated when the tablespaces and indexes are created.

DB2 Contingency Planning Guidelines

When developing your DB2 disaster recovery plan be sure to consider the following tips and techniques.

Plan Before a Disaster Strikes

Ensure that an adequate disaster recovery plan is in place for the DB2 subsystem. This involves backing up system data sets and system tablespaces and integrating the timing of the backups with the needs of each DB2 application.

Remember, the absolute worst time to devise a disaster recovery plan is *during* a disaster!

Create a Schedule to Ship Vital Image Copies Offsite Regularly

Remember that the RECOVER utility can recover only with the backup tapes sent to the remote site. Updates on the active log at the time of the disaster are lost, as are all archive logs and image copy backup tapes not sent offsite.

Ensure that every tablespace has a valid offsite image copy backup.

Do Not Forget to Back Up Other Vital DB2 Data

Copying DB2 tablespace data is not sufficient to ensure a complete disaster recovery plan. Be sure to back up and send offsite all related DB2 libraries, such as

- Any DB2 DDL libraries that might be required
- JCL and proc libraries
- DBRM libraries
- Application program load libraries
- Libraries and passwords for critical third-party DB2 products
- Stored procedure program load libraries
- Application program, stored procedure source code, and copy book libraries

Use SHRLEVEL REFERENCE for Offsite Copies

When running the COPY utility for offsite backup needs:

- Stop concurrent data modification to all tablespaces in the tablespace set using the STOP command or START ... ACCESS(RO).
- Use the SHRLEVEL REFERENCE clause.

Running COPY with SHRLEVEL CHANGE could result in inconsistent data and might cause the RECOVER utility to take longer to execute.

Beware of Compression

If your site uses tape-compression software, be sure that the offsite location to be used for disaster recovery uses the same tape-compression software. If it does not, specify the following JCL parm for any offsite image copy data set:

```
DCB=TRTCH=NOCOMP
```

Document Your Strategy

Document the backup strategy for each tablespace (sledgehammer, scalpel, DSN1COPY, or some other internally developed strategy). Document the state of each DB2 application and the DB2 subsystem by producing DB2 Catalog, DB2 Directory, and BSDS reports after producing your offsite backups. Send this information daily to your remote site.

Use an Appropriate Active Log Size

Keep the active log relatively small, but not so small that it affects system performance. Active logging poses a logistical problem. If a disaster strikes, the active log will be lost. Therefore, you will not be able to restore all DB2 data to its state just prior to the disaster. Remember, a disaster implies total loss of your machine or site. At best, data can be restored only back to the last archive log sent offsite. This is one reason to have small active logs, thereby forcing more frequent log archival. If DB2 provided the capability to remote log and remote copy, it would be technically possible to recover data back to its most recent state using remote logs and remote copies.

Automate Use of the ARCHIVE LOG Command

The ARCHIVE LOG command can be used within a job that is submitted periodically, forcing an archive log and creating a copy of the archive log for offsite recovery. This is an important component of the DB2 disaster recovery plan because the BSDS and the SYSIBM.SYSCOPY table, which play a substantial role in the recovery process, are backed up at log archival time. Be sure to put the appropriate procedures in place to move the archive log copies offsite as soon as feasible after the job completes. A tape that is still sitting in the shop when a disaster strikes will be useless for disaster recovery purposes.

Copy Each Tablespace After an Offsite Recovery

Back up each application's tablespaces at the remote site immediately after each application has been recovered.

Validate Your Offsite Recovery

Run a battery of SELECT statements against the recovered application tables to validate the state of the data.

Test Your Offsite Recovery Plan

Test your disaster recovery plan before a disaster occurs. This gives you time to correct problems before it is too late. It is wise to schedule at least yearly disaster recovery tests in which disaster conditions are mimicked. The DB2 environment should be recovered at the offsite location minimally once a year to ensure that the plan is up-to-date and able to be implemented in case of a disaster.

Appropriate Copying Is Dependent Upon Each Application

DB2 disaster recovery is a complex topic that deserves substantial attention. Each application must be analyzed to uncover its optimal disaster recovery strategy. The frequency of copying will be dependent upon the volatility of the data, the size of the batch window, the length of time allowable for an eventual recovery, and the frequency of log archival.

Summary

The guidelines in this chapter, combined with a comprehensive DB2 subsystem disaster plan, will provide a satisfactory disaster recovery mechanism for your corporation.

VII

The Ideal DB2 Environment

Until now, this book has concentrated on DB2 database management, design, and programming. It has delved into the components of DB2 and some of the complementary software packages used by most DB2 shops (such as QMF and DB2-PM). An ideal DB2 environment, however, consists of much more than DB2, QMF, and DB2-PM.

Section VII of this book expands the scope of discussion to include topics outside the general framework of DB2. In particular, this section discusses the features missing from DB2 and the many organizational issues that must be addressed in using DB2 at your shop.

This discussion includes also a categorization of software toolsets that alleviate the problems caused by DB2's lack of certain features, and a summary of some of the major vendors and the types of products they supply. This section also provides checklists to refer to in evaluating and implementing these value-added tools.

Finally, with the recent explosion of information available on the Internet and the World Wide Web, it is inevitable that many unique and useful sources of DB2 information can be accessed via the Web. As such, a description of what is available and how to find it is also provided.

32

Components of a Total DB2 Solution

DB2, as delivered out of the box, is a relatively complete, full-function relational database management system. An organization can install DB2 as delivered, but it will realize quickly that the functionality needed to adequately support large-scale DB2 development is not provided by DB2 alone.

The administration and maintenance of DB2 applications is time-consuming if you use the standard features of the DB2 database management system as supplied by IBM. Fortunately, a host of tools enhance the functionality of DB2, thereby easing the administrative burden and reducing the possibilities of error.

DB2 Tools

The need for these tools can be seen by the number of them available. Most DB2 shops implement one or more add-on tools for DB2. Of these, IBM's QMF and DB2-PM are among the most popular. Many more tools from other vendors fill market niches not adequately supported by IBM. Table 32.1 provides a rundown of the categories of products.

Table 32.1. Categories of DB2 products.

Abbrev.	*Tool Category Definition*
ALT	Tools that administer the SQL necessary to change DB2 objects without losing either authorization or other, dependent objects.
AUD	Tools that read the DB2 logs and report on data modification and database changes. May also create re-apply SQL from log images.
CAT	Tools that enable panel-driven (or GUI-based) access to the DB2 Catalog without having to code actual SQL queries.
COM	Tools that reduce data storage requirements using compression algorithms.
C/S	DB2-related client/server tools for building applications, connecting databases, or enabling remote access. Include middleware and gateways.
DBA	Database administration and analysis tools that enable a DBA to determine when to reorganize tablespaces and indexes. Useful for implementing proactive tuning.
DES	Database modeling and design tools such as upper CASE tools, entity-relationships diagramming tools, and tools to enable logical to physical model translation.
DSD	Tools that monitor and manage DB2 DASD and space management.
EDT	Tools that provide an ISPF (or GUI-based) editor for accessing,

Abbrev.	*Tool Category Definition*
	manipulating, and modifying data in DB2 tables. Data is typically displayed using a spreadsheet-like interface and can be modified simply by over-typing (instead of issuing SQL statements).
INT	Tools that manage and implement data integrity (check constraints) and referential integrity (RI).
MIG	Tools that create and administer the requisite SQL to migrate DB2 objects from one DB2 subsystem to another.
MOV	Tools that move data from environment to environment, such as from IMS to DB2.
MSC	Miscellaneous tools (do not fit into one of the other categories).
NET	Tools that enable DB2 databases to be connected to the Internet, an intranet, and the World Wide Web.
OPR	Operational support tools, such as on-line DB2 standards manuals, change control systems, and schedulers.
PC	PC- and workstation-based DBMSs that mimic DB2 execution such that application development chores can be offloaded from the mainframe.
PLN	Tools that analyze and evaluate the access paths for individual SQL statements and SQL in plans and packages. May also provide suggestions for how to improve the SQL.
PM	DB2 performance monitors.
PRF	Products to enhance performance.
PRG	Tools that assist the application developer, such as lower CASE tools, 4GLs, SQL generation tools, SQL formatting tools, and application testing tools.
QMF	Tools that augment the functionality and/or enhance the performance of QMF. Examples include query compilers and QMF object administration tools.
QRY	Tools that provide an integrated environment for developing and issuing queries against DB2 tables. May be ISPF- or GUI-based.
REP	Tools that store, manage, and enable access to metadata (such as repositories and data dictionaries).
SEC	Security tools.
UTL	Tools that generate DB2 utility JCL or enhance DB2 utility functions by providing faster, more efficient execution.

These types of add-on tools can significantly improve the efficiency of DB2 application development. In the following sections, each category is described, along with a checklist of features. In evaluating products, look for features important to your organization. These lists are not comprehensive, but they provide a starting point for the evaluation process.

Table Altering Tools (ALT)

DB2 provides the capability to modify the structure of existing objects using the ALTER DDL statement. The ALTER statement, however, is a functionally crippled statement. You should be able to alter all the parameters that can be specified for an object when it is created, but DB2 does not support this. For example, you can add columns to an existing table (only at the end), but you can never remove columns from a table. The table must be dropped and then re-created without the columns you want to remove.

Another problem that DBAs encounter in modifying DB2 objects is the cascading drop effect. If a change to a tablespace mandates its being dropped and re-created (for example, changing the limit keys of a partitioned tablespace), all dependent objects are dropped when the tablespace is dropped. This includes the following:

- All tables in the tablespace
- All information in SYSCOPY (including image copy information)
- All indexes on the tables
- Primary and foreign keys
- Check constraints
- Synonyms and views
- Labels and comments
- FIELDPROC and EDITPROC assignments
- RUNSTATS values
- All authorization below the tablespace level statistics

Ensuring that DDL is issued after the modification to reverse the effects of cascading drops can be a tedious, complex, and error-prone procedure.

Many types of DB2 object alteration cannot be performed using the generic DB2 ALTER statement. Several examples follow:

- You cannot change the name of a database, alias, view, column, constraint, tablespace, or index.
- You cannot create a database based on the attributes of an existing database.
- You cannot create a tablespace based on the attributes of an existing tablespace.
- You cannot change the database in which the tablespace exists.
- You cannot change the number of tablespace partitions.
- You cannot remove a tablespace (or index) partition.
- You cannot change the tablespace type (for example, changing a simple tablespace to a segmented or partitioned tablespace).
- You cannot change the SEGSIZE of a segmented tablespace.

You cannot copy primary and foreign keys using `CREATE LIKE`; this command creates a new table based on the columns of another table.
You cannot move a table from one tablespace to another.
You cannot rearrange column ordering.
You cannot change a column's data type and length.
You cannot remove columns from a table.
You cannot change the primary key without dropping and adding the primary key.
You cannot add to a table a column specified as `NOT NULL`.
You cannot add any columns to a table defined with an `EDITPROC`.
You cannot add columns to a table defined with an `EDITPROC`.
You cannot change a table's `EDITPROC` or a column's `VALIDPROC`.
You cannot create a view based on another view.
You cannot add columns to, or remove columns from, a view.
You cannot change the `SELECT` statement on which the view is based.
You cannot create an index based on another index.
You cannot change the index columns.
You cannot change the partitioning information (`LIMITKEY`).
You cannot change the clustering specification.
You cannot change the number of index subpages (Type 1 indexes).
You cannot change the index order (ascending or descending).
You cannot create an alias based on another alias.
You cannot change the location of the alias.
You cannot change the table on which the alias is based.

This list provides all the justification needed to obtain an alter tool. A tool provides an integrated environment for altering DB2 objects. The burden of ensuring that a change to a DB2 object does not cause other implicit changes is moved from the DBA to the tool.

At a minimum, an alter tool should perform the following functions:

- Maintain tables easily without manually coding SQL.
- Retain or reapply all dependent objects and security affected by the requested alter if a drop is required.
- Retain or reapply all statistical information for dropped objects.
- Navigate hierarchically from object to object, making alterations as it goes.
- Provide panel-driven modification showing before and after definitions of the DB2 objects before the changes are applied.
- Batch requested changes into a work list that can be executed in the foreground or the background.
- Analyze changes to ensure that the requested alterations do not violate any DB2 DDL rules. For example, if a series of changes is requested and one change causes a subsequent change to be invalid (an object is dropped, for instance), this should be flagged before execution.

- Control the environment in which alters are executed.
- Be capable of monitoring changes as they are applied.

Refer to Checklist 1 for a form you can use to evaluate DB2 object altering tools. Each section provides a similar evaluation form for the tool category being discussed. The forms can be copied as needed. Blank lines are provided so that you can add features needed by your shop, and space is provided to evaluate as many as four vendors.

NOTE

All evaluation checklists appear at the end of this chapter.

I favor assigning each row a weight. For example, the feature in the first row could be worth 6 points, whereas the feature in the second row could be worth 20 points. You can then evaluate the features of each tool, assigning values in the assigned range. The tool with the highest cumulative score (adding each column) provides the best product for your needs.

Auditing Tools (AUD)

An audit is the examination of a practice to determine its correctness. DB2 auditing software therefore should help in monitoring the data control, data definition, and data integrity in the DB2 environment. Several mechanisms provided by DB2 enable the creation of an audit trail, but this trail can be difficult to follow.

The primary vehicle provided by DB2 for auditing is the audit trace. This feature enables DB2 to trace and record auditable activity initiated by specific users. When the DB2 audit trace is activated, the following type of information can be captured to the trace destination:

Authorization failures
Grant and revoke SQL statements
DDL issued against auditable tables
DML issued against auditable tables
Bind requests involving auditable tables
Authorization ID changes requested by the `SET CURRENT SQLID` statement
Utility executions

An *auditable table* is any table defined to DB2 with the `AUDIT` clause of the `CREATE TABLE` statement. There are three options for table auditing: `NONE`, `CHANGES`, and `ALL`. Specifying `AUDIT NONE`, which is the default, disables table auditing so that the audit trace does not track that table. Specifying `AUDIT CHANGES` indicates that the first `DELETE`, `INSERT`, or `UPDATE` statement issued against that table in every application unit of work (`COMMIT` scope) is recorded. `AUDIT ALL` records the first DML statement of any type accessing this table in each application unit of work. Note, however, that this information is tracked only if the appropriate audit trace is activated. Refer o Chapter 17, "Traditional DB2 Performance Monitoring," for more information on DB2 udit traces.

'his information is written to the output trace destination specified for the audit trace. DB2 race records can be written to GTF, SMF, or an OP buffer. After the information has been vritten to the specified destination, the problem of how to read this information still exists. If ou have DB2-PM, you can run the appropriate audit reports, but even these can be insuffiient for true auditing.

n audit tool should provide five important features that DB2's audit tracing capability does ot. DB2 auditing requires a trace to be activated, and this can quickly become expensive if nany tables must be audited. The first feature an auditing tool should provide is the capability o read the DB2 logs, which are always produced, and report on update activity as needed. 'his reduces overhead because it uses the regular processing features of DB2 rather than an dditional tracing feature, which increases overhead.

'he DB2 audit trace records a trace record only for the first statement in a unit of work. The econd feature of the auditing tool is reporting all data modification from the DB2 logs.

'he DB2 audit trace facility does not record the specifics of the data modification. The third eature of an auditing tool is reporting who (by authorization ID) makes each change, and also howing a before and after image of the changed data.

'he fourth feature the auditing tool should provide is the capability to report on the DB2 audit race data if so desired.

fifth feature of a DB2 auditing tool is to access the DB2 logs to create re-do SQL scripts that an be run to re-apply data modifications that occurred during a specific timespan. Although his feature is optional for the auditing functionality of such tools, it is a common feature since uditing tools by their very nature must access the DB2 logs.

inally, the auditing tool should provide both standard reports and the capability to create sitepecific reports (either from the log or from the DB2 audit trace data).

f your shop has strict auditing requirements, an auditing tool is almost mandatory because of)B2's weak inherent auditing capabilities. Refer to Checklist 2 for the auditing tools evaluaon form.

)B2 Catalog Query and Analysis Tools (CAT)

'he DB2 Catalog contains a wealth of information essential to the operation of DB2. Infornation about all DB2 objects, authority, and recovery is stored and maintained in the DB2 'atalog. This system catalog is composed of DB2 tables and can be queried using SQL. The ata returned by these queries provides a base of information for many DB2 monitoring and dministrative tasks.

'oding SQL can be a time-consuming process. Often, you must combine information from nultiple DB2 Catalog tables to provide the user with facts relevant for a particular task. This can be verified by reexamining the DB2 Catalog queries presented in Chapter 19, "DB2 Object Monitoring Using the DB2 Catalog."

Add-on tools can ease the burden of developing DB2 Catalog queries. The basic feature common to all DB2 Catalog tools is the capability to request DB2 Catalog information using a screen-driven interface without coding SQL statements. Analysts can obtain rapid access to specific facts stored in the DB2 Catalog without the burden of coding (sometimes quite complex) SQL. Furthermore, procedural logic is sometimes required to adequately query specific types of catalog information.

DB2 V2.3 introduced Catalog Visibility, a screen-driven interface to DB2 that enabled users to access DB2 Catalog data, without coding SQL. This feature provided some of the rudimentary DB2 Catalog querying features needed by most shops, but it was far from complete. Most DB2 Catalog tools provide much more capability than Catalog Visibility (which is no longer available as of DB2 V3). Instead of merely enabling data access, many DB2 Catalog tools can do one or more of the following:

- Create syntactically correct DDL statements for all DB2 objects by reading the appropriate DB2 Catalog tables. These statements are generally executed immediately or saved in a sequential data set for future reference or use.
- Modify the "updateable" DB2 Catalog statistical columns using an editor interface (for example, a non-SQL interface).
- Create syntactically correct DCL statements from the DB2 Catalog in the same way that DDL is generated.
- Perform "drop analysis" on a `SQL DROP` statement. This analysis determines the effect of the cascading drop by detailing all dependent objects and security that will be deleted as a result of executing the `DROP`.
- Provide a hierarchical listing of DB2 objects. For example, if a specific table is chosen, the tool can migrate quickly up the hierarchy to show its tablespace and database, or down the hierarchy to show all dependent indexes, views, synonyms, aliases, referentially connected tables, and plans.
- Create and drop DB2 objects, and grant and revoke DB2 security from a screen without coding SQL. Additionally, some tools log all drops and revokes so that they can be undone in the event of an inadvertent drop or revoke execution.
- Specify the ISOLATION clause to access DB2 data using cursor stability, repeatable read, read stability, or uncommitted read processing.
- Operate on the DB2 Catalog or on a copy of the DB2 Catalog to reduce system-wide contention.

These features aid the DBA in performing his day-to-day duties. Furthermore, a catalog query tool can greatly diminish the amount of time required for a junior DBA to become a productive member of the DBA team.

The evaluation form for DB2 Catalog management tools is presented in Checklist 3.

Compression Tools (COM)

A standard tool for reducing DASD costs is the compression utility. This type of tool operates by applying an algorithm to the data in a table so that the data is encoded in a more compact area. By reducing the amount of area needed to store data, DASD costs are decreased. Compression tools must compress the data when it is added to the table and subsequently modified, then expand the data when it is later retrieved. (See Figure 32.1.)

Third-party compression routines are specified for DB2 tables using the `EDITPROC` clause of the `CREATE TABLE` statement. The load module name for the compression routine is supplied as the parameter to the `EDITPROC` clause. A table must be dropped and re-created to apply an `EDITPROC`.

In general, a compression algorithm increases CPU costs while providing benefits in the areas of decreased DASD utilization and sometimes decreased I/O costs. This trade-off is not beneficial for all tables. For example, if a compression routine saves 30 percent on DASD costs but increases CPU without decreasing I/O, the trade-off is probably not beneficial.

FIGURE 32.1.
A DB2 table compression routine at work.

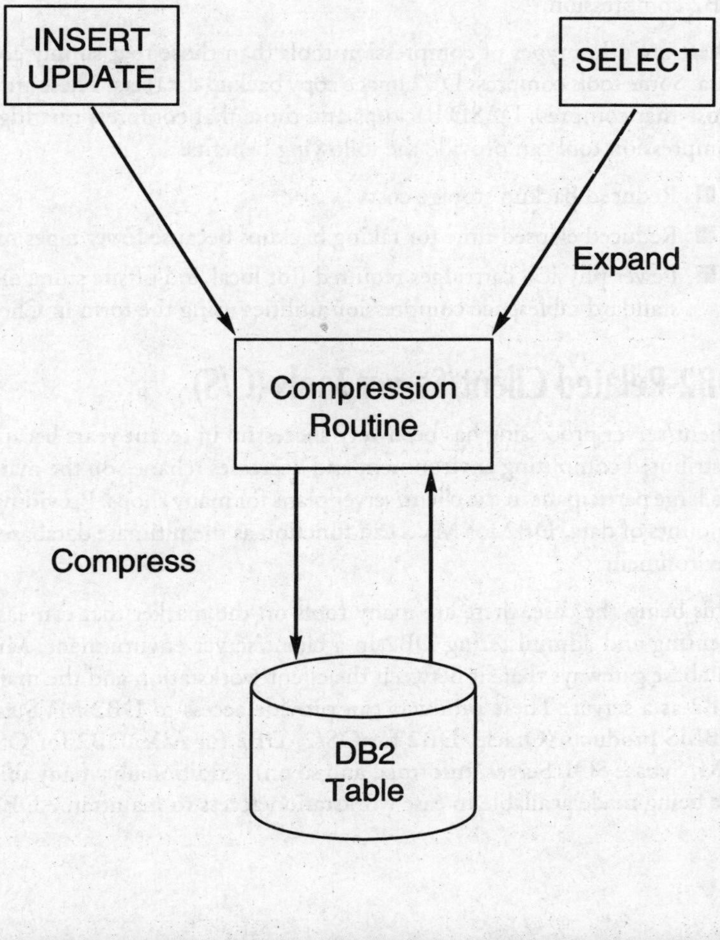

A compression tool can decrease DASD by reducing the size of the rows to be stored. CPU use usually increases because additional processing is required to compress and expand the row. I/O costs, however, could decrease.

Enhancements to DB2 since V2.3 have made most third-party compression tools of little added value. DB2 V2.3 provided a basic compression routine called DSN8HUFF. Still, most third-party compression tools provided more efficient compression algorithms and advanced analysis to determine the costs and benefits of compression for a specific table. This changed dramatically with DB2 V3. The internal compression capabilities of DB2 since V3 have caused DB2 compression to outperform most third-party compression tools. Even when a third-party compression tool can provide benefit to an organization (perhaps because it offers multiple compression routines geared for different types of data), the return on investment is such that most shops typically stick with internal DB2 compression for new tables. The third-party compression tools, however, are here to stay as legacy compression tools. This phenomenon exists because most shops are too busy with production work (and Year 2000 conversions) to support the additional work required to remove the third party EDITPROC and replace it with internal DB2 compression.

There are other types of compression tools than those that simply compress DB2 tablespace data. Some tools compress DB2 image copy backup data sets. These are divided into two camps: those that compress DASD backups and those that compress cartridge backups. This type of compression tool can provide the following benefits:

- Reduced backup storage costs
- Reduced elapsed time for taking backups because fewer tapes must be loaded
- Fewer physical cartridges required (for local and offsite storage). You can evaluate standard tablespace compression utilities using the form in Checklist 4.

DB2-Related Client/Server Tools (C/S)

Client/server processing has been very successful in recent years because it provides a flexible, distributed computing environment and decreases reliance on the mainframe. However, DB2 is a large participant in the client/server plans for many shops. Providing efficient access to large amounts of data, DB2 for MVS can function as the ultimate database server in a client/server environment.

This being the case, there are many tools on the market that can ease the burden of implementing and administering DB2 in a client/server environment. Middleware products and database gateways that sit between the client workstation and the mainframe enable access to DB2 as a server. These products can provide access to DB2 MVS as well as to other server DBMS products (Oracle, DB2 for OS/2, DB2 for AIX, DB2 for OS/400, DB2 for VSE & VM, Sybase SQL Server, Informix, and so on). Additionally, many third-party ODBC drivers are being made available to ease workstation access to mainframe DB2 data.

Another valid type of client/server tool is a 4GL programming environment that provides seamless access to DB2. These types of products typically split the application workload between the workstation and the server aiding the programmer to rapidly develop DB2 client/server applications.

You can evaluate client/server tools using the form in Checklist 6.

Database Analysis Tools (DBA)

DB2 does not provide an intelligent database analysis capability. Instead, a database administrator or performance analyst must keep a vigilant watch over DB2 objects using DB2 Catalog queries or a DB2 Catalog tool. This is not an optimal solution, because it relies on human intervention for efficient database organization, opening up the possibility of human error, forgetting to monitor, and misinterpreting analyzed data.

Fortunately, database analysis tools can proactively and automatically monitor your DB2 environment. This monitoring can perform the following functions:

- Collect statistics for DB2 tablespaces and indexes. These statistics can be standard DB2 RUNSTATS information, extended statistics capturing more information (for example, data set extents), or a combination of both.
- Read the VSAM data sets for the DB2 objects to capture current statistics, read RUNSTATS from the DB2 Catalog, read tables unique to the tool that captured the enhanced statistics, or any combination of these three.
- Set thresholds, whereby the automatic scheduling of the REORG utility is invoked based on current statistics.
- Provide a series of canned reports detailing the potential problems for specific DB2 objects.

Checklist 7 is the evaluation form for DB2 database analysis tools.

Database Modeling and Design Tools (DES)

Database modeling and design tools do not have to be unique to DB2 design, although many are. Application development should be based on sound data and process models. The use of a tool to ensure this is a good practice.

Database modeling and design tools may be referred to as CASE tools. CASE, or computer-aided software engineering, is the process of automating the application development life cycle. A CASE tool, such as a data modeling tool, supports portions of that life cycle. A comprehensive checklist of features to look for in a CASE tool is presented in Chapter 8, "Alternative DB2 Application Development Methods." Although CASE tools were very popular in the late 1980s and early 1990s, they have not been in vogue during the latter half of the 1990s.

Many excellent database design and modeling tools are not specifically designed for DB2 but can be used to develop DB2 applications. Tools developed specifically to support DB2 development, however, add another dimension to the application development effort. They can significantly reduce the development timeframe by automating repetitive tasks and validating the models. If your organization decides to obtain a CASE tool that specifically supports DB2, look for one that can do the following:

- Provide standard features of logical data modeling (such as entity-relationship diagramming and normalization).
- Create a physical data model geared to DB2. This model should support all features of DB2, such as the capability to depict all DB2 objects, referential integrity, VCAT and STOGROUP-defined tablespaces, and capacity planning.
- Provide an expert system to verify the accuracy of the physical data model and to suggest alternative solutions.
- Cross-reference the logical model to the physical model, capturing text that supports physical design decisions such as denormalization and the choice of tablespace type.
- Automatically generate DB2-standard DDL to fully implement the database defined in the physical data model.
- Interface with application development tools and data dictionaries available to the organization.

DASD and Space Management Tools (DSD)

DB2 provides basic statistics for space utilization in the DB2 Catalog, but the in-depth statistics required for both space management and performance tuning are woefully inadequate. The queries presented in Chapter 16, "Locking DB2 Data," form a basis for DB2 DASD management, but critical elements are missing.

Chief among the missing elements of DASD space management in DB2 is the capability to monitor the space requirements of the underlying VSAM data sets and to maintain historical growth information. When these data sets go into secondary extents, performance suffers. Without a DASD management tool, the only way to monitor secondary extents is to periodically examine LISTCAT output. This is a tedious exercise.

Additionally, the manner in which DB2 allocates space can result in the inefficient use of DASD. Often space is allocated but DB2 does not use it. Although the STOSPACE utility, combined with DB2 queries, provides limited out-of-the-box DASD management, this capability is far from robust. A DASD management tool is the only answer for ferreting out the amount of allocated space versus the amount of used space.

DASD management tools often interface with other DB2 and DASD support tools such as standard MVS space management tools, database analysis tools, DB2 Catalog query and management tools, and DB2 utility JCL generators. The evaluation of DASD management tools can be administered using Checklist 8.

DB2 Table Editors (EDT)

The only method of updating DB2 data is with the SQL data manipulation language statements `DELETE`, `INSERT`, and `UPDATE`. Because these SQL statements operate on data a set at a time, multiple rows—or even all of the rows—can be affected by a single SQL statement. Coding SQL statements for every data modification required during the application development and testing phase can be time-consuming.

A DB2 table editing tool reduces the time needed to make simple data alterations by providing full-screen edit capability for DB2 tables. The user specifies the table to edit and is placed in an edit session that resembles the ISPF editor. The data is presented to the user as a series of rows, with the columns separated by spaces. A header line indicates the column names. The data can be scrolled up and down, as well as left and right. To change data, the user simply types over the current data.

This type of tool is ideal for supporting the application development process. A programmer can make quick changes without coding SQL. Also, if properly implemented, a table editor can reduce the number of erroneous data modifications made by beginning SQL users.

CAUTION

Remember that the table editor is issuing SQL in the background to implement the requested changes. This can cause a lag between the time the user updates the data and the time the data is committed. Table editor updates usually are committed only when the user requests that the data be saved or when the user backs out of the edit session without canceling.

Remember too that table editors can consume a vast amount of resources. Ensure that the tool can limit the number of rows to be read into the editing session. For example, can the tool set a filter such that only the rows meeting certain search criteria are read? Can a limit be set on the number of rows to be read into any one edit session? Without this capability, large tablespace scans can result.

A DB2 table editor should be used only in the testing environment. End users or programmers might request that a table editor be made available for production data modification. This should be avoided at all costs. The data in production tables is critical to the success of your organization and should be treated with great care. Production data modification should be accomplished only with thoroughly tested SQL or production plans.

When a table editor is used, all columns are available for update. Thus, if a table editor is used to change production data, a simple miskeying can cause unwanted updates. Native SQL should be used if you must ensure that only certain columns are updated.

Tested SQL statements and application plans are characterized by their planned nature. The modification requests were well-thought-out and tested. This is not true for changes implemented through a table editor.

Additionally, tested SQL statements and application plans are characterized by their planned nature. The modification requests were well-thought-out and tested. This is not true for changes implemented through a table editor.

Checklist 9 is the tool evaluation form for DB2 table editors.

Integrity Tools (INT)

Referential integrity has been available on DB2 since DB2 V2.1. However, it has always been difficult to administer and implement. RI tools eliminate the difficulty by performing one of the following functions:

- Analyzing data for both system- and user-managed referential integrity constraint violations
- Executing faster than the IBM-provided CHECK utility
- Enabling additional types of RI to be supported; for example, analyzing primary keys for which no foreign keys exist and deleting the primary key row

Version 4

Check constraints for data integrity have been available with DB2 since V4. Tools can help implement and maintain check constraints in the following ways:

- Analyzing data for both system- and user-managed data integrity constraint violations
- Executing faster than the IBM-provided CHECK utility
- Enabling additional types of data integrity to be supported; for example, analyzing the compatibility of check constraints and user-defined DEFAULT clauses

DB2 Object Migration Tools (MIG)

DB2 does not provide a feature to migrate DB2 objects from one subsystem to another. This can be accomplished only by manually storing the CREATE DDL statements (and all subsequent ALTER statements) for future application in another system. Manual processes such as this are error-prone. Also, this process does not take into account the migration of table data, DB2 security, plans, packages, statistics, and so on.

DB2 object migration tools facilitate the quick migration of DB2 objects from one DB2 subsystem to another. They are similar to a table altering tool but have a minimal altering capability (some interface directly with an alter tool or are integrated into a single tool). The migration procedure is usually driven by SPF panels that prompt the user for the objects to migrate.

Migration typically can be specified at any level. For example, if you request the migration of a specific database, you also could migrate all dependent objects and security. Minimal renaming capability is provided so that database names, authorization IDs, and other objects are renamed according to the standards of the receiving subsystem. When the parameters of the migration have been specified completely, the tool creates a job stream to implement the requested DB2 objects in the requested DB2 subsystem.

A migration tool reduces the time required by database administrators to move DB2 databases from environment to environment (for example, from test to production). Quicker turnaround results in a more rapid response to user needs, thereby increasing the efficiency of your business.

Typically, migration tools are the second DB2 tool that an organization acquires (right after a DB2 Catalog query product).

To evaluate DB2 migration utilities, refer to Checklist 10.

Data Movement Tools (MOV)

At times, multiple database management systems coexist in data processing shops. This is increasingly true as shops embark on client/server initiatives. Additionally, the same data might need to be stored in each of the databases. In a multiple DBMS environment, the movement of data from DBMS to DBMS is a tedious task. The need to move data from one environment to another is increasing with the overwhelming acceptance and implementation of data warehouses.

Data movement tools ease the burden because the tool understands the data format and environment of each DBMS it works with. The data movement and warehousing tool(s) that a shop chooses depends on the following factors:

- How many DBMS products need to be supported?
- To what extent is the data replicated across the DBMS products?
- What transformations need to occur as the data is moved from one environment to another? For example, how are data types converted for DBMSs that do not support date, time, and timestamp date (or that support these data types using a different format)?
- Does the data have to be synchronized across DBMS products?
- Is the data static or dynamic?
- If it is dynamic, is it updated online, in batch, or both?

The answers to these questions help determine the type of data conversion tool necessary.

Two basic types of conversion tools are popular in the market today:

Replication tools	These tools extract data from external application systems and other databases for population into DB2 tables. This type of tool can extract data from VSAM, IMS, Sybase, Oracle, flat files, or other structures and insert the data into DB2.
Propagation tools	Inserts data from external applications and other database products into DB2 tables. A propagation tool is similar in function to an extract tool, but propagation tools are active. They constantly capture updates made in the external system, either for immediate application to DB2 tables or for subsequent batch updating. This differs from the extract tool, which captures entire data structures, not data modifications.

You can evaluate data movement tools using the form in Checklist 5.

Miscellaneous Tools (MSC)

Many types of DB2 tools are available. The categories in this chapter cover the major types of DB2 tools, but not all tools can be easily pigeonholed. For example, consider a DB2 tablespace calculator. It reads table DDL and information on the number of rows in the table to estimate space requirements. A space calculator is often provided with another tool, such as a DASD management tool or a database design and modeling tool.

Internet Enabling Tools (NET)

The Internet is the hottest technology trend of the 1990s. Every organization is looking for ways to increase their competitive advantage by making corporate data available to customers, partners, and employees over the Internet, intranets, and extranets.

A specialized category of tools is available to hook DB2 data to the Web. These tools are referred to as Internet-enabling tools. For more information on the Internet and IBM's tools for connecting the Web to DB2, refer to Chapter 10, "DB2 and the Internet."

Operational Support Tools (OPR)

Many avenues encompass operational support in a DB2 environment, ranging from standards and procedures to tools that guarantee smoother operation. This section describes tools from several operational support categories.

One type of operational support tool provides online access to DB2 standards and procedures. These tools are commonly populated with model DB2 standards and procedures that can be modified or extended. Tools of this nature are ideal for a shop with little DB2 experience that wants to launch a DB2 project. As the shop grows, the standards and procedures can grow with it.

Another type of product delivers online access to DB2 manuals. With this tool, you avoid the cost of purchasing DB2 manuals for all programmers, and DB2 information and error messages are always available online. In addition, analysts and DBAs who dial in to the mainframe from home can reference DB2 manuals online rather than keeping printed copies at home. IBM's Book Manager is an example of this type of tool.

Products also exist that provide "canned" standards for implementing, accessing, and administering DB2 databases. These tools are particularly useful for shops new to DB2. By purchasing an online standards manual, these shops can quickly come up-to-speed with DB2. However, mature DB2 shops can also benefit from these types of products if the third-party vendor automatically ships updates whenever IBM ships a new release of DB2. This can function as cheap training in the new DB2 release. A product containing DB2 standards should fulfill the following requirements:

- Provide online access via the mainframe or a networked PC environment, so all developers and DBAs can access the manual
- Be extensible, so additional standards can be added
- Be modifiable, so the provided standards can be altered to suit prior shop standards (naming conventions, programming standards, and so on)

Tools also exist to enable a better batch interface to DB2. Standard batch DB2 programs run under the control of the TSO terminal monitor program, IKJEFT01. Another operational support tool provides a call-attach interface that enables DB2 batch programs to run as a standard MVS batch job without the TSO TMP.

DB2, unlike IMS, provides no inherent capability for storing checkpoint information. Tools that store checkpoint information that can be used by the program during a subsequent restart are useful for large batch DB2 applications issuing many `COMMIT`s.

One final type of operational support tool assists in managing changes. These tools are typically integrated into a change control tool that manages program changes. Change control implemented for DB2 can involve version control, plan and package management, and ensuring that timestamp mismatches (`SQLCODE -818`) are avoided. Some tools can even control changes to DB2 objects.

PC-Based DB2 Emulation Products (PC)

Personal computers are everywhere now. Most data processing professionals have one on their desk. Most end users do, too. As such, the need to access DB2 from the PC is a viable one. However, not everyone needs to do this in a *client/server* environment.

Sometimes, just simple access from a PC will suffice. For this, a PC query tool can be used. Data requests originate from the PC workstation. The tool sends the requests to the mainframe for processing.

When processing is finished, the data is returned to the PC and formatted. These types of tools typically use a graphical user interface with pull-down menus and point-and-click functionality. These features are not available on mainframe products.

Another increasingly popular approach to developing DB2 applications is to create a similar environment on the PC. This can be done using a PC DBMS that works like DB2 and other similar PC products that mimic the mainframe (COBOL, IMS/TM, CICS, JCL, and so on).

Quite often, tools that can be used in a straight PC environment also can be used in a client/server environment.

Plan Analysis Tools (PLN)

The development of SQL to access DB2 tables is the responsibility of an application development team. With SQL's flexibility, the same request can be made in different ways. Because some of these ways are inefficient, the performance of an application's SQL could fluctuate wildly unless it is analyzed by an expert before implementation.

The DB2 `EXPLAIN` command provides information about the access paths used by SQL queries by parsing SQL in application programs and placing encoded output into a DB2 `PLAN_TABLE`. To gauge efficiency, a DBA must decode the `PLAN_TABLE` data and determine whether a more efficient access path is available.

SQL code reviews are required to ensure that optimal SQL design techniques are used. SQL code walkthroughs are typically performed by a DBA or someone with experience in SQL coding. This walkthrough must consist of reviews of the SQL statements, the selected access paths, and the program code in which the SQL is embedded. It also includes an evaluation of the `RUNSTATS` information to ascertain whether production-level statistics were used at the time of the `EXPLAIN`.

A line-by-line review of application source code and `EXPLAIN` output is tedious and prone to error, and it can cause application backlogs. A plan analysis tool can greatly simplify this process by automating major portions of the code review process. A plan analysis tool can typically perform the following functions:

- Analyze the SQL in an application program, describing the access paths chosen in a graphic format, an English description, or both.
- Issue warnings when specific SQL constructs are encountered. For example, each time a sort is requested (by `ORDER BY`, `GROUP BY`, or `DISTINCT`), a message is presented informing the user of the requisite sort.
- Suggest alternative SQL solutions based on an "expert system" that reads SQL statements and their corresponding `PLAN_TABLE` entries and poses alternate SQL options.
- Extend the rules used by the "expert system" to capture site-specific rules.

- Analyze at the subsystem, application, plan, package, or SQL statement level.
- Store multiple versions of EXPLAIN output and create performance comparison and plan history reports.

Currently, no tool can analyze the performance of the COBOL code in which the SQL is embedded. For example, consider an application program that embeds a singleton SELECT inside a loop. The singleton SELECT requests a single row based on a predicate, checking for the primary key of that table. The primary key value is changed for each iteration of the loop so that the entire table is read from the lowest key value to the highest key value.

A plan analysis tool will probably not flag the SQL statement because the predicate value is for the primary key, which causes an indexed access. It could be more efficient to code a cursor, without a predicate, to retrieve every row of the table, and then fetch each row one by one. This method might use sequential prefetch or query I/O parallelism, reducing I/O and elapsed time, and thereby enhancing performance. This type of design problem can be caught only by a trained analyst during a code walkthrough. Plan analysis tools also miss other potential problems, such as when the program has two cursors that should be coded as a one-cursor join. Although a plan analysis tool significantly reduces the effort involved in the code review process, it cannot eliminate it.

Following are some required features for a plan analysis tool:

- It must be capable of interpreting standard DB2 EXPLAIN output and present the information in an easy to understand (preferably graphical) format.
- It must automatically scan application source code and PLAN_TABLEs, reporting on the selected access paths and the predicted performance.
- It must be able to provide a historical record of access paths by program, package, plan, or SQL statement.

Checklist 11 provides an evaluation form for plan analysis tools.

Performance Monitors (PM)

Performance monitoring and tuning can be one of the most time-consuming tasks for large or critical DB2 applications. This topic was covered in depth in Parts V, "DB2 Performance Monitoring," and VI, "DB2 Utilities and Commands." DB2 performance monitoring and analysis tools support many features in many ways. For example, DB2 performance tools can operate as follows:

- In the background mode as a batch job reporting on performance statistics written by the DB2 trace facility
- In the foreground mode as an online monitor that either traps DB2 trace information using the instrumentation facility interface or captures information from DB2 control blocks as DB2 applications execute

- By sampling the DB2 and user address spaces as the program runs and by capturing information about the performance of the job independent of DB2 traces
- By capturing DB2 trace information and maintaining it in a history file (or table) for producing historical performance reports and for predicting performance trends
- As a capacity-planning device by giving the tool statistical information about a DB2 application and the environment in which it will operate
- As an after-the-fact analysis tool on a PC workstation for analyzing and graphing all aspects of DB2 application performance and system-wide DB2 performance

DB2 performance tools support one or more of these features. The evaluation of DB2 performance monitors is a complex task. Often more than one performance monitor is used at a single site. The evaluation form in Checklist 12 should be adapted to the type of DB2 performance monitor or monitors that your organization requires. For more information on DB2 performance monitoring and tuning, refer to Parts V and VI.

Products to Enhance Performance (PRF)

Performance is an important facet of DB2 database administration. Many shops dedicate several analysts to tweaking and tuning SQL, DB2, and its environment to elicit every performance enhancement possible. If your shop falls into this category, several tools on the market enhance the performance of DB2 by adding functionality directly to DB2. These DB2 performance tools can interact with the base code of DB2 and provide enhanced performance. Typically, these products take advantage of known DB2 shortcomings.

For example, products exist to perform the following functions:

- Enable DSNZPARMs to be changed without recycling DB2
- Enhance the performance of reading a DB2 page
- Enhance DB2 bufferpool processing

Care must be taken when evaluating DB2 performance tools. New releases of DB2 might negate the need for these tools because functionality was added or a known shortcoming was corrected. However, this does not mean that you should not consider performance tools. They can pay for themselves after only a short period of time. Discarding the tool when DB2 supports its functionality is not a problem if the tool has already paid for itself in terms of better performance.

CAUTION

Because these tools interact very closely with DB2, be careful when migrating to a new release of DB2 or a new release of the tool. Extra testing should be performed with these tools because of their intrusive nature.

DB2 Programming and Development Tools (PRG)

Often times, application development efforts require the population and maintenance of large test beds for system integration, unit, and user testing. A category of testing tools exists to facilitate this requirement. Testing tools enable an application developer or quality assurance analyst to issue a battery of tests against a test base and analyze the results. Testing tools are typically used for all types of applications and are extended to support testing against DB2 tables.

Many other types of tools enhance the DB2 application development effort. These DB2 programming and development tools can perform as follows:

- Compare two DB2 tables to determine the differences. These tools enable the output from modified programs to be tested to determine the impact of code change on application output.
- Enable the testing of SQL statements in a program editor as the programmer codes the SQL.
- Explain SQL statements in an edit session.
- Generate complete code from in-depth specifications. Some tools even generate SQL. When code generators are used, great care should be taken to ensure that the generated code is efficient before promoting it to production status.
- Use 4GLs (fourth-generation languages) that interface to DB2 and extend the capabilities of SQL to include procedural functions (such as looping or row-at-a-time processing).

Due to the variable nature of the different types of DB2 programming tools, they should be evaluated case by case.

QMF Enhancement Tools (QMF)

A special category of tool, supporting QMF instead of DB2, automatically creates COBOL programs from stored QMF queries. QMF provides a vehicle for the ad hoc development, storage, and execution of SQL statements. When an ad hoc query is developed, it often must be stored and periodically executed. This is possible with QMF, but QMF can execute only dynamic SQL. It does not support static SQL. A method of running critical stored queries using static SQL would be beneficial, because static SQL generally provides better performance than dynamic SQL.

QMF enhancement tools convert the queries, forms, and procs stored in QMF into static SQL statements embedded in a COBOL program. The COBOL program does all the data retrieval and formatting performed by QMF, providing the same report as QMF would. However, the report is now created using static SQL instead of dynamic SQL, thereby boosting performance.

See Checklist 13 for items to consider in evaluating QMF enhancement tools.

Query Tools (QRY)

DB2 provides DSNTEP2 and the SPUFI query tool bundled with the DBMS. Most organizations find these inadequate, however, in developing professional, formatted reports or complete applications. It can be inadequate also for inexperienced users or those who want to develop or execute ad hoc queries.

QMF addresses each of these deficiencies. The capability to format reports without programming is probably the greatest asset of QMF. This feature makes QMF ideal for use as an ad hoc query tool for users.

Another important feature is the capability to develop data manipulation requests without using SQL. QMF provides QBE and Prompted Query in addition to SQL. QBE, or Query By Example, is a language in itself. The user makes data manipulation requests graphically by coding keywords in the columns of a tabular representation of the table to be accessed. For example, a QBE request to retrieve the department number and name for all departments that report to 'A00' would look like the following:

DSN8510.DEPT	DEPTNO	DEPTNAME	MGRNO	ADMRDEPT
	P.	P.		'A00'

Prompted Query builds a query by prompting the end user for information about the data to be retrieved. The user selects a menu option and Prompted Query asks a series of questions, the answers to which are used by QMF to build DML. Both QBE and Prompted Query build SQL "behind the scenes" based on the information provided by the end user.

QMF can also be used to build application systems. A QMF application accesses DB2 data in three ways:

- Using the QMF SAA Callable Interface from an application program
- Using the QMF Command Interface (QMFCI) in a `CLIST` to access QMF
- Using a QMF procedure

Why would you want to call QMF from an application? QMF provides many built-in features that can be used by application programs to reduce development cost and time. For example, QMF can display online reports that scroll not only up and down but also left and right. (Coding left and right scrolling in an application program is not a trivial task.) QMF also can issue the proper form of dynamic SQL, removing the burden of doing so from the novice programmer. Refer to Chapter 6, "Dynamic SQL Programming," for an in-depth discussion of dynamic SQL techniques.

Another benefit of QMF is that you can use inherent QMF commands to accomplish tasks that are difficult to perform with a high-level language such as COBOL. Consider, for example, the following QMF commands:

`EXPORT` Automatically exports report data to a flat file. Without this QMF command, a program would have to allocate a data set and read the report line by line, writing each line to the output file.

DRAW	Reads the DB2 Catalog and builds a formatted SQL SELECT, INSERT, UPDATE, or DELETE statement for any table.
SET	Establishes global values for variables used by QMF.

MF, however, is not the only game in town. Other vendors provide different DB2 table query ad reporting tools that can be used to enhance DB2's ad hoc query capabilities. Some of these oducts are similar in functionality to QMF but provide additional capabilities. They can do e following:

- Use static SQL rather than dynamic SQL for stored queries
- Provide standard query formats and bundled reports
- Provide access to other file formats such as VSAM data sets or IMS databases in conjunction with access to DB2 tables
- Provide access from IMS/TM (QMF is supported in TSO and CICS only)
- Execute DB2 commands from the query tool

onsult Checklist 14 for features to look for in a DB2 query tool.

ools that operate on workstations and PCs are becoming more popular than their mainframe unterparts (such as QMF). This is because the PC provides an environment that is more nducive to quickly creating a report from raw data. Using point-and-click, drag-and-drop chnology greatly eases the report generation process.

dditionally, data warehousing is driving the creation of tools that enable rapid querying along usiness dimensions. These tools provide OLAP, or on-line analytical processing. For an overew of data warehousing and OLAP please refer to Chapter 37, "Data Warehousing with DB2."

inally, fourth-generation languages (4GLs) are gaining more and more popularity for accessg DB2 data. Though not a typical type of DB2 add-on tool, these products provide more nctionality than a report writing tool, but with the GUI front-end that makes them easier to se than 3GL programming languages such as COBOL and C. 4GL tools typically work in ne of three ways:

- Queries are developed using 4GL syntax, which is then converted "behind the scenes" into SQL queries.
- SQL is embedded in the 4GL code and executed much like SQL embedded in a 3GL.
- A hybrid of these two methods, in which the executed SQL is either difficult or impossible to review.

general, you should avoid 4GLs that require a hybrid approach. When a hybrid method is andatory, exercise extreme caution before using that 4GL. These methods are usually diffilt to implement and maintain, and they typically provide poor performance.

If you do use a 4GL to access DB2 data, heed the following cautions:

- Many 4GLs provide only dynamic SQL access, which is usually an inefficient way to develop entire DB2 applications. Even if the 4GL provides static SQL access, often the overhead associated with the DB2 interface is high. For this reason, use 4GLs to access DB2 data only for ad hoc or special processing. 4GLs are generally an unacceptable method of developing complete DB2 applications.
- Be wary of using the syntax of the 4GL to join or "relate" DB2 tables. Instead, use views that efficiently join the tables using SQL, then access the views using the 4GL syntax. I was involved in an application tuning effort in which changing a "relate" in the 4GL syntax to a view reduced the elapsed time of a 4GL request by more than 250 percent.

Repositories (REP)

A repository stores information about an organization's data assets. Repositories are used to store *metadata*, or data about data. They are frequently used to enhance the usefulness of DB2 application development and to document the data elements available in the data warehouse.

In choosing a repository, base your decision on the metadata storage and retrieval needs of your entire organization, not just DB2. Typically, a repository can perform the following functions:

- Store information about the data, processes, and environment of the organization.
- Support multiple ways of looking at the same data. An example of this concept is the three-schema approach, in which data is viewed at the conceptual, logical, and physical levels.
- Support data model creation and administration. Integration with popular CASE tools is also an important evaluation criterion.
- Scan the operational environment to generate metadata from operational systems.
- Store in-depth documentation, as well as produce detail and management reports from that documentation.
- Support change control.
- Enforce naming conventions.
- Generate copy books from data element definitions.

These are some of the more common functions of a data dictionary. When choosing a data dictionary for DB2 development, the following features are generally desirable:

- The data stores used by the repository are in DB2 tables. This enables DB2 applications to directly read the data dictionary tables.
- The repository can directly read the DB2 Catalog or views on the DB2 Catalog. This ensures that the repository has current information on DB2 objects.

- If the repository does not directly read the DB2 Catalog, an interface is provided to ease the population of the repository using DB2 Catalog information.
- The repository provides an interface to any modeling and design tools used.

This section is a brief overview of repositories—an extended discussion of data dictionaries is beyond the scope of this book.

Security Tools (SEC)

DB2 security is provided internally to DB2 with the GRANT and REVOKE data control language components of SQL. Using this mechanism, authorization is granted explicitly and implicitly to users of DB2. Authorization exits enable DB2 to communicate with other security packages such as IBM's RACF and Computer Associate's Top Secret and ACF2. This eases the administrative burden of DB2 security by enabling the corporate data security function to administer groups of users. DB2 authorization is then granted to the RACF groups, instead of individual userids. This decreases the volume of security requests that must be processed by DB2.

DB2's implementation of security has several problems. Paramount among these deficiencies is the effect of the cascading REVOKE. If an authority is revoked from one user who previously granted authority to other users, all dependent authorizations are also revoked. For example, consider Figure 32.2. Assume that Bob is a SYSADM. He grants DBADM WITH GRANT OPTION to Ron and Dianne. Ron then grants the same to Rick and Bill, as well as miscellaneous authority to Chris, Jeff, and Monica. Dianne grants DBADM WITH GRANT OPTION to Dale, Carl, and Janet. She grants miscellaneous authority to Mike and Sue also. Rick, Bill, Dale, Carl, and Janet now have the authority to grant authority to other users. What would be the effect of revoking Ron's DBADM authority? Chris, Jeff, and Monica would lose their authority. In addition, Rick and Bill would lose their authority, as would everyone who was granted authority by either Rick or Bill, and so on.

This problem can be addressed by a DB2 security add-on tool. These tools typically analyze the effects of a REVOKE. For example, the implications of revoking Ron's DBADM authority would have been clearly displayed, showing all implicit REVOKEs. These tools enable the user to revoke the authority and optionally reassign all dependent authority either by storing the appropriate GRANT statements to reapply the authorizations implicitly revoked or by revoking the authority and automatically reapplying all implicit REVOKEs in the background.

These tools provide other functions. Consider the administrative overhead when DB2 users are hired, quit, or are transferred. Security must be added or removed. A good security tool enables a user to issue a GRANT LIKE command, which can copy DB2 authority from one DB2 object to another or from one user to another. Consider two examples.

Suppose that Ron is transferred to another department. A security tool can assign all of Ron's authority to another user before revoking Ron's authority. Or suppose that a new DB2 table is created for an existing DB2 application, and it requires the same users to access its data as can access the other tables in the application. This type of tool enables a user to copy all security from one table to the new table.

There is one other type of DB2 security product. Rather than augment DB2 security, however, this type of product replaces DB2 security with an external package.

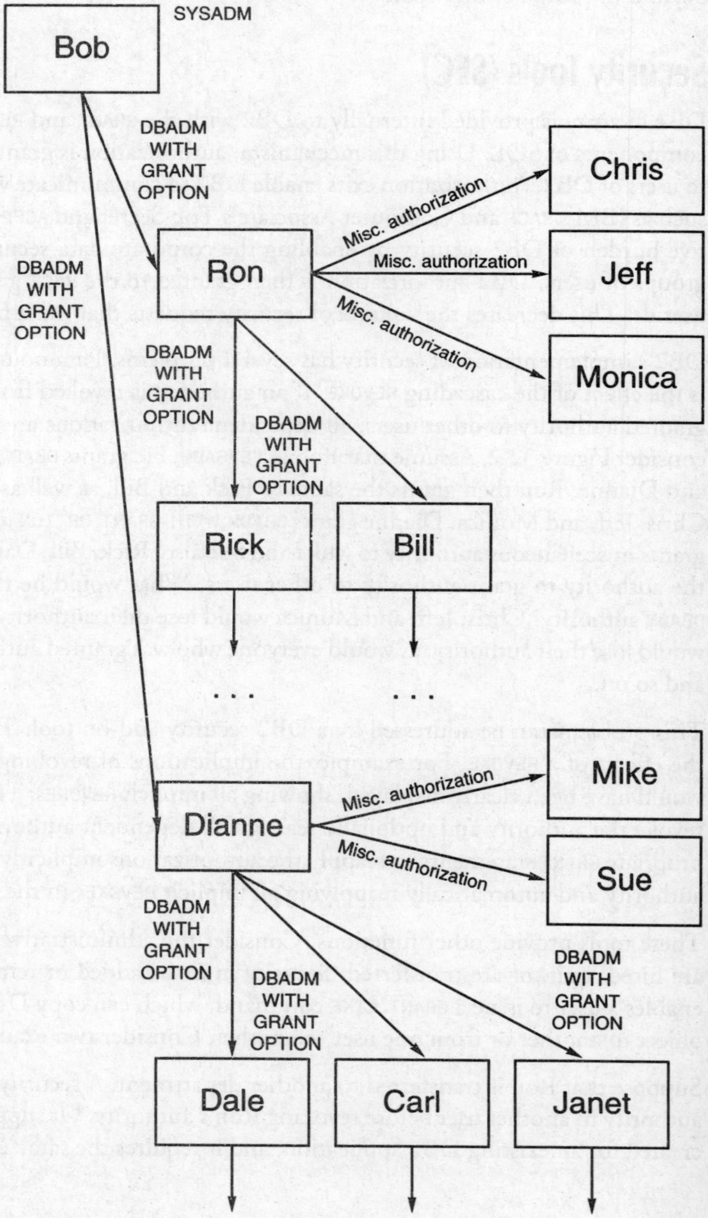

FIGURE 32.2.
DB2 security cascading REVOKE*s.*

The primary benefit is the consolidation of security. If your organization uses a security package from another vendor rather than RACF for regular data security, security administration for regular data security and DB2 security can be consolidated into a single unit. A second benefit is that the cascading revoke effect can be eliminated because MVS data security packages do not cascade security revocations.

The weaknesses of this type of tool, however, outweigh the benefits. These tools do not conform to the rigorous definition of the relational model, which states that the DBMS must control security. Some do not provide all types of DB2 security. For example, INSTALL SYSADM is still required in DB2 for installation of DB2 and DB2 Catalog and Directory recovery.

Another weakness is that if the external security package fails, DB2 data is unprotected. Finally, these types of external security packages do not use supported DB2 exit control points. As such, they may be unable to provide support for new releases of DB2 in a timely fashion.

I recommend that you avoid packages that replace DB2 security in favor of a package that enhances DB2 security. To evaluate DB2 security packages, use Checklist 15.

Utility Enhancement Tools (UTL)

The DB2 COPY, LOAD, RECOVER, REORG, and UNLOAD utilities are notorious for their inefficiency, sometimes requiring more than 24 hours to operate on very large DB2 tables. These utilities are required to populate, administer, and organize DB2 databases.

Several vendors provide support tools that replace the DB2 utilities and provide the same functionality more efficiently. For example, one vendor claims that its REORG utility executes six to ten times faster than the DB2 REORG utility. These claims must be substantiated for the applications at your organization, but enough inefficiencies are designed into the IBM DB2 utilities to make this claim believable.

Before committing to an alternate utility tool, be sure that it conforms to the following requirements:

- Does not subvert the integrity of the data in the DB2 tables.
- Minimally provides the same features as the corresponding DB2 utility. For example, if the DB2 REORG utility can reorganize both indexes and tablespaces, the enhanced REORG tool must be capable of doing the same.
- Does not subvert standard DB2 features, when possible. For example, DB2 image copies are maintained in the DB2 Catalog. The enhanced COPY tool, therefore, should store its image copies there as well.
- Provides an execution time at least twice as fast as the corresponding DB2 utility. For example, if the DB2 LOAD utility requires 20 minutes to load a table, the enhanced LOAD tool must load the same table in at least 10 minutes. (This should not be a hard-and-fast rule. Sometimes even a moderate increase in processing time is sufficient to cost-justify a third-party utility tool.)

- Corrects the deficiencies of the standard DB2 utilities, when possible. For example, the DB2 `LOAD` utility will not load data in sequence by the clustering index. The enhanced tool should provide this capability.

When testing utility tools from different vendors, ensure that you are conducting fair tests. For example, always reload or recover prior to testing `REORG` utilities so that you don't skew your results due to different levels of tablespace organization. Additionally, always run the tests for each tool on the same object with the same amount of data.

CAUTION

IBM utility I/O is charged to the DB2 subsystem. The third-party tool will most likely charge I/O to the batch utility job.

CAUTION

Third-party utility information cannot be monitored using the `-DISPLAY UTILITY` command.

Checklists 16 through 20 are the evaluation forms for the DB2 utility enhancement tools for the `COPY`, `LOAD`, `RECOVER`, `REORG`, and `UNLOAD` utilities.

One last category of the DB2 utility tool is the utility manager. This type of tool provides administrative support for the creation and execution of DB2 utility jobstreams. These utility generation and management tools can do the following:

- Automatically generate DB2 utility parameters and JCL, with correct workspace assignments
- Monitor DB2 utility jobs as they execute
- Automatically schedule DB2 utilities when exceptions are triggered
- Assist in the scheduling of DB2 utilities to kick off the most important ones first, or to manage the available batch window
- Restart utilities with a minimum of intervention. For example, if a utility cannot be restarted, the tool automatically issues a `-TERM UTIL` command and resubmits the utility.

Refer to Checklist 21 for an evaluation form for the utility management tool.

The DB2 add-on tool market is one of the most lucrative and expanding markets in the realm of mainframe software products. This chapter provides an overview of the major DB2 add-on tool vendors. Chapter 29, "DB2 Commands," outlined the types of tools and suggested ways to evaluate their functionality. This chapter presents guidelines to assist you in selecting a vendor.

DB2 Tools Vendors

This section contains an extensive listing of vendors who provide DB2 products. This list is not intended to be exhaustive, but lists the major players in the DB2 add-on tool market. It is accurate as of the writing of this book, but the software industry is dynamic; software development companies are buying out one another or selling their assets almost weekly.

Product names are not provided, as names frequently change and some tools provide more than one function. Often these vendors supply software tools for other products (such as MVS or IMS), but the focus of this list is on the DB2 development tools only. This list is a reference, not a recommendation. Each vendor name is accompanied by the type of DB2 add-on tools the company supplies. The tool types are coded based on the abbreviations used in the preceding sections. The abbreviations are repeated here for reference:

ALT	Table alter tools
AUD	Auditing tools
CAT	DB2 Catalog query and analysis tools
COM	Compression tools
C/S	DB2-related client/server tools
DBA	Database analysis tools
DES	Database modeling and design tools
DSD	DASD and space management tools
EDT	DB2 table editors
INT	Data and referential integrity tools
MIG	DB2 object migration tools
MOV	Data movement and data warehousing tools
MSC	Miscellaneous tools
NET	Internet, intranet, and Web-enabling tools
OPR	Operational support tools
PC	PC-based DB2-related products
PLN	Plan analysis tools
PM	Performance monitors
PRF	Products to enhance performance
PRG	DB2 programming and development tools
QMF	QMF enhancement tools
QRY	Query tools
REP	Repositories and data dictionaries
SEC	Security tools
UTL	Utility enhancement, generation, and management tools

Some tools provide features that support more than one tool category. In most cases, the category shown in the listing indicates the tool's primary purpose. If no single tool dominates the product, however, the tool is listed with multiple categories.

Organize your evaluations of DB2 tools by tool category. Then concentrate on only the features of each tool integral to the category you are evaluating. This is the recommended approach to DB2 tool evaluation because many tools support multiple features. For example, an alter tool could also provide table editing capability. If you are evaluating alter capabilities and do not need table editing, do not let the additional feature of table editing influence your decision. Judge products based solely on the features you need. It is usually less costly (in the long run) to purchase two tools that fully support the required features (for example, altering and editing) than to purchase a single tool that only partially supports two (or more) capabilities.

This does not mean that tools that integrate multiple features always provide fewer capabilities than single-function tools. One integrated tool could provide all the features a small shop needs. Just be sure that a product supports your basic needs before looking at its additional "bells and whistles."

In general, it is wise to realize that third-party add-on tools can significantly improve the efficiency of DB2 application development. When evaluating products, look for features important to your organization. Consider adopting checklists for product comparisons based upon the features discussed in this article. And remember, although DB2 is a fantastic RDBMS, it leaves quite a bit to be desired in the administration, data access, performance monitoring, and application development areas.

The Vendor List

Vendor/Address	Product Categories
Andyne Computing Limited 552 Princess St. Kingston, ON K7L 1C7 (613) 548-4355 fax: (613) 548-7801 `http://www.andyne.com`	C/S, QRY
Aonix 595 Market St., 10th Floor San Francisco, CA 94105 (415) 543-0900 fax: (415) 543-0145	C/S, DES, PRG, QRY
BGS Systems Inc. 128 Technology One First Ave. Waltham, MA 02254-9111 (617) 891-0000 fax: (617) 890-0000 `http://www.bgs.com`	PM

Vendor/Address	**Product Categories**
BMC Software 2101 CityWest Blvd. Houston, TX 77042 (713) 918-8800 fax: (713) 918-8000 `http://www.bmc.com`	ALT, AUD, CAT, COM, C/S, DBA, DSD, INT, MIG, MSC, OPR, PLN, PM, PRF, UTL
Boole & Babbage Inc. 3131 Zanker Rd. San Jose, CA 95134-1933 (408) 526-3484 fax: (408) 526-3053 `http://www.boole.com`	CAT, COM, DSD, MSC, OPR, PM
Brio Technology 3950 Fabian Way, Suite 200 Palo Alto, CA 94303 (415) 856-8000 fax: (415) 856-8020 `http://www.brio.com`	C/S, QRY
BusinessObjects, Inc. 2870 Zanker Rd. San Jose, CA 95134 (408) 953-6000 fax: (408) 953-6001 `http://www.businessobjects.com`	C/S, QRY
Candle Corporation 2425 Olympic Blvd. Santa Monica, CA 90404 (310) 829-5800 fax: (310) 582-4287 `http://www.candle.com`	CAT, DBA, DSD, MIG, PLN, PM, PRG
Cayenne Software 8 New England Executive Park Burlington, MA 01803 (617) 273-2388 fax: (617) 229-9904 `http://www.cayennesoft.com`	DES, MSC, PM, PRG

Vendor/Address	Product Categories
CDB Software Inc. P.O. Box 771624 Houston, TX 77215 (713) 780-2382 fax: (713) 784-1842 `http://www.cdbsoftware.com`	PRG, UTL
Centura Software Corp. 1060 Marsh Rd. Menlo Park, CA 94025 (415) 617-4782 fax: (415) 617-4640 `http://www.centurasoft.com`	C/S, PC, PRG, QRY
Chicago Soft Products Ltd. 45 Lyme Rd., #307 Hanover, NH 03755 (603) 643-4002 fax: (603) 643-4571 `http://www.quickref.com`	OPR
Cognos Inc. 3775 Riverside Drive P.O. Box 9707, Station T Ottawa, ON Canada K1G 4K9 (613) 738-1440 fax: (613) 738-0002 `http://www.cognos.com`	C/S, MSC, PRG, QRY
Computer Associates One Computer Associates Pl. Islandia, NY 11788 (516) 342-5224 fax: (516) 342-5329 `http://www.cai.com`	ALT, AUD, C/S, EDT, MOV, MSC, NET, OPR, PLN, PM, PRG, QRY, SEC
Compuware Corporation 31440 Northwestern Highway Farmington Hills, MI 48334 (248) 737-7300 fax: (248) 737-7119 `http://www.compuware.com`	ALT, CAT, C/S, DBA, EDT, INT, MIG, MSC, OPR, PRG, SEC

Vendor/Address	**Product Categories**
Coromandel Industries Inc. 70-15 Austin St. Forest Hills, NY 11375 (718) 997-0699 `http://www.tile.net/vendors/coromandel.html`	QRY
Cross Access Corp. One Tower Lane Suite 2410 Oakbrook Terrace, IL 60181 (630) 954-0500 fax: (630) 954-0554 `http://www.crossaccess.com`	C/S, MOV
Data Junction 2201 Northland Drive Austin, TX 78756 (512) 459-1308 fax: (512) 459-1309 `http://www.datajunction.com`	MOV
DBE Software, Inc. 7601 Lewisville Rd., Suite 200 McLean, VA 22102 (703) 847-9500 fax: (703) 556-0089 `http://www.dbesoftware.com`	DES, MSC
DSIMS Corporation 510 Water St. Waxahachie, TX 75165 (972) 923-2087 fax: (972) 923-2301 `http://www.psgdsims.com/dsims.html`	PRG, REP
Evolutionary Technologies 4301 Westbank Drive Building B, Suite 100 Austin, TX 78746 (512) 327-6994 `http://www.evtech.com`	MOV

Vendor/Address	Product Categories
GUIdance Technologies, Inc. 800 Vinial St. Pittsburgh, PA 15212 (412) 231-1300 fax: (412) 231-2076 `http://tile.net/vendors/guidance.html`	C/S, PRG
IBM Corporation NET, Santa Teresa Laboratory 555 Bailey Ave. San Jose, CA 95141 (800) 426-4785 fax: (800) 426-4522 `http://www.software.ibm.com/data`	CAT, C/S, DBA, DES, EDT, MOV, MSC, PM, PRG, QMF, QRY, REP, UTL
IMSI 4720 Little John Trail Sarasota, FL 34232 (800) 354-4674 fax: (941) 377-8475 `http://www.imsi-intl.com`	PLN, PRF
Information Builders Inc. 1250 Broadway New York, NY 10020 (212) 736-4433 fax: (212) 967-6406 `http://www.ibi.com`	MOV, PRG, QRY
Infospace 181 2nd Ave., Suite 218 San Mateo, CA 94401 (415) 685-3000 fax: (415) 685-3001 `http://www.infospace-inc.com`	NET
Infotel Corporation 15438 N. Florida Ave. Suite 204 Tampa, FL 33613 (813) 264-2090 fax: (813) 960-5345 `http://www.infotelcorp.com`	COM, DSD, MOV, OPR, PRG, UTL

Vendor/Address	**Product Categories**
Intersolv 9420 Key West Ave. Rockville, MD 20850 (301) 547-4000 `http://www.intersolv.com`	C/S, DES, PRG
JYACC, Inc. 116 John St. New York, NY 10273-0506 (212) 267-7722 fax: (212) 608-6753 `http://www.jyacc.com`	C/S, INT, PRG
Landmark Systems 8000 Towers Crescent Drive Vienna, VA 22182-2700 (703) 902-8000 fax: (703) 893-5568 `http://www.landmark.com`	PM
Logic Works University Square at Princeton 111 Campus Drive Princeton, NJ 08540 (609) 514-1177 fax: (609) 514-1175 `http://www.logicworks.com`	C/S, DES
Mainware, Inc. 601 Carlson Parkway, Suite 620 Minnetonka, MN 55305 (612) 475-8495 fax: (612) 475-8496 `http://www.mainware.com`	MOV, MSC
Manager Software Products 131 Hartwell Ave. Lexington, MA 02173-3126 (617) 863-5800 fax: (617) 861-6130 `http://www.manager-software-products.co.uk`	REP

Vendor/Address	Product Categories
Micro Focus 2465 E. Bayshore Rd. Palo Alto, CA 94303 (415) 856-4161 fax: (415) 856-6134 `http://www.microfocus.com`	C/S, PC, PRG
Microsoft Corporation One Microsoft Way Redmond, WA 9850 (800) 426-9400 fax: (206) 936-7329 `http://www.microsoft.com`	C/S, INT, PRG, QRY
NEON Systems, Inc. 14141 South West Freeway, Suite 6200 Houston, TX 77478 (281) 491-4200 fax: (281) 242-3880 `http://www.neonsys.com`	C/S, MOV, NET, UTL
Oracle Corp. 500 Oracle Parkway Redwood Shores, CA (415) 506-7000 fax: (415) 506-7132 `http://www.oracle.com`	C/S, MOV, PRG
Pine Cone Systems 7430 East Caley Ave., Suite 100 Englewood, CO 80111 (303) 221-4000 fax: (303) 221-4010 `http://www.pine-cone.com`	PRF, MOV
Plasma Technologies 209 Timber Trail East Hartford, CT 06118 (860) 569-2267 `http://www.mjlweb.com/plasma/index.htm`	OPR

Vendor/Address	Product Categories
PLATINUM *technology, inc.* DSD, 1815 South Meyers Rd. Oakbrook Terrace, IL 60181 (630) 620-5000 fax: (630) 691-0710 `http://www.platinum.com`	ALT, AUD, CAT, COM, C/S, DBA, DES, EDT, INT, MIG, MOV, MSC, OPR, PLN, PM, PRF, PRG, QMF, QRY, REP, SEC, UTL
Praxis International 245 Winter St. Waltham, MA 02154-8716 (617) 622-5757 fax: (617) 622-5766 `http://www.praxisint.com`	MOV
Princeton SOFTECH 1060 State Rd. Princeton, NJ 08540-1423 (609) 497-0205 fax: (609) 497-0302 `http://www.princetonsoftech.com`	EDT, INT, MOV
Prism Solutions, Inc. 1000 Hamlin Court Sunnyvale, CA 94089 (408) 752-1888 fax: (408) 752-1875 `http://www.prismsolutions.com`	MOV
Programart Corporation University Place 124 Mount Auburn St. Cambridge, MA 02138 (617) 661-3020 fax: (617) 498-4010 `http://www.programart.com`	C/S, PM
Relational Architects Inc. 33 Newark St. Hoboken, NJ 07030 (201) 420-0400 fax: (201) 420-4080 `http://www.relarc.com`	OPR, PM, PRG, QMF

Vendor/Address	Product Categories
Responsive Systems Co. 281 Highway 79 Morganville, NJ 07751 (908) 972-1261 fax: (908) 972-9416 `http://www.responsivesystems.com`	DSD, OPR, PM
RevealNet 3016 Cortland Place NW Washington, DC 20008 (202) 234-8557 fax: (202) 234-8558 `http://www.revealnet.com`	OPR
Rocket Software Inc. 161 Worcester Rd. Framingham, MA 01701 (508) 875-4321 fax: (508) 875-1335 `http://www.rocketsoft.com`	QMF
SAS Institute Inc. SAS Campus Drive Cary, NC 27513 (919) 677-8200 fax: (919) 677-8123 `http://www.sas.com`	PRG, QRY
SEGUS Inc. 1851 Alexander Bell Drive Reston,VA 20191 (800) 327-9650	CAT, EDT, RI
Softbase Systems Inc. 1664 Hendersonville Highway Asheville, NC 28803 (704) 277-9900 fax: (704) 277-9900 `http://www.softbase.com`	OPR

Vendor/Address	Product Categories
Software AG of North America 11190 Sunrise Valley Drive Reston, VA 22091 (703) 860-5050 fax: (703) 391-6999 `http://www.sagus.com`	C/S, PRG, QRY
Starware Connectivity Software 2150 Shattuck Ave., Suite 600 Berkeley, CA 94704 (510) 704-2000 fax: (510) 704-2001 `http://www.starware.com`	C/S
Sterling Software 300 Crescent Court, Suite 1200 Dallas, TX 75201 (214) 981-1000 fax: (214) 981-1255 `http://www.sterling.com`	C/S, COM, DEC, MOV, PRG, QRY
Sybase Corporation 6475 Christie Ave. Emeryville, CA 94608 (510) 922-3555 fax: (510) 658-9441 `http://www.sybase.com`	C/S, MOV, PRG, QRY
SysData International, Inc. 33-41 Newark St., Suite 4-D Hoboken, NJ 07030 (800) 937-4734 fax: (819) 778-7943 `http://www.sysdata.com`	SEC
Tone Software Corp. 1735 S. Brookhurst Ave. Anaheim, CA 92804 (714) 991-9460 fax: (714) 991-1831 `http://www.tonesoft.com`	COM, OPR

Vendor/Address	Product Categories
Treehouse Software 400 Broad St. Sewickley, PA 15143 (412) 741-1677 fax: (412) 741-7245 `http://www.treehouse.com`	C/S, MOV
Vality Technology One Financial Center, 6th Floor Boston, MA 02111 (617) 338-0300 fax: (617) 338-0338 `http://www.std.com/~Vality/vality.html`	MOV
Vmark Software 50 Washington St. Westboro, MA 01581-1021 (508) 366-3888 fax: (508) 366-3669 `http://www.vmark.com`	C/S, MOV, PRG
Viasoft Corporation 2022 N. 44th St., Suite 101 Phoenix, AZ 85018 (602) 952-0050 fax: (602) 840-4068 `http://www.viasoft.com`	PRG, REP, TST
Wall Data, Inc. 11332 N.E. 122nd Way Kirkland, WA 98034 (415) 856-9255 `http://www.walldata.com`	C/S, NET, PRG, QRY
XDB Systems, Inc. 14700 Sweitzer Lane Laurel, MD 20707-9896 (301) 317-6800 fax: (301) 317-7701 `http://www.xdb.com`	C/S, NET, PC, PRG, QMF, QRY

Evaluating DB2 Tools Vendors

Although the most important aspect of DB2 tool selection is the functionality of the tool and the way it satisfies the needs of your organization, the nature and stability of the vendor that provides the product is important also. This section provides suggested questions to ask when you are selecting a DB2 tool vendor.

1. How long has the vendor been in business? How long has the vendor been supplying DB2 tools?
2. Does your company have other tools from this vendor? How satisfied are the users of those tools?
3. Are other organizations satisfied with the tool you are selecting? Obtain a list of other organizations who use the same tool, and contact several of them.
4. Does the vendor provide a 24-hour support number? If not, what are its hours of operation? Does the vendor have a toll-free number? If not, how far away is the company from your site? You want to avoid accumulating long distance charges when you are requesting customer support from a vendor. (If an 800 number is not shown in the vendor list, that does not mean that the vendor does not have a toll-free customer support line.)
5. Does the vendor provide a newsletter? How technical is it? Does it provide information on DB2 and the vendor's tools, or just on the vendor's tools? Does the vendor provide a bulletin board service? Can you access it before establishing a relationship with the vendor to evaluate its usefulness? If so, scan some of the questions and reported problems for the tools before committing to the vendor's product.
6. Does this vendor supply other DB2 tools that your organization might need later? If so, are they functionally integrated with this one? Does the vendor supply a full suite of DB2 products or just a few?
7. Does the vendor integrate its tools with other tools? For example, a product that analyzes databases to determine whether a REORG is required should integrate the REORG job with your shop's job scheduler.
8. Does the vendor provide training? Is it on-site training? Does the vendor supply DB2 training as well as training for its tools? Are installation, technical, and user manuals provided free of charge? How many copies? Is mainframe- or PC-based training available for the vendor's tools?
9. Evaluate the response of the technical support number. Call the number with technical questions at least four times throughout the day: before 8:00 a.m., at noon, just before 5:00 p.m., and again after 9:00 p.m. These are the times when you could find

problems with the level of support provided by the vendor. Was the phone busy? Were you put on hold? For how long? When you got a response, was it accurate and friendly? Did the person who answered the phone have to find someone with more technical knowledge? (This can indicate potential problems.)

10. Will the vendor answer DB2 questions free of charge in addition to questions about its product? Sometimes vendors will, but they do not advertise the fact. Try it out by calling the technical support number.
11. Does the vendor have a local office? If not, are technicians readily available for on-site error resolution if needed? At what price?
12. Will the vendor deliver additional documentation or error-resolution information by overnight mail? Does it publish a fax number?
13. How are software fixes provided?—Electronically? By tape? On the WWW? Is a complete reinstallation required? Are fixes typically accomplished using zaps?
14. How many man hours, on a short notice, is the vendor willing to spend to solve problems? Is there a guaranteed time limit?
15. Is the vendor willing to send a sales representative to your site to do a presentation on the product tailored to your needs?
16. Is the vendor an IBM business partner? How soon will the vendor's tools be modified to support new DB2 releases and versions?
17. Have the vendor's tools been reviewed or highlighted in any industry publications recently? If so, obtain the publications and read the articles.
18. Will the vendor assist in developing a cost justification? Most tool vendors are eager for your business and will be more than willing to provide cost justification to help you sell upper management on the need for the tool.
19. Does the vendor provide sample JCL to run its product?—Skeleton JCL? A panel-driven JCL generator?
20. Does the vendor charge an upgrade fee when the processor is upgraded? How flexible are the terms and conditions for the contract?
21. If the vendor is sold or goes out of business, will the vendor supply the source code of the tool?
22. Is the vendor willing to set a ceiling for increases in the annual maintenance charge?
23. Does the vendor supply database administration tools for other DBMSs used at your shop? Can the same tool, using the same interface, be used to manage multiple databases across multiple operating systems?
24. How does the vendor rank enhancement requests?

These 24 questions provide a basis for evaluating DB2 tool vendors. Judge for yourself which criteria are most important to your organization.

CHECKLIST 1.
Table alter tool evaluation.

Table Alter Tool Evaluation Form	#1	#2	#3	#4
Provides Support for On-Line, Panel-Driven Alteration of DB2 Object				
Supports all DB2 Objects				
Complete Support for Referential Integrity				
Shows Before and After Images for Changes				
Restores Authorization				
Supports DB2 Utility Processing				
Provides Change Impact Evaluation				
Uses DB2 DDL				
Interfaces to a Migration Tool				
Logs all Changes				
Provides Automated Recovery for Inadvertantly Dropped Objects				
Implements Changes in Foreground				
Implements Changes in Background				
Runs Directly Against DB2 Catalog				
Runs Against a Copy of the DB2 Catalog				
Preserves Data Integrity				
Performs Data Type Conversion				
GUI and/or Web Interface Available				
Compares Database Schemata				

Number	Vendor Name	Contact	Phone
#1			
#2			
#3			
#4			

CHECKLIST 2.
Auditing tool evaluation.

Auditing Tool Evaluation Form	#1	#2	#3	#4
Estimated Overhead (I/O)				
Estimated Overhead (CPU)				
Provides Formatted Reports of DB2 Audit Trace Data				
Identifies and Reports on the Execution of Data Modification SQL				
Identifies and Reports on the Execution of SQL SELECT statements				
Captures Updates from DB2 Logs				
Updates Not Captured from DB2 Logs				
Captures the Authorization ID of the Data Modification Requestor				
Provides Before and After Image of Data				
Extensible Reporting Capability				
On-Line Reporting Capability				
Batch Reporting Capability				
Generates Re-do SQL				

Number	Vendor Name	Contact	Phone
#1			
#2			
#3			
#4			

CHECKLIST 3.
DB2 Catalog tool evaluation.

DB2 Catalog Tool Evaluation Form	#1	#2	#3	#4
Runs Directly Against DB2 Catalog				
Runs Against a Copy of the DB2 Catalog				
Provides On-Line Access to DB2 Catalog Without Requiring SQL				
Provides Reporting for all DB2 Objects				
Provides Security Reporting				
Provides Recovery Information Reporting				
Recreates DDL for DB2 Objects				
Recreates DCL for Security				
Provides Security Cloning Capability				
Generates Utility Parameters				
Provides Support for AMS				
Provides Object Hierarchy Reporting				
Provides REVOKE Analysis Prior to Revoking any Security				
Provides DROP Analysis Prior to Dropping any Objects				
Provides Automated Recovery for Inadvertantly Dropped Objects				
Provides Automated Recovery for Inadvertantly Revoked Security				
Provides the Ability to Individually Update All Modifiable DB2 Catalog Statistics				
GUI and/or Web Interface Available				
Recreates RUNSTATS statistics				
Recreates DDL for switching compression on and off				

Number	Vendor Name	Contact	Phone
#1			
#2			
#3			
#4			

CHECKLIST 4.
Compression tool evaluation.

Compression Tool Evaluation Form	#1	#2	#3	#4
Speed Relative to DSN8HUFF (V2.3)				
Speed Relative to ESA Compression (V3+)				
Estimated Cost Overhead (CPU)				
Estimated Cost Savings (I/O)				
Estimated Cost Savings (DASD)				
Average Compression Percentage				
Provides Multiple Compression Routines				
Optimized for Various Types of Data				
Provides Ability to Analyze Compression Prior to Implementation				
Foreground Compression Analysis				
Background Compression Analysis				
Externalized Routines Required?				
Intelligent Compression Routines Generation (based upon analysis)				

Number	Vendor Name	Contact	Phone
#1			
#2			
#3			
#4			

CHECKLIST 5.
Conversion tool evaluation.

Movement Tool Evaluation Form	#1	#2	#3	#4
Provides Conversion to [ ]				
Provides Conversion from [ ]				
Provides Conversion to [ ]				
Provides Conversion from [ ]				
Provides Conversion to [ ]				
Provides Conversion from [ ]				
GUI and/or Web Interface Available				
ASCII to EBCDIC				
EBCDIC to ASCII				
Works as a Propagator				
Works as an Extractor				
Works as a Replicator				
Provide data transformation capability				
Interfaces to Repository [ ]				
Asynchronous movement capability				
Synchronous movement capability				

Number	Vendor Name	Contact	Phone
#1			
#2			
#3			
#4			

CHECKLIST 6.

Client/server tool evaluation.

Client/Server Tool Evaluation Form	#1	#2	#3	#4
DRDA-Compliant				
Works as Middleware				
Works as Gateway				
Provides Access to DB2 Universal Database				
Provides Access to DB2 for AS/400				
Provides Access to DB2 for VSE and VM				
Provides Access to Oracle				
Provides Access to Sybase SQL Server				
Provides Access to Microsoft SQL Server				
Provides Access to Informix				
Provides Access to [ ]				
Provides Access to [ ]				
Provides a web interface				

Number	Vendor Name	Contact	Phone
#1			
#2			
#3			
#4			

CHECKLIST 7.

Database analysis tool evaluation.

Database Analysis Tool Evaluation Form	#1	#2	#3	#4
Runs Directly Against DB2 Catalog				
Reads DB2 RUNSTATS				
Provides Enhanced Statistics				
Provides Automatic Utility Scheduling				
Provides Alerting Capability				
Provides Canned Reports				
Provides Integrity Checking				
Enables Page Zapping				
Analyzes DB2 Catalog Objects				
Reads image copies				
Maintains historical RUNSTATS information for trend analysis				
Tracks the effectiveness of compression				
Interfaces to IBM Utilities				
Interfaces to [ ] Utilities				

Number	Vendor Name	Contact	Phone
#1			
#2			
#3			
#4			

CHECKLIST 8.
DASD management tool evaluation.

DB2 DASD Manager Evaluation Form	#1	#2	#3	#4
Analyzes DB2 DASD Space Statistics				
Analyzes DB2 Object Organization Statistics				
Executable On-Line				
Executable in Batch Mode				
Monitors Tablespace DASD Space Usage				
Monitors Index DASD Space Usage				
Monitors Underlying VSAM Dataset Extents				
Automatically Triggers REORG to Redefine Space Allocation				
Provides Comprehensive Standard Reports				
Provides Extensible Reporting Capabilities				
Reads DB2 Object Space Maps				
Compares Allocated Space vs. Actual Space Used by DB2 Data				
Tracks EXCP Statistics				

Number	Vendor Name	Contact	Phone
#1			
#2			
#3			
#4			

CHECKLIST 9.

Table editor evaluation.

Table Editor Evaluation Form	#1	#2	#3	#4
Provides On-Line Editing of DB2 Tables				
Provides On-Line Browsing of DB2 Tables				
Mimics ISPF Editor Functions				
Provides Multi-Row at a Time Editing				
Provides Single Row (row by row) Editing				
Optionally Prompts User Before Applying Changes				
Propagates RI Changes				
Can Cancel Accumulated Changes				
Can Periodically Save Changes Without Exiting Editor				
Provides Table Unload Capability				
Provides Table Load Capability				
Provides Table to Table Copying				
Interfaces With Available Testing Tools				
Can Apply Filters to Rows Before Displaying in an Edit Session				
Can Display SQL for Accumulated Changes				
Can Save SQL for Accumulated Changes				
Can Issue SQL Within an Edit Session				
Interfaces With Program Editor				
GUI and/or Web Interface Available				
Optionally migrates RUNSTATS statistics				
Provides data comparison capability				

Number	Vendor Name	Contact	Phone
#1			
#2			
#3			
#4			

CHECKLIST 10.
Migration tool evaluation.

DB2 Object Migration Evaluation Form	#1	#2	#3	#4
Runs Directly Against DB2 Catalog				
Runs Against a Copy of the DB2 Catalog				
Executable in Foreground				
Executable in Background				
Migrates all DB2 Objects				
Migrates DB2 Plans and Packages				
Optionally Migrates Data				
Optionally Migrate Security				
Provides Renaming Capabilities				
Can Specify Migration Cascading (i.e. specify database name and migrate all dependent objects)				
Operates for Multiple DB2 Subsystems				
Recreates DDL Without Executing It				
Provides a Change Control Facility				
Provides Object Comparison Facility				
Versioning Capabilities				
GUI and/or Web Interface Available				
Restartable Change Strategies				

Number	Vendor Name	Contact	Phone
#1			
#2			
#3			
#4			

CHECKLIST 11.
Plan analyzer evaluation.

Plan Analyzer Evaluation Form	#1	#2	#3	#4
Extensible SQL Knowledge Base				
Accessible On-Line				
Accessible in Batch				
Accessible from QMF				
Suggests Alternate SQL Formulations				
Analyzes Embedded SQL				
Analyzes Stand-Alone SQL				
Works with Plans				
Works with Packages				
Works with Compressed Data				
Works with Query I/O Parallelism				
Provides EXPLAIN History				
Compares EXPLAIN Output				
Provides What-If Scenarios				
Reads Standard PLAN_TABLE				
Modifies DB2 Catalog Statistics				
GUI and/or Web Interface Available				

Number	Vendor Name	Contact	Phone
#1			
#2			
#3			
#4			

CHECKLIST 12.

Performance monitor evaluation.

Performance Monitor Evaluation Form	#1	#2	#3	#4
Tracks CPU Time at Various Levels (plan, transaction, auth ID, correlation ID)				
Tracks Elapsed Time at Various Levels				
Tracks I/O at Dataset & System Level				
Tracks Memory Usage and Paging				
Tracks Multiple DB2 Subsystems				
Tracks Bufferpool Utilization				
Monitors Critical Threshholds				
Provides Triggers to Notify Appropriate Personnel When a Treshold is Reached				
Supports Capacity Planning/Benchmarking				
Supports On-Line Monitoring				
Supports Batch Monitoring				
Uses IFI				
Samples DB2 Control Blocks				
Samples Address Space(s) at Run Time				
Provides Extensible Batch Reports				
Provides Extensible On-Line Environment				
Compatible With DB2-PM Report Formats				
Supports Historical Reporting				
Runs When DB2 is Down				
Monitors Locking at Various Levels				
Provides Detailed Deadlock Information				
Interfaces With Allied Agent Monitors (MVS, VTAM, DASD, CICS, IMS/DC)				
Provides EXPLAIN Capability				
Monitors Distributed Data Requests				
Automatically Starts DB2 Traces Based Upon Menu Picks				
Automatically Generates JCL for Batch Performance Reporting				
Identifies Runaway Ad Hoc Queries				
GUI and/or Web Interface Available				

Number	Vendor Name	Contact	Phone
#1			
#2			
#3			
#4			

CHECKLIST 13.

QMF enhancement tool evaluation.

QMF Enhancement Tool Evaluation Form	#1	#2	#3	#4
Creates Batch COBOL Programs Using QMF Queries and Forms				
Creates CICS COBOL Programs Using QMF Queries and Forms				
Creates IMS/DC COBOL Programs Using QMF Queries and Forms				
Supports Code Generation Using QMF Procs				
Generates Static SQL Code				
Generates Dynamic SQL Code				
Supports Distributed Databases				
Requires a Run-Time Interface				
Speed of Generated Program Relative to Previous QMF Query				
Provides Object Administration Facilities				
Provides Query Analysis Facilities				
Provides Runaway Query Controls				

Number	Vendor Name	Contact	Phone
#1			
#2			
#3			
#4			

CHECKLIST 14.
SQL Query tool evaluation.

Query Tool Evaluation Form	#1	#2	#3	#4
Accesses DB2 tables				
Access Other RDBMS tables				
Accesses non-DB2 datasets (VSAM, QSAM, IMS, others)				
Automatically Generates SQL				
Can Edit Automatically Generated SQL				
Provides Extensive Formatting Capabilities				
Error Checking (Flags Potential Problems)				
Prompted Query Support				
QBE Support				
Menu-driven Interface				
Supports Dynamic and Static SQL				
Can be Invoked From a Program				
Provides Ability to Control and/or Limit Resource Consumption				
Provides Global Variables				
Can Group Multiple Queries Together				
GUI and/or Web Interface Available				
Runs Under Windows				
Runs Under UNIX				
Provides Drag & Drop Query Capability				
Query Analysis Component Available				
ODBC Interface				

Number	Vendor Name	Contact	Phone
#1			
#2			
#3			
#4			

CHECKLIST 15.
Security tool evaluation.

Security Tool Evaluation Form	#1	#2	#3	#4
Provides Ability to Clone Security for a Particular Authid				
Provides Ability to Clone Security for a Particular DB2 Object				
On-Line Security Reporting Capabilities				
Batch Security Reporting Capabilities				
Recreates SQL DCL Statements				
Provides REVOKE Analysis Prior to Revoking any Security				
Provides REVOKE Without Cascade				
Provides Automated Recovery for Inadvertantly Revoked Security				
Completely Replaces DB2 Security				
Augments or Enhances DB2 Security				
Provides Grouping of Authids for Simplified Security Administration				
Integrated with MVS Security Product				
Provides Security Within the Tool				
Supports RACF groups				
Supports DCE Security				

Number	Vendor Name	Contact	Phone
#1			
#2			
#3			
#4			

CHECKLIST 16.
Enhanced Copy Utility evaluation.

COPY Utility Evaluation Form	#1	#2	#3	#4
Speed Relative to IBM COPY				
Can Produce Dual Copies				
Can Produce Off-Site Copies				
Can Produce Standard DB2 Image Copies				
Can Produce Incremental Copies				
Can Produce DSN1COPYs				
Optional Setting of Change Bit				
Can copy all DB2 data sets on a volume with a single command				
Integrated With ICF Catalog Backups				
Provides Facility to Copy Sets of Tablespaces				
Is the COPY recorded in the SYSIBM.SYSCOPY table ?				
Sets/Resets Copy Pending Flag				
Interacts With Other Utility Tools				
Interacts With Standard DB2 Utilities				
Restartable by Phase				
Supports SHRLEVEL REFERENCE				
Supports SHRLEVEL CHANGE				
Optimizes output blocksize				
Elapsed Time				
CPU Time				
EXCP Time				
CPU Service Units				
Trackable Using -DISP UTIL				
Backs up Partitions in Parallel				
Copies Multi-Dataset Simple and Segmented Tablespaces				
Records History of Change Bits Modified by Image Copy				
Fails when Tablespace is in a Pending State				
Supports Parallel Sysplex				

Number	Vendor Name	Contact	Phone
#1			
#2			
#3			
#4			

CHECKLIST 17.
Enhanced Load utility evaluation.

LOAD Utility Evaluation Form	#1	#2	#3	#4
Speed Relative to IBM LOAD				
Supports LOAD REPLACE				
Supports LOAD RESUME(YES)				
Provides Data Conversion				
Provides Data Verification				
Provides Purge Capability				
Provides Sorting by Clustering Key				
Is the LOAD recorded in the SYSIBM.SYSCOPY table ?				
Sets/Resets Check Pending Flag				
Sets Copy Pending after LOAD LOG NO				
Provides FIELDPROC Support				
Loads From Various Sources (VSAM, DB2 Table, QSAM, etc.)				
Interacts With Other Utility Tools				
Interacts With Standard DB2 Utilities				
Restartable by Phase				
Work Files are Blocked Optimally				
Collects and Applies RUNSTATS During the LOAD				
Elapsed Time				
CPU Time				
EXCP Time				
CPU Service Units				
Uses DB2 Authority				
Trackable Using -DISP UTIL				
Reads DSNTIAUL Load Cards				
Accepts DSNTIAUL and REORG UNLOAD ONLY data				
Supports multi-dataset simple and segmented tablespaces				
Supports large tablespaces				
Supports Parallel Sysplex				

Number	Vendor Name	Contact	Phone
#1			
#2			
#3			
#4			

CHECKLIST 18.
Enhanced Reorg utility evaluation.

REORG Utility Evaluation Form	#1	#2	#3	#4
Speed Relative to IBM REORG				
Can REORG Multi-dataset Tablespaces and indexes				
Can REORG Large Tablespaces				
Restartable				
Provides Purge Capability				
Optional Unload by Clustering Index				
Optional Sort for Clustering				
Is the REORG recorded in the SYSIBM.SYSCOPY table ?				
Sets/Resets Copy Pending Flag				
Optionally Produces an Image Copy				
Interacts With Other Utility Tools				
Interacts With Standard DB2 Utilities				
Restartable by REORG Phase?				
Sets/Resets Check Pending Flag				
Multi-tasking?				
Elapsed Time				
CPU Time				
EXCP Time				
CPU Service Units				
Uses DB2 Authority				
Trackable Using -DISP UTIL				
Optimally Blocks Work Files				
Maintains a History of REORG Elapsed Time				
Provides Parallel Sysplex Support				

Number	Vendor Name	Contact	Phone
#1			
#2			
#3			
#4			

CHECKLIST 19.
Enhanced Recover utility evaluation.

RECOVER Utility Evaluation Form	#1	#2	#3	#4
Speed Relative to IBM RECOVER				
Can RECOVER Multi-dataset Tablespaces and Indexes				
Can RECOVER Large Tablespaces				
Can RECOVER from any DB2 Copy				
Can RECOVER from a DSN1COPY				
Support for Incremental Copy Recovery				
Provides Support for Disaster Recovery				
Allocates VSAM datasets ?				
Is a partial recovery recorded in the SYSIBM.SYSCOPY table ?				
Does the utility use the standard DB2 Catalog and DB2 Directory recovery information?				
Sets/Resets Recover Pending Flag				
Provides Facility to Recover Sets of Tablespaces				
Interacts With Other Utility Tools				
Interacts With Standard DB2 Utilities				
Elapsed Time				
CPU Time				
EXCP Time				
CPU Service Units				
Can Recover Using Absolute or Relative GDGs				
Restartable by Phase				
Uses DB2 Security				
Trackable Using -DISP UTIL				
Optimally Blocks Work Files				
Supports Parallel Sysplex				

Number	Vendor Name	Contact	Phone
#1			
#2			
#3			
#4			

CHECKLIST 20.
Enhanced Unload utility evaluation.

UNLOAD Utility Evaluation Form	#1	#2	#3	#4
Speed Relative to DSNTIAUL				
Unload in Readable (EBCDIC) Format				
Unloads from DB2 table				
Unloads from Image Copy				
Unloads from DSN1COPY				
Unloads DB2 Catalog				
Unload to Multiple Datasets				
Produces Load Control Cards				
Provides Data Conversion				
FIELDPROC Support				
Provides Selective Unload Capability				
Provides Facility to Unload Sets of Tables				
Interacts With Other Utility Tools				
Interacts With Standard DB2 Utilities				
Supports ORDER BY				
Supports Multiple Unload Formats				
Restartable				
Trackable Using -DISP UTIL				
Optimally Blocks Work Files				
Unloads from Views				
Elapsed Time				
CPU Time				
EXCP Time				
CPU Service Units				
Uses DB2 security				
Supports Parallel Sysplex				

Number	Vendor Name	Contact	Phone
#1			
#2			
#3			
#4			

CHECKLIST 21.
Utility management tool evaluation.

Utility Mgmt Tool Evaluation Form	#1	#2	#3	#4
Sets Triggers to Kick Off Utilities				
Schedules Utilities for Execution				
Monitors Utility Execution				
Interfaces With Enhanced Utility Tools				
Generates Utility JCL				
Calculates Utility Work File Sizes				
Calculates VSAM Files Sizes				
Provides Automated Restart Capabilities				
Interfaces With DB2 Catalog Information				
Maintains Utility History				
Schedules REORGs by Importance				
Estimates Utility Execution Times for Placement within the Batch Window				

Number	Vendor Name	Contact	Phone
#1			
#2			
#3			
#4			

Summary

In this chapter, you learned about the additional tools that are available to make DB2 easier to use, manage, and administer. Not every shop will have (or need) all of these tools. However, when you need to acquire or implement DB2 add-on tools, use the information in this chapter to guide your way.

33

Organizational Issues

Although you must jump many technical hurdles to use DB2 successfully, the organizational issues of implementing and supporting DB2 are not insignificant. Each corporation must address the organizational issues involved in supporting DB2. Although the issues are common from company to company, the decisions made to address these issues can vary dramatically.

This chapter outlines the issues. Your organization must provide the answers as to how it will support these issues. This chapter can be used in any of the following ways:

- As a blueprint of issues to address for organizations that will implement DB2
- As a checklist for current DB2 users to ensure that all issues have been addressed
- As a resource for programmers who need a framework for accessing their organization's standards and operating procedures

Education

Education is the first issue that should be addressed after your organization decides to implement DB2. Does your organization understand what DB2 is? How it works? Why (and if) it is needed at your shop? How it will be used?

After addressing the basics of DB2 education, you must deal with ongoing support for DB2 education. This support falls into three categories. The first is in-house, interactive education in the form of videos, computer-based training, and instructor-led courses.

The second category of support is external education for special needs. This support includes education for database administrators, technical support personnel, and performance analysts. Additionally, your organization needs to plan for ongoing education to keep appropriate personnel up-to-date on new versions and releases of DB2. Although IBM typically offers the earliest courses for new DB2 releases, several third-party vendors such as PLATINUM *technology, inc.* and Themis regularly offer release-specific DB2 courses.

The final category of support is reference material—for example, IBM's DB2 manuals, DB2 books such as this one, vendor-supplied white papers, and industry publications and periodicals. Refer to Appendix E, "DB2 Manuals," for the current IBM manuals for DB2 and DB2-related products. Providing online access to the DB2 and related manuals using BookManager Library Reader on the mainframe (as shown in Figure 33.1), the workstation (as shown in Figure 33.2), or both is a good idea.

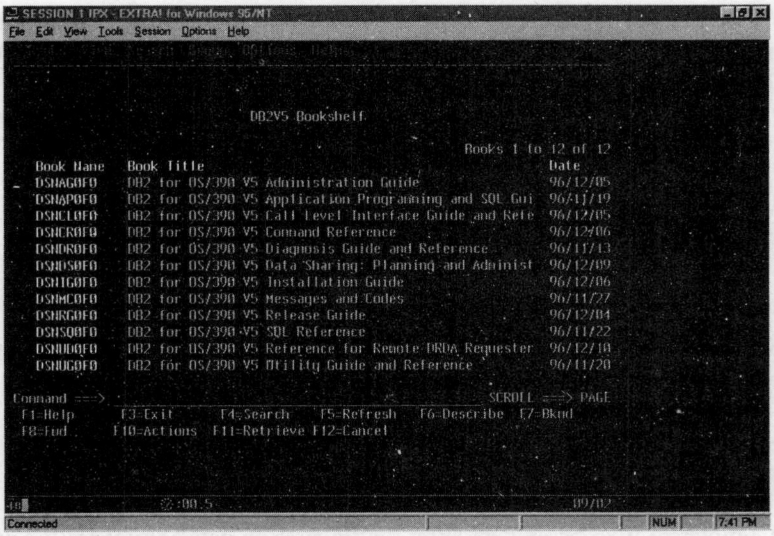

FIGURE 33.1.
IBM BookManager Library Reader on the mainframe.

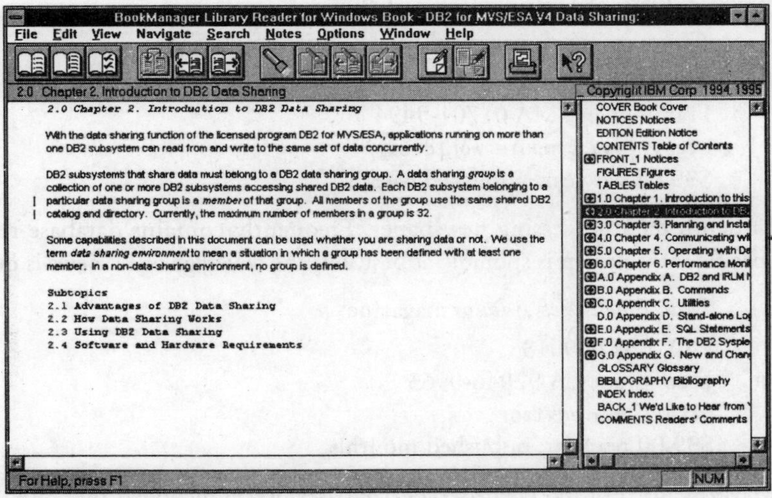

FIGURE 33.2.
IBM BookManager Library Reader for Windows.

Vendors are another rich source of DB2 information. The major vendors provide in-depth technical papers on features of DB2 that would be difficult for most shops to research in the same detail. BMC, Candle, and PLATINUM *technology, inc.* are the best sources for DB2-related white papers.

The final type of reference material is industry periodicals and publications. Many trade magazines describe database management in general and DB2 specifically. A listing of recommended industry publications that cover DB2 on a regular basis follows.

Candle Computer Report
Candle Corporation
2425 Olympic Boulevard
Santa Monica, CA 90404
`http://www.candle.com`
Free to customers and potential customers; published monthly

Contains in-depth technical information about MVS-related platforms and products, including many technical DB2 articles.

The Data Administration Newsletter online newsletter

Free with e-mail reminders; published quarterly

`http://www.sgi.net/tdan`

Completely Web-based newsletter that focuses on data administration and database administration topics.

Computer World newsweekly
375 Cochituate Road
Framingham, MA 01701-9494
`http://www.computerworld.com`
$39.95 per year; published weekly

In-depth data processing newspaper. Frequently contains database-related articles. DB2-specific information is sporadic at best, but the coverage of IT news is outstanding.

Data Based Web Advisor magazine
P.O. Box 469013
Escondido, CA 92046-9963
`http://www.advisor.com`
$39.00 per year; published monthly

Magazine for PC and client/server databases. Recently added the "Web" moniker to its title and provides frequent coverage of Web-based database access. Regular SQL coverage, but only rarely discusses DB2.

Data Management Review magazine
Powell Publishing, Inc.
617 South 94th Street
West Allis, WI 53214-1222

http://www.dm-review.com
http://www.data-warehouse.com
Free to qualified subscribers; published monthly

Interesting publication addressing all types of database management system issues. Highlights include a monthly DB2 column, a large product review section, and occasional additional DB2-related articles. Recent editorial focus is heavily oriented toward data warehousing topics.

Database Programming & Design magazine
Miller Freeman Publications
P.O. Box 51247
Boulder, CO 80321-1247
http:.//www.dbpd.com
$39.00 per year and worth every penny; published monthly

Still the best general-purpose monthly publication for DBAs and DAs. Provides extensive coverage of all aspects of database development. Contains a regular column by Chris Date and occasional coverage of DB2.

Database Newsletter
Database Research Group
One State Street
Boston, MA 02109
$129.00 per year; published bimonthly

Provides current information about the entire database marketplace, with specific emphasis on data administration, business rules, and database design.

Datamation magazine
P.O. Box 7529
Highlands Ranch, CO 80163-9329
http://www.datamation.com
Free to qualified subscribers; published monthly

Provides coverage of news affecting the data processing community. Frequent coverage of IBM, DB2, and CASE.

DBMS magazine
P.O. Box 50096
Boulder, CO 80321-0096
http://www.dbmsmag.com
Free to qualified subscribers; published monthly

Magazine for client/server database administration and development; regular SQL coverage and occasional DB2 client/server articles. The product reviews are usually thoroughly researched and well written.

DB2 magazine
Miller Freeman Publications
P.O. Box 51247
Boulder, CO 80321-1247
`http://www.db2mag.com`
Free to *DBMS* and *Database Programming & Design* subscribers; published quarterly

Provides in-depth, technical articles focused on the DB2 family of products. Useful for DB2 shops.

DB2 Family newsletter
IBM Canada Ltd.
Database Technology Planning
31/110/895/TOR
895 Don Mills Road
North York, Ontario
Canada M3C 1W3
Free publication

Published by IBM's Toronto labs (where DB2 for Common Servers was developed), each issue is devoted entirely to DB2. Provides the latest breaking news on all members of the DB2 family—straight from the horse's mouth.

DB2 Update technical journal
Xephon Publications
1301 West Highway 407
Suite 201-450
Lewisville, TX 75067
`http://www.xephon.com`
$340.00 per year; published monthly

Each issue is devoted to DB2. Provides technical articles on all areas of DB2 administration, design, and development. Each issue contains 20 to 30 pages, with no advertisements.

Enterprise System Journal magazine
Cardinal Business Media
P.O. Box 3051
Northbrook, IL 60065
`http://www.esj.com`
Free to qualified subscribers; published monthly

Provides in-depth technical articles focusing on all areas of IBM mainframe development. Contains sporadic coverage of DB2. Also periodically covers client/server development, CICS, and IMS.

IBM System Journal technical journal

IBM Corporation
P.O. Box 3033
Southeastern, PA 19398
$49.50 per year; published quarterly

Technical articles written by IBM staff about IBM products and architectures. Sometimes covers DB2 topics. Every IBM shop should subscribe to this journal.

IDUG Solutions Journal

IDUG Headquarters
401 N. Michigan Avenue
Chicago, IL 60611-4267
Free to qualified DB2 professionals; published quarterly

A journal specifically for DB2 professionals using DB2 or any platform. Published by IDUG.

InfoDB technical journal

InfoIT
P.O. Box 310
Morgan Hill, CA 95038
`http://www.infoit.com`
$475.00 per year; published quarterly

Provides detailed technical articles on all areas of data administration, database development, and database management. No advertisements. Typical articles average 10 to 20 pages.

Information Week newsweekly

CMP Publications, Inc.
600 Community Drive
Manhasset, NY 11030
Free to qualified data processing professionals; published weekly

In addition to timely DP news, contains frequent user-focused articles related to DBMS technology.

Software magazine

Sentry Technology Group
P.O. Box 5269
Pittsfield, MA 01203-5269
`http://www.software.com`
Free to qualified subscribers; published monthly

Provides coverage of the software development and support industry with particular emphasis on enterprise software including DBMS, software development, and systems management software.

All these components—in-house education, external education, and industry publications—are useful for explaining how you can use DB2 effectively. You would be wise to have a mix of material that supports one or more of the categories outlined previously. In this way, you provide a varied learning environment that meets the needs of all students. This varied learning environment allows each student to learn in the most conducive way for him or her. Plan to provide an on-site library of educational material addressing the following subjects:

Introduction to relational databases
Introduction to DB2 and SQL
Advanced SQL
Programming DB2 in batch
Programming DB2 using TSO, CICS, and IMS
Creating DB2 stored procedures
Programming DB2 in a Distributed Environment
QMF usage guidelines

You also might want to have an introductory DB2 database administration course to train new DBAs. In addition to this basic education library, plan to provide advanced education for technical DB2 users, such as DBAs, technical support personnel, and technical programmers and analysts. Advanced DBA topics (such as data sharing, performance management, and backup/recovery) should be left to instructor-led training courses because of the complex nature of DB2 database administration. Additional advanced topics to consider include system administration (for systems programmers) and disaster recovery. These classes are offered by many vendors, including IBM, Themis, and PLATINUM *technology, inc.* Searching for smaller consulting firms and local resources is also prudent; these firms usually provide courses tailored to your installation needs.

The advanced education program should include allocating time to attend area user groups meetings, the annual DB2 Technical Conference supported by IBM, and/or the International DB2 Users Group (IDUG). When DB2 users get together to share experiences at such forums, they uncover undocumented solutions and ideas that would be difficult to arrive at independently.

Standards and Procedures

To implement DB2 effectively, you must have a set of standards and procedures that are the blueprint for DB2 development in your organization. *Standards* are common practices that provide an environment that is consistent, efficient, or understandable (for example, a naming standard for DB2 objects). *Procedures* are scripts that outline the way a proscribed event should be handled, such as a disaster recovery plan.

DB2 standards and procedures are usually developed together and stored in a common place. Standards and procedures are usually part of a corporate-wide (or MIS) standards and procedures document. They can be stored in written format and online for easy access. Several vendors offer "canned" standards and procedures (both hard copy and online). Examples include Guide/Online from PLATINUM *technology, inc.* and RevealNet's DB2 Knowledge Base.

This section describes the items that should be addressed by DB2 standards and procedures.

Roles and Responsibilities

Running DB2 requires a large degree of administrative overhead. Not only must the DB2 subsystem be installed and then maintained, but the functionality of DB2 must also be administered. This work constitutes the bulk of the administrative burden.

A matrix of DB2 functions and who will support them is necessary. The matrix can be at the department level or at the job description level. Table 33.1 shows a sample matrix you can use as a template for your organization.

Table 33.1. DB2 roles and responsibilities.

Role	*DA*	*DBA*	*PGM*	*ANL*	*TS*	*DSD*	*SEC*	*MGT*	*EU*	*OPR*
Budgeting for DB2		X			X			X	X	X
DB2 Installation		X			X	X	X		X	
DB2 System Support					X					
DB2 System Security					X		X			
System-Wide Performance Monitoring		X			X					X
System-Wide Tuning		X				X				
DB2 System Backup and Recovery Procedures	X	X	X	X	X	X	X	X	X	X
Hardware Planning		X			X	X		X		
Capacity Planning		X		X	X				X	
Utility Development		X			X					
Data Analysis	X	X	X					X	X	
DB2 Object Creation		X								
DB2 Database Performance Monitoring		X			X					X
DB2 Database Performance Tuning	X	X		X	X					

continues

Table 33.1. continued

Role	*DA*	*DBA*	*PGM*	*ANL*	*TS*	*DSD*	*SEC*	*MGT*	*EU*	*OPR*
DB2 Application Design	X	X		X						X
DB2 Program Coding			X	X						
DB2 Program Testing			X	X						
Stored Procedure Coding		X	X	X						
Stored Procedure Testing		X	X	X						
Stored Procedure Support		X	X	X						X
DB2 Application Security		X					X		X	
DB2 Application Turnover		X	X	X					X	X
DB2 Application Performance Monitoring		X		X	X					
DB2 Application Database Backup and Recovery		X		X				X	X	X
DB2 Job Scheduling			X	X					X	X
DB2 Design Reviews	X	X	X	X	X	X	X	X	X	X
DB2 Tool Selections	X	X	X	X	X	X	X	X		
Implementing DDF		X			X		X			
Distributing DB2 Data	X	X	X	X	X	X	X			
DB2 Data Sharing		X			X	X	X	X		X
QMF Installation					X					
QMF Administration		X			X					
QMF Tuning		X		X	X				X	

DA	Data administrator
DBA	Database administrator
PGM	Programmer
ANL	Analyst
TS	Technical support
DSD	DASD support
SEC	Data security
MGT	Management
EU	End user
OPR	Operations

The matrix in Table 33.1 represents a sampling of roles and responsibilities for the DB2 environment. Each block of the matrix represents a portion of the total responsibility for the given role.

Your organization might have different roles responsible for different areas. Additionally, you might have more categories or a further breakdown of the categories (for example, dividing the *Utility Development* line into a single line for each utility).

Each position on the matrix should be accompanied by in-depth text as follows:

- A description of the resources encompassing this combination of role and responsibility.
- A definition of the role in terms of what needs to be performed. This information should include a detailed list of tasks and a reference to the supporting organizational procedures that must be followed to carry out these tasks.
- A definition of the responsibility in terms of who should do the tasks. In addition to primary and secondary contacts for the people performing the task, this description should provide a management contact for the department in charge of the responsibility.

Remember, Table 33.1 is only an example. It is not uncommon for DB2 administrative tasks to be assigned to departments or jobs different from the ones shown in the table. Each shop should have a document appropriately modified to reflect the needs and organization of the company.

This document will eliminate confusion when DB2 development is initiated. Analysts, programmers, and management will have an organized and agreed-on delineation of tasks and responsibilities before the development and implementation of DB2 applications.

Based on the roles and responsibilities matrix in use at your shop, you might need to augment or change the following procedures. Certain functions may move to a different area, but all the necessary standards are covered.

Data Administration

Data administration is beyond the scope of this book, but this section lists some basic guidelines. All DB2 applications must be built using the techniques of logical database design. This design involves the creation of a normalized, logical data model that establishes the foundation for any subsequent development. It documents the data requirements for the organization. Each piece of business data is defined and incorporated into the logical data model. All physical DB2 tables should be traceable to the logical data model.

The data administration standards should outline the following:

- Corporate policies dictating that information is to be managed as a vital business resource
- Who is responsible for creating the logical data model

- How the logical data model will be created, stored, and maintained
- Who is responsible for maintaining and administering the logical data model
- The integration of application data models with an enterprise data model
- Data sharing issues (this does not refer to DB2 data sharing but refers to the sharing of data in general)
- How physical databases will be created from the logical data model
- How denormalization decisions will be documented
- The tools used by the data administrator (modeling tools, data dictionaries, repositories, and so on)
- Rules for data creation, data ownership, and data stewardship
- Meta-data management policy
- The communication needed between data administration and database administration to ensure the implementation of an effective DB2 application

Database Administration Guide

A database administration guide is essential to ensure the ongoing success of the DBA function. The guide serves as a cookbook of approaches to be used in the following circumstances:

- Converting a logical model to a physical implementation
- Choosing physical DB2 parameters when creating (or generating) DDL
- DB2 utility implementation procedures and techniques
- DB2 application monitoring schedules
- DB2 application and database tuning guidelines

This document, although geared primarily for DBA staff, is useful for the programming staff as well. If the program developers understand the role of the DBA and the tasks that must be performed, more effective communication can be established between DBA and application development, thereby increasing the chances of achieving an effective and efficient DB2 application system.

System Administration Guide

The DB2 system administrator is considered to be at a higher level than the database administrator. It is not unusual, though, for a DBA to be the system administrator also. A system administration guide is needed for many of the same reasons that a DBA guide is required. It should consist of the following items:

- DB2 installation and testing procedures
- Procedures to follow for applying fixes to DB2 (APARs)

- A checklist of departments to notify of impending changes
- Interface considerations (CICS, IMS/TM, TSO, CAF, RRSAF, DDF, and other installation-specific interfaces)
- A DB2 system monitoring schedule
- DB2 system tuning guidelines
- DB2 data sharing policy and implementation
- System DASD considerations

Application Development Guide

The development of DB2 applications differs from typical program development. Providing an application development guide specifically for DB2 programmers is therefore essential. It can operate as an adjunct to the standard application development procedures for your organization. This guide should include the following topics:

- An introduction to DB2 programming techniques
- Shop SQL coding standards
- SQL tips and techniques
- DB2 program preparation procedures
- Interpretations of SQLCODEs and DB2 error codes
- References to other useful programming materials for teleprocessing monitors (CICS and IMS/TM), programming languages (such as COBOL and PL/I), and general shop coding standards
- The procedure for filling out DB2 forms (if any) for database design, database implementation, program review, database migration, and production application turnover

DB2 Security Guide

The DBA unit often applies and administers DB2 security. However, at some shops, the corporate data security unit handles DB2 security. You must provide a resource outlining the necessary standards and procedures for administering DB2 security. It should consist of the following:

- A checklist of what to grant for specific situations. For example, if a plan is being migrated to production, it should list the security that must be granted before the plan can be executed.
- A procedure for implementing site-specific security. It must define which tools or interfaces (for example, secondary authorization IDs) are being used and how they are supported.

- An authoritative signature list of who can approve authorization requests.
- Procedures for any DB2 security request forms.
- Procedures for notifying the requester that security has been granted.
- Procedures for removing security from retiring, relocating, and terminated employees.

SQL Performance Guide

The SQL performance guide can be a component of the application development guide, but it should also exist independently. This document should contain tips and tricks for efficient SQL coding. It is useful not only for application programmers but also for all users of DB2 who regularly code SQL.

QMF Guide

If QMF (or another query tool) is in use at your site, a QMF guide must be available. It should contain information from the simple to the complex so that all levels of QMF users will find it useful. This guide should cover the following topics, in increasing order of complexity:

- What QMF is
- Who is permitted to use QMF
- When QMF can be used (such as hours of operation and production windows)
- How to request QMF use
- How to call up a QMF session
- A basic how-to guide for QMF features
- QMF limitations
- References to further documentation (for example, CBT and IBM manuals)

Naming Conventions

All DB2 objects should follow a strict naming convention. You learned some basic guidelines for DB2 naming conventions in Chapter 3, "Data Definition Guidelines." This section details the rules to follow in naming a DB2 object.

Make names as English-like as possible. In other words, do not encode DB2 object names, and avoid abbreviations unless the name would be too long otherwise.

Do not needlessly restrict DB2 object names to a limited subset of characters or a smaller size than DB2 provides. For example, do not forbid an underscore in table names, and do not restrict DB2 table names to eight characters or fewer (DB2 allows as many as 18 characters).

Another rule in naming objects is to standardize abbreviations. Use the abbreviations only when the English text is too long.

In most cases, provide a way to differentiate types of DB2 objects. For example, start indexes with *I*, tablespaces with *S*, and databases with *D*. In two cases, however, this approach is inappropriate. You should not constrain tables in this manner; you need to provide as descriptive a name as possible. The second exception is that views, aliases, and synonyms should follow the same naming convention as tables. In this way, DB2 objects that operate like tables can be defined similarly. The type of object can always be determined by querying the DB2 Catalog using the queries presented in Chapter 19, "DB2 Object Monitoring Using the DB2 Catalog."

Provide naming conventions for the following items:

Databases
Tablespaces
Tables
Indexes
Views
Aliases
Synonyms
DCLGEN Members
DCLGEN Libraries
DB2 COPYLIB Members
DB2 Subsystems
Application DB2 data sets
System DB2 data sets
Locations
Constraints
DSNZPARM
DB2 group name
Location name
DB2 member name
Command prefixes
STOGROUPs
Plans
Packages
Collections
Versions
DBRMs
DBRM Libraries
Transactions
Programs
DB2 Load Libraries
DB2 Address Spaces
RCTs
Data sets for DB2 Tools
Creators
DB2 data sets (tools—general for DB2 subsystem; specific for each tool)
RACF groups
IRLM group name
Group attach name
Workfile DB name

Migration and Turnover Procedures

The minimum number of environments for supporting DB2 applications is two: test and production. Most shops, however, have multiple environments. For example, a shop could have the following DB2 environments to support different phases of the development life cycle:

Unit testing
Integration testing
User acceptance testing
Quality assurance
Education

Having multiple environments requires a strict procedure for migrating DB2 objects and moving DB2 programs and plans from environment to environment. Each shop must have guidelines specific to its environment because all sites do not implement these different environments in the same way. For example, both test and production DB2 could be supported using either a single DB2 subsystem or two DB2 subsystems. (Two are recommended to increase efficiency and turnaround time, but having two is a luxury some smaller shops cannot afford.)

Dual versions of these procedures should exist to describe what is entailed from the point of view of both the requester and the person implementing the request. For the requester, the procedures should include what will be migrated, why and when it will be migrated, who is requesting the migration, and the authorization for the migration. For the person implementing the request, the procedures should include who is responsible for which portions of the migration and a description of the methods used to migrate.

Design Review Guidelines

All DB2 applications, regardless of their size, should participate in a design review both before and after they are implemented. Design reviews are critical for ensuring that an application is properly designed to achieve its purpose.

Design reviews can take many forms. Some of the areas that can be addressed by a design review include the following:

- A validation of the purpose of the application
- An assessment of the logical and physical data models
- A review and analysis of DB2 physical parameters
- A prediction of SQL performance

Before discussing the different types of DB2 design reviews, I must first outline who must participate to ensure a successful review of all elements of the application. The following personnel should engage in the design review process:

AA	Representatives from other applications affected by the application being reviewed (because of the need to interface with the new application, shared data requirements, scheduling needs, and so on)
AD	Application development personnel assigned to this development effort
DA	Data administration representatives
DBA	Database administration representatives
EU	End-user representatives
EUM	End-user management
IC	Information center representatives
MM	MIS management for the new application and all affected applications
OLS	Online support representatives (CICS or IMS/TM unit)
OS	Operational support management
TS	Technical support and systems programming representatives

Each of these participants does not need to take part in every facet of the design review. Holding more than one design review is best, with each one focusing on an aspect of the design. The scope of each design review should be determined before the review is scheduled so that only the appropriate participants are invited.

You can break down the design review into seven distinct phases, which are described in the following sections.

Phase 1

The first phase of the design review process is the Conceptual Design Review (CDR). This review validates the concept of the application. This review involves a presentation of the statement of purpose as well as an overview of the desired functionality.

A CDR should be conducted as early as possible to determine the feasibility of a project. Failure to conduct a CDR can result in projects that provide duplicate or inadequate functionality—projects that are canceled because of lack of funds, staffing, planning, user participation, or management interest; or projects over budget.

Participants should include AA, AD, DA, DBA, EU, EUM, and MM.

Phase 2

Phase 2 of the design review process is the Logical Design Review (LDR). This phase should be conducted when the first cut of the logical data model has been completed. A thorough review of all data elements, descriptions, and relationships should occur during the LDR. The LDR should scrutinize the following areas:

- Is the model in (at least) third normal form?
- Are all data elements (entities and attributes) required for this application identified?
- Are the data elements documented accurately?
- Are all relationships defined properly?

Failure to hold an LDR can result in a failure to identify all required pieces of data, a lack of documentation, and a database that is poorly designed and difficult to maintain. This failure results in the development of an application that is difficult to maintain. If further data modeling occurs after the logical design review is held, further LDRs can be scheduled as the project progresses.

Participants should include AA, AD, DA, DBA, EU, EUM, and IC.

Phase 3

The third phase of the design review process is the Physical Design Review (PDR). Most DB2 developers associate this component with the design review process. In this phase, the database is reviewed in detail to ensure that all the proper design choices were made. In addition, the

DA and DBA should ensure that the logical model was translated properly to the physical model, with all denormalization decisions documented.

In addition, the overall operating environment for the application should be described and verified. The choice of teleprocessing monitor and a description of the online environment and any batch processes should be provided. Data sharing and distributed data requirements should be addressed during this phase.

At this stage, the SQL that will be used for this application might be unavailable. General descriptions of the processes, however, should be available. From the process descriptions, a first-cut denormalization effort (if required) should be attempted or verified.

Because the PDR phase requires much in-depth attention, it can be further divided. The PDR, or pieces of it, can be repeated before implementation if significant changes occur to the physical design of the database or application.

Participants should include AA, AD, DA, DBA, EU, EUM, IC, MM, OLS, OS, and TS.

Phase 4

Phase 4 is the Organization Design Review (ODR). It is smaller in scope—but no less critical—than the Physical Design Review. This review addresses the enterprise-wide concerns of the organization with respect to the application being reviewed. Some common review points follow:

- How does this system interact with other systems in the organization?
- Has the logical data model for this application been integrated with the enterprise data model (if one exists)?
- To what extent can this application share the data of other applications? To what extent can other applications share this application's data?
- How will this application integrate with the current production environment in terms of DB2 resources required, the batch window, the online response time, and availability?

Participants should include AA, AD, DA, DBA, EU, EUM, IC, MM, OLS, OS, and TS.

Phase 5

Phase 5, the SQL Design Review (SDR), must occur for each SQL statement before production turnover. This phase should consist of the following analyses.

An `EXPLAIN` should be run for each SQL statement using production statistics. The `PLAN_TABLE` should then be analyzed to determine whether the most efficient access paths have been chosen. If a plan analysis tool is available, the output from it should be analyzed as well.

Every DB2 program should be reviewed to ensure that inefficient COBOL constructs were not used. In addition, efficient SQL implemented inefficiently in loops should be analyzed for its appropriateness.

All dynamic SQL should be reviewed whether it is embedded in an application program or earmarked for QMF. The review should include multiple EXPLAINs for various combinations of host variables. Be sure to EXPLAIN combinations of host variable values so that you test both values that are not one of the 10 most frequently occurring values and values that are one of the 10 most frequently occurring values.. These values can be determined by running the column occurrence query as presented in Chapter 19.

Different access paths can be chosen for the same query based on differing column value distributions. Values within and outside these top 10 values must be explained and analyzed to avoid performance surprises with dynamic SQL queries.

Suggestions for performance improvements should be made and tested before implementation to determine their effect. If better performance is achieved, the SQL should be modified.

Participants should include AD, DBA, EU, and IC.

Phase 6

Phase 6 is the Pre-Implementation Design Review (PreIDR). This phase is simply a review of the system components before implementation. Loose ends from the preceding five phases should be taken care of, and a final, quick review of each application component should be performed.

Participants should include AA, AD, DA, DBA, EU, EUM, IC, MM, OLS, OS, and TS.

Phase 7

The last design review phase is phase 7, the Post-Implementation Design Review (PostIDR). This phase is necessary to determine whether the application is meeting its performance objectives and functionality objectives. If any objective is not being met, a plan for addressing the deficiency must be proposed and acted on. Multiple PostIDR phases can occur.

Participants should include AA, AD, DA, DBA, EU, EUM, IC, MM, OLS, OS, and TS.

Operational Support

When you're implementing a DB2 environment, sufficient operational support must be available to administer the environment effectively. *Operational support* is defined as the elements of the organization responsible for supporting, maintaining, and running the applications.

This first major operational concern is the establishment of a staff that can support DB2. You can choose from four approaches to staffing for DB2 support. The first is to develop all DB2 expertise using the existing staff. This approach requires a significant amount of training and can result in slow DB2 implementation as your staff comes up to speed with DB2.

The second approach is to hire outside expertise. This approach usually results in a much faster implementation of DB2, but it can breed resentment from your current staff and result in a workplace where it is difficult to accomplish much because of a lack of cooperation between the old staff and the new.

The third approach is to entrust all DB2 development to an outside contracting or consulting firm. This approach is the worst. Although it results in quick development, no one is left to support the application after it is developed.

The fourth and best approach is to combine these strategies. Plan to train your brightest and most eager staff members, while augmenting that staff with several outside experts, temporary consultants, and contract programmers.

Expertise (obtained outside or inside the organization) is required in each of the following areas:

Programmers	In addition to basic coding skills, must know SQL coding techniques and the teleprocessing monitor in your shop.
Systems analysts	Must know DB2 development techniques, data modeling, and process modeling. Should be able to use the CASE tools in your shop.
Data analysts	Must be able to work with data administration and database administration to develop application-level models.
DBA	Must be knowledgeable in all aspects of DB2, with emphasis on the physical implementation of DB2 objects, DB2 utilities, SQL efficiency, and problem solving.
Technical support	Must have basic systems programming skills in addition to an understanding of DB2 installation, DB2 recovery, and day-to-day technical support.
Production control	In addition to basic job scheduling skills, must understand how DB2 is integrated into the organization. Must minimally be able to understand and issue DB2 commands when a problem occurs.
Help desk	Must be able to provide SQL expertise.

Another operational concern is the integration of DB2 standards, policies, procedures, and guidelines with existing ones. These two sets of standards could conflict. For example, DB2 data sets must conform to a rigid standard, but it usually does not agree with the organization's current data set naming standards.

Another operational concern is enabling the production control personnel who submit and monitor production jobs to execute DB2 commands. Enabling operational personnel in this manner could conflict with the current nature of production support as a facilitator and not a doer.

Scheduling of and responsibility for DB2 utilities might pose a problem for your shop. Some utilities lend themselves more toward being developed and supported by a DBA or a technical support area, whereas others are more application-oriented. Sometimes great debates can ensue over who should have responsibility for each utility.

Political Issues

The technical hurdles in supporting a DB2 environment sometimes pale in comparison to the political issues. Technical problems can always be addressed by a combination of outside expertise, enhanced hardware, add-on tools, and overtime. Political issues are more difficult to overcome because they typically rely on human nature, which is fragile at best.

Of paramount importance to the health of your DB2 support structure is keeping the valuable employees with DB2 skills. Although doing so is not always easy, you can do it by packaging jobs with a healthy mix of job challenge, fair salaries, and merit-based promotions.

When this type of workplace is achieved, however, problems occur when other employees learn that junior personnel with advanced DB2 skills are being paid more than senior personnel without those skills. However, DB2 skills are in high demand in the marketplace, so failure to compensate your DB2 employees could result in their leaving. You can take either of two approaches to dealing with the problem, but neither is pleasurable. Either underpay DB2 professionals and risk losing them to firms willing to pay the going rate, or pay the going rate for DB2 expertise and risk resentment from the rest of your application development personnel.

Following are some other political issues that you must deal with in a DB2 workplace. If 24-hour availability and support is required, your personnel might have to adjust their attitude toward shift work and carrying pagers.

Often many programmers will clamor for the opportunity to work on DB2 projects for the chance to learn DB2. They are aware of the monetary rewards that can result if DB2 skills are added to their repertoire. Choosing which of your valued personnel should be given this chance can be difficult. With the advent of client/server technology and the Internet, many shops now have the opposite problem: skilled DB2 professionals wanting to expand their horizons are looking to move out of the DB2 arena into other projects using newer (and resume-enhancing) technology.

Another type of political problem that you can encounter is the direct opposite of the preceding one: ambivalence. People are sometimes afraid of change, and DB2 forces change on an organization. This change can scare MIS personnel and create a resistance movement against DB2 development efforts. This resistance can be assuaged with education and time.

Finally, many organizations have an "island unto themselves" attitude. This attitude should be avoided regarding DB2 development and support. DB2 is complex and dynamic, which makes it difficult to master. Do not be shy about attending user groups meetings, contracting expert consultants to assist with difficult or critical tasks, or contacting other local companies that have experienced the same problems or developed a similar system. Most DB2 professionals are willing to share their experiences to develop a contact that might be useful in the future. And, by all means, share your experiences with other shops. The more informed everyone is, the better.

Environmental Support

The organization must ensure that adequate levels of support are available for the online environments of choice (CICS, TSO, IMS/TM, or other in-house teleprocessing monitors). Usually, the addition of DB2 development to these environments adds considerable growth to the number of developers and end users of these monitors. Be sure that this explosion in use is planned and that appropriate staffing is available to support the growth.

Additionally, if performance monitors are unavailable for these environments, the addition of DB2 should cause your organization to rethink its position. When DB2 is added to the puzzle, tracking certain types of performance problems can be nearly impossible without a performance monitor available in each environment.

Tool Requirements

DB2 implementation is not quite as simple as installing DB2 alone. Your organization must budget for not just DB2 but also DB2, QMF, and tools from the categories deemed most important by your organization. As time goes on and DB2 use grows, your organization should plan to acquire more tools. Budgeting for DB2 tools should be an annual process.

Summary

As you can see, establishing the ideal DB2 environment is not an easy undertaking. It involves not only the installation and mastering (if such a thing is possible) of DB2 but also much organizational change and political maneuvering. This chapter should help you deal with these sometimes frustrating issues.

VIII

Distributed DB2

The final section of this book covers using DB2 in a distributed environment.

DB2 can function as a distributed database management system (DDBMS). A DDBMS is a collection of data spread across multiple computers, and possibly, multiple geographic locations. The distributed components communicate with one another by means of a network. In addition, the DDBMS controls data access and modification requests across the network. Indeed, users of a distributed database should not be aware that the data is distributed to several disparate locations.

The implementation of a distributed database is only one phase of implementing distributed processing. Other stages allocate tasks to available locations (or nodes) to balance the workload across the distributed environment. Involving several computing environments in a distributed network enables optimal utilization of a company's computing resources. These resources may include mainframes, midranges, workstations, and PCs.

Two other types of processing being bandied about in the trades these days can be considered components of distributed processing:

- **Client/server processing** is a specialized form of distributed processing in which one node acts as the supplier of information (the server) and the other nodes act as requesters of information (clients).
- **Cooperative processing** is also a type of distributed processing. Applications running on multiple computing platforms each perform a piece of the overall work in a cooperative processing application.

The Advantages of Data Distribution

Distributed data is fast becoming a fact of life for data processing professionals. Unarguably, a distributed DBMS is more complex, more prone to error, and more susceptible to performance degradation than a non-distributed DBMS. Why then is everyone rushing to distribute their data?

Given these very real precautions, distributing data across multiple sites provides some major advantages, such as the following:

- Eliminating the single point of failure. When data is distributed across multiple locations, no single location is a bottleneck. With portions of the data (and application) residing at multiple sites, each constitutes a point of failure, but none cripples the entire system.
- Moving data to its "home" location can enhance performance. By modeling distributed data such that the data is stored at the location that will access it most frequently, network transmission can be reduced. This should bolster performance.

- Distributing data to multiple sites increases overall availability because when one site is unavailable, the others can still function.
- Establishing multiple, distributed processing sites can aid disaster recovery planning. A remote system can be configuring to handle the bulk of the transaction load in the event of a disaster, thereby reducing down-time.
- Capacity management is easier because growth can occur across the network on all nodes, instead of on a single (potentially overloaded) node only.

DB2 Data Distribution

The purpose of this section, however, is not to delve into an exhaustive definition of distributed processing, but to describe how DB2 can operate in a distributed fashion. As such, it will encompass:

- A description of DRDA, IBM's Distributed Relational Data Architecture. DRDA is the framework upon which IBM has based its distributed relational database management systems.
- A description of DB2's current level of support for data distribution, including DB2 private protocol, DB2's current level of support for DRDA, and distributed two-phase commit.
- Tips and techniques to follow when implementing distributed DB2 databases and applications.

DB2 Data Warehousing

A topic related to data distribution is the burgeoning acceptance of developing DB2-based data warehouses and data marts. Although distributed DB2 is not a requirement for data warehousing, many of the techniques required to build a data warehouse are similar.

Techniques and guidelines for designing, populating, managing, and accessing DB2 data warehouses are provided in the final chapter of the book.

So, turn the page to begin your voyage into the realm of distributed DB2 data!

34

DRDA

When discussing distributed DB2 data, it is necessary to cover Distributed Relational Database Architecture (DRDA)—an architecture developed by IBM that enables relational data to be distributed among multiple platforms. Both *like* and *unlike* platforms can communicate with one another. For example, one DB2 subsystem can communicate to another DB2 subsystem (like). Alternately, a DB2 subsystem can communicate with a third-party RDBMS (unlike). The platforms do not need to be the same. As long as they both conform to the DRDA specifications, they can communicate. DRDA can be considered a sort of universal, distributed data protocol.

This chapter describes DRDA. Keep in mind that no vendor, not even IBM, has implemented an RDBMS that fully supports all DRDA functionality. Chapter 33, "Organizational Issues," describes the components of DRDA currently supported by DB2 V3.

What Is DRDA?

DRDA is a set of *protocols,* or rules, that enable a user to access distributed data, regardless of where it physically resides. It provides an open, robust heterogeneous distributed database environment. DRDA provides methods of coordinating communication among distributed locations. This enables applications to access multiple remote tables at various locations and have them appear to the end user as if they constituted a logical whole.

A distinction should be made, however, between the architecture and the implementation. DRDA describes the architecture for distributed data and nothing more. It defines the rules for accessing the distributed data, but it does not provide the actual application programming interfaces (APIs) to perform the access. Thus, DRDA is not an actual program but is similar to the specifications for a program.

When a DBMS is said to be *DRDA-compliant,* it follows DRDA specifications. DB2 is a DRDA-compliant RDBMS product.

Benefits of DRDA

DRDA is only one protocol for supporting distributed RDBMS. Of course, if you are a DB2 user, DRDA is probably the only protocol that matters.

The biggest benefit provided by DRDA is a clearly stated set of rules for supporting distributed data access. Any product that follows these rules can seamlessly integrate with any other DRDA-compliant product. Furthermore, DRDA-compliance RDBMSs support full data distribution, including multi-site update. The biggest advantage, however, is that DRDA is available today, and an ever-increasing number of vendors are jumping on the DRDA-compliance bandwagon.

An alternative to using DRDA is to utilize a *gateway* product to access distributed data. Gateways are comprised of at least two components—one for each distributed location. These parts communicate with one another. With DB2, a host-based gateway component is necessary. It functions as another mainframe DB2 application. Most gateway products that access DB2 execute using CICS (and sometimes VTAM). Gateways, however, typically support dynamic SQL only.

Thus, there are two more advantages of DRDA surface in the performance arena:

- The removal of the overhead associated with the gateway and its code
- The removal of reliance upon dynamic SQL and the potential performance degradation associated with it

What About RDA?

Although DRDA is the distributed architecture utilized by DB2, it is not the only architecture in the industry. Remote Database Access (RDA) is a competing set of protocols developed by the ISO and ANSI standard committees.

As a DB2 developer, DRDA is the method you'll use to implement distributed data with DB2. However, knowing a bit about RDA cannot hurt:

- RDA was built to work with a standard subset of SQL, available from DBMS to DBMS. DRDA was built to function with platform-specific extensions to SQL.
- Static SQL can be used with DRDA. With RDA, only dynamic SQL is currently available.

DRDA Functions

Three functions are utilized by DRDA to provide distributed relational data access:

- Application Requester (AR)
- Application Server (AS)
- Database Server (DS)

These three functions interoperate to enable distributed access. See Figure 34.1.

The following sections examine these three functions.

FIGURE 34.1.
The three DRDA functions.

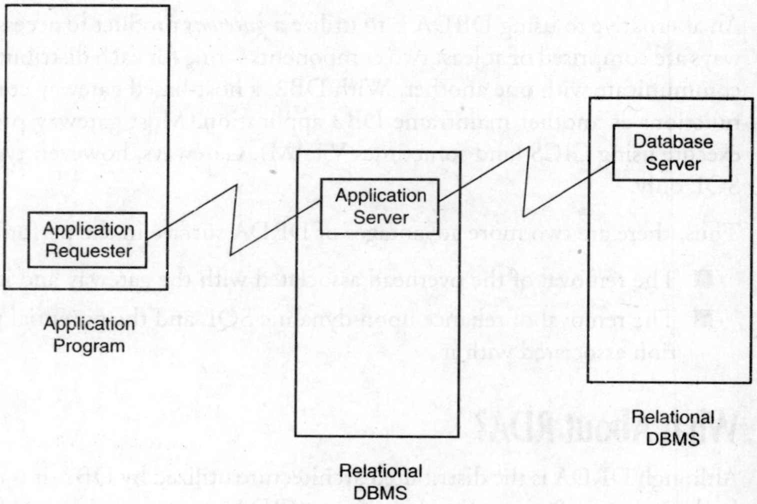

Application Requester

The DRDA application requester (AR) function enables SQL and program preparation requests to be requested by application programs. The AR accepts SQL requests from an application and sends them to the appropriate application server (or servers) for subsequent processing. Using this function, application programs can access remote data.

In theory, if all the data you are interested in is physically located somewhere else (that is, at a *remote* location), there may not be any need for a local RDBMS. DRDA does not require the requester to run on a system with a local RDBMS.

For the DB2 family, the DRDA AR function is implemented as follows:

DBMS	DRDA Facility
DB2 MVS	Distributed Data Facility (DDF)
DB2/2	Distributed Database Connection Services/2 (DDCS/2)
DB2/6000	Distributed Database Connection Services/6000 (DDCS/6000)

Application Server

The DRDA application server (AS) function receives requests from application requesters and processes them. These requests can be either SQL statements or program preparation requests. The AS acts upon the portions that can be processed and forwards the remainder to DRDA database servers for subsequent processing. This is necessary if the local RDBMS cannot process the request.

The AR is connected to the AS using a communication protocol called the Application Support Protocol. The Application Support Protocol is responsible for providing the appropriate level of data conversion. This is only necessary when different data representations are involved in the request. An example of this is the conversion of ASCII characters to EBCDIC (or vice versa).

Database Server

The DRDA database server (DS) function receives requests from application servers or other database servers. These requests can be either SQL statements or program preparation requests. Like the application server, the database server processes what it can and forwards the remainder to another database server.

It is important to note that a database server request may be for a component of an SQL statement. This would occur if data is distributed across two subsystems and a join is requested. The join statement accesses data from tables at two different locations. As such, one portion must be processed at one location and the other portion at a different location.

Because the database servers involved in a distributed request don't need to be the same, the Database Support Protocol is used. It exists for the following reasons:

- To connect an application server to a database server
- To connect two database servers

Like the Application Support Protocol, the Database Support Protocol is used to ensure compatibility of requests between different database servers.

What Is Returned?

When a request is completely processed, the application server must inform the requesting process—the application requester. How is this accomplished?

The AS passes a return code and a result set (if one was produced) back to the AR. The return code is the SQLSTATE (or SQLCODE in DB2). A result set is not generated under the following circumstances:

- INSERT
- UPDATE
- DELETE
- SELECT when no rows qualify
- DCL and DDL requests

This protocol is used unless a cursor is employed. When rows are fetched from a read-only cursor, *limited block protocol* can be used. Limited block protocol passes multiple rows across the network at a time, even though one fetch can process only a single row at a time. Limited block protocol enhances overall performance by minimizing network traffic. If the cursor is not read-only (that is, rows can be updated), limited block protocol is not employed.

DRDA Architectures and Standards

In order for DRDA to exist, it must rely on other established protocols. Refer to Figure 34.2. These architectures are examined in the following sections.

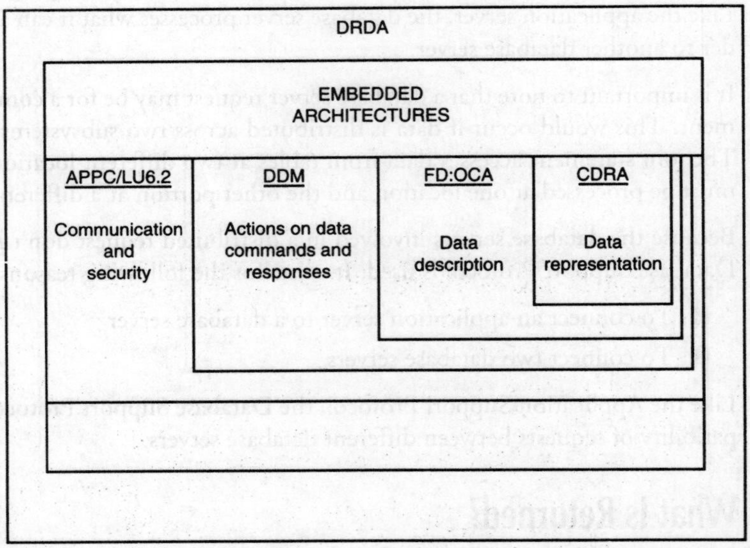

FIGURE 34.2.
DRDA's supporting architectures.

Advanced Program-to-Program Communication (APPC)

Advanced Program-to-Program Communication provides peer-level communication support based on LU 6.2 protocols. LU 6.2 is an advanced communication architecture that defines the formats and protocols for message transmission between functionally equivalent logical units.

APPC/LU 6.2 provides communication and transaction processing facilities needed for cooperative processing and distributed transaction processing.

Distributed Data Management (DDM)

The Distributed Data Management architecture defines facilities for accessing distributed data across a network using APPC and LU 6.2. With DDM, the distributed data to be accessed can reside in either files or relational databases. An RDBMS is implied, however, within the context of DRDA.

Formatted Data: Object Content Architecture (FD:OCA)

FD:OCA is an architecture that provides for the distribution and exchange of field-formatted data. Using FD:OCA, both the data and its description are packaged together so that any DRDA-compliant DBMS can understand its structure and content.

Character Data Representation Architecture (CDRA)

Character Data Representation Architecture is the architecture utilized to ensure that any symbol or character used on any SAA relational DBMS has the same meaning, regardless of the underlying coded character set. CDRA provides a method of unambiguously identifying data from any SAA platform.

CDRA is necessary particularly when data is transferred between a PC work-station (using ASCII code) and a mainframe (using EBCDIC code). Theoretically, CDRA can be extended to support other codes, such as Unicode—a new character encoding scheme that is gaining support.

The Five DRDA Levels

There are five levels within DRDA. Each level represents an increasing level of distributed support. Additionally, the levels reflect the following:

- The number of requests and RDBMSs per unit of work
- The number of RDBMSs per request

In order of increasing complexity, the five DRDA levels are

- User-Assisted Distribution
- Remote Request
- Remote Unit of Work (RUW)
- Distributed Unit of Work (DUW)
- Distributed Request

See Table 34.1 for a synopsis of the DRDA levels.

Table 34.1. The five DRDA levels.

DRDA Level	*SQL Stmts per UOW*	*DBMS per UOW*	*DBMS per SQL Stmt*
User-Assisted			
Remote Request	1	1	1
Remote Unit of Work	>1	1	1

continues

Table 34.1. continued

DRDA Level	SQL Stmts per UOW	DBMS per UOW	DBMS per SQL Stmt
Distributed Unit of Work	>1	>1	1
Distributed Request	>1	>1	>1

The result of moving up the levels is additive. For example, distributed request capability implies distributed unit of work (which in turn implies remote unit of work). The reverse, however, is not implicitly true.

These levels are discussed at greater length in the following sections.

User-Assisted Distribution

User-assisted distribution is the simplest form of data distribution. However, under this DRDA level, the end user is aware of the distribution and participates in accomplishing the distributed access. To accomplish user-assisted distribution, the user must

- Extract the needed data from the original system
- Load the extracted data to the requesting system

This is an intensive procedure that should not be taken lightly. Because it involves replicated data, care must be taken to document the system of record and the date of extraction in case future modification is permitted.

Even given its many limitations, user-assisted distribution is useful for producing snapshot tables and satisfying one-time requests. However, to many, user-assisted distribution is not truly distributed data access. I tend to agree with them.

Often, user-assisted distribution is not included in a formal discussion of DRDA. However, a discussion of it is included here for completeness.

Remote Request

Remote request is the first level of true distribution within DRDA. When a DBMS supports DRDA remote request capability, a single SQL statement can be issued to read or modify a single remote RDBMS within a single unit of work.

Simply stated, remote request enables developers to operate within one RDBMS and refer to a different RDBMS. Furthermore, it is possible to utilize remote request capability to access a remote RDBMS, even if a local RDBMS is not being used.

DRDA remote request provides the capability of issuing only one SQL request per unit of work, and only one RDBMS per SQL request.

Remote Unit of Work

The remote unit of work (RUW) DRDA level adds to the functionality of remote request. RUW enables multiple SQL statements. However, the SQL can only read and modify a single remote RDBMS within a single a unit of work.

Within the scope of a commit, RUW can access only one RDBMS.

Therefore, DRDA remote unit of work provides the capability of issuing multiple SQL requests per unit of work but still can access only one RDBMS per SQL request.

Distributed Unit of Work

Distributed unit of work (DUW) builds onto the functionality of remote unit of work. More than one RDBMS can be accessed per unit of work.

Simply stated, DRDA DUW enables multiple SQL statements to read and modify multiple RDBMSs within a single unit of work. However, only one RDBMS can be specified per SQL statement.

As with any unit of work, all SQL statements within the commit scope either succeed or fail. This requires a two-phase commit protocol to be established. Distributed two-phase commit is functionally equivalent to the two-phase commit DB2 performs when executing under CICS or IMS/TM. When a DUW program issues a COMMIT, the two-phase commit protocol must synchronize the commit across all affected platforms.

Distributed Request

DRDA distributed request capability enables complete data distribution. Using distributed request, the DUW restriction of one RDBMS per SQL statement is removed. Additionally, multiple SQL requests, both distributed and nondistributed can be contained within a single unit of work.

Simply stated, distributed request enables a single SQL statement to read and update multiple RDBMSs at the same time.

No RDBMS products currently provide DRDA distributed request capability.

Putting It All Together

Consider a scenario in which three remote-processing locations are set up, each with an RDBMS: Pittsburgh, Chicago, and Jacksonville. See how each of the four DRDA options could access distributed data from these locations. (See Figure 34.3.)

Consider a situation wherein you need to access specific columns from tables at each remote location. Furthermore, assume that the requests are emanating from Chicago.

FIGURE 34.3.
DRDA remote request.

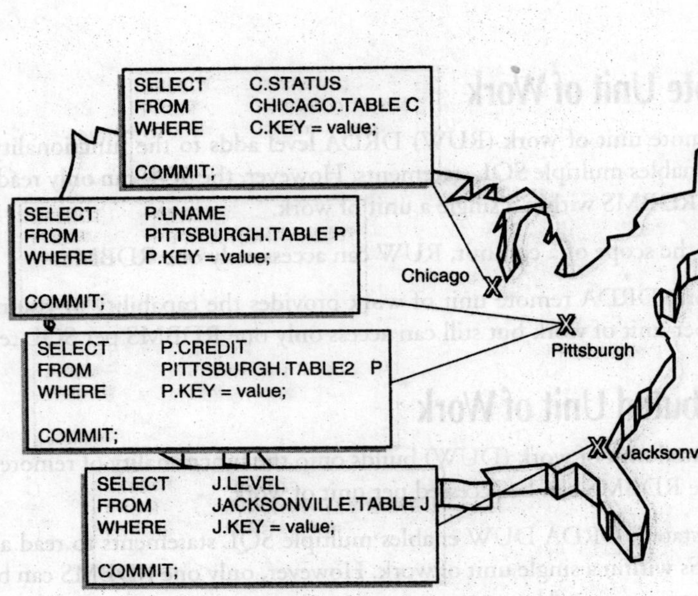
SELECT C.STATUS
FROM CHICAGO.TABLE C
WHERE C.KEY = value;
COMMIT;
SELECT P.LNAME
FROM PITTSBURGH.TABLE P
WHERE P.KEY = value;
COMMIT;
SELECT P.CREDIT
FROM PITTSBURGH.TABLE2 P
WHERE P.KEY = value;
COMMIT;
SELECT J.LEVEL
FROM JACKSONVILLE.TABLE J
WHERE J.KEY = value;
COMMIT;
Chicago
Pittsburgh
Jacksonville

Refer to Figure 34.3 for a depiction of remote request distributed access. In this scenario, you can access only a single RDBMS from a single location in a single unit of work. The request to the Chicago table is a local request; the Pittsburgh and Jacksonville requests are remote. Each request is within a single unit of work (indicated by the `COMMIT`).

Remote unit of work functionality is depicted in Figure 34.4. Contrast this diagram with remote request. Instead of a single statement per unit of work, multiple statements can be issued. (See the Pittsburgh example.)

FIGURE 34.4.
DRDA remote unit of work.

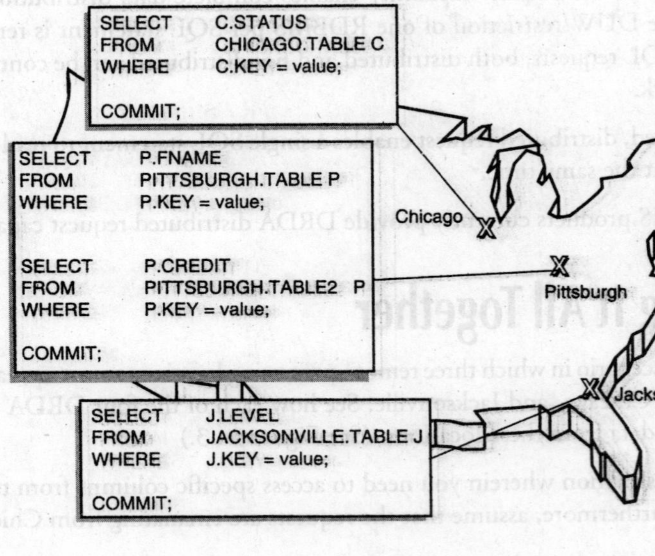
SELECT C.STATUS
FROM CHICAGO.TABLE C
WHERE C.KEY = value;
COMMIT;
SELECT P.FNAME
FROM PITTSBURGH.TABLE P
WHERE P.KEY = value;
SELECT P.CREDIT
FROM PITTSBURGH.TABLE2 P
WHERE P.KEY = value;
COMMIT;
SELECT J.LEVEL
FROM JACKSONVILLE.TABLE J
WHERE J.KEY = value;
COMMIT;
Chicago
Pittsburgh
Jacksonville

Distributed unit of work enables multiple RDBMSs per unit of work. This is shown in Figure 34.5.

All four tables from all three locations can be accessed within one unit of work using DRDA DUW functionality.

Finally, Figure 34.6 depicts distributed request. Using distributed request, multiple RDBMSs from multiple locations can be accessed using a single SQL statement. In this scenario, the application requester sends a request to the Chicago application server, which in turn sends the request to the Chicago database server. It processes what it can and passes it to one of the other database servers (for example, to Pittsburgh) and so on.

FIGURE 34.5.
DRDA distributed unit of work.

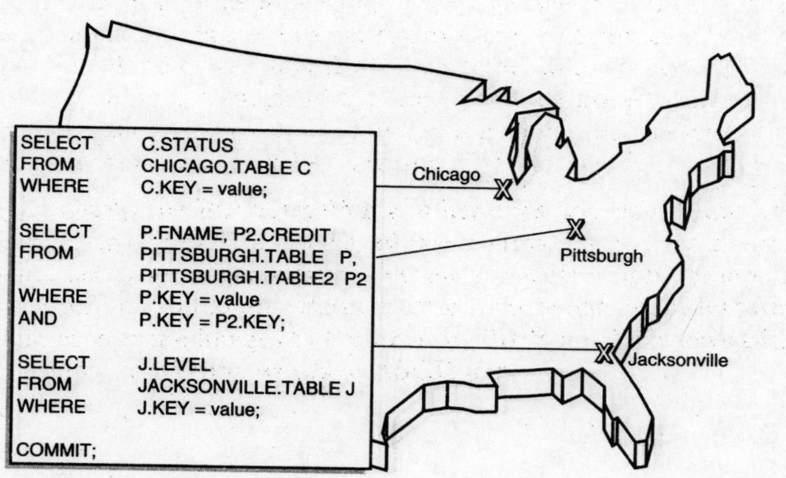
SELECT C.STATUS
FROM CHICAGO.TABLE C
WHERE C.KEY = value;
SELECT P.FNAME, P2.CREDIT
FROM PITTSBURGH.TABLE P,
PITTSBURGH.TABLE2 P2
WHERE P.KEY = value
AND P.KEY = P2.KEY;
SELECT J.LEVEL
FROM JACKSONVILLE.TABLE J
WHERE J.KEY = value;
COMMIT;
Chicago
Pittsburgh
Jacksonville

FIGURE 34.6.
DRDA distributed request.

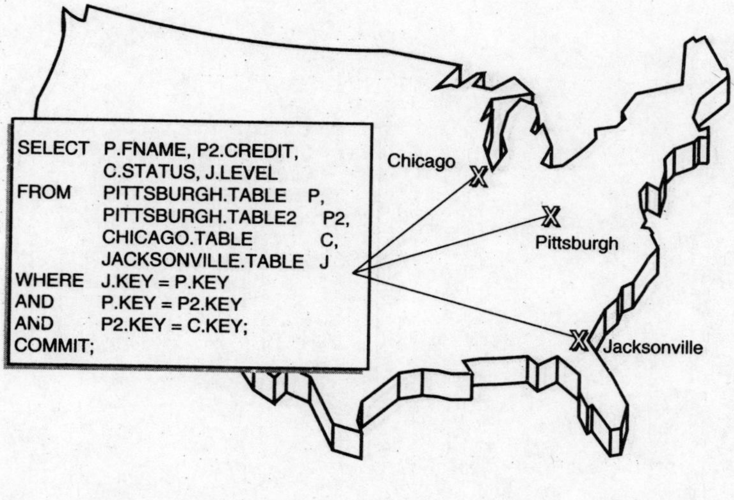
SELECT P.FNAME, P2.CREDIT,
C.STATUS, J.LEVEL
FROM PITTSBURGH.TABLE P,
PITTSBURGH.TABLE2 P2,
CHICAGO.TABLE C,
JACKSONVILLE.TABLE J
WHERE J.KEY = P.KEY
AND P.KEY = P2.KEY
AND P2.KEY = C.KEY;
COMMIT;
Chicago
Pittsburgh
Jacksonville

Summary

This chapter has covered the DRDA framework only. It has not discussed actual implementation in DB2. For this information, see Chapter 35, "Distributed DB2."

35

Distributed DB2

In the preceding chapter, I discussed DRDA from a purely theoretical perspective. DB2 distributes data following the DRDA architecture. However, you will find major differences in some aspects of DB2's implementation of distributed data.

Distributing Data Using DB2

DB2 can distribute data following three of the DRDA levels: remote request, remote unit of work, and distributed unit of work. As of DB2 V5, distributed request capability is not available. Additionally, DB2 V5 supports application requester and application server functions. The database server function is not available under DB2 V5.

DB2 also provides the capability to access distributed data using a non-DRDA private protocol. This capability was introduced to DB2 prior to the existence of DRDA.

The Basics

The Distributed Data Facility (DDF) is required for accessing distributed data through DB2. The DDF is an optional DB2 address space. (Recall from Chapter 13, "DB2 Behind the Scenes," that the others are the DBAS, SSAS, and IRLM.)

The Communication Database

Distributed DB2 connections are defined using system tables defined to DB2. For DB2 V4 and prior releases, connection information is stored in the Communications Data Base (CDB). The CDB is created either during or after DB2's installation. Just like any other DB2 database, the CDB is created using DDL and is maintained using DML `INSERT`, `UPDATE`, and `DELETE` statements. The DDF reads the CDB to perform authid name translations and to map DB2 objects to VTAM objects. As of DB2 V5, the CDB tables were renamed and moved to the DB2 Catalog. The CDB is still required when DB2 V5 subsystems communicate with pre-V5 subsystems.

In a distributed environment, each DB2 subsystem is identified by a unique location name of up to 18 characters. A location can be explicitly accessed using `CONNECT` or three-part table names.

`DSNDDF` is the name of the DB2 database in which the CDB is contained. It consists of six tables in one tablespace (`SYSDDF`). The six tables contain the following information:

`SYSIBM.SYSLOCATIONS`	Maps location names to VTAM `LUNAME`s. Contains a row for each remote DB2 subsystem to which SQL statements can be sent.
`SYSIBM.SYSLULIST`	Assigns `LUNAME`s to locations.
`SYSIBM.SYSLUMODES`	Defines session/conversation limits.

SYSIBM.SYSLUNAMES	Defines the attributes of LUNAMEs. Contains a row for each remote DB2 to which SQL statements can be sent or from which SQL statements can be received.
SYSIBM.SYSMODESELECT	Defines the mode for an individual user.
SYSIBM.SYSUSERNAMES	Translates local usernames.

For DB2 V5, the DB2 Catalog contains seven tables that control distributed DB2 database connections. The seven tables contain thefollowing information:

SYSIBM.IPNAMES	Defines the remote servers that DB2 can access using TCP/IP.
SYSIBM.LOCATIONS	Specifies the location for every accessible remote server.
SYSIBM.LULIST	Assigns LUNAMEs to locations.
SYSIBM.LUMODES	Defines session/conversation limits.
SYSIBM.LUNAMES	Specifies each remote SNA client or server that communicates to DB2.
SYSIBM.MODESELECT	Defines the mode for an individual user.
SYSIBM.USERNAMES	Specifies outbound and inbound ID translations.

Refer to Appendix B, "The DB2 Catalog Tables," for a complete description of the tables used to define distributed DB2 connections.

Distributed Terms

In addition to the DRDA terms from the preceding chapter, I use the following terms in the remainder of this chapter:

- A *location* is a single DB2 subsystem. Locations are also called *sites* or *instances.*
- A *unit of work* describes the activity that occurs between commits. It is also called a *unit of recovery* or *commit scope.*
- A *request* is a single SQL statement.

In the remainder of this chapter, I describe the data distribution options that exist for DB2 V3.

DB2 Support for the DRDA Levels

DB2 provides support for distributed requests using three of the DRDA levels: remote request, remote unit of work, and distributed unit of work.

Remote Request

Applications can implement remote request capability by issuing a single request to a single location within a single unit of work. This approach is the easiest but least flexible method of coding distributed DB2 access.

Remote Unit of Work (RUW)

To utilize RUW within an application program, these rules must be followed:

- Each request must be for a single location.
- Each unit of work can contain multiple requests.
- Each unit of work must access data from a single location only.

A single application program can access data from multiple locations using RUW but not within the same unit of work. The programmer must be cognizant of this fact and therefore code the program appropriately.

Distributed Unit of Work (DUW)

An application utilizes DUW if these rules are followed:

- Each request must be for a single location.
- Each unit of work can contain multiple requests.
- Each unit of work can access data at multiple locations.

Distributed data support was added to DB2 as of V2.2. At that point, IBM had not yet formu lated its DRDA framework. The DUW capability was provided solely through a private pro tocol that did not support any industry standards. Furthermore, it was not full DUW suppor because data could be read from multiple sites and updated only at a single site.

For DB2 V3 and later releases, both the private protocol DUW and full DRDA DUW ar supported. Additionally, the restrictions on multi-site updates are removed because of the ac dition of a distributed two-phase commit.

Methods of Accessing Distributed Data

You should note that the developer of a distributed application does not have to know t descriptions of remote request, RUW, and DUW. Ensuring that the application does not a cess multiple locations within a single request is sufficient. DB2 handles the distributed acc based on the nature of the request(s).

Of course, an informed programmer is an efficient programmer. To enhance performance, application developers should be aware of the location at which the data to be accessed exists.

A DB2 application developer has two choices for the manner in which distributed data is accessed:

- Application-directed access
- System-directed access

In the following sections, you will examine these two methods of distributed data access.

Application-Directed Data Access

Application-directed data access is the more powerful of the two options. With this access, explicit connections are required. Furthermore, application-directed distributed access conforms to the DRDA standard.

Establishing Connections

When implementing application-directed distribution, the application must issue a `CONNECT` statement to the remote location, prior to accessing data from that location. Consider this example:

```
CONNECT TO CHICAGO;
```

This statement connects the application to the location named `CHICAGO`. The connection must be a valid location, as defined in the `SYSIBM.LOCATIONS` (or `SYSBM.SYSLOCATIONS`) table . Multiple locations can be connected at once. For example, an application can issue the following:

```
CONNECT TO CHICAGO;
        .
        .
        .
CONNECT TO JACKSONVILLE;
        .
        .
        .
CONNECT TO PITTSBURGH;
```

In this scenario, three connections have been established—one each to Chicago, Jacksonville, and Pittsburgh. The `CONNECT` statement causes a VTAM conversation to be allocated from the local site to the specified remote location. Therefore, if the preceding example were to be issued from Seattle, three VTAM conversations would be established:

- One from Seattle to Chicago
- One from Seattle to Jacksonville
- One from Seattle to Pittsburgh

However, only one connection can be active at any one time. You use the SET CONNECTION statement to specify which connection should be active. Now look at this example:

```
SET CONNECTION PITTSBURGH;
```

This statement sets the active connection to Pittsburgh. Additionally, the SET CONNECTION statement places the previously active connection into a dormant state.

In all the preceding examples (for both CONNECT and SET CONNECTION), you could have used a host variable in place of the literal, as in this example:

```
SET CONNECTION :HV;
```

This statement sets the active connection to be whatever location was stored in the host variable at the time the statement was executed.

Releasing Connections

After it is established, a connection is available for the duration of the program unless it is explicitly released or the DISCONNECT BIND option was not set to EXPLICIT (which is the default).

Connections are explicitly released using the RELEASE statement, as shown here:

```
RELEASE PITTSBURGH;
```

This statement releases the connection to the Pittsburgh location. Valid options that can be specified on the RELEASE statement are

- A valid location specified as a literal or a host variable
- CURRENT, which releases the currently active connection
- ALL, which releases all connections
- ALL PRIVATE, which releases DB2 private connection and is discussed in the next section

The DISCONNECT BIND option also affects when connections are released. You can specify this option for plans only. It applies to all processes that use the plan and have remote connections of any type. The following DISCONNECT parameters are valid:

EXPLICIT	This option is the default. It indicates that only released connections will be destroyed at a COMMIT point.
AUTOMATIC	This option specifies that all remote connections are to be destroyed at a COMMIT point.
CONDITIONAL	This option specifies that all remote connections are to be destroyed at a COMMIT point unless a WITH HOLD cursor is associated with the conversation.

System-Directed Data Access

In addition to application-directed distribution, DB2 also provides system-directed access to distributed DB2 data. The system-directed access is less flexible than application-directed access because of the following reasons:

- It does not use the open DRDA protocol but uses a DB2-only, private protocol.
- It is viable for DB2-to-DB2 distribution only.
- Connections cannot be explicitly requested but are implicitly performed when distributed requests are initiated.

Although system-directed access does not conform to DRDA, it does provide the same levels of distributed support as application-directed access—remote request, RUW, and DUW.

System-directed access is requested using three-part table names, as shown in this example:

```
SELECT   COL1, COL2, COL7*
FROM     PITTSBURGH.OWNER.TABLE
WHERE    KEY = :HV
```

Issuing this request causes an implicit connection to be established to the Pittsburgh location. DB2 determines the location by using the high-level qualifier of the three-part name. This type of distribution is called system-directed because the system (DB2), not the application, determines to which location to connect.

Optionally, you can create an alias for the three-part table name. The alias enables users to access a remote table (or view) without knowing its location. Here's an example:

```
CREATE ALIAS EMP
FOR PITTSBURGH.OWNER.EMPLOYEE;

SELECT COL1, COL2
FROM    EMP;
```

The first statement creates the alias EMP for the EMPLOYEE table located in Pittsburgh. The second statement requests the data from the Pittsburgh EMPLOYEE table using the alias. Note that the three-part name is avoided.

CAUTION

IBM will eventually phase out system-directed distribution in subsequent releases of DB2. IBM continues to support system-directed distribution to provide support for legacy applications written using the private protocol before DRDA support was provided. You therefore should avoid implementing new applications using system-directed distribution.

DB2 V3 Provides Full DUW Capability

Prior to DB2 V3, system-directed distribution provided only a partial implementation of distributed unit of work capability. The implementation was incomplete because the capability to update multiple sites within a unit of work was not available. Multiple sites could be read, but only a single site could be updated. Of course, DB2 V3 rectified this problem by supplying a distributed two-phase commit capability.

Furthermore, prior to DB2 V3, updates could be requested only through local CICS and IMS subsystems. Remote updates were forbidden. DB2 V3 lifted this restriction as well. Multi-site update is possible, regardless of how you attach to DB2:

- CAF
- CICS
- IMS/TM
- TSO

See Figure 35.1 for a synopsis of the distributed capabilities of DB2 V2.3 compared to DB2 V3.

FIGURE 35.1.
Distributed data capabilities.

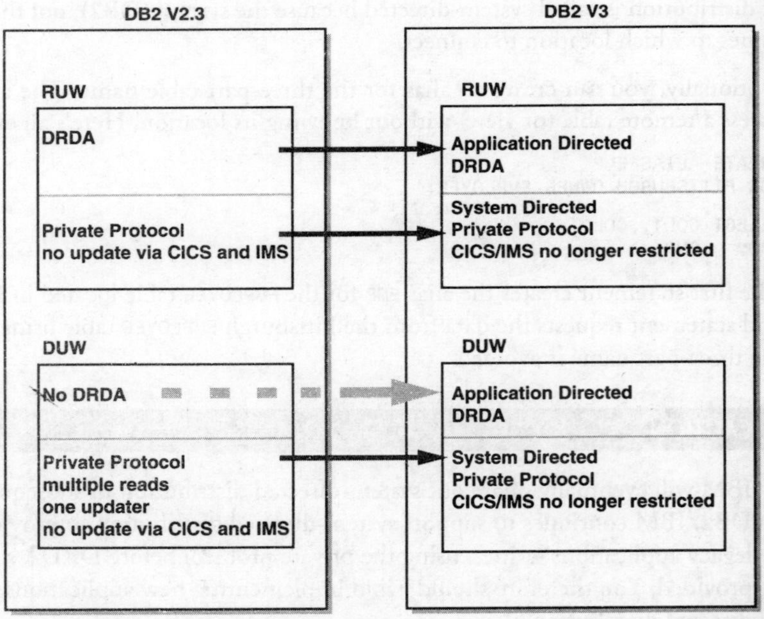

System-Directed Versus Application-Directed

Which is better: system-directed or application-directed access? Both have their benefits and drawbacks. For a short comparison of the two methods, refer to Table 35.1.

Table 35.1. Application-directed versus system-directed access.

	Application-Directed	*System-Directed*
Explicit connections	Yes	No
Three-part table names	No	Yes
Can issue DCL	Yes	No
Can issue DDL	Yes	No
Can issue DML	Yes	Yes
Static SQL using packages	Yes	No
Dynamic SQL at the server	No	Yes
DB2 to any server	Yes	No
DB2 to DB2	Yes	Yes
Open DRDA protocol	Yes	No
DB2 Private protocol	No	Yes
Distributed request support	No	No
Read and update at remote locations from CAF	Yes	Yes
Read and update at remote locations from TSO	Yes	Yes
Read and update at remote locations from CICS	Yes	Yes
Read and update at remote locations from IMS/TM	Yes	Yes

Regardless of the relative merits of system-directed versus application-directed distribution, favor application-directed distribution because it is IBM's strategic direction for DB2 data distribution.

Packages for Static SQL

Static SQL is supported in distributed applications by packages. To access remote locations using SQL embedded in an application program, the program must be precompiled and then bound into a package. The application program calls the SQL API, which executes the package at the RDBMS.

If the application program requires access to multiple RDBMSs, multiple packages must be bound, one at each location. Packages enable a request originating from one location to execute static SQL at remote locations. Of course, dynamic SQL is also supported using system-directed distribution.

Two-Phase Commit

Distributed two-phase commit enables application programs to update data in multiple RDBMSs within a single unit of work. The two-phase commit process coordinates the commits across the multiple platforms. The two-phase commit provides a consistent outcome, guaranteeing the integrity of the data across platforms, regardless of communication or system failures.

A distributed two-phase commit process did not exist prior to DB2 V3. Therefore, it was not possible to update multiple locations within a single unit of work.

Two-Phase Commit Terminology

A syncpoint tree is built by the coordinator of a unit of work. The syncpoint tree determines which process is in control of the commit/abort decision.

Each node in the syncpoint tree is the coordinator of its own resources and of the nodes below it on the syncpoint tree. Additionally, a node is a participant of the node directly above it in the syncpoint tree.

Figure 35.2 shows an example of a syncpoint tree. In this example, `DB2V` is the coordinator for `DB2W`, `DB2X`, and `DB2Y`. In addition, `DB2W` is the coordinator for `DB2Z`.

Keep these terms in mind as I discuss the two-phase commit process in this chapter.

What Are the Two Phases?

The two phases in the two-phase commit process are

1. Preparation
2. Actual commit

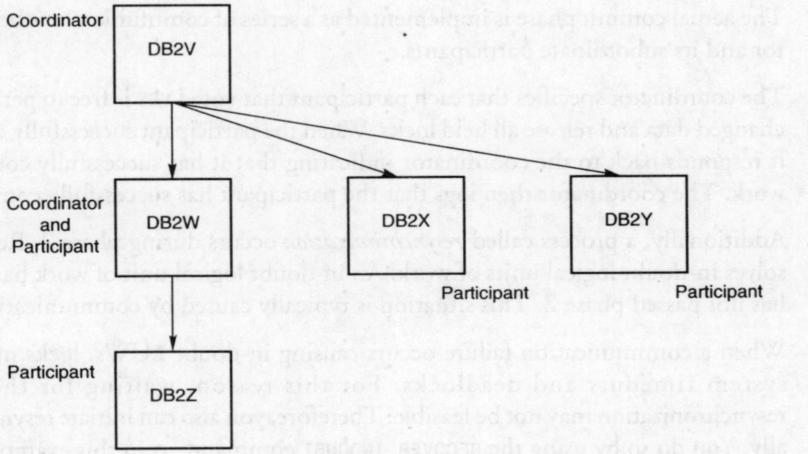

FIGURE 35.2.
A two-phase commit syncpoint tree.

The first phase is the preparation phase. Each participant in the two-phase commit process is informed to get ready to commit. The preparation phase uses the *presumed abort* protocol. Therefore, all affected modifications at all locations within the unit of work are rolled back if an error is encountered.

Each participant informs the coordinator when it has successfully written the appropriate log records and is therefore ready to commit (or roll back) all changes. Usually, this process is followed by a commit. However, if any participant fails to commit, the coordinator may need to back out all changes for all participants.

During phase 1, each participant returns a "vote" on whether commit can proceed. Each participant returns one of the following votes:

`YES`	The participant and all dependent nodes are ready for `COMMIT` or `ABORT` processing.
`READ-ONLY`	The participant and all dependent nodes are read-only and do not need to participate in the two-phase commit process.
`NO`	One or more nodes in the syncpoint tree failed to return a `YES` or `READ-ONLY` vote. A communication failure or error is recorded as a `NO` vote.

If all votes are `READ-ONLY`, a `COMMIT` is not necessary because no updates were performed. If all the votes are `YES` and `READ-ONLY`, the `COMMIT` can be processed. If any vote is `NO`, the unit of work is rolled back.

After all the participants are ready to commit, phase 1 is complete. Therefore, the second phase—the actual commit—is initiated. During phase 2, success is presumed, even in the case of system failure. Because all participants have elected to continue the commit, success can be presumed with no danger of data integrity violations.

The actual commit phase is implemented as a series of communications between the coordinator and its subordinate participants.

The coordinator specifies that each participant that voted YES is free to permanently record the changed data and release all held locks. When the participant successfully completes this work, it responds back to the coordinator indicating that it has successfully committed the unit of work. The coordinator then logs that the participant has successfully committed.

Additionally, a process called *resynchronization* occurs during phase 2. Resynchronization resolves in-doubt logical units of work. An in-doubt logical unit of work has passed phase 1 but has not passed phase 2. This situation is typically caused by communication failures.

When a communication failure occurs causing in-doubt LUWs, locks may be held, causing system timeouts and deadlocks. For this reason, waiting for the automatic DB2 resynchronization may not be feasible. Therefore, you also can initiate resynchronization manually. You do so by using the RECOVER INDOUBT command, as in this example:

```
RECOVER INDOUBT ACTION(COMMIT) ID(1031)
```

This command schedules a commit for the threads identified by the correlation ID of 1031. The ACTION parameter can be either COMMIT or ABORT. The decision whether to commit or abort must be made by the analyst issuing the RECOVER. For this reason, manual resynchronization should be initiated only when absolutely necessary. Automatic DB2 resynchronization is generally more efficient and accurate.

When resynchronization is complete for all the two-phase commit participants, the two-phase commit is complete.

Multi-Site Updating

The presence of the two-phase commit process within DB2 enables multi-site updating capability. The two-phase commit occurs when data at more than one remote location is modified (INSERT, UPDATE, and/or DELETE).

The two-phase commit process ensures that data at all remote locations is consistent and recoverable.

One-Phase or Two-Phase Commit

Two-phase commit is optional. However, if you need to implement applications that perform multi-site updates within a single unit of work, two-phase commit is mandatory. The SYNCLVL=SYNCPT parameter must be specified on the VTAM APPL definition statement to configure DB2's communication support for two-phase commit.

Distributed Thread Support

Successive versions of DB2 have provided enhanced thread support specifically to increase the performance and functionality of distributed applications.

Inactive DBATS

Prior to DB2 V3, remote distributed applications would repeatedly connect, perform the appropriate processing, commit, and then disconnect. This process generated a significant amount of overhead to support each connect and disconnect request. For DB2 V3 and later releases, each database access thread (DBAT) can be made inactive instead of disconnecting. A DBAT becomes inactive when *all* the following are true:

- A commit or rollback was the last task performed.
- No locks are being held by the thread.
- The package being executed was bound specifying `RELEASE(COMMIT)`.
- `INACTIVE` was specified for the DDF `THREAD` install parameter.

Inactive DBATs become active when they receive a message from VTAM. When the remote application shuts down, the thread is disconnected.

Thread Limit Changes

By enabling threads to become inactive instead of disconnecting, DB2 provides a valuable service. However, the existence of inactive threads may cause the number of concurrent DB2 threads to increase substantially.

Version 4

In DB2 V3, the number of concurrent threads was limited to 10,000. As of DB2 V4, this limit is increased to 25,000. This number provides greater flexibility by allowing more connections to be supported by the distributed applications at your shop. The maximum concurrent threads (`MAXDBAT` + `CONDBAT`) can be 25,000, of which only 2,000 (`CTHREAD` + `MAXDBAT`) can be active. See Table 35.2 for a synopsis of the affected `DSNZPARMs`.

Table 35.2. Thread parameters.

Definition	DSNZPARM
Local Threads	CTHREAD
Active DBATs	MAXDBAT
Inactive DBATs	CONDBAT

Miscellaneous Distributed Topics

The following assortment of tips might prove to be helpful as you develop your distributed DB2 applications.

Combining DRDA and Private Protocol Requests

By combining CONNECT statements and SQL statements that access three-part tables names, you can issue application-directed and system-directed requests from within a single unit of work. However, having a system-directed and an application-directed request to the same location is not possible. The requests must be to different locations.

Consider the following piece of code:

```
CONNECT TO JACKSONVILLE;
            .
            .
            .
SELECT COL7
INTO   :HV7
FROM   DEPT;
            .
            .
            .
SELECT COL1, COL2
INTO   :HV1, :HV2
FROM   CHICAGO.OWNER.EMPLOYEE;
            .
            .
            .
COMMIT;
```

The application connects to Jacksonville using application-directed access (CONNECT). At the Jacksonville location, the DEPT table is accessed. Within the same unit of work, a request is made for Chicago data using system-directed access (three-part table name).

Combining DB2 Releases

You can access different release levels of DB2 within a single unit of work. As you might expect, this capability has the following restrictions as well:

- When you're connecting V5 and pre-V5 servers, be sure to keep the CDB. Further, be sure to keep the information in the CDB synchronized with the corresponding DB2 V5 Catalog tables.
- Updates are not permitted to V2.3 servers when accessed from CICS or IMS/TM.
- DB2 V2.2 requesters cannot access DB2 V3 servers.
- When accessing DB2 V2.3, only one phase commit is available.

Workstation DB2

In addition to DB2 for OS/390, IBM also provides versions of DB2 for Windows NT, UNIX, and OS/2 workstations. Of course, these DB2 implementations are not 100-percent compatible with DB2 for OS/390. Also, each DB2 uses SQL, but different SQL features are provided by each. For example, DB2/2 supports the EXCEPT clause for performing relational division and the INTERSECT clause for performing relational intersection. DB2 for OS/390 does not.

At the time of publication, DB2 implementations were available for the following platforms:

AS/400
OS/2
Windows NT
IBM VM
IBM VSE
IBM AIX
Siemens Nixdorf SINIX
Sun Solaris
Hewlett-Packard HP-UX

The edition of DB2 that runs on Windows NT, OS/2, and UNIX variants is called DB2 for Common Servers or DB2 Universal Database. The workstation DB2 products do not internally support DRDA. DRDA support is provided by an additional product, Distributed Data Connection Services (DDCS). This is somewhat analogous to the manner in which DB2 for OS/390 supports distributed access—not internally, but via DDF.

For additional information on how the workstation DB2 products support DRDA, refer to the appropriate IBM manuals for DDCS and the workstation DB2 product of interest.

Developing Client/Server Applications

Client/server processing is fast becoming a *de facto* standard for accessing remote data. DB2 is an ideal candidate for functioning as the server in the client/server framework. It can accept requests from multiple IBM and non-IBM RDBMS products.

ASCII Server Support

IBM mainframes use a different encoding scheme for alphanumeric characters than most other computers. The IBM encoding scheme is known as EBCDIC. When non-IBM computers communicate with IBM computers, it is necessary to translate the EBCDIC encoding scheme to ASCII, the standard encoding scheme used by these other devices.

DB2, as of V5, enables an entire subsystem, database, tablespace, or table to be defined to use ASCII instead of EBCDIC. You can enhance performance by creating ASCII objects for distributed applications because characters will not need to be converted to EBCDIC when communicating with other ASCII servers.

Before creating ASCII objects, consider the following caveats:

- You can specify a different encoding scheme for DB2 objects using the `CCSID` parameter of the `CREATE DATABASE`, `CREATE TABLESPACE`, `CREATE GLOBAL TEMPORARY TABLE`, or `CREATE TABLE` statement.
- The encoding scheme of an object cannot be altered after the object is created.
- Only type 2 indexes are supported for ASCII-encoded tables.
- MVS applications that display ASCII-encoded data actually receive the data as EBCDIC, but sort the data using the ASCII collating sequence.

Native TCP/IP Support

DB2 V5 provides native TCP/IP support for distributed connections. Previous versions of DB2 supported TCP/IP requesters, but only with additional software and configuration. TCP/IP enables direct connections to DB2 from client applications without the overhead and expense of the additional software.

As of V5, you can choose to use SNA, TCP/IP, or mixed networks for distributed DB2 applications.

Summary

In this chapter, you examined the how-to aspect of accessing distributed DB2 data. But what about the practical implications, such as administration and performance? Turn to the next chapter for practical DB2 data distribution hints, tips, and techniques.

36

Distribution Guidelines

In the preceding two chapters, I introduced both the distributed architecture employed by DB2 and the manner in which the architecture is implemented. In this chapter, I discuss some practical guidelines to follow as you develop distributed DB2 applications.

Distribution Behind the Scenes

Distributed DB2 requests are carried out through the Distributed Data Facility (DDF). The DDF is implemented as an address space in the same manner as the other DB2 address spaces: DBAS, SSAS, and IRLM. Refer to Chapter 13, "DB2 Behind the Scenes," for additional information on these three address spaces.

To more fully understand the workings of distributed data, see Figure 36.1 for a brief description of the components of the DDF.

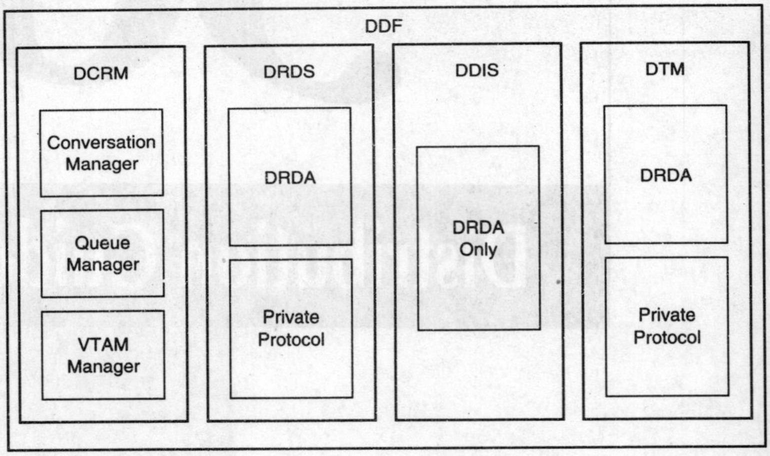

FIGURE 36.1.
The Distributed Data Facility.

The DDF is composed of four components:

DCRM	Distributed Communication Resource Manager
DRDS	Distributed Relational Data System
DDIS	Distributed Data Interchange System
DTM	Distributed Transaction Manager

The DCRM manages the interfaces to other resources with which the DDF must interact. The DCRM is the component that actually manages the connections. (See Figure 36.2.) The DCRM of the requester creates conversations to communicate to the server. The DCRM of the server accepts requests and creates a database access thread (DBAT) to handle distributed requests.

Three different managers within the DCRM enable you to perform these tasks: the conversation manager, the queue manager, and the VTAM manager.

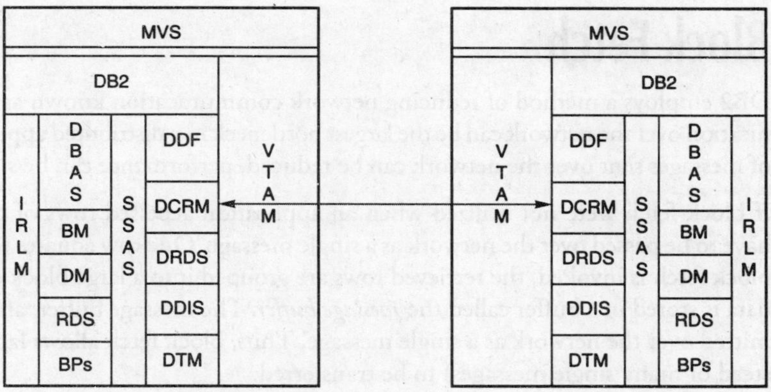

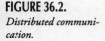

FIGURE 36.2.
Distributed communication.

Connections are managed by the *conversation manager* (CM). The CM is responsible for managing the receipt of messages from remote clients and sending messages from the server back to the requester. Furthermore, the CM manages the creation and termination of connections to support DRDA and private protocol requests.

The *queue manager* (QM) creates and routes work requests for allied agents. Requests from allied agents are queued by the QM and then routed for further processing.

The third and final component of the DCRM is the *VTAM manager.* The CM uses the VTAM manager to communicate with other DBMSs in the network. This component reads the CDB to determine how communication resources are to be used by the DDF.

The second component of the DDF is the *Distributed Relational Data System* (DRDS). It performs tasks similar to those performed by the RDS (in the DBAS). For private protocol requests, the DRDS receives remote requests and invokes the local DCRM to communicate with the remote server DCRM. The server DCRM receives the request and passes it to the RDS of the server. For DRDA requests, the DRDS enables the requester to perform remote binds. The bind request is passed to the server, which uses its DRDS to kick off the bind.

The *Distributed Data Interchange System* (DDIS) is the third component of the DDF. It is used only for DRDA requests. The DDIS performs object mapping of remote objects. Object mapping occurs at both the requester and server.

The final DDF component is the *Distributed Transaction Manager* (DTM). As its name implies, the DTM manages distributed transactions. It performs tasks such as monitoring for errors, controlling commits and aborts, and managing recovery.

A firm understanding of the functionality embedded within each of these components can help the application developer or database analyst more fully comprehend the underlying operations required for supporting a distributed environment.

Block Fetch

DB2 employs a method of reducing network communication known as *block fetch.* Communication over the network can be the largest bottleneck in a distributed application. If the number of messages sent over the network can be reduced, performance can be significantly increased.

If block fetch were not utilized when an application accessed rows of data, each one would have to be passed over the network as a single message. One row equates to one message. When block fetch is invoked, the retrieved rows are grouped into a large block of data. This block of data is stored in a buffer called the *message buffer.* The message buffer, after it is filled, is transmitted over the network as a single message. Thus, block fetch allows large blocks of data (instead of many single messages) to be transferred.

Figure 36.3 shows the difference between blocked and unblocked data access. Obviously, the amount of network communication diminishes when blocks of data are transmitted instead of single rows of data.

FIGURE 36.3.
Block fetch.

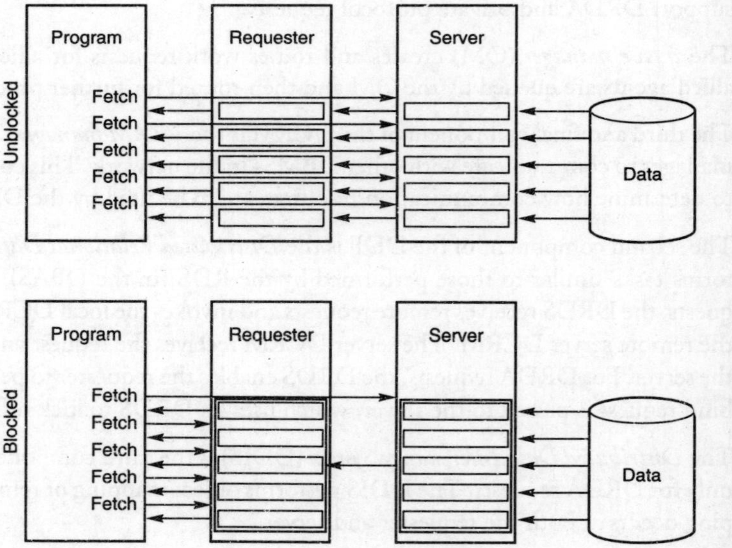

Coding Cursors to Encourage Block Fetch

Block fetch can be used only by read-only cursors. If data can be updated through the cursor, DB2 must send the data over the network one row at a time.

Sometimes, DB2 cannot properly determine whether a cursor is read-only. This type of cursor is called an *ambiguous cursor.* However, there are techniques you can use when coding cursors in an application program to ensure that read-only cursors are known to DB2 to be read-only. These types of cursors are called *unambiguous cursors.*

You can ensure that a cursor is unambiguous in three ways: using the `FOR READ ONLY` (or `FOR FETCH ONLY`) clause, using certain SQL constructs, or when the semantics dictate that the cursor is not updateable.

`FOR READ ONLY` or (`FOR FETCH ONLY`)

You can append the `FOR READ ONLY (or FOR FETCH ONLY)` clause to a cursor to indicate that the cursor is read-only. As a rule of thumb, always specify `FOR READ ONLY` when a distributed query is identified as being read-only. Even if the query is read-only by nature (see the next section), it is still best to code the cursor using `FOR READ ONLY`, thereby ensuring that the cursor is unambiguous and can utilize block fetch.

NOTE

Version 4

> As of DB2 V4, the `FOR READ ONLY` clause provides the same function as `FOR FETCH ONLY`, and it may be preferable because it is ODBC-compliant.

Cursors That Are Read-Only by Nature

Certain cursors, by definition, are always read-only. Any of the following conditions causes a read-only cursor:

- Joining tables
- Specifying the `DISTINCT` keyword in the first `SELECT` clause
- Using either `UNION` or `UNION ALL`
- Specifying a subquery in which the same table is specified in the `FROM` clauses of both the subquery and the outer query
- Using a scalar function in the first `SELECT` clause
- Using either a `GROUP BY` or `HAVING` clause in the outer `SELECT` clause
- Specifying an `ORDER BY` clause

Even though these conditions cause the cursor to be read-only, you should still specify the `FOR READ ONLY` clause. Doing so enhances clarity and is helpful for documentation purposes.

Semantically Non-Updateable Cursors

Certain types of cursors are semantically not updateable, even when not defined using `FOR READ ONLY` or `FOR FETCH ONLY`. They are read-only cursors because they are included within an application program that avoids updates. This type of cursor exists within a program that conforms to the following guidelines:

- No static DELETE WHERE CURRENT OF statements
- No static UPDATE WHERE CURRENT OF statements
- No dynamic SQL

Avoid Ambiguous Cursors

Avoiding ambiguous cursors greatly reduces the administrative burden of identifying updateable and read-only cursors. Likewise, it makes tuning easier because the identification of cursors that are candidates for block fetch becomes easier.

Avoiding ambiguous cursors is simple. To do so, you should establish a global shop standard that requires the specification of the FOR clause on *every* cursor. Read-only cursors should specify the FOR FETCH ONLY clause. Updateable cursors should specify the FOR UPDATE OF clause.

Data Currency

Block fetch is used as the default for *ambiguous* cursors if the package or plan was bound with the CURRENTDATA(NO) parameter. CURRENTDATA(NO) indicates that data currency is not a prerequisite for this package or plan, thereby enabling DB2 to use block fetch.

To disable block fetch for ambiguous cursors, specify CURRENTDATA(YES). However, doing so is not generally recommended.

To determine which plans and packages were bound with CURRENTDATA(NO), issue the following queries against the DB2 Catalog:

```
SELECT   NAME, CREATOR, BINDDATE, EXPREDICATE
FROM     SYSIBM.SYSPLAN P
ORDER BY NAME

SELECT   COLLID, NAME, VERSION, CREATOR,
         BINDTIME, DEFERPREP
FROM     SYSIBM.SYSPACKAGE
ORDER BY COLLID, NAME, VERSION
```

For plans, when the EXPREDICATE column is set to B, blocking is enabled. For packages, when the DEFERPREP column is set to B, blocking is enabled. In both cases, a value of C indicates that CURRENTDATA(YES) was specified.

Specify CURRENTDATA(NO)

Binding packages and plans with the CURRENTDATA(NO) parameter encourages the use of block fetch. This use, in turn, should enhance the overall performance of distributed queries. Fortunately, the DB2 default value for the CURRENTDATA option is CURRENTDATA(NO).

Limited Versus Continuous Block Fetch

The two types of block fetch are limited and continuous. Each method of block fetching has its benefits and drawbacks.

Limited Block Fetch

Limited block fetch can be used by application-directed DRDA units of work. (See Figure 36.4.) When limited block fetch is used, synchronous processing occurs.

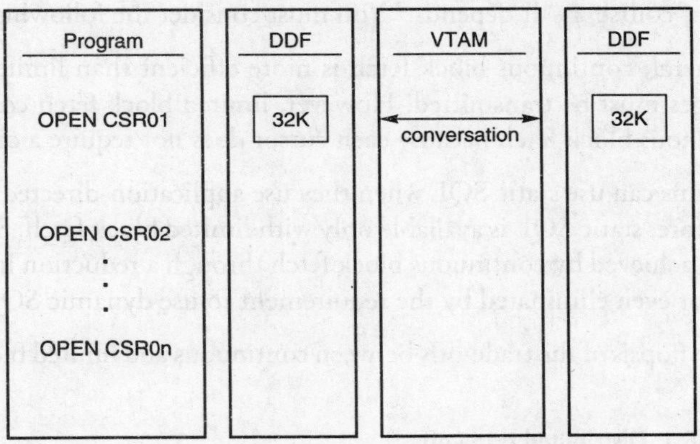

FIGURE 36.4.
Limited block fetch.

Limited block fetch uses a single conversation to facilitate communication between the requester and the server subsystems.

Continuous Block Fetch

Continuous block fetch operates asynchronously. Only system-directed, private-protocol units of work can use it. Each open cursor is assigned a separate conversation when continuous block fetch is used. (See Figure 36.5.)

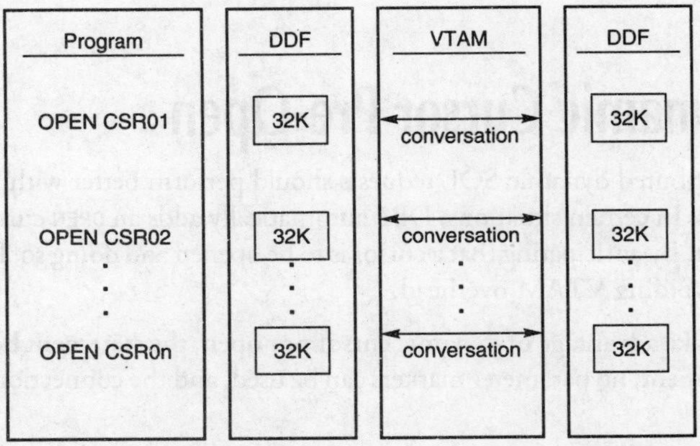

FIGURE 36.5.
Continuous block fetch.

Each open cursor has a buffer area on both the server and the requester. The server continues to fill its buffers with results and transmit them to the requester until it reaches VTAM pacing limits. In other words, the server continues processing behind the scenes.

When a sufficient number of conversations are not available to DB2 (one per open cursor), processing reverts to limited block fetch.

A Comparison of Continuous and Limited Block Fetch

The big question is "Which is the better type of block fetch: continuous or limited?" The answer, of course, is "It depends." You must consider the following two trade-offs.

In general, continuous block fetch is more efficient than limited block fetch because fewer messages must be transmitted. However, limited block fetch consumes fewer resources than continuous block fetch because each cursor does not require a conversation.

Programs can use static SQL when they use application-directed DRDA distributed requests. Therefore, static SQL is available only with limited block fetch. So, the performance gain that can be achieved by continuous block fetch through a reduction in network traffic can be mitigated or even eliminated by the requirement to use dynamic SQL.

For a synopsis of the trade-offs between continuous and limited block fetch, refer to Table 36.1.

Table 36.1. Distributed trade-offs.

Continuous Block Fetch	*Limited Block Fetch*
Resource-intensive	Network-intensive
System-directed	Application-directed
Private DB2 protocol	Open DRDA protocol
DB2 to DB2 distribution only	Open distribution to any DRDA-compliant RDBMS
Dynamic SQL	Static SQL

Dynamic Cursor Pre-Open

Version 5

Distributed dynamic SQL requests should perform better with DB2 V5 than for previous versions. In certain situations, DB2 automatically adds an OPEN cursor request to the PREPARE statement. By anticipating that a cursor is to be opened and doing so, DB2 V5 optimizes performance by avoiding VTAM overhead.

To take advantage of dynamic cursor pre-open, the statement being prepared must be a SELECT statement, no parameter markers can be used, and the connection must be a DRDA connection.

Distributed Performance Problems

Recall the definition of performance given in Part IV, "DB2 Performance Monitoring." Performance in a distributed environment also can be defined in terms of throughput and response time. The server and the requester each place a different degree of emphasis on these two aspects.

The server views performance primarily in terms of throughput. Remember that throughput is the amount of work that can be done in a unit of time.

The requester views performance more in terms of response time. Response time is more visible to the end user. Recall that response time is the amount of time required to accomplish a predefined set of work.

Analyzing Distributed Throughput

When analyzing the throughput of a given distributed DB2 implementation, you must examine each component of the implementation. Failure to analyze every component may result in an overall performance degradation caused by a single weak link.

The combination of all components used to process a transaction is called the *throughput chain.* A sample throughput chain can include a combination of the following components:

- Requester hardware
- Local/requester operating system (OS/2, AIX, MVS, and so on)
- Local DB2
- Network operating system
- Actual network (or LAN)
- Middleware (or gateway)
- Mainframe
- MVS
- Server DB2
- DASD

Each link in the chain may be necessary to complete a given transaction. The best throughput that any given configuration can achieve is always confined by the slowest component on the chain.

To achieve optimal performance, you should spend more tuning and optimization effort on the weaker links in the throughput chain.

Factors Affecting Throughput

The three biggest factors affecting throughput in a distributed environment are hardware, contention, and availability.

The processing speed of the *hardware* used in the distributed environment has a big impact on throughput. Factors such as processor speed (MIPS), available memory, physical configuration, and DASD speed have an impact on the throughput component of performance.

When the demand for a particular resource is high, *contention* results. When two or more processes attempt to utilize a particular resource in a conflicting manner, contention degrades overall performance. In a distributed environment, the number of locations that can utilize a resource increases; thus, contention problems usually increase.

The final factor is *availability*. In a distributed environment, multiple computing platforms are used. If one of these platforms breaks down or becomes otherwise unavailable (such as with a communication problem), throughput is affected. Depending on application design, throughput may

- Increase, if transactions continue to be processed. Work targeted for the unavailable component must be saved so that it can be applied later when the unavailable component becomes available.
- Decrease, if logic has not been coded to handle unavailable components, and transactions start to "hang."
- Become nonexistent, if all work is suspended until the unavailable component is made available again.

NOTE

Plan for periods of resource unavailability in a distributed environment and code distributed DB2 application programs accordingly.

Analyzing Distributed Response Time

Response time is typically easier to comprehend than throughput. Usually, a throughput problem comes to light as a result of a complaint about response time.

End users are the typical bearers of bad news about response-time problems. As the actual patrons of the system, they understand its basic performance patterns. When response time suffers, end users tend to voice their dissatisfaction quickly.

Online performance monitoring tools and performance reports are other means of gauging response-time problems.

General Distributed Performance Guidelines

When developing distributed DB2 applications, implement the following techniques to ensure optimal performance.

Standard DB2 Performance Tuning Techniques

Follow standard DB2 performance tuning techniques, as outlined in Part V, "DB2 Performance Tuning."

Minimize the SQL Result Set

Be sure to access only the data that is actually required by the application. Do not access more data than is necessary and filter it out in the application program. Although this tip is a standard SQL tuning rule of thumb, it is particularly applicable in a distributed environment. When fewer rows qualify, less data is sent over the communication lines. And remember, network-related problems tend to be a significant obstacle in distributed environments.

Distributed Bufferpool

The bufferpool that will hold the distributed data, after it has been sent from the server to the client, is the bufferpool in which the CDB is defined. Ensure that adequate space has been allocated to accommodate distributed data access in the aforementioned bufferpool.

NOTE

As of DB2 V5, the CDB tables were moved to the DB2 Catalog. This means that these tables must use BP0. This is not the case for previous releases of DB2, though.

Version 5

DDF Dispatching Priority

When DB2 is used as a database server in a distributed environment, the dispatching priority of the DDF address space should be reanalyzed.

The general recommendation made in Chapter 20, "Tuning DB2's Environment," (refer to Figure 20.3) is to code the dispatching priority of `DSNDDF` on a par with IMS MP regions (below short-running TSO requests but above medium-running TSO requests). However, in a distributed environment with critical distributed transactions, consider changing the dispatching priority of `DSNDDF` to a higher position in the hierarchy. (See Figure 36.6.)

You should set the dispatching priority of `DSNDDF` so that it is not so high as to affect overall system performance but not so low as to degrade the performance of distributed DB2 requests.

In general, higher dispatching priorities should be reserved for I/O-bound applications. Because `DSNDDF` is a low CPU consumer, setting a higher `DPRTY` may prove to be advantageous.

FIGURE 36.6.
Distributed dispatching priority hierarchy.

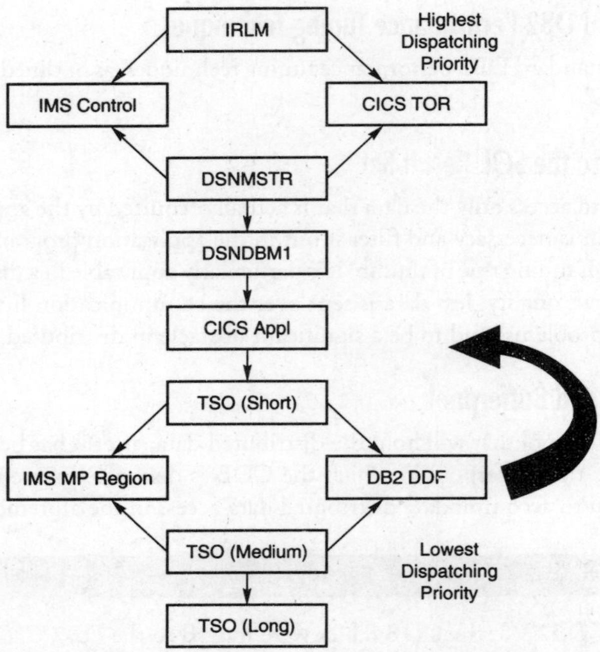

CAUTION

Ensure that a higher DSNDDF dispatching priority does not cause excessive resource consumption. If you decide to experiment with the dispatching priority of DSNDDF, thoroughly test different priority hierarchies in your shop until you're satisfied that the DDF is at an appropriate level.

Tuning VTAM Parameters

Before you implement distributed DB2 applications, buy your VTAM systems programmer lunch! (Most system programmers have a ravenous appetite; buy them food, and they'll be your friends for life.)

The performance of DB2 in a distributed environment depends heavily on ensuring that the appropriate VTAM parameters are coded for the type of distributed applications to be implemented.

The following VTAM parameters are important:

- If the VTAM is set high, and your application retrieves multiple rows, the communication channels can become flooded, consuming an inordinate amount of system resources.

- Avoid the VTAM DELAY parameter when your application is coded to retrieve single rows. The DELAY parameter causes a planned wait that would impede performance.
- Queuing of conversations can greatly increase response time. Consider increasing CONVLIMIT if the number of queued conversations is high. Likewise, if the number of queued conversations is very low or zero, consider decreasing CONVLIMIT. Start the DB2 global trace, IFCID 167, to collect information on queued conversation requests.

  The number of conversations that a remote DB2 subsystem can be handle is controlled in the SYSIBM.LUMODES table. You use the CONVLIMIT column of LUMODES to set the limit of conversations per DB2 subsystem (in the LUNAME column) per VTAM logon mode (in the MODENAME column).

  For a change to CONVLIMIT to take place, the DDF address space must be recycled. Whenever you're making these types of changes, be sure to keep your VTAM systems programmer in the loop, because setting these values overrides the VTAM DSESLIM parameter, and the VTAM systems programmer usually has a much better idea (than a DB2 DBA or analyst) of what these numbers should be.

Distributed Database Design Issues

When you're designing databases in a distributed environment, follow the standard database design rules of thumb provided in Chapter 3, "Data Definition Guidelines." However, you might need to take a more rigorous approach regarding denormalization. For more information, refer to the exhaustive discussion of denormalization in Chapter 3. Use Table 36.2 to recall the types of denormalization covered in Chapter 3.

Table 36.2. Types of denormalization.

Denormalization	*Use*
Prejoined Tables	When the cost of joining is prohibitive
Report Tables	When specialized critical reports are needed
Mirror Tables	When tables are required concurrently by two types of environments
Split Tables	When distinct groups use different parts of a table
Combined Tables	When one-to-one relationships exist
Redundant Data	To reduce the number of table joins required
Repeating Groups	To reduce I/O and (possibly) DASD
Derivable Data	To eliminate calculations and algorithms
Speed Tables	To support hierarchies

Denormalization can be a useful technique in a distributed environment. In the following sections, I discuss several methods of distributed denormalization. Along the way, I make references to the denormalization types already discussed to clarify the distributed denormalization concepts.

Fragmentation

Fragmentation is a specialized form of distributed denormalization that resembles split tables. To implement fragmentation, a table must be separated into separate parts, or fragments. Each fragment is then stored at a different location. Fragmentation can enhance performance because each fragment can be stored at the location that accesses it most frequently.

As with split tables, fragmentation avoids data duplication. Each fragment must contain a logical subset of the data.

Multiple fragments can be created from a single source table. The methodology used to determine where and how to split the table depends on the data access needs of the distributed applications that must access the data.

Two types of fragmentation can be implemented: horizontal and vertical. *Horizontal fragmentation* splits the data by rows, whereas *vertical fragmentation* splits the data by columns. Tables are horizontally fragmented using ranges of values to create distinct fragments. Tables are vertically fragmented by assigning specific columns to specific fragments.

Vertical fragmentation requires a certain amount of data duplication because the key column(s) must be stored at each site to defragment the data. Without the redundant key stored at each location, joining the tables back together so that the data returned is the unfragmented, original data would be impossible.

Ensure Lossless Joins and Unions

You must take care to ensure that fragmentation is accomplished such that defragmenting the tables does not result in additional data or a loss of data.

For horizontal fragmentation, rows must be wholly contained within one, and only one, fragment. In other words, the result of selecting all rows from every fragment and combining them together using `UNION ALL` must provide the same result as a `SELECT` of all rows from the original, unfragmented table:

```
SELECT    *
FROM      FRAGMENT1
UNION ALL
SELECT    *
FROM      FRAGMENT2
UNION ALL
SELECT    *
FROM      FRAGMENTn
```

Of course, this statement cannot be successfully executed until DB2 supports distributed request capability.

For vertical fragmentation, only the key columns are permitted to be duplicated in multiple fragments. The key columns must reside in every fragment. Even when no data is actually associated with a particular key for a particular fragment, a row must be stored in the fragment for that key to facilitate defragmentation. Nulls (or default values) can be used to indicate that the other columns contain no valid data for the particular key at that particular location.

Simply stated, the result of joining all fragments together should provide the same result as selecting from the original, unfragmented table:

```
SELECT   F1.KEY, F1.COL1, F2.COL2, Fn.COLn
FROM     FRAGMENT1  F1,
         FRAGMENT2  F2,
         FRAGMENTn  Fn
WHERE    F1.KEY = F2.KEY
AND      F2.KEY = Fn.KEY
```

If certain keys are not included, an outer join must be used. Until such time, because DB2 provides native outer join support, always propagating keys across locations is wise.

Replication

Another type of distributed denormalization is *replication*. In its implementation, it is similar to mirror tables.

When data is replicated, redundant data is stored at multiple distributed locations. Because replication causes copies of the data to be stored across the network, performance can be enhanced by eliminating the need for distributed data access.

Replication can be implemented simply by copying entire tables to multiple locations. Alternatively, replicated data can be a subset of the rows and/or columns. The general rule of thumb is to copy only what is needed to each remote location.

Furthermore, each replica should contain accurate, up-to-date information. Whenever possible, you should update all replicated copies at the same time. This way, you can eliminate the administrative burden of having to know the state of each replica. Additionally, replication transparency is ensured when the data is accurate at each location.

To achieve optimal performance, you should always read from the closest replica. A replica may not exist at every location. By always reading from the closest replica (which supports the current requirements), you can enhance performance by reducing the communication path.

You can tune replicas independently of one another. Different clustering strategies, different indexes, and different tablespace parameters might be appropriate at different locations.

Finally, do not create more replicas than are required. The more replicas, the more complicated the process of updating them.

Snapshots

Similar to mirror tables, *snapshot tables* are read-only copies of tables. Snapshot tables also are similar to replicas, but the data currency requirements for each snapshot table can differ. Data in snapshot tables usually represents a "point in time" and is not accurate up-to-the-second.

Decision-support applications typically use snapshot tables. Snapshots are most useful for optimizing performance when data does not have to be entirely accurate.

As with the other types of distributed denormalization, snapshots tend to optimize performance when they are stored at the location that accesses them most frequently.

Multiple snapshot tables can be created—each representing a different "point in time." The number of snapshots required depends on the nature of the data and the needs of the applications that must access them.

To achieve optimal performance, always read from the closest snapshot. A snapshot may not exist at every location. By always reading from the closest replica (which supports the current requirements), you can enhance performance by reducing the communication path.

Be sure to send all updates to the *system of record,* which is the master table (or tables) that always contains accurate, up-to-date information. Application updates should never be made to snapshots, only to the system of record. The snapshot tables need to be refreshed periodically with data from the system of record. You should develop a reliable, systematic method of refreshing snapshot data.

By their very nature, snapshot tables do not contain up-to-the-second information. Ad hoc users, programmers, and anyone else requiring access to snapshot tables need to be informed of the following:

- The data is not current; for current data, the system of record should be accessed.
- The date and time for which the data is accurate.
- The next scheduled refresh date and time.

Distributed Data Placement

A key aspect of distributed performance and functionality lies in the application of proper data placement techniques. To perform proper data placement, you should understand the manner in which each piece of data is accessed within the distributed environment. Analyzing which application or program accesses the data is not sufficient. Analyzing is merely one portion of the distributed data placement puzzle. You also need to analyze and understand the access patterns from each location on the network.

Normal data placement revolves around a single subsystem. The access patterns of programs and applications are recorded; based on that information, portions of the data are placed on DASD devices. Access-based data placement still must be done in the distributed environment.

However, location access patterns must be analyzed also. Based on these patterns, portions of data can be placed at the appropriate locations within the distributed network.

The primary goal of distributed data placement is to optimize performance by reducing network transmission costs. Each piece of data should be stored at the location that accesses it most frequently. For example, storing Pittsburgh data at the Pittsburgh server makes more sense than storing it at the Chicago server. Such decisions are easy to make. Problems arise when

- A location has no server
- The frequency of access is (relatively) evenly divided between two or more servers

If the location does not have a server, place the data to the closest location on the network. For example, Pittsburgh data would be better stored in Cleveland than in Chicago, because Cleveland is physically closer to Pittsburgh than Chicago. For scenarios too close to call, the best approach is to choose a location and monitor performance. If performance is not up to par, consider migrating the data to another location.

Distributed Optimization

Optimization in DB2 is usually a clear-cut matter. The DB2 optimizer is a state-of-the-art optimizer that, more often than not, can be relied upon to produce properly optimized access paths for SQL statements. The rule of thumb is to code as much work as possible into the SQL and let the optimizer figure out the best way to access the data. However, in a distributed environment, optimization is not quite so simple.

To understand this difference, consider a distributed implementation of the DB2 sample tables PROJ, PROJACT, and ACT. A project (PROJ) can have many activities, and each activity (ACT) can be a part of many projects. The PROJACT table resolves the many-to-many relationship. For more information on these tables, refer to Appendix D, "DB2 Sample Tables."

Assume that the PROJ and PROJACT tables exist at one location (say, Pittsburgh), and the ACT table exists at a different location (say, Chicago).

The task at hand is to retrieve a list of documentation activities for projects started after January 1, 1998. If DB2 provides distributed request support, the following query would satisfy this request:

```
SELECT   A.ACTNO, A.ACTDESC
FROM     ACT      A,
PROJ     P,
PROJACT  J
WHERE    A.ACTNO = J.ACTNO
AND      J.PROJNO = P.PROJNO
AND      A.ACTKWD = "DOC"
AND      P.PRSTDATE > "01/01/1998";
```

However, DB2 does not provide distributed request. Therefore, issuing this particular join is not possible. Lacking distributed request, what is the best way to satisfy this request? You can optimize this three-table join in (at least) six different ways:

- Join PROJ and PROJACT at Pittsburgh, selecting only projects starting after January 1, 1998. For each qualifying row, move it to Chicago to be joined with ACT to see whether any design activities exist.
- Join PROJ and PROJACT at Pittsburgh, selecting only projects starting after January 1, 1998. Then move the entire result set to Chicago to be joined with ACT, checking for design activities only.
- At Chicago, select only design activities from ACT. For each of them, examine the join of PROJ and PROJACT at Pittsburgh for post-January 1, 1998 projects.
- Select only design activities from ACT at Chicago. Then move the entire result set to Pittsburgh to be joined with PROJ and PROJACT, checking for projects started after January 1, 1998 only.
- Move ACT to Pittsburgh and proceed with a local three-table join.
- Move PROJ and PROJACT to Chicago and proceed with a local three-table join.

Determining which of these six optimization choices will perform best is a difficult task. Usually, performing multiple smaller requests to a remote location is worse than making a single larger request to the remote location. In general, the fewer messages, the better performance will be. However, this rule of thumb is not always true. Try different combinations at your site to arrive at the optimal method of performing distributed queries. The optimal choice will depend on the following:

- The size of the tables
- The number of qualifying rows
- The type of distributed request being made
- The efficiency of the network

Distributed Security Guidelines

Several techniques can enhance the security of distributed DB2 implementations. The following guidelines will assist the developer in securing distributed DB2 data.

Come-From Checking

At times, ensuring that a specific userid has the appropriate authorization to access distributed data is not sufficient. Using the CDB tables, you can use DB2 to institute what is known as *come-from checking*. When come-from checking is established, the requesting location and requesting userid are checked in combination.

Suppose that userid DBAPCSM exists at several locations: Chicago, Jacksonville, and Pittsburgh. By populating the SYSIBM.USERNAMES table appropriately, you can implement come-from checking to effectively disable specific combinations of userid and location.

By inserting the appropriate rows into SYSIBM.LUNAMES and SYSIBM.USERNAMES, you can implement come-from checking to enable a specific user to access data from any location or to enable any user to access data from a specific location. By default, come-from checking is not implemented. Analysis and specific action must be taken to use come-from checking.

Come-from checking is particularly useful when multiple authids may be logging in from multiple locations. Additional control is available with come-from checking.

Authid Translation

Another possibility in a distributed environment is to translate authids automatically for distributed requests. One authid can be translated to another completely different authid.

Authids can be translated by the requesting location, the server location, both locations, or neither location.

Inbound authid translation happens when authids are translated by the server. This term is used because the authid is not changed until it is received by the server (as an inbound request). By contrast, *outbound authid translation* is performed by the requester, prior to the request being sent.

Consistent Authids

You can use authid translation to implement consistent authids for each user on the network, regardless of location. Consider, for example, a situation in which authids are assigned so that they are unique across the network. Perhaps the location is embedded in the name. So, maybe DBAPCSM exists in Pittsburgh; DBAJCSM, in Jacksonville; and DBACCSM, in Chicago.

Authid translation can be used to convert any of these valid authids to a single, consistent authid such as DBACSM. Doing so greatly reduces the administrative burden of implemented distributed security.

Network Specific Authids

Sometimes assigning all requests from a single location the same consistent authid is useful. If you impose outbound authid translation, all outbound requests can be translated to one specific authid, thereby reducing complexity (of course, at the expense of security).

Password Encryption

If outbound authid translation is implemented, DB2 requires that a valid password is sent along with each authid. If you choose this option, be sure to encrypt the passwords in the SYSUSERNAMES CDB table using one of the following methods:

- Specify Y in the ENCRYPTPSWDS column of the SYSLUNAMES table (for that LU).
- Code an EDITPROC on SYSUSERNAMES to encrypt the password.

Miscellaneous Security Guidelines

Utilize the following security guidelines as you develop distributed DB2 applications.

PUBLIC AT ALL LOCATIONS

If a particular table is to be made accessible by anyone on the network—regardless of authid or location—security can be granted specifying PUBLIC AT ALL LOCATIONS. Of course, it is applicable to only the INSERT, UPDATE, DELETE, and SELECT table privileges.

Miscellaneous Distributed Guidelines

Keep the following guidelines in mind as you implement distributed DB2 applications and databases.

Favor Type-2 Connections

Application-directed distribution is implemented using the CONNECT statement. DB2 V3 supports two different types of CONNECTs:

- Type 1 CONNECT: Multiple CONNECT statements cannot be executed within a single unit of work.
- Type 2 CONNECT: Multiple CONNECT statements can be executed within a single unit of work.

Type 2 CONNECTs allow updates to be made to multiple locations within a single unit of work. If you connect to a system using a Type 1 CONNECT, or if the system is at a level of DRDA that does not support two-phase commit, you can update at only one system within a single unit of work. Only one Type 1 CONNECT statement is permitted within a single unit of work; however, multiple Type 2 CONNECT statements can be executed within a single unit of work.

The type of CONNECT being utilized is determined by a precompiler option and the type of processing being performed by the program.

First, DB2 V3 provides a new precompiler option to set the type of connect: CONNECT. Specifying CONNECT(1) indicates that the program is to use Type 1 CONNECTs; CONNECT(2), which is the default, specifies Type 2 CONNECTs are to be used.

Second, the type of connect to be used can be determined by the type of processing within your application. If the first CONNECT statement issued is a Type 1 CONNECT, Type 1 CONNECT rules apply for the duration of the program. If a Type 2 CONNECT is executed first, Type 2 CONNECT rules apply.

Choose Appropriate Distributed Bind Options

Several bind parameters affect the distributed environment. Ensuring that the proper parameters are used when binding plans and packages can greatly influence the performance of distributed applications. Refer to Table 36.3.

Table 36.3. Distributed bind parameter recommendations.

Parameter	*Recommendation*	*Default*	*Applies**
CURRENTDATA	CURRENTDATA(NO)	CURRENTDATA(NO)	B
DEFER	DEFER(PREPARE)	NODEFER(PREPARE)	P
CURRENTSERVER	Depends	Local DBMS	P
SQLRULES	Depends	SQLRULES(DB2)	P
DISCONNECT	DISCONNECT(EXPLICIT)	DISCONNECT(EXPLICIT)	P
SQLERROR	Depends	SQLERROR(NOPACKAGE)	K

*The Applies column indicates whether the parameter applies to plans (P), packages (K), or both (B).

Review the information in Table 36.3. Block fetch is used as the default for *ambiguous* cursors if the package or plan was bound with the CURRENTDATA(NO) parameter. CURRENTDATA(YES) is not recommended because block fetch would be disabled.

When system-directed dynamic access is requested, specifying DEFER(PREPARE) causes only a single distributed message to be sent for the PREPARE, DESCRIBE, and EXECUTE statements. A plan bound specifying DEFER(PREPARE) generally outperforms one bound as NODEFER(PREPARE). The default, of course, is NODEFER.

The CURRENTSERVER parameter specifies a connection to a location before the plan is executed. The server's CURRENT SERVER register is set to the location specified in the CURRENTSERVER option, and a Type 1 CONNECT is issued. This way, the connection can be established prior to making a request. However, debugging an application without an explicit CONNECT is more difficult.

If adherence to the ANSI/ISO standards for remote connection is essential, you should bind using SQLRULES(STD). The ANSI/ISO standard does not allow a CONNECT to be issued against an existing connection, whereas DB2 does. Always specify SQLRULES(DB2) if conformance to the ANSI/ISO standard is not required.

The DISCONNECT parameter determines when connections are to be released. Three options exist: EXPLICIT, AUTOMATIC, and CONDITIONAL. Refer to Chapter 35, "Distributed DB2," for a discussion of these parameters.

Finally, the SQLERROR option indicates what is to happen when SQL errors are encountered when binding a package. If SQLERROR(CONTINUE) is specified, a package is created even if some of the objects do not exist at the remote location. This way, the package can be bound before objects are migrated to a remote location. The default, `SQLERROR(NOPACKAGE)`, is the safer option.

Remove the Distributed Factor

A wise first step when investigating an error within a distributed environment is to remove the remote processing from the request and try again.

Trying to execute the request directly on the server instead of from a remote client eliminates potentially embarrassing problem scenarios. For example, consider an application in which two DB2 subsystems, DB2S and DB2R, are connected via the DDF. An application executing from DB2R is unsuccessful in requesting data from DB2S. The recommended first step in resolving the problem is to ensure that the same request executes properly on DB2S as a *local* request.

Distributed problem determination should ensue only if the request is successful.

Maintain a Problem Resolution Log

Keep a written record of problems encountered in the distributed environment. You should establish and strictly maintain this problem resolution log. You should include every unique problem, along with its solution, in the log. A sample problem resolution log form is shown in Figure 36.7.

FIGURE 36.7.
Distributed problem resolution log.

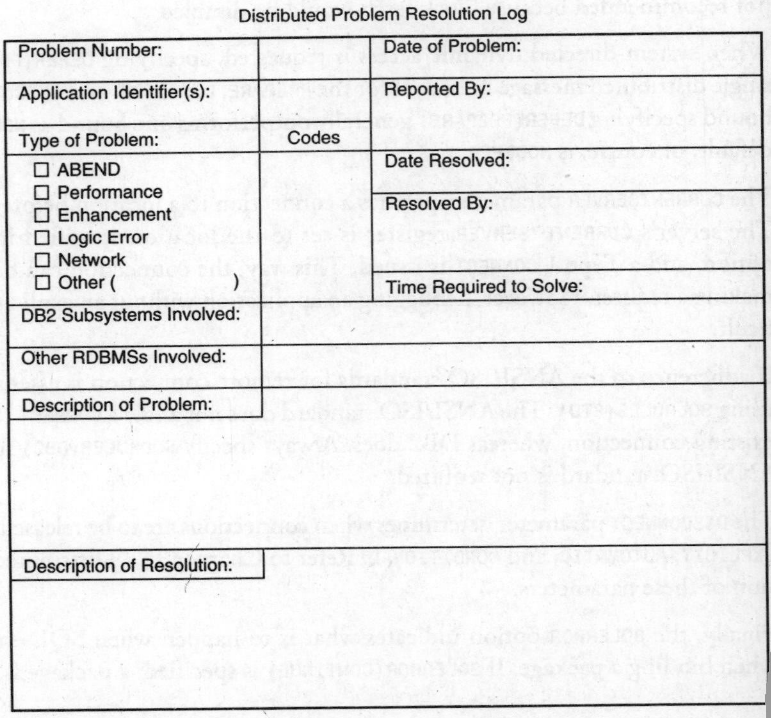
Distributed Problem Resolution Log
Problem Number:
Date of Problem:
Application Identifier(s):
Reported By:
Type of Problem:
Codes
Date Resolved:
☐ ABEND
☐ Performance
☐ Enhancement
☐ Logic Error
☐ Network
☐ Other ( )
Resolved By:
Time Required to Solve:
DB2 Subsystems Involved:
Other RDBMSs Involved:
Description of Problem:
Description of Resolution:

For optimum effectiveness, the log should be automated for ease of maintenance. Anyone involved in distributed problem determination should be permitted to access and update the log. The log should be readily available and stored in a central location. If you review past problems, you can more easily resolve current problems and avoid future problems.

Summary

Implementing applications in a distributed DB2 environment can be a complex and taxing ordeal. However, if you approach the endeavor in a practical manner and follow the guidelines in this chapter, distributing DB2 data need not be an overwhelming task.

37

Data Warehousing with DB2

Data warehousing is not a particularly new idea. The basic idea behind data warehousing is one that has been performed by IT professionals throughout the years: enabling end users to have access to corporate operational data to follow and respond to business trends. You might be tempted, therefore, to shrug off data warehousing as another of the many industry buzzwords that rise and fall every few years. However, doing so would be a mistake.

The true benefit of data warehousing lies not with the conceptual components embodying the data warehouse, but in the combination of these concepts into a single, unified implementation that is novel and worthwhile. Consider the typical DP shop. Data is stored in many locations, in many different formats, and is managed by many different DBMSs from multiple vendors. It is difficult, if not impossible, to access and use data in this environment without a consistent blueprint from which to operate. This blueprint is the data warehouse.

Data warehousing enables an organization to make information available for analytical processing and decision making. The data warehouse defines the manner in which data

- Is systematically constructed and cleansed (or scrubbed)
- Is transformed into a consistent view
- Is distributed wherever it is needed
- Is made easily accessible
- Is manipulated for optimal access by disparate processes

In this chapter, I provide a basic overview of data warehousing concepts and terms. However, I do not provide comprehensive coverage of all that is implied by data warehousing. Additionally, I provide useful guidelines for developers who are building data warehouses using DB2. Some of the guidelines are generally applicable to any RDBMS; however, many of them are tailored specifically to DB2 for OS/390 (or MVS).

Defining the Basic Terms

Although data warehousing is a pervasive term, used throughout the IT industry, there is a lot of misunderstanding as to what a data warehouse actually is. This section will provide a good introductory treatment of data warehousing and the terminology used when discussing data warehouses.

What Is a Data Warehouse?

A *data warehouse* is best defined by the type and manner of data stored in it and the people who use that data. The data warehouse is designed for decision support providing easier access to data and reducing data contention. It is separated from the day-to-day OLTP applications that drive the core business. A data warehouse is typically read-only with the data organized according to the business rather than by computer processes. The data warehouse classifies information by subjects of interest to business analysts, such as customers, products, and accounts. Data in the warehouse is not updated; instead, it is inserted (or loaded) and then read multiple times.

Warehouse information is historical in nature, spanning transactions that have occurred over the course of many months and years. For this reason, warehouse data is usually summarized or aggregated to make it easier to scan and access. Redundant data can be included in the data warehouse to present the data in logical, easily understood groupings.

Data warehouses contain information that has been culled from operational systems, as well as possibly external data (such as third-party point-of-sale information). Data in the data warehouse is stored in a singular manner for the enterprise, even when the operational systems from which the data was obtained store it in many different ways. This fact is important because the analyst using the data warehouse must be able to focus on using the data instead of trying to figure out the data or question its integrity.

A typical query submitted to a data warehouse is: "What was the total revenue produced for the central region for product 'x' during the first quarter?"

To summarize, a data warehouse is a collection of data that is

- Separate from operational systems
- Accessible and available for queries
- Subject-oriented by business
- Integrated and consistently named and defined
- Associated with defined periods of time
- Static, or non-volatile, such that updates are not made

Operational Data Versus the Data Warehouse

The purpose and intent of a data warehouse differ substantially from operational databases supporting OLTP and production systems, such as order entry, shipping, and inventory control. (See Table 37.1.) Operational databases are typically used by clerical or line workers doing the day-to-day business of an organization. Additionally, operational data is atomic in nature, continually changes as updates are made, and reflects only the current value of the last transaction.

Table 37.1. Operational data versus warehouse data.

Operational Data	*Warehouse Data*
Atomic	Summarized
Production Support	Analytical

continues

Table 37.1. continued

Operational Data	*Warehouse Data*
Application-Oriented	Subject-Oriented
Current	Historical
Dynamic	Static

What Is a Data Mart?

The term *data mart* is used almost as often as the term *data warehouse*. But how is a data mart different from a data warehouse? A data mart is basically a departmental data warehouse defined for a single (or limited number of) subject area(s).

Data in data marts need not be represented in the corporate data warehouse, if one even exists. Breadth of data in both data marts and corporate data warehouses should be driven by the needs of the business. Therefore, unless the departmental data is required for enterprise-wide analysis, it may not exist in the corporate data warehouse.

A data mart is not necessarily smaller in size than an enterprise data warehouse. It may be smaller, but size is determined based on business needs. Departmental analysis at the business unit level may require more historical information than cross-department, enterprise-wide analysis.

What Is an Operational Data Store?

An Operational Data Store (ODS) provides a centralized view of near real-time data from operational systems. The ODS is optional in a data warehousing environment. If used, it is populated from multiple operational databases or may be used directly as the data store for multiple operational applications. The ODS can then be used as a staging area for data warehouse population (as shown in Figure 37.1).

FIGURE 37.1.
The Operational Data Store.

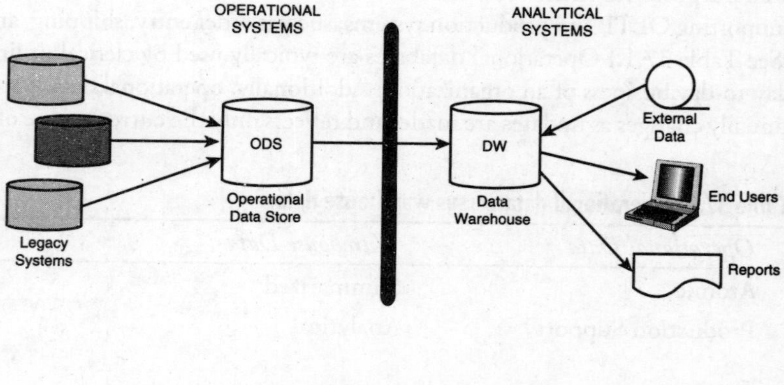

An ODS is a collection of data that is

- Used by operational systems
- Subject-oriented by business
- Integrated and consistently named and defined
- Current, up-to-date (as opposed to historical)
- At the detail level (as opposed to summarized)
- Dynamic, or volatile, to support operational systems

What Is OLAP?

OLAP stands for On-Line Analytical Processing. OLAP technology is often used in conjunction with a data warehouse. OLAP technology enables high-level end users (analysts, managers executives, and so on) to derive intelligence from data through interactive and iterative access to multiple views of information (typically stored in a data warehouse).

OLAP uses a multidimensional view of detail, summary, and aggregate data to access information for further analysis. The key term here is *multidimensional*. A dimension is a structural attribute viewed as similar by the end user. For example, months, quarters, years, and so on make up a time dimension; likewise, all cities, regions, countries, and so on could comprise a geography dimension.

Simply stated, a dimension is a modifier of the basic fact that must be analyzed. Examples of facts include sales figures, expenses, and inventory on hand. Multiple dimensions affect the value of these facts. For example, sales differ by geography (for example, sales region), time (for example, first quarter), product (for example, widgets versus flanges), and any other number of factors.

OLAP is characterized by dynamic multidimensional analysis, enabling complex calculations applied across dimensions, across components of a dimension, and/or through hierarchies. Additionally, OLAP provides analysis and trending capabilities over time, subsetting of data, drill-down through varying levels of detail, reach-through to operational data, and methods for comparing different analytical views of data.

OLAP calculations are usually more complex than simple data summarization and aggregation. For example, the following is a typical OLAP query: "What would be the effect on net revenue if account maintenance fees for demand deposit accounts went up by 3 percent in conjunction with a customer affinity program that reduced the fee by 1 percent for every additional account held by the customer?" Answering this question is not simple.

The technology used to store the aggregate data on which OLAP operates can be relational or a proprietary multidimensional format. If the data is stored in a relational database, such as DB2, the term *ROLAP*, or Relational OLAP, is used; if a multidimensional database is deployed, such as Essbase (which IBM has licensed from Arbor Software), the term *MOLAP*, or Multidimensional OLAP, is used.

This introduction covers the basics of OLAP but is necessarily brief. To cover OLAP in depth could take an entire book.

Designing a Data Warehouse

When you're designing a data warehouse, be sure to drive the project from a plan. This plan should include methods to accomplish each of the following components of data warehouse development:

- Document the business drivers in the marketplace, spearheading the need for a data warehouse.
- Secure an executive sponsor to ensure the overall success of the project.
- Define the scope of the data stored in the data warehouse in terms of subject areas.
- Document the business reasons for the data warehouse; they are typically related to the business drivers in terms of reacting to the identified market trends.
- Develop a detailed analysis of the requirements. Plan to produce a prototype of the data warehouse before proceeding into full-scale development.
- Define the facts and dimensions required. Determine the source systems for acquiring the data that will be populated into the data warehouse. You can have internal and external sources.
- Describe the technology used including client and server hardware, operating systems, DBMS, networking software, data transformation tools, repository technology, middleware, message queuing system, query tools, and other software.
- Define the development approach taken. Is the project staged into smaller manageable projects with defined deliverables? Is it an iterative process with clear milestones? Or is it a monolithic development endeavor (try to avoid these endeavors if possible)?
- Document the resources available and the roles they will be assuming for the project.
- Develop a project timeline and document status of the project as it progresses.

Many of these steps are similar to any application development project that is undertaken. However, the success of the data warehouse is contingent on all of these steps being planned and implemented in a consistent and manageable fashion.

Several design issues, however, are somewhat unique to the data warehouse including metadata management and developing star and snowflake schemas.

The Role of Metadata

When you're designing a data warehouse, incorporating repository technology into the plans is a good idea. In addition to the standard role of a repository (storing the metadata and the data model for the corporation), it can act a single, centralized store to assist in the movement of data into the data warehouse. Furthermore, a repository can help end users as they access data by providing definitions of all data elements stored in the data warehouse.

Alas, many shops do not own a repository. Even worse, some of them that do own a repository neglect the product, causing it to become "shelfware." There it sits on the shelf, and the metadata in the product is either outdated, inaccurate, or non-existent. This lack of use does not negate the value of repository products; it simply depicts the cavalier attitude that many organizations take toward their data. If you own a repository, the single most important thing that you can do to enhance the value of your data is to keep the metadata in the repository up-to-date. Doing so requires a lot of effort, a budget, and most of all, commitment.

See Figure 37.2 for a synopsis of the role a repository can play in data warehousing and how it fits in with the other, traditional duties of the repository.

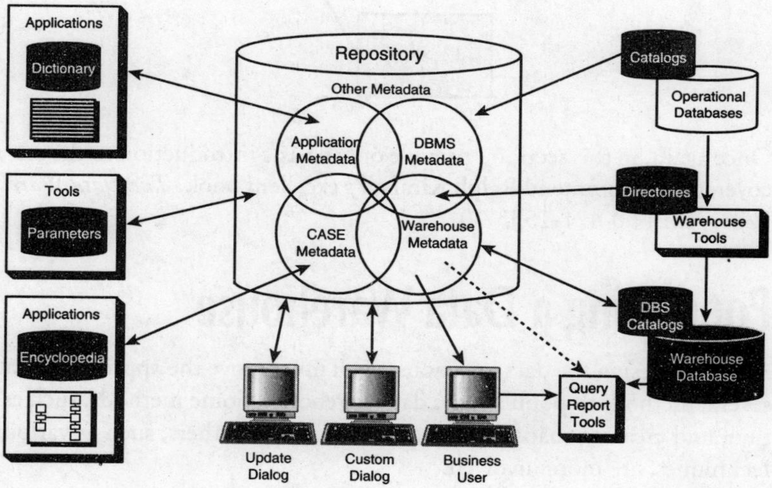

FIGURE 37.2.
The role of the repository.

Star Schema

The *star schema* concept is common within a data warehousing environment. The star schema is also sometimes called a star-join schema, data cube, or multidimensional schema. The name *star schema* comes from the pattern formed by the data model when it is graphically depicted (see Figure 37.3).

Typically, a central fact table stores the primary business activity at the center of the star. The fact table is encircled by the dimensions that affect the activity. You can think of them as the points of the star.

A variation on this theme is the snowflake schema, in which the dimension tables can have additional relationships. In essence, in a snowflake schema each dimension table is a mini-star itself.

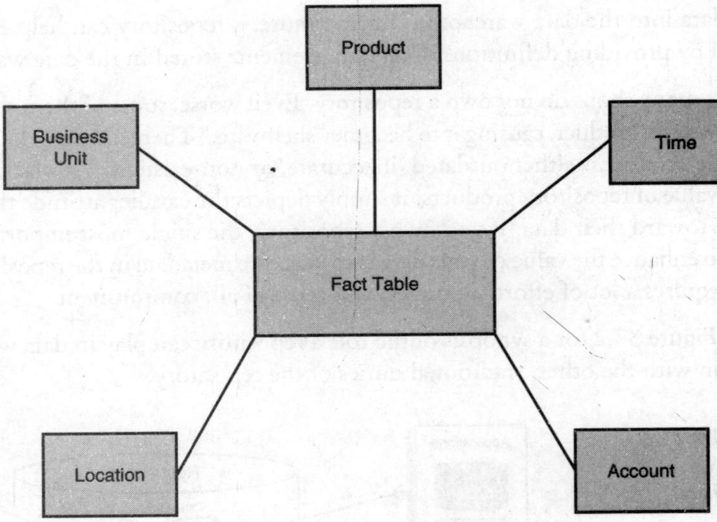

FIGURE 37.3.
Star schema.

Once again, in this section I provide only a basic introduction to the star schema. For in-depth coverage, I recommend Ralph Kimball's excellent book, *The Data Warehouse Toolkit* (1996, J. Wiley, ISBN 0-471-15337-0).

Populating a Data Warehouse

After you design the data warehouse, you must move the appropriate data into it. You can use several methods to populate the data warehouse. Some methods, such as replication, propagation, and creating snapshots are relatively simple; others, such as various data transformation techniques, are more involved.

Replication Versus Propagation

You learned about replication in Chapter 36, "Distribution Guidelines." To review, when data is replicated, one data store is copied to one or more locations. Replication can be implemented simply by copying entire tables to multiple locations. Alternatively, replicated data can be a subset of the rows and/or columns.

You can tune replicas independently of one another. Different clustering strategies, different indexes, and different tablespace parameters might be appropriate at different locations.

Propagation, on the other hand, is the migration of only changed data. Typically, propagation is implemented by scanning the transaction log and applying the results of the `INSERT`, `UPDATE`, and `DELETE` statements to another data store. Figure 37.4 shows the difference between replication and propagation.

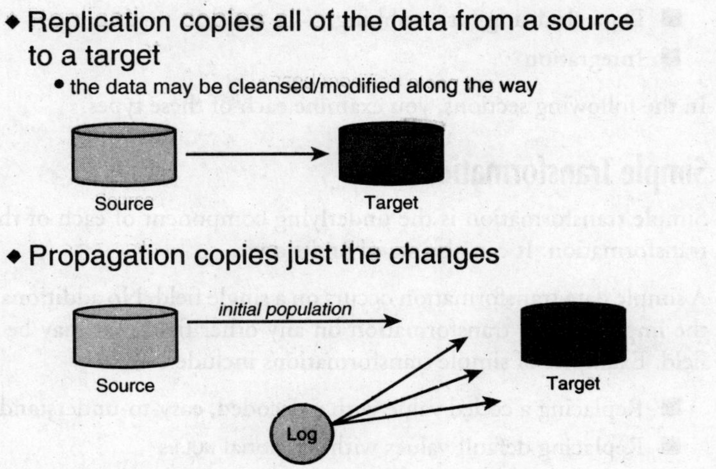
◆ Replication copies all of the data from a source to a target
• the data may be cleansed/modified along the way
Source
Target
◆ Propagation copies just the changes
initial population
Source
Target
Log

FIGURE 37.4.
Replication versus propagation.

Data warehouses can use both of these techniques to remain consistent with source data stores. Initial population of a data warehouse can be achieved by replication and subsequent population of changes by either replication (if the data is very dynamic) or propagation of changes only.

Snapshots

Snapshots, also discussed in Chapter 36, are read-only copies of entire tables. A snapshot table is useful in a data warehouse only when the entire table is needed in exactly the same format as is used in the operational environment.

Because data warehouses are integrated and optimized for query, you should not use snapshots very often. However, there is a major exception. The most popular type of data warehouse is an exact copy of the operational database duplicated for analytical querying. This type of data warehouse consists entirely of snapshot tables. The major benefit of the operational database copy is its ease of implementation. The drawbacks are myriad, including lack of integration, data not optimized for query, much of the data is codified and not easy to access, and so on. Yet, because of the relative simplicity of creating copies of operational tables, this type of data warehouse is sure to prosper.

Data Transformation

Data transformation is the process of modifying data as it is moved from the operational and external sources to the target data warehouse or data mart. The four basic types of data transformation follow:

- Simple transformation
- Aggregation and summarization

- Data cleansing (or scrubbing)
- Integration

In the following sections, you examine each of these types.

Simple Transformation

Simple transformation is the underlying component of each of the other three types of data transformation. It can also stand on its own.

A simple data transformation occurs on a single field. No additional analysis is performed as to the impact of the transformation on any other field that may be related to the transformed field. Examples of simple transformations include:

- Replacing a coded value with a decoded, easy-to-understand value
- Replacing default values with relational `NULL`s
- Changing the data type of a field to a more appropriate type (for example, from `CHAR(6)` to `DATE`)

Aggregation and Summarization

Data stored in data warehouses is usually summarized and aggregated at some level because of the vast size of most data warehouses coupled with the analytical processing that occurs on the warehouse data. Although summarization and aggregation are sometimes used interchangeably, you will find a subtle difference between the two.

Summarization is the addition of like values along one or more business dimensions. An example of summarization is adding up detail revenue values by day to arrive at weekly totals (or by week to arrive at monthly totals, by month to arrive at quarterly totals, and so on).

Aggregation refers to a summarization coupled with a calculation across different business elements. An example of aggregation is the addition of bimonthly salary to monthly commission and bonus to arrive at monthly employee compensation values.

Depending on the data requirements of the warehouse, both summarization and aggregation can be deployed during data transformation. Summarization and aggregation are typically used for the following reasons:

- They are required when the lowest level of detail stored in the data warehouse is at a higher level than the detail arriving from the source. This situation occurs when data warehouse queries do not require the lowest level of detail or sometimes when sufficient disk space is not available to store all the data for the time frame required by the data warehouse.
- They can be used to populate data marts from the data warehouse where the data mart does not require the same level of detail as is stored in the warehouse.

- They can be used to roll up detail values when the detail is removed from the warehouse because it is not being used or because it has aged past its useful life in the data warehouse.

Therefore, the data warehouse can consist of detail data as well as multiple levels of summarized and aggregated data across multiple dimensions. For example, revenue is stored at the detail level, as well as by month and by quarter, and also by product group and product type.

Data Cleansing

Before data is moved to the data warehouse, it almost always must be cleansed (or scrubbed). Do not take this statement lightly. The true scope of a data cleansing project is enormous. Much of production data is dirty, and you don't even want to consider what work cleaning it up would take. By "dirty," I mean that it does not conform to proper domain definitions or "make sense." The age old adage "garbage in, garbage out" still applies, and you can do nothing about it short of analyzing and correcting the corporate data. Failure to do so results in poorly made business decisions.

Basically, the two types of data cleansing are value validation and reformatting.

Value Validation

Value validation is the process of ensuring that each value that is sent to the data warehouse is ccurate. You've probably had that experience in which you look at the contents of one of your najor flat files or database structures and intuitively know that the data is incorrect. No way ould that employee be born in 1995. You know your company doesn't hire toddlers (even if ome of your coworkers seem to act like children)! And that next record looks bad, too. How ould she have been born in 1978 but hired in 1977? Most companies don't hire unborn emryos.

ll too often, these types of data integrity problems are glossed over. "No one would actually ake that information seriously, would they?" Well, maybe people won't, but computerized ystems will. That information can be summarized, aggregated, and/or manipulated in some ay, and then populated into another data element. And when that data element is moved ito the data warehouse, analytical processing will be performed on it that can affect the way our company does business. What if warehouse data is being analyzed to overhaul hiring pracces? That data may make an impact on the business decisions if enough of the hire and birth ates are inaccurate.

nall data discrepancies can become statistically irrelevant when large volumes of data are avaged. But averaging is not the only analytical function that is employed by analytical data arehouse queries. What about sums, medians, max/min, and other aggregate and scalar funcons? Even further, can you actually prove that the scope of your data problems is as small as u think it is? The answer is probably "no."

And the preceding is just one small example of the scope of the data integrity violations that many application systems allow to be inserted into production data stores. Some of the integrity violations may seem to be inexcusable. For example, you probably have discovered the `SEX` column (or field) that is supposed to store `M` or `F`. Frequently, you might see `SEX` data that defies imagination—everything from `*` to `!` to a blank. These designations typically do not refer to a third sex; they are incorrect data values. Shouldn't programmatically forcing the values to be either `M` or `F` be a simple matter? The short answer is "yes," but this answer simplifies the matter too much. Many systems were designed to record this information, if available, but not to force the user to enter it. If you are a telephone marketer, the reasons for this are clear. Not everyone wants to reveal personal information, and acquiring the information independently is not always an easy matter. However, the organization would rather record incomplete information than no information.

The organization is correct in wanting incomplete information over nothing. However, one problem is still ignored. The true problem is that a systematic manner of recording "unknown" values was not employed. Every program that can modify data should be forced to record a special "unknown" indicator if a data value is not readily available at the time of data entry. Most relational DBMS products allow data columns to store a "null," indicating "unknown" or "unavailable" information. Prerelational DBMS products and flat files do not have this option. However, you can choose some specific, standard default value. The trick is to *standardize* on the default value.

One of the key components of value validation should be the standardization of "unknown" values. This process can be tedious. The primitive examples outlined in the preceding paragraphs use data elements with a domain of two valid values. Most data elements have domains that are considerably more complex. Determining which are valid values and which are not can be difficult for someone who is not intimately aware of the workings of the application systems that allowed the values to be inserted in the first place. Is `1895-01-01` a valid date for a field or is it a default for an "unknown" value?

Nineteenth century dates may be valid for birth dates, stock issuance dates, account inception dates, publication dates, and any number of other dates with long periods of "freshness." Just because the program allows it to be put there, though, that does not mean it is actually a valid date. A user can easily type 1895 instead of 1995. If the data entry program is not intelligen enough to trap these types of errors, the systems will insert dirty data into production data stores This type of data integrity problem is the most difficult to spot. Likely, only the business person who understands the data and the business requirements can spot these types of problems

Reformatting

The format of data in the source system does not always conform to the desired format of dat in the data warehouse. Examples include storing addresses as they would appear on an enve lope as opposed to a group of separate address lines or atomic address fields (that is, city, state zip). Other examples include the formatting of orders with associated items or the formattin of any type of data to look like forms used by the analysts accessing the data warehouse.

Automating Data Transformation

Data transformation is typically implemented using a third-party tool that eases the definition and implementation of the various forms of transformation. However, creating home-grown programs to perform data transformation is possible, though time consuming. When you're deciding which approach to use, keep the following five questions in mind:

- What is the time frame for the project, and is it possible to create all the data transformation programs necessary in the time allotted with the available staff?
- What is the budget for the data warehouse project, and how much do the third-party tools cost? Keep in mind that a data transformation tool, once acquired, can be used across multiple projects. Also, be sure to factor in the cost of maintaining home-grown data transformation programs before analyzing the cost of a third-party solution.
- What is the size of the data warehouse being implemented? If it is very small, a tool may not be cost justifiable. If it is large, however, a tool could be less costly than a home-grown solution.
- What other data warehouse projects are on the horizon, and can the cost of the tool be spread across multiple projects? Vendors usually provide discounts when you purchase software in volume.
- What are the skills of the data warehouse development staff? The more savvy the team, the less need you have for a third-party data transformation tool.

As for the cleansing process, you truly cannot avoid human interaction completely when attempting to clean dirty data. The best approach is to clean the data at the source. If you don't clean the data there, dirty data will continue to be stored in the organization and sent to the data warehouse. Of course, the data transformation tool can catch and correct some of these values, but it is impractical to assume that all data anomalies can be captured if they are not corrected at the source.

Integration

The fourth, and final, type of data transformation is integration. Integration can be the most difficult component of the transformation process.

Data warehouses are populated with data from multiple sources, both local and remote; internal and external. Integration is the process of rationalizing data elements received from multiple disparate sources. It is possible that a single data element in the data warehouse can be populated from more than one source. For example, competitive pricing information might be received from multiple research firms. One firm might store the data in a decimal format, another in an integer format, and yet another in decimal format, but with more significant digits. Before the pricing data can be moved to the data warehouse, it must be modified to conform to a single definition.

Another integration problem can occur when data from multiple sources must be combined into a single data element in the data warehouse. This frequently takes the form of a calculated or derived result.

The different types of integration that you might encounter are indeed impossible to predict. Data elements in different applications, systems, and organizations will follow different business rules, be impacted by different administration and coding practices, and, in general, be different. Therefore, you must implement flexible integration procedures to be prepared for the many different data types and formats that you will encounter when populating your data warehouse.

Accessing the Data Warehouse

After you design the data warehouse, you can use data access tools (also known as business intelligence tools) to access the data. You can use many types of data access tools, including the following:

- GUI or Web-based database query tools
- Complex report writers
- OLAP tools that analyze data along dimensions
- Data mining tools
- CASE tools
- Program generation tools

Most data warehouses deploy only the first three categories of data access tools for end-use querying and analysis. Additionally, data mining is gaining acceptance. Data mining is th practice of automatic and systematic analysis of data to find patterns and trends. The topic o data mining is beyond the scope of this book.

Managing the Data Warehouse

After the data warehouse environment is built and users rely on it for their data analysis need you must be prepared to manage the environment like any other mission-critical applicatio Managing implies creating a systems management plan for the data warehouse that shoul include the plans to support the following:

Operations

- 24 × 7 support (help desk)
- Automation
- Chargeback

- Capacity planning
- Securing access

Administration

- Maintenance of database structures
- Data availability
- Backup and recovery

Performance Management

- Proactive automation
- Predictive performance modeling
- Server performance optimization
- Network performance optimization
- Database performance optimization

Additionally, you should manage change throughout the application life cycle for operational systems that can affect the warehouse because they are data sources, as well as for any application that accesses warehouse data directly.

The Big Picture

Now that you have learned about the basics of data warehousing, I will tie all this information together with a single picture. Figure 37.5 contains all the core components of a data warehouse environment.

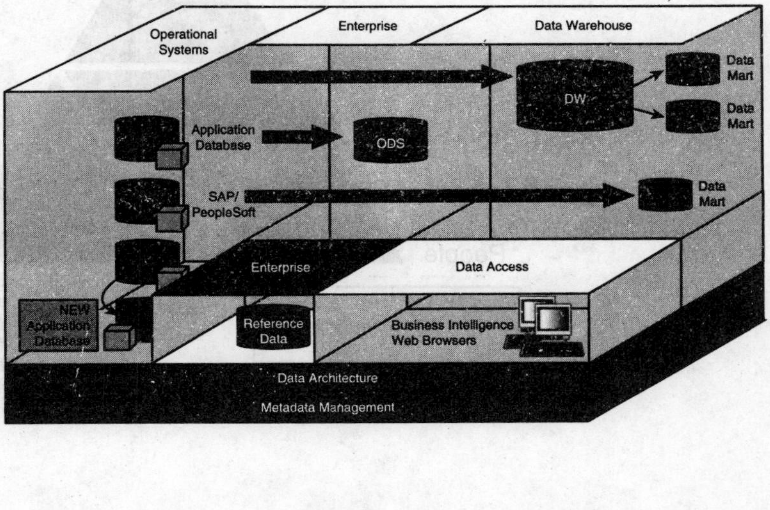

FIGURE 37.5.
Data warehousing: the big picture.

Data Warehouse Guidelines

You can use the following guidelines as rules of thumb when you're designing, implementing, and using your DB2-based data warehouse.

Do Not Implement a Data Warehouse as a Panacea

Many data warehouse development projects begin with "pie in the sky" expectations. One of the biggest problems with a data warehouse project is a situation in which the data warehouse is viewed as a "magic bullet" that will solve all of management's information problems.

To alleviate these types of problems, you should manage expectations by securing an executive sponsor, limiting the scope of the project, and implementing the data warehouse in stages (or possibly by implementing multiple data marts for each department).

Incorporate All Three Sides of the Pyramid

When you're developing a data warehouse, be sure to include tools, people, and methods in your warehouse blueprint (see Figure 37.6). Too often, the focus is solely on the tools component. To be successful, a data warehouse project requires more than just tools. You need careful planning and implementation (methods) as well as a means to learn from the efforts of others (people) through mentoring, consulting, education, seminars, and user groups.

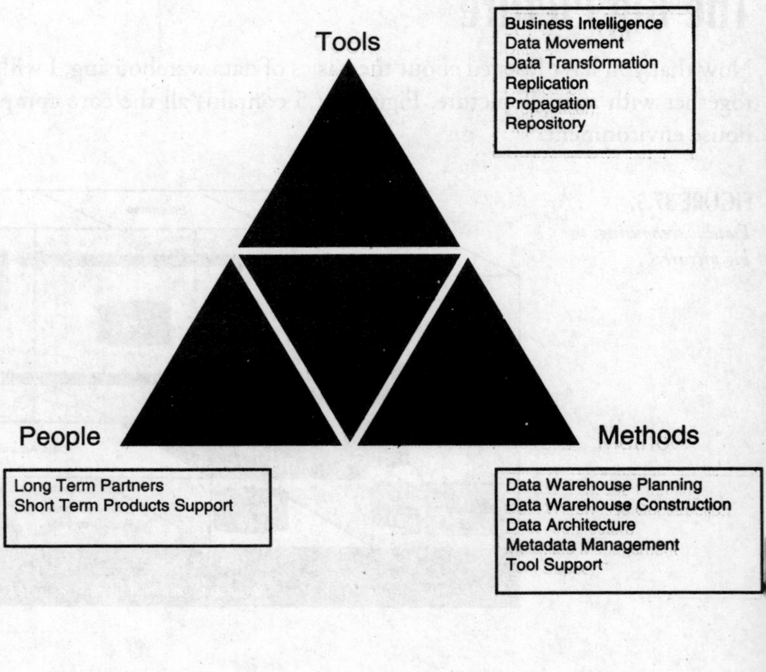

FIGURE 37.6.
The data warehousing pyramid of success.

Do Not Mix Operational Needs into the Data Warehouse Project

When a data warehousing project is first initiated, it may have a mixture of operational and analytical/informational objectives. This mixture is a recipe for disaster. Redefine the project to concentrate on non-operational, informational needs only. The primary reason for the existence of the data warehouse in the first place is to segregate operational processing from reporting.

Ensure Read-Only Data

Create the data warehouse as a decision support vehicle. The data should be periodically updated and summarized. If your design calls for a data warehouse in which all the data is modified immediately as it is changed in production, you need to rethink your data warehouse design.

Consider starting DB2 data warehouse databases as `ACCESS(RO)` to ensure read-only access. Doing so has the additional effect of eliminating locking on the read-only databases. When the data warehouse is refreshed, the databases have to be restarted in read/write mode.

Consider Using Dirty Reads

Because the data warehouses are read-only in nature, locking is not truly required. You can specify `ISOLATION(UR)` for all plans, packages, and queries used in the data warehouse environment. With `ISOLATION(UR)`, DB2 will take fewer locks, thereby enhancing performance. However, DB2 might read uncommitted data when `ISOLATION(UR)` is specified. This should not be a major concern in the read-only data warehouse.

Do Not Underestimate the Complexity of Implementing a Data Warehouse

Moving data into a data warehouse is a complex task. Detailed knowledge of the applications accessing the source databases that feed the data warehouse must be available. Be sure to allot development time for learning the complexities of the source systems. Frequently, the systems documentation for production system is inadequate or non-existent.

Additionally, be sure to analyze the source data to determine what level of data scrubbing is required. As I mentioned earlier, this process can be an immense, time-consuming task.

Prepare to Manage Data Quality Issues Constantly

Maintaining data quality will be an ongoing concern. Both the end users and the data warehouse construction and maintenance team are responsible for promoting and fostering data quality. Data problems will be discovered not only throughout the development phase of the data warehouse, but throughout the useful life of the data warehouse.

Be sure to establish a policy for how data anomalies are to be reported and corrected before the data warehouse is made generally available to its end users. Additionally, be sure to involve the end users in the creation and support of this policy; otherwise, it is doomed to fail. The end users understand the data better than anyone else in the organization, including the data warehouse developers and DBAs.

Do Not Operate in a Vacuum

As business needs change, operational systems change. When operational data stores change, the data warehouse will be affected as well. When a data warehouse is involved, however, both the operational database and the data warehouse must be analyzed for the impact of changing any data formats. This is true because the data warehouse stores historical data that you might not be able to change to the new format. Before the change is made to the operational system, the data warehouse team must be prepared first to accept the new format as input to the data warehouse, and second, to either maintain multiple data formats for the changed data element or to implement a conversion mechanism as part of the data transformation process. Conversion, however, can result in lost or confusing data.

Prepare to Tackle Operational Problems During the Data Warehousing Project

You will encounter problems in operational systems that feed the data warehouse. These problems may have been in production for year, running undetected. The data warehousing project will uncover many such errors. Be prepared to find them and have a plan for handling them. Only three options are available:

- Ignore the problem with the understanding that the problem will exist in the data warehouse if not corrected.
- Fix the problem in the operational system.
- If possible, fix the problem during the data transformation phase of data warehouse population.

Of course, the second and third options are the favored approaches.

Determine When Data Is to Be Purged

Even in the data warehouse environment, when certain thresholds are reached, maintaining certain data in the data warehouse does not make sense. This situation may occur because of technology reasons (such as reaching a capacity limit), regulatory reasons (change in regulations or laws), or business reasons (restructuring data, instituting different processes, and so on).

Plan to arrange for methods of purging data from the data warehouse without dropping the data forever. A good tactic is to prepare a generic plan for offloading warehouse data to tape or optical disk.

Use Denormalization Strategies

Experiment with denormalized tables. Because the data warehouse is a read-only database, you should optimize query at the expense of update. Denormalization takes care of this situation. Analyze the data access requirements of the most frequent queries, and plan to denormalize to optimize those queries.

Refer to Chapter 3, "Data Definition Guidelines," for an in-depth discussion on the types of denormalization.

Be Generous with Indexes

The use of indexes is a major factor in creating efficient data retrieval. You usually can use indexes more liberally in the read-only setting of the data warehouse. Remember, though, you must make a trade-off between data loading and modification and the number of indexes, as shown in Figure 37.7.

FIGURE 37.7.
Indexes and the performance of query versus modification.

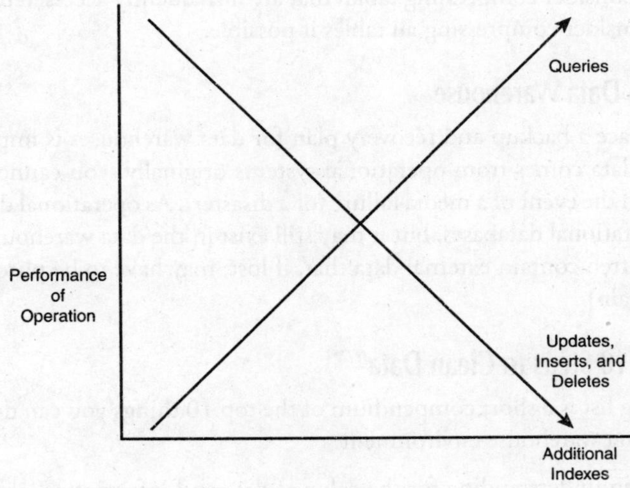

These indexes do not have to be the same indexes that exist in the operational system, even if the data warehouse is nothing more than an exact replica or snapshot of the operational databases. You should optimize the indexes based on the access patterns and query needs of the decision support environment of the data warehouse.

Also, use type 2 indexes to remove index locking as a consideration for the data warehouse.

Avoid Referential Integrity and Check Constraints

Because data is cleansed and scrubbed during the data transformation process, implementing data integrity mechanisms such as referential integrity (RI) and check constraints on data warehouse tables is not efficient. Even without a comprehensive cleansing during data transformation, the data in the warehouse will be as good as the data in the source operational systems (which should utilize RI and check constraints).

Encourage Parallelism

Use partitioned tablespaces and specify `DEGREE(ANY)` to encourage I/O, CPU, and Sysplex parallelism. Parallelism helps to reduce overall elapsed time when accessing large databases such as those common in a data warehouse.

Consider partitioning simple and segmented tablespaces to take advantage of DB2's parallelism features. Additionally, consider repartitioning partitioned tablespaces to take full advantage of DB2 parallelism based on the usage patterns of your data warehouse access.

Consider Data Compression

DB2's hardware-based data compression techniques are optimal for the data warehousing environment. Consider compressing tables that are infrequently accessed to save disk space. Furthermore, consider compressing all tables if possible.

Back Up the Data Warehouse

Putting in place a backup and recovery plan for data warehouses is imperative. Even though most of the data comes from operational systems originally, you cannot always rebuild data warehouses in the event of a media failure (or a disaster). As operational data ages, it is removed from the operational databases, but it may still exist in the data warehouse. Furthermore, data warehouses often contain external data that, if lost, may have to be purchased again (creating a financial drain).

Follow "The 10 Steps to Clean Data"

The following list is a short compendium of the top 10 things you can do to ensure data quality in your data warehouse environment:

1. Foster an understanding for the value of data and information within the organization. In short, treat data as a corporate asset. What does this mean? Consider the other assets of your organization. The capital assets ($) are modeled using a chart of accounts. Human resources (personnel) are modeled using management structures, reporting hierarchies, and personnel files. From building blueprints to item bills of material, every asset that is truly treated as an asset is modeled. If your corporation does not model data, it does not treat data as an asset and is at a disadvantage.

   Acceptance of these ideals can be accomplished through lobbying the users and managers you know, starting an internal newsletter, circulating relevant articles and books throughout your company, and treating data as a corporate asset yourself. A great deal of salesmanship, patience, politics, and good luck will be required, so be prepared.

2. Never cover up data integrity problems. Document them and bring them to the attention of your manager and the users who rely on the data. Usually, the business units using the data are empowered to make changes to it.
3. Do not underestimate the amount of time and effort that will be required to clean up dirty data. Understand the scope of the problem and the process required to rectify it. Take into account the politics of your organization and the automated tools that are available. The more political the battle, the longer the task will take. The fewer tools available, the longer the task will be. Even if you have tools, if no one understands them properly, the situation will probably be worse than having no tools at all as people struggle to use what they do not understand.
4. Understand what is meant by "data warehouse" within the context of your projects. What is the scope of the "warehouse": enterprise or departmental? What technology is used? If OLAP is a component of the environment, is it ROLAP or MOLAP?
5. Educate those people implementing the data warehouse by sending them to courses and industry conferences, purchasing books, and encouraging them to read periodicals. A lack of education has killed many potentially rewarding projects.
6. Physically design the data stores for the data warehouse differently than the similar, corresponding production data stores. For example, the file and table structures, indexes, and clustering sequence should be different in the warehouse because the data access requirements are different.
7. You will often hear that denormalization is desirable in the data warehouse environment, but proceed with caution. Because denormalized data is optimized for data access, and the data warehouse is "read-only," you might think that denormalization is a natural for this environment. However, the data must be populated into the data warehouse at some point. Denormalized data is still difficult to maintain and should be avoided if performance is acceptable.
8. Understand the enabling technologies for data warehousing. Replication and propagation are different technologies with different availability and performance effects on both the production (OLTP) and the warehouse (OLAP) systems.
9. Only after you understand the basics should you delve into the more complex aspects of data warehousing such as implementing an ODS, very large databases, or multidimensional databases.
10. Reread steps 1 through 9 whenever you think you are overworked, underpaid, or both!

Data in the warehouse is only as good as the sources from which it was gleaned. Failure to clean dirty data can result in the creation of a data outhouse instead of a data warehouse.

Use Good DB2 Database Design Techniques

Use the DB2 DDL design techniques presented in Chapter 3 in conjunction with the guidelines presented in this chapter to ensure an optimal DB2 data warehouse implementation.

Summary

Data warehouses can provide organizations with a competitive advantage as users begin to analyze data in conjunction with business trends. After a data warehouse is implemented, you cannot turn back because your users will be hooked, your organization will be more profitable, and you'll have the satisfaction of contributing to the success of the business (and, just maybe, a big fat raise).

IX

Appendixes

A

DB2 SQLCODE and SQLSTATE Values

This appendix lists the SQLCODEs and SQLSTATEs that DB2 returns to indicate the success or failure of each SQL statement. Simply remember the following rules:

- An SQLCODE of 0 indicates that the SQL statement completed successfully.
- A negative SQLCODE value indicates that the SQL statement was not successful. An error that hindered DB2 from performing the requested action occurred.
- An SQLCODE of +100 indicates that no row was found. This value can be returned by any SQL statement that expects to process a row but cannot acquire the row.
- Any other positive SQLCODE value indicates that the SQL statement completed, but with a warning. Warnings might require subsequent attention, or they may be inconsequential.
- You also can use SQLSTATE, a character string value, to determine the success or failure of an SQL statement. The values assigned to SQLSTATE are consistent across platforms (DB2 for Common Servers, DB2 for AS/400, DB2 for VSE & VM, and DB2 for MVS).
- SQLSTATE values do not necessarily have a one-to-one correspondence with SQLCODE values. For example, one SQLCODE can have many corresponding SQLSTATEs, and one SQLSTATE can correspond to many SQLCODEs.
- SQLSTATE values are made up of a two-character class code and a three-character subclass code. The class code indicates the type of error, and the subclass code details the explicit error within that error type. The following list details each SQLSTATE class code and the type of error it relates to:

Class Code	*Type of Error*
00	Unqualified Successful Completion
01	Warning
02	No Data
07	Dynamic SQL Error
08	Connection Exception
16	Feature Not Supported
21	Cardinality Violation
22	Data Exception
23	Constraint Violation
24	Invalid Cursor State
26	Invalid SQL Statement Syntax
2D	Invalid Transaction Termination
34	Invalid Cursor Name
37	Syntax Error
39	External Function Call Exception
40	Serialization Failure
42	Access Violation

44	`WITH CHECK OPTION` Violation
51	Invalid Application State
52	Duplicate or Undefined Name
53	Invalid Operand or Inconsistent Specification
54	SQL or Product Limit Exceeded
55	Object Not in Prerequisite State
56	Miscellaneous SQL or Product Restriction
57	Resource Unavailable or Operator Intervention
58	System Error

- You can gear your program to check for general SQL error types by checking only the two-digit `SQLSTATE` class code.
- In general, you should gear your application programs to check for `SQLCODE`s because checking for negative values is easier. Check the `SQLSTATE` value, however, when you must check for a group of `SQLCODE`s associated with a single `SQLSTATE` or when your program runs on multiple platforms.

Three comprehensive `SQLCODE` and `SQLSTATE` lists follow. Tables A.1 and A.2 list the basic `SQLCODE` and `SQLSTATE` values returned by embedded SQL applications. Table A.1 is in order by `SQLCODE`; Table A.2 is in `SQLSTATE` order. Table A.3 lists the special `SQLSTATE` values returned by DB2 CLI applications. You can use these tables as references when you're writing DB2 application programs or issuing ad hoc SQL statements.

CAUTION

Be aware that IBM changed the `SQLSTATE` values for many errors and warnings as of DB2 V4. The changes were made to better conform to ANSI/ISO standards. However, programs that checked for explicit `SQLSTATE` values may not operate as you want without your making changes after migrating from DB2 V3 to V4.

able A.1. DB2 error messages (sorted by `SQLCODE`).

SQLCODE	*SQLSTATE*	*Description*
000	00000	The SQL statement finished successfully.
	01xxx	The SQL statement finished successfully, but with a warning.
+012	01545	The unqualified column name was interpreted as a correlated reference.
+098	01568	A dynamic SQL statement ends with a semicolon.
+100	02000	No rows found to satisfy the SQL statement.

continues

Table A.1. continued

SQLCODE	*SQLSTATE*	*Description*
+110	01561	Update to a table defined using DATA CAPTURE was not signaled to originating subsystem. (DPROP)
+111	01590	The SUBPAGES clause was specified (and ignored) for a Type 2 index.
+117	01525	The number of values being inserted does not equal the number of columns in the table being inserted to.
+162	01514	Named tablespace placed in check pending status.
+203	01552	The named qualified column was resolved using a non-unique name.
+204	01532	Named object is not defined to DB2.
+206	01533	Named column does not exist in any table named in the SQL statement.
+218	01537	EXPLAIN cannot be executed for the SQL statement as it references a remote object.
+219	01532	The named PLAN_TABLE does not exist.
+220	01546	Improperly defined PLAN_TABLE; check definition of named column.
+304	01515	Value cannot be assigned to host variable because it is out of range for the data type.
+331	01520	String cannot be translated so it has been assigned to null.
+339	01569	Character conversion problem may exist due to connection to a DB2 V2.2 subsystem.
+402	01521	Unknown location.
+403	01522	CREATE ALIAS object does not exist locally.
+464	01609	Named stored procedure exceeded the limit on the number of query results sets it can return.
+466	01610	Specifies the number of query results sets returned by the named stored procedure. Successful completion.
+494	01614	Number of results sets returned by a stored procedure exceeds the number of results set locators as specified by the ASSOCIATE LOCATORS statement.
+535	01591	A positioned update of a primary key or a delete from a table with a self-referencing constraint was requested.

SQLCODE	SQLSTATE	Description
+541	01543	Named foreign key is a duplicate referential constraint.
+551	01548	Named authorization ID lacks authority to perform the named operation on the named DB2 object.
+552	01542	Named authorization ID lacks authority to perform the named operation.
+558	01516	Already granted to PUBLIC so WITH GRANT OPTION not applicable.
+561	01523	PUBLIC AT ALL LOCATIONS not valid for ALTER and INDEX privileges.
+562	01560	One or more of the privileges was ignored because the GRANTEE already possesses that privilege.
+610	01566	The named index is in RECOVER PENDING status due to creating and index specifying DEFER YES.
+625	01518	Table definition marked incomplete because primary key index was dropped.
+626	01529	Index to enforce UNIQUE constraint has been dropped; uniqueness no longer enforced.
+645	01528	WHERE NOT NULL was ignored because the key for the index being created cannot contain NULLs.
+650	01538	Cannot alter or create the named table as a dependent table.
+653	01551	Partitioned index for the named table in the named partitioned tablespace has not been created yet, so it is unavailable.
+658	01600	Cannot specify SUBPAGES clause when creating a catalog index; SUBPAGES will be ignored and default to 1.
+664	01540	Limit key for the partitioning index exceeds the maximum value.
+738	01530	The change to the named object may require like changes for the objects in read-only systems.
+802	01519	Data exception error caused by data overflow or divide exception.
+806	01553	ISOLATION(RR) conflicts with LOCKSIZE PAGE.
+807	01554	Overflow may result due to decimal multiplication.
+863	01539	Connection successful, but only SBCS will be supported.

continues

Table A.1. continued

SQLCODE	*SQLSTATE*	*Description*
+2000	56094	Type 1 indexes where SUBPAGES does not equal 1 cannot become group bufferpool dependent in a data sharing environment.
+30100	01558	Distribution protocol error detected. Original SQLCODE and SQLSTATE provided.
-007	42601	Illegal character in SQL statement.
-010	42603	String constant not terminated properly; check for missing quotation marks.
-029	42601	INTO clause required.
-060	42815	Invalid length or scale specification for the specified data type.
-084	42612	SQL statement cannot be executed because it is invalid for dynamic SQL or is not valid for DB2 for MVS.
-101	54001	SQL statement exceeds an established DB2 limit; that is, too many tables, too many bytes in statement, and so on.
-102	54002	String constant is too long.
-103	42604	Invalid numeric literal.
-104	42601	Illegal symbol encountered in SQL statement.
-105	42604	Invalid character string format; usually refers to an improperly formatted graphic string.
-107	42622	Object name is too long.
-108	42601	Incorrect name specified for the RENAME statement; cannot use a qualifier.
-109	42601	Invalid clause specified; for example: CREATE VIEW may not contain an ORDER BY clause.
-110	42606	Invalid hexadecimal literal encountered.
-111	42901	Column function specified without a column name.
-112	42607	Invalid column function syntax; column function cannot operate on another column function.
-113	42602	Invalid character encountered.
-114	42961	Location name for this statement must match the current server, but it does not.
-115	42601	Invalid predicate encountered because comparison operator not followed by an expression or list.

SQLCODE	*SQLSTATE*	*Description*
-117	42802	Number of inserted values not equivalent to number of columns for the inserted row.
-118	42902	Table or view is illegally named in both data modification clause (INSERT, UPDATE, or DELETE) and the FROM clause.
-119	42803	Column list in HAVING clause does not match column list in the GROUP BY clause.
-120	42903	WHERE clause is not allowed to reference column function.
-121	42701	A column is illegally referenced twice in an INSERT or UPDATE statement.
-122	42803	Column function applied illegally because all columns not applied to a column function are not in the GROUP BY clause.
-125	42805	Invalid number specified in the ORDER BY clause; number is either less than 1 or greater than the number of columns selected.
-126	42829	An ORDER BY clause may not be specified for an UPDATE statement.
-127	42905	DISTINCT may only be specified once in a subselect.
-128	42601	NULL used improperly in an SQL predicate.
-129	54004	The SQL statement contains more than 15 tables.
-130	22019	Escape clause must be one character.
	22025	Invalid escape pattern.
-131	42818	The LIKE predicate may only be applied to character data.
-132	42824	First operator of LIKE predicate must be a column and the second operator must be a character string.
-133	42906	Invalid correlated subquery reference.
-134	42907	Column larger than 254 bytes used improperly.
-136	54005	Sort key length is greater than 4,000 bytes.
-137	54006	Concatenated string is too large; maximum is 32,767 for pure character or 16,382 for graphic.

continues

Table A.1. continued

SQLCODE	*SQLSTATE*	*Description*
-138	22011	The second or third operator of the SUBSTR column function is invalid.
-144	58003	Named section number is invalid.
-148	42809	RENAME cannot be used to rename a view or an active RLST table.
-150	42807	Invalid view update requested.
-151	42808	Invalid column update requested; trying to update either a non-updateable view column, a DB2 Catalog table column, or the key of a partitioning index.
-152	42809	DROP CHECK tried to drop a referential constraint, or DROP FOREIGN KEY tried to drop a check constraint.
-153	42908	Invalid view creation required; must provide a name for an unnamed or duplicate column listed in the select list.
-154	42909	Cannot create a view using UNION, UNION ALL, or a remote table.
-156	42809	It is invalid to create an index on a view or specify an object other than a table on the ALTER TABLE, DROP TABLE, or LOCK TABLE statements.
-157	42810	Must specify a table name on the FOREIGN KEY clause.
-158	42811	View columns do not match columns in the select list.
-159	42809	Invalid DROP or COMMENT ON statement.
-160	42813	WITH CHECK OPTION invalid for this view.
-161	44000	The WITH CHECK OPTION clause of the view being updated prohibits this row from being inserted or updated as specified.
-164	42502	User does not have the authority to create this view.
-170	42605	Invalid number of arguments specified for the scalar function.
-171	42815	Invalid data type length or value for the scalar function.
-173	42801	Isolation level UR cannot be specified on a cursor that is not read only.
-180	22007	Invalid syntax for the string representation of a date, time, or timestamp value.

SQLCODE	SQLSTATE	Description
-181	22007	Not a valid date, time, or timestamp value.
-182	42816	Invalid date/time value in an arithmetic expression.
-183	22008	Result of arithmetic expression returns a date/time value that is not within the range of valid values.
-184	42610	Improper usage of parameter marker for date/time values.
-185	57008	No local date/time exits defined.
-186	22505	Local date/time exit changed, causing invalid length for this program.
-187	22506	MVS returned invalid current date/time.
-188	22503	Invalid string representation.
-189	22522	The named coded character set ID is invalid or undefined.
-191	22504	String contains invalid mixed data.
-197	42877	Qualified column names cannot be used in an ORDER BY clause when two or more tables are unioned and then ordered.
-198	42617	Trying to issue a PREPARE or EXECUTE IMMEDIATE statement on a blank string.
-199	42601	Illegal keyword used in SQL statement.
-203	42702	Ambiguous column reference.
-204	42704	Undefined object name.
-205	42703	Invalid column name for specified table.
-206	42703	Column name not in any table referenced in the FROM clause.
-208	42707	Cannot ORDER BY specified column because it is not in the select list.
-219	42704	EXPLAIN cannot be executed because PLAN_TABLE does not exist.
-220	55002	Invalid PLAN_TABLE column encountered.
-221	55002	If any optional columns are defined for the PLAN_TABLE, all of them must be defined.
-240	428B4	The PART clause of a LOCK TABLE statement is invalid.
-250	42718	Local location name is not defined.

continues

Table A.1. continued

SQLCODE	*SQLSTATE*	*Description*
-251	42602	Invalid token.
-300	22024	String in host variable or parameter is not null-terminated.
-301	42895	Invalid host variable data type.
-302	22001	The value of an input variable is invalid for the specified column.
	22003	The value of an input variable is too large for the specified column.
-303	42806	Value cannot be assigned because of incompatible data types.
-304	22003	Value cannot be assigned because it is out of range.
-305	22002	Null indicator variable is missing.
-309	22512	Invalid predicate due to referenced host variable set to null.
-310	22023	Decimal host variable or parameter cannot contain non-decimal data.
-311	22501	Invalid length of input host variable; either negative or too large.
-312	42618	Undefined or unusable host variable.
-313	07001	Number of host variables does not equal number of parameter markers.
-314	42714	Ambiguous host variable reference.
-327	22525	Cannot INSERT row outside the bounds of the last partition key range.
-330	22021	String cannot be translated successfully.
-331	22021	String cannot be assigned to a host variable because of unsuccessful translation.
-332	57017	Translation not defined for the two named coded character set IDs.
-333	56010	Subtype invalid, causing translation to fail.
-338	42972	Invalid ON clause; must refer to joined columns.
-339	56082	Access to DB2 V2.2 subsystem was denied because ASCII to EBCDIC translation cannot occur.
-351	56084	Unsupported data type.

SQLCODE	SQLSTATE	Description
-400	54027	Cannot define more than 100 user-defined indexes in the DB2 Catalog.
-401	42818	The operands of an arithmetic or comparison operator are not compatible.
-402	42819	Arithmetic function cannot be applied to character or date/ time data.
-404	22001	Update or insert statement specified a string that is too long.
-405	42820	Numeric literal is out of range.
-406	22003	A calculated or derived numeric value is out of range.
-407	23502	Cannot insert a null value into a column that is defined as NOT NULL.
-408	42821	Value cannot be inserted or updated because it is incompatible with the column's data type.
-409	42607	COUNT function specified invalid operand.
-410	42820	Floating point literal longer than maximum allowable length of 30 characters.
-411	56040	Invalid CURRENT SQLID usage.
-412	42823	Multiple columns encountered in the select list of a subquery.
-413	22003	Overflow condition when converting a numeric data type.
-414	42824	The LIKE predicate may not operate on columns defined with a numeric or date/time data type.
-415	42825	The select lists specified for the UNION operation are not union-compatible.
-416	42907	Long string columns are not allowed in SQL statements containing the UNION operator.
-417	42609	Two parameter markers specified as operands on both sides of the same predicate.
-418	42610	Invalid usage of parameter markers.
-419	42911	Invalid decimal division.
-420	22018	Character string argument value did not conform to the function's requirements.
-421	42826	Same number of columns not supplied in the select lists for a UNION operation.

continues

Table A.1. continued

SQLCODE	*SQLSTATE*	*Description*
-423	0F001	Invalid result set locator value.
-426	2D528	COMMIT not permitted for an application server where updates are not permitted.
-427	2D529	ROLLBACK not permitted for an application server where updates are not permitted.
-440	42884	Number of parameters in the parameter list for a stored procedure does not match the number expected.
-444	42724	Program associated with the called stored procedure could not be found.
-450	39501	The stored procedure overwrote storage beyond a parameter's declared length.
-469	42886	Host variable must be provided on the CALL statement for parameters defined as OUT or INOUT.
-470	39002	Null parameter specified but stored procedure does not support NULLs.
-471	55023	Stored procedure failed; reason code provided.
-480	51030	DESCRIBE PROCEDURE and ASSOCIATE LOCATORS cannot be issued until the stored procedure has been CALLed.
-482	51030	Stored procedure returned no locators.
-496	51033	Statement cannot be executed because the current server is different than the server that called a stored procedure.
-497	54041	Named database exceeded the limit of 32,767 OBIDs.
-499	24516	Named cursor already assigned to a result set from named stored procedure.
-500	24501	A WITH HOLD cursor was closed because the connection was destroyed.
-501	24501	Must open a cursor before attempting to fetch from it or close it.
-502	24502	Cannot open a cursor twice without first closing it.
-503	42912	Column cannot be updated because it was not specified in the FOR UPDATE OF clause of the cursor from which it was fetched.

SQLCODE	SQLSTATE	Description
-504	34000	Cannot reference cursor because it is not defined to the program.
-507	24501	Must open a cursor before attempting to update or delete WHERE CURRENT OF.
-508	24504	Cannot update or delete because the referenced cursor is not currently positioned on a data row.
-509	42827	Cannot update from a different table than the one specified on the cursor referenced by the WHERE CURRENT OF clause.
-510	42828	Table or view cannot be modified as requested.
-511	42829	FOR UPDATE OF is invalid for non-modifiable tables or views.
-512	56023	Invalid reference to a remote object.
-513	42924	An alias cannot be defined on another alias.
-514	26501	Cursor has not been prepared.
-516	26501	Describe attempted for an unprepared SQL statement.
-517	07005	Cursor is invalid because the SQL statement has not yet been prepared.
-518	07003	Execute attempted for an unprepared SQL statement.
-519	24506	Cursor cannot be open when issuing a prepare statement for its SQL statement.
-525	51015	Cannot execute SQL statement within named package because it was invalid at bind time.
-526	42995	Global temporary table cannot be used in the given context.
-530	23503	Invalid foreign key value specified for the specified constraint name.
-531	23504	As of V5, multi-row update of a parent key attempted to remove a parent key value on which a foreign key was dependent. Prior to V5, attempting to update a primary key value when foreign keys currently exist that reference that value.
-532	23504	Deletion violates the named referential constraint.
-533	21501	Invalid multiple row insert; attempted to insert multiple rows into a self-referencing table.

continues

Table A.1. continued

SQLCODE	*SQLSTATE*	*Description*
-534	21502	An update statement changing the value of a primary key column cannot be used to update more than one row at a time.
-535	21502	Cannot specify WHERE CURRENT OF when deleting from a self-referencing table or updating primary key column(s). This code will be raised only by non-V5 subsystems.
-536	42914	Invalid delete statement due to referential constraints existing for the specified table.
-537	42709	A single column may not appear more than once in a foreign key or primary key clause specification.
-538	42830	Invalid foreign key; does not conform to the definition of the referenced table's primary key.
-539	42888	Foreign key cannot be defined because the referenced table does not have a primary key.
-540	57001	Table definition is incomplete until a unique index is created for the primary key.
-542	42831	Nullable columns are not permitted to be included as part of a primary key.
-543	23511	DELETE cannot occur because the table is a parent table in a referential constraint specifying the SET NULL delete rule, but the check constraint does not allow NULLs.
-544	23512	Cannot add this check constraint using ALTER because an existing row violates the check constraint.
-545	23513	INSERT or UPDATE caused a check constraint violation.
-546	42621	Invalid check constraint specified in CREATE or ALTER TABLE.
-548	42621	Invalid check constraint due to named column.
-549	42509	Invalid SQL statement for DYNAMICRULES(BIND) plan or package.
-551	42501	User is attempting to perform an operation on the specified object for which he is not authorized or the table does not exist.
-552	42502	User is attempting to perform an operation for which he is not authorized.

SQLCODE	SQLSTATE	Description
-553	42503	Cannot set CURRENT SQLID because the user has not been set up to change to that id.
-554	42502	Cannot grant a privilege to yourself.
-555	42502	Cannot revoke a privilege from yourself.
-556	42504	Cannot revoke a privilege that the user does not possess.
-557	42852	Inconsistent grant or revoke key word specified.
-558	56025	Invalid clause or clauses specified for the grant or revoke statement.
-559	57002	The DB2 authorization mechanism has been disabled. Grant and revoke may not be issued.
-567	42501	Named authorization ID lacks the authority to bind the named package.
-571	25000	Multiple site updates are not permitted.
-573	42890	Referential constraint cannot be defined because the named parent table does not have a unique key on the specified column.
-574	42894	Specified default conflicts with the column definition.
-580	42625	Result expressions of a CASE expression cannot all be null.
-581	42804	Incompatible data types in the result expressions of a CASE expression.
-582	42625	Search condition in a searched when clause specifies a quantified, IN, or EXISTS predicate.
-601	42710	Attempting to create an object that already exists.
-602	54008	Too many columns specified in the CREATE INDEX statement.
-603	23515	Unique index cannot be created because duplicates were found.
-604	42611	Invalid length precision or scale specified for a column in a CREATE or ALTER TABLE statement.
-607	42832	The INSERT, UPDATE, or DELETE statement specified cannot be issued as written against the DB2 Catalog tables.
-611	53088	When LOCKSIZE is TABLE or TABLESPACE, LOCKMAX must be 0.

continues

Table A.1. continued

SQLCODE	*SQLSTATE*	*Description*
-612	42711	Duplicate column names not permitted within a single table.
-613	54008	Invalid primary key; is either longer than 254 bytes or contains more than 40 columns.
-614	54008	Maximum internal key length of 254 for indexes has been surpassed.
-615	55006	Cannot drop this package because it is currently executing.
-616	42893	The specified object may not be dropped because other objects are dependent upon it.
-617	56089	Type 1 index cannot be defined with LOCKSIZE ROW or LARGE tablespace.
-618	42832	Requested operation not permitted for DB2 Catalog tables.
-619	55011	DSNDB07 may not be modified unless it has first been stopped.
-620	53001	The specified key word is not permitted for a tablespace in DSNDB07.
-621	58001	Duplicate DBID encountered; system problem encountered.
-622	56031	Cannot specify FOR MIXED DATA because the mixed data option has not been installed.
-623	55012	Cannot define more than one clustering index for a single table.
-624	42889	Cannot define more than one primary key for a single table.
-625	55014	A unique index is required for a table defined with a primary key.
-626	55015	Cannot issue an alter statement to change PRIQTY, SECQTY, or ERASE unless the tablespace has first been stopped.
-627	55016	Cannot issue an alter statement to change PRIQTY, SECQTY, or ERASE unless the tablespace has first been defined to use storage groups.
-628	42613	CREATE TABLESPACE clauses specified are mutually exclusive (for example, cannot partition segmented tablespace).
-629	42834	SET NULL is invalid because the foreign key cannot contain null values.

SQLCODE	SQLSTATE	Description
-630	56089	WHERE NOT NULL cannot be specified for Type 1 indexes.
-631	54008	Invalid foreign key; is either longer than 254 bytes or contains more than 40 columns.
-632	42915	The specified delete rules prohibit defining this table as a dependent of the named table.
-633	42915	Invalid delete rule; the specified mandatory delete rule must be used.
-634	42915	DELETE CASCADE is not allowed in this situation.
-635	42915	The delete rule cannot be different or cannot be SET NULL.
-636	56016	The partitioning index must be consistent in its specification of ascending or descending for the partitioning index key.
-637	42614	Duplicate key word encountered.
-638	42601	Missing column definition in CREATE TABLE statement.
-639	56027	A nullable column of a foreign key with a delete rule of SET NULL cannot be a column of the key of a partitioning index.
-640	56089	LOCKSIZE ROW cannot be specified for this tablespace because a Type 1 index is defined on a table in the tablespace.
-642	54021	Unique constraint contains too many columns.
-643	54024	Check constraint exceeds maximum length of 3,800 characters.
-644	42615	Invalid value specified for key word in the SQL statement.
-646	55017	The table cannot be created in the specified partitioned or default tablespace because the specified tablespace already contains a table.
-647	57003	The specified bufferpool is invalid because it has not been activated.
-650	56090	ALTER INDEX cannot be executed; reason code provided.
-651	54025	Table object descriptor (OBD) would exceed maximum size (32K) if the CREATE or ALTER TABLE were allowed.
-652	23506	Violation of EDITPROC or VALIDPROC encountered.

continues

Table A.1. continued

SQLCODE	*SQLSTATE*	*Description*
-653	57004	A table in a partitioned tablespace is unavailable because the partitioning index has not been created yet.
-655	56036	STOGROUP cannot specify both specific and non-specific (that is, "*") volumes in the volume list.
-660	53035	Improper partitioning index specification; must define limit keys for the clustering index.
-661	53036	Partitioning index does not specify the proper number of partitions.
-662	53037	Attempted to create a partitioning index on a non-partitioned (segmented or simple) tablespace.
-663	53038	Invalid number of key limit values specified for the partitioning index.
-665	53039	Invalid PART clause specified for ALTER TABLESPACE statement.
-666	57005	SQL statement cannot be processed because the specified function is currently in progress.
-667	42917	Cannot explicitly drop the clustering index for a partitioned tablespace; must drop the partitioned tablespace to drop index.
-668	56018	Cannot add a column to a table defined with an EDITPROC.
-669	42917	Cannot explicitly drop a table in a partitioned tablespace; must drop the partitioned tablespace to drop the table.
-670	54010	The row length for the table exceeds the page size.
-671	53040	Cannot alter the bufferpool for the specified tablespace because it would change the page size of the tablespace.
-672	55035	DROP not allowed on named table.
-676	53041	BP32K cannot be used for an index.
-677	57011	Bufferpool expansion failed due to insufficient amount of available virtual storage.
-678	53045	The literal specified for the limit key in the partitioning index does not conform to the data type of the key value.
-679	57006	Cannot create the specified object because a drop is currently pending for that object.

SQLCODE	SQLSTATE	Description
-680	54011	No more than 750 columns may be specified for a DB2 table.
-681	23507	Column violates specified FIELDPROC.
-682	57010	FIELDPROC could not be loaded.
-683	42842	Invalid column type specified for FIELDPROC or FOR BIT DATA option.
-684	54012	The specified literal list cannot exceed 254 bytes.
-685	58002	FIELDPROC returned an invalid field description.
-686	53043	A column defined with a FIELDPROC cannot be compared to a column defined with a different FIELDPROC.
-687	53044	A column cannot be compared to a column with an incompatible field type.
-688	58002	Incorrect data returned by the FIELDPROC.
-689	54011	Dependent table defined with too many columns.
-690	23508	Data definition control support rejected this statement.
-691	57018	The named registration table does not exist.
-692	57018	The named index does not exist, but is required for the named registration table.
-693	55003	The named column for the named registration table/index is invalid.
-694	57023	Drop is pending on the named registration table.
-713	42815	The special register value specified is invalid.
-715	56064	The named program cannot be run because it depends upon features of a release of DB2 that your shop has installed, but backed off.
-716	56065	The named program was precompiled with an incorrect level for this release.
-717	56066	BIND failed because it depends upon features of a release of DB2 that your shop has installed, but backed off.
-718	56067	REBIND failed because IBMREQD column is invalid.
-719	42710	Cannot BIND ADD a package that already exists.

continues

Table A.1. continued

SQLCODE	SQLSTATE	Description
-720	42710	Cannot BIND REPLACE a package version that already exists.
-721	42710	Consistency token must be unique for package.
-722	42704	Bind error due because the named package does not exist.
-726	55030	Cannot bind this package because of SYSPKSYSTEM entries.
-730	56053	Invalid referential integrity definition for a table in a read-only shared database.
-731	56054	VSAM dataset must be defined using SHAREOPTION(1,3).
-732	56055	Read-only database defined but the owning DB2 subsystem has not defined the tablespace or index space.
-733	56056	Inconsistent read-only shared database definition.
-734	56057	Once a database has been defined as ROSHARE READ, it cannot be altered to a different ROSHARE state.
-735	55004	The database identified by the named DBID is no longer a read-only shared database.
-736	53014	The named OBID is invalid.
-737	56056	Cannot create an implicit tablespace under these circumstances.
-741	55030	Work file database already defined for named data sharing group member.
-742	53004	DSNDB07 is the implicit work file database.
-750	42986	Cannot rename the named table because it is referenced in at least one existing view.
-751	42987	Stored procedure placed in MUST_ROLLBACK state due to named SQL operation.
-752	0A001	Invalid CONNECT statement.
-802	22012	Exception error has occurred for the specified operation. Divide by zero.
	22003	Exception error has occurred for the specified operation. Other than divide by zero.
-803	23505	Cannot insert row because it would violate the constraints of a unique index.

SQLCODE	*SQLSTATE*	*Description*
-804	07002	The call parameter list for the SQLDA is in error.
-805	51002	The DBRM or package name not found in plan.
-807	23509	Package not enabled for the named environment and connection.
-808	08001	The CONNECT statement is not consistent with the program's first CONNECT statement.
-811	21000	Must use a cursor when more than one row is returned as the result of an embedded select statement.
-812	22508	Collection-Id is blank in the CURRENT PACKAGESET; statement cannot be executed.
-815	42920	A GROUP BY or HAVING clause is implicitly or explicitly specified in an embedded select statement or a subquery of a basic predicate.
-817	25000	Execution of the SQL statement would result in a prohibited update to user data or the DB2 Catalog.
-818	51003	Plan <—> load module timestamp mismatch. The DBRM in the executing plan was not created from the same precompilation as the load module.
-819	58004	View cannot be recreated because the length of the parse tree stored in the DB2 Catalog is zero.
-820	58004	Invalid value encountered in DB2 Catalog for this DB2 release.
-822	51004	Invalid address encountered in the SQLDA.
-840	54004	Too many items returned in a select list or insert list.
-842	08002	A connection to the named location already exists.
-843	08003	The SET CONNECTION or RELEASE statement cannot be executed because the connection does not exist.
-870	58026	The number of host variable descriptors does not equal the number of host variables in the statement.
-872	51032	A valid CCSID has yet to be specified for this subsystem.
-873	53090	Cannot refer to a column defined in an ASCII table in the same SQL statement as a column defined in an EBCDIC table.
-874	53091	The encoding scheme for the table does not match the encoding scheme for its tablespace.

continues

Table A.1. continued

SQLCODE	*SQLSTATE*	*Description*
-875	42988	Specified operand cannot be used with ASCII data.
-876	53092	Object cannot be created for the specified reason; reason code provided.
-877	53093	ASCII not permitted for the database or tablespace; EBCDIC must be used.
-878	53094	This PLAN_TABLE cannot be ASCII; EBCDIC must be used.
-879	53095	GRAPHIC, VARGRAPHIC, and LONG VARGRAPHIC columns cannot be used in an ASCII table.
-900	08003	Application process is not connected to an application server; statement cannot be executed.
-901	58004	Intermittent system error encountered that does not inhibit subsequent SQL statements from being executed.
-902	58005	Internal control block pointer error; rebind required.
-904	57011	The specified resource is unavailable.
-905	57014	Resource limit has been exceeded.
-906	51005	SQL statement cannot be executed because of prior error.
-908	23510	Current Resource Limit Facility specification or Auto-Rebind system parameter does not permit the BIND, REBIND, or AUTO-REBIND.
-909	57007	The object has been deleted.
-910	57007	Cannot access an object for which a drop is pending.
-911	40001	The current unit of work has been rolled back.
-913	57033	Unsuccessful execution caused by either a deadlock or a timeout.
-917	42969	Bind package has failed.
-918	51021	SQL statement cannot be executed because connection was lost.
-919	56045	A ROLLBACK is required
-922	42505	Connection authorization failure. Attempting to access DB2 from TSO, CICS, or IMS and appropriate attachment facility is inactive.

SQLCODE	SQLSTATE	Description
-923	57015	Connection not established because DB2 is unavailable.
-924	58006	DB2 internal connection error encountered; reason code provided.
-925	2D521	The SQL COMMIT statement cannot be issued from CICS or IMS/DC.
-926	2D521	The SQL ROLLBACK statement cannot be issued from CICS or IMS/DC.
-927	51006	The language interface was called when the connecting environment was not established. Invoke the program using the DSN command.
-929	58002	Data capture exit has failed. (DPROP)
-939	51021	Rollback is required due to unrequested rollback of a remote server.
-947	56038	SQL statement failed because update cannot be propagated. (DPROP)
-948	56062	DDF not started; distributed operation is invalid.
-950	42705	Location specified in the SQL statement not defined in SYSIBM.LOCATIONS.
-965	51021	Stored procedure terminated abnormally.
-981	57015	Attempt to execute SQL in the RRSAF when it was not in a state to allow SQL.
-991	57015	Call attach was not able to establish an implicit connect or open to DB2.
-2001	53089	Number of host variable parameters specified for a stored procedure does not equal the expected number of parameters.
-30000	58008	DRDA distribution protocol error; processing can continue.
-30020	58009	DRDA distribution protocol error; conversation deallocated.
-30021	58010	DRDA distribution protocol error; processing cannot continue.
-30030	58013	Distribution protocol violation; COMMIT unsuccessful, conversation deallocated. (AS)
-30040	57012	Execution failed due to unavailable resource(s); processing can continue. (AS)

continues

Table A.1. continued

SQLCODE	*SQLSTATE*	*Description*
-30041	57013	Execution failed due to unavailable resource(s); processing cannot successfully continue.
-30050	58011	Execution unsuccessful; statement cannot be executed during the BIND process.
-30051	58012	Failure caused by specific BIND process not being active. (Remote BIND)
-30052	42932	Program preparation assumption incorrect.
-30053	42506	Authorization failure encountered for package owner.
-30060	08004	Authorization failure encountered for RDB.
-30061	08004	Invalid or non-existent RDB specified.
-30070	58014	Target subsystem does not support this command.
-30071	58015	Target subsystem does not support this object.
-30072	58016	Target subsystem does not support this parameter.
-30073	58017	Target subsystem does not support this parameter value.
-30080	08001	SNA communication error.
-30081	58019	TCP/IP communication error.
-30082	08001	Communication failed due to security violation; reason code provided.
-30090	25000	Specified operation invalid for remote execution.
-30104	56095	Error in bind option and bind value.
-30105	56096	The specified bind options are incompatible.

Table A.2. DB2 error messages (sorted by SQLSTATE).

SQLSTATE	*SQLCODE*	*Description*
00000	000	The SQL statement finished successfully.
01xxx	000	The SQL statement finished successfully, but with a warning.
01514	+162	Named tablespace placed in check pending status.
01515	+304	Value cannot be assigned to host variable because it is out of range for the data type.

SQLSTATE	*SQLCODE*	*Description*
01516	+558	Already granted to PUBLIC, so WITH GRANT OPTION not applicable.
01518	+625	Table definition marked incomplete because primary key index was dropped.
01519	+802	Data exception error caused by data overflow or divide exception.
01520	+331	String cannot be translated, so it has been assigned to null.
01521	+402	Unknown location.
01522	+403	CREATE ALIAS object does not exist locally.
01523	+561	PUBLIC AT ALL LOCATIONS not valid for ALTER and INDEX privileges.
01525	+117	The number of values being inserted does not equal the number of columns in the table being inserted to.
01528	+645	WHERE NOT NULL was ignored because the key for the index being created cannot contain NULLs.
01529	+626	Index to enforce UNIQUE constraint has been dropped; uniqueness no longer enforced.
01530	+738	The change to the named object may require like changes for the objects in read-only systems.
01532	+204	Named object is not defined to DB2.
	+219	The named PLAN_TABLE does not exist.
01533	+206	Named column does not exist in any table named in the SQL statement.
01537	+218	EXPLAIN cannot be executed for the SQL statement as it references a remote object.
01538	+650	Cannot alter or create the named table as a dependent table.
01539	+863	Connection successful, but only SBCS will be supported.
01540	+664	Limit key for the partitioning index exceeds the maximum value.
01542	+552	Named authorization ID lacks authority to perform the named operation.
01543	+541	Named foreign key is a duplicate referential constraint.

continues

Table A.2. continued

SQLSTATE	*SQLCODE*	*Description*
01545	+012	The unqualified column name was interpreted as a correlated reference.
01546	+220	Improperly defined PLAN_TABLE; check definition of named column.
01548	+551	Named authorization ID lacks authority to perform the named operation on the named DB2 object.
01551	+653	Partitioned index for the named table in the named partitioned tablespace has not been created yet, so it is unavailable.
01552	+203	The named qualified column was resolved using a non-unique name.
01553	+806	ISOLATION(RR) conflicts with LOCKSIZE PAGE.
01554	+807	Overflow may result due to decimal multiplication.
01558	+30100	Distribution protocol error detected. Original SQLCODE and SQLSTATE provided.
01560	+562	One or more of the privileges was ignored because the GRANTEE already possesses that privilege.
01561	+110	Update to a table defined using DATA CAPTURE was not signaled to originating subsystem. (DPROP)
01566	+610	The named index is in RECOVER PENDING status due to creating and index specifying DEFER YES.
01568	+098	A dynamic SQL statement ends with a semicolon.
01569	+339	Character conversion problem may exist due to connection to a DB2 V2.2 subsystem.
01590	+111	The SUBPAGES clause was specified (and ignored) for a Type 2 index.
01591	+535	A positioned update of a primary key or a delete from a table with a self-referencing constraint was requested.
01600	+658	Cannot specify SUBPAGES clause when creating a catalog index; SUBPAGES will be ignored and default to 1.
01609	+464	Named stored procedure exceeded the limit on the number of query results sets it can return.
01610	+466	Specifies the number of query results sets returned by the named stored procedure. Successful completion.

SQLSTATE	SQLCODE	Description
01614	+494	Number of results sets returned by a stored procedure exceeds the number of results set locators as specified by the ASSOCIATE LOCATORS statement.
02000	+100	No rows found to satisfy the SQL statement.
07001	-313	Number of host variables does not equal number of parameter markers.
07002	-804	The call parameter list for the SQLDA is in error.
07003	-518	Execute attempted for an unprepared SQL statement.
07005	-517	Cursor is invalid because the SQL statement has not yet been prepared.
08001	-808	The CONNECT statement is not consistent with the program's first CONNECT statement.
	-30080	SNA communication error.
	-30082	Communication failed due to security violation; reason code provided.
08002	-842	A connection to the named location already exists.
08003	-843	The SET CONNECTION or RELEASE statement cannot be executed because the connection does not exist.
	-900	Application process is not connected to an application server; statement cannot be executed.
08004	-30060	Authorization failure encountered for RDB.
	-30061	Invalid or non-existent RDB specified.
0A001	-752	Invalid CONNECT statement.
0F001	-423	Invalid result set locator value.
21000	-811	Must use a cursor when more than one row is returned as the result of an embedded select statement.
21501	-533	Invalid multiple row insert; attempted to insert multiple rows into a self-referencing table.
21502	-534	An update statement changing the value of a primary key column cannot be used to update more than one row at a time.
	-535	Cannot specify WHERE CURRENT OF when deleting from a self-referencing table or updating primary key column(s). This code will be raised only by non-V5 subsystems.

continues

Table A.2. continued

SQLSTATE	*SQLCODE*	*Description*
22001	-302	The value of an input variable is invalid for the specified column.
	-404	Update or insert statement specified a string that is too long.
22002	-305	Null indicator variable is missing.
22003	-302	The value of an input variable is too large for the specified column.
	-304	Value cannot be assigned because it is out of range.
	-406	A calculated or derived numeric value is out of range.
	-413	Overflow condition when converting a numeric data type.
	-802	Exception error has occurred for the specified operation. Other than divide by zero.
22007	-180	Invalid syntax for the string representation of a date, time, or timestamp value.
	-181	Not a valid date, time, or timestamp value.
22008	-183	Result of arithmetic expression returns a date/time value that is not within the range of valid values.
22011	-138	The second or third operator of the SUBSTR column function is invalid.
22012	-802	Exception error has occurred for the specified operation. Divide by zero.
22018	-420	Character string argument value did not conform to the function's requirements.
22019	-130	Escape clause must be one character.
22021	-330	String cannot be translated successfully.
	-331	String cannot be assigned to a host variable because of unsuccessful translation.
22023	-310	Decimal host variable or parameter cannot contain non-decimal data.
22024	-300	String in host variable or parameter is not null-terminated.
22025	-130	Invalid escape pattern.
22501	-311	Invalid length of input host variable; either negative or too large.

SQLSTATE	*SQLCODE*	*Description*
22503	-188	Invalid string representation.
22504	-191	String contains invalid mixed data.
22505	-186	Local date/time exit changed, causing invalid length for this program.
22506	-187	MVS returned invalid current date/time.
22508	-812	Collection-Id is blank in the CURRENT PACKAGESET; statement cannot be executed.
22512	-309	Invalid predicate due to referenced host variable set to null.
22522	-189	The named coded character set ID is invalid or undefined.
22525	-327	Cannot INSERT row outside the bounds of the last partition key range.
23502	-407	Cannot insert a null value into a column that is defined as NOT NULL.
23503	-530	Invalid foreign key value specified for the specified constraint name.
23504	-531	As of V5, multi-row update of a parent key attempted to remove a parent key value on which a foreign key was dependent. Prior to V5, attempting to update a primary key value when foreign keys currently exist that reference that value.
	-532	Deletion violates the named referential constraint.
23505	-803	Cannot insert row because it would violate the constraints of a unique index.
23506	-652	Violation of EDITPROC or VALIDPROC encountered.
23507	-681	Column violates specified FIELDPROC.
23508	-690	Data definition control support rejected this statement.
23509	-807	Package not enabled for the named environment and connection.
23510	-908	Current Resource Limit Facility specification or Auto-Rebind system parameter does not permit the BIND, REBIND, or AUTO-REBIND.
23511	-543	DELETE cannot occur because the table is a parent table in a referential constraint specifying the SET NULL delete rule, but the check constraint does not allow NULLs.

continues

Table A.2. continued

SQLSTATE	SQLCODE	Description
23512	-544	Cannot add this check constraint using ALTER because an existing row violates the check constraint.
23513	-545	INSERT or UPDATE caused a check constraint violation.
23515	-603	Unique index cannot be created because duplicates were found.
24501	-500	A WITH HOLD cursor was closed because the connection was destroyed.
	-501	Must open a cursor before attempting to fetch from it or close it.
	-507	Must open a cursor before attempting to update or delete WHERE CURRENT OF.
24502	-502	Cannot open a cursor twice without first closing it.
24504	-508	Cannot update or delete because the referenced cursor is not currently positioned on a data row.
24506	-519	Cursor cannot be open when issuing a prepare statement for its SQL statement.
24516	-499	Named cursor already assigned to a result set from named stored procedure.
25000	-571	Multiple site updates are not permitted.
	-817	Execution of the SQL statement would result in a prohibited update to user data or the DB2 Catalog.
	-30090	Specified operation invalid for remote execution.
26501	-514	Cursor has not been prepared.
	-516	Describe attempted for an unprepared SQL statement.
2D521	-925	The SQL COMMIT statement cannot be issued from CICS or IMS/DC.
	-926	The SQL ROLLBACK statement cannot be issued from CICS or IMS/DC.
2D528	-426	COMMIT not permitted for an application server where updates are not permitted.
2D529	-427	ROLLBACK not permitted for an application server where updates are not permitted.
34000	-504	Cannot reference cursor because it is not defined to the program.

SQLSTATE	SQLCODE	Description
39002	-470	Null parameter specified but stored procedure does not support NULLs.
39501	-450	The stored procedure overwrote storage beyond a parameter's declared length.
40001	-911	The current unit of work has been rolled back.
42501	-551	User is attempting to perform an operation on the specified object for which he is not authorized or the table does not exist.
	-567	Named authorization ID lacks the authority to bind the named package.
42502	-164	User does not have the authority to create this view.
	-552	User is attempting to perform an operation for which he is not authorized.
	-554	Cannot grant a privilege to yourself.
	-555	Cannot revoke a privilege from yourself.
42503	-553	Cannot set CURRENT SQLID because the user has not been set up to change to that ID.
42504	-556	Cannot revoke a privilege that the user does not possess.
42505	-922	Connection authorization failure. Attempting to access DB2 from TSO, CICS, or IMS and appropriate attachment facility is inactive.
42506	-30053	Authorization failure encountered for package owner.
42509	-549	Invalid SQL statement for DYNAMICRULES(BIND) plan or package.
42601	-007	Illegal character in SQL statement.
	-029	INTO clause required.
	-104	Illegal symbol encountered in SQL statement.
	-108	Incorrect name specified for the RENAME statement; cannot use a qualifier.
	-109	Invalid clause specified; for example, CREATE VIEW may not contain an ORDER BY clause.
	-115	Invalid predicate encountered because comparison operator not followed by an expression or list.
	-128	NULL used improperly in an SQL predicate.

continues

Table A.2. continued

SQLSTATE	*SQLCODE*	*Description*
	-199	Illegal keyword used in SQL statement.
	-638	Missing column definition in CREATE TABLE statement.
42602	-113	Invalid character encountered.
	-251	Invalid token.
42603	-010	String constant not terminated properly; check for missing quotation marks.
42604	-103	Invalid numeric literal.
	-105	Invalid character string format; usually refers to an improperly formatted graphic string.
42605	-170	Invalid number of arguments specified for the scalar function.
42606	-110	Invalid hexadecimal literal encountered.
42607	-112	Invalid column function syntax; column function cannot operate on another column function.
	-409	COUNT function specified invalid operand.
42609	-417	Two parameter markers specified as operands on both sides of the same predicate.
42610	-184	Improper usage of parameter marker for date/time values.
	-418	Invalid usage of parameter markers.
42611	-604	Invalid length precision or scale specified for a column in a CREATE or ALTER TABLE statement.
42612	-084	SQL statement cannot be executed because it is invalid for dynamic SQL or is not valid for DB2 for MVS.
42613	-628	CREATE TABLESPACE clauses specified are mutually exclusive (that is, cannot partition a segmented tablespace).
42614	-637	Duplicate key word encountered.
42615	-644	Invalid value specified for key word in the SQL statement.
42617	-198	Trying to issue a PREPARE or EXECUTE IMMEDIATE statement on a blank string.
42618	-312	Undefined or unusable host variable.
42621	-546	Invalid check constraint specified in CREATE or ALTER TABLE.
	-548	Invalid check constraint due to named column.

SQLSTATE	SQLCODE	Description
42622	-107	Object name is too long.
42625	-580	Result expressions of a CASE expression cannot all be null.
	-582	Search condition in a searched when clause specifies a quantified, IN, or EXISTS predicate.
42701	-121	A column is illegally referenced twice in an INSERT or UPDATE statement.
42702	-203	Ambiguous column reference.
42703	-205	Invalid column name for specified table.
	-206	Column name not in any table referenced in the FROM clause.
42704	-204	Undefined object name.
	-219	EXPLAIN cannot be executed because PLAN_TABLE does not exist.
	-722	Bind error due because the named package does not exist.
42705	-950	Location specified in the SQL statement not defined in SYSIBM.LOCATIONS.
42707	-208	Cannot ORDER BY specified column because it is not in the select list.
42709	-537	A single column may not appear more than once in a foreign key or primary key clause specification.
42710	-601	Attempting to create an object that already exists.
	-719	Cannot BIND ADD a package that already exists.
	-720	Cannot BIND REPLACE a package version that already exists.
	-721	Consistency token must be unique for package.
42711	-612	Duplicate column names not permitted within a single table.
42714	-314	Ambiguous host variable reference.
42718	-250	Local location name is not defined.
42724	-444	Program associated with the called stored procedure could not be found.
42801	-173	Isolation level UR cannot be specified on a cursor that is not read only.

continues

Table A.2. continued

SQLSTATE	*SQLCODE*	*Description*
42802	-117	Number of inserted values not equivalent to number of columns for the inserted row.
42803	-119	Column list in HAVING clause does not match column list in the GROUP BY clause.
	-122	Column function applied illegally because all columns not applied to a column function are not in the GROUP BY clause.
42804	-581	Incompatible data types in the result expressions of a CASE expression.
42805	-125	Invalid number specified in the ORDER BY clause; number is either less than 1 or greater than the number of columns selected.
42806	-303	Value cannot be assigned because of incompatible data types.
42807	-150	Invalid view update requested.
42808	-151	Invalid column update requested; trying to update either a non-updateable view column, a DB2 Catalog table column, or the key of a partitioning index.
42809	-148	RENAME cannot be used to rename a view or an active RLST table.
	-152	DROP CHECK tried to drop a referential constraint, or DROP FOREIGN KEY tried to drop a check constraint.
	-156	It is invalid to create an index on a view or specify an object other than a table on the ALTER TABLE, DROP TABLE, or LOCK TABLE statements.
	-159	Invalid DROP or COMMENT ON statement.
42810	-157	Must specify a table name on the FOREIGN KEY clause.
42811	-158	View columns do not match columns in the select list.
42813	-160	WITH CHECK OPTION invalid for this view.
42815	-060	Invalid length or scale specification for the specified data type.
	-171	Invalid data type length or value for the scalar function.
	-713	The special register value specified is invalid.
42816	-182	Invalid date/time value in an arithmetic expression.

SQLSTATE	SQLCODE	Description
42818	-131	The LIKE predicate may only be applied to character data.
	-401	The operands of an arithmetic or comparison operator are not compatible.
42819	-402	Arithmetic function cannot be applied to character or date/time data.
42820	-405	Numeric literal is out of range.
	-410	Floating point literal longer than maximum allowable length of 30 characters.
42821	-408	Value cannot be inserted or updated because it is incompatible with the column's data type.
42823	-412	Multiple columns encountered in the select list of a subquery.
42824	-132	First operator of LIKE predicate must be a column and the second operator must be a character string.
	-414	The LIKE predicate may not operate on columns defined with a numeric or date/time data type.
42825	-415	The select lists specified for the UNION operation are not union-compatible.
42826	-421	Same number of columns not supplied in the select lists for a UNION operation.
42827	-509	Cannot update from a different table than the one specified on the cursor referenced by the WHERE CURRENT OF clause.
42828	-510	Table or view cannot be modified as requested.
42829	-126	An ORDER BY clause may not be specified for an UPDATE statement.
	-511	FOR UPDATE OF is invalid for non-modifiable tables or views.
42830	-538	Invalid foreign key; does not conform to the definition of the referenced table's primary key.
42831	-542	Nullable columns are not permitted to be included as part of a primary key.
42832	-607	The INSERT, UPDATE, or DELETE statement specified cannot be issued as written against the DB2 Catalog tables.
	-618	Requested operation not permitted for DB2 Catalog tables.

continues

Table A.2. continued

SQLSTATE	*SQLCODE*	*Description*
42834	-629	SET NULL is invalid because the foreign key cannot contain null values.
42842	-683	Invalid column type specified for FIELDPROC or FOR BIT DATA option.
42852	-557	Inconsistent grant or revoke key word specified.
42877	-197	Qualified column names cannot be used in an ORDER BY clause when two or more tables are unioned and then ordered.
42884	-440	Number of parameters in the parameter list for a stored procedure does not match the number expected.
42886	-469	Host variable must be provided on the CALL statement for parameters defined as OUT or INOUT.
42888	-539	Foreign key cannot be defined because the referenced table does not have a primary key.
42889	-624	Cannot define more than one primary key for a single table.
42890	-573	Referential constraint cannot be defined because the named parent table does not have a unique key on the specified column.
42893	-616	The specified object may not be dropped because other objects are dependent upon it.
42894	-574	Specified default conflicts with the column definition.
42895	-301	Invalid host variable data type.
428B4	-240	The PART clause of a LOCK TABLE statement is invalid.
42901	-111	Column function specified without a column name.
42902	-118	Table or view is illegally named in both data modification clause (INSERT, UPDATE, or DELETE) and the FROM clause.
42903	-120	WHERE clause is not allowed to reference column function.
42905	-127	DISTINCT may only be specified once in a subselect.
42906	-133	Invalid correlated subquery reference.
42907	-134	Column larger than 254 bytes used improperly.
	-416	Long string columns are not allowed in SQL statements containing the UNION operator.

SQLSTATE	SQLCODE	Description
42908	-153	Invalid view creation required; must provide a name for an unnamed or duplicate column listed in the select list.
42909	-154	Cannot create a view using UNION, UNION ALL, or a remote table.
42911	-419	Invalid decimal division.
42912	-503	Column cannot be updated because it was not specified in the FOR UPDATE OF clause of the cursor from which it was fetched.
42914	-536	Invalid delete statement due to referential constraints existing for the specified table.
42915	-632	The specified delete rules prohibit defining this table as a dependent of the named table.
	-633	Invalid delete rule; the specified mandatory delete rule must be used.
	-634	DELETE CASCADE is not allowed in this situation.
	-635	The delete rule cannot be different or cannot be SET NULL.
42917	-667	Cannot explicitly drop the clustering index for a partitioned tablespace; must drop the partitioned tablespace to drop index.
	-669	Cannot explicitly drop a table in a partitioned tablespace; must drop the partitioned tablespace to drop the table.
42920	-815	A GROUP BY or HAVING clause is implicitly or explicitly specified in an embedded select statement or a subquery of a basic predicate.
42924	-513	An alias cannot be defined on another alias.
42932	-30052	Program preparation assumption incorrect.
42961	-114	Location name for this statement must match the current server, but it does not.
42969	-917	Bind package has failed.
42972	-338	Invalid ON clause; must refer to joined columns.
42986	-750	Cannot rename the named table because it is referenced in at least one existing view.
42987	-751	Stored procedure placed in MUST_ROLLBACK state due to named SQL operation.

continues

Table A.2. continued

SQLSTATE	*SQLCODE*	*Description*
42988	-875	Specified operand cannot be used with ASCII data.
42995	-526	Global temporary table cannot be used in the given context.
44000	-161	The WITH CHECK OPTION clause of the view being updated prohibits this row from being inserted or updated as specified.
51002	-805	The DBRM or package name not found in plan.
51003	-818	Plan <—> load module timestamp mismatch. The DBRM in the executing plan was not created from the same precompilation as the load module.
51004	-822	Invalid address encountered in the SQLDA.
51005	-906	SQL statement cannot be executed because of prior error.
51006	-927	The language interface was called when the connecting environment was not established. Invoke the program using the DSN command.
51015	-525	Cannot execute SQL statement within named package because it was invalid at bind time.
51021	-918	SQL statement cannot be executed because connection was lost.
	-939	Rollback is required due to unrequested rollback of a remote server.
	-965	Stored procedure terminated abnormally.
51030	-480	DESCRIBE PROCEDURE and ASSOCIATE LOCATORS cannot be issued until the stored procedure has been CALLed.
	-482	Stored procedure returned no locators.
51032	-872	A valid CCSID has yet to be specified for this subsystem.
51033	-496	Statement cannot be executed because the current server is different than the server that called a stored procedure.
53001	-620	The specified key word is not permitted for a tablespace in DSNDB07.
53004	-742	DSNDB07 is the implicit work file database.
53014	-736	The named OBID is invalid.

SQLSTATE	SQLCODE	Description
53035	-660	Improper partitioning index specification; must define limit keys for the clustering index.
53036	-661	Partitioning index does not specify the proper number of partitions.
53037	-662	Attempted to create a partitioning index on a non-partitioned (segmented or simple) tablespace.
53038	-663	Invalid number of key limit values specified for the partitioning index.
53039	-665	Invalid PART clause specified for ALTER TABLESPACE statement.
53040	-671	Cannot alter the bufferpool for the specified tablespace because it would change the page size of the tablespace.
53041	-676	BP32K cannot be used for an index.
53043	-686	A column defined with a FIELDPROC cannot be compared to a column defined with a different FIELDPROC.
53044	-687	A column cannot be compared to a column with an incompatible field type.
53045	-678	The literal specified for the limit key in the partitioning index does not conform to the data type of the key value.
53088	-611	When LOCKSIZE is TABLE or TABLESPACE, LOCKMAX must be 0.
53089	-2001	Number of host variable parameters specified for a stored procedure does not equal the expected number of parameters.
53090	-873	Cannot refer to a column defined in an ASCII table in the same SQL statement as a column defined in an EBCDIC table.
53091	-874	The encoding scheme for the table does not match the encoding scheme for its tablespace.
53092	-876	Object cannot be created for the specified reason; reason code provided.
53093	-877	ASCII not permitted for the database or tablespace; EBCDIC must be used.
53094	-878	This PLAN_TABLE cannot be ASCII; EBCDIC must be used.

continues

Table A.2. continued

SQLSTATE	*SQLCODE*	*Description*
53095	-879	GRAPHIC, VARGRAPHIC, and LONG VARGRAPHIC columns cannot be used in an ASCII table.
54001	-101	SQL statement exceeds an established DB2 limit; that is, too many tables, too many bytes in statement, and so on.
54002	-102	String constant is too long.
54004	-129	The SQL statement contains more than 15 tables.
	-840	Too many items returned in a select list or insert list.
54005	-136	Sort key length is greater than 4,000 bytes.
54006	-137	Concatenated string is too large; maximum is 32,767 for pure character or 16,382 for graphic.
54008	-602	Too many columns specified in the CREATE INDEX statement.
	-613	Invalid primary key; is either longer than 254 bytes or contains more than 40 columns.
	-614	Maximum internal key length of 254 for indexes has been surpassed.
	-631	Invalid foreign key; is either longer than 254 bytes or contains more than 40 columns.
54010	-670	The row length for the table exceeds the page size.
54011	-680	No more than 750 columns may be specified for a DB2 table.
	-689	Dependent table defined with too many columns.
54012	-684	The specified literal list cannot exceed 254 bytes.
54021	-642	Unique constraint contains too many columns.
54024	-643	Check constraint exceeds maximum length of 3,800 characters.
54025	-651	Table object descriptor (OBD) would exceed maximum size (32K) if the CREATE or ALTER TABLE were allowed.
54027	-400	Cannot define more than 100 user-defined indexes in the DB2 Catalog.
54041	-497	Named database exceeded the limit of 32,767 OBIDs.
55002	-220	Invalid PLAN_TABLE column encountered.
	-221	If any optional columns are defined for the PLAN_TABLE, all of them must be defined.

SQLSTATE	SQLCODE	Description
55003	-693	The named column for the named registration table/index is invalid.
55004	-735	The database identified by the named DBID is no longer a read-only shared database.
55006	-615	Cannot drop this package because it is currently executing.
55011	-619	DSNDB07 may not be modified unless it has first been stopped.
55012	-623	Cannot define more than one clustering index for a single table.
55014	-625	A unique index is required for a table defined with a primary key.
55015	-626	Cannot issue an alter statement to change PRIQTY, SECQTY, or ERASE unless the tablespace has first been stopped.
55016	-627	Cannot issue an alter statement to change PRIQTY, SECQTY, or ERASE unless the tablespace has first been defined to use storage groups.
55017	-646	The table cannot be created in the specified partitioned or default tablespace because the specified tablespace already contains a table.
55023	-471	Stored procedure failed; reason code provided.
55030	-726	Cannot bind this package because of SYSPKSYSTEM entries.
	-741	Work file database already defined for named data sharing group member.
55035	-672	DROP not allowed on named table.
56010	-333	Subtype invalid, causing translation to fail.
56016	-636	The partitioning index must be consistent in its specification of ascending or descending for the partitioning index key.
56018	-668	Cannot add a column to a table defined with an EDITPROC.
56023	-512	Invalid reference to a remote object.

continues

Table A.2. continued

SQLSTATE	*SQLCODE*	*Description*
56025	-558	Invalid clause or clauses specified for the grant or revoke statement.
56027	-639	A nullable column of a foreign key with a delete rule of SET NULL cannot be a column of the key of a partitioning index.
56031	-622	Cannot specify FOR MIXED DATA because the mixed data option has not been installed.
56036	-655	STOGROUP cannot specify both specific and non-specific (that is, "*") volumes in the volume list.
56038	-947	SQL statement failed because update cannot be propagated. (DPROP)
56040	-411	Invalid CURRENT SQLID usage.
56045	-919	A ROLLBACK is required
56053	-730	Invalid referential integrity definition for a table in a read-only shared database.
56054	-731	VSAM dataset must be defined using SHAREOPTION(1,3).
56055	-732	Read-only database defined but the owning DB2 subsystem has not defined the tablespace or index space.
56056	-733	Inconsistent read-only shared database definition.
	-737	Cannot create an implicit tablespace under these circumstances.
56057	-734	Once a database has been defined as ROSHARE READ, it cannot be altered to a different ROSHARE state.
56062	-948	DDF not started; distributed operation is invalid.
56064	-715	The named program cannot be run because it depends upon features of a release of DB2 that your shop has installed, but backed off.
56065	-716	The named program was precompiled with an incorrect level for this release.
56066	-717	BIND failed because it depends upon features of a release of DB2 that your shop has installed, but backed off.
56067	-718	REBIND failed because IBMREQD column is invalid.
56082	-339	Access to DB2 V2.2 subsystem was denied because ASCII to EBCDIC translation cannot occur.

SQLSTATE	SQLCODE	Description
56084	-351	Unsupported data type.
56089	-617	Type 1 index cannot be defined with LOCKSIZE ROW or LARGE tablespace.
	-630	WHERE NOT NULL cannot be specified for Type 1 indexes.
	-640	LOCKSIZE ROW cannot be specified for this tablespace because a Type 1 index is defined on a table in the tablespace.
56090	-650	ALTER INDEX cannot be executed; reason code provided.
56094	+2000	Type 1 indexes where SUBPAGES does not equal 1 cannot become group bufferpool dependent in a data sharing environment.
56095	-30104	Error in bind option and bind value.
56096	-30105	The specified bind options are incompatible.
57001	-540	Table definition is incomplete until a unique index is created for the primary key.
57002	-559	The DB2 authorization mechanism has been disabled. Grant and revoke may not be issued.
57003	-647	The specified bufferpool is invalid because it has not been activated.
57004	-653	A table in a partitioned tablespace is unavailable because the partitioning index has not been created yet.
57005	-666	SQL statement cannot be processed because the specified function is currently in progress.
57006	-679	Cannot create the specified object because a drop is currently pending for that object.
57007	-909	The object has been deleted.
	-910	Cannot access an object for which a drop is pending.
57008	-185	No local date/time exits defined.
57010	-682	FIELDPROC could not be loaded.
57011	-677	Bufferpool expansion failed due to insufficient amount of available virtual storage.
	-904	The specified resource is unavailable.
57012	-30040	Execution failed due to unavailable resource(s); processing can continue. (AS)

continues

Table A.2. continued

SQLSTATE	*SQLCODE*	*Description*
57013	-30041	Execution failed due to unavailable resource(s); processing cannot successfully continue.
57014	-905	Resource limit has been exceeded.
57015	-923	Connection not established because DB2 is unavailable.
	-981	Attempt to execute SQL in the RRSAF when it was not in a state to allow SQL.
	-991	Call attach was not able to establish an implicit connect or open to DB2.
57017	-332	Translation not defined for the two named coded character set IDs.
57018	-691	The named registration table does not exist.
	-692	The named index does not exist, but is required for the named registration table.
57023	-694	Drop is pending on the named registration table.
57033	-913	Unsuccessful execution caused by either a deadlock or a timeout.
58001	-621	Duplicate DBID encountered; system problem encountered.
58002	-685	FIELDPROC returned an invalid field description.
	-688	Incorrect data returned by the FIELDPROC.
	-929	Data capture exit has failed. (DPROP)
58003	-144	Named section number is invalid.
58004	-819	View cannot be recreated because the length of the parse tree stored in the DB2 Catalog is zero.
	-820	Invalid value encountered in DB2 Catalog for this DB2 release.
	-901	Intermittent system error encountered that does not inhibit subsequent SQL statements from being executed.
58005	-902	Internal control block pointer error; rebind required.
58006	-924	DB2 internal connection error encountered; reason code provided.
58008	-30000	DRDA distribution protocol error; processing can continue.
58009	-30020	DRDA distribution protocol error; conversation deallocated.

SQLSTATE	*SQLCODE*	*Description*
58010	-30021	DRDA distribution protocol error; processing cannot continue.
58011	-30050	Execution unsuccessful; statement cannot be executed during the BIND process.
58012	-30051	Failure caused by specific BIND process not being active. (Remote BIND)
58013	-30030	Distribution protocol violation; COMMIT unsuccessful, conversation deallocated. (AS)
58014	-30070	Target subsystem does not support this command.
58015	-30071	Target subsystem does not support this object.
58016	-30072	Target subsystem does not support this parameter.
58017	-30073	Target subsystem does not support this parameter value.
58019	-30081	TCP/IP communication error.
58026	-870	The number of host variable descriptors does not equal the number of host variables in the statement.

Table A.3. DB2 CLI SQLSTATE messages.

Version 5

SQLSTATE	*Description*
01000	The SQL statement finished successfully, but with a warning.
01002	Disconnect error.
01004	Data truncated.
01504	The UPDATE or DELETE statement does not specify a WHERE clause.
01508	Statement is disqualified for blocking.
01S00	Invalid connection string attribute.
01S01	Error in the row.
01S02	Option value changed.
07001	Wrong number of parameters.
07002	Too many columns specified.
07005	The statement did not return a result set.
07006	Invalid conversion.
08001	Not able to connect to data source.

continues

Table A.3. continued

SQLSTATE	*Description*
08002	Connection in use.
08003	Connection is closed.
08004	The application server rejected the connection.
08007	Connection failure during transaction.
21S01	Value list for INSERT does not match column list.
21S02	Degrees of derived table do not match column list.
22002	Invalid output or indicator buffer specified.
22003	Numeric value out of range.
22005	Error in assignment.
22008	Datetime field overflow.
22012	Division by zero is invalid.
23000	Integrity constraint violation.
24000	Invalid cursor state.
24504	The cursor in the UPDATE, DELETE, SET, or GET statement is not positioned on a row.
25500	Invalid transaction state.
25501	Invalid transaction state.
28000	Invalid authorization specification.
34000	Invalid cursor name.
37xxx	Invalid SQL syntax.
38552	Error in function listed in SYSFUN schema.
40001	Transaction ROLLBACK.
40003	Communication link failure.
42xxx	Syntax error or access rule violation.
425xx	Syntax error or access rule violation.
42601	Syntax error in PARMLIST.
42895	The value of a host variable in the EXECUTE or OPEN statement cannot be used because of its data type.
44000	Integrity constraint violation.

SQLSTATE	*Description*
56084	Large Object (LOB) data is not supported in DRDA.
58004	Unexpected system failure.
S0001	Database object already exists.
S0002	Database object does not exist.
S0011	Index already exists.
S0012	Index not found.
S0021	Column already exists.
S0022	Column not found.
S1C00	Driver not capable.
S1000	General error.
S1001	Memory allocation failure.
S1002	Invalid column number.
S1003	Program type out of range.
S1004	SQL data type out of range.
S1009	Invalid argument value.
S1010	Function sequence error.
S1011	Operation is currently invalid.
S1012	Invalid transaction code.
S1013	Unexpected memory handling error.
S1014	No more handles.
S1090	Invalid string or buffer length.
S1091	Descriptor type out of range.
S1092	Option type out of range.
S1093	Invalid parameter number.
S1094	Invalid scale value.
S1096	Information type out of range.
S1097	Column type out of range.
S1098	Scope type out of range.
S1099	Nullable type out of range.

continues

Table A.3. continued

SQLSTATE	*Description*
S1100	Uniqueness option type out of range.
S1101	Accuracy option type out of range.
S1103	Direction option out of range.
S1104	Invalid precision value.
S1105	Invalid parameter type.
S1106	Fetch type out of range.
S1107	Row value out of range.
S1110	Invalid driver completion.
S1501	Invalid data source name.
S1503	Invalid filename length.
S1506	Error closing a file.
S1509	Error deleting a file.

B

The DB2 Catalog Tables

The DB2 Catalog is contained in a single database (DSNDB06). The 54 tables in the DB2 Catalog collectively describe the objects and resources available to DB2. You can find a comprehensive description of the DB2 Catalog and its purpose in Chapter 15, "The Table-Based Infrastructure of DB2."

Prior to DB2 Version 5, an additional database (called the Communication Database, or CDB) was used for establishing and documenting distributed DB2 connections. The CDB tables have been renamed and rolled into the DB2 Catalog as of DB2 V5, as follows:

Old CDB Table Name	*New DB2 Catalog Table Name*
SYSIBM.SYSLOCATIONS	SYSIBM.LOCATIONS
SYSIBM.SYSLULIST	SYSIBM.LULIST
SYSIBM.SYSLUMODES	SYSIBM.LUMODES
SYSIBM.SYSLUNAMES	SYSIBM.LUNAMES
SYSIBM.SYSMODESELECT	SYSIBM.MODESELECT
SYSIBM.SYSUSERNAMES	SYSIBM.USERNAMES

Note that the definitions for the CDB tables have changed, in some case, substantially.

This appendix presents each DB2 Catalog table, outlining the following information:

- A description of the table
- The name of the tablespace in which the table resides
- The indexes for each table, the index columns, and whether the indexes are unique
- A listing of the DB2 Catalog links and/or relationships (RI) for each table. A *link* is a physical pointer used by the DB2 Catalog to provide enhanced data access.
- A description of the columns in each table

DB2 developers can use this information to query the status of their DB2 subsystem and applications.

SYSIBM.IPNAMES

SYSIBM.IPNAMES contains a single row for each LU associated with one or more other systems accessible to the local DB2 subsystem.

Tablespace	DSNDB06.SYSDDF	
Indexes	DSNFPX01	[unique]
	(LINKNAME)	
Relationship	None	

Column Definitions

`LINKNAME`	Must match the `LINKNAME` of the associated row in `SYSIBM.LOCATIONS`.
`SECURITY_OUT`	An indicator specifying the DRDA security option used when DB2 SQL applications connect to any remote server associated with this TCP/IP host. Contains the following: `A` Outbound connection requests do not require passwords; the authid used for outbound requests is either the DB2 authid or a translated ID, depending on the value of the `USERNAMES` column. It is the default. `R` Outbound connection requests contain a userid and an `RACF` PassTicket; the authid used for outbound requests is either the DB2 authid or a translated ID, depending on the value of the `USERNAMES` column. `P` Outbound connection requests contain an authid and a password; the password is obtained from `SYSIBM.USERNAMES` or `RACF`; the `USERNAMES` column must contain `B` or `O`.
`USERNAMES`	Indicates whether outbound authid translation is to occur. Contains the following: *blank* No translation. `O` Outbound requests subject to ID translation.
`IBMREQD`	An indicator specifying `Y` if the row was supplied by IBM, or `N` if it was not.
`IPADDR`	Contains the IP address or domain name of a remote TCP/IP host.

SYSIBM.LOCATIONS

`SYSIBM.LOCATIONS` contains a single row for each accessible server, equating a location with its SNA or TCP/IP network attributes.

Tablespace	`DSNDB06.SYSDDF`
Indexes	`DSNFCX01[unique]` `(LOCATION)`
Relationship	None

Column Definitions

`LOCATION`	A unique location name, to be used by the local DB2 subsystem, for the accessible server.
`LINKNAME`	Identifies the VTAM or TCP/IP attributes for the specified location. Must have a corresponding row in either `SYSIBM.IPNAMES` or `SYSIBM.LUNAMES`.
`IBMREQD`	An indicator specifying `Y` if the row was supplied by IBM, or `N` if it was not.
`PORT`	For TCP/IP, specifies a port number as follows: *blank* Default DRDA port is used. `value` Either a TCP/IP port number or a TCP/IP service name.
`TPN`	Indicates the SNA LU 6.2 transaction program name that will allocate the conversation.

SYSIBM.LULIST

`SYSIBM.LULIST` enables you to specify multiple `LUNAMES` for any given `LOCATION`.

Tablespace	`DSNDB06.SYSDDF`

Indexes	`DSNFLX01[unique]`
	`(LINKNAME, LUNAME)`
	`DSNFLX02[unique]`
	`(LUNAME)`

Relationship	`DSNFN@FL REFERENCES LUNAMES`

Column Definitions

`LINKNAME`	Corresponds to a `SYSIBM.LOCATIONS LINKNAME`.
`LUNAME`	Contains the `VTAM LUNAME` of the remote system. Must not exist in `SYSIBM.LUNAMES`.
`IBMREQD`	An indicator specifying `Y` if the row was supplied by IBM, or `N` if it was not.

SYSIBM.LUMODES

`SYSIBM.LUMODES` contains conversation limits for a specific `LUNAME` / `MODENAME` combination. It is used to control change-number-of-sessions (CNOS) negotiations at DDF startup.

Tablespace	DSNDB06.SYSDDF
Indexes	DSNFMX01[unique] (LUNAME, MODENAME)
Relationship	DSNFN@FM REFERENCES SYSIBM.LUNAMES

Column Definitions

LUNAME	Name of the LU involved in CNOS processing.
MODENAME	Logon mode description name as defined in the VTAM logon mode table.
CONVLIMIT	Conversation limit (maximum number of conversations) between the local DB2 and the server.
IBMREQD	An indicator specifying Y if the row was supplied by IBM, or N if it was not.

SYSIBM.LUNAMES

SYSIBM.LUNAMES contains a single row for each LU associated with one or more other systems accessible to the local DB2 subsystem.

Tablespace	DSNDB06.SYSDDF
Indexes	DSNFNX01 [unique] (LUNAME)
Relationship	None

Column Definitions

LUNAME	Name of the LU for one or more accessible systems. Blank if requester is undefined.
SYSMODENAME	Identifies the mode used to establish system to system conversations. Blank indicates default IBMDB2LM mode.
SECURITY_IN	An indicator specifying the security acceptance option when an SNA client connects to DB2. Contains the following: V An incoming connection must contain a userid and a password; or a userid and RACF PassTicket; or a DCE security ticket. A Requests do not require passwords; can contain just a userid or any of the options described previously; if the USERNAMES column contains B or I, RACF is not invoked to validate incoming connection requests. It is the default.

SECURITY_OUT — An indicator specifying the security acceptance option when local DB2 SQL applications connect to any remote server associated with this LUNAME. Contains the following:

- A — Outbound connection requests do not require passwords; the authid used for outbound requests is either the DB2 authid or a translated ID, depending on the value of the USERNAMES column. It is the default.
- R — Outbound connection requests contain a userid and an RACF PassTicket; the authid used for outbound requests is either the DB2 authid or a translated ID, depending on the value of the USERNAMES column.
- P — Outbound connection requests contain an authid and a password; the password is obtained from SYSIBM.USERNAMES or RACF; the USERNAMES column must contain B or O.

ENCRYPTPSWDS — Indicator specifying whether passwords are encrypted. Value applies to DB2 systems only. Contains the following:

- N — Not encrypted (default)
- Y — Encrypted

MODESELECT — Indicates whether the SYSIBM.MODESELECT table is to be used. Contains the following:

- N — Uses default modes: IBMDB2LM (private protocol) and IBMRDB (DRDA). It is the default.
- Y — Searches SYSIBM.MODESELECT for mode name.

USERNAMES — Indicates whether the SYSIBM.USERNAMES table is to be used for "come from" checking and userid translation. Contains the following:

- *blank* — No translation
- B — Both inbound and outbound requests subject to ID translation.
- I — Inbound requests subject to ID translation.
- O — Outbound requests subject to ID translation.

GENERIC — Indicates whether DB2 should use its real LU name or a generic LU name. Contains the following:

- N — Real VTAM LU name. It is the default.
- Y — Generic LU name.

IBMREQD — An indicator specifying Y if the row was supplied by IBM, or N if it was not.

SYSIBM.MODESELECT

SYSIBM.MODESELECT assigns mode names to conversations supporting outgoing SQL requests.

Tablespace	DSNDB06.SYSDDF
Indexes	DSNFDX01 [unique]
	(LUNAME, AUTHID, PLANNAME)
Relationship	DSNFN@FD REFERENCES SYSIBM.LUNAMES

Column Definitions

AUTHID	Authid of the SQL request. Blank is the default, which indicates the MODENAME for the row is to apply to all authids.
PLANNAME	Plan name containing the SQL request.
LUNAME	LU name associated with the SQL request.
MODENAME	Logon mode description name, as defined in the VTAM logon mode table, to be used in support of the SQL request.
IBMREQD	An indicator specifying Y if the row was supplied by IBM, or N if it was not.

SYSIBM.SYSCHECKDEP

SYSIBM.SYSCHECKDEP contains a row for each reference to a column in a check constraint.

Tablespace	DSNDB06.SYSSTR
Indexes	DSNSDX01 [unique]
	(TBOWNER, TBNAME, CHECKNAME, COLNAME)
Relationship	DSNSC@SD REFERENCES SYSIBM.SYSCHECKS

Column Definitions

TBOWNER	The owner of the table named in TBNAME.
TBNAME	The table name to which this check constraint applies.
CHECKNAME	The name of the check constraint.
COLNAME	The name of the column referenced by the check constraint.
IBMREQD	An indicator specifying Y if the row was supplied by IBM, or N if it was not.

SYSIBM.SYSCHECKS

SYSIBM.SYSCHECKS contains one row for each check constraint.

Tablespace	DSNDB06.SYSSTR
Indexes	DSNSCX01 [unique] (TBOWNER, TBNAME, CHECKNAME)
Relationship	DSNDT@SC REFERENCES SYSIBM.SYSTABLES

Column Definitions

TBOWNER	The owner of the table named in TBNAME.
CREATOR	The authid of the creator of this check constraint.
DBID	Internal identifier of the database for this check constraint.
OBID	Internal identifier for this check constraint.
TIMESTAMP	Date and time when this check constraint was created.
RBA	The log RBA when this check constraint was created.
IBMREQD	An indicator specifying Y if the row was supplied by IBM, or N if it was not.
TBNAME	The table name to which this check constraint applies.
CHECKNAME	The name of the check constraint.
CHECKCONDITION	The actual text of the check constraint.

SYSIBM.SYSCOLAUTH

SYSIBM.SYSCOLAUTH contains the UPDATE privileges held by DB2 users on single table columns or view columns.

Tablespace	DSNDB06.SYSDBASE
Indexes	None
Links	DSNAT#AF REFERENCES SYSIBM.SYSTABAUTH

Column Definitions

GRANTOR	A userid, the literal PUBLIC, or the literal PUBLIC*. This user granted update authority to the GRANTEE.
GRANTEE	The authid of the user who possesses the privileges described in this row, the name of a plan or package that uses the privileges, the literal PUBLIC to indicate that all users have these privileges, or the literal PUBLIC* to indicate that all users at all distributed locations hold these privileges.
GRANTEETYPE	A value indicating the type of GRANTEE. Contains the following: P GRANTEE is a plan. *blank* GRANTEE is a userid.

CREATOR	The owner of the view or table named in TNAME.
TNAME	The view or table name in which the COLNAME indicated in this row exists.
TIMESTAMP	An internal timestamp representing when authority was granted. Do not use because it is unreadable.
DATEGRANTED	The date on which authority was granted (*yymmdd*).
TIMEGRANTED	The time at which authority was granted (*hhmmssth*).
COLNAME	The authority in this row applies to this column name.
IBMREQD	An indicator specifying Y if the row was supplied by IBM, or N if it was not.
LOCATION	Not currently used (DB2 V3).
COLLID	The collection name, if GRANTEE is a package.
CONTOKEN	The consistency token, if GRANTEE is a package.
PRIVILEGE	Indicates which privilege this row describes. Contains the following: R REFERENCES privilege. *blank* UPDATE privilege.
GRANTEDTS	Time the GRANT was executed.

SYSIBM.SYSCOLDIST

SYSIBM.SYSCOLDIST contains non-uniform distribution statistics (NUDS). One row exists for each column on which RUNSTATS was executed.

Tablespace	DSNDB06.SYSSTATS
Index	DSNTNX01 [nonunique] (TBOWNER, TBNAME, NAME)
Relationship	DSNDC@TN REFERENCES SYSIBM.SYSCOLUMNS

Column Definitions

FREQUENCY	The percentage (* 100) that the value specified in COLVALUE exists in the column if the row will hold statistics (V4 and previous; not used in V5).
STATSTIME	Timestamp indicating the date and time that RUNSTATS was executed to produce this row.
IBMREQD	An indicator specifying Y if the row was supplied by IBM, or N if it was not.
TBOWNER	The owner of the table named in TBNAME.

TBNAME	The table name to which this statistical row applies.
NAME	The column name; if NUMCOLUMS is > 1, this column identifies the first column name of the set of columns associated with the statistics.
COLVALUE	Contains the actual data of a frequently occurring value.
TYPE	Type of statistics generated: C Cardinality F Frequent value
CARDF	Number of distinct values for the column group; valid only if TYPE = "C".
COLGROUPCOLNO	Identifies the set of columns associated with the statistics. For single column stats, the column is of zero length.
NUMCOLUMNS	Number of columns associated with the statistics.
FREQUENCYF	The percentage (* 100) that the value specified in COLVALUE exists.

SYSIBM.SYSCOLDISTSTATS

SYSIBM.SYSCOLDISTSTATS contains partition-level, non-uniform distribution statistics. Zero, one, or many rows exist for the key columns of each partitioned index.

Tablespace	DSNDB06.SYSSTATS
Index	DSNTPX01 [nonunique] (TBOWNER, TBNAME, NAME, PARTITION)
Relationship	DSNDC@TP REFERENCES SYSIBM.SYSCOLUMNS

Column Definitions

FREQUENCY	The percentage (* 100) that the value specified in COLVALUE exists in the column if the row will hold statistics (V4 and previous; not used in V5).
STATSTIME	Timestamp indicating the date and time that RUNSTATS was executed to produce this row.
IBMREQD	An indicator specifying Y if the row was supplied by IBM, or N if it was not.
PARTITION	The partition number indicating the physical partition of the tablespace to which this statistical row applies.
TBOWNER	The owner of the table named in TBNAME.

TBNAME	The table name to which this statistical row applies.
NAME	The column name.
COLVALUE	Contains the actual value to which the statistic contained in the FREQUENCY column applies.
TYPE	Type of statistics generated: C Cardinality F Frequent value
CARDF	Number of distinct values for the column group; valid only if TYPE = "C".
COLGROUPCOLNO	Identifies the set of columns associated with the statistics. For single column stats, the column is of zero length.
NUMCOLUMNS	Number of columns associated with the statistics.
FREQUENCYF	The percentage (* 100) that the value specified in COLVALUE exists.

SYSIBM.SYSCOLSTATS

SYSIBM.SYSCOLSTATS contains one row of general partition-level statistics for each column specified to RUNSTATS.

Tablespace	DSNDB06.SYSSTATS
Index	DSNTCX01 [unique] (TBOWNER, TBNAME, NAME, PARTITION)
Relationship	DSNDC@TC REFERENCES SYSIBM.SYSCOLUMNS

Column Definitions

HIGHKEY	A number generated by the RUNSTATS utility or explicitly specified by an authorized user indicating the highest value in this column. If RUNSTATS has not been run for this column, COLCARD is set to -1.
HIGH2KEY	A number generated by the RUNSTATS utility or explicitly specified by an authorized user indicating the second highest value in this column. If RUNSTATS has not been run for this column, COLCARD is set to -1.
LOWKEY	A number generated by the RUNSTATS utility or explicitly specified by an authorized user indicating the lowest value contained in this column. If RUNSTATS has not been run for this column, COLCARD is set to -1.

LOW2KEY	A number generated by the RUNSTATS utility or explicitly specified by an authorized user indicating the second lowest value contained in this column. If RUNSTATS has not been run for this column, COLCARD is set to -1.
COLCARD	A number generated by the RUNSTATS utility or explicitly specified by an authorized user indicating the number of distinct values in this column. If RUNSTATS has not been run for this column, COLCARD is set to -1.
STATSTIME	Timestamp indicating the date and time that RUNSTATS was executed to produce this row.
IBMREQD	An indicator specifying Y if the row was supplied by IBM, or N if it was not.
PARTITION	The partition number indicating the physical partition of the tablespace to which this statistical row applies.
TBOWNER	The owner of the table named in TBNAME.
TBNAME	The table name to which this statistical row applies.
NAME	The column name.
COLCARDDATA	Internal use only.

SYSIBM.SYSCOLUMNS

SYSIBM.SYSCOLUMNS contains one row for every column of every table and view defined to DB2.

Tablespace	DSNDB06.SYSDBASE	
Index	DSNDCX01	[unique]
	(TBCREATOR, TBNAME, NAME)	
Links	DSNDT#DF REFERENCES SYSIBM.SYSTABLES	

Column Definitions

NAME	The column name.
TBNAME	The table name that contains the column identified by NAME.
TBCREATOR	The owner of the view or table named in TBNAME.
COLNO	A small integer identifying the position of the column in the table. For example, 3 indicates the third column in the table.
COLTYPE	The data type of the column.
LENGTH	The length of the column as it is physically stored.
SCALE	The scale if the column is the DECIMAL data type; otherwise, it contains 0.

NULLS	An indicator specifying Y if the column is nullable, or N if it is not.
COLCARD	For V4 and previous releases, a number generated by the RUNSTATS utility or explicitly specified by a SYSADM indicating the number of distinct values in this column. If RUNSTATS has not been run for this column, COLCARD is set to -1. (Not used as of V5.)
HIGH2KEY	A number generated by the RUNSTATS utility or explicitly specified by a SYSADM indicating the second highest value in this column. If RUNSTATS has not been run for this column, COLCARD is set to -1.
LOW2KEY	A number generated by the RUNSTATS utility or explicitly specified by a SYSADM indicating the second lowest value contained in this column. If RUNSTATS has not been run for this column, COLCARD is set to -1.
UPDATES	An indicator specifying Y if this column is updateable, or N if it is not.
IBMREQD	An indicator specifying Y if the row was supplied by IBM, or N if it was not.
REMARKS	Documentation describing the column as specified by the COMMENT ON SQL statement.
DEFAULT	An indicator specifying the characteristic default values for this column. Valid values are as follow: N No default value. Y If NULLS is Y, the default is NULL; otherwise, it is the system default based on the data type. B The column uses the system default based on the data type. 1 The default is string data. 2 The default is a floating-point number. 3 The default is a decimal value. 4 The default is an integer value. 5 The default is a hex string. S The default is the SQL ID of the process. U The default is the USER special register (at execution time).
KEYSEQ	A small integer indicating the column's position in the table's primary key. If the column is not part of the primary key, KEYSEQ is 0.

FOREIGNKEY — An indicator specifying the characteristics of character columns. Contains the following:

B — If the column can contain bit data.

S — If the MIXED DATA installation option is YES and the column contains SBCS data.

Any other character indicates SBCS if the MIXED DATA installation option is NO, or MIXED data if the MIXED DATA installation option is YES.

FLDPROC — An indicator specifying Y if the column has a field procedure, or N if it does not.

LABEL — The label of the column as specified by the LABEL ON SQL statement.

STATSTIME — Timestamp indicating the date and time that RUNSTATS was executed for the named column.

DEFAULTVALUE — When the DEFAULT column equals 1, 2, 3, 4, or 5, DEFAULTVALUE contains the actual default value.

COLCARDF — Estimated number of distinct values in the column. If RUNSTATS has not been run for this column, COLCARD is set to -1.

SYSIBM.SYSCOPY

SYSIBM.SYSCOPY contains information on the execution of the DB2 COPY, QUIESCE, LOAD, and REORG utilities. DB2 uses this information to manage data recovery scenarios.

Tablespace	DSNDB06.SYSCOPY	
Index	DSNUCH01	[nonunique]
	(DBNAME, TSNAME, STARTRBA, TIMESTAMP)	
Index	DSNUCX01	[nonunique]
	(DSNAME)	
Links	None	

Column Definitions

DBNAME — The database name.

TSNAME — The tablespace name.

DSNUM — The tablespace data set number: the partition number of partitioned tablespaces, 1 for non-partitioned tablespaces using a single data set, or the data set number of large non-partitioned tablespaces residing in more than one data set.

`ICTYPE`	The type of utility information stored in this row. Refer to Chapter 28, "Miscellaneous Utilities," for a listing of valid `ICTYPE` values.
`ICDATE`	The date (*yymmdd*) when this row was added to `SYSCOPY`. Do not reference this column; use `TIMESTAMP` instead.
`START_RBA`	A 48-bit positive integer containing the LRSN of point in the DB2 log. (The LRSN is the RBA if you're not using data sharing.)
`FILESEQNO`	The sequence number of the tape for this copy.
`DEVTYPE`	The device type for the copy as specified in the `COPY` parameters.
`IBMREQD`	An indicator specifying `Y` if the row was supplied by IBM, or `N` if it was not.
`DSNAME`	Contains the data set name if `ICTYPE` is `I`, `F`, or `P` (`RECOVER TOCOPY` only). For other `ICTYPE`s, `DSNAME` contains the database and tablespace (or is blank for pre-V4 rows).
`ICTIME`	The time (*hhmmss*) when this row was added to `SYSCOPY`. Do not reference this column; use `TIMESTAMP` instead.

`SHRLEVEL`	The share level used when creating full and incremental image copies (`ICTYPE = F` or `I`). Valid values are as follow:
	`C` `SHRLEVEL CHANGE`
	`R` `SHRLEVEL REFERENCE`
	blank Not applicable; row does not describe an image copy.

`DSVOLSER`	A list of the volume serial numbers used by the image copy data set. When more than one volume exists, the volume serial numbers are strung together in this column and separated by commas.
`TIMESTAMP`	The date and time when this row was added to `SYSCOPY`.
`ICBACKUP`	An indicator specifying the type of image copy in this row: `LB` `LOCALSITE` backup copy `RB` `RECOVERYSITE` backup copy `RP` `RECOVERYSITE` primary copy *blank* `LOCALSITE` primary copy
`ICUNIT`	Media type used for the image copy: `D` DASD `T` Tape *blank* Either not DASD or tape, row generated prior to DB2 V2.3, or row does not pertain to an image copy.

STYPE	When ICTYPE="T", valid STYPE indicates which type of copy was terminated by TERM UTIL or START DATABASE ACCESS(FORCE); values are as follow: F COPY FULL YES I COPY FULL NO When ICTYPE="F", valid values are as follow: C DFSMS concurrent copy R LOAD REPLACE(YES) S LOAD REPLACE(NO) W REORG LOG(NO) X REORG LOG(YES) *blank* DB2 image copy When ICTYPE="P", the only valid value is as follows: L RECOVER TORBA LOGONLY When ICTYPE="Q", valid values are as follow: W WRITE(YES) in effect when QUIESCE was taken. For any other ICTYPE, STYPE is blank.
PIT_RBA	Contains the LRSN for the point in the DB2 log (for RECOVER TOCOPY and RECOVER TORBA rows). The LRSN is the RBA when data sharing is not being used.
GROUP_MEMBER	The DB2 data-sharing member name of the DB2 subsystem that performed the operation; or blank if the DB2 susbsystem was not in a data-sharing environment.

SYSIBM.SYSDATABASE

SYSIBM.SYSDATABASE contains information about every DB2 database.

Tablespace	DSNDB06.SYSDBAUT	
Index	DSNDDH01 (NAME)	[unique]
Index	DSNATX02 (GROUP_MEMBER)	[nonunique]
Links	None	

Column Definitions

NAME	The database name.
CREATOR	The owner of the database named in NAME.
STGROUP	The name of the default storage group specified in the CREATE DATABASE DDL.
BPOOL	The name of the default bufferpool specified when this database was created.
DBID	An internal identifier assigned to this database by DB2.
IBMREQD	An indicator specifying the following: Y Row was supplied by IBM. N Not supplied by IBM. E Not supplied by IBM; V2.3 dependent. G Not supplied by IBM; V4 dependent.
CREATEDBY	The primary authorization ID of the individual who created this database.
ROSHARE	An indicator specifying whether the database is shared with another DB2 subsystem: O Shared database with local DB2 as the owner. R Shared database with local DB2 as read-only user. *blank* Database is not shared.
TIMESTAMP	The date and time when the database was made shareable on the owning system. If the database is not shared, it contains 0001-01-01-00.00.00.000000.
TYPE	The type of the database: W Work file database. *blank* Not a work file database.
GROUP_MEMBER	The DB2 data-sharing member name of the DB2 subsystem that uses this work file database; or blank if the work file database was not created in a data-sharing environment or if the database is not a work file database.
CREATEDTS	The date and time when the database was created.
ALTEREDTS	The date and time of the last ALTER for this database. ALTEREDTS equals CREATEDTS when no ALTER has been issued.

ENCODING_SCHEME	Default encoding scheme for the database. Valid values are as follow: A ASCII E EBCDIC *blank* For DSNDB04 and work files
SBCS_CCSID	Default SBCS CCSID.
DBCS_CCSID	Default DBCS CCSID.
MIXED_CCSID	Default mixed CCSID.

SYSIBM.SYSDBAUTH

SYSIBM.SYSDBAUTH contains database privileges held by DB2 users.

Tablespace	DSNDB06.SYSDBAUT
Index	DSNADH01 [nonunique] (GRANTEE, NAME)
Index	DSNADX01 [nonunique] (GRANTOR, NAME)
Links	DSNDD#AD REFERENCES SYSIBM.SYSDATABASE

Column Definitions

GRANTOR	Authid of the user who granted the privileges described in this row.
GRANTEE	The authid of the user who possesses the privileges described in this row, the name of a plan that uses the privileges, or the literal PUBLIC to indicate that all users have these privileges.
NAME	The database name.
TIMESTAMP	The date and time (in the internal format) when the privileges were granted.
DATEGRANTED	The date when the authority was granted (*yymmdd*).
TIMEGRANTED	The time when the authority was granted (*hhmmssth*).
GRANTEETYPE	Internal use only.
AUTHHOWGOT	The authorization level of the GRANTOR: C DBCTRL D DBADM L SYSCTRL

	M	DBMAINT
	S	SYSADM
	blank	Not applicable
CREATETABAUTH	The privilege to create tables in the named database:	
	G	GRANTEE holds the privilege and can grant it to others.
	Y	GRANTEE holds the privilege.
	blank	GRANTEE does not hold the privilege.
CREATETSAUTH	The privilege to create tablespaces in the named database:	
	G	GRANTEE holds the privilege and can grant it to others.
	Y	GRANTEE holds the privilege.
	blank	GRANTEE does not hold the privilege.
DBADMAUTH	The DBADM privilege on the named database:	
	G	GRANTEE holds the privilege and can grant it to others.
	Y	GRANTEE holds the privilege.
	blank	GRANTEE does not hold the privilege.
DBCTRLAUTH	The DBCTRL privilege on the named database:	
	G	GRANTEE holds the privilege and can grant it to others.
	Y	GRANTEE holds the privilege.
	blank	GRANTEE does not hold the privilege.
DBMAINTAUTH	The DBMAINT privilege on the named database:	
	G	GRANTEE holds the privilege and can grant it to others.
	Y	GRANTEE holds the privilege.
	blank	GRANTEE does not hold the privilege.
DISPLAYDBAUTH	The DISPLAY DATABASE privilege on the named database:	
	G	GRANTEE holds the privilege and can grant it to others.
	Y	GRANTEE holds the privilege.
	blank	GRANTEE does not hold the privilege.
DROPAUTH	The privilege to alter or drop the named database:	
	G	GRANTEE holds the privilege and can grant it to others.
	Y	GRANTEE holds the privilege.
	blank	GRANTEE does not hold the privilege.

IMAGCOPYAUTH	The privilege to execute the COPY, MERGECOPY, MODIFY, and QUIESCE utilities for the named database:	
	G	GRANTEE holds the privilege and can grant it to others.
	Y	GRANTEE holds the privilege.
	blank	GRANTEE does not hold the privilege.
LOADAUTH	The privilege to execute the LOAD utility for the named database:	
	G	GRANTEE holds the privilege and can grant it to others.
	Y	GRANTEE holds the privilege.
	blank	GRANTEE does not hold the privilege.
REORGAUTH	The privilege to execute the REORG utility for the named database:	
	G	GRANTEE holds the privilege and can grant it to others.
	Y	GRANTEE holds the privilege.
	blank	GRANTEE does not hold the privilege.
RECOVERDBAUTH	Privilege to execute the RECOVER and REPORT utilities for the named database:	
	G	GRANTEE holds the privilege and can grant it to others.
	Y	GRANTEE holds the privilege.
	blank	GRANTEE does not hold the privilege.
REPAIRAUTH	The privilege to execute the REPAIR and DIAGNOSE utilities for the named database:	
	G	GRANTEE holds the privilege and can grant it to others.
	Y	GRANTEE holds the privilege.
	blank	GRANTEE does not hold the privilege.
STARTDBAUTH	The privilege to issue the START command for the named database:	
	G	GRANTEE holds the privilege and can grant it to others.
	Y	GRANTEE holds the privilege.
	blank	GRANTEE does not hold the privilege.
STATSAUTH	The privilege to execute the RUNSTATS and CHECK utilities for the named database:	
	G	GRANTEE holds the privilege and can grant it to others.
	Y	GRANTEE holds the privilege.
	blank	GRANTEE does not hold the privilege.

STOPAUTH	The privilege to issue the STOP command for the named database: G GRANTEE holds the privilege and can grant it to others. Y GRANTEE holds the privilege. *blank* GRANTEE does not hold the privilege.
IBMREQD	An indicator specifying Y if the row was supplied by IBM, or N if it was not.
GRANTEDTS	Time the GRANT was executed.

SYSIBM.SYSDBRM

SYSIBM.SYSDBRM contains DBRM information only for DBRMs bound into DB2 plans.

Tablespace	DSNDB06.SYSPLAN
Indexes	None
Links	DSNPP#PD REFERENCES SYSIBM.SYSPLAN

Column Definitions

NAME	The name of the Database Request Module bound into the plan identified by PLNAME.
TIMESTAMP	The date and time (in the internal format) when the privileges were granted.
PDSNAME	The named DBRM is a member of the partitioned data set named in this column.
PLNAME	The plan name.
PLCREATOR	The owner of the plan named in PLNAME.
PRECOMPTIME	The time the DBRM was precompiled [*HHMMSSTH*] unless the LEVEL precompiler option was specified.
PRECOMPDATE	The date the DBRM was precompiled [*YYMMDD*], unless the LEVEL precompiler option was specified.
QUOTE	An indicator specifying Y if the SQL escape character is a quotation mark, or N if it is an apostrophe.
COMMA	An indicator specifying Y if the SQL decimal point is a comma, or N if it is a period.
HOSTLANG	An indicator specifying the host language used for the DBRM: B BAL (assembler) C VS/COBOL D C

	F FORTRAN
	P PL/I
	2 COBOL II
	3 IBM COBOL
	4 C++
IBMREQD	An indicator specifying Y if the row was supplied by IBM, or N if it was not.
CHARSET	An indicator specifying K if the Katakana character set was specified at precompile time, or A if alphanumeric was used.
MIXED	An indicator specifying Y if the mixed precompiler option was specified, or N if it was not.
DEC31	An indicator specifying Y if the 31-byte decimal precompiler option was specified, or blank if it was not.
VERSION	The version specified at precompile time.
PRECOMPTS	Time when the DBRMS was compiled.

SYSIBM.SYSDUMMY1

SYSIBM.SYSDUMMY contains a single row. It is designed to be used in SQL statements in which a table reference is needed but the table contents are unimportant.

Tablespace	DSNDB06.SYSSTR
Indexes	None
Links	None

Column Definitions

IBMREQD	An indicator specifying Y if the row was supplied by IBM, or N if it was not.

SYSIBM.SYSFIELDS

SYSIBM.SYSFIELDS contains information on field procedures implemented for DB2 tables. It also holds the non-uniform distribution statistics collected by RUNSTATS.

Tablespace	DSNDB06.SYSDBASE
Indexes	None
Links	DSNDF#FD REFERENCES SYSIBM.SYSCOLUMNS

Column Definitions

TBCREATOR	The owner of the table named in TBNAME.
TBNAME	The name of the table that contains the column specified in NAME.
COLNO	The position of the column in the table.
NAME	The column name.
FLDTYPE	The data type of the column.
LENGTH	The physical length of the column, not including varchar length fields and null indicators.
SCALE	The scale of columns when FLDTYPE is DECIMAL, or 0 if FLDTYPE is not DECIMAL.
FLDPROC	The name of the field procedure.
WORKAREA	The size of the work area used by the FLDPROC.
IBMREQD	An indicator specifying Y if the row was supplied by IBM, or N if it was not.
EXITPARML	The length of the parameter list used by the FLDPROC.
PARMLIST	The actual parameter list used by the FLDPROC.
EXITPARM	The parameters used by the FLDPROC.

SYSIBM.SYSFOREIGNKEYS

SYSIBM.SYSFOREIGNKEYS contains information about all columns participating in foreign keys.

Tablespace	DSNDB06.SYSDBASE
Indexes	None
Links	DSNDR#DF REFERENCES SYSIBM.SYSRELS

Column Definitions

CREATOR	The owner of the table named in TBNAME.
TBNAME	The table name containing the foreign key column.
RELNAME	The referential constraint name.
COLNAME	The column name that participates in the foreign key.
COLNO	The sequence of the column in the table definition.
COLSEQ	The sequence of the column in the foreign key definition.
IBMREQD	An indicator specifying Y if the row was supplied by IBM, or N if it was not.

SYSIBM.SYSINDEXES

SYSIBM.SYSINDEXES contains information about every DB2 index.

Tablespace	DSNDB06.SYSDBASE
Index	DSNDXX01 [unique] (CREATOR, NAME)
Index	DSNDXX02 [unique] (DBNAME, INDEXSPACE)
Index	DSNDXX03 [nonunique] (TBCREATOR, TBNAME, CREATOR, NAME)
Links	DSNDT#DX REFERENCES SYSIBM.SYSTABLES

Column Definitions

NAME	The index name.
CREATOR	The owner of the index named in NAME.
TBNAME	The table name for which the index was created.
TBCREATOR	The owner of the table named in TBNAME.
UNIQUERULE	Describe if the index is unique: C Unique and used to enforce a UNIQUE constraint. D Duplicates are allowed. N UNIQUE WHERE NOT NULL. P Unique and supports a primary key. R Unique and used to enforce uniqueness of a non-primary parent key. U Unique (but no UNIQUE constraint).
COLCOUNT	The number of columns defined for the key.
CLUSTERING	Y if the index was created with the CLUSTER option, or N if it was not.
CLUSTERED	Y if the table is more than 95 percent clustered by the key of this index, or N if it is not.
DBID	An internal database identifier.
OBID	An internal object identifier for the index.
ISOBID	An internal object identifier for the index space.
DBNAME	The database name containing this index.

INDEXSPACE	An 8-byte index space name. It differs from the index name when the index name is greater than 8 bytes, or when more than one index has the same name (with a different CREATOR) in the same database.
FIRSTKEYCARD	For V4 and prior releases, a value indicating the number of distinct values in the first column of the index key, or -1 if RUNSTATS has not been run. Value is an estimate if updated while collecting statistics on a single partition only. (Not used for V5.)
FULLKEYCARD	For V4 and prior releases, a value indicating the number of distinct values in the entire index key, or -1 if RUNSTATS has not been run. (Not used for V5.)
NLEAF	The number of active leaf pages, or -1 if RUNSTATS has not been run.
NLEVELS	The number of levels in the index b-tree structure, or -1 if RUNSTATS has not been run.
BPOOL	The bufferpool name specified when this index was created.
PGSIZE	The size of the index subpages: 256 16 subpages 512 8 subpages 1024 4 subpages 2048 2 subpages 4096 1 subpage
ERASERULE	Y if the index was created with the ERASE YES option, or N if it was created with ERASE NO.
DSETPASS	The index data set password; only for indexes created using a STOGROUP.
CLOSERULE	Y if the index was created with the CLOSE YES option, or N if it was created with CLOSE NO.
SPACE	The space in kilobytes allocated for this index, or 0 if STOSPACE has not been run, or for indexes not created using a STOGROUP.
IBMREQD	An indicator specifying whether the row was supplied by IBM: Y Yes, row was supplied by IBM. N No. C No; V2.1 dependent. D No; V2.2 dependent. E No; V2.3 dependent. G No; V4 dependent.

CLUSTERRATIO	Indicates the percentage of table rows that are in clustered order by this index key, or 0 if RUNSTATS has not been run.
CREATEDBY	The primary authorization ID of the individual who created this index.
IOFACTOR	Not currently used.
PREFETCHFACTOR	Not currently used.
STATSTIME	Timestamp indicating the date and time that RUNSTATS was executed for the named index.
INDEXTYPE	The type of index: *blank* Type 1 index 2 Type 2 index
FIRSTKEYCARDF	A value indicating the number of distinct values in the first column of the index key, or -1 if RUNSTATS has not been run. Value is an estimate if updated while collecting statistics on a single partition only.
FULLKEYCARDF	A value indicating the number of distinct values in the entire index key, or -1 if RUNSTATS has not been run.
CREATEDTS	The date and time when the index was created.
ALTEREDTS	The date and time of the last ALTER for this index. ALTEREDTS equals CREATEDTS when no ALTER has been issued.
PIECESIZE	Maximum size of the data set storage piece (for non-partitioned indexes only).

SYSIBM.SYSINDEXPART

SYSIBM.SYSINDEXPART contains information about the physical structure and storage of every DB2 index.

Tablespace	DSNDB06.SYSDBASE
Index	DSNDRX01 [unique] (IXCREATOR, IXNAME, PARTITION)
Links	DSNDX#DR REFERENCES SYSIBM.SYSINDEXES

Column Definitions

PARTITION	The partition number for partitioned indexes, or 0 if the index is not partitioned.
IXNAME	The index name.
IXCREATOR	The owner of the index named in IXNAME.

PQTY	The primary space quantity, in 4KB pages, specified when the index was created.
SQTY	The secondary space quantity, in 4KB pages, specified when the index was created.
STORTYPE	E for explicit VCAT-defined indexes, or I for implicit STOGROUP-defined indexes.
STORNAME	The storage group name for STOGROUP-defined indexes, or a VCAT identifier for VCAT-defined indexes.
VCATNAME	The name of the VCAT used to allocate the index, regardless of how the index was defined (STOGROUP or VCAT).
CARD	For V4 and prior releases, the number of rows this index references, or -1 if RUNSTATS has not been run. (Not used as of V5.)
FAROFFPOS	For V4 and prior releases, the number of rows located "far off" from their optimal position, or -1 if RUNSTATS has not been run. (Not used as of V5.)
LEAFDIST	The average number of pages (multiplied by 100) between consecutive index leaf pages, or -1 if RUNSTATS has not been run.
NEAROFFPOS	For V4 and prior releases, the number of rows located "near off" from their optimal position, or -1 if RUNSTATS has not been run. (Not used as of V5.)
IBMREQD	An indicator specifying Y if the row was supplied by IBM, or N if it was not.
LIMITKEY	The high key value used to limit partitioned indexes, or 0 if the index is not partitioned.
FREEPAGE	The number of consecutive pages to be loaded before loading a blank page, or 0 for no free pages.
PCTFREE	The percentage of each page (or leaf subpage) to leave free at load time.
SPACE	Amount of DASD storage allocated to the index partition (in KB).
STATSTIME	Timestamp indicating the date and time that RUNSTATS was executed for the named index partition.
INDEXTYPE	Not currently used.
GBPCACHE	Group bufferpool cache option used: *blank* Only changed pages are cached. A Changed and unchanged pages are cached in the group bufferpool.

FAROFFPOSF	The number of rows located "far off" from their optimal position, or -1 if RUNSTATS has not been run.
NEAROFFPOSF	The number of rows located "near off" from their optimal position, or -1 if RUNSTATS has not been run.
CARDF	The number of rows this index (or partition) references, or -1 if RUNSTATS has not been run.

SYSIBM.SYSINDEXSTATS

SYSIBM.SYSINDEXSTATS contains one row of partition-level statistics for each index partition.

Tablespace	DSNDB06.SYSSTATS
Index	DSNTXX01 [unique] (OWNER, NAME, PARTITION)
Relationship	DSNDX@TX REFERENCES SYSIBM.SYSINDEXES

Column Definitions

FIRSTKEYCARD	A value indicating the number of distinct values in the first column of the index key, or -1 if RUNSTATS has not been run.
FULLKEYCARD	A value indicating the number of distinct values in the entire index key, or -1 if RUNSTATS has not been run.
NLEAF	The number of active leaf pages, or -1 if RUNSTATS has not been run.
NLEVELS	The number of levels in the index b-tree structure, or -1 if RUNSTATS has not been run.
IOFACTOR	Not currently used (DB2 V3).
PREFETCHFACTOR	Not currently used (DB2 V3).
CLUSTERRATIO	A number indicating the percentage of table rows in clustered order by this index key, or 0 if RUNSTATS has not been run.
STATSTIME	Timestamp indicating the date and time that RUNSTATS was executed to produce this row.
IBMREQD	An indicator specifying Y if the row was supplied by IBM, or N if it was not.
PARTITION	The partition number indicating the physical partition of the index to which this statistical row applies.
OWNER	The owner of the index named in NAME.
NAME	The index name to which this statistical row applies.
KEYCOUNT	Total number of rows in the partition.

SYSIBM.SYSKEYS

SYSIBM.SYSKEYS contains information about every column of every DB2 index.

Tablespace	DSNDB06.SYSDBASE
Indexes	DSNDKX01 [unique] (IXCREATOR, IXNAME, COLNAME)
Links	DSNDX#DK REFERENCES SYSIBM.SYSINDEXES

Column Definitions

IXNAME	The index name.
IXCREATOR	The owner of the index named in IXNAME.
COLNAME	The column name.
COLNO	The sequence of the column in the table definition.
COLSEQ	The sequence of the column in the index key definition.
ORDERING	A for an index key column ordered in ascending sequence, or D if the sequence is descending.
IBMREQD	An indicator specifying Y if the row was supplied by IBM, or N if it was not.

SYSIBM.SYSLINKS

SYSIBM.SYSLINKS contains information about the table-to-table links that make up the physical structure and storage of the DB2 Catalog. Links are internal structures similar to RI relationships. Not all catalog tables use links.

Tablespace	DSNDB06.SYSDBASE
Indexes	None
Links	DSNDR#DL REFERENCES SYSIBM.SYSRELS

Column Definitions

CREATOR	The owner of the dependent table named in TBNAME.
TBNAME	The dependent table name for this link.
LINKNAME	The name of this link.
PARENTNAME	The parent table name for this link.
PARENTCREATOR	The owner of the parent table named in PARENTNAME.
CHILDSEQ	A number indicating the clustering order of the dependent table in the parent table.

DBNAME	The database name containing this link.
DBID	The internal database identifier.
OBID	The internal object identifier assigned to this link by DB2.
COLCOUNT	The number of columns defined for the link.
INSERTRULE	An indicator specifying how rows will be inserted into the DB2 Catalog tables for this link: F FIRST L LAST O ONE U UNIQUE
IBMREQD	An indicator specifying Y if the row was supplied by IBM, or N if it was not.

SYSIBM.SYSPACKAGE

SYSIBM.SYSPACKAGE contains information on DB2 packages.

Tablespace	DSNDB06.SYSPKAGE
Index	DSNKKX01 [unique] (LOCATION, COLLID, NAME, VERSION)
Index	DSNKKX02 [unique] (LOCATION, COLLID, NAME, CONTOKEN)
Links	None

Column Definitions

LOCATION	Blanks.
COLLID	The collection name.
NAME	The package name.
CONTOKEN	The consistency token for the package.
OWNER	The owner specified for the package named in NAME.
CREATOR	The creator of the package named in NAME. Differs from OWNER in that this is the primary authorization ID of the user who binds the package.
TIMESTAMP	The date and time when the package was created.
BINDTIME	The time that the package was bound (*hhmmssth*).
QUALIFIER	A qualifier to be used for all tables, views, synonyms, and aliases referenced in the program.

PKSIZE	The size of the package base section (in bytes).
AVGSIZE	The average size of the sections of the package containing DML (in bytes).
SYSENTRIES	The number of enabled/disabled entries for this package (as recorded in SYSIBM.SYSPKSYSTEM).
VALID	An indicator specifying the state of the package: A An object that the plan depends on has been altered; rebind is not required. H Table (or base table of a view) description was ALTERed, invalidating the package. N The plan must first be rebound. Y The plan can be run without rebinding.
OPERATIVE	Y if the package can be allocated, or N if it cannot.
VALIDATE	Specifies when validity checking will be accomplished: B Checking performed at BIND time. R Checking performed at RUN time.
ISOLATION	Isolation level for the plan: R Repeatable Read. S Cursor Stability. T Read Stability. U Uncommitted Read. *blank* Default to the isolation level of the plan into which this package is bound.
RELEASE	An indicator specifying when resources for this package will be released: C Resources are released at each COMMIT point. D Resources not released until the plan is deallocated. *blank* Default to the release level of the plan into which this package is bound.
EXPLAIN	An indicator specifying Y if the package was bound with EXPLAIN YES, or N if it was bound with EXPLAIN NO.
QUOTE	An indicator specifying Y if the SQL escape character is a quotation mark, or N if it is an apostrophe.
COMMA	An indicator specifying Y if the SQL decimal point is a comma, or N if it is a period.

`HOSTLANG`	An indicator specifying the host language used for the `DBRM` for this package: `B` BAL (assembler) `C` VS/COBOL `D` C `F` FORTRAN `P` PL/I `2` VS COBOL II `3` IBM COBOL `4` C++ *blank* Remote bound package
`CHARSET`	An indicator specifying `K` if the Katakana character set was used at precompile time, or `A` if alphanumeric was used.
`MIXED`	An indicator specifying `Y` if the mixed precompiler option was used, or `N` if it was not.
`DEC31`	An indicator specifying `Y` if the 31-byte decimal precompiler option was used, or `N` if it was not.
`DEFERPREP`	`Y` if the package was bound with `DEFER(PREPARE)`, or `N` if it was bound with `NODEFER(PREPARE)`.
`SQLERROR`	An indicator specifying the SQL error option chosen at bind time: `C` `CONTINUE` on error `N` `NOPACKAGE`
`REMOTE`	An indicator specifying the package source: `C` Created by `BIND COPY` command. `N` Created from a local `BIND PACKAGE` command. `Y` Created from a remote `BIND PACKAGE` command.
`PCTIMESTAMP`	Indicates the date and time when the program was precompiled.
`IBMREQD`	An indicator specifying whether the row was supplied by IBM: `Y` Yes, row was supplied by IBM. `N` No. `E` No; V2.3 dependent. `F` No; V3 dependent. `G` No; V4 dependent. `H` No; V5 dependent.

VERSION	The package version.	
PDSNAME	The DBRM for the package named by NAME is a member of the partitioned data set named in this column. For remote packages, PDSNAME contains an identifier for the remote location.	
DEGREE	The degree of parallelism chosen for this package:	
	ANY	Bound as DEGREE(ANY).
	1	Bound as DEGREE(1) or default.
	blank	Migrated from a prior release.
GROUP_MEMBER	The DB2 data-sharing member name of the DB2 subsystem that performed the most recent bind for this package; or blank if DB2 subsystem was not in a DB2 data-sharing environment when the bind was performed.	
DYNAMICRULES	Indicates dynamic SQL treatment:	
	S	Dynamic SQL statements are handled like static SQL statements at runtime.
	blank	Dynamic statements are handled like dynamic SQL statements at runtime.
REOPTVAR	Indicator specifying if access path is to be determined again at runtime using explicit values for host variables or parameter markers. Valid values are as follow:	
	N	No, access path determined at bind time.
	Y	Yes, access path may be redetermined at runtime.
DEFERPREPARE	Indicator specifying whether PREPARE is deferred until OPEN. Valid values are as follow:	
	N	No, PREPARE is not deferred.
	Y	Yes, PREPARE is deferred.
	blank	Bind option not specified; inherited from plan.
KEEPDYNAMIC	Indicator specifying whether dynamic statements are to be kept past a commit point. Y = yes; N = no.	

SYSIBM.SYSPACKAUTH

SYSIBM.SYSPACKAUTH contains the privileges held by DB2 users on packages.

Tablespace	DSNDB06.SYSPKAGE
Index	DSNKAX01 [nonunique]
	(GRANTOR, LOCATION, COLLID, NAME)
Index	DSNKAX02 [nonunique]

	`(GRANTEE, LOCATION, COLLID, NAME, BINDAUTH, COPYAUTH, EXECUTEAUTH)`
Index	`DSNKAX03 [nonunique]` `(LOCATION, COLLID, NAME)`
Links	None

Column Definitions

GRANTOR	The authid of the user who granted the privileges described in this row.
GRANTEE	The authid of the user who possesses the privileges described in this row, the name of a plan that uses the privileges, or the literal PUBLIC to indicate that all users have these privileges.
LOCATION	The package location.
COLLID	The collection name.
NAME	The package name.
CONTOKEN	The consistency token for the package.
TIMESTAMP	The date and time that these privileges were granted.
GRANTEETYPE	A value indicating the type of GRANTEE: P GRANTEE is a plan. *blank* GRANTEE is a userid.
AUTHHOWGOT	The authorization level of the GRANTOR: C DBCTRL D DBADM L SYSCTRL M DBMAINT S SYSADM *blank* Not applicable
BINDAUTH	The privilege to BIND or REBIND the named package: G GRANTEE holds the privilege and can grant it to others. Y GRANTEE holds the privilege. *blank* GRANTEE does not hold the privilege.
COPYAUTH	The privilege to COPY the named package: G GRANTEE holds the privilege and can grant it to others. Y GRANTEE holds the privilege. *blank* GRANTEE does not hold the privilege.

EXECUTEAUTH	The privilege to execute the named package: G GRANTEE holds the privilege and can grant it to others. Y GRANTEE holds the privilege. *blank* GRANTEE does not hold the privilege.
IBMREQD	An indicator specifying Y if the row was supplied by IBM, or N if it was not.

SYSIBM.SYSPACKDEP

SYSIBM.SYSPACKDEP contains a cross-reference of DB2 objects on which each given package is dependent.

Tablespace	DSNDB06.SYSPKAGE
Index	DSNKDX01 [nonunique] (DLOCATION, DCOLLID, DNAME, DCONTOKEN)
Index	DSNKDX02 [nonunique] (BQUALIFIER, BNAME, BTYPE)
Links	DSNKK@KD REFERENCES SYSIBM.SYSPACKAGE

Column Definitions

BNAME	The name of the object upon which the package depends.
BQUALIFIER	A qualifier for the object named in BNAME. If BTYPE is equal to R, BCREATOR is a database name; otherwise, it is the owner of the object named in BNAME.
BTYPE	Type of object named in BNAME: A Alias I Index P Partitioned Tablespace R Tablespace S Synonym T Table V View
DLOCATION	The location of the package.
DCOLLID	The name of the collection.
DNAME	The name of the package.
DCONTOKEN	The consistency token for the package.
IBMREQD	An indicator specifying Y if the row was supplied by IBM, or N if it was not.

SYSIBM.SYSPACKLIST

SYSIBM.SYSPACKLIST lists the DB2 packages that have been bound into application plans.

Tablespace	DSNDB06.SYSPKAGE
Index	DSNKLX01 [nonunique] (LOCATION, COLLID, NAME)
Index	DSNKLX02 [unique] (PLANNAME, SEQNO, LOCATION, COLLID, NAME)
Links	DSNPP@KL REFERENCES SYSIBM.SYSPLAN

Column Definitions

PLANNAME	The plan name.
SEQNO	A sequence number used to identify the order of the packages in the package list for this plan.
LOCATION	The location of the package.
COLLID	The name of the collection.
NAME	The name of the package. If this column contains an asterisk (*), the entire collection applies.
TIMESTAMP	The date and time when this package list was created.
IBMREQD	An indicator specifying Y if the row was supplied by IBM, or N if it was not.

SYSIBM.SYSPACKSTMT

SYSIBM.SYSPACKSTMT contains the SQL statements for every DB2 package.

Tablespace	DSNDB06.SYSPKAGE
Index	DSNKSX01 [unique] (LOCATION, COLLID, NAME, CONTOKEN, SEQNO)
Links	DSNKK@KS REFERENCES SYSIBM.SYSPACKAGE

Column Definitions

LOCATION	Always contains blanks.
COLLID	The name of the collection.
NAME	The name of the package.
CONTOKEN	The consistency token for the package.
SEQNO	A sequence number used to identify SQL statements that span multiple rows of this table.

STMTNO	A statement number for the SQL statement as stored in the source for the application program.
SECTNO	The DBRM section number.
BINDERROR	An indicator specifying Y if an SQL error was encountered when this package was bound, or N if an SQL error was not encountered.
IBMREQD	An indicator specifying Y if the row was supplied by IBM, or N if it was not.
VERSION	The package version.
STMT	Up to 254 characters of the SQL statement text. For SQL statements that comprise more than 254 characters, multiple rows with ascending SEQNO values exist.
ISOLATION	Isolation level for the SQL statement: L RS with KEEP UPDATE LOCKS. R Repeatable Read. S Cursor Stability. T Read Stability. U Uncommitted Read. X RR with KEEP UPDATE LOCKS. *blank* WITH clause not specified; isolation level defaults to package isolation level.
STATUS	Indicator specifying the status of the bind. Valid values are as follow: A Distributed statement uses DB2 private protocol; statement will be parsed and executed at the server using defaults for input variables. B Distributed statement uses DB2 private protocol; statement will be parsed and executed at the server using values for input variables. C Compiled statement was bound successfully using defaults. D Interpretive statement will be interpreted at execution time; usually DDL. E EXPLAIN. F Parsed statement not bound successfully; VALIDATE(RUN) was used. The statement will be parsed and executed at the server using values for input variables.

G	Compiled statement was bound successfully with REOPT specified. The statement will be parsed and executed at the server using defaults for input variables.
I	Indefinite; statement is dynamic. The statement will be parsed and executed at the server using defaults for input variables.
J	Indefinite; statement is dynamic. The statement will be parsed and executed at the server using values for input variables.
K	CALL statement.
L	Error in statement.
blank	Non-executable statement, or was bound prior to V5.

SYSIBM.SYSPKSYSTEM

SYSIBM.SYSPKSYSTEM contains the systems (for example, CICS or IMS/DC) that have been enabled or disabled for specific packages.

Tablespace	DSNDB06.SYSPKAGE
Index	DSNKYX01 [nonunique] (LOCATION, COLLID, NAME, CONTOKEN, SYSTEM, ENABLE)
Links	DSNKK@KY REFERENCES SYSIBM.SYSPACKAGE

Column Definitions

LOCATION	The location of the package.
COLLID	The name of the collection.
NAME	The name of the package.
CONTOKEN	The consistency token for the package.
SYSTEM	A value indicating the environment that will be disabled or enabled. Valid values are as follow:

BATCH	TSO Batch
CICS	CICS
DB2CALL	Call Attach Facility
DLIBATCH	DL/I Batch (IMS)
IMSBMP	IMS/DC BMP
IMSMPP	IMS/DC MPP
REMOTE	Remote package

`ENABLE`	An indicator specifying `Y` if the row will enable access, or `N` if it will disable access.
`CNAME`	A name identifying the connection or connections to which this row is applicable.
`IBMREQD`	An indicator specifying `Y` if the row was supplied by IBM, or `N` if it was not.

SYSIBM.SYSPLAN

`SYSIBM.SYSPLAN` contains information on every plan known to DB2. The plan name is unique in the DB2 subsystem.

Tablespace	`DSNDB06.SYSPLAN`
Index	`DSNPPH01` `[unique]` `(NAME)`
Links	None

Column Definitions

`NAME`	The plan name.
`CREATOR`	The owner of the plan named in `NAME`.
`BINDDATE`	The date (*yymmdd*) when the plan was bound.
`VALIDATE`	`B` if validity checking is performed at bind time, or `R` if checking is performed at runtime.
`ISOLATION`	Isolation level for the plan: `R` Repeatable Read `S` Cursor Stability `T` Read Stability `U` Uncommitted Read
`VALID`	An indicator specifying the state of the plan: `A` An object upon which the plan depends has been altered; rebind not required. `H` The table (or base table of a view) was `ALTER`ed. The change invalidates the plan. `N` The plan must first be rebound. `Y` The plan can be run without rebinding.
`OPERATIVE`	`Y` if the plan can be allocated, or `N` if it cannot.
`BINDTIME`	The time (*hhmmssth*) that the plan was bound.

PLSIZE	The number of bytes in the base section of the plan.
IBMREQD	An indicator specifying whether the row was supplied by IBM: Y Yes, row was supplied by IBM. N No. B No; V1.3 dependent. C No; V2.1 dependent. D No; V2.2 dependent. E No; V2.3 dependent. F No; V3 dependent. G No; V4 dependent. H No; V5 dependent.
AVGSIZE	The average number of bytes for the non-base sections of the plan.
ACQUIRE	An indicator specifying when resources for this plan will be acquired: A All resources are acquired when the plan is allocated. U Resources are not acquired until they are used by the plan.
RELEASE	An indicator specifying when resources for this plan will be released: C Resources are released at each COMMIT point. D Resources are not released until the plan is deallocated.
EXREFERENCE	Not currently used.
EXSTRUCTURE	Not currently used.
EXCOST	Not currently used.
EXPLAN	Y if the plan was bound specifying EXPLAIN YES, or N if it was bound specifying EXPLAIN NO.
EXPREDICATE	Not currently used.
BOUNDBY	The primary authorization ID of the individual who bound this plan.
QUALIFIER	A qualifier specified to be used for all tables, views, synonyms, and aliases referenced in the program.
CACHESIZE	The size of the cache to be acquired for the named plan.
PLENTRIES	The number of package list entries (from SYSIBM.SYSPKLIST) for this plan.

DEFERPREP	Y if the plan was bound specifying DEFER(PREPARE), or N if it was bound specifying NODEFER(PREPARE).
CURRENTSERVER	The location name of the current server.
SYSENTRIES	The number of enabled/disabled entries for this plan (as recorded in SYSIBM.SYSPLSYSTEM).
DEGREE	The degree of parallelism chosen for this plan: ANY Bound as DEGREE(ANY). 1 Bound as DEGREE(1) or default. *blank* Migrated from a prior release.
SQLRULES	Valid values are as follow: D Bound as SQLRULES(DB2). S Bound as SQLRULES(STD). *blank* Migrated from a prior release.
DISCONNECT	Valid values are as follow: A Bound DISCONNECT(AUTOMATIC). C Bound DISCONNECT(CONDITIONAL). E Bound DISCONNECT(EXPLICIT). *blank* Migrated from a prior release.
GROUP_MEMBER	The DB2 data-sharing member name of the DB2 subsystem that performed the most recent bind for this plan; or blank if DB2 subsystem was not in a DB2 data-sharing environment when the bind was performed.
DYNAMICRULES	Indicates dynamic SQL treatment: S Dynamic SQL statements are handled like static SQL statements at runtime. *blank* Dynamic statements are handled like dynamic SQL statements at runtime.
BOUNDTS	Date and time the plan was bound.
REOPTVAR	Indicator specifying whether access path is to be determined again at runtime using explicit values for host variables or parameter markers. Valid values are as follows: N No, access path determined at bind time. Y Yes, access path may be redetermined at runtime.
KEEPDYNAMIC	Indicator specifying whether dynamic statements are to be kept past a commit point. Y = yes; N = no.

SYSIBM.SYSPLANAUTH

SYSIBM.SYSPLANAUTH contains the plan privileges (BIND and EXECUTE authorities) held by DB2 users.

Tablespace	DSNDB06.SYSPLAN
Index	DSNAPH01 [nonunique]
	(GRANTEE, NAME, EXECUTEAUTH)
Index	DSNAPX01 [nonunique]
	(GRANTOR)
Links	DSNPP#AP REFERENCES SYSIBM.SYSPLAN

Column Definitions

GRANTOR	The authid of the user who granted the privileges described in this row.
GRANTEE	The authid of the user who possesses the privileges described in this row, the name of a plan that uses the privileges, or the literal PUBLIC to indicate that all users have these privileges.
NAME	The name of the plan.
TIMESTAMP	The date and time (in the internal format) when the privileges were granted.
DATEGRANTED	The date (*yymmdd*) that authority was granted.
TIMEGRANTED	The time (*hhmmssth*) that authority was granted.
GRANTEETYPE	Not currently used.
AUTHHOWGOT	The authorization level of the GRANTOR: C DBCTRL D DBADM L SYSCTRL M DBMAINT S SYSADM *blank* Not applicable
BINDAUTH	The privilege to BIND or REBIND the named plan: G GRANTEE holds the privilege and can grant it to others. Y GRANTEE holds the privilege. *blank* GRANTEE does not hold the privilege.

EXECUTEAUTH	The privilege to execute the named plan: G GRANTEE holds the privilege and can grant it to others. Y GRANTEE holds the privilege. *blank* GRANTEE does not hold the privilege.
IBMREQD	An indicator specifying Y if the row was supplied by IBM, or N if it was not.
GRANTEDTS	Time the GRANT was executed.

SYSIBM.SYSPLANDEP

SYSIBM.SYSPLANDEP contains a cross-reference of DB2 objects used by each plan known to the DB2 subsystem.

Tablespace	DSNDB06.SYSPLAN
Index	DSNGGX01 [nonunique] (BCREATOR, BNAME, BTYPE)
Links	DSNPP#PU REFERENCES SYSIBM.SYSPLAN

Column Definitions

BNAME	The name of the object upon which the plan depends.
BCREATOR	A qualifier for the object named in BNAME. If BTYPE is equal to R, BCREATOR is a database name; otherwise, it is the owner of the object named in BNAME.
BTYPE	Type of object named in BNAME: A Alias I Index P Partitioned Tablespace R Tablespace S Synonym T Table V View
DNAME	The name of the plan.
IBMREQD	An indicator specifying Y if the row was supplied by IBM, or N if it was not.

SYSIBM.SYSPLSYSTEM

SYSIBM.SYSPLSYSTEM contains the systems (for example, CICS or IMS/DC) that have been enabled or disabled for specific plans.

Tablespace	DSNDB06.SYSPKAGE
Index	DSNKPX01[nonunique]
	(NAME, SYSTEM, ENABLE)
Links	DSNPP@KP REFERENCES SYSIBM.SYSPLAN

Column Definitions

NAME — The name of the plan.

SYSTEM — A value indicating the environment that will be disabled or enabled. Valid values are as follow:

BATCH	TSO Batch
CICS	CICS
DB2CALL	Call Attach Facility
DLIBATCH	DL/I Batch (IMS)
IMSBMP	IMS/DC BMP
IMSMPP	IMS/DC MPP
REMOTE	Remote package

ENABLE — An indicator specifying Y if the row will enable access, or N if it will disable access.

CNAME — The name identifying the connection or connections to which this row is applicable. Blank if SYSTEM=BATCH or SYSTEM=DB2CALL.

IBMREQD — An indicator specifying Y if the row was supplied by IBM, or N if it was not.

SYSIBM.SYSPROCEDURES

SYSIBM.SYSPROCEDURES contains one row for each DB2 stored procedure. This table differs from most other DB2 Catalog tables in that rows must be explicitly inserted, updated, and deleted from this table by the DBA (instead of implicitly by DB2 when a DCL or DDL statement is issued).

Tablespace	DSNDB06.SYSPKAGE
Index	DSNKCX01[unique]
	(PROCEDURE, AUTHID DESC,LUNAME DESC)
Links	None

Column Definitions

PROCEDURE	The name of the stored procedure.
AUTHID	The authid of the user running the SQL application that issued the CALL. If blank, applies to all authids.
LUNAME	The LUNAME of the system that issued the CALL. If blank, applies to all systems.
LOADMOD	The MVS load module to use for this stored procedure.
LINKAGE	The linkage convention used for passing parameters to the stored procedure: N SIMPLE WITH NULLS *blank* SIMPLE (input parameters cannot be null)
COLLID	Collection ID of the package for this stored procedure.
LANGUAGE	Programming language used. Valid values are ASSEMBLE, PLI, COBOL, or C.
ASUTIME	Specifies the number of service units permitted before an execution of the stored procedure is canceled.
STAYRESIDENT	Indicates whether the module is to remain in memory after the stored procedure finishes execution: Y Load module remains resident when stored procedure ends. *blank* Load module is removed from memory when stored procedure ends.
IBMREQD	An indicator specifying Y if the row was supplied by IBM, or N if it was not.
RUNOPTS	Specified the LE/370 runtime options to be used by this stored procedure.
PARMLIST	The list of parameters expected by this stored procedure.
RESULT_SETS	Maximum number of query result sets that can be returned by this procedure.
WLM_ENV	Name of the WLM environment used to run this procedure. A blank indicates that the procedure is to run in the DB2-established SPAS.
PGM_TYPE	Indicates whether the stored procedure is a main routine (M) or a subroutine (S).

EXTERNAL_SECURITY	Indicates whether a special RACF environment is needed to control access to non-SQL resources. Values are as follow: N Not required Y Required
COMMIT_ON_RETURN	Indicator specifying whether work is to be committed upon successful completion of the stored procedure. Valid values are as follow: N Do not commit; continue UOW Y Commit null Same as N

SYSIBM.SYSRELS

SYSIBM.SYSRELS contains information on the foreign key and link relationships for all DB2 tables.

Tablespace	DSNDB06.SYSDBASE
Index	DSNDLX01[nonunique] (REFTBCREATOR, REFTBNAME)
Links	DSNDT#DR REFERENCES SYSIBM.SYSTABLES DSNDT@DR REFERENCES SYSIBM.SYSTABLES

Column Definitions

CREATOR	The owner of the dependent table named in TBNAME.
TBNAME	The dependent table name.
RELNAME	The referential constraint name.
REFTBNAME	The parent table name.
REFTBCREATOR	The owner of the parent table named in REFTBNAME.
COLCOUNT	The number of columns defined for this referential constraint.
DELETERULE	The referential DELETE RULE specified for this constraint: A NO ACTION C CASCADE N SET NULL R RESTRICT
IBMREQD	An indicator specifying Y if the row was supplied by IBM, or N if it was not.
RELOBID1	An internal object identifier for the parent table.

RELOBID2	An internal object identifier for the dependent table.
TIMESTAMP	A DB2 timestamp indicating the date and time that the referential constraint was defined.
IXOWNER	Owner of the unique non-primary key used as the parent key.
IXNAME	Name of the unique non-primary key used as the parent key.

SYSIBM.SYSRESAUTH

SYSIBM.SYSRESAUTH contains privileges held by DB2 users over DB2 resources.

Tablespace	DSNDB06.SYSGPAUT
Index	DSNAGH01[nonunique]
	(GRANTEE, QUALIFIER, NAME, OBTYPE)
Index	DSNAGX01[nonunique]
	(GRANTOR, QUALIFIER, NAME, OBTYPE)
Links	None

Column Definitions

GRANTOR	The authid of the user who granted the privileges described in this row.
GRANTEE	The authid of the user who possesses the privileges described in this row, the name of a plan that uses the privileges, or the literal PUBLIC to indicate that all users have these privileges.
QUALIFIER	If this row defines a privilege for a tablespace, this column is the name of the database in which this tablespace resides; otherwise, it is blank.
NAME	The name of the resource for which the privilege has been granted. This is the name of a bufferpool, a storage group, or a tablespace.
GRANTEETYPE	Not currently used.
AUTHHOWGOT	The authorization level of the GRANTOR:

C	DBCTRL
D	DBADM
L	SYSCTRL
M	DBMAINT
S	SYSADM
blank	Not applicable

OBTYPE	The type of object defined in this row: B Bufferpool S STOGROUP R Tablespace
TIMESTAMP	The date and time (in the internal format) when the privileges were granted.
DATEGRANTED	The date (*yymmdd*) that authority was granted.
TIMEGRANTED	The time (*hhmmssth*) that authority was granted.
USEAUTH	The privilege to use the resource named in NAME: G GRANTEE holds the privilege and can grant it to others. Y GRANTEE holds the privilege.
IBMREQD	An indicator specifying Y if the row was supplied by IBM, or N if it was not.
GRANTEDTS	Time the GRANT was executed.

SYSIBM.SYSSTMT

SYSIBM.SYSSTMT contains the SQL statements for every plan known to DB2.

Tablespace	DSNDB06.SYSPLAN
Indexes	None
Links	DSNPD#PS REFERENCES SYSIBM.SYSDBRM

Column Definitions

NAME	The DBRM name.
PLNAME	The plan name.
PLCREATOR	The owner of the plan named in PLNAME.
SEQNO	The sequence number used to identify SQL statements that span multiple rows of this table.
STMTNO	The statement number for the SQL statement as stored in the source for the application program.
SECTNO	The DBRM section number.
IBMREQD	An indicator specifying Y if the row was supplied by IBM, or N if it was not.
TEXT	Up to 254 characters of the SQL statement text. For SQL statements that comprise more than 254 characters, multiple rows with ascending SEQNO values exist.

ISOLATION	Isolation level for the SQL statement:	
	L	RS with KEEP UPDATE LOCKS.
	R	Repeatable Read.
	S	Cursor Stability.
	T	Read Stability.
	U	Uncommitted Read.
	X	RR with KEEP UPDATE LOCKS.
	blank	WITH clause not specified; isolation level defaults to plan isolation level.
STATUS	Indicator specifying the status of the bind. Valid values are as follow:	
	A	Distributed statement uses DB2 private protocol; statement will be parsed and executed at the server using defaults for input variables.
	B	Distributed statement uses DB2 private protocol; statement will be parsed and executed at the server using values for input variables.
	C	Compiled statement was bound successfully using defaults.
	D	Interpretive statement will be interpreted at execution time; usually DDL.
	E	EXPLAIN.
	F	Parsed statement not bound successfully; VALIDATE(RUN) was used. The statement will be parsed and executed at the server using values for input variables.
	G	Compiled statement was bound successfully with REOPT specified. The statement will be parsed and executed at the server using defaults for input variables.
	I	Indefinite; statement is dynamic. The statement will be parsed and executed at the server using defaults for input variables.
	J	Indefinite; statement is dynamic. The statement will be parsed and executed at the server using values for input variables.
	K	CALL statement.
	L	Error in statement.
	blank	Non-executable statement, or was bound prior to V5.

SYSIBM.SYSSTOGROUP

SYSIBM.SYSSTOGROUP contains information on DB2 storage groups.

Tablespace	DSNDB06.SYSGROUP
Indexes	DSNSSH01[unique] (NAME)
Links	None

Column Definitions

NAME	The storage group name.
CREATOR	The owner of the storage group named in NAME.
VCATNAME	The name of the VCAT specified to the STOGROUP when it was created.
VPASSWORD	The ICF catalog password; if no password is used, this column is blank.
SPACE	The DASD space allocated for data sets defined to this storage group. If STOSPACE has not been run, this column contains 0.
SPCDATE	The Julian date (*yyddd*) indicating the last execution of the STOSPACE utility.
IBMREQD	An indicator specifying Y if the row was supplied by IBM, or N if it was not.
CREATEDBY	The primary authorization ID of the individual who created this STOGROUP.
STATSTIME	Not used.
CREATEDTS	The date and time when the storage group was created.
ALTEREDTS	The date and time of the last ALTER for this storage group. ALTEREDTS equals CREATEDTS when no ALTER has been issued.

SYSIBM.SYSSTRINGS

SYSIBM.SYSSTRINGS contains information on converting from one coded character set to another.

Tablespace	DSNDB06.SYSSTR
Index	DSNSSX01[unique] (OUTCCSID, INCCSID, IBMREQD)
Links	None

Column Definitions

INCCSID	An input-coded character set identifier.
OUTCCSID	An output-coded character set identifier.
TRANSTYPE	An indicator specifying the nature of the conversion.
ERRORBYTE	An error byte for the translation table stored in TRANSTAB.
SUBBYTE	The substitution character for the TRANSTAB.
TRANSPROC	The name of the translation procedure module.
IBMREQD	An indicator specifying Y if the row was supplied by IBM, or N if it was not.
TRANSTAB	The coded character set translation table (or any empty string).

SYSIBM.SYSSYNONYMS

SYSIBM.SYSSYNONYMS contains information on DB2 synonyms.

Tablespace	DSNDB06.SYSDBASE
Index	DSNDYX01[unique]
	(CREATOR, NAME)
Links	DSNDT#DY REFERENCES SYSIBM.SYSTABLES

Column Definitions

NAME	The synonym name.
CREATOR	The owner of the synonym named in NAME.
TBNAME	The table name on which the synonym is based.
TBCREATOR	The owner of the table named in TBNAME.
IBMREQD	An indicator specifying Y if the row was supplied by IBM, or N if it was not.
CREATEDBY	The primary authorization ID of the individual who created this synonym.
CREATEDTS	The date and time when the synonym was created.

SYSIBM.SYSTABAUTH

SYSIBM.SYSTABAUTH contains information on the table privileges held by DB2 users.

Tablespace	DSNDB06.SYSDBASE
Index	DSNATX01[nonunique]
	(GRANTOR)

Index DSNATX02[nonunique]
(GRANTEE, TCREATOR, TTNAME, GRANTEETYPE, UPDATECOLS, ALTERAUTH, DELETEAUTH, INDEXAUTH, INSERTAUTH, SELECTAUTH, UPDATEAUTH, CAPTUREAUTH, REFERENCEAUTH, REFCOLS)

Index DSNATX03[unique]
(GRANTEE, GRANTEETYPE, COLLID, CONTOKEN)

Links DSNDT#AT REFERENCES SYSIBM.SYSTABLES

Column Definitions

GRANTOR — The authid of the user who granted the privileges described in this row.

GRANTEE — The authid of the user who possesses the privileges described in this row, the name of a plan that uses the privileges, the literal PUBLIC to indicate that all users have these privileges, or the literal PUBLIC* to indicate that all users at all distributed locations hold these privileges.

GRANTEETYPE — A value indicating the type of GRANTEE:

- P — GRANTEE is a plan or package.
- *blank* — GRANTEE is a userid.

DBNAME — The database name over which the GRANTOR possesses DBADM, DBCTRL, or DBMAINT authority, if this privilege was granted by a user with this type of authority. Otherwise, the column is blank.

SCREATOR — For views, SCREATOR contains the owner of the view named in STNAME. If the row defines a table and not a view, SCREATOR is equal to TCREATOR.

STNAME — For views, STNAME contains the view name. If the row defines a table and not a view, STNAME is equal to TTNAME.

TCREATOR — The owner of the table or view named in TTNAME.

TTNAME — The table or view name.

AUTHHOWGOT — The authorization level of the GRANTOR:

- C — DBCTRL
- D — DBADM
- L — SYSCTRL

	M DBMAINT
	S SYSADM
	blank Not applicable
TIMESTAMP	The date and time (in the internal format) when the privileges were granted.
DATEGRANTED	The date (*yymmdd*) that authority was granted.
TIMEGRANTED	The time (*hhmmssth*) that authority was granted.
UPDATECOLS	If the UPDATEAUTH column applies to all columns in this table, UPDATECOLS is blank. Otherwise, this column contains an asterisk (*), indicating that the value of UPDATEAUTH applies to some columns but not all. SYSIBM.SYSCOLAUTH contains details in which PRIVILEGE = blank.
ALTERAUTH	The privilege to alter the named table: G GRANTEE holds the privilege and can grant it to others. Y GRANTEE holds the privilege. *blank* GRANTEE does not hold the privilege.
DELETEAUTH	The privilege to delete rows from the named table: G GRANTEE holds the privilege and can grant it to others. Y GRANTEE holds the privilege. *blank* GRANTEE does not hold the privilege.
INDEXAUTH	The privilege to create indexes for the named table: G GRANTEE holds the privilege and can grant it to others. Y GRANTEE holds the privilege. *blank* GRANTEE does not hold the privilege.
INSERTAUTH	The privilege to insert rows into the named table: G GRANTEE holds the privilege and can grant it to others. Y GRANTEE holds the privilege. *blank* GRANTEE does not hold the privilege.
SELECTAUTH	The privilege to select rows from the named table: G GRANTEE holds the privilege and can grant it to others. Y GRANTEE holds the privilege. *blank* GRANTEE does not hold the privilege.
UPDATEAUTH	The privilege to update rows in the named table: G GRANTEE holds the privilege and can grant it to others. Y GRANTEE holds the privilege. *blank* GRANTEE does not hold the privilege.

IBMREQD	An indicator specifying Y if the row was supplied by IBM, or N if it was not.
GRANTEELOCATION	Not currently used.
LOCATION	Not currently used.
COLLID	The package location (if the privilege was granted by a package).
CONTOKEN	The consistency token for the package (if the privilege was granted by a package).
CAPTUREAUTH	Not currently used.
REFERENCESAUTH	An indicator specifying whether the GRANTEE can create or drop referential constraints in which the table is a parent: *blank* No G Yes, WITH GRANT OPTION Y Yes
REFCOLS	If the REFERENCESAUTH column applies to all columns in this table, REFCOLS is blank. Otherwise, this column contains an asterisk (*), indicating that the value of REFERENCESAUTH applies to some columns but not all. SYSIBM.SYSCOLAUTH contains details in which PRIVILEGE = "R".
GRANTEDTS	Time the GRANT was executed.

SYSIBM.SYSTABLEPART

SYSIBM.SYSTABLEPART contains information on tablespace partitions and the physical storage characteristics of DB2 tablespaces.

Tablespace	DSNDB06.SYSDBASE
Index	DSNDPX01[unique] (DBNAME, TSNAME, PARTITION)
Links	DSNDS#DP REFERENCES SYSIBM.SYSTABLESPACE

Column Definitions

PARTITION	The partition number for partitioned tablespaces, or 0 for simple and segmented tablespaces (that is, not partitioned).
TSNAME	The tablespace name.
DBNAME	The database name.
IXNAME	The partitioned index name, or blank for simple and segmented tablespaces.

IXCREATOR	The owner of the index named in IXNAME.
PQTY	The primary space quantity, in 4KB pages, specified when the tablespace was created.
SQTY	The secondary space quantity, in 4KB pages, specified when the tablespace was created.
STORTYPE	E for explicit VCAT-defined tablespaces, or I for implicit STOGROUP-defined tablespaces.
STORNAME	The storage group name for STOGROUP-defined tablespaces; a VCAT identifier for VCAT-defined tablespaces.
VCATNAME	The name of the VCAT used to allocate the tablespace, regardless of how the tablespace was defined (STOGROUP or VCAT).
CARD	The number of rows contained in this tablespace or partition, or -1 if RUNSTATS has not been run.
FARINDREF	A value indicating the number of rows relocated far from their initial page.
NEARINDREF	A value indicating the number of rows relocated near to their initial page.
PERCACTIVE	A percentage indicating the amount of space utilized by active tables in this tablespace partition.
PERCDROP	A percentage indicating the amount of space utilized by dropped tables in this tablespace partition.
IBMREQD	An indicator specifying Y if the row was supplied by IBM, or N if it was not.
LIMITKEY	The high key value used to limit partitioned tablespaces, or 0 if the tablespace is not partitioned.
FREEPAGE	The number of consecutive pages to be loaded before loading a blank page, or 0 for no free pages.
PCTFREE	The percentage of each page to leave free at load time.
CHECKFLAG	C if the tablespace partition is in check pending status, or blank if it is not. May have been caused by referential constraint violations, check constraint violations, or both.
CHECKRID	For DB2 V4 and prior releases, a blank if the tablespace partition is not in check pending status or if the tablespace is simple or segmented. Otherwise, contains the RID of the first row that can contain a referential constraint violation, a check constraint violation, or both; or the value X'00000000' to indicate that any row may be in violation. (Not used as of DB2 V5.)

SPACE	The DASD space, in KB, allocated for the tablespace partition. If STOSPACE has not been run, this column contains 0.
COMPRESS	Indicates whether compression has been specified in the DDL. Contains Y if compression is defined, blank if not.
PAGESAVE	Percentage of pages (multiplied by 100) saved by specifying compression. Takes overhead, free space, and dictionary pages into account.
STATSTIME	Timestamp indicating the date and time that RUNSTATS was executed for the named tablespace partition.
GBPCACHE	Group bufferpool cache option used: *blank* Only changed pages are cached. A Changed and unchanged pages are cached in the group bufferpool.
CARDF	The number of rows contained in this table, or -1 for temp tables, views, aliases, or if RUNSTATS has not been run.
CHECKRID5B	Blank if the table or partition is not in a check pending state, or if the tablespace is not partitioned; otherwise, it contains the RID of the first row that can violate referential and/or check constraints.

SYSIBM.SYSTABLES

SYSIBM.SYSTABLES contains information on every table known to the DB2 subsystem.

Tablespace	DSNDB06.SYSDBASE
Index	DSNDTX01[unique] (CREATOR, NAME)
Index	DSNDTX02[unique] (DBID, OBID, CREATOR, NAME)
Links	DSNDS#DT REFERENCES SYSIBM.SYSTABLESPACE

Column Definitions

NAME	The table name.
CREATOR	The owner of the table, view, or alias named in NAME.
TYPE	Indicator specifying the table type. Valid values are as follow: A Alias G Temporary table T Table V View

DBNAME	The name of the database associated with the tablespace named in TSNAME; for an alias, temp table, or view, the value is always DSNDB06.
TSNAME	The name of the tablespace in which the table was created; if the row defines a view based on tables, the value is the name of the tablespace for one of the tables. If the row defines a temporary table, the value is SYSPKAGE. If the row defines a view based on other views, the value is SYSVIEWS. If the row defines an alias, the value is SYSDBAUT.
DBID	The internal database identifier; 0 for a view, temp table, or alias.
OBID	The internal object identifier assigned to this table by DB2; 0 for a view, temp table, or alias.
COLCOUNT	The number of columns defined for this table.
EDPROC	The name of the EDITPROC used by the table, if any; always blank for aliases and views.
VALPROC	The name of the VALIDPROC used by the table, if any; always blank for aliases and views.
CLUSTERTYPE	Indicator describing whether RESTRICT ON DROP is specified: *blank* No Y Yes
CLUSTERRID	Not currently used.
CARD	For DB2 V4 and prior releases, the number of rows contained in this table, or -1 for temp tables, views, aliases, or if RUNSTATS has not been run. (Not used as of DB2 V5.)
NPAGES	The number of tablespace pages that contain rows for this table, or -1 for temp tables, views, aliases, or if RUNSTATS has not been run.
PCTPAGES	The percentage of tablespace pages that contain rows for this table, or -1 for a temp table, view, or alias, or if RUNSTATS has not run.
IBMREQD	An indicator specifying whether the row was supplied by IBM: Y Yes, row was supplied by IBM. N No. B No; V1.3 dependent. C No; V2.1 dependent. D No; V2.2 dependent.

	E No; V2.3 dependent.
	F No; V3 dependent.
	G No; V4 dependent.
	H No; V5 dependent.
REMARKS	The table comments as specified by the COMMENT ON statement.
PARENTS	The number of referential constraints in which this table is a dependent table, or 0 for temp tables, views, and aliases.
CHILDREN	The number of referential constraints in which this table is a parent table, or 0 for temp tables, views, and aliases.
KEYCOLUMNS	The number of columns in this table's primary key, or 0 for temp tables, views, and aliases.
RECLENGTH	A value indicating the absolute maximum length for any row of this table.
STATUS	An indicator representing the status of this table's primary key situation: I Primary key incomplete because a parent index is not yet created for the key. X Parent index exists for this table's primary key. *blank* No parent index defined, or row defines a temp table, view, or alias.
KEYOBID	The internal object identifier assigned to this table's primary key by DB2.
LABEL	A label as specified by the LABEL ON statement.
CHECKFLAG	C if the tablespace containing the table is in check pending status, or blank if it is not. May have been caused by referential constraint violations, check constraint violations, or both.
CHECKRID	For DB2 V4 and prior releases, this column is blank if the table is not in check pending status, if the tablespace is partitioned, or if the row describes an alias or view. Otherwise, contains the RID of the first row that can contain a referential constraint violation, a check constraint violation, or both; or the value X'00000000' to indicate that any row may be in violation. (Not used as of DB2 V5.)
AUDITING	An indicator specifying the auditing option for the named table: A AUDIT ALL C AUDIT CHANGE *blank* AUDIT NONE, or row defines a temp table, view, or alias

CREATEDBY	The primary authorization ID of the individual who created this table.
LOCATION	The location name for an alias defined for a remote table or view. Otherwise, this column is blank.
TBCREATOR	For aliases, contains the owner of the table named in TBNAME.
TBNAME	For aliases, contains the table name on which the alias is based.
CREATEDTS	The date and time when the table, view, or alias was created.
ALTEREDTS	For tables, ALTEREDTS indicates the date and time when the table was altered. If the table has not been altered, or the row defines a view or alias, this column equals the value of CREATEDTS.
DATACAPTURE	Records the value of the DATA CAPTURE option: Y Yes *blank* No (always blank for temp table)
RBA1	The log RBA when the table was created.
RBA2	The log RBA when the table was last altered.
PCTROWCOMP	Percentage of active table rows compressed; or -1 if RUNSTATS was not executed or the row is for a temp table, view, or alias.
STATSTIME	Timestamp indicating the date and time that RUNSTATS was executed for the named table.
CHECKS	The number of check constraints defined on the table; 0 if no check constraints are defined or if the row describes a temp table, view, or alias.
CHECKRID5B	Blank if the table or partition is not in a check pending state, or if the tablespace is not partitioned; otherwise, it contains the RID of the first row that can violate referential and/or check constraints.
ENCODING_SCHEME	Default encoding scheme for the database. Valid values are as follow: A ASCII E EBCDIC *blank* For remote aliases

SYSIBM.SYSTABLESPACE

SYSIBM.SYSTABLESPACE contains information on every tablespace known to the DB2 subsystem.

Tablespace	DSNDB06.SYSDBASE
Index	DSNDSX01[unique] (DBNAME, NAME)
Links	None

Column Definitions

NAME	The tablespace name.
CREATOR	The owner of the tablespace named in NAME.
DBNAME	The database name.
DBID	The internal database identifier.
OBID	The internal object identifier assigned to this tablespace by DB2.
PSID	The internal page set identifier assigned to this tablespace by DB2.
BPOOL	The bufferpool name specified when this tablespace was created.
PARTITIONS	The number of partitions for a partitioned tablespace; 0 for segmented and simple tablespaces.
LOCKRULE	An indicator specifying the LOCKSIZE parameter for the tablespace: A ANY P PAGE R ROW S TABLESPACE T TABLE
PGSIZE	The size of the tablespace pages, in bytes. Can be 4K or 32K.
ERASERULE	Y if the tablespace was created with the ERASE YES option, or N if it was created specifying ERASE NO.
STATUS	An indicator specifying the current status of the tablespace: A Available. C Definition incomplete, no partitioning index defined.

	P	Check pending for entire tablespace.
	S	Check pending for less than the entire tablespace.
	T	Definition incomplete; no table yet created.
IMPLICIT	Y if the tablespace was created implicitly, or N if it was not.	
NTABLES	The number of tables defined for this tablespace.	
NACTIVE	The number of active pages for this tablespace. A page is active if it is formatted (even if it contains no rows).	
DSETPASS	The index data set password; only for indexes created using a STOGROUP.	
CLOSERULE	Y if the tablespace was created with the CLOSE YES option, or N if it was created specifying CLOSE NO.	
SPACE	The space in kilobytes allocated for this tablespace; 0 if STOSPACE has not been run, or for tablespaces not created using a STOGROUP.	
IBMREQD	An indicator specifying Y if the row was supplied by IBM, or N if it was not. Additional values are used for the IBMREQD column in this table indicating specific DB2 version/release dependencies:	
	C	V2R1
	F	V3R1
	H	V5R1
ROOTNAME	Internal DB2 use only.	
ROOTCREATOR	Internal DB2 use only.	
SEGSIZE	The number of pages per segment for segmented tablespaces; 0 for simple or partitioned tablespaces.	
CREATEDBY	The primary authorization ID of the individual who created this tablespace.	
STATSTIME	Timestamp indicating the date and time that RUNSTATS was executed for the named tablespace.	
LOCKMAX	Maximum number of locks per user or tablespace before lock escalation occurs:	
	0	No lock escalation.
	n	The maximum number of locks before lock escalation occurs.
	-1	Use LOCKMAX SYSTEM.

TYPE — Indicator specifying whether tablespace is large. Valid values are as follow:

L	Large
blank	Not large

CREATEDTS — The date and time when the tablespace was created.

ALTEREDTS — The date and time of the last ALTER for this tablespace. ALTEREDTS equals CREATEDTS when no ALTER has been issued.

ENCODING_SCHEME — Default encoding scheme for the database. Valid values are as follow:

A	ASCII
E	EBCDIC
blank	For DSNDB04 and work files

SBCS_CCSID — Default SBCS CCSID.

DBCS_CCSID — Default DBCS CCSID.

MIXED_CCSID — Default mixed CCSID.

MAXROWS — Maximum number of rows per page.

LOCKPART — Indicator specifying whether selective partition locking is used. Valid values are as follow:

Y	LOCKPART YES
blank	LOCKPART NO (or not partitioned)

SYSIBM.SYSTABSTATS

SYSIBM.SYSTABSTATS contains one row of partition-level statistics for each tablespace partition.

Tablespace	DSNDB06.SYSSTATS
Index	DSNTTX01[unique]
	(OWNER, NAME, PARTITION)
Relationship	DSNDT@TT REFERENCES SYSIBM.SYSTABLES

Column Definitions

CARD — The number of rows contained in this partition.

NPAGES — The number of tablespace pages on which rows of the partition appear.

PCTPAGES — The percentage of tablespace pages that contain rows for this partition.

NACTIVE — The number of active pages for this tablespace partition.

PCTROWCOMP	Percentage of active rows compressed in the partition.
STATSTIME	Timestamp indicating the date and time that RUNSTATS was executed to produce this row.
IBMREQD	An indicator specifying Y if the row was supplied by IBM, or N if it was not.
DBNAME	The database name containing the tablespace.
TSNAME	The tablespace name to which this statistical row applies.
PARTITION	The partition number indicating the physical partition to which this statistical row applies.
OWNER	The owner of the table named in NAME.
NAME	The table name to which this statistical row applies.

SYSIBM.SYSUSERAUTH

SYSIBM.SYSUSERAUTH contains information on system privileges held by DB2 users.

Tablespace	DSNDB06.SYSUSER
Index	DSNAUH01[nonunique] (GRANTEE)
Index	DSNAUX01[nonunique] (GRANTOR)
Links	None

Column Definitions

GRANTOR	The authid of the user who granted the privileges described in this row.
GRANTEE	The authid of the user who possesses the privileges described in this row, the name of a plan that uses the privileges, or the literal PUBLIC to indicate that all users have these privileges.
TIMESTAMP	The date and time (in the internal format) when the privileges were granted.
DATEGRANTED	The date (*yymmdd*) that authority was granted.
TIMEGRANTED	The time (*hhmmssth*) that authority was granted.
GRANTEETYPE	Not currently used.
AUTHHOWGOT	The authorization level of the GRANTOR: C DBCTRL D DBADM

	L	SYSCTRL
	M	DBMAINT
	S	SYSADM
	blank	Not applicable
ALTERBPAUTH	Not currently used.	
BINDADDAUTH	The privilege to issue the BIND ADD command:	
	G	GRANTEE holds the privilege and can grant it to others.
	Y	GRANTEE holds the privilege.
	blank	GRANTEE does not hold the privilege.
BSDSAUTH	The privilege to issue the -RECOVER BSDS command:	
	G	GRANTEE holds the privilege and can grant it to others.
	Y	GRANTEE holds the privilege.
	blank	GRANTEE does not hold the privilege.
CREATEDBAAUTH	The privilege to create databases resulting in the creator obtaining DBADM over the new database:	
	G	GRANTEE holds the privilege and can grant it to others.
	Y	GRANTEE holds the privilege.
	blank	GRANTEE does not hold the privilege.
CREATEDBCAUTH	The privilege to create databases resulting in the creator obtaining DBCTRL over the new database:	
	G	GRANTEE holds the privilege and can grant it to others.
	Y	GRANTEE holds the privilege.
	blank	GRANTEE does not hold the privilege.
CREATESGAUTH	The privilege to create STOGROUPs:	
	G	GRANTEE holds the privilege and can grant it to others.
	Y	GRANTEE holds the privilege.
	blank	GRANTEE does not hold the privilege.
DISPLAYAUTH	The privilege to issue -DISPLAY commands:	
	G	GRANTEE holds the privilege and can grant it to others.
	Y	GRANTEE holds the privilege.
	blank	GRANTEE does not hold the privilege.
RECOVERAUTH	The privilege to issue the -RECOVER INDOUBT command:	
	G	GRANTEE holds the privilege and can grant it to others.
	Y	GRANTEE holds the privilege.
	blank	GRANTEE does not hold the privilege.

STOPALLAUTH	The privilege to issue the -STOP DB2 command:	
	G	GRANTEE holds the privilege and can grant it to others.
	Y	GRANTEE holds the privilege.
	blank	GRANTEE does not hold the privilege.
STOSPACEAUTH	The privilege to execute the STOSPACE utility:	
	G	GRANTEE holds the privilege and can grant it to others.
	Y	GRANTEE holds the privilege.
	blank	GRANTEE does not hold the privilege.
SYSADMAUTH	SYSADM privilege:	
	G	GRANTEE holds the privilege and can grant it to others.
	Y	GRANTEE holds the privilege.
	blank	GRANTEE does not hold the privilege.
SYSOPRAUTH	SYSOPR privilege:	
	G	GRANTEE holds the privilege and can grant it to others.
	Y	GRANTEE holds the privilege.
	blank	GRANTEE does not hold the privilege.
TRACEAUTH	The privilege to issue -START TRACE and -STOP TRACE commands:	
	G	GRANTEE holds the privilege and can grant it to others.
	Y	GRANTEE holds the privilege.
	blank	GRANTEE does not hold the privilege.
IBMREQD	An indicator specifying Y if the row was supplied by IBM, or N if it was not.	
MON1AUTH	The privilege to read IFC serviceability data:	
	G	GRANTEE holds the privilege and can grant it to others.
	Y	GRANTEE holds the privilege.
	blank	GRANTEE does not hold the privilege.
MON2AUTH	The privilege to read IFC data:	
	G	GRANTEE holds the privilege and can grant it to others.
	Y	GRANTEE holds the privilege.
	blank	GRANTEE does not hold the privilege.
CREATEALIASAUTH	The privilege to create aliases:	
	G	GRANTEE holds the privilege and can grant it to others.
	Y	GRANTEE holds the privilege.
	blank	GRANTEE does not hold the privilege.

SYSCTRLAUTH	SYSCTRL privilege:
	G GRANTEE holds the privilege and can grant it to others.
	Y GRANTEE holds the privilege.
	blank GRANTEE does not hold the privilege.
BINDAGENTAUTH	BINDAGENT privilege:
	G GRANTEE holds the privilege and can grant it to others.
	Y GRANTEE holds the privilege.
	blank GRANTEE does not hold the privilege.
ARCHIVEAUTH	The privilege to issue -ARCHIVE commands:
	G GRANTEE holds the privilege and can grant it to others.
	Y GRANTEE holds the privilege.
	blank GRANTEE does not hold the privilege.
CAPTURE1AUTH	Not currently used.
CAPTURE2AUTH	Not currently used.
GRANTEDTS	Time the GRANT was executed.
CREATETMTABAUTH	The privilege to create temporary tables:
	G GRANTEE holds the privilege and can grant it to others.
	Y GRANTEE holds the privilege.
	blank GRANTEE does not hold the privilege.

SYSIBM.SYSVIEWDEP

SYSIBM.SYSVIEWDEP contains a cross-reference of DB2 objects on which each view depends.

Tablespace	DSNDB06.SYSVIEWS
Indexes	DSNGGX02[nonunique] (BNAME, BNAME, BTYPE)
Links	DSNVT#VU REFERENCES SYSIBM.SYSVTREE

Column Definitions

BNAME	The table or view name on which the view named in DNAME is dependent.
BCREATOR	The owner of the view or table named in BNAME.
BTYPE	T if the object is a table, or V if it is a view.
DNAME	The view name.

DCREATOR	The owner of the view named in DNAME.
IBMREQD	An indicator specifying Y if the row was supplied by IBM, or N if it was not.

SYSIBM.SYSVIEWS

SYSIBM.SYSVIEWS consists of one or more rows for each DB2 view, containing the actual text of the DDL view creation statement.

Tablespace	DSNDB06.SYSVIEWS
Index	DSNVVX01[unique] (CREATOR, NAME, SEQNO)
Links	DSNVT#VW REFERENCES SYSIBM.SYSVTREE

Column Definitions

NAME	The view name.
CREATOR	The owner of the view named in NAME.
SEQNO	The sequence number used to identify the view components.
CHECK	Indicator specifying whether CHECK OPTION is in effect. Valid values are as follow: A Yes, with cascaded semantic N No Y Yes, with local semantic
IBMREQD	An indicator specifying whether the row was supplied by IBM: Y Yes, row was supplied by IBM. N No. B No; V1.3 dependent. C No; V2.1 dependent. D No; V2.2 dependent. E No; V2.3 dependent. F No; V3 dependent. G No; V4 dependent. H No; V5 dependent.
TEXT	The SQL for the view CREATE statement.

SYSIBM.SYSVLTREE

SYSIBM.SYSVLTREE contains the extra portion of the internal representation of very large views. It is used in conjunction with SYSIBM.SYSVTREE.

Tablespace	DSNDB06.SYSVIEWS
Indexes	None
Links	DSNVT#VL REFERENCES SYSIBM.SYSVTREE

Column Definitions

IBMREQD	An indicator specifying Y if the row was supplied by IBM, or N if it was not.
VTREE	When SYSIBM.SYSVTREE cannot hold the entire view parse tree, the bytes in excess of 4,000 are stored here.

SYSIBM.SYSVOLUMES

SYSIBM.SYSVOLUMES contains the list of DASD volumes assigned to DB2 storage groups.

Tablespace	DSNDB06.SYSGROUP
Indexes	None
Links	DSNSS#SV REFERENCES SYSIBM.SYSSTOGROUP

Column Definitions

SGNAME	The storage group name.
SGCREATOR	The owner of the storage group named in SGNAME.
VOLID	A volume serial number assigned to the storage group named in SGNAME.
IBMREQD	An indicator specifying Y if the row was supplied by IBM, or N if it was not.

SYSIBM.SYSVTREE

SYSIBM.SYSVTREE contains the first 4,000 bytes of the internal representation of each view known to the DB2 subsystem. This internal representation is called a *view parse tree.*

Tablespace	DSNDB06.SYSVIEWS
Index	DSNVTH01[unique] (CREATOR, NAME)
Links	None

Column Definitions

NAME	The view name.
CREATOR	The owner of the view named in NAME.
TOTLEN	The length of the parse tree.
IBMREQD	An indicator specifying whether the row was supplied by IBM: Y Yes, row was supplied by IBM. N No. B No; V1.3 dependent. C No; V2.1 dependent. D No; V2.2 dependent. E No; V2.3 dependent. F No; V3 dependent. G No; V4 dependent. H No; V5 dependent.
VTREE	The first 4,000 bytes of the parse tree. If the entire view parse tree is 4,000 bytes or fewer, the entire parse tree can be stored here; if it is larger, additional rows are stored in SYSIBM.SYSVLTREE.

SYSIBM.USERNAMES

SYSIBM.USERNAMES is used to enable outbound and inbound ID translation.

Tablespace	DSNDB06.SYSDDF
Indexes	DSNFEX01 [unique] (TYPE, AUTHID, LUNAME)
Relationship	LUNAME REFERENCES SYSIBM.LUNAMES

Column Definitions

TYPE	Indicator specifying how the row is to be used. Contains the following: I Inbound translation and "come from" checking O Outbound translation
AUTHID	Authorization ID to be translated.

LINKNAME	The VTAM or TCP/IP network locations associated with this row:	
	blank	The name translation rule applies to any TCP/IP or SNA partner.
	nonblank	Row exists in either SYSIBM.LUNAME or SYSIBM.IPNAMES for this LINKNAME.
NEWAUTHID	Translated value for the authid. Blank indicates no translation to occur.	
PASSWORD	If passwords are not encrypted, contains the password for the outbound request. Not used if row is for an inbound request or if passwords are encrypted.	
IBMREQD	An indicator specifying Y if the row was supplied by IBM, or N if it was not.	

C

The QMF Administrative Tables

QMF administers and controls its system using a series of seven tables. Authorized personnel can query each table to obtain a comprehensive view of the status and use of QMF.

This appendix provides the definition DDL for each table, along with a brief description of the table and its columns. This information can be helpful in QMF error tracking; in determining the effects of database changes on dynamic SQL stored in QMF queries; and in monitoring, tracking, and limiting the use of QMF.

Q.COMMAND_SYNONYMS

Q.COMMAND_SYNONYMS contains synonyms for installation-defined commands.

Table DDL

```
CREATE TABLE Q.COMMAND_SYNONYMS
 (VERB                  CHAR(18)       NOT NULL ,
  OBJECT                VARCHAR(31),
  SYNONYM_DEFINITION    VARCHAR(254)   NOT NULL ,
  REMARKS               VARCHAR(254)
)
IN DSQDBCTL.DSQTSSYN ;
```

Column	*Definitions*
VERB	The name of the installation-defined command
OBJECT	An optional name of an object upon which the command in VERB acts
SYNONYM_DEFINITION	The command or commands invoked by the synonym
REMARKS	Descriptive comments for the command synonym

Q.ERROR_LOG

Q.ERROR_LOG contains a log of information on QMF system errors, resource errors, and unexpected condition errors.

Table DDL

```
CREATE TABLE Q.ERROR_LOG
 (DATESTAMP    CHAR(8)         NOT NULL ,
  TIMESTAMP    CHAR(5)         NOT NULL ,
  USERID       CHAR(8)         NOT NULL ,
  MSG_NO       CHAR(8)         NOT NULL ,
  MSGTEXT      VARCHAR(254)    NOT NULL
)
IN DSQDBCTL.DSQTSLOG ;
```

Column	*Definitions*
DATESTAMP	The date the error was recorded
TIMESTAMP	The time the error was recorded
USERID	The logon ID of the user who encountered the error
MSG_NO	The QMF internal error message number
MSGTEXT	A textual description of the error

Q.OBJECT_DATA

Q.OBJECT_DATA contains the text that defines each stored QMF object. Valid QMF objects are queries, forms, and procedures.

Table DDL

```
CREATE TABLE Q.OBJECT_DATA
 (OWNER        CHAR(8)           NOT NULL ,
  NAME         VARCHAR(18)       NOT NULL ,
  TYPE         CHAR(8)           NOT NULL ,
  SEQ          SMALLINT          NOT NULL ,
  APPLDATA     LONG VARCHAR
)
IN DSQDBCTL.DSQTSCT3 ;
```

Column	*Definitions*
OWNER	The authorization ID for the QMF object owner
NAME	The name of the QMF object
TYPE	An indicator specifying the type of QMF object (query, form, or proc)
SEQ	The row sequence number to order the APPLDATA data
APPLDATA	The text defining the QMF object

Q.OBJECT_DIRECTORY

Q.OBJECT_DIRECTORY contains general information on all stored QMF queries, forms, and procedures.

Table DDL

```
CREATE TABLE Q.OBJECT_DIRECTORY
 (OWNER        CHAR(8)           NOT NULL ,
  NAME         VARCHAR(18)       NOT NULL ,
  TYPE         CHAR(8)           NOT NULL ,
  SUBTYPE      CHAR(8),
  OBJECTLEVEL  INTEGER           NOT NULL ,
  RESTRICTED   CHAR(1)           NOT NULL ,
  MODEL        CHAR(8)
)
IN DSQDBCTL.DSQTSCT1 ;
```

Column	Definitions
OWNER	The authorization ID for the QMF object owner
NAME	The name of the QMF object
TYPE	An indicator specifying the type of QMF object (query, form, or proc)
SUBTYPE	The subtype of the QMF object
OBJECTLEVEL	The version of the internal representation of the QMF object
RESTRICTED	An indicator as to whether QMF users other than the OWNER can access this QMF object
MODEL	The indicator specifying whether the query uses SQL, QBE, or Prompted Query format, if the QMF object is a query

Q.OBJECT_REMARKS

Q.OBJECT_REMARKS contains comments saved for QMF queries, forms, and procedures.

Table DDL

```
CREATE TABLE Q.OBJECT_REMARKS
 (OWNER        CHAR(8)          NOT NULL ,
  NAME         VARCHAR(18)      NOT NULL ,
  TYPE         CHAR(8)          NOT NULL ,
  REMARKS      VARCHAR(254)
)
IN DSQDBCTL.DSQTSCT2 ;
```

Column	Definitions
OWNER	The authorization ID for the QMF object owner
NAME	The name of the QMF object
TYPE	An indicator specifying the type of QMF object (query, form, or proc)
REMARKS	Descriptive text about the QMF object

Q.PROFILES

Q.PROFILES contains profile information used by QMF to help manage user sessions.

Table DDL

```
CREATE TABLE Q.PROFILES
 (CREATOR      CHAR(8)          NOT NULL ,
  CASE         CHAR(18),
  DECOPT       CHAR(18),
  CONFIRM      CHAR(18),
  WIDTH        CHAR(18),
  LENGTH       CHAR(18),
```

```
  LANGUAGE        CHAR(18),
  SPACE           CHAR(50),
  TRACE           CHAR(18),
  PRINTER         CHAR(8),
  TRANSLATION     CHAR(18)         NOT NULL ,
  PFKEYS          VARCHAR(31),
  SYNONYMS        VARCHAR(31),
  RESOURCE_GROUP  CHAR(16),
  MODEL           CHAR(8)
)
IN DSQDBCTL.DSQTSPRO ;
```

Column	*Definitions*
CREATOR	Either a logon ID for a QMF user or SYSTEM
CASE	Either UPPER or LOWER, specifying the default for user input
DECOPT	The specification for numeric decimal output
CONFIRM	An indicator specifying whether to confirm data change
WIDTH	The default width for the PRINT command
LENGTH	The default length for the PRINT command
LANGUAGE	The query language to be used
SPACE	The tablespace name used for saving tables with SAVE DATA
TRACE	The type of QMF trace to be used
PRINTER	The GDDM printer nickname for use with the PRINT command
TRANSLATION	The language environment for the user
PFKEYS	The PF key definition table name
SYNONYMS	The synonym definition table name
RESOURCE_GROUP	The RESOURCE GROUP name to be used by the QMF Governor
MODEL	The indicator specifying whether the query uses SQL, QBE, or Prompted Query format, if the QMF object is a query

Q.RESOURCE_TABLE

Q.RESOURCE_TABLE contains resource and limit values for the QMF Governor.

Table DDL

```
CREATE TABLE Q.RESOURCE_TABLE
 (RESOURCE_GROUP    CHAR(16)         NOT NULL ,
  RESOURCE_OPTION   CHAR(16)         NOT NULL ,
  INTVAL            INTEGER,
  FLOATVAL          FLOAT,
  CHARVAL           VARCHAR(80)
)
IN DSQDBCTL.DSQTSGOV ;
```

Column	*Definitions*
RESOURCE_GROUP	The RESOURCE GROUP name used by the QMF Governor
RESOURCE_OPTION	The RESOURCE OPTION name associated with the RESOURCE GROUP
INTVAL	The integer value for a RESOURCE OPTION
FLOATVAL	The floating-point value for a RESOURCE OPTION
CHARVAL	The character value for a RESOURCE OPTION

D

DB2 Sample Tables

This appendix provides information on the DB2 sample tables used in most of the figures and examples in this book. You learned about the DB2 sample tables because they are bundled with DB2, installed at most DB2 shops, and generally available for everyone's use.

An understanding of the data in the sample tables and the relationship between these tables is imperative to understanding the SQL in this book. The DB2 sample tables primarily contain information about projects and the entities involved in working on these projects. Figure D.1 shows these entities and the relationships between them.

FIGURE D.1.
DB2 sample table relationships.

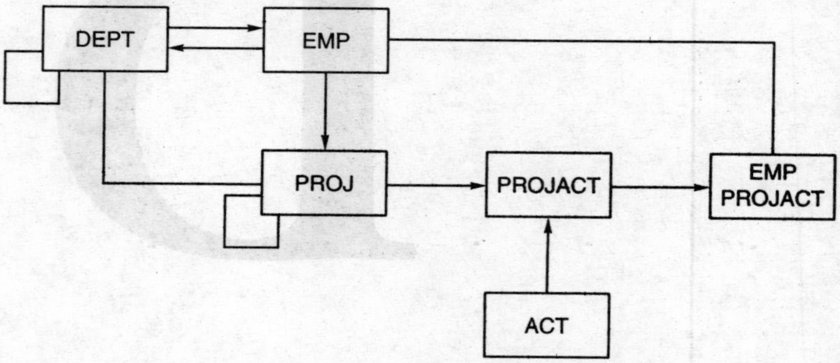

The six tables represent departments, employees, projects, activities, activities assigned to a project, and employees assigned to a project's activities. In the following sections, you can find a general description of each table, its columns, and its relationship to the other sample tables, along with its table creation DDL.

The Activity Table: DSN8510.ACT

DSN8510.ACT describes activities that can be performed for projects. This table simply provides activity information. It does not tie each activity to a project. The following information about an activity is recorded: the activity number, the activity keyword, and the activity description. The activity number (ACTNO) is the primary key for this table.

DSN8510.ACT is a parent table for DSN8510.PROJACT. Two indexes have been built for this table: DSN8510.XACT1 is a primary key index on ACTNO, and DSN8510.XACT2 is a unique index on ACTKWD.

DSN8510.ACT Table DDL

```
CREATE TABLE DSN8510.ACT
 (ACTNO              SMALLINT         NOT NULL,
  ACTKWD             CHAR(6)          NOT NULL,
  ACTDESC            VARCHAR(20)      NOT NULL,
  PRIMARY KEY (ACTNO)
)
IN IN DSN8D51A.DSN8S51P;
```

The Department Table: DSN8510.DEPT

DSN8510.DEPT describes information about departments that might be participating in projects. The following information is stored for each department: the department number, the department name, the employee number for the manager of the department, and the department number for the department to which this department reports. The department number is the primary key.

Referential integrity is used to implement a self-referencing constraint for ADMRDEPT. This referential constraint establishes the higher level department to which this department reports. A constraint also exists for MGRNO to EMPNO, the primary key of the DSN8510.EMP table. It ensures that the manager of a department is a valid employee.

Three indexes have been built for this table: DSN8510.XDEPT1 is a primary key index on DEPTNO, DSN8510.XDEPT2 is an index on MGRNO, and DSN8510.XDEPT3 is an index on ADMRDEPT.

DSN8510.DEPT Table DDL

```
CREATE TABLE DSN8510.DEPT
 (DEPTNO            CHAR(3)          NOT NULL,
  DEPTNAME          VARCHAR(36)      NOT NULL,
  MGRNO             CHAR(6),
  ADMRDEPT          CHAR(3)          NOT NULL,
  LOCATION          CHAR(16),
  PRIMARY KEY (DEPTNO)
)
IN DSN8D51A.DSN8S51D;
ALTER TABLE DSN8510.DEPT
  FOREIGN KEY RDD (ADMRDEPT)
    REFERENCES DSN8510.DEPT ON DELETE CASCADE;
ALTER TABLE DSN8510.DEPT
  FOREIGN KEY RDE (MGRNO)
    REFERENCES DSN8510.EMP ON DELETE SET NULL;
```

The Employee Table: DSN8510.EMP

DSN8510.EMP describes employees in the organization. This table is in a partitioned tablespace. The following information is retained about employees: the employee's number, first name, middle initial, and last name; the department where this employee works; the employee's phone number; the date the employee was hired; and the employee's job description, education level, sex, birth date, salary, commission, and bonus data. The primary key is the employee number.

This table is a child of DSN8510.DEPT by the WORKDEPT column and a parent table for DSN8510.PROJ. Two indexes have been built for this table: DSN8510.XEMP1 is a primary unique, partitioning index on EMPNO, and DSN8510.XEMP2 is an index on WORKDEPT.

DSN8510.EMP Table DDL

```
CREATE TABLE DSN8510.EMP
 (EMPNO          CHAR(6)          NOT NULL,
  FIRSTNME       VARCHAR(12)      NOT NULL,
  MIDINIT        CHAR(1)          NOT NULL,
  LASTNAME       VARCHAR(15)      NOT NULL,
  WORKDEPT       CHAR(3),
  PHONENO        CHAR(4) CONSTRAINT NUMBER CHECK
                 (PHONENO >= '0000' AND
                  PHONENO <= '9999'),
  HIREDATE       DATE,
  JOB            CHAR(8),
  EDLEVEL        SMALLINT,
  SEX            CHAR(1),
  BIRTHDATE      DATE,
  SALARY         DECIMAL(9,2),
  BONUS          DECIMAL(9,2),
  COMM           DECIMAL(9,2),
  PRIMARY KEY (EMPNO)
  FOREIGN KEY RED (WORKDEPT)
    REFERENCES DSN8510.DEPT ON DELETE SET NULL
)
EDITPROC DSN8EAE1
IN DSN8D51A.DSN8S51E;
```

The Employee Assignment Table: DSN8510.EMPPROJACT

DSN8510.EMPPROJACT details which employee performs which activity for each project. It effectively records the assignment of employees to a given activity for a given project. To accomplish this assignment, the table stores an employee number, a project number, and an activity number on every row, along with information about the employee's assignment. This additional information consists of the percentage of time the employee should spend on this activity, the date the activity starts, and the date the activity ends. No primary key is implemented, but a unique index is used on the combination of PROJNO, ACTNO, EMSTDATE, and EMPNO.

The table is a child of both DSN8510.PROJACT and DSN8510.EMP. Two indexes exist for this table: DSN8510.XEMPPROJACT1 is a unique index on PROJNO, ACTNO, EMSTDATE, and EMPNO; and DSN8510.XEMPPROJACT2 is an index on EMPNO.

DSN8510.EMPPROJACT Table DDL

```
CREATE TABLE DSN8510.EMPPROJACT
 (EMPNO          CHAR(6)          NOT NULL,
  PROJNO         CHAR(6)          NOT NULL,
  ACTNO          SMALLINT         NOT NULL,
  EMPTIME        DECIMAL(5,2),
  EMSTDATE       DATE,
  EMENDATE       DATE,
```

```
  FOREIGN KEY REPAPA (PROJNO, ACTNO, EMSTDATE)
    REFERENCES DSN8510.PROJACT ON DELETE RESTRICT,
  FOREIGN KEY REPAE (EMPNO)
    REFERENCES DSN8510.EMP ON DELETE RESTRICT
)
IN DSN8D51A.DSN8S51P;
```

The Project Table: DSN8510.PROJ

DSN8510.PROJ defines all the projects for the organization. It contains information on the project's number; the project's name; the responsible department number and employee number; the project's staffing requirements, start date, and end date; and the project number of any related, superior project. The primary key is PROJNO.

DSN8510.PROJ is a self-referencing table because one project can relate to another by the MAJPROJ column, which identifies a parent project. It is also a parent table because it has relationships to DSN8510.DEPT for the responsible department and to DSN8510.EMP for the responsible employee.

Two indexes exist for this table: DSN8510.XPROJ1 is a primary key index on PROJNO, and DSN8510.XPROJ2 is an index on RESPEMP.

DSN8510.PROJ Table DDL

```
CREATE TABLE DSN8510.PROJ
 (PROJNO        CHAR(6) PRIMARY KEY NOT NULL,
  PROJNAME      VARCHAR(24)         NOT NULL WITH DEFAULT
                                    'PROJECT NAME UNDEFINED',
  DEPTNO        CHAR(3)             NOT NULL
                REFERENCES DSN8510.DEPT ON DELETE RESTRICT,
  RESPEMP       CHAR(6)             NOT NULL
                REFERENCES DSN8510.EMP ON DELETE RESTRICT,
  PRSTAFF       DECIMAL(5, 2),
  PRSTDATE      DATE,
  PRENDATE      DATE,
  MAJPROJ       CHAR(6)
)
IN DSN8D51A.DSN8S51P;
ALTER TABLE DSN8510.PROJ
  FOREIGN KEY RPP (MAJPROJ)
    REFERENCES DSN8510.PROJ ON DELETE CASCADE;
```

The Project Activity Table: DSN8510.PROJACT

DSN8510.PROJACT records the activities for each project. It stores the following information: the project's number, the activity's number, the number of employees needed to staff the activity, and the estimated activity start date and end date.

DSN8510.PROJACT is a parent of the DSN8510.EMPPROJACT table and functions as a child table for DSN8510.ACT and DSN8510.PROJ. This table has one index: DSN8510.XPROJAC1 is a unique primary key index on PROJNO, ACTNO, and ACSTDATE.

DSN8510.PROJACT Table DDL

```
CREATE TABLE DSN8510.PROJACT
 (PROJNO              CHAR(6)          NOT NULL,
  ACTNO               SMALLINT         NOT NULL,
  ACSTAFF             DECIMAL(5,2),
  ACSTDATE            DATE             NOT NULL,
  ACENDATE            DATE,
  MAJPROJ             CHAR(6),
  PRIMARY KEY (PROJNO, ACTNO, ACSTDATE),
  FOREIGN KEY RPAP (PROJNO)
    REFERENCES DSN8510.PROJ ON DELETE RESTRICT,
  FOREIGN KEY RPAA (ACTNO)
    REFERENCES DSN8510.ACT ON DELETE RESTRICT
)
IN DSN8D51A.DSN8S51P;
```

The Sample STOGROUP

The storage group used by the sample database is DSN8G410. The following statement is provided by IBM to define the sample STOGROUP. (Of course, the VOLUMES, VCAT, and PASSWORD information is usually modified prior to the creation of the storage group.)

```
CREATE STOGROUP DSN8G510
  VOLUMES (DSNV01)
  VCAT     DSNC510
  PASSWORD DSNDEFPW;
```

Sample Databases and Tablespaces

Tables D.1 and D.2 provide a synopsis of the databases and tablespaces used for the sample tables.

Table D.1. Sample databases.

Database Name	*Storage Group*	*Bufferpool*
DSN8D51A	DSN8G510	BP0
DSN8D51P	DSN8G510	BP0

Table D.2. Sample tablespaces.

Tablespace Name	*Database Name*	*Buffer-pool*	*Tablespace Type*	*Lock Size*	*Close Rule*
DSN8S51D	DSN8D51A	BP0	SIMPLE	ANY	NO
DSN8S51E	DSN8D51A	BP0	PARTITIONED	ANY	NO
DSN8S51C	DSN8D51P	BP0	SEGMENTED	TABLE	NO
DSN8S51R	DSN8D51A	BP0	SIMPLE	ANY	NO

E

DB2 Manuals

IBM supplies two types of DB2 manuals. The first type is the standard issue DB2 manual. The standard manuals contain core information necessary to administer and use DB2, such as SQL syntax, command syntax, utility syntax, installation instructions, error codes, and high-level overviews of programming and design issues. However, the standard issue manuals contain few implementation guidelines on the day-to-day use of DB2. Every installation that uses DB2 should have at least one set of standard issue manuals.

The second type of DB2 manual offered by IBM is called a *redbook* (because of its red cover). These manuals are limited to a specific subject and provide practical information and examples, such as usage and design guidelines, performance information, and implementation examples. You should obtain a library of relevant redbooks because they contain information not readily available elsewhere. They are not always current, however, so use caution before relying on information from redbooks.

In addition to printed manuals, an online version of the manuals should be made available at your site on Book Manager (either accessible using TSO on the mainframe or on CD-ROM for Windows-based access). You might also want to consider owning the following two CD-ROM collections for personal use at home or when away from the office:

- Transaction Processing and Data Collection (SK2T-0730)—Contains all the DBMS and TP manuals for IBM products across multiple release levels (for example, CICS, DB2, MQ Series, IMS).
- System Center Publications S/390 "Rainbow Books" Collection (SK2T-2177)—Contains a wide range of IBM ITSO redbooks across numerous topics.

IBM also offers many products that enhance the capabilities of DB2. I refer to these as *DB2-related products.* The most popular of these products is QMF, IBM's Query Management Facility. It provides the capability to quickly and easily retrieve DB2 data in a formatted report. Other popular DB2-related products include CSP, Data Propagator, and DB2-PM. Each of these products enhances the functionality of DB2.

Similar to the two types of manuals that IBM provides for DB2, two types of manuals are supplied by IBM for most of the DB2-related products: standard issue manuals and redbooks. These manuals are also available in both a printed and online version.

The rest of this appendix lists the most pertinent manuals for DB2 and DB2-related products.

DB2 Standard Issue Manuals

The order numbers listed for the standard issue manuals are the DB2 version 5 order numbers (unless specifically stated otherwise).

;C26-8970—*Installation Guide*

he *Installation Guide* is an instruction manual for installing and upgrading DB2 and is useful •r systems programmers and DBAs who install DB2 subsystems.

C26-3394—*DB2 V4 Release Guide* and SC26-8965—*DB2 V5 Release* ;uide

he *Release Guide* provides a basic overview of the new features for new DB2 releases. A *Release uide* is available for both DB2 V4 and V5. It is useful for all DB2 users who are migrating to new version of DB2.

C26-8971—*What's New in DB2?*

'hat's New in DB2? is a very high-level overview of the new features of the latest version or ease of DB2. It is most useful for non-technical managers and end users.

:26-8957—*Administration Guide*

ıe *Administration Guide* provides information on planning and installing DB2, designing 32 databases, and performance monitoring and tuning. It is very technical and usually stops ɔrt of providing implementation-specific information. This standard manual is beneficial DBA and system programming staffs, but technical analysts and anyone interesting in learn- ; more about the technical details of DB2 can glean useful information by reading or refer- :ing this guide.

26-8958—*Application Programming and SQL Guide*

application programmers will find the *Application Programming and SQL Guide* useful. It ıtains most of the information necessary to code embedded SQL programs. The manual :s not cover the teleprocessing environments in which DB2 runs (TSO, CICS, or IMS/TM), gramming languages, or SQL, but it does provide information on how DB2 uses these nents. Every programmer who needs to code DB2 application programs should have a copy his guide handy.

26-8959—*Call Level Interface Guide and Reference*

: *Call Level Interface Guide and Reference* is a guide to using the DB2 call level interface .I), new as of DB2 V5. It is useful for DB2 programmers and developers writing applica- ıs using CLI.

SC26-8966—*SQL Reference*

The *SQL Reference* is a complete reference for IBM standard SQL syntax. This is the bible DB2 SQL. It is not an implementation guide, though, and will not help you code efficie SQL. A description of the DB2 Catalog tables is provided in an appendix to this manual.

SC26-8967—*Utility Guide and Reference*

The *Utility Guide and Reference* helps technical programmers and DBAs in the development DB2 utility jobs. The manual contains utility syntax descriptions and a detailed narrative each DB2 utility. It does not contain implementation advice such as scheduling recommend tions and usage guidelines.

SC26-8960—*Command Reference*

The *Command Reference* contains syntax and usage information for DB2 commands. It is m useful to DBAs, system administrators, and systems programmers.

SC26-8979—*Messages and Codes*

The *Messages and Codes* manual contains a detailed reference for all SQL return codes, D error messages, and DB2 reason codes. Testing and debugging of DB2 applications, SC development, and DB2 database support is impossible without this manual. No applicati programmer, system programmer, DBA, or DB2 technical support staff should be caught wi out a copy of it.

SX26-3842—*Reference Summary*

The *Reference Summary* is a smaller, spiral-bound summary of syntax for SQL statements, D commands, and DB2 utilities. It is useful for quick SQL syntax checking and SQL error c investigation. Every DB2/SQL programmer should have a copy of this manual.

SC26-8961—*Data Sharing: Planning and Administration*

Data Sharing: Planning and Administration describes DB2's data-sharing capabilities and gi guidance on how to implement DB2 data sharing. It is most useful for DBAs and systems p grammers preparing to implement and support DB2 in a Sysplex environment.

LY27-9659—*Diagnosis and Reference Guide*

The *Diagnosis and Reference Guide* contains elaborate information about DB2 subsystem c ponents, diagnostic aids and techniques, formats of physical DB2 objects, and other techn information. This manual is difficult to digest and is targeted to system programmers.

SC26-8964—*Reference for Remote DRDA Requesters and Servers*

The *Reference for Remote DRDA Requesters and Servers* provides a handy reference for programmers and administrators setting up the distributed environment and implementing distributed applications.

SK2T-9092—DB2 Server for OS/390 Online Library

This provides the entire DB2 manual library on a CD-ROM in Book Manager format for easy online browsing. The only exception is the *Diagnosis Guide and Reference*, which is only available to licensed users of DB2 (CD-ROM order number LK2T-9075).

DB2 Redbooks

The listing of redbooks in this section shows the DB2 release level to which each redbook is guaranteed to be accurate and the audience to whom the redbook should appeal. The redbooks are grouped in eight categories:

Concepts	DB2 concepts at basic levels. These manuals are useful for DB2 beginners or managers requiring an overview of DB2 functionality.
Control	DB2 from an audit and security perspective.
Distributed	Distributed database management techniques, specifically as available through DB2 and SAA.
Environment	Establishing connections between DB2 and other environments.
Implementation	Practical advice on coding SQL, implementing DB2 programs and tables, and general application development guidelines and techniques.
Performance	Achieving better DB2 subsystem performance, monitoring DB2 performance, and tuning DB2 applications.
Release	Issues pertaining to a particular version and release of DB2.
Utilities	Developing and executing DB2 utilities.

Some of these manuals are outdated, and as such, are not recommended. Outdated manuals are so marked. Also, a few redbooks in this section do not apply specifically to DB2 but are useful for DB2 users. The DB2 release level is not supplied for these types of manuals.

There is a redbook that catalogs all of the redbooks that are currently available. It is a good idea to keep a copy of this redbook on hand. The IBM order number is SG24-4580. Additionally, IBM provides a searchable Web site of redbooks currently available, which can be found at `http://www.redbooks.ibm.com/redbooks`.

Concepts

The following manuals discuss DB2 and relational database concepts at basic levels.

GG24-1581—*Relational Concepts*

The *Relational Concepts* redbook presents relational database management systems concepts. The discussion includes a definition of RDBMS, a comparison of relational and hierarchical databases, the advantages of relational databases, and DB2's conformance to the relational model. Though originally published in 1983, this manual provides an excellent starting point for those new to relational technology and is also useful for those familiar with IMS who need a quick introduction to the relational way of thinking.

Release level:	V1.1
Audience:	Application developers, database administrators, end users, information center staff, non-technical, managerial, and systems programmers

GG24-1582—*DB2 Concepts & Facilities Guide*

The *DB2 Concepts & Facilities Guide* provides an overview of the components of DB2. It is outdated but still useful as a nonauthoritative introductory guide to DB2.

Release level:	V1.1
Audience:	Application developers, end users, nontechnical, and managerial

Control

The following manuals cover DB2 from an audit and security perspective.

GE20-0783—*Audit and Control in the DB2 Environment*

Audit and Control in the DB2 Environment was provided by IBM in conjunction with the Institute of Internal Auditors and Price Waterhouse. This document is useful as a guide for auditing a DB2 environment, providing an overview of DB2 and the relational model, a discussion of security and audit functions, and an overview of systems that can interface with DB2.

Release level:	V1.2
Audience:	Application developers, database administrators, end users, and systems programmers

GG24-1599—*Security and Authorization Guide*

The authorization features of DB2 are detailed in the *Security and Authorization Guide.* Usage guidelines are provided for different levels of DB2 users as well as for different types of operational environments. This manual is useful despite its age, but keep in mind that DB2 security features have expanded since the first release of DB2. Some of these features are secondary authorization IDs, the `SET SQLID` command, the `OWNER` parm of the `BIND` command, `BINDAGENT`, and the new `SYSCTRL` and `PACKADM` group-level authorities.

Release level: V1.1

Audience: Application developers, database administrators, information center staff, and systems programmers

GG24-3299—*Security & Authorization Extensions Guide*

The *Security & Authorization Extensions Guide* provides an in-depth description of the security features added to DB2 V2.1. In conjunction with GG24-1599, this guide provides a comprehensive description of DB2 security as of DB2 V2.2.

Release level: V2.1

Audience: Application developers, database administrators, information center staff, and systems programmers

GG24-3300—*Audit Trace Usage Guide*

The *Audit Trace Usage Guide* describes the audit functions added to DB2 V2.1. It is still relevant as of DB2 V5 because no new audit features have been added since DB2 V2.1.

Release level: V2.1

Audience: Application developers, auditors, database administrators, information center staff, non-technical, managerial, and systems programmers

Distributed

The manuals in this section provide coverage of DRDA and the distributed database techniques available to DB2.

GG24-2500—*DB2 for MVS DRDA Server: Security Considerations*

DB2 for MVS DRDA Server: Security Considerations discusses client/server and distributed security concepts. The manual specifically details the security issues involved when accessing DB2 for MVS from DDCS on OS/2 and AIX.

Release level: V4

Audience: Database administrators and systems programmers

GG24-3200—*Introduction to Distributed Relational Data*

Although *Introduction to Distributed Relational Data* is not a DB2 manual, it does provide valuable insight into IBM's distributed database ideology. It provides an overview of a possible implementation of a distributed relational database architecture, and it explains the functions of a DDBMS and the benefits of distributed data. This manual is highly recommended for shops that use or are considering the use of distributed DB2 databases.

Release level:	—
Audience:	Database administrators and systems programmers

GG24-3400—*DB2 Distributed Database Application Implementation and Installation Primer*

DB2 Distributed Database Application Implementation and Installation Primer provides design solutions and guidelines for implementing distributed database applications. It includes examples for TSO, IMS/VS, and CICS environments.

Release level:	V2.2
Audience:	Application developers, database administrators, and systems programmers

GG24-3513—*Distributed Relational Database—Application Scenarios*

The *Distributed Relational Database—Application Scenarios* redbook is another document that is not DB2-specific, but it is helpful in assisting readers in their understanding of DB2 distributed database functionality. This manual provides four examples of application and database designs that can benefit from SAA distributed database implementations.

Release level:	—
Audience:	Application developers, database administrators, and systems programmers

GG24-3600—*DB2-APPC/VTAM Distributed Database Usage Guide*

Consult the *DB2-APPC/VTAM Distributed Database Usage Guide* to gain an understanding of DB2, APPC, and VTAM concepts. It can also assist in distributed database problem determination.

Release level:	V2.2
Audience:	Database administrators and systems programmers

GG24-3755—*Distributed Relational Database Planning & Design Guide for DB2 Users*

The *Distributed Relational Database Planning & Design Guide for DB2 Users* provides information about accessing distributed data from DB2 and other IBM relational databases.

Release level:	V2.3
Audience:	Database administrators and systems programmers

GG24-4333—*Access to the DB2 Family with ODBC*

Access to the DB2 Family with ODBC describes experiences using DB2 DOS CAE 1.2 and Microsoft Access with ODBC to access DB2 data. It is mostly geared to DB2 for OS/2 and AIX, but some concepts are helpful in general.

Release level:	—
Audience:	Application developers

SG24-4311—*Distributed Relational Database Cross Platform Connectivity*

Distributed Relational Database Cross Platform Connectivity discusses the impact of connecting multiple DB2s on multiple platforms. This redbook is based on actual experiences IBM encountered during a project that connected DB2 for OS/2, DB2 for AIX, DB2 for OS./400, DB2 for VM and VSE, and DB2 for MVS. At times, it requires knowledge of networking.

Release level:	V4
Audience:	Database administrators and systems programmers

SG24-4558—*DB2 for MVS Connections with AIX and OS/2*

DB2 for MVS Connections with AIX and OS/2 discusses the latest and greatest distributed capabilities of DB2 for MVS, DB2 common server V2.1, and DDCS V2.3. It also provides a basic overview of DRDA concepts.

Release level:	V4
Audience:	Application developers, database administrators, and systems programmers

Environment

The following manuals provide information on establishing connections between DB2 and other environments.

GG24-3202—*CICS-DB2 Interface Guide*

Although the *CICS-DB2 Interface Guide* was written for DB2 V1.3, an appendix covers DB2 V2.1 features. The information in this guide is relevant for CICS MVS V2.1 and CICS OS/VS V1.7. Everything from installation instructions to advice on monitoring, recovery, security, and programming is offered in this comprehensive introduction to the CICS-DB2 connection. Be sure to consult this guide before attempting to develop any DB2 application that uses CICS as the teleprocessing monitor.

Release level:	V2.1
Audience:	Application developers, CICS support staff, database administrators, information center staff, and systems programmers

GG24-3203—*IMS/VS: A Planning Guide for DB2*

The information in *IMS/VS: A Planning Guide for DB2* is accurate as of DB2 V2.1 and IMS/VS V2.2. It contains information on the attachment of DB2 to an existing IMS/VS environment. Pertinent details covered by this redbook include parameters and JCL changes, restart/recovery information, monitoring advice, application design considerations, and logging details.

Release level:	V2.1
Audience:	Application developers, database administrators, information center staff, IMS support staff, IMS DBAs, and systems programmers

Implementation

The following manuals provide practical advice on coding SQL, implementing DB2 programs and tables, and general application development guidelines and techniques.

GG24-1583—*SQL Usage Guide*

The *SQL Usage Guide* offers a good overview of the syntax and nature of SQL. It progresses from simple to complex SQL and is useful for all DB2 users. This document is still worthwhile even though it is very outdated.

Release level:	V1.1
Audience:	Application developers, database administrators, end users, information center staff, non-technical, managerial, and systems programmers

GG24-3056—*Storage Management Usage Guide*

The *Storage Management Usage Guide* touches on both application and system storage topics, addressing the issues of DB2 data storage, space management, and migration. Most of the information in this redbook is still applicable to DB2 V5, but many changes have been made to DB2 since V1.2 (including VSAM linear data set support and better STOGROUP administration functions).

Release level:	V1.2
Audience:	Application developers, DASD support group, database administrators, information center staff, and systems programmers

GG24-3180—*Operation & Recovery Sample Procedures*

Most of the strategies for DB2 operation, maintenance, recovery, and restart in the *Operation & Recovery Sample Procedures* manual are still viable. The procedures, however, should be augmented to incorporate forced log archival, local and offsite dual image copies, and enhanced utility processing.

Release level:	V1.3
Audience:	Database administrators, information center staff, and systems programmers

GG24-3312—*Referential Integrity Usage Guide*

The *Referential Integrity Usage Guide* is one of the most valuable redbooks about DB2 produced by IBM. It should be read by anyone planning to develop DB2 applications using referential integrity. Topics covered by this manual include a definition of referential integrity, DB2's support for the RI of the relational model, recommendations for RI usage, DB2 Catalog queries to administer RI-related tables, and many great examples detailing the dos and don'ts of implementing RI delete rules.

Release level:	V2.2
Audience:	Application developers, database administrators, and information center staff

GG24-3317—*DB2 Usage in the DFSMS Environment*, Part 1

Parts 1 and 2 of *DB2 Usage in the DFSMS Environment* describe the interaction of DB2 with DFSMS (Data Facility Storage Management Subsystem). Part 1 is an overview of DB2 and DFSMS and includes preliminary planning guidelines for implementing the two products to work together.

Release level:	V2.1
Audience:	DASD support group, database administrators, information center staff, and systems programmers

GG24-3371—*DB2 Usage in the DFSMS Environment, Part 2*

Parts 1 and 2 of *DB2 Usage in the DFSMS Environment* describe the interaction of DB2 with DFSMS (Data Facility Storage Management Subsystem). Part 2 provides in-depth guidelines and examples for using DB2 and DFSMS.

Release level:	V2.1
Audience:	DASD support group, database administrators, information center staff, and systems programmers

GG24-3383—*Design Guidelines for High Performance*

Design Guidelines for High Performance provides various tips and tricks for increasing performance. The advice in this document is application-specific and should not be followed unless you completely understand the ramifications. Many good ideas are presented, but sometimes the enhanced performance results in decreased flexibility.

Release level:	V2.2
Audience:	Application developers, database administrators, information center staff, and systems programmers

GG24-3512—*Capacity Planning for DB2 Applications*

Capacity Planning for DB2 Applications details and defines DB2 capacity planning. This manual provides techniques for determining the resources that will be consumed by an application, a methodology for DB2 capacity planning, information on using ANDB2 as an aid in capacity planning, and many examples.

Release level:	V2.2
Audience:	Application developers, database administrators, information center staff, and systems programmers

GG24-3601—*DB2 Offsite Recovery Sample Procedures*

The procedures in *DB2 Offsite Recovery Sample Procedures* can be used or modified to develop a disaster recovery plan for your DB2 installation. The procedures in this guide are based on DB2 V2.2 and V2.3.

Release level:	V2.2
Audience:	Application developers, auditors, DBAs, end users, information center staff, non-technical, managerial, and systems programmers

GG24-4001—*Implementing and Using DB2 Packages*

If you do not already use packages, be sure to read this redbook before you do anything else. It contains many useful tips and techniques for optimally implementing DB2 packages.

Release level:	V2.3
Audience:	Application developers, database administrators, systems programmers, and bind agents

GG24-4445—*Planning for Conversion to the DB2 Family*

Planning for Conversion to the DB2 Family provides an overview of the steps required to convert legacy systems to use DB2.

Release level:	V4
Audience:	Application developers, database administrators, and technical managers

GG66-3117—*DB2 Implementation Primer*

The *DB2 Implementation Primer* was written with the first-time user of DB2 in mind. It provides an overview of DB2, touching on the way DB2 stores data, SQL, DB2 project management, training, required and optional hardware and software, application design, DB2 operational support, recovery, and performance.

Release level:	V2.1
Audience:	Application developers, database administrators, information center staff, non-technical, managerial, and systems programmers

GH20-7562—*DBMS Conversion Guide: IDMS to DB2*

GH20-7563—*DBMS Conversion Guide: Adabas to DB2*

GH20-7564—*DBMS Conversion Guide: Datacom/DB to DB2*

GH20-7565—*DBMS Conversion Guide: Model 204 to DB2*

GH20-7566—*DBMS Conversion Guide: VSAM to DB2*

GH21-1083—*IMS-DB and DB2 Migration & Coexistence Guide*

The *DBMS Conversion Guides* are useful when converting non-DB2 applications to DB2. Before converting from any of these platforms, read these manuals for advice and guidance, particularly the sections listing sources for conversion assistance. These manuals are no longer published and might be difficult to track down.

Release level:	V2.2/V2.3
Audience:	Application developers and database administrators

GH20-9255—*Data Portability Guide*

The *Data Portability Guide* was written for DB2 V1.2 and is not very useful as of DB2 V5. It contains information on moving DB2 data from system to system and migrating to and from different types of DASD devices. It provides useful information but at times provides it within the context of tools that are no longer available (such as DBMAUI). The DSN1COPY and DSNTIAUL/LOAD information is still somewhat relevant.

Release level:	V1.2
Audience:	DASD support group, database administrators, and systems programmers

G320-0160—*DB2 Design Review Guidelines*

The *DB2 Design Review Guidelines* redbook is not usually useful when preparing a DB2 V5 design review. Many enhancements have been made to DB2 since 1984, including data/time/timestamp data types, segmented tablespace support, referential integrity, packages, query parallelism, distributed data support, data sharing, stored procedures, row-level locking, Type 2 indexes, and so on.

Release level:	V1.1
Audience:	Application developers and database administrators

SG24-2072—*DB2 for OS/3490 Terabyte Database: Design and Build*

DB2 for OS/3490 Terabyte Database: Design and Build provides assistance with implementing large tablespaces to store up to a terabyte of data in a parallel Sysplex environment. It provides hints and tips for dealing with VLDB.

Release level:	V5
Audience:	Database administrators and systems programmers

SG24-4693—*Getting Started with DB2 Stored Procedures: Give Them a Call Through the Network*

Getting Started with DB2 Stored Procedures: Give Them a Call Through the Network is an in-depth treatment of how to implement stored procedures in a DB2 environment. This redbook discusses both DB2 for MVS and DB2 common servers.

Release level:	V4
Audience:	Application developers and database administrators

SG24-4725—*Locking in the DB2 for MVS/ESA Environment*

Locking in the DB2 for MVS/ESA Environment is a detailed description of locking in the DB2 for MVS environment. It includes several examples of the impact of locking on application design and performance.

Release level:	V4
Audience:	Application developers and database administrators

SG24-4791—*DB2 for MVS/ESA V4 Data Sharing Implementation*

DB2 for MVS/ESA V4 Data Sharing Implementation provides detailed coverage of how to implement DB2 data sharing. It discusses planning techniques, global locking, bufferpool management, creating data-sharing groups, installation considerations, procedures, recovery, tuning, and more.

Release level:	V4
Audience:	Database administrators and systems programmers

Performance

The following manuals provide techniques and guidelines for DB2 performance monitoring and tuning.

GG09-1008—*Segmented Tablespace Analysis*

The *Segmented Tablespace Analysis* document provides an evaluation of the performance of segmented tablespaces. A variety of benchmarks demonstrate the benefits of segmented tablespaces for administering multiple tables in a single tablespace. Because this redbook was published in 1989, these numbers are useful for historical purposes only.

Release level:	V2.1
Audience:	Application developers, database administrators, and information center staff

GG24-1600—*Performance Design and Tuning Guide*

The *Performance Design and Tuning Guide* discusses performance and design from both application and system perspectives. It is helpful for providing an overview of these issues, but the information is too dated to be of much practical value.

Release level:	V1.1
Audience:	—

GG24-3004—*Application Design and Tuning Guide*

The *Application Design and Tuning Guide* covers information on designing a DB2 application (not subsystem) for performance and application tuning issues. Some of the information in this manual is obsolete, but the basic ideas are still sound.

Release level:	V1.2
Audience:	Application developers, database administrators, and information center staff

GG24-3005—*System Monitoring and Tuning Guide*

The *System Monitoring and Tuning Guide* covers information on designing a DB2 subsystem (not application) for performance, system monitoring, and performance problem investigation. Although this document was published in 1986, it still contains useful information, some of which is not outdated.

Release level:	V1.2
Audience:	Database administrators and systems programmers

GG24-3413—*DB2 Performance Monitor Usage Guide*

The *DB2 Performance Monitor Usage Guide* is valid for DB2-PM V2.1. This manual covers an older release of DB2-PM; the *DB2-PM Usage Guide Update* should be used instead.

Release level:	V2.2
Audience:	Database administrators and systems programmers

GG24-4308—*DDCS/2 to DB2 Performance Benchmarks*

DDCS/2 to DB2 Performance Benchmarks describes the results of a series of benchmark tests done by IBM using DDCS/2 2.0.1 and DB2 V3. It is of value to performance analysts.

Release level:	V3
Audience:	Database administrators and systems programmers

SG24-2549—*DB2 Quick Upper Bound Estimate*

This redbook outlines an application design method, QUBE, that enables developers to make reasonably accurate performance-oriented design decisions.

Release level:	V4
Audience:	Application developers and database administrators

SG24-2584—*DB2 Performance Monitor Usage Guide Update*

The *DB2 Performance Monitor Usage Guide Update* is valid for DB2-PM V4. It contains an easy-to-read synopsis of the DB2-PM reports, a discussion of the DB2 monitoring environments, the approaches to using DB2-PM, and appendixes on trace types and potential anomalies. This manual should be used in conjunction with, not as a replacement for, the official DB2-PM documentation.

Release level:	V5
Audience:	Database administrators and systems programmers

Release

The following manuals cover issues pertaining to a particular version and release of DB2.

GG24-3146—*Performance Report*

This *Performance Report* is an outdated manual that is useful only from a historical perspective or to gain insight into DB2 performance benchmarking methods.

Release level:	V1.2
Audience:	—

GG24-3182—*DB2 Release 3 Notebook*

DB2 Release 3 Notebook is an introductory discussion of features new to DB2 as of V1.3. These features include data/time/timestamp data types, the `UNION ALL` operator, and miscellaneous performance enhancements.

NOTE

Do not confuse Release 3 (which refers to DB2 V1.3) with version 3.

Release level:	V1.3
Audience:	Application developers, database administrators, and information center staff

GG24-3261—*Presentation Guide, Volume 1*

Presentation Guide, Volume 1 provides an overview of referential integrity. Both volumes consist mostly of overhead transparency foils and are not easy to read.

Release level: V2.1

Audience: Database administrators and information center staff

GG24-3263—*Presentation Guide, Volume 2*

Presentation Guide, Volume 2 provides information on operational considerations, utility enhancements, and potential DB2 V2.1 performance gains. Together with Volume 1 it provides a comprehensive overview of the new features added to DB2 for V2.1. Both volumes consist mostly of overhead transparency foils and are not easy to read.

Release level: V2.1

Audience: Database administrators and information center staff

GG24-3331—*Usage Guide*

The *Usage Guide* provides advice on DB2 application design and implementation for novice users. Although this guide was developed for DB2 V2.1, its value has not been significantly diminished by subsequent DB2 releases. Topics covered include DB2 and QMF installation, the establishment of administrative functions, the adoption of naming conventions, security administration, and database recovery. None of the topics are covered in great depth, but this manual is indispensable as an introduction to DB2.

Release level: V2.1

Audience: Application developers, database administrators, information center staff, and systems programmers

GG24-3461—*Performance Report*

The *Performance Report* redbook provides information specific to V2.2. It compares DB2 V2.1 performance with DB2 V2.2 performance, and it also provides useful data on benchmarking procedures such as table sizes, workload, the type of SQL to process, and EXPLAIN interpretations. It is helpful for determining DB2 performance based on well-defined workloads. The workloads outlined in the book can be used for developing your own performance benchmarks.

Release level: V2.2

Audience: Database administrators and information center staff

GG24-3823—*DB2 V2.3 Nondistributed Performance Topics*

DB2 V2.3 Nondistributed Performance Topics discusses the performance enhancements that were applied to DB2 as of V2.3. This redbook explains the details of sequential detection, index lookaside, RDS sort enhancements, join enhancements (including hybrid join), and other miscellaneous enhancements.

Release level:	V2.3
Audience:	Application developers, database administrators, and systems programmers

GG24-4284—*DB2 V3 Performance Topics*

DB2 V3 Performance Topics discusses the performance enhancements that were applied to DB2 as of V3. This redbook explains the details of I/O parallelism, multiple bufferpools, data compression, utility enhancements, and other performance-related improvements to V3.

Release level:	V3
Audience:	Application developers, database administrators, and systems programmers

SG24-4562—*DB2 for MVS/ESA V4 Non-Data Sharing Performance Topics*

This redbook discusses the performance enhancements made to V4 outside the scope of data sharing. It discusses CP parallelism, type 2 indexes, partition independence improvements, stored procedures, and other performance improvements.

Release level:	V4
Audience:	Database administrators and systems programmers

SG24-4611—*DB2 for MVS/ESA V4 Data Sharing Performance Topics*

This redbook discusses the performance impact of data sharing in a DB2 V4 environment. It discusses how to measure performance and gives tips and guidelines for enhancing the performance of data sharing.

Release level:	V4
Audience:	Database administrators and systems programmers

Utilities

The manuals discussed in this section cover how to properly implement and execute DB2 utilities.

GG09-1013—*Utility Analysis*

DB2 V2.1 provided many significant performance enhancements for utility processing. The *Utility Analysis* document details those modifications with a series of benchmarks displaying potential performance gains in the LOAD, REORG, RECOVER, CHECK, COPY, and RUNSTATS utilities.

Release level:	V2.1
Audience:	Application developers, database administrators, information center staff, and systems programmers

GG24-3390—*Utilities Guide*

The GG24-3390 *Utilities Guide*, which replaced the outdated GG24-3130 *Utilities Guide*, is the DB2 utility user's bible. Each utility has a separate section that contains considerations and recommendations for usage. Unfortunately, this redbook does not reflect the significant changes made to most utilities since DB2 V2.3.

Release level:	V2.2
Audience:	Application developers, database administrators, information center staff, and systems programmers

Redbook Subscriptions

If you are a DB2 professional, you should consider subscribing to the ITSO redbooks for DB2. After providing IBM with the subscription number GBOF-6330, you will receive all the DB2-related redbooks automatically when they are published. You will also, of course, be billed for them.

Other DB2-Related Manuals

Many add-on products are used in conjunction with DB2. Several of these products, such as QMF and DB2-PM, are provided by IBM and are used in many DB2 shops. This section provides basic information on the most popular DB2 add-on products that are provided by IBM.

QMF V3.2 Standard Manuals

QMF, IBM's Query Management Facility for DB2, is very heavily used by many DB2 shops for the creation of ad hoc queries and formatted reports. The following manuals are available for QMF.

GC26-4713—*Introducing Query Management Facility*

This general information manual should be used by anyone interested in a very high-level introduction to QMF concepts and facilities. This manual is suitable for all levels of MIS personnel, including management and end users.

SC26-8078—*Using QMF*

This introductory-level manual can be used as a learner's guide to QMF. It is a well-organized manual that teaches the basics of QMF. This manual is recommended for beginning programmers, technicians, and end users who want to learn about the features and functionality provided by QMF.

SC26-4719—*Installing QMF on MVS*

Installing QMF on MVS is usually used by the technical support personnel who install the QMF product. It is not intended for the casual QMF user.

SC26-4721—*Managing QMF for MVS*

This manual is most useful for those planning and administering the QMF environment. It is usually used only by the DBA, systems programmer, or information center analyst responsible for QMF.

SC26-4722—*Developing QMF Applications*

Developing QMF Applications provides comprehensive information on designing and developing QMF applications. A QMF application is any application that calls QMF and uses QMF functions.

SC26-4716—*QMF Reference*

QMF Reference provides a complete reference for QMF commands and syntax. This is the one QMF document that all QMF users should have ready access to.

SC26-4717—*Query-By-Example Guide & Reference*

Not for every QMF user, the *Query-By-Example Guide & Reference* provides the information necessary to write queries using the Query-By-Example (QBE) language, as well as a description of QBE syntax.

SX26-3783—*Reference Summary*

The *Reference Summary* is a smaller, spiral-bound summary of the *QMF Reference.* It is useful for quick QMF syntax checking and as a general QMF reference.

DB2-PM Manuals

DB2-PM, IBM's DB2 performance monitor, is very heavily used by many DB2 shops for batch reporting of DB2 performance statistics. Traditionally, DB2-PM has not provided strong online monitoring support, but IBM has made substantial improvements to DB2-PM in the most recent versions. The manuals below apply to DB2-PM V4.1:

SH12-6164	*DB2-PM Batch User's Guide*
SH12-6163	*DB2-PM Report Reference*
SH11-6167	*DB2-PM Command Reference*
SH12-6168	*DB2-PM Messages Manual*
SH12-6165	*DB2-PM Online Monitor User's Guide*

F

Valid DB2 Data Types

Data Type	Physical Storage	Value Range	COBOL Picture
SMALLINT	2 bytes	–32,768 to +32,767	PIC S9(4) COMP
INTEGER	4 bytes	–2,147,483,648 to +2,147,483,647	PIC S9(9) COMP
REAL	4 bytes	5.4E –79 to 7.2E+75	PIC USAGE COMP -1
FLOAT(1..21)	4 bytes	5.4E –79 to 7.2E+75	PIC USAGE COMP -1
DOUBLE PRECISION	8 bytes	5.4E –79 to 7.2E+75	PIC USAGE COMP -2
FLOAT(22..53)	8 bytes	5.4E –79 to 7.2E+75	PIC USAGE COMP -2
DECIMAL(*m*,*n*)	(*m*/2)+1 bytes	1 -10^{31} to $10^{31}-1$	PIC S9(*m*-*n*)V9(*n*) COMP -3
CHARACTER(*n*)	n bytes	254 characters maximum	PIC X(*n*)
VARCHAR(*n*)	2 to *n*+2 bytes	4,046 bytes maximum 32,704 for 32KB pages	01 VARCHAR. 49 LTH PIC S9(4)COMP. 49 COLUMN PIC X(*n*).
GRAPHIC(*n*)	2*n* bytes	127 double-byte characters maximum	PIC G(*n*) DISPLAY -1
VARGRAPHIC(*n*)	2 to 2*n*+2 bytes	2,023 double-byte characters maximum 32,704 for 32KB pages	01 VGRAPHIC. 49 LENGTH PIC S9(4) 49 COLUMN PIC G(n) DISPLAY -1
DATE	4 bytes	0001-01-01 to 9999-12-31	PIC X(10)
TIME	3 bytes	00.00.00 to 24.00.00	PIC X(8)
TIMESTAMP	10 bytes	0001-01-01.00.00.00.000000 to 9999-12-31.24.00.00.000000	PIC X(10)

G

DB2 Limits

You can use this appendix as a handy reference for the various physical and structural limitations to which DB2 must conform.

Item	*Limit*
STOGROUP name	8 bytes
Volumes per STOGROUP	133
Database name	8 bytes
Maximum number of databases	65,279
Authorization ID	8 bytes
Tablespace name	8 bytes
Partitions per tablespace	
(non-LARGE)	64
(LARGE)	254
Partition size (non-LARGE)	
1 to 16 parts	4 gigabytes
17 to 32 parts	2 gigabytes
33 to 64 parts	1 gigabyte
Partition size (LARGE)	
1 to 254 parts	4 gigabytes
Segment size	64 pages
Tablespace size	1,016 gigabytes
Table name	18 bytes
View name	18 bytes
Alias name	18 bytes
Synonym name	18 bytes
Column name	18 bytes
Referential constraint name	8 bytes
Check constraint name	18 bytes
Maximum length of the check constraint text	3,800 bytes
Cursor name	18 bytes
Host identifier	64 bytes
Server name	16 bytes
Location name	16 bytes

Item	*Limit*
Number of base tables per view	15
Maximum number of columns in the table or view	750 *
Index name	18 bytes (8 recommended **)
Columns per index	64
Index columns size	
(Partitioned)	40 bytes (number of nullable columns ***)
(Non-partitioned)	254 bytes (number of nullable columns)
Plan name	8 bytes
Package name	8 bytes
Collection name	18 bytes
Version name	64 bytes
DBRM name	8 bytes
Maximum length of CHAR	254 bytes
Largest VARCHAR	
(4KB pages)	4,046 bytes
(32KB pages)	32,704 bytes
Maximum length of GRAPHIC	127 characters
Largest VARGRAPHIC	
(4KB pages)	4,046 bytes
(32KB pages)	32,704 bytes
Largest SMALLINT	32,767 bytes
Smallest SMALLINT	–32,768 bytes
Largest INTEGER	2,147,483,647
Smallest INTEGER	–2,147,483,648
Largest DECIMAL	$10^{31} - 1$
Smallest DECIMAL	$1 - 10^{31}$
Largest FLOAT	7.2×10^{75}
Smallest FLOAT	-7.2×10^{75}
Smallest positive FLOAT	5.4×10^{-79}
Largest negative FLOAT	-5.4×10^{79}
Smallest DATE	0001-01-01

Item	*Limit*
Largest DATE	9999-12-31
Smallest TIME	00.00.00
Largest TIME	24.00.00
Smallest TIMESTAMP	0001-01-01-00.00.00.000000
Largest TIMESTAMP	9999-12-31-24.00.00.000000
	Physical Storage
SMALLINT	2 bytes
INTEGER	4 bytes
REAL	4 bytes
DOUBLE PRECISION	8 bytes
DECIMAL (*p*, *m*)	(TRUNCATE (p/2)+1) bytes
CHAR (*n*)	*n* bytes
VARCHAR (*n*)	*n* + 2 bytes
LONG VARCHAR	size of tablespace page
GRAPHIC (*n*)	2 * *n*
VARGRAPHIC (*n*)	(2 * *n*) + 2 bytes
LONG VARGRAPHIC	Size of tablespace page
DATE	4 bytes
TIME	3 bytes
TIMESTAMP	10 bytes
Row length	
(4KB pages)	4,056 bytes
(32KB pages)	32,714 bytes
Row length (with EDITPROC)	
(4KB pages)	4,046 bytes
(32KB pages)	32,704 bytes
Maximum number of rows per page	
(user tables)	255
(DB2 Catalog & Directory)	127
Maximum number of tables or views per subselect	15

	Physical Storage
Largest SQL statement	32,765 bytes
Columns**** per SELECT	750
SQL correlation ID	18 bytes
Predicates per WHERE clause	750
Predicates per HAVING clause	750
Length of columns in ORDER BY	4,000
Length of columns in GROUP BY	4,000
Maximum length of host and indicator variables pointed to in SQLDA	32,767 bytes
Maximum number of parms per stored procedure	limited by size of PARMLIST in SYSPROCEDURES (3,000 bytes)
Maximum size of a single stored procedure parm	32,765 bytes
Concurrent users	2,000
Open data sets	10,000
Largest active log data set	2 gigabytes
Largest archive log data set	2 gigabytes
Maximum active log copies	2
Maximum archive log copies	2
Maximum active log data sets	31
Maximum archive log volumes	1,000
Maximum DBRM entry size	131,072 bytes

* If the table is a dependent, it can contain a maximum of 749 columns. The value (749 or 750) depends on the complexity of the CREATE VIEW statement.

** If the index name is longer than 8 bytes, DB2 derives an index space name using the index name. An index space name must be unique in the given database. The index space name that DB2 generates for index names of nine characters or more may be hard to track when you're performing DASD management and object monitoring.

*** For both partitioning and nonpartitioning indexes, you must subtract 1 for each nullable column in the index to determine the maximum length of the columns that can be assigned to the index. Although you can specify up to 254 bytes for a partitioning index, only the first 40 are used to determine actual partitioning.

**** The maximum is for all items in the SELECT list, not just columns. For example, expression and constants can be included in the SELECT list.

H

Regional DB2 User Groups

The best way to keep up-to-date on DB2 and to learn more tricks of the trade is to attend a DB2 user group meeting. Many regional DB2 user groups are located throughout North America and the world.

International DB2 User Group

401 North Michigan Avenue
Chicago, IL 60611-4267
Phone: 312/644-6610 or 312/527-6677
Fax: 312/321-6869
Web: `http://www.idug.org`
E-mail: `idug@compuserve.com`

The International DB2 User Group (IDUG) is an independent, not-for-profit, user-run organization whose mission is to support and strengthen the information systems community by providing education and services to promote the effective utilization of the DB2 family of products. IDUG hosts three annual user conferences: one in the USA, one in Europe, and one in the Pacific Rim.

Regional User Groups

The following lists provide contact information so that you can participate in a DB2 user group in your area. For the most up-to-date information on who to contact, when meetings are planned, and how to attend, you can visit the IDUG Web site at `http://www.idug.org/regional`.

USA: Eastern Time Zone

Atlanta DB2 Users Group

Patrick Ross
Total System Services, Inc.
7374 Wood Hollow Way
Stone Mountain, GA 30087
Phone: 404/319-2977

Baltimore/Washington DB2 Users Group

Teresa Pascal
P.O. Box 18554
BWI Airport, MD 21240
Phone: 301/803-6144
E-mail: `tpascal@vnet.ibm.com`

Boston DB2 Technology Exchange

Nate Murphy
Nate Murphy and Associates
5 Lancelot Court
Mount Laurel, NJ 08054
Phone: 609/234-2353
Fax: 609/234-0182
CompuServe: 105174,1470

Central Ohio DB2 Users Group

John Cochran 3-13-3
Nationwide Insurance
Plaza III, P.O. Box 1559
Columbus, OH 43216-1559
Phone: 614/249-3187
Fax: 614/249-4442
Web: http://ourworld.compuserve.com/homepages/schulzp/codug.htm

Central Pennsylvania DB2 Users Group

Cathy L. Peck
Pennsylvania Blue Shield
1800 Center Street CHC-200 L3
P.O. Box 890089
Camp Hill, PA 17089
Phone: 717/975-7396
Fax: 717/975-5001
E-mail: cpeck@pabs.com

Delaware Valley DB2 and SQL/DS Users Group

Don Baker
2126 Guernsey Avenue
Abington, PA 19001
Phone: 215/466-8364
Fax: 215/563-0517

Indiana DB2 User Group (INDUG)

John Hsu
Eli Lilly & Company, DC 2029
Lilly Corporate Center
Indianapolis, IN 46825
Phone: 317/276-8635
Fax: 317/276-5507

Kentucky DB2 Users Group

Mara Kleczinski
Ashland Oil
3475 Dabney Drive
Lexington, KY 40512
Phone: 606/357-7777
Fax: 606/357-2229

Michigan DB2 Users Group

Carol Little
Michigan DB2 Users Group
30600 Telegraph Road
Suite 2340
Bingham Farms, MI 48025
Phone: 810/646-1342
Fax: 810/646-1275

New England DB2 Users Group

Carol Gagne-Cestone
ITT Sheraton Corporation
1505 Washington Street
Braintree, MA 02184
Phone: 617/380-4267
Fax: 617/849-1273

North Florida Database Users Group

Michael McBride
Florida Department of Transportation
605 Swannee Street
Mail Station 43
Tallahassee, FL 32399-0450
Phone: 904/488-1954
Fax: 904/922-4143
E-mail: `mcbridm@dot.state.fl.us`

Northeast Florida Relational Users Group

Dick Sheltz
Barnett System Technologies
9000 South Side Boulevard
Building 300, Mail Code 576335
Jacksonville, FL 32256

Phone: 904/987-7737
Fax: 904/464-6478
E-mail: rpsheltz@jax-inter.net

Northeast Ohio DB2 Users Group

Michael James
S & P Solutions, Inc.
730 Som Center Road
Suite 100
Cleveland, OH 44143
Phone: 216/646-9111
Fax: 216/646-1429
E-mail: sales@sps-solutions.com

Northern New England DB2 Users Group

Collin Fay
National Semiconductor
333 Western Avenue
Mail Stop 01-20
South Portland, ME 04106
Phone: 207/775-4612
Fax: 207/761-6067

Pittsburgh Large Users Group (PLUG)

Ronald Shirey
Duquesne Light
One Oxford Centre
301 Grant Street
Pittsburgh, PA 15279
Phone: 412/393-6546

Richmond DB2 Users Group

Ken Hynes
Blue Cross Blue Shield
Maildrop [illegible]
2221 Edward Holland Drive
Richmond, VA 23230
Phone: 804/354-4586
Fax: 804/354-2885
CompuServe: 73733,2770

Southeastern IBM Relational Database Users Group

Bing Sinski
First Union National Bank of NC
1525 West W.T. Harris Blvd (2B2)
Charlotte, NC 28288-0078
Phone: 704/590-1373

South Florida Database Users Group

Johnnie Phillips
Pratt & Whitney
P.O. Box 109600
M/S 712-08
West Palm Beach, FL 33410-9600
Phone: 407/796-7622
Fax: 407/796-4780

Tampa Bay Relational Users Group

Bill Schray
Time Customer Services
1 North Dale Mabry Highway
Tampa, FL 33609-2700
Phone: 813/878-6479
Fax: 813/878-6350

Triangle DB2 Users Group

Mike Dempsey
UNC Hospitals
Information Services Division, 2nd Floor
Carr Mill Mall
Carrboro, NC 27510
Phone: 919/966-4696
Fax: 919/966-2110
E-mail: `mdempse.isd1@mail.unch.unc.edu`

Tri-State DB2 Technology Exchange (TRIDEX)

Nate Murphy
Nate Murphy and Associates
5 Lancelot Court
Mount Laurel, NJ 08054

Phone: 609/234-2353
Fax: 609/234-0182
CompuServe: `105174,1470`

Tri-State DB2 Users Group

Peter McDonough
Cincinnati Gas & Electric
139 East 4th Street
Room 651 A
Cincinnati, OH 45202
Phone: 513/287-3892
Fax: 513/287-3812

Upstate New York Open Database Users Group

Jill Werner
34 Church St.
Pittsford, NY 14534
Phone: 716/647-7878
Email: `jill_werner@mc.xerox.com`

USA: Central Time Zone

Alabama DB2 Users Group (ADUG)

Blane McCarthy
Big B, Inc.
2600 Morgan Road
Bessener, AL 35023
Phone: 205/424-3421 x495
Fax: 205/426-8748

Arkansas DB2 Users Group

Paul Hartjen
PLATINUM *technology, inc.*
850 Warrenville Road
3rd Floor
Lisle, IL 60532
Phone: 800/442-6861 x8047
Fax: 630/241-8200

Central Illinois Relational Database Users Group

Mike Friedrich
Illinois Department of Revenue
101 West Jefferson
Springfield, IL 62974
Phone: 217/785-6512
Fax: 217/524-2552

Database User Association of Iowa

Rick Reger
Farm Bureau
5400 University Avenue
West Des Moines, IA 50266
Phone: 515/225-5952
Fax: 515/226-6063

DB2 Forum: Dallas

Gabrielle Wiorkowski
Gabrielle & Associates
9922 Lincolnshire Court
Rockwall, TX 75087
Phone: 214/412-8866
Fax: 214/412-8867
CompuServe: 74732,2627

Great Plains DB2 Forum, Inc.

Carol Beck
U.S. West Communications
1299 Farnam
Room 505
Omaha, NE 68102
Phone: 402/422-4030
Pager: 402/977-7927
Fax: 402/422-8216
E-mail: croseno@creighton.edu

Green Country DB2 Users Group

Ann Darks
Amoco Production
P.O. Box 591

4502 East 41st St., 1H12
Tulsa, OK 74102-0591
Phone: 918/581-4493
Fax: 918/581-3203

Gulf South Association of DB2 Professionals

Fred Lavens
Lockheed Martin
13800 Old Gentilly Road
New Orleans, LA 70129
Phone: 504/257-1144
Fax: 504/257-4465

Heart of America DB2 Users Group

Tim White
Yellow Technology Services
10990 Row Avenue
P.O. Box 7950
Overland Park, KS 66207-0950
Phone: 913/344-3819
Fax: 913/344-3523

ILLINOIS STATE GOVERNMENT DB2 USERS GROUP

Alice Christensen
Illinois Department of Central Management Services
201 West Adams
Springfield, IL 62706
Phone: 217/785-0145
Fax: 217/524-0945

Midwest DB2 Users Group

Madeline Lebedow
676 North St. Clair
Suite 1765
Chicago, IL 60611
Phone: 312/951-9600
Fax: 312/951-9854

Mississippi Ultimate DB2 User Group

Martin McKay
Southern Farm Bureau Life Insurance
P.O. Box 78
1401 Livingston Lane
Jackson, MS 39205-0078
Phone: 601/981-5332 x326

Nashville DB2 Users Group

Elizabeth Moore
American General Center
Mail Code 0720
Nashville, TN 37250
Phone: 615/749-1492
Fax: 615/749-2421

Relational Database Exchange

Betty Petty
12121 Northwest Freeway
Suite 309
Houston, TX 77092

St. Louis DB2 Users Group

Linda Buechler
Southwestern Bell Telephone
801 Chestnut, 6-8-N4
St. Louis, MO 63101-2501
Phone: 314/340-0977
Fax: 314/340-9441

Twin Cities Database Users Group

Barbara Burkey
Target Corp.
33 South 6th Street
Minneapolis, MN 55402
Phone: 612/375-7041
Fax: 612/375-4628

Wisconsin DB2 Users Group

Debbie Lechmaier
MNI Data Services
Wisconsin DB2 Users Group
P.O. Box 83292
Milwaukee, WI 53223-8592
Phone: 414/357-3803
Fax: 414/357-5725

USA: Mountain Time Zone

Boise DB2 Users Group

Sue Belcher
Boise Cascade
P.O. Box 50
Boise, ID 83728
Phone: 208/384-6161
Fax: 208/384-7199

Colorado DB2 User Group

Amy Swanson
Stanford Place 3
Raymond James Consulting
4582 South Ulster Street
Suite 100
Denver, CO 80237
Phone: 303/770-7200
Fax: 303/770-5452

New Mexico DB2 Users Group

Sandra Ulibarri
State of New Mexico
715 Alta Vista
P.O. Drawer 26110
Santa Fe, NM 87502
Phone: 505/827-2087
Fax: 505/827-2325
Internet: `sulibar@isd.state.nm.us`

Southwest Area Relational Users Group

Daniel Mueller
Salt River Project
P.O. Box 52025
Phoenix, AZ 85072-2025
Phone: 602/236-6899
Fax: 602/236-6541

USA: Pacific Time Zone

Los Angeles Area DB2 Users Group

Tom Glass
City of Long Beach
Information Services
333 West Ocean Boulevard
Long Beach, CA 90802
Phone: 310/570-6317
Fax: 310/570-6511
E-mail: `toglass@ci.long-beach.ca.us`

Northern Oregon DB2 Exchange

Ricardo Chu
Fred Meyer, Inc.
3800 SE 22nd Avenue
M/S: MO/SDV
Portland, OR 97202
Phone: 503/797-3940
Fax: 503/797-3822
E-mail: `chucrew@telestream.com`
Web: `http://www.geocities.com/researchtriangle/5522`

Sacramento DB2 Users Group

Ira Trepper
State of California
Teale Data Center
2005 Evergreen
Sacramento, CA 95815
Phone: 916/263-1750
Fax: 916/263-1346

San Francisco Bay Area DB2 Users Group

Alex Schwab
Systems Partners
2 Theatre Square
Orinda, CA 94563
Phone: 510/254-3110
Fax: 510/253-2576
E-mail: `aschwab@syspart.com`

Canada

Central Canada DB2 Users Group

Tim Johnson
Central Canada DB2 Users Group
2175 Sheppard Avenue East
Ste. 309
North York
Ontario, Canada M2J 1W8
Phone: 416/920-5777 x719
Fax: 416/920-3532
CompuServe: `75114,2740`
E-mail: `ccdb2@interlog.com`
Web: `http://www.interlog.com/~ccdb2`

Ottawa DB2 Users Group

Mike Giovinazzo
DRT Systems International
P.O. Box 55063
240 Sparks Street
Ottawa, Ontario, Canada K1P 1A1
Phone: 613/723-7311
Fax: 613/723-7117

Quebec DB2 Users Group

Gilles Belanger
Canadian National Railway
C.P. 5661
Succursale B
Montreal, PQ
Canada M2J 1W8
Phone: 514/399-5682
Fax: 514/399-6526
E-mail: belang09@cn.ca

Asia Pacific

Adelaide DB2 Users Group

Colin Best
Electoral Trust of South Australia
#1 Anzac Highway
Keswick, South Australia
Australia
Phone: 61 8 301 2250
Fax: 61 8 404 5058

Brisbane DB2 Users Group

Peter Spinoglio
Metway Bank
36 Wickham Terrace
Brisbane 4000
Australia
Phone: 61 7 836 1105
Fax: 61 7 835 5637

Canberra DB2 Users Group

Frank Ryan
Australia Tax Office
P.O. Box 900
#2 Constitution Avenue
Civic Square

Canberra ACT 2601
Australia
Phone: 61 6 216 5644
Fax: 61 6 216 5040

Hong Kong Computer Society

Joseph Fong/Brian Siu
Unit D, 1/Fl Luckifast Building
No. 1 Stone Nullah Lane
Wanchai, Hong Kong

India DB2 Users Group

Nitin Shah
Wipro Systems
88, M.G. Road, S.B. Towers
Banglore 560001
India
Phone: 91 80 5588613
E-mail: nitinr@putnam.wipsys.soft.net

Johannesburg DB2 Users Group

Hennie Mynhardt
First National Bank
Johannesburg
South Africa
Phone: 27 11 889 4251
Fax: 27 11 889 4660

Malaysia DB2 Users Group

Eric Vesely
Analyst Workbench Consulting SDN BHD
No 272A Jalan 5/51 Petaling Garden
46000 Petaling Jaya
Selangor Darul Ehsan
Kuala Lumpur
Malaysia
Phone: 60 3 791 5986

Melbourne DB2 Users Group

John H'ng
Infopro Consulting Pty. Ltd.
27 Wakley Crescent
Wantirna South, Vic 3152
Australia
Phone: 61 412 411 114
Fax: 61 3 9800 1052
E-mail: jhng@vitgaxis.telecom.com.au or mdug@mdug.org.au
Web: http://www.mdug.org.au

Middle-East DB2 Users Group

Tung Nguyen
National Bank of Kuwait S.A.K.
P.O. Box 95
Safat 13001
Kuwait
Phone: 965 242 2011 ext. 2540
Fax: 965 246 4773
E-mail: tung58@nbk.com

New Zealand DB2 Users Group

Denis Martin
IBM
171 Featherston Street
Wellington 6001
New Zealand
Phone: 64 4 576 5995
Fax: 64 4 576 5915
Internet: dmartin@sydvm1 or db2nzl@vnet.ibm.com

Perth DB2 Users Group

Chris Benthien
HBF
125 Murray Street
Perth, WA 6000
Australia
Phone: 61 9 265 6271
Fax: 61 9 265 6380
E-mail: chris_benthien@hbf.com.au

Singapore DB2 Users Group

Peter Gaik-Sun Ong
PLATINUM *technology, inc.*
30 Bideford Road
#03-03 Thongsia Building
Singapore
Phone: 65 738 6891
Fax: 65 738 3931

Sydney DB2 Users Group

Bruce Allen
36 Austin Street
Lane Cove, NSW 2066
Australia
CompuServe: `100352,733`

Western Cape DB2 Users Group

John Green
P.O. Box 1
Sanlamhof 7532
Capetown, South Africa
Phone: 27 21 947 3312
Fax: 27 21 947 2791

Europe

DB2 Users Group: UK

Trevor Hackett
Amdahl UK
Windsor House
Britannia Road
Walthamcross
Herts, England EN8 7NX
Phone: 44 99 278 7999
Fax: 44 81 577 2871

Dutch DB2 Users Group

Klaus Brant
BMC Software
P.O. Box 1050
3430 BB Nieuwegein
The Netherlands

East Pennines Regional User Group

Hamid Houman
IBM U.K. Ltd.
11 Albion Street
Leeds LS1 5EU
United Kingdom
Phone: 44 53 235 6757
Fax: 44 53 242 5890

Finland DB2 Users Group

Anne Lesell
FD Finanssidata
P.O. Box 308
00101 Helsinki
Finland
Phone: 358 9 404 3383
Fax: 358 9 404 3007
E-mail: `anne.lesell@finanssidata.fd.mailnet.fi`

Great Britain DB2 Users Group

David Harris-White
Turnberry House
30 Caldegotte Lake Drive
Milton Keynes MK7 8LE
England
Phone: 44 90 827 4274
Fax: 44 90 827 4999

Manchester DB2 Users Group

Steve Crocker Tel
OPS/DBSS
Barclays Computer Operations
Radbroke Hall
Cheshire

Knutsford WA1 6 9EU
United Kingdom
Phone: 44 742 730 161

Midland DB2 Users Group

Grant Payne
Taylan Consultancy
Wrens Park House
Tobys Hill, Draycott in the Clay
Ashbourne, Dubshire D65 BT
England
Phone: 44 28 354 5320
Fax: 44 28 353 9891

Scottish Relational Users Forum

Hugh Levey
IBM UK Ltd
Inverkip Road
Spango Valley
Greenock PA16 OAH
Scotland, UK
Phone: 44 47 589 8819
Fax: 44 57 589 8904

SQLADRIA: Croatia

Zeljen Stanic
CTK - SQLADRIA
51 000 Rijeka
Croatia
Pomerio 29/I
Phone: 385 51 338 531
Fax: 385 51 338 531

Swedish DB2 Users Group

Lars Svanberg
RFV
S-851 93 Sundsvall
Sweden
Phone: 46 60 18 72 96
Fax: 46 60 18 73 74
E-mail: `lars.svanberg@svall.rfv.sfa.se`

UK-Computer Measurement Group

Caroline Wagstaff
Pound Court
Pound Street
Newbury, Berkshire RG14 6AA
England
Phone: 44 1635 32338
Fax: 44 1635 43275
E-mail: caroline@ukcmg.org.uk
Web: http://www.ukcmg.org.uk/ukcmg/

South America

GUDB2: Brazil

Sergio Roberto Ricupero
Dept: GSI/GPT
Pirelli Adm. & Ser. LTDA
Avenue Alexandre de Gusmao, 177
CEP: 09110
Santo Andre - Sao Paulo
Brazil
Phone: 55 11 411 2703
Fax: 55 11 411 2698

South American I/S Brazil DB2 User Group

Marcelo da Silva Fernandes
Av. Pres. Vargas, 824/VA15
Rio de Janeiro - RJ
Brazil 20071-001
Phone: 55 21 271 3367
Fax: 55 21 276 2797

I

DB2 on Other Platforms

Although DB2 began its life on the mainframe, the advent of client/server technology caused IBM to create versions of DB2 for additional platforms. In short, DB2 is no longer just a mainframe product.

The DB2 Family

Versions of DB2 exist for a large array of platforms, of which MVS (or OS/390) is only one (see Table I.1). These products are now all collectively referred to by IBM as *DB2*. The proper way to refer to any individual offering in the DB2 family is *DB2 for (operating system)* (for example, DB2 for OS/390 or DB2 for AIX).

Many shops implement applications on several different platforms and interconnect them using client/server development methods.

Table I.1. The DB2 family of products.

Platform	*Operating System*	*AKA (Old Name)*
AS/400	OS/400	SQL/400
Mainframe	MVS, OS/390	DB2
Mainframe	VM	SQL/DS
Mainframe	VSE	SQL/DS
Workstation Manager	OS/2	OS/2 Database
Workstation	Windows NT	—
IBM (server)	AIX	DB2/6000
Hewlett-Packard	HP-UX	—
Sun	Solaris	—
Seimens-Nixdorf	SINIX	—

However, these products are not simply "plug and play" commodities simply because they al share the name *DB2*. There are some big differences among these products in their curren releases. The biggest differences are relatively easy to detect and include the following:

- Differences imposed due to operating system constraints (OS/2 versus MVS versus AIX)
- Back-level compatibility issues (that is, ensuring that DB2 for OS/2 will work with code developed for OS/2 Database Manager)
- Workstation orientation differences such as GUI interfaces and drag-and-drop menus
- Subsystem-centric implementation (OS/390) versus database-centric implementation (workstation)

However, there are some "gotchas" lurking under the covers that might be more difficult to find.

Some Major Differences

Of the basic differences mentioned earlier, the only one that might not be obvious is the focus of the DBMS implementation. DB2 for common servers (the group name for the workstation and UNIX server flavors of DB2) is database-centric. This implies that each new database carries its own system catalog with it. Additionally, it is not possible to simply access tables across different databases; distributed access is required.

On OS/390, DB2 is subsystem-centric. A single system catalog spans databases. Each subsystem has a unique identification, and you can create multiple databases within it. Distributed requests are not required to access databases within the same subsystem (or, indeed, across multiple subsystems in a data-sharing environment).

Directories

Another concept that is different at the workstation level is that of a directory. The DB2 for MVS Directory houses DBMS system-related information regarding DBD structure, skeleton plan and skeleton package table, RBA log ranges, and utility control data. The information cannot be updated by the user but is managed and controlled by DB2.

At the workstation level, a directory is another matter altogether. For example, the directory structure used by DB2 for OS/2 controls the overall environment. The directories used by DB2 for OS/2 are as follow:

- The *System Database Directory* identifies the databases that can be accessed from the workstation and contains an entry for each local and remote one. Each database entry contains the database name, alias, entry type, and location.
- One *Volume Database Directory* is allocated per disk drive that contains a workstation database. Each entry identifies the location of a specific database on the drive.
- The *Workstation Directory* is used to make a connection to a remote database server. It is used in conjunction with the Database Connection Services Directory to make a connection to a remote host server.
- The *Database Connection Services Directory* is used by DDCS/2 to make a connection to a remote host server.

Not only is it possible for the user to update these directories, but it is required. The workstation directories define the environment for DB2/2. Without the proper information recorded in these directories, DB2/2 might not function in the desired manner. The information in these directories is somewhat analogous to DB2 for MVS DSNZPARMs and SYSDDF.

Database Structures

Not all the objects available to DB2 for OS/390 users are supported at the workstation level. For example, hardware-specific DB2 objects such as tablespaces and storage groups are not available for DB2 on other platforms. As such, partitioning and segmenting as it is done on the OS/390 flavor of DB2 is not possible. However, DB2 for common servers does provide a feature known as a segmented table. But this is not the same concept as a DB2 for OS/390 segmented tablespace. Common server segmented tables are used to span volumes, enabling DB2 to get around the 2 gigabyte file size limitations under AIX.

The file structure used for databases differs from platform to platform. For example, DB2 for OS/390 use VSAM Linear Data Sets (LDS) or Entry Sequenced Data Sets (ESDS). A database deployed on DB2 for common servers uses two files for table data: one for normal data and a second to store long fields. These workstation files are flat files, not VSAM files.

Although tables are basically the same for all of the DB2 environments, not all of the DDL options are provided in all of the environments. For example, DB2 for OS/390 does not support triggers, and DB2 for common servers does not allow `VALIDPROCs`, `FIELDPROCs`, and `EDITPROCs`.

Optimizer Differences

One of the most significant benefits of relational databases is that they provide built-in optimization. The DB2 for OS/390 optimizer is well-known to mainframe DB2 users, but how similar are the other DB2 optimizers?

The DB2 for common servers product uses the latest and greatest optimization technology from IBM's Almaden labs: the Starburst optimizer. Starburst is a database optimization research project that has been covered quite extensively in the academic press. Although some Starburst technology will find its way to DB2 for OS/390, the DB2 for OS/390 optimizer will never be completely replaced by Starburst technology. The DB2 for OS/390 optimizer has been finely tuned for its environment over the course of more than a decade.

Another interesting tidbit is that DB2 for OS/400 provides an access method for programmers in which they can bypass the relational engine. This is not encouraged, but it is available.

Summary

The intent of this appendix is not to criticize IBM or to provide an exhaustive listing of differences among the DB2 family product offerings. Instead, its purpose is to inform you that DB2 is available on multiple platforms and to prepare you for the inevitable differences from DB2 for OS/390 that you will encounter.

For more extensive coverage of the differences between IBM's various SQL implementations and DB2 products, consult your local IBM representative and the IBM manuals. Another good reference manual is the IBM *SQL Reference*, Volumes 1 and 2 (SC26-8416). It provides an up-to-date comparison of the SQL implementation within each of IBM's database management systems.

J

Summary of Version 4 and Version 5 Changes

This appendix provides short checklists of features for the versions of DB2 introduced by IBM since the publication of the previous edition of this book. This book has been updated to include information on two new DB2 versions:

- DB2 version 4 (also known as DB2 V4 or DB2 V4.1)
- DB2 version 5 (also known as DB2 V5 or DB2 V5.1)

DB2 Version 4 Features

Version 4

IBM introduced many new and useful features with DB2 V4, available since December 1995. Most large shops are using DB2 V4 in production today (while planning to move to DB2 V5).

Database Administration Features

DB2 Catalog REORG

User-defined DB2 Catalog Indexes

COPY, RECOVER, and REORG Improvements

Dynamic SQL Security Improvements

REFERENCES Privilege

Data Sharing

Type 2 Indexes

User-defined Defaults

Check Constraints

UNIQUE WHERE NOT NULL Indexes

Row-level Locking

Multi-character Command Prefixes

Tracking DFSMS Concurrent Copies in the DB2 Catalog

Client/Server Features

Stored Procedures

Support for 25,000 Distributed Connections

Performance Features

Partition Scanning (Page Range Scan)

Query CP Parallelism

Uncommitted Read (Read-through Locks)

No Locks on Type 2 Indexes

Programming Features

Outer Join

In-line Views (Nested Tables)

COALESCE Function

Column Renaming Using AS

DCLGEN Improvements

DB2 Catalog Impact

Communications Database Moved to the DB2 Catalog Database

3 New Tables

16 Tables Have One or More New or Changed Columns

18 Total New Columns

21 Total Revised Columns

DB2 Version 5 Features

Version 5

DB2 V5 was first announced by IBM as V4.2. However, late in 1996 IBM changed plans and switched from a point release to a full-fledged new version. DB2 V5, generally available since June 1997, is laden with new features.

Database Administration Features

Large Tables (up to 254 partitions; approx. 1 TB)

Multiple Stored Procedure Address Spaces

Table Renaming

ASCII Server Support

Native TCP/IP

DCE Security

DDL-based Support Rows Per Page (up to 255)

Workstation GUI Install

Utility Features

Online REORG

LOAD and REORG Improvements

COPY with Thresholds

RUNSTATS Using Sampling

Programming Features

CASE Expressions

Stored Procedure Result Sets

Temporary Tables

RRSAF

Call-level Interface (ODBC)

NULLIF Function

STRIP Function

Visual EXPLAIN

Performance Features

Optimization Changes

Skip Partition Scanning

Changes to Stage 1 and Indexable Predicates

SQL Caching

Persistent Dynamic BIND

Query Sysplex Parallelism

Partition Locking

Data Sharing Improvements

DB2 Catalog Impact

Communications Database Moved to the DB2 Catalog Database

8 New or Renamed Tables

31 Tables Have One or More New or Changed Columns

65 Total New Columns

59 Total Revised Columns

I

Index

Symbols

A

E

O

T

U

V

W

X-Z

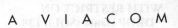

MACMILLAN COMPUTER PUBLISHING USA

A VIACOM COMPANY

Technical Support:

If you need assistance with the information in this book or with a CD/Disk accompanying the book, please access the Knowledge Base on our Web site at **http://www.superlibrary.com/general/support.** Our most Frequently Asked Questions are answered there. If you do not find the answer to your questions on our Web site, you may contact Macmillan Technical Support (317) 581-3833 or e-mail us at **support@mcp.com.**

What's on the Disc

The companion CD-ROM contains all of the author's source code and samples from the book, as well as many third-party software products.

Windows 3.1 and Windows NT 3.5.1 Installation Instructions

1. Insert the CD-ROM into your CD-ROM drive.
2. From File Manager or Program Manager, choose Run from the File menu.
3. Type `<drive>\SETUP.EXE` and press Enter, where `<drive>` corresponds to the drive letter of your CD-ROM. For example, if your CD-ROM is drive D:, type `D:\SETUP.EXE` and press Enter.
4. Installation creates a program named DB2 Developer's Guide. This group will contain icons to browse the CD-ROM.

Windows 95 and Windows NT 4.0 Installation Instructions

1. Insert the CD-ROM into your CD-ROM drive.
2. From the Windows 95 desktop, double-click the My Computer icon.
3. Double-click the icon representing your CD-ROM drive.
4. Double-click the icon titled `SETUP.EXE` to run the installation program.
5. Installation creates a program group named DB2 Developer's Guide. This group will contain icons to browse the CD-ROM.

NOTE

If Windows 95 is installed on your computer and you have the AutoPlay feature enabled, the `SETUP.EXE` program starts automatically whenever you insert the disc into your CD-ROM drive.

Techmedia-COMPUTER BOOKS

TITLE	PRICE
◆3D STUDIO / ANIMATION	**PRICE**
INSIDE 3D STUDIO MAX Vol I (W/CD)	**Rs.** 499/-
INSIDE 3D STUDIO MAX Vol II (W/CD)	350/-
INSIDE 3D STUDIO MAX Vol III (W/CD)	399/-
INSIDE 3D STUDIO Rel. 4 (W/CD)	450/-
3D STUDIO MAX Fundamentals (W/CD)	350/-
3D STUDIO for Beginners (W/CD)	240/-
3D GRAPHICS & ANIMATION From Starting up to Standing Out (W/CD)	399/-
TEACH YOURSELF 3D STUDIO MAX IN 14 DAYS (W/CD)	**MAY'98**
◆ABAP	
TEACH YOURSELF ABAP IN 21 DAYS (W/CD)	**JUN'98**
◆ACTIVE SERVER	
ACTIVE SERVER PAGES UNLEASHED (W/CD)	**399/-**
TEACH YOURSELF ACTIVE SERVER PAGES IN 14 DAYS	**165/-**
◆ACTIVE X	
DEVELOPING ACTIVE X COMPONENTS WITH VISUAL BASIC 5 (W/CD)	**450/-**
Teach Yourself ACTIVE X PROGRAMMING in 21 Days (W/CD)	270/-
TEACH YOURSELF ACTIVE X CONTROL Programming with VISUAL BASIC 5 in 21 Days (W/CD)	275/-
◆ACCESS 97	
Peter Norton's guide to ACCESS 97 PROGRAMMING (W/CD)	399/-
ALISON BALTER'S **MASTERING ACCESS 97 DEVELOPMENT-SECOND EDITION (W/CD)**	**399/-**
Teach Yourself ACCESS 97 IN 24 HOURS	135/-
◆ADOBE	
Adobe WEB DESIGN & PUBLISHING Unleashed (W/CD)	450/-
◆AUTOCAD	
AUTOCAD 14 Fundamentals	195/-
Inside AUTOCAD 14 (W/CD)	450/-
◆BACKOFFICE	
MICROSOFT **BACKOFFICE UNLEASHED (W/CD) (SECOND EDITION)**	**499/-**
(Covers NT SERVER 4.0, SQL SERVER 6.5, TRANSACTION SERVER 1.0, EXCHANGE SERVER 5.0, IIS 3.0, PROXY SERVER 1.0)	
◆BROADBAND	
CISCO SYSTEMS RESIDENTIAL BROADBAND	**495/-**
◆C	
Teach Yourself C in 24 Hours (W/CD)	165/-

TITLE	PRICE
◆C	
TEACH YOURSELF C IN 21 DAYS - FORTH EDITION	**195/-**
◆C++	
C++ Interactive Course (W/CD)	399/-
C++ UNLEASHED (W/CD)	**JUN'98**
C++ PRIMER PLUS : MITCHELL WAITE SIGNATURE SERIES (3RD -REVI. EDN.)-(W/CD)	**450/-**
Teach Yourself ANSI C++ in 21 Days	399/-
Teach Yourself C++ in 21 Days	225/-
Teach Yourself C++ in 24 Hours (W/CD)	165/-
◆CGI	
CGI HOW — TO (W/CD)	399/-
Teach Yourself CGI PROG. with PERL 5 in a week (W/CD)	275/-
TEACH YOURSELF CGI PROGRAMMING IN A WEEK	**150/-**
◆CLIENT / SERVER	
CLIENT / SERVER Unleashed (W/CD)	399/-
◆COBOL	
COBOL UNLEASHED	**JUN'98**
Teach Yourself COBOL in 21 Days (with YEAR 2000 problems solutions)	300/-
◆DIGITAL PHOTOGRAPHY	
Teach Yourself DIGITAL PHOTOGRAPHY in 14 Days	180/-
◆CORELDRAW 8	
TEACH YOURSELF CORELDRAW 8 IN 24 HOURS	**135/-**
◆DATA COMMUNICATION	
UNDERSTANDING DATA COMMUNICATION - FIFTH EDITION (COVERS PDA'S, ISDN, SNMP, TCP/IP)	**150/-**
◆DOS	
Peter Norton's COMPLETE GUIDE TO DOS 6.22	399/-
◆DB2	
DB2 DEVELOPER'S GUIDE (Also cover V4 and V5) (W/CD) - 3RD ED.	**495/-**
TEACH YOUSELF DB2 UNIVERSAL SERVER IN 21 DAYS (W/CD)	**JUN'98**
◆DIRECTOR - MACROMEDIA	
Inside MACROMEDIA DIRECTOR 6 with Lingo (W/CD)	450/-
MACROMEDIA WEB PUBLISHING Unleashed (W/CD)	450/-

TITLE	PRICE
◆EXCHANGE SERVER	
MS EXCHANGE SERVER 5 Unleashed (W/CD)	450/-
◆EXCEL 97	
Teach Yourself MS EXCEL 97 in 24 Hours	135/-
◆FRONTPAGE 98	
TEACH YOURSELF MS FRONT PAGE 98 IN A WEEK	**180/-**
◆HARDWARE	
Winn Rosch HARDWARE BIBLE (W/CD)	450/-
◆HOMEPAGE	
Teach Yourself to create HOMEPAGE in 24 Hours (W/CD)	180/-
◆HTML	
HTML 4 Unleashed (W/CD)	450/-
HTML 4 HOW TO (W/CD) - WAITE GROUP	**399/-**
Teach Yourself DYNAMIC HTML in a week	195/-
Teach Yourself WEB PUBLISHING with HTML in 14 Days (W/CD)	570/-
Teach Yourself HTML 4 in 24 Hours	120/-
DYNAMIC HTML UNLEASHED	**300/-**
◆ILLUSTRATOR 7	
TEACH YOURSELF ILLUSTRATOR 7 IN 24 HOURS	**135/-**
◆INFORMIX	
INFORMIX Unleashed (W/CD)	499/-
◆INTRANETS	
INTRANETS Unleashed (W/CD)	499/-
◆INTERNET	
Teach Yourself THE INTERNET in 24 Hours	150/-
◆INTERNET EXPLORER 4	
Teach Yourself INTERNET EXPLORER 4 in 24 Hours	120/-
◆INTERNET-NETWORKING	
CISCO SYSTEMS INTERNETWORKING TECHNOLOGIES HANDBOOK	**499/-**
◆INTERNET SECURITY	
INTERNET SECURITY Professional Ref. (W/CD)	499/-
MAXIMUM SECURITY : A Hacker's Guide to Protecting Your Internet Site and Network (W/CD)	**499/-**
◆JAVA	
JAVA 1.1 Interactive Course (W/CD)	495/-
JAVA 1.1 Developer's Guide (W/CD)	499/-
JAVA 1.1 CERTIFICATION TRAINING GUIDE-(W/CD)	**399/-**
JAVA INDUSTRIAL STRENGTH-(W/CD)	**450/-**
JAVA 1.1 UNLEASHED - 3RD REVISED EDITION (W/CD)	**499/-**
MAXIMUM JAVA 1.1-(W/CD)	**450/-**

TITLE	PRICE
◆JAVA	
PETER NORTON's Guide to JAVA Programming (W/CD)	450/-
TEACH YOURSELF MORE JAVA 1.1 IN 21 DAYS	**165/-**
TEACH YOURSELF JAVA 1.1 IN 21 DAYS - SECOND EDITION (W/CD)	**225/-**
MITCHELL Waite Object-Oriented Programming in JAVA (W/CD)	450/-
Teach Yourself JAVA 1.1 Programming in 24 Hours (W/CD)	165/-
◆JAVA SCRIPT	
JAVA SCRIPT Interactive Course (W/CD)	450/-
◆JDBC	
Teach Yourself DATABASE Programming with JDBC in 21 Days (W/CD)	275/-
◆LDAP	
LDAP PROGRAMMING	**499/-**
◆LINUX	
LINUX Unleashed (W/CD)	499/-
RED HAT LINUX UNLEASHED (REVISED 2ND EDITION) (W/CD)	**399/-**
TEACH YOURSELF LINUX IN 24 HOURS (W/CD)	**MAY'98**
◆LOTUS NOTES	
LOTUS NOTES & DOMINO SERVER 4.5 Unleashed (W/CD)	450/-
Teach Yourself LOTUS NOTES 4.5 in 14 Days	195/-
◆MFC	
Microsoft FOUNDATION CLASS 4 BIBLE (W/CD)	499/-

MICROSOFT CERTIFIED SOFTWARE ENGINEERS

TITLE	PRICE
◆MCSE : TEACH YOURSELF	
TEACH YOURSELF MCSE WINDOWS NT SERVER 4.0 IN 14 DAYS	**195/-**
TEACH YOURSELF MCSE WINDOWS NT WORKSTATION IN 14 DAYS	**APR'98**
◆MCSE STUDY GUIDE	
MCSE: STUDY GUIDE WINDOWS 95 & NETWORKING ESSENTIALS (W/CD)	425/-
MCSE: STUDY GUIDE TCP/IP SYSTEM MANAGEMENT SERVER (W/CD)	425/-
MCSE: STUDY GUIDE WINDOWS NT SERVER & WORKSTATION 4 (W/CD)	425/-
◆MCSE: TRAINING GUIDE	
MCSE TRAINING GUIDE: SQL SERVER 6.5 ADMINISTRATION (W/CD)	**425/-**
MCSE TRAINING GUIDE: SQL SERVER 6.5 DESIGN & IMPLEMENTATION (W/CD)	**425/-**
MCSE TRAINING GUIDE: WINDOWS NT WORKSTATION 4 (W/CD)	**425/-**
MCSE: Training Guide WINDOWS 95 (W/CD)	425/-
MCSE TRAINING GUIDE: IIS 4 (W/CD)	**APR'98**

TITLE	PRICE
◆MCSE: TRAINING GUIDE	
MCSE: Training Guide WINDOWS NT SERVER 4 (W/CD)	425/-
MCSE: Training Guide WINDOWS NT SERVER 4 ENTERPRISE (W/CD)	425/-
MCSE TRAINING GUIDE: EXCHANGE SERVER 5 (W/CD)	**APR'98**
MCSE TRAINING GUIDE: SYSTEMS MANAGEMENT SERVER (W/CD)	**APR'98**
MCSE TRAINING GUIDE: TCP/IP (W/CD)	**APR'98**
MCSE Training Guide: NETWORKING ESSENTIALS (W/CD)	425/-
◆MCSE: TEST PREPARATION GUIDE	
MCSE TEST PREPARATION CORE EXAMS	**APR'98**
MCSE TEST PREPARATION GUIDE: TCP/IP	**APR'98**
MICROSOFT CERTIFIED PRODUCTSPECIALIST	
◆MCP STUDY GUIDE	
Netwroking with Microsoft TCP/IP (W/CD)	450/-
◆MS-OFFICE 4.3 / WIN	
Inside MS-OFFICE 4.3 Professional for WINDOWS (W/DISK)	450/-
◆MS-OFFICE 97 / WIN 95	
MS OFFICE 97 Interactive Course	399/-
MS OFFICE 97 Unleashed (W/CD)	399/-
Teach Yourself MS OFFICE 97 in 24 Hours	135/-
◆NETSCAPE COMMUNICATOR 4	
Teach Yourself NETSCAPE COMMUNICATOR 4 in 24 Hours	150/-
TEACH YOURSELF NETWORKING IN 24 HOURS	**MAY'98**
◆NETWORK COMPUTING	
NC Guide Development Strategies for Network Computer	499/-
◆ODBC	
Teach Yourself ODBC Programming in 21 Days	225/-
◆OLE DB & ADO	
Teach Yourself OLE DB AND ADO in 21 Days (W/CD)	275/-
◆ORACLE	
TEACH YOURSEFL ORACLE DEVELOPER/2000 IN 21 DAYS	**JUN'98**
TEACH YOURSELF ORACLE 8 IN 21 DAYS	**195/-**
Teach Yourself ORACLE 8 DATABASE Development in 21 Days (W/CD)	270/-
Teach Yourself PL/SQL in 21 Days (W/CD)	275/-
ORACLE 8 SERVER UNLEASHED	**JUN'98**
ORACLE 8 HOW TO - WAITE GROUP	**300/-**
ORACLE UNLEASHED (W/CD)-(Second Revised Edition also Cover Oracle 8)	**599/-**

TITLE	PRICE
◆ORACLE	
FREE ORACLE 7 Trial Version CD with Following Books Till Stock Lasts	
Developing CLIENT/SERVER Applications with ORACLE DEVELOPER/2000 (W/CD)	423/-
Developing Personal ORACLE 7 for WINDOWS 95 Applicaitons (W/CD)	360/-
ORACLE 7.3 Developer's Guide (W/CD)	399/-
ORACLE DBA SURVIVAL GUIDE (W/CD)	399/-
ORACLE 8 DATA WAREHOUSING Unleashed	450/-
ORACLE PERFORMANCE TUNING & OPTIMIZATION (W/CD)	423/-
ORACLE HOW - TO (W/CD)	375/-
ORACLE ELECTRONIC RESOURCE KIT (W/3CDS)	**799/-**
◆PAGEMAKER	
PAGEMAKER 6.5 Complete	360/-
◆PC	
PETER NORTON's INSIDE THE **PC, 7th Edn .**	**240/-**
TEACH YOURSELF PCs IN 24 HOURS	**150/-**
◆PC - SERVICING	
PETER NORTON's GUIDE TO UPGRADING & REPAIRING PCS	**240/-**
◆PERL	
PERL 5 HOW - TO (W/CD)	399/-
PERL 5 Interactive Course (W/CD)	495/-
Teach Yourself PERL 5 in 21 Days (W/CD)	300/-
◆PHOTOSHOP-ADOBE	
ADOBE PHOTOSHOP 4 Interactive Course (W/CD)	495/-
Inside ADOBE PHOTOSHOP (W/CD)	399/-
PHOTOSHOP 4 Complete (W/CD)	450/-
PHOTOSHOP 4 STUDIO SKILLS (W/CD)	**195/-**
Teach Yourself PHOTOSHOP 4 in 24 Hours	120/-
TEACH YOURSELF PHOTOSHOP 4 IN 14 DAYS (W/CD)	**180/-**
◆POWER BUILDER 5.0	
POWER BUILDER 5 Unleashed (W/CD)	450/-
POWER BUILDER 5 HOW - TO (W/CD)	399/-
◆POWER BUILDER 6.0	
POWER BUILDER 6.0 UNLEASHED (W/CD)	**450/-**
◆POWER POINT 97	
Teach Yourself MS POWER POINT 97 in 24 Hours	135/-
◆PL / SQL	
Teach Yourself PL/SQL in 21 Days (W/CD)	275/-
◆MS-PROJECT	
TEACH YOURSELF MS - PROJECT 98 IN 24 HOURS	**JUN'98**
◆QUARK EXPRESS	
TEACH YOURSELF QUARK EXPRESS 4 IN 14 DAYS (W/CD)	**180/-**

TITLE	PRICE
◆SYBASE	
SYBASE SQL SERVER 11 Unleashed (W/CD)	499/-
◆SQL	
MS SQL SERVER 6.5 Unleashed (W/CD)	450/-
SQL Unleashed (W/CD)	499/-
TEACH YOURSELF MS-SQL SERVER IN 21 DAYS	**MAY'98**
Teach Yourself SQL in 21 Days	180/-
TEACH YOURSELF SQL IN 24 HOURS	**APR'98**
◆TRANSACT - SQL	
Teach Yourself TRANSACT - SQL in 21 Days	225/-
◆TCP/IP	
INSIDE TCP/IP - 3RD EDITION	**300/-**
Networking with Microsoft TCP/IP (W/CD)	450/-
Teach Yourself TCP/IP in 14 Days (Second Edn.)	150/-
TCP/IP BLUEPRINTS (W/CD)	**350/-**
TEACH YOURSELF TCP/IP IN 24 HOURS	**MAY'98**
◆TURBO C++	
Teach Yourself TURBO C++ 4.5 for WINDOWS in 21 Days	270/-
◆UNIX	
EXPLORING THE UNIX SYSTEM - THIRD REVISED EDITION	**150/-**
Teach Yourself UNIX in 24 Hours	180/-
UNIX SYSTEM V PRIMER - WAITE GROUP	**150/-**
UNIX SYSTEM ADMINISTRATOR'S Unleashed (W/CD)	599/-
UNIX UNLEASHED, INTERNET EDN. (W/CD)	**450/-**
◆VISUAL BASIC	
DEVELOPING ACTIVE X COMPONENTS WITH VISUAL BASIC 5-(W/CD)	**450/-**
DOING OBJECTS IN MS VISUAL BASIC 5 -(W/CD)	**360/-**
Teach Yourself VISUAL BASIC 5 in 24 Hours (W/CD)	180/-
Teach Yourself DATABASE Programming with VISUAL BASIC 5 in 21 Days (W/CD)	330/-
◆VISUAL BASIC	
Teach Yourself VISUAL BASIC 5 in 21 Days	270/-
TEACH YOURSELF MORE VISUAL BASIC 5 IN 21 DAYS	**MAY'98**
TEACH YOURSELF OOP WITH VB IN 21 DAYS (W/CD)	**MAY'98**
VISUAL BASIC for Applications Unleashed (W/CD) (Covers Office 97, Internet, Active X)	399/-
VISUAL BASIC 5 Interactive Course (W/CD)	495/-
WAITE GROUP **VISUAL BASIC 5 SUPER BIBLE - SET - 2 VOLs. (W/CD)**	**795/-**
VISUAL BASIC 5 CLIENT/SERVER HOW-TO (W/CD)	450/-
VISUAL BASIC 5 Developer's GUIDE (W/CD)	399/-
VISUAL BASIC 5 Fundamentals Unleashed (W/CD)	360/-

TITLE	PRICE
◆VISUAL BASIC	
WAITE GROUP **VISUAL BASIC 5 HOW TO (W/CD)**	**375/-**
WAITE GROUP **VISUAL BASIC 5 DATABASE HOW TO (W/CD)**	**450/-**
VISUAL BASIC 5 DEVELOPMENT UNLEASHED (W/CD)	**300/-**
VISUAL BASIC 5 PROG GUIDE TO THE WIN 32 API-(W/CD)	**599/-**
◆VBSCRIPT	
VBSCRIPT Interactive Course (W/CD)	495/-
◆VISUAL C++	
TEACH YOURSELF VISUAL C++ 5 IN 24 HOURS	**150/-**
Teach Yourself VISUAL C++ 5 in 21 Days	270/-
VISUAL C++ 5 DEVELOPER'S Guide	450/-
VISUAL C++ 5 Unleashed (W/CD)	450/-
◆VRML	
Teach Yourself VRML 2 in 21 Days (W/CD)	210/-
◆WORD 97	
Teach Yourself MS WORD 97 in 24 Hours	135/-
◆WINDOWS 95	
Peter Norton's Complete Guide to WIN 95	360/-
Paul Mcfedries WIN95 Unleashed (W/CD)	499/-
INSIDE WIN 95 DELUXE EDN. - (W/2CDS)	**450/-**
WINDOWS 95 API Bible Book - 1 WIN 32 Programming (W/CD)	499/-
WINDOWS 95 API Bible Book - 2 Common Controls & Messages (W/CD)	499/-
WINDOWS 95 API Bible Book - 3 MULTIMEDIA & ODBC (W/CD)	499/-
Teach Yourself WINDOWS 95 in 24 Hours	135/-
◆WINDOWS 98	
INSIDE WINDOWS 98 (W/CD)	**MAY'98**
PETER NORTON'S MAXIMIZING WINDOWS 98 ADMINISTRATION	**JUN'98**
PETER NORTON'S COMPLETE GUIDE TO WINDOWS 95	**JUN'98**
PAUL MCFEDRIES WINDOWS 98 UNLEASHED PREMIER (W/CD)	**JUN'98**
TEACH YOURSELF WIN 98 IN 21 DAYS	**JUN'98**
TEACH YOURSELF WIN 98 IN 24 HOURS	**JUN'98**
WINDOWS 98 UNLEASHED	**JUN'98**
◆WINDOWS NT 4 - SERVER & WORKSTATION	
INSIDE WINDWOS NT SERVER 4 (W/CD)	**450/-**
Peter Norton's MAXIMIZING WINDOWS NT SERVER 4	399/-
PETER NORTON'S COMPLETE GUIDE TO WINDOWS NT 4 WORKSTATION	**450/-**
TEACH YOURSEFL NT WORKSTATION 4 IN 24 HOUR	**165/-**
TEACH YOURSELF NT SERVER 4 IN 14 DAYS	**225/-**

BPB-COMPUTER BOOKS

TITLE	PRICE
➢80386/80486 & HARDWARE	
Microprocessor Data Handbook	180/-
MODERN - All About Hard Disk drive.	150/-
MODERN - All About Floppy Disk & Drives	120/-
MODERN - All About Mother Board	150/-
MODERN - All About Keyboard & Mouse	120/-
Programming the 80386	180/-
The 386/486 PC : A Power User's Guide	99/-
The PC DATA Handbook	99/-
PC Magazine Programmer's Technical Ref.	180/-
➢A+ CERTIFICATION PROGRAMME	
A+: Core Module CERTIFICATION Study Guide	299/-
A+: Windows / DOS CERTIFICATION Study Guide	JUL'98
A+ Certification Kit	JUL'98
➢ACCESS	
ABCs of MS ACCESS	99/-
Learn MS ACCESS for Windows in a day	45/-
PCLL Teaches MS ACCESS (W/D)	180/-
➢ACCESS 2	
PCLL-Teaches ACCESS 2.0 (W/D)	150/-
➢ACCESS 7.0 / WIN 95	
Teach Yourself ACCESS for Windows 95	165/-
Learn MS ACCESS 7.0 for Win 95 in a day	45/-
➢ACCESS 97	
ACCESS 97 Developers Hand Book (W/CD-ROM)	499/-
ACCESS 97 - No Experience Required	150/-
Mastering ACCESS 97 for Win 95 / NT (W/CD-ROM)	450/-
Teach Yourself ACCESS 97 /WIN 95	180/-
➢ACTIVE X	
Active X - No Experience Required	180/-
Mastering ACTIVE X and COM (W/CD)	MAY'98
➢AMIPRO	
Learn AMIPRO 3.0 in a day	45/-
➢ANIMATION	
Graphics Programming & ANIMATION	180/-
➢ARTIFICIAL INTELLIGENCE	
Knowledge Engineering & EXPERT Systems	90/-
NEURO-INTELLIGENT Systems	150/-
Understanding ARTIFICIAL INTELLIGENCE	120/-
➢ACCOUNTING	
Computerised ACCOUNTING	135/-

TITLE	PRICE
➢ACCOUNTING	
Financial Management and Accounting System (W/D)	300/-
➢MAIN – AS/400	
AS/400 Disk Saving Tips & Techniques	120/-
AS/400 Companion	90/-
Navigating the AS/400 A Hands on Guide	180/-
➢ASSEMBLER	
Learn MS-ASSEMBLER in a day	45/-
Teach Yourself ASSEMBLER (W/D)	180/-
➢ASSEMBLY LANGUAGE	
ASSEMBLY LANGUAGE Techniques IBM for PC	150/-
Developing Utilities in ASSEMBLY LANGUAGE (W/D)	99/-
➢ASTROLOGY	
Computer ASTROLOGY (W/D)	345/-
➢AUTOCAD	
Inside AUTOCAD	180/-
Encyclopedia AUTOCAD	450/-
Learn AUTOCAD in a Day	45/-
Mastering AUTOCAD	240/-
➢AUTOCAD 11	
AUTOCAD 11 Instant Reference	54/-
Illustrated AUTOCAD (Release 11)	195/-
Mastering AUTOCAD (Release 11)	300/-
➢AUTOCAD 12	
ABCs of AUTOCAD (Release 12)	150/-
Advanced AUTOCAD (Release 12)	195/-
Mastering AUTOCAD Release 12 (W/D)	350/-
AUTOCAD 12 Instant Reference	60/-
Learn AUTOCAD 12 in a Day	45/-
Mastering AUTOCAD Release 12 for Windows	775/-
➢AUTOCAD 13	
AUTOCAD 13 for DOS & WINDOWS Inst. Reference	66/-
Teach Yourself AUTOCAD 13 (W/D)	150/-
Mastering AUTOCAD 13 /WIN / WIN 95 / NT (W/CD-ROM)	450/-
➢AUTOCAD 14	
AUTOCAD 14 instant reference	54/-
Mastering AUTOCAD 14 (W/CD)	450/-
Mastering AUTOCAD 14 for Mechanical Engineers (W/CD)	499/-
AUTOCAD 14 - No Experience Required	APR'98

TITLE	PRICE

➢AUTOCAD – CAD/CAM

Understanding CAD/CAM	150/-

➢AUTOLISP

ABCs of AUTOLISP	120/-
AUTOLISP & Customisation Made Simple	150/-
Illustrated AUTOLISP	120/-

➢BAR CODES

Understanding BAR CODES	120/-

➢BASIC

BASIC : Step by Step Programming	45/-
BASIC : Work Book	36/-
BASIC For Beginners	30/-
BASIC for Schools	54/-
BASIC Programming Lab Workbook	75/-
Computer Programming in BASIC — The Easy Way	75/-
Electrical Engineering Computation by Computer Graphics Aided Basic Programming	150/-
Programming Expertise in BASIC	90/-
Your First BASIC Program	60/-
Learning IBM BASIC	120/-

➢BORLAND C/C++

BORLAND C++ 3.0 for Windows 3.1	195/-
BORLAND C++ Techniques & Utilities (W/D)	240/-
BORLAND C++ 4.0 Upgrade Book	99/-
Clean Coding in BORLAND C++	150/-
Illustrated BORLAND C++ 3.1	150/-
Programming Output Drivers Using BORLAND C++	54/-
Windows Programming with BORLAND C++	300/-

➢C

AL Stevens Teaches C (W/D)	195/-
Advanced Fractal Programming in C	225/-
C - DATA BASE Development	120/-
C Language for Programmers	120/-
C Pearls	150/-
C Projects (With 2 Disks)	300/-
C Under DOS Test	54/-
C with Assembly Language	150/-
Database Management Using C (W/D)	195/-
Data Structure Using C Lab Workbook (W/D)	150/-
ENCYCLOPEDIA C	495/-
EXPLORING C	150/-
GRAPHIC USER INTERFACE Programming With C	180/-
GRAPHICS Programming in C	300/-
Illustrated C	120/-
Illustrated C Programming	120/-
Image Processing in C (W/D)	350/-
Learn C in Three Days	45/-
Let us C	135/-
Programming with ANSI C	120/-

TITLE	PRICE

➢C

Mastering C	120/-
Numerical Techniques in C	75/-
Question Bank unix C Programming	66/-
Teach Yourself - C	99/-
The Hidden Treasures of C	75/-
Test your C Skils	150/-
Understanding C	90/-
Understanding Pointers in C (2nd Revi. ed.)	150/-
Undocumented DOS Through C	195/-
Working With C (For DOE — 'A' & 'B' Level)	150/-
Writing TSR's through C	225/-
Writing Utilities in C	JUL'98
The C Odyssey - Vol. I DOS	250/-
The C Odyssey - Vol. II Advanced DOS	250/-
The C Odyssey - Vol III UNIX	250/-
The C Odyssey - Vol. IV Networks RDBMS	250/-
The C Odyssey - Vol. V C++ & Graphics	250/-
The C Odyssey - Vol. VI Windows	250/-
The C Odyssey - Vol. VII OS/2	250/-
The Complete ANSI C	252/-

➢C++

A Comprehensive Guide to C++	99/-
Advanced GRAPHICS Programming In C & C++	350/-
Applying C++ (W/D)	225/-
Black Belt C++ : Master Collection for Programmers	150/-
C - Elements of Style for C & C++	90/-
C++ - No Experience Required	165/-
C/C++ Programmer's Guide (W/D)	240/-
C/C++ Programming Lab Workbook	120/-
C++ COMMUNICATIONS UTILITIES (W/D)	300/-
C++ An Intro. of Experienced C Programmers	75/-
C++ COMPONENTS & ALGORITHMS (W/D)	300/-
C++ Database Development (W/D)	225/-
C++ Neural Networks & Fuzzy Logic (W/D)	300/-
Convert To C & C++	120/-
Learn MFC C++ Classes (W/2 Disks)	180/-
Mastering C++ (From C to C++ in 2 Weeks) (W/D)	295/-
Object Oriented Programming with C++	120/-
Programming On-Line Help Using C++	180/-
Teach Yourself C++ (W/D) (Revised Edition)	150/-
Write Your Own Programming Language Using C++	54/-
Your First C/C++ Program (W/D)	180/-

➢COMPUSERVE

Learn COMPUSERVE for Windows in a day	54/-

➢CARTOONS

Laughing Bytes (Hilarious Cartoons)	36/-

➢CASE TOOLS

CASE TOOLS : Concepts & Applications	180/-

TITLE	PRICE

➢CLIENT/SERVER

CLIENT/SERVER Computing SYBASE SQL SERVER 225/-
CLIENT/SERVER Computing with ORACLE 225/-
Developing CLIENT/SERVER Applications 275/-
Guide to CLIENT/SERVER Databases (2nd Ed.) 180/-
Mastering ORACLE 7 & CLIENT/SERVER Computing (W/D) 345/-
NOVELL's CLIENT-SERVER Applications & Architecture 350/-

➢CLIPPER

111 CLIPPER Functions (W/D) 150/-
CLIPPER - 5 & 5.01 Programming Guide 195/-
CLIPPER 5 & 5.01: A Developers Guide 450/-
CLIPPER 5.01/87 Test 45/-
CLIPPER 5.2 Power Programming Guide (W/D) . 250/-
CLIPPER Applications 75/-
CLIPPER Programming Guide (Summer 87) ... 180/-
Illustrated CLIPPER 5.0 & 5.01 .... 135/-
Learn CLIPPER..... Fast 45/-
Writing Applications with CLIPPER (W/D) 225/-

➢CNA

CNA Study Guide (W/2D) 1399/-
CNA Study Guide (Revi. Edn.) W/CD 1925/-

➢CNE

CNE -4 Study Guide for Netware 4.1 Certification (W/CD) 495/-

➢COBOL

COBOL : Language of Business 75/-
COBOL Programming Lab Workbook 99/-
Structured Programming in COBOL 99/-

➢COMPUTER - TEXTBOOKS

A First Course in Computer SCIENCE (ICSE Class IX TO XII) 120/-
Computers Don't Byte: A Beginners Guide to Understanding Computers 45/-
Computer Basics 30/-
COMPUTER Concepts & Facts 36/-
COMPUTER Fundamentals 99/-
COMPUTER Programming 54/-
Basic Computing - Book A to F .... EACH 33/-
Basic Computing Principles 54/-
COMPUTER Fundamentals and C++ Programming VOL.I (CBSE-XI) 81/-
COMPUTER FUNDAMENTALs AND C++ PROGRAMMING vol.Ii (CBSE-XII) 150/-
COMPUTER TUTOR 24/-
Fun with Computers Vol. I to Vol. VI 36/-
Introducing COMPUTERS - Part - I REVISED .. 39/-
Introducing COMPUTERS - Part - II REVISED . 39/-
Introducing COMPUTERS - Part - III 39/-

TITLE	PRICE

➢COMPUTER - TEXTBOOKS

Introduction to COMPUTER SCIENCE Vol.-I 99/-
Introduction to COMPUTER SCIENCE Vol.-II 99/-
Let us Learn COMPUTER (REVISED EDN.) 45/-
Programming in PASCAL -Volume I 75/-
Programming in PASCAL -Volume II 60/-
Questions & Answers on Computer 120/-
We can use the COMPUTERS - A to F . EACH 33/-
Your First Computer 120/-

➢COREL DRAW - 4 - 5 - 6 - 7 - 8

Learn COREL DRAW In a Day 45/-
Looking Good with COREL DRAW (4&5) 150/-
Teach Yourself - COREL DRAW 4.0 .... 120/-
Teach Yourself - COREL DRAW 5.0 .... 120/-
Teach Yourself - COREL DRAW 6.0 .... 135/-
Mastering COREL DRAW 6 (W/CD-ROM) 450/-
Mastering COREL DRAW 7 (W/CD-ROM) 450/-
Mastering COREL DRAW 8 (W/CD-ROM) 450/-

➢CD RECORDABLE

CD Recordable Hand Book (W/CD-ROM) 399/-
Complete Recordable CD Guide (W/CD-ROM) 390/-

➢CROSSTALK

Mastering CROSSTALK XVI 120/-

➢DATABASE

Relational DATABASE — Theory & Practice 99/-
The Database Dictionary 150/-

➢DBASE III PLUS

ABCs of dBASE III PLUS 81/-
Advanced Techniques in dBASE III PLUS 180/-
dBASE III Plus/dBASE IV Test 39/-
dBASE Workbook 36/-
dBASE III PLUS: A Comprehensive Users Manual 90/-
dBASE Programmers Utilities (W/D) 150/-
dBASE III PLUS Instant Reference 60/-
dBASE III PLUS Programmers Reference Guide 275/-
dBASE III PLUS Programming Tips & Techniques 180/-
dBASE III PLUS Students & Instructor Work Book 99/-
dBASE III PLUS Tips & Tricks 99/-
Illustrated dBASE III PLUS Book 99/-
Learn dBASE Programming in a Day 45/-
Mailing List Using dBASE 45/-
Mastering dBASE III PLUS 99/-
Quick Guide to dBASE 90/-
Understanding dBASE III PLUS 99/-

➢DBASE IV

Illustrated dBASE IV 1.1 .... 120/-
Teach Yourself dBASE V for Windows 120/-
Understanding dBASE IV 1.5 .... 275/-

TITLE	PRICE

➤DBASE V

Understanding dBASE V for Windows 640/-

➤DATA COMPRESSION

DATA COMPRESSION Book 2nd Edn. (W/D) . 225/-

➤DELPHI - 2 / 3

From DELPHI 2 you (W/D) 180/-
Mastering DELPHI 2 for Win 95 & NT (W/CD-ROM) 399/-
Mastering DELPHI 3 (W/CD) 495/-
Teach Yourself DELPHI (W/D) 150/-

➤DICTIONARY

Computer DICTIONARY 36/-
The PC User's Pocket DICTIONARY 66/-
DICTIONARY of Networking 75/-

➤DTP

DESKTOP PUBLISHING on PC 99/-

➤ELECTRONIC MAIL

CC : MAIL Plain & Simple 150/-

➤EXCEL

Murphy's Laws of EXCEL 225/-
Mastering EXCEL - 4 for Windows 195/-

➤EXCEL 5 / WIN

EXCEL 5 for Windows Instant Reference 45/-
Learn EXCEL 5.0 For Windows In a Day 45/-
MS EXCEL 5.0 For Windows at a Glance 60/-
Mastering EXCEL - 5 for Windows 225/-
PCLL-Teaches EXCEL 5.0 for Windows (W/D) 150/-

➤EXCEL 7 / WIN 95

Learn MS EXCEL 7.0 for Win 95 in a day 45/-
PCLL-Teaches EXCEL 7.0 for Win 95 (W/D) .. 165/-
Teach Yourself EXCEL 7.0 for Win 95 (W/D) .. 150/-

➤EXCEL 97

Abcs of EXCEL 97 .... 120/-
Mastering EXCEL 97 .... 399/-

➤EXCHANGE SERVER

Mastering MS Exchange Server 5 .... 450/-

➤FLOPPY DISK

FLOPPY DISK : INTERNALS 54/-
Modern All About FLOPPY DISK & DRIVES ... 120/-

➤FORTRAN-77

Programming in MS FORTRAN 77 for IBM PC & Compatibles (2nd Edn.) 99/-
Programming Through FORTRAN 77 - A Practical Approach 75/-

➤FOXBASE+

Illustrated FOXBASE+ 2.1 .... 99/-
FOXBASE+ 2.1:Programming & AppLications. .. 60/-

➤FOXPRO — 2

FOXPRO 2 - A Developers Guide 120/-

➤FOXPRO — 2

FOXPRO 2 - The Art of Visual Programming 99/-
FOXPRO 2 - C & MULTIUSER -Programming 150/-
Illustrated FOXPRO 2 .... 120/-
Mastering FOXPRO 2 .... 150/-
Learn FOXPRO 2.0 in A Day 45/-

➤FOXPRO — 2.5

FOXPRO 2.5 Made Simple 165/-
FOXPRO 2.5 for DOS at a Glance 60/-
FOXPRO 2.5 for WINDOWS at a Glance 75/-
Learn FOXPRO 2.5 for WINDOWS in a day...... 45/-
Complete FOXPRO 2.5 Language Reference 99/-
PCLL-Teaches FOXPRO 2.5 for Win (W/D) 150/-

➤FOXPRO — 2.6

Developing & Distributing FOXPRO 2.5/2.6 / Win Appl. (W/D) 99/-
Mastering FOXPRO 2.5 & 2.6 (Special Edn.) .. 345/-
Programming FOXPRO 2.5 & 2.6 (W/D) 480/-
Programmers Guide to FOXPRO 2.5/2.6 (W/D) .. 375/-
FOXPRO 2.6 Code Book 180/-

➤VISUAL – FOXPRO—3

Mastering Visual FOXPRO 3 Special Edition ... 345/-
PCLL Teaches Visual FOXPRO 3.0 (W/D) 180/-
Teach Yourself VISUAL FOXPRO 3 /Win (W/D) .. 180/-

➤VISUAL – FOXPRO— 5

Teach Yourself Visual FoxPro 5.0 /WIN (W/D) 195/-

➤FRACTALS

Advanced FRACTAL Programming in C 275/-
Fun With FRACTALS (W/D) 375/-

➤FRONT PAGE 97

ABCs of FRONT PAGE 97 .... 150/-
Learn MS FRONT PAGE 97 (W/D) 99/-
Mastering FRONT PAGE 97 (W/CD) 450/-

➤FRONT PAGE 98

FRONT PAGE 98 - No Experience Required .. 150/-
Mastering MS-FRONT PAGE 98 (W/CD) 450/-

➤GENERAL BOOKS

ALMOST PERFECT : How a Bunch of Regular Guys Built WORDPERFECT Corporation (Hard Bound) 150/-
SILICON SAMURAI : How Japan Conquered the World's I.T. Industry (Hard Bound) 225/-
कम्प्यूटर - एक पूर्ण परिचय (द्वितीय संस्करण) 45/-
Little Book On Computer 45/-
Learn Computers in a Day 54/-

➤GRAPHICS

Computer GRAPHICS Secrets & Solutions 120/-
Designing GUI Applications for Windows (W/D) 225/-

➤GW BASIC

Programming in GW-BASIC (2nd Edn.) 54/-

TITLE	PRICE
➢GW BASIC	
MODERN All About GW-BASIC for Schools & Colleges	180/-
➢HARD DISK	
HARD DISK Management - PC & PS/2	90/-
Modern All About of HARD DISK Drive	150/-
HARD DISK Survival Guide (W/D)	225/-
HARD DISK Technical Guide (W/CD)	450/-
➢HARVARD GRAPHICS	
Learn HARVARD GRAPHICS 3.0 in a Day	54/-
Presentation with HARVARD GRAPHICS	60/-
➢HEALTH & FITNESS	
Your Personal FITNESS Trainer with Interactive (W/CD-ROM)	450/-
➢HUMAN COMMUNICATION	
HUMAN Communication	99/-
➢HTML	
Mastering HTML 4.0 (W/CD-ROM)	450/-
HTML 4.0 - No Experience required	180/-
HTML Example Book	150/-
Dynamic HTML: Master the Essentials	MAY/-
➢IBM PC-AT	
Mastering XENIX on the IBM PC AT	150/-
➢IBM PS/2	
IBM PS/2 Handbook	99/-
➢IBM PC-XT	
IBM XT Clone Handbook	99/-
➢IBM-PC/XT/AT	
ABCs of IBM PC's & Compatibles	60/-
IBM PC & PS/2 GRAPHICS Handbook	135/-
New PETER NORTON Programmer's Guide to the IBM PC & PS/2	345/-
PC Buyer's Survival Guide	195/-
PC Companion	120/-
PC Power—Boosting Your PC's Performance	150/-
Programmers' Guide To PC & PS/2 VIDEO Sys.	300/-
➢IBM-PC/XT/AT — SERVICING	
Build Your Own Computer (2nd Edition)	54/-
Exploring and Upgrading your PC	399/-
How Computer Works with Interactive CD-ROM	480/-
How Computer Works (Without CD)	300/-
Inside The Grey Box-Choosing, Building & Upgrading PC	120/-
PC Upgrade Guide for Everybody	90/-
PC Upgrade & Maintenance : No Experience Required	150/-
Complete PC Upgrade & Maintenance Guide 8th edition (W/2CD-ROM'S)	599/-

TITLE	PRICE
➢IBM-PC/XT/AT — SERVICING	
UPGRADING, MAINTAINING & SERVICING IBM PC's & Compatibles (W/D)	275/-
➢INGRES-RDBMS	
INGRES and Relational Databases	150/-
Introduction to INGRES	225/-
Mastering INGRES	225/-
➢GENERAL – INTERNET	
ABCs of the INTERNET (2nd Rev. Edn.)	99/-
INTERNET Basic Reference from A to Z	180/-
INTERNET Dictionary	99/-
INTERNET Instant Reference (3rd Edn.)	90/-
INTERNET Roadmap	90/-
INTERNET Toolkit	120/-
INTERNET For Kids	54/-
INTERNET - No Experience Required	150/-
Learn INTERNET Relay Chat	60/-
Learning to use the INTERNET	120/-
Learning Guide to the INTERNET (W/CD)	225/-
Mastering the INTERNET (W/CD-ROM)	450/-
Mastering WEB DESIGN (W/CD-ROM)	450/-
MASTERING NETSCAPE FAST TRACK SERVER	225/-
Surfing the INTERNET with NETSCAPE NAVIGATOR 2 (W/D)	150/-
Surfing the INTERNET with NETSCAPE NAVIGATOR 3 (W/CD-ROM)	240/-
➢INTERNET EXPLORER	
ABC of MS Internet Explorer 3	99/-
ABC of MS INTERNET EXPLORER 4 (With Free MS-INTERNET EXPLORER 4.0 CD)	150/-
Mastering INTERNET EXPLORER 4 (With Free MS-INTERNET EXPLORER 4.0 CD)	450/-
➢IIS	
Developing Internet Information Server	MAY'98
Mastering MS INTERNET INFORMATION SERVER	399/-
MCSE: Internet Info Server 3 Study Guide (W/CD)	450/-
➢INTRANETS	
ABCs OF INTRANETS	120/-
Building INTRANETS on NT, Netware and Solaris	399/-
INTRANETS: The Surf Within (W/CD)	270/-
Mastering Intranets FOR win 95 /NT (W/CD-ROM)	450/-
Practical Guide to Intranet Client Server Applications Using the Web (W/CD)	225/-
➢ISDN	
Mastering ISDN	300/-

TITLE	PRICE
➢ISO 9000	
Getting ISO 9000 for a Software Organisation	225/-
➢JAVA	
JAVA 1.1 certification study guide (W/CD)	450/-
JAVA 1.1 DEVELOPERS HandBook(W/CD)	450/-
JAVA 1.1 : No Experience Required (W/CD)	225/-
Java Workshop Programming (W/D)	150/-
Mastering JAVA 1.1 (W/CD)	450/-
Mastering Java (W/CD)	399/-
➢JAVA SCRIPT	
ABCs of JAVA Script	150/-
Mastering JAVA Beans (W/CD-ROM)	399/-
Mastering JAVA Scripts (W/CD-ROM)	450/-
Learn Advance JAVA Script Programming (W/CD)	399/-
➢PRINTERS – LASERJET	
LASERJET Unlimited	180/-
➢LINUX	
Complete LINUX Kit (W/CD-ROM)	450/-
LINUX Configuration & Installation (Including SLAckware) (W/2CD's)	300/-
Mastering LINUX - Internet edition (W/CD)	MAY'98
➢LOGO	
LOGO Work Book	36/-
The School LOGO Book	45/-
Working with LOGO	36/-
➢LOTUS 1-2-3	
ABCs of 1-2-3 (Release 2.2)	90/-
ABCs of 1-2-3 (Release 3)	90/-
Illustrated LOTUS 1-2-3 (Release 2.2)	99/-
Illustrated LOTUS 1-2-3 (Release 3)	135/-
Illustrated LOTUS 1-2-3 Book	120/-
Learn LOTUS 1-2-3 in a Day (Revised Edition)	45/-
Learn LOTUS 1-2-3 Rel. 4 for Windows In a Day	45/-
Learn LOTUS 1-2-3 Rel. 5 for Windows in a day	54/-
LOTUS 1-2-3 (Students & Instructor Work Book)	99/-
LOTUS 1-2-3 Instant Reference 2.3 & 2.4	45/-
LOTUS 1-2-3 Release 5 Quick & Easy	360/-
LOTUS 1-2-3 Release 5 For WIN Instant Ref.	54/-
LOTUS 1-2-3 For Windows at a Glance	75/-
Mastering 1-2-3	150/-
Mastering 1-2-3 (Release 3)	180/-
Manual LOTUS 1-2-3	54/-
Teach Yourself LOTUS 1-2-3	120/-
Up & Running with LOTUS 1-2-3 (Release 2.3)	180/-
Understanding 1-2-3 Release 4.0 for Windows	540/-
Understanding LOTUS 1-2-3 Release 5 / WIN	640/-
➢LOTUS SMARTSUITE	
Compact Guide to LOTUS SMARTSUITE	180/-
Mastering LOTUS SMARTSUITE 97 / WIN 95	450/-

TITLE	PRICE
➢LOTUS-NOTES 4.5 & DOMINO	
ABCs OF LOTUS NOTES 4.5	120/-
Learn LOTUS DOMINO (w/d)	99/-
LOTUS NOTES 4.5 Administrator Guide	300/-
Lotus Notes Developer's Guide for Users Rel 4.0-4.5 (W/CD-ROM)	275/-
LOTUS NOTES Plain & Simple	180/-
Mastering LOTUS NOTES 4 (W/CD-ROM)	399/-
Mastering LOTUS NOTES 4.5 & DOMINO (W/CD-ROM)	450/-
Teach Yourself Lotus Notes 4.5 (W/D)	225/-
➢MACROMEDIA	
Mastering MACROMEDIA DIRECTOR 5 (W/CD-ROM)	450/-
Mastering MACROMEDIA Director 6 (W/CD-ROM)	450/-
➢MAPI	
Inside MAPI (W/CD ROM)	1078/-
➢MATHS	
Computer Related MATHEMATICS	120/-
MATHEMATICS for Computer Students	120/-
➢MEMORY	
The One Minute MEMORY MANAGER	180/-
➢MICROPROCESSORS	
MICROPROCESSORS & Microcomputers Technology	120/-
MICROPROCESSORS Data Handbook	180/-
MICROPROCESSORS X86 Programming	180/-
➢MCSE - MICROSOFT CERTIFIED SYSTEMS ENGINEER	
NT Workstation Study Guide 4 (W/CD-ROM)	450/-
NETWORKING ESSENTIALS STUDY GUIDE (W/CD ROM)	450/-
NT SERVER 4 in ENTERPRISE STUDY GUIDE (W/CD-ROM)	450/-
NT SERVER 4 STUDY GUIDE (W/CD-ROM)	450/-
MCSE Core Requirements (4 Books & 4 CDs)	1650/-
➢MCSE - ELECTIVE STUDY GUIDES	
MCSE: Windows 95 Study Guide (W/CD-ROM)	450/-
MCSE: TCP/IP for NT Server 4 Study Guide (W/CD-ROM)	450/-
MCSE: INTERNET Information Server 3 Study Guide (W/CD)	450/-
MCSE: INTERNET Information Server 4 Study Guide (W/CD)	MAY'98
MCSE: EXCHANGE 5 STUDY GUIDE (W/CD-ROM)	450/-
MCSE: Exchange 5.5 Study Guide (W/CD)	MAY'98
MCSE: SQL Server 6.5 Administration Study Guide (W/CD)	450/-
MCSE: PROXY Server 2 Study Guide (W/CD)	MAY'98

TITLE	PRICE
➢MCSE - TEST SUCCESSS	
MCSE Test Success: NT Server 4	150/-
MCSE Test Success: Networking Essentials	MAY'98
MCSE Test Success: NT Server 4 in the Enterprise	MAY'98
MCSE Test Success: NT Workstation 4	MAY'98
MCSE Test Success: Exchange Server 5.5	MAY'98
MCSE Test Success: TCP/IP for NT4	MAY'98
MCSE Test Success:Windows 95	MAY'98

➢MCSE - TESTING GUIDES

These are companion books to the Study guides. These Contain sample questions & answers for practicing for the exams.

TITLE	PRICE
Networking Essentials Testing Guide (W/CD)	MAY'98
NT Server 4 Testing Guide	MAY'98
NT Workstation 4 Testing guide	MAY'98
NT server 4 testing guide (W/CD)	MAY'98
NT SERVER 4 WITH ENTERPRISE TESTING GUIDE	MAY'98
Exchange Server 5.5 Testing Guide (W/CD)	MAY'98
PROXY Server 2 Study Guide (W/CD)	MAY'98
➢MCSE - TESTING GUIDES	
MCSE: TCP/IP for NT 4 Testing Guide (W/CD)	MAY'98
MCSE:Windows 95 Testing Guide (W/CD)	MAY'98
NT Server 4 in the Enterprise Testing Guide (W/CD)	MAY'98
➢MCPS / MCSE	
Internet System Specialist	APR'98

TITLE	PRICE
➢MCSD	
MCSD: Visual Basic 5 Certificaiton Study Guide (W/CD)	MAY'98
MCSD: Visual C++ Certification Study Guide (W/CD)	MAY'98
➢HARDWARE – KEYBOARD AND MOUSE	
Modern All About Keyboard and Mouse	120/-
➢HARDWARE – MODEM	
Learn to use your MODEM in a Day	60/-
The MODEM Technical Guide (W/CD)	450/-
Your first MODEM	150/-
➢HARDWARE – MONITORS	
MODERN-All About MONITORS	60/-
MODERN-MONITOR Circuits & FAULT-FINDING VOl. I	45/-
MODERN-MONITOR Circuits & FAULT-FINDING VOl. II	45/-
MODERN-MONITOR Circuits & FAULT-FINDING VOl. III	54/-
मॉडर्न कम्प्यूटर मानीटर सर्विसिंग मेन्युल (M-Tek & Vintron)	45/-
MODERN-Colour VGA MONITOR Servicing Manual	45/-
मॉडर्न कम्प्यूटर मानीटर सर्विसिंग मेन्युल (TRL - DUAL)	45/-
मॉडर्न कम्प्यूटर मानीटर सर्विसिंग मेन्युल (M-Tek - DUAL)	45/-
Programmer's Guide to the EGA/VGA	275/-
➢HARDWARE – SMPS	
A Complete Guide to SMPS for PC (HardWare & Software)	45/-
Modern - Computer SMPS Servicing Manual Pioneer, Power, TVSE (हिन्दी)	45/-
Modern - Computer SMPS Servicing Manual Vintron, Microtek, Bull Power (हिन्दी)	45/-
Modern - Computer SMPS Circuits & Faults Finding Vol. I	45/-
➢MS-DOS	
ABCs of DOS 5	90/-
Advanced MS DOS Programming	275/-
DOS (3.3 & 5) Instant Reference	45/-
DOS 3.3 & 5.0 Test	45/-
DOS 6 Running Start	75/-
DOS 6.0 & 6.22 Companion	99/-
DOS 6.0 & 6.2 Instant Reference	54/-
DOS Quick Reference Manual - Volume I (upto ver.-5)	45/-
DOS Quick Reference Manual - Volume II (upto ver.-6.2)	45/-
Illustrated MS-DOS 5 (Upto Version - 5)	99/-
Illustrated MS DOS 6.22	99/-
DOS A Developers Guide (upto ver:-5)	225/-
Learn DOS in a Day (Upto 6.2)	45/-
MS-DOS 5 Power User's Guide	60/-
PCLL Teaches DOS 6 & 6.2	150/-

TITLE	PRICE
➢MS-DOS	
MS-DOS System Programming (W/D)	225/-
Mastering DOS 6 & 6.2 - Special Edition	325/-
Murphy's Laws of DOS-6	99/-
Teach Yourself - DOS	90/-
MS-DOS Handbook	99/-
➢MULTIMEDIA/SOUND BLASTER/CD-ROM	
Choosing & Using Your First CD-ROM Drive -(W/CD-ROM)	350/-
Multimedia on the PC (W/D)	120/-
SOUND BLASTER Book	300/-
THE DICTIONARY OF MULTIMEDIA (TERMS & ACRONYMS)	MAY'98
➢NORTON UTILITIES	
Learn NORTON UTILITIES in a Day	45/-
NORTON Desktop for Windows Instant Ref.	240/-
Understanding NORTON UTILITIES 6	299/-
➢NETWORKING	
ABCs of LOCAL AREA NETWORKS	99/-
Complete Encyclopedia Of Networking (W/CD-ROM)	495/-
Dictionary of NETWORKING	75/-
Fix Your own LAN	270/-
Introduction to LOCAL AREA NETWORKS (REVISED EDITION)	150/-
LAN Security Handbook (W/D)	225/-
LAN Troubleshooting Handbook (W/D)	240/-
LOCAL AREA NETWORKS	99/-
Multiprotocol Network Design & Troublshooting	450/-
NT Network Security	APR'98
NETWORK Concepts & Architectures	150/-
PC Magazine - Guide to CONNECTIVITY	225/-
The NETWORK Technical Guide (W/CD)	450/-
Welcome to NETWORKING - A Guide to LAN's	99/-
➢NOVELL NETWARE	
Learn NOVELL NETWARE in A Day	45/-
NETWARE 2.2 & 3.11 Users Guide	240/-
NETWARE 3.12 Administrator's Handbook	180/-
NETWARE Programmer's Guide for 286/386	180/-
NOVELL's Guide to Netware 3.12 Networks	270/-
NOVELL NETWARE - Tips, Tricks & Techniques	225/-
NOVELL NETWARE 386-3.11 User's Perspective	195/-
NOVELL's Applications Notes for NETWARE 4.01	350/-
NOVELL's CLIENT/SERVER Applications & Architecture	350/-
NOVELL's Guide to NETWARE 4.01 NETWORKS	225/-
NOVELL's Guide to Personal NETWARE	360/-

TITLE	PRICE
➢NOVELL NETWARE	
NOVELL's Problem Solving Guide for NETWARE Systems (For Version 3.X/4.X)	180/-
PCLL-Teaches NETWARE (W/D)	150/-
The Official NOVELL NETWARE Little Hand Book	180/-
Troubleshooting NETWARE For The 286	275/-
NOVELL's Quick Access Guide to NETWARE 3.11 Networks	60/-
Troubleshooting NETWARE For The 386	350/-
Troubleshooting Netware Systems (W/2 CD ROMs)	499/-
➢NOVELL NETWARE 4.11	
Complete Guide to Netware 4.11 / INTRANETWARE	450/-
Managing Small Netware 4.11 Networks	180/-
➢NUMERICAL METHODS	
NUMERICAL METHODS: A Computer Oriented Approach	99/-
➢NETSCAPE NAVIGATOR / COMMUNICATOR	
Mastering NETSCAPE FAST TRACK SERVER	225/-
Surfing the Internet with NETSCAPE NAVIGATOR-2 (W/D)	150/-
Surfing the Internet with NETSCAPE NAVIGATOR-3 (W/CD)	240/-
Surfing the INTERNET with NETSCAPE COMMUNICATOR 4 (W/CD)	275/-
Mastering NETSCAPE COMMUNICATOR 4 (W/CD-ROM)	399/-
➢NT SERVER	
NT NETWORK Security (W/CD)	450/-
➢'O' LEVEL - TEXT BOOKS - OLD SYLLABUS	
'O' LEVEL- Module I- COMPUTERS FUNDAMENTALS	120/-
'O' LEVEL- Module II- Section A - PROGRAMMING CONCEPTS & SYSTEMS	120/-
'O' LEVEL -Module II- Section B - SOFTWARE PACKAGES	180/-
'O' LEVEL - Module IV Section A - Problem Solving & Programming in BASIC	120/-
'O' LEVEL Module IV - Section B Problem Solving & Programming in COBOL	120/-
Solved Papers-'O' LEVEL Examinations Module I- COMPUTER FUNDAMENTALS	150/-
'O' LEVEL Made Simple - Module I- COMPUTER FUNDAMENTALS	120/-
'O' LEVEL Made Simple - Module II- Volume 1 Programming Concepts	120/-
'O' LEVEL Made Simple Module II - Vol. 2 Software Packages	195/-

TITLE	PRICE

➢'O' LEVEL - TEXT BOOKS - NEW SYLLABUS

Quan Book 'O' LEVEL 99/-
Quan Book 'A' LEVEL Vol. 1 .... 123/-
Quan Book 'A' LEVEL Vol. 2 .... JUN'98
'O' LEVEL Made Simple Module I - Information Technology 150/-
'O' Level Module I - Information Technology ... 150/-
'O' Level Module II - Section A Personal Computer software 150/-
Question with Answer 'O' Level Module-I Information Technology 150/-
Question with Answer 'O' Level Module- II Personal Computing Software 150/-

➢OBJECT ORIENTED

OBJECT ORIENTED Programming in C++ 120/-
OBJECT ORIENTED Programming : A new way of thinking 75/-

➢MS – OFFICE 4.2/4.3/WIN

MS-OFFICE 4.3 Professional Instant Reference 66/-
MS-OFFICE Question Bank 36/-
PCLL-Teaches MS-OFFICE (W/D) 150/-
Pushbutton guide to MS Office for Windows 350/-
Compact Guide to MS OFFICE 4.2 .... 225/-
Compact Guide to MS OFFICE 4.3 Professional 399/-

➢MS – OFFICE 7.0 / WIN 95

Mastering MS OFFICE Professional 7.0/ Win 95 . 375/-
MS OFFICE Professional / Win 95 Instant Ref. . 75/-
Point & Click Guide to MS OFFICE STD / Win 95 150/-

➢MS – OFFICE 97

ABCs OF MS OFFICE 97 PROFESSIONAL 150/-
Teach yourself Office 97 for Windows 360/-
Learn MS OFFICE 97 (W/D) 180/-
Mastering MS Office 97 Web Publishing 360/-
Mastering MS OFFICE 97 Professional 399/-
Mastering MS OFFICE 97 Internet Edition (W/2CDs) 570/-
MS OFFICE 97 - No Experience Required 240/-
Microsoft OFFICE 97 user Certification Study Guide (W/CD) 399/-

➢OPERATING SYSTEMS

OPERATING SYSTEMS 120/-

➢OLE-2

OLE-2 Programmer's Reference Vol. I 805/-
OLE-2 Programmer's Reference Vol. II 670/-
Mastering OLE 2 (W/D) 180/-

➢ORACLE

Client Server Computing with ORACLE 225/-
Commercial Application Development Using ORACLE Developer 2000 .... 240/-

TITLE	PRICE

➢ORACLE

Mastering ORACLE 6.0.... .... 180/-
ORACLE : Building High Performance On-line Systems 150/-
ORACLE 6.0: The Basics 150/-
ORACLE 7 : The Complete Reference 180/-
ORACLE 6/7 - SQL Report Writer 180/-
The ORACLE Cook Book (W/D) 225/-
Understanding ORACLE 250/-
Mastering ORACLE 7 & Client/Server Computing (W/D) 2nd Edition 345/-
The First Step to ORACLE 75/-

➢OUTLOOK 97

ABCs OF OUTLOOK 97 .... 120/-

➢PAGEMAKER

Learn PAGEMAKER 5.0 for Windows in a Day . 54/-
Mastering PAGEMAKER 4 on IBM PC 150/-
Mastering PAGEMAKER 5.0 / Windows (W/D) 300/-
PAGEMAKER 5.0 by Example (W/D) 345/-
Mastering PAGEMAKER 6 for Win 95 (W/CD-ROM) 399/-
Teach Yourself PAGEMAKER 6.5 for WIN & MAC(W/CD) 240/-

➢PARADOX

Mastering PARADOX 4.5 for Windows 396/-

➢PASCAL

Data Structure Using PASCAL LAB Workbook (W/D) 120/-
Introductory PASCAL 60/-
Learn PASCAL in three days 45/-
PASCAL : An Introduction 45/-
PASCAL Programming — 2nd Edition 150/-
PASCAL Programming Lab Workbook 99/-
Programming in Borland PASCAL (W/D) 525/-
Programming in PASCA -Volume I (CBSE-XI) .. 75/-
Programming in PASCAL-Volume II (CBSE-XII) 60/-

➢PC TOOLS

Learn PC TOOLS in a Day 45/-
PC TOOLS 7.1..... .... 99/-
Up & Running with PC TOOLS Deluxe 6 .... 45/-
PC TOOLS 7.1 Instant Reference 45/-

➢PERL / CGI

PERL/CGI : No Experience Required 150/-

➢PFS : FIRST CHOICE

Understanding PFS: FIRST CHOICE 150/-

➢PHOTOSHOP

Adobe PHOTOSHOP Handbook 300/-
Teach Yourself Photoshop 4 for Win/Mac (W/CD) 240/-

TITLE	PRICE

➢POWER BUILDER

TITLE	PRICE
Commercial Applications in POWER BUILDER	225/-
POWER BUILDER : Concepts & Applications	225/-
POWER BUILDER 4:A Developer's Guide (W/D)	350/-
POWER BUILDER 4.0 (W/D)	325/-

➢POWER BUILDER 5

TITLE	PRICE
Power Builder 5.0:A Developer's Guide (W/CD)	450/-
Teach Yourself Power Builder 5.0 (W/D)	225/-

➢POWER POINT

TITLE	PRICE
Learn MS POWER POINT 7.0 /Win 95 in a day	45/-
Mastering POWER POINT 97	195/-
Teach Yourself POWER POINT for Win 95	180/-

➢PRINTSHOP

TITLE	PRICE
The Official PRINTSHOP Deluxe H/B	180/-

➢PRINTER

TITLE	PRICE
Getting the Most FROM your HP Laserjet (W/D)	150/-
Laser PRINTER Unlimited	150/-
Modern all about PRINTER	99/-
Winn L. Rosch's PRINTER Bible (W/CD-ROM)	450/-

➢PROCOMM PLUS

TITLE	PRICE
Learn PROCOMM PLUS 2.0 /Windows in a day	54/-
Mastering PROCOMM PLUS	150/-

➢PROGRAMMING

TITLE	PRICE
Foundations of PROGRAMMING	60/-
Mixed Language PROGRAMMING (W/D)	225/-
PROGRAMMING Techniques for PC's	66/-
Plug & Play PROGRAMMING (W/D)	180/-
Structured Programming: go to Controversy to OBJECT ORIENTED PROGRAMMING	120/-
Welcome to PROGRAMMING (W/D)	180/-

➢PROJECT

TITLE	PRICE
PCLL-Teaches MS PROJECT 4.0 / Win (W/D)	150/-
Teach Yourself MS PROJECT /Win 95 (W/D)	180/-

➢QUATTRO PRO

TITLE	PRICE
Learn QUATTRO PRO 5.0 in a Day	45/-
Mastering QUATTRO PRO 5 for Windows	295/-
Mastering QUATTRO PRO for Windows	396/-

➢RS-232

TITLE	PRICE
The RS-232 Solution	150/-

➢SAP's

TITLE	PRICE
Developing SAP's R/3 Applications with ABAP/4 (W/CD-ROM)	499/-

➢SERIAL COMMUNICATION

TITLE	PRICE
Mastering SERIAL COMMUNICATIONS	180/-
SERIAL COMMUNICATIONS:A C++ Development Guide (W/D)	275/-

➢SGML FILTERS

TITLE	PRICE
PRACTICAL GUIDE TO SGML FILTERS (W/2 DISKS)	180/-

➢SOFTWARE

TITLE	PRICE
ALMOST PERFECT : How a Bunch of Regular Guys Built WORDPERFECT CORPORATION	150/-
Getting ISO 9000 for SOFTWARE Organizations (2nd Revised Edition)	225/-
How Computer Works (W/CD-ROM)	480/-
SOFTWARE FACTORY : Managing SOFTWARE Development & Maintenance	150/-

➢SOFTWARE ENGINEERING

TITLE	PRICE
Object Oriented SOFTWARE ENGINEERING	150/-

➢SQL

TITLE	PRICE
Optimizing SQL (W/D)	180/-
SQL Spoken Here	120/-
Understanding SQL	225/-

➢SYBASE

TITLE	PRICE
CLIENT/SERVER Computing SYBASE SQL Server	225/-

➢SYSTEM ANALYSIS & DESIGN

TITLE	PRICE
Introducing SYSTEMS ANALYSIS - NCC	90/-
Introducing SYSTEMS DESIGN - NCC	90/-

➢TCP/IP & SNA

TITLE	PRICE
Demystifying TCP/IP	90/-
Integrating TCP/IP into SNA	225/-
Troubleshooting TCP/IP	399/-

➢TSR

TITLE	PRICE
Write TSR's Now	99/-
Writing TSR's Through C	225/-

➢TURBO C

TITLE	PRICE
Mastering TURBO C	180/-
TURBO C Programming Techniques	99/-
Programming Guide to TURBO C2	180/-

➢TURBO C++

TITLE	PRICE
Illustrated TURBO C++	150/-
Object Oriented Programming Using TURBO C++	45/-
TURBO C ++ Techniques & Applications	180/-

➢TURBO PASCAL

TITLE	PRICE
Advanced Techniques in TURBO PASCAL	90/-
Mastering TURBO PASCAL	150/-
Mastering TURBO PASCAL - 6	150/-
TURBO PASCAL 6.0	75/-
TURBO PASCAL Companion	75/-

➢TURBO PROLOG

TITLE	PRICE
Illustrated TURBO PROLOG	120/-
Introduction to TURBO PROLOG	120/-

➢UNIX/XENIX

TITLE	PRICE
Advanced UNIX : A Programmer's Guide	180/-
Illustrated UNIX System V	195/-

TITLE	PRICE
➢UNIX/XENIX	
Inside XENIX	96/-
Peter Norton Guide to UNIX	180/-
Question Bank UNIX C Programming	66/-
Teach Yourself...UNIX .	99/-
Test Your UNIX Skills	81/-
ABCs of SCO UNIX	90/-
Running UNIX	180/-
UNIX ... Power ... UNLEASHED	120/-
UNIX C SHELL Desk REFERENCE	120/-
UNIX Power UTILITIES	150/-
UNIX Desk Reference – Guide to Commands, Concepts of Latest Release of UNIX Linux BSD	135/-
UNIX Quick !	99/-
Understanding UNIX	270/-
UNIX Programming On the 80286/80386	150/-
UNIX Power Tools (W/CD-ROM)	395/-
UNIX Shells Bourne-Korn-C	150/-
UNIX Shell Programming	175/-
Working With UNIX	150/-
➢VENTURA	
Learn VENTURA 4.0 in A Day	45/-
Mastering VENTURA 3.0	150/-
VENTURA Publisher Test	54/-
➢VIRUS	
Computer VIRUS Protection HandBook (W/D)	180/-
SCIENCE OF VIRUSES & VACCINES (W/2 DISKS)	300/-
➢VISUAL BASIC	
VISUAL BASIC Utilities (W/D)	240/-
Visual Basic Certification Study Guide (W/CD)	MAY'98
Programming in VISUAL BASIC	75/-
Teach Yourself ... VISUAL BASIC 3.0 (W/D)	195/-
➢VBA	
VBA Developer's Handbook (W/CD-ROM)	495/-
➢VISUAL BASIC 4	
Developing Utilities in VISUAL BASIC 4.0 (W/D)	99/-
Learn VISUAL BASIC 4.0 in three days	45/-
PCLL - Teaches MS VISUAL BASIC 4 (W/D)	165/-
The VISUAL BASIC 4.0 Example Book (W/D)	120/-
Teach Yourself VISUAL BASIC 4.0 for Windows 95 (W/D)	195/-
The Fast Track to VISUAL BASIC 4	120/-
➢VISUAL BASIC 5	
VISUAL BASIC 5 : No Experience Required	135/-
Visual Basic 5 Developer's Handbook (W/CD)	450/-
Learn VISUALBASIC 5.0 in three days (W/D)	66/-
Mastering VISUAL BASIC 5 (W/CD)	450/-

TITLE	PRICE
➢C – VISUAL C++	
MS Visual C++ 5 No Experience Required	180/-
Mastering MS VISUAL C++ 4 (W/CD-ROM)	450/-
Teach Yourself VISUAL C++ 4	180/-
Visual C++ Certification Study Guide (W/CD)	MAY'98
Visual C++ A Developer's Guide (W/D)	225/-
➢VISUAL C++	
Writing Visual Basic Controls Using VISUAL C++	180/-
➢VISUAL J++	
Mastering Visual J++ (W/CD-ROM)	450/-
Visual J++ 1.1 No Experience Required	135/-
➢CLIPPER – VISUAL OBJECTS	
Rick Spence'S Guide to CA-VISUAL OBJECTS	225/-
➢INTERNET – WORLD WIDE WEB	
Learning to Use the WORLDWIDE WEB	150/-
Mastering OFFICE 97 WEB PUBLISHING	360/-
➢WORLD WIDE WEB DESIGN	
WorlD Wide Web Bible (W/CD Rom)	399/-
Mastering WEB Design (W/CD-ROM)	450/-
THE WEB PAGE WORKBOOK (W/D)	150/-
Building Business Web Sites (W/CD-ROM)	450/-
Effective WEB Design: Master the Essentials	MAY'98
Web Pages that Suck: Learn Good Design by Looking at Bad Design	APR'98
Web by Design: The complete Guide	APR'98
➢WIN FAX	
Just the Fax All about WIN FAX	150/-
➢WINDOWS	
ABCs of WINDOWS 3.1	99/-
Compact Guide To WINDOWS, WORD & EXCEL	180/-
Advanced Tools for WINDOWS Developers (W/D)	540/-
Creating Help for WINDOWS Applications (W/D)	99/-
Designing GUI Applications /WINDOWS (W/D)	225/-
Illustrated WINDOWS 3.1	150/-
PC Computing Customizing Win 3.1 (W/D)	180/-
Learn WINDOWS in a Day	45/-
Programming WINDOWS 3.1 (W/D)	345/-
Making WINDOWS Application Work Together (W/D)	240/-
Mastering WINDOWS 3.1 (Special Edition)	250/-
MS WINDOWS At A Glance	60/-
PCLL-Teaches WINDOWS 3.1 (W/D)	150/-
Programming for WINDOWS	45/-
Teach Your Self WINDOWS 3.1	120/-